online resource centre

www.oxfordtextbooks.co.uk/orc/roach/

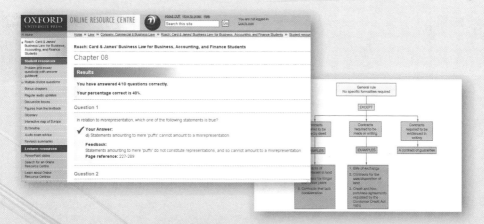

Wherever you see this icon @ remember to visit the accompanying **Online Resource Centre** where you will find a wealth of resources which will help further your study of business law, including:

Self-assessment exercises:
- Problem and essay questions with answer guidance
- Multiple choice questions

Revision aids:
- Revision summaries
- Audio exam advice
- Regular audio updates

For lecturers:
- PowerPoint presentations

Additional materials:
- Bonus chapters on business ethics, corporate governance, credit transactions, and sale of goods
- Discussion boxes
- Glossary of the key terms
- Figures from the textbook
- EU timeline - delineating the development of the European Union
- Map of Europe - providing useful details on each country, and its legal standing

! Remember to check the Online Resource Centre regularly for updates on the recent developments and major e

D1098792

CARD & JAMES'

BUSINESS LAW

FOR BUSINESS, ACCOUNTING, & FINANCE STUDENTS

Lee Roach LLB, PhD, FHEA

Senior Lecturer in Law,
Portsmouth Business School,
University of Portsmouth

OXFORD

UNIVERSITY PRESS

OXFORD

UNIVERSITY PRESS

Great Clarendon Street, Oxford OX2 6DP

Oxford University Press is a department of the University of Oxford.
It furthers the University's objective of excellence in research, scholarship,
and education by publishing worldwide in

Oxford New York

Auckland Cape Town Dar es Salaam Hong Kong Karachi
Kuala Lumpur Madrid Melbourne Mexico City Nairobi
New Delhi Shanghai Taipei Toronto

With offices in

Argentina Austria Brazil Chile Czech Republic France Greece
Guatemala Hungary Italy Japan Poland Portugal Singapore
South Korea Switzerland Thailand Turkey Ukraine Vietnam

Oxford is a registered trade mark of Oxford University Press
in the UK and in certain other countries

Published in the United States
by Oxford University Press Inc., New York

British Library Cataloguing in Publication Data

Data available

Library of Congress Cataloging in Publication Data

Data available

Typeset by Newgen Imaging Systems (P) Ltd., Chennai, India
Printed in Great Britain
on acid-free paper by
Ashford Colour Press Ltd., Gosport, Hampshire

ISBN 978–0–19–928921–9

1 3 5 7 9 10 8 6 4 2

For Tom and Sandra Roach

preface

Business law is an unusual topic, largely because it is aimed at students who may have no prior desire to study the law. There are doubtless many students studying finance and business-related degrees who, upon discovering that they are required to study law, justifiably ask: 'Why am I studying law when I do not wish to be a lawyer?' It is an excellent question, deserving of an answer. The answer lies in the pervasiveness of law, and the close relationship between law and business. Any field of financial or business activity will be subject to extensive legal regulation and a full understanding of any business-related field can only be obtained if one understands the legal environment within which businesses operate. That numerous professional bodies mandate the study of business law is evidence of this. It is hoped, however, that this book does more than simply help students to understand why the law is so important: a good law textbook should make its reader *want* to study the law and it is my hope that, in some small way, this book will cultivate a desire for a deeper understanding of the topic, even amongst those with no prior desire to study the law.

Although this text is a new work, it owes its existence to *Law for Accountancy Students* by Richard Card and Jennifer James. The final edition of that text was published in 2002, and it gained a reputation amongst business law texts in terms of its detailed exposition and faultless accuracy. Since then, much has moved on, not only in terms of the content of law, but also in the way in which law is taught. The law is a complex animal, even more so for non-law students. Accordingly, this text has been written with accessibility and clarity in mind. Key legal terms are prominently defined and example boxes are used to provide clarity to more complex areas of the law. But clarity should not come at the expense of depth and analysis, and it is hoped that this book continues the tradition of providing a level of detailed discussion and faultless accuracy that was a hallmark of Card and James' original text.

Business law is an extremely broad topic and tends to get broader each year. In recent years, the topic has expanded to encompass topics that have not traditionally been covered in business law texts. With that in mind, the Online Resource Centre that accompanies this book contains chapters on topics not normally covered by business law texts, but which have risen to prominence in recent years—notably, corporate governance and business ethics.

I offer my thanks to Richard Card and Jennifer James for inviting me to author this book. The feedback and comments offered by Richard Card, in particular, have been invaluable, and this book would have been all the poorer but for his encyclopaedic knowledge of the law and immaculate eye for detail. My thanks also go to all of the publishing team at OUP for all of their hard work. In particular, I would like to express my sincere gratitude to Eleanor Williams and Jacqueline Senior, whose aid and encouragement was a crucial factor in completing this book within the agreed schedule. Finally, my thanks go out to my parents, my friends, and my colleagues, whom I doubtless neglected while I locked myself away writing this book. Your patience and support are appreciated more than you will ever know.

The Interpretation Act 1978, s 6, provides that, in relation to statutory interpretation, unless otherwise stated, the masculine shall also indicate the feminine. This text follows the same rule and, accordingly, 'he', 'his', and 'him' shall, unless otherwise indicated, also be taken to mean 'she', hers', and 'her', respectively.

I have attempted to state the law as at 16 February 2009. With the kind indulgence of the publisher, minor amendments have been made to accommodate subsequent changes in the law.

LRR
Portsmouth
February 2009

approach of the book

Referencing: Most business, finance, and accounting degrees will use a referencing system called Harvard APA. However, the predominant referencing system in law (and a referencing system your lecturer may require you to use) is called OSCOLA (the Oxford Standard for the Citation of Legal Authorities). Accordingly, to enable you to become comfortable with this referencing system, this textbook references sources in accordance with OSCOLA. The full OSCOLA document can be found at <http://www.competition-law.ox.ac.uk/published/oscola.shtml>.

Footnotes: Whereas Harvard APA cites sources in-text, law textbooks and journal articles use footnotes, and OSCOLA also states that footnotes must be used. Accordingly, in this textbook, authority is cited using footnotes. The Online Resource Centre contains a document entitled 'The Referencing of Authority' which will provide students with guidance on the correct use of footnotes, and the advantages of using footnotes.

More details on OSCOLA can be found on the Online Resource Centre where a document entitled 'The Referencing of Authority' provides guidance on when and how to cite authority

guide to the book

This guide outlines the features that have been devised to make the learning experience easier and more enjoyable for you. This brief overview explains the features and how to make the most of them for effective study of the law.

Features to aid learning

INTRODUCTION

The need for commercial certainty goes beyond the form
need to be aware in what circumstances validly formed c
removed from existence. The business may engage in activ
being formed that can subsequently cause the contract to become
resulting in the business sustaining a substantial loss, or the loss of
future business. In order to avoid a contract being vitiated, businesses
what type of pre-contract activity should be avoided—whether it be the

Introductions at the start of each chapter explain why that area of law is particularly relevant and how it will relate to you as a business, accounting or finance student.

‹› Key points summary

- Currently, the European Union (EU) and European Convention
  are completely independent of each other, with separate courts a
  Membership of one is not dependent upon being a signatory of the c
  versa.
- The EU currently has twenty-seven member States, whereas forty
  (including the twenty-seven EU member states) have signed up to the EC

Summary boxes throughout highlight the essential areas of the law using summaries of key points. These also help you to focus your study, not to mention making great revision aids!

➜ **subjective:** relating to the thoughts or characteristics of an individual

➜ **precedent:** an authoritative and binding decision in a case used to decide a later case with similar facts

emerge. Firstly, because natural law
it is a highly subjective theory. If o
result would be severe inconsisten
regard as moral might be consider
ignore the law and base their decision
precedent would become redundant and
ability would be lost.
    Secondly, it could be argued that natural law is
of thought, in that an unjust law is just as likely to
one. Judges do not ignore the law simply because t

Definition boxes highlight and explain all of the new terms that you will come across within the text. They are also collated on the Online Resource Centre in a searchable glossary.

g into force of the Human Rights
ts contained in the Convention can

ort, is probably the most significant
ublic authority to act in a way which
refore, if any public body infringes
ay bring a claim against that public
emedy that is 'just and appropriate',
ortious cases succeeding under the
e probably failed prior to the Act's

🔗 The Human Rights Act 1998, s 6, is discussed in more detail at p 122

Cross references direct you to other areas of the textbook with page references to highlight fundamental connections across the chapters, thereby aiding your understanding of the overarching themes.

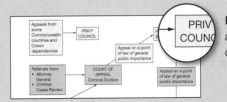

Diagrams summarise the more complex areas of the law to provide a clear and concise visual overview.

Key cases which are integral to an effective understanding of the law are clearly explained and discussed to emphasise their relevance.

Case analysis boxes provides links to articles in which academics discuss and debate the landmark cases in detail. Be sure to follow these links to journal articles for a more detailed discussion of the case; particularly useful for essays!

Example boxes help to explain the sometimes complex and unfamiliar aspects of the law by contextualising the theory via an everyday example.

Self test questions are provided at the end of each chapter to help you to check your understanding of the chapter and assess your progress.

Further reading references conclude each chapter. Annotated, they point you in the direction of articles, textbooks, reports and websites which develop the issues discussed in the chapter, and how each one is relevant to your study.

guide to the Online Resource Centre

This book is accompanied by a fully integrated Online Resource Centre which provides a whole host of additional resources to support you in your studies, and to advance your understanding of the topics.

Problem and essay questions with answer guidance

Try the further problem and essay questions for each chapter to practice the technique of answering problem questions, then check the author's answer guidance.

Multiple choice questions

Test yourself with the multiple choice questions written for each chapter. Feedback for each question and page references to the textbook are provided to direct you back to the content.

Regular audio updates

Ensure that you keep up to date with developments on the move by downloading the audio updates. Written transcripts are also available.

Revision summaries

Use these summaries of the key points to test yourself when revising the topics, and as useful key points to remember.

Audio exam advice

Audio advice on principal exam topics talks you through the key points you need to remember, and provides some handy hints and tips.

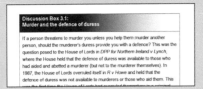

Discussion boxes

Discussion boxes on areas of the law which have incited debate – use these boxes to pause and reflect on the legal provisions.

Glossary

Over 600 legal terms from the textbook are collated in this searchable glossary as a complete reference for all the terms you will need to be familiar with.

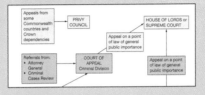

Diagrams

All of the diagrams used in this book are freely available for download.

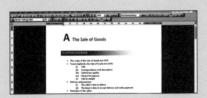

Bonus chapters

Bonus chapters on business ethics, corporate governance, credit transactions, and sale of goods help you gain a more holistic appreciation of law, especially for those studying for CIMA or ACCA.

These chapters are available free of charge to all readers of the book. To access them please follow the instructions below:

1. Go to: www.oxfordtextbooks.co.uk/orc/roach/
2. Click on the 'Bonus chapters' link
3. Enter the login details opposite (case sensitive)

Username: Roach1e
Password: businesslaw

For Lecturers

The following resources are password-protected and only available for lecturers who have adopted the textbook to assist their teaching. Registering is easy: click on 'Lecturer resources' on the Online Resource Centre and complete a simple registration form which allows you to use your own username and login.

PowerPoint Presentations

Each chapter of the book has an accompanying PowerPoint presentation which can be downloaded and customized for your lectures.

contents in brief

Business ethics

Visit the **Online Resource Centre** that accompanies this book to access these chapters and other useful materials: <http://www.oxfordtextbooks.co.uk/roach>

PART V: **Employment Law**

PART VI: **Elements of Commercial Law**

Consumer credit

The sale of goods

Visit the **Online Resource Centre** that accompanies this book to access these chapters and other useful materials: <http://www.oxfordtextbooks.co.uk/roach>

detailed contents

PART III: The Law of Torts

Visit the **Online Resource Centre** that accompanies this book to access these chapters and other useful materials: <http://www.oxfordtextbooks.co.uk/roach>

PART V: Employment Law

PART VI: Elements of Commercial Law

The sale of goods

Visit the **Online Resource Centre** that accompanies this
book to access this chapter and other useful materials:
<http://www.oxfordtextbooks.co.uk/roach>

list of abbreviations

The following is a list of abbreviations used in this text, including the abbreviations of law reports and journals.

AC or App Cas	Appeal Cases
ACAS	Advisory, Conciliation and Arbitration Service
ADR	alternative dispute resolution
AG	Attorney General
AGM	annual general meeting
All ER	All England Law Reports
All ER (Comm)	All England Law Reports (Commercial Cases)
All ER Rep	All England Law Reports Reprint
AML	additional maternity leave
art/Art	article (domestic)/Article (supranational)
Atk	Atkyns Law Reports
B & Ald	Barnewell & Adolphus Law Reports
B & CR	Bankruptcy and Companies Winding Up
BCC	British Company Cases
BCLC	Butterworths' Company Law Cases
Beav	Beavan Law Reports
BERR	Department for Business, Enterprise and Regulatory Reform
Bing	Bingham Law Reports
BLR	Building Law Reports
BPMMR 2008	Business Protection from Misleading Marketing Regulations 2008
CA	Court of Appeal
CA 1985	Companies Act 1985
CA 2006	Companies Act 2006
CARICOM	Caribbean Community
CAT	Competition Appeal Tribunal
CC	Competition Commission
CCRC	Criminal Cases Review Commission
CDDA 1986	Company Directors Disqualification Act 1986
CDO	Competition Disqualification Order
CEO	chief executive officer
CFI	Court of First Instance
CFSP	Common Foreign and Security Policy
Ch	Chancery Division of the High Court
ch	chapter
Ch App	Chancery Appeal Law Reports
Ch or Ch D	Chancery Division Law Reports
CIC	community interest company
CIO	charitable incorporated organization
CJQ	Civil Justice Quarterly

cl	clause
CLJ	Cambridge Law Journal
CML	compulsory maternity leave
CMLR	Common Market Law Reports
Co Law	Company Lawyer
Colum LR	Columbia Law Review
Comm	Commercial Court
Cowp	Cowper Law Reports
Cox CC	Cox Criminal Cases
CPA 1987	Consumer Protection Act 1987
CPC	Community protection cooperation
CPS	Crown Prosecution Service
CPUTR 2008	Consumer Protection from Unfair Trading Regulations 2008
CRTPA 1999	Contracts (Rights of Third Parties) Act 1999
CVA	company voluntary arrangement
DDA 1995	Disability Discrimination Act 1995
DGFT	Director General of the Office of Fair Trading
DPP	Director of Public Prosecutions
DTI	Department of Trade and Industry
EAT	Employment Appeal Tribunal
EC	European Community
ECHR	European Convention on Human Rights
ECJ	European Court of Justice
ECR	European Court Reports
ECSC	European Coal and Steel Community
ECtHR	European Court of Human Rights
EEA	European Economic Area
EEAR 2006	Employment Equality (Age) Regulations 2006
EEC	European Economic Community
EERBR 2003	Employment Equality (Religion or Belief) Regulations 2003
EESOR 2003	Employment Equality (Sexual Orientation) Regulations 2003
EG, or Est Gaz	Estates Gazette
EHRC	Equality and Human Rights Commission
EHRR	European Human Rights Reports
EMLR	Entertainment and Media Law Reports
ENE	early neutral evaluation
EPA 1970	Equal Pay Act 1970
ERA 1996	Employment Rights Act 1996
ET	employment tribunal
EU	European Union
EWC	expected week of childbirth
EWCA Civ	Civil Division of the Court of Appeal (England and Wales)
EWCA Crim	Criminal Division of the Court of Appeal (England and Wales)
EWHC	High Court (England and Wales)
Ex	Court of Exchequer
ex p	*ex parte*
Fam	Family Division of the High Court

FTER 2002	Fixed-Term Employees (Prevention of Less Favourable Treatment) Regulations 2002
Harv LR	Harvard Law Review
HL	Appellate Committee of the House of Lords
HL Cas	House of Lords Cases
HMRC	Her Majesty's Revenue and Customs
HMSO	Her Majesty's Stationery Office
HSE	Health and Safety Executive
HSWA 1974	Health and Safety at Work etc. Act 1974
IA 1986	Insolvency Act 1986
ICR	Industrial Cases Reports
ILEX	Institute of Legal Executives
IRLR	Industrial Relations Law Reports
IT	industrial tribunal
J/JJ	Mr/Mrs Justice(s)
JAC	Judicial Appointments Commission
JHA	Co-operation in Justice and Home Affairs
JP	Justice of the Peace
KB	King's Bench Division of the High Court
LC	Lord Chancellor
LCJ	Lord Chief Justice
LJ/LJJ	Lord/Lady Justice(s)
LLA	liability limitation agreement
Lloyd's Rep	Lloyd's List Law Reports
LLP	limited liability partnership
LLPA 2000	Limited Liability Partnerships Act 2000
LMCLQ	Lloyd's Maritime and Commercial Law Quarterly
LQR	Law Quarterly Review
LR CP	Law Reports: Common Pleas
LR Eq	Law Reports: Equity
LR Ex	Law Reports: Exchequer
LR HL	Law Reports: English and Irish Appeals
LR QB	Law Reports: Queen's Bench
LSB	Legal Services Board
LT	Law Times
MEP	member of the European Parliament
MLR	Modern Law Review
MP	member of Parliament
MR	Master of the Rolls
NI	National Insurance
NIRC	National Industrial Relations Court
NLJ	New Law Journal
NMWA 1998	National Minimum Wage Act 1998
NPC	New Property Cases
OFT	Office of Fair Trading
OLA 1957	Occupiers' Liability Act 1957
OLA 1984	Occupiers' Liability Act 1984

OLC	Office for Legal Complaints
OML	ordinary maternity leave
P	Probate (Law Reports)
P & CR	Property, Planning and Compensation Reports
PCP	provision, condition, or practice
p/pp	page(s)
PA 1890	Partnership Act 1890
PC	Judicial Committee of the Privy Council
PJC	Police and Judicial Co-operation in Criminal Matters
PMB	private member's Bill
Pt	Part
PTWR 2000	Part-Time Workers (Prevention of Less Favourable Treatment) Regulations 2000
QB, or QBD	Queen's Bench Division of the High Court or Queen's Bench Law Reports
QC	Queen's Counsel
r/rr	rule(s)
R	Regina (Queen) or Rex (King)
reg	regulation
RRA 1976	Race Relations Act 1976
s/ss	section(s)
Sch	Schedule
SDA 1975	Sex Discrimination Act 1975
SE	Societas Europaea
SGA 1979	Sale of Goods Act 1979
SGITA 1973	Supply of Goods (Implied Terms) Act 1973
SI	statutory instrument
SJ or Sol Jo	Solicitors' Journal and Reporter
Stat LR	Statute Law Review
TLR	Times Law Reports
TUPE	Transfer of Undertakings (Protection of Employment) Regulations 2006
UCPD	Unfair Commercial Practices Directive
UCTA 1977	Unfair Contract Terms Act 1977
UKHL	House of Lords (UK)
UKPC	Judicial Committee of the Privy Council
UTCCR 1999	Unfair Terms in Consumer Contracts Regulations 1999
VAT	value-added tax
WLR	Weekly Law Reports
WTRs	Working Time Regulations 1998

PART I

the English legal system

1

What is law?

- Theoretical conceptualizations of law
- Classifying the law
- Defining the 'English legal system'

INTRODUCTION

An ordered society is premised upon the adherence to rules. Rules exist in many forms, whether social rules (for example, hats should not be worn in church), scientific rules (for example, $E = MC^2$), sporting rules (for example, in basketball, players may not run with the ball), or legal rules (for example, it is a crime to steal the property of others). Whilst it could be said that all laws are rules, it is certainly not the case that all rules are laws. So why are some rules elevated to legal status and others not? What are the defining characteristics that make a rule a law? What is the geographical limit of English law? These are a few of the issues that will be explored in this opening chapter.

The purpose of this chapter is to provide students with a rounded conception of what law is. Whilst much of what is discussed is not of crucial importance in the context of how businesses operate, it will aid the students in developing a more thorough appreciation of the theories that underpin English law, as well as in understanding the various ways in which English law can be classified and the parameters of English law. Much of the terminology used in this discussion is embedded in our legal system and will be of considerable aid in later chapters, when we discuss the law as it applies specifically to businesses.

Theoretical conceptualizations of law

For several millennia, jurisprudence and legal philosophy have struggled to find answers to the above questions. Given the scope of the arguments involved, a detailed discussion will be beyond the scope of this text. A brief discussion of the principal schools of thought will, however, be of significant aid to any student who is interested in exploring the question of 'what is law'. It may be considered that such theories offer little to a person seeking to understand how the law applies to businesses, but it should not be thought that business law operates in a vacuum. The legal theories that underpin the law apply to all laws, whether they are applicable to natural persons or businesses. Further, an appreciation of the theory behind the

→ jurisprudence: the study of the theory and philosophy of law

law will result in a more rounded understanding of the operation of the law. Oliver Wendell Holmes Jr, a Justice of the US Supreme Court from 1902 to 1932 and one of the most highly regarded jurists ever, stated that:

> If a man goes into law it pays to be a master of it, and to be a master of it means to look straight through all the dramatic incidents and to discern the true basis for prophecy. Therefore, it is well to have an accurate notion of what you mean by law…[1]

Natural law

In terms of chronology, the earliest identifiable theory discussing the issue of what is law concerns the role of 'natural law'. The first major natural law writings can be traced back to the works of Plato (427–347 BCE) and his pupil, Aristotle (384–322 BCE), but the theory gained prominence during the Judaeo-Christian period with the works of St Augustine (AD 354–430) and St Thomas Aquinas (AD 1225–74). Augustine was the Bishop of Hippo (a city in Algeria, North Africa) and in *De Civitate Dei* ('The City of God'), he postulated the existence of the *lex aeterna* (eternal law), an unchanging form of law that derived directly from the will of God. The *lex aeterna* was the highest form of law and, in *De Libero Arbitrio* ('On Free Will'), Augustine infamously stated '*lex iniusta non est lex*' ('an unjust law is no law at all'), meaning that any man-made laws that conflicted or failed to uphold the *lex aeterna* were unjust and need not be obeyed. A similar viewpoint was expressed by St Thomas Aquinas when he stated '*lex tyrannica cum non sit secundum rationem non est simpliciter lex sed magis est quadam perversitas legis*' ('a tyrannical law made contrary to reason is not straightforwardly a law, but rather a perversion of true law'). Therefore, for a natural lawyer, when discussing the issue of what is law, the relationship between law and morality is the crucial factor.

In time, the influence of natural law waned as a number of weaknesses began to emerge. Firstly, because natural law places great emphasis on the morality of the law, it is a highly subjective theory. If our legal system were to embrace natural law, the result would be severe inconsistency in decisions, because what one judge would regard as moral might be considered immoral by another. If judges were free to ignore the law and base their decisions on their own sense of morality, the doctrine of precedent would become redundant and much of the law's consistency and predictability would be lost.

Secondly, it could be argued that natural law is not a particularly realistic school of thought, in that an unjust law is just as likely to be applied by the courts as a just one. Judges do not ignore the law simply because they view it as unjust or immoral.

One should not, however, conclude that natural law has no role to play in the English legal system. Judges may not be free to ignore the law if they consider it immoral (although, as we shall see, they do have ways in which to avoid precedent and considerable discretion in the interpretation of statutes), but there does exist a group of persons who can—namely, juries. As we shall see in Chapter 2, there are numerous examples of cases in which juries have blatantly and unashamedly delivered a verdict contrary to the law on the basis that an application of the law would produce an unjust result. Further, although judges cannot act overtly on the basis of what is considered moral, the system of law known as 'equity' (which is discussed

➡ subjective: relating to the thoughts or characteristics of an individual

➡ precedent: an authoritative and binding decision in a case used to decide a later case with similar facts

🔗 The doctrine of precedent and the interpretation of statutes are discussed in Chapter 3

---

1. O Wendell-Holmes Jr, 'The Path of the Law' (1896–97) 10 Harv LR 457, 475.

later in this chapter) is concerned with notions of fairness, equality, and justice—notions that lie at the heart of classic natural law theory.

Ultimately, however, natural law theories do not help us to understand what the law is, but rather what the law should aspire to be. A number of legal philosophers became disenchanted with natural law due to its inherent subjectivity, and sought to propound a theory that was more objective and which better defined what the law actually was. This resulted in the birth of 'legal positivism'.

➡ objective: unbiased, impartial, and detached; not affected by personal feelings or opinions

Legal positivism

From a philosophical standpoint, positivism is a school of thought that states that true knowledge can only derive from the perception of our senses—notably, observation. Only that which can be observed and empirically evaluated can be regarded as proven. Accordingly, judgments based on values, morals, or perceptions of good and evil are irrelevant, because they cannot be measured scientifically. From a legal point of view, the fathers of legal positivism were Jeremy Bentham (1748–1832) and John Austin (1790–1859). Bentham objected to the predominant naturalistic legal philosophy of the day and, in a prophetic passage written over ten years before the events of the French Revolution, Bentham stated 'the natural tendency of such [naturalist] doctrine is to impel a [person]..., by the force of conscience, to rise up in arms against any law whatever that he happens not to like'.[2]

Bentham and Austin's answer was to devise the 'command theory of law'. According to this theory, a law can be viewed as a command issued by an unfettered sovereign that is backed up by the imposition of a sanction. The views of Bentham and Austin have come to be doubted by modern legal positivists who argue that:

- not all laws are in the form of commands;
- the command theory is based upon an unfettered sovereign, but in many modern countries, the 'rule of law' is dependent upon the State's powers being limited; and
- only breaches of criminal law are backed with sanctions.

Accordingly, the command theory fell out of favour and more modern positivist theories have emerged, the most prominent of which derived from HLA Hart's 1961 text, *The Concept of Law*. Hart chose to base his definition of law on rules, as opposed to commands, and he argued that rules were of two types. Primary rules set out the basic rights of obligations of citizens (that is, what they should and should not do). Hart recognized, however, that a body of primary rules would be ineffective in itself, in that there would be no mechanism for their interpretation, alteration, and enforcement. Accordingly, there also had to exist secondary rules, which would determine the operation of the primary rules.

But just as Hart rejected 'commands' in favour of rules, so, in turn, have recent theories rejected 'rules' in favour of 'rights'. Notably, Ronald Dworkin has argued against legal positivism, partly on the ground that it is too preoccupied with rules. Dworkin argued that a legal system is not only made up of rules, but also of rights, principles, and policies, and that very often, these rights, principles, and policies are

---

2. J Bentham, *A Fragment on Government* (Basil Blackwell, Oxford, 1967) ch 4, [19].

more important than the rules. As an example, Dworkin cites the case of a man who murders his grandfather in order to claim his inheritance early.[3] According to the strict letter of the law, the murderer would be entitled to the inheritance, but the courts denied his claim, applying the public policy principle that a person should not be allowed to profit from his own crime. Accordingly, under Dworkin's 'rights thesis', policies and principles determine the operation of the law.

 Key points summary

- Natural law theories concentrate on the relationship between law and morality.

- Legal positivists are not concerned with morality or values that cannot be scientifically evaluated. Provided that laws are validly created, a law is a law, irrespective of its content.

- Bentham and Austin's command theory of law contends that a law is the command of a sovereign, backed up by a sanction.

- Hart argued that laws consisted of primary rules and secondary rules.

- Dworkin argued that a legal system was made up not only of rules, but also of policies and principles, which were often more fundamental and influential than rules.

Classifying the law

Criminal law and civil law

Perhaps the most fundamental legal distinction is that between criminal law and civil law. Understanding whether a particular act constitutes a crime or a civil wrong (or both) is fundamental in determining in what court the case will be tried, what will need to be established by the parties, what procedural rules apply, and what the potential outcome may be. Fortunately, in practice, distinguishing between civil and criminal acts is straightforward, because civil and criminal law cases are tried in different courts, and have different procedures, outcomes, and terminology. Table 1.1 clearly outlines the fundamental differences between criminal law and civil law cases.

Based on Table 1.1, it can be deduced that the most effective way in which to determine if an act is a crime or a civil wrong is not to focus on the act itself, but rather to focus on the consequences of the act. For example, if the legal consequence of an act is the prosecution and punishment of the perpetrator of the act, then the act will constitute a crime. If an individual is seeking compensation for an act, the case is likely to be a civil one.

It should, however, be noted that the criminal/civil distinction is not mutually exclusive (that is, that an act can result in both criminal and civil liability), as the following example demonstrates.

---

3. The case in question, *Riggs v Palmer* 115 NY 506 (1889), was a US case, but the English case of *R v National Insurance Commissioner, ex p Connor* [1981] QB 758 (DC) has almost identical facts and came to the same decision.

TABLE 1.1 Distinguishing criminal law and civil law

	Criminal	Civil
Purpose of the case	To preserve social order by punishing wrongdoers and deterring others from committing crimes	To compensate a person who has suffered loss or injury due to the acts of another
Parties in the case	The State (*R—Regina* or *Rex*, meaning 'Queen' or 'King' respectively) prosecutes the defendant, e.g. *R v James*	The claimant (the person who has suffered loss) initiates a claim against the defendant (the person alleged to have caused the loss) e.g. *Card v James*
Outcome of the case	If innocent, the defendant is acquitted If guilty, the defendant is convicted and sentenced	The claimant either wins his case and is awarded a remedy, or loses and is not awarded a remedy
Courts involved	First heard in either a magistrates' court or the Crown Court	First heard in either a county court or the High Court
Burden/standard of proof	The prosecution must prove the guilt of the defendant beyond a reasonable doubt	The claimant must prove his case on a balance of probabilities
Examples	Murder; manslaughter; theft; rape; drink-driving	Negligence; breach of contract; cases involving the sale of goods; cases involving property disputes

Eg Crimes and civil wrongs

Joanne leaves her coat at a cloakroom in a nightclub. Andrew, the cloakroom attendant, searches through Joanne's coat and steals her mobile phone, which is secreted in one of the pockets. In such a case, Andrew would be guilty of the crime of theft. He would also have committed several civil wrongs—namely, the tort of conversion (as Andrew's acts are inconsistent with Joanne's ownership of the phone) and breach of contract (he would have breached his contract with his employer).

➡ conversion: interfering with goods in a manner that is inconsistent with another's right to possession (see p 457)

The distinction between criminal law and civil law is further blurred by the existence of 'hybrid' offences that combine criminal and civil legal proceedings. For example, the Protection from Harassment Act 1997 provides that it is a criminal offence to act in a manner that causes another person to fear, on at least two occasions, that violence will be used against him.[4] Section 3 goes on to provide a civil remedy for victims of harassment that can result in the payment of damages or the imposition of a restraining order. Although such an order is a civil remedy, its breach will result in the commission of a criminal offence.[5]

Public law and private law

This textbook is overwhelmingly concerned with private law topics—but in order to understand what we mean by 'private law', it is important to explain how it differs

---

4. Protection from Harassment Act 1997, ss 1 and 4(1).
5. Ibid, s 3(6).

→ legal persons: persons created by the law (e.g. companies)

from public law. At its simplest level, public law concerns laws that regulate the relationship between the State and its citizens (this would include legal persons, as well as natural persons). Examples of public law topics would therefore include criminal law (the State prosecutes and punishes citizens who have breached the criminal law), human rights (persons may initiate proceedings against the State if their human rights have been breached), and administrative law (which deals with disputes between persons and government agencies).

Conversely, private law concerns laws that regulate the relationships between persons. In private law cases, the role of the State is limited to providing a forum within which to remedy disputes and the subsequent enforcement of that forum's decision. Examples of private law topics include family law (laws regulating disputes between spouses, children, etc.), contract law (laws governing the rights and obligations of contracting parties), and company law (laws governing the rights and responsibilities of directors, shareholders, etc.). Table 1.2 illustrates the significant differences between public law and private law.

TABLE 1.2 Distinguishing between public law and private law

	Public law	Private law
Regulates the relationship between	The State and persons	Persons
Purpose	Focuses on conduct that the State wishes to discourage	Focuses on enforcing the rights and obligations of persons
Case initiated by	The State	The person alleging wrongdoing
Role of the State	Undertakes responsibility for detection, prosecution, and (if relevant) punishment Also provides a forum for dispute resolution and mechanisms to enforce the forum's decisions	Limited to providing a forum for dispute resolution and enforcement of that forum's decision
Examples	Criminal law; human rights breaches; constitutional law; administrative law	Contract law; tort; company law; property law; trusts

In recent years, however, the line between public law and private law has become blurred, because the State has become increasingly involved in traditional private law disputes. For example, historically, contract law has been a quintessentially private law topic, with little, to no, State involvement. But as consumer protection became an increasing priority for governments, the State's role in contract law has grown considerably—notably, through statutory measures, such as the imposition of implied terms in consumer contracts. For example, the Sale of Goods Act 1979, s 14(2), implies a term into sale of goods contracts that provides that such goods will be of 'satisfactory quality'.

→ implied terms: terms added to the contract by the law, which usually serve to protect consumers

Common law and civil law

To understand fully the operation of the English legal system and its place within the legal systems of the world, it is necessary to understand the various meanings of the term 'common law'. Matters are complicated, however, by the fact that the phrase has three different meanings. At its broadest level, it refers to those countries around the world that have based their legal system on that of England—namely, the Commonwealth countries (notably, Australia, New Zealand, and Canada) and the USA (at both federal and state level).[6]

Juxtaposed with common law systems are civil law systems. Just as the phrase 'common law' has several different meanings, so too does the term 'civil law'. We have already noted that it can refer to laws that are not criminal in nature. A second meaning refers to those legal systems that are based largely on Roman law—especially Emperor Justinian's *Corpus Juris Civilis* ('Body of Civil Law').

The civil law system is undoubtedly the most widespread legal system in the world and is especially dominant in Continental Europe. In fact, the only common law systems in Europe belong to the UK and the Republic of Ireland. Civil law systems are characterized by a codified written body of laws that will attempt to set out the entire law in a certain area (for example, all of the crimes that may be committed may be found in a single Code).[7] Such Codes tend to be less specific and more abstract than legislation in common law systems. The reason for this is that, in civil law systems, the judiciary and the legislature appear to cooperate more harmoniously than in common law systems. Civil law judges view their role as simply interpreting the various Codes in line with the intention of the legislature and do not seek to create law. Conversely, the role of judges in common law countries tends to go beyond interpretation into law creation, and when common law judges do interpret legislation, it has not always been consistent with the legislature's intentions. Because judges in civil law countries cooperate more closely with the legislature, there is no pressing need for a system of binding precedent, and many civil law systems lack a system of precedent, although the decisions of 'higher' judges do tend to be followed.

The role of the judiciary when interpreting legislation is discussed at p 62

Table 1.3 sets out the main differences between common law and civil law systems.

Common law and statute law

The second meaning of the term 'common law' refers to the body of laws and procedures created by the judiciary and applied via the doctrine of precedent. Conversely, statute law concerns laws created by Parliament in the form of legislation. The last century has witnessed a substantial increase in the amount of legislation passed by Parliament, due largely to the increasing role played by the State in certain areas. But this legislation still needs to be interpreted and applied, and Parliament relies upon the judiciary to interpret legislation in a manner that is consistent with the intention of Parliament.

These sources of law are discussed in detail in Chapter 3

Common law and equity

The third meaning of the term 'common law' relates to the system of law that emerged following the Norman Conquest in 1066. Prior to this, England lacked a unified legal system; instead, different regions of the country had their own system of laws, based on a mixture of custom and the incorporation of laws imposed by

---

6. Except the state of Louisiana, which, being a former French and Spanish colony, has a civil law system.

7. It should, however, be noted that common law systems may also have certain areas of the law codified.

TABLE 1.3 Distinguishing between common law and civil law legal systems

	Common law system	Civil law system
Origins	The seeds of our common law tradition were sown during the Norman Conquest in 1066, but it was during the reign of Henry II that the foundations of the modern common law system were put into place	Originated in Roman law—notably, the *Corpus Juris Civilis* created by Emperor Justinian during the period AD 529–34
Location of laws	The bulk of the law is to be found in case law, but statute plays an increasing role	All laws tend to be set out in a number of written documents known as 'codes'
Role of the judiciary	It is acknowledged that judges in common law systems both interpret and create law	To interpret the law in line with the legislature's intentions and not to create law
Role of precedent	Common law systems have a well-established system of binding precedent	Civil law systems tend not to have a doctrine of binding precedent, but, in practice, the decisions of 'higher' judges are usually followed
Authority of academic writings	Rarely cited and of little weight	Not a source of law, but accorded significant weight—often greater weight than previous judicial decisions
Recruitment of judiciary	Normally recruited from ranks of legal practitioners	Civil law systems tend to have a career judiciary, who are trained to be judges straight from university

invading forces. For example, Viking invaders who had settled in northern England during the ninth century caused the northern counties of England to have a system of laws that was based heavily on Danish law.

The Norman Conquest brought about a legal revolution that paved the way for the system in place today. Although William the Conqueror is often credited with commencing the process that led to the establishment of the common law, it was actually a century later, during the reign of Henry II, that we find the genesis of our modern legal system. When Henry took the throne in 1154, there were only eighteen judges in England.[8] Five of those judges remained in Westminster and established the Court of King's Bench. The remaining judges travelled the country[9]—but applying what laws? It is generally believed that the most appropriate customs of the counties of England were selected to form the basis of a unified, national body of laws. In reality, the travelling judges applied laws that were created predominantly by the King's Bench and many local customs were replaced by a body of laws deriving from Westminster that were soon being applied throughout the country. For the first time in England's history, its people were subject to a body of laws that were common to all (hence the 'common law'). The decisions of the judges were recorded and applied in similar cases throughout the country, thereby creating the beginnings of our system of precedent.

---

8. Today, there are close to 4,000 full-time and part-time judges, and over 28,000 magistrates.
9. This system, whereby a core group of judges remained in London and the remaining judges travelled the country, was to continue for over 800 years. It was finally abolished in 1971.

But as the system grew, a number of problems began to emerge.

1. Initially, the only remedy at common law was an award of **damages**—but damages are not always an appropriate remedy. For example, imagine a landowner who is plagued by ramblers who unlawfully enter his land. In such a case, recovering damages from the ramblers would be of little use. The landowner would prefer a court order prohibiting the ramblers from entering his land—but such a remedy was not available under the common law.

➡ **damages:** an award of money designed to compensate loss

2. To commence an action in the common law courts, the claimant needed to obtain a **writ**, with different writs existing based upon the different types of case. The claimant would need to demonstrate that his case fell within the parameters of an existing writ. If it did not, he would be unable to proceed with his claim. Further, during the reign of Henry III, the passing of the Provisions of Oxford meant that new forms of writ could not be created, thereby hampering the expansion of the common law.

➡ **writ:** a written command from the court requiring either the performance of, or abstention from, an act

3. Even if the claimant could obtain a writ, the slightest defect in the writ's wording would defeat the claim.

4. The common law was a system of laws that was designed to be applied countrywide. Whilst such a broad-brush approach made the law certain, it also made it inflexible and, in a number of cases with idiosyncratic facts, following previous decisions could often lead to an unjust result.

The result was that many individuals with legitimate grievances could not obtain justice. The response was to permit individuals to petition the King directly for a remedy. As the number of such cases grew, the cases were delegated to the **Lord Chancellor** and a specific court created to hear them—the Court of Chancery. The important point to note is that these cases were not based upon obtaining writs, or following strict procedures and precedents; rather, these cases were decided based upon fairness, morality, and natural justice. For this reason, this supplementary system of law became known as 'equity'.

➡ **Lord Chancellor:** historically, the highest-ranking judge in the English legal system; no longer exercises judicial capacity following the Constitutional Reform Act 2005

In time, equity developed new remedies (notably, **injunctions** and **specific performance**) for situations in which damages were inappropriate. Crucially, however, unlike at common law, winning a case did not guarantee a remedy. Because equity was based upon fairness, the claimant would only be granted a remedy if he had acted fairly. The famous equitable maxims were developed, chief among them being 'He who comes to Equity must come with clean hands', meaning that a claimant seeking an equitable remedy must himself have behaved equitably. To ensure that the principles of equity could not be defeated by the rigidity of the common law, the courts held that where equity and the common law conflicted, equity would prevail.[10]

➡ **injunction:** a court order restraining an act, or requiring an act to be performed

➡ **specific performance:** a court order requiring performance of an act, normally to fulfil a contract

Although equity was never intended to be a rival system to the common law, in time, it came to be regarded as such. Because the common law was based upon consistency and predictability, and equity was based upon morality and flexibility, it was inevitable that conflict would arise. Further, the administrative and procedural rigidity that plagued the common law courts soon came to affect the Court of Chancery too, and equity cases soon gained a reputation for being overly lengthy and expensive. The problems largely derived from having the two systems of law being based in separate courts. Therefore, the Judicature Acts 1873–75 merged the

---

10. *Earl of Oxford's Case* (1615) 1 Rep Ch 1.

courts to create the modern court structure that we have today. The administration of the common law and equity was fused, but the systems of law themselves continued to exist separately. Any court could apply common law or equitable principles and, if a claimant had a cause of action in common law and equity, he could bring his case in a single action, as opposed to two.

Equity as a supplementary system of law is still of crucial importance. In fact, the continuing importance of the system of equity is demonstrated in that the rule that equity prevails has now been codified.[11] As time progressed, new equitable remedies have been developed, but it is still a fundamental principle that they are discretionary and the courts will not hesitate in denying a claimant with a valid claim a remedy if his conduct does not meet with equitable principles, as the following case demonstrates.

D&C Builders Ltd v Rees [1965] 3 All ER 837 (CA)

FACTS: Rees owed £482 to D&C Builders. Knowing that the company was in financial difficulty, Rees' wife offered it £300 in settlement of the debt, adding that if it refused, it would receive nothing. The company accepted, but later sued for the remaining £182. Rees' wife attempted to rely on the doctrine of promissory estoppel.

HELD: The Court of Appeal did not permit Rees to rely on the equitable doctrine of promissory estoppel, because his wife's conduct had been improper (that is, she had not come to equity with clean hands).

The doctrine of promissory estoppel is discussed at p 194

Table 1.4 clarifies the main differences between equity and the common law.

TABLE 1.4 Distinguishing the common law from equity

	Common law	Equity
Origin	Derived from the body of precedent created by circuit judges following the Norman Conquest in 1066	Derived from decisions of Lords Chancellor in cases in which the application of the common law would be unjust or common law remedies deemed inadequate
Status	A complete system of law	A supplementary system of law created to remedy the harshness of the common law, but which could not exist without the common law
Availability of a remedy	Claimant acquires a remedy as of right upon winning the case	Remedies are granted at the discretion of the court, and subject to maxims, including: 'He who comes into Equity must come with clean hands' 'Delay defeats equity' 'Equity suffers not a right without a remedy' 'Equity regards that as done which ought to be done'
Examples of remedies	Damages	Injunctions; specific performance; estoppel; rectification; rescission

---

11. Supreme Court Act 1981, s 49.

Key points summary

- The term 'common law' has three meanings:
    - a legal system that is based on the system existing in England and Wales;
    - the body of law created by the judges via case law; and
    - the body of law that operates alongside the system of equity.

- The term 'civil law' has two meanings:
    - the body of law that regulates the rights and obligations existing between individuals;
    - a system of law that is based upon Roman law and is characterized by a codified set of laws.

- Public law regulates the relationship between the State and persons. Private law regulates the relationship between persons.

- Equity is a supplementary system of law designed to mitigate against the perceived harshness of the common law.

Defining the 'English legal system'

Laws have geographical limitations. A person resident in England would not be subject to the laws of France whilst he is present in England—he is subject to the laws of what judges, academics, and practitioners universally refer to as the 'English legal system'. Those not familiar with the historical, political, and cultural factors that led to the creation of the UK could be forgiven for thinking that the laws of the English legal system apply only to those within England, but the truth is somewhat more complex, leading to the term 'English legal system' being somewhat inaccurate. Having discussed what law is and how it may be classified, it is equally important to understand to whom the laws of the English legal system apply.

Geographically, the UK[12] consists of four countries (Wales, England, Scotland, and Northern Ireland).[13] From a legal point of view, however, the United Kingdom is anything but united, with three separate legal systems existing within the UK—namely:

- the legal system of England and Wales;
- Scots law; and
- the legal system of Northern Ireland.

England and Wales

Although England and Wales may constitute two separate countries, they essentially constitute one legal system. The Law in Wales Acts 1535–42 provided that the laws of England would also apply fully in Wales, thereby legally annexing Wales

---

12. Or, to give it its full title, the 'United Kingdom of Great Britain and Northern Ireland'.

13. There is debate as to whether Wales is a country or is still regarded as a principality (that is, a state ruled by a prince). Current weight of opinion would appear to lean towards it being a country.

to England. Therefore, when we refer to the 'English legal system', we are actually discussing the laws that apply to both England *and Wales*.

Recent developments have complicated matters slightly. Although the move towards devolution in Wales has not been as pronounced as that in Scotland and Northern Ireland, significant steps have still been taken. The Government of Wales Act 1998 created the National Assembly of Wales (see Photo 1.1), but did not grant it legislative competence. This has been redressed in part by the Government of Wales Act 2006, which allows the Assembly to pass delegated legislation in relation to specified devolved areas.[14] Potentially more significant is the fact that, upon the passing of a referendum in Wales, the Assembly would gain the ability to pass primary legislation,[15] thereby bringing the Welsh Assembly onto a footing similar to that of the Scottish Parliament. The Assembly has indicated, however, that it has no current plans to hold a referendum on this issue. Therefore, for the foreseeable future, Wales will remain legally tied to England, and the term 'English legal system' will continue to refer to the system in England and Wales.[16]

➡ devolution: the transfer of power to a lower level, i.e. from central government to local government

➡ delegated legislation: legislation made by those authorized by Parliament to create legislation (subordinate legislation—of which delegated legislation is the principal form—is discussed at p 56)

PHOTO 1.1 The Welsh Assembly
Source: Matthew Dixon/iStock

---

14. Government of Wales Act 2006, Pt 3. The list of devolved matters can be found in Sch 5.
15. Ibid, Pt 4. As with delegated legislation, the ability to pass primary legislation would be limited to certain devolved areas—see Sch 7.
16. Compare TH Jones, JH Turnbull, and JM Williams, 'The Law of Wales and the Law of England and Wales?' (2005) 23 Stat LR 135, 145, arguing that it may be time to recognize formally the 'law of Wales'.

➡ primary legislation: legislation passed by Parliament in the form of an Act (Acts of Parliament are discussed further at p 55)

Scotland

Unlike Wales, which has only recently gained its own Assembly, Scotland can trace the existence of its own Parliament back to the mid-thirteenth century. Prior to the Acts of Union 1707, England and Scotland had their own Parliaments creating and administering their own laws. The 1707 Acts joined the kingdoms of Scotland and England to form the 'United Kingdom of Great Britain'. The Acts also dissolved the Parliaments of England and Scotland, and replaced them with the UK Parliament, based in Westminster. Crucially, whilst the 1707 Acts dissolved the Scottish Parliament, they preserved Scots law, with the result that, to this day, Scotland has its own legal system and set of laws. Following a referendum in Scotland in 1997, a new Scottish Parliament was created (under the Scotland Act 1998), which has the power to create legislation in certain devolved areas. Note however, that the Parliament at Westminster remains the supreme legislature in Scotland, and can pass laws that apply to Scotland with the same force of law as in England and Wales. Indeed, the presumption is that laws passed by Parliament apply throughout the UK, unless the Act itself specifies otherwise.

Northern Ireland

In 1801, the United Kingdom of Great Britain became the 'United Kingdom of Great Britain and Ireland' when the Acts of Union 1800 were passed. As with Scotland, Ireland retained its own legal system and laws, but dissatisfaction soon grew with the union and there were increasing calls for Irish independence. Following numerous failures to achieve Home Rule, the Government of Ireland Act 1920 was eventually passed, which split Ireland into two distinct regions: six predominantly Protestant counties became Northern Ireland, and the remaining twenty-six predominantly Catholic counties became Southern Ireland. Whilst Northern Ireland became a fully functioning region with its own Parliament and executive, in Southern Ireland, no government was ever established and its Parliament never passed any laws, with the result that whilst Southern Ireland may have existed *de jure*, it never really existed *de facto*.

➡ Home Rule: the granting of independence or self-government to a constituent part of a state or country

➡ *de jure*: 'in law'
➡ *de facto*: 'in fact'

The passing of the Anglo-Irish Treaty 1921 created an independent Irish republic, although the Parliament of Northern Ireland exercised its treaty right to opt out of the republic and remain part of the UK, thereby creating the current United Kingdom of Great Britain and Northern Ireland.

The Government of Ireland Act 1920 was eventually repealed by the Northern Ireland Act 1998, which provided for a process of devolution in Northern Ireland similar to that in Scotland. The Northern Ireland Assembly, like the Welsh Assembly and the Scottish Parliament, has the power to legislate in certain devolved areas.

Key points summary

- The UK consists of three legal systems:
  - England and Wales;
  - Scotland; and
  - Northern Ireland.

- The phrase 'English legal system' really means the legal system of England and Wales.

- Wales, Scotland, and Northern Ireland all have their own bodies with various legislative powers, but the Parliament at Westminster retains legislative supremacy.

- Legislation created by the Westminster Parliament will apply throughout the UK, unless such legislation expressly states otherwise.

Chapter conclusion

A sound understanding of what is law is fundamental to understanding the legal topics that will be discussed throughout this text. It may be thought that much that was discussed in this chapter is of limited relevance to those seeking to understand the laws that regulate businesses, but this is not the case. For example, in an era dominated by increasing globalization and the prevalence of multinational corporations, many businesses will operate in, or import or export goods to, countries all around the world. In such cases, understanding the geographical limitations of a country's legal system is crucial.

Having discussed in this chapter what law is, how it is classified, and its geographical extent, the next chapter moves on to discuss the practical issue of how the law is administered, by discussing those persons and bodies that are responsible for applying, interpreting, and debating what the law is, and how their decisions are put into practice.

Self-test questions

1. Define the following:
   (a) positivism;
   (b) common law;
   (c) civil law;
   (d) equity;
   (e) public law;
   (f) private law;
   (g) devolution.

2. Explain and critically evaluate natural law theory. Does legal positivism provide a more attractive definition of what law is and, if so, why?

3. Parliament passes the (fictional) Punishment of Terrorists Act 2009. Section 10 of the Act allows suspected members of Al Qaeda to be detained, questioned, and executed without charge or trial. How would a natural lawyer and a legal positivist view the Act?

4. What are the three domestic legal systems operating in the UK?

5. TeleBuild plc manufactures flat-screen televisions. Although TeleBuild is based in England, it exports all of the televisions that it manufactures to India. The televisions are built in an unsatisfactory manner and do not comply with the standards laid down by English product safety law, although they do comply with Indian product safety law. A hotel in New Delhi purchases several televisions from TeleBuild. John, an English holidaymaker staying in the hotel, is electrocuted by the television and sustains severe burns on his hand. Advise John.

Further reading

Gillespie, A, *The English Legal System* (2nd edn, OUP, Oxford, 2009) ch 1
Provides a clear and lucid account of what is the 'English legal system', focusing on the meaning of the words 'English', 'legal', and 'system'

Jones, TH, Turnbull, JH, and Williams, JM, 'The Law of Wales and the Law of England and Wales?' (2005) 23 Stat LR 135
Discusses how statutes that apply only to Wales can be reconciled with the notion that England and Wales comprise a unified legal system and contends that the time may be right to recognize the 'law of Wales'

Mcleod, I, *Legal Theory* (4th edn, Palgrave, Basingstoke, 2007) chs 3 and 4
Provides a clear and well-structured discussion regarding the basics of natural law and legal positivism

Slapper, G, and Kelly, D, *The English Legal System* (10th edn, Routledge, Oxford, 2009) ch 1
Contains a particularly clear discussion of how the law is classified

Websites

<http://new.wales.gov.uk>
The website of the Welsh Assembly government

<http://www.niassembly.gov.uk>
The website of the Northern Ireland Assembly

<http://www.scottish.parliament.uk>
The website of the Scottish Parliament

 Remember to visit the **Online Resource Centre** at **<http://www.oxfordtextbooks.co.uk/roach>** to access the following resources for Chapter 1, 'What is law?': more **practice questions** and answers; a **glossary** of key terms; **multiple-choice questions**; **revision summaries**; and **audio updates** when relevant.

2 The administration of the law

- The courts
- Tribunals
- Alternative dispute resolution
- The legal profession

INTRODUCTION

Laws can only be as effective as the mechanisms put in place to administer them. We saw, in the previous chapter, that Hart argued that an effective legal system needs primary rules and secondary rules—but, in reality, it could be argued that much more is required. Courts are required to adjudicate on disputes that arise—but what should the jurisdiction and function of these courts be? Where should these courts be located? The decisions of lower courts may need to be re-examined, thereby requiring that a robust appeals process exists. We need to establish a system of legal representation for defendants and claimants. It can therefore be seen that the administration of the law is an extremely complex issue. In this chapter, we will aim to clarify how—and by whom—the law is administered.

The courts

An understanding of the functions, jurisdiction, and composition of the various courts is vital in order to appreciate the operation of the English legal system (especially in relation to the doctrine of precedent, which is discussed in the next chapter). Some courts hear only civil cases; others hear only criminal cases; some will hear both. Certain courts are largely courts of **first instance**, whereas others will only hear **appeals**. It is crucial to understand which types of case the various courts will hear and how a case can proceed through the court hierarchy. Figures 2.1 and 2.2 help to explain the court hierarchy and the appeal routes through the courts: Figure 2.1 focuses on criminal cases; Figure 2.2 focuses on civil cases.

➜ **first instance:** cases tried for the first time are said to be heard 'at first instance'

➜ **appeals:** the process whereby a losing party, seeking to reverse or modify a first-instance decision, may apply to have the case reheard on certain grounds

Magistrates' courts

The 330 magistrates' courts throughout England and Wales are predominantly courts of first instance, and have both a criminal and civil jurisdiction. Whereas all other courts are composed of professional, legally qualified, judges, the vast majority[1]

---

1. There are approximately 140 professional district judges and 170 deputy district judges who also hear cases in magistrates' courts.

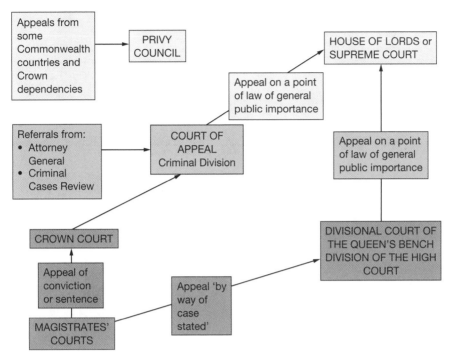

FIGURE 2.1 The structure of the criminal courts

of the 28,000 or so magistrates—or 'Justices of the Peace' (JP), to give them their correct title—are usually laypersons with no legal qualifications. In this sense, the English legal system is unique: no other country in the world has such a high proportion of criminal cases decided by laypersons. The rationale behind putting laypersons on the bench is the same as that behind the use of the jury: it allows everyday members of the community to become involved in the justice system and reinforces the notion of a participatory democracy. Magistrates usually hear cases in benches of three, with a legally qualified clerk present to provide advice when needed. District judges will sit on their own. Magistrates receive an allowance for expenses and loss of earnings, but are otherwise unpaid, resulting in the system being relatively cheap. In 2003–04, the total expenses for all magistrates amounted to £15 million (which equates to about £500 each).[2] Interestingly, because district judges are, at the time of writing, paid £102,921 per year, their remuneration amounts to almost as much as the total expenses of their 30,000 lay colleagues. But such a comparison may be unfair, because research has indicated that one district judge can handle the annual workload of thirty magistrates.[3]

Anyone between the ages of 18 and 70 years old may apply to be a magistrate, although, in practice, anyone over the age of 65 will not usually be appointed. The

---

2. Hansard HC, vol 425, col WA773W (20 October 2004).

3. R Morgan and N Russell, *The Judiciary in the Magistrates' Courts* (Home Office RDS Occasional Paper No 66, HMSO, London, 2000) [6.1.3].

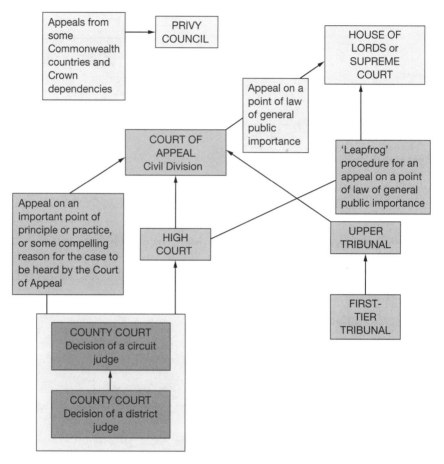

FIGURE 2.2 The structure of the civil courts and tribunals

Lord Chancellor appoints magistrates in the name of the monarch. In the future, however, it is anticipated that the Judicial Appointments Commission (JAC) will undertake the appointment of magistrates.

The JAC was the third major reform contained in the Constitutional Reform Act 2005 (alongside the reform of the office of Lord Chancellor and the creation of the Supreme Court). Traditionally, a group within the Lord Chancellor's Department called the 'Judicial Group' carried out judicial appointments. The process for appointment was secretive: objective criteria for appointment did not exist and there was suspicion that an 'old boys' network was in place. The first step to remedy this occurred in 2001 when the government established the Commission for Judicial Appointments—a body that exercised only an advisory and supervisory function, and which was not actually involved in the appointments process. Accordingly, the government indicated its intention to establish a more powerful body that would have a direct role in judicial appointments.[4] The

---

4. Department of Constitutional Affairs, *Constitutional Reform: A New Way of Appointing Judges* (CP 10/03, HMSO, London, 2003).

2005 Act thereby created the JAC, which began work on the 3 April 2006. The JAC comprises six lay members, five judges, one barrister, one solicitor, a tribunal member, and a magistrate.[5] It is worth noting that the chair of the JAC must be one of the lay members.

The process for appointment depends upon the rank of judge. For puisne judges and below, the JAC will recommend a single candidate to the Lord Chancellor.[6] The Lord Chancellor can then accept the candidate, reject the candidate, or ask the JAC to reconsider its choice of candidate.[7] The Lord Chancellor has the right to reject a candidate once and to request the JAC to reconsider its selection once.[8] After this, the Lord Chancellor must accept a recommended candidate. If asked to reconsider its selection, the JAC may recommend the same candidate again,[9] but cannot recommend the same candidate if the Lord Chancellor has made a rejection.[10] The result of these rules is that the JAC will never have to recommend more than three candidates and that one of its chosen candidates will have to be accepted.

To combat the middle-class domination of the bench, vacancies in the magistrates' courts are advertised widely, including in newspapers such as *The Sun* and even magazines such as *Inside Soap*. Magistrates are required to retire at the age of 70, but may be removed prior to retirement on a number of grounds, including incapacity and misbehaviour.[11]

Visit the Online Resource Centre for the discussion box 'Replacing lay persons with professional judges'

Criminal jurisdiction

The vast majority of cases heard by magistrates are criminal cases—in fact, over 95 per cent of all criminal cases commence in magistrates' courts and, in 2007, an estimated 1.7 million defendants were proceeded against.[12]

All criminal cases can be divided into one of three types:

1. *Summary offences*   Ninety-eight per cent of all criminal cases relate to summary offences that must be tried in a magistrates' court. Summary offences tend to be the more minor criminal offences and this is reflected in the magistrates' limited sentencing powers. Currently, the magistrates' sentencing powers are limited to six months for one offence, and twelve months for two or more offences to be served consecutively (if those offences are either-way offences).[13] The maximum fine that can be imposed in a magistrates' court is a Level 5 fine (currently £5,000),[14] although in the case of certain offences committed by businesses, the maximum fine is £20,000.

2. *Offences triable on indictment only*   Indictable offences are more serious and cannot be heard in a magistrates' court. In such cases, the case may still commence in a magistrates' court, but the magistrates will have no option but to send the case to the Crown Court for trial.

indictment: a formal document setting out charges against the defendant

5. Constitutional Reform Act 2005, Sch 12, Pt 1.   6. Ibid, ss 88 and 89.

7. Ibid, s 90(2).   8. Ibid, s 90(2) and (3).

9. Ibid, s 92(3)(a).   10. Ibid, s 92(2)(a).

11. Criminal Justice Act 2003, s 168(1)(b).

12. Ministry of Justice, *Judicial and Court Statistics 2007* (Cm 7467, HMSO, London, 2008) 137.

13. The Criminal Justice Act 2003, ss 154–155, increased the sentencing powers of magistrates to fifty-one weeks for one offence and sixty-five weeks for two or more offences, to be served consecutively. These sections are yet to come into force and have been suspended indefinitely.

14. Criminal Justice Act 1982, s 37.

3. *Offences triable either way* These are offences that are triable either summarily in a magistrates' court or on indictment in the Crown Court. A strict procedure is in place[15] to determine the most appropriate venue and failure to adhere to the procedure could cause the decision to be declared **ultra vires** and quashed. The procedure is as illustrated in Figure 2.3.

➡ ultra vires: acting 'beyond one's powers'

The above procedures generally apply to defendants aged 18 or over. Where the defendant is aged 10 or over,[16] but under the age of 18, he will normally be tried—irrespective of whether the offence is summary, indictable,[17] or either way—by a panel of magistrates constituted as a youth court (formerly known as a 'juvenile court'). The procedures in a youth court are much less formal than in a standard magistrates' court. Whereas cases in a standard magistrates' court are open to the public, only specified persons may be present at a youth court.[18] The name, address, or school of the defendant may not be reported, nor can a picture of the defendant be published.[19]

Defendants convicted in a magistrates' court have a number of possible avenues of appeal. All defendants have the right to appeal either their conviction or sentence (or both) to the Crown Court. If their appeal fails, however, it is possible that their sentence might actually be increased. In cases in which either party feels that the magistrates were wrong in law or exceeded their jurisdiction, an appeal may lie 'by way of case stated' to the Divisional Court of the Queen's Bench Division of the High Court.

Civil jurisdiction

A magistrates' court also has a limited, but nonetheless significant, civil jurisdiction in the following cases.

➡ inter alia: 'amongst others'

- *Family proceedings* Sitting as a 'family proceedings court', the magistrates have an extensive jurisdiction in relation to family law cases. This could include, inter alia, determining maintenance payments through making contribution orders, making protection orders in cases of domestic violence, and the making of numerous court orders in relation to the care of children.[20]

- *Debt recovery* The court will enforce measures designed to collect unpaid Council Tax, as well as unpaid gas, water, and electricity bills.

- *Licensing* The responsibility for licensing entertainment and gambling establishments is placed upon local authorities,[21] but the decision of the local authority can be appealed to a magistrates' court.[22]

The decisions of magistrates in relation to family proceedings can be appealed to the Divisional Court of the Family Division of the High Court.

---

15. This procedure can be found in the Magistrates' Courts Act 1980, ss 17A–21.

16. The defence of *doli incapax* ('incapable of crime') is extended to all children under the age of 10 by virtue of the Children and Young Persons Act 1933, s 50.

17. Except in the case of homicide, in which the defendant must be tried on indictment.

18. Children and Young Persons Act 1933, s 47(2), stipulates such persons as the officers of the court, the parties, and their legal representatives, witnesses, bona fide members of the press, and any other person that the court authorizes to be present.

19. Ibid, s 49(1).

20. For a list of family proceedings that must be commenced in a magistrates' court, see the Allocation and Transfer of Proceedings Order 2008, SI 2008/2836, art 5.

21. Licensing Act 2003, s 3; Gambling Act 2005, s 2.

22. Licensing Act 2003, s 181; Gambling Act 2005, s 207.

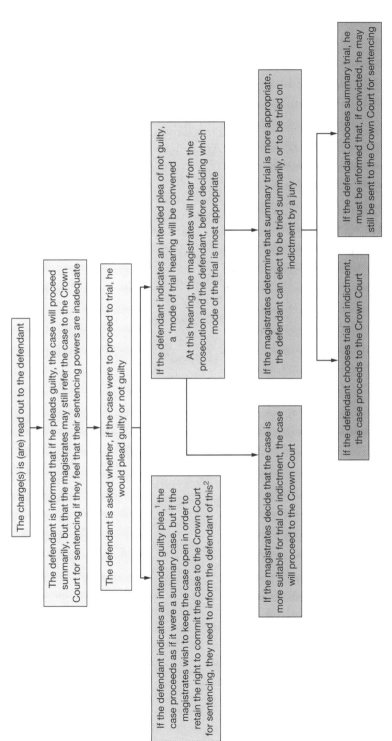

The charge(s) is (are) read out to the defendant

The defendant is informed that if he pleads guilty, the case will proceed summarily, but that the magistrates may still refer the case to the Crown Court for sentencing if they feel that their sentencing powers are inadequate

The defendant is asked whether, if the case were to proceed to trial, he would plead guilty or not guilty

If the defendant indicates an intended guilty plea,[1] the case proceeds as if it were a summary case, but if the magistrates wish to keep the case open in order to retain the right to commit the case to the Crown Court for sentencing, they need to inform the defendant of this[2]

If the defendant indicates an intended plea of not guilty, a 'mode of trial hearing will be convened

At this hearing, the magistrates will hear from the prosecution and the defendant, before deciding which mode of the trial is most appropriate

If the magistrates decide that the case is more suitable for trial on indictment, the case will proceed to the Crown Court

If the magistrates determine that summary trial is more appropriate, the defendant can elect to be tried summarily, or to be tried on indictment by a jury

If the defendant chooses trial on indictment, the case proceeds to the Crown Court

If the defendant chooses summary trial, he must be informed that, if convicted, he may still be sent to the Crown Court for sentencing

[1] The Court of Appeal has indicated that defendants who plead guilty at this stage should receive the maximum discount—see *R v Barber* [2001] EWCA Civ 2267, [2002] Cr App (S) 548

[2] *R v Wirral Magistrates Court, ex p Jermyn* [2001] Crim LR 45 (DC)

FIGURE 2.3 Offences triable either way

The Crown Court

The Courts Act 1971 introduced the Crown Court system to replace the inefficient system of assize courts and quarter sessions. It is often stated that there are a number of crown courts around the country, but this is not strictly true. There is only one Crown Court—but its business may be conducted anywhere in England and Wales.[23] Currently, the Crown Court sits in ninety-two locations throughout England and Wales, and, in 2007, it held 82,721 trials.[24] The Crown Court is a court of almost exclusive criminal jurisdiction, holding trials for all indictable offences[25] and those either way offences that have been sent to the Crown Court for trial. The Crown Court will also deal with either way cases that have been determined in a magistrates' court, but then sent for sentence to the Crown Court due to the limited sentencing powers of the magistrates. The Crown Court also hears appeals from those summarily convicted in a magistrates' court. These appeals involve a complete rehearing of the case, and if the appeal is dismissed, the judge may impose any sentence that the magistrates could have imposed, in addition to a harsher sentence than the one originally imposed.

Cases in the Crown Court normally take place in front of a single judge and a jury of twelve—but a jury is not used:

- where the defendant pleads guilty;
- in appeal cases; and
- where the case has been sent to the Crown Court for sentence.

The judge involved will depend upon the class of the crime, as illustrated in Table 2.1.[26]

A decision of the Crown Court heard on appeal from a magistrates' court can be appealed to the High Court. Appeals against a conviction or sentence of the Crown Court are made to the Criminal Division of the Court of Appeal. The right of appeal is not automatic: leave to appeal is required and this can either be obtained from the trial judge or from the Court of Appeal itself.[27] Clearly, it would be odd for a trial judge to declare a case fit for appeal as soon as it has been decided. Accordingly, the Court of Appeal has stated that leave to appeal should only be granted by the trial judge in exceptional circumstances.[28]

Trial by jury

In practice, the role of the jury forms a minor part of the English legal system. As noted, 95 per cent of criminal trials are heard in magistrates' courts and, of the remaining 5 per cent that are heard in the Crown Court, the majority of defendants will plead 'guilty' and no jury will be required. The result is that juries decide less than 1 per cent of criminal cases. In relation to civil cases, trial by jury is becoming increasingly obsolete. But despite the practical limitations of the jury, it is still

---

23. Supreme Court Act 1981, s 78(1).
24. Secretary of State for Justice, *Judicial and Court Statistics 2007* (Cm 7464, HMSO, London, 2008) 103.
25. Supreme Court Act 1981, s 46.
26. The full list of crimes and their corresponding classes can be found in the *Consolidated Criminal Practice Direction* [21.1].
27. Criminal Appeal Act 1968, s 1(2).   28. *R v Bansal* [1999] Crim LR 484 (CA).

TABLE 2.1 The classification and allocation of cases

Class of offence	Examples	Heard by
Class 1	• Treason • Murder • Offences under the War Crimes Act 1991 • Torture • Infanticide and child destruction • Manslaughter	Almost always heard by a High Court judge, but can also be released to a circuit judge who has been authorized by the Lord Chief Justice to hear Class 1 cases
Class 2	• Rape • Rape/sexual intercourse/incest with a girl under the age of 13 • Inducement to procure sexual activity with a mentally disordered person	Usually heard by a High Court judge, but can also be released to a circuit judge who has been authorized by the Lord Chief Justice to hear Class 2 cases
Class 3	• All other offences not listed in Class 1 or 2	Will be tried by a circuit judge, recorder, or assistant recorder (High Court judges can act in a Class 3 case, but this is rare)

regarded as symbolically fundamental. Lord Devlin famously described jury service as 'the lamp that shows freedom lives'[29] and Lord Denning stated that jury service gives 'ordinary folk their finest lesson in citizenship'.[30]

It is argued that juries add certainty to the law—their decisions are not open to dispute, because they provide no reasons for the verdict that they deliver:[31] they simply find the accused 'guilty' or 'not guilty'.[32] It follows that, because juries do not have to justify their verdict, they are free to decide a case based on any factors they wish, including their own personal beliefs or the dictates of their conscience. They may even ignore the law completely and deliver a verdict contrary to that required by the law.

The extent to which this ability to depart from the law and base a verdict on conscience is beneficial or detrimental has been a matter of substantial academic debate. Some regard the ability of the jury to depart from the law as a fundamental ingredient in the pursuit of justice.[33] Others argue that it demonstrates a lack of

---

29. Lord Devlin, *Trial by Jury* (Steven & Sons, London, 1956) 164.

30. Lord Denning, *What Next in the Law?* (Butterworths, London, 1982) 33.

31. In fact, jurors who disclose their reasoning will be held in contempt of court (Contempt of Court Act 1981, s 8), as will any newspaper that publishes such disclosures: *Attorney General v Associated Newspapers* [1994] 2 WLR 227 (HL).

32. It could be legitimately argued that convicting a defendant without justifying the decision is a breach of the defendant's right to a fair trial under the European Convention on Human Rights, Art 6. To date, this issue has not arisen before the courts.

33. See Lord Devlin, *Trial by Jury* (Steven & Sons, London, 1956) 160, who argues that the ability to act on conscience ensures 'that the criminal law will conform to the ordinary man's idea of what is fair and just'.

competence[34] on the part of the jury and constitutes a 'blatant affront to the legal process'.[35]

Below are several infamous cases in which the jury clearly decided the case based upon its conscience; whether their verdicts could be regarded as just or perverse is very much a matter of personal opinion. Would you have decided differently to the jury?

R v Owen, The Times 12 December 1991

FACTS: Owen's son was run over and killed by a drink-driver. The driver had prior convictions for drink-driving and had never taken a driving test. At the trial, he showed no remorse for his actions, and was duly convicted of drink-driving and sentenced to eighteen months' imprisonment. Upon his release, he continued to drive unlawfully. Feeling that justice had not been done, Owen located the driver and shot him with a shotgun, severely injuring him.

HELD: Despite the substantial amount of evidence against him, the jury acquitted Owen of attempted murder.

R v Ponting [1985] Crim LR 318

FACTS: Ponting was a senior civil servant at the Ministry of Defence. He passed two confidential documents to a member of Parliament (MP) in contravention of the Official Secrets Act 1911, s 2. The MP, in turn, passed them on to a national newspaper and they were published. The documents indicated that the government had lied to the public in relation to the sinking of the ship *General Belgrano* during the Falklands War.[36] Ponting admitted handing over the documents, but argued that his actions were in the public interest.

HELD: Despite a direction from the judge indicating that the government was to decide what was in the public interest, the jury acquitted Ponting.

County courts

The majority of cases involving businesses will be heard in a county court. These courts were first established by the County Courts Act 1846 and were designed to provide a forum for the resolving of minor civil cases—especially the recovery of small debts. Today, the 218 county courts in England and Wales still exercise an exclusively civil jurisdiction, and hear the vast majority of non-family civil claims

---

34. An often-cited case backing up this contention is *R v Young* [1995] QB 324 (CA), in which a murder case had to be retried following revelations that the jury based its decision to convict on answers that it received from the deceased via the use of a Ouija board.

35. Lord Justice Auld, *Review of the Criminal Courts of England and Wales* (HMSO, London, 2001) [105].

36. The Argentine warship *General Belgrano* was sunk in 1982 by the British submarine *HMS Conqueror*, with the loss of 323 lives. A 200-mile exclusion zone had been established and any Argentine ship found within it would be attacked. The *Belgrano* was not within the exclusion zone, but the then Prime Minister Margaret Thatcher authorized the attack on the ground that the ship was sailing towards the Royal Navy taskforce, presumably intending to attack. The documents leaked by Ponting revealed that the *Belgrano* was actually moving *away* from the taskforce when it was attacked and sunk.

(in 2007, just over two million non-family civil cases were commenced in county courts).[37] Cases are heard by circuit judges and district judges, with the former hearing more complex cases or cases worth more than £15,000.

The types of case that may be heard in a county court are set out in statute and includes the following.

- *Actions in contract and tort*[38] All small claims and fast-track cases, and certain multi-track cases in contract and tort, will be heard by county courts. The majority of actions in a county court involve contractual and tortious issues. But certain tortious cases (for example, defamation) will not be heard in a county court and will instead by heard in the High Court.

- *Equity proceedings* Equity cases (such as the granting of specific performance, the administration of a deceased person's estate, and the dissolution of a partnership), in which the value of the property is below £30,000, will be heard in a county court.[39]

- *Contentious probate* County courts will hear contentious cases in relation to wills and the administration of estates, provided that the value of the estate does not exceed £30,000.[40]

- *Family proceedings* County courts designated as 'divorce courts' may hear cases relating to divorce, nullity of marriage, or judicial separation,[41] and any accompanying custody issues. County courts designated as 'civil partnership proceeding county courts' may hear any civil partnership cases.[42]

- *Bankruptcy* Only those county courts granted a bankruptcy jurisdiction may hear bankruptcy cases, but their jurisdiction is not limited in amount.[43]

- *Patents* Courts designated as 'patents county courts' may hear smaller, and less complex, patent and design cases.[44]

The division of work between the county courts and the High Court

Over the last twenty years, the division of work between the county courts and the High Court has altered radically. The first major reform came with the passing of the Courts and Legal Services Act 1990, which aimed to transfer a significant number of cases being heard in the High Court to the county courts. The Act allowed the Lord Chancellor to pass delegated legislation that determined the allocation of cases between the county courts and the High Court. A year later, such legislation was passed and provided that a case may only be commenced in the High Court if its financial value was over £15,000, except for personal injury claims, which would need to be over £50,000.[45] The reforms quickly had the desired effect. In 1990–91, 1,828 trials resulting in awards of £25,000 or less were heard in the Queen's Bench Division. Three years later, this had fallen to 346 trials.[46] The civil justice system overall, however, was still extremely inefficient and cumbersome, with one report stating that 'expense is often

---

37. Secretary of State for Justice, *Judicial and Court Statistics 2007* (Cm 7464, HMSO, London, 2008) 54.

38. County Courts Act 1984, s 15.   39. Ibid, s 23.

40. Ibid, s 32.   41. Matrimonial and Family Proceedings Act 1984, s 33.

42. County Courts Act 1984, s 36A.   43. Civil Courts Order 1983, SI 1983/713, art 9.

44. Copyright, Designs and Patents Act 1988, s 287. The Patents Court, which is part of the Chancery Division of the High Court, will hear larger, more complex cases.

45. High Court and County Courts Jurisdiction Order 1991, SI 1991/724, arts 4A and 5.

46. Lord Chancellor's Department, *Court Service Annual Report 1993–94* (HC 568, HMSO, London, 1993–94) 49.

excessive, disproportionate and unpredictable; and delay is frequently unreasonable'.[47] The result was a review of the civil justice system by Lord Woolf, whose final report[48] advocated a raft of reforms, almost all of which were implemented.

In terms of the allocation of cases, by far the most significant reform was the introduction of the track system, whereby all civil cases would be allocated to one of three tracks, as follows.

1. *Small claims* Any claim for less than £5,000 will be allocated to the small claims track and will be heard in a county court. There are several exceptions to this—namely:
   - personal injury claims in which the claim for pain and suffering or loss of amenity does exceed £1,000, and the full value of the claim does not exceed £5,000; and
   - claims against landlords requiring repairs costing over £1,000.[49]

2. *Fast track* Any claim for more than £5,000, but less than £15,000, will be allocated to the fast track, unless the trial is expected to last longer than one day, or substantial amounts of oral evidence are likely to be presented.[50] Fast-track cases should be completed within thirty weeks of allocation and the trial should last no more than one day. The majority of fast-track claims will be heard in a county court.

3. *Multi-track* A case that does not fit into either of the above tracks will be allocated to the multi-track.[51] These will be cases of higher complexity and/or value, and will generally be heard in the High Court. Personal injury cases worth less than £50,000 will be heard in a county court. Procedures will be considerably more flexible than for the previous tracks, because cases could involve any sum over £15,000: a case involving sums of £15,500 will need to be handled very differently from a case worth £15.5 million.

Appeals routes from the county courts depend upon the presiding judge. If a district judge heard the case, an appeal will remain in a county court, but will be heard by a circuit judge. Decisions of circuit judges may be appealed to the High Court. An exception to this occurs where the appeal raises important points of principle or practice, or there is some compelling reason why it should be heard by the Court of Appeal: in such cases, decisions of a county court can be appealed directly to the Civil Division of the Court of Appeal.[52] Permission to appeal is normally required.[53]

The High Court of Justice

The High Court was created by the Judicature Acts 1873–75 and consists of three divisions—namely, the Chancery Division, the Queen's Bench Division, and the Family Division. Each division has a substantial first-instance jurisdiction, as well as an appellate role via two judges sitting as a Divisional Court (in some cases, a single judge can sit as a Divisional Court). Finally, a number of specialist courts exist within the various divisions. The High Court has an unlimited civil jurisdiction, and the Queen's Bench Division also has an important criminal jurisdiction and supervisory

---

47. Lord Woolf, *Interim Report on Access to Justice* (HMSO, London, 1995) 7.
48. Lord Woolf, *Final Report on Access to Justice* (HMSO, London, 1996).
49. Civil Procedure Rules, Pts 26.6(1) and 27. 50. Ibid, Pts 26.6(4)–(5) and 28.
51. Ibid, Pts 26.6(6) and 29. 52. Ibid, Pt 52.14.
53. Ibid, Pt 52.3.

PHOTO 2.1 The Royal Courts of Justice
Source: Tony Bagget/Stockxpert

jurisdiction. Cases in the High Court are normally heard by a single High Court judge, known as a 'puisne' (pronounced 'puny', meaning 'lesser') judge.

The High Court is based at the Royal Courts of Justice in London (see Photo 2.1), but it can also sit at twenty-seven centres based in provincial towns and cities throughout England and Wales.

The Chancery Division

The senior division of the High Court is the Chancery Division, which currently consists of the Chancellor of the High Court[54] and eighteen High Court judges. Like all divisions of the High Court, the jurisdiction of the Chancery Division can be found in the Supreme Court Act 1981, Sch 1, and includes:

- the sale, exchange, or partition of land, or the raising of charges on land;
- the redemption or foreclosure of mortgages;
- the execution of trusts;
- the administration of the estates of deceased persons;
- bankruptcy; and
- the dissolution of partnerships, or the taking of partnership or other accounts.

---

54. The Chancellor of the High Court was formerly known as the 'Vice-Chancellor', but following the passing of the Constitutional Reform Act 2005 and the removal of the Lord Chancellor as head of the Chancery Division, the office of Vice-Chancellor had to be replaced.

In addition, there is a specialist Patents Court that settles disputes relating to patents and designs, and a Companies Court that deals with certain corporate matters—notably, liquidation. Judges sitting as the Chancery Divisional Court can hear appeals from circuit judges in county courts on matters such as bankruptcy, and will hear appeals from Her Majesty's Commissioners of Revenue and Customs (HMRC) on income tax disputes. The Chancery Division hears cases not only in London, but also in eight designated provincial High Court centres around the country.

The Queen's Bench Division

The largest division of the High Court is the Queen's Bench Division (QBD, which becomes the King's Bench Division, or KBD, when a male is monarch) and comprises the President of the Queen's Bench,[55] the Vice-President, and sixty-nine High Court judges. Its jurisdiction can be divided into four sections, as follows.

1. *First-instance civil jurisdiction* A judge of the QBD will hear a large number of first-instance common law civil claims, predominantly in contract and tort. The Commercial Court—a specialist court that exists within the QBD, which is discussed in more detail below—will hear commercial cases. Similarly, disputes involving ships and aircraft will be heard by the Admiralty Court, and disputes involving building, construction, computers, and software will be heard by the Technology and Construction Court.

2. *Appellate civil jurisdiction* A judge of the QBD will hear appeals from the decisions of circuit judges in the county courts.

3. *Appellate criminal jurisdiction* The QBD will hear appeals on points of law or jurisdiction by way of case stated from magistrates' courts. It will also hear appeals on points of law or jurisdiction from decisions of the Crown Court, except in relation to cases tried on indictment.

4. *Judicial review* A single judge sitting as an Administrative Court can hear cases relating to alleged ultra vires acts committed by magistrates' courts, the Crown Court (except in relation to matters concerning trial on indictment), county courts, public bodies (for example, local authorities), and individuals such as police officers and government ministers. The court may issue:

   (a) a quashing order, which will nullify any ultra vires decision;

   (b) a mandatory order, which will compel the defendant to do something; or

   (c) a prohibition order, which will require the defendant to refrain from doing something in the future.

As noted, several specialist courts exist within the QBD, of which particular mention should be made of the Commercial Court. The Commercial Court was formed in 1970,[56] although its origins can be traced back to a Commercial List that was established in 1895. The Commercial Court currently consists of around fourteen nominated judges, and hears cases relating to both national and international business disputes, with specific emphasis on cases involving international trade, banking, and arbitration disputes. The procedures[57] of the Commercial Court tend to be more flexible than those of the High Court generally (for example, many of the rules relating to case management in the

---

55. Like the Chancellor of the High Court, the post of 'President of the Queen's Bench' was also created by the Constitutional Reform Act 2005. Prior to 2005, the Lord Chief Justice was head of the QBD.
56. Administration of Justice Act 1970, s 3(1).
57. The procedural rules of the Commercial Court can be found in the Civil Procedure Rules, Pt 58.

High Court[58] do not apply to the Commercial Court).[59] The work of the Commercial Court is often extremely complex, with around 80 per cent of cases involving a claimant or defendant that derives from outside the jurisdiction of the Court.[60] That many parties choose to resolve their dispute in the Commercial Court is a testament to how highly the Court is regarded worldwide. Accordingly, it is inundated with work, which provides another reason why it is granted its own more flexible rules of procedure. To alleviate the workload, the Civil Procedure Rules provide that less complex commercial cases can be dealt with in a Mercantile Court. The London Mercantile Court operates within the structure of the Commercial Court, and to spare the cost and inconvenience of travelling to London, Mercantile Courts may also sit in seven other locations around England and Wales.[61] Mercantile Court cases are heard by mercantile judges, who are specialist circuit judges authorized to sit in a Mercantile Court.

The Family Division

The Family Division was created by the Administration of Justice Act 1970 and consists of the President, nineteen High Court judges, and around twenty district judges. Its jurisdiction is entirely civil, and will hear first-instance cases involving matrimonial matters, cases involving the legitimacy, custody, and maintenance of children, adoption cases, and cases concerning the exclusion of a violent spouse. In addition, the Divisional Court (or, in some cases, a single judge) will hear appeals from magistrates' courts and from circuit judges in county courts on family issues.

Jury trial in civil cases

The decline of trial by jury is evidenced starkly in relation to civil cases, where jury trial has been abolished in all but a handful of case types. Prior to 1854, virtually all civil trials would have been conducted in front of a jury, but the Common Law Procedure Act 1854 began a lengthy process that has all but eradicated the use of juries in civil trials. Today, the role of the jury in civil trials taking place in the QBD is governed by the Supreme Court Act 1981, s 69, which provides for a qualified right to hear a case before a jury and also provides the court with a discretion to order a jury trial in certain cases.

Section 69(1) provides that there exists a qualified right to trial by jury in cases concerning fraud, libel, slander, malicious prosecution, and false imprisonment. Because this is a qualified right, however, it is subject to a limitation—namely, that the court will not order a jury trial where the case involves 'a prolonged examination of documents or accounts or any scientific or local examination which cannot conveniently be made with a jury'.[62] In practice, the only substantial use of juries in civil cases is in relation to defamation cases and, as we shall see below, recommendations have been made to limit the use of juries in such cases.

➜ defamation: a statement that lowers the claimant in the estimation of right-thinking members of society generally, or which would tend to make them shun or avoid him (see p 487)

58. These can be found in the Civil Procedure Rules, Pts 26 and 29.
59. Ibid, r 58.13.
60. Judiciary of England and Wales, *Report of the Commercial Court and Admiralty Court 2005–06* (2006) 2, available online at <http://www.hmcourts-service.gov.uk>.
61. Birmingham, Bristol, Cardiff, Chester, Leeds, Liverpool, and Manchester.
62. Supreme Court Act 1981, s 69(1).

In all other civil cases, there is a presumption against trial by jury, but the court has discretion to grant a jury trial.[63] But whilst this discretion might once have been unlimited,[64] today, it is heavily restricted and is used exceptionally. In *Ward v James*,[65] the Court of Appeal stated that, unless special circumstances were present, juries should not be used in personal injury cases. The Court's advice has been followed: since *Ward*, only one reported personal injury case has involved a jury.[66]

The final point to note is that juries in civil trials not only determine the victor, but also the level of damages to be awarded. This has proved to be extremely controversial, especially in defamation cases, in which juries have awarded excessive damages. For example, in 1990, the jury awarded £600,000 in damages to the defamed wife of Peter Sutcliffe, the serial killer known as the 'Yorkshire Ripper'.[67] In one case,[68] the award of damages was so high (£1.5 million) that it was held to amount to a breach of the defendant's rights under the European Convention on Human Rights, Art 10 (freedom of expression). Such awards resulted in two developments, as follows.

1. Where a jury awards damages that are excessive or inadequate, the Court of Appeal may grant a new trial, or substitute the sum awarded with a sum that the Court thinks proper.[69]

2. The Faulks Committee[70] recommended that the qualified right to jury trial for defamation cases be abolished and defamation cases be subject to the same discretion as all other civil cases. To date, this recommendation has not been acted upon.

Appeals

In relation to civil cases, decisions of the High Court may be appealed to the Civil Division of the Court of Appeal. It is possible, however, to appeal directly to the House of Lords or Supreme Court via what is known as the 'leapfrog' procedure. For this to occur, certain conditions must be met.[71] The trial judge must grant a certificate indicating that the various conditions have been met—namely, that the case involves a point of law of general public importance that either involves the interpretation of a statute, or is one that derives from the House of Lords or Court of Appeal and would bind the High Court. In addition, all of the parties involved in the case will need to agree to the case proceeding directly to the House of Lords or Supreme Court.

Regarding criminal cases, before 1960, there was no further right to appeal the decision of a single judge or Divisional Court of the QBD. The Administration of Justice Act 1960 altered this and stated that decisions of a single judge or Divisional Court of the QBD may be appealed to the House of Lords, provided that the appeal is based on a point of law of general public importance and that leave to appeal has been obtained from either the single judge or the Divisional Court that heard the appeal, or the House of Lords.[72]

---

63. Ibid, s 69(3).
64. *Hope v Great Western Rly Co* [1937] 2 KB 130 (CA).   65. [1966] 1 QB 273 (CA).
66. *Hodges v Harland & Wolff Ltd* [1965] 1 WLR 523 (CA).
67. *Sutcliffe v Pressdram Ltd* [1991] 1 QB 153 (CA). The wife eventually settled for £60,000 after the Court of Appeal indicated that it would reduce the award.
68. *Tolstoy Miloslavsky v UK*, App no 18139/91 (1995) 20 EHRR 442.
69. Courts and Legal Services Act 1990, s 8.
70. *Report of the Committee on Defamation* (Cmnd 5909, HMSO, London, 1975).
71. Administration of Justice Act 1969, ss 12–15.
72. Administration of Justice Act 1960, ss 1–2.

The Court of Appeal

The Criminal Appeal Act 1966 split the Court of Appeal into the two divisions that exist today—namely, the Civil Division and the Criminal Division. The Court consists of the Master of the Rolls (who is President of the Civil Division), the Vice-President of the Civil Division, the Lord Chief Justice (who is President of the Criminal Division), the heads of the three divisions of the High Court, and up to thirty-eight Lords/Lady Justices of Appeal. In addition, any High Court judge or circuit judge may be required to sit in the Court of Appeal, although circuit judges may only sit in the Criminal Division.[73] The appointment of the Lord Chief Justice, Heads of Division, and Lords and Lady Justices is subject to a similar procedure as that previously discussed in relation to High Court judges and below. One notable difference is that a selection panel will need to be convened, which will consist of specified senior judges, the Chairman of the Judicial Appointments Commission, and a lay member of the Commission designated by the Chairman.[74]

> 🔗 The procedures for appointing High Court judges and below are discussed at p 21

The Court of Appeal is, like the High Court, based at the Royal Courts of Justice in London (with an increasing number of regional sittings), which can hear up to twelve cases at any one time. A panel of three judges normally hears cases, with cases of particular importance occasionally being heard by a panel of five. In order to reduce waiting times, since 1982, it has been possible to hear cases with a panel of two judges. In the event of a split decision, the case can be reheard with a panel of three or five. As a result of the above measures, the Court of Appeal hears considerably more cases than the House of Lords: in 2007, the House of Lords heard eighty-two cases, compared with some 8,000 heard by the Court of Appeal.[75]

The Civil Division

The Civil Division hears appeals from the High Court and can also hear appeals directly from a county court if the appeal raises important points of principle or practice, or if there is some compelling reason why the Court of Appeal should hear it.[76] The Court of Appeal also has the power to reopen any case if it feels that it is necessary to do so to avoid a real injustice, that the circumstances are exceptional, and that there is no alternative effective remedy.[77] Decisions of the Civil Division may be appealed to the House of Lords or Supreme Court, provided that leave to appeal is obtained from either the Court of Appeal, or the House of Lords or Supreme Court, and that the appeal is lodged within three months of the date of the order appealed from (although statute or the Court of Appeal may order otherwise).

The Criminal Division

The Criminal Division hears cases from a number of different sources, as follows.

- *The Crown Court* Defendants convicted of an offence on indictment in the Crown Court may appeal to the Criminal Division against their conviction or

---

73. Supreme Court Act 1981, s 9.
74. Constitutional Reform Act 2005, ss 71 and 80.
75. Secretary of State for Justice, *Judicial and Court Statistics 2007* (Cm 7467, HMSO, London, 2008) 22–6. Note that this figure also includes cases determining leave to appeal.
76. Civil Procedure Rules, r 52.14
77. Ibid, r 52.17(1).

against sentence,[78] unless the sentence is fixed by law (for example, murder).[79] A defendant who appeals against conviction will either have his conviction quashed or his appeal will be dismissed.[80] Defendants who appeal against sentence may have their sentences confirmed or reduced, but not increased.[81] In both cases, permission to appeal is required, either from the trial judge or the Criminal Division.

- *The Criminal Cases Review Commission (CCRC)* The Home Secretary used to have the power to refer cases to the Criminal Division,[82] but this power proved to be extremely controversial and so, in 1995, the power was transferred to a newly created independent public body called the Criminal Cases Review Commission.[83] The CCRC can refer convictions on indictment[84] to the Criminal Division, provided that the CCRC believes that there is 'a real possibility that the conviction...or sentence would not be upheld were the reference to be made'.[85] As of 30 April 2009, the CCRC had received 11,686 applications and referred 385 to the Criminal Division, of which 273 resulted in the conviction being quashed.[86]

- *Appeals against acquittal* It is a cardinal principle of the UK's criminal justice system that no one should be tried twice for the same offence (known as the 'double jeopardy' rule). The murder of Stephen Lawrence provided a catalyst for a reappraisal of the rule. The Criminal Justice Act 2003 created a significant inroad into the rule by permitting prosecutors to apply to the Criminal Division for an order quashing the acquittal and ordering a retrial, where new and compelling evidence comes to light. The acquittal will need to be in relation to a 'qualifying offence'[87] and the prosecutor will need to obtain the written permission of the Director of Public Prosecutions (DPP), who will need to satisfy himself that new evidence is available, that it is in the public interest to rehear the case, and that the trial will not break the European Union's equivalent of the double jeopardy rule.[88]

- *Attorney General's references* In two instances, the Attorney General has the power to refer a case to the Court of Appeal. Firstly, he may, in relation to certain offences, refer a point of law to the Court of Appeal that arose in a case in which the defendant was convicted.[89] Secondly, where he considers that a defendant has been sentenced leniently, he may, with the leave of the Court of Appeal, refer the case to the Criminal Division, which may impose a more severe sentence.[90] The aim of both procedures is to remedy quickly a mistake made at trial by providing a more authoritative Court of Appeal ruling.

Either the prosecution or defence may appeal the decision of the Criminal Division to the House of Lords or Supreme Court, provided that the case involves a point of law of

---

78. Criminal Appeal Act 1968, ss 1 and 9.

79. In relation to a murder conviction, the defendant can appeal against the minimum term imposed.

80. Criminal Appeal Act 1968, s 2.   81. Ibid, s 11(3).

82. Ibid, s 17 (repealed).   83. Criminal Appeal Act 1995, Pt II.

84. The CCRC can refer summary convictions to the Crown Court.

85. Criminal Appeal Act 1995, s 13(1).

86. Statistics obtained from the CCRC website, <http://www.ccrc.gov.uk>.

87. The list of qualifying offences can be found in the Criminal Justice Act 2003, Sch 5, and are all extremely serious, including murder, rape, manslaughter, kidnapping, importing Class A drugs, arson, and genocide.

88. Criminal Justice Act 2003, s 76(4).

89. Criminal Justice Act 1972, s 36. It should be noted that the reference will have no effect upon the original acquittal.

90. Criminal Justice Act 1988, s 36.

general public importance, and that permission to appeal has been granted by either the Court of Appeal or the House of Lords or Supreme Court. The application for leave to appeal must be made within fourteen days of the Criminal Division's decision.[91]

The Appellate Committee of the House of Lords and the Supreme Court

The Appellate Committee of the House of Lords

Until October 2009, the Appellate Committee of the House of Lords[92] is the final court in the UK in relation to cases of a purely domestic nature. The House of Lords hears both criminal and civil cases, and, whilst it does have an extremely limited first-instance jurisdiction,[93] it is predominantly an appellate court (that is, it hears appeals from lower courts). It hears around eighty or ninety cases in total each year[94] from the Court of Appeal, the High Court (using the so-called 'leapfrog' procedure), the Court of Session (the final civil court in Scotland),[95] and the Court of Appeal and High Court of Justice in Northern Ireland.

An appeal to the House of Lords is dependent upon two conditions being satisfied:

1. the lower court must grant leave to appeal to the House of Lords; and
2. the point of law involved in the appeal must be of general public importance.

Appeal cases in the House of Lords are predominantly heard by the Lords of Appeal in Ordinary and any peer who holds, or has held, high judicial office.[96] There are currently twelve Lords of Appeal in Ordinary, one of whom is appointed as the Senior Law Lord—a position of considerable influence in determining the panels of judges who hear appeals. Although cases may be heard by a minimum of three Lords of Appeal in Ordinary, practice is to hear appeals with a bench of five, although important cases may be heard with a bench of seven, or even nine. Because the House of Lords is the final appeal court in civil cases from the Scottish Court of Session and the Court of Appeal in Northern Ireland, it is customary that one or two judges are appointed from Scotland, and one from Northern Ireland.

---

91. Criminal Appeal Act 1968, s 34 (appeal from the Court of Appeal); Administration of Justice Act 1960, s 2 (appeal from the High Court).

92. Not to be confused with the House of Lords as the second chamber of Parliament. In this chapter, unless otherwise stated, the term 'House of Lords' shall refer to the court, and not the parliamentary chamber.

93. For example, the House will hear first-instance cases relating to impeachment (the commission of a crime against the State, usually by a public official, who is removed from office upon conviction)—but the last time that the House exercised this function was in 1806, when Viscount Melville was charged (but acquitted) with the misappropriation of public funds.

94. In 2007, the House of Lords disposed of eighty-two appeals: see Secretary of State for Justice, *Judicial and Court Statistics 2007* (Cm 7467, HMSO, London, 2008) 7.

95. No appeal will lie to the House of Lords from the High Court of Justiciary (the final criminal court in Scotland): see House of Lords, *Practice Directions and Standing Orders Applicable to Criminal Appeals* (2007–08 edn) [1.7].

96. Appellate Jurisdiction Act 1876, s 5. The Lord Chancellor was removed from this list via the Lord Chancellor (Transfer of Functions and Supplementary Provision) (No 2) Order 2006, SI 2006/1016.

PHOTO 2.2 The Middlesex Guildhall
Source: Arpingstone

The Supreme Court

From October 2009, the Supreme Court of the UK will replace the House of Lords. The initial announcement in 2003 came as something of a surprise, because it was not preceded with a consultation document; instead, the consultation document[97] was published *after* the decision to abolish the House of Lords was announced. This is extremely unusual, especially given the constitutional importance of the decision, and understandably led to significant judicial criticism, especially from six of the twelve Lords of Appeal in Ordinary, who believed that the reform was 'unnecessary and will be harmful'.[98] The consultation document emphasizes that the catalyst for the reform was the need to comply with the doctrine of separation of powers.[99]

The Supreme Court will consist of a President, a Deputy President, and ten Justices of the Court. The twelve Lords of Appeal in Ordinary of the House of Lords will become the first Justices of the Supreme Court, with the Senior Lord becoming the President and the second senior becoming the Deputy President.[100] They will remain members of the second chamber of Parliament, but future appointees will not.[101] Therefore, the ties between the judiciary and the legislature are not

⌘ Visit the Online Resource Centre ⓦ for the discussion box, 'The separation of powers, the Lord Chancellor, and the Supreme Court'

---

97. Department for Constitutional Affairs, *Constitutional Reform: A Supreme Court for the United Kingdom* (CP 11/03, HMSO, London, 2003).

98. House of Lords, *The Law Lords' Response to the Government Consultation Paper on Constitutional Reform: A Supreme Court for the United Kingdom* (CP 11/03, 2003) [1], available online at <http://www.parliament.uk/documents/upload/JudicialSCR071103.pdf>.

99. Ibid, [10]–[11].   100. Constitutional Reform Act 2005, s 24.

101. Ibid, s 137.

yet fully severed. The monarch will appoint future Justices,[102] following a recommendation by the prime minister.[103] The prime minister's recommendation is based upon the selection made by the Lord Chancellor, which will in turn be based upon recommendations made by the Judicial Appointments Commission. The Lord Chancellor's ability to reject or require reconsideration is the same as that discussed previously.[104]

The jurisdiction of the Supreme Court differs slightly from that of the House of Lords. Its appellate jurisdiction will remain the same,[105] but it will take over devolution cases that were previously dealt with by the Judicial Committee of the Privy Council.[106]

Despite the somewhat inappropriate way in which the abolition of the Appellate Committee of the House of Lords was announced, the ultimate decision to replace the House of Lords with a Supreme Court is arguably the correct one. Aside from the principal benefit in terms of separation of powers, other notable benefits include the following.

> ✎ The Lord Chancellor's powers to reject a candidate or require reconsideration are discussed further at p 21

- *Independence* Article 6(1) of the European Convention on Human Rights provides the right to a fair trial and states that courts should be independent. It could be argued that judges who are also involved in the lawmaking process via their membership of the legislature lack the requisite independence. Although conventions are in place that aim to prevent judges from adjudicating on cases involving legislation upon which they have commented in Parliament, the appearance of a lack of independence may still exist—the notable example being Lord Scott, a master of foxhounds, who, in 2001, spoke out against the proposed ban on hunting that was to become the Hunting Act 2004. Even though Lord Scott stated that he would not sit on any cases involving the hunting ban, it still creates the appearance of a lack of independence.

- *Practicality* The Appellate Committee of the House of Lords shares accommodation with a number of other departments in the Palace of Westminster, resulting in one Lord of Appeal in Ordinary not even having his own room. Accordingly, the Appellate Committee does not compare well with other final courts around the world. Having a Supreme Court housed in its own building will provide the Justices with much-needed facilities.[107]

- *Clarity* Having the Privy Council as the final court in relation to devolution cases created the appearance of two top courts. The new arrangements leave no doubt as to which is the supreme court in the UK.

But it could also be argued that introduction of the Supreme Court has a number of disadvantages, as follows.

- *Cost* The costs of establishing and maintaining the new system will be significantly higher than those at present. The Minister of Justice has estimated that the Supreme Court will cost around £60 million to set up and another £12.3 million per year to run.[108] Running the Appellate Committee of the House of Lords costs an estimated £3.2 million per year.[109]

---

102. Ibid, s 23(2).   103. Ibid, s 26(2).

104. Ibid, s 29.   105. Ibid, s 40.

106. Ibid, s 40(4)(b).

107. But see Lord Hope, 'A Phoenix From the Ashes? Accommodating a New Supreme Court' (2005) 121 LQR 253, who argues that the chosen location of the Supreme Court, the Middlesex Guildhall, is unsuitable.

108. Hansard HC, vol 479, col 1251W (22 July 2008).

109. G Dymond, *The Appellate Jurisdiction of the House of Lords* (House of Lords Library Note 2007/008, 2007) 23.

- *Lack of change* Virtually every innovation was rejected, leaving a Supreme Court that is virtually identical to the Appellate Committee of the House of Lords, leading one Lord of Appeal in Ordinary to describe the Supreme Court as 'a receptacle into which the existing package...could be placed with as little disruption to the existing system as possible'.[110] Lord Woolf stated that the planned Supreme Court would be a 'poor relation'[111] compared with other supreme courts around the world. Given this and the increased costs mentioned above, half of the current Lords of Appeal in Ordinary have expressed the opinion that 'the cost of the change would be wholly out of proportion to any benefit'.[112]

- *Hastiness* There is little doubt that the decision to abolish the House of Lords was made in a hasty and inappropriate manner. The decision to abolish the House and replace it with a Supreme Court was announced in 2003, yet as recently as 2001, in a White Paper on House of Lords reform, the government stated: 'The Government is committed to maintaining judicial membership within the House of Lords.'[113] Such a dramatic change of mind within the space of two years indicates that the decision may not have received the due consideration that it deserved.

The Judicial Committee of the Privy Council

The Judicial Committee of the Privy Council (hereinafter referred to as the 'Privy Council') was formally created by the Judicial Committee Act 1833 to better deal with appeals arising from cases in British colonies and Crown dependencies. Today, the Privy Council still acts as the final appeal court for a number of Crown dependencies (for example, the Isle of Man and the Channel Islands), British overseas territories (for example, Bermuda and Gibraltar), and Commonwealth countries[114] (for example, the Bahamas and Jamaica).[115] In 2007, the Privy Council heard seventy-one such cases.[116] The Privy Council is currently the final appeal court in relation to devolution issues in Wales,[117] Scotland,[118] and Northern Ireland,[119] but from October 2009 onwards, this function will be undertaken by the Supreme Court.[120]

---

110. Lord Hope, 'A Phoenix From the Ashes? Accommodating a New Supreme Court' (2005) 121 LQR 253, 253.

111. F Gibb and P Webster, 'Ministers are Breaking the Law, Say Judges', *The Times*, 4 March 2004.

112. House of Lords, *The Law Lords' Response to the Government Consultation Paper on Constitutional Reform: A Supreme Court for the United Kingdom* (CP 11/03, 2003) [2].

113. White Paper, *The House of Lords: Completing the Reform* (Cm 5291, HMSO, London, 2001) [82].

114. Initially, all Commonwealth countries could appeal to the Privy Council. But as time progressed, many of these countries abolished the right to appeal and created their own final appeal courts. Examples include (year of abolition follows): Canada (1949); Malaysia (1985); Australia (1986); Singapore (1994); Hong Kong (1997); and New Zealand (2003).

115. But in 2001, the Caribbean Community (CARICOM) established the Caribbean Court of Justice to act as a final appeal court in Caribbean countries. At the time of writing, two Caribbean countries (Guyana and Barbados) have passed legislation removing the Privy Council as the final appeal court. Jamaica attempted to pass legislation, but it was ruled (by the Privy Council) that the procedure used to pass the legislation was unconstitutional.

116. Statistics derived from the website of the Privy Council, <http://www.privycouncil.org.uk>.

117. Government in Wales Act 1998, Sch 8, para 32.   118. Scotland Act 1998, s 103(1).

119. Northern Ireland Act 1998, s 82(1).

120. Constitutional Reform Act 2005, s 40(4)(b) and Sch 9.

Only the Law Lords and those who hold (or have held) 'high judicial office'[121] may sit on the Privy Council. Further, due to the court's overseas appellate jurisdiction, judges from Commonwealth countries are also eligible to sit.[122] Privy Council judges do not hand down individual judgments; instead (except for devolution cases), one judgment will be handed down for unanimous decisions, while for split decisions, one judgment is handed down for the majority and one for each dissenting judge.

⟨⟩ Key points summary

- Civil cases will commence in either a county court or the High Court. All criminal cases will commence in a magistrates' court.

- Criminal offences are either summary (triable in the magistrates' court), indictable only (triable only in the Crown Court), or triable either way (capable of being heard in either).

- Civil cases will be allocated to either the small claims track (usually those valued at £0–£5,000), the fast track (usually those valued at £5,001–£15,000), or the multi-track (usually those valued at more than £15,000).

- The three divisions of the High Court are the Chancery Division, the Queen's Bench Division, and the Family Division.

- In civil cases, county court decisions can be appealed to the High Court. High Court decisions can be appealed to the Civil Division of the Court of Appeal.

- In criminal cases, the defendant can appeal magistrates' court decisions to the Crown Court. Either party can appeal the decision to the High Court. Crown Court convictions or sentences can be appealed to the Criminal Division of the Court of Appeal.

- The Supreme Court will replace the Appellate Committee of the House of Lords in October 2009.

- The Judicial Committee of the Privy Council is the final appeal court for a number of Crown dependencies and Commonwealth countries. Until October 2009, it is also the final appeal court in devolution cases. After this date, the Supreme Court takes over.

Tribunals

Although tribunals have existed for over two hundred years,[123] it is only within the last century that they have experienced a dramatic increase in importance. In fact, the importance of tribunals has increased so much that Carnwarth LJ, the Senior President of Tribunals, has stated that 'more people bring a case before a tribunal than

---

121. The Appellate Jurisdiction Act 1876, ss 5 and 25, indicate that this can include judges who normally sit in the High Court and Court of Appeal, provided that they have been appointed as a Privy Councillor.

122. Judicial Committee Amendment Act 1895, s 1.

123. The first identifiable tribunal, the General Commissioners of Income Tax Tribunal, was established in 1799.

go to any other part of the justice system'.[124] Today, well over a hundred tribunals exist in England, Wales, and Scotland, in a number of specialized areas[125]—notable examples being the Competition Appeal Tribunal, employment tribunals, the General Commissioners of Income Tax Tribunal, and the Social Security and Child Support Appeals Tribunal. Tribunals usually consist of a panel of three: a legally trained chairperson and two laypersons with expertise in the area in question.

The Competition Appeal Tribunal is discussed at p 1008

The work of employment tribunals and the Employment Appeal Tribunal is discussed at p 777

A major review of tribunals, known as the Franks Report, was carried out in 1957,[126] but no further review of the system was carried out until 2001,[127] by which time a number of problems had started to emerge. Key among these was the fact that the number of tribunals had grown considerably since the previous review, and that each tribunal had developed its own set of complex rules and procedures. This lack of a coherent framework had made the tribunal system inaccessible, incoherent, and needlessly complex. Further, a significant number of tribunals were set up by the very government departments that they were established to regulate; of such tribunals, the Legatt Review states that 'plainly, they are not independent'.[128] The Review's main recommendation was to transfer responsibility for the administration of all tribunals to a single body, thereby ensuring that the tribunals were independent of the bodies they were regulating. This body is known as the 'Tribunals Service'[129] and it was established on 1 April 2006 as an executive agency of the Ministry of Justice. At the time of writing, twenty-seven tribunals are administered by the Tribunals Service.

The Tribunals, Courts and Enforcement Act 2007

The establishment of the Tribunals Service was but one part of the Legatt Review's reforms. It was also important that an effective framework of rules and procedures was put in place to complement the new administrative framework. These rules are to be found in the Tribunals, Courts and Enforcement Act 2007, of which the main points are as follows.

- All tribunals are either classified as First-tier Tribunals or Upper Tribunals.[130] Decisions of First-tier Tribunals may be appealed to an Upper Tribunal.[131] Decisions of Upper Tribunals can be appealed on a point of law to the Court of Appeal.[132]

- Legally qualified members of tribunals are to have the title of 'judge'.[133]

- A Tribunal Procedures Committee was to be set up to create Tribunal Procedure Rules, which will apply to all First-tier and Upper Tribunals.[134]

---

124. Quoted in T Buck, 'Precedent in Tribunals snd the Development of Principle' (2006) 25 CJQ 458, 459.
125. A full list can be found in Council on Tribunals, *Annual Report 2006/07* (HC 733, HMSO, London, 2007) 60–71.
126. *Report of the Committee on Administrative Tribunals and Enquiries* (Cmnd 218, HMSO, London, 1957).
127. Sir A Legatt, *Tribunals for Users: One System, One Service* (2001), available online at <http://www.tribunals-review.org.uk>.
128. Ibid, [1.19].
129. For more on this body, see <http://www.tribunals.gov.uk>.
130. Tribunals, Courts and Enforcement Act 2007, s 3.   131. Ibid, s 11.
132. Ibid, s 13.   133. Ibid, ss 4–5.
134. Ibid, s 22.

Tribunals—an evaluation

When compared to resolving disputes in courts, tribunals are seen to have a number of advantages, as follows.

- *Cost*   Tribunals tend to operate much more cheaply than the courts for several reasons:
    - in many tribunals, legal representation is not needed;
    - tribunals can take place in any building—a specialist building is not required;
    - tribunal panels are much cheaper to employ than judges;
    - tribunals do not charge for their services; and
    - unlike in court (where the loser pays all costs), parties involved in tribunal hearings pay their own costs.
- *Time*   From application to decision, tribunals tend to decide cases notably more quickly than the courts. Further, tribunals will supply the parties with a definite date for the hearing, thereby allowing the parties to plan their affairs around that date.
- *Accessibility*   Because many persons at tribunals will represent themselves, it is essential that tribunals should operate in a manner that is informal and not intimidatory. To that end, wigs are rarely worn, and the evidential and procedural rules tend to be substantially more relaxed than those in court.[135]
- *Flexibility*   Tribunals do not have a system of precedent akin to that of the courts, which can afford the tribunal panel considerable flexibility in reaching an acceptable decision. It should be noted, however, that because tribunals are inferior to the courts, they are governed by binding precedents made by courts.
- *Expertise*   Because two members of the tribunal panel will normally be experts in the area in dispute, tribunals are likely to have on hand access to expertise that courts do not.
- *Privacy*   It is often claimed that tribunal proceedings lack the publicity that can arise from a court battle. Whilst this may be true, it cannot be attributed to the procedural rules of tribunals. Many tribunals work in open and may be observed by members of the public in very much the same way that courts may be.

The above should not, however, be taken to mean that tribunals operate in a superior manner to the courts, because tribunals suffer from a number of notable weaknesses, as follows.

- *Openness*   It was noted above that there is a perception that the operation of tribunals is more private than litigating through the courts. Whilst many tribunals operate openly, there are a number of closed tribunals that sit in private and will not admit members of the public (for example, the Investigatory Powers Tribunal, which hears complaints about the conduct of the intelligence services, especially in relation to communications issues, such as covert surveillance).
- *Inequality*   Research has indicated that individuals who bring legal representation to a tribunal stand a much better chance of succeeding than those who represent themselves,[136] especially if the issue in question is a technical and

---

135. See A Gillespie, *The English Legal System* (OUP, Oxford, 2007) 460–1, who argues that the perceived informality of tribunals may not be so apparent in practice and that tribunal procedures are analogous to procedures in court.

136. See the study by H Genn and Y Genn, *The Effect of Representation at Tribunals* (Lord Chancellor's Department, London, 1989).

complex one. This could mean that the result of a tribunal is not based on the strength of a claim, but on whether or not a party has the resources to obtain legal representation.

- *Funding* Linked to the issue of inequality is the issue of funding. Currently, funding for legal representation is only available in the Employment Appeal Tribunal, the Mental Health Review Tribunal, the Proscribed Organisations Appeal Commission, the Special Immigration Appeals Commission,[137] and the Asylum and Immigration Tribunal.[138] Outside of these tribunals, individuals who cannot afford representation may have to represent themselves and, as seen above, that will have an adverse impact upon their chances of success.

‹› Key points summary

- Tribunals exist to resolve disputes in certain specialist areas (for example, employment disputes, tax disputes, etc.).

- Tribunals usually consist of a legally qualified chairman and two laypersons who have expertise in the tribunal's specialist area.

- The Tribunals Service was set up in 2006 to provide a unified administration system for tribunals. At the time of writing, it covers the work of twenty-seven tribunals.

- Tribunals are either First-tier Tribunals or Upper Tribunals. Decisions of First-tier Tribunals can be appealed to an Upper Tribunal. Decisions of Upper Tribunals can be appealed on a point of law to the Court of Appeal.

Alternative dispute resolution

We have spent a considerable amount of time discussing how disputes may be formally resolved via the courts, but, in practice, the vast majority of disputes are resolved 'out of court' by a number of differing methods that are collectively known as 'alternative dispute resolution' (ADR). Before discussing the various forms of ADR, it is worth briefly identifying several reasons why parties may wish to avoid formal legal proceedings.

- *Cost* Despite the reforms introduced into the civil justice system, taking a dispute to court can still be extremely costly. Further, the cost-saving reforms introduced by the Woolf Report do not yet appear to have had a significant impact.

- *Time* There is little doubt that the Woolf reforms have reduced the time that it takes for a case to reach court and the length of trial, but cases can still be protracted.

- *Salvaging a business relationship* Taking another person to court will almost certainly destroy any chance of being able to transact with him again in the future. The use of ADR is more likely to result in disputing parties working together again once the dispute is resolved.

---

137. Access to Justice Act 1999, Sch 2, para 2(1).
138. Nationality, Immigration and Asylum Act 2002, s 103D.

- *Polarization* Court proceedings result in a winner and a loser; ADR is more concerned with reaching a compromise that is acceptable to both parties. Again, parties are more likely to contract with each other following a dispute if an amicable, compromised resolution was reached.

- *Publicity* For large, well-known companies, becoming involved in a bitter and public legal battle may reflect poorly and result in adverse publicity, causing a loss of reputation, a drop in sales, or a reduction in share price. Further, confidential details of the company and its practices may be revealed to competitors.

Accordingly, in a 1998 White Paper entitled *Modernising Justice*, the government stated that 'in civil matters, for most people, most of the time, going to court is, and should be, the last resort'.[139] Parties who wish to avoid the potential consequences discussed above would do well to consider ADR. In fact, the courts themselves have recognized this to the extent that the law strongly encourages (but cannot compel)[140] parties to use ADR before resorting to legal proceedings. This is codified in the Civil Procedure Rules, which state that effective case management is to include 'encouraging the parties to use an ADR procedure if the court considers that appropriate'.[141] The court's encouragement can, however, be 'in the strongest terms'[142] and parties who unreasonably refuse ADR may find that costs are awarded against them.

Types of ADR

An exhaustive analysis of the many different forms of ADR is beyond the scope of this text. Here, we will briefly discuss the operation of only the principal forms of ADR, before discussing the advantages and disadvantages of such out-of-court procedures.

Arbitration

Arbitration is the oldest and one of the most formal types of ADR. The purpose of arbitration is 'to obtain the fair resolution of disputes by an impartial tribunal without necessary delay or expense'.[143] To this end, instead of taking their dispute to the courts, the parties involved will let their case be decided by an independent third party, known as an 'arbitrator'. An arbitrator may or may not be legally qualified, but he will usually be an expert in the area in question.

In several respects, arbitration is similar to litigation:

- the rules of procedure may be similar to rules in court;
- lawyers will act in almost the same way that they would in court;

---

139. Lord Chancellor, *Modernising Justice: The Government's Plans for Reforming Legal Services and the Courts* (Cm 4155, HMSO, London, 1998) [1.10].

140. In *Halsey v Milton Keynes General NHS Trust* [2004] EWCA Civ 576, [2004] 1 WLR 3002, the Court of Appeal held that to compel a person to use ADR would be to deny him the right to a fair trial, as provided for by the European Convention on Human Rights, Art 6.

141. Civil Procedure Rules, r 1.4(2)(e).

142. *Halsey v Milton Keynes General NHS Trust* [2004] EWCA Civ 576, [2004] 1 WLR 3002, [9] (Dyson LJ).

143. Arbitration Act 1996, s 1(a).

- the decision of the arbitrator is legally binding and may be enforced by a court order;[144] and

- the arbitrator's decision may be appealed to the courts, but on limited grounds— namely, that:
  - the arbitrator lacked jurisdiction to decide the case;[145]
  - there was a procedural irregularity;[146] or
  - there is contention on a point of law.[147]

The upshot of this is that, whilst the case may be decided more quickly and with more privacy, it is unlikely to be significantly cheaper than resolving the issue through the courts.

Arbitration is used most commonly in commercial cases—notably, where a contract contains an arbitration clause (commonly known as a '*Scott v Avery*[148] clause'). The aim of such a clause is to ensure that, in the event of a dispute, the parties refer the matter to arbitration before commencing legal proceedings. The courts have long held that such clauses are perfectly valid and will not be defeated easily.[149] Where such a valid clause exists, if one party initiates legal proceedings before referring the dispute the arbitration, the other party may apply to the court for an order staying the proceedings.[150]

Mediation

Arbitration can be extremely useful, but, like a decision of the court, it still involves the imposition of a decision upon the parties. Alternatively, the parties could employ a mediator, whose function is to help the parties reach a mutually acceptable agreement. The mediator's function is not to impose a resolution (if the mediation is 'facilitative', he may not even suggest one), but to facilitate the negotiation between the parties so that they can resolve the matter themselves. It may very well be the case that no resolution is reached, in which case, the parties may resort to legal proceedings. Therefore it could be argued that mediation is a less certain form of ADR than arbitration, in which a resolution is guaranteed. To combat this, a hybrid form of ADR entitled 'mediation-arbitration' ('med-arb') has been introduced that involves the parties undertaking mediation, but moving onto arbitration if mediation fails.

Because mediation is less confrontational than litigation or arbitration, it is much more suitable for resolving disputes between parties who need, or desire, to maintain a legal relationship once the issue is resolved. Obvious examples include divorcing couples who will need to remain in contact due to custody issues, employment cases in which the parties involved will continue to work together, and disputes between neighbours (for example, excessive noise or boundary issues).

The work of the Commercial Court is discussed at p 30

The value of mediation has been recognized formally by the courts. Since 1993, the Commercial Court (part of the Queen's Bench Division of the High Court) has operated an official mediation scheme, whereby it identifies cases suitable for

---

144. Ibid, s 66.   145. Ibid, s 67.

146. Ibid, s 68.

147. Ibid, s 69. Note that this ground of appeal can only be pleaded if both parties agree.

148. (1856) 5 HL Cas 811.

149. See, e.g., *Cable & Wireless plc v IBM United Kingdom Ltd* [2002] EWHC 2059, [2002] 2 All ER (Comm) 1041.

150. Arbitration Act 1996, s 9(1).

mediation and strongly urges the parties involved to attempt mediation before issuing proceedings. In 1996, a similar scheme was introduced in the Civil Division of the Court of Appeal, except that cases are not preselected for mediation; rather, a letter is sent to all parties involved informing them of the procedure. Parties who refuse mediation must provide their reasons for refusal. If both parties consent to mediation, a mediator will be arranged by the court who will provide his services free of charge.

Conciliation

Conciliation is virtually identical to mediation, except that the conciliator will take a much more proactive role and will actually suggest solutions to the dispute. A notable form of conciliation is that provided by the Advisory Conciliation and Arbitration Service (ACAS). Before an employment case is heard by the courts or employment tribunal, an ACAS member will attempt to resolve the case via conciliation. In the majority of instances, the conciliation is successful and litigation is avoided.[151]

Expert involvement

There are two other forms of ADR that involve appointing certain experts, as follows.

1. *Expert determination* The parties jointly appoint an independent expert to rule on their dispute and agree to be bound by his decision.
2. *Early neutral evaluation (ENE)* This is similar to expert determination, except that the parties are not bound by the decision of the expert. The Commercial Court offers such a service, with a judge providing his opinion. If litigation ensues, the judge will be barred from taking part in the case.

Ombudsmen

Ombudsmen operate to resolve disputes arising between citizens and public bodies. The Parliamentary Commissioner Act 1967 established the first ombudsman, the Parliamentary Commissioner for Administration, whose function is to investigate alleged maladministration in governmental departments. Since then, the ombudsman scheme has been extended beyond governmental activities to include, inter alia, the provision of legal services (the Legal Services Ombudsman), complaints against the judiciary (the Judicial Appointment and Complaints Ombudsman), the provision of financial services (the Financial Ombudsman Service), and complaints regarding pensions (the Pensions Ombudsman).

ADR—an evaluation

The increased popularity of ADR in recent years is a testament to the undoubted advantages that it has over litigation, in terms of the following.

- *Cost* ADR tends to be significantly cheaper than litigation, because many ADR procedures do not require legal representation.

---

151. In relation to collective disputes, 90 per cent of cases reach a successful outcome: see ACAS, *Annual Report and Accounts 2006–07* (HMSO, London, 2007) 8.

- *Time*   When discussing the court system, we noted that the civil justice system suffers from significant delays and it is not uncommon for more complex cases to take years to resolve, especially if appeals are involved. There is no doubt that, generally, ADR can provide a speedier resolution than litigation.
- *Privacy*   ADR is a private procedure—certainly much more so than litigation. Accordingly, disputes can be resolved without revealing commercially sensitive information to competitors, or information that could potentially damage a party's reputation.
- *Compromise*   With the exception of arbitration, most forms of ADR are about reaching a compromise, which, from an objective perspective, may be preferable to the polarized result in which litigation results. It also is more likely to preserve the parties' relationship post-ADR.
- *Expertise*   Arbitrators, mediators, and conciliators will usually be experts in the area of dispute, which increases the likelihood of their efforts being fair, efficient, and in line with commercial practice.

But ADR can only ever complement litigation; it can never replace it, because ADR suffers from several disadvantages of its own.

- *Cost*   We note above that ADR tends to be cheaper than litigation—but this is only the case if ADR is successful. Where ADR fails and litigation subsequently ensues, the overall costs of obtaining a resolution will ultimately be increased.
- *Time*   As with costs, if ADR fails and litigation is required, the overall time taken to resolve a dispute will be increased.
- *Uncertainty*   With the exception of arbitration, med-arb, and expert determination, there is no guarantee that ADR will result in a dispute being resolved.
- *Inequality of power*   The avoidance of litigation does not mean that a mutually beneficial result has been achieved. One party may be substantially stronger than the other and can devote more resources to advocating its case—an obvious example of an unequal relationship being that between employer and employee.
- *Inconsistency*   Unlike legal decisions, which are (theoretically) consistent, decisions in ADR cases may lack consistency due to the lack of any form of precedent.

‹› Key points summary

- ADR tends to be cheaper, quicker, and more private than litigation. It is also more likely to preserve the relationship between the parties.

- ADR may be voluntarily entered into by the parties, but its use may also be encouraged by legislation or the courts.

- Some forms of ADR will produce a binding result—namely, arbitration and expert determination.

- Arbitrators impose a decision; mediators and conciliators attempt to get the parties to resolve their own disputes.

- ADR can be quick, cheap, and private, and is more likely to reach a mutually beneficial resolution. But where ADR fails, it can increase costs and delays. Further, avoiding litigation does not necessarily mean that a fair result was reached.

The legal profession

The *Oxford English Dictionary* defines the word 'lawyer' as '[o]ne versed in the law; a member of the legal profession, one whose business it is to conduct suits in the courts, or to advise clients'.[152] Unfortunately, this definition is somewhat imprecise, because the differing strands of the definition could include differing professions. University lecturers who teach law could be regarded as 'versed in the law', but it would be a stretch to regard them as 'members of the legal profession', because the vast majority of lecturers do not practise law in any capacity. Accordingly, the word 'lawyer' will be avoided and 'members of the legal profession' used instead. The English legal system is one of only a few systems in the world that splits its legal profession into two distinct occupations: solicitors and barristers.[153] It is also important to consider the role of other persons within the legal profession—namely, legal executives and paralegals.

Solicitors

As of 31 July 2008, there were 139,666 solicitors in England and Wales, with 112,433 holding a practising certificate.[154] Unlike barristers, solicitors are permitted to incorporate or form partnerships, and the most recent statistics indicate there are 14,673 organizations employing solicitors in England and Wales.[155] These organizations may be firms of solicitors (usually in the form of a partnership or limited liability partnership), but it is also common for larger commercial organizations to have their own in-house solicitors. Solicitors firms can range from a small, high-street firm with one or two solicitors in a single office, to massive multinational law firms (the largest being known as the 'Magic Circle') with offices all over the world and thousands of practising solicitors.[156]

The type of work undertaken by a solicitor very much depends on the nature of the firm for which they work. A solicitor working in a high-street firm may have general expertise and undertake work in a variety of areas; a solicitor working for a larger firm will be much more likely to specialize in a particular field (for example, solicitors working for the larger firms in London will specialize almost exclusively in corporate and commercial matters).

Solicitors are usually the first point of contact for anyone with a legal issue. It used to be the case that barristers could only be contacted through a solicitor, but, as we will see, this rule is no more. It may, however, be the case that a solicitor will have to refer a client to a barrister because the solicitor may lack expertise in a particular area, or the case may need to be heard in a court in which the solicitor is not qualified to litigate. A solicitor has a right to litigate in any court,[157] but his right

➡ litigate: pursue or defend a legal action

---

152. Definition derived from the Oxford English Dictionary Online, <http://www.oed.com>.
153. Other systems that have a split legal profession include Scotland, the Republic of Ireland, Hong Kong, and the Australian states of Queensland and New South Wales.
154. Law Society, *Trends in the Solicitors' Profession: Annual Statistical Report 2008* (The Law Society, London, 2009) 5.
155. Ibid.
156. For example, Clifford Chance LLP has thirty-one offices in twenty-two countries and over 3,800 legal advisers.
157. Courts and Legal Services Act 1990, s 119.

➡ rights of audience: rights that determine in which court one may appear as an advocate

to advocate in higher courts is limited (the courts in which a member of the legal profession may advocate are known as his rights of audience). Upon qualification, solicitors only have rights of audience in magistrates' courts and county courts, and highly limited rights in the Crown Court. Historically, solicitors could not gain rights of audience for the higher courts at all (subject to a limited exception whereby solicitors could appear in certain Crown Court centres), but following the Courts and Legal Services Act 1990, solicitors can now acquire rights of audience to higher courts by qualifying as solicitor-advocates.

The Law Society is the professional body for solicitors, and has undergone substantial changes in recent years. Previously, the Law Society both represented the interests of solicitors and regulated their professional activity. But it was decided that these two functions could not stand with each other and so, in 2005, the Law Society ceased to be the regulatory body for solicitors—this function being handed over to the Solicitors Regulation Authority.[158]

Barristers

The majority of barristers in the UK are self-employed. Bar Council rules prohibit barristers from incorporating or forming partnerships, but instead they can coalesce into loose organizations known as 'chambers'. Currently, there are 12,136 self-employed barristers practising in 690 chambers.[159] There are, however, a significant number (3,046) of barristers who are not self-employed and who are instead employed in companies, local government, or the Crown Prosecution Service (CPS). In addition, there are currently around 3,721 non-practising barristers.

The functions of a barrister are several, as follows.

- *Advocacy*   Representing clients in court is a major function of a barrister. Qualified barristers have rights of audience in any court and,[160] until 1990, only barristers could act as advocates in the higher courts, but, as we have seen, this monopoly was abolished by the Courts and Legal Services Act 1990.

- *Writing opinions*   Prior to trial, barristers will provide a written opinion advising the client and the instructing solicitor on the significant points of law, the evidential requirements, the likelihood of success, and the potential liability of the client. Alternatively, written opinions may also be provided where litigation is not intended (for example, the extent of private rights).

- *Drafting documents*   These can include general legal documents such as contracts and wills, as well as specific claim litigation documents such as claim forms.

Traditionally, a barrister could only receive instructions from a solicitor; clients could not approach barristers directly. Further, via what is known as the 'cab rank' rule, barristers must (with some exceptions)[161] take any case referred to them. Whilst the 'cab rank' rule still exists, the rules regarding the receipt of instructions were

---

158. Information on the Solicitors Regulation Authority can be found online at <http://www.sra.org.uk>.

159. Statistics derived from the Bar Council website, <http://www.barcouncil.org.uk/about/statistics>.

160. Courts and Legal Services Act 1990, s 31(1).

161. These exceptions can be found in paras 603–606 of the Code of Conduct of the Bar of England and Wales, available online at <http://www.barstandardsboard.org.uk/standardsandguidance/codeofconduct>.

relaxed in 2004 and barristers may now receive instructions directly from professional clients (via the Licensed Access Rules)[162] and the public (via the Public Access Rules).[163]

Barristers will be either juniors or Queen's Counsel (QCs). All newly qualified barristers are juniors and will remain so, unless they become QCs (a process known as 'taking silk' due to the silk robes worn by QCs). There are currently 1,273 QCs in England and Wales, and, in 2008, 104 barristers took silk. Historically, only barristers could become QCs, but this was changed in 1996 to permit solicitors also to take silk, although the majority of QCs are still barristers (of 2008's new QCs, only three were solicitors).

The Bar Council is the professional body for barristers. Like the Law Society, the Bar Council used to represent and regulate its members, but it has split these functions in the same manner as the Law Society has. The Bar Council continues to represent the interests of barristers, but its regulatory responsibility has been transferred to the Bar Standards Board.

Legal executives and paralegals

Increasingly, persons who are not qualified solicitors or barristers are undertaking legal work. Specific mention must be made of legal executives and paralegals.

Legal executives

There are currently around 24,000 trainee and practising legal executives in the UK.[164] Legal executives are legally authorized to engage in 'reserved legal activities' that are very similar to the activities of solicitors, including:

- exercising a right of audience;
- conducting litigation;
- engaging in probate activities;
- notarial activities; and
- the administration of oaths.[165]

Legal executives, like solicitors and barristers, will often specialize in a certain field and, to that end, legal executives may engage in tasks as diverse as engaging in civil and criminal litigation, advising and drafting documents for the conveyancing of properties, drafting wills, and advising on company incorporations and drafting the articles of association. It can be seen that legal executives can engage in much of the same work as a qualified solicitor. Like solicitors, they can be fee-earners, and legal executives are now eligible to be appointed as judges.[166]

---

162. The Licensed Access Rules can be found in the Code of Conduct, Annex F1.

163. The Public Access Rules can be found in the Code of Conduct, Annex F2.

164. See <http://www.ilex.org.uk>.

165. Legal Services Act 2007, s 12(1).

166. Tribunals, Courts and Enforcement Act 2007, s 50(2). At the time of writing, the highest judicial post available to a legal executive is that of deputy district judge, but in 2010, legal executives will become eligible to apply to become district judges.

The Institute of Legal Executives (ILEX) is the professional body for legal executives, and it establishes the requirements to become a legal executive. Becoming a legal executive is a three-stage process, as follows.

1. The person wishing to become a legal executive must complete the ILEX Diploma in Law and Practice, which will provide a basic introduction to law and the skills needed to become a legal executive.

2. The Professional Higher Diploma in Law must be completed. The qualification is equivalent to an honours degree and, once attained, will make the holder a Qualified Member of ILEX, and will entitle him to use the designatory letters 'M Inst L Ex'.

3. Fellowship of ILEX is only attained after the Qualified Member has completed a minimum of five years' employment experience in legal work. Only Fellows may call themselves 'legal executives'.

Paralegals

The Institute of Paralegals defines a paralegal as '[s]omeone who is not a lawyer who does legal work that would previously have been done by a solicitor or barrister' and '[s]omeone who does legal work that a solicitor might do, and if he/she did it would charge for their time'.[167] It is a generic term for someone who engages in legal work, but who is not a solicitor, barrister, or legal executive. The Institute estimates that there are around 500,000 persons engaged in paralegal work (meaning that paralegals form the largest group within the legal profession), but only 50,000 of those work in law firms or in-house legal departments. The remainder work in companies, trade unions, governmental departments, local council and finance, and the insurance sectors.

Paralegals have yet to acquire the recognition afforded to other members of the legal profession. Unlike a solicitor, barrister, or legal executive, anyone can call themselves a 'paralegal' and there are no formal qualifications needed. A professional qualification is offered by the Institute of Paralegals whereby persons can become 'certified paralegals' and only such persons can become Fellows of the Institute of Paralegals.

The Legal Services Act 2007

In 2004, Sir David Clementi carried out a review of the provision of legal services. The final report highlighted three significant problems:

1. the regulatory framework of the legal profession was outdated, rigid, overly complex, and lacked transparency;

2. the complaints procedure was inefficient and unsatisfactory; and

3. the business structures used by the legal profession were unduly restrictive.[168]

---

167. See <http://www.instituteofparalegals.org>.
168. D Clementi, *Review of the Regulatory Framework for Legal Services in England and Wales: Final Report* (2004) 1–3, available online at <http://www.legal-services-review.org.uk>.

The review recommended a number of reforms, which were eventually implemented by the Legal Services Act 2007. The three major criticisms noted will hopefully be remedied via three main reforms, as follows.

- Instead of barristers and solicitors being regulated by different bodies, a new body, called the Legal Services Board (LSB), will be established to regulate all legal services.[169] The Solicitors Regulation Authority and the Bar Standards Board will, however, continue to act as 'front-line' regulators, with the LSB supervising their regulation. The LSB will consist of a president, a chief executive, and between seven and ten other persons. The 'regulatory objectives' of the LSB include improving access to justice, protecting and promoting the interests of consumers, encouraging an independent, strong, diverse, and effective legal profession, and promoting and maintaining adherence to the professional principles.[170] The LSB should be fully operational by early 2010.

- Any complaints relating to the provision of legal services will be dealt by a newly established Office for Legal Complaints (OLC).[171] All legal services providers would have to put in place in-house complaints procedures that meet the requirements of the LSB. Before an individual could complain to the OLC, he would first need to pass through the in-house procedures. The OLC should be fully operational by late 2010.

- The most significant part of the 2007 Act is undoubtedly Pt 5, which allows legal services to be provided through 'alternative business structures'. These structures could consist solely of lawyers (for example, a single firm could contain a mixture of solicitors and barristers); alternatively, it could consist of lawyers and non-lawyers (for example, lawyers could work with accountants or bankers). As a result, legal services are now even offered by supermarkets.[172]

Given that the key reforms will not be fully implemented and operational until late 2010, it is too early to predict the exact effects of the Act—but from a theoretical viewpoint, the potential for change in the way in which legal services are provided is enormous.

⟨•⟩ Key points summary

- The legal profession in the UK is rare in that it is split into two branches: solicitors and barristers.

- Traditionally, barristers could not form partnerships, but could coalesce to form chambers. Solicitors may form partnerships, limited liability partnerships, or even incorporate. The Legal Services Act 2007 will allow providers of legal services to form 'alternative business structures'.

- Barristers may appear in any court. Solicitors normally can only appear in magistrates' court and county courts, but solicitor-advocates have rights of audience in any court.

---

169. Legal Services Act 2007, s 2 and Sch 1.
170. Ibid, s 1(1).
171. Ibid, s 114 and Sch 15.
172. At the time of writing, The Co-op has established a group known as 'The Co-operative Legal Services'. Tesco has indicated that it has plans to offer conveyancing services to the public.

- Although clients may approach barristers directly, solicitors still tend to be the first point of contact for those with legal problems.

- Increasingly, legal executives are undertaking much of the work that was formerly carried out by solicitors. Legal executives are eligible for certain judicial appointments.

- Paralegals are persons who engage in legal work, but who are not solicitors, barristers, or legal executives.

- Currently, different bodies regulate solicitors and barristers, but this will change in 2010, when the Legal Services Board becomes fully operational.

Chapter conclusion

Laws would be largely ineffective without an effective system in place that provides for their application. As we have seen, the court system in England and Wales is relatively complex, but one can only begin to understand the law (and its binding nature) if one has an understanding of the court system.

The cost of taking a dispute to court may, however, be prohibitively expensive. Increasingly, therefore, parties are looking for more informal, non-legal mechanisms with which to resolve their disputes. Parties not wishing to take their dispute to court have a number of other options, which, in many circumstances, may produce a more acceptable compromise than if the dispute was litigated in court, where one party wins and the other loses. In recent years, the use of tribunals and alternative dispute resolution has grown considerably and many businesses will make wise use of ADR before taking their dispute to court—largely because the various ADR procedures are cheaper than litigation and because the working relationship between the two parties might be salvaged. Of course, ADR will not always work and, in such cases, resort to the courts may be unavoidable. In such a case, the parties involved will usually wish to avail themselves of the services of a member of the legal profession. Solicitors and barristers are an integral part of the law's administration, and it is vital to understand the extent of the services that they offer

Having discussed how the law is administered, the next two chapters discuss the various sources of law, beginning with domestic sources of law.

Self-test questions

1. Define the following:
   (a) magistrate;
   (b) first instance;
   (c) appeal;
   (d) judicial review;
   (e) separation of powers;
   (f) alternative dispute resolution;
   (g) rights of audience.

2. Explain the distinction between offences: (i) heard summarily; (ii) tried on indictment only; and (iii) triable either way.

3. Answer the following.
   (a) Tom has been arrested for the suspected murder of his wife, Helen. In which court will Tom's case be heard? If he is convicted, to which court could he appeal the decision?
   (b) Pablo has been convicted of theft in the magistrates' court, but he feels that the judges have made a mistake regarding the law. What options does Pablo have?

4. Explain the operation of the track system as regards the allocation of civil cases.

5. 'The time has come to merge the county courts and the High Court into one single civil court system.' Do you agree? Provide arguments for and against merging the two courts.

6. Explain the distinction between: (i) arbitration; (ii) mediation; and (iii) conciliation.

Further reading

Bailey, SH, Ching, JPL, and Taylor, NW, *The Modern English Legal System* (5th edn, Sweet & Maxwell, London, 2007) chs 2 and 3
A detailed, but accessible and analytical, account of the court system and the legal profession

Clementi, D, *Review of the Regulatory Framework for Legal Services in England and Wales: Final Report* (Department for Constitutional Affairs, London, 2004)
Discusses several problems relating to the regulation of the legal profession and suggests reforms, now implemented by the Legal Services Act 2000

Gillespie, A, *The English Legal System* (2nd edn, OUP, Oxford, 2009) ch 14
Provides an accessible and interesting account of the function and operation of tribunals

Leggatt, A, *Tribunals for Users: One System, One Service* (Department for Constitutional Affairs, London, 2001)
Provides a review of the use of tribunals in the UK and suggests a number of reforms that were implemented by the Tribunals, Courts and Enforcement Act 2007

Websites

<http://www.barcouncil.org.uk>
The website of the Bar Council, the body that represents the interests of barristers

<http://www.barstandardsboard.org.uk>
The website of the Bar Standards Board, the body that regulates barristers

<http://www.hmcourts-service.gov.uk>
The website of Her Majesty's Court Service; provides a substantial amount of accessible information concerning the court system and the various forms of legal proceeding

<http://www.judiciary.gov.uk>
The website of the judiciary of England and Wales; provides an impressive amount of information concerning the role and composition of the judiciary

<http://www.justice.gov.uk/whatwedo/alternativedisputeresolution.htm>
The Ministry of Justice's website on ADR; provides access to reports relating to ADR, as well as links to other useful websites

<http://www.lawsociety.org.uk>
The website of the Law Society, the body that represents the interests of solicitors

<http://www.sra.org.uk>
The website of the Solicitors Regulation Authority, the body that regulates the conduct of solicitors

<http://www.tribunals.gov.uk>
The website of the Tribunals Service, the administrative body for a substantial number of tribunals in England, Wales, and Scotland

 Remember to visit the **Online Resource Centre** at **<http://www. oxfordtextbooks.co.uk/roach>** to access the following resources on Chapter 2, 'The administration of the law': more **practice questions** and answers; a **glossary** of key terms; **multiple-choice questions**; **revision summaries**; **audio updates** when relevant; **diagrams** in pdf; **discussion boxes,** and audio exam advice on this key topic.

Domestic sources of law

- Legislation
- Case law
- Custom

INTRODUCTION

Having discussed in Chapter 1 what law is, we now move on to examine the various types of law and their sources. Understanding the sources of law and the complex relationships that exist between them is crucial in understanding the operation of the English legal system. To simplify matters, the principal sources of law have been split into two chapters: in Chapter 4, we will examine European sources of law and their effect upon domestic law; in this chapter, we will discuss the three principal sources of domestic law—namely, legislation, case law, and custom.

Legislation

Legislation comes in one of three forms:

1. Acts of Parliament;
2. subordinate legislation; and
3. legislation deriving from the European Union (EU).

European legislation is discussed in Chapter 4. This chapter will concentrate on domestic legislation—namely, Acts of Parliament and subordinate legislation.

Types of legislation

Acts of Parliament

Acts of Parliament (also known as 'primary legislation', or 'statute law') constitute the supreme source of domestic law in the English legal system, and cannot be overruled or modified by the courts. Parliament is the supreme lawmaking body within the UK and, according to the doctrine of parliamentary sovereignty, can create any law that it wishes (except laws that would bind future Parliaments). An Act of Parliament will consist of sections and subsections, with technical details coming in the form of Schedules at the end of the Act. Acts can range from minor pieces of legislation containing a few short sections, to massive statutes, such as the Companies Act 2006, which contains 1,300 sections and sixteen Schedules, and a combined total of over 305,000 words. Acts are immortal, in that they will continue to be good law until they are repealed, and, with the exception of legislative reform orders (which are discussed shortly), only Parliament has the power to repeal an Act.

In terms of their function, Acts of Parliament may be classified as:

- *original* Acts, which create completely new law;
- *codifying* Acts, which aim to take all of the existing law (statute and case law) and set it out anew in a single Act, with notable examples being the Partnership Act 1890 and the Sale of Goods Act 1893 (now consolidated into the Sale of Goods Act 1979);
- *consolidating* Acts, which bring together into one Act provisions that were previously contained in a series of Acts. Such Acts usually simplify the law without necessarily bringing about any real reform (which could also be said to be the aim of a codifying Act). Notable large-scale consolidations include the Companies Act 1985 (now largely repealed and replaced by the Companies Act 2006), the Income and Corporation Taxes Act 1988, and the Trade Union and Labour Relations (Consolidation) Act 1992;
- *amending* Acts, which simply alter existing legislation. Such Acts do not usually constitute free-standing Acts in their own right. For example, the Consumer Credit Act 2006 significantly reforms the Consumer Credit Act 1974, but the 1974 Act is still the governing statute.

Subordinate legislation

Acts of Parliament may be the prime form of legislation in the UK, but numerically, the volume of subordinate legislation (also known as 'secondary legislation')[1] passed each year greatly exceeds the number of Acts that make it onto the statute book. In 2008, thirty-three public Acts and three private Acts were passed, compared to 3,296 statutory instruments.[2] As we shall see, creating an Act of Parliament can be a time-consuming process and the parliamentary timetable is so crowded that not all of the laws that require passing can be passed as Acts of Parliament. Instead, Parliament will pass an Act (known as an 'enabling' Act) setting out the broad principles and aims of the legislation, but delegating the specifics to another body. Thus, Parliament can delegate its lawmaking function to outside bodies that are better qualified to legislate the technical detail.

These bodies may include governmental departments, ministers, local authorities, the Crown, companies, and devolved legislative bodies (for example, the National Assembly for Wales). Once authorized, they may create subordinate legislation of various types that have the same force of law as an Act of Parliament, as follows.

- *Statutory instruments* The vast majority of subordinate legislation comes in the form of statutory instruments. Statutory instruments permit governmental ministers to make regulations on areas specified by the enabling Act. Controversially, in

---

1. Very often, it is contended that subordinate legislation is also known as 'delegated legislation', but there is a difference, in that not all subordinate legislation is delegated. For example, Orders in Council made under the royal prerogative do not always derive their authority from an enabling Act. Accordingly, such orders may be subordinate, but not delegated.

2. Statistics derived from the website of the Office of Public Sector Information, <http://www.opsi.gov.uk>.

recent years, the legislative power of ministers has grown considerably. In 1994, ministers were given the power to change Acts of Parliament (including repealing sections) via the passing of a form of statutory instrument known as a 'deregulation order' if they felt that provisions of the Act imposed an inappropriate burden on businesses or individuals.[3] The Regulatory Reform Act 2001 extended these powers. Much more controversial was the Legislative and Regulatory Reform Bill, which gave ministers significant legislative powers, including, via the passing of a legislative reform order,[4] the ability to repeal *any* legislation and to create new criminal offences (provided that they were punishable by less than two years' imprisonment). The controversy was such that the government reduced considerably the proposed new powers of ministers, and limited them to promoting business regulation and efficiency, but many still regard the Legislative and Regulatory Reform Act 2006 as a substantial shifting of power from a democratically elected body to the government.

- *Orders in Council*   These are made by the monarch upon advice from the Privy Council,[5] and tend to be used in times of emergency to create legislation and to provide direct effect to EU provisions that lack **direct effect**. In practice, the advice given to the monarch derives from Cabinet ministers, and many of the members of the Privy Council play no part in its legislative function.

➜ direct effect: an EU provision has direct effect if it can be relied on in a domestic court

- *By-laws*   These are, subject to approval from a government minister, legally binding laws created by local authorities, and certain public and nationalized bodies. The majority of by-laws relate to local issues of relatively minor importance. Breaching a by-law is a criminal offence.

- *Professional regulations*   These allow certain professional bodies to create rules that regulate the conduct of their profession (for example, the Solicitors Act 1974 allows the Law Society to create subordinate legislation regulating the conduct of solicitors).

The advantages of subordinate legislation are well known and often lauded—but what is not made so prominent is that these advantages often come hand in hand with some notable disadvantages.

- *Convenience vs constitutionality*   There is little doubt that Parliament cannot carry out its full legislative programme via primary legislation alone. The convenience of delegating its law making function is crucial. But the fact is that, via the use of subordinate legislation, the majority of legislation created in the UK is not created by the democratically elected Parliament, but by the various bodies discussed above. One could question whether this is constitutionally correct, especially amidst a growing belief that the recent Conservative and Labour governments have used subordinate legislation to implement policy.

- *Speed vs scrutiny*   Subordinate legislation is not dependent upon finding time in the crowded parliamentary timetable, and can therefore be introduced, created, and altered quickly, enabling it to respond to changes much more effectively and speedily than primary legislation. But the speed with which subordinate legislation can be enacted can result in a lack of effective scrutiny. The need for

---

3. Deregulation and Contracting Out Act 1994, ss 1 and 4.

4. Legislative and Regulatory Reform Act 2006, s 12(1), indicates that such orders must be made by statutory instrument.

5. A body consisting primarily of all members of the Cabinet (past and present), but also includes ambassadors, members of the royal family, senior judges, archbishops, and other notable figures. At the time of writing, membership stands at 420.

close scrutiny by members of Parliament (MPs) is essential, especially given the constitutional problems highlighted above. Unfortunately, given the sheer bulk of subordinate legislation, and the fact that it may be highly detailed and technical, it is unlikely that the vast majority of subordinate legislation receives any parliamentary scrutiny.

- *Expertise vs bias* Because legislative power is delegated to specialist bodies with expertise of the area in question, subordinate legislation should be more effective and cost-efficient than primary legislation created by MPs who lack the requisite expertise. Especially in the case of professional regulations, however, there is always the danger that the body will create legislation that best serves itself or members of the profession that it should be regulating. Such a danger is more likely given the aforementioned lack of detailed scrutiny.

Creating legislation

The origins of a piece of legislation

A piece of legislation may originate from a number of different sources. The political party with the highest number of seats in the House of Commons will form the government, and will seek to implement its policies and election manifesto pledges via the passing of legislation. The majority of legislation passed derives from governmental proposals and, since 1965, the government has been assisted hugely by the Law Commission—an independent body with a statutory duty to:

> review all the law…with a view to its systematic development and reform, including in particular the codification of such law, the elimination of anomalies, the repeal of obsolete and unnecessary enactments, the reduction of the number of separate enactments and generally the simplification and modernisation of the law…[6]

As of April 2009, the Law Commission had published 315 reports, more than two-thirds of which have been implemented by Parliament. But not all legislation derives from the government. Individual MPs (from any party) may also propose legislation via what is known as a 'private member's Bill'.

Irrespective of the source of the legislative proposal, the ultimate aim of the proposal is the creation of a Bill. A Bill is simply a draft piece of legislation, and it comes in three main forms, as follows.

1. *Public Bills* These deal with matters of public interest that affect the entire UK. They will therefore apply to England, Wales, Scotland, and Northern Ireland, unless (as is often the case) a specific provision states otherwise.[7] Public Bills come in one of two forms:
   - government Bills, which are introduced by a minister of the government and which, accordingly, almost always pass through Parliament; and
   - private member's Bills, which are introduced by a single non-ministerial MP of any political party. The majority of private member's Bills fail, largely due to

---

6. Law Commission Act 1965, s 3(1).

7. For example, the Supply of Goods and Services Act 1982, s 1, specifically states that it only applies to England, Wales, and Northern Ireland.

lack of governmental support or a lack of time, but a number of notable Acts began life as private member's Bills, including the Adoption Act 1964, the Murder (Abolition of Death Penalty) Act 1965, and the Abortion Act 1967.

2. *Private Bills*   Not to be confused with private member's Bills, these affect specific individuals, groups of individuals, companies, or localities. The individual or group desiring the Bill will present it to Parliament. Historically, private Bills were common during the nineteenth century and were used to grant construction rights to companies to build railways, canals, etc. Today, private Bills are largely sought by local authorities that wish to extend the powers granted to them via public Acts.

3. *Hybrid Bills*   As their name suggest, hybrid Bills mix the qualities of public Bills and private Bills. They usually relate to works that affect the general population, but are likely to have more significant impacts upon specific persons or groups. For example, the Channel Tunnel Act 1987, which authorized construction of the Channel Tunnel, was of clear importance to the UK in general, but particularly affected the south east of England via specific provisions permitting extensive building works in that region.

The legislative process

In order to become an Act of Parliament, a Bill must pass through Parliament, which comprises the House of Commons, the House of Lords, and the monarch. Most Bills are introduced in the House of Commons, but any Bill (except money Bills) may also be introduced in the House of Lords. Irrespective of into which House the Bill is introduced, the legislative stages are the same. Because the majority of Bills are introduced in the House of Commons and the majority of such Bills are public Bills, the following discussion will focus on the process by which a public Bill is passed, following its introduction in the House of Commons.

➜ money Bills: Bills that concern national taxation, public money or loans, and their management

1. *First reading*   This is a purely formal stage at which the Bill is introduced, its title read out, and a date set for the second reading. The purpose of the first reading is simply to inform MPs that a Bill is coming up for discussion. There is no debate and no vote, so all Bills automatically pass through this stage and onto the second reading.

2. *Second reading*   This is the first crucial stage of the Bill. The purpose of the Bill is stated to the House and its main principles debated, although no amendments may be made. To save parliamentary time, certain Bills will not be debated by the full House, but will instead be referred to a standing second reading committee, which will report to the House on whether the Bill should receive a second reading or not. The House will vote on whether the Bill should proceed to the next stage. Unsurprisingly, the vast majority of government Bills pass their second reading[8] and pass onto the Committee stage.

3. *Committee stage*   The Bill is passed onto a public Bill committee (formerly known as a 'standing committee') of between sixteen and fifty MPs (usually around seventeen), who scrutinize the Bill clause by clause. The reason for this delegation is that a smaller group of MPs can have a more productive debate than the entire House of 646 MPs. The entire House may, however, debate

---

8. In fact, since 1905, only three government Bills have been voted down at their second reading—the last being in 1986, when the Shops Bill (which aimed to relax the laws relating to Sunday trading) was defeated.

controversial Bills, or Bills of constitutional importance.[9] For the first time, amendments may be proposed. Once the desired amendments are made, the amended Bill then progresses onto the report stage.

4. *Report stage* The public Bill committee reports back to the full House, high-lighting any amendments made during the committee stage. MPs who were not part of the public Bill committee will have the opportunity to propose their own amendments. Alternatively, the House may reject or replace amendments made during the committee stage. Once the desired amendments are made, the Bill passes onto its third reading.

5. *Third reading* The final stage in the House of Commons is the third reading, which usually happens immediately after the report stage. Further debate may occur, but, in practice, will usually be very short. In the Commons, no fur-ther amendments can be made. The final Bill is voted on and, if successful, progresses on to the House of Lords (or the House of Commons, if the Bill was introduced in the House of Lords).

Once the House of Commons has passed the Bill, it is passed on to the House of Lords, (or vice versa, if the Bill was introduced into the House of Lords), where it will pass through the exact same stages as in the Commons—with three notable differences in procedure:

- the committee stage will usually involve the entire House;
- there are no restrictions on debates regarding amendments; and
- amendments may be made during the third reading.

Both Houses must agree the text of the Bill. Therefore, if the Lords propose any amendments, the Bill is referred back to the Commons for its approval. The Commons may accept the amendments, in which case the Bill can progress to the final stage—namely, Royal Assent. But if the House of Commons rejects the amendments or proposes new ones, the Bill will once again be referred to the Lords for further consideration. A Bill may travel between the two Houses several times (a process known as 'ping pong') before one of a possible number of outcomes is reached:

- agreement is reached between the two Houses and the Bill may progress to the monarch to receive Royal Assent;

➡ parliamentary session: the period between the State Opening of Parliament (usually November) and Parliament's prorogation (closing) (again, usually in November)

- because, normally, public Bills must be passed within their current parliamen-tary session (although private and hybrid Bills may carry over into another), if agreement cannot be reached before the end of a session, the Bill will lapse and will need to pass through the entire legislative process again when Parliament reconvenes. A process now exists, however, whereby public Bills can be carried over by agreement.[10]

Special provision has been made to deal with the case in which the two Houses cannot reach an agreement and the House of Lords remains opposed to a Bill passed by the House of Commons. In such a case, the Bill will not lapse at the end of the parliamentary session and will be passed in the next session without

---

9. For example, the European Union (Amendment) Act 2008, which ratified the Treaty of Lisbon, was debated by a committee of the whole House.

10. HC Standing Order No 80A. Notable Bills that have used this process include the Financial Services and Markets Bill, the Constitutional Reform Bill, and the Corporate Manslaughter and Corporate Homicide Bill.

the consent of the House of Lords.[11] This ability to pass a Bill without the Lords' consent was first granted to the Commons by the Parliament Act 1911, which was passed following the Lords' initial refusal to pass the 'People's Budget' of 1909.[12] The 1911 Act removed the Lords' power of veto and replaced it with the power to delay a Bill by up to two years. The power of delay was reduced further to one year by the Parliament Act 1949, but the Parliament Act 1949 itself was passed without the consent of the Lords using the 1911 Act procedure (the importance of this will be seen when the case of *R (Jackson) v Attorney General*[13] is discussed below).

But the ability to pass legislation without the consent of the Lords is limited in two key ways: firstly, the Parliament Acts do not apply in the case of private member's Bills; secondly, the Parliament Acts cannot be used in respect of Bills that were introduced in the House of Lords. Since 1949, only four Acts have been passed without the consent of the Lords—the most recent being the Hunting Act 2004,[14] which resulted in a seminal case attacking the legality of the Parliament Acts themselves.

 R (Jackson) v HM Attorney General [2005] UKHL 56

FACTS: The Hunting Act 2004 banned the hunting of animals (notably, foxes) with dogs. The Bill was rejected by the House of Lords and so was passed without its consent using the Parliament Acts procedures. The Countryside Alliance challenged the validity of the 2004 Act by challenging the validity of the Act that allowed it to be passed—namely, the Parliament Act 1949. The Alliance argued that using the 1911 Act to pass the 1949 Act was invalid, because the 1949 Act amended the 1911 Act: in effect, the 1911 Act was used to amend itself. The Countryside Alliance argued that the 1911 Act could not be used for this purpose. Accordingly, the 1949 amendments were invalid, which consequently invalidated the Hunting Act 2004, because it was not passed in accordance with the unamended 1911 Act.

HELD: The High Court, the Court of Appeal, and a nine-strong bench in the House of Lords all unanimously rejected the Countryside Alliance's claims, and upheld the validity of the Parliament Act 1949. The key issue was what were the limits of the 1911 Act—specifically, could it be used to amend itself? The Lords held that it could be used for such a purpose (although they did note that there were some limitations on this power, which did not arise in this case).

---

11. Parliament Act 1911, s 2, as amended by the Parliament Act 1949.
12. The 1909 Budget aimed to introduce a radical programme of welfare reform by increasing the top rate of income tax and imposing a land tax, which would have hit large landowners hardest. Unsurprisingly, the Conservative-dominated House of Lords (which included some of the largest landowners in the country) was violently opposed to the Budget and vetoed it—the first time that it had done so since the seventeenth century.
13. [2005] UKHL 56, [2006] 1 AC 262.
14. The other three were the War Crimes Act 1991, the European Parliamentary Elections Act 1999, and the Sexual Offences (Amendment) Act 2000.

COMMENT: Whilst the decision of the Lords might have been unanimous, they did not agree on all aspects of this case. An interesting issue in this case was what were the limitations on the exercise of the power contained in the 1911 Act and, specifically, whether future courts could imply further limitations upon the exercise of that power. On this issue, the House appeared divided, with four judges[15] stating that no further limitations could be implied, whilst another four[16] contended that further future limitations might be possible. In a key passage, Lord Steyn stated:

> the supremacy of Parliament is still the *general* principle of our constitution. It is a construct of the common law. The judges created this principle. If that is so, it is not unthinkable that circumstances could arise where the courts may have to qualify a principle established on a different hypothesis of constitutionalism.[17]

★ See R Cooke, 'A Constitutional Retreat' (2006) 122 LQR 224

Once a Bill passes through both Houses (either with the Lords' consent or via the Parliament Acts procedure), the Bill is submitted to the monarch for Royal Assent. Although the monarch can personally grant Assent,[18] today, it is granted either by Lord Commissioners in the presence of both Houses, or (as is more common) via simple notification to each House that the Bill has been Assented.[19] Constitutionally, there is no rule that states that the monarch must grant assent to a Bill, but today, Assent is regarded as an automatic process and no monarch would dare refuse it for fear of jeopardizing the position of the monarchy.[20] Unless otherwise stated, as soon as Assent is granted, the Bill becomes an Act of Parliament—but this does not mean that the Act immediately comes into effect. Many Acts are brought into effect months, or even years,[21] after Assent, via the passing of a commencement order, which may bring the entire Act into effect, or via multiple commencement orders, with each one bringing specific sections of the Act into effect.[22]

Figure 3.1 demonstrates the legislative process of a public Act.

Statutory interpretation

Whilst Royal Assent may mark the conclusion of the legislative process, in practical terms, it merely commences the infancy of a statute that may remain on the statute book for years, decades, or possibly even centuries.[23] The effectiveness of a statute is dependent upon how it is interpreted and applied—a major role of the judiciary.

---

15. Lords Bingham, Nicholls, and Steyn, and Baroness Hale.
16. Lords Hope, Walker, Carswell, and Brown.
17. *R (on the Application of Jackson) v HM Attorney General* [2005] UKHL 56, [2006] 1 AC 262, [102].
18. The last monarch to Assent a Bill personally was Queen Victoria in 1854.
19. Royal Assent Act 1967, s 1(1)(b).
20. The last monarch to refuse Assent was Queen Anne, who refused to Assent the Scottish Militia Bill 1707.
21. The Easter Act 1928, which aimed to establish a fixed date for Easter, has yet to come into force.
22. An extreme example of this is the Town and Country Planning Act 1971, which had seventy-five separate commencement orders.
23. The oldest piece of UK legislation still in force is the Distress Act 1267 (part of the Statute of Marlborough), which provides that damages cannot be lawfully obtained other than through the courts.

P **A** **R** **L** **I** **A** **M** **E** **N** **T**	House of Commons	First reading	The title of the Bill is read out and a date set for the second reading The Bill is then printed and published
		Second reading	The purpose of the Bill is explained to the House and its main principles debated No amendments may be made at this stage The House votes on whether the Bill progresses to the committee stage
		Committee stage	The Bill is scrutinized clause by clause by a public Bill committee of 16–50 MPs (except in the House of Lords, where the entire House will take part) Amendments may be made at this stage in the House of Commons only and will be voted on before proceeding to the report stage
		Report stage	The public Bill committee reports to the House on any amendments made during the report stage The House may suggest its own amendments
		Third reading	The third reading usually happens immediately after the report stage Debate will be short In the Commons, no further amendments may be made, but amendments may be made in the Lords The final Bill is voted on and, if successful, passes onto the next House
	House of Lords	Same as above	The stages are identical in both Houses, subject to the differences noted above If amendments are made, the Bill is sent back to the Commons so that the amendments can be approved
	Monarch	Royal Assent	The monarch grants Royal Assent and the Bill becomes an Act of Parliament, although it may not come into force until a later date Bringing the Act into force can be achieved by passing a commencement order, which brings the whole, or specific provisions, of the Act into force

FIGURE 3.1 The passing of a public Bill

Constitutionally, the role of the judges is simply to interpret statue and apply it to the case before them. Unlike judges in countries with written constitutions (notably, the US Supreme Court), judges in the English legal system have no power to strike down legislation as unconstitutional. One would therefore assume that the judges have little influence over the application of a statute. In reality, however, judges may, through their interpretive function, play a massive role in the application of a statute. The interpretative role of the judiciary becomes more important the higher up the court hierarchy a case progresses. Over half of the cases reaching the Court of Appeal and three-quarters of those reaching the House of Lords involve issues of statutory interpretation.

The problem

The problem (or opportunity, depending on your viewpoint) facing judges is that, despite the highly skilled nature of statutory draftsmen,[24] they are still limited to using words as a means of communicating the law. The English language, despite being the most descriptive language in the world (with around three times as many words as any other), is still something of an imprecise tool and the inherent complexity of the law means that, in many cases, the precise meaning of a statute may be unclear or ambiguous, as the following example demonstrates.

Eg The Wills Act 1837, s 9

Originally, the Wills Act 1837, s 9, stated that in order for a will to be validly executed, the signature must appear 'at the foot or end' of the will. At first glance, this appears to be relatively straightforward—but closer scrutiny reveals a significant ambiguity in that the word 'end' could mean, among other things:

1. that the signature must appear at the end of the content of the will, but that sections of the will can be inserted at a later date; or

2. that the signature is the last thing written on the will, but can be written anywhere.

Judges were unable to interpret the phrase consistently, leading some judges to permit signatures anywhere on the will, while other judges required the signature to be physically at the end of the will. As a result of the ambiguity, the phrase was removed and replaced in 1852.

A statute may contain clear and unambiguous wording that is subsequently rendered unclear by developments that could not have been foreseen when the statute was enacted. In such a case, the judges will be required to interpret and apply statute to novel cases that the statute was never designed to cover.

---

24. For an account of the problems faced by draftsmen when drafting statutes, see FAR Bennion, *Bennion on Statute Law* (3rd edn, Longman, Harlow, 1990).

R v Ireland (Burstow) [1998] AC 147 (HL)

FACTS: The Offences Against the Person Act 1861 was enacted to deal with all instances of physical attack, except murder, including the well-known crimes of 'actual bodily harm' and 'grievous bodily harm'. The first defendant made repeated telephone calls to a number of women, but remained silent when they answered. The effect of the calls was eventually to cause the women to suffer psychological damage and the court had to determine whether this constituted 'bodily harm'.

HELD: Although 'psychiatry was in its infancy in 1861'[25] and therefore the 1861 Act was not passed with psychiatric harm in mind, it nevertheless was within the definition of 'bodily harm'. Lord Steyn stated that, in some cases, judges should interpret legislation as 'if one were interpreting it the day after it was passed'.[26] In many cases, however, a statute 'should be deemed to be always speaking'[27] and therefore the courts must be 'free to apply the current meaning of the statute to present day conditions'.[28]

COMMENT: Lord Steyn was not particularly clear on when the court should apply an historical interpretation and when it should apply a current interpretation. Subsequent courts have aimed to clarify matters and have limited Lord Steyn's 'always speaking' rule by emphasizing that, before a court applies a new interpretation to a statute, it 'must be very clear that the new situation falls within the Parliamentary intention'.[29]

★ See S Gardner, 'Stalking' (1998) 114 LQR 33

Aids to interpretation

The interpretive function of the judges is rendered slightly easier by the presence of certain interpretive aids. Interpretive aids come in one of three types:

- presumptions;
- intrinsic aids; and
- extrinsic aids.

In certain unclear cases, the court may apply certain presumptions in order to ascertain what Parliament intended the provision in question to mean. Note, however, that they are presumptions only and may be rebutted by the statute itself.

It is impossible to list all of the presumptions, because they may be 'modified or even abandoned with the passage of time, and with the modification of the social values which they embody'.[30] Below therefore is a selection of the principal presumptions. Note, however, that they are in no particular order and that the lack of a hierarchy can create problems where multiple presumptions conflict.

- *Presumption against alteration of the common law* Parliament is presumed to know the common law and not to intend to change it, unless the wording of the statute clearly and unmistakably indicates that the common

---

25. *R v Ireland (Burstow)* [1998] AC 147 (HL) 150 (Lord Steyn).   26. Ibid, 158.

27. Ibid.   28. Ibid.

29. *Victor Chandler International Ltd v Customs and Excise Commissioners* [2000] 1 WLR 1296 (CA) 1304 (Sir Richard Scott V-C).

30. Law Commission, *Interpretation of Statutes: Report by the Two Commissions* (Law Com No 21, HMSO, London, 1969) [34].

law is to be changed.[31] Given that the specific purpose of much modern legislation is to alter the common law, this presumption is one of the more controversial.

- *Presumption against legislation having retrospective effect* It is presumed that statute will not affect factual situations and cases that arose before the statute was passed, unless it indicates the contrary.[32] This presumption is especially strong in relation to the creation of criminal offences—indeed, today, the creation of retrospective criminal offences would breach the European Convention on Human Rights, Art 7.

- *Presumption against the ousting of the court's jurisdiction* The courts tend to act in a hostile manner towards any statute that seeks to oust their jurisdiction. The courts tend to interpret such statutes narrowly, or to find ways in which to evade them altogether.

- *Presumption that statutes do not affect the Crown* It is presumed that statutes do not apply to the Crown unless expressly stated,[33] or if it is necessary to imply that the Crown is bound. Note that 'the Crown' here refers not only to the monarch personally, but also to certain employees and agents of the Crown.

Intrinsic aids refer to aids contained within the statute itself. A fundamental principle of statutory interpretation is that the statute should be read as a whole.[34] Therefore, judges may look at any part of a statute in order to interpret a difficult section. This may involve an analysis of any or all of the following.

- *The Preamble* Older statutes used to contain a Preamble, which would set out, often at some length, the purposes for which the statute was enacted. Judges may use the Preamble to interpret any section in the Act, but it may not be used to defeat the clear wording of a provision. In more modern statutes (except private Acts), the Preamble has been replaced by the long title.

- *The long title* Statutes are almost always known by their short title, but all statutes also have a long title that explains in more detail the purposes of the Act. For example, the long title of the Companies Act 2006 is 'An Act to reform company law and restate the greater part of the enactments relating to companies; to make other provision relating to companies and other forms of business organisation; to make provision about directors' disqualification, business names, auditors and actuaries; to amend Part 9 of the Enterprise Act 2002; and for connected purposes'. Judges are free to use the long title to interpret unclear provisions,[35] but it may not be used to defeat the clear wording of a provision.

- *Punctuation, side notes, and headings* Although these are not voted on by Parliament and may be altered any time before Royal Assent, they may still be used to aid interpretation. Punctuation and side notes carry little weight, but headings can, in theory, be useful in determining the scope of a section. In

---

31. *Black-Clawson International Ltd v Papierwerke Waldhof-Aschaffenburg AG* [1975] AC 591 (HL).
32. *L'Office Cherifien des Phosphates v Yamashita-Shinnihon Steamship Co Ltd* [1994] 1 AC 486 (HL). Legislation that does have specific retrospective effect includes the War Damage Act 1965 and the War Crimes Act 1991.
33. For example, the Crown Proceedings Act 1947 provided, for the first time, that the Crown could be subject to a civil action.
34. *Attorney General v Prince Ernest Augustus of Hanover* [1957] AC 436 (HL).
35. *Fielding v Morley Corporation* [1900] AC 133 (HL).

reality, because sections may be widened by subsequent amendments, headings are most useful to determine the purpose of a section as opposed to its scope.[36]

- *Interpretive sections*   Many statutes will provide their own interpretation(s) of key words and phrases, usually via a dedicated section(s). For example, the Sale of Goods Act 1979, s 61, defines twenty-seven words and phrases that appear throughout the Act.

Unlike courts in Continental Europe, English and Welsh courts historically have been unable to examine material outside the confines of the Act itself. In certain circumstances, however, the courts do have access to a range of extrinsic material to aid interpretation, as follows.

- *The Interpretation Act 1978*   This Act defines terms that commonly appear in statute and imposes these definitions on all statutes, unless the Act in question states that an alternative definition is to be used.[37] The Act also states that, unless otherwise stated, 'he' will also mean 'she' (and vice versa), and terms in the singular tense will also include the plural (and vice versa).[38]

- *Dictionaries and textbooks*   The courts regularly use dictionaries to define words that have a non-legal meaning. Textbooks are increasingly being used, although their use is still not as common as in civil law systems.

- *Official reports*   As noted, the Law Commission produces reports proposing legislation or recommending the reform of current legislation. A Royal Commission is a governmental inquiry into an issue of public importance. For the purpose of ascertaining the 'mischief' that an Act was meant to remedy, judges may examine these official reports—but because Parliament may not have accepted the findings of these reports, they cannot be used to ascertain the intention of Parliament.[39]

- *Explanatory Notes*   Since 1999, Explanatory Notes must accompany all Bills and Acts, and may be used to aid interpretation, even if there is no ambiguity.[40]

- *Parliamentary materials*   As noted earlier, a Bill will be debated in Parliament several times before it becomes an Act. These debates are recorded and reported in the official record of parliamentary debates (known as **Hansard**).[41] Historically, the courts have held that they may not refer to parliamentary materials when interpreting statutes.[42] As time progressed, the rule was relaxed and judges were permitted to utilize certain parliamentary materials. Using Hansard was, however, still prohibited on the grounds that to permit recourse to it would lead to a significant increase in the length and cost of litigation, and also because Hansard does not necessarily indicate the intention of Parliament, but rather the views of the MPs who took part in the debate. The prohibition was lifted in the following seminal and controversial case.

➜ Hansard: the official report of parliamentary debates

---

36. *DPP v Schildkamp* [1971] AC 1 (CA).
37. Interpretation Act 1978, s 5 and Sch 1.   38. Ibid, s 6.
39. *Eastman Photographic Materials Co Ltd v Comptroller General of Patents* [1898] AC 571 (HL).
40. *R (on the Application of Westminster City Council) v National Asylum Support Service* [2002] UKHL 38, [2002] 1 WLR 2956.
41. Named after Thomas Hansard, who purchased the rights to print parliamentary debates in the early nineteenth century.
42. *Davis v Johnson* [1979] AC 264 (HL).

Pepper (Inspector of Taxes) v Hart [1993] AC 593 (HL)

FACTS: The facts of the case are not directly relevant.

HELD: The House of Lords held that if a provision is ambiguous or unclear, or if applying a literal meaning would lead to absurdity, then the courts may have recourse to Hansard if:

1. Hansard discloses the mischief that the provision was meant to remedy, or the legislative intention behind the provision in question;

2. the statements relied on were made by a minister or other promoter of the Bill; and

3. such statements are clear.

COMMENT: The above conditions indicate that Hansard was never intended to be referred to routinely. In the vast majority of cases, Hansard will provide little, if any, clarification of an ambiguous provision.[43] Despite this, *Pepper v Hart* remains an extremely controversial decision—especially the second condition stated by the House. Reference to Hansard should be used to ascertain the intention of Parliament—why therefore is such reference limited to statements of ministers and promoters of the Bill? The voice of a minister is not the voice of Parliament, and it could be argued that the second condition provides an unfair preference for the views of the government that could ultimately result in 'a real danger of the courts becoming too close to the executive's intentions'.[44] A growing consensus also seems to be that permitting reference to Hansard has increased the costs of litigation,[45] leading one commentator to conclude that 'the *pragmatic* reasons for overruling or restricting *Pepper v Hart* are now very strong'.[46]

⭐ See B Davenport, 'Perfection—But at What Cost?' (1993) 109 LQR 149

In addition to presumptions, and intrinsic and extrinsic aids, the courts have also developed several contextual linguistic rules to aid interpretation, of which three need be noted. The first is expressed by the Latin maxim *expressio unius est exclusio alterius* ('to express one thing is to exclude another'). This rule applies where a statute provides a list and states that only those items listed will be within the scope of the provision. The following case demonstrates this rule in practice.

 R v The Inhabitants of Sedgely (1831) 2 B & Ald 65

➡ poor rate: a form of tax levied on certain persons, the proceeds of which were used to help the poor

FACTS: The Poor Relief Act 1601, s 1, provided that a **poor rate** be levied on the occupiers of 'lands, houses, tithes and coal mines'. The limestone mine of the Earl of Dudley was charged the poor rate and he applied to the court, arguing that his mine was not within the definition contained in s 1 and so he was not liable to pay the poor rate.

---

43. The House in *Pepper v Hart* itself admitted this: see [1993] AC 593 (HL) 634, in which Lord Browne-Wilkinson stated that '[i]n many…cases reference to Parliamentary material will not throw any light on the matter' and would be unlikely to yield a 'crock of gold'.

44. D Miers, 'Taxing Perks and Interpreting Statutes: *Pepper v Hart*' (1993) 56 MLR 695, 708.

45. See Lord Steyn, '*Pepper v Hart*: A Re-examination' (2001) 21 OJLS 59, 64, where he stated: 'It remains my view that *Pepper v Hart* has substantially increased the cost of litigation to very little advantage. Many appellate judges share this view.'

46. SH Bailey, JPL Ching, and NW Taylor, *The Modern English Legal System* (5th edn, Sweet & Maxwell, London, 2007) 454.

> **HELD:** Whilst coal mines were listed in s 1, limestone mines were not. The *expressio unius* rule provided that only those items listed were within the scope of the provision and so the limestone mine was not rateable under the 1601 Act.

It is common, however, for a statute to provide a list of specific words and then follow it with a general phrase (for example, 'this Act will apply to X, Y, Z, and any other relevant items'). The addition of the general phrase means that the *expressio unius* rule cannot be used and so a second rule is used, which is known as the *ejusdem generis* ('of the same class') rule. This simply means that the general phrase will relate only to things of the same class or type as the specific words, and is demonstrated by the following case.

 Powell v Kempton Park Racecourse Co Ltd [1899] AC 143 (HL)

FACTS: The Betting Act 1853 made it an offence to use a 'house, office, room or other place for betting' ('house, office and room' constituted the specific class, and 'other place' constituted the general phrase). The defendant operated Tatersall's Ring, an outdoor enclosure in which betting took place. The defendant was charged with breach of the 1853 Act.

HELD: The House of Lords held that no contravention of the 1853 Act had occurred. The specific words used were all related to indoor locations and, accordingly, the phrase 'other place' could only include locations of the same class. Because Tatersalls' Ring was outside, it was not an 'other place' for the purposes of the 1853 Act.

The third rule to be discussed is represented by the maxim *noscitur a sociis* ('it is known from its associates'). This rule provides that the words of a statute should be interpreted in the context of the words surrounding them and the neighbouring provisions. The application of this rule can be seen in the following case.

 Pengelley v Bell Punch Co Ltd [1964] 1 WLR 1055 (CA)

FACTS: The Factories Act 1961, s 28, provided that 'floors, steps, stairs, passageways and gangways' should be kept clear of obstruction. The defendant used a section of the factory floor to store reels of paper. The claimant injured himself whilst reaching over these reels and alleged that the defendant had breached s 28.

HELD: The Court of Appeal held that s 28 had not been breached. The word 'floor' in s 28 should be interpreted in context with the words around it. The words around it clearly indicated that 'floor' was being used in the sense of a passageway; the floor on which the reels were stored was not a passageway, but was used for storage. Accordingly, it did not fall within the definition of 'floor' contained in s 28.

Presumptions, intrinsic and extrinsic aids, and linguistic rules may be useful in specific cases, but, generally, their usefulness is limited. It has therefore largely been left to the judges themselves to determine the most appropriate methods to interpret legislation. Over time, the judiciary has formed what are known as the 'canons of interpretation'—three rules that are designed to provide the judiciary with the flexibility to interpret legislation effectively and in line with the intention of Parliament:

- the literal rule;
- the golden rule; and
- the mischief rule.

Unfortunately, the precise relationship between the three rules has never been clarified and, as we shall see, the rules can produce vastly different outcomes. The general belief appears to be that the rules are hierarchical (that is, that the court will use the literal rule first, and, if that produces an unacceptable result, it will move onto the golden rule, etc.)—but there is no conclusive evidence to indicate that such a belief is justified and it is actually more accurate to state that:

> a court invokes whichever of the rules produces a result that satisfies its sense of justice in the case before it. Although the literal rule is the one most frequently referred to in express terms, the courts treat all three as valid and refer to them as occasion demands...[47]

The literal rule

Under the literal rule, the words of a statute are given their literal, normal, every-day meaning, irrespective of the result that such an interpretation produces. So, for example, in *Whitely v Chapell*,[48] the Poor Law Amendment Act 1851, s 3, made it a criminal offence to personate at an election 'any person entitled to vote'. The defendant was found 'not guilty' after he personated a dead voter, because a dead person is not *entitled* to vote.

The literal rule is the most constitutionally acceptable rule, because it focuses on the actual words that Parliament chose to use and if Parliament chooses words that produce unacceptable results, it is for Parliament to rectify the law, not the judges. As Lord Esher stated: 'If the words of an Act are clear, you must follow them, even though they lead to a manifest absurdity. The court has nothing to do with the question of whether the legislature has committed an absurdity.'[49] Whilst such an approach may respect the principle of parliamentary sovereignty, that will provide little comfort to the litigant who loses his case due to a literal, but absurd, interpretation. In criminal law cases, the results of an overly literal interpretation can be even more severe, as seen in the following case.

---

47. J Willis, 'Statute Interpretation in a Nutshell' (1938) 16 Can Bar Rev 1, 6.
48. (1869) 4 QB 147.
49. *R v Judge of the City of London Court* [1892] 1 QB 273 (CA) 290.

🔓 *R v Maginnis* [1987] 1 All ER 907 (HL)[50]

FACTS: The police had discovered a package containing cannabis resin in Maginnis' car. He claimed that the package was not his, but was left in his car by a friend, who intended to collect it later. Despite this, Maginnis was charged under the Misuse of Drugs Act 1971, s 5(3), which makes it a criminal offence for 'a person to have a controlled drug in his possession, whether lawfully or not, with intent to supply it to another'.

HELD: The key words were 'intent to supply'. Applying their literal meaning, a four-to-one majority (Lord Goff dissenting) in the House of Lords upheld Maginnis' conviction. He intended to give the drugs back to his friend; ergo he intended to supply them.

COMMENT: This case demonstrates a fundamental flaw of the literal rule—namely, the presumption that all words have a single, literal, normal meaning. In reality, few words will have a single everyday meaning; they will usually have several. None of the judges involved in *Maginnis* could agree on what was the literal definition of the word 'supply': judges in the majority and minority were both able to point to dictionary definitions that upheld their respective viewpoints. This case also demonstrates that a literal interpretation can actually run counter to the intention of Parliament. There is little doubt that the offence contained in s 5(3) was aimed at drug 'pushers' (a point made by Lord Goff), as opposed to drug users, who were subject to a less serious offence under s 5(1)—namely, being in possession of a controlled drug. By convicting Maginnis of the more serious offence, there is little doubt that the courts had applied the Act in a way that Parliament had not intended.

As time progressed, criticisms of the literal rule began to emerge. In 1969, the Law Commission stated:

> To place undue emphasis on the literal meaning of the words of a provision is to assume an unattainable perfection in draftsmanship…Such an approach ignores the limitations of language, which is not infrequently demonstrated even at the level of the House of Lords when Law Lords differ as to the so-called 'plain meaning' of words.[51]

Clearly, the literal rule could not be the sole governing rule for the interpretation of statutes. A rule was needed that could be used where the literal interpretation was insufficient, and such a rule was created in 1857—namely, the golden rule.

The golden rule

The golden rule was first advanced by Lord Wensleydale when he stated 'the grammatical and ordinary sense of the words is to be adhered to, unless that would lead to some absurdity…in which case the grammatical and ordinary sense of words may be modified, so as to avoid that absurdity…but no farther'.[52] Based on this, it could validly be argued that the golden rule is nothing more than an evolution of the literal rule. The courts have since categorically stated that the literal rule will not be used

---

50. Another case universally regarded as producing an absurd result is *London and North Eastern Railway v Berriman* [1946] AC 278 (HL).

51. Law Commission, *Interpretation of Statutes: Report by the Two Commissions* (Law Com No 21, HMSO, London, 1969) [30].

52. *Grey v Pearson* (1857) 6 HL Cas 61, 106.

where it would produce an absurd result;[53] instead, the courts will use an alternative meaning of the relevant words that 'though less proper, is one which the Court thinks the words will bear'.[54] In other words, the court will endeavour to find the meaning that the words should bear, as opposed to the meaning that they actually do bear. The use of the golden rule to avoid an absurd result can be seen in the following cases.

 ### Adler v George [1964] 2 QB 7 (QB)

FACTS: The defendant obtained access to a Royal Air Force station and, within the station, he obstructed a member of the Her Majesty's forces. The Official Secrets Act 1920, s 3, made it an offence to obstruct a member of Her Majesty's forces 'in the vicinity of' a prohibited place, which the station was. The defendant argued that he had not obstructed the member of the forces 'in the vicinity of' the prohibited place, but had carried out the obstruction *inside* the prohibited place, and that being inside a place was not the same as being in its vicinity. He was convicted and he appealed.

HELD: The High Court dismissed his appeal. Lord Parker CJ stated that to read the provision literally in the way that the defendant contended would be absurd and that the phrase should be read as '*in or* in the vicinity of'.

 ### R v Allen (1872) 1 CCR 367

FACTS: Allen had married another woman whilst his existing wife was still alive. He was charged with the crime of bigamy under the Offences Against the Person Act 1861, s 57, which states: 'Whosoever being married shall marry any other person during the life of the former husband or wife...shall be guilty of bigamy.' Allen argued that, because he was already married, it was technically impossible to marry someone else: he may take part in a marriage ceremony, but he would not be lawfully marrying the second 'wife'; ergo he was not guilty under the 1861 Act.

HELD: Allen's defence failed and he was convicted. From a literal point of view, he was correct—but a literal interpretation of s 57 would have rendered it completely useless. Therefore, the court held that the words 'shall marry' would be interpreted to mean shall 'go through the form and ceremony of marriage with another person'.[55]

It should be noted that the court cannot abandon the literal rule in favour of the golden rule whenever it wishes. The golden rule can be used only where the literal rule would produce 'an inconsistency, or an absurdity or inconvenience so great as to convince the Court that the intention could not have been to use [the words of the statute] in their ordinary signification'.[56] This limitation can lead to

---

53. *McMonagle v Westminster City Council* [1990] 2 AC 716 (HL).
54. *River Wear Commissioners v Adamson* (1877) 2 App Cas 743 (HL) 765 (Lord Blackburn).
55. *R v Allen* (1872) 1 CCR 367, 375 (Cockburn CJ).
56. Ibid, 764–5 (Lord Blackburn).

situations in which the court is bound to adopt a literal interpretation when it would desperately wish not to. This occurred in the decision of the High Court in *R v Human Fertilisation and Embryology Authority, ex p Blood*,[57] in which Diane Blood wished to be inseminated with sperm taken from her husband before he died. Unfortunately for her, the Human Fertilisation and Embryology Act 1990, Sch 3(1), provided that the donor would need to provide written consent, which was obviously impossible. In dismissing her appeal against the decision of the Human Fertilisation and Embryology Authority's decision not to allow her to be inseminated, Sir Stephen Brown described the case as 'most anxious and moving [and that his] heart went out to this applicant who wishes to preserve an essential part of her late beloved husband'.[58] The requirement for written consent was, however, clear and, as a matter of statutory construction, the court had no option but to dismiss her appeal.[59]

Whilst an application of the golden rule may be preferable to the literal rule in certain cases, this does not mean that the golden rule is without problems. The Law Commission noted that the application of the golden rule is based upon the literal rule producing an 'absurdity, inconsistency or inconvenience, but provides no clear means to test the existence of these characteristics or to measure their quality or extent'.[60] Often, the justification behind an application of the golden rule is to apply a rule of public policy, with such rules being notoriously vague and amorphous. The golden rule would appear to provide a measure of flexibility to statutory interpretation, but at the cost of reducing certainty.

The mischief rule and the purposive approach

The final rule to be examined was actually the first to be established. The mischief rule was laid down in 1584 in *Heydon's Case*[61] and basically states that, where a statute was enacted to remedy a problem (mischief), the court will, if possible, adopt an interpretation of the statute that corrects that mischief. More specifically, the court in *Heydon's Case* stated that four factors needed to be considered.

1. What was the common law before the enactment of the Act?
2. What was the defect (mischief) that the common law failed to remedy?
3. What remedy had Parliament implemented to cure the mischief?
4. What was the true reason for the adoption of the remedy?

The following case demonstrates the mischief rule in action.

---

57. [1996] 3 WLR 1176 (QB).
58. Ibid, 1191.
59. Fortunately for Diane Blood, whilst the Court of Appeal agreed with the interpretation of the trial judge, it reversed his decision ([1999] Fam 151) on the ground that the EC Treaty, Arts 59 and 60, provided Mrs Blood with the right to receive medical treatment in another member State. Accordingly, she was permitted to receive *in vitro* fertilization (IVF) treatment in Belgium using her dead husband's sperm. She subsequently gave birth to two sons (on separate occasions) and won another legal battle to have Mr Blood legally recognized as the boys' father.
60. Law Commission, *Interpretation of Statutes: Report by the Two Commissions* (Law Com No 21, HMSO, London, 1969) [32].
61. (1584) 3 Co Rep 7a.

Royal College of Nursing v DHSS [1981] AC 800 (HL)

FACTS: The Abortion Act 1967, s 1(1), provided that no criminal offence is committed 'when a pregnancy is terminated by a registered medical practitioner'. When the Act was passed, abortions were carried out surgically by doctors, but in 1972, chemical abortions were introduced, which involved a doctor inserting a catheter and a nurse pumping a chemical into the womb. The introduction of the chemical was carried out while the doctor was on call, but not actually present. The Royal College of Nursing sought a declaration from the court that the new procedure was in breach of s 1(1).

HELD: The House of Lords, by a majority of three to two, held that the new procedure was lawful. Lord Diplock focused on the mischief behind the 1967 Act, which was to clarify and remedy the uncertain nature of the law prior to 1967, and to render unlawful the 'back-street abortions' that many women undertook due to the law's lack of clarity. The 1967 Act achieved this by broadening the grounds upon which a lawful abortion may be obtained and ensuring that the abortion is carried out in hygienic conditions with the requisite skill. Given this, a nurse in a hospital administering a chemical under the instruction of a doctor is clearly not what s 1(1) was enacted to prevent.

COMMENT: Clearly, in order to reach their verdict, the majority had to reject a literal interpretation of s 1(1). Much of the confusion in this case could be seen to be the result of the drafting of s 1(1), which was described as 'far from elegant'.[62] But is the poor drafting of a provision reason enough to reject a literal interpretation? The two dissenting judges (Lords Wilberforce and Edmund-Davies) thought not. Both judges adopted a literal interpretation and found the procedure to be unlawful, because the pregnancy was clearly not terminated by a 'registered medical practitioner', but by a nurse. Lord Edmund-Davies was particularly critical of the majority, arguing that they had engaged in 'redrafting with a vengeance'.[63] It is interesting to note that, of the nine judges who were involved in this case in the various courts, only four believed the new procedure to be lawful.

Whilst the mischief rule may be the preferred rule of the Law Commission, it still acknowledges that the legal environment today has changed hugely since *Heydon's Case*.[64] When the rule was conceived, parliamentary sovereignty was not yet fully established and statute was a much less important source of law than it is today. Accordingly, a rule that, in essence, allows the judges to rectify the meaning of a statute to allow it to remedy the mischief that it was intended to was appropriate. Today, when parliamentary sovereignty is well established and statute a primary source of law, allowing judges such a quasi-legislative role is less constitutionally justifiable. Further, when the rule was conceived, judges played a prominent role in the drafting of statutes; they were therefore well placed to identify the mischief that a statute was meant to remedy. Today, skilled parliamentary draftsmen draft statutes and the judges may not be as well placed to identify the mischief that an Act was designed to remedy.

---

62. *Royal College of Nursing v DHSS* [1981] AC 800 (HL) 827 (Lord Diplock).
63. Ibid, 831.
64. Law Commission, *Interpretation of Statutes: Report by the Two Commissions* (Law Com No 21, HMSO, London, 1969) [33].

Much modern legislation is not concerned with remedying a particular mischief, but rather with achieving some other, more general, purpose. For this reason, in recent decades, the 'pendulum has swung towards purposive methods of construction',[65] whereby the courts will interpret the statute by reference to its context and purpose. The following case demonstrates the court's application of the purposive approach.

> ## Attorney General's Reference (No 1 of 1988) [1989] AC 971 (HL)
>
> **FACTS:** The defendant wished to purchase a particular company—but before the purchase could be made, an adviser to the company in question informed him that the company had agreed to accept a rival offer. Within ten minutes of discovering this, the defendant began purchasing shares in the company, which he subsequently sold at a substantial profit. The issue arising was whether he had engaged in insider dealing. The relevant statute provided that insider dealing was committed where the defendant had inside information that he 'knowingly obtained'.[66] The defendant argued that, because he took no positive steps to acquire the information, but had merely received it, he had not actually 'obtained' the information.
>
> **HELD:** Whilst the defendant had not obtained information according to the primary definition of the word ('to procure by one's own efforts'), he had obtained information according to the word's secondary definition ('to acquire something without effort on one's part'). The House stated that it should not be bound by the primary, literal definition of a word, and should apply a definition that is in line with the statute's purpose. On this basis, the secondary definition was more in line with the Act's purpose (that is, to prevent insider dealing) and therefore the defendant had obtained inside information within the meaning of the Act.

⭐ See 'A Simple Matter of Statutory Interpretation' (1990) Crim LR 1

This purposive approach is universally accepted and judges will frequently refer to their interpretation of a statute being 'purposive'. This approach is wider than the golden rule, because it does not depend on the literal approach producing an absurd result, or a result that Parliament could not have intended. It is also wider than the mischief rule, because it does not focus on a particular mischief, but rather the broad aims and purposes of the statute.

The courts' reliance on the use of the purposive approach is demonstrated in that the courts have held that a statute that fails to fulfil its purpose due to a drafting error, it can be rectified by the courts by adding, removing, or substituting words. But before the court remedies a drafting error, it must be sure:[67]

- of the intended purpose of the statute or provision;
- that the draftsmen and Parliament have, inadvertently, failed to give effect to that purpose; and

---

65. *R (Quintavalle) v Secretary of State for Health* [2003] 2 AC 687 (HL) 700 (Lord Steyn).
66. Company Securities (Insider Dealing) Act 1985, s 1.
67. *Inco Europe Ltd v First Choice Distribution* [2000] 1 WLR 586 (HL) 592 (Lord Nicholls).

- of the substance (although not the precise working) of the provision that Parliament would have enacted, had it noticed the error.

These three rules impose clear limits on the courts' ability to remedy a statute using the purposive approach. Where a case involves a *casus omissus* (that is, something for which statute should provide, but which it does not), the court cannot fill the gap in the statute; to do so would attribute an intention that Parliament clearly did not have and would constitute 'naked usurpation of the legislative function under the thin disguise of interpretation'.[68] Where statute does contain a gap, it is for Parliament to fill it by passing an amending Act.

Can the three rules of interpretation be unified?

Although it is traditional to discuss statutory interpretation by reference to the three rules discussed above, it is worth noting the possibility of unifying the above rules. In 1976, Sir Rupert Cross published *Statutory Interpretation*,[69] which has since become a seminal work on statutory interpretation. In it, he postulated a unified approach to statutory interpretation that has, in later editions of the text, become known as the unified 'contextual' approach.[70]

This approach was based on four rules, of which the first three are of key importance. But instead of providing three alternative rules, Cross' contextual theory provides three progressive rules that should be followed in order.

1. The judge should give effect to the ordinary and grammatical meaning of the words within the general context of the statute.
2. If the judge is of the opinion that applying the ordinary and grammatical meaning of the words would produce a result contrary to the purpose of the statute, he may apply to those words a secondary meaning that they are capable of bearing.
3. The judge has a limited power to add, alter, or ignore words, but only to prevent a statute from becoming unintelligible, absurd, unreasonable, unworkable, or irreconcilable with the rest of the statute.

The above rules provide the judges with substantial flexibility to 'rescue' a statute the effect of which could be compromised by its drafting. In many cases, Cross' rules have been evidenced (if not overtly identified) as effecting minor changes to a statute that could have important effects in practice, as the following case demonstrates.

 Federal Steam Navigation Co Ltd v Department of Trade and Industry [1974] 1 WLR 505 (HL)

FACTS: A ship had discharged oil into a prohibited sea area. The Oil in Navigable Waters Act 1955, s 1(1), provided that, where this occurred, 'the owner or master of the ship shall be guilty of an offence'. The owner of the ship was convicted and, shortly after, so was

---

68. *Magor and St Mellons Rural District Council v Newport Corporation* [1952] AC 189 (HL) 191 (Lord Simonds).
69. Sir R Cross, *Statutory Interpretation* (Butterworths, London, 1976).
70. Sir R Cross, J Bell, and Sir G Engle, *Cross on Statutory Interpretation* (3rd edn, OUP, Oxford, 1995) 49.

the master. The master argued that the use of the words 'owner *or* master' meant that the prosecution could only proceed against one of them and could not prosecute both.

HELD: The House of Lords rejected the master's argument. It held that Parliament clearly intended that both master and owner should be liable, and the words in s 1(1) could be read as if they stated 'owner *and/or* master'.

It should be noted, however, that where the words of a statute are clear and are not capable of an alternative interpretation, the court should apply a literal interpretation, even if it produces an absurd result.[71] Such statutes are 'beyond judicial redemption'.[72]

 Key points summary

- Domestic legislation comes in two forms: Acts of Parliament and subordinate legislation.

- Acts of Parliament (also known as 'primary legislation', or 'statute law') are the highest form of UK law.

- Subordinate legislation is legislation created by bodies authorized by Parliament to legislate. It is also known as 'secondary legislation'.

- In order to become an Act of Parliament, a Bill will need to pass though both Houses of Parliament (Commons and Lords) and receive royal assent from the monarch.

- The stages that a public Bill will pass though in both Houses are:
  - first reading;
  - second reading;
  - committee stage:
  - report stage; and
  - third reading.

- A Bill can become an Act of Parliament without the consent of the Lords under the procedure found in the Parliament Acts 1911 and 1949.

- The three 'canons of statutory interpretation' are the literal rule, the golden rule, and the mischief rule. In more recent times, the purposive approach has come to be used more by the courts.

---

71. *Inland Revenue Commissioners v Hinchy* [1960] AC 748 (HL).
72. SH Bailey, JPL Ching, and NW Taylor, *The Modern English Legal System* (5th edn, Sweet & Maxwell, London, 2007) 426.

Case law

Although the amount of legislation passed by Parliament has increased in recent years, largely due to Parliament legislating in areas that have traditionally been regulated by the common law, the bulk of law within the English legal system is still largely derived from cases and the English legal system is still very much a common law system. 'Case law' refers to the body of law that is created and reformed via the decisions of judges.

The doctrine of precedent

Central to our common law system is what is known as the doctrine of 'precedent'. The *Oxford English Dictionary* defines 'precedent' as '[a] previous instance taken as an example or rule by which to be guided in similar cases or circumstances'.[73] In legal terms, it simply refers to the process whereby cases are decided based upon previous judicial decisions.

In terms of precedent, cases come in three varieties, as follows.

- *No precedent value*   Certain cases will not set a precedent at all and can be ignored in subsequent cases. For example, decisions in magistrates' courts do not establish precedent.

- *Persuasive authority*   Certain cases, although not needing to be followed in later cases, may nevertheless be regarded as persuasive. The persuasiveness of a case will depend upon its source. For example, decisions of the Judicial Committee of the Privy Council are regarded as extremely persuasive,[74] largely because this court consists of former Law Lords. Less persuasive precedents include *obiter dicta* (which are discussed later),[75] the decisions of lower courts (for example, decisions of the Court of Appeal will constitute persuasive authority in the House of Lords), the decisions of Irish, Scottish, Commonwealth, and US courts, and binding decisions that have been distinguished.[76]

- *Binding authority*   Certain cases are regarded as binding authority, meaning that they lay down principles that must be followed by later courts (unless the court is not bound by that precedent or the case can be distinguished).

Having established that cases may be binding on later courts, two questions need to be answered.

1. *When* is a case binding?
2. Exactly *what* aspect of a case binds later courts?

---

73. Definition derived from Oxford English Dictionary Online, <http://www.oed.com>.

74. For example, the law relating to remoteness of damages is based upon the Privy Council case *Overseas Tankships (UK) Ltd v Morts Dock Engineering Co Ltd* [1961] AC 388 (known as *The Wagon Mound (No 1)*). This case and the rule of remoteness is discussed in more depth at p 436.

75. Although *obiter dicta* deriving from higher courts or prestigious judges may be strongly persuasive, the best example being the 'neighbour principle' set down by Lord Atkin in *Donoghue v Stevenson* [1932] AC 562 (HL) 580, which has become the basis for the tort of negligence. The neighbour test is discussed at p 381.

76. Especially if it a House of Lords' decision: see *Re House Property and Investment Co Ltd* [1954] Ch 576.

The court hierarchy

The extent to which a court is bound by precedent (and can bind other courts) is dependent upon where it sits in the court hierarchy. The UK court system is made up of seven main courts (eight, if we count the Divisional Courts as distinct from the High Court). The general rule is that higher courts bind lower courts, but, as we shall see, there are exceptions to this and one court, the Judicial Committee of the Privy Council, does not sit easily within the hierarchy.

Table 3.1 demonstrates in brief the court hierarchy in relation to the doctrine of precedent.

The jurisdiction, operation, and composition of each court is discussed in Chapter 2

The Appellate Committee of the House of Lords and the Supreme Court

The highest domestic court in the UK is the Appellate Committee of the House of Lords.[77] Decisions of the House of Lords are binding on all other UK courts in civil matters, and on all other courts in England, Wales, and Northern Ireland in criminal matters. It used to be the case that the House of Lords was also bound by its own decisions[78]—but the unfortunate effect of this was to entrench House of Lords' decisions, making them unalterable except by statute. Recognizing that 'too rigid adherence to precedent may lead to injustice in a particular case and…unduly restrict the proper development of the law',[79] the House of Lords issued a Practice Statement indicating that it was no longer bound by its own decisions and would depart from them 'when it appears right to do so'.[80] Although the House of Lords is now free to overrule its own decisions, it does so rarely.

It is well established that the House will not overrule a previous decision simply because it is 'wrong'.[81] So when will the House of Lords overrule itself? Should the House only be allowed to overrule itself in set circumstances, or should it have full discretion? Authority exists for both positions. In *Vestey v Inland Revenue Commissioners*,[82] Lord Wilberforce stated that the House's power to overrule itself should be 'governed by stated principles'.[83] Conversely, in *The Hannah Blumenthal*,[84] Lord Roskill stated that instances in which the House can overrule itself 'cannot be categorized'.[85] Currently, there are no set criteria in place establishing when the House will exercise the power granted to it by the Practice Statement, but it has been argued[86] that an analysis of the cases in which the power has been used reveals some common principles, as follows.

The extent to which the House of Lords is bound by decisions of the European Court of Justice will be considered at p 110

---

77. Not to be confused with the House of Lords as the second chamber of Parliament. In this chapter, unless otherwise stated, 'House of Lords' will refer to the court and not the parliamentary chamber.

78. *London Tramways v London County Council* [1898] AC 375 (HL). An exception to this was provided where the decision was *per incuriam* ('through want of care'), meaning that the House of Lords had decided the case without being made aware of an important case or statute.

79. *Practice Statement (Judicial Precedent)* [1966] 3 All ER 77 (HL).

80. Ibid.

81. *R v National Insurance Commissioner, ex p Hudson* [1972] AC 944 (HL) 966.

82. [1980] AC 1148 (HL).   83. Ibid, 1150.

84. [1983] 1 AC 845 (HL).   85. Ibid, 922.

86. See Sir R Cross and JW Harris, *Precedent in English Law* (4th edn, OUP, Oxford, 1991) 135–43.

TABLE 3.1 Precedent and the court hierarchy

Court	Bound by	Binds
House of Lords or Supreme Court	• No domestic court can bind the House of Lords or Supreme Court	• Every court below, except the Privy Council in relation to common law issues
Court of Appeal	• House of Lords or Supreme Court • Court of Appeal (subject to exceptions)	• Court of Appeal (subject to exceptions) • Every court below
Divisional Courts	• House of Lords or Supreme Court • Court of Appeal • Divisional Courts (subject to exceptions)	• Divisional Courts (subject to exceptions) • Every court below (including the High Court)
High Court	• House of Lords or Supreme Court • Court of Appeal • Divisional Courts	• Every court below
County courts Crown Court Magistrates' courts	• All courts above	• No court—these cannot create binding precedent, but Crown Court decisions constitute persuasive authority
Judicial Committee of the Privy Council	• House of Lords or Supreme Court, in relation to non-common law issues	• Every other court (except itself) in relation to appeals from specialist courts • Every other court (except itself) in relation to devolution issues (until October 2009—after this date, the Supreme Court will assume this function)

- The House must be of the opinion that '[t]he present law, all things considered, would be improved'[87] by overruling a previous decision.
- The House will not overrule a previous decision where no new reasons or arguments are advanced.
- The House will not overrule a previous decision where 'a class of the citizenry'[88] has justifiably relied upon the previous decision and ordered its affairs based upon it.
- The House will not overrule a previous decision where Parliament has enacted legislation based upon the assumption that the previous decision is the law.
- In criminal cases, the House should not overrule a previous decision where the issue is moot (that is, having no practical significance).

🔗 The Supreme Court is discussed at p 36

In October 2009, the House of Lords will be replaced by a Supreme Court, following the passing of the Constitutional Reform Act 2005. From the point of view of the doctrine of precedent, however, little will change, except that the Supreme Court will assume the devolution function of the Privy Council.

87. JW Harris, 'Towards Principles of Overruling: When Should a Final Court of Appeal Second Guess?' (1990) 10 OJLS 135, 149.
88. Ibid, 169.

The Court of Appeal

The Court of Appeal consists of two divisions—namely, the Civil Division and Criminal Division—and it is necessary to consider them separately. Decisions of the Civil Division of the Court of Appeal bind all lower civil courts (namely, the High Court, the county courts, and, in respect of its civil jurisdiction, the magistrates' courts). The Civil Division is bound by its own decisions, as well as those of the House of Lords or Supreme Court—but the ability of the Civil Division to bind itself is subject to a number of exceptions, as laid down in the following case.

Young v Bristol Aeroplane Co Ltd [1944] KB 718 (CA)

FACTS: The facts of the case are not directly relevant.

HELD: The Court of Appeal reiterated that it is usually bound by its own decisions, but stated that three exceptions exist to this principle, as follows.

1. If two previous Court of Appeal decisions conflict, the Court must choose which case to follow. The other case is automatically overruled.

2. The Court of Appeal may ignore its own previous decision, which 'although not expressly overruled, cannot stand with a subsequent decision of the House of Lords'.[89]

3. If a Court of Appeal decision is *per incuriam* ('through want of care'), it need not be followed. An example of a decision being *per incuriam* is where a key case or statute was overlooked and, had the Court known of this case or statute, it would have reached a contrary decision.

Since *Young*, a number of other exceptions have been established, including:

- Court of Appeal judgments in relation to the granting of permission to appeal are not binding;[90]
- the decision of a two-judge Court of Appeal in relation to an interlocutory appeal will not bind a future three-judge Court of Appeal;[91]
- if a Court of Appeal decision is appealed to the House of Lords and the Lords decide the appeal on different grounds from those argued in the Court of Appeal, then the Court of Appeal decision will not be binding on itself;[92]
- there is authority indicating that a Court of Appeal decision may not be binding on itself (or, indeed, on a first-instance judge)[93] if it is inconsistent with a decision of the Privy Council,[94] although this issue is far from settled;[95]

---

89. *Young v Bristol Aeroplane Co Ltd* [1944] KB 718 (CA) 722 (Lord Greene MR); *Great Peace Shipping Ltd v Tsavliris Salvage (International) Ltd* [2002] EWCA Civ 1407, [2003] QB 679.

90. *Clark v University of Lincolnshire and Humberside* [2000] 3 All ER 752 (CA).

91. *Boys v Chaplin* [1968] 2 QB 1 (CA).

92. *Al-Mehdawi v Secretary of State for the Home Department* [1990] 1 AC 876 (CA).

93. See *Daraydan Holdings Ltd v Solland International Ltd* [2004] EWHC 622, [2005] Ch 119.

94. *Doughty v Turner Manufacturing Co Ltd* [1964] 1 QB 518 (CA); *Worcester Works Finance Ltd v Cooden Engineering Co Ltd* [1972] 1 QB 210 (CA).

95. See, e.g., *Davis v Johnson* [1979] AC 264 (CA).

- although not overtly established, it is highly probable that a Court of Appeal decision will not be binding on itself if it is inconsistent with a decision of the European Court of Justice (ECJ). This is because the European Communities Act 1972, s 3(1), imposes a duty upon all domestic courts either to refer cases involving European law to the ECJ, or, if a referral is not made, to determine the case in accordance with principles and decisions of the ECJ.

Decisions of the Criminal Division of the Court of Appeal bind all lower criminal courts (namely, the Queen's Bench Division of the High Court, the Crown Court, and magistrates' courts). The Criminal Division is bound by its own decisions, as well as by those of the House of Lords or Supreme Court. The above exceptions that apply to the Civil Division also apply to the Criminal Division, except that relating to an inconsistent decision of the Privy Council.[96] Because criminal cases involve the potential to deprive defendants of their liberty, precedent is not followed as strictly as it is in the Civil Division and the discretion of the Criminal Division to ignore its own decisions is wider. So, for example, the Criminal Division may ignore an earlier case if it believes that the earlier case 'misapplied or misunderstood'[97] the law.

The Divisional Courts

Judges in each of the three divisions of the High Court may also sit as a Divisional Court. Decisions of a Divisional Court bind other Divisional Courts and all lower courts, including the standard High Court, if a judge sits alone. The Divisional Courts are bound by the decisions of the House of Lords or Supreme Court, the Court of Appeal,[98] and themselves. In civil cases, however, the *Young v Bristol Aeroplane Co Ltd* exceptions outlined above apply to a Divisional Court.[99] In criminal cases and cases involving judicial review, the Court may depart from previous decisions where it feels that 'the previous decision was plainly wrong'.[100]

The High Court

High Court decisions are binding upon all lower courts. The High Court is bound by decisions of the House of Lords or Supreme Court, the Court of Appeal, and its Divisional Courts. The High Court is not bound by itself, although decisions by other High Court judges are considered extremely persuasive and are departed from reluctantly. It has been argued that a High Court judge should only depart from a previous High Court decision if he is convinced that it was incorrect,[101] and that deputy High Court judges should follow the decisions of High Court judges.[102] If two High Court decisions conflict, the practice is to follow the later decision, provided that the later decision fully considered the earlier decision.[103]

---

96. *R v Campbell* [1997] Cr App R 199 (CA).

97. *R v Gould* [1968] 2 QB 65 (CA) 69 (Diplock LJ).

98. Unless the Court of Appeal decision was *per incuriam* and the missing authority was a House of Lords' decision: *R v Northumberland Compensation Appeal Tribunal, ex p Shaw* [1952] 1 KB 338 (CA).

99. *Huddersfield Police Authority v Watson* [1947] KB 842 (DC).

100. *Hornigold v Chief Constable of Lancashire* [1986] Crim LR 792 (DC).

101. *Re Hillas-Drake, National Provincial Bank v Liddell* [1944] Ch 235.

102. *R v Hertsmere Borough Council, ex p Woolgar* (1996) HLR 703 (QB).

103. *Colchester Estates (Cardiff) v Carlton Industries plc* [1986] Ch 80.

The Crown Court

Although legal rulings of the Crown Court are not binding, they do constitute per-suasive authority. The Crown Court is bound by decisions of the House of Lords or Supreme Court, Court of Appeal, and the High Court. It was held in *R v Colyer*[104] that the Crown Court is not bound by decisions of a Divisional Court, but given that the High Court and Divisional Courts themselves are bound by decisions of a Divisional Court, such an assertion is unlikely ever to be accepted.

The inferior courts

County courts and magistrates' courts are referred to collectively as the 'inferior courts'. Neither of these courts can produce binding precedent. Consequently, deci-sions of these courts bind no one, including themselves. These courts are all bound by decisions of the House of Lords or Supreme Court, Court of Appeal, and High Court (including Divisional Courts).

The Judicial Committee of the Privy Council

One court that does not fit neatly into the court hierarchy is the Judicial Committee of the Privy Council. As a general rule, its decisions are not binding on any court, except in relation to appeals from certain specialist courts[105] and devolution issues, in which case its decisions bind even the House of Lords[106] (although deci-sions of the Privy Council are not binding on itself).[107] Even when not binding, Privy Council decisions are regarded as extremely persuasive, largely due to the fact that it comprises current and former Law Lords. In fact, in one extremely controversial decision,[108] it was decided that, in extremely exceptional (if not unique) circumstances,[109] a ruling of the Privy Council can take precedence over (that is, overrule) a previous decision of the House of Lords or Supreme Court, and that the Court of Appeal and courts below will be bound to follow the ruling of the Privy Council. Furthermore, in relation to common law issues, the Privy Council is not bound by decisions of the House of Lords or Supreme Court,[110] although such decisions will be extremely persuasive. The reason for this is that the Privy Council acts as a final appeal court for Commonwealth countries and that such countries may require the law to develop in a manner different from that of the UK.

---

104. *R v Colyer* [1974] Crim LR 243.

105. This would include the Ecclesiastical Court, which hears disputes relating to religious matters, and the Prize Court, which hears cases on whether ships have been lawfully captured in times of war.

106. See Scotland Act 1998, s 103(1), Government of Wales Act 1998, Sch 8, para 32, and Northern Ireland Act 1998, s 82(1). When the Supreme Court comes into operation, it will assume the devolution jurisdiction of the Privy Council.

107. *Gibson v Government of the United States of America* [2007] UKPC 52, [2007] 1 WLR 2367.

108. *R v James* [2006] EWCA Crim 14, [2006] QB 588.

109. In *R v James*, the Privy Council decision that was followed was decided by a bench of nine Law Lords. Over half of them were Law Lords at the time that the case was decided and, had the case been appealed to the House of Lords, the result would have been a foregone conclusion.

110. See, e.g., *Australian Consolidated Press Ltd v Uren* [1969] 1 AC 590 (PC).

Stare decisis and ratio decidendi

Once it has been established that the decisions of one court bind another, it then needs to be determined exactly which aspect of a case is binding. The UK system of binding precedent is based upon the Latin maxim *stare decisis* ('keep to what has been decided previously').[111] This is, however, a shortened version of the full maxim and its abbreviation is unfortunate, because the full phrase is descriptively more accurate. The full maxim *stare rationibus decidendis* ('keep to the reasoning of what has been decided previously') indicates that it is the *reasoning* behind the court's decision that is binding upon later courts, not the actual decision itself, nor the specific facts of the case. The facts of a case cannot be binding on future courts: if this were the case, the application of precedent would be dependent upon two cases having identical facts—something that virtually never happens in practice. By making the reasoning the binding element, the court can apply this reasoning to cases with a wide range of facts. This reasoning is known as the *ratio decidendi*. Unfortunately, in practice, identifying the *ratio* of a case can be extremely difficult, especially because judges will never overtly state 'the *ratio* of this case is ...' To make matters more complicated, a case may have more than one *ratio* (known as *rationes*).

The following example demonstrates how the *ratio* differs from the facts, but is still influenced by the facts.

Eg Identifying the *ratio*

Andrew is driving down the road in his black BMW. He takes his eyes off the road in order to tune in the car's radio. He does not notice that Ceri is trying to cross the road at a zebra crossing and he runs her over, injuring her severely. Ceri sues Andrew in negligence and is successful. Possible *rationes* could be any of the following.

1. *Men who drive black BMWs and who run over women at zebra crossings are liable in negligence* This *ratio* is far too narrow and could only be applied in cases with identical facts to our case. Does the sex of the driver and victim matter? Does the colour and make of car matter? The answer to both of these questions is 'no'.

2. *Drivers of cars are liable if they negligently run over a person at a zebra crossing* This *ratio* is better, but is still too narrow. Why are only drivers of cars liable? What if I negligently run over someone by mounting the pavement instead of at a zebra crossing?

3. *Drivers of motor vehicles who drive without due care and attention may be liable in negligence for injuries caused to another as a result of such negligence* This seems like a much more sensible *ratio*, but may still be too narrow. What if Andrew ran over Ceri on a bicycle? What if he did not collide with her, but ran over her handbag, which contained an expensive mobile phone? This *ratio* would not cover these situations.

4. *Drivers of vehicles who operate their vehicle without due care and attention may be liable in negligence for losses sustained as a result of such negligence* This is an effective *ratio* that could be used to cover cases with wide-ranging facts, including all of the hypothetical situations mentioned above.

---

111. Sir R Cross and JW Harris, *Precedent in English Law* (4th edn, OUP, Oxford, 1991) 3.

The *ratio* of a case may be the only aspect of a case that provides binding authority, but persuasive authority may derive from what are known as *obiter dicta*. *Obiter dicta* are statements of law that do not form part of the *ratio* and can arise in several ways, as follows.

➔ *obiter dicta*: 'statements said by the way'

- The judge may apply the law to a hypothetical case with facts that differ from those of the case before him. As we shall see in Chapter 6, Denning J's seminal statement on the application of promissory estoppel in *Central London Property Trust Ltd v High Trees House Ltd*[112] was *obiter dictum*.
- The judge may state a legal principle that is wider than necessary to deal with the current case. In such a situation, the *ratio* will be limited to the part of the principle that applies to the facts. The remainder of the principle will be *obiter dictum*.[113]
- Statements of law in dissenting judgments constitute *obiter dicta*.

The application of precedent

Once a binding precedent is established, there are a number of possible ways in which it can be applied and used by later courts, as illustrated by Table 3.2.

TABLE 3.2 The application of precedent

Application	Meaning
Followed (or applied)	Provided that the facts of the current case sufficiently resemble those of the precedent, the *ratio* of the precedent will be applied to the current case
Overruled	If the court is not bound by the precedent, it may overrule it, in which case, the old precedent ceases to be good law and a new precedent is created
Distinguished	If the court feels that the facts of the current case differ materially from the facts of the case that established the precedent, it can distinguish the precedent and will not need to follow it The judge will need to justify why he is distinguishing the precedent and an insufficient justification is likely to lead to the case being criticized or reversed

Advantages and disadvantages of precedent

The doctrine of precedent is something of a paradox, in that it can produce, simultaneously, an advantage and its opposing disadvantage. For example, perhaps the most touted advantage of precedent is that, by applying like cases in a consistent manner, the law becomes more certain. There is no doubt that the doctrine of precedent does promote certainty, but the UK system of precedent can also result in uncertainty. The ability of judges to distinguish cases, often based upon minute and illogical distinctions of fact, can render the law increasingly uncertain.

Other potential combinations of advantages and disadvantages include the following.

---

112. [1974] KB 130.
113. *Cassidy v Ministry of Health* [1951] 2 KB 343 (CA).

- *(Un)predictability* It is argued that the fact that the law is rendered more certain by the existence of an established precedent makes the law more predictable. This is certainly true—but, for two reasons, there is also a strong element of chance and unpredictability:
  - the aforementioned ability to distinguish cases can render the law more unpredictable, because litigants will not know if the judge will attempt to distinguish an established precedent;
  - case law can only be reformed by cases actually reaching court (unless Parliament decides to legislate in the area in question). There are numerous examples of areas of the law that require a definitive House of Lords' judgment, but have not received one, because a relevant case has not reached the House. This introduces an element of chance into the law and increases its unpredictability.

- *(In)efficiency* Because the law is rendered more predictable, people can discover the relevant precedents and organize their affairs so as not to breach the law, thereby reducing the number of cases and making the legal system more efficient. Furthermore, if an individual does intend to initiate proceedings, he can locate the precedent to use it to gauge the likelihood of success, further reducing the number of weak cases being brought. But the sheer bulk of case law and precedent significantly affects the efficiency of the system. An individual seeking a definitive statement of law on his legal position may have to wade through hundreds of cases. These cases may often run to hundreds of pages and, as stated earlier, the *ratio* is never clearly stated.

- *(In)flexibility* As discussed above, creating and reforming legislation can be a lengthy affair. Conversely, case law can continually adapt to meet the changing needs of society, thereby keeping the law up to date. If a previous precedent is no longer effective, it can be overruled and replaced. But the doctrine of precedent can also make the law rigid and inflexible: lower courts cannot overrule higher courts and will be forced to apply a precedent, even if it produces a manifestly unacceptable decision. Further, as noted, precedent can only evolve if cases reach the appropriate court. There are numerous examples of anachronistic House of Lords' precedents remaining good law because a similar case took a long time to reach the Lords—the obvious example being the perpetuation of the marital rape exemption that was eventually abolished in *R v R*.[114]

One final criticism can be made regarding the doctrine of precedent—that is, it is retrospective. As noted, in virtually all cases, legislation changes the law only from the date on which it comes into effect. Conversely, case law is retrospective, as can be demonstrated in the following infamous case.

⚿ *R v R* [1992] 1 AC 599 (HL)

FACTS: The defendant assaulted and attempted to have sexual intercourse with his wife against her will after the couple had been separated for three weeks. They had separated, inter alia, because he had tried to force sex on her before and both parties were considering divorce. The husband contended that, at the time that he forced sex upon his wife, the

---

114. [1992] 1 AC 599 (HL).

law still stated that (with some limited exceptions) marriage granted perpetual consent to sexual intercourse and that therefore a husband who forced sex upon his wife had not committed rape (this was known as the 'marital exemption'). At first instance, he was convicted and the Court of Appeal upheld the conviction.

HELD: The House of Lords abolished the marital exemption and upheld the husband's conviction for rape.

COMMENT: Irrespective of how contemptible the acts of the husband were, the simple fact is that, at the time that he forced sex upon his wife, the marital exemption still existed and marriage was deemed to provide perpetual consent to sexual intercourse. At the time that the forced sex was committed, it was not technically rape—yet the courts retrospectively deemed it so. The European Convention on Human Rights, Art 7(1), prohibits imposing criminal liability upon a person when the act in question did not constitute a crime when it was committed. The European Court of Human Rights held that Art 7 was not breached in R's case,[115] stating that a development in the law would not breach Art 7 provided that it was reasonably foreseeable. Because the marital exemption had been eroded over time, it was foreseeable that it could be abolished.

 See M Giles, 'Judicial Lawmaking in the Criminal Courts: The Case of Marital Rape' (1992) Crim LR 407

Do judges make law?

The final issue to be discussed is the extent to which judges make law. Blackstone's declaratory theory of law states that judges are 'not delegated to pronounce a new law, but to maintain and expound the old one'.[116] In other words, the role of the judges is to interpret and apply law, not to create it, because judges lack the constitutional legitimacy of Parliament and therefore the right to create law. Although the judiciary has reiterated the declaratory theory of law on countless occasions, it is universally accepted that judges do, in fact, make law. A principal reason for this is historical: historically, statute law was not a major source of law and it was therefore left to the judges, via the common law, to create much of the law of the English legal system. Even today, a court may be faced with a situation in which there is no legislative guidance. In such a case, the court cannot wait for Parliament to legislate on the issue; it must make a decision.

Airedale NHS Trust v Bland [1993] AC 789 (HL)

FACTS: As a result of injuries sustained during the Hillsborough disaster, Anthony Bland had remained in a persistent vegetative state for three years. All medical practitioners involved in the case agreed that there was no hope of improvement or recovery. Accordingly, the Hospital Trust, with the full backing of Bland's parents, sought a declaration from the court that it could lawfully discontinue Bland's treatment, thereby allowing him to die. The Official

---

115. *SW v UK*, App no 20166/92 (1996) 21 EHRR 363.
116. See W Blackstone, *Commentaries on the Laws on England: Volume 1* (University of Chicago Press, Chicago, IL, 1979) 69–70.

➡ guardian *ad litem*: a person who protects the rights and property of a person who lacks capacity, or who is incapable of managing his own affairs

Solicitor of the Supreme Court, acting as Bland's guardian *ad litem*, opposed the Trust's application, arguing that such discontinuance of treatment would amount to murder.

HELD: During the course of their judgments, all of the judges involved in this case stressed repeatedly that this case raised entirely new moral and ethical issues that should not be addressed by the courts, but by Parliament. Despite this, the House of Lords was obliged to rule on the case and held that the treatment could be lawfully discontinued. The purpose of medical care was to benefit the patient, but the treatment being administered to Bland conferred no benefit at all. The duty placed upon the doctors to treat had come to an end and, consequently, they could lawfully end the treatment of the patient. Given the importance of the issue, and the need to protect both doctors and patients, however, the House stated that, before discontinuing treatment, an application should be made to the Family Division of the High Court. Several judges also urged that the issue required urgent consideration by Parliament.

COMMENT: The law has moved little since *Bland*. A doctor who ends a patient's life at his request will have committed murder. Anyone who aids another person in committing suicide will commit a crime punishable by a maximum of fourteen years' imprisonment.[117] Doctors may withdraw treatment, but only where the patient cannot communicate his wishes. This is an area in which legislation is needed, but, to date, the only development has been the passing of the Mental Capacity Act 2005, which allows for the creation of living wills.[118] A living will is a document that indicates in what situations a person wishes to discontinue treatment. Such documents are legally binding and doctors who ignore them could be subject to legal action.

⭐ See J Keown, 'Doctors and Patients: Hard Case, Bad Law, "New" Ethics' (1993) 52 CLJ 209

Even where statute does dominate, the lawmaking ability of the judiciary is not curtailed completely. As noted earlier, legislation needs to be interpreted and applied, and, given the aforementioned imperfections of the English language, this legislation may very well contain provisions that are ambiguous or vague. A court faced with an ambiguous or vague provision cannot ask Parliament for guidance, or wait until Parliament reforms the Act in question; the court has to make a decision.

Therefore, as time progressed, it became universally accepted that judges do make law, and even the judges themselves have started to admit this—albeit with some reluctance, Lord Radcliffe stating that judges 'will serve the public interest better if they keep quiet about their legislative function'.[119] The next step in the issue was stated forcefully by Lord Reid: 'We do not believe in fairy tales any more. So we must accept the fact that for better or worse judges do make law, and tackle the question how do they approach their task and how they should approach it.'[120] The House of Lords attempted to answer this question in *C (a Minor) v DPP*,[121] in which, having examined the relevant authorities, Lord Lowry established five propositions.[122]

1. If the solution is doubtful, the judges should beware of imposing their own remedy.

---

117. Suicide Act 1961, s 2.   118. Mental Capacity Act 2005, ss 24–26.
119. Lord Radcliffe, *Not in Feather Beds* (Hamilton, London, 1968) 271.
120. Lord Reid, 'The Judge as Lawmaker' (1972) 12 JSPTL 22, 22.
121. [1996] AC 1 (HL).   122. Ibid, 28.

2. Caution should prevail if Parliament has rejected opportunities of clearing up a known difficulty or has legislated, while leaving the difficulty untouched.

3. Disputed matters of social policy are less suitable areas for judicial intervention than purely legal problems.

4. Fundamental legal doctrines should not be lightly set aside.

5. Judges should not make a change unless they can achieve finality and certainty.

The above list would indicate the adoption of a cautious approach by the courts that pays due respect to the principle of parliamentary sovereignty. In practice, however, judges have, on occasions, not followed the above rules too closely and have been a touch zealous in the exercise of their lawmaking function, with one commentator referring to a 'growing appetite of some judges for changing the law themselves, rather than waiting for Parliament to do it'.[123] The case of *R v R*[124] (discussed above) provides a classic example of this. At the time of the case, rape was defined in statute as 'unlawful sexual intercourse with a woman who at the time of the intercourse does not consent to it'.[125] It had been long accepted by both the courts[126] and academics[127] that Parliament had included the word 'unlawful' specifically to preserve the marital exemption. When the 1976 Act was being debated in Parliament, there existed a clause in the Bill that would have abolished the marital exemption, but Parliament rejected it. Despite this, the House of Lords held that the word 'unlawful' was mere surplusage, even though it was well established by the courts that 'it was the duty of the court to give a meaning to every word in the section'.[128] The case has been summed up well by Glanville Williams, who describes it as 'high-handed judicial action taken for a praiseworthy purpose',[129] but goes on to question 'whether the praiseworthiness redeemed the high-handedness'.[130] It is contended that, despite the honourable motives of the House, it ultimately stepped over its constitutional boundaries and adopted a quasi-legislative role. If the word 'unlawful' and its consequent preservation of the marital exemption were regarded as inappropriate, it was for Parliament, and not the courts, to remove it.

➡ surplusage: in law, a word or phrase that is superfluous or useless to the case in question

‹› Key points summary

- The doctrine of precedent states that the reasoning behind decisions of higher courts is binding upon lower courts. This is based on the principle of *stare decisis* ('keep to what has been decided previously').

- Only the reasoning behind a court's decision (the *ratio decidendi*) is binding upon lower courts. Cases may have multiple *rationes*.

---

123. F Bennion, 'A Naked Usurpation?' (1999) 149 NLJ 421, 421.
124. [1992] 1 AC 599 (HL).   125. Sexual Offences (Amendment) Act 1976, s 1(1).
126. *R v Chapman* [1959] 1 QB 100 (CA).
127. See G Williams, 'Rape is Rape' (1992) 142 NLJ 11, 11, who states that '[e]very criminal lawyer knew in 1976, when the relevant statute was passed, that this phrase meant fornication, coition outside marriage, which was the meaning intended in the Act'.
128. *R v Williams* [1953] 1 QB 660 (CA) 663 (Goddard CJ).
129. G Williams, 'Rape is Rape' (1992) 142 NLJ 11, 11.   130. Ibid.

- Only the Court of Appeal and the Divisional Courts of the High Court are bound by their own decisions (subject to exceptions).

- The inferior courts (magistrates' courts and county courts) cannot create binding precedents.

- A binding precedent can be distinguished if the facts of the present case differ materially from those of the precedent.

- Although, from a constitutional point of view, the role of judges should be limited to interpreting and applying the law (known as the 'declaratory theory of law'), it is universally acknowledged that judges do, in fact, make law.

Custom

The third—and, today, the least important—source of domestic law is custom. In Anglo-Saxon times, custom (that is, patterns of behaviour recognized and enforced by the courts) was the principal source of law. Today, custom, as a source of laws that can apply throughout the land, is largely non-existent, save for those customs that have been absorbed into statute or the common law (for example, the prohibition against bigamy found in the Offences Against the Person Act 1861, s 57, derived from custom). Local customs still, however, have a role to play and it is not unheard of for the courts to give legal effect to a particular local custom, even if it conflicts with the common law. As we shall see in Chapter 7, it may be possible for a local custom to be implied into a contract. But in order for a local custom to be recognized by the courts, it will need to comply with a number of strict conditions, as follows.

- The local custom must have existed since 'time immemorial'. This rather vague phrase has, for historical reasons, been fixed by statute[131] at the 3 September 1189.[132] Initially, it would appear almost impossible to prove this, but provided that it can be shown that the custom has existed in the locality for a substantial time, the court will presume that it has existed since time immemorial,[133] provided that the custom was possible in 1189.

- The custom must have existed continuously since that date. This does not mean that the custom has not been exercised,[134] but that the ability to exercise it has not been interrupted.

- The custom must not be unreasonable.[135]

- The custom must be certain in nature and scope, and must be specific to a defined locality.

---

131. Statute of Westminster I 1275.
132. This was the date of the coronation of Richard I (Richard the Lionheart).
133. *Mercer v Denne* [1905] 2 Ch 538 (CA). In order to prove the existence of the custom for a substantial time, the court will often call as a witness the locality's oldest living inhabitant.
134. In *New Windsor Corporation v Mellor* [1975] Ch 380 (CA) the court recognized a custom even though it had not been exercised for a hundred years.
135. *Wolstanton Ltd v Newcastle-Under-Lyme Borough Council* [1940] AC 860 (HL).

- The custom must be compulsory (for example, if the custom grants someone a discretion to do something, it will not be compulsory).
- The custom must not conflict with a statutory provision.

 Key points summary

- Custom, as a general source of law that affects England and Wales, no longer exists (although many current statutory and common law principles derive from customary rules).

- A local rule of custom may be recognized and enforced by the court, provided that it has existed continuously since 1189, is reasonable, is certain in nature and scope, is compulsory, and does not conflict with a statutory provision.

Chapter conclusion

It is impossible to have a thorough understanding of the law applicable to businesses without also having an understanding of the sources of such laws and the relationships between the different sources. Acts of Parliament constitute the highest form of domestic law and businesses should ensure that their activities comply with any statutory obligations placed upon them. Whilst one or several statutes dominate some areas of the law, these statutes will need applying and interpreting. Therefore, an understanding of the relevant common law provisions is also vital. Some areas of the law derive almost entirely from the common law, with little or no statutory intervention. In such areas, a thorough knowledge of the key cases is advisable. Custom as a general source of law is non-existent today, but the court may still recognize local customs. Local businesses may have evolved a custom regarding their dealings, but, in order to give effect to such a custom, the court will require strict conditions to be complied with.

Domestic law cannot, however, be fully appreciated without an understanding of how it is affected by laws that derive from outside England and Wales. In particular, European Union law and the European Convention on Human Rights have had a huge impact upon domestic law. Both of these sources of European law, and the extent to which they affect domestic law, are discussed in the next chapter.

Self-test questions

1. Define the following:
   (a) subordinate legislation;
   (b) Hansard;
   (c) *stare decisis*;
   (d) *ratio decidendi*;
   (e) *obiter dicta*.

2. Explain the process by which a Bill becomes an Act.

3. Explain the difference between an Act of Parliament that is: (i) original; (ii) consolidating; (iii) codifying; and (iv) amending.

4. Explain the rules of statutory interpretation. For each rule, provide a case that demonstrates the use of that rule in practice.

5. Explain the distinction between:
   (a) a public Bill and a private Bill;
   (b) binding precedent and persuasive precedent;
   (c) primary legislation and subordinate legislation.

6. In relation to precedent, explain what is meant by: (i) following a decision; (ii) overruling a decision; (iii) reversing a decision; and (iv) distinguishing a case.

7. Explain how the doctrine of precedent would operate in the following situations.
   (a) The Court of Appeal is hearing an appeal. There are two previous Court of Appeal decisions on the issue and they were both decided on the same day— but their decisions conflict. Which decision should the Court of Appeal follow? What happens to the decision that was not followed?
   (b) An either-way offence is being heard summarily in the magistrates' court. There is a decision of the Crown Court that involves similar facts. Are the magistrates obliged to follow the decision of the Crown Court?

8. Do you think that judges should have the ability to make law? Provide reasons for your answer.

Further reading

Bennion, FAR, *Statutory Interpretation* (5th edn, Butterworths, London, 2008)
The definitive text on statutory interpretation

Finch, E and Fafinski, F, *Legal Skills* (2nd edn, OUP, Oxford, 2009) chs 3 and 6
Provides a practical account of how best to use domestic sources of law, including how to interpret statutes and how to find the ratio of a case

Gillespie, A, *The English Legal System* (2nd edn, OUP, Oxford, 2009) chs 2 and 3
Provides a clear account of domestic sources of law, backed up with a number of extremely interesting examples

Websites

<http://business.timesonline.co.uk/tol/business/law/reports/>
The website of The Times Law Reports; very up to date and often contains cases not reported elsewhere

<http://www.justice.gov.uk/whatwedo/supremecourt.htm>
The official website of the new Supreme Court

<http://www.opsi.gov.uk>
The website of the Office of Public Sector Information; provides access to original and revised legislation, which appears on this website within twenty-four hours of it becoming available in printed form

\<http://www.parliament.uk/business/bills_and_legislation.cfm\>
Parliament's official Bills and legislation page; provides the text and progress of all Bills before Parliament

\<http://www.publications.parliament.uk/pa/cm/cmhansrd.htm\>
The official website of the House of Commons debates (Hansard)

\<http://www.publications.parliament.uk/pa/ld/ldjudgmt.htm\>
Contains the full text of all House of Lords judgments since 1996

\<http://www.statutelaw.gov.uk\>
Contains the official revised edition of primary legislation, so you can be sure that it is up to date

Remember to visit the **Online Resource Centre** at **\<http://www.oxfordtextbooks.co.uk/roach\>** to access the following resources on Chapter 3, 'Domestic sources of law': more **practice questions** and answers; a **glossary** of key terms; **multiple-choice questions**; **revision summaries**; **audio updates** when relevant; **discussion boxes**; and **audio exam advice** on this key topic.

4 Europe and the English legal system

- The relationship between the European Union and the European Convention on Human Rights

- The European Union

- The European Convention on Human Rights and the Human Rights Act 1998

INTRODUCTION

In Chapters 2 and 3, we discussed the administration of the English legal system and the domestic sources of English law. Increasingly, however, laws that do not derive from domestic legal sources affect the English legal system. Since 1973, European law (hereafter referred to as 'EU law') has taken precedence over domestic law to such an extent that Acts of Parliament that fail to comply with EU law can be suspended by the courts. Since 1953, the UK has had to ensure that its domestic laws do not breach the rights protected by the European Convention on Human Rights, although UK citizens have only been able to enforce these rights in the European Court of Human Rights since 1966, and in domestic courts since October 2000. Accordingly, in order to obtain a full appreciation and understanding of the operation of the English legal system, it is essential that students understand the full impact of European law upon the domestic legal system. This will involve a discussion of the various aspects of EU law and the effects of the Human Rights Act 1998, before which, we need to establish the differences between these two sources of European law.

The relationship between the European Union and the European Convention on Human Rights

It is common for students to fail to understand the relationship between the European Union (EU) and the European Convention on Human Rights (ECHR). Students tend to assume that membership of the EU automatically brings about ratification of the ECHR, or vice versa. Currently, however, this is not the case: the EU is not a party to the ECHR (although, as we shall see, this is likely to change) and has no administrative role as regards the European Court of Human Rights (ECtHR).

This is borne out by the fact that the EU currently comprises twenty-seven member States,[1] whereas the ECHR has forty-seven signatories (including all twenty-seven EU member States).

Even though the EU and ECHR may be separate, however, a strong relationship does exist between them in two ways. Firstly, accession to the EU is dependent upon satisfying what are known as the 'Copenhagen Criteria', named after the European Council meeting at which they were created. The respect for human rights is one of the criteria laid down and whilst being a signatory of the ECHR is not currently a legal requirement of EU membership (although it may be regarded as a political requirement), becoming a signatory will be compelling evidence that a candidate country does have the requisite respect for human rights.

Secondly, prior to the Treaty of Lisbon of 2007, the Treaty of Rome, Art 6(2), stated that '[t]he Union shall respect fundamental rights, as guaranteed by the European Convention for the Protection of Human Rights and Fundamental Freedoms'. Certainly, the European Court of Justice (ECJ) has been heavily influenced by decisions of the ECtHR, especially where there is no EU law on a topic. But EU law in relation to human rights is not exactly the same as that under the ECHR, leading to situations in which similar facts produce different outcomes in the different courts.

Visit the Online Resource Centre for the discussion box 'Contraception and the European courts'

It has been argued forcefully that, in order to remedy such inconsistencies, the EU itself should actually accede to the ECHR. The Fourteenth Protocol amended the ECHR to allow the EU to accede and, following the Treaty of Lisbon in 2007, the Treaty of Rome, Art 6(2), was amended to state that '[t]he Union shall accede to the European Convention for the Protection of Human Rights and Fundamental Freedoms'. Therefore, the amended Art 6(2) goes further than the Fourteenth Protocol by actually requiring, rather than permitting, the EU to accede to the ECHR.

The process of EU accession to the ECHR has, however, been held up by two developments:

1. before the EU can accede, the Fourteenth Protocol needs to come into effect and this will only happen once all ECHR signatories have ratified it (at the time of writing, the Russian Federation has yet to ratify the Protocol);[2]

2. the Treaty of Lisbon will only come into effect once all twenty-seven EU member States have ratified it. Following a referendum in June 2008, Ireland rejected the Treaty and is unlikely to ratify it in the absence of a successful referendum. The Irish government has agreed to hold a second referendum by November 2009. The Czech Republic and Poland also have yet to ratify the Treaty.

---

1. Three countries currently are candidates for accession to the EU—namely, Croatia, the Former Yugoslav Republic of Macedonia, and Turkey. It is expected that Croatia will become a member State at some time during 2009 or 2010.

2. This may be related to the fact that Russia has arguably been the ECHR signatory that has the least respect for human rights. Russia is easily the state that has the most complaints levelled against it. At the end of 2008, 27,246 cases were pending against the Russian Federation. The second highest number of cases was against Turkey, with 11,085 cases pending: see European Court of Human Rights, *Annual Report 2008* (Registry of the European Court of Human Rights, Strasbourg, 2008) 126.

Key points summary

- Currently, the European Union (EU) and European Convention on Human Rights (ECHR) are completely independent of each other, with separate courts and institutions. Membership of one is not dependent upon being a signatory of the other, and vice versa.

- The EU currently has twenty-seven member States, whereas forty-seven states (including the twenty-seven EU member States) have signed up to the ECHR.

- The European Court of Justice (ECJ) will take into account decisions of the European Court of Human Rights (ECtHR), but is in no way bound by them.

- The Treaty of Lisbon of 2007 provides for EU accession to the ECHR, but has been delayed due to the failure of several countries to ratify it.

The European Union

In 1950, the French Foreign Minister Robert Schuman put forward a proposal that was to form the foundations of the current European Union, and which was designed to ensure that the events of World War I and World War II could never happen again. Because the waging of war was heavily dependent upon heavy industry (notably, coal and steel), Schuman proposed that the production of coal and steel should be placed under the control of a single supranational organization. A year later, Schuman's vision became a reality, with six countries[3] signing the Treaty of Paris, which established the 'European Coal and Steel Community'. In 1957, the same six countries signed the Treaty of Rome (known as the 'EC Treaty'), thereby establishing the 'European Economic Community' (EEC). The UK joined in 1973, following the passing of the European Communities Act 1972. As time progressed, further measures were passed that were designed to increase European cooperation and integration. The Single European Act 1986 (which is a European treaty and not a UK Act of Parliament) indicated the member States' commitment to the creation of an internal (or single) market by the end of 1992. The Treaty on European Union (commonly known as the 'Maastricht Treaty') was signed in 1992 and created the European Union,[4] and further advanced the cause of monetary and economic union, via the establishment of a single European currency (the euro). The 1997 Treaty of Amsterdam renumbered and simplified the Treaty of Rome, introduced a number of provisions aimed at benefiting citizens, and, for the first time, made reference to the ECHR. The 2000 Treaty of Nice paved the way for the enlargement of the EU from fifteen States to twenty-seven. Finally, in 2007, the Treaty of Lisbon was signed and provides for a number of institutional reforms designed to improve the workings of the EU and its institutions. Crucially, it also incorporates the EU's Charter for

---

3. Belgium, France, Italy, Luxembourg, the Netherlands, and West Germany.
4. Note that the EU has not replaced the EEC, but has renamed it. The EEC is now known as the European Community (EC) and is but one pillar of the European Union, the other two being the Common Foreign and Security Policy (CFSP), and Police and Judicial Co-operation in Criminal Matters (PJC), which was formerly known as 'Co-operation in Justice and Home Affairs' (JHA).

PHOTO 4.1 The European Flag
Source: Bestmoose/Stockxpert

Fundamental Freedoms into EU law (although this Charter will not apply fully to the UK because it secured an opt-out), and provides for the EU's compulsory accession to the ECHR. As noted, however, the Treaty has yet to be ratified by all twenty-seven member States and, at the time of writing, its future is somewhat precarious.

To understand the operation of the EU and its effect upon the English legal system, we need to discuss the various institutions of the EU, the differing types of EU legislation and their effects on national law, and the operation of the European Court of Justice.

Institutions of the EU

The EC Treaty, Art 7, states that five bodies, the functions of which can be categorized as financial, legal, or political, shall carry out the functions of the Community. The financial body is the Court of Auditors, the function of which is to 'examine the accounts of all revenue and expenditure of the Community'.[5] The legal body is the European Court of Justice, which will be discussed later. In this section, we will focus on the three 'political' institutions—namely, the European Commission, the Council of the European Union, and the European Parliament.

---

5. EC Treaty (Treaty of Rome), Art 248(1).

The European Commission

The Commission can be thought of as the executive of the EU. The four main functions of the Commission are set out in the EC Treaty, Art 211. Firstly, the Commission is responsible for ensuring that Treaty obligations are met and that EU law is enforced. To that aim, the Commission is granted extensive powers to investigate and punish breaches of EU law committed by member States and companies. These powers exist in all areas of EU law, but one area in which the Commission has been especially active is in relation to breaches of competition law.

 Competition law is discussed further at p 1004

 T-214/04 *Microsoft Corporation v Commission* **[2007] 5 CMLR 11**

FACTS: The EC Treaty, Arts 81 and 82, give the Commission extensive powers to investigate and punish those in breach of competition law. Sun Microsystems, a competitor of Microsoft, complained that Microsoft had not provided adequate information to enable it to interoperate its server operating systems with Windows, thereby preventing Sun from offering certain services to clients using Windows. In 2004, the Commission found that by failing to disclose adequate interoperability information, Microsoft was abusing its dominant position in the market. Microsoft appealed to the Court of First Instance.

HELD: The Court of First Instance upheld the decision of the Commission and also the remedies imposed—namely, a fine of €497.2 million (around £420 million) and an order requiring Microsoft to disclose the relevant interoperability information within 120 days. In October 2007, the Commission announced that Microsoft had taken the necessary steps to remedy its breaches of Art 82 and had also indicated that it would not appeal the Court of First Instance's decision.

COMMENT: Microsoft's failure to adhere to EU competition law continues. In February 2008, the Commission fined Microsoft €899 million (£841.4 million) for failure to adhere to a previous ruling handed down in 2004. In January 2008, the Commission announced that two further complaints that been made against Microsoft, both concerning further potential breaches of Art 82 and both relating to interoperability issues of Microsoft products. In January 2009, the Commission announced its preliminary view, stating that the bundling of Internet Explorer with Windows constituted a violation of EU competition law.

See L Penny and A Edwards, 'The Microsoft Investigations' (2008) 19 Ent LR 77

The second function of the Commission is to provide opinions and recommendations where the EC Treaty or the Commission considers it necessary.

Thirdly, the Commission implements rules laid down by the Council of Ministers.

Finally, and perhaps most importantly, the Commission plays a massive role in the EU's legislative process. The Commission has the sole right to legislative initiative, which means that only the Commission can propose and initiate legislation (although other bodies can request that the Commission proposes legislation in certain areas). For this reason, the Commission is often referred to as the 'motor of integration'.

The Commission is based in Brussels and comprises twenty-seven Commissioners (one from each member State). Commissioners are appointed for terms of five years and they tend to be senior politicians. Commissioners may resign, but they cannot be individually dismissed; only the Commission as a whole can be dismissed and whilst this has yet to happen, in 1999, the

Santer[6] Commission did resign amidst allegations of fraud, corruption, nepotism, and incompetence. Had the Commission not resigned, there is little doubt that the European Parliament would have filed a motion of censure that would ultimately have led to the Commission's dismissal.

The Council of the European Union

The Council of the European Union[7] consists of a ministerial representative from each member State.[8] The minister in question will, however, depend upon the issue that the Council is discussing. So, for example, if the Council is discussing security and defence issues, it will be composed of the twenty-seven member States' Ministers of Defence. Presidency of the Council rotates amongst member States, with each state having a term of six months. The position of the President has assumed increased importance in recent years, because the President has substantial control over the setting of meetings and the agenda of Council activity during his presidency. The Council meets around eight times a year, with meetings taking place in Brussels and Luxembourg.

The role of the Council is set out in the EC Treaty, Art 202, but this provision is somewhat vague and does little to explain the Council's functions, which can be summarized as follows.

- The Council plays a major role in the passing of EU legislation. Although it cannot propose legislation, virtually all EC legislation requires the Council's approval in order to become law. The Council's inability to propose legislation is offset in that the Council can 'request the Commission to undertake any studies the Council considers desirable for the attainment of the common objectives, and to submit to it any appropriate proposals'.[9]
- The Council can delegate its lawmaking function to the Commission, allowing the latter to pass delegated legislation.
- The Council, along with the European Parliament, plays a significant role in approving the EU's budget.

Because the Council consists of national ministers, it strongly represents national interests, as opposed to the interests of the EU. For this reason, the Council has not always had an amicable relationship with the 'motor of integration'—namely, the Commission. To ensure that the advocacy of national interest does not bog down discussion, the Council has a robust decision-making process in place. Initially, many decisions of the Council required unanimity, but this system soon came to be unworkable, because smaller countries were able to veto proposals that the majority desired. Accordingly, the present system was devised whereby most decisions of the Council require a 'qualified majority'. Under this system, a total of 345 votes are allocated to the twenty-seven member States, with countries with larger populations having more votes.

In order to pass a qualified majority vote, three conditions need to be met:

- 255 out of 345 votes are required;

---

6. Commissions tend to be named after their president—in this case, Jacques Santer, the former prime minister of Luxembourg.
7. Not to be confused with the Council of Europe, which is a body that also works towards European integration, but which is not part of the EU. The Council of Europe oversees the European Convention on Human Rights and the European Court of Human Rights.
8. EC Treaty (Treaty of Rome), Art 203.   9. Ibid, Art 208.

- a majority of member States (that is, fourteen) must approve; and
- votes cast in favour must represent at least 62 per cent of the EU's population.

If the Treaty of Lisbon comes into force, these rules will be relaxed, but, as noted, it has yet to be ratified by several member States. Even if the Treaty is ratified, the new system will not be fully in place until 2017.

Related to the Council of the European Union is the European Council. This body consists of the President of the Commission, the twenty-seven heads of State or government, and the Foreign Ministers of member States, and meets at least twice a year.[10] Although the various treaties mention little of the European Council and it has no formal power, its role is a crucial one. In fact, it has been argued that 'since 1975, most of the major political decisions of the European Community have been taken in the European Council'.[11] In recognition of this, the Treaty of Lisbon, if or when it comes into effect, fully recognizes the European Council as a full institution and provides it with a permanent President, who will hold office for two-and-a-half years.

The European Parliament

Of all the EU institutions, the European Parliament has undergone the most change. Created by the Treaty of Paris in 1952, it began life as the relatively powerless Assembly. As time has progressed, however, its power has grown to reflect its democratic nature and, today, it is one of the most powerful bodies in the EU. The European Parliament is the only democratically elected body in the EU, and currently consists of 736 members of the European Parliament (MEPs), who are directly elected by the citizens of their member States every five years.

Unlike the Council, allotment of seats in the European Parliament is not based upon population size and the smaller countries are currently over-represented. The Treaty of Amsterdam therefore provides that if the number of MEPs changes in the future, the allotment of MEPs will change to reflect the populations of the member States.[12] MEPs do not sit in Parliament according to their nationality, but rather according to their membership of one of the seven political groupings.

The various roles of the European Parliament include the following.

- The European Parliament plays an increasingly strong legislative role. Initially, Parliament only had a consultative role, but following the passing of the Single European Act and the creation of the cooperation procedure, the European Parliament now enjoys a legislative role broadly similar to that of the Council. Like the Council, it may also request that the Commission proposes legislation.

- The European Parliament supervises the activities of the other EU institutions. It can censure the Commission and, if required, require its to resign. It can investigate the activities of any institution via the establishment of a committee of inquiry and, following the Maastricht Treaty, it can appoint an ombudsman to investigate complaints made by EU citizens in relation to maladministration.

- The European Parliament shares joint responsibility with the Council in approving the EU's budget, although the Council's view is still dominant.

- The European Parliament has the power to veto the admission of a new member State.

---

10. Treaty on European Union (Maastricht Treaty), Art 4.
11. M Westlake and D Galloway, *The Council of the European Union* (3rd edn, Harper, London, 2004) 177.
12. EC Treaty (Treaty of Rome), Art 190(2).

PHOTO 4.2 The European Parliament
Source: Lullabi/Stockxpert

There is little doubt that, over time, the powers of the European Parliament have increased significantly. Initially, it had very little real power, but it soon came to be viewed as incongruous that the only democratically elected EU institution was the least powerful—this was known as the 'democratic deficit'. To remedy this, each new treaty has increased the power of the European Parliament significantly to reflect its democratic status, thereby lessening the democratic deficit.

Key points summary

- There are five institutions in the EU:

  - the European Commission;
  - the Council of the European Union;
  - the European Parliament;
  - the Court of Auditors; and
  - the European Court of Justice.

- The Commission consists of twenty-seven Commissioners, and is responsible for ensuring that Treaty obligations are met and that EU law is enforced. Only the Commission can propose legislation.

- The Council consists of one minister per member State, the minister's identity being dependent upon the issue under discussion. The Council's role is to pass legislation and to approve the budget.

- Heads of State or government and Foreign Ministers form the European Council. Although this body is currently not a formal institution like the official five institutions, it exercises significant decision-making power in practice.

- The European Parliament plays a strong role in the approval of legislation. It also monitors the other EU institutions and has a role in relation to approval of the EU's budget.

- The European Parliament is the only directly democratically elected EU institution.

Legislation of the European Union

In the above section, we discussed the roles of the various EU institutions, including their input to the legislative process. Here, we will discuss the differing types of EU legislation. The EC Treaty, Art 249, defines the three different types of Community legislation—namely, regulations, directives, and decisions.[13] In addition, we also need to understand the role of treaty provisions. But before we can discuss these types of legislation, we need to discuss how they affect UK law and in order to do that, we need to explain the concepts of direct applicability and direct effect.

- *Direct applicability* Normally, in order for any piece of international law to become part of the UK law, it will need to be incorporated into UK law (normally via the passing of legislation)—but EU legislation that is directly applicable (namely, regulations) is automatically incorporated into domestic law as soon as it is passed, without the need for any action by the member State. This does not mean, however, that individuals will be able to enforce the legislation in domestic courts: in order for them to do that, the legislation will need to have direct effect. As we shall see, not all directly applicable legislation will be directly effective.

- *Direct effect* Legislation that can be relied on (either as a cause of action or defence) in a domestic court is said to have 'direct effect'. In order for a provision to be directly effective, the case of *van Gend en Loos*[14] established that a number of conditions must be met: the obligations laid down by it must be clear; it must be unconditional (that is, subject to no limitations);[15] and it must not require the implementation of domestic legislation. The situation is further complicated by the existence of two types of direct effect.

  - *Vertical direct effect* A provision will have vertical direct effect if it creates legal obligations only between member States and individuals.

  - *Horizontal direct effect* A provision will have horizontal direct effect if it creates legal obligations only between individuals.

Treaty provisions

Treaty provisions form the primary source of EU law and are directly effective, provided that they meet the conditions discussed above.[16] Many treaty provisions do not

---

13. Article 249 also includes recommendations and opinions, but these cannot be regarded as legislative, because they have no binding force.
14. C-26/62 *NV Algemene Transporten Expeditie Onderneming van Gend en Loos v Nederlandse Administratie der Belastigen* [1963] ECR 1.
15. This requirement has since been relaxed and the court is more willing to accept justifiable limitations: see C-41/74 *Van Duyn v Home Office* [1974] ECR 1337.
16. C-26/62 *NV Algemene Transporten Expeditie Onderneming van Gend en Loos v Nederlandse Administratie der Belastigen* [1963] ECR 1.

satisfy the criteria, because they provide only broad and vague statements of intent; such treaty provisions will require implementing legislation in order to be domestically enforced. Numerous key treaty provisions do have direct effect, however, an obvious example being the EC Treaty, Art 141, which states: 'Each Member State shall ensure that the principle of equal pay for male and female workers for equal work or work of equal value is applied.' This obligation is clear, unconditional, and is not dependent upon domestic implementation. Accordingly, in *Macarthys Ltd v Smith*,[17] a female worker who was paid less than her male predecessor was able to enforce Art 141, even though domestic legislation provided her with no right to equal pay.[18]

The effect of ECHR, Art 141, on domestic employment law is discussed at p 802

Treaty provisions that meet the criteria for direct effect usually have both vertical and horizontal direct effect, but the wording of a provision may indicate otherwise. For example, the EC Treaty, Art 28, states: 'Quantitative restrictions on imports and all measures having equivalent effect shall be prohibited between Member States.' Because this obligation is imposed only upon member States (and not individuals), it follows that Art 28 has only vertical direct effect and not horizontal.

Regulations

Regulations can be thought of as the EU equivalent of Acts of Parliament. The EC Treaty, Art 249, specifically states that regulations are directly applicable and therefore become part of domestic law upon coming into force. Provided that the conditions for direct effect are met, regulations have both vertical and horizontal direct effect. It is clear that regulations are used in order to provide uniformity across the laws of member States and, accordingly, must be enforced by a domestic court, even if the regulation conflicts with domestic law.[19]

Directives

Whilst regulations are extremely useful for securing uniformity of the law, they ignore the fact that the twenty-seven EU member States have vastly differing legal systems, each with their own idiosyncrasies. A particular regulation may be extremely simple to enforce in one state, but may produce massive legal difficulties in another. In such a case, it may be preferable to use a directive. Directives are not as specific as regulations and tend to set out broad aims and goals. The member State is then free to implement these goals in any way that it sees fit, thereby allowing it to tailor a response that is most appropriate given the features of its legal system. The member State will be given a period of time in order to implement the directive (usually two years). Consequently, because directives are dependent upon implementation by member States, they cannot be said to be directly applicable—but do they have direct effect? Because directives are designed to allow states to implement them in their own way, it follows that they will not have direct effect during the implementation period. Once they have been implemented by a particular member State, they will have full effect in accordance with the implementing legislation of that state. If the member State fails to implement a directive by the implementation date, however, it will become directly

---

17. C-129/79 [1980] ECR 1275.
18. At the time, the Equal Pay Act 1970 required equality only as between men and women working together contemporaneously; it did not apply in the case of successive employment.
19. C-93/71 *Leonesio v Ministero dell'Agricoltura e Foreste* [1972] ECR 287.

effective, and may be relied on by individuals and companies in a domestic court (provided that they comply with the *van Gend en Loos* conditions).[20] The ECJ explained the rationale behind this: if this were not the case, member States could avoid troublesome directives simply by refusing to implement them—in effect, their inactivity would protect them.[21] Thus, in *Marshall v Southampton and South West Hampshire Area Health Authority*,[22] the claimant alleged discrimination under the Sex Discrimination Act 1975 and the Equal Treatment Directive. Unfortunately, the 1975 Act did not apply in her particular case, and the UK had not implemented the Directive and the implementation date had passed. The ECJ held that, once the implementation date had passed, the Directive became directly effective; ergo the claimant could rely on it. But the Court imposed a limitation: because directives impose obligations upon member States (and not individuals), they would have only vertical direct effect, which means that they would provide rights only to individuals and not the State itself (or emanations of the State). Thus, when Westminster Council attempted to rely on a directive[23] to challenge the introduction of the congestion charge, its claim failed, because the directive did not confer rights upon emanations of the State.[24]

The *Marshall* case is discussed in more detail at p 111

The failure to implement a directive on time may have further consequences. The Commission can bring proceedings against any member State that fails to implement a directive within the implementation period. The UK was subject to such proceedings in respect of its failure to implement the Equal Pay Directive, discussed above in relation to the *Marshall* case.[25] Further, any individual who suffers loss due to a member State's failure to implement a directive properly is able to sue the State for damages for non-implementation or defective implementation.[26] Indeed, this could be used to circumvent the limitation imposed in *Marshall*: instead of relying on a directive to claim damages from another individual (which would fail), a claimant could instead seek damages against the State for non-implementation.

Decisions

A decision is an instrument of law created by one of the EU institutions. Unlike regulations and directives, which are addressed to all member States, decisions may be addressed to a single member State, company, or individual. Under Art 249, a decision is to be 'binding upon those to whom it is addressed'. Provided that a decision satisfies the *van Gend en Loos* conditions, it will be vertically directly effective against its addressee.[27]

The supremacy of EU law

Finally, we need to examine the effect that all of the above legislation has on the English legal system. The doctrine of parliamentary sovereignty states that Acts of Parliament constitute the highest form of law. Parliament is free to legislate in any

---

20. C-41/74 *Van Duyn v Home Office* [1975] 1 CMLR 1.
21. C-148/78 *Pubblico Ministero v Tullio Ratti* [1980] 1 CMLR 96, 110.
22. C-152/84 [1986] ECR 723.
23. Council Directive 85/337 EEC on the assessment of the effects of certain public and private projects on the environment [1985] OJ L175/40.
24. *R (on the Application of Westminster City Council) v Mayor of London* [2002] EWHC 2440 (Admin), [2003] BLGR 611.
25. C-165/82 *Re Equal Treatment: EC Commission v UK* [1983] ECR 3431.
26. C-6/1990 and C-9/1990 *Francovich and Bonifaci v Italy* [1991] ECR I-5357.
27. C-9/70 *Franz Grad v Finanzamt Traunstein* [1970] ECR 825.

TABLE 4.1 The general effect of EU legislation

Legislation	Direct applicability	Direct effect (provided that conditions are met)	
		Vertical	Horizontal
Treaty provisions	No	Yes	Yes (if wording permits)
Regulations	Yes	Yes	Yes
Directives	No	Yes (once implementation date has passed)	No
Decisions	No	Yes (only upon addressee)	No

manner[28] that it wishes and its legislation cannot be called into question by the courts. As one commentator stated, the doctrine of parliamentary sovereignty provides the principle 'upon which the whole system of legislation hangs'.[29] The question is, then, to what extent has this principle been affected by the UK's membership of the EU?

Prior to 1972, EU law constituted foreign law and, as such, the UK was in no way bound by it. Further, the Treaty of Rome itself did not contain a provision stating that EU law was to take precedence over domestic law. The issue was therefore left to the ECJ, which, in the seminal case of *Costa v ENEL*,[30] stated that 'the EEC Treaty has created its own legal system which, on the entry into force of the Treaty, became an integral part of the legal systems of the Member States and which their courts are bound to apply'.[31] This, in turn, brought about 'a permanent limitation of their sovereign rights'.[32] Although the ECJ in *Costa* provided several reasons why EU law should be supreme, the issue ultimately is one of practicality: if the member States of the EU were free to ignore EU law, the EU would become entirely impotent. Accordingly, by the time that the UK joined the EC in 1973, the supremacy of EU law was well established, and this was reflected in the European Communities Act 1972, s 2(1), which states:

> All such rights, powers, liabilities, obligations and restrictions from time to time created or arising by or under the Treaties, and all such remedies and procedures from time to time provided for by or under the Treaties, as in accordance with the Treaties are *without further enactment* to be given legal effect or used in the United Kingdom shall be recognised and available in law, and be enforced, allowed and followed accordingly... [Emphasis added]

Therefore, directly applicable or effective EU law was to take precedence over domestic law and, if domestic law were incompatible with EU law, domestic law would have to be changed. Thus, in *R v Secretary of State for Employment, ex p Equal Opportunities Commission*,[33] the House of Lords held that the Employment Protection (Consolidation) Act 1978 was discriminatory and incompatible with the EC Treaty,

---

28. The only exception to this is that Parliament cannot pass legislation that binds future Parliaments.
29. HWR Wade, 'The Basis of Legal Sovereignty' [1955] CLJ 172, 188.
30. C-14/64 [1964] ECR 585.
31. Ibid, 593.
32. Ibid.
33. [1995] 1 AC 1 (HL).

Art 119 (now Art 141, which provides for equal pay between men and women), on the ground that the 1978 Act provided fewer rights for part-time workers. Because the majority of part-time workers in the UK were women, the 1978 Act indirectly discriminated against them. As a result of this case, the law was changed and the rights of part-time workers were greatly increased.

But what should the court do if faced with a piece of legislation that was incompatible with directly applicable or effective EU law? Could the court ignore the domestic law, or was it bound to apply it, but indicate to Parliament that domestic law was incompatible? The answer came in the following seminal case.

 R v Secretary of State for Transport, ex p Factortame (No 2) [1991] AC 603 (HL)

FACTS: EC fishing policy stated that member States had exclusive rights to fish within 12 miles of their own coastline and subjected each member State to fishing quotas. Factortame, a Spanish fishing firm, attempted to avoid these limitations by registering its vessels in the UK and fishing in UK waters (thereby contributing to the UK quota). In response, Parliament passed the Merchant Shipping Act 1988, which stated that, in order to register as a British vessel, legal title to the vessel had to be vested wholly in a British citizen or company, and a company would only be classified as British if 75 per cent of its directors and shareholders were British citizens.[34] Ninety-five Spanish vessels could not meet these requirements, and so they challenged the 1988 Act, arguing that it breached the EC Treaty, Arts 7 (now Art 12, relating to the prohibition of discrimination) and 58 (now Art 43, relating to the freedom of establishment).

HELD: The ECJ held that it was a requirement of the EC Treaty that domestic courts enforce any provision that has direct effect, and, if a national law constituted an obstacle to this, the national law should be set aside and subsequently amended by the member State's legislature. Accordingly, the House of Lords issued an injunction suspending the operation of the Merchant Shipping Act 1988. Subsequently, the Spanish fishermen were able to sue and obtain damages from the government for their loss.[35] The offending sections of the 1988 Act were removed.

COMMENT: It could be argued that this decision severely emasculates the principle of parliamentary sovereignty for two reasons: firstly, the House acknowledged that EU law was supreme to domestic law; secondly, it permitted an English court to overrule an Act of Parliament. For this second reason, Atiyah describes *Factortame* as a 'revolutionary decision'. Other commentators were more critical: Lord Denning stated '[n]o longer is European law an incoming tide flowing up the estuaries of England. It is now like a tidal wave bringing down our sea walls and flowing inland over our fields and houses—to the dismay of all'.[36] The House of Lords, however, did not regard this case as weakening the sovereignty of Parliament. Lord Bridge stated that the supremacy of EU law was established by Parliament itself via the 'entirely voluntary'[37] passing of the European

---

34. Merchant Shipping Act 1988, s 14.
35. *R v Secretary of State for Transport, ex p Factortame (No 5)* [2000] 1 AC 524 (HL).
36. Lord Denning, *Introduction to the European Court of Justice: Judges or Policy Makers?* (Bruges Group, London, 1990) 8.
37. [1991] AC 603 (HL) 658.

Communities Act 1972. Accordingly, Parliament retains supremacy in that it could repeal the 1972 Act whenever it wished. Whilst this may be legally true, in political and economic terms, it is highly unlikely that the UK would ever wish, or be able, to leave the EU.

⭐ See HWR Wade, 'Sovereignty: Revolution or Evolution?' (1996) 112 LQR 568

The supremacy of EU law can also be seen in relation to the interpretation of EU law in domestic courts. In Chapter 3, we discussed the canons of interpretation adopted by domestic courts when interpreting statute—namely, the literal rule, the golden rule, and the mischief rule, or purposive approach. Whereas domestic legislation tends to be drafted in a very specific, detailed manner, EU law tends to be drafted in a much more open manner, focusing on general principles, with the detailed application left to the European courts. Accordingly, when domestic courts interpret EU law, the domestic canons of interpretation may not be suitable and domestic courts should use a method of interpretation that is consistent with that of the European courts. European courts (and the courts of most civil law systems) adopt what is known as the 'teleological approach' when interpreting legislation, whereby the courts will seek to give effect to the 'spirit' of the legislation, taking into account any relevant social, cultural, or economic considerations. The supremacy of EU law requires that domestic courts adopt a similar approach when interpreting EU law, and the following case provides an example of the House of Lords interpreting domestic legislation broadly in order to comply with the spirit of EU law.

🔗 *Litster v Forth Dry Dock and Engineering Co Ltd* [1990] 1 AC 546 (HL)

FACTS: A directive protecting the jobs of employees during the transfer of a business was implemented in the UK by the Transfer of Undertakings (Protection of Employment) Regulations 1981.[38] The claimant employees were dismissed one hour before the business that employed them was transferred. The claimants alleged that their dismissal was unfair under the Regulations. The defendants (the former and new owners of the business) contended that the claimants were not protected by the Regulations, because they were not employed at the time of the transfer.

🔗 The protection afforded to employees upon a transfer of business is discussed at p 815

HELD: Applying the literal rule would have resulted in the claimants losing, because the Regulations applied to persons employed at the time of the transfer—but this would clearly not be in keeping with the spirit of the Directive, the aim of which was to safeguard the jobs of employees during a transfer. Accordingly, the House of Lords adopted a strong purposive approach and held that the Regulations applied to those employed at the time of the transfer and also to those 'who would have been so employed if [they] had not been unfairly dismissed before the transfer for a reason connected with the transfer'.[39] The dismissals were therefore unfair.

⭐ See H McLean, 'Dosing the Transfer of Undertakings Regulations with European Medicine' (1989) 48 CLJ 383

---

38. SI 1981/1794. Now repealed and replaced by the Transfer of Undertakings (Protection of Employment) Regulations 2006, SI 2006/246.

39. [1990] 1 AC 546 (HL) 558 (Lord Templeman).

Key points summary

- The principal forms of EU legislation are treaty provisions, regulations, directives, and decisions.

- Legislation that is directly applicable automatically forms part of domestic law, without the need for further implementation. Only regulations are directly applicable.

- Legislation capable of having direct effect can be enforced in a domestic court, provided that it is clear and unconditional, and that does not require further implementation.

- Legislation that has vertical direct effect can be enforced only against the state, or an emanation of the State. Legislation that has horizontal direct effect can be enforced between individuals.

- Directives that have not been implemented within the implementation period can have vertical direct effect, but not horizontal.

- Decisions have vertical direct effect upon the parties to whom they are addressed.

- Directly applicable or effective EU law takes precedence over domestic law, and incompatible domestic legislation may be suspended by the courts. Such legislation will need to be changed by Parliament to make it compatible.

The European Court of Justice and Court of First Instance[40]

The European Court of Justice (ECJ) was set up as part of the Treaty of Paris in 1952 and—unlike all other all EU institutions, which are based in Brussels—it is based in Luxembourg. It consists of twenty-seven judges[41] and eight Advocates General, each being appointed for a term of six years (which can be renewed). The role of an Advocate General is 'with complete impartiality and independence, to make, in open court, reasoned submissions on cases which…require his involvement'.[42] In other words, following an examination of the claims of either party, the Advocate General will provide a neutral view of how the law should be applied in the case. The judges are free to disregard the opinions of their Advocates General, but, in practice, they are usually followed.[43] Cases in the ECJ are heard either before a chamber (comprising three or five judges), a Grand Chamber (comprising thirteen judges), or in full session (comprising all twenty-seven judges). Unlike UK courts, there are no majority and minority opinions, and each judge does not provide an individual judgment; rather, one judgment is issued for the entire court, and if there are any dissenters, this will be indicated within the language of the judgment.

Due to an increased caseload, in 1974, the ECJ requested the establishment of a secondary court to deal with less important cases. Nothing was done, however,

---

40. The Treaty of Lisbon, if or when it is finally ratified, will rename both courts. The European Court of Justice will become known as the 'Court of Justice' and the Court of First Instance will become known as the 'General Court'. Collectively, both courts will be known as the 'Court of Justice of the European Union'.
41. One for each member State: EC Treaty (Treaty of Rome), Art 221.
42. Ibid, Art 222.
43. A Dashwood, 'The Advocate General in the Court of Justice of the European Communities' (1982) 2 LS 202, 212, contends that judges follow the opinion of the Advocate General in about 70 per cent of cases.

PHOTO 4.3 The European Court of Justice
Source: Kolvenbach/Alamy

until the passing of the Single European Act, which amended the Treaty of Rome to allow for the creation of a Court of First Instance (CFI). The CFI was eventually established in 1988. Like the ECJ, the CFI consists of one judge per member State[44] and judges are appointed for a (renewable) term of six years. Decisions of the CFI may be appealed to the ECJ.

Jurisdiction of the CFI and ECJ

The CFI has jurisdiction to hear a wide range of cases, including:

- direct actions brought by natural or legal persons against acts of Community institutions (addressed to them or directly concerning them as individuals), or against a failure to act on the part of those institutions;
- actions brought by the member States against the Commission;
- actions seeking compensation for damage caused by the Community institutions or their staff;
- actions based on contracts made by the Communities that expressly give jurisdiction to the CFI.

The jurisdiction of the ECJ involves the following six areas.

1. *Preliminary references* Domestic courts may refer questions of EU law to the ECJ. These will be examined in the next section.

2. *Actions against member States* If a member State has failed to comply with a treaty or any other piece of Community legislation, proceedings in the ECJ may be initiated by the Commission or another member State.[45] If the breach is upheld, the ECJ will make an order indicating a breach has been made. The member State is then required to take the necessary steps to comply with the ECJ's judgment.[46] The Treaty on European Union now allows the ECJ to fine

---

44. EC Treaty (Treaty of Rome), Art 224.   45. Ibid, Arts 226–227.
46. Ibid, Art 228.

member States that breach EU law. For example, in 2005, France was held to be breaching EC fishing rules by failing to prevent its fishermen from catching undersized fish.[47] The ECJ imposed an initial fine of €20 million and an additional fine of €57,761,250 for every six months that France continued to allow its fishermen to breach EU law.

3. *Actions against Community institutions*   Articles 230 and 232 provides that the ECJ will review the legality of the acts (or omissions) of the various EU institutions. Applications may be made by member States, other EU institutions, and, in some cases, by individuals. The ECJ has the power to:

   – annul acts of the Council or Commission;

   – declare that, contrary to the Treaty, an institution has failed to act;

   – review fines and penalties imposed by the Commission; and

   – require the payment of compensation to those who suffer loss due to the unlawful actions of the EU institutions.

4. *Community employee disputes*   Article 236 grants the ECJ jurisdiction to hear disputes between the Community and any of its employees.

5. *Opinion regarding agreements*   Under Art 300(6), an EU institution or member State may seek the ECJ's opinion regarding the compatibility with EU law and any agreement into which it is considering entering.

6. *Appeals from the CFI*   Decisions of the CFI can be appealed to the ECJ, provided that the appeal is made within two months of the CFI's decision.[48] Appeals are limited to points of law.[49]

Domestic courts and the ECJ

Perhaps the principal function of the ECJ is ensuring the consistent application of EU law throughout the EU. To this end, Art 234 permits domestic courts to apply to the ECJ for a preliminary ruling in relation to the interpretation of Community legislation, or the acts of Community institutions. It should be noted that an Art 234 reference is not an appeal, because the decision to refer belongs to the domestic court and not the parties. Further, the possibility of a reference only arises where the case involves Community law.

The stages of a reference are as follows.

1. Any court or tribunal recognized by the ECJ *may* make a reference, but courts or tribunals 'against whose decisions there is no judicial remedy under national law'[50] *must* make a reference if a point of EU law is involved (except in certain circumstances). At first glance, this would indicate that only the House of Lords or Supreme Court must make a reference, but the issue is more complex. For example, an appeal to the House of Lords requires leave to appeal from either the Lords themselves or the Court of Appeal. If leave is not granted, the Court of Appeal becomes the final appeal court and is subject to the mandatory requirement to refer. The key issue to be determined is whether the court's decision is subject to appeal *in the particular case*.[51]

---

47. C-304/02 *Re Control Measures for Fishing Activities: Commission of the European Communities v France* [2005] ECR I-6263.

48. Statute of the Court of Justice, Art 56.   49. Ibid, Art 58.

50. EC Treaty (Treaty of Rome), Art 234(3).

51. C-99/00 *Criminal Proceedings Against Lyckescog* [2002] ECR I-4839.

2. The ECJ will decide whether or not to accept the reference. The ECJ has reserved the right to reject a reference where the questions raised are not articulated clearly,[52] where the questions raised are not substantially relevant to the action in the domestic court[53] or are hypothetical,[54] and where the facts of the case lack clarity.[55]

3. If the ECJ accepts the reference, proceedings are suspended in the domestic court until the ECJ completes the reference.

4. The ECJ will interpret the relevant legislation. Note that it will not apply the legislation: that is still the function of the domestic court (although, in practice, the distinction between interpretation and application can be extremely thin). Once the ECJ has interpreted a provision, that interpretation is binding on all courts within the EU.

5. Once the ECJ has provided a reference, it will refer the case back to the domestic court. The reference does not compel the national court to decide the case in a certain way; the decision is still a matter for the national court. In practice, however, the ruling of the ECJ is always followed, unless the ECJ oversteps its authority under Art 234.[56] If the preliminary ruling indicates that domestic legislation conflicts with EC law, the domestic legislation is usually changed.

 C-152/84 *Marshall v Southampton and South West Hampshire Area Health Authority* [1986] ECR 723

FACTS: The local area authority employed Marshall as a dietician. The authority required employees to retire when social security pensions became payable. For men, this was at the age of 65, and for women, this was at the age of 60. Because Marshall was 62 years old, she was dismissed. Marshall argued that this amounted to sex discrimination under the Sex Discrimination Act 1975 and the Equal Treatment Directive,[57] because a man would have been able to continue working until the age of 65. The Court of Appeal dismissed her claim under the 1975 Act, because that Act specifically did not apply to cases concerning retirement. In relation to the Directive, the Court referred her case to the ECJ under Art 234.

HELD: Marshall had been discriminated against under the Directive. Further, the ECJ stated that the Sex Discrimination Act 1975, s 6(2)(b) (which excluded discrimination relating to retirement), was in conflict with the provisions of the Equal Treatment Directive.

COMMENT: Following this case, the Sex Discrimination Act 1986 was passed, which amended the 1975 Act to require employers to set a retirement age that did not discriminate on grounds of sex. Several years later, Marshall was once again in the ECJ, successfully arguing that the statutory limit on compensation recoverable for sex discrimination under the 1975 Act was in breach of EU law.[58] The limits under both the 1975 Act and the Race Relations Act 1976 were subsequently removed.

★ See S Atkins, 'Equal Treatment and Retirement Age' (1986) 49 MLR 508

---

52. C-88/99 *Roquette Frères SA v Direction des Services Fiscaux du Pas-de-Calais* [2000] ECR I-10465.
53. C-83/91 *Wienland Meilicke v ADV/ORGA FA Meyer AG* [1992] ECR I-4871.
54. C-467/04 *Criminal Proceedings Against Gasparini and Ors* [2006] ECR I-9199.
55. C-320–322/90 *Telemarsicabruzzo SpA v Circostel, Ministero delle Poste e Telecommunicazioni and Ministerio della Difesa* [1993] ECR I-393.
56. *Arsenal Football Club plc v Reed* [2003] EWCA Civ 696, [2003] 3 All ER 865.
57. Council Directive EEC 76/207 [1976] OJ L039/40.
58. C-271/91 *Marshall v Southampton and South West Hampshire Area Health Authority* [1993] ECR I-4367.

> ### Key points summary
>
> - Each of the European Court of Justice (ECJ) and the Court of First Instance (CFI) comprise twenty-seven judges. The ECJ is assisted by eight Advocates General.
>
> - The CFI was established in 1988 to ease the caseload of the ECJ.
>
> - The ECJ will hear preliminary references, actions against member States that breach EU law, actions against EU institutions, cases involving disputes between EU institutions and their employees, and appeals from the CFI.
>
> - A preliminary reference is the referral of a case to the ECJ for an authoritative and conclusive interpretation of a point of EU law. The ECJ will not apply the law to the case; that is still the responsibility of the domestic court.

The European Convention on Human Rights and the Human Rights Act 1998

Many countries throughout the world protect the rights of their citizens via a specific physical document, the most obvious example being the US Constitution. It is often stated that the English legal system has no equivalent document, but this is not strictly true. The UK may not have a written constitution, but there are documents that serve to protect the rights of citizens, as follows.

➡ Magna Carta: 'Great Charter'

➡ *habeas corpus*: 'you have the body'; a writ whereby an individual can challenge the lawfulness of his detention

- *Magna Carta 1215* This is the first statute ever,[59] the 1297 version of which remains in force today, albeit with most of its provisions repealed. It aimed to reduce the power of the monarch, as well as to provide citizens with certain fundamental rights, the most significant of which—the writ of *habeas corpus*—is still in force today.

- *The Bill of Rights 1689* Passed following the tyrannical reign of James II, the Bill of Rights laid down a collection of rights, largely in relation to abuses of power by the monarch and Parliament. It remains in force today and is regarded as a significant influence on the US Constitution and Bill of Rights.

Of course, neither of these documents can be regarded as indicative of modern human rights, but they do still contain important (albeit limited) rights that are occasionally relied upon today. The modern source of human rights protection can be found in the ECHR[60] and accompanying Protocols.

The European Convention on Human Rights

Keen to ensure that the horrific events of World War II could not happen again, Winston Churchill proposed in 1946 that a Council of Europe be created to further the cause of European integration. In 1949, his proposal became a reality and

---

59. It should be stated that Magna Carta would not be regarded as a statute based on the modern definition of the term (that is, an Act of Parliament), because Parliament did not exist in 1215.
60. Or to give it its full title, the 'European Convention on Human Rights and Fundamental Freedoms'.

the Statute of the Council of Europe (known as the 'Treaty of London') came into force and was signed by ten countries.[61] Article 3 stated that '[e]very member of the Council of Europe must accept the principles of the rule of law and of the enjoyment by all persons within its jurisdiction of human rights and fundamental freedoms' and to fulfil this aim, in 1950, the ECHR was adopted by the Council of Europe. Although it was ratified by the UK in 1951, it did not come into force until 1953.

The ECHR itself comprises fifty-nine Articles, of which Arts 2–14 are the most important, because they contain the various human rights upon which citizens of the signatory countries may rely. They include rights such as the right to life (Art 2), freedom from torture (Art 3), freedom from slavery and forced labour (Art 4), the right to liberty and security (Art 5), the right to a fair trial (Art 6), the right to respect of private and family life (Art 8), freedom of expression (Art 10), and freedom from discrimination (Art 14). In addition, the rights protected by the ECHR have been expanded over time by the addition of Protocols, most of which provide additional human rights (for example, the First Protocol provides for, inter alia, the right to education and the right to free elections). It should be noted, however, that the protection offered by the ECHR is not always absolute: certain human rights can be limited or qualified, and it is important to know the extent of any particular right.

- *Absolute rights* can never be limited or withheld by the state.
- *Limited rights* may be limited by the state in finite and express circumstances. These limitations are usually found in the Article itself, but the right may also be limited via a **derogation** made by the state.

  ➡️ derogation: the ability to opt out in certain circumstances

- *Qualified rights* are those rights in relation to which the rights of the citizen need to be balanced with the rights of other parties, the Community, or the State. The qualification must have a clear legal basis, must be used for a legitimate purpose (usually specified in the Article itself), and must be necessary in a democratic society. Qualified rights may also be derogated from.

A significant number of Convention rights are therefore not absolute and may either be subject to derogations (which disapply rights completely) or reservations (which limits a right). The UK government has made a reservation only once, whereas derogations have been used more often—especially in relation to the prevention of terrorism.

🔗 Visit the Online Resource Centre for the discussion box 'Derogations and the prevention of terrorism'

The ECHR and businesses

The title of the ECHR is somewhat inaccurate. The use of the word 'human' indicates that the protection afforded is limited to natural human persons, thereby excluding businesses. This is most certainly not the case and, unlike other human rights regimes,[62] the text of the ECHR makes it clear that the rights embodied apply to legal persons (for example, companies), as well as natural persons. Sometimes, the Convention states this overtly, as is the case with Art 1 of the First Protocol, which states: 'Every natural or legal person is entitled to the peaceful enjoyment of

---

61. They were Belgium, Denmark, France, Ireland, Italy, Luxembourg, Netherlands, Norway, Sweden, and the UK. Today, the Council of Europe's membership stands at forty-seven full members, with five other countries having 'observer' status.

62. The United Nations' International Bill of Human Rights applies only to natural persons, as does the US Convention on Human Rights.

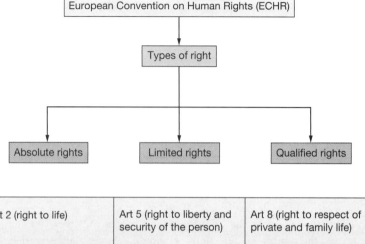

Art 2 (right to life)	Art 5 (right to liberty and security of the person)	Art 8 (right to respect of private and family life)
Art 3 (prohibition of torture)	Art 6 (right to a fair trial)	Art 9 (freedom of thought, conscience, and religion)
Art 4 (prohibition of slavery and forced labour)	Art 12 (right to marry)	Art 10 (freedom of expression)
Art 7 (no punishment without law)	Art 14 (prohibition of discrimination)	Art 11 (freedom of assembly and association)

FIGURE 4.1 The status of ECHR rights

his possessions.' Other provisions do not overtly include legal persons, but state that the protection is afforded to 'everyone'. Article 34, which identifies which parties can petition the European Court of Human Rights (ECtHR), provides that '[t]he Court may receive applications from any person, non-governmental organisation or group of individuals claiming to be the victim of a violation…of the rights set forth in the Convention or the protocols thereto'. There is no doubt that, for the purposes of Art 34, businesses qualify as non-governmental organizations[63] and therefore can freely petition the ECtHR. But it was not until 1980 that the first business petitioned the ECtHR[64] and, even today, claims deriving from individuals far outweigh those from businesses. Between 1998 and 2003, the ECtHR delivered 3,307 judgments— only 126 of which related to claims filed by companies.[65]

---

63. It could be argued that businesses could qualify as persons. But the authentic French text of the ECHR refers to a *personne physique* ('physical person'). Accordingly, businesses would not qualify as persons and must be categorized as non-governmental organizations.

64. *Sunday Times v UK* (1980) 2 EHRR 245.

65. M Emberland, *The Human Rights of Companies: Exploring the Structure of ECHR Protection* (OUP, Oxford, 2006) 14–15.

Not all of the rights contained in the ECHR will apply to businesses. For example, Art 3 of the Convention provides that '[n]o one shall be subjected to torture or to inhuman or degrading treatment or punishment'. Clearly, it is impossible to torture a business. In practice, human rights cases involving businesses tend to concentrate around a few key provisions of the ECHR, as follows.

- *Article 6 (right to a fair trial)* Businesses are entitled to the right to a fair trial, including the right to bring a case in the first place. Depriving a business of access to the court may constitute a breach of Art 6, as occurred in the late 1980s and early 1990s when Belgium attempted to deny a group of shipowners access to the Belgian courts.[66]

- *Article 10 (freedom of expression)* Article 10 cases involving businesses have almost universally focused on businesses involved in the media industry, which contend that certain acts of censorship or other State-imposed restrictions breach their Art 10 right to free expression. Alternatively, Art 10 is often pleaded as a defence in cases in which the claimant contends that publication or disclosure has breached his right to privacy under Art 8. For example, when the *News of the World* published stories accusing Max Mosely (president of the Formula 1 governing body) of engaging in Nazi-themed activities with a number of prostitutes, the newspaper's publisher sought (unsuccessfully) to justify publication under Art 10.[67]

- *Article 1 of the First Protocol (protection of property)* This provides, inter alia, that everyone is entitled to peaceful enjoyment of their property and that the State will not deprive persons of their property, unless it is in the public interest.

The European Court of Human Rights

The European Court of Human Rights (ECtHR), based in Strasbourg, was created in 1959. Initially, due to the relatively low number of cases, the Court only sat part-time. As time progressed, new states acceded to the ECHR and the number of cases increased substantially, with the result that the Court was unable to cope with the caseload. Therefore, in 1998, the Eleventh Protocol was passed, which replaced the old administration with a new, full-time Court. The reform was well timed, because the number of cases immediately exploded. In 1998, the Court had disposed of 5,979 applications; in 2001, it dealt with 13,858—a rise of 130 per case.[68] In 2008, the ECtHR disposed of 32,044 applications.[69]

The ECtHR currently consists of forty-seven judges (equal to the number of signatory states, although it is not a requirement that each state appoints one judge), a registrar, and a deputy registrar. The number of judges sitting in each case depends upon the importance of the case: a committee consists of three judges, chambers consist of seven judges, and a Grand Chamber consists of seventeen judges.[70] Just like a domestic court, the role of the ECtHR is to interpret and apply the law—namely,

66. *Pressos Compania Naviera SA v Belgium,* App no 17849/91 (1996) 21 EHRR 301.
67. *Mosely v News Group Newspapers Ltd* [2008] EWHC 1777 (QB), [2008] EMLR 20.
68. Statistics derived from the ECtHR website, <http://www.echr.coe.int>.
69. European Court of Human Rights, *Annual Report 2008: Provisional Edition* (Registry of the European Court of Human Rights, Strasbourg, 2009) 125.
70. ECHR, Art 27(1).

PHOTO 4.4 The European Court of Human Rights
Source: Jon Arnold Images Ltd/Alamy

the ECHR. The decisions of the ECtHR form a significant source of law in relation to human rights. The ECHR itself is relatively brief, so the judges of the ECtHR have considerable discretion in the forming of human rights law. Unlike UK judges who, due to the doctrine of precedent, have a reputation for being conservative and favouring the status quo, judges in the ECtHR have to be flexible enough to adapt to changes in society and a consequent change in the nature of human rights. Such flexibility often produces an impetus for UK law to change when, normally, it would be slow to respond, as the following example demonstrates.

Eg The right to marry

Developments in relationship types have forced the court to reconsider which relationships attract the protection of the ECHR. In the case of *Rees v UK*,[71] the ECtHR limited the protection provided by Art 12 (the right to marry) to different-sex heterosexual couples and upheld Matrimonial Causes Act 1973, s 11(c), which prohibited post-operative transsexuals from marrying by rendering *void ab initio* any marriage not between a male and a female. Sixteen years later, in *Goodwin v UK*,[72] the ECtHR reversed its previous position and stated that prohibiting transsexuals to marry constituted a breach of Art 12. The Court cited 'major social changes in the institution of marriage' and 'dramatic changes brought about by developments in medicine and science in the field of transsexuality'[73] as compelling reasons for the recognition of the transsexual's right to marry. Less than a year later, in the case of *Bellinger v Bellinger*,[74] the House of Lords held that the Matrimonial Causes Act 1973, s 11(c), was incompatible with ECHR, Art 12.

➔ *void ab initio*: 'invalid from the beginning'

---

71. App no 9532/81 (1986) 9 EHRR 56. Confirmed in *Cossey v UK*, App no 10843/84 (1990) 13 EHRR 622, and *Sheffield and Horsham v UK*, App nos 22885/93 and 23390/94 (1998) 27 EHRR 163, although, in the latter case, the ECtHR was critical of the UK's apparent failure to keep this area of the law under review.
72. App no 28957/95 [2002] 35 EHRR 18.   73. Ibid, [100].
74. [2003] UKHL 21, [2003] 2 AC 467.

UK law was subsequently amended and the Gender Recognition Act 2004, s 9(1), now allows transsexuals to live permanently according to their acquired gender[75] and, consequently, to marry.[76] The requirement that a marriage must be between a male and female was not removed, however, meaning that same-sex marriages are still not possible in the UK, although same-sex couples may form a civil partnership under the Civil Partnership Act 2004.

In the above example, the decision of the ECtHR provided the catalyst for legislative reform. It should be noted, however, that whilst domestic courts are required to take into account decisions of the ECtHR,[77] they are not required to follow them. Therefore, whilst the UK courts may be bound by the ECHR, they are not bound by decisions of the ECtHR.

The Human Rights Act 1998

Although the ECHR came into force in 1953, it was not until 1966 that UK citizens could take their case to the ECtHR. The process was, however, notoriously difficult: petitioners would first have to exhaust all domestic rights of appeal[78] (an extremely expensive and time-consuming process in itself) before being allowed to petition the ECtHR directly. Unlike other signatory states, the UK did not incorporate the ECHR into domestic law, nor are Convention rights directly applicable or effective in the way that EU legislation can be. The result was that there was no mechanism to enforce the ECHR in an English or Welsh court; claimants would therefore have to take their case to the ECtHR in Strasbourg, further increasing the time and expense. A governmental White Paper discovered that, on average, it took five years for a case to reach the ECtHR, by which time costs would have, on average, reached £30,000.[79] Accordingly, the Labour government indicated its intention to allow claimants to enforce their rights in a domestic court.

The Human Rights Act 1998, which came into force on October 2000, consists of only twenty-two sections and four short Schedules, but its importance cannot be overstated. The immediate effect of the Act was, to use the language of the White Paper that led to the 1998 Act, to 'bring rights home'[80] by allowing certain Convention rights to be enforced in a domestic court,[81] rather than in the ECtHR (although a direct application is still possible). But the full effect of the Act was much wider. Although the Act did not permit domestic courts to strike down primary

---

75. The transsexual seeking gender reassignment will first need to apply for a full gender recognition certificate, including evidence specified in s 3.

76. But according to s 4(3), parties who are married at the time of their application will only be provided with an interim gender recognition certificate, which lasts six months. In order to obtain a full gender recognition certificate, the marriage will have to be annulled: s 5(2). This is to avoid the Act having retrospective effect.

77. Human Rights Act 1998, s 2(1)(a).

78. ECHR, Art 35(1).

79. Secretary of State for the Home Department, *Bringing Rights Home: The Human Rights Bill* (Cm 3782, HMSO, London, 1997) [1.14].

80. Ibid.

81. Human Rights Act 1998, s 7.

legislation that was incompatible with Convention rights, the court can issue a declaration of compatibility. The Act also had a profound effect upon how judges are to interpret domestic legislation. Finally, the Act provides that it is unlawful for public authorities to act in a manner that is incompatible with a Convention right.

Enforcing the ECHR in a domestic court

The principal effect of the Human Rights Act 1998 was to give domestic effect to the ECHR, thereby permitting individuals to enforce it in a domestic court. It is important to note, however, that not all of the rights contained within the Convention can be enforced; only those rights contained in the ECHR, Arts 2–12 and 14, Arts 1–3 of the First Protocol, and Art 1 of the Thirteenth Protocol.[82] Domestic proceedings are governed by s 7 of the Act and s 7(1) states that the protected rights may be used to commence a claim or to defend a claim. But in order to enforce a Convention right under s 7, the individual will need to demonstrate that he is a 'victim' within the meaning of Art 34.[83] Unfortunately, Art 34 does not provide a definition of 'victim', other than to state it can include 'any person, non-governmental organisation or group of individuals claiming to be the victim of a violation' by the State. The exact definition has therefore been left to the judges, who, through various cases, have established that a victim is someone who has been 'directly or indirectly affected by the alleged infringement of the Convention...[or]...those who are potentially at risk of an infringement of their rights'.[84] Proceedings must be brought within one year of the date on which the alleged infringement took place, although the court may permit a longer period if it considers it equitable to do so.[85] Finally, if an individual can establish that his Convention rights have been breached, the court 'may grant such relief or remedy, or make such order, within its powers as it considers just and appropriate'.[86]

Mention should be made to the 'margin of appreciation'—a concept that has long been recognized by the ECtHR, but which is increasingly being taken into account in domestic cases involving human rights. Because the ECHR is an international convention, it will be applied amongst states with vastly differing cultures and legal systems. Accordingly, the ECtHR has been careful not to enforce certain rights too rigidly and will give signatory States a margin of appreciation to take into account the State's idiosyncrasies. Thus, when a particular book was prohibited from being sold in England for breaching the Obscene Publications Acts 1959 and 1964, but could be purchased in many other countries in Europe, the ECtHR held that the prohibition in England did not breach the publisher's right to freedom of expression, because each country is better placed to determine what is obscene based on its own culture and traditions.[87] The margin of appreciation therefore allows each state to determine how far the Convention rights should be protected and indicates that the Convention need not be applied uniformly throughout all signatory states. Domestic

---

82. Ibid, s 1.
83. Ibid, s 7(7).
84. R Stone, *Textbook on Civil Liberties and Human Rights* (7th edn, OUP, Oxford, 2008) 40.
85. Human Rights Act 1998, s 7(5).
86. Ibid, s 8(1).
87. *Handyside v UK* (1979–80) 1 EHRR 737.

recognition of the margin of appreciation arrived prior to the 1998 Act coming into force when Lord Hope stated that:

> difficult choices may have to be made by the executive or the legislature between the rights of the individual and the needs of society. In some circumstances it will be appropriate for the courts to recognise that there is an area of judgment within which the judiciary will defer, on democratic grounds, to the considered opinion of the elected body or person whose act or decision is said to be incompatible with the Convention.[88]

Human rights and statutory interpretation

In Chapter 3, we noted the various rules created by the judges to aid in the interpretation of statutes. With the passing of the Human Rights Act 1998, a new rule[89] was created and can be found in s 3(1), which states: 'So far as it is possible to do so, primary legislation and subordinate legislation must be read and given effect in a way which is compatible with the Convention rights.'

The effect of this section is significant for several reasons, as follows.

- Although the 1998 Act came into force in October 2000, s 3 also applies to all legislation passed before that date[90] (that is, it has retrospective effect). In relation to legislation passed after that date, s 19 states that the minister responsible for a Bill must, before the second reading, make a statement indicating to what extent the Bill is compatible with the ECHR.[91]

- The statutory rule in s 3 outranks the doctrine of precedent. Therefore an inferior court may validly refuse to follow a precedent established by a higher court if it feels that the precedent is incompatible with a Convention right. This could be regarded as a potentially substantial erosion of the doctrine of precedent.

Section 3 requires the judiciary to walk an extremely thin line between legislative interpretation and legislative alteration. In the majority of cases, the courts have been able to interpret legislation in a way that complies with the Convention, yet still pays respect to Parliament's intentions. For example, in *Ghaiden v Godin-Mendoza*,[92] the House of Lords was able to extend the protection offered under the Rent Act 1977 to same-sex couples by interpreting the phrase 'as his or her wife or husband' to mean 'as if they were his or her wife or husband'. In several cases, however, the courts have strayed from this line and have interpreted a statute in a way

---

88. *R v DPP, ex p Kebilene* [2000] 2 AC 326 (HL) 381.

89. The rule cannot be regarded as an extension of the previous rules, because it permits the court to reject a literal interpretation if it is incompatible with the ECHR. Further, it cannot be regarded as an example of the golden or mischief rules, because they are concerned with the intention of Parliament at the time that the legislation was passed, which may have been many years before the Human Rights Act 1998 came into effect.

90. Human Rights Act 1998, s 3(2)(a).

91. It has become common to include this statement on the cover of the Bill. But such statements are usually very short and uninformative (for example, the Secretary of State promoting the Terrorism Bill 2005 simply stated '[i]n my view the provisions of the Terrorism Bill are compatible with the Convention rights'). Accordingly, such statements do not even constitute persuasive authority in court: *R v A* [2001] 3 All ER 1 (HL).

92. *Ghaiden v Godin-Mendoza* [2004] UKHL 30, [2004] 2 AC 557.

that Parliament clearly did not intend in order to ensure forcefully that it complies with Convention rights.

🔑 R v A (No 2) [2001] UKHL 25

FACTS: A common tactic of defence lawyers in rape cases is to attempt to discredit the alleged victim by cross-examining her about her past sexual experiences. The public exposure of such intimate, but often evidentially worthless, details could be extremely harrowing, and so the Youth Justice and Criminal Evidence Act 1999 was passed, with s 41 providing for a so-called 'rape shield', which prohibited the asking of questions or provision of evidence concerning the victim's previous sexual history, except for in a number of very narrow and exhaustive instances. The defendant argued that by making such evidence inadmissible, he was denied the right to a full defence and, consequently, a fair trial, as provided for by ECHR, Art 6.

HELD: To avoid s 41 compromising the defendant's Art 6 rights, the House of Lords held that s 41 should be 'subject to the implied provision that evidence or questioning which is required to ensure a fair trial under article 6 of the Convention should not be treated as inadmissible'.[93]

COMMENT: In R v A, the House used the duty imposed upon it by s 3 of the 1998 Act to override the intention of Parliament completely. The House basically held that an alleged rape victim could not be questioned about her past sexual history, unless the court felt that it was fair to do so. A principal aim of s 41 was to provide a narrow and exhaustive list of instances in which the victim may be questioned regarding her sexual history, thereby removing the issue from the discretion of the judge. The decision in R v A places the issue firmly back in the judge's hands, because he will determine what is 'fair'. Accordingly, the judges granted themselves a discretion that Parliament clearly intended they should not have and, in doing so, potentially weakened the protection afforded to victims of rape.

⭐ See P Mirfield, 'Human Wrongs?' (2002) 118 LQR 20

It should be remembered that s 3 is subject to limits. The opening words of s 3—'So far as it is possible to do so'—indicate that there will be occasions on which the courts cannot interpret primary legislation in line with the ECHR. In addition, s 19(1)(b) preserves the right of Parliament to pass legislation that is incompatible with the ECHR. Therefore, if, in order to render a statutory provision compatible with the ECHR, the court has to adopt an interpretation that is 'intellectually indefensible, or would amount to a usurpation of Parliament's legislative function',[94] then certain courts (namely, the House of Lords or Supreme Court, the Court of Appeal, the High Court, and the Privy Council) are free to abandon their duty under s 3 and instead may (*not* must) issue a declaration of incompatibility under s 4. In relation to subordinate legislation, a declaration if incompatibility need not be made; the court can simply quash incompatible subordinate legislation, provided that its parent Act does not expressly prevent removal of the incompatibility.[95]

---

93. *R v A (No 2)* [2001] UKHL 25, [2002] 1 AC 45, [45] (Lord Steyn).

94. Lord Irvine, 'The Impact of the Human Rights Act: Parliament, the Courts and the Executive' (2003) PL 308, 320.

95. Human Rights Act 1998, ss 3(2)(c) and 4(4).

Declarations of incompatibility

A declaration of incompatibility is just that: a declaration by a domestic court indicating that it considers a piece of domestic legislation to be incompatible with a Convention right. Declarations of incompatibility have been relatively few in number and a significant proportion of them are overturned on appeal. Those declarations that did stand, however, have been of notable importance, with perhaps the most noteworthy being the declaration issued by the House of Lords in the following case.

A v Secretary of State for the Home Department [2004] UKHL 56

FACTS: In response to the events of 11 September 2001, Parliament passed the Anti-Terrorism, Crime and Security Act 2001, s 23 of which allowed certain non-UK citizens suspected of being terrorists to be detained indefinitely without charge or trial. Clearly, this was in breach of ECHR, Art 5 (right to liberty and security), and so the government passed a derogation order[96] excluding certain provisions of the 2001 Act from Art 5 in relation to suspected Al Qaeda terrorists. Whilst the order took care of any possible breach of Art 5, it did not cover Art 14 (prohibition of discrimination), and, given that the indefinite power of detention was aimed solely at non-UK citizens, those who were detained argued that it was discriminatory.

HELD: A nine-strong panel of the House of Lords held, by a majority of eight to one, that s 23 was discriminatory and therefore incompatible with Art 14, as well as Art 5. The Act concentrated on non-UK suspects, but did nothing to address the threat posed by UK nationals. Accordingly, a declaration of incompatibility was issued and the derogation order was quashed.

COMMENT: This case is notable for the scathing and undisguised attack levelled at the government's anti-terrorism policies by the House of Lords. At various points, the notion of a power to hold suspects indefinitely was described as 'anathema in any country which observes the rule of law',[97] '[t]he real threat to the life of the nation',[98] and 'the stuff of nightmares'.[99] In response, the government passed the Prevention of Terrorism Act 2005, which provided for a system of 'control orders' that could be levelled at any suspected terrorist, irrespective of his nationality. Further, these orders will last for a maximum of twelve months, although they can be renewed if the Secretary of State considers it necessary.[100]

⭐ See DM Dwyer, 'Rights Brought Home?' (2005) 121 LQR 359

The key feature of a declaration of incompatibility, however, is that it in no way affects the legality of the statute in question and that the court must still enforce it. A declaration is merely a statement of the court indicating that it believes that a breach of the ECHR has occurred. Given this, it has been argued that declarations

---

96. Human Rights 1998 (Designated Derogation) Order 2001, SI 2001/3644.
97. [2004] UKHL 56, [2005] 2 AC 68, [74] (Lord Nicholls).
98. Ibid, [97] (Lord Hoffmann).
99. Ibid, [155] (Lord Scott).
100. Prevention of Terrorism Act 2005, s 2(4).

of incompatibility will be of little use.[101] From a purely legal perspective, this may be true. But as Lord Scott stated, '[t]he import of such a declaration is political not legal',[102] meaning that whilst a declaration of incompatibility may not compel Parliament to change the law, the political embarrassment in which it can result can provide a strong impetus for reform. The 1998 Act itself recognizes this by permitting the government to remedy the breach via a fast-track process known as a 'Henry VIII order', which basically allows primary legislation to be reformed via subordinate legislation.[103]

Acts of public authorities

The Human Rights Act 1998, s 6(1), states that '[i]t is unlawful for a public authority to act in a way which is incompatible with a Convention right' unless the authority is acting in such a manner in order to comply with primary legislation.[104] The phrase 'public authority' is not exhaustively defined, but it will include a court or tribunal, or any person whose functions are of a public nature.[105] Either House of Parliament is excluded from the definition of 'public authority', because Parliament expressly retains the right to act in contravention of the ECHR.

It has been judicially accepted [106] that, apart from courts and tribunals, there are two forms of public authority, as follows.

- *'Core' authorities* These are authorities that *always* act in a public capacity (for example, the police and governmental departments). Such authorities must comply with the ECHR in relation to every act that they undertake.

- *'Hybrid' authorities* These are authorities that *sometimes* act in a public manner and sometimes act in a private manner (for example, non-governmental organizations and privatized utility companies). Such authorities need only comply with the ECHR in relation to their public activities.[107]

Because s 6 places the duty upon 'public authorities', it is clear that an individual may initiate a claim against a public authority that has violated his Convention rights (known as 'vertical effect'). But does this mean that non-public authorities (that is, individuals) can breach the ECHR without fear of being sued? In other words, can one individual sue another individual for a breach of the ECHR (known as 'horizontal effect')? It has been argued that, because a court is a public authority, for it to deny private parties the right to enforce the ECHR against each other would put the court itself in breach of s 6.[108] Although this argument does have a certain logic to it, it has been resisted to date, largely on the ground that it appears contrary to the intention of Parliament. Despite this, there are indications that the courts are slowly

---

101. D Feldman, 'Remedies for Violations of Convention Rights Under the Human Rights Act' (1998) EHRLR 691, 699.

102. *A v Secretary of State for the Home Department* [2004] UKHL 56, [2005] 2 AC 68, [142].

103. Human Rights Act 1998. s 10.

104. Ibid, s 6(2).

105. Ibid, s 6(3).

106. *Aston Cantlow and Wilmcote with Billesley Parochial Church Council v Wallbank* [2003] UKHL 37, [2004] 1 AC 546.

107. See, e.g., *L v Birmingham City Council* [2007] UKHL 27, [2008] 1 AC 95.

108. Sir W Wade, 'The United Kingdom's Bill of Rights' in J Beatson et al (eds), *Constitutional Reform in the United Kingdom: Practice and Principles* (Cambridge Centre for Public Law, Cambridge, 1998) 61.

and cautiously considering that the scope of s 6 can include actions between individuals, notably in cases concerning breaches of privacy.

 Celebrities, the right to privacy, and horizontal effect

In two notable privacy cases, the courts have exhibited a cautious recognition of the possibility that the ECHR can potentially produce horizontal effects, although it is still a long way from overt recognition. Both cases concerned the publication of private information: in one case, photographs illicitly obtained at the wedding of Michael Douglas and Catherine Zeta-Jones;[109] in the other case, photographs and other materials pertaining to treatment received from Narcotics Anonymous by the supermodel Naomi Campbell.[110]

In the *Douglas* case, Keene LJ stated that the court's duty in upholding s 6 'arguably includes their activity in interpreting and developing the common law, even where no public authority is a party to the litigation'.[111] Unfortunately, he did not expand upon this and indicate to what extent this created a new cause of action, and instead determined the case based upon the tort of breach of confidence.

In the *Campbell* case, Lord Hoffmann stated:

> I can see no logical ground for saying that a person should have less protection against a private individual than he would have against the state for the publication of personal information for which there is no justification. Nor, it appears, have any of the other judges who have considered the matter.[112]

The other judges involved—notably, Baroness Hale—clearly stated, however, that they felt that s 6 did not create a new cause of action between individuals.

The issue is still unresolved, but it cannot be denied that certain judges in the higher courts are open to an imminent possibility that the ECHR can acquire some form of horizontal effect.

The future of human rights protection in the UK

At the time of writing, the Human Rights Act 1998 has been in force for over eight years. The obvious questions to ask are:

- what has the Act achieved?
- does it require reform?

In relation to the first question, in 2006, the Department of Constitutional Affairs (now replaced by the Ministry of Justice) carried out a review of the implementation of the 1998 Act. The most interesting conclusion reached was that the Act 'involved the courts in a much more active and intense scrutiny of the Executive

---

109. *Douglas, Zeta-Jones and Northern & Shell Plc v Hello! Ltd* [2001] QB 967 (CA).
110. *Campbell v Mirror Group Newspapers Ltd* [2004] UKHL 22, [2004] 2 AC 457.
111. *Douglas, Zeta-Jones and Northern & Shell Plc v Hello! Ltd* [2001] QB 967 (CA) 1011.
112. *Campbell v Mirror Group Newspapers Ltd* [2004] UKHL 22, [2004] 2 AC 457, [50].

than they had been required to do prior to October 2000'.[113] The review argued that '[t]he Human Rights Act has not significantly altered the constitutional balance between Parliament, the Executive and the Judiciary'.[114] Whilst the 1998 Act may not have altered the *constitutional* relationship between these three organs of the State, there is little doubt that the relationship between them has been altered. It surely is no coincidence that, in the years in which the 1998 Act has been in force, the UK has witnessed a stark deterioration in the relationship between the judiciary and the executive that, on occasions, has bordered on open hostility.[115] In the case of *A v Secretary of State for the Home Department*,[116] discussed above, it was noted how the House of Lords launched a scathing attack on the government's anti-terrorism policies. The Home Secretary who attempted to pilot in much of the government's anti-terrorism legislation, David Blunkett, was involved in an unprecedented number of run-ins with the judiciary over attempts to limit civil rights. A significant contributory factor to this deterioration in relations was doubtless the fact that the courts, through the 1998 Act, were 'rather too successful at challenging the executive for the government's comfort'.[117]

As a result, a Parliament that was once very much in favour of the Human Rights Act 1998 has now tempered its support somewhat and momentum has increased to replace it with a Bill of Rights akin to that of the USA. On 10 May 2006, the High Court stopped the Home Secretary from deporting nine Afghan hijackers.[118] Four days later, it was reported that Tony Blair was considering reforming the 1998 Act to allow the government to veto court rulings.[119] In June 2006, the Leader of the Opposition, David Cameron, pledged to repeal the Human Rights Act 1998 and replace it with a British Bill of Rights.[120] In July 2007, the government published a Green Paper in which it rejected repeal of the Human Rights Act 1998, but then went on to suggest that 'the Human Rights Act should not necessarily be regarded as the last word on the subject' and that it was merely 'the first step in a journey'.[121] The Paper then proposes the next step—namely, the creation of a 'Bill of Rights and Duties' that would

→ Green Paper: a governmental report, inviting consultation on the development of the law or creation of new legislation

> provide explicit recognition that human rights come with responsibilities and must be exercised in a way that respects the human rights of others. It would

---

113. Department of Constitutional Affairs, *Review of the Implementation of the Human Rights Act* (HMSO, London, 2006) 35.
114. Ibid, 1.
115. It is acknowledged that the unsatisfactory manner with which the government announced the creation of the Supreme Court doubtless also contributed to this tension.
116. [2004] UKHL 56, [2005] 2 AC 68.
117. F Klug, 'A Bill of Rights: Do We Need One or Do We Already Have One?' [2007] PL 701, 714.
118. *R (on the Application of S) v Secretary of State for the Home Department*, The Times 14 June 2006 (QB). The decision was upheld by the Court of Appeal: The Times 9 October 2006 (CA).
119. N Temko and J Doward, 'Revealed: Blair Attack on Human Rights Law', *The Observer*, 14 May 2006.
120. Reported in W Woodward, 'Cameron Promises UK Bill of Rights to Replace Human Rights Act', *The Guardian*, 26 June 2006.
121. Secretary of State for Justice and Lord Chancellor, *The Governance of Britain* (Cmnd 7170, HMSO, London, 2007) [208].

build on the basic principles of the Human Rights Act, but make explicit the way in which a democratic society's rights have to be balanced by obligations.[122]

In a speech given in January 2008, Jack Straw reiterated the government's commitment to the now renamed 'Bill of Rights and Responsibilities', but also stated that 'we wish to have the widest possible debate on it before we come to final conclusions'.[123] A major criticism of the 1998 Act was that it 'appeared like a bolt out of the blue to most people'[124] and that, like the governmental document that led to the Constitutional Reform Act 2005, there was no prior consultation before the government announced its proposals. In August 2008, a joint committee of the House of Commons and House of Lords published a report[125] recommending the creation of a Bill of Rights to operate alongside the Human Rights Act 1998. The Bill of Rights would be used to update and provide additional rights to those contained in the ECHR. As regards the future of the 1998 Act, however, the committee did state that there should be no question of repealing the 1998 Act until such time as the Bill of Rights is firmly in place.[126]

 Key points summary

- The European Convention on Human Rights (ECHR) was created in 1950 and ratified by the UK in 1953. UK citizens have been able to petition the European Court of Human Rights (ECtHR) directly since 1966. Almost all of the rights contained provided for by the ECHR can be enforced in a UK domestic court following the implementation of the Human Rights Act 1998 in October 2000.

- ECHR rights may be absolute, limited, or qualified. Certain rights can be excluded via a derogation, or limited via a reservation.

- The ECtHR was created in 1959 and currently consists of forty-seven judges. Cases are heard by a committee, a chamber, or a Grand Chamber.

- Domestic courts are not bound by decisions of the ECtHR, although they must take them into account.

- The Human Rights Act 1998, s 3, places a duty upon domestic courts to interpret domestic legislation, as far as possible, in line with the ECHR. If the court feels that it cannot do this, however, it may issue a declaration of incompatibility.

- Declarations of incompatibility have no effect upon legislation, so the court will still have to apply the incompatible provision.

- The Human Rights Act 1998, s 6, places a duty on public authorities not to act in a manner that is incompatible with the ECHR.

---

122. Ibid, [210].
123. Full text of speech available online at <hhtp://www.justice.gov.uk/news/sp210108a.htm>.
124. F Klug, 'A Bill of Rights: Do We Need One or Do We Already Have One?' [2007] PL 701, 713.
125. Joint Committee on Human Rights, *A Bill of Rights for the UK?* (HMSO, London, 2008).
126. Ibid, [63].

Chapter conclusion

The impact that EU membership has had upon the English legal system cannot be overstated. The creation of the EU resulted in a new legal order that takes priority over domestic laws. From a business perspective, the creation of a Europe-wide system of law can be seen as extremely beneficial. A system of laws that applies uniformly throughout the EU will be of considerable benefit to businesses that operate in several EU countries. Such business would previously need to be aware of the laws of every country within which they operated or with which they had commercial dealings. In cases involving directly applicable law, such laws will apply uniformly throughout the EU, thereby reducing the need to understand fully the laws of numerous countries.

Similarly, ratifying the ECHR has had an appreciable and often unpredictable effect upon the operation of businesses in the UK, especially since the enactment of the Human Rights Act 1998, which permits much of the ECHR to be enforced in a domestic court. The extension of many human rights to cover legal persons is accepted without dispute, but determining the exact scope and application of human rights principles to businesses has proved to be an extremely controversial and problematic issue. The effect of the 1998 Act in relation to the interpretation and application of statutes has already been felt, and will continue to be so for some time as the judges reinterpret statutes in light of the obligations imposed by the 1998 Act. As seen, however, the long-term future of the Act may be in doubt and, once the proposed Bill of Rights becomes law, it is possible that the 1998 Act will be repealed.

Self-test questions

1. Explain the relationship between the EU and the ECHR. Explain the reasons behind the creation of the EU and the ECHR.

2. Explain the composition and functions of:
    (a)   the Council of the European Union;
    (b)   the European Council;
    (c)   the European Commission;
    (d)   the European Parliament;
    (e)   the European Court of Justice.

3. Explain the difference between 'direct applicability' and 'direct effect'. How does vertical direct effect differ from horizontal direct effect?

4. Do all directly applicable provisions also have direct effect?

5. How do directives differ from regulations?

6. In August 2007, the (fictional) Employee Records Directive is passed. It provides that 'all employees have a right to see their personnel records, subject to this right being excluded by the employee's contract of employment'. Peter requests to see his personnel record, but his employer refuses, arguing that Peter's employment contract contains a term stating that he does not have the right to see his personnel record. Advise Peter.

7. How has the enactment of the Human Rights Act 1998 affected: (i) the enforcement of the ECHR; and (ii) the way in which legislation is interpreted?

8. Can the UK, having ratified the ECHR, pass legislation that infringes upon the rights enshrined in the ECHR?

Further reading

Craig, P, and De Búrca, G, *EU Law: Text, Cases and Materials* (4th edn, OUP, Oxford, 2008) chs 1–3
Provides an in-depth, but easy-to-understand, account of the development and institutions of the European Union, as well as a well-chosen selection of relevant materials

Emberland, M, *The Human Rights of Companies* (OUP, Oxford, 2006)
Provides a detailed analysis of the protection offered to companies by the European Convention on Human Rights and the Human Rights Act 1998

Stone, R, *Civil Liberties and Human Rights* (7th edn, OUP, Oxford, 2008) chs 1 and 2
Provides a clear and accessible account of the ECHR and the Human Rights Act 1998

Websites

<http://curia.europa.eu>
The official website of the European Court of Justice and Court of First Instance; contains extensive and up-to-date information on the working of both courts, as well as providing access to court decisions

<http://eur-lex.europa.eu>
Provides full access to EU treaties, legislation, and case law

<http://europa.eu>
The official website of the EU; contains a massive amount of accessible and up-to-date information on all of the workings of the EU, including detailed information on the workings of all of its institutions

<http://www.echr.coe.int/echr>
The official website of the European Court of Human Rights; contains up-to-date information on the ECHR and the ECtHR, as well as providing access to decisions of the ECtHR

Remember to visit the **Online Resource Centre** at **<http://www.oxfordtextbooks.co.uk/roach>** to access the following resources on Chapter 4, 'Europe and the English legal system': more **practice questions** and answers; a **glossary** of key terms; **multiple-choice questions**; **revision summaries**; **audio updates** when relevant; **diagrams** in pdf; and **discussion boxes**.

PART II

the law of contract

5 An introduction to the law of contract

- Why are contracts enforced?
- Formalities
- The capacity to contract
- Privity of contract and third-party rights

INTRODUCTION

Most laypersons do not appreciate the significance that contracts play in their everyday lives. We are all aware of the importance of a contract when we buy a house or a car and we have to 'sign on the dotted line', but apart from such obvious instances, we tend not to think about the role that contracts play. Put simply, contracts dominate our ability to transact: whenever you purchase goods from a shop, watch a film in a cinema, take a ride on a bus, or pay another to perform a service for you, you are entering into a contract. Becoming a shareholder in a company creates a contract between the shareholder and the company. For businesses, the importance of contract is even more pronounced, because virtually every transaction and relationship will be governed by contract. When all goes well, our ignorance of the contractual relationships into which we enter is not a problem—but when things do not go well and one party fails to deliver what it has promised, the dispute can only be resolved by reference to the contract that has been created. It is therefore of paramount importance that we know what a contract actually *is*.

Unfortunately, in English law, there is no legally accepted, formal definition of the word 'contract'. In the absence of a legal definition, the issue has been left largely to academics and, whilst individual definitions differ, the majority of definitions broadly cover the same ground. Perhaps the most straightforward and well-known definition is that provided by Treitel, who defines a contract as 'an agreement giving rise to obligations which are enforced or recognized by law'.[1] Whilst such a definition provides an adequate understanding of what a contract is, it does not provide an understanding of why the law enforces such agreements, or the role of contract law. At its most basic level, the role of contract law is to determine which contractual obligations can be enforced and which cannot. It is therefore important to understand the theoretical justifications behind the enforcement of contracts.

---

1. E Peel, *Treitel on the Law of Contract* (12th edn, Sweet & Maxwell, London, 2007) 1.

Why are contracts enforced?

For centuries, contract theorists have argued and debated the theoretical justifi-cations behind why some promises are enforced by the law and others are not. A detailed account of these theories is well beyond the scope of this text; the follow-ing notes in brief only some of the theoretical and practical justifications behind the enforcement of certain agreements.

- *The moral argument* On a moral level, enforcing contracts simply ensures that we keep our promises.[2] In this sense, the law is not imposing an obligation on us; rather, it is simply giving effect to obligations that we voluntarily undertook ourselves.

- *The efficiency argument* It is argued that enforcing contractual promises maxi-mizes efficiency. When negotiating, individuals will attempt to reach a conclusion that maximizes their own benefit (known as 'utility' in economic terms). A freely negotiated contract produces an outcome that maximizes the benefit of both parties. If all parties act this way, societal wealth will be maximized.

- *The reliance argument* Numerous prominent academics[3] have contended that the principal modern theory for enforcing contractual obligations is based upon the notion of 'reliance'. According to this theory, it is not the making of the promise that justifies enforcement, but the other party's reliance on it.

- *The relationship argument* Some have argued that the role of contract law is not to enforce promises, but to encourage and protect the forming of valuable relationships.[4]

Having highlighted the theoretical justifications for enforcing contracts, we will now examine three practical issues relating to the enforcement of contracts:

- what formalities are required to create a contract?
- who has the legal ability to enter into a contract?
- who can enforce a contract?

Formalities

It is a common belief amongst laypersons that, in order to be valid, a contract must be in writing and both parties must 'sign on the dotted line'. In reality, however, this is a complete misconception and, in the vast majority of cases, the law imposes no requirements regarding the form that a contract takes, although there are clear advantages to putting a contract into writing—namely, that it will render less likely the possibility of the parties subsequently disagreeing over what was agreed.

---

2. C Fried, *Contract As Promise: A Theory of Contractual Obligation* (Harvard University Press Cambridge, Cambridge, MA, 1981) 14–17.

3. See, e.g., G Gilmore, *The Death of Contract* (Ohio State University Press, Columbus, OH, 1974); P Atiyah, *The Rise and Fall of the Freedom of Contract* (Clarendon Press, Oxford, 1979).

4. J Raz, 'Promises in Morality and Law' (1982) 95 Harv LR 916.

Generally, a contract made orally is just as valid in law as a written contract signed by both parties.

Whilst it could legitimately be argued that, from an evidential perspective, it would be desirable that all contracts were in writing, one could also argue that, from a practical viewpoint, imposing formality requirements could be unworkable for several reasons:

- given the sheer number of contracts entered into daily, the task of determining which contracts should be subject to formality and which should not would be an unduly burdensome task;
- ensuring that the text and form of a contract complies with formality can be an extremely time-consuming task;
- requiring strict adhesion to a set of formalities could be regarded as out of touch in an era increasingly dominated by electronic commerce.

Accordingly, the general rule that contracts require no particular formalities is one of efficiency and convenience, and the law will only impose requirements as to formality when 'there is some good reason for doing so'.[5] For example, in some contracts (for example, consumer contracts), there is considerable inequality of bargaining power between the parties and the setting of certain formalities helps to protect the weaker party against the stronger party abusing its dominant position.

Three principal forms of formality can be identified:

1. contracts required to be made by deed;
2. contracts required to be in writing; and
3. contracts required to be evidenced in writing.

Contracts required to be made by deed

Certain contracts must be made in the form of a deed. A deed is simply a legal document that is subject to more formal requirements than a normal contract. It is often said the deeds must be 'signed, sealed and delivered', but the requirement that a deed be sealed was abolished in 1989.[6] Today, the validity of a deed is dependent upon it indicating that it is a deed (although the word 'deed' need not be used),[7] and that the deed is signed in the presence of a witness and then delivered.[8] If one of the parties to a deed is a company, the formalities are different. Corporate deeds can be signed by affixing the company's seal, if it has retained one. Failing that, it will need to be signed by two 'authorized signatories' (defined as either a director or company secretary), or signed by one director in the presence of a witness.[9]

Examples of contracts that must be made by deed include the following.

- A lease for more than three years will be void *ab initio* for the purpose of creating a lease if not made by deed.[10] A contract to grant a lease of over three

> **deed:** a legal document that is used to create a right; similar it is subject to stricter formalities

> **void *ab initio*:** void 'from the beginning'; a void contract is treated as though it never existed

---

5. H Kotz, *European Contract Law Volume 1: Formation, Validity and Content of Contracts—Contract and Third Parties* (OUP, Oxford, 1997) 80.

6. Law of Property (Miscellaneous Provisions) Act 1989, s 1.　　7. Ibid, s 1(2).

8. Ibid, s 1(3).　　9. Companies Act 2006, s 44.

10. Law of Property Act 1925, s 54(2).

years in length need not be executed by deed, however, but must be evidenced in writing.[11]

- We shall see in Chapter 6 that an agreement that lacks consideration will not normally constitute a binding contract. A contract that lacks consideration will, however, be binding if made by deed.[12]

Contracts required to be made in writing

In order to be valid and enforceable, certain types of contract must be made in writing, including the following.

- A bill of exchange must be in writing and signed.[13] A bill of exchange is simply a written instruction from one person to pay a specified sum of money to another.
- Contracts for the sale or disposition of an interest in land must be made in writing and all of the terms agreed by the parties must be in one document.[14] This requirement is, however, waived in the case of:
  - contracts involving a lease not exceeding three years, taking effect in possession at the best rent reasonably obtainable;
  - contracts made in the course of a public auction; and
  - contracts regulated by the Financial Services Act 1986.
- Regulated consumer credit agreements and regulated consumer hire-purchase agreements under the Consumer Credit Act 1974 must comply with certain requirements, or they will be unenforceable unless a court order is obtained. The requirements are that the express terms must be set out in a prescribed order and that certain rights are drawn to the attention of the debtor. Both parties must sign the document and the debtor must be supplied with a copy.[15]

Visit the **Online Resource Centre** for more on the law relating to consumer credit agreements in the chapter entitled 'Consumer credit'

Contracts required to be evidenced in writing

A contract of guarantee is simply 'a promise to answer for the debt, default or miscarriage of another person'.[16] A contract of guarantee does not need to be in writing, but it will be unenforceable against the party providing the guarantee unless it is evidenced in writing. 'Evidenced in writing' simply means that there must be written evidence that the agreement has been made.

Two points should be noted:

1. only the contract of guarantee need be evidenced in writing;
2. this rule of formality only applies to guarantees—it does not apply to indemnities.

The following example explains the operation of these two points.

---

11. Ibid, s 40(1). Note that this section has been repealed, but its provisions are not retrospective.
12. *Rann v Hughes* (1778) 7 Term Rep 350n (HL).
13. Bills of Exchange Act 1882, ss 3(1) and 17(2).
14. Law of Property (Miscellaneous Provisions) Act 1989, s 2(1).
15. Consumer Credit (Agreements) Regulations 1983, SI 1983/1553, regs 2–3.
16. Statute of Frauds 1677, s 4.

> ## (Eg) Guarantees and indemnities
>
> Tom and Dave walk into a BMW showroom. Tom chooses a car and enters into a contract with BMW to purchase the car. Dave enters into an agreement with BMW, stating that he will pay for the car if Tom fails to do so. The contract between Tom and BMW is a normal contract, and so would require no formality (unless Tom bought the car on credit, in which case, it may need to be in writing, as discussed above). The contract between Dave and BMW is a contract of guarantee, and so would need to be evidenced in writing. This evidence would need to identify the parties,[17] describe the subject matter of the contract,[18] contain the material terms of the contract[19] (other than implied terms or the consideration),[20] and be signed by the person giving the guarantee (Dave), or his agent.[21] Failure to evidence the contract would not render it void or voidable, but would render it unenforceable.
>
> Note that if Tom were to enter into the contract with BMW, but Dave agreed to pay for the car, the contract between Dave and BMW would not be a contract of guarantee—it would be a contract of indemnity—and the agreement would not need to be evidenced in writing. A guarantee is a promise by A to pay for another (B), if B fails to pay. In such a case, B remains liable under the contract and A is only liable if B defaults. An indemnity is simply the promise to pay for another (B), irrespective of B's liability (that is, A is liable in any event).

Formalities and e-commerce

The advent of e-commerce has created problems regarding the formality of contract. For example, how can one sign an electronic document? Will printing off a contract satisfy the requirement that it be in writing? With the passing of the Electronic Commerce Directive, the issue became one that had to be addressed. Article 9(1) states:

> Member States shall ensure that their legal system allows contracts to be concluded by electronic means. Member States shall in particular ensure that the legal requirements applicable to the contractual process neither create obstacles for the use of electronic contracts nor result in such contracts being deprived of legal effectiveness and validity on account of their being made by electronic means.[22]

As a result, three major reforms have been introduced in order to ensure that UK laws relating to formalities do not fall foul of Art 9(1), as follows.

1. The Electronic Commerce (EC Directive) Regulations 2002[23] were made in order to implement the Electronic Commerce Directive.

2. The Electronic Communications Act 2000, s 7, recognizes the validity of 'electronic signatures' and provides that they will fulfil the same function as

---

17. *William v Jordan* (1877) 6 Ch D 517.
18. *Burgess v Cox* [1951] Ch 383 (Ch).
19. *Cook v Taylor* [1942] Ch 349 (Ch).
20. *Laythoarp v Bryant* (1836) 2 Bing NC 735.
21. Mercantile Law Amendment Act 1856, s 3.
22. European Parliament Directive (EC) 2000/31 OJ L178/1, Art 9(1).
23. SI 2002/2013.

a handwritten signature, provided that they meet the test of authenticity in s 15(2).

3. The Electronic Communications Act 2000, s 8, empowers the Secretary of State to amend legislation 'for the purpose of authorising or facilitating the use of electronic communications or electronic storage'.

The Law Commission has contended that s 8 will only need to be used in 'very rare cases',[24] because, in the majority of cases, existing legislation will comply with Art 9(1). Further, where the legislation is vague, it can be interpreted in such a way as to permit the use of e-commerce, thereby avoiding the need to amend it. Thus, in *Pereira Fernandes SA v Mehta*,[25] the court held that a contractual offer sent by email satisfied the requirement of being in 'writing' for the purposes of the Statute of Frauds 1677, and that by including his name in the email text, the sender had successfully 'signed' the document.

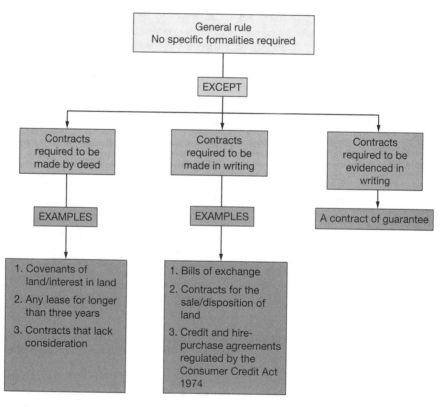

FIGURE 5.1 The formality of contracts

---

24. Law Commission, *Electronic Commerce: Formal Requirements in Commercial Transactions* (2001), [3.49], available online at <http://www.lawcom.gov.uk/docs/e-commerce.pdf>.
25. [2006] EWHC 813 (Ch), [2006] 1 WLR 1543.

Key points summary

- As a general rule, contracts require no special formalities in order to be valid and binding.
- Certain contracts are subject to formalities—namely:
  - contracts required to be made by deed;
  - contracts required to be in writing; and
  - contracts required to be evidenced in writing.
- EU member States are under a duty to ensure that their laws permit the making of contracts electronically. The Electronic Communication Act 2000 was passed to ensure that electronic signatures are as effective as handwritten ones for the purposes of authentication and to permit easy alterations to any law that makes difficult the process of electronic contracting.

The capacity to contract

An individual who has the ability to enter into a binding contract is said to have 'contractual capacity'. Prima facie the law assumes that all living, sober adults of sound mind have contractual capacity. It follows that individuals who do not fall within this description may lack the ability to enter into binding contracts. The determination of contractual capacity can be a delicate one, because the law is required to balance two justifiable aims:

➡ prima facie: 'at first glance'; initially

1. the need to protect vulnerable or incapacitated individuals; and
2. the need to protect those who fairly enter into contracts with persons who may lack capacity.

Note that the following is concerned with the ability of natural persons to contract; the contractual capacity of bodies corporate will be examined in Chapter 17.

Minors

Any person below the age of 18 is legally regarded as a minor[26] and lacks the capacity to makes many types of contract. Where the minor does lack capacity, however, this does not mean that the contract is void *ab initio.* Although the party contracting with the minor will be unable to enforce the contract, the minor may be able to enforce the contract, so that the other party will be unable to escape the contract by relying on the minor's incapacity.

The principle that minors lack the capacity to contract cannot be absolute for several reasons. Firstly, in recent years, the prominence of young entertainers and sportspersons has meant that the capacity of a minor to enter into contracts of service has become an increasingly important issue. Secondly, the need to protect the minor must be balanced against the need to deal equitably with those who have contracted

---

26. Family Law Reform Act 1969, s 1.

fairly with a minor. Accordingly, in a number of limited instances, minors may have contractual capacity, resulting in contracts that are either binding or voidable.

Binding contracts

In two situations, a minor will acquire full contractual capacity and can enter into binding contracts. The first situation concerns contracts for necessaries, which are held to be binding 'not for the benefit of the tradesman who may trust the infant, but for the benefit of the infant himself'.[27] A minor will acquire full contractual capacity when purchasing goods or hiring services that are 'necessary' to maintain him, given his circumstances. In relation to goods, this rule has been codified in the Sale of Goods Act 1979, s 3(3), which states that 'necessaries' include 'goods suitable to the condition in life of the minor and to his actual requirements at the time of the sale and delivery' and that a minor will be required to pay a reasonable price for such goods.[28] Clearly, goods such as food, drink, and clothing will be regarded as necessaries, but it is important to note that, in determining what is necessary, the court will have regard to characteristics of the minor in question.[29] This has resulted in the term 'necessaries' receiving a somewhat wide definition and has been held to include a selection of rings, breast pins, and watch chains for the child of a rich member of Parliament,[30] and a uniform for a minor's servant.[31] It can accordingly be seen that the word 'necessaries' is not to have the same meaning as the word 'necessities', although the courts have stated that 'mere luxuries' will not constitute necessaries.[32] This principle applies to services as well as goods, and will include the provision of education,[33] legal advice,[34] and medical services.[35] A significant problem with this exception to the normal rule is, however, that the person contracting with the minor is unlikely to be aware of the minor's circumstances, thereby making it impossible for him to judge whether or not the goods or services in question are 'necessaries'. To remedy this, the Law Commission considered limiting the principle to cover 'necessities', not necessaries, but the proposal was omitted from the final report.[36] Where a contract for the supply of necessary goods or services contains harsh or onerous terms that operate against the minor, then the contract will be void.[37]

The second situation in which a minor acquires full contractual capacity is in relation to contracts for service—namely, employment or apprenticeship. The rationale behind holding such contracts valid is that the law should not prevent a minor from pursuing an occupation. Such contracts will be binding where they are for the minor's benefit as a whole. Accordingly, a contract that benefits the minor overall will not be called into question simply because one or two terms are disadvantageous,[38] but if the disadvantageous terms outweigh the benefit of the contract, the contract will be unenforceable.

---

27. *Ryder v Wombwell* (1868) LS 4 EX 32, 38.
28. Sale of Goods Act 1979, s 3(2).
29. *Chapple v Cooper* (1844) 13 M & W 253 (Ex).
30. *Peters v Fleming* (1840 6 M & W 42 (Ex).
31. *Hands v Slaney* (1800) 8 TR 578.
32. *Peters v Fleming* (1840 6 M & W 42 (Ex).
33. *Walter v Everard* [1891] 2 QB 369 (CA).
34. *Helps v Clayton* (1864) 29 JP 263.
35. *Huggins v Wiseman* (1690) Carth 110.
36. Law Commission, *Law of Contract: Minor's Contracts* (Law Com No 134, HC 494, HMSO, London, 1984).
37. *Fawcett v Smethurst* (1914) 84 LJKB 473.
38. *Clements v London and North Western Railway Company* [1894] 2 QB 482 (CA).

De Francesco v Barnum (1890) 45 Ch D 430 (Ch)

FACTS: A contract provided that a minor would, for a period of seven years, learn to dance under the tutelage of Signor De Francesco. During this period, he was not obliged to maintain her or provide employment for her. Further, she could not marry or obtain any professional work without obtaining permission from De Francesco. Finally, De Francesco had the right to terminate the contract without notice at any time.

HELD: The High Court held that the contract was unenforceable. The terms of the contract were unduly harsh and unreasonable, and, overall, were not for the minor's benefit.

The following case provides a recent and interesting example of a situation in which the court held that a contract of service was not a contract for necessaries and applied the general rule that a contract with a minor is voidable at the minor's option.

 Proform Sports Management Ltd v Proactive Sports Management Ltd [2006] EWHC 2903 (Ch)

FACTS: The claimant and defendant firms acted as executive agents for football players. The claimant entered into an agreement to act as Wayne Rooney's agent. At the time that the contract was formed, Rooney was 15 years old and was already at a football club. But because Football Association rules prohibited players under the age of 17 from becoming professional footballers, Rooney was employed at the club as a trainee. Rooney then entered into an agreement with the defendant whereby the defendant would act as Rooney's agent. The claimant brought an action alleging that the defendant had unlawfully interfered with the claimant's contract and/or had induced Rooney to breach the contract.

HELD: The High Court summarily dismissed the claimant's action. The general rule is that a minor is not bound by a contract, unless the contract was one for necessaries, or one of employment or apprenticeship. This was not such a contract. Because Rooney was not bound by the contract, the defendant could not be liable for inducing Rooney to breach it, because Rooney had the right to set aside the contract at any point.

> The torts of unlawful interference with contract and inducing breach of contract are discussed in Chapter 13

Voidable contracts

In four situations, a minor can create a voidable contract. This means that it will bind both parties, but that the minor is free to **repudiate** the contract at any time before he reaches the age of 18, or within a reasonable time afterwards.[39] The other party cannot repudiate the contract.[40]

> ➡ repudiate: to refuse to honour or fulfil a contract

- *Contracts concerning land* This could include contracts to rent property,[41] or contracts to purchase or sell land.[42]

---

39. *Edwards v Carter* [1893] AC 360 (HL).
41. *Keteley's Case* (1613) 1 Brownl 1.
40. *Clayton v Ashdown* (1714) 2 Eq Ca Arb 516.
42. *Whittingham v Murdy* (1889) 60 LT 956 (QB).

➡ marriage settlement: an agreement made in contemplation of a marriage, which usually operates to benefit any children of the marriage

- *Marriage settlements* Marriage settlements will bind a minor, unless he repudiates.[43]
- *Shares* Minors who purchase or subscribe for shares are liable to pay for them, unless they repudiate.[44]
- *Partnerships* A minor may become a partner, but will not be made liable for the partnerships losses whilst he remains a minor.[45]

The effect of repudiation is to free the minor from all future obligations—but obligations may have accrued prior to repudiation and whether the minor is bound by such obligations is unclear. The weight of authority appears to favour the view that the repudiation rescinds the contract and, because repudiation is retrospective, the minor will not be bound by any obligations that have accrued.[46] Authority also exists, however, for the view that minors are bound by obligations that accrue prior to repudiation.[47] A definitive decision on the matter is required.

𝒫 The law relating to consideration is discussed at p 183

Where a minor has paid money or transferred property to the other party and then repudiates the contract, the general rule is that the minor can recover the money or property only if there has been a total failure of consideration (that is, if the minor has received no benefit from the contract).[48] Where the minor has gained property from the contract prior to repudiation, the court has the discretion to require the minor to return any property gained where it is 'just and equitable' to do so.[49]

Ratification and restitution

➡ ratifies: approves or sanctions, even though it may be in breach of the law

Even if a contract does not come within one of the above instances, a minor may still be bound if, upon reaching the age of 18, he expressly or impliedly ratifies it. Prior to ratification, however, the contract would not be binding on the minor, but the minor may choose to enforce it. Further, the minor may have received a benefit from the purported contract. The court has the discretion to require the minor to return any property gained where it is 'just and equitable' to do so;[50] this will usually be used where the minor has acquired property without paying for it. As with voidable contracts, if a minor has expended money in relation to a contract that he later repudiates, he will only be permitted to claim back the money if there has been a total failure of consideration.

Mental incapacity

The law presumes that a person has mental capacity unless the contrary is established.[51] The Mental Capacity Act 2005, s 2(1), states that a person will lack capacity in relation to a matter if 'at the material time he is unable to make a decision for himself in relation to a matter because of an impairment of, or a disturbance of the functioning of, the mind or brain'. The impairment can be permanent or temporary.[52]

---

43. *Duncan v Dixon* (1890) 44 Ch D 211.
44. *Steinberg v Scala (Leeds) Ltd* [1923] 2 Ch 452 (CA). 45. *Goode v Harrison* (1821) 5 B & Ald 147.
46. See, e.g., *North Western Rly Co v McMichael* (1850) 5 Exch 114.
47. See, e.g., *Blake v Concannon* (1870) IR 4 CL 323. 48. *Corpe v Overton* (1833) 10 Bing 252.
49. Minors' Contracts Act 1987, s 3(1). 50. Ibid.
51. Mental Capacity Act 2005, s 1(2). 52. Ibid, s 2(2).

Despite this, a contract with a person who is proved to lack capacity under s 2(1) will normally be binding, except:

- when the other party knew of the mental incapacity. In such a case, the contract is voidable at the option of the mentally incapacitated party.[53] If the incapacitated person sets aside the contract, it will cease to bind either party;

- when the mentally incapacitated person's affairs are subject to the control of the Court of Protection, any contract that interferes with the court's control of said property will not bind the incapacitated individual,[54] although it will bind the other party.

➡ Court of Protection: a court set up to deal with the affairs of adults (and some children) who lack capacity

A mentally incapacitated person who enters into a contract for 'necessaries' will be liable for the full contract price if:

1. the other person is not aware of the incapacity; and

2. the incapacitated person's affairs are not under the control of the Court of Protection.[55]

If these two conditions are not met, the action is limited to recovery of a reasonable price.[56]

Intoxication

If, at the time of making a contract, one party is intoxicated (through drink or drugs) to such an extent that he is unable to understand the transaction and the other party knows this, the contract is voidable at the intoxicated party's discretion.[57] If, however, he does not avoid the contract, he must pay a reasonable price for any necessary *goods* (not services) delivered under the contract.[58]

Figure 5.2 clarifies the rules relating to a person's contractual capacity.

‹› Key points summary

- The legal ability to enter into a contract is known as 'capacity'.

- As a general rule, all living, sober adults of sound mind have the legal right to enter into contracts.

- Contracts created with a minor are generally not binding on the minor, but are binding on the other party.

- Generally, persons under the age of 18 lack capacity to contract, but have full contractual capacity in relation to 'necessaries' (that is, necessary goods or services) and beneficial contracts for service.

- Minors have the capacity to make certain voidable contracts (for example, certain contracts concerning land and contracts subscribing for shares).

---

53. *Molton v Camroux* (1849) 4 EX 17. 54. *Re Walker* [1905] 1 Ch 160 (CA).
55. *Baxter v Portsmouth* (1826) 5 B & C 170. 56. Mental Capacity Act 2005, s 7(1).
57. *Gore v Gibson* (1843) 13 M & W 623, as qualified by *Matthews v Baxter* (1873) LR 8 Exch 132.
58. Sale of Goods Act 1979, s 3(2)—but he will not be liable to pay the contract price, only a reasonable sum.

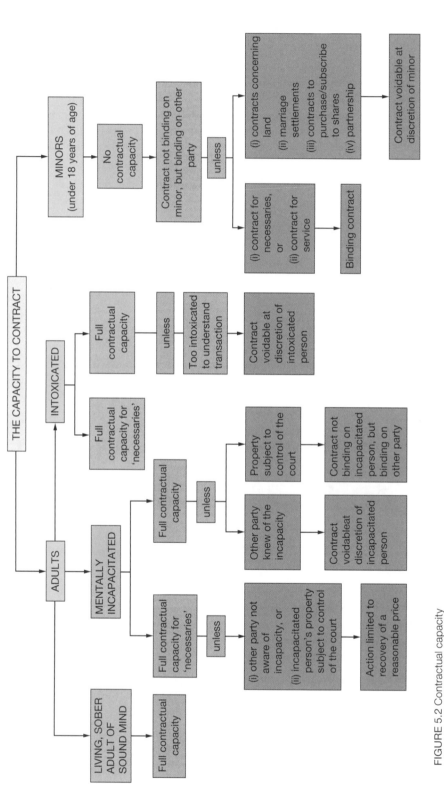

FIGURE 5.2 Contractual capacity

- Upon reaching the age of 18, a minor can ratify a contract entered into while he was a minor.

- Generally speaking, a person who lacks capacity on the ground of mental incapacity will still be bound by a contract unless:
  - the other party knew of the incapacity; or
  - the incapacitated person's property is subject to court control.

- Contracts with intoxicated persons who are so intoxicated as to be unable to understand the transaction are voidable, provided that the other person knew of the intoxication.

Privity of contract and third-party rights

Privity of contract is a long-established doctrine in contract law that consists of two rules. The first rule provides that only the parties to a contract may enforce the contract. Third parties have no right to enforce the contracts of others or to sue if the contract is breached, even if they have an interest in such contracts, as can be seen in the case below.

 ## Tweddle v Atkinson (1831) 1 B & S 393

FACTS: John Tweddle's son (the claimant) was marrying William Guy's daughter. John Tweddle and William Guy contracted with each other to pay the claimant a sum of money (Tweddle would pay £100 and Guy would pay £200). William Guy died without paying the claimant the £200 promised and the claimant sued Guy's personal representatives for the money.

HELD: The claimant's action failed. He was not a party to the contract and so could not enforce it. John Tweddle would be able to sue Guy's representatives for the failure to pay, but because Tweddle had not actually suffered any loss, he would only be able to recover nominal damages.

The second rule provides that a contract only imposes obligations on the parties to it. Contracts do not impose obligations on third parties. The following example demonstrates this rule in practice.

 ## Eg Privity of contract

Rhian, Ceri, and Steve are shareholders of OmniTech plc. Rhian and Ceri enter into a contract with each other, which provides that either Rhian or Ceri can require Steve to sell them half of his shares. This obligation on Steve will be unenforceable, and neither Rhian nor Ceri will be able to compel Steve to sell his shares, because he is not a party to the contract.

🔗 The law of agency is discussed in more depth in Chapter 27

Exceptions to the doctrine of privity did exist, but they were few. Perhaps the most notable was where there was a relationship of agency. A relationship of agency is one in which one party (the principal) instructs another (the agent) to carry out some task on his behalf. An agent has the power to bind his principal contractually to a third party, provided that the agent acts within his authority. The following example demonstrates how agency works.

Eg **Privity and agency**

John employs Elen to act as his agent. He instructs her to locate a 1956 Rolls Royce Phantom and to purchase it for him, provided that it costs no more than £100,000. Ricardo has such a car and offers to sell it to Elen for £95,000. She accepts. Although Elen and Ricardo created the contract, it will be binding between John and Ricardo, because Elen was acting as John's agent and was acting within her authority.

As time progressed, the doctrine (especially the first rule) became subject to a major criticism from judges,[59] the Law Commission,[60] and academics[61]—namely, that preventing third parties with an interest in the contract from being able to enforce the contract could be criticized for several reasons, chief among them being that it defeats the entire purpose of a contract that both the parties and the third party would normally wish to see enforced. As far back as 1937, the Law Revision Committee recommended that:

> Where a contract by its express terms purports to confer a benefit directly on a third party it shall be enforceable by a third party in his own name subject to any defence that would have been valid between the contracting parties.[62]

But this recommendation was not taken any further until 1996, when the Law Commission published a report[63] that contained a draft Bill, which would implement the Law Revision Committee's recommendation. The Bill was introduced into Parliament and, with some amendments, became the Contracts (Rights of Third Parties) Act 1999.

The Contracts (Rights of Third Parties) Act 1999

The Contracts (Rights of Third Parties) Act 1999 (CRTPA 1999) provides an important exception to the first rule of the privity doctrine. But this exception will apply only to those contracts covered by the Act. Where a contract is not covered by the Act (excluded situations are discussed later), the privity doctrine will apply, unless one of the other exceptions discussed later applies. The exception contained

---

59. For example, *Woodar Investment Development Ltd v Wimpey Construction UK Ltd* [1980] 1 WLR 277 (HL) 291 (Lord Salmon).
60. Law Commission, *Contracts for the Benefit of Third Parties* (Law Com No 3329, HMSO, London, 1996) [3.2].
61. For example, MP Furmston, 'Return to *Dunlop v Selfridge*' (1960) 23 MLR 373.
62. Law Revision Committee, *Sixth Interim Report* (Cmnd 5449, HMSO, London, 1937) [48].
63. Law Commission, *Contracts for the Benefit of Third Parties* (Law Com No 3329, HMSO, London, 1996).

in the Act is found in s 1(1), which states that, subject to the provisions of the Act, a third party may enforce a term of the contract if:

(a) the contract expressly provides that he may, or

(b) the term purports to confer a benefit on him.

As a result of s 1(1), had *Tweddle v Atkinson* been decided today, the claimant would have been able to recover the £200 from Guy's estate. But the exception contained in s 1(1)(b) will not operate where, on a proper construction of the contract, it appears that the parties did not intend the term to be enforceable by a third party.[64] The effect of this is to provide that the default position (or, as the Law Commission termed it, a 'rebuttable presumption')[65] is that third parties may enforce terms that confer a benefit upon them, unless the contract indicates otherwise.

The exception contained in s 1(1) does not provide that all third parties can enforce the contract; only third parties expressly[66] identified in the contract by name, as a member of a class (for example, 'employees' of a certain business), or by reference to a description (for example, the party of a particular sale of goods contract) may enforce the term.[67] Where an identified third party does come within s 1(1), he will be able to obtain any remedy that would be available for breach of contract had he actually been a party to the contract[68] (for example, damages, injunction, or specific performance). Further, a third party can also rely on an exclusion or limitation clause that is contained in the contract[69]—but where the exclusion clause could not be relied on even by a party to the contract (for example, because it has been deemed unenforceable for contravening the Unfair Contract Terms Act 1977), then the third party will also be unable to rely on the clause.[70]

🔗 The Unfair Contract Terms Act 1977 is discussed at p 977

Discharge and variation

The third party's right to enforce the term of the contract would be worthless if the original parties to the contract were able simply to discharge the contract or to vary it to remove the third party's rights. Conversely, the third party acquiring the right to enforce a term of the contract should not unduly restrict the original parties' rights to discharge or vary the contract. Section 2(1) aims to strike this balance by providing that the contracting parties' right to discharge or vary the contract remains intact, except where such discharge or variation would extinguish the third party's rights under the term and:

(a) the third party has communicated his assent to the term to the promisor,

(b) the promisor is aware that the third party has relied on the term, or

---

64. CRTPA 1999, s 1(2).
65. Law Commission, *Contracts for the Benefit of Third Parties* (Law Com No 3329, HMSO, London, 1996) [7.5].
66. The CRTPA 1999 does not require express identification, but in *Avraamides v Colwill* [2006] EWCA Civ 1533, [2007] BLR 76, the Court of Appeal held that implied identification would not suffice.
67. CRTPA 1999, s 1(3). Provided that the third party is identified, he does not need to exist at the time that the contract was entered into. Therefore, unborn children and companies awaiting incorporation are also able to enforce the term.
68. Ibid, s 1(5).   69. Ibid, s 1(6).
70. Ibid, s 3(6).

(c) the promisor can reasonably be expected to have foreseen that the third party would rely on the term and the third party has in fact relied on it.

In relation to s 2(1)(c), the discharge or variation will only be effective if the third party gives his consent.

If the third party cannot be located, or if he lacks mental capacity, a court or tribunal may waive the requirement of consent.[71] Where this occurs, the court or tribunal may impose whatever conditions it deems fair, including a requirement to pay compensation to the third party.[72]

But this limitation on the contracting parties' right to discharge or vary the contract will not apply where the contract expressly provides that the parties may vary or discharge the contract without the third party's consent, or where the consent of the third party is required in circumstances that are different from those stated in s 2(1).[73]

The defences available to the promisor

Where a third party acquires the right to enforce a term under s 1(1), then the promisor (that is, the party against whom the term is being enforced) has available any defences or set-offs that arise from or in connection with the contract, and would have been available to him had the proceedings been brought by the promisee.[74] Therefore, the third party does not acquire any more rights than the promisee would have and if the promisor has a defence that would render the contract void, discharged, or unenforceable, then this defence will work just as well against the third party as it would against the promisor.

Whilst the third party will be no better off than the promisee, there is one notable situation in which the third party is worse off than the promisee: where the promisor is protected by a clause that excludes or limits liability for acts of negligence, the promisee can challenge such a clause by arguing that it is unreasonable.[75] The third party cannot challenge the clause on this ground,[76] meaning that a promisor can rely on an unreasonable exclusion or limitation clause.

The scope of the CRTPA 1999

As noted above, the exception contain in s 1(1) will apply only to contracts that come within the scope of the Act. The Act itself provides a number of instances in which s 1 will not apply, as follows.

- Contracts containing a bill of exchange, promissory note, or any other negotiable instruments confer no rights on third parties.[77]
- The contract between a company and its members by virtue of the articles of association confers no rights on third parties.[78] The same would apply to an incorporation document of a limited liability partnership.[79]

---

71. Ibid, s 2(4).

72. Ibid, s 2(6).

73. Ibid, s 2(3).

74. Ibid, s 3(2).

75. Unfair Contract Terms Act 1977, s 2(2).

76. CRTPA 1999, s 7(2).

77. Ibid, s 6(1).

78. Ibid, s 6(2). This contract existed by virtue of the Companies Act 1985, s 14 (now the Companies Act 2006, s 33(1)).

79. Ibid, s 6(2A).

- A third party cannot enforce any term in a contract of employment against an employee or worker[80] (for example, a term in an employment contract requiring the employee not to divulge trade secrets supplied by a third party could not be enforced by the third party, but could be enforced by the employer).

Other exceptions

In addition to the 'general and wide-ranging'[81] exception contained in the 1999 Act, a number of other common law and statutory exceptions exist. Section 1 of the 1999 Act does not affect these pre-existing exceptions.[82]

Statute

Because the privity rule is a creation of the common law, it follows that it can be excluded by statute. Examples of such statutes include:

- a third party who is injured in a road traffic accident can enforce the driver's insurance policy against the insurance company, under the Road Traffic Act 1988, s 148(7);
- the beneficiaries of a husband or wife's life insurance policy (that is, the spouse and/or children) can, under the Married Women's Property Act 1882, s 11, enforce payment upon the husband or wife's death, even though they are not parties to the insurance contract.

Collateral contracts

A collateral contract is not really an exception to the privity rule, but is rather a means of avoiding the privity rule. The effect of a collateral contract is to create a contract between the promisor and a third party, as the following case demonstrates.

 Shanklin Pier Ltd v Detel Products Ltd [1951] 2 KB 854 (KB)

FACTS: The claimant (the third party) employed a firm of contractors to paint a pier. The claimant required that the contractors use a special type of paint manufactured by the defendant (the promisor). The defendant promised that this paint would last for seven to ten years. The contractors purchased the paint from the defendant and applied it to the pier. The paint lasted only three months. The claimant sued. The defendant argued that, because the contract was between itself and the contractors, the claimant could not sue.

HELD: The High Court held that whilst the claimant could not sue on the contract of sale (because it was between the contractor and the defendant), a collateral contract existed between the claimant and the defendant. The contract arose due to the defendant's promise that the paint would last for seven to ten years. The claimant had provided consideration for this promise by requiring the contractors to use the defendant's paint.

---

80. Ibid, s 6(3).
81. Law Commission, *Contracts for the Benefit of Third Parties* (Law Com No 3329, HMSO, London, 1996) [5.16].
82. CRTPA 1999, s 7(1).

Actions in tort

A third party prevented from bringing a claim in contract due to the privity rule may always have a claim in tort if one of the parties to the contract owes a duty of care to the third party. The following example provides a situation in which such a duty may occur.

The concept of the duty of care is discussed at p 381

Eg Privity and tort

MicroCom plc employs Price & Young to audit its financial accounts, stating that a copy of the audit report should be sent to Emily, a local billionaire, who is considering purchasing a large number of shares in MicroCom. The audit report indicates that MicroCom is very profitable and so Emily purchases a 10 per cent stake in the company. It transpires that the audit was conducted negligently and that MicroCom is actually close to insolvency. Emily could not sue Price & Young in contract, because she was not party to the audit contract, but it may be the case that Price & Young owed Emily a duty of care, which it breached in conducting the audit in a negligent manner.

Assignment

assignment: the transferring of contractual rights

Assignment simply refers to a situation in which one party transfers his contractual rights to another. Therefore, if a party to a contract transfers his rights to a third party, that third party will acquire the right to sue on the contract.

Eg The assignment of contractual rights

Under an existing contract, Gus owes Damon £1,000. Damon owes £1,000 to Marcus. Damon could therefore assign to Marcus the contractual right to the £1,000 owed by Gus in full satisfaction of his debt to Marcus. If Gus agrees to the assignment, Damon will have no right to recover the debt from Gus, because it will be owed to Marcus, who will have the contractual right to enforce it.

At common law, contractual rights cannot be assigned, but both equity[83] and statute[84] have recognized that assignment can occur, subject to certain limitations (for example, the right to the salary of a public officer cannot be assigned)[85] and compliance with certain formalities (for example, see the four requirements for statutory assignment as set out in the Law of Property Act 1925, s 136(1)).

---

83. *Crouch v Martin* (1707) 2 Vern 595.
84. Law of Property Act 1925, s 136(1).
85. *Grenfell v Dean and Canons of Westminster* (1840) 2 Beav 544.

Key points summary

- Privity of contract consists of two rules:
  - only parties to a contract may enforce the contract; and
  - contracts do not impose obligations on third parties.
- A third party may enforce a term of a contract where the contract expressly states that he can or where the term confers a benefit on him.
- Only third parties identified in the contract can enforce its terms.
- In addition to enforcing a contract and obtaining a remedy, the third party can also obtain protection from an exclusion clause contained in the contract.
- Where a third party acquires a right to enforce a term of the contract, the original parties to the contract cannot alter the contract or discharge it without the third party's consent.
- Exceptions to the privity rule include where the rule is excluded by statute, where there is a collateral contract, where a third party has a remedy in tort, and where a party to a contract assigns his rights to a third party.

Chapter conclusion

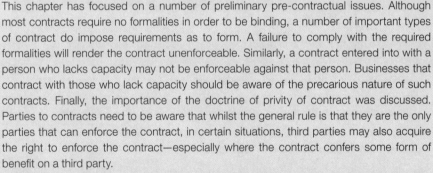

This chapter has focused on a number of preliminary pre-contractual issues. Although most contracts require no formalities in order to be binding, a number of important types of contract do impose requirements as to form. A failure to comply with the required formalities will render the contract unenforceable. Similarly, a contract entered into with a person who lacks capacity may not be enforceable against that person. Businesses that contract with those who lack capacity should be aware of the precarious nature of such contracts. Finally, the importance of the doctrine of privity of contract was discussed. Parties to contracts need to be aware that whilst the general rule is that they are the only parties that can enforce the contract, in certain situations, third parties may also acquire the right to enforce the contract—especially where the contract confers some form of benefit on a third party.

Compliance with formality and having contractual capacity is not enough to bring a contract into existence. In order for a legally binding contract to be created, a number of ingredients must be present. It is these ingredients that are examined in detail in the next chapter.

Self-test questions

1. Define the following:
   (a) deed;
   (b) capacity
   (c) void *ab initio*;
   (d) voidable;

    (e) repudiate;

    (f) ratification;

    (g) privity of contract.

2. Why should the law enforce contractual obligations?

3. Hamish offers to sell his car to Ross for £5,000, with payment to be made by the end of the month. Ross agrees, but nothing is put into writing. The end of the month arrives and Ross is refusing to accept or pay for the car. Advise Hamish.

4. Louise decides to leave school at the age of 16, once she hears that a friend is looking for an apprentice for his carpentry firm. Louise enters into a contract that states that she shall be an apprentice of the firm. A week before she is due to start, she changes her mind and decides to complete her A levels. Does the carpenter have a right of action against Louise?

5. 'Third parties should never be allowed to enforce the contracts of others and the Contracts (Rights of Third Parties) Act 1999 should therefore be repealed.' Do you agree?

6. 'The law relating to contractual capacity is confusing and in dire need of reform.' Discuss.

Further reading

Chen-Wishart, M, *Contract Law* (2nd edn, OUP, Oxford, 2008) ch 1
An excellent discussion of the theoretical underpinnings behind contract law

Koffman, L, and Macdonald, E, *The Law of Contract* (6th edn, OUP, Oxford, 2007) ch 17
*A clear and straightforward account of the various persons who normally lack full
   contractual capacity*

Law Commission, *Contracts for the Benefit of Third Parties* (Law Com No 3329,
   HMSO, London, 1996)
Provides a clear account of the law of privity and criticisms of the pre-1999 law

Poole, J, *Textbook on Contract Law* (9th edn, OUP, Oxford, 2008) 176–88
A clear account of the law relating to contractual formalities

Stevens, R, 'The Contracts (Rights of Third Parties) Act 1999' (2004) 120 LQR 292
*Discusses the reasons behind, and the effectiveness of, the Contracts (Rights of Third
   Parties) Act 1999*

 Remember to visit the **Online Resource Centre** at <http://www. oxfordtextbooks.co.uk/roach> to access the following resources for Chapter 5, 'An introduction to the law of contract': more **practice questions** and answers; a **glossary** of key terms; **multiple-choice questions**; **revision summaries**; **audio updates** when relevant; and **diagrams** in pdf.

6 The formation of the contract

- The objective nature of agreement
- Bilateral and unilateral contracts
- Offer
- Acceptance
- Certainty
- Consideration
- Intention to create legal relations

INTRODUCTION

Having discussed in Chapter 5 what a contract is, we now turn our attention to what ingredients are required in order to create a legally binding contract. This is a crucial issue. The law needs to be able to distinguish between those promises that may be enforced in a court of law and those that cannot. For businesses, the importance of this distinction is even more important, because virtually every transaction in which a business engages will be via contract. Businesses need to know that the parties with whom they enter into agreements will fulfil their obligations and that, if these obligations are not fulfilled, the court will grant the business a legal remedy. Accordingly, businesses will wish to ensure that the agreements into which they enter have contractual force.

So, how can we distinguish between binding, contractual promises and non-contractual promises? Put simply, a contract consists of a series of ingredients that, if all present, will create legally enforceable obligations. We have already discussed in the previous chapter certain preliminary ingredients, such as formality and capacity. To use a sporting metaphor, these preliminary ingredients can be thought of as entry requirements that allow a party onto the starting line. To complete the race and create a binding contract, five further ingredients are needed:

1. offer;
2. acceptance;
3. certainty;
4. consideration;[1] and
5. intention to create legal relations.

The first two requirements (offer and acceptance) are collectively known as 'agreement', and once agreement is reached, a valid contract usually comes into existence.

---

1. As we mentioned in Chapter 5, a valid contract can be created without consideration being present, provided that it is executed by deed.

Accordingly, the determination of agreement is crucial. Therefore, before examining the individual requirements in detail, we need to discuss briefly the court's approach to determining whether agreement is present or not.

The objective nature of agreement

In many cases, it will be easy to determine whether or not agreement is present. Both parties will have signed a written document and agreement will therefore be overt. But this is not always the case and a situation may arise in which one party contends that an agreement was reached and a contract created, whereas the other party denies that agreement was reached. In such a case, the law will have to determine whether agreement was present—but how will the law determine this? It used to be said that, in order for agreement to arise, the law would require *consensus ad idem* ('agreement as to the same thing', but more loosely translated as 'a meeting of the minds'). This would seem to require that the parties actually and subjectively agree on the terms of the contract, but this is not the case. The law is more concerned with the objective appearance of agreement, based upon the available evidence, than with the actual intentions of the parties. As Lord Denning MR stated:

> In contracts you do not look into the actual intent in a man's mind. You look at what he said and did. A contract is formed, when there is, to all outward appearances, a contract. A man cannot get out of a contract by saying: 'I did not intend to contract,' if by his words he has done so.[2]

The reason for a rejection of subjective agreement is simple. Evidentially, it is almost impossible to know what a person is thinking or intending. Accordingly, we determine agreement on the basis not of what the parties actually intended, but on what their words or actions objectively inferred. This could result in a court finding that an agreement has been concluded on terms that one of the parties clearly did not intend. For example, in *Centrovincial Estates plc v Merchant Investors Assurance Co Ltd*,[3] a landlord wrote to a prospective tenant offering to rent commercial property to it for £65,000 per annum. The tenant wrote back accepting, but the landlord then wrote back informing it that a mistake had been made and that the true figure was £126,000 per annum. The Court of Appeal held that there was a valid contract for £65,000. The words and conduct of the landlord and tenant objectively indicated that they had reached agreement, even though the landlord clearly did not intend to rent the property for so low a sum. Therefore, 'the judicial task is not to discover the actual intentions of each party; it is to decide what each was reasonably entitled to conclude from the attitude of the other'.[4]

---

2. *Storer v Manchester City Council* [1974] 1 WLR 1403 (CA) 1408.
3. [1983] Com LR 158 (CA).
4. **WM** Gloag, *Gloag on Contract* (2nd edn, W Green, Edinburgh, 1929) 7, approved by Lord Reid in *McCutcheon v David Macbrayne Ltd* [1964] 1 WLR 125 (HL) 128.

Bilateral and unilateral contracts

Before discussing the various ingredients that make a binding contract, it is important that we distinguish between bilateral and unilateral contracts. The importance of the distinction lies in that many of the general rules that apply to bilateral contracts do not apply, or are modified, in the case of unilateral contracts (for example, unilateral offers do not require communication of acceptance).

The distinction is relatively simple and can be deduced from the contract's names. A bilateral contract is a contract in which both[5] parties are legally bound to perform their side of the agreement (that is, both parties exchange promises). Conversely, in a unilateral contract, only one[6] party is obliged to perform (that is, one party makes a promise in exchange for the performance by the other party of an act, but the other party does not promise to perform that act). Put simply, bilateral contracts consist of two promises, whereas unilateral contracts consist of one.

The following example demonstrates the difference.

Eg **Bilateral and unilateral contracts**

Bilateral contract

Adam walks into his local BMW showroom. He enters into negotiations to buy a new car. A contract is presented to Adam, which states that the car will cost £25,000 and will be delivered before the end of the month. Full payment is due within ten working days of signing the contract. Adam signs the contract. This is a bilateral contract, because both parties have made promises and are therefore legally bound to perform their respective obligations. Adam must pay the purchase price within ten days of signing the contract and BMW must deliver the car to Adam before the end of the month. If either party fails to perform, it will constitute breach of contract.

Unilateral contract

After buying the car, Adam leaves it parked outside his house. One night, it is stolen. Adam puts an advertisement in his local newspaper stating that anyone who locates the car, or provides the police with information leading to the recovery of the car, will receive from him a reward of £100. This is a unilateral offer: only Adam is bound, because only he has made a promise. No one is legally obliged to search for the car and no one can be sued for failing to find the car. But if somebody does locate the car or provides information leading to its recovery, Adam is legally obliged to pay him the £100 reward and if he fails to do so, he will be in breach of contract.

We will now turn to the five ingredients identified above.

---

5. Hence the prefix 'bi-', which derives from the Latin *bis*, meaning 'two' or 'twice'.
6. Hence the prefix 'uni-', which derives from the Latin *unus*, meaning 'one'.

Offer

Treitel defines an offer as 'an expression of willingness to contract on specified terms, made with the intention that it is to become binding as soon as it is accepted by the person to whom it is addressed'.[7] The person making an offer is known as the 'offeror' and the person to whom an offer is addressed is known as the 'offeree'. An offer may be made in writing, may be made orally, or may be inferred through the conduct of a party. An offer may be made to a specific person, a group of persons, or to the entire world.[8] An offer made to a specific person cannot be accepted by anyone other than that person.[9] An offer will only be valid if it is communicated to the intended offeree.[10] This is a logical requirement: how can an offeree accept an offer about which he knows nothing?

As noted above, the courts will adopt an objective approach when determining the existence of agreement. Accordingly, the courts may hold that a valid offer was made, when, in fact, the offeror had no intention of making an offer, but had acted in such a way as to make a reasonable person believe that an offer was being made.

 Moran v University College Salford (No 2), The Times 23 November 1993 (CA)

FACTS: Moran applied to gain entry onto a physiotherapy course. His application was rejected, but, due to a clerical error, he was sent an unconditional offer by the college, which he accepted. When Moran phoned the college to make enquiries about the course, he was told that his application was rejected and a place on the course was not available for him.

HELD: The Court of Appeal held that a binding agreement existed between Moran and the college to enrol him on the course, because, despite the college's error, the unconditional offer was capable of acceptance by him.

Offers and invitations to treat

In the course of negotiations, the parties will make a number of preliminary statements, and it is important to be able to identify which statements amount to an offer and which do not. For example, if Pat asks Charlotte, 'at what price would you be prepared to sell your car?', to which Charlotte replies '£5,000', has Charlotte made an offer to Pat to sell her car for £5,000? The answer is 'no'. Charlotte is not making an offer; rather, she is inviting Pat to make an offer. Such preliminary statements that do not amount to offers are known as 'invitations to treat'. The word 'treat' in this sense means '[t]he action or an act of treating, or discussing terms;

---

7. E Peel, *Treitel on the Law of Contract* (12th edn, Sweet & Maxwell, London, 2007) 9.

8. *Carlill v Carbolic Smoke Ball Co* [1893] 1 QB 256 (CA).

9. *Cundy v Lindsay* (1877–78) LR 3 App Cas 459 (HL).

10. *Taylor v Laird* (1856) 25 LJ Ex 329.

parley, negotiation; agreement'.[11] Accordingly, an invitation to treat is an invitation to negotiate, or to make an offer.

Distinguishing between an offer and an invitation to treat can sometimes be extremely difficult, because the distinction is often based upon the intention of the parties; the issue to determine is whether one of the parties has indicated a willingness to be bound and, like all matters involving agreement, this issue will be determined objectively. Use of the word 'offer' by one of the parties may indicate an intention to be bound, but it is not conclusive.[12] In order to assist the courts in identifying whether a particular statement amounts to an offer or an invitation to treat, the courts have created a number of presumptions in relation to certain commonly occurring transactions, the principal examples being as follows.

Advertisements

The general presumption is that advertisements are regarded as invitations to treat, as the following case demonstrates.

🔑 *Partridge v Crittenden* **[1968] 1 WLR 1204 (QB)**

FACTS: The defendant placed an advertisement in a magazine, which stated 'bramblefinch cocks, bramblefinch hens, 25s each'. Bramblefinches were a protected species and it was a criminal offence to 'offer to sell' a protected species of bird.[13] Therefore, the issue that the court had to determine was whether or not the advertisement amounted to an offer.

HELD: The High Court held that the advertisement was merely an invitation to treat. Accordingly, the defendant was not guilty of the offence under the 1954 Act.

COMMENT: In Chapter 1, we discussed the distinction between civil law and criminal law, and noted that the two are not mutually exclusive. *Partridge* is an excellent example of this: in order to determine whether a crime had been committed, the court had to discuss a point of civil law.

⭐ See 'Offers for Sale' (1968) 32 J Crim L 223

The rationale behind this general presumption is based upon two practical considerations.

1. If advertisements were regarded as offers, sellers of goods would be in breach of contract if they could not supply the advertised goods to anyone who wanted them, even if they had a legitimate reason (for example, the goods were out of stock).[14] Sellers will often protect themselves by providing that any claims made in the advertisement will only apply 'while stocks last', but such action is not actually necessary.

2. Prices and conditions stated in advertisements may not be final; further bargaining may be desirable or necessary. For example, a company that places an

---

11. Definition derived from the Oxford English Dictionary Online, <http://www.oed.com>.
12. *Spencer v Harding* (1869–70) LR 5 CP 561.   13. Protection of Birds Act 1954, s 6(1).
14. The House acknowledged such a rationale in *Grainger & Son v Gough* [1896] AC 325 (HL) 334 (Lord Herschell).

advertisement indicating that purchases of its goods made on credit will attract 0 per cent finance will still want to carry out credit checks on potential customers to determine the likelihood of repayment. If advertisements were regarded as offers, further bargaining could not take place.

This principle is, however, only a presumption and can be rebutted if the facts indicate a willingness to be bound. More specifically, the presumption only tends to apply in the case of bilateral contracts. In the case of unilateral contracts, the above rationales do not apply: further bargaining is not envisaged, or even possible. Accordingly, in the case of unilateral contracts, the presumption is reversed and an advertisement will be presumed to constitute an offer, as the following case demonstrates.

 Carlill v Carbolic Smoke Ball Co [1893] 1 QB 256 (CA)

FACTS: The defendant (Carbolic) manufactured the 'Carbolic Smoke Ball'. It placed an advertisement in the *Pall Mall Gazette*, stating that it would pay £100 to anyone who correctly used the smoke ball, but still contracted influenza. To demonstrate its sincerity, it deposited £1,000 into a bank. The claimant (Mrs Carlill) purchased a smoke ball, used it correctly, and still caught influenza. Accordingly, the claimant sought her £100, but the defendant refused to pay on the grounds that the advertisement was a 'mere puff' that was not meant to be taken seriously or intended to be binding, and that it was impossible to make a contract with the entire world.

HELD: The Court of Appeal rejected the defendant's arguments and found in favour of the claimant. The £1,000 deposit indicated that the advertisement was not a mere puff and demonstrated that the defendant intended to be bound. Further, offers made to the whole world were perfectly valid. Accordingly, the advertisement constituted an offer, which Mrs Carlill accepted by purchasing and using the smoke ball, and she was therefore entitled to the £1000.

Displays of goods

The rationale behind classifying advertisements as invitations to treat also applies to displays of goods. Displays of goods within shops or shop windows constitute the most common form of invitation to treat. Thus, in *Fisher v Bell*,[15] the defendant displayed a flick knife in his shop window and was charged under the Restriction of Offensive Weapons Act 1959, s 1(1)(a), which made it an offence to offer to sell a flick knife. He was acquitted, because the display amounted to an invitation to treat and not an offer.

The rationale for holding displays of goods as invitations to treat was stated in the following case.

---

15. [1961] 1 QB 394 (DC).

Pharmaceutical Society of Great Britain v Boots Cash Chemists (Southern) Ltd [1953] 1 QB 401 (CA)

FACTS: Boots had opened one of the first 'self-service' shops in the country. The goods were displayed on shelves and customers would choose which goods they wanted, before taking them to a cashier near the exit. A registered pharmacist was adjacent to the cashier. Boots was prosecuted under the Pharmacy and Poisons Act 1933, s 18, which made it an offence to sell certain drugs unless the sale was supervised by a registered pharmacist. The Pharmaceutical Society argued that the display of goods amounted to an offer, which was accepted by placing the goods in the basket. Accordingly, the Society argued, the sale took place when the customer put the goods in the basket and not at the cash desk under the supervision of the pharmacist.

HELD: The Court of Appeal rejected the Pharmaceutical Society's argument and held that the display of goods constituted an invitation to treat. The customer made the offer by presenting the goods to the cashier and the cashier accepted the offer by taking the customer's money. Because the pharmacist was present at the cash desk, he supervised the transaction, and therefore s 18 was not contravened.

COMMENT: The Court justified its decision in the following way: if the display of goods were to amount to an offer, the customer would accept the goods by placing them in his basket. At this point, a binding contract would exist, so that if the customer were to change his mind and put the goods back, he would technically be in breach of contract.[16] Clearly, this would negate the whole purpose of a self-service store.

See J Unger, 'Self-service Shops and the Law of Contract' (1959) 16 MLR 369

Transactions effected through machines

Particular problems can arise when transactions are effected through machines (for example, vending machines or 'pay and go' petrol pumps). The problem that arises is, if we take the traditional view that such displays of goods amount only to invitations to treat, that the customer would make an offer by proffering payment. How would the machine accept? When exactly is the contract formed? These are not easy questions to answer, based upon the orthodox approach. At a self-service store, if we change our mind, we can put the goods back on the shelf; once we have obtained goods from a machine, they cannot be put back. Further, there is no possibility of negotiations taking place with a machine. Therefore, in relation to sales effected through a machine, the courts are likely to take a different approach from that which applies to sales effected through a person.

 Thornton v Shoe Lane Parking Ltd [1971] 2 QB 163 (CA)

FACTS: The claimant drove his car into an automatic car park. A sign at the entrance of the car park indicated the cost of parking and also stated that all cars were 'parked at owner's risk'. The claimant drove up to a machine, took the offered ticket, and parked his

16. *Pharmaceutical Society of Great Britain v Boots Cash Chemists (Southern) Ltd* [1953] 1 QB 401 (CA) 406 (Somervell LJ).

car. Upon returning, there was an accident and he was injured. The defendant argued that the exclusion clause at the car park's entrance prevented it from being liable. The validity of the clause depended upon when the contract was concluded—that is, on who made the offer and who accepted.

HELD: In the Court of Appeal, Lord Denning MR stated:

> The customer pays his money and gets a ticket. He cannot refuse it. He cannot get his money back. He may protest to the machine, even swear at it. But it will remain unmoved. He is committed beyond recall. He was committed at the very moment when he put his money into the machine. The contract was concluded at that time. It can be translated into offer and acceptance in this way: the offer is made when the proprietor of the machine holds it out as being ready to receive the money. The acceptance takes place when the customer puts his money into the slot.[17]

★ See R Brownsword, 'Incorporating Exemption Causes' (1972) 35 MLR 179

Accordingly, in such situations, the machine makes the offer, which the customer accepts by committing himself fully. In the case of a vending machine, this would occur when the customer puts the money into the machine. At a petrol pump, this would occur when the customer puts the petrol into his car.[18]

E-commerce

For many people, purchasing goods via the Internet is as natural as purchasing goods from a high-street shop. From a contractual point of view, however, e-commerce can be problematic. EU legislation exists that aims to harmonize and facilitate e-commerce,[19] but this legislation does not indicate at what point a contract is created, nor does it indicate the legal status of displays of goods found on websites. The issue can be problematic, as evidenced by a significant number of recent cases concerning websites displaying incorrect prices. Poole[20] cites a number of examples, including:

- in September 1999, Argos' website advertised Sony television sets for £3 instead of £299;
- on New Year's Eve 2001, the Kodak website incorrectly stated that a certain camera cost £100 when it actually cost £329;[21]
- in March 2003, Amazon offered a pocket PC for sale at £7.32 instead of £274.99.

In all of the above examples, customers, keen to secure a bargain, quickly ordered the mispriced items. The issue was whether, when the online retailers refused to sell the goods at the incorrect price, they were acting in breach of contract.

To answer this question, it is necessary to determine the identities of the offeror and offeree. A number of arguments would operate in the online retailer's favour, as follow.

---

17. *Thornton v Shoe Lane Parking Ltd* [1971] 2 QB 163 (CA) 169.
18. *Re Charge Card Services* [1989] Ch 497 (CA).
19. The Electronic Commerce (EC Directive) Regulations 2002, SI 2002/2013, implementing Council Directive (EC) 2000/31 on electronic commerce.
20. J Poole, *Textbook on Contract Law* (9th edn, OUP, Oxford, 2008) 49.
21. On this, see K Rogers, 'Snap! Internet "Offers" Under Scrutiny' (2002) 23 BLR 70.

- In the above cases, the websites in question were simply virtual shops and the goods displayed would almost certainly be regarded the same as displays of goods in an actual store (that is, as invitations to treat). On such websites, instead of examining a selection of goods on a shelf, the customer is examining a selection of goods on a computer screen. Instead of putting goods into a physical basket or trolley, he adds goods to a virtual basket or trolley. Most telling of all, irrespective of whether the goods are bought physically or online, once the customer has decided which goods he wishes to purchase, he pays for them at the 'checkout'. Given this, the online retailers would be free to reject the customer's offers.

- In many cases, the online retailers emailed the customers 'accepting' their order. But it is highly likely that this will not constitute legal acceptance and will simply constitute a confirmation of the customer's order.

- The courts have made clear that they will not assist a purchaser who is aware that a pricing mistake has been made and is attempting to obtain a bargain.[22] The situation would be less clear if a more modest pricing mistake were made.

The conclusion is that, in the absence of a definitive higher court ruling or a statutory clarification, displays of goods on websites are likely to constitute invitations to treat. Many online retailers now make this absolutely clear by indicating to the customer at exactly what point the customer becomes bound. Such clarification is now a legal requirement under the Electronic Commerce (EC Directive) Regulations 2002,[23] reg 9(1). In addition, reg 11(1)(a) provides that the seller shall acknowledge receipt of the order without undue delay and by electronic means. It should be noted that regs 9 and 11 do not apply where the parties are not consumers and have agreed otherwise.

Auctions

The general rule in relation to auctions is that when an auctioneer calls for bids, he is not making an offer to sell the goods to the highest bidder; he is merely making an invitation to treat.[24] Bidders make the offer, which the auctioneer is free to accept or reject.[25] It would appear that the making of a higher bid destroys an offer. Items may be sold at auction advertised as 'with reserve'—meaning that the item will not be sold unless it reaches a minimum price. If the bidding fails to reach the reserve price, no contract exists. Further, no contract of sale will exist where the auctioneer mistakenly accepts a bid lower than the reserve price.[26] Where an item does reach the reserve price, the auctioneer is still not bound to sell, because bids above the reserve price still amount only to invitations to treat. The seller of the goods may therefore withdraw the goods from auction at any time before the fall of the auctioneer's hammer.

Where an auction is advertised as 'without reserve' (that is, where there is no minimum price and the bid of the highest bona fide bidder will be accepted), the situation is slightly more complex. Three parties are involved: the seller of the

---

22. *Hartog v Colin & Shields* [1939] 3 All ER 566 (KB).   23. SI 2002/2013.

24. *Payne v Cave* [1775] All ER Rep 492.

25. Sale of Goods Act 1979, s 57(2), indicates that the offer is accepted by the auctioneer on the 'fall of the hammer, or in any other customary manner'.

26. *McManus v Fortescue* [1907] 2 KB 1 (CA).

goods; the bidder; and the auctioneer. In the case of a sale 'without reserve', if the auctioneer fails to accept the highest bid, no contract of sale will exist between the seller and the highest bidder. There will, however, be a collateral contract between the highest bidder and the auctioneer. The rationale behind this is that, in advertising the sale as 'without reserve', the auctioneer is making an offer to accept the bid of the highest bidder, which is then accepted by the highest bidder.[27] The auctioneer is therefore obliged to accept the highest bona fide bid. This obligation arises under a collateral contract between the auctioneer and the highest bidder.

Barry v Davies (t/a Heathcote Ball & Co) [2000] 1 WLR 1962 (CA)

FACTS: The defendant auctioneer was auctioning without reserve two engine analysers, each one costing £14,251 new. The highest bid derived from the claimant and was for £400 for both machines. Unable to secure a higher price, the auctioneer withdrew the machines from the auction. The claimant sued the auctioneer, arguing that the auctioneer legally had to accept the highest bid.

HELD: The Court of Appeal stated that there was no contract between the claimant and the owners of the machines. There did, however, exist a collateral contract between the claimant and the defendant, which the defendant breached by withdrawing the goods. Accordingly, the claimant was awarded £27,600 damages.

COMMENT: One initial reaction may be to think that the claimant received something of a windfall, but, as will be seen when we discuss the calculation of damages for non-delivery in sale of goods cases, this is not the case.

 See F Meisel, 'What Price Auctions Without Reserve?' (2001) 64 MLR 468

Tenders

Tenders are a common mechanism in larger commercial and construction contracts, whereby a company that is seeking to purchase an expensive item (for example, a piece of heavy machinery), or requires the performance of a substantial service (for example, the construction of a building), will invite tenders from interested parties. As a general rule, inviting tenders does not constitute an offer,[28] but will form an invitation to treat. Therefore, there is no obligation to accept the most competitive tender. Such a rule could be regarded as unfair, because the preparation of tenders can be time-consuming and costly, but, like many of the rules discussed in relation to offer and acceptance, the role of the law is to assign the risk fairly, and it would appear to be fair that the risk is placed on those submitting the tender.

It follows that, because the invitation to tender does not constitute the offer, the parties make the offer in submitting tenders. The party who invited the tenders is then free to accept or reject any tender made based on any considerations that it deems relevant. But his rule is subject to qualification, as follows.

1. If the party inviting the tenders indicates that it will accept the most competitive tender, this will amount to a unilateral offer whereby the party seeking the tender

---

27. *Warlow v Harrison* (1859) 1 El & El 309.   28. *Spencer v Harding* (1870) LR 5 CP 561.

promises to accept the most competitive tender. This offer will be accepted by the party that submits the highest or lowest tender, and the person seeking the tender will then be contractually obliged to accept that tender.[29]

2. When an invitation to tender is made to only a small, selected group of persons and is accompanied by conditions (for example, tenders must be in writing, or submitted by a certain date), it will be held to be accompanied by an offer to consider all tenders that comply with the conditions. Parties accept the offer by submitting a tender that complies with the conditions and the party seeking the tenders will thereby commit a breach of contract if it fails to consider conforming tenders.[30]

Termination of an offer

An offer may be terminated in a number of different ways:

- by the offeree's rejection;
- through the lapse of time;
- via the death of either party;
- via the failure to comply with a condition precedent; or
- via revocation by the offeror.

Once an offer has been effectively terminated, it cannot subsequently be accepted, because it is no longer in existence.

Rejection

An offer will be terminated if the offeree rejects it.[31] As we shall see when we discuss acceptance, if the offeree purports to accept the offer, but based on new or differing terms to the offer, this will serve to reject the original offer and will constitute a counter-offer.[32]

Although there is no settled law on the point, it appears to be the case that a rejection is only effective once it is communicated to the offeror. Further, it would appear (but again, there is no established authority) that the postal rule (the rule providing that acceptance by post occurs as soon as the letter is posted) would not apply to rejection by post, so that a postal rejection seems to take effect only when the offeror received the letter. Accordingly, assuming that this is the law, it has been contended that if an offeree rejects an offer by post, but before the letter reaches the offeror, the offeree accepts the offer (for example, by phoning the offeror or visiting him), the acceptance will be effective and the rejection letter will have no effect.[33]

🔗 The postal rule is discussed further at p 172

Lapse of time

Offerors are perfectly free to attach an expiry date to their offer; if the offer is not accepted before this date, it will cease to exist. In the majority of cases, offers do not normally have a stipulated expiry date, but this does not mean that such offers last

---

29. *Harvela Investments Ltd v Royal Trust Co of Canada* [1986] AC 207 (HL).
30. *Blackpool and Fylde Aero Club Ltd v Blackpool Borough Council* [1990] 1 WLR 1195 (CA).
31. *Tinn v Hoffman & Co* (1873) 29 LT 271.
32. *Hyde v Wrench* (1840) 3 Beav 334.
33. E Peel, *Treitel on the Law of Contract* (12th edn, Sweet & Maxwell, London, 2007) 46.

forever. As the following case shows, an offer that does not have an expiry date will still lapse after a reasonable time.

> ### 🔑 *Ramsgate Victoria Hotel Co Ltd v Montefiore* (1866) LR 1 Ex 109
>
> **FACTS:** The two defendants applied (offered) to purchase shares in the claimant company on 8 June. Hearing nothing from the claimant, one of the defendants withdrew his application on 8 November. The other defendant did not withdraw his application. On 23 November, the claimant allotted shares to both defendants and requested that the balance be paid. Both defendants refused to pay and the claimant commenced proceedings.
>
> **HELD:** The defendants were justified in refusing the shares. Once the defendants had made the offer, acceptance (the allotment of the shares) should have occurred within a reasonable time. Because it had not, the defendants' offer had lapsed and so they were not bound to accept the shares.

What is reasonable will depend upon the facts of the case and, in particular, the subject matter of the contract. If the quality of the subject matter of the contract is in some way time-sensitive (for example, perishable goods), then a shorter period of time will be regarded as reasonable. Thus, if John were selling a consignment of apples that he had acquired and was also looking to sell his car, the offer to sell the apples would lapse long before the offer to sell the car.

Death of offeror or offeree

The effect of the death of the offeror or offeree on an offer is unclear. What is clear is that once an offer has been accepted, the death of either party will not terminate the offer, although it may lead to the contract being frustrated. It is less clear what the effect would be if a party were to die after the offer has been made, but before it has been accepted. It is contended that the death of either party does not automatically terminate the offer, but that termination may be justified depending upon the nature of the contract.

 The doctrine of frustration is discussed at p 311

It is likely that the death of the offeror will result in the termination of the offer if the contract is one of personal service. For example, if an opera singer were to offer to perform at an opera house, but then die, the offer would lapse regardless of whether the offeree knew of the death. If, however, the contract is not one for personal service, the effect of the offeror's death is less clear. It has been argued that, in such a case, the offer is terminated automatically,[34] but this would appear to be a minority view. The more accepted view appears to be that if the offeree knows of the offeror's death, then acceptance will not be effective.[35] On the other hand, if the offeree is ignorant of the offeror's death, then acceptance will be effective,

---

34. *Dickinson v Dodds* (1876) 2 Ch D 463 (CA) 475 (Mellish LJ).
35. *Coulthart v Clementson* (1870) 5 QBD 42.

the contract will stand, and the contract will have to be performed by the deceased offeror's personal representatives.[36]

There is no conclusive law on the effect of the death of the offeree, but uncontradicted *dicta* favour the view that the offeree's death will cause the offer to lapse (that is, that the offer, being made to a living person, cannot survive his death and be accepted by someone else).[37] It has, however, been contended that, in such a case, the same rule could apply as regards the offeror's death (that is, that the offer would stand, provided that it was not for the supply of a personal service and could therefore be accepted the offeree's personal representatives).[38] This would appear to breach the rule that an offer made to a specific person cannot be accepted by any other person, but it has been argued that, provided that the contract is not one for personal services, the offer is said to be made to the offeree and his personal representatives.[39]

➡ personal representative: an administrator or executor whose function it is to settle the affairs of deceased persons

Failure of a condition precedent

We noted above than an offer may be subject to a time limit. It is also possible for the offeror to stipulate that the offer will only exist based on other considerations, and such stipulations are known as conditions precedent. It may be the case that the offeror stipulates that, upon the occurrence of some event, the offer will lapse. Once this event has occurred, the offer cannot be accepted, as the following example demonstrates.

➡ conditions precedent: conditions that must be complied with before an offer can be accepted, or before a contract becomes operational

---

Eg Offers and conditions precedent

Cathy offers to purchase a car from Jill, but states that the offer will only exist while the car is roadworthy. A day later, before Jill has accepted the offer, she is involved in a minor accident and the car requires repairs in order for it to function. This would constitute a breach of the condition precedent and so Cathy's offer would lapse.

It should be noted that conditions precedent need not be express; they may also be implied (for example, an offer to sell life insurance to a person cannot be accepted after that person is seriously injured by falling off a cliff).[40]

Revocation

Because acceptance of an offer will bring about a binding contract, it follows that the revocation of an offer post-acceptance will constitute a breach of contract. But before acceptance has occurred, the offeror is perfectly free to revoke any offer made.[41] Once revoked, the offer is destroyed and acceptance is impossible, unless there exists a sep-

---

36. *Bradbury v Morgan* (1862) 1 H & C 249.
37. See, e.g., *Reynolds v Atherton* (1921) 125 LT 690; *Kennedy v Thomassen* [1929] 1 Ch 426.
38. See, e.g., E Peel, *Treitel on the Law of Contract* (12th edn, Sweet & Maxwell, London, 2007) 48; J Poole, *Textbook on Contract Law* (9th edn, OUP, Oxford, 2008) 77.
39. E Peel, *Treitel on the Law of Contract* (12th edn, Sweet & Maxwell, London, 2007) 48.
40. *Canning v Farquhar* (1885) 16 QBD 722 (CA).
41. *Payne v Cave* (1789) 3 Term Rep 148.

arate contract to keep the offer open for a specified period. This applies even where the offeror has indicated that an offer will remain open for a certain time. For example, in *Routledge v Grant*,[42] the defendant offeror offered to purchase the claimant offeree's house and stated that the offer was to last for six weeks. The offeror revoked the offer after only three weeks and the court held that he was perfectly free to do this.

In order for revocation of an offer to be valid, it must be communicated to the offeree. As we shall see when we discuss acceptance, acceptance may occur before it is received by the offeror (for example, by posting a letter). This rule does not apply to revocation of offers: in order for revocation to be valid, it must be received by the offeree.

⚷ *Byrne & Co v Van Tienhoven & Co* (1880) 5 CPD 344

FACTS: The defendant offered to sell goods to the claimant. The offer was made by letter on 1 October 1879. On 8 October, the defendant revoked its offer by post. The claimant received the letter making the offer on 11 October and accepted by telegram on the same day. It also posted a letter of acceptance on 15 October. On the 20 October, the claimant received the letter revoking the offer. The defendant refused to supply the goods on the ground that the offer had been revoked before it was accepted. The claimant brought an action.

HELD: The claimant accepted the offer on 11 October and this was when a valid contract came into being. The claimant did not receive the defendant's revocation of the offer until 20 October. Because acceptance had already occurred, the revocation was invalid and the defendant was therefore in breach of contract.

It should, however, be noted that whilst communication of the revocation must be communicated to the offeree, it does not follow that the revocation must come from the offeror. Provided that acceptance has not taken place, an offeree who hears about the revocation of the offer from a reliable third party and thereby knows beyond all question of the revocation will then be unable to accept that offer.[43]

Applying the above rules poses little problem in relation to bilateral contracts. In relation to unilateral contracts, however, the issue is more problematic. The essence of the problem is demonstrated in the following example.

Eg **Revocation of an offer of a unilateral contract**

Roger says to Les: 'If you climb to the summit of Mount Everest, I will pay you £10,000.' This is clearly an offer of a unilateral contract, because Les is under no obligation to climb the mountain, but Roger is under an obligation to pay if Les does climb the mountain. Les indicates that he will climb the mountain. He spends £1,000 on climbing gear and mountain-climbing tuition. Les begins to climb the mountain. When he is 100 metres short of the summit, Roger phones Les on his mobile phone and states that he is revoking the offer.

---

42. (1828) 4 Bing 653.   43. *Dickinson v Dodds* (1876) 2 Ch D 463 (CA).

As we shall see when we discuss acceptance, an offeree accepts an offer of a unilateral contract by fully performing the act in question (that is, by climbing Mount Everest). In other words, acceptance and performance occur at the same time. Until the act is fully performed, acceptance has not taken place. According to this logic, Roger is free to revoke when he did, because Les has not fully accepted Roger's offer—but, as we shall see, this does not represent the current legal position.

🔗 On the rules relating to acceptance of offers of a unilateral contract, see p 177

In the above example, an application of the standard revocation rule would be extremely harsh on Les. Accordingly, the courts have adapted the rule by distinguishing between commencement of the specified act and completion of the specified act.[44] As soon as the offeree commences performance of the specified act, the offeror cannot withdraw the unilateral offer, but the offeror will only be required to perform his side of the contract once the act is fully performed.

⚖ *Errington v Errington & Woods* [1952] 1 KB 290 (CA)

FACTS: A father purchased a house in his own name, but his son and daughter-in-law occupied it. The father stated that, provided that the couple continued to pay the mortgage instalments, once the mortgage was paid off, he would transfer title of the house to them. Subsequently, the father died, and the son and daughter-in-law split up, but the daughter-in-law continued to live in the house and pay the mortgage instalments. The father's widow wished to evict the daughter-in-law and claim possession of the house.

HELD: The Court of Appeal held that the father's promise could not be revoked. Denning LJ (as he then was) stated:

> The father's promise was a unilateral contract—a promise of the house in return for their act of paying the instalments. It could not be revoked by him once the couple entered on performance of the act, but it would cease to bind him if they left it incomplete and unperformed, which they have not done. If that was the position during the father's lifetime, so it must be after his death. . . . They have acted on the promise, and neither the father nor his widow, his successor in title, can eject them in disregard of it.[45]

COMMENT: The conceptual justification behind this decision is elusive. How did the Court of Appeal justify moving away from the traditional view? Three justifications have been advanced, as follows, but none are wholly satisfactory.

1. *Commencement constitutes acceptance* The case could be justified on the basis that commencement of performance constitutes acceptance.[46] The fatal flaw of this approach is that once commencement of performance occurs, the offeree is bound and cannot change his mind. This is clearly unacceptable. Such a justification would mean that the daughter-in-law would be held in breach of contract if she were to fail to meet a mortgage instalment.

---

44. This rule appears to have been extended to cover omissions as well as acts: see *Soulsbury v Soulsbury* [2007] EWCA Civ 969, [2008] 2 WLR 834.

45. *Errington v Errington & Woods* [1952] 1 KB 290 (CA) 295, 300.

46. E Peel, *Treitel on the Law of Contract* (12th edn, Sweet & Maxwell, London, 2007) 41.

Promissory estoppel is discussed at p 194

2. *Promissory estoppel* The above passage hints that Denning LJ based the decision on promissory estoppel. The father made a promise on which the daughter-in-law relied. Accordingly, it would be inequitable to allow the promise to be taken back and the law will stop (hence 'estoppel') any party who attempts to renege on this promise. The problem with this justification is that, in order for promissory estoppel to arise, there must be an existing legal relationship, and there will usually be no such relationship in the case of unilateral contracts. Certainly, there was no existing legal relationship between the father and the daughter-in-law.

3. *Collateral contract* The third possible justification is that the main unilateral contract exists alongside an implied collateral contract. This collateral contract provides that the offeror impliedly promises not to revoke the unilateral offer once the offeree has begun performance.[47] Once performance has commenced, revocation of the offer would amount to a breach of the collateral contract. Whilst such an approach has a conceptual logic, it has been described on more than one occasion as 'artificial'.[48]

Ultimately, the lack of a conceptual justification may not prove problematic in practice. It is clear that the courts' policy is not to permit revocation of an offer of a unilateral contract once performance has been commenced. Accordingly, the lack of single conceptual justification does not render the law uncertain in practical terms, but the fact that a decision of such practical significance could potentially run counter to certain well-established principles is nevertheless a cause for concern.

One final problem regarding the revocation of offers of a unilateral contract is that such offers are often made to the whole world (for example, the offer of a reward). As noted, revocation of an offer is normally effective only upon its communication to the offeree, but clearly this rule cannot be applied to offers made to the whole world. Although there is no English authority on the issue, the consensus is that we would follow the approach taken in the USA, whereby the revocation of an offer of a unilateral contract would be valid if the revocation were communicated in the same manner as the offer was made[49] (for example, if the offer was made in a newspaper, the revocation should be made in the same newspaper).

‹› Key points summary

- An offer is a willingness to contract on specified terms that will become binding once accepted by the person to whom it is addressed.

- Offers may be spoken, made in writing, or made by conduct. They may be addressed to a specific person, a group of persons, or the entire world.

- An invitation to treat is not an offer, but an invitation to negotiate or to make an offer.

---

47. DO McGovney, 'Irrevocable Offers' (1914) 27 Harv LR 644, 659.

48. E Peel, *Treitel on the Law of Contract* (12th edn, Sweet & Maxwell, London, 2007) 41; J Poole, *Textbook on Contract Law* (9th edn, OUP, Oxford, 2008) 83.

49. *Shuey v US* 92 US 73 (1875).

- Advertisements, displays of goods (in stores or online), calls for bids at auctions, and invitations to tender are all generally regarded as invitations to treat.

- Offers may be terminated by rejection, the lapse of time, the death of either party, the failure of a condition precedent, or by revocation.

- An offer of a bilateral contract cannot be revoked once it has been accepted. An offer of a unilateral contract cannot be revoked once the offeree has commenced performance of the act or omission required for acceptance.

Acceptance

In order for agreement to exist and a binding contract to be formed, the offeree must accept the offer. This leads us to ask: 'What exactly is acceptance?' There appears to be no judicially accepted definition, but Treitel's formulation is generally regarded as authoritative. He defined acceptance as 'a final and unqualified expression of assent to the terms of an offer'.[50]

From this simple definition, a number of consequences flow.

- Because the offeree must 'assent' to the terms of the offer, it follows that he must know of the existence of the offer in the first place. Acceptance will not be valid where the offeree accepted an offer the he did not know existed. Thus, a person who discovers the offeror's lost dog cannot claim an offered reward if he did not know of the reward at the time that he found the dog.[51]

- The phrase 'expression of assent' indicates that, generally, the offeree's acceptance must be communicated to the offeror in order to be valid.

- The words 'final' and 'unqualified' mean that the acceptance must match precisely the terms of the offer. Any variation will not amount to valid acceptance and may even constitute a counter-offer. This is a result of what is known as the 'mirror image' rule, which is discussed next.

The rules relating to communication of acceptance are discussed at p 171

The 'mirror image' rule and counter-offers

The 'mirror image' rule basically states that the acceptance must mirror the offer (that is, that the acceptance must precisely and unequivocally match the terms of the offer). It follows that if, in accepting the offer, the offeree adds a new term or varies an existing term, this will not constitute valid acceptance and will be regarded as a counter-offer.

A counter-offer has two effects, as follows.

1. A new offer is created by the former offeree, who now becomes the offeror, and the original offeror now becomes the offeree.

2. The original offer is destroyed, so that the former offeree cannot subsequently accept it.

---

50. E Peel, *Treitel on the Law of Contract* (12th edn, Sweet & Maxwell, London, 2007) 18.
51. *R v Clarke* (1927) 40 CLR 227 (High Court of Australia).

Hyde v Wrench (1840) 3 Beav 334

FACTS: The defendant offered to sell a farm to the claimant for £1,000. The claimant sent a letter, indicating that he would pay £950, but the defendant was not willing to sell at this price and did not reply to the letter. Subsequently, the claimant attempted to accept the original offer of £1,000 and the court had to determine whether this was valid acceptance.

HELD: The court held that the acceptance was not valid. The claimant's letter amounted to a counter-offer, which destroyed the defendant's original offer, meaning that the claimant could not subsequently accept it.

Care must be taken when determining the status of an offeree's reply to an offer. In certain cases, what may initially appear to be a counter-offer may actually be a mere request for information. In the next section, we discuss the importance of this distinction.

Distinguishing counter-offers from requests for information

It is important that we distinguish counter-offers from requests for information, because the former will destroy the original offer and create a new offer capable of acceptance by the former offeror, whereas the latter will have no effect upon the original offer and will not create a new offer. The following case demonstrates the distinction.

 Stevenson, Jacques & Co v McLean (1880) LR 5 QBD 346 (QB)

FACTS: The defendant offered to sell a consignment of iron at a fixed price of 40 shillings per ton. The claimant sent a telegram, asking whether the defendant would accept payment of the 40 shillings over a two-month period. The claimant received no reply and purported to accept the original offer. By this time, however, the defendant had already sold the iron to a third party. The claimant sued for non-delivery. The defendant argued that the claimant's telegram amounted to a counter-offer, so it was perfectly free to reject the counter-offer and sell the iron to someone else.

HELD: The High Court held that the telegram did not constitute a counter-offer: it was merely an inquiry. Accordingly, the original offer was still open for the claimant to accept. The claimant could therefore recover damages for non-delivery.

'Battle of the forms'

Determining if and when acceptance has occurred has been complicated by the commercial prevalence of standard terms. Standard terms (or 'standard-form contracts', as they are known) are simply terms that are drafted specifically to cater for the company's needs. The advantages of using such terms are obvious. Standard terms obviate the need for lengthy and expensive negotiations, and, because they are drafted to meet the company's needs, such terms will strongly favour the company.

The problem arises when two commercial entities wish to contract with each other and each has its own set of standard terms. Which set of terms will form the basis of the contract?

This has come to be known as the 'battle of the forms' and it has resulted in a major problem. The problem is that, given the complexity of many business transactions, it may be extremely difficult to determine exactly when acceptance occurred, and both parties may be under the belief that their standard terms are governing the contract. For example, *A* offers to sell goods to *B* and accompanies the offer with a copy of his standard terms. *B* purports to accept the offer, but includes a set of his standard terms. Both parties perform the contract believing that their terms are governing the contract. If both parties perform as planned, no problem arises, but should a dispute occur, the court would seek to resolve the dispute by looking to the contract. The problem is that, under the mirror image rule, such a mistaken belief may result in a lack of agreement and no contract will exist, because it cannot be established objectively that there has been an offer on a party's standard terms that has been accepted by the other.

Despite this unfortunate outcome, the courts have tended to stick to the orthodox position, as the following case demonstrates.

 ### *Butler Machine Tool Co Ltd v Ex-Cell-O Corporation (England) Ltd* [1979] 1 WLR 401 (CA)

FACTS: The seller offered to sell a piece of machinery to the buyer. The seller's offer was accompanied by its standard terms and conditions, which were to 'prevail over any terms and conditions in the buyer's order'. The seller's terms contained a price-variation clause, which allowed the seller to increase the price quoted if its costs were increased at the date of delivery. The buyer placed an order for the machine using its own order form, which did not contain a price-variation clause. This order form was sent to the seller. At the bottom of the order form was a tear-off slip, which was to be signed by the seller and returned to the buyer. This slip stated that the seller accepted the order 'on the terms and conditions stated therein'—that is, on the buyer's terms. The seller signed and returned the slip to the buyer. Upon delivery of the machine, the seller exercised the price-variation clause and charged an extra £2,892. The buyer argued that the contract was based on its own terms and that, because these terms contained no price-variation clause, the seller was not entitled to the extra £2,892. Both sets of terms claimed primacy over the other. Which terms were to prevail?

HELD: The Court of Appeal unanimously agreed that the buyer's terms prevailed. When the seller signed and returned the tear-off slip, it accepted the terms of the buyer's offer. The buyer had got in the 'last shot'. Because the buyer's terms contained no price-variation clause, the seller had no contractual right to claim the extra £2,892.

COMMENT: Lawton and Bridge LJJ decided the case based upon the mirror image rule—namely, that whichever party gets in the 'last shot' will win the battle of the forms, provided that the other party acknowledges the terms of the last shot[52] and unequivocally accepts them. The obvious advantage of this approach is that it promotes certainty.

---

52. *Sterling Hydraulics Ltd v Dichtomatik Ltd* [2006] EWHC 2004 (QB), [2007] 1 Lloyd's Rep 8.

The principal disadvantage of this approach is that, if the last shot is not unequivocally accepted, there will be no contract. To avoid this, Denning MR suggested a different approach. He argued that, where the principal terms do not materially differ, the court should reconcile those terms that do differ to create a harmonious compromise contract. If the terms cannot be reconciled, the court should scrap those terms and replace them with terms of 'reasonable implication'.[53] Such an approach is commercially flexible and will avoid the finding that no contract exists between the parties, but it lacks the certainty of the last-shot approach. Further, many members of the judiciary would not relish the interventionist role that Lord Denning's approach envisages. For these reasons, subsequent courts have not embraced Lord Denning's approach and the mirror image rule is still the general approach to be used.

 See R Rawlings, 'The Battle of the Forms' (1979) MLR 715

It would appear that the key determinant of the battle of the forms is the drafting of the standard terms. As Treitel notes, 'it is possible by careful draftsmanship to avoid losing the battle of the forms, but not (if the other party is equally careful) to win it'.[54] Where both parties have well-drafted standard terms, the result would appear to be a stalemate and the mirror image rule would seem to dictate that the judge rule that no contract exists.

Acceptance by conduct

In many cases, acceptance will be express and communicated orally or in writing. But it is also possible to accept an offer by conduct. This most commonly occurs in contracts for the sale of goods in which the offeree accepts the offer by dispatching the ordered goods.[55] In order for acceptance by conduct to be valid, however, it must be objectively established that the offeree knew of the offer, and performed and acted in reliance on it.[56]

The following case demonstrates these principles.

Brogden v Metropolitan Railway Company (1877) 2 App Cas 666 (HL)

FACTS: Brogden (the defendant) had, for many years, supplied the Metropolitan Railway Company (the claimant) with coal—but no formal agreement had ever existed between the two parties. They finally decided to formalize their relationship. The claimant drafted a contract, but left certain areas blank for Brogden to fill in (for example, the identity of the arbitrator). Brogden completed the blank areas, signed it, and wrote 'approved' at the end of the contract, before returning it to the claimant. The claimant received the contract and its manager placed it in his desk. The parties continued trading on the basis of the contract, but a dispute subsequently arose and Brogden refused to supply any more coal, claiming that there was no contract between them. The claimant sued.

---

53. *Butler Machine Tool Co Ltd v Ex-Cell-O Corporation (England) Ltd* [1979] 1 WLR 401 (CA) 405.
54. E Peel, *Treitel on the Law of Contract* (12th edn, Sweet & Maxwell, London, 2007) 23.
55. *Harvey v Johnston* (1848) 6 CB 295.
56. *Taylor v Allon* [1966] 1 QB 304 (DC).

HELD: The House of Lords held that a contract had come into existence either when the claimant had ordered the first supply of coal, or when the defendant supplied it. Sending the draft contract to Brogden amounted to an offer. Because Brogden added a term (by adding the arbitrator's name), the return of the contract constituted a counter-offer. The issue was whether the claimant accepted Brogden's offer. Initially, it would appear that simply placing the contract in a desk would not amount to acceptance, but this was not the case. The claimant did not object to Brogden's choice of arbitrator and both parties continued to transact on the basis of the contract. Accordingly, the claimant's conduct amounted to acceptance of the defendant's counter-offer.

Communication of acceptance

It is a general rule that, in order for acceptance to be effective, it must be communicated to the offeror. The rationale behind this general principle is that if acceptance could be valid without being communicated to the offeror, this would place the offeror in an extremely difficult position, because he would not able to determine whether or not he could make offers to others. It follows that the communication of acceptance need not come from the offeree,[57] but can be made by a third party authorized by the offeree (for example, his agent).

As a general rule, the communication of acceptance must actually be brought to the offeror's attention. Attempted communication will be insufficient, even where the reasons for failure are not attributable to the offeree (for example, if a plane flies overhead and drowns out his voice, or if the telephone line goes dead as he is communicating acceptance).[58] The contract will be concluded at the time and place of the receipt of communication of acceptance. In the case of cross-border contracts, determining the exact time and place that a contract came into being can often be crucial in determining which legal system has jurisdiction.

Entores Ltd v Miles Far East Corporation [1955] 2 QB 327 (CA)

FACTS: The claimant company was based in London. It telexed (the forerunner to email) the defendant, which was based in Holland, and offered to purchase a quantity of copper cathodes. The defendant replied by telex, accepting the claimant's offer. Later, a dispute arose and the claimant initiated an action for breach of contract in an English court. The defendant argued that the contract was concluded in Holland and that the English courts therefore lacked the jurisdiction to decide the case.

HELD: The Court of Appeal held that the contract was concluded in England. Acceptance may have taken place in Holland, but it only became valid once it was communicated to the offeror. Because this took place in England, that was where the contract was concluded and so the English courts had jurisdiction.

⭐ See EH Scamell, 'Offer and Acceptance by Teleprinter' (1956) 19 MLR 89

---

57. *Bloxham's Case* (1864) 33 Beav 529.
58. *Entores Ltd v Miles Far East Corporation* [1955] 2 QB 327 (CA) 332 (Denning LJ).

The rule that communication of acceptance must be received by the offeror is not, however, absolute. As we shall see in the following sections, in some cases, the rule is modified; in other cases, it is reversed.

Prescribed methods of acceptance

If the offeror is concerned that he may be bound by a contract before he has notice of acceptance (as is usually the case when the postal rule applies—see the next section), it is always open for him to prescribe a specific form of acceptance. The offeror could require the offeree to deliver acceptance personally, in writing, thereby removing all doubt as to where and when acceptance took place. The general rule is that if the offeror states that acceptance may *only* occur via the prescribed means, then acceptance will only be effective if it complies with the offeror's specifications. Accordingly, if the offeror requires acceptance in writing to be sent to a particular place and it is sent elsewhere, he will not be bound.[59] Similarly, if he states that acceptance must be in writing, but it is delivered orally, the offeror will not be bound.[60] The offeror may, however, indicate that a form of acceptance should be used, but not prescribe that it is the *only* way in which acceptance can occur. In such a case, an alternative method of acceptance will be effective, provided that it is no less advantageous to the offeror than the prescribed method.[61]

The following example demonstrates this.

 Prescribed methods of acceptance

Paul offers to sell a consignment of goods to Marc, stating that acceptance should be 'by return of mail'. In many cases, 'return of mail' does not literally mean that acceptance should only be sent in the post; it merely indicates that acceptance should be communicated quickly. Accordingly, if Marc were to accept Paul's offer via email, it could be argued that Marc would have complied with Paul's intention.

The 'postal rule'

In the absence of a prescribed method of acceptance, one of the most common forms of acceptance is by post, and postal acceptance constitutes perhaps the most important exception to the rule that acceptance is not valid until it is communicated to the offeror. The 'postal rule' states that, where it applies, acceptance takes place as soon as the letter is posted, not when the offeror receives it.

 Adams v Lindsell (1818) 1 B & Ald 681

FACTS: On 2 September, the defendant posted a letter offering to sell wool to the claimant, requesting a reply 'in the course of post'. Due to the defendant's letter being misdirected, it was delivered to the claimant two days later than expected, on the evening

---

59. *Frank v Knight* (1937) OQPD 113.   60. *Financings Ltd v Stimson* [1962] 1 WLR 1184 (CA).
61. *Tinn v Hoffmann* (1873) 29 LT 271.

of 5 September. The claimant posted his acceptance on the same day and it was delivered to the defendant on 9 September. Had the defendant's original letter of offer not been misdirected, he would have expected to receive acceptance on 7 September. Because he did not, he sold the wool to someone else. The claimant alleged that there existed a binding contract, which the defendant breached by selling the wool to another party.

HELD: The court held that as soon as the claimant posted his acceptance on 5 September, a binding contract was created and the defendant was therefore in breach.

COMMENT: It is apparent that the postal rule can be extremely harsh upon the offeror. Suppose that the acceptance letter is lost in the post. The offeror may sell the goods to a third party, completely unaware that he is party to a binding contract for the goods with the offeree. The offeror would have acted completely honestly and innocently, yet would be in breach of contract.[62]

Clearly, the postal rule favours the offeree at the expense of the offeror. Why is this so? Several justifications have been advanced, as follows.

- If the offeror expressly or impliedly (for example, by making the offer by post) indicates that postal acceptance is acceptable, he should bear the risks associated with the postal system.

- The postal rule prevents an offeree from taking advantage of the market (for example, by posting a letter of acceptance and then, if the market changes, retracting the acceptance—perhaps by email—before the letter reaches the offeror, and then contracting based on the new favourable market conditions).

- The postal rule facilitates the provision of evidence, because it is easier to prove that a letter has been posted than it is to prove that it has been received.

In several situations, the postal rule will not apply to acceptance sent by post.

- The harshness of the postal rule can be completely avoided by a prudent offeror, in so much as the offeror is free to contract out of the postal rule. We saw in the previous section that an offeror is free to specify the form of acceptance. Accordingly, the offeror is free to specify that post may not be used or that, if post is used, acceptance will not be effective until the offeror actually receives the offeree's letter of acceptance.[63]

- The postal rule will not apply where it is not reasonable to use the post to accept,[64] or where acceptance by post would give rise to a manifest inconvenience or absurdity.[65] In these cases, the normal rule of acceptance will apply and acceptance will occur when the letter is received.

Electronic forms of communication

The advent of electronic forms of communication has necessitated the application of the acceptance rules to novel and developing situations. In many cases, this poses no problems. In the case of instantaneous forms of electronic communication, the

---

62. *Household Fire and Carriage Accident Insurance Co v Grant* (1879) 4 Ex D 216 (CA).
63. *Holwell Securities v Hughes* [1974] 1 WLR 155 (CA).
64. *Henthorn v Fraser* [1892] 2 Ch 27 (CA).
65. *Holwell Securities v Hughes* [1974] 1 WLR 155 (CA).

standard rule that acceptance must be communicated to the offeror will continue to apply, because in such cases, although the parties might be thousands of miles apart, the fact that communication is instantaneous means that it is *as if* they were in each other's presence. Accordingly, the standard rules of acceptance normally apply to contracts created by telephone,[66] telex,[67] and fax.[68]

But problems can arise and, due to technological difficulties, instantaneous forms of communication may not prove so instantaneous in practice (for example, a fax machine might malfunction, or a mobile phone may lose a signal). What is the outcome in such situations?

The answer came from Denning LJ in *Entores v Miles Far East Corporation*.[69]

- Where the offeree knows that his acceptance has not been received (for example, if his phone goes dead, or his fax machine malfunctions whilst midway through sending a message), there will be no contract. The offeree will need to repeat acceptance.

- Where the offeree believes that his acceptance has been communicated, but, in fact, it has not (for example, the offeror's fax malfunctions and does not receive the offeree's acceptance), then unless the offeror asks for the message to be repeated, a contract will exist. This is because the offeror is at fault for his failure to receive the acceptance.

- If no party is at fault and neither party is aware of the communication problem (so that the offeror believes that acceptance was not received, and the offeror believes that it was), then there will be no contract.

Aside from technological malfunctions, there is another reason to believe that instantaneous forms of communication may not be received instantly—namely, that businesses may work within set office hours.

- If communication is received during office hours, acceptance will occur when the acceptance was received on the machine, not when it was actually read.[70] The rationale behind this is that, during office hours, fax machines, etc. should be regularly monitored and therefore offerees who do not monitor such machines should not be able to rely on the standard communication of acceptance rule.

- If acceptance was received outside office hours, then acceptance will be deemed to have taken place at the start of the next working day.[71]

The above rules do not apply to all situations of electronic communication. In particular, there has been much discussion and deliberation on how the rules of acceptance should apply to contracts created via email. Although email is invariably quicker than postal mail, it is not an instantaneous form of communication, because the email is stored on a server before being sent to the recipient. This may lead us to believe that the standard rules should not apply and that emails should be treated as postal mails—that is, that acceptance occurs when the 'send' button is clicked. But it appears that the weight of opinion is against such a result and most commentators

66. *Entores v Miles Far East Corporation* [1955] 2 QB 327 (CA).   67. Ibid.
68. *JSC Zestafoni Nikoladze Ferroalloy Plant v Ronly Holdings Ltd* [2004] EWHC 245 (Comm), [2004] 2 Lloyd's Rep 335.
69. *Entores v Miles Far East Corporation* [1955] 2 QB 327 (CA).
70. *Brinkibon v Stahag Stahl und Stahlwarenhandelsgesellschaft GmbH* [1983] 2 AC 34 (HL).
71. *Mondial Shipping and Chartering BV v Astarte Shipping Ltd* [1995] 2 Lloyd's Rep 249 (QB).

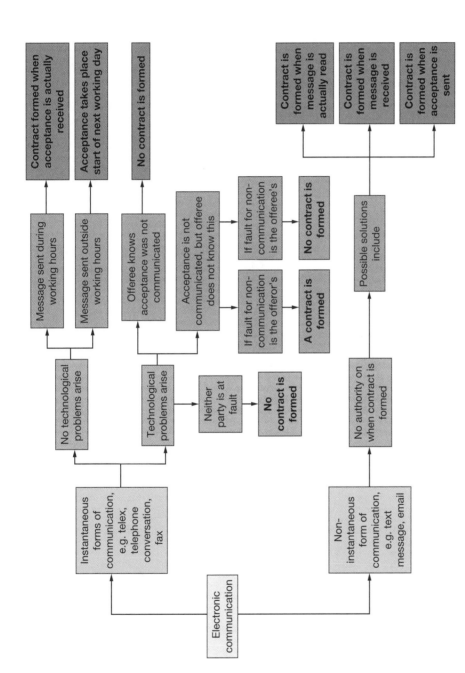

FIGURE 6.1 Electronic communication of acceptance

prefer acceptance to occur when the email is received. So what does 'received' mean? An email could be 'received' when it is delivered to the recipient's inbox; it could also be said to be 'received' once the recipient actually reads the message. It would appear that the weight of academic opinion favours the former interpretation,[72] but until the issue is definitively determined by statute or the courts, uncertainty will remain.

Acceptance through silence

We saw above that the offeror can specify the method of communication of acceptance. Does it follow that an offeror can choose to waive the requirement of communication of acceptance if he so wishes? The general answer appears to be 'no'.

 Felthouse v Bindley (1862) 11 CB NS 869

FACTS: An uncle (the claimant) sent a letter to his nephew, offering to buy a horse from him. The letter stated: 'If I hear no more about him, I will consider the horse mine.' The horse was due to be sold at auction, but the nephew, apparently happy with his uncle's offer, instructed the auctioneer (the defendant) to withdraw the horse from auction. Mistakenly, the horse was not withdrawn and was sold to a third party. The uncle argued that the horse belonged to him when the auctioneer sold it and so sued under the tort of **conversion**.

HELD: The uncle's claim failed. The court held that silence could not constitute valid acceptance. Therefore, the nephew never accepted the uncle's offer and no contract came into being. Accordingly, when the horse was sold, it still belonged to the nephew.

COMMENT: It could be argued that this was not a case of acceptance by silence, but rather acceptance by conduct. The uncle could have validly contended that, by removing the horse from auction, the nephew's conduct indicated acceptance. But the counter-argument to this would be that the nephew never informed the uncle that he was withdrawing the horse from the auction and so the conduct was not communicated to the offeror.

➡ conversion: the act of interfering with goods in a manner inconsistent with another's rights of possession (see p 457)

Accordingly, the general rule is that silence cannot constitute valid acceptance. There is, however, a growing belief that this rule is not absolute. In *Vitol SA v NorElf Ltd*,[73] Lord Steyn stated that silence could constitute valid acceptance in 'exceptional cases'.[74] Possible exceptions could include the following.

- In *Felthouse*, the court held that no contract existed where the offeror attempted to argue that the offeree's silence constituted acceptance. It has been argued that if the offeree had been attempting to enforce the contract by contending that his silence was valid acceptance, this would be acceptable. In such a case, all that the offeree is doing is relying upon the conditions of the offer stated by the offeror.[75]

---

72. See, e.g., D Capps, 'Electronic Mail and the Postal Rule' (2004) 15 ICCLR 207, 212.
73. [1996] AC 800 (HL).
74. Ibid, 812.
75. E Peel, *Treitel on the Law of Contract* (12th edn, Sweet & Maxwell, London, 2007) 35; J Poole, *Textbook on Contract Law* (9th edn, OUP, Oxford, 2008) 67.

- Judicial *dicta* exist that indicate that if the offeree states that his silence will constitute acceptance, a valid contract will exist.[76]
- Where there has been a previous course of dealing, silence may constitute acceptance. A good example of this is car insurance. Several weeks before motor insurance policies are due to expire, insurance companies will inform customers of the expiry date and the renewal premium. This will be accompanied by instructions that, if customers do nothing, the insurance coverage will continue as normal upon payment of the premium. Of course, one could argue that payment of the premium amounts to acceptance by conduct, but because many customers pay by direct debit, it could be argued that simply allowing the money to be taken out of a bank account would not constitute the requisite level of positive assent needed for acceptance by conduct. The more likely argument is that driving a car in reliance of an offer of renewal would constitute acceptance of the renewal offer.[77]

Unilateral contracts

We discussed above why the general rules relating to contractual offers needed to be modified, or even disapplied, in the case of unilateral contracts. The same is true in relation to the rules of acceptance. The following example demonstrates how and why the rules differ.

Eg Acceptance and unilateral contracts

Kirsty has lost her dog. She places an advertisement in her local newspaper stating that she will pay £100 to any person who finds her dog and returns it to her. This is clearly a unilateral offer, because no one is compelled to search for the dog, but if anyone does comply with the advertisement, Kirsty will be bound to pay the £100.

Two issues arise, as follows.

1. How is such an offer accepted?

2. Is communication of acceptance required?

The answers to both of these questions are relatively well established. Regarding the first question, although there has been academic debate on the subject (as we saw when we discussed the revocation of unilateral offers), it is still the accepted view that unilateral offers are accepted by fully performing the stipulated act.[78] Accordingly, someone finding her dog and returning it to her would accept Kirsty's offer. The rationale behind this is that, at any time, the offeree is free to give up searching for Kirsty's dog without fear of penalty. If offerees are free to abandon performance at any time, then the offeror should be similarly free to retract the offer at any time prior to full performance being completed. As we have seen above, however, the courts have significantly limited the offeror's ability to revoke a unilateral offer once performance has commenced.

76. *Re Selectmove Ltd* [1995] 1 WLR 474 (CA) 478 (Peter-Gibson J).

77. *Taylor v Allon* [1966] 1 QB 304 (DC).

78. *Daulia Ltd v Four Millbank Nominees Ltd* [1978] Ch 231 (CA).

Regarding the second question, it is also settled law that, in the case of unilateral offers, the offeree does not have to communicate acceptance of the offer.[79] The reason for this is one of practicality. Because unilateral offers may be made to the entire world, it would be impractical to require every person who decided to look for Kirsty's dog first to contact her and inform her that they were going to search for the dog. Accordingly, the requirement for communication of acceptance is waived.

Revocation of acceptance

All textbooks discuss the laws relating to revocation of offers, but the possibility of revocation of acceptance is often overlooked. The assumption behind this lack of analysis is the belief that upon acceptance taking place, a binding contract is created and so acceptance cannot be retracted. But the possibility of revocation of acceptance should not be so swiftly dismissed. The possibility arises in the case of postal acceptance: if an offeree posts his acceptance, should he be able to revoke that acceptance before the letter reaches the offeror? There is no English law on the point and the one Scottish case that appeared to hold that revocation of postal acceptance is possible if communicated before the letter of acceptance arrives[80] is somewhat dubious authority.

There are, however, two plausible reasons why such revocation of postal acceptance should be valid, as follows.

1. Because the law of agreement is based upon the objective determination of the intentions of the parties, it would seem odd to permit an offeror to rely on a postal acceptance when the evidence clearly indicates that both parties are fully aware that such acceptance had been revoked. The counter-argument to this is that, upon the letter being posted, agreement has already taken place and cannot be revoked; to do so would constitute a repudiatory breach of contract.

2. Provided that the offeror is clearly aware that acceptance has been revoked before the acceptance letter arrives, he suffers no detriment.[81]

‹ › Key points summary

- Treitel defined acceptance as 'a final and unqualified expression of assent to the terms of the offer'.[82] It can be spoken, in writing, or by conduct.

- As soon as the offer is accepted and (generally) communicated, a contract is created. The requirement of communication of acceptance does not apply to unilateral contracts.

- Acceptance that varies a term of the offer or adds a new term will amount to a counter-offer.

---

79. *Carlill v Carbolic Smoke Ball Co* [1893] 1 QB 256 (CA).

80. *Countess of Dunmore v Alexander* (1830) 9 S 190 (Ct of Session).

81. DM Evans, 'The Anglo-American Mailing Rule: Some Problems of Offer and Acceptance in Contracts by Correspondence' (1966) 15 ICLQ 553, 563.

82. E Peel, *Treitel on the Law of Contract* (12th edn, Sweet & Maxwell, London, 2007) 41.

- A counter-offer destroys the original offer and creates a new offer capable of acceptance by the former offeror.
- Acceptance by post takes place as soon as the letter is posted.
- Silence does not constitute valid acceptance.

Certainty

Even where agreement is present, there will not be a binding contract if the agreement lacks sufficient certainty. An agreement that lacks certainty will not be rewritten by the courts and will instead be declared invalid. Where possible, however, the courts prefer to uphold the validity of contracts (especially where performance has commenced), rather than be perceived as 'the destroyer of bargains'.[83] Uncertain contracts can fall into one of two categories, although there is significant potential for overlap.

Vague agreements

Where the words of a contract are vague, the court will attempt to uphold the contract by divining the intention of the parties. Where the intention cannot be divined, the court will deny the existence of a legally binding contract.

G Scammell and Nephew Ltd v Ouston [1941] AC 251 (HL)

FACTS: The defendant wrote to the claimant offering to sell it a van for £286 and also offering to take its Bedford van for £100 in part exchange. The agreement provided that 'this order is given on the understanding that the balance of purchase price can be had on hire-purchase terms over a period of two years'. The relationship deteriorated when the defendant refused to accept the Bedford van, due to its poor condition. The claimant sued for breach of contract.

HELD: The claim failed. The House of Lords held that there was no contract between the parties, because the phrase 'on hire-purchase terms' was so vague and had so many possible interpretations that it was impossible to determine which interpretation the parties had intended.

It may, however, be the case that whilst the terms of the contract are vague, the contract itself might provide some implied mechanism through which to determine the precise nature of the vague terms. In such a case, the courts will apply the maxim *id certum est quod certum reddi potest* ('that is certain which may be rendered certain'— that is, if the courts can make the contract certain, then it will become certain). An

---

83. *Hillas & Co Ltd v Arcos Ltd* (1932) 43 Ll L Rep 359 (HL) 364 (Lord Tomlin).

example of the court using the contract to imply certainty can be seen in the following case.

 Hillas & Co Ltd v Arcos Ltd (1932) 43 Ll L Rep 359 (HL)

FACTS: The claimant had entered into an agreement with the defendant whereby it would, in the 1930 season, purchase 22,000 standards of timber 'of fair specification'. The contract also provided the claimant with the option to purchase another 100,000 standards of timber in 1931, but did not provide details relating to the size and quality of the timber. Come 1931, the claimant decided to exercise this option, but the defendant had already sold all of its timber. The claimant sued for breach of contract. The defendant contended that the agreement was so vague that it did not give rise to a contract.

HELD: The claimant succeeded. The House of Lords held that, even though the option did not specify the size and quality of the timber, this information could be implied by reference to the previous season's dealing and by reference to the normal practices of the timber trade.

Where a particular term is vague, it may also be possible for the court to sever that term and enforce the remaining agreement.

 Nicolene Ltd v Simmonds [1953] 1 QB 543 (CA)

FACTS: The claimant ordered 3,000 tons of reinforced steel bars from the defendant. The agreement was subject to 'the usual conditions of acceptance', but no usual conditions existed. The defendant failed to deliver the goods and the claimant sued. The defendant argued that, because there were no usual conditions of acceptance, the contract was too vague to be enforced.

HELD: The Court of Appeal held that the clause was meaningless and could be severed from the contract. The remaining agreement was certain and complete, and could be enforced. Denning LJ (as he then was) was quick to draw a distinction between:

> a clause which is meaningless and a clause which is yet to be agreed. A clause which is meaningless can often be ignored, whilst still leaving the contract good; whereas a clause which has yet to be agreed may mean that there is no contract at all, because the parties have not agreed on all the essential terms.[84]

The courts will also have regard to whether performance has commenced. Where the parties have wholly or partially performed their obligations under the contract (known as 'executed performance'), it will be:

> difficult to submit that the contract is void for vagueness or uncertainty. Specifically, the fact that the transaction is executed makes it easier to imply a term resolving any uncertainty, or alternatively, it may be possible to treat a matter not finalised in negotiations as inessential.[85]

---

84. *Nicolene Ltd v Simmonds* [1953] 1 QB 543 (CA) 551.
85. *G Percy Trentham Ltd v Archital Luxfer Ltd* [1993] 1 Lloyd's Rep 25 (CA) 27 (Steyn LJ).

Incomplete agreements

The parties may agree on broad terms, but may wish to leave certain matters for future negotiation. Provided that the essential terms of the contract have been agreed upon and that the parties agree to be bound immediately, the fact that further terms require negotiation will not prevent the court from finding a concluded agreement, as the following case demonstrates.

 Bear Stearns Bank plc v Forum Global Equity Ltd [2007] EWHC 1576 (Comm)

FACTS: The defendant wished to purchase from the claimant loan notes in respect of companies within the Parmalat group (the notes would entitle the holder to be regarded as a creditor of Parmalat). The parties entered into negotiations and reached an agreement on price, but several more minor terms were not agreed on. It was decided that the remainder of the terms would be negotiated by the parties' lawyers, but, believing that an agreement had been made, the claimant agreed to sell the loan notes to the defendant. Before the lawyers had finalized terms, the defendant decided not to proceed with the purchase. The claimant sued for breach of contract and the defendant argued that no agreement was ever made.

HELD: The Commercial Court held that a contract existed, which the defendant had breached. The essential term of the contract—namely, price—had been agreed. Andrew Smith J stated:

> If parties have shown an intention to be contractually committed, albeit while deferring discussion of some aspect or aspects of the deal, then the court will recognise a contract unless what remains outstanding is not merely important but essential in the sense that without it the contract is too uncertain or incomplete to be enforced.[86]

⭐ See P Nicholls, 'My Word is My Bond' (2008) 158 NLJ 122

This case indicates the courts' commitment to give effect to business dealings wherever possible. But the courts will only go so far. Where essential terms are missing, or are yet to be agreed upon by the parties, there will be no contract; there will be merely an 'agreement to agree'.

 May and Butcher Ltd v R [1934] 2 KB 17n

FACTS: The claimant entered into an agreement with the defendant to purchase surplus war equipment. The agreement stated that the price to be paid and the date of payment would be decided 'from time to time'. The relationship between the parties broke down and the claimant sought to enforce the agreement at a 'reasonable price'.

HELD: The High Court held that there was no contract. Because an essential term was left open for future negotiation, the contract was therefore too incomplete to enforce.

---

86. *Bear Stearns Bank plc v Forum Global Equity Ltd* [2007] EWHC 1576 (Comm) [155].

As with uncertain agreements, the presence of certain factors will make the court more willing to conclude that a contract exists—namely:

- if performance has already begun; or
- if the contract provides for some effective form of mechanism to resolve the lack of agreement.

Both of these factors were present in the following case.

 Foley v Classique Coaches Ltd **[1934] 2 KB 1 (CA)**

FACTS: The claimant sold a piece of land to the defendant, who was to use it to run its coach business. It was a term of the agreement that the defendant enter into a second agreement with the claimant, whereby it agreed to purchase all of its petrol from the claimant at a price to be agreed from 'time to time'. The second agreement also provided that, in the event of a lack of agreement, the parties would aim to resolve their dispute through arbitration. For three years, the agreement continued, until the defendant decided to repudiate the second agreement. The claimant sued and the defendant argued that there was no contract due to the uncertain price clause.

HELD: The Court of Appeal held that the second agreement was binding and enforceable. The Court implied a term that the petrol should be sold to the defendant at a reasonable price.

COMMENT: Initially, this case appears very similar to *May and Butcher*, discussed above, yet the Court reached the opposite result. But closer inspection reveals two crucial differences between the cases.

1. The parties had acted on the agreement for three years—which was not the case in *May and Butcher*.

2. The contract provided that, in the absence of agreement, the issue was to be determined by arbitration.

Key points summary

- A contract will only be binding if it is sufficiently certain.
- If the terms of a contract are vague, the court will generally attempt to hold the contract valid by divining the intentions of the parties.
- It may also be possible to sever a vague term and enforce the remaining agreement.
- Where the parties have completed or commenced performance, the court will be extremely reluctant to hold a contract void on the ground of uncertainty.
- There will be no contract where an agreement is incomplete because essential terms are missing, or are yet to be agreed upon by the parties.
- The court may be prepared to hold an incomplete contract valid if performance has already commenced, or if the contract contains some mechanism through which to resolve the incomplete area.

Consideration

A promise in a contract must be supported by consideration (unless executed by deed) from the person to whom the promise is made (that is, the promisee). The requirement of consideration reinforces the notion of reciprocity and that a contract is designed to be a bargain. It follows that (unless made by deed) gratuitous promises cannot be enforced.[87] For example, if I promise to donate £100 to charity and then change my mind, the charity cannot sue me to recover the donation, because the charity has not provided any consideration for my promise; my promise is only a gratuitous one.

➡ gratuitous promises: promises for which consideration is not given

Various attempts have been made to define 'consideration'. Historically, consideration was viewed in terms of benefit and detriment, as the following definition of Lush J indicates:

> A valuable consideration in the sense of the law may consist either in some right, interest, profit or benefit accruing to one party, or some forbearance, detriment, loss or responsibility given, suffered or undertaken by the other.[88]

The following example demonstrates this definition in practice, and also its principal weakness.

Eg Benefit and detriment

Martin purchases goods online from Expensivestuff.co.uk. He pays £100 for the goods. Martin will suffer a detriment (payment of the £100) and the seller will gain a benefit (receipt of the £100). At the same time, Martin will gain a benefit (receipt of the goods) and the seller will suffer a detriment (loss of the goods).

The problem with this approach is that, at the time that the contract is concluded, neither party has gained or lost anything: the above benefits and detriments will take place in the future, once both parties have performed their obligations. Therefore, in normal bilateral contracts, defining consideration purely in terms of benefit and detriment is descriptively inaccurate.

For this reason, Lush J's definition has fallen out of favour and has been replaced, with the approval of the House of Lords,[89] by the more accurate description of Sir Frederick Pollock (1845–1937), an eminent academic, who defined consideration as '[a]n act of forbearance of one party, or the promise thereof, is the price for which the promise of the other is bought, and the promise thus given for value is enforceable'.[90]

---

87. *Re Hudson* (1885) 54 LJ Ch 811.
88. *Currie v Misa* (1875) LR 10 Ex 153, 162.
89. *Dunlop Pneumatic Tyre Co Ltd v Selfridge Ltd* [1915] AC 847 (HL) 855 (Lord Dunedin).
90. Sir P Winfield, *Pollock's Principles of Contract* (13th edn, Stevens, London, 1950) 133.

Forms of consideration

Consideration can be classified into one of three forms:

- executed;
- executory; and
- past.

As a general rule, executed and executory consideration constitutes valid consideration, whereas past consideration does not.

Executory and executed consideration

Executory consideration is consideration that is yet to be provided, whereas executed consideration is consideration that has already been provided. The following examples demonstrate the distinction.

> **Eg Executory and executed consideration**
>
> **Executory consideration**
>
> Heavy Construction plc orders 2,000 tonnes of steel girders from Steel Smelting Co Ltd at a price of £250,000. A contract is drawn up to reflect this. At the time that the contract is drawn up, neither party has performed its obligations—but this does not mean that they have not provided consideration, because their promises to perform constitute valid consideration. Because each party has yet to perform (execute) its obligations, their consideration is not executed, but executory. Put simply: the whole agreement is to take place in the future. All bilateral contracts will feature executory consideration, because at the time of concluding the contract, neither party will have fulfilled their obligations.
>
> **Executed consideration**
>
> Gareth loses his Rolex watch at the gym. He puts up posters at the gym indicating that he will pay £100 to anyone who finds the watch and returns it to him. Melanie finds the watch and returns it to Gareth. By finding the watch and returning it to Gareth, Melanie has performed (executed) her obligation. Accordingly, Melanie's consideration for Gareth's promise is executed.

Past consideration

Normally, the parties will each make a promise and then carry out the promised act. In this case, the promise constitutes consideration and, because it occurs before performance of the act, it will be valid. Conversely, where a party performs an act that is then followed by a promise, that act will normally constitute past consideration, which generally does not provide good consideration for a promise. The following example demonstrates this.

Eg Past consideration

Greg loses his wallet on a train. Two days later, Charles finds Greg's wallet and returns it to him. Greg is overjoyed and promises to pay Charles a reward of £50. Two weeks later, Greg has yet to pay the reward and indicates to Charles that he is not going to do so. Can Charles sue to recover the promised reward? The answer is 'no'. Charles has provided no consideration for the reward, because his act was not undertaken in exchange for a promise: his act pre-dated the promise, ergo his consideration was past.

The phrase 'past consideration' is somewhat misleading, because the general rule is that past consideration is no consideration at all, as the following case demonstrates.

Re McArdle [1951] Ch 669 (CA)

FACTS: A father died and his will provided that his five children would inherit his house upon the death of their mother. The mother lived in the house, along with her son and his wife (the claimant). The claimant carried out alterations to the house worth £488, although she had not been asked to do this. A year later, all five children agreed to reimburse her, out of the estate, for the work done. The mother died and the house was sold. The children refused to pay the claimant the promised £488. The claimant sought to enforce the agreement.

HELD: The Court of Appeal held that the agreement was unenforceable. The work that the claimant undertook pre-dated the promise to reimburse. Accordingly, she had provided no consideration for the £488.

⭐ See OM Stone, 'Assignment and Consideration in Action' (1951) 14 MLR 330

There are, however, a number of instances in which what appears to be past consideration will, in fact, be regarded as good consideration by the courts. Lord Scarman stated the requirements for this to occur:

> An act done before the giving of a promise to make a payment or to confer some other benefit can sometimes be consideration for the promise. The act must have been done at the promisors' request: the parties must have understood that the act was to be remunerated either by a payment or the conferment of some other benefit: and payment, or the conferment of a benefit, must have been legally enforceable had it been promised in advance.[91]

It can be seen that Lord Scarman imposed a three-stage test:

1. the act in question must have been requested by the promisor;
2. both parties must have understood (if not expressly agreed) that the act was to be remunerated in some way so that a promise of prior remuneration can be implied; and
3. the promise must have been enforceable, had it been promised in advance of the act.

---

91. *Pao On v Lau Yiu Long* [1980] AC 614 (PC) 630.

If the test is satisfied, the subsequent promise of payment of a specified sum merely quantifies the amount payable.

The following two cases demonstrate this test in practice.

 Lampleigh v Braithwait (1615) Hob 105

FACTS: Braithwait (the defendant) had killed a man and requested that Lampleigh (the claimant) petition the King for a pardon. At considerable effort and expense, Lampleigh secured the pardon, and Braithwait then promised to pay Lampleigh £100 for his efforts. Braithwait subsequently refused to pay the £100, so Lampleigh sued.

HELD: Lampleigh could recover the £100. The court held that Braithwait's request to obtain a pardon and his subsequent promise were so closely connected as to form essentially part of the same transaction. Further, given the obvious time and expense through which Lampleigh would have to go to obtain a pardon, the court held that there was an implied promise to pay Lampleigh a reward for his efforts.

 Re Casey's Patents (Stewart v Casey) [1892] 1 Ch 104 (CA)

FACTS: Two men, named Mr Stewart and Mr Charlton, owned the patent rights to a particular invention. For two years, the claimant promoted this invention. Stewart and Charlton then wrote to the claimant promising to pay him a one-third share of the patent rights, in return for his prior services. Stewart died, and Charlton and Stewart's executor, keen to avoid sharing the patent rights, argued that the claimant had no right to a share of the patent rights, because he provided no consideration for the agreement. The claimant sued.

HELD: The claimant succeeded. The Court of Appeal held that, when the claimant undertook work for Stewart and Charlton, there was an implied promise that he would be paid for such work. The subsequent promise simply clarified the price that he would be paid.

Adequacy of consideration

The general rule is that consideration for another's promise must be sufficient, but need not be adequate. The word 'adequate' is being used in a legal sense to refer to consideration being equal in value. Accordingly, the consideration of both parties need not be equal in value, provided that it is legally sufficient.

 Mountford v Scott [1975] Ch 258 (CA)

FACTS: The defendant granted the claimant a six-month option to purchase his house for £10,000, in return for which the claimant provided £1. The defendant purported to withdraw the offer, but two months later, the claimant exercised the option. The defendant argued that a binding agreement existed, because the claimant had not provided sufficient consideration.

HELD: Despite the obvious inequality of the bargain, the £1 had value in the eyes of the law and so the Court of Appeal held that it constituted good consideration.

Forbearance not to sue

If a person who could sue another promises not to pursue his claim, that constitutes good consideration for a promise by the other person to pay a sum of money as a final settlement of the claim. In return, the person promising to pay that sum thereby provides consideration for the other's promise not to pursue his claim. The court will require, however, that the person relying upon the surrendering of the claim prove:

- that the claim is reasonable in itself;
- that he genuinely believed that the claim stood a chance of succeeding;
- that he genuinely intended to pursue the claim; and
- that he was not concealing from the other party facts that would constitute a defence to the claim.[92]

Where the party providing the forbearance is unaware that he has a right to claim, the court will be unlikely to uphold the forbearance, as the following case demonstrates.

Bank of Credit and Commerce International v Ali (No 1) [2001] UKHL 8

FACTS: The defendant bank made the claimant redundant in 1990. In addition to statutory redundancy pay and an *ex gratia* payment, he would receive a month's salary if he signed a document indicating that the month's salary was in full and final satisfaction of any statutory, common law, or equitable claim that he might have, or would ever have. Unknown to the claimant, at the time of the redundancy, the bank's management were engaged in fraudulent and criminal activity. Seven years later, a number of former employees of the defendant bank obtained 'stigma' damages for the damage that was caused to their reputation by the defendant's activities. The claimant sought to recover such 'stigma' damages. The defendant argued that he was prevented from doing so by the agreement that he had signed.

HELD: The House of Lords held that the agreement did not cover the recovery of 'stigma' damages and that 'the court will be very slow to infer that a party intended to surrender rights and claims of which he was unaware and could not have been aware'.[93]

> The ability to claim 'stigma' damages is discussed at p 335

> See K Wheat, *'Bank of Credit and Commerce International v Ali and Others'* (2002) 65 MLR 425

Consideration must be sufficient

In determining what constitutes sufficient consideration, the court generally refuses to recognize the sufficiency of certain promises. These promises can be classified into two groups:

- promises to perform, or performance of, an existing duty; and
- promises to pay in part, or part-payment of, a debt.

> The rules relating to part-payment are discussed at p 192

---

92. *Horton v Horton (No 2)* [1961] 1 QB 215 (CA).
93. *Bank of Credit and Commerce International v Ali (No 1)* [2001] UKHL 8 (Lord Bingham) [10].

To clarify discussion, this section will focus on the former—namely, a promise to perform an existing legal duty—which can arise where:

- the party performs, or promises to perform, an existing legal duty;
- the party performs, or promises to perform, an existing contractual duty that is owed to the other party; and
- the party performs, or promises to perform, an existing contractual duty owed to a third party.

Performance, or promise of performance, of an existing legal duty

The law places a number of obligations and duties upon all of us. The question here is whether the performance (actual or promised) of an existing legal duty can provide sufficient consideration for the promise of another. The general answer is 'no', as can be seen in the following case.

 Collins v Godefroy (1831) 1 B & Ad 950

→ subpoena: a writ compelling a person to attend a trial as a witness; now known as a 'witness summons'

FACTS: The defendant issued a **subpoena**, requiring the claimant to attend a civil trial and give evidence. The claimant attended court for six days, but was not required to give any evidence. After the trial, the defendant agreed to pay the claimant a fee of one guinea (£1.05) per day. The defendant never paid this fee and the claimant sued.

HELD: The claim failed. Once subpoenaed, the claimant was legally obliged to attend court and give evidence if required. Because he was doing no more than was required by the law, he had not provided consideration for the six guineas.

COMMENT: The decision in this case no longer represents the law. A subpoena (witness order) must now be accompanied by a tender of 'conduct money' to defray the costs and expenses (for example, loss of time) borne by the witness in attending the trial. A witness who fails to comply with a witness summons cannot be proceeded against for contempt of court unless such conduct money has been tendered.[94]

Where a party has done more than is required by the law, however, this will constitute good consideration for the other party's promise.

 Glasbrook Bros v Glamorgan County Council [1925] AC 270 (HL)[95]

FACTS: The owner of a colliery feared that striking employees might cause violence and property damage. He therefore requested extra protection from the police, adding that the colliery could only be protected properly if the police were actually billeted on the premises. The police did not think that this was necessary, because regular police patrols

---

94. Supreme Court Act 1981, s 36(4).

95. See also *Harris v Sheffield United Football Club* [1988] QB 77 (CA); *Ward v Byham* [1956] 1 WLR 496 (CA).

would be adequate. Nevertheless, the police agreed to billet a number of police officers at the colliery, provided that the owner agreed to pay for this, which he did. After the strike had ended, the police presented the colliery owner with a bill for £2,300. He refused to pay, contending that the police had a legal duty to protect his premises and that therefore they had not provided sufficient consideration for the £2,300.

HELD: The House of Lords ordered the colliery owner to pay the £2,300. The police were free to choose which method of protection was most effective. Because, at the insistence of the colliery owner, they had provided more protection than was deemed necessary, they had gone beyond the obligations imposed upon them and had therefore provided good consideration for the £2,300.

The case of *Williams v Roffey Bros & Nicholls (Contractors) Ltd*[96] (discussed below) established that performance of an existing contractual duty can provide good consideration if it provides the other party with a practical benefit, or avoidance of a disbenefit. It is now clear that this principle also applies to cases in which a duty is imposed by the law.[97] Therefore, the performance of a legal duty can constitute good consideration if it provides a practical benefit, or avoids a disbenefit, to the other party.

Performance, or promise of performance, of a contractual duty owed to the other party

The following example demonstrates the type of situation that we will discuss in this section.

Eg **Existing contractual duty owed to the other party**

Keith is a sculptor who has agreed to provide a large, granite sculpture to be placed in the lobby of the new corporate headquarters of MicroTech plc. Keith will be paid £50,000 and will deliver the sculpture in time for the new building's opening in three months' time. One month later, Keith informs the board of MicroTech that he cannot complete the sculpture at the contracted price and will require an extra £10,000. MicroTech promises to pay Keith the extra £10,000.

The question that we will discuss here is whether Keith has provided consideration for the extra £10,000. In other words: does the performance of his existing contractual duty provide sufficient consideration for the extra sum?

Traditionally, the answer to the question posed in this example has been 'no'. The mere performance, or promise of performance, of an existing contractual duty will not provide sufficient consideration for a new promise by the person to whom the contractual duty is owed—a rule that was established in the following case.

---

96. [1991] 1 QB 1 (CA).   97. *Re Selectmove Ltd* [1995] 1 WLR 474 (CA).

Stilk v Myrick (1809) 2 Camp 317

FACTS: The claimant was a crewman aboard a ship chartered to transport goods from London to the Baltic and back. For this trip, the eleven-man crew was paid a lump sum. During the voyage, two crewmen deserted, leaving the ship short-handed. The captain of the ship promised that if the remaining crew got the ship back to England, he would divide the deserting crewmen's wages amongst them. Upon returning to London, the captain refused to pay the crewmen extra.

HELD: The claimant (and the other crewmen) had not done any more than they were already contractually obliged to do. Accordingly, they had provided no consideration for the extra wages and so the claim failed.

COMMENT: This case can be contrasted with *Hartley v Ponsonby*,[98] which had almost identical facts to *Stilk*, except that seventeen crewmen out of thirty-six deserted. Given that the remaining crew would have to undertake considerably more work than they were contractually obliged to do, their claim for the extra £40 promised was upheld.

The principle in *Stilk v Myrick* has its advantages and disadvantages. It does create a measure of certainty and prevents a party placing undue pressure on the other once performance has commenced. Certainly, in *Stilk*, this was the principal policy reason behind the court's decision. To permit recovery of the extra wages would invite crewmen to hold their captains to ransom when far from home. The problem with the rule is that it is out of line with commercial reality, in so much as it is reasonably common to make new promises in order to secure timely performance. Perhaps for this reason, a limitation to the principle in *Stilk* was created in the following case.

 Williams v Roffey Bros & Nicholls (Contractors) Ltd [1991] 1 QB 1 (CA)

FACTS: The defendant was contracted to refurbish a block of twenty-seven flats. It subcontracted the carpentry work to the claimant, who would be paid £20,000 in a series of instalments. The claimant commenced performance, but realized soon afterwards that he could not complete the work for £20,000 (this was due to a combination of an unrealistic estimate and a failure to supervise the workforce adequately). The defendant was subject to a substantial time penalty clause if the flats were not completed on time. In order to secure timely performance and avoid the financial penalty, the defendant agreed to pay the claimant a further £10,300, payable at the rate of £575 per flat completed. The claimant completed a number of flats, but did not receive the extra payment. The issue arising was whether the claimant had provided consideration for the extra payment.

HELD: The Court of Appeal held that the claimant could recover the extra payment. The claimant had provided consideration for the extra money, this consideration coming in the form of 'practical benefits'[99] (or avoidance of disbenefits) that the defendant obtained by

---

98. (1857) 7 E & B 872.
99. *Williams v Roffey Bros & Nicholls (Contractors) Ltd* [1991] 1 QB 1 (CA) 11 (Glidewell LJ).

paying the extra amount. These benefits were the avoidance of the penalty clause and the avoidance of having to engage substitute carpenters. The Court did, however, state that had the extra money been secured via duress or fraud, the 'practical benefit' principle would not apply.

COMMENT: What effect does this case have on *Stilk v Myrick*? Given that a new promise will never be made unless some form of 'practical benefit' is derived, it could be argued that, in practical terms, the principle established in *Williams* obliterates the principle in *Stilk*. Soon after *Williams* was decided, two commentators argued that the principle in *Stilk* now existed in name only.[100] The Court in *Williams* denied that it was overruling the principle in *Stilk*, with Purchas LJ describing *Stilk* as 'a pillar stone of the law of contract'.[101] Glidewell LJ stated that the principle established in *Williams* is designed to 'refine and limit'[102] the principle in *Stilk*. With all due respect to their Lordships, it is contended that the decision in *Williams* goes far beyond mere refinement.

⭐ See R Halson, 'Sailors, Subcontractors and Consideration' (1990) 106 LQR 183

In *Re Selectmove Ltd*,[103] the Court of Appeal indicated a restrictive approach to its decision in *Williams*, saying that it did not apply where the existing obligation was one to pay money. It held that a promise to pay money already due could not be good consideration. Other cases have gone further and have openly criticized the decision in *Williams*. In *South Caribbean Trading v Trafalgar Beheer BV*,[104] Coleman J stated *obiter* that '[b]ut for the fact that *Williams v Roffey Bros* was a decision of the Court of Appeal, I would not have followed it'.[105]

Although the Court's reasoning has proven to be highly controversial, there is a significant body of opinion that contends that, in terms of commercial reality, the result is a beneficial one. The Court in *Williams* was concerned with making businessmen keep their promises and demonstrated a willingness to give effect to commercial reality—namely, that once contracts are concluded, subsequent renegotiation may be beneficial. The decision 'signals that the courts, in deciding whether or not to enforce a promise, may be guided less by technical questions of consideration than by questions of fairness, reasonableness and commercial utility'.[106]

Performance of, or the promise to perform, a contractual duty owed to a third party

It is accepted that a party to a contract may provide sufficient consideration for the promise of the other party by fulfilling a contractual duty owed to a third party, or by promising to fulfil it. This would occur where *A* makes a promise to *B* and, in return, *B* promises to do an act that he is already contractually obliged to perform for *C* (the third party). *B* will have provided sufficient consideration for *A*'s promise, by performing his contractual obligation towards *C*, as the following case demonstrates.

---

100. NJ Hird and A Blair, 'Minding Your Own Business: *Williams v Roffey* Re-visited—Consideration Reconsidered' (1996) JBL 254, 255.
101. *Williams v Roffey Bros & Nicholls (Contractors) Ltd* [1991] 1 QB 1 (CA) 20.
102. Ibid, 16.
103. [1995] 1 WLR 474 (CA).
104. [2004] EWHC 2676 (Comm), [2005] 1 Lloyd's Rep 128.
105. Ibid, [108].
106. J Adams and R Brownsword, 'Contract, Consideration and the Critical Path' (1990) 53 MLR 536, 537.

Scotson v Pegg (1861) 6 H & N 295

FACTS: The claimant entered into a contract with X to deliver coal to X, or to a party of X's choice. X required the coal to be delivered to the defendant. The defendant then promised to the claimant that, if he delivered to coal to him, he would unload it at the rate of 49 tonnes per day. The claimant delivered the coal to the defendant, but the defendant failed to unload it at the promised rate. When the claimant sued, the defendant argued that the claimant had not provided good consideration for the promise, because he was already obliged to deliver the coal under the contract with X.

HELD: The claimant succeeded. The claimant had provided good consideration for the defendant's promise, by carrying out the obligation that he already owed to X.

COMMENT: *Scotson* was a first-instance decision, but the Privy Council has since affirmed it on two occasions.[107]

Therefore, it can be seen that the principle in *Stilk v Myrick* discussed earlier only applies to existing contractual obligations of the other party; it does not apply to existing contractual obligations owed to third parties.

Promises of payment in part, or part-payment of, a debt

The following example provides the factual circumstances in which part-payment will occur.

 Part-payment of debt

Black Horse Bank plc lends £2 million to Welsh Petroleum Ltd—but Welsh Petroleum Ltd soon suffers significant financial difficulties. It informs Black Horse Bank plc that it will be unable to repay the loan in full when it is due. It will, however, be able to pay back £1.5 million, provided that Black Horse Bank plc promises to forgo the remainder of the loan.

The question with which we are concerned below is this: if Black Horse Bank plc does promise to forgo the remainder of the loan, will that promise be legally binding, or can it accept the £1.5 million and then sue for the remainder? In other words, does part-payment of a debt provide sufficient consideration for Black Horse Bank plc's promise to accept the lesser sum?

Common law

Part-payment of a debt does not provide sufficient consideration and, according to the common law, a creditor is not bound by any promise to accept a lower sum. This rule was established in 1602 in *Pinnel's Case*,[108] in which the court stated: 'Payment of

---

107. See *New Zealand Shipping Co Ltd v AM Satterthwaite & Co Ltd (The Eurymedon)* [1975] AC 154 (PC); *Pao On v Lau Yiu Long* [1980] AC 614 (PC).
108. (1602) 5 Co Rep 117a.

a lesser sum on the day in satisfaction of a greater sum cannot be any satisfaction for the whole.' The House of Lords approved this rule in the following case.

🔑 *Foakes v Beer* (1884) 9 App Cas 605 (HL)

FACTS: In a previous legal action, Dr Foakes (the defendant) had been ordered to pay Mrs Beer (the claimant) £2,090. She was entitled to this money immediately and, for every day it remained unpaid, she was also entitled to interest. Foakes was unable to pay and asked Beer for more time. She replied that if he were to paid £500 immediately, he could pay the balance in instalments and she would 'not take any proceedings whatever on the said judgment'. In accordance with this agreement, Foakes paid the £2,090, but Beer then sued Foakes for £360 interest. Foakes argued that she had promised not to sue, provided that he paid the instalments, which he did.

HELD: Because Foakes had only paid the £2,090 judgment debt and not the accompanying interest (to which Beer was legally entitled), he had not provided sufficient consideration for Beer's promise not to sue. Accordingly, the House of Lords held that Beer could recover the £360 interest.

The common law provides for a number of exceptions to this principle. Firstly, part-payment of a debt will constitute sufficient consideration if it is accompanied by something else requested by the creditor. In *Pinnel's Case*, Lord Coke referred to 'the gift of a horse, hawk or robe', but more modern examples would include early payment in part of the debt, payment in kind, or part-payment in a different location. It used to be the case that part-payment by cheque could satisfy the whole debt, but this is no longer the case.[109] It is important to note that the creditor, not the debtor, must request the new element.[110] This is to ensure that financially vulnerable creditors cannot be bullied by debtors who are aware of the creditor's financial troubles (although, today, such creditors would be protected by the doctrine of economic duress).

The following two common law exceptions are more specific and their conceptual justification for not being subject to the general rule is somewhat elusive. The second exception occurs where a debtor has multiple creditors and he enters into an arrangement (known as a 'composition agreement') with them, whereby he promises to pay them all a percentage of what they are owed. In this case, the percentage paid will satisfy the full debt and no creditor can recover more than that percentage.[111] The final common law exception is that where the debtor's debt is paid in part by a third party, the creditor cannot recover the balance from the debtor.[112]

The strict rule laid down in *Pinnel's Case* and evidenced in *Foakes v Beer* has been criticized on a number of grounds. Firstly, it is arguably unfair to permit a creditor

 Economic duress is discussed at p 267

---

109. *Hirachand Punamchand v Temple* [1911] 2 KB 330 (CA).

110. *D & C Builders Ltd v Rees* [1966] 2 QB 617 (CA).

111. *Good v Cheesman* (1831) 2 B & Ad 328.

112. *Welby v Drake* (1825) 1 C & P 557; *Hirachand Punamchand v Temple* [1911] 2 KB 330 (CA).

to recover full payment when he has freely promised to accept part-payment (as was the case in *Foakes v Beer*).

Secondly, the rule appears to be commercially unrealistic. Businesses will often accept part-payment of a debt in full satisfaction, provided that payment is made early. They regard certain part-payment now to be preferable to possible part-payment later.

To mitigate the harshness of the common law rule in *Pinnel's Case*, equity has provided a means to evade the part-payment rule where it appeared just to do so—namely, the doctrine of promissory estoppel. As we shall see, however, promissory estoppel is a second-best solution, because it merely suspends the creditor's rights, whereas a finding of sufficient consideration extinguishes the creditor's rights completely.

Promissory estoppel

The distinction between the common law and equity is discussed at p 9

As we noted in Chapter 1, equity exists as supplementary system of law to mitigate the harshness of common law rules. Nowhere is this more evident than in relation to the part-payment of debt, where the equitable doctrine of promissory estoppel has significant mitigated the harshness of the rule in *Pinnel's Case*. Promissory estoppel applies where *A* promises not to enforce his strict legal rights, and *B* relies on this promise. If *A* goes back on his promise and tries to enforce his strict legal rights against *B*, he will be estopped (prevented) from doing so, although normally *A* can revert to his strict legal rights after a period of reasonable notice has elapsed.

The application of promissory estoppel to the part-payment of debt was first established in the following case.

Central London Property Trust Ltd v High Trees House Ltd [1947] KB 130 (KB)

FACTS: In September 1937, the claimant let a block of flats to the defendant for ninety-nine years at a ground rent of £2,500 per year. The defendant would generate a profit by subletting the flats to others, which it was able to do for several years. But by January 1940, due to wartime conditions, many of the flats were empty and the defendant could not afford the ground rent. The claimant agreed to halve the ground rent to £1,250, but no time limit was established for this arrangement. Come September 1945, the flats were once again full. In 1946, the claimant initiated friendly proceedings to recover full rent from September 1945 onwards.

HELD: The High Court held that the reduced rent arrangement was meant to apply only when wartime conditions rendered the flats empty. Once this ended, the claimant was once again entitled to full rent. Accordingly, its claim succeeded. It was clear, however, that this was merely a test claim and that the claimant intended to attempt to recover the full rent for the period 1940–45, which, under the rule in *Pinnel's Case*, it would be entitled to do. Denning J (as he then was), relying on the already existing doctrine of equitable estoppel established by the House of Lords in *Hughes v Metropolitan Railway Company*,[113] pre-empted this by stating *obiter* that the doctrine of promissory estoppel would prevent the claimant from claiming full rent for the period. It is this *dictum*, and not the actual decision, that forms the most important and most controversial element of this case.

---

113. (1877) 2 App Cas 439 (HL).

It could be argued that Denning J's *obiter* was inconsistent with *Foakes v Beer*. Denning circumvented this criticism (not entirely successfully) by stating that the House in *Foakes v Beer* had not considered applying the doctrine of equitable estoppel and, had it done so, the case might have been decided differently. The problem with this reasoning is that *Hughes v Metropolitan Railway Company* was decided only seven years before *Foakes*, and Lords Selborne and Blackburn sat on both cases. Therefore, it would seem more likely that the House of Lords did not consider equitable estoppel to be relevant, as opposed to them merely forgetting to consider it.

In *High Trees*, Denning J's account of promissory estoppel lacked accuracy. In 1951, he therefore set out the requirements for promissory estoppel in more detail:

> where one party has, by his words or conduct, made to the other a promise…which was intended to affect the legal relations between them and to be acted on accordingly, then, once the other party has taken him at his word and acted on it, the one who gave the promise or assurance cannot afterwards be allowed to revert to the previous legal relations as if no such promise or assurance had been made by him, but he must accept their legal relations subject to the qualification which he himself has so introduced, even though it is not supported in point of law by any consideration but only by his word.[114]

From this statement and subsequent cases, it is generally regarded that the requirements for promissory estoppel are as follows.

1. There must be a clear and unequivocal promise, by words or conduct, that strict legal rights will not be enforced.
2. The promise must have been intended to have legal effect and to be relied on.
3. The promisee must rely on the promise.
4. It must be inequitable for the promisor to go back on his promise.

The first requirement is that one of the parties must clearly and unequivocally promise that he will not enforce his strict legal rights under the contract.[115] In *High Trees*, the claimant was entitled to £2,500 rent per year under the contract, but he clearly promised to accept £1,250. The promise must be clear and precise, but need not be express. A promise may be implied if sufficiently clear,[116] but silence or inaction will usually not suffice, because these are equivocal acts.[117]

The second and third requirements are that the promise must have been intended to have legal effect and to be relied on, and that the promisee must rely on the promise. There has been debate on what exactly constitutes 'reliance'. It is often assumed that, in order for reliance to be present, the promisee must have acted to his detriment, but there is no convincing authority for this proposition. Certainly, in *High Trees*, the defendant did not suffer any detriment by accepting half-rent for five years. Therefore it has come to be accepted that the promisee does not need to have suffered a detriment, but that he does need to have 'altered [his] position' in reliance

---

114. *Combe v Combe* [1951] 2 KB 215 (CA) 220.
115. *Woodhouse Israel Cocoa Ltd v Nigerian Produce Marketing Co Ltd* [1972] AC 741 (HL).
116. *Hughes v Metropolitan Railway Company* (1877) 2 App Cas 439 (HL).
117. *Allied Marine Transport Ltd v Vale do Rio Doce Navegacao SA (The Leonidas D)* [1985] 1 WLR 925 (CA).

of the promise.[118] Denning MR later interpreted this to mean that the promisee 'must have been led to act differently from what he otherwise would have done'.[119] It follows that if the promisee does nothing in reliance of the promise and continues to do what would have been done anyway, promissory estoppel will not arise.[120]

The fourth requirement is that it must be inequitable for the promisor to go back on his promise and enforce his strict legal rights.[121] Going back on a promise will not always be inequitable, as the following case demonstrates.

 D & C Builders Ltd v Rees [1966] 2 QB 617 (CA)

FACTS: The claimant had carried out repair work on the defendant's shop, for which it was owed £482. The claimant was close to insolvency. Knowing this, the defendant offered it £300 in full satisfaction of the debt, adding that if it were to refuse, it would get nothing. The claimant accepted this, but later sued for the remaining £182. The defendant pleaded promissory estoppel as a defence.

HELD: The Court of Appeal held that the claimant could recover the balance of the debt. Whilst the claimant had promised not to enforce its strict legal rights and had gone back on that promise, it was not inequitable for it to go back on that promise and enforce its strict legal rights. It was the defendant who had acted inequitably by attempting to take advantage of the claimant's financial vulnerability.

In addition to these four requirements, the courts have imposed an additional limitation on the use of promissory estoppel—namely, that it can only be used as a 'shield' and not as a 'sword'. This means that it can only be used as a defence and cannot be used to found a cause of action.

 Combe v Combe [1951] 2 KB 215 (CA)

FACTS: The claimant and defendant divorced. Shortly before the divorce, the defendant (the husband) promised to pay his soon-to-be ex-wife annual maintenance payments of £100. In reliance on this, she did not make a formal application to the court for maintenance payments. He failed to make any payments. Nearly seven years later, the claimant initiated proceedings to recover the maintenance owed to her. She had not provided any consideration for her husband's promise, so she based her claim on promissory estoppel. Her husband made a promise, on which she relied and altered her position (by not applying for maintenance to the court). By not paying, her husband had gone back on his promise and she contended that he should be estopped from doing so.

HELD: Although she met the requirements for promissory estoppel, she was attempting to use it as a sword (to found a cause of action). Because it cannot be used this way, the Court of Appeal rejected her claim.

---

118. *WJ Alan & Co Ltd v El Nasr Export & Import Co* [1972] 2 QB 189 (CA).
119. Ibid, 213.
120. *Scandinavian Trading Tanker Co AB v Flota Petrolera Ecuatoriana (The Scaptrade)* [1983] QB 529 (CA).
121. *Hughes v Metropolitan Railway Company* (1877) 2 App Cas 439 (HL).

COMMENT: The 'shield, not sword' rule does not mean that promissory estoppel can only be used by defendants and not claimants. Promissory estoppel may be used by a claimant who has an independent cause of action against *X* to prevent *X* from setting up by way of defence a strict legal right that he (*X*) has promised the claimant not to enforce.

Having discussed the conditions under which promissory estoppel will arise, we now need to discuss the effect of promissory estoppel.

Generally, the effect of promissory estoppel is to suspend rights, not extinguish them. In *High Trees* (discussed above), the finding of promissory estoppel was not to extinguish the right to full payment of rent, but merely to suspend it until the war-time conditions had passed. It follows that the promisor may, on giving due notice, reassert his strict legal rights.[122]

Tool Metal Manufacturing Co v Tungsten Electric Co Ltd (No 3) [1955] 1 WLR 761 (HL)

FACTS: The claimant owned the patent rights to certain metal alloys. It granted the defendant the right to import, manufacture, use, and sell the patented alloys, in return for royalty payments. The agreement also provided that the defendant could only manufacture a certain volume of alloy per month and that, if this volume were exceeded, it would have to pay compensation to the claimant. Following the outbreak of World War II, the claimant agreed to suspend the compensation clause. In 1945, the claimant claimed to have revoked the suspension and was once again entitled to receive compensation. This action failed, because adequate notice was not provided to the defendant. In 1951, the claimant commenced proceedings, claiming compensation from 1 January 1947.

HELD: By the time of the 1951 claim, the defendant was clearly aware that the claimant wished to revert to the original agreement. Therefore, the House of Lords held that the claimant had provided sufficient notice and effectively revoked its promise, thereby entitling it to the compensation for the period claimed.

⭐ See JC Smith, 'Waiver of Contractual Rights' (1955) 18 MLR 609

Despite the general rule that promissory estoppel is suspensory, it does appear that, in certain cases, the operation of promissory estoppel will extinguish rights. Such a case would be where, following the promise, 'the promisee cannot resume his position'[123] (that is, he cannot revert to his strict contractual position).

‹› Key points summary

- Consideration can be simply defined as the price for which the promise of the other is bought.

- Both parties are required to provide consideration in order to create a binding contract (unless the contract is made by deed).

---

122. *Birmingham and District Land Co v London & North Western Railway Co* (1888) 40 Ch D 268 (CA).

123. *Ajayi v RT Briscoe (Nigeria) Ltd* [1964] 1 WLR 1326 (PC) 1330 (Lord Hodson).

- Consideration may be executory (yet to be completed), executed (completed), or past (where the promise follows the act).

- Past consideration is no consideration. Where the promisor requested an act and it was understood by both parties that the act would be remunerated, the consideration will not be past.

- Consideration must be sufficient (that is, of value in the eyes of the law), but it need not be adequate (that is, of equal value).

- Performance of, or the promise to perform, an existing legal duty or an existing contractual obligation does not generally constitute good consideration, but it may where the other party obtains a 'practical benefit' or avoids a disbenefit.

- Generally, part-payment of a debt is not sufficient consideration—but a party who promises to accept part-payment may be estopped from going back on that promise if the court considers it inequitable to allow him to do so.

Intention to create legal relations

The fifth and final ingredient of a binding contract is that the parties must have an objective intention to create legal relations. This requirement is clearly based on public policy—notably, the desire to avoid opening the floodgates of litigation by giving legal effect to every form of agreement. Speaking specifically of familial agreements, Atkin LJ stated that 'the small Courts in this country would have to be multiplied one hundredfold if these arrangements were held to result in legal obligations'.[124] It is open to the parties specifically to indicate in the agreement that there is an intention to create legal relations. In the absence of such an agreement, the courts rely on two rebuttable presumptions in order to determine the existence of intention.

Social and domestic agreements

The presumption is that social, domestic, or family agreements will not have contractual force, because the parties will clearly not intend a contract to be created. But it is only a presumption, which, on the facts of the case, may be rebutted.

The following two cases demonstrate this: the first case demonstrates the presumption in action; the second case demonstrates its rebuttal.

 Balfour v Balfour [1919] 2 KB 571 (CA)

FACTS: The defendant worked as a civil servant in Ceylon (now Sri Lanka). The claimant (his wife) remained in England due to health problems. The husband agreed to pay his wife £30 maintenance every month. Their relationship soon broke down and the husband ceased payment of the £30. The wife sued.

---

124. *Balfour v Balfour* [1919] 2 KB 571 (CA) 579.

HELD: Her claim failed. The presumption was that such a familial agreement contained no contractual intention, unless the wife could rebut this presumption. On the facts, the Court of Appeal held that she had failed to do this.

 ***Merritt v Merritt* [1970] 1 WLR 1211 (CA)**

FACTS: In 1941, a husband and wife married. In 1949, they built a matrimonial home, which, in 1966, was put into their joint names. Shortly afterwards, the husband left to live with another woman. The husband agreed to pay the wife £40 per month, out of which the wife agreed to pay off the mortgage. The husband then signed a document stating that, in consideration of the wife paying all of the charges in connection with the house until the mortgage repayments were completed, he would transfer the house to the wife's sole ownership. The wife paid off the mortgage, but the husband refused to transfer the house. The wife sued. The husband stated that, because the agreement was a domestic one, it was presumed that there was no intention to create legal relations.

HELD: In *Balfour*, the agreement between the parties was made when the parties' relationship was amicable, thereby creating the presumption that there was no intention to be legally bound. Conversely, in *Merritt*, the agreement was made when the couple was separated. Where a couple is separated, or is about to separate, the presumption will be rebutted and an intention to create legal relations will be presumed. Accordingly, the Court of Appeal held that the house should be transferred to the claimant.

Although both of the above cases concerned familial agreements, the presumption equally applies to other social or domestic agreements, such as:

- a 'car pool' agreement whereby a group of persons contribute to the petrol costs of one person who drives them all to work;[125]
- the right to take part in a golf club's tournament;[126]
- an agreement between a group of friends who had formed a band (Spandau Ballet) and had agreed to play a number of musical performances.[127]

Commercial agreements

One of the aims of contract law is to create an environment in which businesses can contract efficiently and inexpensively, without undue interference from the law. Requiring businesses to establish an intention to create legal relations would be an undue and unnecessary obstacle, so the law presumes that commercial agreements are to have contractual force.

---

125. *Coward v Motor Insurers' Bureau* [1963] 1 QB 259 (CA).
126. *Lens v Devonshire Club*, The Times, 4 December 1914.
127. *Hadley v Kemp* [1999] EMLR 589 (Ch).

Edwards v Skyways Ltd [1964] 1 WLR 349 (QB)

FACTS: The defendant employed the claimant as an airline pilot. He was made redundant, and his employment contract gave him two options regarding his pension:

1. he could either recover the contributions that he had made; or

2. he could receive his full pension when he reached the age of 50.

The British Airline Pilots Association had obtained a further agreement that, if the claimant chose the first option, the defendant would make the claimant an *ex gratia* payment equal to his pension contribution. The claimant accepted this, but the defendant failed to make the *ex gratia* payment, contending that the agreement was not intended to create legal relations. The claimant sued for breach of contract.

HELD: The claimant was successful. Because the agreement was a commercial one, there was a heavy onus placed on the defendant to argue that there was no intention to create legal relations. The High Court held that the defendant had failed to establish this. The fact that the payment was described as *ex gratia* was not enough to rebut the presumption.

It can therefore be seen that this presumption is extremely difficult to rebut and that a party will need to adduce strong evidence in order to do so. A party in a commercial relationship does, however, have options available to it if it wishes to rebut the intention that the agreement is a binding one.

- *Honour clauses*   An honour clause is a clause inserted into the agreement that states that the agreement simply records the intention of the parties and is binding in honour, but not in law. Generally, the inclusion of such a clause will effectively negative any intention to create legal relations.[128]

- *Agreements 'subject to contract'*   Very often, agreements will be entered into 'subject to contract'. The phrase is usually used to indicate that the agreement is simply an 'agreement to agree', pending the creation of the formal contract. As such, the inclusion of the phrase will normally rebut the presumption and no contract will exist.

Finally, we need briefly to discuss an exception to this presumption—namely, collective bargaining agreements. A collective bargaining agreement is an agreement between employers and trade unions, and usually relates to working conditions, rates of pay, etc. The common law provided that, even though such agreements are clearly commercial in nature, they are not intended to be prima facie binding.[129] The reason for this is that such agreements are often merely expressions of aspirations, and are usually written in extremely general and imprecise language. The Trade Union and Labour Relations (Consolidation) Act 1992, s 179, now states that such agreements are 'conclusively presumed' not to be binding, unless expressly stated otherwise in writing. The incorporation of a collective bargaining

---

128. *Rose and Frank Co v JR Crompton and Bros Ltd* [1925] AC 445 (HL).
129. *Ford Motor Co Ltd v Amalgamated Union of Engineering and Foundry Workers* [1969] 2 QB 303 (QB).

agreement into an employee's employment contract will, however, be presumed to be binding.[130]

 Key points summary

- A contract will only be valid if both parties have an objective intention to create legal relations.

- Where the agreement is social or domestic, there is a rebuttable presumption that there is no intention to create legal relations.

- Where the agreement is commercial, there is a very strong rebuttable presumption that the agreement was intended to create legal relations.

- The use of 'honour clauses' or the phrase 'subject to contract' is usually enough to rebut the presumption that a commercial agreement is to have legal effect.

- Collective bargaining agreements are not legally binding, unless they expressly indicate otherwise.

Chapter conclusion

Business is conducted through a series of voluntary exchanges and transactions entered into with other parties. Accordingly, what constitutes a contract and exactly when a contract comes into existence are crucial to the running of a business. Ultimately, a contract is little more than a series of ingredients, which, if present, create binding rights and obligations that can be enforced in court. To ensure that a business has the right to hold others to account for a failure to provide it with what was agreed, it will wish to ensure that the transactions into which it enters have legally binding status. This, in turn, will require those who run businesses to have a thorough appreciation of what ingredients are needed to create legally binding obligations. In most cases, should one of the five ingredients discussed be lacking, a contract will fail to exist and businesses will be unable to enforce the terms of the agreement. This could prove extremely costly—especially where obtaining goods and services from others is central to the operation of the business, and these goods and services are not supplied.

Self-test questions

1. Define the following:
    (a) offer;
    (b) acceptance;
    (c) consideration;
    (d) promissory estoppel.

2. Explain the distinction between a bilateral and a unilateral contract.

---

130. *Robertson v British Gas Corporation* [1983] ICR 351 (CA).

3. Expensive Gadgets Ltd operates a website (ExpensiveGadgets.co.uk) specializing in selling new mobile phones. The website offers customers the opportunity to pre-order an iPhone, but due to a mistake by the web designer, the phone is advertised for £9.99, instead of £99.99. Thousands of customers pre-order the phone and receive an email confirming their pre-order. A day later, customers receive another email, informing them that the stated price was incorrect and that the phone actually costs £99.99; it also confirms that their order has been cancelled and that they will need to re-order at the correct price. Can the customers hold Expensive Gadgets Ltd to the £9.99 price?

4. Steel Smelting Ltd offers to sell 1,000 tonnes of reinforced steel girders to Rees Construction Ltd. Rees Construction Ltd accepts the offer by letter, the letter also informing Steel Smelting where the girders should be delivered. The letter is lost in the post and Steel Smelting Ltd sells the girders to a third party. Has acceptance occurred in this situation and, if so, when did it occur?

5. Read the case of *Williams v Roffey Bros & Nicholls (Contractors) Ltd*[131] and answer the following.
   (a) What effect do you think this case has had on the principle in *Stilk v Myrick*?
   (b) Could the Court have reached the same decision using the doctrine of promissory estoppel? If so, why did it not do so?
   (c) Do you think the 'practical benefit' approach should apply to cases involving part-payment of a debt? Why has it not done so to date?

6. Every year, Tom, Helen, and Dave (who are friends) each contribute £100 and place a £300 bet on a horse in the Grand National, with any winnings being split equally three ways. Dave is at the betting shop, and Tom and Helen send him a text message stating that if he puts in their £100, they will pay him back later. Dave places a £300 bet on a horse at five to one. The horse wins and Dave collects £1,500 from the betting shop—but he refuses to share the winnings with Tom and Helen, and is refusing to accept the £100 that they claim to owe him. Does a binding contract exist in this situation?

7. Will an agreement that has terms missing always be held not to be a contract on the grounds of uncertainty?

Further reading

Beale, HG, Bishop, WD, and Furmston, MP, *Contract: Cases and Materials* (5th edn, OUP, Oxford, 2008) ch 6
Provides a detailed account of the law relating to consideration and contains a number of extracts from cases discussed in this chapter

Capps, D, 'Electronic Mail and the Postal Rule' (2004) 15 ICCLR 207
Discusses when acceptance occurs in relation to contracts by email and argues that the postal rule should not apply to such contracts

Hepple, BA, 'Intention to Create Legal Relations' [1970] CLJ 122
Discusses the purpose and effect of the requirement of an intention to create legal relations

---

131. [1991] 1 QB 1 (CA).

Howarth, W, 'The Meaning of Objectivity in Contract' (1984) 100 MLR 265
Discusses what is meant by 'objectivity' in contract, and rejects promisor and promisee
  objectivity in favour of an entirely objective approach

Koffman, L, and Macdonald, E, *The Law of Contract* (6th edn, OUP, Oxford, 2007) ch 2
A clear and accessible account of the law relating to offer and acceptance

O'Sullivan, J, 'In Defence of *Foakes v Beer'* (1996) 55 CLJ 219
Provides an excellent analytical discussion of Williams v Roffey Bros, *and argues that*
  the law relating to existing contractual performance and part-payment should be
  harmonized by reverting to the strict rule in Foakes v Beer

Poole, J, *Textbook on Contract Law* (9th edn, OUP, Oxford, 2008) ch 5
Discusses how the law determines the existence of an intention to create legal relations

Remember to visit the **Online Resource Centre** at **<http://www.
oxfordtextbooks.co.uk/roach>** to access the following resources on
Chapter 6, 'The formation of the contract': more **practice questions** and
answers; a **glossary** of key terms; **multiple-choice questions**; **revision
summaries**; **audio updates** when relevant; **diagrams** in pdf; and **audio
exam advice** on this key topic.

7 The terms of the contract

- Express terms
- Implied terms
- Conditions, warranties, and innominate terms
- Exclusion clauses
- The interpretation of contractual terms

INTRODUCTION

In the previous two chapters, we focused on the pre-contractual process—namely, who has the ability to contract, what formalities are required, and what are the necessary ingredients for a valid contract. In this chapter, we move on to discuss the actual contents of a contract. Contracts are made up of terms, which will set out the rights and obligations of all of the parties involved. These terms come in a number of different forms and derive from a number of different sources. The parties may expressly agree terms, but other terms may be imposed upon the parties by statute, the courts, or through custom. Because businesses conduct virtually all transactions through contract, it is vital that they appreciate all of the sources from which terms can potentially derive.

Terms may be fundamental to the operation of the contract, or they may be ancillary and relatively minor. Terms can be classified in a number of different ways, but from the point of view of determining the origin and extent of a contract's terms, the crucial classification that needs to be understood is the distinction between express and implied terms. Only by having a thorough understanding of express and implied terms can a business meet its obligations, and protect itself should the contract not proceed as smoothly as planned.

Express terms

Terms that the parties have specifically negotiated should form part of the contract are known as 'express terms', because they are included at the express wishes of the parties. Where the terms of a contract are in writing, identifying the express terms poses little problems and, in the event of a dispute, all that the court is required to do is to interpret and apply the terms as written. Problems arise, however, when a contract is made orally, based upon the negotiations of the parties. Not every promise made during negotiations will amount to a term: certain oral statements will be 'mere puffs' that will have no legal standing and will never provide any form of remedy.

Many advertisements that we see contain statements that are clearly not meant to be taken seriously (for example, washing powders that clean 'whiter than white'); clearly, such statements are not meant to be taken literally and relied upon, and so will amount to unactionable 'puffs'. But other statements may constitute more than a puff and may amount to either a term or a mere representation. As we shall see, the ability to distinguish between terms and mere representations is fundamental in determining the extent of the rights and obligations imposed under a contract.

➡ representation: a pre-contractual statement concerning some fact or belief that is designed to induce a party into entering a contract

Terms and mere representations

Terms are contractual undertakings that set out the rights and obligations of the parties, which, if not complied with, can result in an action for breach of contract. Conversely, mere representations are simple statements made to induce the other party to contract, but which are not intended to form part of the contract and which will not give rise to an action for breach of contract (although, as we shall see in Chapter 8, they may result in the contract being set aside on the ground of misrepresentation).

➡ breach of contract: failure to comply with a term of the contract

Distinguishing between terms and representations can be extremely difficult in practice, as the following example demonstrates.

➡ misrepresentation: a false statement that induces a party to enter into a contract

---

Eg **Terms and representations**

Tom hears that his friend, Dave, is selling his car. Tom visits Dave to inspect the car. During the inspection, Dave says: 'That is an excellent car. Only 20,000 miles on the clock, has never broken down, and has never been involved in an accident.' Tom carries out a thorough inspection of the car and, when he is finished, Dave states: 'The car is yours for £5,000.' Tom accepts. Tom later discovers that the car's odometer has actually been once around the clock and has therefore done 120,000 miles, and that three years previously, it was involved in a serious accident. Two weeks after Tom purchases the car, it starts to develop serious mechanical faults. Tom wishes to return the car and recover his money, but Dave refuses.

There is little doubt that Dave's offer is a valid term, as is Tom's acceptance. But because Tom has paid the £5,000 and Dave has delivered the car, neither term has been breached. The issue is whether the statements made by Dave regarding the quality of the car are terms or mere representations. If they are terms, Tom will have a valid claim for breach of contract. If they are mere representations, Dave will not have breached the contract and Tom will have to base his claim in misrepresentation.

➡ exclusion clause: a term in a contract that excludes or limits liability for breach of contract or other civil wrong

---

The practical importance of the distinction lies in the determination of a remedy. The remedies for breach of contract differ from those for misrepresentation. Subject to an effective exclusion clause, breach of contract automatically entitles the claimant to damages and he may also be able to obtain other remedies to enforce the contract—notably, specific performance. Conversely, an actionable misrepresentation does not provide an automatic right to damages and specific performance is not available. But if the claimant wishes to escape from a contract, then misrepresentation provides greater opportunity, because all forms of misrepresentation permit

➡ damages: an award of money that is designed to compensate loss

➡ specific performance: a court order requiring performance of an act, normally to fulfil a contract

➡ rescission:
the termination of a
contract

rescission, whereas only breaches of fundamental terms will give rise to the right to terminate. Accordingly, from a remedial viewpoint, the distinction is of considerable practical importance.

The courts, when determining whether a particular statement is a term or a representation, will look objectively at the words and conduct of the parties in order to determine whether the parties intended the representation to amount to a term or not.[1] Note that the test is objective, not subjective. Therefore, the courts are not concerned with the actual intentions of the parties, but rather their intentions, as evidenced by their words and conduct. As Denning LJ (as he then was) stated, the status of a representation 'depends on the conduct of the parties, on their words and behaviour, rather than on their thoughts'.[2] The reason for this is that, in the majority of cases, the parties will not have an intention concerning the legal status of a particular statement and so a subjective intention will not exist.[3] This objectivity of the test can be seen in the following case.

Thake v Maurice [1986] QB 644 (CA)

FACTS: Mr and Mrs Thake (the claimants) did not wish to conceive any more children, and so approached the defendant surgeon to enquire about Mr Thake having a vasectomy. The surgeon explained that the procedure was irreversible, but failed to inform the Thakes that, in a small number of cases, the vasectomy might reverse itself naturally. The operation was performed. Believing the operation to be a success, the Thakes had unprotected sex and gave no thought to the possibility that Mrs Thake might become pregnant. The procedure naturally reversed itself and, by the time that Mrs Thake realized she was pregnant, it was too late to abort the pregnancy. The Thakes sued, alleging that it was a term of the contract that the procedure would render Mr Thake sterile and that, because he was not, the surgeon had breached the contract.

HELD: The Court of Appeal noted that this case demonstrated why the subjective intentions of the parties cannot be the relevant test. The Thakes believed that the statements made by the surgeon would guarantee Mr Thake's sterility, whereas, from the surgeon's point of view, no such promise was made. Accordingly, a subjective test would have been no use. Applying an objective test, the Court held that a reasonable person would know that 'the results of medical treatment are to some extent unpredictable'[4] and that therefore 'such a person would not have left thinking that the defendant had given a guarantee that Mr. Thake would be absolutely sterile'.[5] Accordingly, the Thakes' claim for breach of contract failed, but the Court did hold that, in failing to warn the Thakes of the risk of natural reversal, the surgeon had acted negligently, and so the Court awarded the Thakes £11,177.

★ See A Grubb,
'Failed Sterilisation: Is
a Claim in Contract
or Negligence
a Guarantee of
Success?' [1986] 45
CLJ 197

---

1. *Heilbut, Symons & Co v Buckleton* [1913] AC 30 (HL).
2. See *Oscar Chess Ltd v Williams* [1957] 1 WLR 370 (CA) 375.
3. SA Smith, *Atiyah's Introduction to the Law of Contract* (6th edn, Clarendon Press, Oxford, 2005) 134.
4. *Thake v Maurice* [1986] QB 644 (CA) 685 (Neill LJ).
5. Ibid.

In practice, the objective test has proved problematic to apply, so, in order to ensure greater consistency, the courts have identified a number of factors that can be taken into account. It should be noted, however, that the courts have made clear that these various factors:

> cannot be said to furnish decisive tests, because it cannot be said as a matter of law that the presence or absence of those features is conclusive of the intention of the parties. The intention of the parties can only be deduced from the totality of the evidence, and no secondary principles of such a kind can be universally true.[6]

Timing

The timing of the statement in relation to the date on which the contract was created may be relevant. As a general rule, the longer the time between the making of the statement and the entering into of the contract, the less likely it will be that the statement was intended to be a term.

 Bannerman v White (1861) 10 CBNS 844

FACTS: Two parties were negotiating for the sale of hops. During negotiations, White (the defendant) indicated that he would not purchase hops that had been treated with sulphur and Bannerman (the claimant) assured White that sulphur had not been used. A short time later, a contract was concluded. It transpired that 5 of the 300 acres had been treated with sulphur. White argued that a term had been breached, thereby allowing him to terminate the contract and not pay the agreed price. Bannerman argued that, because the issue of sulphur had arisen in negotiations immediately prior to the contract being entered into, it could not constitute a term. Accordingly, Bannerman sued White for the contract price.

HELD: The importance of the statement, and the short period of time between its making and the contract being concluded, indicated that both parties objectively intended it to amount to a term. Accordingly, White was entitled to repudiate the contract.

This principle is not absolute, however, and cases exist in which the courts have found a statement to be a term, even though a protracted period existed between the statement and the contract's conclusion.[7] Similarly, the courts have found a statement to be a mere representation, even though it was only made one day before the contract was entered into.[8] Clearly, each case must be decided on its own facts.

The importance of the statement

The more important a statement is to one of the parties, the more likely it is to be a term. *Bannerman v White* (discussed above) provides a good example. If a statement is of such importance that the **representee** would not have entered into the contract

➡ **representee:** the party hearing the statement

---

6. *Heilbut, Symons & Co v Buckleton* [1913] AC 30 (HL) 50, 51 (Lord Moulton).
7. *Schawel v Reade* [1913] 2 IR 64 (HL).
8. *Hopkins v Tanqueray* (1854) 15 CB 130.

but for the making of the statement, then the statement will almost certainly amount to a term. The following case demonstrates this in practice.

> ### 🔑 J Evans & Son (Portsmouth) Ltd v Andrea Merzario Ltd [1976] 1 WLR 1078 (CA)
>
> **FACTS:** The claimant, an English company, had purchased some machinery from Italy. It employed the defendant to arrange transport, because they had had previous dealings. Because the machinery was prone to rusting, it was always stowed in crates or trailers below deck. The defendant changed its standard terms to indicate that items would be shipped in containers, not crates. The claimant agreed to the change in terms, provided that the containers were held below deck, and the defendant's representative gave oral assurances that this would be the case—but this oral assurance was never included in any subsequent written agreements. It transpired that the containers containing the claimant's goods were stored on deck, and, owing to rough seas, two containers fell overboard and were lost. The defendant argued that it had not breached the contract, because the oral assurance that its representative gave never amounted to a term.
>
> **HELD:** It was clear that the claimant only agreed to contract with the defendant on the basis that the containers were shipped below deck. Given the importance attached to the oral assurance of the defendant's representative, it was therefore held by the Court of Appeal to be a term of the contract (with Lord Denning believing it to be a term of a collateral contract), and the claimant could therefore recover damages for breach of contract.

⭐ See JN Adams, 'Exemption Clauses Overboard! Oral Assurance and Written Exemptions: Which Wins?' (1977) 40 MLR 223

The knowledge of the parties

Another relevant factor is the respective knowledge of the parties. In many contracts (especially consumer contracts), one party will rely considerably on the knowledge of the other. Parties with specialist knowledge are much more likely to be able to ascertain the truth of a statement than a party with no knowledge. Accordingly, statements made by parties with specialist knowledge are more likely to be regarded as terms, and statements made by those without specialist knowledge are more likely to amount to mere representations, as the following contrasting cases demonstrate.

> ### 🔑 Oscar Chess Ltd v Williams [1957] 1 WLR 370 (CA)
>
> **FACTS:** The defendant purchased a car from the claimant car dealer and traded in his old car in part-exchange. The registration book of the old car indicated that it was a Morris 10, first registered in 1948. Based on this, the claimant offer £290 part-exchange and this was accepted by the defendant. It transpired that the car was made in 1939 (there was no evidence that the defendant knew this) and so would have been worth only £175. On this basis, the claimant sued for breach of contract to recover the £115 difference.
>
> **HELD:** The Court of Appeal held that the statement indicating the car's age was a representation and not a term. The claimant had specialist knowledge, whereas the defendant did not, and so it was the claimant who was better placed to discover the true age of the car.

⭐ See O Daly, 'Innocent Misrepresentation or Term of the Contract?' (1957) 20 MLR 410

CHAPTER 7 **THE TERMS OF THE CONTRACT** | **209**

> ### Dick Bentley (Productions) Ltd v Harold Smith (Motors) Ltd [1965] 1 WLR 623 (CA)
>
> **FACTS:** The claimant approached the defendant car dealer and informed it that it wished to purchase a quality British second-hand car. The defendant confirmed that it had found such a car—namely, a Park Ward drop-head Bentley coupé. The defendant stated that the car had been fitted with a new engine and gearbox, and that, since then, it had only done 20,000 miles (the odometer reading confirmed this). The claimant purchased the car, whereupon mechanical faults developed almost immediately. It transpired that the car had done closer to 100,000 miles, although there was no evidence that the defendant knew this. The claimant sought damages for breach of contract.
>
> **HELD:** The defendant, being a specialist car dealer, was in a much better position to verify the car's history and determine the accuracy of the odometer reading than the claimant. Accordingly, the Court of Appeal held that the statement amounted to a term and the claimant's action succeeded.

★ See LS Sealy, 'Representations, Warranties, and the Reasonable Man' (1965) CLJ 178

Statements of opinion

As we shall see in Chapter 8, the general rule is that statements of opinion do not even amount to representations,[9] although they may do so where the court is of the opinion that a reasonable man possessing all of the knowledge of the **representor** could not have honestly held such an opinion.[10] In limited cases, however, it would appear that a statement of opinion might even amount to a term—namely, where the opinion states a fact that is difficult to verify.[11]

➡ **representor:** the party making a statement

✎ The legal status of statements of opinion is discussed at p 229

Statements inviting verification

If the representor invites the other party to verify the validity of the statement, it is highly unlikely that the statement will be regarded as a term. Thus, in *Ecay v Godfrey*,[12] the seller of a boat assured the buyer that it was seaworthy, but advised a survey nonetheless. The buyer bought the boat and a survey subsequently discovered that it was not seaworthy. The court held that the statement advising the buyer to verify the seaworthiness of the boat negatived any intention that he might have that such statement was to be a term. Accordingly, the statement amounted to a representation.

If, however, the representor specifically states that his statement can be relied upon and that no verification is required, the court will be likely to regard such a statement as a term. In *Schawel v Reade*,[13] the claimant required a horse for stud purposes. Whilst inspecting a horse belonging to the defendant, the defendant said: 'You need not look for anything; the horse is perfectly sound. If there was anything the matter with the horse I would tell you.' Satisfied by this, the claimant purchased the horse. The horse turned out to be violent and unsuitable as a stud, and the claimant sought his money back, alleging breach of contract. Because the defendant's

---

9. *Bisset v Wilkinson* [1927] AC 177 (PC).
10. *Smith v Land and House Property Corporation* (1884) 2 Ch D 7 (CA).
11. *Power v Barham* (1836) 4 A & E 473; cf *Jendwine v Slade* (1797) 2 Esp 571.
12. (1947) 80 Ll L Rep 286 (KB).   13. [1913] 2 IR 64 (HL).

statement was designed to prevent the claimant from discovering the truth, the House of Lords held it to be a term and the claimant's action succeeded.

The parol evidence rule

As noted above, where a contract is wholly in writing, identifying the express terms will be simple. But even though there is a written document, one party may still argue that it does not contain all of the terms and that additional terms were intended to be included. In order to establish this, the party will need to provide evidence indicating that additional terms were intended to form part of the contract. The ability to adduce such evidence is determined by what is known as the '**parol** evidence' rule, which provides that 'evidence cannot be admitted to add to, vary or contradict a deed or other written document'.[14] It has been correctly pointed out, however, that to describe this as a 'rule' is somewhat misleading, because, in reality, it merely establishes a presumption that a written contractual document contains all of the terms of the contract[15]—albeit a very strong one.[16] Accordingly, the presumption that a written document contains all of the terms can be rebutted if one party can show that other terms were intended to form part of the contract.

➜ **parol:** oral; not to be confused with 'parole', which means the early release of a prisoner

The rationale behind the rule is clearly to promote contractual certainty, by imposing a presumption that the only terms that can be relied on are those contained within the written document. But the rigid adherence to such a rule could result in injustice in certain individual cases. Accordingly, the courts have created a substantial number of exceptions, so many, in fact, that a Law Commission Working Paper stated that 'the exceptions were so numerous and so extensive that it might be wondered whether the rule itself had not been largely destroyed'.[17]

Exceptions or qualifications to the rule include the following.

- *Incompleteness*   If the court is of the opinion that the written document was not intended to represent the full extent of the agreement between the parties, then it will permit extrinsic evidence to be adduced.[18]

- *Implied terms*   The parol evidence rule applies only in the case of express terms. It does not exclude evidence being adduced that indicates that the contract contains an implied term.[19]

- *Invalidity*   The rule does not apply to any evidence that casts doubt upon the validity of the written contract (for example, lack of consideration or intention,[20] incapacity, misrepresentation, or mistake).[21]

---

14. *Jacobs v Batavia and General Plantations Trust Ltd* [1924] 1 Ch 287 (CA) 295 (Lawrence J).
15. L Koffman and E Macdonald, *The Law of Contract* (6th edn, OUP, Oxford, 2007) 115.
16. *Gillespie Bros & Co v Cheney, Eggar & Co* [1896] 2 QB 59 (QB).
17. Law Commission, *Law of Contract: The Parol Evidence Rule* (Law Com No 154, Cmnd 9700, HMSO, London, 1986) [1.3], citing Law Commission, *Law of Contract: The Parol Evidence Rule* (Working Paper No 70, HMSO, London, 1976).
18. *J Evans & Son (Portsmouth) Ltd v Andrea Merzario Ltd* [1976] 1 WLR 1078 (CA).
19. *Gillespie Bros & Co v Cheney Eggar & Co* [1896] 2 QB 59 (QB).
20. *Kleinwort Benson Ltd v Malaysia Mining Corporation Berhad* [1989] 1 WLR 379 (CA).
21. *Campbell Discount Co v Gall* [1961] 1 QB 431 (CA).

- *Rectification*   The written document may have failed to reflect the true intentions of the parties. In such a case, evidence can be adduced to indicate the party's true intentions[22] and, if accepted, the court will rectify the contract accordingly.

➜ rectification: the correction by the court of an error in a written document

- *Conditions precedent*   Extrinsic evidence can be adduced to establish that no contract exists because a condition precedent was not complied with.[23]

➜ condition precedent: a condition that must be complied with before a contract becomes operational

Two qualifications to the parol evidence rule deserve more detailed discussion—namely, the finding of a collateral contract and the use of 'entire agreement' clauses.

Collateral contracts

If, for some reason, a party cannot establish that a particular statement is a term of the contract (for example, because the parol evidence rule bars them from submitting evidence), the court may hold that the statement actually creates a second contract, known as a '**collateral** contract'. Breach of a term in a collateral contract is just as actionable as a breach of the main contract. Thus, in *Birch v Paramount Estates (Liverpool) Ltd*,[24] the defendant housing estate developers offered a house to the claimant, claiming that it would be of the same quality as the show home. Accordingly, the claimant entered into an agreement, but the contract made no mention of the developer's statement. The house was not of the same quality as the show home and the claimant initiated proceedings. The Court of Appeal held that the oral statement created a collateral contract, alongside the contract of sale, and accordingly awarded the claimant damages. The terms of a collateral contract can be enforced even when they conflict with the terms of the main contract.[25]

➜ collateral: parallel; running side by side

The device of the collateral contract has been described as 'a fudge, a cheat…[and an]…escape route'.[26] There is little doubt that it has been used effectively by the courts to avoid certain inconvenient principles of law—notably, the parol evidence rule,[27] with one commentator stating that '[i]t could be argued that the collateral contract device largely destroys the parol evidence rule'.[28] In the case of *Shanklin Pier Ltd v Detel Products Ltd*,[29] the High Court even used a collateral contract to avoid the doctrine of privity of contract.

🔗 The case of *Shanklin Pier* is discussed at p 147

The House of Lords has held that courts should not be too quick to find that a collateral contract exists and that such contracts 'must from their very nature be rare'.[30] There must be evidence adduced that objectively indicates an intention that the statement should form a collateral contract and not a mere representation. Failure to take a strict approach would have 'the effect of lessening the authority of written contracts by making it possible to vary them by suggesting the existence of verbal collateral agreements relating to the same subject-matter'.[31]

---

22. *Murray v Parker* (1854) 19 Beav 305.   23. *Pym v Campbell* (1856) 6 E & B 370.

24. (1956) 167 Estates Gazette 396 (CA).

25. *City and Westminster Properties (1934) Ltd v Mudd* [1959] Ch 129 (Ch).

26. R Taylor and D Taylor, *Contract Law: Directions* (OUP, Oxford, 2007) 110.

27. See Lord Wedderburn, 'Collateral Contracts' (1959) CLJ 58, 69, who states that the collateral contract 'eases the consciences of those who believe that the parol evidence rule is a strict and meaningful prohibition'.

28. E Peel, *Treitel on the Law of Contract* (12th edn, Sweet & Maxwell, London, 2007) 222.

29. [1951] 2 KB 854 (KB).

30. *Heilbut, Symons & Co v Buckleton* [1913] AC 30 (HL) 47 (Lord Moulton).

31. Ibid.

'Entire agreement' clauses

Parties who wish to ensure that oral statements do not become terms may attempt to do so by inserting an 'entire agreement' clause. Such a clause will normally state that the written document contains the entire terms of the contract and that no further terms can be added. An effectively drafted clause should prevent parol evidence being adduced and should also prevent any oral statements being regarded as the basis of a collateral contract. One commentator has, however, argued that such clauses do not prevent evidence being adduced that establishes the existence of a collateral contract[32]—but the High Court has since rejected this argument and stated overtly that, where a contract has a well-drafted entire agreement clause: 'It is unnecessary...to decide whether the alleged collateral warranty was ever given. Indeed it is...the whole purpose of the entire agreement clause that this further exercise should not have to be undertaken.'[33] Accordingly, a statement that would have had contractual effect as a term in a collateral contract will be deprived of such effect by the existence of an entire agreement clause.

It can be seen that there are numerous exceptions to the parol evidence rule. The number of exceptions initially caused the Law Commission to recommend abolition of the rule.[34] Following consultation, however, the Law Commission altered its position and recommended its retention—but noted, correctly, that the rule 'no longer has either the width or effect once attributed to it'.[35]

 Key points summary

- Express terms are those terms that have been specifically agreed upon by the parties.

- We need to be able to be able to distinguish between statements that amount to terms and statements that amount to representations. The former can give rise to an action in breach of contract. The latter can give rise to an action in misrepresentation.

- When distinguishing between terms and representations, the courts will try to ascertain the objective (not the actual) intentions of the parties. Relevant factors include the timing of the statement, the importance of the statement, the respective knowledge of the parties, and whether the representor invited the representee to verify the statement.

- The parol evidence rule states that evidence cannot be submitted that would seek to add to, or vary, the terms of a contract. But this rule only establishes a presumption that can be rebutted, and the courts have established a number of exceptions and qualifications

- An oral statement may be deemed not to be a term of the main contract, but it may establish a parallel, collateral contract.

---

32. H Beale, *Chitty on Contracts, Vol 1* (28th edn, Sweet & Maxwell, London, 1999) [12.102].

33. *Inntrepreneur Pub Co v East Crown Ltd* [2000] 2 Lloyd's Rep 611 (Ch) 615 (Lightman J).

34. See Law Commission, *Law of Contract: The Parol Evidence Rule* (Working Paper No 70, HMSO, London, 1976).

35. Law Commission, *Law of Contract: The Parol Evidence Rule* (Law Com No 154, Cmnd 9700, HMSO, London, 1986) [1.7].

- Parties who wish to provide that the written document contains all of the terms of the contract, and that such terms cannot be added to or varied, can do so by including an 'entire agreement' clause in the contract. Such a term can exclude the possibility of an oral statement forming a collateral contract.

Implied terms

The majority of terms in a contract will usually be express, but the ability of the parties to foresee and plan for eventualities and contingencies is limited. Parties may regard certain issues as so obvious that they do not need to be included in the contract. Parties may both operate within an industry or trade that has a set procedure or custom, and such procedures may be so well known and well established that the parties fail to include them in the contract. Accordingly, even carefully drafted contracts may be incomplete and, in reality, virtually all contracts will contain gaps of some kind. If the gaps are too large, the contract will be unenforceable on the grounds of uncertainty; if the gaps are not unacceptably substantial, they may be filled in by implying terms into the contract.

The rules relating to uncertainty are discussed at p 179

But the implication of terms runs counter to classical contract theory, which strongly advocates the exclusive right of the parties to determine the content of a contract. Accordingly, if classical theory is to be departed from, the courts will require a strong justification. The chosen justification of the court for its ability to imply terms into contracts has been 'necessity', but it can be argued that, in a number of the cases that will be examined, the implication of a term was by no means necessary. Consequently, a number of prominent commentators have argued that the rationale behind the implication of terms is not necessity, but rather the need to protect the reasonable expectations of the parties (or the courts' view of what the parties' reasonable expectations should be).[36]

Principally, implied terms fall under one of two headings:

- terms implied in law; and
- terms implied in fact.

The distinction between the two was set out neatly by Lord Denning:

[Implied terms in law concern] all those relationships which are of common occurrence. Such as the relationship of seller and buyer, owner and hirer, master and servant, landlord and tenant, carrier by land or by sea, contractor for building works, and so forth. In all those relationships the courts have imposed obligations on one party or the other, saying they are "implied terms". These obligations are not founded on the intention of the parties, actual or presumed, but on more general considerations…In such relationships the problem is not to be solved by asking what did the parties intend? Or would they have unhesitatingly agreed to it, if asked? It is to be solved by asking: has the law already

---

36. See Lord Steyn, 'Contract Law: Fulfilling the Reasonable Expectations of Honest Men' (1997) 113 LQR 433, 441; H Collins, *The Law of Contract* (4th edn, Butterworths, London, 2003) 246.

defined the obligation or the extent of it? If so, let it be followed. If not, look to see what would be reasonable in the general run of such cases.

[Implied terms in fact concern] those cases which are not within the first category. These are cases—not of common occurrence—in which from the particular circumstances a term is to be implied. In these cases the implication is based on an intention imputed to the parties from their actual circumstances...Such an imputation is only to be made when it is necessary to imply a term to give efficacy to the contract and make it a workable agreement in such manner as the parties would clearly have done if they had applied their mind to the contingency which has arisen...In such cases a term is not to be implied on the ground that it would be reasonable: but only when it is necessary and can be formulated with a sufficient degree of precision.[37]

From a theoretical perspective, the implication of terms is problematic. As noted, classical contract law theory is based upon the notion that the terms of a contract are to be determined by the parties and not by the courts. In respect of terms implied in fact, no problem arises, because such terms are implied based on the imputed intentions of the parties. But terms implied by the law may be completely at odds with the intentions of the parties and therefore appear to be theoretically irreconcilable with classical theory. In effect, the implication of terms in law involves the judges actually making a contract for the parties.[38]

Terms implied in fact

It may be that the court is of the opinion that the facts of a particular case merit the implication of a term. In such a case, the court will imply a term on the basis that the parties meant to include the term, but for some reason did not. Therefore, the implication of terms in fact is the court giving recognition to the unexpressed intentions of the parties and, accordingly, can be reconciled with classical contract theory.

Over the years, the courts have established a number of tests to determine whether to imply a term in fact, with the two principal tests being the 'business efficacy' test and the 'officious bystander' test, which were established respectively in the following two cases.

The Moorcock (1889) LR 14 PD 64 (CA)

FACTS: The claimant owned as ship called *The Moorcock*. The defendant owned a wharf and contracted with the claimant permitting him to dock his ship at a jetty, so that goods could be loaded and unloaded. The claimant did not have to pay for use of the jetty, but did have to pay for use of the cranes to load and unload goods, and the defendant earned commission from such usage. The jetty extended into the Thames and, at low tide, the ship would be grounded (would touch the river bed)—a fact known to both parties. At low tide, the ship was grounded on a ridge of hard ground and was damaged. The defendant

---

37. *Shell UK Ltd v Lostock Garage Ltd* [1976] 1 WLR 1187 (CA) 1196, 1197.
38. SA Smith, *Contract Theory* (OUP, Oxford, 2004) 280.

denied liability on the ground that there was no term in the contract guaranteeing the safety of the ship.

HELD: The defendant was liable for the damage caused. The defendant knew that the ship would be grounded at low tide and therefore the Court of Appeal implied a term into the contract providing that the defendant would take 'reasonable care to find out that the bottom of the river is reasonably fit for the purpose for which they agree that their jetty should be used'.[39] But the Court stated that a term should only be implied where it is necessary to 'give such business efficacy to the transaction as must have been intended at all events by both parties who are business men'.[40]

COMMENT: Bowen LJ's 'business efficacy' test has subsequently been interpreted to mean that the term must be 'necessary' to give a contract business efficacy. Whilst it can be argued that the term implied in *The Moorcock* was reasonable, it does not appear to be the case that the term was necessary to give the contract business efficacy. The contract would probably have been just as valid without the implied term. It could therefore be argued that the main issue to be determined in *The Moorcock* was which of the two parties should bear the loss. Did the Court really have to resort to implying a term into the contract to answer this question?

 Shirlaw v Southern Foundries (1926) Ltd [1939] 2 KB 206 (CA)

FACTS: In 1933, Shirlaw (the claimant) entered into a contract with Southern Foundries (the defendant), which provided that he would be managing director for ten years. In 1936, Southern Foundries was taken over by another company, which changed Southern Foundries' articles of association to allow it to remove Shirlaw from the company, which it did.

HELD: The Court of Appeal implied a term that Shirlaw would not be removed in this manner before the ten-year period had expired. MacKinnon LJ stated that the court will only imply a term if it is:

> something so obvious that it goes without saying; so that, if, while the parties were making their bargain, an officious bystander were to suggest some express provision for it in their agreement, they would testily suppress him with a common "Oh, of course!" [41]

The relationship between the two tests is somewhat unclear. It is certainly true that, in the majority of cases, the tests will produce the same result, leading commentators[42] and numerous judges[43] to argue that there is little difference between the two tests. In some cases, the courts have failed to comment on the relationship

---

39. *The Moorcock* (1889) LR 14 PD 64 (CA) 67 (Escher MR).
40. Ibid, 68 (Bowen LJ).
41. *Shirlaw v Southern Foundries (1926) Ltd* [1939] 2 KB 206 (CA) 227.
42. For example, A Phang, 'Implied Terms, Business Efficacy and the Officious Bystander: A Modern History' [1998] JBL 1, 24.
43. For example, *Reigate v Union Manufacturing Company (Ramsbottom) Ltd* [1918] KB 592 (CA) 605 (Scrutton LJ); *Lister v Romford Ice and Coal Storage Co Ltd* [1957] AC 555 (HL) 594 (Lord Tucker).

between the two tests, preferring to state vaguely that both tests provide 'a route to the presumed intention of the parties'.[44] In other cases, however, the courts have indicated that:

- they are 'distinct tests with the result that a term may sometimes be implied on the basis of one but not of the other'[45] and that, accordingly, satisfying either test will suffice;
- both tests must be satisfied before a term will be implied;[46]
- both tests can be merged and that a term will be implied where it would give 'such efficacy to the contract as the parties must have intended, as interpreted by the officious bystander'.[47]

Whilst the exact nature of the test may be unclear, what is clear is that the courts will not quickly imply a term into a contract. The above tests are relatively stringent and, as a consequence, the court has stated that, in certain circumstances, a term will not be implied in fact, as follows.

- A term will not be implied if it would conflict with an express term of the contract.[48]
- A term will not be implied if one party is ignorant of the facts on which the implied term would have been based.[49]
- The court is unlikely to imply a term where 'the parties have entered into a carefully drafted written contract containing detailed terms agreed between them'.[50]
- The court is unlikely to imply a term where it is unclear whether or not both parties would have agreed to the term, at the time that the contract was made.[51]
- The court is reluctant to imply a term in order to resolve a 'bitter and contentious' dispute.[52]

Terms implied in law

Terms implied by the courts

We have seen above that the courts may imply terms into a contract depending upon the facts of the case. In addition to implying terms in fact, the court can also imply terms in law, which leads us to question the difference between the two. Two main differences can be advanced.

1. When courts imply terms in fact, they do so on the basis of the idiosyncratic facts of the case. Accordingly, the term is what Atiyah called an 'individualized

---

44. *Richco International Ltd v Alfred C Toepfer International GmbH (The Bonde)* [1991] 1 Lloyd's Rep 136 (QB) 144 (Potter J).
45. *Ashmore v Corporation of Lloyd's (No 2)* [1992] 2 Lloyd's Rep 620 (QB) 627 (Gatehouse J).
46. *Stubbs v Trower Still and King* [1987] IRLR 321; *Association of British Travel Agents v British Airways plc* [2000] 1 Lloyd's Rep 169 (CA).
47. *Dellacassa and Associates Ltd v Wren Homes Ltd*, 8 December 1982 (CA) (Fox LJ).
48. *Duke of Westminster v Guild* [1985] QB 688 (CA).
49. *Spring v National Amalgamated Stevedores and Dockers Society* [1956] 1 WLR 585 (Ch).
50. *Shell UK Ltd v Lostock Garages Ltd* [1976] 1 WLR 1187 (CA) 1200 (Ormrod LJ).
51. *Luxor (Eastbourne) Ltd v Cooper* [1941] AC 108 (HL).
52. *Nicholson v Markham* (1998) 75 P & CR 428 (CA) 433 (Otton LJ).

implied term',[53] meaning that it is a 'one-off' or an 'individualized gap filler',[54] and does not establish a precedent that such terms should be implied in all contracts of that type in the future. Conversely, a term implied by law will establish a precedent that such a term should be implied in all similar contracts in the future (what Atiyah termed a 'standardized implied term'),[55] unless the term is validly excluded by, or is inconsistent with, the contract.[56]

2. Terms implied in fact are implied based upon the unexpressed intentions of the parties. Conversely, terms implied in law are not based upon the intentions of the parties at all, but are obligations that are imposed upon certain commonly arising contracts as necessary incidents of them (for example, employment contracts, sale of goods contracts, etc.).

These two points are evidenced in the following case.

 Liverpool City Council v Irwin [1977] AC 239 (HL)

FACTS: Liverpool City Council (the claimant) owned a dilapidated block of flats, within which Mr Irwin (the defendant) and his wife lived. The tenancy agreement imposed a number of obligations on the Irwins, but none on the Council. The lifts did not work, vandalism was rife, stair lighting was inadequate, and the rubbish chutes were often blocked. The Irwins therefore decided to withhold their rent as a protest, on the ground that the Council had breached an implied term of the contract—namely, to maintain adequately the common areas of the building.

HELD: The House of Lords agreed with the Irwins and implied a duty on the Council 'to take reasonable care to keep in reasonable repair and usability'[57] the communal areas of the building. On the facts, however, the House did not believe that the term had been breached.

COMMENT: It is clear that this was a term implied in law and not a term implied in fact for two reasons.

1. Terms implied in fact are only implied in the case in question, whereas in *Liverpool*, the House stated that such a term was to be implied into all contracts involving local authority and private lettings.

2. Terms implied in fact are based upon the imputed intentions of the parties, yet it was clear that the Council did not intend such a term to be implied.

★ See D McIntyre, 'Implied Obligations of Landlords: High-rise Blocks' (1976) 35 CLJ 25

Whilst the court may have unanimously agreed that a term should be implied, it could not agree on when such a term should be implied. Lord Denning in the Court of Appeal and Lord Cross in the House of Lords thought that a term should be implied in law where 'in the general run of such cases the term in question would be one which it would be reasonable to insert'.[58] But Lords Edmund-Davies, Salmon,

---

53. SA Smith, *Atiyah's Introduction to the Law of Contract* (6th edn, Clarendon Press, Oxford, 2005) 157.

54. *Society of Lloyd's v Clementson* [1995] CLC 117 (CA) 131 (Steyn LJ).

55. SA Smith, *Atiyah's Introduction to the Law of Contract* (6th edn, Clarendon Press, Oxford, 2005) 159.

56. *Lynch v Thorne* [1956] 1 WLR 303 (CA).

57. *Liverpool City Council v Irwin* [1977] AC 239 (HL) 256 (Lord Wilberforce).

58. Ibid, 258 (Lord Cross).

and Wilberforce were of the opinion that the 'touchstone is always necessity and not merely reasonableness'.[59] Subsequent authority has indicted that the test of necessity has prevailed, and it is now clear that two requirements must be fulfilled before the court will imply a term in law: '[T]he first requirement is that the contract in question should be a contract of a defined type...The second requirement is that the implication of the term should be necessary.'[60]

'[C]ontracts of a defined type' refers to certain commonly occurring contracts, the main examples being employment contracts, contracts involving the sale of goods, and contracts between landlord and tenant. Determining whether such a contract exists is normally a straightforward matter. The test of 'necessity' is slightly more complex. What is clear is that the test of necessity in relation to terms implied in law is nowhere near as strict as the necessity test in relation to terms implied in fact. The distinction is clearly stated by Phang:

> In the category of terms implied in fact, the criterion of necessity is a truly narrow one, having regard to the specific position of the contracting parties themselves. Where terms implied in law are concerned, however, the criterion of necessity is a much broader one: the presence (or absence) of necessity is ascertained by reference to not only the category of contract concerned but also to broader policy factors.[61]

Given this, it has been argued that, to avoid 'semantic and terminological confusion'[62] and better differentiate implied terms in law and implied terms in fact, the court should adopt a reasonableness test when implying terms in law.[63] There is evidence that the courts may be starting to acknowledge this. In *Crossley v Faithful & Gould*,[64] Dyson LJ stated:

> rather than focus on the elusive concept of necessity, it is better to recognise that, to some extent at least, the existence and scope of standardised implied terms raise questions of reasonableness, fairness and the balancing of competing policy considerations.[65]

Such comments have led one commentator to conclude that the test is 'somewhere in between "reasonableness" and "necessity." Thus it might be said that it must be "reasonably necessary" to imply the term into the contract.'[66]

Terms implied by statute

It is often the case that terms that have been implied into contracts by the court will eventually be placed on a statutory footing. The classic example is the implied terms contained in the Sale of Goods Act 1979, ss 12–15. The number of statutorily implied terms is too numerous to discuss in depth, but notable examples include the following.

---

59. Ibid, 266 (Lord Edmund-Davies).
60. *El Awadi v Bank of Credit and Commerce International SA* [1990] 1 QB 606 (QB) 624 (Hutchison J).
61. A Phang, 'Implied Terms in English Law: Some Recent Developments' [1993] JBL 242, 246.
62. Ibid, 246.   63. Ibid, 245.
64. *Crossley v Faithful & Gould* [2004] EWCA Civ 293, [2004] ICR 1615.   65. Ibid, [36].
66. E McKendrick, *Contract Law: Text, Cases and Materials* (3rd edn, OUP, Oxford, 2008) 353.

Visit the **Online Resource Centre** for more on the implied terms contained in the Sale of Goods Act 1979 in the chapter entitled 'The sale of goods'

- The Supply of Goods and Services Act 1982, s 13, implies a term into contracts for the supply of services that services provided in the course of a business will be carried out with reasonable skill and care.
- The Late Payment of Commercial Debts (Interest) Act 1998, s 1, implies a term into a qualifying contract that parties who owe a qualifying debt are also liable to pay interest on that debt.
- The Partnership Act 1890 implies a number of terms into the partnership agreement that are aimed at regulating the relationship between the partners. These implied terms will form part of the partnership agreement, unless the agreement contains a contrary express provision.

The terms implied by the Partnership Act 1890 are discussed at p 564

Just as statute implies these terms, it can also limit the extent of their scope. It is common for statutes implying terms to set out detailed rules regarding which contracts will qualify and which will not. Certain implied terms will apply only to contracts between certain parties (for example, businesses and consumers). The implication of certain terms may be avoided by inserting an exclusion clause, but certain implied terms are incapable of exclusion. It should be remembered that a term will only be imposed within the confines and requirements of the statute that implies it.

Terms implied by trade usage, previous dealings, or local custom

Although terms implied in fact and terms implied in law constitute the two principal sources of implied terms, a third class is also of significant importance—namely, terms implied by trade usage, a consistent course of previous dealings, or local custom. The rationale behind such implication is that, if both parties are aware of a term that is commonly included through trade custom, etc. they must have intended it to be a term of the contract.

- *Trade usage* A term may be implied because it is customary within a particular trade or profession. In *British Crane Hire Corporation Ltd v Ipswich Plant Hire Ltd*,[67] the defendant hired a crane from the claimant. After the contract was concluded, the claimant sent out a document containing the terms (which were based on model terms of the relevant trade association), but the defendant never signed this document. One of the terms stated that the defendant would be responsible for recovering the crane if it were to sink on soft ground, which was what happened. The claimant sought to recover the cost of recovering the crane from the defendant. The defendant argued that, because it had not agreed to the relevant term, it was not binding upon it. The Court held that, because the terms sent out were customary within the trade, it was implied into the contract and the claimant could obtain damages covering the cost of recovery.
- *Consistent course of previous dealings* The court may imply terms based on the party's previous dealings. In *Motours Ltd v Euroball (West Kent) Ltd*,[68] the claimant and defendant had contracted with each other fourteen times over an eighteen-month period, based on the defendant's standard terms—but the

---

67. [1975] QB 303 (CA). 68. [2003] EWHC 614 (QB), [2003] All ER (D) 165.

claimant had never read the terms (largely because the terms were in small print using difficult language). Accordingly, the claimant was not aware of a clause excluding the defendant of all liability for consequential loss caused by breach of contract or negligence. When problems arose, the claimant initiated a claim and the defendant sought to rely on the exclusion clause. The High Court held that, even though the claimant had never seen the exclusion clause, it was implied into the contract based on their previous dealings: after eighteen months, the defendant was entitled to believe that the claimant knew of the clause.[69] It is important to note that terms based on a previous course of dealings will only be implied where such dealings are consistent. Where the parties' dealings change from one course of dealing to the next, no term will be implied.[70]

- *Locality* A term may be customary within a certain geographical area. In *Hutton v Warren*,[71] a tenant of a farm in Lincolnshire was given notice to quit by his landlord. Given that the landlord would benefit from the produce planted by the tenant, the tenant argued that he should be compensated for the money spent on purchasing seeds and also for the hours of labour that he had invested in the farm. Although such a term was not in the contract, it was regarded as a local custom, and so the court implied a term requiring the landlord to pay an allowance to the tenant.

It should be noted that, for three reasons, it is not easy to establish that a term should be implied by custom.

1. A term based on trade usage, etc. will not be implied if it conflicts with the express wording of the contract.[72]
2. A well-drafted entire agreements clause will prevent the implication of terms based on trade usage, etc.[73]
3. The trade usage, etc. must be certain, notorious, and reasonable.[74]

The requirement of notoriety appears especially difficult to establish, because it will require 'evidence of a universal and acknowledged practice of the market'.[75]

Key points summary

- Terms may be implied into a contract by the court, statute, or by custom. Terms implied by the court can be split into:

  - terms implied in fact; and
  - terms implied in law.

- The courts will only imply terms in law and in fact where they feel that it is 'necessary' to do so. It is clear, however, that the 'necessity' test is less stringent in relation to terms implied in law.

---

69. Ultimately, although the exclusion clause was implied into the contract, it could not be relied upon by the defendant, because it was deemed unreasonable under the Unfair Contract Terms Act 1977.
70. *McCutcheon v David Macbrayne Ltd* [1964] 1 WLR 125 (HL).
71. (1836) 1 M & W 466.
72. *Les Affréteurs Réunis Société Anonyme v Walford* [1919] AC 801 (HL).
73. *Exxonmobil Sales and Supply Corporation v Texaco Limited (The Helene Knutsen)* [2003] EWHC 1964 (Comm), [2003] 2 Lloyd's Rep 686.
74. *Cunliffe-Owen v Teather & Greenwood* [1967] 1 WLR 1421 (Ch).
75. *Baker v Black Sea and Baltic General Insurance Ltd* [1998] 2 All ER 833 (HL).

- The courts will imply terms in fact to give effect to the unexpressed intention of the parties. Conversely, implied terms in law are not based on the party's intentions.

- Implied terms in fact apply only to the case in question (that is, they do not establish a precedent). Conversely, implied terms in law will be implied into all future contracts of the same type, unless inconsistent with the contract or validly excluded.

- The courts will only apply a term in law if the contract in question falls within a number of commonly occurring contracts, and the implication of the term is 'necessary'. The courts have, however, taken a generous view regarding what is necessary.

- Terms may be implied into contracts by statute (for example, the terms implied by the Sale of Goods Act 1979).

- Terms implied by trade usage, consistent course of dealing, or local custom may be based on customs that occur within a particular trade or profession, locality, or between customs that have arisen between the parties.

Conditions, warranties, and innominate terms

We have noted above that the main distinction between contractual terms is between express terms and implied terms. For the purposes of determining the content and extent of a contract, this classification is paramount—but in relation to determining the consequences following the breach of a term, the crucial distinction is between conditions, warranties, and innominate terms. All terms (express or implied) will constitute either a condition, a warranty, or an innominate term. Because this distinction is relevant to the issue of breach, it will be examined in detail when we discuss the various methods by which a contract can be discharged.

The distinction between conditions, warranties, and innominate terms is discussed in detail at p 303

Exclusion clauses

In this chapter, we have discussed the broad classification of terms. One specific term is, however, worth mentioning at this point—namely, the exclusion clause. Exclusion clauses aim to exclude or limit the liability of one of the parties in the event of breach of contract, or the commission of some other civil wrong (for example, negligence). The regulation of such terms is a key issue for businesses and consumers alike, and will be examined in Chapter 28, when we discuss unfair commercial practices.

The regulation of exclusion clauses is discussed in detail at p 969

The interpretation of contractual terms

Once the terms of the contract have been identified, they will need to be interpreted. The aim of the courts when interpreting contracts is to ascertain and put into practice the intentions of the parties. Historically, as a result of the parol evidence rule, the courts adopted a largely literal approach, whereby courts would ascertain the parties' intentions by reference to the contract itself, giving the words used their everyday, grammatical meaning[76] and deeming extrinsic evidence inadmissible. As with statutory interpretation, however, the courts acknowledged that a literal approach was not always appropriate or helpful, and, in certain situations, the court could look outside the contract itself and take into account extrinsic factors.

- Where a word has a technical or specialist meaning, the court could look outside the contract to determine that meaning.
- Where a word is ambiguous, or if giving it its everyday, grammatical meaning would produce an inconsistency or absurdity, then the court may examine the surrounding circumstances to the contract (known as the 'matrix of fact') and interpret the contract in a manner consistent with those surrounding circumstances.

This original approach was therefore principally literal, with a more purposive secondary approach in evidence where a literal approach was inappropriate or would produce an absurdity. In the case of *Investors Compensation Scheme Ltd v West Bromwich Building Society*,[77] however, Lord Hoffmann restated the principles by which contracts are to be interpreted and advocated a much more purposive approach. Lord Hoffmann's restatement consisted of five principles. Before discussing these principles, we should be wary of allowing them too much weight: how a contract is interpreted is heavily dependent on the facts of the particular case, so much so that Lord Goff (who sat in the House of Lords in *Investors Compensation Scheme*) has stated extrajudicially that when interpreting contracts, examining previous case law would provide little help.[78]

Lord Hoffmann's restatement

Lord Hoffmann's first principle stated that:

> Interpretation is the ascertainment of the meaning which the document would convey to a reasonable person having all the background knowledge which would reasonably have been available to the parties in the situation in which they were at the time of the contract.[79]

The first principle indicates that the courts should take an objective approach to interpreting contracts. What the parties actually intended or understood is irrelevant; what is important is what a reasonable person would have understood the words to mean.

More importantly, the reasonable person can take into account 'background knowledge' and Lord Hoffmann's second principle demonstrates the breadth of such knowledge. He states that:

> The background was famously referred to by Lord Wilberforce as the 'matrix of fact,' but this phrase is, if anything, an understated description of what

---

76. *Lovell and Christmas Ltd v Wall* (1911) 104 LT 85 (CA).

77. [1998] 1 WLR 896 (HL).

78. Lord Goff, 'Commercial Contracts and the Commercial Court' [1984] LMCLQ 382, 385.

79. *Investors Compensation Scheme Ltd v West Bromwich Building Society* [1998] 1 WLR 896 (HL) 912.

the background may include. Subject to the requirement that it should have been reasonably available to the parties and to the exception to be mentioned next, it includes absolutely anything which would have affected the way in which the language of the document would have been understood by a reasonable man.[80]

Lord Hoffmann defines 'background knowledge' extremely widely. In fact, it could be argued that his definition is too wide and, in a subsequent case, he sought to place a limit on his second principle, stating that when he restated the principles of interpretation, he 'did not think it necessary to emphasise that [he] meant anything which a reasonable man would have regarded as *relevant*'[81] and that he 'was certainly not encouraging a trawl through "background" which could not have made a reasonable person think that the parties must have departed from conventional usage'.[82]

A further limit on what constitutes background information is found in Lord Hoffmann's third principle, which states that '[t]he law excludes from the admissible background the previous negotiations of the parties and their declarations of subjective intent'.[83] Given the objective nature of the interpretive role, this limitation is unsurprising, but excluding evidence regarding negotiations has proven extremely divisive, with both judges[84] and academics[85] arguing that there are instances in which such evidence can be extremely valuable.

Lord Hoffmann's first three principles clearly indicate that the courts are no longer confined to examining only the contract itself and that taking into account wider background knowledge forms an essential part of their interpretive role. This would appear to indicate that the courts are no longer limited to a literal approach and can instead interpret the words of the contract in line with relevant background information. Lord Hoffmann's fourth principle emphasizes this point:

> The meaning which a document (or any other utterance) would convey to a reasonable man is not the same thing as the meaning of its words. The meaning of words is a matter of dictionaries and grammars; the meaning of the document is what the parties using those words against the relevant background would reasonably have been understood to mean. The background may not merely enable the reasonable man to choose between the possible meanings of words which are ambiguous but even (as occasionally happens in ordinary life) to conclude that the parties must, for whatever reason, have used the wrong words or syntax.[86]

This fourth principle makes absolutely clear that 'contextualism is now king and is to be preferred to literalism'[87]—a sentiment that has been echoed by the judges

---

80. Ibid, 912, 913.   81. *BCCI v Ali* [2001] UKHL 8, [2001] 1 AC 251, [39].

82. Ibid.

83. *Investors Compensation Scheme Ltd v West Bromwich Building Society* [1998] 1 WLR 896 (HL) 913.

84. Lord Nicholls, 'My Kingdom for a Horse: The Meaning of Words' (2005) 121 LQR 577.

85. G McMeel, 'Prior Negotiations and Subsequent Conduct: The Next Step Forward for Contractual Interpretation?' (2003) 119 LQR 272.

86. Ibid.

87. M Furmston, *Cheshire, Fifoot & Furmston's Law of Contract* (15th edn, OUP, Oxford, 2007) 161.

themselves, who have stated that '[t]he tendency should therefore generally speaking be against literalism'.[88]

But this does not mean that a literal interpretation of the words used should be abandoned, because, as Lord Hoffmann's fifth and final principle states:

> The 'rule' that words should be given their 'natural and ordinary meaning' reflects the common sense proposition that we do not easily accept that people have made linguistic mistakes, particularly in formal documents. On the other hand, if one would nevertheless conclude from the background that something must have gone wrong with the language, the law does not require judges to attribute to the parties an intention which they plainly could not have had.[89]

The fifth principle establishes that establishing the grammatical and ordinary meaning of the words used is the first step in determining the objective intentions of the parties. The courts should then take into account the relevant background information to determine whether this information would convey to a reasonable man a different meaning from that provided by a literal approach. Lord Hoffmann's restatement is clearly more focused on the commercial realities of a situation, as opposed to the literal wording used by the parties. That this was the role of the judiciary when interpreting contracts was recognized long before Lord Hoffmann's restatement, when, in 1984, Lord Goff stated that:

> We are there to help businessmen, not to hinder them: we are there to give effect to their transactions, not to frustrate them: we are there to oil the wheels of commerce, not to put a spanner in the works, or even grit in the oil.[90]

‹› Key points summary

- The courts take an objective approach when interpreting contracts and interpret words based on how a reasonable person would understand them, taking into account relevant background information.

- Background information does not include evidence regarding pre-contractual negotiations.

- Although a contextual or purposive approach is preferred to a literal one, the first step for the court is to determine the meaning of the words based upon their ordinary grammatical usage. The courts may depart from such a literal meaning if the background information would lead a reasonable man to believe that a literal meaning was not what the parties intended.

---

88. *Sirius International Insurance Co (Publ) v FAI General Insurance Ltd* [2004] UKHL 54, [2004] WLR 3251, [19].
89. *Investors Compensation Scheme Ltd v West Bromwich Building Society* [1998] 1 WLR 896 (HL) 913.
90. Lord Goff, 'Commercial Contracts and the Commercial Court' [1984] LMCLQ 382, 391.

Chapter conclusion

The layperson's conception of a contract is a written document that contains the totality of the terms affecting the parties. In this chapter, we have seen that the truth is very different and that a contract can consist of more than express terms. A spoken statement of a party can become a term of a contract and additional terms can be implied into the contract from a number of different sources. It is vital that businesses are aware that they may have rights, obligations, and duties outside those specifically negotiated with the other party. Many implied terms or terms implied through trade usage, etc. can be excluded via an express provision, and businesses would do well to have a thorough understanding of such terms, so that they can exclude them if they so desire.

Self-test questions

1. Define the following:
   (a) representation;
   (b) the parol evidence rule;
   (c) collateral contract;
   (d) entire agreement clause.

2. Dean is an antique dealer specializing in ancient Greek manuscripts. He acquires a painting that he is told is a genuine Constable. Matthew, a renowned expert in Constable paintings, walks into Dean's antique shop. Although Dean has little knowledge of Constable paintings, he states to Matthew: 'This is a genuine Constable painting and one of his finest.' Matthew purchases the painting for £3 million. It transpires that the painting is a forgery. Is Dean in breach of contract? What is the legal status of Dean's statement?

3. Why do you think the courts regard the collateral contract as such a useful device? Back up your answer with examples from case law.

4. 'The exceptions to the parol evidence rule are now so numerous that the rule should be abandoned.' Do you agree with this assertion?

5. Explain the distinction between:
   (a) express terms and implied terms;
   (b) terms and representations;
   (c) terms implied in fact and terms implied in law.

Further reading

Koffman, L, and Macdonald, E, *The Law of Contract* (6th edn, OUP, Oxford, 2007) ch 7
A very clear and lucid account of the law relating to express and implied terms

Law Commission, *Law of Contract: The Parol Evidence Rule* (Law Com No 154, Cmnd 9700, HMSO, London, 1986)
A clear, yet indepth, examination of the parol evidence rule; over twenty years old, so may not reference more modern cases or include all of the exceptions

Lord Nicholls, 'My Kingdom for a Horse: The Meaning of Words' (2005) 121
  LQR 577
*Discusses the law's approach to the interpretation of contracts; provides arguments for
  and against allowing evidence of prior negotiations to be adduced, and argues that such
  evidence can be useful*

Phang, A, 'Implied Terms, Business Efficacy and the Officious Bystander:
  A Modern History' [1998] JBL 1
*This article explores the 'business efficiency' and 'officious bystander' tests, and examines
  the relationship between them*

Phang, A, 'Implied Terms in English Law: Some Recent Developments' [1993]
  JBL 242
Discusses the distinction between terms implied in fact and terms implied in law

Lord Wedderburn, 'Collateral Contracts' [1959] CLJ 58
*An indepth discussion of the operation of the collateral contract, including how it has been
  used to evade the parol evidence rule*

 Remember to visit the **Online Resource Centre** at **<http://www.
oxfordtextbooks.co.uk/roach>** to access the following resources on
Chapter 7, 'The terms of the contract': more **practice questions** and
answers; a **glossary** of key terms; **multiple-choice questions**; **revision
summaries**; and **audio updates** when relevant.

8 Vitiating factors

- Misrepresentation
- Mistake
- Duress
- Undue influence
- Unconscionable bargains
- Illegality and public policy

INTRODUCTION

The need for commercial certainty goes beyond the formation of a contract. Businesses need to be aware in what circumstances validly formed contracts may be set aside or removed from existence. The business may engage in activities prior to the contract being formed that can subsequently cause the contract to become unenforceable, resulting in the business sustaining a substantial loss, or the loss of reputation and future business. In order to avoid a contract being **vitiated**, businesses need to know what type of pre-contract activity should be avoided—whether it be the making of false statements, the infliction of improper pressure, or the taking advantage of another's weakness. As we shall see, however, there are instances in which a contract will, or can be, set aside even though no reprehensible conduct has taken place. Businesses need to be aware that innocent activities can render a contract void or voidable, so that measures can be taken to avoid such conduct.

➜ vitiate: render incomplete, imperfect, or faulty

Situations such as those mentioned above are said to 'vitiate' the contract. Certain vitiating factors (for example, mistake) will render a contract void, whereas others (for example, misrepresentation) will merely render the contract voidable. Therefore, before discussing the various vitiating factors, it is first important to understand the difference between a contract that has become 'void' and a contract that has become 'voidable'.

- Void is an abbreviation of **void *ab initio*** ('invalid from the beginning'). Accordingly, a contract held to be void is treated as if it never existed, and the parties have no discretion as to whether the contract should continue to exist.

➜ void *ab initio*: 'invalid from the beginning'

- **Voidable** contracts are not wiped from existence. A voidable contract will continue to be valid and enforceable until such time as the relevant party sets it aside. As we shall see, however, there are instances in which the relevant party will be barred from setting the contract aside.

➜ voidable: valid until set aside

Having established the difference between a void and voidable contract, we can now turn our attention to the various vitiating factors, as follows.

- *Misrepresentation* Where a party to a contract makes a false statement that induces the other party to enter the contract, the contract may be voidable.

- *Mistake*   A contract may be held void where the contracting parties have contracted based upon some form is mistake.

- *Duress*   Where a party is forced into entering a contract due to some form of illegitimate pressure or threat, the contract may be voidable.

- *Undue influence*   Where the relationship between the parties is one that could result in one party having improper influence or a dominant role over the other, the contract may be held to be voidable.

- *Unconscionable bargains*   Where one party takes advantage of the weakness of another party, the contract may be voidable.

- *Illegality and public policy*   Illegal contracts are generally unenforceable (subject to several important exceptions). A lawful contract may be declared void on the ground that it offends public policy.

Misrepresentation

 The distinction between terms and representations is discussed more fully at p 205

In Chapter 7, we noted that certain statements can become terms of the contract and, if proven to be untrue, can form the basis of a claim for breach of contract. Conversely, other statements will not be regarded as terms: they will amount to mere representations and cannot found a cause of action for breach. A false representation may, however, result in an action for misrepresentation, which will usually entitle the innocent party to **rescind** the contract and, depending upon the type of misrepresentation, also claim damages for misrepresentation. An action in misrepresentation can lie irrespective of whether a representation has become a term of the contract or not.

➡ rescind: terminate a contract, either by an act of the parties or the court

For an action in misrepresentation to succeed, the defendant (or his agent) must be proved to have satisfied three requirements, as follows.

1. There must be a false statement of past or existing fact, or of law.
2. The false statement of fact or law must have been addressed to the person misled.
3. The statement must have induced the other person to enter into the contract.

A false statement of fact or law

 Statements of law are discussed at p 231

Traditionally, only false statements of fact could normally constitute a misrepresentation, but it would now appear that false statements of law may also constitute misrepresentations. Although a statement will normally be made by words, it is possible for a statement to be made by conduct, as the following case demonstrates.

Spice Girls Ltd v Aprilia World Service BV [2002] EWCA Civ 15[1]

FACTS: The Spice Girls' world tour was to be sponsored by the defendant, a motor scooter manufacturer. Prior to the contract being signed, all five members of the band

---

1. See also *Crystal Palace Football Club (2000) Ltd v Dowie* [2007] EWHC 1392 (QB), [2007] IRLR 682.

engaged in advertising activities (for example, photo shoots, television commercials, etc.) for the Spice Sonic scooter. At the time that they engaged in these activities, the band knew that Geri Halliwell would be leaving the group before the sponsorship agreement ended, but the defendant was not told of this. When she left the group, the defendant argued that it had paid for the right to use the image of all five members of the band. As a result, it withheld the next sponsorship fee instalment. The band sued.

HELD: The Court of Appeal held that, by appearing in the promotional material, the Spice Girls' conduct constituted a representation that the Spice Girls did not know or have reasonable grounds to believe that any of them intended to leave the group before the minimum term of the advertising contract. Because the band already knew that Geri would leave before the end of the transaction, that statement was false.

Proving that a statement is false is not normally problematic, but it may be difficult where the statement is ambiguous and has several meanings, some being true and others being false. In such a case, provided that the representor's interpretation of the statement was reasonable, it will not be regarded as false.[2]

'Mere puffs'

Statements that constitute sales talk, or which are so vague as to be almost meaningless, will not be regarded as representations and will instead amount to 'mere puffs'. Thus, in *Dimmock v Hallet*,[3] an auctioneer described a piece of land as 'fertile and improvable', whereas, in fact, it was abandoned and useless. The Court of Appeal held that the statement did not amount to a representation, because it was 'a mere flourishing description by an auctioneer'.[4]

Statements of opinion

A statement of opinion does not, in itself, constitute a misrepresentation if the opinion turns out to be incorrect, because opinions are not facts.

Bisset v Wilkinson [1927] AC 177 (PC)

FACTS: The seller of a farm told a prospective purchaser that, in his opinion, the farm could support 2,000 sheep. Based upon this, the representee purchased the farm and discovered that the farm could not support anywhere near 2,000 sheep. The representee alleged that the representor's statement amounted to a misrepresentation.

HELD: The Privy Council held that because the seller had never been a sheep farmer and the farm had never reared sheep, his statement was a mere statement of opinion aimed at providing an honest estimate. As such, it did not constitute a statement of fact and consequently did not amount to a misrepresentation.

It does not follow, however, that a statement of opinion will never form the basis of a misrepresentation action. In two situations, a statement of opinion can involve

---

2. *McInerny v Lloyd's Bank Ltd* [1974] 1 Lloyd's Rep 246 (CA).
3. (1867) 2 Ch App 21 (CA).   4. Ibid, 21 (Turner LJ).

a misrepresentation of fact. Firstly, if the representor states an opinion that he knows that he does not believe in, this constitutes a misrepresentation of fact because he falsely represents the fact that he holds a particular opinion.[5]

Secondly, if the representor represents an opinion for which he does not have reasonable grounds, and he impliedly represents that he has such grounds, this will constitute a misrepresentation of fact.

Smith v Land and House Property Corporation (1884) 28 Ch D 7 (CA)

FACTS: The claimant wished to sell a hotel and he described the hotel as let to a 'Mr Frederick Fleck (a most desirable tenant) … for an unexpired term of 27½ years, thus offering a first class investment'. The defendant purchased the hotel, but discovered that Fleck had not paid rent for the last quarter and, shortly after the sale, the business that Fleck was running went into liquidation. The defendant refused to complete the sale and the claimant sought an order for specific performance. The defendant counterclaimed, alleging that the contract was voidable, because the claimant's statement regarding Fleck amounted to a misrepresentation. The claimant argued that the statement was merely one of opinion and so was not actionable.

HELD: The Court of Appeal held that the claimant's statement was not merely one of opinion, but also involved a misrepresentation of fact, because the claimant had impliedly stated that it had reasonable grounds for the opinions expressed regarding Fleck. That the claimant actually knew of Fleck's financial difficulties meant that the statement amounted to a misrepresentation and the defendant was therefore entitled to rescind the contract.

Statements of intention or prediction

Statements concerning the future (the notable example being statements of intention) are generally not actionable, because such statements are not factual. Accordingly, if the representor makes a statement concerning a future state of affairs and that state of affairs does not occur, the representor will normally not have committed a misrepresentation. But if a representor makes a statement concerning a future state of affairs, this will constitute a misrepresentation of fact if, *at the time that the statement was made,* he either knows or does not believe that the state of affairs will arise.

Edgington v Fitzmaurice (1885) 29 Ch D 459 (CA)

prospectus: a document providing information concerning a company, issued when the company wishes to raise money

FACTS: The directors of a company issued a **prospectus** in order to raise money. The prospectus stated that any money raised would be used to purchase goods to expand and develop the company's business. In fact, the money was going to be used to pay off the company's debts. The claimant advanced money and then discovered the real reason behind the issuing of the prospectus.

---

5. *Jendwine v Slade* (1797) 2 Esp 571.

HELD: The Court of Appeal held that the statement in the prospectus constituted a misrepresentation. Although it was a statement of intention, at the time that the statement was made, the defendant knew that it was not going to act in accordance with the statement. The claimant therefore recovered damages for the defendant's fraudulent misrepresentation.

Statements of law

The traditional view is that neither the common law[6] nor equity[7] would regard a false statement as to the state of the law as a misrepresentation, unless the representation relates to foreign law.[8] But this traditional view needs elaboration. What is true is that pure or abstract statements of law (that is, statements of law that did not relate to the facts of the case) were not actionable, but that statements of law related to the facts of a particular case (known as a 'misrepresentation of private rights') may be regarded as statements of fact.[9]

The rule that pure statements of law cannot constitute misrepresentation needs to be reassessed in light of more recent cases. In *Kleinwort Benson Ltd v Lincoln City Council*,[10] the House of Lords abolished the rule that stated that monies could not be recovered where a *mistake* of law had been made. The question arising is whether this would be extended to cover situations in which there had been a *misrepresentation* of law.

In *Pankhania v Hackney London Borough Council*,[11] the High Court stated that the rule preventing misstatements of law from being actionable 'has not survived the decision in Kleinwort Benson'.[12] This would appear to abolish the distinction between law and fact mentioned above, but we should remain cautious. The decision in *Pankhania* was only a first-instance decision and, whilst the High Court is free to depart from higher authorities under the rule in *Young v Bristol Aeroplane Co Ltd*,[13] it is still open to a higher court to affirm the traditional rule. Due to the difficulty in distinguishing between statements of law and statements of fact, however, the higher courts are likely to follow the decision in *Pankhania*: both Maurice Kay LJ and Bodey J in the Court of Appeal in *Brennan v Bolt Burdon*,[14] speaking *obiter*, expressed approval for the decision in *Pankhania*. But in another case in the Court of Appeal, Rix LJ stated *obiter*, in a dissenting judgment regarding the main point in the case, that in cases involving the tort of deceit,[15] a statement of fact is still required.[16] Rix LJ did not, however, consider *Pankhania* or *Brennan*, so his *dictum* is of doubtful authority. Therefore, one can cautiously state that false statements of law are likely to be just as actionable as false statements of fact.

The rules established in *Young* are discussed at p 81

---

6. *Beattie v Lord Ebury* (1872) 7 Ch App 777.   7. *Rashdall v Ford* (1866) LR 2 Eq 750.

8. *André & Cie SA v Ets Michel Blanc & Fils* [1979] 2 Lloyd's Rep 427 (CA).

9. *Solle v Butcher* [1950] 1 KB 671 (CA).   10. [1999] 2 AC 349 (HL).

11. [2002] EWHC 2441 (Ch), [2002] NPC 123.   12. Ibid, [57] (Rex Tedd QC).

13. [1946] AC 163 (HL).   14. [2004] EWCA Civ 303, [2005] QB 303.

15. A claim for damages for fraudulent misrepresentation is brought for the tort of deceit, but that tort is not limited to a fraudulent misrepresentation resulting in a contract.

16. *AIC Ltd v ITS Testing Services (UK) Ltd* [2006] EWCA Civ 1601, [2007] 1 Lloyd's Rep 555, [255].

Can silence constitute a false statement?

The general rule is that silence cannot constitute a misrepresentation, because parties to a contract are not under a duty to disclose relevant facts to one another. A consequence of the principle of *caveat emptor* is that parties are free to profit from their superior knowledge.

 caveat emptor: 'let the buyer beware'

 Fletcher v Krell (1873) 42 LJ QB 55

FACTS: The defendant agreed to employ the claimant as a governess for three years. She had been described to the defendant as a spinster and, upon this basis, he employed her. In fact, she was a divorcee and, had the defendant known this, he would not have employed her. When he discovered the truth, he rescinded the contract of employment (that is, he refused to employ her), claiming that she had misrepresented her position. The claimant alleged breach of contract.

HELD: The claimant was under no obligation to reveal that she was divorced, nor had she been asked if she had been married before. Accordingly, there had been no misrepresentation. The defendant was therefore not entitled to rescind the contract and the claimant could recover damages for the breach of contract resulting from the wrongful rescission.

This principle is not absolute, however, and silence can constitute a false statement in five principal situations. Firstly, the Court of Appeal has stated that a failure to disclose by *A* could amount to negligence, where *A* voluntarily assumed the responsibility of making such a disclosure to *B* and *B* relied on that assumption.[17] The application of this rule to misrepresentation can be seen in the following case.

 Hamilton v Allied Domecq plc [2007] UKHL 33

FACTS: The claimant was a shareholder in a company called Gleneagles that had begun to produce bottled water. Gleneagles could not develop this business by itself, so it sought a company that could invest in it and provide it with a distribution network. The claimant wanted first to distribute the bottled water on-trade in restaurants and hotels, before moving into off-trade markets. To that end, the claimant entered into a subscription agreement with the defendant, whereby the defendant became the majority shareholder in Gleneagles. Contrary to the claimant's wishes, the defendant launched the bottled water in off-trade markets, with on-trade distribution to follow. The venture did not succeed and Gleneagles entered administration, by which time, the claimant's shares were virtually worthless. The claimant sued the defendant, on the ground that the defendant had represented that it would distribute the water on-trade from the beginning and that its failure to inform the claimant that it would be distributing off-trade first amounted to a misrepresentation.

HELD: The House of Lords dismissed the claimant's action. There was nothing in the subscription agreement indicating that the defendant should distribute the water on-trade

17. *Banque Keyser Ullmann SA v Skandia (UK) Insurance Co Ltd* [1990] 1 QB 665 (CA).

first and, because the general rule is that silence cannot constitute misrepresentation, the defendant's failure to inform the claimant that it would distribute off-trade first did not amount constitute a misrepresentation. There was also no liability in negligence, because the defendant had not voluntarily assumed responsibility to the defendant. Lord Rodger stated that, in cases such as this, in which the parties engage in arm's-length commercial negotiations, establishing an assumption of responsibility will prove extremely difficult.

 See S Jackson, 'Silence is Golden' (2007) 157 NLJ 1332

Secondly, where a representation that is true when it is made subsequently becomes untrue to the representor's knowledge due to a change of circumstances, the representor is under a duty to notify the representee of the change. A failure to do so may amount to a misrepresentation.

 With v O'Flanagan [1936] Ch 575 (CA)

FACTS: A doctor, seeking to sell his medical practice, made representations to a prospective buyer that the practice generated £2,000 per year. At the time that the statement was made, this figure was correct. Some five months later, the representee purchased the practice. By the time that the contract was signed, however, the income that the practice was generating had fallen to around £5 per week (due to the illness of the doctor) and the majority of the practice's patients had left. The claimant, upon discovering this, alleged misrepresentation.

HELD: The Court of Appeal held that representation inducing the other party into entering into a contract is to be regarded as continuing until the contract is signed. Accordingly, where a change of circumstances renders a previously true representation untrue, the representor should disclose the change to the representee and failure to do so may constitute a misrepresentation.

Thirdly, where a statement is literally true, but fails to convey the whole truth by omitting certain facts (that is, it is a half-truth), the non-disclosure of the key facts may amount to a misrepresentation.

Nottingham Patent Brick and Tile Co v Butler (1886) 16 QBD 778 (CA)

FACTS: The defendant contracted to sell a piece of land to claimant. The claimant's solicitor asked the defendant's solicitor whether the land was subject to any restrictive covenants. The defendant's solicitor stated that he was not aware of any covenants, but did not disclose that this was because he had not read the title deeds. It transpired that the land was subject to restrictive covenants. The claimant alleged misrepresentation.

HELD: Although the defendant's solicitor's statement was literally true, it omitted key facts that the claimant would wish to know. This omission changed the statement of fact into a misstatement of fact. Accordingly, the Court of Appeal held that the statement amounted to a misrepresentation.

➡ *uberrimae fidei*:
'utmost good faith'

Fourthly, certain contracts are classified as *uberrimae fidei*. Under such contracts, the parties are under a duty to disclose all material facts to one another. The classic example of an *uberrimae fidei* contract is a contract of insurance. Accordingly, a contract of insurance is voidable if a party fails to disclose a material fact before the contract was entered into and if that non-disclosure induced the making of the contract[18] (for example, failure to disclose motoring offences in a contract for motor insurance, or the failure to disclose a terminal medical condition in a life insurance contract).

The final instance in which silence can constitute a misrepresentation is where the parties are in a fiduciary relationship. A fiduciary relationship is one of trust and confidence. It tends to arise only in certain professional relationships, such as principal and agent, partner and partner, solicitor and client, and trustee and beneficiary. Where such a relationship exists, there is a duty to disclose all material facts and non-disclosure may therefore amount to a misrepresentation.

The statement must be addressed to the person misled

In order for misrepresentation to be founded, the statement must have been addressed to the person misled or his agent.[19] This does not mean, however, that a statement must be specifically addressed to a particular person, because statements can be made to the public. Further, it may be the case that the representor makes a statement that he intends or knows will be passed on to others. In such a case, provided that the person alleging misrepresentation falls within the class of persons on to whom the representor intends or knows the information could be passed, this requirement will be satisfied.[20]

Inducement

Once the existence of an actionable statement has been established, the party misled will need to prove[21] that the statement induced him[22] to enter the contract (that is, he relied on the statement). From this requirement, it follows that misrepresentation will not be established where the representee:

- was not aware of the representor's false statement at the time that he entered into the contract;[23]
- knew that the statement was false,[24] or the representee's agent knew the statement was false;[25]

---

18. *St Paul Fire and Marine Insurance Co (UK) Ltd v McConnell Dowell Constructors Ltd* [1995] 2 Lloyd's Rep 116 (CA).

19. *Peek v Gurney* (1873) LR 6 HL 377 (HL).   20. *Andrews v Mockford* [1896] 1 QB 372 (CA).

21. *Arkwright v Newbold* (1880) 17 Ch D 301 (CA) established that the party misled bears the burden of proof.

22. Provided that the statement was a genuine inducement, it is irrelevant that other factors also induced the representee into entering the contract: *Edgington v Fitzmaurice* (1885) 29 Ch D 459 (CA).

23. *Re Northumberland and Durham District Banking Co, ex p Biggs* (1858) 28 Ch 50.

24. *Begbie v Phosphate Sewage Co* (1875) LR 10 QB 491 (CA); *Eurocopy v Teesdale* [1992] BCLC 1067 (CA).

25. *Strover v Harrington* [1988] Ch 390 (Ch).

- would have entered into the transaction, even if he knew the truth;[26]
- relied upon his own information (of which the following case provides an example).

⊙ Attwood v Small (1838) 6 Cl & F 232

FACTS: The defendant offered to sell a mine and made exaggerated statements about the mine's earning potential. The claimant agreed to purchase the mine on the condition that his agent could investigate the validity of the defendant's statements. The defendant agreed and the agent carried out an investigation. The agent failed to discover the falsity of the statement and verified the defendant's statement. The claimant purchased the mine and discovered the truth.

HELD: The contract could not be rescinded for misrepresentation, because the claimant was not induced into entering the contract by the defendant's statement. It was the statement of the claimant's own agent that had induced him into purchasing the mine.

It should be noted that whilst the representee's own investigation into the validity of the representor's statement might result in a failure to establish inducement, the mere fact that the representee could have discovered the truth, but failed to do so, will not cause his claim to fail.[27]

Materiality

In order for a statement to induce a party, it must be shown to be material.[28] A material statement has been defined as:

> one which would have affected the judgment of a reasonable person in deciding whether, or on what terms, to enter into the contract; or one which would induce him into entering the contract without making such enquiries as he would otherwise make.[29]

In practice, the requirement of materiality is usually a formality, simply existing in order to filter out trivial claims that, even if successful, would most likely only result in an award of nominal damages.

Figure 8.1 illustrates the actionability of a false statement.

Remedies for misrepresentation

Once the representee has established the existence of an actionable (or operative) misrepresentation, the next step is to determine what remedy will be awarded. This is largely determined by the type of misrepresentation that was committed.

---

26. *JEB Fasteners Ltd v Marks Bloom & Co* [1983] 1 All ER 583 (CA).
27. *Redgrave v Hurd* (1881) 20 Ch D 1 (CA).
28. *McDowell v Fraser* (1779) 1 Dougl 247.
29. E Peel, *Treitel on the Law of Contract* (12th edn, Sweet & Maxwell, London, 2007) 367.

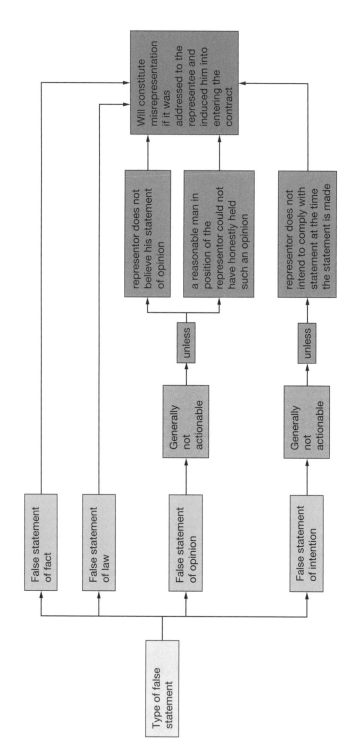

FIGURE 8.1 The actionability of a statement

Misrepresentations come in one of four types and are determined by the state of mind of the representee:

- fraudulent misrepresentation;
- common law negligent misrepresentation;
- statutory negligent misrepresentation; and
- innocent misrepresentation.

Fraudulent misrepresentation

A fraudulent misrepresentation will give rise to an action in the tort of deceit. The classic definition of fraudulent misrepresentation was made in the case of *Derry v Peek*,[30] in which Lord Herschell stated:

> [I]n order to sustain an action in deceit, there must be proof of fraud, and nothing short of that will suffice.... [F]raud is proved when it is shown that a false representation has been made, (1) knowingly, or (2) without belief in its truth, or (3) recklessly, careless whether it be true or false.[31]

It follows that a statement will not be fraudulent if:

- the representor honestly believes it to be true, even if there are no reasonable grounds for such belief;[32]
- the statement is merely negligent. Even gross negligence will not suffice.[33] What is required is that the representor knew the statement to be untrue, or, if he did not know that it was untrue, that he had no grounds for believing it to be true.

The motive of the representor is irrelevant; the lack of dishonesty or the intent to deceive or cause another loss does not need to be established.[34] But, provided that the representor believed the statement was true, an unreasonable interpretation will not be regarded as a fraudulent misrepresentation.[35]

If the representee can establish that a fraudulent misrepresentation has been made, he will have access to several remedies, as follows.

- He will be able to **affirm** the contract and then recover damages.
- Alternatively, he may choose to rescind the contract and then recover damages.
- If the representee does rescind or **repudiate** the contract, and the representor claims damages for breach of contract or tries to obtain specific performance, the representee may plead the representor's fraud as a defence, and counterclaim for damages.

➡ **affirm**: continue with a voidable contract, or continue with a contract that has been breached by the other party

➡ **repudiate**: refuse to honour or fulfil a contract

Although misrepresentation is a contractual concept, an action for fraudulent misrepresentation is based in the tort of deceit. Accordingly, damages are not assessed on the normal contractual basis (that is, the amount required to put the claimant in the position in which he would have been had the representation been true), but are assessed on the tortious basis (that is, the amount required to put the claimant in the position in which he would have been had the misrepresentation not been made).

30. (1889) 14 App Cas 337 (HL).   31. Ibid, 374.
32. Ibid.   33. *Angus v Clifford* [1891] 2 Ch 449 (CA).
34. *Bradford Third Equitable Benefit Building Society v Borders* [1941] 2 All ER 205 (HL).
35. *Akerhielm v De Mare* [1959] AC 789 (PC).

Damages for breach of contract are discussed in Chapter 10, and damages in tort generally are discussed in Chapter 15

This provides a very wide measure of damages, because it permits the representee to claim for all losses flowing directly from the misrepresentation, even losses that are not reasonably foreseeable.[36] Further, damages will not be reduced on the ground of contributory negligence, because this defence cannot be pleaded in actions in deceit.[37]

The above rules are demonstrated in the following case.

The defence of contributory negligence is discussed at p 529

Smith New Court Securities Ltd v Scrimgeour Vickers (Asset Management) Ltd [1997] AC 254 (HL)

FACTS: The defendant owned shares in a company named Ferranti Inc. It offered to sell the shares to the claimant, stating that two other parties were interested in purchasing the shares. This was a lie, but it caused the claimant to raise its bid from 78 pence to 82.25 pence per share. This offer was accepted and the claimant bought just over 28 million shares at this price. Some time later, it was discovered that Ferranti had been the victim of a fraud committed by a third party, causing the share price to plummet to just over 40 pence per share. The claimant eventually sold the shares at a massive loss. The Court of Appeal awarded damages of just under £1.2 million, basing this figure on the difference between the price paid (82.25 pence) and the value of the shares at the date of the contract (78 pence). The claimant appealed the quantum of damages.

HELD: The House of Lords stated that, in cases of fraudulent misrepresentation, the claimant could recover damages for all losses flowing from the breach. Accordingly, damages were recalculated based on the difference between the price paid for the shares (82.25 pence) and the price for which the claimant was able to sell them (44 pence). On this calculation, the claimant recovered just under £10.8 million.

See J Payne, 'Measure of Damages for Fraudulent Misrepresentation' (1997) 56 CLJ 17

It should, however, be noted that whilst the rules regarding remoteness are relaxed, given that the claimant is alleging fraud, the standard of proof required is likely to be higher than the usual civil standard of proof. Further, the rules relating to mitigation of loss will apply fully to a representee who has sustained loss due to a fraudulent misrepresentation.[38]

The rules relating to mitigation of loss are discussed at p 340

Common law negligent misrepresentation (negligent misstatement)

Prior to 1964, negligent misrepresentation did not exist and any misrepresentation that was not fraudulent was classified as innocent. The lack of a specific form of misrepresentation covering negligent statements was problematic, in so much as whilst the victim of an innocent misrepresentation could rescind the contract, he could not normally recover any damages. This changed following the case of *Hedley Byrne & Co Ltd v Heller & Partners Ltd*,[39] in which the House of Lords created a new category of misrepresentation to cover negligent misstatements. But the House made clear

---

36. *Doyle v Olby (Ironmongers) Ltd* [1969] 2 QB 158 (CA).
37. *Standard Chartered Bank v Pakistan National Shipping Corporation* [2001] QB 167 (CA).
38. Ibid.   39. [1964] AC 465 (HL).

that establishing the requirements of negligence would not be enough to establish the existence of a negligent misstatement. The usual requirements would need to be established (for example, existence of a duty of care, breach of duty, causation, and remoteness), but the representee would also need to show that a 'special relationship' existed between himself and the representor. The case of *Hedley Byrne* and what constitutes a special relationship is discussed in depth in Chapter 12; it will therefore not be repeated here.

The remedies for common law negligent misrepresentation are largely the same as those for fraudulent misrepresentation, but with one crucial difference. Whilst damages are still measured on the tortious basis (because the action is based on negligent misstatement), only losses that are reasonably foreseeable can be recovered.

The case of Hedley Byrne and the law relating to negligent misstatement is discussed at p 399

Statutory negligent misrepresentation

In 1962 (one year before *Hedley Byrne* established negligent misstatement), the Law Reform Committee published a report recommending the creation of a Misrepresentation Act, which would fill in the gap in the law by providing a remedy for those who sustain loss due to a negligent misrepresentation. With the creation of common law negligent misrepresentation in *Hedley Byrne*, one would suspect that the Law Reform Committee's proposals would become redundant. But in the years following *Hedley Byrne*, subsequent courts severely restricted the scope of negligent misstatement by placing an extremely strict interpretation upon the requirement of a 'special' relationship. Accordingly, the recommendations of the Law Reform Committee were implemented and the Misrepresentation Act 1967 was passed.

Section 2(1) of the 1967 Act states:

> Where a person has entered into a contract after a misrepresentation has been made to him by another party thereto and as a result thereof he has suffered loss, then, if the person making the misrepresentation would be liable to damages in respect thereof had the misrepresentation been made fraudulently, that person shall be so liable notwithstanding that the misrepresentation was not made fraudulently, unless he proves that he had reasonable ground to believe and did believe up to the time the contract was made the facts represented were true.

Four notable points can be made about s 2(1), as follows.

- Establishing negligent misrepresentation under s 2(1) is not dependent upon the existence of a duty of care or a special relationship. The only requirement of 'proximity' is the existence of a contract between representor and representee.
- Section 2(1) only applies where the other party to the contract is the representor. Accordingly, the three-party situation in *Hedley Byrne* (where the contract is entered into on the basis of a third party's representation) is not within the scope of s 2(1).
- Section 2(1) only applies where a contract is formed. Where contractual negotiations do not result in a contract, but the representee suffers loss in reliance of a misrepresentation, the representee will have to rely on the common law to obtain a remedy.
- The burden of proof is reversed. Accordingly, the representor is liable unless he had reasonable grounds to believe that his statement was true.

The pro-representee nature of s 2(1) extends into the assessment of damages. As with fraudulent and common law negligent misrepresentations, damages are assessed on a tortious basis[40] (that is, an amount that would put the claimant in the position in which he would have been had the representation not been made). The question arising is whether such damages should be limited to those losses that are reasonably foreseeable (as under common law negligent misrepresentation), or whether the claimant should be able to recover for all losses that flow from the misrepresentation (as under fraudulent misrepresentation).

The relevant portion of s 2(1) indicates that it is the latter:

> [...] if the person making the representation would be liable to damages in respect thereof had the misrepresentation been made fraudulently, that person shall be so liable notwithstanding that the misrepresentation was not made fraudulently [...]

The reference to fraud in s 2(1) led the Court of Appeal in *Royscot Trust Ltd v Rogerson*[41] to conclude that damages under s 2(1) are calculated in the same way as damages for fraudulent misrepresentation, even though the misrepresentation is not fraudulent (this is known as the 'fiction of fraud'). Unsurprisingly, the fiction of fraud has attracted considerable criticism on the ground that it is objectionable in principle to 'treat the foolish but honest man as if he were dishonest'.[42] Whilst the decision in *Royscot* has not been judicially doubted, there is evidence of dissatisfaction with the fiction of fraud. For example, Lord Steyn has stated that 'it is a rational and defensible strategy to impose wider liability on an intentional wrongdoer',[43] arguing that such an approach 'serves a deterrent purpose in discouraging fraud'.[44] It is submitted that the fiction of fraud is yet another example of the Act's poor drafting and numerous academics have validly argued that the Act should be amended to remove the reference to fraud.

A representor who is ordered to pay damages under s 2(1) can plead the defence of contributory negligence, provided that he is also liable in tort for negligence.[45]

Innocent misrepresentation

With the creation of negligent misrepresentation, it now follows that innocent misrepresentations include only those that are wholly innocent (that is, those that include no fraud or negligence whatsoever).

As with other misrepresentations, the claimant may affirm or rescind the contract. Damages are not available as of right, but, as we shall see in the next section, the court does have the power to award damages in lieu of rescission.[46] Where damages are not granted in lieu of rescission, the representee may be able to obtain an indemnity. An indemnity is an ancillary order[47] requiring the representor to reimburse the

---

40. *Sharneyford Supplies v Edge* [1987] Ch 305 (CA).   41. [1991] 2 QB 297 (CA).
42. R Hooley, 'Damages and Misrepresentation Act 1967' (1991) 107 LQR 547, 549.
43. *Smith New Court Securities Ltd v Citibank NA* [1997] AC 254 (CA) 279.
44. *Ibid.*
45. *Gran Gelato Ltd v Richcliff (Group) Ltd* [1992] Ch 560 (Ch).
46. Misrepresentation Act 1967, s 2(2).
47. As an indemnity order will be ancillary to a rescission order, it follows that an indemnity cannot be recovered where rescission is barred.

representee for any payments made arising from obligations necessarily created by the contract. Indemnities are much more limited than an award of damages, as the following case demonstrates.

 ### *Whittington v Seale-Hayne* (1900) 82 LT 49 (Ch)

FACTS: The defendant owned premises that the claimant wished to use for the purposes of breeding poultry. To this end, the defendant represented that the premises were completely sanitary and in a good state of repair. Relying on this, the claimant took up a lease on the premises. The lease required the claimant to execute such work as might be required by a local or public authority. In reality, due to unsanitary conditions, the premises' water supply was poisoned, resulting in the farm manager becoming ill and a large number of poultry dying, with those that did survive rendered useless for the purposes of breeding. The premises were subsequently condemned by the local authority, which required the claimant to repair them. The claimant sought an indemnity for the loss of the dead birds, loss of profits on sales, recovery of rent payments, recovery of medical expenses in respect of the manager, and the cost of repairing any defects in the premises.

HELD: The High Court rescinded the lease—but it held that the claimant's action was in reality a claim for damages, not an indemnity. Accordingly, whilst the claimant could recover an indemnity for those expenses that were a necessary obligation created by the lease— namely, the rates and rent payments, and repair costs—the claimant could not recover an indemnity for the loss of stock, loss of profits, and medical expenses, because the lease did not oblige the claimant to carry on business as a poultry farm or to employ a manager.

Because an award of damages will naturally cover the losses recoverable under an indemnity, it follows that an indemnity order is pointless where damages are awarded. For this reason, indemnity orders are usually made only where the misrepresentation is innocent and the court does not exercise the power to award damages in lieu of rescission.

Rescission

Misrepresentation renders a contract voidable,[48] which means that it will continue until such time as the representee sets it aside (this is known as 'rescission'). Rescission has the effect of setting aside the contract as if it had never been made. Accordingly, its principal aim is to return the parties to their pre-contract position (this is known as *restitutio in integrum*). In essence, both parties simply give back what they gained from the other.

➡ *restitutio in integrum*: 'restoration to the original position'

The representee can rescind in one of two ways, as follows.

- The representee can apply to the court for a rescission order. Where a formal document (for example, a lease) is to be rescinded, a rescission order might be necessary. A rescission order might also be necessary if one party fails to return what is due.

---

48. *Clough v L & NW Rly* (1871) LR 7 Ex 26.

- In many cases, a court order will not be necessary. The representee can rescind the contract simply by indicating to the representor that he is no longer bound by the contract. Whilst communication of rescission is normally required, where the misrepresentation is fraudulent and the representor has since absconded, communication of rescission is not required, provided that the representee performs some overt act that indicates his intention to rescind.[49]

Whilst rescission is normally available for all forms of misrepresentation, in a number of instances, the representee will be barred from exercising the right to rescind.

Affirmation

It may be the case that the representee does not wish the contract to come to an end. In such a case, he may decide to waive his right to rescind—known as 'affirmation'. Once the representee has expressly or impliedly indicated affirmation, the right to rescind is lost. But affirmation will only be valid if the representee knew that the representor's statement was false and that he had the right to rescind.[50] Following the acquisition of this knowledge, the representee may find that his subsequent action or inaction is enough to indicate affirmation,[51] as the following example demonstrates.

Eg Rescission and affirmation

BioCorp Ltd issues a prospectus, describing the company as one of the top ten pharmaceutical companies in the UK, and states that any money raised through the selling of shares will be used to expand the business, with a view to increasing future profitability. Relying on the prospectus, Richard purchases a large number of shares in BioCorp. Richard then discovers that BioCorp is not one of the UK's top ten pharmaceutical companies and that the money raised from selling shares is to be used to pay off BioCorp's substantial debt. Upon discovering the truth, however, Richard takes no further action and continues to accept dividend payments. Some time later, when BioCorp's financial position worsens and insolvency looms, Richard decides that he wishes to rescind the contract.

In such a case, it is likely that Richard will be barred from rescinding. His failure to act (for example, by removing his name from the register of shareholders)[52] and his continued acceptance of dividend payments[53] would be likely to amount to affirmation. In any event, depending on the length of time that passed between becoming aware of the truth and attempting to rescind, the court may also bar rescission on the basis that too much time has passed.

Lapse of time

Lapse of time provides evidence of affirmation in cases of inaction by the representee. In addition, the right to rescind will be lost if the falsity is not discovered within

---

49. *Car and Universal Finance Co Ltd v Caldwell* [1965] 1 QB 525 (CA).
50. *Peyman v Lanjani* [1985] Ch 457 (CA).
51. See *Long v Lloyd* [1958] 1 WLR 753 (CA).
52. *Re Scottish Petroleum Co (No 2)* (1883) 23 Ch D 413 (CA).
53. *Scholey v Central Railway Co of Venezuela* (1867) LR 9 Eq 266

a reasonable time. Where the misrepresentation is fraudulent, a lapse of time will not probably bar rescission.[54]

 Leaf v International Galleries [1950] 2 KB 86 (CA)

FACTS: The defendant innocently represented that a painting that it wished to sell was a genuine Constable. Relying on this, the claimant purchased the painting. Five years later, the claimant attempted to sell the painting, whereupon it was discovered that the painting was not by Constable. The claimant sought to rescind the contract based on the defendant's innocent misrepresentation.

HELD: The claimant had sought rescission promptly after discovering the falsity of the statement. Therefore, the lapse of time did not indicate that he had affirmed the contract. Despite this, the Court of Appeal held that the right to rescind was lost due to the fact that the claimant did not discover the falsity of the statement within a reasonable time.

★ See LCB Gower, 'Contract: Sale of Goods—Innocent Misrepresentations and Conditions' (1950) 13 MLR 362

Third-party rights

The right to rescind may be lost where an innocent third party (that is, one who does not know of the falsity of the statement) acquires, by purchase, rights in the subject matter of the contract. Because misrepresentation renders a contract voidable only, this means that good title can be passed to an innocent third-party purchaser at any time before the representee rescinds the contract,[55] as the following case demonstrates.

 White v Garden (1851) 10 CB 919

FACTS: A rogue bought 50 tonnes of iron from Garden. The rogue paid for the iron using a fraudulent **bill of exchange**. The rogue then sold the iron to White, who was unaware of the rogue's prior fraudulent activities. When the bill of exchange was dishonoured, Garden removed some of the iron that had been delivered to White, alleging that he had the right to rescind the contract due to the rogue's misrepresentation. White alleged that, in removing the iron, Garden had committed the tort of **conversion**.

HELD: Garden was held liable for the tort of conversion. White had acquired good title to the goods, because he had no knowledge of the rogue's misrepresentation. Garden had therefore lost the right to rescind.

COMMENT: In this case, White acquired rights in the goods before Garden attempted to rescind. If rescission takes place before the third party acquires the rights, the rescission will be valid.[56]

➡ **bill of exchange:** a document that promises to pay the bearer a sum of money at a future date

➡ **conversion:** interfering with goods in a manner inconsistent with another's rights (see p 457)

---

54. *Clough v LNW Railway* (1871) LR 7 Ex 26.

55. In the case of contracts involving the sale of goods, this rule is statutory: see Sale of Goods Act 1979, s 23.

56. *Car and Universal Finance Co Ltd v Caldwell* [1965] 1 QB 525 (CA).

Impossibility of restitutio in integrum

As noted, the principal aim of rescission is to place the claimant into his pre-contract position[57] (*restitutio in integrum*). This is usually achieved by each party giving back what was gained from the other party. It follows that if *restitutio in integrum* is impossible, the right to rescind will be lost.[58] But because rescission is an equitable remedy, the courts will not enforce this requirement strictly in cases in which it would cause unfairness or injustice. Accordingly, rescission will not be barred:

- simply because the subject matter of the contract has deteriorated in some way or lessened in value;[59]
- where *restitutio in integrum* becomes impossible due to a fraudulent representee's own dealings;[60]
- simply because one party has spent the money that he received;
- because precise *restitutio in integrum* is impossible. Provided that substantial *restitutio in integrum* is possible (for example, where the subject matter of the contract has deteriorated in some way or lessened in value),[61] this will suffice and rescission will not be barred.[62]

Awarding damages in lieu of rescission

 in lieu of: instead of, or in place of

The right to rescind will be lost if the court exercises its power under the Misrepresentation Act 1967, s 2(2), and awards damages in lieu of rescission. This power can only be exercised in relation to negligent and innocent misrepresentations, and is exercised where 'it would be equitable to do so, having regard to the nature of the misrepresentation and the loss that would be caused by it if the contract were upheld, as well as to the loss that rescission would cause to the other party'. The existence of this provision recognizes that rescission is a serious remedy and in cases in which the misrepresentation is trivial,[63] damages are a much more appropriate remedy. The exercise of s 2(2) is not pleaded by the parties; its use is entirely at the court's discretion.

The following case demonstrates the court's approach to the use of s 2(2).

 William Sindall plc v Cambridgeshire County Council [1994] 1 WLR 1016 (CA)

FACTS: The claimant purchased a piece of land from the defendant Council, for the purposes of property development, for £5 million. It took eighteen months to obtain planning permission, by which time the value of the land had dropped to £2 million. When the builders began development of the land, they discovered a sewer running throughout the land. This sewer meant that the proposed development could not go ahead unless drainage work costing £18,000 was carried out. The claimant alleged that the defendant's

---

57. *Spence v Crawford* [1939] 3 All ER 271 (HL).   58. *Clarke v Dickson* (1858) EB & E 148.
59. *Armstrong v Jackson* [1917] 2 KB 822 (KB).   60. *Spence v Crawford* [1939] 3 All ER 271 (HL).
61. *Armstrong v Jackson* [1917] 2 KB 822 (KB).
62. *Erlanger v New Sombrero Phosphate Co* (1873) 3 App Cas 1218 (HL).
63. The law never regards fraud as trivial, hence the reason why s 2(2) does not apply in cases of fraudulent misrepresentation.

failure to disclose the existence of the sewer amounted to a misrepresentation and sought rescission. The defendant argued that it did not know the sewer existed.

HELD: The Court of Appeal held that there was no misrepresentation. Hoffmann LJ went on to state *obiter* that, if a misrepresentation were present, the Court would have exercised its power under s 2(2) to prevent rescission for the following reasons.

1. Because remedying the problem would have cost a mere £18,000, this seems trivial in comparison to a sale involving £5 million. Remedying the problem would not have had an impact upon development or the resale value of the property.

2. Had rescission been allowed, the defendant would have suffered enormously. It would have to return the purchase price with interest (around £8 million) and, in return, it would recover land worth less than £2 million.

COMMENT: It was clear that the claimant was trying to use misrepresentation and the remedy of rescission to escape what turned out to be a bad bargain. Had the misrepresentation caused the bargain to be bad, then it is doubtless that rescission would be an appropriate remedy, but this was not the case here.

★ See H Beale, 'Damages in Lieu of Rescission for Misrepresentation' (1995) 111 LQR 60

Section 2(2) awards damages in lieu of rescission. Because it applies where 'the representee [...] would be entitled to rescind', it would appear that, where the representee cannot rescind (that is, because rescission is barred), s 2(2) should have no application. The courts have struggled with this issue. Certain cases have followed a literal interpretation and denied the use of s 2(2) where rescission is barred.[64] This approach was branded 'unattractive' by one judge,[65] but in more recent cases, it is the literal approach that has been favoured.[66] The disparity of opinion is not a product of judicial indecisiveness, but is rather more indicative of the Act's poor drafting.

Finally, several differences between s 2(1) and (2) should be noted, as follows.

- Damages cannot be awarded under s 2(1) in the absence of negligence. Negligence does not need to be established to receive damages under s 2(2).
- Under s 2(1), damages and rescission can be awarded; under s 2(2), damages are awarded instead of rescission.
- Under s 2(1), damages are available as of right; under s 2(2), damages are at the court's discretion.
- Section 2(3) indicates that damages granted under s 2(1) are likely to be greater than those granted under s 2(2) (for example, *dicta* indicate that damages under s 2(2) cannot include consequential loss).[67]

---

64. For example, *Zanzibar v British Aerospace (Lancaster House) Ltd* [2000] 1 WLR 2333 (QB); *Floods of Queensferry Ltd v Shand Construction Ltd (No 3)* [2000] BLR 81 (QB).

65. *Thomas Witter Ltd v TBP Industries Ltd* [1996] 2 All ER 573 (Ch) 590 (Jacob J).

66. *Pankhania v Hackney London Borough Council* [2002] EWHC 2441 (Ch), [2002] NPC 123.

67. *William Sindall plc v Cambridgeshire County Council* [1994] 1 WLR 1016 (CA).

Representations that have become contractual terms

The above discussion has concerned those situations in which a statement amounts to a mere representation (that is, it does not become a term of the contract). If a misrepresentation has become a contractual term, then the claimant has a choice between two courses of action.

🔗 Breach of contract is discussed at p 298 and damages for breach are discussed at p 327

🔗 The ability to terminate a contract on the ground of breach is discussed at p 302

1. He may commence a claim for breach of contract. If he does so, the claimant will recover damages for breach of contract and not for misrepresentation. In addition, if the term breached is a condition, or an innominate term, the breach of which deprives the claimant of substantially the whole benefit of the contract, then the claimant can also terminate the contract on the ground of the breach.

2. Alternatively, the claimant can make use of the Misrepresentation Act 1967, s 1(a). This provides that where a person enters into a contract after a misrepresentation has been made to him, and the misrepresentation becomes a term of the contract, then that person can rescind the contract, subject to the bars to rescission discussed above. But if that person does rescind, he cannot then recover damages for breach of contract, because rescission sets aside not only the contract, but also any right to claim damages for its breach. The right to claim damages for misrepresentation may still exist, depending on the circumstances.

Excluding liability for misrepresentation

The ability to exclude liability for misrepresentation is regulated by both the common law and statute. In addition to the common law requirements relating to notice and incorporation, the courts have established that liability cannot be excluded for losses resulting from a fraudulent misrepresentation.[68]

Three pieces of legislation regulate the ability to exclude liability for misrepresentation contractually. The Unfair Contract Terms Act 1977 and the Unfair Terms in Consumer Contracts Regulations 1999[69] will be examined in a later chapter. Here, we will focus on the Misrepresentation Act 1967, s 3, which provides that any term in a contract that seeks to exclude or restrict liability or any remedy for misrepresentation will only be valid in so far as it satisfies the requirement of reasonableness. Therefore, the effect of s 3 is to make such terms prima facie unenforceable unless the representor can establish that the clause is reasonable.

🔗 The Unfair Contract Terms Act 1977 and the Unfair Terms in Consumer Contracts Regulations 1999 are examined in detail in Chapter 28

The courts have not been entirely consistent in their application of the reasonableness test. In particular, two issues have tested the courts. The first issue is whether an exclusion clause will be unreasonable because it could potentially exclude liability for unreasonable or fraudulent behaviour. In several cases, the courts have held that an exclusion clause that is capable of covering such behaviour is unreasonable.[70] Conversely, other cases have held that, because fraud cannot be excluded, any

---

68. *S Pearson and Son Ltd v Dublin Corp* [1907] AC 351 (HL).
69. SI 1999/2083.
70. *Thomas Witter Ltd v TBP Industries Ltd* [1996] 2 All ER 573 (Ch).

clause that could potentially exclude liability for fraud would not actually intend to exclude liability for fraud and, as such, could be reasonable.[71]

The second issue concerns the applicability of s 3 to 'entire agreement clauses'. Entire agreement clauses do not so much exclude liability for misrepresentation as attempt to avoid committing misrepresentation altogether. These clauses provide that the entire agreement is contained in the contract and that the parties have not relied on any representations made prior to, or during, negotiations. Because such agreements do not expressly seek to 'exclude or restrict' liability for misrepresentation, the court has held that s 3 does not apply to such agreements. The rationale for this approach was stated by Chadwick LJ:

> Liability in damages under the Misrepresentation Act 1967 can arise only where the party who has suffered the damage has relied on the misrepresentation. Where both parties to the contract have acknowledged, in the document itself, that they have not relied on any pre-contract representation, it would be bizarre…to attribute to them an intention to exclude a liability which they must have thought could never arise.[72]

But the problem is that a very fine line exists between entire agreement clauses (to which s 3 will not apply) and clauses merely stating that statements made are not to be construed as assertions of fact or are statements of opinion only (which will be subject to s 3).[73] In such cases, the application of s 3 may depend on technical constructions of the contract, but this will do little to aid predictability and a party to a contract may find that his exclusion clauses are subject to regulation that he specifically wished to avoid.

⟨·⟩ Key points summary

- Misrepresentation occurs where a party is induced into entering into a contract by another's false statement of fact or law.

- A statement of opinion will not constitute a misrepresentation unless the representor does not honestly believe the opinion that he states, or the representor represents an opinion for which he does not have reasonable grounds and impliedly represents that he has such grounds.

- A statement of intention will not constitute a misrepresentation unless the representor, at the time that the statement was made, does not believe that the intended state of affairs will occur.

- Subject to several exceptions, silence cannot constitute misrepresentation.

- A fraudulent misrepresentation occurs where a party makes a false statement knowingly, without belief in its truth, or recklessly careless of whether it is true or false.

- Negligent misrepresentation exists at both common law and in statute.

---

71. *Zanzibar v British Aerospace (Lancaster House) Ltd* [2000] 1 WLR 2333 (QB) 2347 (Raymond Jack QC).
72. *Watford Electronics Ltd v Sanderson CFL Ltd* [2001] EWCA Civ 317, [2001] All ER (Comm) 696, [41].
73. *Cremdean Properties Ltd v Nash* (1977) 244 EG 547 (CA).

- An innocent misrepresentation is one that is completely devoid of fraud or negligence. Damages are not available as of right where the misrepresentation is innocent.

- Misrepresentation renders a contract voidable, but in certain circumstances, the representee will be barred from rescinding the contract.

- In cases of negligent and innocent misrepresentation, the court can award damages in lieu (instead) of rescission.

Mistake

In Chapter 6, we noted that, in order for a valid and enforceable contract to exist, classical contract law required there to be a *consensus ad idem* ('agreement as to the same things'). It followed that where the parties have contracted based on some form of mistake, the required meeting of minds would not be present and the courts would invalidate the contract.[74]

Today, the courts are much more reluctant to invalidate a contract on the ground of mistake, for several reasons.

- The finding of mistake can result in the contract being declared void. Given that a principal aim of the English system of contract law is to uphold contracts where possible, the courts should not be quick to erase contracts from existence. In certain cases (for example, contracts involving the sale of goods), declaring a contract to be void can adversely affect innocent third parties who subsequently contract with the party to a mistaken contract.

- Businesses require a measure of commercial certainty in their dealings. If contracts were regularly declared void due to the discovery of a fact that was unknown to the parties when they contracted, certainty would be considerably reduced. The contractual process could become burdensome, because parties would be forced to investigate every facet of the agreement to ensure that no mistakes existed.

- A party who had made a bad bargain could attempt to use the doctrine of mistake to avoid the adverse consequences of the bargain.

There are many different forms of mistake, but their classification is a matter of considerable debate, with different commentators taking different approaches. In this text, mistake is divided into the traditional three categories, as follows.

- *Common mistake* Common mistake occurs where both parties have made the same mistake.
- *Mutual mistake* Mutual mistake occurs where both parties have made a mistake, but they have made a different mistake.
- *Unilateral mistake* Unilateral mistake occurs where only one party is mistaken and the other party knows, or can be taken to know, of the mistake.

---

74. See, e.g., *Smith v Wheatcroft* (1878) 9 Ch D 223 (Ch).

Common mistake

Common mistake occurs where both parties to a contract have made the same mistake. As we shall see, in many cases of common mistake, the law provides that the contract will be rendered void. But this only applies if the contract does not, expressly or impliedly, allocate the risk of a common mistake to one party or the other, or provide some other solution. In many cases, the contract will provide for this and the solution as specified in the contract will dictate the effect of a common mistake. The law discussed in this section can therefore be thought of as a fallback position for those situations in which the contract is silent on this issue.

Categories of common mistake include the following.

Mistake as to existence of the subject matter

This form of mistake occurs where:

- the subject matter of the contract may never have existed; or
- the subject matter of the contract did exist, but has subsequently ceased to exist (this is known as *res extincta*).

➡ *res extincta*: 'the thing has ceased to exist'

In cases involving a mistake regarding the existence of the subject matter, performance of the contract is impossible[75] and so the contract will be held void.

The following case demonstrates this form of mistake in practice.

🔘 *Galloway v Galloway* (1914) 30 TLR 531 (KB)

FACTS: Following the wedding ceremony of the claimant and defendant, they entered into a contract known as a 'separation agreement', whereby the defendant agreed to pay the claimant £1 per week, which would be used to support their three children. It transpired that the defendant's first wife, who both the defendant and claimant believed to be dead, was, in fact, still alive. The defendant fell behind on his payments under the separation agreement and the claimant sued.

HELD: The High Court held that the separation agreement was void, because it was based on a common mistake—namely, that the defendant and claimant believed that they were married. The marriage was the subject matter of the contract and, because the defendant's first wife was still alive, the marriage between the claimant and defendant was invalid. Accordingly, at the time that the separation agreement was entered into, the subject matter of the contract did not exist.

Galloway demonstrates that the subject matter of the contract need not be a physical object. But the majority of cases in this area do relate to goods that, at the time the contract was made, do not exist.

---

75. This is why *res extincta* is also known as 'initial impossibility'. Where the subject matter is destroyed after the contract has been formed, the contract will be frustrated on the ground of 'subsequent impossibility'.

Couturier v Hastie (1856) 5 HL Cas 673

FACTS: The claimant sold a cargo of corn to the defendant. At the time that the contract was made, both parties believed the corn to be on board a ship on its way to London. Unknown to both parties, however, whilst in transit, the corn began to ferment and, shortly before the contract was made, had been sold by the ship's captain whilst in port at Tunis. The defendant argued that, because this was a simple contract for the sale of goods and because the corn had 'perished'[76] at the time of the contract, the contract was void and he was not required to pay the contract price. The claimant disagreed and argued that the contract was not a simple contract for the sale of goods, but was a contract for the entire 'adventure', which would include any risks faced by the shipment of the cargo.

HELD: The House of Lords held that, on the construction of the contract, it was a contract for the sale of goods and that, because the goods did not exist at the time that the contract was made, the contract was held void and the defendant was not required to pay the contract price.

In *Couturier*, Lord Cranworth LC stated: 'The whole question turns upon the construction of the contract ...'[77] This would seem to indicate that cases involving mistake as to the existence of the subject matter will not automatically result in the contract being held void, but that the result will depend upon the construction of the contract (as stated above). Even if this is the case, however, statute would appear to indicate that the construction of the contract is irrelevant where the contract is one for the sale of goods. The Sale of Goods Act 1979, s 6, states that:

> Where there is a contract for the sale of specific goods, and the goods without the knowledge of the seller have perished at the time the contract is made, the contract is void.

Several commentators have, however, argued that s 6 merely establishes the prima facie position,[78] or that where one party expressly agrees to bear the risk that the goods may not exist, then s 6 should not serve to render the contract void.[79] Whilst such conclusions would result in a more commercially flexible position and some ingenious sophistry may be able to lead to such conclusions, the wording of s 6 does seem to clearly indicate that Parliament did not intend s 6 to be the prima facie position. Further, the fact that certain sections of the Sale of Goods Act 1979[80] can be expressly excluded by a contractual term would lead to the conclusion that, if Parliament had intended s 6 to be capable of exclusion, it would have expressly stated as much.

---

76. In law, 'perishing' not only includes destruction of goods, but also includes situations in which they are so damaged that they cease to comply with their contractual description or purpose.

77. *Couturier v Hastie* (1856) 5 HL Cas 673 (HL) 681.

78. PS Atiyah, '*Couturier v Hastie* and the Sale of Non-Existent Goods' (1957) 73 LQR 340.

79. E Peel, *Treitel on the Law of Contract* (12th edn, Sweet & Maxwell, London, 2007) 316.

80. For example, the Sale of Goods Act 1979, s 55(1), provides that certain terms implied by law may be negatived or varied by express agreement.

Mistake as to title

Mistake as to title is also known as *res sua*, which is an abbreviation of *nulli enim res sua servit jure servitutis* ('no one can have a servitude over his own property'). Mistake as to title occurs where a buyer purchases an item that he already owns, but neither he nor the seller is aware of this. Both parties labour under the mistaken belief that the seller owns the goods (hence the mistake is common). Where there is a mistake as to title, the contract will be void. But if the contract provides, expressly or impliedly, that the seller has the right to sell the goods (the right to sell is known as title), then the rules regarding mistake as to title will not apply and the seller can be liable for breach of contract. Such a term is implied into sale of goods contracts by the Sale of Goods Act 1979, s 12.

➡ title: the right to sell goods to another

Mistake as to quality

In cases involving mistakes as to title or the existence of the subject matter, the nature of the mistake is so fundamental that it is justifiable to hold the contract void. Where the parties are mistaken regarding the quality of the subject matter of the contract, the issue is slightly more complex, because the mistake as to quality can be of varying degrees. Before discussing the law in this area, it is important to note that, in many cases, the issue of mistake as to quality will not arise, because one party (normally the seller) will bear the risk of the subject matter lacking quality. For example, the Sale of Goods Act 1979, s 14(2), implies a term into sale of goods contracts providing that goods sold will be of 'satisfactory quality' and that, should the goods not be of satisfactory quality, the buyer will normally have the right to reject the goods. Where the risk of a lack of quality is not contractually allocated, the starting point will be to examine the following leading case in this area.

 Visit the Online Resource Centre for more on this implied term in the chapter entitled 'The sale of goods'

⊙ *Bell v Lever Bros Ltd* [1932] AC 161 (HL)

FACTS: The defendants (Bell and Snelling) were employed by the claimant on a fixed-term contract. In 1926, the defendants' contracts were renewed for another five years, but in 1929, the claimant company merged with another and the defendants' services were no longer required. Accordingly, the defendants contracted with the claimant to pay them £50,000 compensation (Bell received £30,000 and Snelling received £20,000) for the early termination of their employment contracts. It was subsequently discovered that the defendants had acted in breach of their employment contracts, which would have allowed the claimant to terminate their contracts without paying any compensation. The claimant brought an action alleging that the contract providing for the payment of compensation was void on the grounds of common mistake (that is, both parties mistakenly believed that the defendants were entitled to compensation) and that it could therefore recover the £50,000 paid. The court at first instance and the Court of Appeal held that the contract was void due to fundamental mistake, and that the £50,000 could be recovered.

HELD: The House of Lords, by a majority of three to two, held that the contract was valid and the defendants could keep the compensation paid. Lord Atkin, providing what is regarded as the leading judgment, stated that the mistake was not a fundamental one, but was rather one of quality, and mistakes as to quality will not affect the contract 'unless it is a mistake of both parties, and is as to the existence of some quality which makes the thing without the quality essentially different from the thing it was believed to be'.[81] Applying this test, the mistake had not rendered the contract essentially different from what it was believed to be. The contract was one to terminate early the employment of the defendants and that is exactly what the contract did. The fact that it could have been achieved without paying the defendants compensation did not render the contract 'essentially different'.

⭐ See C Macmillan, 'How Temptation Led to Mistake: An Explanation of *Bell v Lever Brothers Ltd*' (2003) 119 LQR 625

COMMENT: The test laid down by Lord Atkin is extremely strict. In fact, no case has ever satisfied it. If mistake as to quality was not established in *Bell*, it is difficult to see when it will ever be established. Some have gone further and argued that *Bell* is so stringent that it does not provide authority for the existence of mistake as to quality as a separate class of mistake.[82]

The result of *Bell* is that, unlike mistake as to title or the existence of the subject matter, mistake as to quality will not normally render a contract void. In fact, it is still not clear that a mistake as to quality will ever render a contract void. Lord Atkin's test above was merely *obiter*, and whilst a number of judges (for example, Steyn J, as he then was, in the following case) have stated that a sufficiently fundamental mistake as to quality may render the contract void, these comments were *obiter* too.

🔐 Associated Japanese Bank (International) Ltd v Credit Du Nord SA [1989] 1 WLR 255 (QB)

FACTS: The fraudster, a man named Bennett, entered into a transaction with the claimant bank whereby the bank would purchase four textile machines, which would then be leased to Bennett. Before entering into the agreement, the claimant required that Bennett obtain a guarantor (a party who would pay the rental payments should Bennett not pay). The defendant bank agreed to act as guarantor. Bennett was given just over £1 million to purchase the machines on the bank's behalf, but the machines did not exist. Bennett absconded with the £1 million and, of course, never paid any of the rental instalments. Bennett was subsequently caught and charged with fraud, but by this time, he was bankrupt. Accordingly, the claimant sought to enforce the guarantee against the defendant.

➡️ condition precedent: a condition that must be complied with before an offer can be accepted, or before a contract becomes operational

HELD: In the High Court, Steyn J held that, on the construction of the contract, the existence of the machines was a condition precedent and that, because the machines did not exist, the defendant was not liable to act as guarantor. But he then proceeded to discuss *obiter* whether the contract would have been void on the ground of common mistake. Echoing the words of Lord Atkin in *Bell*, Steyn J stated that the mistake as to quality must render the contract essentially different from that which the parties believed it to be, and that the current facts would pass this test and render the contract void.

⭐ See GH Treitel, 'Mistake in Contract' (1988) 104 LQR 501

COMMENT: It may be thought that this was a case of mistake as to the existence of the subject matter, but it was not. The subject matter of the contract was not the machines themselves, but Bennett's representations regarding his use of the machines and his obligations once they were purchased.

---

81. *Bell v Lever Bros Ltd* [1932] AC 161 (HL) 256.
82. M Furmston, *Cheshire, Fifoot & Furmston's Law of Contract* (15th edn, OUP, Oxford, 2007) 292–3.

It can therefore be seen that if mistake as to quality is an established category of common mistake, it will be extremely difficult to establish. As noted in Chapter 1, in some cases, the harshness of the common law is mitigated by the supplementary system of equity. As we will see, for a time, the harshness of the approach in *Bell* was indeed mitigated by the existence of common mistake in equity.

The distinction between equity and the common law is discussed at p 9

Common mistake as to a fundamental assumption

A contract is void if the parties have made their agreement on the basis of a particular assumption that turns out to be untrue, provided that the assumption was fundamental to the continued validity of the contract, or was a foundation essential to its existence.[83] This was accepted by the House of Lords in *Bell*, although their Lordships were divided on whether or not the assumption in question was sufficiently fundamental and did not find the contract in that case void for mistake on this or any other ground.

Common mistake as to possibility of performance

A contract is void if it is made under a common mistaken belief that it is possible to perform it, unless the risk of impossibility of performance is allocated to a party or the contract provides for some other solution. Thus, a contract whereby one party agreed to cut and process a certain tonnage of a particular crop on a specific piece of land was held to be void when it was discovered that the land could not yield the tonnage of the crop stated in the contract.[84]

Common mistake in equity

The above categories of common mistake were created by the common law. For a time, however, there also existed a separate doctrine of common mistake in equity, and there existed two notable differences between common mistake at common law and in equity, as follows.

- Mistake in equity could be established in situations in which mistake at common law could not.
- Common mistake at common law would render the contract void, whereas common mistake in equity merely rendered the contract voidable.

The doctrine of common mistake in equity appears to have been created by Lord Denning in the case of *Solle v Butcher*.[85] The decision in *Solle* was followed numerous times over the course of the next fifty years[86] and the existence of a doctrine of common mistake in equity was well accepted, although there were judges[87] who argued that *Solle* was incompatible with the House of Lords' decision in *Bell v Lever Bros Ltd* (discussed above). In *Associated Japanese Bank (International) Ltd v Credit Du Nord SA* (discussed above), Steyn J took time to explain the relationship between the doctrines of common mistake at common law and in equity. He stated:

> Where common law mistake has been pleaded, the court must first consider this plea. If the contract is held to be void, no question of mistake in equity arises.

---

83. *Grains & Fourrages SA v Huyton* [1997] 1 Lloyd's Rep 628 (QB).
84. *Sheikh Bros v Ochsner* [1957] AC 136 (PC).　　85. [1950] 1 KB 671 (CA).
86. See, e.g., *Grist v Bailey* [1967] Ch 532 (Ch); *Magee v Pennine Insurance Co Ltd* [1969] 2 QB 507 (CA).
87. See, e.g., Winn LJ (dissenting) in *Magee v Pennine Insurance Co Ltd* [1969] 2 QB 507 (CA).

But if the contract is held to be valid, a plea of mistake in equity may have to be considered.[88]

Despite this, there was always a tension and uncertainty regarding the relationship between common mistake at common law and in equity. Reconciling the separate doctrines was an extremely difficult task. For example, if a contract could be set aside on the ground of common mistake in equity, why did the House in *Bell* not consider this? Accordingly, in the following case, the Court of Appeal decided that the decision in *Solle* could not stand alongside the decision in *Bell*, thereby abolishing the doctrine of common mistake in equity.

Great Peace Shipping Ltd v Tsavliris Salvage (International) Ltd (Great Peace) [2002] EWCA Civ 1407

FACTS: Whilst in the Indian Ocean, a ship, the *Cape Providence*, sustained structural damage and was in danger of sinking. The defendant offered to salvage the ship and the shipowners accepted. The defendant located a tug that could salvage the *Cape Providence*, but it was at least five days away, by which time it was feared that the *Cape Providence* would have sunk. The defendant therefore consulted with various parties to try to locate a ship that was closer to the *Cape Providence*. A ship, the *Great Peace*, was located that was believed to be only 35 miles away from the *Cape Providence*. Accordingly, the defendant contracted with the owners of the *Great Peace* (the claimant) to salvage the *Cape Providence*. At the time that the contract was formed, both parties believed that the *Great Peace* was 35 miles away from the *Cape Providence*; shortly after, it was discovered that the *Great Peace* was, in fact, 410 miles away and would take over three days to reach the *Cape Providence*. The defendant therefore cancelled the contract and located a closer ship to perform the salvage. The claimant sued to recover the hire price and succeeded at first instance. On appeal, the defendant argued that the contract was void at common law on the ground of common mistake or, if that argument failed, that the contract was voidable in equity.

HELD: The Court of Appeal held that there was no mistake at common law. Applying the test established by Lord Atkin in *Bell v Lever Bros*, the Court held that the mistake had not rendered the contract essentially different from what the parties believed it to be. The contract was still one of salvage: the mistake as to distance did not render the contract 'essentially different'. The *Great Peace* could still have performed the contract and, had the defendant not located a closer ship, the *Great Peace* probably would have performed the salvage.

Turning to common mistake in equity, the Court expressed sympathy for Lord Denning's desire to mitigate the harshness of the approach in *Bell*. But after 'full and mature consideration',[89] the Court concluded that there is 'no way that *Solle v Butcher* can stand with *Bell v Lever Bros*'.[90] Accordingly, the defendant's appeal was dismissed.

★ See FMB Reynolds, 'Reconsider the Contract Textbooks' (2003) 119 LQR 177

---

88. *Associated Japanese Bank (International) Ltd v Credit Du Nord SA* [1989] 1 WLR 255 (QB) 268.
89. *Great Peace Shipping Ltd v Tsavliris Salvage (International) Ltd (Great Peace)* [2002] EWCA Civ 1407, [2003] QB 679, [160].
90. Ibid.

The immediate effect of the decision in *Great Peace* is to abolish the doctrine of common mistake in equity. Whilst this will result in the law relating to common mistake (especially mistake as to quality) becoming considerably more certain, it also means that the flexibility evidenced in cases such as *Solle v Butcher* has been lost. The Court in *Great Peace* acknowledged this, with Lord Phillips stating that:

> An equitable jurisdiction to grant rescission on terms where a common funda-mental mistake has induced a contract gives greater flexibility than a doctrine of common law which holds the contract void in such circumstances.[91]

The Court went on to state that there is 'scope for legislation to give greater flexibil-ity to our law of mistake than the common law allows'.[92] Legislation might not even be required if a future House of Lords or Supreme Court is of the opinion that com-mon mistake in equity can exist alongside the common law, or that *Bell* should be overruled. For the time being, however, common mistake exists at common law only and the court will adopt an 'all or nothing approach', whereby if mistake is estab-lished, the contract will be void, and if no mistake exists, the contract will be valid.

Mutual mistake

Mutual mistake occurs where both parties are mistaken regarding the essence of the subject matter of the contract (as opposed to the quality of it), but they have made a different mistake (unlike common mistake, where both parties make the same mis-take). This is usually expressed by stating that the parties are 'at cross-purposes' (for example, *A* makes an offer to sell a Ferrari, but *B* accepts the offer believing it to be for the sale of a Porsche). Such a mistake can render a contract void.

 Scriven Bros & Co v Hindley & Co [1913] 2 KB 564 (KB)

FACTS: The claimant put up for auction a number of bales of hemp and of tow. All of the bales had the same shipping mark and the auction catalogue failed to mention that the bales were of differing commodities. The defendant inspected the hemp, but not the tow. It accordingly believed that all of the bales were of hemp and made a bid (which was successful) based on this. Because hemp was more expensive than tow, the result was that the defendant paid well over the odds for the bales of tow. The defendant refused to pay for the tow, and the claimant commenced proceedings.

HELD: The High Court held that the contract was void, because there was no agreement.

When determining whether or not mutual mistake is present, the courts will require that the agreement between the parties contain an element of ambiguity. Whether this ambiguity is enough to warrant rendering the contract void is based on an objective test. It will need to be established that a reasonable man could not have chosen between the view of the offeror or the offeree. If a reasonable man would have

---

91. Ibid, [161].   92. Ibid (Lord Phillips MR).

thought that the view of the offeror or offeree was intended to form the basis of the contract, then no mutual mistake will exist. This can be seen in the following case.

 Smith v Hughes (1871) LR 6 QB 597

FACTS: The defendant wished to purchase a quantity of oats to feed to his racehorses. The claimant demonstrated a sample of oats to the defendant, who agreed to purchase a larger quantity. When the oats were delivered, the defendant discovered that the oats were new oats, whereas he had wanted—and had thought that he was buying—old oats. Accordingly, the defendant rejected the oats and refused to pay. The claimant sued for price.

HELD: The claimant succeeded and recovered the contract price. The court held that the claimant had never described the oats as old and that there was no evidence to indicate that the age of the oats was a term of the contract. Accordingly, a reasonable man would have understood the contract in the way that the claimant understood it and so there was no mistake.

COMMENT: This case also indicates that mistake regarding quality of the subject matter is not enough to establish mutual mistake (and unilateral mistake, which is examined next).

Unilateral mistake

Common and mutual mistake occurs where both parties are mistaken. Conversely, unilateral mistake occurs where only one party is mistaken and the other party is aware, or is taken to be aware, of the mistake. Unilateral mistake operates at common law to render a contract void within extremely narrow boundaries and tends be found in mistakes involving the identity of the person, or the terms of the contract.

Mistake as to identity of the person

Mistake as to the identity of the person can be a somewhat complex issue and typically occurs in situations similar to that in the following example.

 Mistake as to identity of the person

Isaac owns a small high-street jewellery business. He is approached by an individual claiming to be Lord Bill Sugar, a well-known entrepreneur. Being aware of Lord Sugar's reputation, Isaac allows him to purchase on credit a number of necklaces and several expensive wristwatches. It transpires that the man is not Lord Bill Sugar, but an impostor (these characters are known in such cases as 'rogues'). Consequently, the credit is dishonoured. The rogue sells the necklaces and watches to Vicki, an innocent purchaser, and then disappears with his ill-gotten money. Isaac, having discovered that the rogue was an impostor, discovers that his property was sold to Vicki. Isaac will obviously wish to recover his property from Vicki, usually via the tort of **conversion**. The problem is that both Isaac and Vicki are innocent parties—so who should bear the loss?

➡ conversion: interfering with goods in a manner that is inconsistent with another's rights (see p 457)

Isaac will need to establish that the contract between himself and the rogue was void on the ground of unilateral mistake as to identity. If this is established, it follows that the rogue did not acquire good title to the goods and so cannot lawfully pass good title onto Vicki, even though she bought them in good faith.[93] Vicki will therefore have to return the goods to Isaac. Conversely, Vicki would try to establish that the contract between Isaac and the rogue was valid. This would result in the rogue acquiring good title, which he could in turn pass onto Vicki, who could then keep the goods.[94]

An alternative approach for Isaac would be to argue that the contract between himself and the rogue was voidable on the ground of fraudulent misrepresentation. But whilst fraudulent misrepresentation would almost certainly be established, it will be remembered that rescission may be barred where an innocent third party (such as Vicki) acquires an interest in the goods. Accordingly, Isaac would probably be unable to rescind the contract.

The bars to rescission are discussed at p 242

As can be seen from the above example, the question that the courts face is whether they should favour the innocent owner of the property (Isaac) or the innocent third party (Vicki). Either way, an innocent party will suffer, which is why this area of the law has become so controversial and complex. It is generally regarded that the law in this area is unsatisfactory, and the validity of a contract depends on a number of complex, technical, and (arguably) artificial distinctions.

A crucial requirement of mistake as to identity is that the mistake should relate to the *identity* of the person, not merely to some *attribute* of the person. In practice, this distinction can be extremely difficult to discern. The following two cases demonstrate the distinction. In the first case, the mistake related to identity and so the contract was held void, whereas in the second case, the mistake related to the attributes of the person and so the contract was held not to be void.

Cundy v Lindsay (1878) 3 App Cas 459 (HL)

FACTS: A rogue by the name of Alfred Blenkarn hired premises at 37 Wood Street. He placed an order with the claimant linen manufacturer for a consignment of linen handkerchiefs. The rogue signed his name on the order so that it looked like 'Blenkiron & Co', which was a respectable business known to the claimant that was based at 123 Wood Street. Relying on the respectable reputation of Blenkiron & Co, the claimant sent the handkerchiefs to 37 Wood Street, with payment to follow at some point in the future. The payment was never made. The rogue then sold a number of handkerchiefs to the defendant and fled (he was later caught and convicted of obtaining goods by deception). The claimant sought the recovery of the handkerchiefs in conversion.

HELD: The House of Lords held that the contract between the claimant and the rogue was void. In this case, the identity of the person was crucial to the claimant. He intended to deal with a respectable business man (Blenkiron), but instead had dealt with a rogue (Blenkarn). Because this mistake was known to the rogue, there was clearly a unilateral mistake as to identity.

---

93. Sale of Goods Act 1979, s 21(1). The common law also provides that *nemo dat quod non habet* ('no one gives who possesses not').

94. Ibid, s 23.

King's Norton Metal Co Ltd v Edridge, Merrett & Co Ltd (1897) 14 TLR 98 (CA)

FACTS: A rogue named Wallis set up a company called Hallam & Co, the sole purpose of the company being to defraud the claimant metal manufacturer. Hallam & Co sent a letter to the claimant ordering a quantity of brass rivet wire. The letterhead gave the impression that Hallam & Co was a large, successful factory, with multiple depots and agencies around Europe, which, of course, was not the case: the company consisted solely of Wallis. Relying on the letterhead's description of the company, the claimant dispatched the goods on credit to Hallam & Co's (that is, Wallis') address. The goods were never paid for and Wallis sold the goods to the defendant, who knew nothing of the deception. The claimant sought the recovery of the goods.

HELD: The Court of Appeal held that the contract was not void for mistake, but was merely voidable for fraud. The identity of Hallam & Co was not important; what was important was its perceived attributes (for example, its size, success, and creditworthiness). In fact, because Wallis *was* Hallam & Co, subject to the principle of corporate personality, it was probably the case that no mistake of identity was present. Accordingly, the defendant acquired good title to the goods and was entitled to keep them.

🔗 Corporate personality is discussed at p 606

The above cases demonstrate that the distinction between identity and attributes can be extremely fine. This distinction can be even more difficult to discern when the parties contract face to face. In such cases, the courts tend to presume that the party intended to contract with the person in front of him (not the person that the rogue is claiming to be), so that any mistake will be as to that person's attributes as opposed to his identity—unless the case is exceptional.

The following case demonstrates this presumption and its consequences.

Lewis v Averay [1972] 1 QB 198 (CA)

FACTS: The claimant placed an advertisement in a local newspaper stating that he wished to sell his car. The rogue came to inspect the car, introduced himself as the then famous actor Richard Green, and offered to purchase the car. The claimant agreed and the rogue wrote a cheque for the advertised price of £450. The rogue signed the cheque 'RA Green' and indicated that he wished to take the car immediately. Understandably, the claimant was cautious and asked the rogue if he had any proof of identification. The rogue produced a Pinewood Studios admission pass, which bore his photograph. The claimant therefore permitted the rogue to take the car before the cheque had cleared. The rogue was not Richard Green and the cheque failed to clear. The rogue sold the car to the innocent defendant. The claimant sought recovery of the car, contending that the contract between himself and the rogue was void for unilateral mistake as to identity.

HELD: The Court of Appeal held that the claimant had intended to contract with the person in front of him, irrespective of his identity. Accordingly, the Court held that the contract was not void for mistake; it was merely voidable for misrepresentation. Because the contract had not been rescinded (nor could it be, because rescission would be barred) when the defendant acquired the car, his title was good and he could keep the car.

COMMENT: The distinction between identity and attributes was not wholly accepted in this case. Lord Denning stated that it was:

> a distinction without a difference. A man's very name is one of his attributes. It is also a key to his identity. If then, he gives a false name, is it a mistake as to his identity? Or a mistake as to his attributes? These fine distinctions do no good to the law.[95]

It is contended that Lord Denning's view is correct. The distinction creates considerable uncertainty and inconsistency in the law. The mistake in *Lewis* was extremely similar to the mistake in *Cunday v Lindsay*, yet in the latter case, the contract was held void, whereas in the former, it was merely voidable.

★ See CC Turpin, 'Mistake of Identity' (1972) 30 CLJ 19

It follows that, when parties deal face to face, mistake as to identity will only be established in exceptional cases—but the presumption that the party deals with the person in front of them can be rebutted, as occurred in the following case.

Ingram v Little [1961] 1 QB 31 (CA)

FACTS: The claimants, two elderly sisters, advertised their car for sale. A rogue approached the claimants and identified himself as 'Hutchinson'. He offered the asking price for the car, which the claimants accepted. But when the rogue produced a chequebook, one of the claimants stated that payment by cheque was not acceptable. The rogue stated that he was a businessman: 'PGM Hutchinson' of Stanstead House, Caterham. One of the sisters checked the telephone directory and discovered that such a person did, indeed, live at the stated address. On the strength of this, the claimants accepted the cheque. The rogue was not Hutchinson and the cheque was predictably dishonoured. By this time, the rogue had sold the car to the innocent defendant. The claimants sought recovery of the car.

HELD: The Court of Appeal held that the contract between the claimants and the rogue was void. Accordingly, the defendant had to return the car to the claimants. The checking of the telephone directory was evidence that they intended to deal with PGM Hutchinson.

COMMENT: This case has been severely criticized and subsequently doubted by the courts[96] to such an extent that it should now be regarded as wrongly decided. It has been argued that it is 'difficult to escape the conclusion that the court allowed its sympathy for the ladies to cloud its judgment of the issues'.[97]

Where the parties do not deal face to face (for example, in contracts by correspondence), the presumption would appear to be that the party intends to contract with the person identified. Accordingly, the presumption is that identity is crucial and a mistake will render the contract void. The case of *Cunday v Lindsay* discussed earlier is a good example of this presumption in practice.

---

95. *Lewis v Averay* [1972] 1 QB 198 (CA) 206.
96. See, e.g., ibid, 206 (Megaw LJ); *Shogun Finance Ltd v Hudson* [2003] UKHL 62, [2004] 1 AC 919, [87] (Lord Millett).
97. L Koffman and E Macdonald, *The Law of Contract* (6th edn, OUP, Oxford, 2007) 307.

The above discussion indicates that the law relating to mistake as to identity was highly unsatisfactory, because it rested on a number of technical, complex, and arguably unjustifiable distinctions. Accordingly, when the opportunity arose for the House of Lords to re-examine the law relating to mistake as to identity, it was hoped that a measure of much-needed clarity would be introduced. Whether such clarity was introduced is highly doubtful.

Shogun Finance Ltd v Hudson [2003] UKHL 62

FACTS: A rogue visited a Mitsubishi car dealer and indicated that he wished to purchase a certain vehicle on hire-purchase. The rogue identified himself as Dulabh Patel and produced a driving licence bearing this name. The rogue was not Dulabh Patel and had stolen the driving licence from the real Mr Patel. A price of £22,500 was agreed and the rogue signed the draft hire-purchase agreement using a signature that resembled that of the real Mr Patel. The car dealer then faxed a copy of the draft agreement and the driving licence to the claimant finance company[98] to run a credit check. Mr Patel's credit rating was good and so the claimant finance company entered into a hire-purchase agreement with the rogue, believing him to be Mr Patel. Upon payment of a 10 per cent deposit, the rogue took immediate delivery of the vehicle and drove it away. Shortly thereafter, the rogue sold the vehicle to the innocent defendant for £17,000. The rogue disappeared and the claimant finance company brought an action to recover the vehicle from the defendant. The defendant argued that he had acquired good title under the Hire Purchase Act 1964, s 27, which provided that a private purchaser who purchases a vehicle on good faith from a debtor who has obtained possession of the vehicle via hire-purchase would have good title. The claimant finance company contended that, because the defendant had not purchased the car from the debtor, but an impostor, s 27 did not apply.

HELD: By a three to two majority, the House of Lords held that the hire-purchase agreement between the claimant finance company and the rogue was void on the ground of unilateral mistake as to identity. Accordingly, the defendant had to return the car and was left bearing the £17,000 loss.

COMMENT: Lords Phillips and Walker, in the majority, affirmed the view that different presumptions exist where contracts are made face to face (in which case, the presumption is that there is no mistake as to identity) and where contracts are made at a distance (in which case, the presumption is that identity is crucial and so there may be a mistake as to identity). Lords Walker and Hobhouse opined that the face-to-face presumption might also apply to contracts concluded via telephone.

Lords Millett and Nicholls (dissenting) contended that the distinction between face-to-face contracting and distance contracting should be abandoned. Further, they argued that *Cunday v Lindsay* should be overruled and that the principle in *Lewis v Averay* should be followed—namely, that the innocent third-party purchaser should be protected, rather than the original owner.

See A Phang, P Lee, and P Koh, 'Mistaken Identity in the House of Lords' [2004] 63 CLJ 24

---

98. In such contracts, the car dealer sells the vehicle to the finance company and the finance company will then sell or lease the car to the purchaser on its standard terms. This explains why the finance company, and not the car dealer, brought the claim.

It is contended that the approach of the minority is considerably more attractive than the approach favoured by the majority in *Shogun Finance*. In his dissenting judgment, Lord Millett stated:

> It is surely fairer that the party who was actually swindled and who had an opportunity to uncover the fraud should bear the loss rather than a party who entered the picture only after the swindle had been carried out.[99]

This is a powerful argument. In *Shogun Finance*, the defendant was left £17,000 out of pocket, whereas the claimant finance company, which clearly had not taken sufficient steps to verify the identity of the rogue, was permitted to recover the vehicle. Whilst the third-party purchaser might not always be more deserving of protection than the original owner, it is usually the case that 'the person selling to a fraudster is in a stronger position to check their credentials than the person who buys from a fraudster'.[100] The decision in *Shogun Finance*, rather than encouraging parties to check the identity of those with whom they deal, indicates that the law will protect parties whose lax efforts to identify others has resulted in a mistake as to identity.

The minority were also extremely critical of the distinction between face-to-face contracts and contracts at a distance, with Lord Millett describing the distinction as 'the real objection to the present state of the law'.[101] Lord Nicholls agreed, stating that there is 'no magic attaching to a misrepresentation made in writing rather than by word of mouth'.[102] Certainly, it could be argued that the seemingly inconsistent decisions discussed previously are the result of the distinction (for example, *Cunday v Lindsay* and *Lewis v Averay*).

The result is that many commentators believe *Shogun Finance* to be 'a huge disappointment in terms of clarifying the applicable principles'.[103] It has been contended that the clear judicial divergence over the issues might warrant parliamentary intervention, in the same way that Parliament intervened to clarify the law relating to the effects of frustration. The comparison with the rules relating to frustration of a contract is a relevant one, because Devlin LJ (as he then was) has recommended that instead of placing the loss fully on either the original owner or third party, the law could apportion the loss between the two parties, as it does in cases involving frustration.[104] If such an approach could be devised, it would surely provide a more acceptable outcome that that evidenced in *Shogun Finance*.

🔗 The law relating to frustration is discussed at p 311

Mistake as to the terms of the contract

Where one party is mistaken as to the terms of the contract and the other party is aware of this mistake, then the court may hold the contract void for unilateral mistake. It is important to note that a mistake as to the terms is required; a mistake as to quality is not sufficient to establish unilateral mistake.[105] Unlike other forms of mistake, however, there is no requirement that the mistake is fundamental.

---

99. *Shogun Finance Ltd v Hudson* [2003] UKHL 62, [2004] 1 AC 919, [82].
100. C Elliot, 'No Justice for Innocent Purchasers of Dishonestly Obtained Goods: *Shogun Finance v Hudson*' (2004) JBL 381, 386.
101. *Shogun Finance Ltd v Hudson* [2003] UKHL 62, [2004] 1 AC 919, [68].   102. Ibid, [24].
103. J Poole, *Textbook on Contract Law* (9th edn, OUP, Oxford, 2008) 119.
104. *Ingram v Little* [1961] 1 QB 31 (CA) 73, 74.   105. *Smith v Hughes* (1871) LR 6 QB 597.

Hartog v Colin & Shields [1939] 3 All ER 566 (KB)

FACTS: The contract involved the sale of 30,000 hare skins. The defendant offered to sell the hare skins to the claimant, but mistakenly stated the price at 'per pound', when he meant to state 'per piece'. Trade custom was to quote the price 'per piece' and negotiations had been conducted on a 'per piece' basis. The result of the mistake was that the price offered was about one third of what the defendant intended. Unsurprisingly, the claimant accepted the offer. The defendant realized the mistake and refused to deliver the skins at that contract price. The claimant brought an action to enforce the contract.

HELD: Singleton J stated that:

> I am satisfied that it was a mistake on the part of the defendants or their servants which caused the offer to go forward in that way, and I am satisfied that anyone with any knowledge of the trade must have realised that there was a mistake.[106]

Accordingly, the High Court held that the contract was void for unilateral mistake.

Mistakes of law

When we discussed misrepresentation, we noted that traditionally only false representations of fact could constitute misrepresentation, but that, recently, the court had acknowledged that false representations of law could also constitute misrepresentation. The impetus for this extension was the recognition that mistakes of law could be actionable. Historically, only mistakes of fact were actionable and a mistake of law would only be actionable if it also amounted to a mistake of fact.[107] This limitation has now been removed[108] and a mistake of law can now render a contract void. The distinction between mistakes of fact and mistakes of law was not always easy to draw, so the decision to abolish the distinction is a welcome one.

Mistaken documents

Where a contract in writing contains a mistake, two additional remedies may be available—namely, rectification and a plea of *non est factum*.

Rectification

Where the parties have engaged in negotiations that result in a written contract, it may be that key terms may be omitted, or that the final contract is drafted incorrectly, so that it fails to reflect what the parties agreed. In such a case, the equitable remedy of rectification may be available, which will enable the court to rectify the contract so that it accurately reflects what the parties agreed. Because rectification involves adducing oral evidence to amend a contract, it follows that it constitutes an exception to the parol evidence rule.

 The parol evidence rule is discussed at p 210

The following case provides an example of how the courts can rectify a contract.

---

106. *Hartog v Colin & Shields* [1939] 3 All ER 566 (KB) 568.
107. *Solle v Butcher* [1950] 1 KB 671 (CA).
108. *Brennan v Bolt Burdon* [2004] EWCA Civ 1017, [2005] QB 303.

> ## 🔘 *Craddock Brothers v Hunt* **[1923] 2 Ch 136 (CA)**
>
> **FACTS:** The claimant agreed to sell a piece of property to the defendant. Both parties agreed that an adjoining yard would not form part of the sale and would remain the property of the claimant—but the final written contract provided that this yard would also be sold to the defendant. The claimant alleged that the contract was void on the ground of common mistake.
>
> **HELD:** The Court of Appeal rectified the contract to reflect the true agreement of the parties. The defendant would have to convey the adjoining yard back to the claimant.

Traditionally, rectification was only available in cases of common mistake, but it is now clear that rectification is also available in cases of unilateral mistake.[109] In order for rectification to be ordered in cases of common mistake, several requirements must be met, as follows.

- The agreement for which rectification is being sought must fail to reflect accurately the agreement of both parties. It follows that if the agreement omits a term desired by one party, but not the other, then rectification will not be ordered.[110]
- To prevent the courts imposing terms upon parties that they did not desire, the party seeking rectification will need to provide 'convincing proof'[111] that the agreement failed to reflect the parties' intentions.
- It must be equitable to grant rectification.

Where *A* is unaware of the mistake, but *B* is aware of it, or can be taken to be aware of it (that is, the mistake is unilateral), then rectification will only be ordered:

- if *B* knew of[112] that mistake, but nevertheless failed to draw the mistake to *A*'s notice and allowed the document to be executed,[113] or conducted himself as to divert *A* from discovering the mistake;[114] and
- the mistake would inequitably benefit *B* or be detrimental to *A*.[115]

Like rescission, rectification will be barred due to lapse of time[116] or where an innocent third party acquires rights to the subject matter of the contract.[117] The impossibility of achieving *restitutio in integrum* will not, however, bar rectification.[118]

---

109. *Blay v Pollard & Morris* [1930] 1 KB 628 (CA).

110. *Riverlate Properties Ltd v Paul* [1975] Ch 133 (CA).

111. *Joscelyne v Nissen* [1970] 2 QB 86 (CA) 98 (Russell LJ).

112. Knowledge here includes wilfully shutting one's eyes to the obvious, or wilfully and recklessly failing to make reasonable enquiries: *Commission for the New Towns v Cooper (Great Britain) Ltd* [1995] Ch 259 (CA).

113. *Thomas Bates & Son Ltd v Wyndham's (Lingerie) Ltd* [1981] 1 WLR 505 (CA).

114. *Commission for the New Towns v Cooper (Great Britain) Ltd* [1995] Ch 259 (CA).

115. *Thomas Bates & Son Ltd v Wyndham's (Lingerie) Ltd* [1981] 1 WLR 505 (CA).

116. *Bloomer v Spittle* (1872) LR 13 Eq 427.   117. *Smith v Jones* [1954] 1 WLR 1089 (Ch).

118. *Cook v Fearn* (1878) 48 LJ Ch 63.

Non est factum

The effect of a signature is discussed at p 970

→ *non est factum*: 'it is not my deed'

The general rule is that a person who signs a contract is bound by that contract, irrespective of whether he reads it or understands it.[119] In the sixteenth century, when few people could read, the courts developed an exception to this general rule and provided that a contract would not be binding where it was incorrectly read to a person who could not read.[120] Such a person could plead *non est factum*. The rationale behind the doctrine was that there was no *consensus ad idem* in that the signer signed a contract that he did not intend to, or, to put it another way, that 'the mind of the signer did not accompany his signature'.[121]

Today, the doctrine of *non est factum* is no longer limited to those who cannot read, nor is it limited to contracts executed by deed. But because a successful plea of *non est factum* results in the contract being held void, it follows that its use should be restricted. The restricted scope of the plea was established in the following case.

> ### Saunders v Anglia Building Society [1970] AC 1004 (HL)[122]
>
> **FACTS:** The claimant, Gallie, was a 78-year-old widow. She agreed to transfer the title of her house to her nephew, Parkin, to enable him to raise money by using the house as security. The claimant stated that she would only agree to the transfer if she could remain in the house until she died. Parkin and a business associate, Lee (the first defendant), asked the claimant to sign a document that, due to her glasses being broken, she was unable to read. Lee told her that the document would transfer title of the house to Parkin and, relying on this, she signed it. In fact, the document transferred the house to Lee for the price of £3,000, payable to Parkin. Lee failed to pay the £3,000 and mortgaged the house to the building society (the second defendant). The claimant sought to have the contract held void on the ground of *non est factum*. By the time that the case reached the House of Lords, the claimant had died and her action was continued by her executrix.
>
> **HELD:** The House of Lords held that the claimant's plea of *non est factum* should fail and the contract remained valid. The House held that for *non est factum* to succeed, the mistake must render the contract radically, substantially, or fundamentally different from what the party seeking relief intended. In *Saunders*, the contract was designed to enable Parkin to raise money by transferring the house, and that is what the contract did. That it transferred the house to Lee and not Parkin did not render it sufficiently different enough to warrant being held void. Further, *non est factum* could only be pleaded in the absence of carelessness. The claimant had been careless in signing the contract without asking for it to be read to her, or without obtaining professional advice.

→ executrix: a female executor— appointed by the testator (the person making the will) to administer the estate upon the testator's death

★ See CJ Miller, '*Non est Factum* and Mistaken Identity' (1969) 32 MLR 431

---

119. *L'Estrange v Graucob* [1934] 2 KB 394 (KB).
120. *Thoroughgood's Case* (1584) 2 Co Rep 9a.
121. *Foster v Mackinnon* (1869) LR 4 CP 704, 711 (Byles J).
122. This case is also sometimes known as *Gallie v Lee*.

The above requirements place significant limitations upon the doctrine of *non est factum*. Further, Lord Reid stated that the doctrine would apply to:

> Those who are permanently or temporarily unable through no fault of their own to have without explanation any real understanding of the purport of a particular document, whether that be from defective education, illness or innate incapacity.[123]

It follows that persons of full capacity who can read will be unlikely to be able to plead *non est factum* successfully[124] unless they have been tricked in some way into signing the document.[125] As a result of these limitations, *non est factum* will only be successfully pleaded in a small number of cases.

 Key points summary

- Mistakes may be common (both parties have made the same mistake), mutual (both parties have made a different mistake), or unilateral (only one party has made a mistake).

- At common law, mistake can render a contract void *ab initio*. There is no doctrine of common mistake in equity.

- Common mistakes include mistake as to the existence of the subject matter, mistake as to title, mistake as to quality, mistake as to a fundamental assumption, and mistake as to the possibility of performance.

- Mutual mistakes tend to concern mistakes relating to the essence of the subject matter of a contract.

- Unilateral mistakes will either relate to the terms of the contract or the identity of one of the parties.

- Mistakes of law are just as actionable as mistakes of fact.

- Where the parties' mistake is contained in a document, the courts may be prepared to rectify the contract to remedy the mistake.

- A person who signs a mistaken contract may, in exceptional circumstances, be able to have the contract declared void if he did not realize what he was signing.

Duress

As was stated in Chapter 6, classical contract law theory is based upon the notion of consent. It follows that if an individual is, in some way, pressured or forced into entering a contract, the law should provide some form of relief. This was recognized by both the common law (via the concept of duress) and equity (via the concept of

---

123. *Saunders v Anglia Building Society* [1970] AC 1004 (HL) 1016.
124. Ibid.   125. Ibid, 1025 (Lord Wilberforce).

🔗 Undue influence is discussed at p 271

undue influence). Here, we will focus on the law relating to duress. Undue influence will be examined later in the chapter.

Duress occurs where a party enters into a contract as a result of some form of illegitimate pressure or threat, and it is well established that a contract made under duress is voidable under the common law.[126] Because the contract is voidable, it follows that the principal remedy is rescission, but, as we have seen, the right to rescind may be lost and the bars to rescission discussed in misrepresentation cases also apply to cases involving duress.

🔗 The bars to rescission are discussed at p 242

Pressure or threats

Initially, the concept of duress was an extremely narrow one and would only apply where physical violence was threatened against a person.[127] The harshness of this rule was mitigated by equity's establishment of the concept of undue influence, but, eventually, the common law also came to recognize that duress against goods and property could be just as illegitimate as duress against the person.[128] As a result of this, the subject matter of the contract is no longer relevant; all that matters is the legitimacy of the pressure or threat. Provided that it was a reason for the victim contracting, it does not matter that it was not the sole, or even the dominant, reason.[129] The victim, however, must have had no realistic alternative but to enter the contract.[130]

Duress against the person

There is no doubt whatsoever that actual violence or the physical threat of violence will amount to illegitimate pressure, as will the threat of imprisonment.[131]

🔑 *Barton v Armstrong* [1976] AC 104 (PC)

FACTS: The claimant was the managing director of a company. The defendant was the chairman of the same company. Both were major shareholders. The defendant had threatened to kill the claimant unless he executed a deed selling his interest in the company to the defendant. The claimant sought relief on the ground of duress, but the defendant argued that, because the deed was in the commercial interests of the claimant, the claimant would have executed the deed even if the threat had not been made. The New South Wales Court of Appeal accepted this and dismissed the claim. The claimant appealed.

HELD: The Privy Council allowed the claimant's appeal. It was clear that the threat constituted illegitimate pressure and it was irrelevant that it was not the claimant's sole, or even dominant, reason for entering into the contract. Provided that the threat was *a* reason behind the choice to enter into the contract, it does not matter that it was not the sole reason or even a dominant one.

---

126. *Pao On v Lau Yiu Long* [1980] AC 614 (PC); *Universe Tankships Inc of Monrovia v International Transport Workers Federation (The Universe Sentinel)* [1983] 1 AC 366 (HL).

127. *Skeate v Beale* (1840) 11 A & E 983.

128. *Occidental Worldwide Investment Corp v Skibs A/S Avanti (The Siboen and The Sibotre)* [1976] 1 Lloyd's Rep 293 (QB).

129. *Barton v Armstrong* [1976] AC 104 (PC).

130. *B & S Contracts & Design Ltd v Victor Green Publications Ltd* [1984] ICR 419 (CA).

131. *Williams v Bayley* (1886) LR 1 HL 200 (HL).

Duress against property

During the nineteenth century, the courts refused to extend the concept of duress beyond threatened or actual acts of physical violence. The result of this was that if *A* were to unlawfully seize goods belonging to *B* and then force *B* to enter into a contract promising to pay money in return for the goods, such an agreement would held valid.[132] The common law eventually came to realize the harshness of this approach and, in *The Siboen and The Sibotre*,[133] the High Court stated *obiter* that a contract entered into due to threatened or actual violence against goods or unlawful seizure of goods could amount to duress. Subsequent cases affirmed this.[134]

Recognition that threats against property could constitute duress did not, however, completely fill the gaps in the doctrine. Pressure could be placed upon a party's economic interests without threatening his person or property (for example, by taking advantage of a person who is financially vulnerable). To accommodate such cases, the courts developed the concept of economic duress and, today, cases involving duress against property are likely to be regarded as a form of economic duress.[135]

Economic duress

Economic duress concerns those cases in which a party's economic or business interests are threatened. Usually, this will take the form of one party threatening not to perform its contractual obligations unless the other party agrees to forgo, vary, or reduce some benefit owed to them. A classic example of this would be a case that we have discussed several times in previous chapters: *D & C Builders Ltd v Rees*.[136] That case, like many other early cases involving economic duress, was decided based upon a lack of consideration and did not establish economic duress as we know it today. It was in the following case that a formal doctrine of economic duress emerged.

Occidental Worldwide Investment Corp v Skibs A/S Avanti (The Siboen and The Sibotre) [1976] 1 Lloyd's Rep 293 (QB)

FACTS: The claimant chartered two of the defendant's ships. Subsequently, a worldwide recession had caused the charter market to weaken, resulting in charter rates substantially lower than those being paid by the claimant. The claimant therefore attempted to renegotiate its charter rates by falsely informing the defendant that, unless the rates were lowered, it would be unable to pay and would become insolvent. The claimant also knew that the defendant was unlikely to find another party to charter the ships, given the recession. Given this, the defendant amended the charter to reduce

---

132. *Skeate v Beale* (1840) 11 A & E 983.

133. *Occidental Worldwide Investment Corp v Skibs A/S Avanti (The Siboen and The Sibotre)* [1976] 1 Lloyd's Rep 293 (QB).

134. *Pao On v Lau Yiu Long* [1980] AC 614 (PC).

135. *Vantage Navigation Corp v Suhail & Saud Bahwan Building Materials (The Alev)* [1989] 1 Lloyd's Rep 138 (QB).

136. [1966] 2 QB 617 (CA).

the rates payable by the claimant. The defendant subsequently withdrew the ships and chartered them to other parties (making large profits in the process). The claimant alleged that the ships were wrongfully withdrawn. The defendant argued that it had been subject to duress.

HELD: Kerr J, in the High Court, rejected the defendant's plea of duress, stating that duress would only be present where the behaviour complained of constituted 'a coercion of will so as to vitiate consent'.[137] On the facts, this was not present.

COMMENT: The defendant actually succeeded and the court declared the contract voidable—but not on the ground of duress; rather it was on the ground that the claimant had misrepresented its financial position.

This case provided a basis for the establishment of the doctrine of economic duress. In particular, subsequent courts have latched onto Kerr J's test. In *Pao On v Lau Yiu Long*,[138] Lord Scarman stated that, in order for economic duress to exist, two requirements must be present:

1. coercion of the will that vitiates consent; and
2. illegitimate pressure or threat.

No realistic alternative

Early cases relating to economic duress (including *Pao On*) used Kerr J's formulation as the first step in establishing the presence of economic duress. The problem that arose was that these cases stated that the requisite coercion of will would only be present where the victim's act was not voluntary (known as the 'overborne will' theory). The principal criticism of such an approach was first stated by Atiyah,[139] who correctly noted that, in cases involving duress, the victim does voluntarily enter or vary the contract. He may do so because an alternative course of action would cause greater damage, but this does not alter the fact that voluntary consent is present. Due to this, more recent cases have doubted the utility of a test based upon coercion of will and, as a result, the coercion of will requirement has been replaced with a test based upon causation, as follows.

1. Did the illegitimate pressure or threat cause the victim to enter the contract? Such pressure does not need to be the sole cause, but it does need to be a 'significant cause'[140] or 'decisive or clinching'.[141]
2. Did the victim have 'no realistic alternative' but to enter the contract? The following case provides an example of a situation in which this was the case.

---

137. *Occidental Worldwide Investment Corp v Skibs A/S Avanti (The Siboen and The Sibotre)* [1976] 1 Lloyd's Rep 293 (QB) 336.
138. [1980] AC 614 (PC).
139. PS Atiyah, 'Economic Duress and the "Overborne Will"' (1982) 98 LQR 197.
140. *Dimskal Shipping Co SA v International Transport Workers' Federation (The Evia Luck)* [1992] 2 AC 152 (HL) 165 (Lord Goff).
141. *Huyton SA v Peter Cremer GmbH & Co* [1999] 1 Lloyd's Rep 620 (QB) 636 (Mance J).

B & S Contracts & Design Ltd v Victor Green Publications Ltd [1984] ICR 419 (CA)

FACTS: The defendant had let a number of exhibition stands to various exhibitors at a trade show. The stands were to be built by the claimant. The claimant's employees knew that they were to be made redundant following the building of the stands and so they refused to work unless they received £9,000 severance pay between them. The claimant offered their employees £4,500, but this was rejected. The claimant then told the defendant to pay the balance of the £9,000 (£4,500). It indicated that unless the defendant agreed to pay the balance, it would allow the workers to strike. The defendant therefore agreed to pay. When the work was complete, the defendant deducted the £4,500 from the contract price. The claimant argued that it was entitled to the contract price and the £4,500.

HELD: The claimant's indication amounted to a veiled threat. The Court of Appeal therefore held that the defendant did not have to pay the £4,500, because it had acted under duress. It had no realistic alternative but to pay £4,500 up front. It could have refused payment and initiated a claim for breach of contract when the claimant did not build the stands on time—but this would have 'exposed [the defendant] to very heavy claims from the exhibitors'[142] for failing to provide the stands promised.

⭐ See NE Palmer and L Catchpole, 'Industrial Conflict, Breach of Contract and Duress' (1985) 48 MLR 102

Illegitimate pressure or threat

The threat or pressure exerted must be illegitimate. This is a difficult issue, because it is not easy to distinguish illegitimate pressure from 'the rough and tumble of the pressures of normal commercial bargaining'.[143]

The following case provides an example of illegitimate pressure.

Universe Tankships Inc of Monrovia v International Transport Workers' Federation (The Universe Sentinel) [1983] 1 AC 36 (HL)

FACTS: The claimant owned a Liberian ship, which docked in Milford Haven. The defendant trade union considered that the claimant's crewmen were being paid too little and so they 'blacked' the ship. This meant that the tugs that towed the ship out of harbour would not be made available to the claimant unless the claimant paid US$80,000 back pay to the crewmen and US$6,480 to the defendant's welfare fund. The claimant paid the money, but subsequently sued the defendant for recovery of the US$6,480. The defendant argued that its acts were given immunity by statute.

HELD: The House of Lords held that the statute did not apply and therefore the defendant's actions amounted to illegitimate pressure.

⭐ See BW Napier, 'Economic Duress, Restitution and Industrial Conflict' (1983) 42 CLJ 43

---

142. *B & S Contracts & Design Ltd v Victor Green Publications Ltd* [1984] ICR 419 (CA) 426 (Griffiths LJ).
143. *DSND Subsea Ltd v Petroleum Geo Services ASA* [2000] BLR 530 (QB) [131] (Dyson J).

Unsurprisingly, an unlawful act (for example, breach of contract or the commission of a crime) will almost certainly to be regarded as illegitimate. The question that arises is whether a lawful act can constitute illegitimate pressure. In *The Universe Sentinel*, Lord Scarman (dissenting) stated:

> The present is a case in which the nature of the demand determines whether the pressure threatened or applied…was lawful or unlawful. If it was unlawful, it is conceded that the owner acted under duress and can recover. If it was lawful, it is conceded that there was no duress and the sum sought by the owner is irrecoverable.[144]

Lord Scarman appeared to indicate that a lawful act cannot amount to duress, but in the following case, the Court of Appeal conceded that whilst it would be extremely unlikely, a lawful act may constitute duress.

 CTN Cash and Carry Ltd v Gallaher Ltd [1994] 4 All ER 714 (CA)

FACTS: The claimant, a cash-and-carry business, purchased on credit a consignment of cigarettes from the defendant. The defendant mistakenly sent the cigarettes to the wrong warehouse, but before it could collect the cigarettes and redeliver them, they were stolen. The defendant genuinely (but wrongly) believed that the risk of loss was borne by the claimant, and so invoiced the claimant for the price of the cigarettes (around £17,000). Understandably, the claimant refused to pay, whereupon the defendant threatened to withdraw the credit facilities (this was provided for by the contract). Faced with this, the claimant paid the invoice price, but subsequently sought to recover the monies on the ground of duress.

HELD: The Court of Appeal held that there was no duress. The defendant's actions were lawful and whilst a lawful act may amount to duress in certain circumstances, the arm's-length bargaining between the parties and the fact that the defendant believed its actions to be bona fide meant that the defendant's lawful threat was not illegitimate. Steyn LJ (as he then was) said that, in a purely commercial context, it would be relatively rare for a lawful act to constitute duress and would be particularly difficult to establish where the threatener believed bona fide that his demand was valid.

 Key points summary

- Duress occurs where a party enters into a contract due to the presence of some form of illegitimate pressure or threat that causes him to have no realistic alternative other than to enter into the contract.

- Duress can be committed against the person, property, or against economic or business interests.

- Where a contract is entered into as a result of duress, it will be voidable. As with misrepresentation, however, the right to rescind may be barred.

---

144. *Universe Tankships Inc of Monrovia v International Transport Workers' Federation (The Universe Sentinel)* [1983] 1 AC 36 (HL) 401.

Undue influence

As noted above, the common law originally would only find duress in cases involving threats or actual violence to the person. Conversely, equity provided relief in cases concerning wider forms of pressure via the creation of the concept of undue influence. Undue influence traditionally applies to cases in which the pressure exerted is less direct or more subtle than in duress cases. As we shall see, usually, this pressure is created as a result of the relationship between the two parties (in relation to duress, the parties' relationship is largely irrelevant—all that matters being the illegitimacy of the threat or pressure). Undue influence cases are divided into two classes:

1. actual undue influence; and
2. presumed undue influence.

Actual (or Class 1) undue influence

Actual undue influence overlaps considerably with the doctrine of duress. Actual undue influence is present where one party actually causes the other to enter into a contract, or make a gift, via some form of improper pressure or inappropriate use of influence. Examples of such pressure and influence include:

- A threatening to prosecute B, or B's family, unless payment is provided to A;[145]
- taking advantage of a person's religious beliefs;[146]
- husbands who place pressure on their wives to consent to using the matrimonial home as security for a loan;[147]
- an older mentor using his influence over a younger person to cause him to incur certain liabilities.[148]

Actual undue influence is not dependent upon the existence of a particular relationship, or the transaction in question causing a disadvantage.[149] All that need be established is that the requisite level of influence existed and that it was exercised unduly. With the expansion in the scope of duress, the instances of actual undue influence have declined sharply in recent years.

Presumed (or Class 2) undue influence

Presumed undue influence arises where the relationship between the parties gives rise to a 'presumption of undue influence'.[150] Historically, presumed undue influence was divided into two types.[151]

1. *Type 2A*   In this case, some special relationship exists between the parties.
2. *Type 2B*   In this case, no special relationship exists, but the relationship is one of trust and confidence.

---

145. *Williams v Bayley* (1866) LR 1 HL 200 (HL).   146. *Morley v Loughnan* [1893] 1 Ch 736 (Ch).
147. *CIBC Mortgages v Pitt* [1994] 1 AC 200 (HL).   148. *Smith v Kay* (1859) 7 HLC 750 (HL).
149. *CIBC Mortgages v Pitt* [1994] 1 AC 200 (HL).
150. *Barclays Bank plc v O'Brien* [1994] 1 AC 180 (HL) 189 (Lord Browne-Wilkinson).
151. Ibid.

Type 2A—special relationship

Certain types of relationship automatically give rise to a presumption that undue influence is present (the 'relationship presumption'). Examples of such relationships include:

- parent and child;[152]
- doctor and patient;[153]
- trustee and beneficiary;[154]
- solicitor and client,[155] including ex-clients;[156]
- guardian and ward.[157]

It is worth noting that two important relationships do not come within Type 2A—namely, husband and wife[158] and employer and employee.[159]

The presumption in Type 2A cases is limited. In *Royal Bank of Scotland v Etridge (No 2)*,[160] Lord Nicholls stated:

> It would be absurd for the law to presume that every gift by a child to a parent, or every transaction between a client and his solicitor or between a patient and his doctor, was brought about by undue influence unless the contrary is affirmatively proved. Such a presumption would be too far-reaching....So something more is needed before the law reverses the burden of proof, something which calls for an explanation.[161]

➡ per se: 'in itself' What Lord Nicholls is saying is that the existence of a Type 2A relationship is not enough per se to establish a presumption of undue influence; the court will also need to examine the nature of the transaction between the two parties. Where the transaction is suspect to such a degree that it 'calls for an explanation' or is 'not readily explicable by the relationship of the parties',[162] then the 'evidential presumption' will be satisfied and undue influence will be presumed. The burden of proof will then be transferred to the other party, who will need to rebut the presumption. Obviously, only the evidential presumption need be rebutted; the relationship presumption is irrebuttable.

Type 2B—no special relationship

Where a Type 2A relationship does not exist, it used to be the case that undue influence would be presumed where the relationship was one that involved such trust and confidence that one party could exert improper influence over the other (for example, husband and wife).[163] This presumption no longer exists, and the party claiming relief will need to establish that he placed sufficient trust and confidence in the other party. If this is established, he will then need also to establish the evidential presumption (that is, that the transaction is one that calls for an explanation). If this

152. *Powell v Powell* [1900] 1 Ch 243 (Ch).
154. *Benningfield v Baxter* (1886) 12 App Cas 167 (PC).
156. *McMaster v Byrne* [1952] 1 All ER 1362 (PC).
158. *Bank of Montreal v Stuart* [1911] AC 120 (PC).
160. [2001] UKHL 44, [2002] 2 AC 773.
162. Ibid, [21].

153. *Dent v Bennett* (1839) 4 My & Cr 269.
155. *Wright v Carter* [1903] 1 Ch 27 (CA).
157. *Hylton v Hylton* (1754) 2 Ves Sen 547.
159. *Matthew v Bobbins* (1980) 256 EG 603 (CA).
161. Ibid, [24].
163. *Howes v Bishop* [1909] 2 KB 390 (CA).

can also be shown, a prima facie case for undue influence will be established and the burden of proof will shift to the other party.

Transactions 'calling for explanation'

In cases of presumed (or Class 2) undue influence, the party seeking relief will need to show that the transaction was one that called for an explanation. This used to be expressed in terms of requiring the party seeking relief to show that the transaction was one that caused him 'manifest disadvantage',[164] but, following *Etridge*, this term is no longer used. Whether a transaction calls for an explanation will very much depend on the individual facts of the case.

The following case provides an example of such a transaction.

 ### *Hammond v Osborn* [2002] EWCA Civ 885

FACTS: Pritler was a frail 72-year-old man. He became friends with the defendant, who was a neighbour. Pritler was hospitalized following an accident and the defendant visited him regularly. Upon his discharge, the defendant continued to care for him as he became more infirm. The defendant claimed that Pritler told her to cash all of his investments and keep the proceeds (£297,500). This she did, leaving Pritler with hardly any savings. The consequences of this act were never discussed. Pritler died **intestate**, and one of his next of kin (the claimant) sought to have the agreement between Pritler and the defendant rescinded on the ground of undue influence.

→ intestate: having not made a will (on death)

HELD: Ward LJ described Pritler's gift as 'an act of generosity wholly out of proportion to the kindness shown to him. Looking at the matter objectively, it was an irrational decision, not a good one'.[165] Evidence for this could be found in the consequences of the gift: the gift represented 91.6 per cent of his assets, and he became liable to pay tax amounting to £49,670. Accordingly, the transaction was clearly one that called for an explanation. Because the defendant could not rebut the presumption, the Court of Appeal found that undue influence was present.

COMMENT: This decision has been described as 'cruel but correct'.[166] However deserving the actions of the defendant might have been, the simple fact is that Pritler's decision to gift his assets was not 'the product of full, free and independent volition'.[167]

Rescission

Transactions tainted by undue influence are voidable and may therefore be rescinded at the claimant's instance. Rescission may be barred on the same grounds as misrepresentation and duress (that is, affirmation,[168] third-party rights,[169] and impossibility

---

164. *National Westminster Bank plc v Morgan* [1985] AC 686 (HL).

165. *Hammond v Osborn* [2002] EWCA Civ 885, [58].

166. P Birks, 'Undue Influence as Wrongful Exploitation' (2004) 120 LQR 34, 37.

167. *Hammond v Osborn* [2002] EWCA Civ 885, [60] (Ward LJ).

168. *Mitchell v Homfray* (1882) 8 QBD 587 (CA).

169. *Bainbrigge v Brown* (1881) 18 Ch D 188 (Ch).

of *restitutio in integrum*).[170] The sole exception to this is that lapse of time alone will not bar rescission in cases of undue influence.[171] But once the actual or presumed influence has been removed, the party seeking relief must do so within a reasonable time.[172] Although damages are not available to those unduly influenced, where rescission has been barred, the court may make an award of equitable compensation to compensate the victim for his loss.[173]

 Key points summary

- Undue influence is a creation of equity, designed to provide a party with relief in cases in which the narrow common law rules of duress did not apply.

- Actual undue influence exists where one party causes another party to enter into a contract, or make a gift, via the use of some form of improper pressure or inappropriate use of influence.

- Presumed undue influence occurs where the relationship between the parties gives rise to a presumption that undue influence may be present. In order for the presumption to arise, the party seeking relief will need to establish that the transaction was one that calls for an explanation—but there is no need to establish that the transaction was 'manifestly disadvantageous'.

- Where a contract is tainted by undue influence, it will be voidable. Rescission will, however, be barred if:
  - the victim affirms the contract;
  - a bona fide third-party purchaser acquires rights in the contract; or
  - *restitio in integrum* is impossible.

Unconscionable bargains

Whereas duress and undue influence are fully recognized doctrines that operate within reasonably well-defined borders, the law relating to unconscionable bargains is somewhat more unclear. That equity will provide relief to a party who has entered into an unconscionable bargain[174] is clear, but the cases themselves comprise a motley selection of idiosyncratic situations that do not fit neatly into either duress or undue influence. Further, attempts to draw these cases together into one coherent doctrine[175] (entitled either 'unconscionable bargains' or 'inequality of bargaining

---

170. *O'Sullivan v Management Agency & Music Ltd* [1985] QB 428 (CA).
171. *Re Pauling's Settlement Trusts* [1964] Ch 303 (CA).
172. *Allcard v Skinner* (1887) Ch D 145 (CA).
173. *Mahoney v Purnell* [1996] 3 All ER 61 (QB).
174. Because we are dealing with unconscionable bargains, it follows that this doctrine does not apply to gifts. Conversely, both duress and undue influence can apply to gifts.
175. For example, *Lloyds Bank v Bundy* [1975] QB 326 (CA).

power') have been rejected by the House of Lords[176] on the ground that such cases are preferably decided under the doctrine of undue influence.

Establishing an unconscionable bargain does not depend upon the existence of a certain relationship (as is the case with undue influence), nor does it require any illegitimate pressure (as is the case under duress). Unconscionable bargain cases usually involve one party taking advantage of another party who has some form of weakness or deficiency. Examples of transactions set aside on the ground of unconscionability include:

- a poor man who sold, for 200 guineas (£210), a share in an estate worth £1,200;[177]
- an employee, of limited financial means, who guaranteed the £270,000 overdraft of her employer;[178]
- a senile 84-year-old widow who sold paintings worth £6,000–£7,000 for £40;[179]
- moneylenders who take advantage of financially vulnerable 'expectant heirs' (that is, those who will inherit large fortunes);[180]
- pilgrims, whose ship had sunk and who were trapped on a rock, agreeing to pay £4,000 to be rescued.[181]

It should be noted that the courts are not quick to grant relief in such cases. Relief will not be granted merely because the consideration is inadequate,[182] or simply because a transaction is unfair[183] or improvident:[184] 'The courts [will] only interfere in exceptional cases where as a matter of common fairness it was not right that the strong should be allowed to push the weak to the wall.'[185]

The following case laid down guidelines for establishing the existence of an unconscionable bargain.

Boustany v Pigott (1995) 69 P & CR 298 (PC)

FACTS: Pigott leased a flat to the defendant. Pigott was ageing and 'quite slow', so her affairs were dealt with by her cousin (the claimant). The defendant wished to renegotiate the lease with the claimant, but no action was taken. The defendant and her barrister went to see Pigott. They presented her with a new lease, to which she agreed, despite the fact that this new lease contained terms that were unfavourable to Pigott—notably, that the lease was to last ten years, and that the rent payable was relatively low and was unreviewable. When the claimant discovered this, he sought to have the lease set aside.

176. *National Westminster Bank v Morgan* [1985] AC 686 (HL).

177. *Evans v Llewellin* (1787) 1 Cox CC 333.

178. *Credit Lyonnais Bank Nederland NV v Burch* [1997] 1 All ER 144 (CA).

179. *Ayres v Hazelgrove*, unreported 9 February 1984.

180. *Earl of Aylesford v Morris* (1873) 8 Ch App 484 (CA).

181. *The Medina* (1876) 1 P 272.   182. *Collier v Brown* (1788) 1 Cox CC 428.

183. *Alec Lobb (Garages) Ltd v Total Oil (Great Britain) Ltd* [1985] 1 WLR 173 (CA).

184. *Kalsep v X-Flow BV*, The Times, 3 May 2001.

185. *Alec Lobb (Garages) Ltd v Total Oil (Great Britain) Ltd* [1985] 1 WLR 173 (CA) 183 (Dillon LJ).

HELD: The Privy Council viewed the lease as unconscionable and set it aside. Lord Templeman approved several submissions of counsel, as follows.

- Equity will not provide relief simply because the bargain is hard, unreasonable, or foolish. One of the parties must have imposed terms in a morally reprehensible manner.

- 'Unconscionable' relates not only to the terms of the agreement, but also to the stronger party's behaviour, which must demonstrate moral culpability or impropriety.

- Equity will usually not interfere solely because the parties' bargaining power is unequal, or because the terms are unreasonable.

- The party seeking relief will need to establish that the other party's conduct was unconscionable.

- The party seeking relief will need to establish that his weakness or disabling circumstances were taken advantage of by the other party.

COMMENT: After stating the above submissions, Lord Templeman went on to state six factual findings that led the court to its decision. As one commentator has correctly pointed out,[186] however, these findings are not linked to the five submissions that preceded them, and the words used (for example, 'unconscionable', 'moral culpability', and 'morally reprehensible') were vague and no further definition was provided. As a result, the case has been described as 'a prime example of the imprecise approach which must be avoided if unconscionability is to merit support as a vitiating factor'.[187]

 Key points summary

- Equity may provide relief to a party who has entered into an unconscionable bargain.

- The unconscionable bargain does not constitute a vitiating factor per se, but is rather a group of situations and cases that do not it easily into the other categories of vitiating factor.

- An unconscionable bargain will usually be one in which a stronger party has taken advantage of some weakness or deficiency of a weaker party.

- The courts will not interfere merely because a contract is unfair or improvident.

Illegality and public policy

The law places limits on an individual's ability to contract by branding certain contracts illegal or by declaring them contrary to public policy. It is customary in textbooks to attempt to classify the various forms of illegality and public policy. Given the complexity and nature of the topic, however, such classifications are always imperfect. As one commentator stated: 'This area is a minefield for the student of the subject since it has little in the way of uniform structure and what there is produces

---

186. N Bamforth, 'Unconscionability as a Vitiating Factor' [1995] LMCLQ 538, 534.
187. Ibid.

tremendous inconsistencies.'[188] Perhaps the most straightforward (although not necessarily the most accurate) classification is to split the relevant cases into:

- illegal contracts; and
- contracts that are contrary to public policy.

Illegal contracts

Illegal contracts come in a number of different forms. Certrain contracts may be regarded as illegal irrespective of their aims and motives; other contracts may be lawful per se, but become illegal by requiring the parties to perform unlawful acts. Finally, both the contract itself and the acts required may be lawful, but may be performed by the parties in an unlawful manner. Each of these instances will be discussed, but it should be noted that this is not an exhaustive list and that there are many other instances in which a contract may be deemed illegal.

Contracts amounting to a legal wrong

Some contracts are unlawful simply by virtue of their existence; the mere making of such a contract is a legal wrong, irrespective of the lawfulness of the acts to be performed. Examples include the following.

- *Contracts for 'maintenance' and 'champerty'* 'Maintenance' refers to the situation in which a person supports the litigation of another, but has no legitimate interest in such litigation. 'Champerty' occurs if a person 'maintaining' another receives a share of the other's damages. Although civil and criminal liability for champertous acts has been abolished, the general rule is still that champerty is unlawful.[189] There are exceptions to this principle—the most obvious being the validity of **conditional fee agreements**.[190]
- *Contracts to secure the misprision of an arrestable offence*[191] 'Misprision' is accepting a reward in return for not reporting a crime.
- *Contracts that seek to prevent, restrict, or distort competition*[192]
- *Contracts that involve commercial dealings with the enemy during wartime*[193] Trading with the enemy is also a statutory offence.[194]

➡ conditional fee agreement: an agreement made between a lawyer and a client, whereby the lawyer is paid only upon some condition being satisfied (e.g. the lawyer winning the case)

Contracts requiring unlawful acts

A contract that requires the intentional commission of an unlawful act will clearly be unlawful and unenforceable by either party. Examples include:

- a contract requiring the commission of an assault;[195]

188. P Richards, *Law of Contract* (8th edn, Pearson, London, 2007) 308.
189. Criminal Law Act 1967, s 14(2).   190. Courts and Legal Services Act 1990, s 58.
191. Criminal Law Act 1967, s 5(1).   192. Competition Act 1998, s 2.
193. *Sovfracht (V/O) v Van Udens Scheepvaart en Agentuur Maatschppij (NV Gebr)* [1943] AC 203 (HL).
194. Trading with the Enemy Act 1939, s 1(1).   195. *Allen v Rescous* (1676) 2 Lev 174.

- a contract that aims to defraud the shareholders of a company;[196]
- any contract that permits, invites, or causes a child or young person to gamble;[197]
- any contract for the sale of bodily organs or human material for the purposes of transplantation;[198]
- a contract involving the publishing of libellous information.[199]

Further, a contract that does not require the commission of an unlawful act, but which results in a person benefiting from the unlawful act, is similarly unlawful. Thus, in *Beresford v Royal Insurance Co Ltd*,[200] an individual took out an insurance policy that provided for a financial payout of £50,000 upon his committing suicide. Shortly afterwards, he shot himself. His next of kin claimed on the insurance policy, but the claim was rejected, because, at the time, suicide was illegal.

Contracts performed in breach of statute

A lawful contract may exist between the parties, but may be performed in a manner that is in breach of a statute. In such a case, the general rule is that a party who performs a contract unlawfully cannot enforce it,[201] but the innocent party can.

 Archbolds (Freightage) Ltd v S Spanglett Ltd [1961] 1 QB 374 (CA)

FACTS: The claimant employed the defendant to transport a consignment of whisky from Leeds to London. The vans used to transport the whisky were only licensed to carry goods belonging to the defendant, however, not goods belonging to anyone else. Due to the defendant's negligence, the whisky was stolen en route. The claimant sued for breach of contract, but the defendant claimed that the contract was unenforceable on the ground of illegality—namely, the use of vans that were not licensed for the purpose of carrying other people's goods.

HELD: The Court of Appeal stated that the contract itself was clearly not an illegal one. The claimant had no knowledge of the unlawful performance, nor did it play a role in it. Accordingly, it was permitted to claim for the loss of the whisky.

This rule is not absolute, however, for two reasons. Firstly, a party who has acted lawfully will be prohibited from enforcing the contract if he knew that the other party's performance was carried out in an unlawful manner, and allowed that performance to proceed.[202] Secondly, depending on the purpose of the law that was breached, a party who performed in an unlawful manner may still be able to enforce the contract. There does not appear to be a general principle in place and the courts appear to take a

---

196. *Begbie v Phosphate Sewage Co Ltd* (1875) LR 10 QB 491.
197. Gambling Act 2005, s 46.　198. Human Tissue Act 2004, s 32.
199. *Apthorp v Neville & Co* (1907) 23 TLR 575.　200. [1938] AC 586 (HL).
201. *Anderson Ltd v Daniel* [1924] 1 KB 138 (CA).
202. *Ashmore, Benson, Pease & Co Ltd v AV Dawson Ltd* [1973] 1 WLR 828 (CA).

case-by-case approach, with the result heavily dependent upon the wording of the statute that was breached.

Shaw v Groom [1970] 2 QB 504 (CA)

FACTS: The Landlord and Tenant Act 1962, s 4, required that any person leasing a property should be provided with a rent book containing specified information and that failure to comply amounted to a criminal offence. The claimant gave the defendant a rent book, but it did not contain the prescribed information. Some time later, the claimant sued the defendant for unpaid rent amounting to £103. The defendant argued that, because the rent book was incomplete, the contract was unlawful and unenforceable.

HELD: The Court of Appeal allowed the claimant to recover the back rent. Where performance was unlawful, the enforceability test to be applied was whether Parliament intended to prevent the claimant from enforcing the contract. With regards to the 1962 Act, Parliament intended to punish those who breached the legislation, but it did not intend to prevent landlords from recovering unpaid rent.

The effects of illegality

It is impossible to generalize about the effects that illegality can have on a contract, because there are numerous degrees of unlawfulness. Two *general* principles can, however, be stated: firstly, any person who is aware of the illegality of a contract will not be permitted to enforce it;[203] secondly, money or property that has changed hands due to an illegal contract cannot be recovered and the defendant can therefore keep what he has obtained.

Parkinson v College of Ambulance Ltd and Harrison [1925] 2 KB 1

FACTS: The defendant company was set up to teach first aid and ambulance work, and to administer aid to the poor. The president of the company was a member of the royal family. A representative of the company (Harrison, another defendant) informed the claimant, Colonel Parkinson, that if he were to donate a substantial sum of money to the company, the company could arrange for Parkinson to receive a knighthood. An agreement was entered into and Parkinson donated £3,000 to the company, but never received a knighthood. When questioned, the company stated that the money was donated as an act of charity and would not be returned. Parkinson sued.

HELD: A contract to purchase a knighthood is clearly illegal. Because the claimant knew this, he would be unable to enforce the contract. Accordingly, he could not recover the £3,000.

COMMENT: In response to this case, the Honours (Prevention of Abuses) Act 1925 was quickly passed, which makes it a criminal offence to contract for the purchase of an honour.

---

203. *Holman v Johnson* (1775) 1 Cowp 341.

But there are exceptions to the rule and, in several situations, as follows, the courts will permit money or property transferred under a illegal contract to be recovered.

➡ *in pari delicto:* 'in equal fault'

- Where the parties are not *in pari delicto*, the less culpable party may be able to recover money paid or property transferred.[204] This may occur where one party is induced into the illegal contract by a misrepresentation,[205] or is forced into an illegal contract by oppression.[206]

- If a party can argue for the recovery of money or property on the basis of some lawful ground (in other words, not by relying on the illegality), then he will be allowed to recover.[207]

- A party to an illegal contract may be able to recover money or property if he repents and voluntarily withdraws from the contract before the unlawful purpose commences.[208] Note that the repentance must be genuine: recovery will not be permitted where withdrawal is the result of the contract being frustrated[209] or the failure of the other party to perform, or where the illegality is discovered by the authorities.[210]

- A party to an illegal contract who is totally innocent (that is, did not know or take part in the illegality) may be able to recover money or property if there is complete failure of consideration by the other party (that is, if the innocent party has gained no benefit from the contract).[211]

➡ frustration: where a contract becomes illegal, impossible, or radically different from what the parties envisaged, it is said to be frustrated and will be void (see p 311)

Contracts in breach of public policy

A contract that is not illegal may nevertheless be deemed unenforceable by the parties (or, sometimes, one of them) if it involves activity that the law regards as contrary to public policy. Instances in which the courts will declare a contract void on the grounds of public policy are many and the categories are not closed. Below is a selection of the most significant examples, with contracts in restraint of trade being perhaps the most important.

Family agreements

Contracts that serve to affect adversely the institution of marriage, or the status of the family or parental responsibility, will breach public policy. Examples of such contracts include the following.

- Contracts that unjustifiably restrict a person's ability to marry may be invalid (for example, a contract to promise only ever to marry a specific person).[212]

---

204. *Kiriri Cotton Ltd v Dewani* [1960] AC 192 (PC).
205. *Hughes v Liverpool Victoria Legal Friendly Society* [1916] 2 KB 482 (CA).
206. *Atkinson v Denby* (1862) 7 H & N 934.
207. *Bowmakers Ltd v Barnet Instruments Ltd* [1945] KB 65 (CA).
208. *Kearley v Thomson* (1890) 24 QBD 742 (CA).
209. *Bigos v Bousted* [1951] 1 All ER 92 (KB).
210. *Alexander v Rayson* [1936] 1 KB 169 (CA).
211. *Re Cavalier Insurance Co Ltd* [1989] 2 Lloyd's Rep 430 (Ch).
212. *Lowe v Peers* (1768) 2 Burr 2225.

- A contract whereby a person promises to obtain a prospective husband or wife for another in return for payment (known as a 'marriage brokage contract') is unenforceable.[213]
- Separation agreements made by married parties, parties who still live together, or parties who are to be married will be unenforceable on the ground that they disrespect the sanctity of marriage.[214]
- Contracts that require the performance of acts that are inconsistent with the responsibilities of a parent[215] will be invalid. This could include a parent with legal custody of a child contracting that custody away to another,[216] or a contractual agreement entered into by a surrogate mother, purporting to relinquish her parental responsibilities to another.[217]

Sexually immoral contracts

Historically, this principle was absolute and any contract that could be regarded as sexually immoral was regarded as unenforceable. Thus, a carriage owner who knew that a carriage that he had leased out was to be used for the purposes of prostitution was unable to claim when the prostitute refused to pay.[218] Similarly, a contract whereby a woman agrees to become a man's mistress in return for payment is unenforceable.[219] In recent years, however, the attitudes of the courts have undoubtedly started to relax.

Armhouse Lee Ltd v Chappell and Anor, The Times 7 August 1996 (CA)

FACTS: The defendant was a pornographer whose company ran a telephone sex line. The claimant was an advertising agency, which placed advertisements in magazines advertising the defendant's service. The defendant's business became unprofitable and he stopped paying the claimant for its advertising services. As a result, the claimant went into liquidation and eventually initiated proceedings against the defendant, who argued that the contract was unenforceable on the ground of public policy—namely, that the advertisements were obscene and could corrupt public morality.

HELD: The claimant could recover the monies owed. The Court of Appeal was scathing in its attack on the defendant, not for the activities it undertook, but in relation to its hypocrisy. The defendant requested and profited from the advertisements, and provided the very services that it claimed were immoral. The Court therefore, with confessed relief, rejected the claims of the defendant.

Contracts that oust the jurisdiction of the courts

Contracts may seek to avoid justice in an indirect manner—namely, by ousting the jurisdiction of the courts. Such agreements are contrary to public policy and the

---

213. *Cole v Gibson* (1750) 1 Ves Sen 503.   214. *Brodie v Brodie* [1917] P 271.
215. 'Parental responsibility' is defined in the Children Act 1989, s 3.
216. *Vansittart v Vansittart* (1858) D & J 249 (Ch).   217. Surrogacy Arrangements Act 1985, s 1A.
218. *Pearce v Brooks* (1866) LR 1 Ex 213 (Ex).   219. *Franco v Bolton* (1797) Ves 368.

offending parts of the contract will be held void.[220] But agreements that provide that the parties shall resort to alternative dispute resolution before commencing legal proceedings are perfectly valid.

⊙ *Scott v Avery* (1856) 5 HL Cas 811 (HL)

FACTS: An insurance contract provided that if the insured goods were damaged or lost, the question of the amount of compensation would be referred to a committee. If the committee's determination of loss differed from that of the insurance company, the issue could not be decided by the courts until the matter had been referred to arbitration and a decision reached. One party alleged that such a clause ousted the jurisdiction of the courts.

HELD: The House of Lords held that the clause was valid, because it did not oust the jurisdiction of the courts; rather, it imposed a condition that needed to be satisfied before the courts could exercise their jurisdiction.

The relationship between arbitration and legal proceedings must be read in light of the passing of the Arbitration Act 1996. Section 67 allows the parties to challenge the substantive jurisdiction of the tribunal and s 68 allows parties to appeal a decision of an arbitrator to a court in the event of a 'serious irregularity'. Such appeals cannot be excluded by contract.[221] Section 69 allows parties to appeal on points of law, but such an appeal is conditional upon the agreement of the parties. Accordingly, a clause that ousts the jurisdiction of the court in relation to appeals on points of law would appear to be perfectly valid.

Contracts in restraint of trade

The benefits of competition in the marketplace are well known. Healthy competition can result in increased innovation, higher quality goods, and lower prices. Accordingly, contracts that purported to restrict a business or individual's ability to carry on trade were historically regarded as void.[222] As time progressed, however, the courts came to realize that there are actually very good practical reasons to restrain trade in certain circumstances:

> A master might be reluctant to employ and train apprentices if he could not to some extent restrain them from competing with him after the end of their apprenticeship. And a trader might be unable to sell the business he had built up if he could not bind himself not to compete with the purchaser.[223]

Therefore, the law started to regard contracts in restraint of trade as prima facie valid.[224]

---

220. *Thompson v Charnock* (1799) 8 Term Rep 139.
221. Arbitration Act 1996, s 4(1) and Sch 1.
222. *Claygate v Batchelor* (1602) Owen 143 (KB).
223. E Peel, *Treitel on the Law of Contract* (12th edn, Sweet & Maxwell, London, 2007) 498.
224. *Mitchel v Reynolds* (1711) 1 P Wms 181.

Today, the position has reversed and the following case established that the general position is that contracts that restrain trade are prima facie void, but will be valid if they reasonably protect a legitimate interest and do not harm the public interest.

Nordenfelt v Maxim Nordenfelt Guns and Ammunition Co [1894] AC 535 (HL)

FACTS: Nordenfelt was a patentee and manufacturer of guns and ammunition. He transferred all of the guns, ammunition, plant, and patents to another company (MNGA), for which he was paid £237,000 in cash and £50,000 in shares. He also covenanted not to manufacture guns or ammunition for any other company in the world for a period of twenty-five years. Soon thereafter, Nordenfelt began manufacturing guns and ammunition for competing companies. MNGA sought an injunction to enforce the covenant.

HELD: The House of Lords held that the covenant was valid and binding. In a key judgment, Lord Macnaghten stated:

> The public have an interest in every person's carrying on his trade freely: so has the individual. All interference with individual liberty of action in trading, and all restraints of trade of themselves, if there is nothing more, are contrary to public policy, and therefore void. That is the general rule. But there are exceptions: restraints of trade and interference with individual liberty of action may be justified by the special circumstances of a particular case. It is a sufficient justification, and indeed it is the only justification, if the restriction is reasonable—reasonable, that is, in reference to the interests of the parties concerned and reasonable in reference to the interests of the public, so framed and so guarded as to afford adequate protection to the party in whose favour it is imposed, while at the same time it is in no way injurious to the public.[225]

In practice, very few contracts are set aside on the ground that they are not in the public interest, leaving the test of 'reasonableness' as the dominant test to determine validity. When determining reasonableness, the courts will take into account a number of factors—notably, the duration of the restraint and the geographical extent of the restraint. Both of these issues are very much dependent upon the facts of the case.

Although the categories of contracts in relation to which restraint may be justified are open, the court has stated that, in two instances in particular, a legitimate interest may exist that warrants the imposition of a restraint:

- contracts for the sale of a business; and
- contracts of employment.[226]

We will examine both briefly.

A restraint of trade clause in a contract providing for the sale of a business is more likely to be valid than in other contracts, since the new owner has a legitimate interest in preventing the previous owner from setting up a new competing business. It

Visit the Online Resource Centre for the discussion box, 'Reasonableness and the restraint of trade'

---

225. *Nordenfelt v Maxim Nordenfelt Guns and Ammunition Co* [1894] AC 535 (HL) 546.
226. *Herbert Morris Ltd v Saxelby* [1916] AC 688 (HL) 713 (Lord Shaw).

should be emphasized, however, that imposing a restraint simply to prevent competition per se is not enough to rebut the general rule that restraint clauses are void.[227] The factor that justifies the imposition of a restraint clause is the protection of goodwill. When a business is purchased, the price paid does not only reflect the cost of the plant, materials, and tangible goods belonging to the company, it also reflects the cost of the company's reputation, its customer connections, and the potential increase in future customers via word-of-mouth recommendations.[228] Collectively, these intangible assets are known as 'goodwill' and it is this goodwill that must be protected by a restraint clause. In order for goodwill be to be protected validly, two conditions must be present: firstly, the sale of goodwill must relate to an actual business in existence that is then sold;[229] secondly, the restraint must go no further than is reasonably necessary as between the parties and in the public interest to protect the business that has been bought.

The following case provides an example of a restraint that went beyond what was reasonably necessary.

British Reinforced Concrete Engineering Co Ltd v Schelff [1921] 2 Ch 563 (Ch)

FACTS: The defendant carried on a small local business selling (not manufacturing) 'Loop' road reinforcements. He sold this business to a larger company (the claimant) that manufactured and sold 'BRC' road reinforcements throughout the UK. He also covenanted not compete with the company anywhere in the UK (either through setting up a business or joining a competitor) in relation to the manufacture or sale of road reinforcements. Subsequent to the sale, the defendant was employed by a rival company and the claimant sued.

HELD: The High Court held that the covenant was invalid, because it was too wide. The defendant's business concerned only the sale of road reinforcements, yet the covenant prohibited him from engaging in the sale *or manufacture* of road reinforcements. Accordingly, the restraint sought not to protect the business sold, but rather to protect the claimant's own business.

The second type of contract in which a legitimate interest is more likely to be protected by a restraint clause is a contract of employment, wherein restraint of trade clauses may be express or implied. Certainly, during the lifetime of the employment, the employer is quite justified in restricting the actions of its employees (for example, by requiring them to maintain confidentiality, or not work for a rival firm). Problems arise when an employee is subject to a restraint clause after he has left an employer's business. In these cases, the clause will only be valid if it serves to protect a 'proprietary interest' of the employer.

➡ **proprietary:** relating to exclusive ownership, control, or use

---

227. *Vancouver Malt and Sake Brewing Co Ltd v Vancouver Breweries Ltd* [1934] AC 181 (PC).
228. *Allied Dunbar (Frank Weisinger) Ltd v Weisinger* [1988] IRLR 60.
229. *Vancouver Malt and Sake Brewing Co Ltd v Vancouver Breweries Ltd* [1934] AC 181 (PC).

Proprietary interests fall into three categories, as follows.

1. *Trade secrets* Trade secrets are clearly an asset of a company deserving of protection. In *Forster & Sons Ltd v Suggett*,[230] the claimant instructed the defendant in secret methods for the production of glass bottles. Upon leaving the claimant company, the defendant agreed not to work for a rival firm or be involved in glass bottle manufacturing for a period of five years, but he later sought to be released from the restraint. The court held that the restraint was valid and granted an injunction to enforce it. In practice, however, it may be the case that employees are prohibited from disclosing trade secrets at any time after their employment ends, even in the absence of a restraint clause.[231]

2. *Confidential information* The line between trade secrets and confidential information can be thin, but the distinction is important, because the courts appear to afford less protection to confidential information than to trade secrets. The Court of Appeal has indicated that, whilst the duty not to disclose trade secrets continues after employment ends (the court will imply such a term if there is no express term), the duty not to disclose confidential information generally only lasts as long as the employment, unless there exists an express provision to the contrary.[232] The courts will not imply a term protecting confidential information after employment ends. Such protection must be derived from an express term.

3. *Customer connections* In the absence of a restraint clause, the law will only prevent an employee from soliciting his employer's customers during the life of his employment.[233] Once employment has ended, the courts will permit an employer to protect his customer connections via a restraint clause. In *Fitch v Dewes*,[234] a solicitor's clerk (who was himself a solicitor), based in Tamworth, agreed that he would not practice within 7 miles of Tamworth town hall if he were to leave his present employment. The court held that the restraint clause was valid, because the clerk was in a position to gain influence over the firm's clients.

Although contractual restraints relating to the selling of a business and contracts of employment form the main bulk of cases in this area, a third form of restraint has become more common over the last few decades—namely, exclusive trading agreements (also known as 'solus' agreements, or 'vertical' agreements). These occur where a retailer agrees to sell the products of one manufacturer only and not those of its rivals. Such agreements are common between oil companies and petrol station proprietors, and the leading case involves such an arrangement.

Esso Petroleum Co Ltd v Harper's Garage (Stourport) Ltd [1968] AC 269 (HL)

FACTS: The defendant owned two garages (G1 and G2). It entered into an agreement with the claimant, whereby both garages would sell only the claimant's petrol, in return for which the defendant would receive a discount on the price of petrol. The agreement with

---

230. (1918) 35 TLR 87.

232. Ibid.

234. [1921] 2 AC 158 (HL).

231. *Faccenda Chicken Ltd v Fowler* [1987] Ch 117 (CA).

233. *Wessex Dairies Ltd v Smith* [1935] 2 KB 60 (CA).

G1 was to last four years and five months. The claimant had lent the defendant £7,000 and secured the loan via a mortgage over G2. The mortgage agreement also contained the same restriction as in the contract with G1 and was to last for the duration of the mortgage repayments—namely, twenty-one years. The defendant started to sell a rival brand of petrol and the claimant sued. The defendant argued that the agreements were unreasonable.

HELD: The House of Lords noted that solus agreements were not invalid per se, because both parties often benefited from them. But because solus agreements sought to restrain trade, they were prima facie void unless the claimant could establish that they were reasonable.

1. The agreement with G1 was valid. The period involved was reasonable in order to protect the claimant's legitimate interest of securing continuity of sale outlets and ensuring stability of sales. In return, the defendant received cheaper petrol and the financial backing of a major oil company.

2. The agreement with G2 was held void. The period of twenty-one years was unreasonable, in so much as it went well beyond what was necessary in order to protect the claimant's legitimate interests.

⭐ See KL Koh, 'Contract: Doctrine of Restraint of Trade' (1967) CLJ 151

Like with many cases involving restraint of trade, however, it should be noted that the validity of a clause will always be dependent upon the individual facts of the case.

The effects of a breach of public policy

Where a contract breaches public policy, it will be unenforceable, unless those terms that breach public policy can be removed (known as 'severance'), in which case the remainder of the contract may be valid and enforceable. In practice, severance is an important tool in relation to contracts involving restraint of trade clauses, whereby courts will remove the unreasonable restraint, leaving the remainder of the contract valid. But the courts will only sever a term, or part of a term, as follows.

1. The court will not sever a term if the main consideration for the contract derived from the defendant's breach of public policy.[235]

2. An objectionable term will only be severed if it can be cut out of the contract and the rest of the contract remains capable of standing alone.[236] This is known as the 'blue pencil' test, because the court is, in effect, running an editing pencil through the offending words. The court will not sever terms where it would have to rearrange, add, or delete words in order to make the severed contract workable.

3. The court will not sever a term if to do so would alter the nature of the original contract.[237]

---

235. *Lound v Grimwade* (1888) 39 Ch D 605 (Ch).   236. *Goldsoll v Goldman* [1915] 1 Ch 292 (CA).
237. *Attwood v Lamont* [1920] 3 KB 571 (CA).

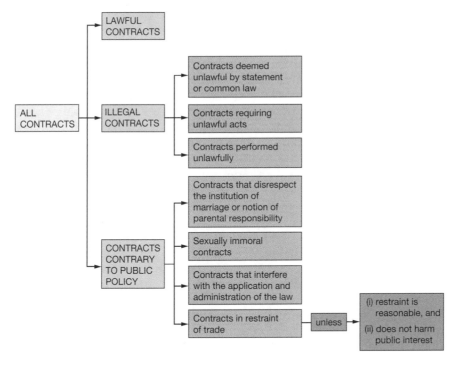

FIGURE 8.2 The legality of contracts

Key points summary

- Illegal contracts include:

  - contracts that amount to a legal wrong;
  - contracts that require the commission of an unlawful act; and
  - contracts that are performed in breach of statute.

- Contracts that offend public policy include:

  - contracts that disrespect the institution of marriage or parental responsibility;
  - contracts that promote sexually immoral behaviour;
  - contracts that interfere with the application or administration of justice; and
  - contracts that restrain trade.

- Contracts that serve to restrain trade are prima facie unenforceable unless it can be established that the restraint is not unreasonable in the public interest and it reasonably protects the legitimate interests of the parties.

- Notable cases involving restraint of trade clauses include:

  - contracts involving the sale of a business;
  - contracts of employment; and
  - exclusive trading contracts.

- Even if a contract is unenforceable or void on the ground of public policy, the court may be able to sever the offending part, thereby leaving the remainder of the contract valid and enforceable.

Chapter conclusion

In Chapter 6, we stated that a contract will be formed provided there is valid agreement and consideration, and an intention to create legal relations. As we have seen, however, in a number of situations, the courts will hold that, despite the validity of the contract's formation, the contract should not be enforceable. Given that the stability of commercial contracts is crucial for businesses, it is essential that those who run businesses are aware of those situations that can result in a contract being declared void or voidable, and take steps to avoid those situations arising. In order to avoid a contract being held voidable for misrepresentation, businesses should either take great care in the pre-contractual statements made, and/or include a suitably worded exclusion clause in the contract. To avoid the contract being held void on the grounds of mistake, the business should take care to ensure that there are no cross-purposes and that the relevant facts behind a contract are well known and verified (for example, that the subject matter of the contract actually exists, that the seller of goods has the right to sell them, and that the buyer does not already own them). The doctrines of misrepresentation and mistake demonstrate that some form of reprehensible conduct is not required in order to vitiate a contract. But we have also seen that reprehensible conduct can often result in a contract being deemed voidable or void. Pressurizing others into entering into contracts or entering into contracts that are illegal or contrary to public policy will usually result in a contract becoming unenforceable.

This chapter has demonstrated that contracts, once formed, are not beyond challenge. In the next chapter, this will be advanced to examine those instances in which a contract will become discharged.

Self-test questions

1. Define the following legal words and phrases:
    (a) vitiate;
    (b) misrepresentation;
    (c) *uberrimae fidei*;
    (d) rescission;
    (e) duress;
    (f) undue influence;
    (g) affirmation.

2. Paul established and has built up a relatively successful, high-street accountancy firm. He is due to retire in six months, so decides to sell the firm. He is approached by Aled, who expresses interest in purchasing the firm and asks why the firm has been so successful. Paul replies that it is because: 'There are no other accountancy firms within 30 miles. This business will make you a fortune. I believe the annual level of profit is around £1.2 million.' Aled asks his accountant, Chloe, to verify Paul's stated level of profits. Chloe confirms Paul's statement, but, in fact, the firm only makes around £100,000 profit per year. Aled asks for a few weeks to think it over. Paul then discovers that Ernst & Waterhouse, a multinational accountancy firm, is due to open an office close to his firm. He does not inform Aled of this. Aled agrees to purchase the firm and subsequently discovers the true level of profit, as well as the opening of the rival office. Aled seeks your advice to his legal options.

3. Explain the distinction between:
   (a) fraudulent, negligent, and innocent misrepresentation;
   (b) actual and presumed undue influence;
   (c) common, mutual, and unilateral mistake;
   (d) initial impossibility and subsequent impossibility;
   (e) illegality and public policy.

4. Alfonso works for a local firm of accountants based in Hampshire. For the last six months, he has been considering setting up his own firm and, to that end, he has been sounding out clients to see which ones would be keen on having their accounts audited by his new firm. He has also been collecting documents belonging to his current firm relating to new and potentially more efficient accounting systems. Alfonso resigns and his former employer draws his attention to a clause in his contract that prevents him from competing in any way with the firm anywhere in the UK for a period of five years. Despite this, Alfonso sets up a new business in London and acquires a number of his old firm's former clients. Alfonso's old firm is seeking an injunction to prevent Alfonso from accepting its prior clients. Discuss.

Further reading

Chandler, A, Devenney, J, and Poole, J, 'Common Mistake: Theoretical Justification and Remedial Inflexibility' [2004] JBL 34
Analyses the law relating to common mistake as to quality, focusing on the decision to abolish common mistake in equity; argues that whilst Great Peace *has clarified the law, it has also made it unduly rigid*

Duxbury, R, *Contract Law* (Sweet & Maxwell, London, 2008) ch 12
An impressively simple and straightforward account of the complex topic of mistake

Koffman, L, and Macdonald, E, *The Law of Contract* (6th edn, OUP, Oxford, 2007) ch 13
A clear and well-structured account of the law relating to misrepresentation; useful discussion of the advantages of claiming based on s 2(1) of the Misrepresentation Act 1967

Peel, E, *The Law of Contract* (12th edn, Sweet & Maxwell, London, 2007) ch 11
A detailed, but accessible and highly interesting, account of the law relating to illegality and public policy

Poole, J, *Textbook on Contract Law* (9th edn, OUP, Oxford, 2008) ch 15
Provides an up-to-date and analytical account of the law relating to duress, undue influence, and unconscionable bargains

Remember to visit the **Online Resource Centre** at **<http://www.oxfordtextbooks.co.uk/roach>** to access the following resources on Chapter 8, 'Vitiating factors': more **practice questions** and answers; a **glossary** of key terms; **multiple-choice questions**; **revision summaries**; **audio updates** when relevant; **diagrams** in pdf; **audio exam advice** on these key topics; and discussion box.

9 Discharge of the contract

- Discharge by performance
- Discharge by agreement
- Discharge by breach
- Discharge by frustration

INTRODUCTION

The importance of contract to the operation of businesses cannot be overemphasized. It is crucial that businesses know at what point a contract is created and what the terms of the contract are. It is equally important to know when the rights and obligations contained in a contract have come to an end. In the previous chapter, we noted that a contract might be rendered void or voidable due to the behaviour of the parties. In this chapter, we discuss in what situations a contract will become discharged. In some cases (for example, frustration), a contract will be automatically discharged with no possibility of continuance. In other cases (for example, breach), the actions of one party may result in the other party being entitled to terminate (discharge) the contract or may simply entitle him to recover damages only.

Given the regularity with which businesses will enter into contractual relations with other persons, it is vital to understand when a contract will become discharged and what the effects of discharge will be. This will depend upon the method of discharge and four methods can be identified:

- discharge by performance;
- discharge by agreement;
- discharge by breach; and
- discharge by frustration.

Discharge by performance

Although much discussion of contract law revolves around situations in which something goes wrong, the simple fact is that the vast majority of contracts are performed straightforwardly, with both parties fulfilling their obligations under the contract. Once both parties have fulfilled their obligations, their liability under the contract ceases and the contract comes to a natural end. This is known as 'discharge by performance'. If only one party performs his side of the contract, he will be discharged from liability under the contract and will acquire a right of action against the other party for breach of contract.

What constitutes performance?

In order for a contract to be discharged by performance, the requisite standard of performance will need to be present. The general rule is that that all of the obligations of the contract must be precisely and completely performed. Sometimes these obligations will be strict (for example, to deliver goods to a specified location by a certain date), and at other times the obligations will be qualified (for example, to exercise reasonable skill and care in the performance of a task). Either way, the requirement for precise and complete performance is a strict one, and parties who depart from their precise obligations will be unable to claim that the contract was discharged by performance. Further, the other party may acquire the right to sue for damages, or may even be able to elect to terminate the contract on the ground of breach.

The following case demonstrates the need for precise and complete performance.

 Arcos Ltd v EA Ronaasen & Son [1933] AC 470 (HL)

FACTS: An English company contracted to purchase a number of timber staves to be used in the making of barrels. The contract stated that the staves should be half an inch thick. Upon the staves' delivery, it was discovered that many of the staves were nine-sixteenths of an inch thick. The one-sixteenth increase in thickness made no difference at all to the company's ability to use them to manufacture barrels, but the company rejected the staves anyway and terminated the contract.

HELD: The House of Lords held that the term that was breached was a condition—namely, a breach of the implied condition regarding description found today in the Sale of Goods Act 1979. Therefore, the company's termination of the contract was valid, even though it suffered no actual loss. Lord Atkin stated: 'A ton does not mean about a ton, or a yard about a yard.'[1]

COMMENT: The ability of non-consumers to reject goods for minor breaches of the contract is now heavily limited by the Sale of Goods Act 1979, s 15A, to such an extent that if this case were to be decided today, the rejection would most likely amount to a breach.

Visit the Online Resource Centre for more on the Sale of Goods Act 1979, s 15A, in the chapter entitled 'The sale of goods'

The de minimis *rule*

The rule that performance must comply precisely and completely with the terms of the contract is subject to an important exception that was stated in *Arcos* itself when Lord Atkin stated: 'No doubt there may be microscopic deviations which business men and therefore lawyers will ignore.'[2] Where the deviation is 'microscopic', performance will be regarded as precise and complete. This is known as the *de minimis* rule, because it based upon the maxim *de minimis non curat lex* ('the law does

1. *Arcos Ltd v EA Ronaasen & Son* [1933] AC 470 (HL) 479.   2. Ibid.

not concern itself with trifles'). Thus, in *Shipton, Anderson & Co v Weil Bros & Co*,[3] a contract provided for the delivery of 4,950 tonnes of wheat. The seller delivered 55 lbs more than the contractual amount, but the court, applying the *de minimis* rule, held that this constituted performance of the contract by the seller.

Divisible obligations

Another important exception to the rule requiring precise and complete performance is in relation to divisible obligations. A divisible obligation is one that is due in intervals or instalments. Examples would include the monthly payment of an employee's wage, or the instalment payments made to a builder. Where an obligation is divisible, a party who has performed the requisite part can recover the accompanying divisible payment, even though the contract as a whole has not been performed,[4] as the following example demonstrates.

Eg **Divisible obligations and performance**

Caroline is hired to work as part of the crew aboard The Fearne, a ship chartered to transport goods between ports in Europe. The charterparty is to last one year. Caroline's employment contract provides that she will work for the entire duration of the charter and will be paid £1,500 per month, but will not be paid until the charter is complete. Accordingly, after one year, she will receive £18,000.

After six months, Caroline decides that she no longer wishes to work aboard The Fearne and leaves. Although she has not completed the contract, because the obligation to pay her is divisible (that is, a monthly rate of £1,500), she can recover her wages for the six months' work completed (£9,000), even though she was not due to be paid until the end of the charter. Of course, her failure to complete the charter period will amount to breach of contract, for which she may be required to pay damages.

Payment

In many contracts, the obligations of one party will amount to no more than to pay the price stipulated in the contract. Where this is the case, the payment of that sum will constitute performance of that party's obligations and discharge his liability. As a general rule, payment must be in legal tender (that is, bank notes and coins of certain denominations),[5] but an alternative method of payment will be acceptable where it is agreed upon (expressly or impliedly) by the parties. In the absence of such an agreement, payment by **negotiable instrument** (such as by cheque) presumptively amounts to conditional discharge only,[6] because such payment methods may be dishonoured. Whilst the instrument is current—that is, where the form of payment (for example, a cheque) has been initiated, but has not been completed (for

➡ **negotiable instruments:** transferable documents that promise to pay the bearer a sum of money at a future date

---

3. [1912] 1 KB 574 (KB).
4. *Ritchie v Atkinson* (1808) 10 East 295.
5. *Official Solicitor v Thomas* [1986] 2 EGLR 1 (CA). What constitutes legal currency can be found in the Currency and Bank Notes Act 1954, s 3, the Coinage Act 1971, s 2, and the Currency Act 1983, s 4.
6. *Sard v Rhodes* (1836) 1 M & W 153.

example, the cheque has not yet cleared)—the creditor impliedly undertakes not to sue for the contract price.[7] Once the instrument is honoured, the contract will be fully discharged, but if the instrument is dishonoured—that is, payment is not completed (for example, the cheque 'bounces')—then the creditor's right to sue revives.[8] Where payment is made by credit or debit card, the presumption is that payment is unconditional (and liability is discharged) unless the contract states otherwise.[9]

A party who claims that he has discharged his obligations by the payment of a sum will need to provide proof of payment. In many cases, this proof will constitute a written receipt, but, contrary to popular belief, other forms of proof are acceptable. In fact, any form of evidence from which payment may be inferred can be valid.[10] In many cases, however, a receipt is the most usual and most easily obtainable form of proof—but a debtor has no legal entitlement to insist on being given a receipt and, even if one is provided, it only provides prima facie evidence of payment.[11] The provider of the receipt can rebut this prima facie presumption by adducing evidence showing that payment was never made, or that the receipt was given mistakenly or obtained by fraud.

Time of performance

Where the contract does not provide that performance must be completed by a certain date, both the courts[12] and statute[13] state that the party's obligations must be performed within a reasonable time. Failure by a party to perform within a reasonable time will not constitute proper performance and that party will be in breach of contract. Where the contract does require the obligations to be performed by a certain date, the issue is slightly more complex and will depend on whether the time stipulation is 'of the essence of the contract'. Where a contract is not specifically enforceable (that is, where equity will not order performance via an order for specific performance), whether or not time is of the essence will depend upon the express or implied intentions of the parties. In determining this, the law does put in place certain presumptions. For example, the Sale of Goods Act 1979, s 10(1), provides that a term as to the time *of payment* for goods is deemed not to be of the essence of the contract, unless the contrary intention appears from the contract.

➡ specific performance: a court order requiring performance of an act, normally to fulfil a contract

Where a contract is specifically enforceable, the common law and equity have historically taken different positions on whether or not time was of the essence. At common law, unless the parties agreed otherwise, the courts would regard a time stipulation as of the essence of the contract and classify it as a condition, with the result that if the obligation was not performed on time, the other party could terminate the contract and claim damages. Conversely, equity did not regard time stipulations as of the essence of the contract, and would grant the equitable remedy of specific performance to parties who had failed to perform their obligations by the contractual date and would decline to order specific performance against a party in

---

7. *Sayer v Wagstaff* (1844) 14 LJ Ch 116.   8. Ibid.

9. *Re Charge Card Services* [1989] Ch 497 (CA).   10. *Eyles v Ellis* (1827) 4 Bing 112.

11. *Wilson v Keating* (1859) 27 Beav 121.

12. *Postlethwaite v Freeland* (1880) 5 App Cas 599 (HL).

13. For example, Sale of Goods Act 1979, s 29(3). Note that this Act only applies to contracts concerning the sale of goods, not to the supply of services, etc.

breach of a time stipulation. When the Supreme Court of Judicature Acts 1873–75 merged the courts of equity and common law, they provided that, where there was a conflict, equity would prevail. Today, this rule is preserved by the Law of Property Act 1925, s 41, which states that:

> Stipulations in a contract, as to time or otherwise, which according to rules of equity are not deemed to be or to have become of the essence of the contract, are also construed and have effect at law in accordance with the same rules.

Because s 41 preserves the rules of equity, it follows that any exceptions created under the rules of equity will also be preserved. Accordingly, a time stipulation will not be regarded as of the essence of the contract, unless it comes within one of the following three categories that equity regarded as of the essence:

- the contract expressly states that time is of the essence;[14]
- the contract itself does not expressly provide that time is of the essence, but upon the passing of the stipulated or implied date, the party subject to the delay gives notice that time has become of the essence and fixes a reasonable time for performance;[15] or
- the subject matter of the contract, or the circumstances surrounding it, indicate that time should be regarded of the essence. Examples include mercantile contracts,[16] contracts for the sale of a business as a going concern,[17] or an option to acquire property.[18]

Where the court holds that time is of the essence, even the slightest delay will constitute failed performance and will entitle the other party to terminate. Thus, in *Union Eagle Ltd v Golden Achievement Ltd*,[19] a party to a contract was entitled to terminate when the other party performed its obligations ten minutes late. Where time is not of the essence, the failure to perform by the date stipulated in the contract will still constitute breach and will entitle the other party to damages.[20]

Contracts concluded over distance

In the case of contracts concluded over distance (for example, email, Internet, letter), the Consumer Protection (Distance Selling) Regulations 2000,[21] reg 19(1), provides that:

> Unless the parties agree otherwise, the supplier shall perform the contract within a maximum of 30 days beginning with the day after the day the consumer sent his order to the supplier.

If the contract is not performed within this period, it is regarded as having not been made, save for any remedies the consumer would normally have for non-performance[22] (for example, the right to claim damages).

---

14. *Steedman v Drinkle* [1916] 1 AC 275 (PC); *Harold Wood Brick Co Ltd v Ferris* [1935] 2 KB 198 (CA).
15. *Stickney v Keeble* [1915] AC 386 (HL); *Behzadi v Shaftesbury Hotels Ltd* [1992] Ch 1 (CA).
16. *Hare v Nicoll* [1966] 2 QB 130 (CA); *Scandinavian Trading Tanker Co AB v Flota Petrolera Ecuatoriana* [1983] 2 AC 694 (HL).
17. *Tadcaster Tower Brewery Co v Wilson* [1897] 1 Ch 705 (Ch); *Lock v Bell* [1931] 1 Ch 35 (Ch).
18. *Hare v Nicoll* [1966] 2 QB 130 (CA).   19. [1997] AC 514 (PC).
20. *Raineri v Miles* [1981] AC 1050 (HL).   21. SI 2000/2334.
22. Ibid, reg 19(5).

Tender

What happens if one party attempts to perform his contractual obligations (known as a tender), but is prevented from doing so by the other party? The answer depends upon whether the attempted performance consists of payment or some other act.

➡ tender: attempted performance of a contractual obligation

Tender of payment

If the debtor attempts to tender payment, but the other party refuses, this does not discharge the debtor from the obligation to pay. The debtor must still be ready to 'find out the creditor and pay him when the debt is due'.[23] But if the creditor initiates a claim for non-payment against the debtor, the debtor can argue that the tender has been made and pay the money into court.[24] If the court holds that the debtor's tender is valid, several consequences follow:

- the debtor will not be liable for his non-payment of debt on the due date;
- any lien that the creditor has will be extinguished;
- the creditor only receives the money originally tendered. Interest and damages cannot be obtained; and
- the creditor will be required to pay the debtor's legal costs.

➡ lien: the right to hold the property of another until an obligation is satisfied

These consequences will put the debtor in the position in which he would have been had the tender been accepted. But these consequences will only follow if the debtor's tender is a valid one, and a series of nineteenth-century cases have imposed extremely strict requirements, as follows.

- The tender must comply with the terms of the contract. Such terms might relate to the time of payment, the place of payment, or the method of payment.
- The tender must be in a legal currency.[25] Therefore, cheques or other negotiable instruments will not suffice.[26]
- The legal currency must actually be produced in the presence of, and made accessible to, the creditor.[27] The rationale behind requiring actual production of the money is that 'it might tempt the creditor to yield'.[28] Where the creditor expressly or impliedly dispenses with the need actually to produce the payment, however, this requirement will be waived.[29]
- If the debtor attempts to tender an amount that is greater than the amount due, the tender will be invalid if the creditor is required to provide change.[30] If the debtor permits the creditor to keep the excess amount, the tender will be valid.[31]

---

23. *Walton v Mascall* (1844) 13 M & W 452, 458 (Parke B).
24. Civil Procedure Rules, r 37.3.
25. The legal definition of currency can be found in the Currency and Bank Notes Act 1954, s 3, the Coinage Act 1971, s 2, and the Currency Act 1983, s 4.
26. *Blumberg v Life Interests and Reversionary Securities Corporation* [1897] 1 Ch 171.
27. *Thomas v Evans* (1808) 10 East 101.
28. *Finch v Brook* (1834) 1 Bing NC 253, 257 (Vaughan J).
29. *Farquharson v Pearl Assurance Co Ltd* [1937] 3 All ER 124 (KB).
30. *Robinson v Cook* (1815) 6 Taunt 336.
31. *Bevans v Rees* (1839) 5 M & W 306; *Wade's Case* (1601) 5 Co Rep 114a.

Tender of acts

Where a party (*A*) is required to perform some act other than payment, a valid tender will occur where he attempts performance of the act in precise accordance with the terms of the contract. If the other party (*B*) then refuses to accept the tendered performance, *A* can sue *B* for damages in breach of contract.[32] Further, if *B*'s refusal of the tender is absolute and unqualified, this will amount to renunciation of the contract, entitling *A* to terminate the contract and claim damages.[33] If, following *A*'s tender, *B* attempts to sue *A* for non-performance, *A* can raise his tender as a defence.[34]

⟨⟩ Key points summary

- Where the parties precisely and completely perform their contractual obligations, the contract will be discharged by performance—but a discharge by performance may still occur where deviations in performance are 'microscopic' (the *de minimis* rule).

- Where a party's obligation is to pay a stipulated amount, payment of that amount will constitute precise and complete performance by him.

- Where the contract does not stipulate a completion date for performance, performance must be completed within a reasonable time. Failure to do so will constitute breach of contract.

- Where a time for performance is stipulated, the ability to discharge the contract for failure to perform on time will depend on whether or not time is of the essence of the contract.

- Attempted performance is known as 'tender', and the effect of a tender depends on whether the tender was the payment of a sum of money or the performance of some other act.

Discharge by agreement

Because a contract is brought into existence upon the parties' agreement, it follows that it can also be brought to an end through the parties' agreement. In many cases, no formality is required: the parties can simply abandon performance and walk away. In order to prevent a party changing his mind and subsequently alleging breach of contract, however, it is desirable that some form of written discharge is obtained.

Consideration

The requirement of consideration not only applies to the formation of a contract, but it also applies to the discharge of a contract. Both parties will need to provide consideration for the other's agreement to discharge (unless the agreement to discharge is executed by deed). This is known as 'accord' and 'satisfaction'. 'Accord'

---

32. *Startup v Macdonald* (1843) 6 Man & G 593.   33. Ibid.
34. Ibid.

refers to the agreement to discharge and 'satisfaction' refers to the need to provide consideration for the other's promise to agree to discharge. The form of this consideration will depend upon whether the contract is executed or executory, as the following example demonstrates.

 The distinction between executed and executory consideration is discussed at p 184

Eg Consideration and discharge by agreement

Executory consideration

Gareth, an art dealer, is looking to sell a genuine Constable painting. Melanie, an avid art collector, wishes to purchase it. A contract is drawn up, stating that payment and delivery will take place within a month. Before payment or delivery occurs, Gareth decides that he wishes to keep the painting and Melanie discovers another Constable painting in better condition elsewhere. The parties therefore decide to discharge their contract. Because the contract is executory (that is, neither party has performed its obligations), Gareth's promise to discharge Melanie's obligations will provide consideration for his own non-performance, and vice versa. There is both accord and satisfaction.

Executed consideration

Imagine that Gareth has delivered the painting (so his consideration is executed), but Melanie is yet to pay (so her consideration will be executory). If the parties then decide to discharge the contract, Melanie would not have provided any consideration for the painting or the agreement to discharge. There is accord, but no satisfaction. In order for the agreement to discharge to be valid, it will either need to be executed via a deed,[35] or Melanie will need to provide fresh consideration (satisfaction)[36] for Gareth's agreement to discharge. This fresh consideration could amount to the payment of a sum of money or some other benefit, but the fresh consideration cannot be less than what was due originally under the contract. This is because, as we have discussed, part-payment of a debt is not normally sufficient consideration.

 The rules relating to part-payment of a debt are discussed at p 192

Formalities

As we discussed in Chapter 5, certain contracts require certain formalities in order to be created (for example, to be executed by deed, or to be made or evidenced in writing). The question arising is whether the discharge needs to comply with the same formalities as the creation. The common law provides that a contract made under deed can only be discharged via a deed, but equity provides that a deed is not required. Because equity prevails,[37] it follows that a contract executed by deed does not require any formality in order to be discharged.[38] The same rule applies to contracts required to be in, or evidenced in, writing.[39]

 The formalities of a contract are discussed at p 132

In many cases, however, the parties may not wish the discharge to be total. The parties may instead merely desire to vary some of the terms within the original

---

35. *Foster v Dawber* (1851) 6 Exch 839.
36. *British Russian Gazette and Trade Outlook Ltd v Associated Newspapers Ltd* [1933] 2 KB 616 (CA).
37. Supreme Court Act 1981, s 49.   38. *Berry v Berry* [1929] 2 KB 316 (KB).
39. *Morris v Baron & Co* [1918] AC 1 (HL).

contract (subject to formalities). In this case, the agreement is to discharge certain terms and replace them with new terms. This is known as 'partial discharge' and will usually be ineffective unless it is complies with the relevant formalities (for example, it must be in writing if the contract itself must be in writing). Thus, if the parties agree orally to vary the terms of a contract, the variation will be ineffective.

◀▶ Key points summary

- A contract may be brought to an end by the mutual consent of the parties.

- A party will need to provide consideration for the other party's promise to discharge in order to be discharged by agreement (unless the agreement to discharge is executed by deed).

- The formalities that apply to the creation of a contract do not apply to its discharge, unless the discharge is partial, in which case, it will be required to comply with the relevant formality.

Discharge by breach

exclusion clause: a contractual term that attempts to exclude or limit liability for breach of contract or some other civil wrong

Damages, injunctions, and specific performance are discussed in Chapter 10

A party will be in breach of contract where, without a lawful excuse, he fails to perform his contractual obligations, or where he performs them in a defective manner. Subject to an effective **exclusion clause** to the contrary, breach of contract will entitle the non-breaching party to damages, and equitable remedies such as an injunction or specific performance may also be available. In addition, the non-breaching party may be entitled to terminate the contract, depending upon the type of breach that has occurred. A breach that entitles the non-breaching party to terminate is known as a 'repudiatory breach'.

Certain types of breach will automatically, subject to an effective exclusion clause to the contrary, give rise to the ability to terminate, whereas others will only give rise to the right to claim damages. There are four types of breach:

- renunciation;
- incapacitation;
- anticipatory breach; and
- defective performance.

Renunciation

Where one party renounces his contractual obligations, the other party may terminate the contract. Renunciation occurs where one party demonstrates an intention not to perform his obligations under the contract. Where a party expressly and unequivocally refuses to perform, establishing an intention not to perform is straightforward and the other party may freely terminate the contract, as the following simple example demonstrates.

> ## Eg Renunciation and termination
>
> Dominic is an employee of Keep Trucking Ltd, a haulage firm. His contract requires him to transport items to designated depots around the country. His manager, Marcus, instructs Dominic to transport a consignment of goods from London to Aberdeen. Not wishing to engage in such a long drive, Dominic refuses and tells Marcus to get one of the other drivers to transport the consignment.
>
> Because Dominic has expressly and unequivocally evinced an intention not to perform his contractual obligations (that is, he has renounced his employment contract), Keep Trucking can terminate his contract of employment and dismiss him.

More problematic are those cases in which an alleged intention not to perform is implied through the actions or conduct of a party. The difficulties can be seen in the following case.

> ## *Woodar Investment Development Ltd v Wimpey Construction UK Ltd* **[1980] 1 WLR 277 (HL)**
>
> **FACTS:** The defendant contracted to purchase a piece of land from the claimant. The defendant subsequently purported to terminate the contract on the basis of an honest, but mistaken, belief that the contract granted it such a right. The claimant alleged that the defendant's conduct (that is, the purported termination of the contract) demonstrated an intention not to perform and that the defendant had therefore renounced the contract, entitling the claimant to obtain damages.
>
> **HELD:** The House of Lords dismissed the claimant's action. The House held that the defendant had not demonstrated an intention not to perform. In fact, the defendant had relied on the contract and invoked one of its provisions (albeit mistakenly and invalidly). Where an express intention is lacking, the crucial issue is whether 'a reasonable person in the position of the respondents would properly infer [from the circumstances and the party's words and conduct] an intention'[40] not to be bound by the contract.

⭐ See JW Carter, 'Regrettable Developments in the Law of Contract?' (1980) 39 CLJ 256

Before terminating a contract on the ground of the other party's renunciation, the non-breaching party should be confident that the other party has, in fact, renounced the contract. If *A* terminates a contract and claims damages on the belief that *B* has renounced it, but that belief is mistaken, *B* is likely to be able to claim damages from *A* for wrongful termination.

Incapacitation

A contract may be regarded as discharged where it is breached due to one party, through his own act or default, incapacitating himself from performing his contractual obligations. Discharge will occur even where the breaching party still wishes to perform.

---

40. *Woodar Investment Development Ltd v Wimpey Construction UK Ltd* [1980] 1 WLR 277 (HL) 296 (Lord Keith).

> ### Universal Cargo Carriers Corporation v Citati [1957] 2 QB 401 (QB)
>
> **FACTS:** The claimant chartered a ship to the defendant. The charterparty provided that the defendant would provide cargo and nominate a shipper by a certain date. Three days before this date, the defendant had provided no cargo and no shipper had been nominated, meaning that, even if the defendant did nominate a shipper before the expiry date, the purpose of the charterparty had become frustrated. Accordingly, the claimant cancelled the charter and chartered the ship to someone else. It then claimed damages for breach of contract. The defendant counterclaimed for wrongful repudiation of the contract.
>
> **HELD:** Although the defendant had not renounced the contract, the High Court held that his own failure to nominate a shipper meant that the purpose of the charterparty had become frustrated. The fact that the defendant still wished to perform did not matter. Devlin J (as he then was) stated: 'To say "I would like to but cannot" negatives intent to perform as much as "I will not".'[41]

The burden of proof is placed upon the non-breaching party to establish that the other party's conduct rendered performance impossible. It should be noted that the insolvency of one of the parties will not constitute incapacitation.[42]

Anticipatory breach

Although anticipatory breach is often considered as a type of breach in its own right, it is probably more accurate to regard it as a form of renunciation or incapacitation. So far, we have discussed actual breaches of contract (that is, breaches that occur at the time when performance is due)—but an anticipatory breach occurs where a party renounces the contract, or incapacitates himself from performing it, *before performance is due*. At this point, the non-breaching party has two options.

The first option is that the non-breaching party may accept the other party's breach and terminate the contract immediately (it is not necessary to wait until the date of performance before terminating). The non-breaching party may also immediately bring a claim for damages, but the normal rules of mitigation of loss apply, so damages may be reduced if the non-breaching party fails to mitigate his loss.

 The rules relating to mitigation of loss in contract cases are discussed at p 340

> ### Hochster v De La Tour (1853) 2 E & B 678
>
> **FACTS:** The defendant employed the claimant for a three-month period. The contract provided that the claimant would begin work on 1 June. On 11 May, the defendant informed the claimant that he no longer needed his services. The claimant sued for damages, but the defendant argued that claimant could only bring an action after 1 June.

---

41. *Universal Cargo Carriers Corporation v Citati* [1957] 2 QB 401 (QB) 437.
42. *Re Agra Bank* (1867) LR 5 Eq 160.

HELD: The claimant became entitled to terminate the contract and claim damages on 11 May. There was no need to wait until the date for performance had passed.

COMMENT: Whilst the court's approach provides the non-breaching party with a quick remedy, it does create certain problems—especially where there is a considerable delay between entering into the contract and performance being due. The court will have to assess damages based on the conditions that would exist at some point in the future. Such assessments might very well under- or overcompensate the claimant.

Once the non-breaching party exercises his right to terminate, the other party cannot tender performance, even if such performance is completed within the due date.[43] If, however, the non-breaching party has acquired the right to terminate but has yet to exercise it, performance can be validly tendered.[44]

The second option available to the non-breaching party is slightly more complex. Instead of accepting the other party's breach, the non-breaching party might reject it and continue to insist on performance (that is, affirm the breach). In such a case, the contract remains in force and both parties are required to fulfil their obligations. Because the non-breaching party has affirmed the anticipatory breach, he will lose his immediate right to terminate the contract and claim damages. These rights will resurrect if the other party fails to perform by the due date.

The following case provides an example of this option.

White and Carter (Councils) Ltd v McGregor [1962] AC 413 (HL)

FACTS: The defendant entered into a contract with the claimant, whereby the claimant would advertise the defendant's business on litter bins for a period of three years. In return, the defendant would pay for the advertising space by instalments. On the same day that the contract was made, the defendant wrote to the claimant cancelling the contract. The claimant refused to accept this anticipatory breach—that is, it affirmed the breach—and proceeded to advertise the defendant's business. The contract provided that, if the defendant were to fail to pay an instalment, the claimant could sue for the full amount due under the contract. Upon missing an instalment, the claimant brought an action for the agreed sum. The defendant argued that, because the claimant had not attempted to sell the advertising space to anyone else, it had failed to mitigate its loss.

The law relating to an action for an agreed sum is discussed at p 346

HELD: The House of Lords allowed the claimant to perform the contract and recover the full contract price. Lord Keith stated that where a party affirms an anticipatory breach, the rules relating to mitigation would not apply (because this was an action for an agreed sum, the rules relating to mitigation did not apply anyway).

COMMENT: The decision of the House has been subject to criticism—namely, that it requires the party in breach to 'engage in performance that is entirely pointless and wasteful'.[45] The House was fully aware of this criticism, with Lord Reid stating that the

---

43. *Xenos v Danube and Black Sea Rly Co* (1863) 13 CBNS 825.

44. *Norwest Holst Group Administration Ltd v Harrison* [1985] ICR 668 (CA).

45. *Stocznia Gdanska SA v Latvian Shipping Co* [2001] 1 Lloyd's Rep 537 (QB) 565 (Thomas J).

non-breaching party could only insist on performance where he had a 'legitimate interest' in doing so, which the claimant in *White* did.[46] Subsequent courts have added a second limitation—namely, that the non-breaching party cannot insist on performance where the cooperation of the party in breach is required in order for performance to continue.[47] In *White*, the claimant clearly did not require the defendant's cooperation to perform.

Defective performance

The most common form of breach is where one party has failed to perform his contractual obligations adequately. Where the performance is defective, it does not automatically follow that the non-breaching party will have the right to terminate the contract. The ability to terminate depends upon the type of term that was breached. In Chapter 7, it was noted that the principal classification of contractual terms is between express and implied terms. For the purposes of determining the remedy for breach of contract due to defective performance, however, there is a more important classification—namely, the distinction between 'conditions', 'warranties', and 'innominate terms'. Specifically, the ability of the non-breaching party to terminate the contract depends heavily upon this distinction.

It may be the case that the classification of the term will be determined by statute. For example, the majority of the implied terms contained in the Sale of Goods Act 1979 are classified as conditions,[48] except where the buyer is a non-consumer, in which case, breach of these implied terms may be regarded as a breach of warranty where the breach is so slight that it would be unreasonable to reject the goods.[49] The parties themselves are free to expressly classify the terms of the contract and whilst such a classification will usually be followed,[50] it will not provide a conclusive classification, as the following case demonstrates.

L Schuler AG v Wickman Machine Tool Sales Ltd [1974] AC 235 (HL)

FACTS: The defendant provided the claimant with the sole right to sell a certain piece of machinery for four-and-a-half years. The contract provided that it was a condition of the contract that the claimant shall send its representatives to visit the six largest UK motor manufacturers at least once a week to solicit orders (over the four-and-a-half-year period, this would amount of around 1,400 visits). The claimant failed to visit the six manufacturers every week and the defendant purported to terminate the contract for breach of the condition.

HELD: The House of Lords held that the term breached was not a condition. If it were a condition, missing a single visit could result in termination and the House did not believe

---

46. This requirement has been adopted by the courts: see *Attica Sea Carriers Corporation v Ferrostaal Poseidon Bulk Reederei GmbH* [1976] 1 Lloyd's Rep 250 (CA).
47. *Hounslow London Borough Council v Twickenham Garden Developments Ltd* [1971] Ch 233 (Ch).
48. See Sale of Goods Act 1979, ss 12(5A) (implied term as to title), 13(1A) (compliance with description), 14(6) (satisfactory quality and fitness for purpose), and 15(3) (sale by sample).
49. Ibid, s 15A(1).
50. *London North Central plc v Butterworth* [1987] QB 527 (CA).

that either party had intended such a consequence. Accordingly, it was held that the parties had used the word 'condition' in a non-legal sense merely to indicate that it was a term.

⭐ See
R Brownsword, 'L Schuler AG v Wickman Machine Tool Sales Ltd: A Tale of Two Principles' (1974) 37 MLR 104

In the absence of classification by statute, by a previous binding decision regarding the particular type of term, or by the parties, the courts will classify the term.

Conditions and warranties

Historically, the principal distinction has been between 'conditions' and 'warranties', as follows.

- *Conditions* are the most important terms that 'go to the root of the contract'. If a condition is breached, the non-breaching may terminate the contract and claim damages.

- *Warranties* are less important terms. Whereas conditions relate to the main purpose of the contract, warranties tend to be 'collateral to the main purpose of...a contract'.[51] Because a warranty is less important and the consequences of its breach usually less severe, it follows that its breach can adequately be compensated by an award of damages and therefore the non-breaching party may not terminate the contract.

The practical distinction between conditions and warranties is extremely important from the perspective of the non-breaching party, as the following example demonstrates.

Eg Breach, conditions, and warranties

MicroTech plc enters into a contract with ViaSoft Ltd. ViaSoft breaches a term of the contract. Three options exist.

1. If the term breached is a condition, MicroTech can terminate the contract and claim damages from ViaSoft.

2. If the term breached is a warranty, MicroTech can recover damages from ViaSoft, but it cannot terminate the contract.

3. The term breached could be an innominate term—in which case, the consequences of breach of such a term will be discussed later and this option can be ignored for now.

MicroTech, believing the term to be a condition, terminates the contract, refuses to perform its obligations, and claims damages for breach. ViaSoft counterclaims for damages, contending that the term that it breached was merely a warranty and that MicroTech's termination of the contract is improper, and therefore itself constitutes a repudiatory breach of contract because it amounts to a renunciation. Should the court agree with ViaSoft, MicroTech will have wrongfully terminated and will be liable for breach. Instead of recovering damages, it will become liable to pay damages.

---

51. *Dawsons Ltd v Bonnin* [1922] 2 AC 413 (HL) 422 (Lord Haldane).

The above example demonstrates how important it can be that the classification of a term is known before the non-breaching party elects to terminate (although, as we shall see, the advent of the innominate term has lessened this importance somewhat).

The distinction between conditions and warranties can be seen in the following two cases with similar facts, which were decided in the same year.

 Poussard v Spiers (1876) 1 QB 410 (DC)

FACTS: Madame Poussard (the claimant) contracted to perform at the defendant's opera house for three months. A few days before the opera's opening night, she became ill and was unable to perform for the first four performances. A substitute was located, but would only perform for the full three-month contract. Given that the defendant did not know how long the claimant would be ill, he terminated Madame Poussard's contract and took on the substitute. Madame Poussard sued.

HELD: The High Court held that the claimant's inability to perform from the opening night onward went to the root of the contract and that therefore the defendant's termination of the contract was valid.

COMMENT: Note that, because the defendant had a lawful excuse for her failure to perform, she had not actually breached the contract; rather the contract had become frustrated. Irrespective of the method of discharge, the key issue was whether the claimant had the right to terminate, and this was dependent upon the term in question being a condition.

 Bettini v Gye (1876) 1 QB 183 (DC)

FACTS: Bettini (the claimant) had agreed to perform in the defendant's opera for three-and-a-half months. It was a term of the contract that he arrive six days before the opening night to take part in rehearsals. Due to illness, the claimant arrived three days before the opening night. The defendant refused to let the claimant sing and obtained a replacement. The claimant sued.

HELD: The High Court held that the defendant was not entitled to terminate the claimant's contract. The term requiring six days' rehearsal time did not go to the root of the contract. Therefore, because the term was a mere warranty, the defendant was not entitled to terminate Bettini's employment. Bettini could therefore recover damages for wrongful termination.

The distinction between *Poussard* and *Bettini* is clear, but this is not always the case and it may be that a term is not so easy to classify. So how will the courts determine the term's status?

Where statute or a binding precedent does not classify the term, the courts will attempt to determine the status of a term by reference to the parties' intentions. In many cases, however, the parties may have given no thought to the legal status of the terms when negotiating them. Accordingly, the court will attempt to ascertain the intentions of the parties, based on the nature, purpose, and construction of the contract. If, based on the context of the whole contract, it is clear that that term is so important that it goes to 'the very root…of the contract'[52] and that an injured party would always want to be entitled to terminate for breach of the term, then it will be regarded as a condition. Thus, where a charterparty provided that a ship was 'now in the port of Amsterdam', when, in fact, it was elsewhere, the term was held to be a condition, because the location of the ship was commercially vital to the charterer.[53] Conversely, where a term of a charterparty provided that the ship should be seaworthy, the court held it was not a condition, because the term could be breached in a number of ways, some of which the parties could not intend to result in termination.[54]

Innominate terms

Classifying terms as either conditions or warranties provided certainty in so far as it gave the parties clarity in relation to whether or not they could terminate if the other party were to commit a breach. But the approach was also unjustifiably rigid in that, once a term was classified as a condition, the non-breaching party could escape the contract irrespective of the seriousness of the breach. The case of *Arcos Ltd v EA Ronaasen & Son* (discussed above) is a stark example of this. Further, this approach allowed parties to escape from a bad bargain by upholding their right to terminate based on a trivial breach of a condition. Accordingly, in the following case, the Court of Appeal established a third type of term—namely, the innominate term (also known as the 'intermediate term').

Hong Kong Fir Shipping Co Ltd v Kawasaki Kisen Kaisha Ltd [1962] 2 QB 26 (CA)

FACTS: The claimant owned a ship, which it chartered to the defendant for a period of two years. The charterparty provided that the claimant would provide a ship that was 'in every way fitted for ordinary cargo service'. The ship was actually in a poor state of repair and the engine crew was incompetent. As a result of this, on the ship's first voyage, significant repairs were needed, resulting in use of the ship being lost for twenty weeks whilst repairs were being made. Shortly before the ship was fully repaired, the defendant purported to terminate the charter for repudiatory breach. Subsequently, the ship was repaired (with seventeen months of the contract left to go) and was completely seaworthy. The claimant brought an action for wrongful termination.

HELD: There was no doubt that the claimant was in breach of contract, but was it a breach that entitled the defendant to terminate? Under the approach in *Arcos*, the answer would almost certainly have been 'yes'—but the Court of Appeal took a different approach. Diplock LJ (as he then was) stated:

> There are, however, many contractual undertakings of a more complex character which cannot be categorised as being 'conditions' or 'warranties,'…Of such undertakings all that can be predicated is that some breaches will and others will not give rise to an event which will deprive the party not in default of substantially

---

52. *Glaholm v Hays* (1841) 2 Man & G 257, 268.
53. *Behn v Burness* (1863) 3 B & S 751.
54. *Hong Kong Fir Shipping Co Ltd v Kawasaki Kisen Kaisha Ltd* [1962] 2 QB 26 (CA).

the whole benefit which it was intended that he should obtain from the contract; and the legal consequences of a breach of such an undertaking, unless provided for expressly in the contract, depend upon the nature of the event to which the breach gives rise and do not follow automatically from a prior classification of the undertaking as a 'condition' or a 'warranty'.[55]

These terms that cannot be categorized as conditions or warranties would be classed as innominate terms, breach of which would only give the non-breaching party the right to terminate if the breach were to deprive him of substantially the whole benefit of the contract. The term in the contract requiring seaworthiness was deemed to be such an innominate term. Because the ship had been fully repaired and the defendant still had seventeen months' potential use, it had not been deprived of substantially the whole benefit, and therefore the defendant's termination was wrongful.

COMMENT: The introduction of the innominate term represents a stark departure from the approach evidenced in previous cases, with one commentator describing the decision as 'revolutionary'.[56] Under the previous approach, the seriousness and effects of the breach were largely inconsequential. Where an innominate term is breached, the seriousness and effects of the breach become all-important in determining the non-breaching party's right to terminate.

 See MP Furmston, 'The Classification of Contractual Terms' (1962) 25 MLR 584

How does the introduction of the innominate term affect the court's approach to the classification of terms? There is little doubt that the courts now rarely classify terms as warranties, given that a classification as an innominate term will provide the court with much more flexibility. The courts will only classify a term as a warranty where there is clear evidence that the parties did not intend a breach to result in the right to terminate, or where statute or a binding precedent classifies a term as such. Accordingly, since *Hong Kong Fir*, the crucial distinction is now between conditions and innominate terms.

The problem that has arisen is that the courts now have to balance two opposing objectives. The first objective is to uphold the validity of contracts where possible. The introduction of the innominate term is clearly evidence of this, because it restricts the non-breaching party's right to terminate. In the absence of clear agreement as to the term being a condition, the courts should 'lean in favour of construing'[57] the term as innominate. This is widely regarded as a beneficial development, because it prevents parties from avoiding contracts for technical or trivial breaches, or where they have simply made a bad bargain, as the following case demonstrates.

Reardon-Smith Line Ltd v Yngvar Hansen Tangen [1976] 1 WLR 989 (HL)[58]

FACTS: To help finance the construction of a tanker, it was chartered before it had even been constructed. The charterers subchartered the tanker to the claimant. Because the

---

55. *Hong Kong Fir Shipping Co Ltd v Kawasaki Kisen Kaisha Ltd* [1962] 2 QB 26 (CA) 70.
56. T Weir, 'Contracts: The Buyer's Right to Reject Defective Goods' [1976] CLJ 33, 35.
57. *Tradax Internacional SA v Goldschmidt SA* [1977] 2 Lloyd's Rep 604 (QB) 612 (Slynn J).
58. See also *Cehave NV v Bremer Hangelsgesellschaft mbH (The Hansa Nord)* [1976] QB 44 (CA).

tanker did not yet have a name, it was referred to in the charterparty by reference to the shipyard at which it was built—namely, 'Yard No. 354 at Osaka'. The ship was too large to be built at Osaka, so it was built at another shipyard in Oshima. Upon completion of the tanker, the charter market had fallen due to an oil crisis, meaning that such tankers could be chartered for much less than the claimant had agreed to pay in the contract. The claimant therefore terminated the contract, on the ground that the tanker was not built at the shipyard specified in the contract.

HELD: Lord Wilberforce described the traditional approach of classifying a term as either a condition or warranty as 'excessively technical and due for fresh consideration in this House'.[59] He stated that the court should have more regard to 'the nature and gravity of a breach or departure rather than in accepting rigid categories which do or do not automatically give a right to rescind'.[60] On this basis, the House of Lords held that the term breached was innominate, and that, because the effect of the breach was minor, the claimant had no right to terminate, and the termination was therefore invalid.

The second objective is the need to provide commercial certainty to the parties' dealings, but the flexibility of the innominate term has resulted in increased uncertainty. Under the pre-*Hong Kong Fir* approach, all that the non-breaching party needed to know was whether the term breached a condition or a warranty, and such information was usually discernable from the wording of the contract. Where a term is innominate, the ability to terminate depends not on the words of the contract, but on events, and these events 'may be in the China Sea rather than in the head office where decisions are taken, and one will probably have to wait for them, since consequences tend to occur after their causes'.[61] Accordingly, where the term is innominate, the non-breaching party cannot terminate with certainty; it will have to 'wait and see' whether the breach is of sufficient gravity to enable it to terminate. Parties who terminate before such knowledge is available risk being subject to a wrongful termination action should the consequences of the breach not be sufficiently serious.

The courts' concern over the uncertainty inherent in the use of the innominate term is evidenced in the following case.

Maredelanto Compania Naviera SA v Bergbau-Handel GmbH (The Mihalis Angelos) [1971] 1 QB 164 (CA)[62]

FACTS: The defendant chartered a ship from the claimant shipowner. Clause 1 of the charterparty provided that the ship would be expected to load cargo at Haiphong on about 1 July 1965. The claimant knew, however, that this expectation was unreasonable (because the ship was engaged elsewhere) and that the ship would not be at Haiphong until around 13–14 July. In the meantime, the defendant had discovered that it could not obtain any of the cargo that it had hoped to transport on the chartered ship. The

---

59. *Reardon-Smith Line Ltd v Yngvar Hansen Tangen* [1976] 1 WLR 989 (HL) 998.
60. Ibid.
61. T Weir, 'Contracts: The Buyer's Right to Reject Defective Goods' [1976] CLJ 33, 35.
62. See also *Bunge Corporation v Tradax Export SA* [1981] 1 WLR 711 (HL).

defendant therefore terminated the charterparty and the claimant sued for damages. The claimant argued that clause 1 was an innominate term and that, because the defendant had not been deprived of substantially the whole benefit of the contract, it had no right to terminate.

HELD: The Court of Appeal declined to follow *Hong Kong Fir* and held the termination by the defendant to be valid. Megaw LJ stated the reason for the Court's decision:

> [S]uch a term in a charterparty ought to be regarded as being a condition of the contract, in the old sense of the word "condition"...One of the important elements of the law is predictability. At any rate in commercial law, there are obvious and substantial advantages in having, where possible, a firm and definite rule for a particular class of legal relationship....It is surely much better, both for shipowners and charterers...to be able to say categorically: "If a breach is proved, then the charterer can put an end to the contract," rather than that they should be left to ponder whether or not the courts would be likely...to decide that in the particular circumstances the breach was or was not such as "to go to the root of the contract." Where justice does not require greater flexibility, there is everything to be said for, and nothing against, a degree of rigidity in legal principle.[63]

COMMENT: The decision does not reject the introduction of the innominate term, but it does indicate that the Court's reasoning in *Hong Kong Fir* is not appropriate in all cases. In certain cases, the need for certainty may outweigh the need for flexibility. In particular, the judicial preference for labelling a term as innominate will need to be balanced with the need for certainty in commercial dealings.

★ See WVH Rogers, 'The Late Ship and the Non-existent Cargo' (1971) 34 MLR 190

A small measure of clarity has been provided by Waller LJ,[64] who expressed approval for the relevant passage in *Chitty on Contracts*, which stated that a term is likely to be regarded as innominate, unless it comes within one of the following situations, when it will likely be classed as a condition:

- if statute expressly classifies a term as a condition;
- if, subject to the rules of precedent, a previous judicial decision classifies a type of term as a condition;
- if the contract itself provides that the term is a condition, or that its breach can result in termination;
- if the nature or the subject matter or the circumstances of the case lead to the conclusion that the parties must have intended that the term's breach would entitle the non-breaching party to terminate.

These situations are relatively narrow and fit in with the widely held judicial belief that 'the courts should not be too ready to interpret contractual clauses as conditions'.[65] Accordingly, we appear to have completely moved away from the traditional position, whereby the effect of the breach was not important, to a position in which, in the majority of cases, the effect of the breach becomes the determining factor.

---

63. *Maredelanto Compania Naviera SA v Bergbau-Handel GmbH (The Mihalis Angelos)* [1971] 1 QB 164 (CA) 205.
64. *BS & N Ltd (BVI) v Micado Shipping Ltd (Malta) (The Seaflower)* [2001] 1 Lloyd's Rep 341 (CA) 348.
65. *Bunge Corporation v Tradax Export SA* [1981] 1 WLR 711 (HL) 715 (Lord Wilberforce).

Termination and affirmation

Unlike frustration, breach does not automatically discharge the contract. As discussed in the previous sections, subject to an effective exclusion clause to the contrary, the non-breaching party *may* have the right to terminate the contract and therefore discharge it, or he may simply have a right to recover damages only. Alternatively, a party that has the right to terminate may instead choose to affirm the contract. Termination and affirmation will now be examined.

Termination

A repudiatory breach does not automatically discharge the contract; rather, the non-breaching party may elect to terminate the contract. The party terminating need not comply with any formalities in order to terminate the contract, but the termination 'must be unequivocal and it must be communicated to the party in breach'[66] (for example, by refusing to accept the other party's performance or by refusing to perform himself).

A valid election to terminate can result in a number of consequences, as follows.

- The party that terminated the contract is released from performing any obligations that remain to be performed. This could include accepting or paying for future performance,[67] paying any future instalments,[68] or adhering to a restrictive covenant contained in the contract.[69] Should the party in breach commence an action for non-performance, the non-breaching party can raise the termination as a defence.

- Termination operates only in relation to future obligations. The obligations of both parties due at the time of termination remain in force and must be performed. For example, if the non-breaching party terminates a contract that requires it to pay for goods in instalments, any instalments unpaid at the time of discharge will still need to be paid, but future instalments need not be paid.

- The above rules also apply to a party in breach, so future obligations will not need to be performed, but obligations accruing at the time of termination remain in force (these are known as 'primary obligations'). But the party in breach will also become subject to a secondary obligation—namely, to pay damages to the non-breaching party.[70]

- The non-breaching party can recover any monies paid if there has been a total failure of consideration. This will occur where the party in breach has not performed any part of its contractual duties in respect of which payment is due under the contract.[71]

- If the non-breaching party has supplied goods or performed a service but, at the time that it exercised the right to terminate, has not been paid, it can sue for a *quantum meruit* (reasonable sum).

---

66. *Sookraj v Samaroo* [2004] UKPC 50, [2005] 1 P & CR DG 11, [17] (Lord Scott).
67. *Photo Production Ltd v Securicor Transport Ltd* [1980] AC 827 (HL).
68. *SCI (Sales Curve Interactive) v Titus SARL* [2001] EWCA Civ 591, [2001] 2 All ER (Comm) 416.
69. *General Billposting Co Ltd v Atkinson* [1909] AC 118 (HL).
70. *R v Ward Ltd v Bignall* [1967] 1 QB 534 (CA).
71. *Stocznia Gdanska SA v Latvian Shipping Co* [1998] 1 WLR 574 (HL).

- A party that exercises the right to terminate a contract cannot subsequently change its mind, affirm the breach, and demand performance.[72] This is a corollary of the rule that, upon termination, all future obligations become discharged.
- Termination does not necessarily discharge the whole contract. Certain terms may impose obligations post-termination (for example, a term requiring that any disputes be referred to arbitration before commencing legal proceedings) and these terms may likely continue to be binding if it was the intention of the parties that this be so.[73] In addition, liquidated damages clauses and valid exclusion clauses are also likely to remain in force.[74]

 Liquidated damages clauses are discussed at p 343

Affirmation

The non-breaching party may not want to contract to end. Accordingly, it may elect to affirm the breach or it may simply decide not to exercise the right to terminate. In either event, several consequences will follow.

- The contract will remain in force and will continue to bind both parties.[75]
- Where the non-breaching party expressly and unequivocally elects to affirm the breach, its right to terminate is lost and it cannot subsequently change its mind. Because affirmation is only effective if it is unequivocal, however, it follows that a non-breaching party that demands that performance continue can still subsequently elect to terminate, because it has not unequivocally affirmed the breach. The ability to change one's mind will also exist where the affirmation is conditional (for example, upon the breaching party discontinuing the breach).
- If the non-breaching party obtains an order for specific performance requiring the party in breach to fulfil its contractual obligations, this will amount to conditional affirmation only. If the party in breach fails to comply with the order or if performance becomes impossible, the non-breaching party may terminate the contract and recover damages.[76]

Exclusion clauses

The contract may contain an exclusion clause that excludes or restricts liability or a remedy for breach of contract. The effect and regulation of such clauses will be discussed in detail in Chapter 28.

⟨⟩ Key points summary

- Breach of contract occurs where a party to a contract, without lawful excuse, fails to perform its contractual obligations or performs them in a defective manner.

---

72. *Johnson v Agnew* [1980] AC 367 (HL).
73. *Heyman v Darwins Ltd* [1942] AC 356 (HL).
74. *Photo Production Ltd v Securicor Transport Ltd* [1980] AC 827 (HL).
75. *BMBF (No 12) v Harland & Wolff Shipbuilding & Heavy Industries Ltd* [2001] EWCA Civ 862, [2001] 2 Lloyd's Rep 227.
76. *Austins of East Ham Ltd v Macey* [1941] Ch 338 (CA).

- There are four types of breach:

    - renunciation;
    - incapacitation;
    - anticipatory breach;
    - defective performance.

- Subject to an effective exclusion clause, a breach of contract always entitles the non-breaching party to damages.

- If the breach is repudiatory, the non-breaching party is entitled (subject to an exclusion clause) to terminate the contract. Renunciation, incapacitation, and anticipatory breach are all repudiatory breaches.

- Where performance is defective, the right to terminate the contract will depend upon the type of term breached. The three types of term are conditions, warranties, and innominate terms. A term can be classified by statute, judicial precedent, or by the parties' intentions as expressed in the contract, or inferred from the subject matter and surrounding circumstances.

- Breach of a condition allows the non-breaching party to terminate the contract and claim damages. Breach of warranty allows the recovery of damages only. Breach of an innominate term will provide a right to terminate where the breach deprives the non-breaching party of substantially the whole benefit of the contract.

- Instead of terminating the contract, the non-breaching party may affirm the breach and continue with the contract.

- Liability or a remedy for breach of contract can be excluded or limited by an exclusion clause.

Discharge by frustration

We noted above that a breach occurs where a party to a contract, without lawful excuse, fails to perform its obligations. We also noted that, generally, the standard of performance is strict, meaning that any failure to perform, no matter how slight, will usually constitute a breach. Where a lack of contractual performance is caused by events outside the control of either party, however, it would be unfair to impose liability for breach. In such a case, the court is likely to hold that the contract has been frustrated, and the effect of frustration is to provide the breaching party with a lawful excuse for its breach of contract.

Frustrating events

Numerous events can bring about a contract's frustration. It should be noted that, in order for a contract to be frustrated, the event must occur after the contract was made (that is, the event must be supervening). Where the event existed at the time that the contract was made, frustration will not apply and the relevant party will need to seek relief via the law relating to illegality or mistake.

The principal categories of frustrating event are:

- physical impossibility;
- frustration of common purpose;
- fundamental change of circumstances; and
- illegality.

Physical impossibility

The most straightforward form of frustrating event is one that occurs after the contract was entered into and which serves to render performance of the contract physically impossible. The obvious example of this would be where the subject matter of the contract has been destroyed.

 Taylor v Caldwell (1863) 3 B & S 826

FACTS: The defendant granted the claimant the use of a music hall in order to put on a series of concerts. Accidentally, and without any fault on the part of either party, the music hall was burnt down. Because the music hall was unavailable, the defendant was in breach of contract and so the claimant sued.

HELD: The claimant's action failed. The contract had become frustrated and so the defendant was not liable to pay damages. One of the judges, Blackburn J, justified this by imposing an implied term into the contract, which provided that liability would not be imposed where performance becomes impossible. It should be noted that this implied term theory is no longer accepted today.

COMMENT: Destruction of the contract's subject matter will not always result in the contract's frustration. Certain contracts (for example, sale of goods contracts) may be governed by rules, or may contain terms, that place the risk of destruction upon one of the parties before performance is completed. In such a case, if the risk has been imposed upon a party before the subject matter is destroyed, then the contract will not be frustrated.

The above principle will also apply where it is not the subject matter of the contract, but rather some other object essential to performance, that is destroyed.[77] Further examples of subsequent impossibility that could cause a contract to become frustrated include the following.

- Where the contract is a personal one and requires performance from a particular person (for example, employment, skilled service), the death of either party will frustrate the contract.[78] The same will apply to a party who is rendered incapable of performing the contract (for example, due to physical or mental disability).[79]
- Where the subject matter of the contract (or something essential to performance) is not destroyed, but becomes unavailable (for example, where a specified ship becomes unavailable to carry out the charterparty at the specified time due to

---

77. *Appleby v Myers* (1867) LR 2 CP 651.
78. *Stubbs v Holywell Railway Co* (1867) LR 2 Ex 311.
79. *Condor v The Barren Knights Ltd* [1966] 1 WLR 87.

strike activity,[80] or where the subject matter of the contract becomes impossible to obtain),[81] the contract is likely to be frustrated. Unavailability is often regarded as a separate head of frustration, but it is contended that it is more appropriate to regard it as a subspecies of impossibility.

Frustration of a common purpose or basic assumption

Where performance is possible and lawful, a contract may still be frustrated where its common purpose, or the basic assumptions upon which it was made, are destroyed by subsequent events.

 Krell v Henry [1903] 2 KB 740 (CA)

FACTS: The defendant hired a flat from the claimant in order to watch the coronation procession of Edward VII. The coronation was cancelled and the claimant claimed the balance of the contract price. The defendant refused to pay.

HELD: The Court of Appeal held the contract to be frustrated, because the fundamental assumption on which both parties contracted had been destroyed. Clearly, the defendant had hired the flat to watch the procession; the claimant had also let the flat for the purpose of watching the procession. This was not stated in the contract, but was inferred from the flat's advertisement, which stated that its windows faced the procession route. The price charged for use of the flat during the procession was also much higher than normal.

It is essential that the purposes or assumptions of both parties must be destroyed; it is not enough that the purposes of one party in making the contract cannot be fulfilled, as the following case demonstrates.

 Herne Bay Steamboat Co v Hutton [1903] 2 KB 683 (CA)

FACTS: The defendant hired a steamship from the claimant for the express purpose of taking fare-paying passengers to observe the King's naval review and for taking a cruise around the fleet. The review was cancelled, but the fleet remained anchored. Hearing this, the claimant contacted the defendant for instructions, but received no reply. The claimant therefore used the steamship himself and made a profit. A day later, the defendant repudiated the contract and the claimant sued to recover the contract price, less the profits made. The defendant argued that the contract had become frustrated.

HELD: The Court of Appeal (in fact, the same three judges who decided *Krell v Henry*) held that the contract was not frustrated. The naval review was not the sole basis of the contract and, even if it was, it was not the claimant's sole basis. Accordingly, the common purpose was not destroyed and so the contract was not frustrated.

---

80. *Pioneer Shipping Ltd v BTP Tioxide Ltd (The Nema) (No 2)* [1982] AC 724 (HL).
81. *CTI Group Inc v Transclear SA* [2008] EWCA Civ 856, [2008] Bus LR 1729.

Fundamental change of circumstances

The general rule is that an event that causes performance of a contractual obligation to become impracticable, or more onerous or expensive, does not cause the contract to become frustrated.

 Davis Contractors Ltd v Fareham Urban UDC [1956] AC 696 (HL)

FACTS: The claimant contractor agreed to build seventy-two houses in eight months, in return for which the defendant local authority would pay it £94,000. Due to shortages in the availability of labour, the houses were not completed until twenty-two months later and had cost the claimant £115,000. The claimant alleged that the shortage of labour had caused the contract to become frustrated, thereby allowing it to claim a *quantum meruit* in excess of the agreed contractual price.

HELD: The House of Lords held that the contract was not frustrated. Lord Radcliffe stated:

it is not hardship or inconvenience or material loss itself which calls the principle of frustration into play. There must be as well such a change in the significance of the obligation that the thing undertaken would, if performed, be a different thing from that contracted for.[82]

Lord Radcliffe's statement in *Davis* indicates that, although a contract could still be physically performed, where a fundamental change of circumstances occurs that results in a situation whereby, if the contract were performed, it would become something radically different from that contracted for, the court may be prepared to regard the contract as frustrated.

The following case demonstrates such a fundamental change of circumstances.

 Metropolitan Water Board v Dick Kerr & Co Ltd [1918] AC 119 (HL)

FACTS: The defendant company contracted to build a reservoir for the claimant water board within six years. The contract contained a term that stated that this time limit would be extended if the defendant were to encounter any difficulties, impediments, or obstructions. When World War I started, the Minister of Munitions, acting under the Defence of the Realm (Consolidation) Act 1914, required the defendant to cease work on the reservoir, and to remove and sell any plant there. The claimant alleged that the contract was still valid, but the defendant argued that the Minister's actions had frustrated the contract.

HELD: The effect of the Minister's prohibition was such that performance of the contract, if resumed at a later date, would be radically different from the contract originally made. Accordingly, the House of Lords held that the contract was frustrated.

---

82. *Davis Contractors Ltd v Fareham Urban UDC* [1956] AC 696 (HL) 729.

Cases such as *Metropolitan Water Board* are rare. The courts are usually extremely reluctant to allow impracticability or financial hardship to result in frustration, as the following case shows.

Tsakiroglou & Co Ltd v Noblee Thorl GmbH [1962] AC 93 (HL)

FACTS: The defendant had agreed to sell to the claimant 300 tonnes of groundnuts. The defendant would also transport the groundnuts from the Sudan to the claimant in Hamburg. This would normally involve passing through the Suez Canal (and, indeed, this is what both parties envisaged, although it was not a term of the contract)—a journey of 4,386 miles. The Canal was, however closed for several months, meaning that the only way to transport the groundnuts was to go around the Cape of Good Hope—a journey of 11,137 miles. The defendant therefore decided not to perform, on the ground that the Canal's closure had frustrated the contract.

HELD: The House of Lords held that the contract was not frustrated. There was no term in the contract indicating that the Canal should be used, nor could a term requiring the Canal be used be implied, because the route used made no difference to the claimant. Therefore, the contract was not physically impossible to perform. In addition, although the closure of the Canal involved a change in performance at considerable expense to the defendant, it did not render performance radically different from the contract as originally made.

★ See CJ Hamson, 'Contract: CIF—Frustration: Closure of Suez Canal' (1961) CLJ 150

Illegality

In Chapter 8, we noted that certain types of contract are classed as illegal. Where the contract is illegal at the time it is made, it will usually be void on the ground of illegality and frustration will therefore not apply. Where a contract entered into is lawful, but, subsequently, its performance becomes illegal, it will become frustrated.

Denny, Mott and Dickson Ltd v James B Fraser & Co Ltd [1944] AC 265 (HL)

FACTS: The claimant was a timber merchant. It agreed to purchase all of its timber from the defendant and also that it would let a timber yard to the defendant, over which the defendant would have an option to purchase in the event of the contract being terminated. With the outbreak of World War II, increased timber was needed for the war effort. Therefore, legislation was passed prohibiting dealing in the timber being sold by the defendant. The defendant therefore terminated the contract and exercised the option to purchase. The claimant brought an action to determine the rights of the parties.

HELD: The House of Lords held that the contract was frustrated. Lord Macmillan stated: 'It is plain that a contract to do what it has become illegal to do cannot be legally enforceable.'[83] The defendant could not therefore exercise the option to purchase the

---

83. *Denny, Mott and Dickson Ltd v James B Fraser & Co Ltd* [1944] AC 265 (HL) 272.

timber yard, because the contract was not terminated; rather, it was frustrated by the prohibition in dealing in timber.

COMMENT: This case also demonstrates that frustration can occur where the illegality (or impossibility or unavailability) is only temporary. Once the war ended, the prohibition on timber trading was removed. In such cases, the courts will need to take into account the likely period that the contractual relations of the parties will be interrupted.[84] The longer the period (relative to the duration of the contract), the more likely it will be that the contract will be frustrated.

The limitations of frustration

Even if a frustrating event occurs, it does not automatically follow that the contract will be frustrated. In three situations, the court is likely to hold that a contract is not frustrated, even though a frustrating event has occurred:

- where the contract expressly states an outcome to occur in the event of a frustrating event occurring;
- where the frustrating event was foreseen or foreseeable;
- where the frustrating event was the fault of one of the parties.

Contractual provision

force majeure:
'superior force'

The principal purpose of the doctrine of frustration is to allocate risk fairly in the event of an unforeseen event that affects a party's ability to perform the contract. But there is nothing stopping the parties from expressly allocating this risk themselves by including a term in the contract (known as a '*force majeure* clause') that states what the outcome will be should a frustrating event occur (for example, one party bears the risk, the contract is suspended, etc.). In effect, this will contractually exclude the doctrine of frustration[85] and prevent the courts' intervention.

There are, however, two limitations on the parties' ability to do this, as follows.

- Where a contract is frustrated due to subsequent illegality, a contractual provision avoiding the effects of frustration will be ineffective.[86]
- Such provisions are restrictively interpreted and, even though it may literally cover the frustrating event, the court may hold that its true construction does not, as the following case shows.

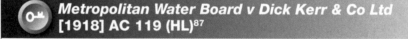

Metropolitan Water Board v Dick Kerr & Co Ltd [1918] AC 119 (HL)[87]

FACTS: The defendant company contracted to build a reservoir for the claimant water board within six years. The contract contained a term that stated that this time limit

---

84. *National Carriers Ltd v Panalpina (Northern) Ltd* [1981] AC 675 (HL).

85. *Joseph Constantine SS Line Ltd v Imperial Smelting Corp Ltd* [1942] AC 154 (HL) 163 (Viscount Simon LC).

86. *Ertel Bieber & Co v Rio Tinto Co Ltd* [1918] AC 260 (HL).

87. See also *Jackson v The Union Marine Insurance Co Ltd* (1874) LR 10 CP 125 (Ex).

would be extended if the defendant were to encounter any difficulties, impediments, or obstructions 'however occasioned'. When World War I started, the Minister of Munitions, acting under the Defence of the Realm (Consolidation) Act 1914, required the defendant to cease work on the reservoir, and to remove and sell any plant there. The defendant argued that the contract was frustrated, but the claimant alleged that the contract itself excluded the doctrine of frustration by providing for an extension.

HELD: The clause failed to exclude the doctrine of frustration. Although the frustrating event was literally within the scope of the clause, the House of Lords held that it was meant to cover temporary difficulties, not events that radically altered the character and duration of the contract.

Foreseeability

If the frustrating event was foreseen or was foreseeable by *one* of the parties, then the doctrine of frustration will not usually apply. The party who foresaw the event should have provided for it in some manner and his failure to do so (and consequent breach) will not be excused by the contract being frustrated.

Walton Harvey Ltd v Walker & Homfrays Ltd [1931] 1 Ch 274 (CA)

FACTS: The defendant had leased a hotel. It granted the claimant (an advertising agency) the right to display electronically illuminated advertisements on top of the hotel for a period of seven years. Before the seven years had expired, the hotel was compulsorily purchased by the local authority and demolished. The claimant brought an action for damages against the defendant, who argued that the contract had been frustrated.

HELD: The Court of Appeal held that the contract was not frustrated and that the defendant was therefore liable to pay damages. The defendant knew that compulsory purchase of the hotel was a possibility, whereas the claimant did not. That the defendant chose not to provide contractually for the risk of compulsory purchase indicated that it undertook the risk of it occurring.

So what degree of foreseeability is required to displace the doctrine of frustration? Given enough time and money, every possible contingency and event could be planned for, but this would be an extremely inefficient use of the parties' resources. Hence, the law will require a reasonably high degree of foreseeability before frustration will cease to apply. Further, the following case demonstrates that the details of the event will also need to be foreseen or foreseeable.

WJ Tatem Ltd v Gamboa [1939] 1 KB 132 (KB)

FACTS: The defendant chartered a ship from the claimant for a period of thirty days. The purpose of the charter was to evacuate refugees of the Spanish Civil War. The rate of hire was £250 per day, payable until the ship was returned—but payment would cease if the ship were to go 'missing'. Two weeks after the ship was chartered, it was seized by Nationalist forces and not returned for two months. The claimant claimed the daily rate for the period of two months and two weeks.

HELD: The High Court held that the contract was frustrated. Whilst the seizure of the ship was foreseeable, it was not foreseeable that it would be held for so long after the charter period. Accordingly, the details of the seizure were not foreseeable enough to displace the doctrine of frustration.

If the frustrating event was foreseen or foreseeable by both parties, then their failure contractually to provide for such an event will ensure that the doctrine of frustration can apply.[88]

Fault

A party cannot rely on the doctrine of frustration if the event was caused by his fault. Otherwise, the law would allow parties to induce frustration themselves and then use it as an excuse for their breach of contract.

Maritime National Fish Ltd v Ocean Trawlers Ltd [1935] AC 524 (PC)

FACTS: The claimant owned a trawler, which was fitted with an otter trawl. Such trawlers required a licence from the Minister of Fisheries. The claimant chartered this trawler to the defendant, which already owned four similar trawlers. The defendant accordingly applied for five licences, but was only granted three. The defendant decided to licence its own trawlers and not those of the claimant. It claimed that the inability to obtain further a licence for the claimant's trawler had frustrated the contract, so that it did not have to pay the claimant. The claimant sued for the contract price.

HELD: The Privy Council held that the contract was not frustrated. The inability to use the claimant's trawler was caused by the defendant's decision not to license it. Therefore, the supervening event was the fault of the defendant, which remained liable for the charter price.

The courts take a very strict approach to self-induced frustration. Provided that a party makes a choice that results in the supervening event, the court will not frustrate the contract, no matter how reasonable or commercially sensible the party's choice might have been.

J Lauritzen AS v Wijsmuller BV (The Super Servant Two) [1990] 1 Lloyd's Rep 1 (CA)

FACTS: The claimant owned an oil rig that it wished to transport from its place of manufacture in Japan to a port near Rotterdam. The defendant agreed to transport the

---

88. *Ocean Tramp Tankers Corporation v V/O Sovfracht (The Eugenia)* [1964] 2 QB 226 (CA).

rig using one or other of two transportation units—namely, the *Super Servant One* or the *Super Servant Two*. The defendant chose to use the *Super Servant Two* to transport the rig and the *Super Servant One* was used to fulfil contracts with other parties. Before transportation of the rig commenced, the *Super Servant Two* sank. Given that the *Super Servant One* was engaged elsewhere, the defendant could not perform the contract and, to avoid being liable for breach, claimed that it had been frustrated.

HELD: The Court of Appeal held that the contract was not frustrated, because the inability to perform was the choice of the defendant. It could have performed the contract by using the *Super Servant One*; the fact that this would have resulted in the defendant breaching its contract with a third party was deemed irrelevant.

COMMENT: Understandably, this case has proven controversial. The result is seen as harsh and many have questioned whether it was true to say that the defendant had a choice. It could be argued that the defendant did not have a real choice, because it would have ended up being in breach of contract to either the claimant or the third parties.

⭐ See E McKendrick, 'The Construction of *Force Majeure* Clauses and Self-induced Frustration' [1990] LMCLQ 153

The above cases were based on deliberate acts. It would also appear that a negligent act that renders contractual performance impossible or illegal will not cause the contract to become frustrated.[89] Therefore, if, in *Taylor v Caldwell*, the concert hall were to have burned down due to the owner's negligence, then the contract would not have been frustrated.

The effects of frustration

To appreciate the legal effects of frustration fully, it is necessary to examine the original position at common law, before discussing the current position under statute. It will be seen that the current position under statute is much more satisfactory than the effect of frustration at common law.

Common law

At common law, the effects of frustration are as follows.

1. The contract is automatically discharged[90] (no election or affirmation may take place). This is not the same as holding the contract void (for example, for mistake), voidable (for example, for misrepresentation), or terminated (for example, for breach), because the discharge is automatic at the point of frustration and the contract cannot survive at the discretion of the parties or the court.
2. Any rights or liabilities that arise after the frustrating event are discharged.[91]
3. Any rights or obligations that arose before the frustrating event remain enforceable.[92] As we shall see, this rule has been significantly amended by statute.

These three effects are demonstrated in the following case (like *Krell v Henry* discussed above, this was concerned with the cancellation of Edward VII's coronation).

---

89. *Joseph Constantine Steamship Line Ltd v Imperial Smelting Corp Ltd* [1942] AC 154 (HL).
90. Except those provisions intended by the parties to apply in the event of frustration: *Heyman v Darwins Ltd* [1942] AC 356 (HL).
91. *Chandler v Webster* [1904] 1 KB 493 (CA).   92. Ibid.

Chandler v Webster [1904] 1 KB 493 (CA)

FACTS: The defendant let a room to the claimant for the purpose of watching the coronation procession. The contract price was £141 15s, payable immediately, but the defendant paid only £100. The coronation was cancelled before he had paid the remaining £41 15s and the contract was accordingly frustrated. The claimant sought recovery of the £100 and the defendant counterclaimed for the remaining £41 15s.

HELD: The frustration automatically discharged the contract. Because the obligation to pay the full contract price arose before the contract was frustrated, the Court of Appeal held that the claimant could not recover the £100 paid and remained liable for the remaining £41 15s.

⭐ See RG McElroy and G Williams, 'The Coronation Cases' (1941) 4 MLR 241 and (1942) 5 MLR 1

The result in *Chandler v Webster* is clearly an extremely harsh one: the claimant received no benefit whatsoever, yet remained liable to pay the full amount. Fortunately, the harshness of *Chandler* was partially remedied in the following case, in which it was held that payments made before the frustrating event could be recovered where there was a 'total failure of consideration'.

Fibrosa Spolka Akcyjna v Fairbairn Lawson Combe Barbour Ltd [1943] AC 32 (HL)

FACTS: The defendant was a company based in Leeds that manufactured machinery. It agreed to provide certain machinery to the claimant, a company based in Poland. The contract price was £4,800 and a term provided that £1,600 was payable immediately, although only £1,000 was paid. Before the machinery could be manufactured, Germany invaded and occupied Poland, thereby frustrating the contract. The claimant requested that the £1,000 be returned. The defendant refused, arguing that, based on *Chandler*, it did not need to return the £1,000.

HELD: The House of Lords held that advance payments could be recovered where there had been a total failure of consideration (that is, where a party had not gained any benefit from the contract). Accordingly, the claimant could recover the £1,000, and Lord Atkin stated *obiter* that it did not need to pay the remainder of what was due at the time of frustration (that is, £600). Obviously, because the contract was discharged, the claimant would not have to pay the remaining contract price either (£3,200).

Whilst the decision in *Fibrosa* can be regarded as a step in the right direction, it still left the law in an unsatisfactory state for two reasons.

- A party could only recover an advance payment where there was a total failure of consideration. Where a party has gained any form of benefit, no matter how small, the advance payment would be irrecoverable.[93]
- Allowing a party to recover an advance payment fully might be harsh where the other party has incurred expenses in preparing to perform.

---

93. *Whincup v Hughes* (1871) LR 6 CP 78.

It was these two criticisms that led to Parliament's intervention in the form of the Law Reform (Frustrated Contracts) Act 1943, which serves to remedy the deficiencies of the common law.

Statute

The Law Reform (Frustrated Contracts) Act 1943 deals solely with the consequences of frustration. As under the common law, an express contractual provision allocating risk can exclude the operation of the Act.[94] Section 1(2) establishes three crucial rules designed to overrule *Chandler v Webster* and to remove the limitation established in *Fibrosa*. In addition to the contract being discharged, s 1(2) provides as follows.

1. Any sums *payable* before the occurrence of the frustrating event cease to be payable, irrespective of whether or not there is a total failure of consideration. This effectively overrules *Chandler v Webster*. Thus, if that case were to be decided today, the defendant's counterclaim for the remaining £41 15s would fail.

2. Any sums *paid* before the occurrence of the frustrating event are recoverable, irrespective of whether or not there has been a total failure of consideration. This removes the limitation established in *Fibrosa* and would mean that the claimant in *Chandler* could recover the £100.

3. Where one party is seeking recovery of sums paid, however, and the other party has incurred expenditure before the contract is discharged, the court has a discretion to set off any expenses incurred against the sum that can be recovered.

The following fictional example demonstrates these three rules in practice.

Eg The effect of frustration

DataCorp plc enters into a contract with Ferrari to provide custom-built laptops that will be used by the Ferrari Formula One team. DataCorp will provide fifty such laptops, for which Ferrari will pay £1 million upon delivery. A term of the contract provides that £250,000 is payable immediately, and that this money must be used by DataCorp to commence research and development on the laptops—but Ferrari pays only £200,000. DataCorp spends £100,000 in research and development, but before production can go ahead, DataCorp's manufacturing facility is the victim of an arson attack and is completely destroyed. The contract is frustrated.

1. At the time of the frustrating event, Ferrari owed DataCorp £50,000 (the contract provided that £250,000 was payable immediately, but Ferrari paid only £200,000). Under the first rule identified above, Ferrari would not be liable to pay the £50,000.

2. Ferrari had already paid £200,000. Under the second rule, Ferrari could recover this money.

3. Because DataCorp had already incurred expenditure of £100,000 preparing for the contract, however, the court has the discretion to offset this against any monies recoverable by Ferrari. Should the court exercise this discretion, Ferrari will not recover the full £200,000; it will recover only £100,000, or whatever sum the court deems reasonable.

---

94. Law Reform (Frustrated Contracts) Act 1943, s 2(3).

But what if the £100,000 spent by DataCorp in research and development were to result in some discovery or technological development that could be used outside of the contract with Ferrari? What is the position where a party to a frustrated contract gains some form of valuable benefit from something done by the other party in, or for the purpose of, performing the contract before it is frustrated? Under the common law, a party could not recover a sum for a valuable benefit gained before frustration,[95] but this has been altered by s 1(3) of the 1943 Act. Section 1(3) provides that:

> Where any party to the contract has, by reason of anything done by any other party thereto in, or for the purpose of, the performance of the contract, obtained a valuable benefit…before the time of discharge, there shall be recoverable from him by the said other party such sum (if any), not exceeding the value of the said benefit to the party obtaining it, as the court considers just, having regard to all the circumstances of the case

The courts' approach to quantifying a sum under s 1(3) can be seen in the following case.

BP Exploration Co (Libya) Ltd v Hunt (No 2) [1979] 1 WLR 783 (QB)[96]

FACTS: The defendant was an extremely wealthy US citizen, who had obtained a concession from the Libyan government to explore for, and exploit, any oil found. He lacked the resources to exploit the oil himself, so he entered into an agreement with the claimant oil company (BP), whereby BP would pay for and conduct the exploratory work, in return for a half-share in the concession. The contract also allowed BP to recover its expenses at a certain rate. A large oil field was found, but, following a revolution, the new Libyan government expropriated the concession, thereby frustrating the contract. BP had only recovered one third of its expenses, so brought a claim against the defendant under s 1(3), arguing that the defendant had received a valuable benefit from it.

HELD: Robert Goff J (as he then was) stated that the correct approach in s 1(3) cases was, firstly, to identify and value the benefit received at the date of frustration. Because an award under s 1(3) cannot exceed the value of the benefit, this would constitute the maximum sum that could be recovered. In the case, the court valued the benefit received by the defendant at US$85 million.

Secondly, the court must decide what is a just sum. The court calculated this by reference to what the claimant had already expended in developing the concession (US$87 million) plus any monies paid to the defendant (US$10 million). From this, it deducted any monies already recovered from the defendant (US$62 million). Using this method, the claimant recovered US$35 million from the defendant.

---

95. *Appleby v Myers* (1867) LR 2 CP 651.
96. Affirmed by both the Court of Appeal ([1981] 1 WLR 232) and the House of Lords ([1983] 2 AC 352).

Finally, it should be noted that the 1943 Act does not apply to all types of contract. Excluded contracts include:

- contracts in which the parties have included an express term providing what will occur in the event of a frustrating event;[97]
- those in which a part of a contract is severable (that is, it contains divisible obligations), in which case, that part will be treated as a separate contract that will not be frustrated—the Act will apply only to remainder of the contract;[98]
- charterparties and contracts for the carriage of goods by sea,[99] meaning that freight due prior to frustration remains due and any freight paid cannot be recovered, even though the voyage cannot be completed or the cargo is lost.[100] But the Act will apply to a time charterparty (that is, a charterparty for a definite duration);
- contracts of insurance,[101] in which case, generally, once the risk has attached, premiums are non-returnable;[102]
- contracts to which the Sale of Goods Act 1979, s 7, applies.[103] Section 7 provides that where there is an agreement to sell specific goods, and subsequently, without any fault on the part of the seller or buyer, the goods perish before the risk passes to the buyer, the agreement is thereby avoided. In such a case, the common law rules laid down in *Fibrosa* will apply.

Divisible obligations are discussed at p 292

❮❯ Key points summary

- Frustration provides the parties with a lawful excuse for breaching their contractual obligations where an event occurred that was outside of their control.

- The frustrating event must be supervening (that is, it must occur after the contract was formed).

- Frustrating events include performance of the contract becoming physically impossible, where a common and fundamental assumption of the parties is destroyed, where performance becoming illegal, where something essential to performance becomes unavailable, and where performance becomes radically different from that for which the parties contracted.

- Frustration cannot be claimed where the contract expressly provides for what should occur in the event of a frustrating event, or where the frustrating event is foreseen or is foreseeable. A party cannot rely on a frustrating event that was its own fault.

- Frustration causes the contract to be discharged automatically. Any money payable ceases to be payable. Any money paid can be recovered, although this may be offset against any expenses incurred by the other party. Any party that gained some form or valuable benefit may have to pay a sum for such benefit.

---

97. Law Reform (Frustrated Contracts) Act 1943, s 2(3).

98. Ibid, s 2(4).

99. Ibid, s 2(5)(a).

100. *Byrne v Schiller* (1871) LR 6 Ex 319.

101. Law Reform (Frustrated Contracts) Act 1943, s 2(5)(b).

102. *Tyrie v Fletcher* (1777) 2 Cowp 666.

103. Law Reform (Frustrated Contracts) Act 1943, s 2(5)(c).

Chapter conclusion

Because discharge causes liability under a contract to cease, it is important that the parties understand when a contract can become discharged. Where the parties fully perform their contractual obligations, the discharge of the contract is relatively straightforward to discern. Similarly, where the parties agree to end a contract, the discharge of the contract is a relatively straightforward affair, provided that the parties have provided consideration for the discharge.

Discharge due to frustration or breach is significantly more complex and the effects are wildly different. A frustrated contract is automatically discharged and cannot be continued or performed simply because the parties so desire. Conversely, breach of contract does not automatically discharge the contract—but, in some instances (that is, in cases of repudiatory breach), it normally provides the non-breaching party with the right to terminate the contract and thereby discharge it. Should the non-breaching party wish to continue to deal with a party in repudiatory breach, it can affirm the breach, in which case, the contract continues in force. Where a contract is frustrated, the law tries to apportion any monetary loss between the two parties in order to achieve a fair result. In cases of breach, the law normally achieves a satisfactory result via granting the non-breaching party a right to terminate in the case of a repudiatory breach and the ability to claim damages (in any event).

The purpose and scope of an award of contractual damages is considered in the next chapter. Damages may not, however, always compensate the claimant for his loss; accordingly, a number of other remedies are also examined.

Self-test questions

1. Define the following legal words and phrases:
   (a) *de minimis*;
   (b) tender;
   (c) breach of contract;
   (d) renunciation;
   (e) anticipatory breach;
   (f) innominate term;
   (g) repudiatory breach;
   (h) frustration.

2. A ship is chartered by BuildCorp Ltd to transport a cargo of 100 tonnes of steel girders from London to New York. The charterparty provides that the shipowner, TransShip plc, will receive £500 for each tonne that arrives in New York. The ship only transports 40 tonnes and, upon arrival, BuildCorp refuses to pay, because the complete cargo was not delivered. Advise TransShip.

3. Explain the differences between conditions, warranties, and innominate terms. What is the effect of breach of these terms?

4. Discuss how the effects of frustration under the Law Reform (Frustrated Contracts) Act 1943 provide a fairer and more satisfactory result than the effects of frustration under the common law. Provide case law examples to back up your arguments.

5.   Woodhouse plc contracts Buildmore to build its new office complex for £1.2 million. Due to a worldwide timber shortage, the cost of building the office complex is increased by £20,000. On completion, Woodhouse plc refuses to pay more than the contracted £1.2 million. Advise Buildmore.

Further reading

Chen-Wishart, M, *Contract Law* (2nd edn, OUP, Oxford, 2008) ch 13
An excellent and highly accessible account of the law relating to breach of contract and termination

Peel, E, *Treitel on the Law of Contract* (12th edn, Sweet & Maxwell, London, 2007) ch 19
A highly detailed and comprehensive, but very readable, account of the law relating to the frustration of contracts

Poole, J, *Textbook on Contract Law* (9th edn, OUP, Oxford, 2008) pp 323–8
A simple and easy-to-understand account of the law relating to discharge by performance and discharge by agreement

Stewart, A, and Carter, JW, 'Frustrated Contracts and Statutory Adjustment: The Case for a Reappraisal' [1992] CLJ 66
Provides an excellent analysis of the effects of frustration at common law and under statute, before discussing how other countries have legislated in this area; contends that none of these statutes have proved successful

Treitel, GH, 'Affirmation After Repudiatory Breach' (1998) 114 LQR 22
Examines the role of affirmation in breach of contract cases, focusing specifically on the ability to revoke affirmation and discharge the contract

Treitel, GH, *Frustration and Force Majeure* (2nd edn, Sweet & Maxwell, London, 2004)
The leading text on the law of frustration; provides an extremely comprehensive account of the law and also a comparative analysis on the law of frustration in the USA

 Remember to visit the **Online Resource Centre** at <http://www.oxfordtextbooks.co.uk/roach> to access the following resources on Chapter 9, 'Discharge of the contract': more **practice questions** and answers; a **glossary** of key terms; **multiple-choice questions**; **revision summaries**; **audio updates** when relevant; and **audio exam advice** on these key topics.

10 Remedies for breach of contract

- Damages
- Action for the price or other agreed sum
- Restitutionary remedies
- Specific performance
- Injunctions
- The relationship between damages, specific performance, and injunctions
- Limitation periods

INTRODUCTION

Once the claimant has established the existence of a breach of contract, the final matter to be determined is the availability of a remedy. It may be the case that the claimant will have a self-help remedy that will avoid the need to initiate legal proceedings (for example, complaining to a local authority trading standards board). In the absence of such a self-help remedy, and provided that the claimant is not subject to an applicable and effective exclusion clause, the claimant may seek one or more (for example, termination and damages) of the following legal remedies.

- *Termination* If the breach is repudiatory, the claimant may terminate the contract and discharge himself from any future obligations. This remedy was discussed in Chapter 9 and so will not be discussed further in this chapter.

- *Damages* The claimant may seek damages to compensate him financially for his loss.

- *Action for price or other agreed sum* Where the breach of contract consists of the other party's failure to pay a debt that is due, instead of, or in addition to, claiming damages, the claimant may bring an action for price to recover the debt owed.

- *Restitutionary remedies* It may be the case that the defendant's breach has resulted in him becoming unjustly enriched. The claimant may be able to recover this unjust enrichment in full or in part, or may be able recover any advance payments or a *quantum meruit*.

➡ *quantum meruit*: 'as much as he has deserved'; a reasonable sum based on services provided

- *Specific performance* The claimant may be able to obtain an order for specific performance, which will compel the defendant to fulfil his contractual obligations.

- *Injunction* The claimant may be able to acquire a court order requiring the defendant to engage in, or to refrain from, the doing of a certain act.

Even where the claimant has a valid claim, however, it may be the case that he will be denied a remedy on the ground that his action was not initiated promptly enough. Therefore, once we have discussed the above remedies in detail, we will examine the relevant limitation periods within which these remedies must be sought.

Damages

Damages are awarded to compensate the claimant.[1] Because we are concerned with compensating the claimant for his actual loss, three consequences follow.

1. The claimant cannot recover more than he actually lost. Therefore, if a breach of contract causes the claimant no loss, he will only receive nominal damages.

2. Because contractual damages are compensatory, damages are not designed to punish the defendant for his behaviour[2] and will not be increased because the defendant behaved in a reprehensible manner (such damages are known as 'exemplary', or 'punitive', damages).

3. Because damages are designed to compensate the claimant, it follows that a claimant cannot normally recover damages for loss sustained to a third party,[3] although there do exist specific exceptions to this rule.

> ➡ nominal damages: damages awarded when no loss has been sustained, which consequently tend to amount to around £2

> 🔗 Exemplary damages are recoverable in tort, as we shall see in Chapter 15

Expectation loss

The general purpose of an award of damages is to put the claimant in the position in which he would have been had the breach not occurred[4] (that is, if the contract had been performed properly). Accordingly, the claimant is being compensated for his 'expectation loss', because the damages will compensate him for the benefits that he would have expected to gain had the defendant not breached the contract. In many cases, this will be relatively straightforward to quantify, because it will involve a simple loss of profit, as the following example demonstrates.

Eg Loss of expected profit

Andrew runs a business selling second-hand luxury cars. Cathryn informs him that she is looking for a second-hand Rolls Royce Phantom in good condition, with less than 30,000 miles on the clock, and that she is willing to pay £50,000 for such a car (which is in line with the market value). Unfortunately, Andrew does not have such a car in stock. Several days later, he discovers that Lawrence has a Phantom that matches Cathryn's specifications. Andrew enters into a contract with Lawrence to purchase the car for £30,000 and informs Cathryn that he has located a car for her. Cathryn is overjoyed. But Lawrence changes his mind and refuses to sell the car to Andrew. Andrew sues.

---

1. *Tai Hing Cotton Mill Ltd v Kamsing Knitting Factory* [1979] AC 91 (PC).
2. *Addis v Gramophone Co Ltd* [1909] AC 488 (HL).
3. *Woodar Investment Ltd v Wimpey Construction Ltd* [1980] 1 WLR 277 (HL).
4. *Robinson v Harman* (1848) 1 Ex 855 (Ex); *Addis v Gramophone Co Ltd* [1909] AC 488 (HL).

> There is no doubt that Lawrence is in breach of contract, but what damages will Andrew receive? Had Lawrence performed his obligations, Andrew would have purchased the car for £30,000 and sold it for £50,000, thereby making an expected profit of £20,000. Accordingly, Lawrence will be ordered to pay Andrew £20,000 compensation.

The above example involves an application of the 'difference in value' approach to quantifying expectation loss. Under this approach, damages are assessed based on the difference between the expected value and the actual value. Such an approach is preferable in cases involving sale of goods—but, in many cases, the claimant will enter into a contract, the purpose of which is not to make a profit (for example, employing a builder to install a swimming pool). In such cases, the difference in value measure is still often used, but an alternative approach exists, whereby the court may instead be prepared to quantify damages based on the 'cost of cure'. In practice, both calculations may result in the same figure, but this is not always the case.

Cost of cure

In certain cases, contracts will not confer a financial benefit upon the claimant, so there will be no difference in value. We do not always enter into contracts to benefit ourselves financially; we may have subjective, non-financial motives for contracting (this is known as the 'consumer surplus'). For example, booking a holiday with a travel agent is a contract that, from the consumer's point of view, is entered into for non-financial reasons. In such cases, a breach will deny us of these non-financial benefits and in order to compensate us fully for our loss, these non-financial benefits should also be taken into account. This can be achieved by quantifying damages based on the cost of securing substitute or remedial performance. This is known as the 'cost of cure', because it quantifies damages based on how much it would cost to cure the defendant's breach. It should be noted that, in many cases, cost of cure will not be an appropriate method to compensate the claimant's loss, as we shall see.

The classic example of cost of cure can be seen in the following case.

 Radford v De Froberville [1977] 1 WLR 1262 (Ch)

FACTS: The claimant owned a piece of land upon which were built a number of flats, but which also contained a plot of land suitable for the building of a house. He obtained planning permission to build a house on this plot, but instead of building the house himself, he sold the plot of land to the defendant, on the condition that, once she had built the house, she would also build a boundary wall to divide her land from the claimant's land. The defendant failed to build the wall. The court had to decide whether to quantify damages based on the difference in value (which would have resulted in nominal damages only, because the failure to build the wall resulted in no difference in value), or on the cost of cure (it would cost £3,000 to have the wall built).

HELD: The High Court awarded damages based on cost of cure. Oliver J stated:

> If [the claimant] contracts for the supply of that which he thinks serves his interests—be they commercial, aesthetic or merely eccentric—then if that which is contracted for is not supplied by the other contracting party I do not see why...he should not be compensated by being provided with the cost of supplying it through someone else or in a different way...[5]

The courts have, however, been cautious in permitting the cost of cure for the reason that, in many cost of cure cases, the cost of curing the defendant's breach is completely out of proportion to the benefit that would be obtained. Accordingly, the court will only permit recovery of the cost of cure where it is reasonable to do so.

 ### *Ruxley Electronics and Construction Ltd v Forsyth* [1996] AC 344 (HL)

FACTS: The claimant entered into a contract with the defendant builder to build a swimming pool in his garden. The contract specified that the pool should be 7 feet 6 inches deep at the diving point. This depth would allow the claimant to dive safely into the pool. The pool was only 6 feet deep at the diving point—but evidence indicated that this would still make the pool perfectly safe to dive into. Because it constituted a breach of contract, however, the claimant sued. The lack of depth caused no difference in value to the pool. Therefore, the claimant claimed for the cost of cure. To remedy the breach, the entire pool would have to be ripped out and a new pool installed at a cost of £21,560.

HELD: The House of Lords refused to award cost of cure and instead awarded £2,500 for loss of amenity. It would be wholly unreasonable to award cost of cure, because it would be completely out of proportion to the benefit obtained. Further, the courts should take into account the intentions of the claimant (that is, if the claimant were awarded cost of cure, whether the damages would actually be used to remedy the defect). In a case such as this, it was doubtful that the claimant would actually use the money to cure the defect.

★ See J O'Sullivan, 'Contract Damages for Failed Fun: Taking the Plunge' (1995) 54 CLJ 496

An application of the reasonableness requirement can be seen in the following case.

 ### *McGlinn v Waltham Contractors Ltd* [2007] EWHC 698 (QB)

FACTS: The defendant contracted to build a house for the claimant. In breach of contract, the house was built with a significant number of non-structural, aesthetic defects. After listening to expert advice, the claimant decided to demolish it and rebuild it, rather than repair it. He claimed the costs of the demolition and rebuilding from the defendant.

---

5. *Radford v De Froberville* [1977] 1 WLR 1262 (Ch) 1270.

> **HELD:** The High Court held that the claimant could recover the cost of repairing the house, but he could not recover the cost of demolishing and rebuilding the house. The act of demolishing the house was not a reasonable one and so it could not be recovered.

Based on the above cases, the current position regarding recovery of cost of cure is that, in cases involving defective construction or contracts to secure a non-financial benefit, the normal measure of damages is the cost of cure. Where the cost of cure is unreasonable (for example, because the cost of cure is wholly out of proportion to the benefit obtained), however, cost of cure will be denied and the difference in value measure shall be applied. If there is no difference in value, the claimant will only receive nominal damages.

Reliance loss

In certain cases, expectation loss may be extremely difficult to assess because the extent of the expected benefit is uncertain or speculative. But the courts will not refuse to award damages based on expectation loss simply because they are difficult to quantify, as the following case demonstrates.

 Chaplin v Hicks [1911] 2 KB 786 (CA)

FACTS: The defendant, an actor and theatrical manager, placed an advertisement in the _Daily Express_, stating that he was looking to employ twelve actresses. Aspiring actresses sent their photographs into the newspaper and, a short time later, three hundred were selected to be published. Readers of the newspaper then selected their favourite fifty and, from those, the defendant would choose the twelve to be employed based on an interview. The claimant was one of the fifty selected by the readers, but the defendant, in breach of contract, made an appointment for the interview that was wholly unreasonable. As a result, the claimant could not attend the interview and lost her chance to gain employment as an actress. She claimed damages for the loss of this chance.

HELD: Although the damages were difficult to quantify, because they were based on the loss of a chance, this did not prevent the Court of Appeal from awarding the claimant £100 damages. Provided that the chance is real and substantial (and not merely speculative), difficulty in quantifying the loss will not prevent a claim. Because the claimant's chance of securing employment was real and substantial (around one in four), she was awarded damages.

In certain cases, however, the expectation loss may be too speculative to quantify. In such cases, the claimant is likely to choose instead to seek to recover his reliance loss. This is based not on the expected benefit of the contract, but on monies already paid out in reliance of performance. Because reliance loss is based on expenditure already paid out and wasted as a result of the breach, it does not place the claimant in the position in which he would have been had the breach not occurred; rather, it places him in the position in which he would have been had the contract never been entered into, as the following case demonstrates.

Anglia Television Ltd v Reed [1972] 1 QB 60 (CA)

FACTS: The defendant, a famous actor named Robert Reed, contracted with the claimant to star in a television film. Relying on this, the claimant expended money on hiring directors, support artists, stage managers, etc. Shortly after, in breach of contract, the defendant withdrew from the contract and it was too late to obtain a replacement actor. The result was that the film was never made. Because there was no way of knowing how successful the film would have been, the claimant elected not to claim for expectation loss and instead based its claim on recovering the wasted expenditure.

HELD: The Court of Appeal held that the claimant was entitled to recover the £2,750 that it had spent in pre-contractual expenditure, which was wasted as a result of the defendant's breach.

⭐ See Al Ogus, 'Damages for Pre-contract Expenditure' (1972) 35 MLR 423

Expectation loss or reliance loss?

As noted above, reliance loss is especially suitable in cases in which the claimant's loss is speculative. But the law does not fetter a claimant's ability to base his claim on whatever form of loss he chooses.[6] The court does, however, have the power to deny the claimant's claim for expectation loss and to award reliance loss instead if it considers it more appropriate. The following Australian case is the seminal example of this.

McRae v Commonwealth Disposals Commission (1951) 84 CLR 377 (High Court of Australia)

FACTS: The defendant invited tenders for the salvage rights to a shipwrecked oil tanker. The claimant's tender was accepted and he incurred substantial expenditure in preparing the salvage expedition. When the claimant arrived at the location provided by the defendant, however, no tanker was found. It transpired that the tanker had never existed. The claimant sought to recover his expectation loss (that is, the amount of profit that he would have gained through the selling of the tanker and any oil within it).

HELD: The Court refused recovery of expectation loss. The defendant had no idea how big the tanker was, nor how much oil it contained. Accordingly, expectation loss was too speculative. Instead, the Court allowed the claimant to recover the wasted expenditure (that is, his reliance loss).

In *McRae*, the Court refused to allow the claimant to recover his expectation loss. In certain cases, the court will not allow a claimant to recover his reliance loss—namely, where the reliance loss exceeds the benefit that would be obtained had the contract been performed. This is demonstrated in the following case—a case that we will also examine later when we discuss causation.

---

6. *CCC Films (London) v Impact Quadrant Films* [1985] QB 16 (QB).

C & P Haulage v Middleton [1983] 1 WLR 1461 (CA)

FACTS: The defendant owned a garage. He contracted with the claimant to let it use his garage for a six-month period. The claimant purchased various pieces of machinery and installed them within the garage. A term of the contract provided that any machinery installed would become the property of the defendant once the claimant stopped using the garage. In breach of contract, the defendant terminated the contract ten weeks early. The claimant used its own garage for the remaining ten weeks. The claimant then initiated a claim to recover the expenditure on the machinery (that is, his reliance loss).

HELD: The Court of Appeal rejected the claim for reliance loss and the claimant recovered only nominal damages. Had the defendant not breached the contract, the machinery would still have become the defendant's property once the six months expired. To permit recovery of the reliance loss would therefore place the claimant in a better position than it would have been in had the contract been properly performed.

There was a second reason for the Court's decision in this case—namely, that claimants should not be allowed to escape from a bad bargain (that is, a situation in which they have spent more than they gained) by permitting the recovery of reliance loss. In such cases in which reliance loss exceeds expectation loss, the court will not permit recovery of reliance loss.

Double recovery

We noted in the previous section that a claimant is free to base his claim on either expectation loss or reliance loss—but is it possible for the claimant to claim both? In *Anglia Television Ltd v Reed*,[7] Lord Denning MR stated: 'It seems to me that a [claimant] in such a case has an election: he can either claim for his loss of profits; or for his wasted expenditure. But he must elect between them. He cannot claim both.'[8] In establishing that the claimant must choose to base his claim on expectation loss or reliance loss, Lord Denning was seeking to ensure that there was no possibility of double recovery in respect of the same loss. Double recovery is the situation in which the claimant is overcompensated by receiving the reliance loss twice.

The following example demonstrates this, and also demonstrates why Lord Denning's prohibition is no longer absolute.

Eg Double recovery

John runs a business that specializes in locating unique and antique first-edition books. Elen contracts with John to locate a rare book, stating that if he finds it, she will purchase it from him for £1 million. John locates the book and purchases it for £500,000. Elen decides that she no longer wishes to purchase the book. John's options are as follows.

1. *To claim his expectation loss* Had Elen performed the contract, John would have made £500,000 profit. Because John is currently £500,000 down (due to purchasing the book), his expectation loss is therefore £1 million (the amount of money that it

---

7. [1972] 1 QB 60 (CA).   8. Ibid, 63, 64.

would take to put him in the position in which he would be had Elen not breached the contract).

2. *To claim his reliance loss*   John may decide to simply claim his reliance loss (that is, the £500,000 that he spent in acquiring the book). Clearly, this will not yield as much compensation as claiming for the expectation loss and will result in John only breaking even.

3. *To claim both*   Claiming both would amount to £1.5 million, and this is clearly more than John would have received had the contract been performed and would constitute double recovery. Accordingly, the courts will not allow John to recover this sum. But this is because John's expectation loss of £1 million constitutes the **gross** amount. The sum of £1 million includes not only the expected profit (£500,000), but also the sum that John has already paid (£500,000). Accordingly, the reliance loss is already part of that sum. Therefore, to allow John to claim the gross expectation loss and his reliance loss would be to pay him his reliance loss twice. Deducting the cost of the book from the gross amount would provide the **net** expectation loss. Claiming the net expectation loss (£500,000) and the reliance loss (£500,000) is not objectionable, because it does not result in double recovery.

➡ **gross:** before deductions are made

➡ **net:** following deductions

Accordingly, the courts have now recognized that recovery of both expectation loss and reliance loss is permissible, provided that expectation loss is calculated on a net basis.[9]

Non-pecuniary loss

Here, we are concerned with the extent to which damages for non-pecuniary losses are recoverable. The word 'pecuniary' simply means 'financial', and, as such, we will focus on the availability of damages for physical inconvenience, disappointment, and loss of reputation.

Physical inconvenience

It is well established that damages may be recovered for a breach of contract that causes physical discomfort, injury, or inconvenience. Accordingly, in *Hobbs v London & South Western Railway*,[10] when a railway company, in breach of contract, transported a married couple to the wrong station, the couple could recover damages for the physical inconvenience caused by having to walk several miles in the rain to their home.

Mental distress and disappointment

The general rule is that contractual damages cannot be recovered for mental distress or disappointment.

---

9. *Western Web Offset Printers Ltd v Independent Media Ltd* [1996] CLC 77 (CA); *Bridge UK Com Ltd v Abbey Pynford plc* [2007] EWHC 728 (QB), [2007] CILL 2465.

10. (1875) LR 10 QB 11 (QB).

Addis v Gramophone Co [1909] AC 488 (HL)

FACTS: The claimant was employed by the defendant to manage a business in Calcutta. His contract of employment provided him with six months' notice of dismissal. The defendant gave him notice of dismissal, but instead of allowing the claimant to work for six months, it immediately appointed his replacement and took steps to prevent the claimant from carrying out his managerial functions. He claimed damages for breach of contract, including an additional amount for the injured feelings that he suffered as a result of the manner of his dismissal.

HELD: Although he could claim damages for his lost salary, the House of Lords held that he could not claim damages for the injured feelings caused by the harsh manner of his dismissal.

The general rule still stands, but the court has since recognized that damages for mental distress or disappointment are recoverable in two situations:[11]

- where the mental distress is directly consequential upon physical injury or inconvenience (for example, mental distress caused by living in a house that was represented as being in good condition, but was actually in poor condition);[12]
- where the purpose of the contract is to provide enjoyment (for example, in relation to a contract for the purchase of a holiday) or to prevent distress.

Jarvis v Swans Tours Ltd [1973] QB 233 (CA)

FACTS: The claimant booked a two-week holiday with the defendant tour operator. The defendant's brochure described the holiday as a 'house party', with excellent entertainment, including skiing, a yodeller evening, and afternoon tea and cakes. It also promised a friendly welcome from the owners of the hotel. For the first week of the holiday, there were thirteen people in the hotel and, in the second week, the claimant was on his own. Further, the hotel owners did not speak English, so he had no one to talk to during the second week. The cakes promised were wholly disappointing, the skiing facilities were only available for two days, and the yodeller was a local man who sang a few songs in his normal clothes. At first instance, the claimant obtained £31.72 in damages based on the difference in value measure. He appealed, claiming an extra amount for the distress and disappointment caused.

HELD: His appeal was allowed and the Court of Appeal awarded him a further £60 to compensate him for his disappointment.

Accordingly, where the very purpose of the contract is to provide enjoyment, not compensating the claimant for disappointment caused by breach will result in under-compensation. Therefore, where the purpose of the contract is to provide enjoyment, damages for disappointment are justifiably awarded. It follows from this

---

11. *Watts v Morrow* [1991] 1 WLR 1421 (CA).
12. *Perry v Sidney Phillips & Son* [1982] 1 WLR 1297 (CA).

that such damages are normally not available in employment or commercial contracts, because providing enjoyment or peace of mind is not a normal purpose of such contracts.

Damages may also be recovered where the purpose of the contract is to prevent distress. For example, damages for mental distress were recoverable where a solicitor failed to take prompt measures against a stalker who was distressing his client.[13]

Loss of reputation

Generally, damages are not recoverable for a breach of contract that damages the claimant's reputation.[14] But where the breach of contract results in a loss of reputation, which in turn causes financial loss, then so-called 'stigma damages' may be recovered.

 ## Malik (or Mahmud) v Bank of Credit and Commerce International SA [1998] AC 20 (HL)

FACTS: The claimants were senior employees of BCCI, a bank that collapsed amidst allegations of fraud and corruption. They claimed that, due to the stigma that was attached to former employees of BCCI, they were unable to obtain employment (the claimants were in no way involved with the events that led to BCCI's collapse). They claimed damages against BCCI for the damage that had been caused to their reputation.

HELD: The House of Lords held that BCCI had breached the implied obligation not, without reasonable excuse, to conduct its business in a way likely to destroy or damage the relationship of confidence between an employer and employee. It went on to hold that if the claimants could prove that this breach had handicapped them in the labour market and thereby caused financial loss as a result of the injury done to the claimant's reputation, they would be entitled to damages for this.

★ See M Jefferson, '"Stigma" Damages Against Corrupt Companies' (1998) 19 Co Law 21

The House of Lords has since extended the principle in *Malik* to cover a loss of reputation caused by an unfair suspension,[15] but the House refused to extend it to cases of unfair dismissal.[16]

Limitations on the recovery of damages

In *British Columbia Saw-Mill Co Ltd v Nettleship*,[17] Willes J clearly indicated why a claimant should not be free to claim damages for any loss caused by the defendant's breach of contract. He referred to an early seventeenth-century case in which the claimant was being transported to marry an heiress. On the journey, his horse lost a shoe, so he employed a blacksmith to forge a new one. The blacksmith's work was of such poor quality that the shoe rendered the horse lame, with the

---

13. *Heywood v Wellers* [1976] QB 446 (CA).
14. *Addis v Gramophone Co* [1909] AC 488 (HL).
15. *Eastwood v Magnox Electric plc* [2004] UKHL 35, [2005] 1 AC 503.
16. *Johnson v Unisys Ltd* [2001] UKHL 13, [2003] 1 AC 518.
17. (1868) LR 3 CP 499, 508.

result that the claimant failed to arrive on time and the heiress married another. The blacksmith was held liable for the claimant's loss caused by the marriage not occurring.

Such a case indicates that there needs to be some limit on the claimant's ability to claim damages and, here, we will discuss four such limitations—namely, the rules relating to:

- causation;
- remoteness;
- mitigation; and
- contributory negligence.

Causation

The recovery of damages is dependent upon the claimant's ability to establish a causal link between the defendant's breach of contract and the loss sustained. Damages will only be awarded where the breach was the effective or dominant cause of the loss.[18] Referring to the case of *C & P Haulage v Middleton*[19] discussed earlier, the claimant was unable to recover damages because it was not the breach of contract that caused his loss, but the term in the contract providing that such property would pass to the defendant.

C & P Haulage is discussed at p 332

In the majority of cases, determining causation will pose little difficulty. Problems begin to arise, however, when the occurrence of an intervening act threatens to break the causal link. This can occur in a number of ways, as follows.

- The defendant breaches the contract, but the claimant's loss is caused entirely by an intervening act or natural event—the latter being described as an 'act of God'. In such a case, the intervening act will constitute a *novus actus interveniens*, which serves to break the chain of causation, thereby rendering the defendant not liable for the claimant's loss. For example, a ship transporting cargo encounters a storm and the ensuing rough seas damage the cargo. If it were to transpire that the ship was in breach of contract because it failed to have proper medical facilities, this breach would not permit the cargo owner to claim damages, because the loss was entirely attributable to the storm.[20]

→ *novus actus interveniens*: 'new intervening act' (discussed in more detail in a tortious capacity in Chapter 12)

- If the claimant's loss is caused partly by the defendant's breach of contract and partly by an intervening act or natural event, then, provided that the two causes are cooperating and contributed equally to the loss, the defendant will still be liable for the loss. Thus, in a contract to transport goods by sea, if the claimant's cargo is damaged partly because of rough weather conditions, but also partly because the shipowner breached the contract and provided an unseaworthy vessel, the shipowner will be liable for the claimant's loss.[21]

- If the claimant's loss is caused partly by the defendant's breach of contract and partly by the intervening act of a third party, the defendant will only be liable for the claimant's loss if the act of the intervening third party was reasonably foreseeable. In *Stansbie v Troman*,[22] a painter breached his contract

---

18. *Galoo Ltd v Bright Grahame Murray* [1994] 1 WLR 1360 (CA).
19. [1983] 1 WLR 1461 (CA).
20. *Monarch Steamship Co Ltd v Karlshamns Oljefabriker (A/B)* [1949] AC 196 (HL) 226 (Lord Wright).
21. *Smith, Hogg & Co Ltd v Black Sea & Baltic General Insurance Co Ltd* [1940] AC 997 (HL).
22. [1948] 2 KB 48 (CA).

by leaving the claimant's house unlocked. Thieves gained easy access and stole a number of the claimant's items. The claimant commenced proceedings in tort, alleging that the painter had breached his contractual duty to exercise reasonable care regarding the state of the premises if they were left during work or at its conclusion. It was reasonably foreseeable that leaving the house unlocked would be a security risk and so the painter was held liable for the claimant's loss.

- If the defendant breaches the contract, but the loss is caused by the claimant's own negligence, the claimant's negligence will constitute a *novus actus interveniens* and the defendant will not be liable. For example, if the defendant breaches the contract by providing a defective machine, but the claimant then repairs it inadequately and puts it back to use without testing the repairs, the defendant will not be liable for any loss caused by the machine exploding.[23]

Remoteness

The claimant may have established that the defendant's breach of contract caused his loss, but it does not follow that the defendant is liable for every loss that his breach causes. Certain losses will be regarded as too remote from the breach and irrecoverable.

The test for determining remoteness was formulated in the following case.

Hadley v Baxendale (1854) 9 Exch 341

FACTS: The claimant owned a mill. A mill shaft broke and the claimant had no spares, so the broken shaft was sent to an engineer in Greenwich to act as a template for the construction of a new shaft. The defendant was employed to transport the broken shaft to Greenwich and to bring the new shaft back to the claimant's mill. In breach of contract, the defendant failed to deliver the broken shaft to the engineer on time, resulting in the mill ceasing production for five extra days. The claimant sought damages for the loss of profits during this period.

HELD: Alderson B stated:

> The damages...should be such as may fairly and reasonably be considered either arising naturally, that is, according to the usual course of things, from such breach of contract itself, or such as may reasonably be supposed to have been in the contemplation of both parties at the time they made the contract as the probable result of the breach.[24]

Applying this test to the facts, the claimant's action failed for two reasons: firstly, the loss did not arise naturally from the breach, because the mill owner might have had a spare mill shaft; secondly, the loss of profits was not within 'the contemplation of both parties at the time they made the contract', because the claimant did not tell the defendant that he had no spare shaft. Accordingly, the claimant could not claim for the loss of profits.

---

23. *Beoco Ltd v Alfa Laval Co Ltd* [1994] 4 All ER 464 (CA).
24. *Hadley v Baxendale* (1854) 9 Exch 341, 354.

It can be seen that the test for remoteness established by Alderson B has two limbs. Accordingly, a loss will not be too remote if it comes within either of the following.

1. *Losses that arise naturally (that is, according to the usual course of things), which are in the reasonable contemplation of both parties at the time they made the contract* This would include losses that are the inevitable result of the breach. These could be regarded as 'normal' or 'ordinary' losses.

2. *Losses that do not arise naturally, but which are in the reasonable contemplation of both parties, based on facts known to both parties* These could be regarded as 'special' or 'exceptional' losses.

The application of the two limbs can be seen in the following case.

Victoria Laundry (Windsor) Ltd v Newman Industries Ltd [1949] 2 KB 528 (CA)

FACTS: The claimant ran a laundry business. Hoping to expand its business, it bought a second-hand boiler from the defendant, which knew that the claimant wanted the boiler for immediate use. When dismantling the boiler to send to the claimant, the boiler was damaged, resulting in the boiler being delivered some five months late. The claimant claimed:

1. £16 per week (which represented the profit that would have been made had the boiler arrived on time); and

2. £262 (which represented the cost of a particularly lucrative government contract it had acquired, but could not fulfil due to the boiler arriving late).

HELD: The Court of Appeal held that the claimant could claim the £16 per week under the first limb, because it was an inevitable loss. It could not, however, claim the £262, because it was not an inevitable loss, nor was it in the contemplation of both parties, because the claimant did not inform the defendant of the government contract.

COMMENT: Asquith LJ slightly reformulated the second limb of the *Hadley* test, stating that a claimant may recover 'such part of the loss actually resulting as was at the time of the contract reasonably foreseeable as liable to result from the breach'.[25] This test is almost identical to the test of remoteness in tort and is more generous than the test established in *Hadley*. This reformulation of the second limb was, however, severely criticized by the House of Lords in the following case.

Koufos v Czarnikow Ltd (The Heron II) [1969] 1 AC 350 (HL)

FACTS: The facts are not directly relevant.

HELD: Lord Reid stated that the test for remoteness in contract is not the same as that in tort and that Asquith LJ was wrong to apply such a test. The tortious test of 'reasonable foreseeability' is more generous than the contractual test of 'reasonable contemplation'. The tortious test could be satisfied by a 'slight possibility', whereas the contractual test

---

25. *Victoria Laundry (Windsor) Ltd v Newman Industries Ltd* [1949] 2 KB 528 (CA) 539.

requires 'a serious possibility'[26] or 'a real danger'[27] of loss. The reason why the test in contract must be stricter is that the parties to a contract are able to protect themselves by informing the other party of the exceptional or special loss. Conversely, in tort cases, the two parties are often strangers.

COMMENT: The decision of the House has attracted criticism, largely because of the different terminology used by their Lordships to indicate the likelihood of loss. Lord Reid used the phrase 'not unlikely'; Lord Morris chose the phrase 'not unlikely to occur'; Lords Pearce and Upjohn stated that there must be a 'serious possibility' or a 'real danger' of loss, although Lord Reid strongly disagreed. All of the judges involved, except Lord Reid, would have accepted 'liable to result'.

⭐ See CJ Hamson, 'Contract and Tort: Measure of Damages' (1968) 26 CLJ 14

In the following case, it was held that, provided that the *type* of loss is not too remote, it does not matter that the *extent* of the loss was greater than could be reasonably contemplated, or that the loss occurred in a manner that could not be reasonably contemplated.

H Parsons Livestock Ltd v Uttley Ingham [1978] QB 791 (CA)

FACTS: The claimant was a pig farmer. He required an animal feed hopper in which to store feed for his pigs. He purchased such a hopper from the defendant, with the hopper in question being described as 'ventilated'. The hopper's ventilation hatch was closed during transit, but, upon delivery, the defendant failed to open it. As a result of this, the pig feed that was placed within it became mouldy and contaminated. Following a subsequent outbreak of E. coli, 254 of the claimant's pigs died. The claimant sued, alleging that the defendant was liable for their deaths. The defendant argued that the extent of the loss was not foreseeable and so was too remote.

HELD: The Court of Appeal held that the type of loss (physical harm to the pigs caused by poor storage conditions) was reasonably contemplatable, even if the extent and manner of the loss were not. Accordingly, the loss was not too remote and the claimant was awarded damages.

COMMENT: The Court also took the opportunity to discuss the remoteness test in contract and tort. Lord Denning MR took an unusual approach, arguing that it was immaterial whether the action was brought in contract and tort; instead, the nature of the damage inflicted was the key factor. A case involving economic loss or loss or profits would be subject to the 'contractual' test (that is, reasonable contemplation), whereas a case involving physical injury or property damage would be subject to the relaxed 'tortious' test (that is, reasonable foreseeability). The other members of the majority rejected this distinction, although Lord Scarman also expressed the view that the test of remoteness should not differ in contract and tort. Ultimately, this was a Court of Appeal decision, so the views of their Lordships in *The Heron II* will remain the most authoritative decision in the issue and the remoteness test in contract will continue to be stricter than the remoteness test in tort.

⭐ See DH Hadjihambis, 'Remoteness of Damage in Contract' (1978) 41 MLR 464

---

26. *Koufos v Czarnikow Ltd (The Heron II)* [1969] 1 AC 350 (HL) 414, 415.
27. Ibid, 425.

Having established that the correct test under both limbs of *Hadley v Baxendale* is one of reasonable contemplation, the final issue to discuss is at what time must the parties have reasonably contemplated that the type of loss could result from the breach. It is now clear that this contemplation must occur when the contract was made and not when the contract was breached.

Jackson v Royal Bank of Scotland plc [2005] UKHL 3

FACTS: The claimant imported a quantity of dog chews from Thailand, marked the price up by 19 per cent, and sold them onto a company called Economy Bag Ltd (EB). EB was not aware of the substantial mark-up in price. Both the claimant and EB shared the same bank (the defendant), and, in breach of contract, the bank revealed to EB the extent of the mark-up charged by the claimant. On discovering the extent of the mark-up, EB decided to obtain the dog chews directly from Thailand. Because EB was the claimant's principal source of business, it soon ceased trading, and claimed damages against the defendant for breach of confidence. Evidence indicated that, had EB not discovered the mark-up and terminated the contract, the contract would have continued for another four years. Accordingly, the trial judge calculated damages based on a four-year period. The Court of Appeal reduced the damages, stating that, based on the bank's knowledge at the time of the breach, the bank could have contemplated a loss of business, but that any damage beyond a year was too remote.

HELD: The House of Lords reversed the Court of Appeal's decision and reinstated the trial judge's decision. Damages should be calculated based upon the reasonable contemplation of the parties *at the time that the contract was made*, not when the breach occurred.

★ See J Morgan, 'Liability for Lost Future Business in Contract' (2005) 64 CLJ 285

The result of the above cases appears to be that, in relation to both limbs of *Hadley v Baxendale*, the claimant can only recover for such loss as would, at the time of the contract, have been within the reasonable contemplation of the parties as a serious possibility as a result of its breach.

Mitigation

A claimant who suffers loss due to a breach of contract cannot just sit back, initiate a claim, and recover compensation: the law expects the claimant to take reasonable steps to mitigate (minimize) his loss. It is often stated by both academics and the courts[28] that the claimant is under a 'duty' to mitigate, but this is not strictly true. Breach of any 'duty' will result in a cause of action, but a failure to mitigate results in no cause of action;[29] it simply results in a claimant being unable to recover those losses that he could have avoided by taking reasonable steps.

The following example demonstrates mitigation in practice.

---

28. See, e.g., *British Westinghouse Electric and Manufacturing Co Ltd v Underground Electric Railways Co of London* [1912] AC 673 (HL) 689 (Lord Haldane).

29. *Sotiros Shipping Inc v Sameiet Solholt (The Solholt)* [1983] 1 Lloyd's Rep 605 (CA) 608 (Donaldson MR); *Empresa Cubana Importada de Alimentos 'Alimport' v Iasmos Shipping Co SA (The Good Friend)* [1984] 2 Lloyd's Rep 586 (QB) 597 (Staughton J).

Eg The mitigation of loss

Tom is appointed as a director of a company. His service contract is to last for three years and he is to receive an annual salary of £120,000. After two years, the company terminates Tom's contract. Accordingly, Tom decides to sue the company for breach of contract and to claim damages of £120,000 (the wages that he would have gained had the contract lasted its final year). But Dave hears that Tom's contract has been terminated and offers Tom an identical job at his company, except that the annual salary will be £110,000. Tom turns down Dave's offer, because he would rather claim the £120,000 and have a year off.

In such a case, the court is likely to hold that Tom taking the alternative job would be a reasonable step in mitigating his loss.[30] Had he done so, his loss of £120,000 would have been mitigated to a loss of only £10,000. Accordingly, if the court were to believe that the acceptance of the alternative job was a reasonable step, Tom would only be able to claim £10,000 in damages from his previous employer.

If the claimant does not mitigate his loss, a number of consequences can follow. The claimant's damages will be reduced according to the extent that he was able to mitigate his loss. If his mitigation is so successful that his losses are completely eradicated, then only nominal damages will be awarded.[31] It may be the case that the claimant's reasonable steps to mitigate actually increase his loss. In such a case, the claimant is entitled to claim the increased loss.[32] But any increased losses incurred due to *unreasonable* attempts at mitigation are not recoverable.[33]

Because the claimant is not under a 'duty' to mitigate, merely an expectation that that he will take reasonable steps to mitigate his loss, the obvious question is what actions constitute 'reasonable steps'. This question is one of fact[34] and the burden of proof is placed upon the defendant to show that the claimant failed to mitigate.[35] Because only reasonable steps are needed, the claimant will not be required to take steps immediately, nor will he be required to engage in extremely difficult, time-consuming, or expensive activities. Accepting some form of substitute performance is regarded as reasonable, provided that it is comparable to the original performance. Thus, in the example that we discussed above, Tom would not be expected to accept employment as a floor sweeper. Similarly, in a contract for sale of goods, the claimant would not be expected to accept goods of vastly inferior quality.

Contributory negligence

In the previous section, we saw that a claimant may have his damages reduced because he failed to mitigate the loss caused by the defendant's breach. A claimant may also have his damages reduced because he actually contributed to the act

---

30. *Brace v Calder* [1895] 2 QB 253 (CA).
31. *British Westinghouse Electric & Manufacturing Co Ltd v Underground Electric Railways Co of London Ltd (No 2)* [1912] AC 673 (HL).
32. *Hoffberger v Ascot International Bloodstock Bureau* (1926) 120 SJ 130 (CA); *Banco de Portugal v Waterlow & Sons Ltd* [1932] AC 452 (HL).
33. *Compania Financiera Soleada SA v Hamoor Tanker Corp Inc (The Borag)* [1981] 1 WLR 287 (CA).
34. *Payzu Ltd v Saunders* [1919] 2 KB 581 (CA) 586.
35. *James Finlay & Co v NV Kwik Hoo Tong TM* [1928] 2 KB 604 (CA) 614.

🔗 We will examine contributory negligence in more detail when we discuss its tortious application in Chapter 15

that caused his loss—this is known as 'contributory negligence'. At common law, contributory negligence could operate as a complete defence, thereby completely defeating the claimant's claim, but as a general rule, it only applied in tort cases and not in contract.[36] It could, however, apply to cases in which a breach of contract also amounted to a tort.

Contributory negligence also exists in statute, and its effects are quite different from those under the common law. The Law Reform (Contributory Negligence) Act 1945, s 1(1), states:

> Where any person suffers damage as the result partly of his own fault and partly of the fault of any other person or persons, a claim in respect of that damage shall not be defeated by reason of the fault of the person suffering the damage, but the damages recoverable in respect thereof shall be reduced to such extent as the court thinks just and equitable having regard to the claimant's share in the responsibility for the damage.

The question arising is to what extent s 1(1) applies to liability for breach of contract. This is dependent upon the interpretation of the word 'fault', which is defined in s 4 as 'negligence, breach of statutory duty or other act or omission which gives rise to a liability in tort or would, apart from this Act, give rise to the defence of contributory negligence'. It is clear that s 4 was drafted with tortious acts in mind, and so applying it to cases involving breach of contract has proven to be a complex and controversial issue.

The extent to which breach of contract comes within s 4 was discussed in the case of *Forsikringsaktieselskapet Vesta v Butcher*,[37] in which the High Court applied s 4 to three classes of cases, as follows.

1. *Where the defendant commits a breach of a contractual term that imposes a strict obligation (that is, not dependent upon a failure to take reasonable care) under the contract, but his conduct does not amount to a tort* Because the breach does not give rise to liability in tort, it will not fall within the definition of 'fault' in s 4 and so the 1945 Act will not apply. Contractual terms normally impose strict obligations and so the 1945 Act will not apply to the majority of breaches.

2. *Where the defendant commits a breach of a contractual duty to take reasonable care (or equivalent), but no corresponding duty exists in tort* Again, because the defendant has not been tortiously negligent and no liability arises in tort, the Act will not apply.

3. *Where the defendant's conduct has breached a contractual duty of care and is also a tort* In this case, the defendant is liable in tort, and so the Act will apply and the court may reduce damages in line with s 1(1).

Accordingly, the current law is that the 1945 Act will apply only where a contractual duty of care has been breached, which also amounts to an independent tort. In 1990, a Law Commission Working Paper provisionally proposed that the Act apply

---

36. *AB Marintrans v Comet Shipping Co Ltd (The Shinjitsu Maru No 5)* [1985] 1 WLR 1270 (QB) 1287.
37. *Forsikringsaktieselskapet Vesta v Butcher* [1986] 2 Lloyd's Rep 179 (QB).

to all three cases identified above.[38] Following consultation, the Law Commission's subsequent recommendation was that the Act should cover instances 2 and 3 (that is, that the Act would not apply in relation to breaches of strict contractual obligations).[39] But the Law Commission's recommendations were not implemented, so that, for the time being, the Act will only apply where a contractual duty of care has been breached and this breach also amounts to an independent tort.

Finally, it should be noted that, in any breach of contract case, where the claimant's contribution to his loss is so great as to prevent the defendant's breach of contract being an effective or dominant cause of the claimant's loss, then the clamant will not be able to recover any damages at all on the ground of a lack of causation.[40] Moreover, if the defendant successfully brings a counterclaim to a successful claim by the claimant, the effect on the damages awarded to each party may be the same as if there were an apportionment of liability on grounds of contributory negligence.[41]

Liquidated damages and penalties

So far, our discussion has been limited to unliquidated damages. Given the complexity and unpredictability of the above rules, it is common for the parties themselves to insert a clause into the contract stating how the quantum of damages will be assessed in the event of breach. This might take one of two forms, as follows.

➡️ unliquidated damages: unascertained damages that will be quantified by the court

- *The level of damages specified represents a genuine pre-estimate of the loss resulting from a breach* This is known as a 'liquidated damages clause' and such clauses will be upheld by the courts, even where the actual loss sustained is more or less than the amount estimated in the clause.

- *The level of damages specified does not represent a genuine pre-estimate of the loss resulting from beach, but is instead an excessive amount designed to intimidate the party into proper performance* This is known as a 'penalty clause' and such a clause will only be enforced to the extent that it is commensurate with the actual loss sustained.[42] Accordingly, if the actual loss sustained is less than the amount specified in the penalty clause, only the loss sustained can be claimed.[43] If the actual loss is greater than that specified, however, the court will ignore the penalty clause and award the greater amount.[44] A penalty clause in a consumer contract will be regulated by the Unfair Terms in Consumer Contracts Regulations 1999, and is very likely to be regarded as an unfair term and so will not be binding on the consumer.

🔗 The Unfair Terms in Consumer Contracts Regulations 1999 are discussed at p 985

Liquidated damages clauses are often found in contracts that have to be completed within a certain time. Thus contracts for building or civil engineering work normally

---

38. Law Commission, *Contributory Negligence as a Defence in Contract* (Law Com Working Paper No 114, HMSO, London, 1990) [5.1].

39. Law Commission, *Contributory Negligence as a Defence in Contract* (Law Com No 219, HMSO, London, 1993) [3.60].

40. *Marintrans AB v Comet Shipping Co Ltd* [1985] 1 WLR 1270 (QB).

41. See, e.g., *Tennant Radiant Heat Ltd v Warrington Development Corporation* [1988] 1 EGLR 41 (CA).

42. Note that this is not the same as saying that the courts will ignore the clause or that it is unenforceable, although, in most cases, the result will be the same.

43. *Wilbeam v Ashton* (1807) 1 Camp 78; *Jobson v Johnson* [1989] 1 WLR 1026 (CA).

44. *Wall v Rederiaktiebolaget Luggude* [1915] 3 KB 66 (KB); *Cellulose Acetate Silk Co v Widnes Foundry (1925) Ltd* [1933] AC 20 (HL).

provide for a specified sum to be paid for every day or week of delay. Similarly, most, if not all, voyage **charterparties** of ships contain a provision for a specified sum per day to be paid by the charterer to the shipowner if the ship is delayed due to the charterer's failure to load or unload within a stipulated period of time—the specified sum being known as 'demurrage'.

→ charterparty: a written agreement whereby a person (known as the 'charterer') leases a ship for the purposes of transporting goods

Distinguishing between liquidated damages and penalties clauses

Given the above, it is vital that the courts are able to distinguish between liquidated damages clauses and penalty clauses. Parties may attempt to evade the rules relating to penalty clauses by labelling a clause as a 'liquidated damages clause'. The courts have indicated that such a label, whilst relevant, is not decisive.[45] The test used by the courts is based upon the party's intentions at the time that the contract was made. The leading case is as follows.

 Dunlop Pneumatic Tyre Co Ltd v New Garage and Motor Co Ltd [1915] AC 79 (HL)

FACTS: The facts are not directly relevant.

HELD: Lord Dunedin established four tests to help to distinguish between a liquidated damages clause and a penalty clause.

1. If the stipulated amount is *extravagant and unconscionable* compared to the maximum loss that could conceivably arise following the breach, the clause will be a penalty clause.

2. If a contract requiring payment of a fixed sum of money stipulates that if that sum is not paid, a larger sum will become payable, the clause will be a penalty clause.

3. A clause is presumed to be a penalty if it provides for the payment of a single lump sum upon the occurrence of a number of different events, some of which are serious, some of which are trifling.

4. The fact that loss is difficult or impossible to pre-estimate will not automatically mean that the pre-estimate is not a genuine one.

In the commercial context—especially in relation to complex commercial contracts—it is crucial that the parties feel that they can rely on damages clauses upon which they have agreed. In such cases, it appears that the courts will not lightly rule that a clause is a penalty clause. In *Philips Hong Kong Ltd v A-G of Hong Kong*,[46] Lord Woolf stated that 'what the parties have agreed should normally be upheld. Any other approach will lead to undesirable uncertainty especially in commercial

---

45. In *Kemble v Farren* (1829) 6 Bing 141, a clause labelled a 'liquidated damages clause' was held to be a penalty. In *Elphinstone v Monkland Iron & Coal Co Ltd* (1886) 11 App Cas 332 (HL), a clause labelled as a 'penalty' was held to constitute a liquidated damages clause.
46. (1993) 61 BLR 41 (PC).

contracts'. In *Meretz Investments NV v ACP Ltd*,[47] Lewison J stated: 'To characterise a clause as a penalty, with the consequence that the court will refuse to enforce it, is a blatant interference with freedom of contract, and should normally be reserved for cases of oppression.'[48]

One final point to note is that the above rules apply only to sums payable upon breach of contract. A penalty payable upon any other event will not be called into question by the courts.[49] It is arguable this rule is unsatisfactory for two reasons. Firstly, it will allow a stronger party to impose an excessive penalty clause on a weaker party, provided that the clause does not come into effect upon breach. Secondly, it leads to the illogical situation in which the weaker party would rather breach the contract than trigger the event that activates the penalty clause.

 Key points summary

- The basic aim of damages is to put the claimant in the position in which he would have been had the breach not occurred. This will compensate the claimant for his 'expectation loss'.

- Alternatively, the claimant may elect to cover his 'reliance loss' (that is, monies already spent in anticipation of the defendant's proper performance).

- Expectation loss and reliance loss cannot both be recovered, unless the expectation loss is calculated on a net basis.

- Damages for mental distress and disappointment caused by physical loss are recoverable. Where physical loss is not present, damages cannot be recovered for mental distress unless the contract was one designed to provide enjoyment, promote peace of mind, or prevent distress.

- Damages can only be recovered where the breach was the effective or dominant cause of the loss.

- Damages that are a natural consequence of the breach can be claimed, provided they are in the reasonable contemplation of both parties. Damages that are not a natural consequence of the breach cannot be claimed, unless such loss is in the reasonable contemplation of both parties at the time that the contract was made.

- A claimant cannot recover damages for losses that could have been avoided by taking reasonable steps (known as 'mitigation').

- Where the defendant's conduct breaches a contractual duty of care and this breach also amounts to an independent tort, then the claimant's damages may be reduced if he contributed to his own loss.

---

47. [2006] EWHC 74 (Ch), [2007] Ch 197.
48. Ibid, [349].
49. *Export Credit Guarantee Department v Universal Oil Products Co* [1983] 1 WLR 399 (HL).

Action for the price or other agreed sum

We have seen above that the rules for calculating the quantum of damages can be complex, resulting in the defendant never being able to predict with certainty how much compensation he will obtain. To remove such uncertainty, in certain circumstances, it is preferable to bring an action for the price or some other agreed sum (hereinafter referred to as an 'action for the price'). Indeed, an action for the price is the most common action following a breach of contract.[50]

The operation and advantages of such an action, and how it differs from an action in damages, can be seen in the following example.

Eg | The action for price or other agreed sum

Charles enters into a contract with Greg, whereby Greg agrees to sell Charles his car in return for £5,000. The car will be delivered to Charles by 12 October. Payment is to take place by 15 October. Greg delivers the car to Charles on 11 October. By the end of October, Charles has yet to pay the £5,000.

Bringing an action for damages

Greg could argue that Charles has breached the contract and should pay Greg damages. In such an action, Greg would need to establish that breach occurred and justify to the court, based on the rules above, why the amount that he is claiming is the appropriate one to compensate him for his loss. He would also need to establish that the loss suffered was caused by, and was not too remote from, the breach and that he had taken reasonable steps to mitigate his loss.

Bringing an action for the price

An action for price or other agreed sum would be much simpler. Greg would still need to establish breach, but would simply claim for the exact amount specified in the contract (£5,000)—no more and no less. Given the simplicity of the claim, it can be dealt with summarily,[51] thereby making the process quick and relatively cheap. Further, because Greg is not claiming damages, but is rather simply claiming the fixed sum owed to him under the contract, the above rules regarding quantum, causation, remoteness, and mitigation do not apply.[52] Greg is simply applying to the court for enforcement of Charles' primary obligation. As such, it is a form of specific performance, but because it involves only the recovery of money, it is not subject to the normal limitations of specific performance actions. Should any additional losses accrue as a result of Charles not paying on time, Greg can also seek damages for these additional losses.[53]

---

50. H Beale, *Remedies for Breach of Contract* (Sweet & Maxwell, London, 1980) 144.
51. Civil Procedure Rules, Pt 24.
52. *White and Carter (Councils) Ltd v McGregor* [1962] AC 413 (HL); *Reichman v Beveridge* [2007] Bus LR 412 (CA); cf E Peel, *The Law of Contract* (12th edn, Sweet & Maxwell, London, 2007) 1097–9, who argues that, in certain circumstances, the rules on mitigation can apply to cases involving an action for price or other agreed sum.
53. *Overstone Ltd v Shipway* [1962] 1 WLR 117 (CA).

An action for the price will arise only once the duty to pay has arisen. An obvious example would be a contract for the sale of goods, in which the price is 'payable on a day certain irrespective of delivery'.[54] Once this date has passed, an action for price can commence, but not before. Problems arise, however, where one party indicates that he has no intention of paying the price and the other party has yet to commence performance. In this case, two possibilities exist, as follows.

- The innocent party may continue to perform the contract (that is, he may affirm it). In such a case, he may succeed in an action for the price when the debt becomes due.
- The innocent party may accept the other party's breach as discharging the contract (that is, he may terminate the contract for repudiatory breach). In such a case, he can only recover damages and cannot succeed in an action for the price.

White and Carter (Councils) Ltd v McGregor [1962] AC 413 (HL)

FACTS: The claimant, an advertising contractor, provided free litter bins to local authorities, the bins being paid for by local companies who would advertise on the bins. The defendant entered into such an arrangement whereby its garage would be advertised on the bins for three years. On the same day that the contract was entered into, the defendant changed its mind and asked the claimant to cancel the contract. The claimant refused to cancel the contract and instead advertised the defendant's business as promised. The defendant failed to pay and the claimant initiated an action for price.

HELD: The majority of the House of Lords held that the claimant could recover the full contract price, even though its performance was completely unwanted and it had made no effort to mitigate its loss by finding another company to advertise on the bins. But this ability to continue to perform and claim the price is limited in two ways, as follows.

1. An action for price will only be permitted if the innocent party can complete performance without the cooperation of the party in breach. If the cooperation of the other party is required, an action for price will not be permitted and the claimant will have to seek damages.

2. The innocent party will only be able to continue performance if he has a legitimate interest, financial or otherwise, in doing so.

COMMENT: This case is a controversial one—a fact evidenced by the three to two split in the House of Lords. The main criticism against the decision is that it indicates a 'willingness to countenance waste purely for the sake of legal principle'.[55] The decision permits a party to continue to perform, even where such performance is entirely unwanted by the other party. It could be argued that this decision is out of line with other principles in contract law—namely, the principle of mitigation, which exists purely to discourage waste by encouraging claimants to lessen their loss. A secondary criticism is that, in effect, the decision of the House amounted to an order for specific performance, but, because this was a contract for service, specific performance would not have been available. Should the court allow parties to circumvent the rules relating to specific performance this way?

⭐ See MP Furmston, 'The Case of the Insistent Performer' (1962) 25 MLR 364

---

54. Sale of Goods Act 1979, s 49(2).
55. PM Nienaber, 'The Effect of Anticipatory Repudiation: Principle and Policy' [1962] CLJ 213, 233.

Restitutionary remedies

Very often, restitution is classified as a third measure of damages alongside expectation loss and reliance loss. But restitution has been specifically recognized by the House of Lords as a separate area of law[56] and so will be examined separately.

Restitution refers to those situations in which the defendant has been unjustly enriched at the claimant's expense. Restitutionary remedies fall into two broad categories.

- *Unjust enrichment by subtraction* This occurs where the defendant has been unjustly enriched at the expense of causing the claimant actual loss.
- *Recovery of profits* This occurs where the defendant has been unjustly enriched, but the claimant, whilst having a wrong committed against him, has suffered no actual loss.

Unjust enrichment by subtraction

Total failure of consideration

A party may make advance payments in anticipation of a contract coming into existence. It may then follow that, due to the other party's breach, that party obtains no benefit whatsoever from the contract. This is known as a 'total failure of consideration' and, where this occurs, any monies paid out in anticipation of the contract can be recovered, even if the other party has not acted in breach.

The failure of consideration must be total. If a party receives even a small proportion of the consideration under the agreement (that is, the failure of consideration is partial), advance monies paid will not be recoverable.[57] If, however, the partial performance is such as to entitle him to terminate the contract and he elects to do so, it is possible to convert a partial failure into total failure by returning the partial benefit that he has obtained. He will then be able to reclaim any advance monies.[58]

Quantum meruit

A party to a contract (*A*) may have completed work under the contract, or supplied certain goods, but then, for some reason, the other party may unjustifiably have prevented performance and *A* may have terminated the contract for this repudiatory breach. In such a case, *A* may be able to obtain a *quantum meruit* ('as much as he has deserved', but more loosely translated to mean a 'reasonable sum').

 Planché v Colburn (1831) 8 Bing 14

FACTS: The claimant was engaged to write a book for 'The Juvenile Library', a series of books being compiled by the defendant. Midway through writing the book, the series was cancelled. The defendant offered to publish the book separately, but the claimant refused and instead claimed for a *quantum meruit*.

---

56. *Lipkin Gorman v Karpnale Ltd* [1991] 2 AC 548 (HL).   57. *Whincup v Hughes* (1871) LR 6 CP 78.
58. *Baldry v Marshall* [1925] 1 KB 260 (CA).

HELD: The claimant was entitled to refuse the offer of separate publication and to terminate the contract for repudiatory breach. He was awarded a *quantum meruit* of 50 guineas (£52.50).

It should be noted that a *quantum meruit* is not an award of damages. Two principal differences exist between an award of damages and a *quantum meruit*, as follows.

1. Damages are dependent upon the existence of a contract and that contract being breached. Because restitution is not a part of contract law, but is an area of law in its own right, a *quantum meruit* can be claimed even where no contract exists (for example, where a party incurs expense or undertakes work in anticipation of a formal contract coming into existence in the future, but no such contract is entered into).[59]

2. As we have seen, damages are compensatory and will aim to put the claimant in the position in which he would have been had the breach not occurred. Conversely, a *quantum meruit* aims to award the claimant an amount equal to the work that he has completed. Normally, an award of damages will be higher than a *quantum meruit*, but where the claimant has made a bad bargain, or where only nominal damages can be recovered, a *quantum meruit* may be preferable.

If the defendant commits a repudiatory breach of the contract, the claimant may elect to discharge the contract and claim damages; he may alternatively claim a *quantum meruit*. As noted above, a *quantum meruit* is calculated in a different manner from damages and, depending on the case, it may be more advantageous to claim a *quantum meruit* instead of damages.

Recovery of profits

Here, we are concerned with cases in which the defendant has committed a breach of contract against the claimant for which he has been unjustly enriched, but the breach has not caused the claimant loss. In this case, can the claimant recover the benefit (or a proportion of the benefit) unjustly gained by the defendant?

In the following case, the High Court answered in the affirmative.

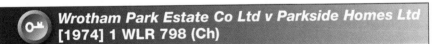

Wrotham Park Estate Co Ltd v Parkside Homes Ltd [1974] 1 WLR 798 (Ch)

FACTS: The defendant purchased a piece of land that was subject to a restrictive covenant, which had been imposed for the benefit of the claimant, who owned land adjacent to the defendant's land. The covenant stated that houses could not be built on the land. The defendant breached the covenant and built houses on the newly acquired land. The claimant sought an injunction to prevent the houses being built and a further mandatory injunction to demolish the houses that had already been built.

---

59. *British Steel Corporation v Cleveland Bridge and Engineering Co Ltd* [1984] 1 All ER 504 (QB).

★ See CT Emery, 'Restrictive Covenants: Annexation to the Whole or to All or Any Parts of the Land' (1974) 33 CLJ 214

HELD: The High Court refused to grant any injunction—but the claimant was awarded damages based on the profit that the defendant had made by breaching the covenant. These damages were based on the hypothetical sum that might have been gained had the defendant bargained with the claimant for the release of the covenant (even though the claimant had no intention of engaging in such bargaining). Accordingly, this has come to be known as the 'hypothetical release' approach.

In the following case, however, *Wrotham Park* was distinguished and the Court of Appeal established the general rule that the claimant can only recover damages for his actual loss.

Surrey County Council v Bredero Homes Ltd [1993] 1 WLR 1361 (CA)

FACTS: The claimant sold a piece of land to the defendant, on the basis that the defendant would only develop the land in accordance with the existing planning permission. The existing planning permission limited the number of houses that could be built on the land to seventy-two. After the sale of the land was completed, the defendant obtained new planning permission, which enabled it to build seventy-seven houses on the land. In deliberate breach of contract, the defendant then built seventy-seven houses on the land. The claimant sought damages based on the profits that the defendant made on the sale of the extra houses.

★ See P Birks, 'Profits in Breach of Contract' (1993) 109 LQR 518

HELD: The Court of Appeal held that the claimant could only recover nominal damages, because it had not suffered any loss as a result of the breach. The Court distinguished *Wrotham Park*, stating that it was not an application of restitutionary principles, but was a case of awarding damages in lieu of injunction, as permitted by the Supreme Court Act 1981, s 50.

The next case to arise constituted a major common law development by allowing full recovery of unjustly acquired profit and was subsequently described as marking 'a new start in this area of the law'.[60]

Attorney General v Blake [2001] 1 AC 268 (HL)

FACTS: The defendant, George Blake, was a British spy, but had become a double agent working for the Soviet Union. In 1961, he was convicted of treason and espionage and sentenced to forty-two years' imprisonment, but five years later, he escaped from prison and fled to Moscow. There, in 1989, he wrote his autobiography, *No Other Choice*. The Crown had no knowledge of the book until it was published, by which time, Blake had received around £60,000 from the British publisher and could expect further payments totalling around £90,000. The Attorney General initiated a claim against Blake to recover

---

60. *Experience Hendrix LLC v PPX Enterprises Inc* [2003] EWCA Civ 323, [2003] EMLR 25, [16] (Mance LJ).

the £60,000 and to prevent him receiving any further payments. The basis of the claim was that Blake's employment contract provided that he would not divulge official information in press or book form. Accordingly, there was no doubt that Blake was in breach of contract. The problem was that, by the time the book was published, the information that he divulged was no longer confidential. Accordingly, the Crown had not suffered any loss and, following *Bredero* (discussed above), the Court of Appeal held that the Crown could only recover nominal damages.

HELD: A majority of the House of Lords held that the Crown could recover the profits from Blake. All the majority judges were, however, keen to emphasize that this would only be permitted in exceptional circumstances. Lord Nicholls stated:

> An account of profits will be appropriate only in exceptional circumstances. Normally the remedies of damages, specific performance and injunction, coupled with the characterisation of some contractual obligations as fiduciary, will provide an adequate response to a breach of contract.[61]

COMMENT: In addition to allowing the recovery of profit, the House also indicated a preference for the approach evidenced in *Wrotham Park* over the approach evidenced in *Bredero*. Lord Nicholls (with whom the majority agreed) described *Bredero* as a 'difficult decision'[62] and commented that strict adherence to it could constitute a 'sorry reflection on the law'.[63] Conversely, he described *Wrotham Park* as:

 See D Fox, 'Restitutionary Damages to Deter Breach of Contract' (2001) 60 CLJ 33

> a solitary beacon, showing that in contract as well as in tort damages are not always narrowly confined to recoupment of financial loss. In a suitable case damages for breach of contract may be measured by the benefit gained by the wrongdoer from the breach.[64]

The House of Lords emphasized that profits could be recovered only in exceptional cases. The obvious question is how future courts are to determine what constitutes an 'exceptional' case. The Court of Appeal in *Attorney General v Blake* attempted to lay down fixed situations in which profits would be recoverable, but the House of Lords rejected this approach, stating that fixed rules should be avoided and that '[e]xceptions to the general principle that there is no remedy for disgorgement of profits against a contract breaker are best hammered out on the anvil of concrete cases'.[65]

The Court did not have to wait long for such a case.

Experience Hendrix LLC v PPX Enterprises Inc [2003] EWCA Civ 323

FACTS: The defendant entered into an agreement, whereby it covenanted not to license certain music in which Jimi Hendrix appeared as a support guitarist alongside another performer. The defendant breached the agreement, and the claimant (the Hendrix estate) sought to recover the profits made from the breach and to restrain future breaches.

---

61. *Attorney General v Blake* [2001] 1 AC 268 (HL) 285. 62. Ibid, 283.
63. Ibid. 64. Ibid, 283, 284.
65. Ibid, 291 (Lord Steyn).

HELD: The Court of Appeal granted an injunction restraining future breaches of the agreement. As for the recovery of profits, the claimant had suffered no actual loss, so the Court was forced to rely on *Blake*—but was the current case as 'exceptional' as *Blake*? The Court concluded that this case was not exceptional in the way that *Blake* was and so the recovery of profits was not allowed. The Court still awarded damages, however, based on the 'hypothetical release' approach evidenced in *Wrotham Park* (that is, damages were assessed based on the hypothetical sum that the defendant would pay the claimant to obtain release from the agreement).

 See M Graham, 'Restitutionary Damages: The Anvil Struck' (2004) 120 LQR 26

It has been argued that the decision in *Experience Hendrix* has 'fully resurrected *Wrotham Park*…a case which until *Blake*, was languishing in the shadow of *Surrey County Council v Bredero Homes Ltd*'.[66] Shortly after the *Experience Hendrix* case, a string of cases occurred in which damages were awarded based on the 'hypothetical release' approach established in *Wrotham Park*.[67] Accordingly, it would appear that the full recovery of profits, as seen in *Blake*, will be seldom be granted and will be limited to exceptional cases. In those cases not deemed exceptional, damages may still be awarded to the claimant based on the 'hypothetical release' approach. It would therefore appear that this approach provides a middle ground between *Bredero* (no recovery of profits is permitted) and *Blake* (full recovery of profits is permitted).

‹› Key points summary

- Restitutionary remedies arise where the defendant has been unjustly enriched by his breach of contract.

- A claimant may be able to claim a *quantum meruit* (reasonable sum) based on work already performed if he has terminated the contract for a repudiatory breach by the defendant.

- In exceptional cases, a claimant may be able to recover profits from a defendant who has benefited from a breach of contract, even though the claimant has suffered no loss.

- Where the defendant has profited through a breach of contract, the courts may award damages to the claimant based on the hypothetical cost that the defendant would have paid to be released from the term that was breached, even though the claimant has suffered no loss.

Specific performance

In the majority of breach of contract cases, an award of damages can adequately compensate a claimant who has suffered loss. But there will always be cases in which damages are an inadequate remedy, as the following example demonstrates.

---

66. M Graham, 'Restitutionary Damages: The Anvil Struck' (2004) 120 LQR 26, 30.
67. For example, *Lane v O'Brien Homes Ltd* [2004] EWHC 303 (QB); *Wynn-Jones v Bickley* [2006] EWHC 1991 (Ch); *Small v Oliver & Saunders* [2006] EWHC 1293 (Ch); *Lunn Poly Ltd v Liverpool & Lancashire Properties Ltd* [2007] L & TR 6 (CA).

> ### Eg The inadequacy of damages
>
> Mike is an avid car collector with a particular passion for rare and unique cars. He enters into a contract with Anna to purchase the last remaining Model T Ford in existence. After the contract is made, however, Anna decides that she wishes to keep the car and informs Mike that he cannot purchase it. In this case, an award of damages will not adequately compensate Mike for his loss: he will want Anna to fulfil her contractual obligations and sell him the car. In such a case, the court might be prepared to grant Mike the remedy of specific performance.

Specific performance is simply a court order requiring a person to fulfil his contractual obligations. Failure to comply with an order for specific performance constitutes contempt of court, which can result in a fine and/or imprisonment.

Instances in which specific performance is not available

Unlike the common law remedy of damages, which claimants acquire as of right upon a successful claim, the remedy of specific performance is equitable, meaning that it is only granted at the discretion of the court. It is granted sparingly and, over the years, the courts have created a number of rules dictating when specific performance may not be granted.

Where damages are adequate

Historically, the equitable courts would only provide a claimant with a remedy if the remedies at common law were inadequate. This rule has survived and specific performance will not be granted where damages provide an adequate remedy[68] (although in certain years, the courts have started to move towards a test based on appropriateness, rather than adequacy).[69] The general test used by the courts to determine the adequacy of damages is whether, if damages were awarded, the claimant would be able to purchase substitute performance. If the claimant would be readily able to purchase a substitute, then clearly damages will be an adequate remedy. Accordingly, in the vast majority of sale of goods cases, specific performance will not be granted, because the claimant can easily obtain the goods elsewhere. To grant specific performance in such circumstances would be completely contrary to the principle of mitigation discussed above.[70]

But where a substitute cannot be obtained, an order of specific performance may be granted. This could include goods that are rare or unique (for example, antiques or rare works of art),[71] the supply of a machine or machine part that is unobtainable elsewhere,[72] or the purchase of shares that would determine the controlling interest

---

68. *Harnett v Yielding* (1805) 2 Sch & Lef 549.
69. See, e.g., *Beswick v Beswick* [1968] AC 58 (HL) 88.
70. *Buxton v Lister* (1746) 3 Atk 383.
71. *Pusey v Pusey* (1684) 1 Vern 273.
72. *Nutbrown v Thornton* (1804) 10 Ves 159; *Land Rover Group Ltd v UPF (UK) Ltd* [2002] EWHC 3183 (QB), [2003] 2 BCLC 222.

in a company.[73] The courts take the view that every plot of land is unique, with the result that contracts involving the sale or lease of land are always specifically enforceable.[74] This has resulted in the rule that, since such a contract is specifically enforceable in favour of the purchaser or lessee, a seller or lessor of land can also obtain specific performance of the contract.[75]

Where the contract is for personal services

It is a long-held rule that, generally, equity will not compel performance of a contract of personal service[76] (for example, a contract of employment). Forcing a person to work for another would be an unjustifiable restriction on personal liberty and contrary to public policy. Statute has now recognized this, and the Trade Union and Labour Relations (Consolidation) Act 1992, s 236, provides that no court shall compel a person to work via an order for specific performance or an injunction. Similarly, the courts will not order specific performance requiring an employer to employ another. This is evidenced in the law relating to unfair dismissal. If an employment tribunal rules that an employee has been unfairly dismissed, it can order the employee to be reinstated—but if the employer chooses not to comply, the tribunal cannot order specific performance; it can only require the employer to pay compensation.[77]

Where the contract would require constant court supervision

In contracts imposing continuous obligations, the court will not order specific performance, if such performance would require constant supervision by the court. In *Ryan v Mutual Tontine Westminster Chambers Association,*[78] a residential block of flats was leased to a group of persons, with a term of the lease providing that the lessors would employ a resident porter who would be 'constantly in attendance'. The person appointed deputized the duty to others, while he was engaged in a second job as a cook at a nearby club. The lessors applied for specific performance, but were refused on the ground that such an order would require the courts' constant supervision.

For this reason, the courts are unlikely to order specific performance compelling a person to carry on the running of a business. Accordingly, for example, specific performance was refused to require a shop owner to his shop open during normal business hours[79] and was similarly refused against a company seeking to keep an airfield open that was due to be demolished to make way for a housing estate.[80]

The following case provides another example of a refusal to order specific performance.

---

73. *Harvela Investments Ltd v Royal Trust Co of Canada* [1986] AC 207 (HL).
74. Unless the claimant elects to claim damages: *Meng Leong Developments Pte Ltd v Jip Hong Trading Co Pte Ltd* [1985] AC 511 (PC).
75. *Walker v Eastern Counties Rly* (1848) 6 Hare 595.
76. *Johnson v Shrewsbury and Birmingham Rly* (1853) 3 DM & G 358.
77. Employment Rights Act 1996, s 117(1).
78. [1893] 1 Ch 116 (CA).
79. *Braddon Towers v International Stores Ltd* [1987] 1 EGLR 209 (Ch).
80. *Dowty Boulton Paul Ltd v Wolverhampton Corporation (No 1)* [1971] 1 WLR 204 (Ch).

Co-operative Insurance Society Ltd v Argyll Stores (Holdings) Ltd [1998] AC 1 (HL)

FACTS: The defendant took out a thirty-five-year lease on a unit in a shopping centre that belonged to the claimant, intending to use the unit as a supermarket. A term of the lease was that the defendant would keep the supermarket open during normal business hours. Unfortunately, the supermarket became unprofitable and so the defendant closed it down. The claimant, believing that the closure of the supermarket would adversely affect trade in the shopping centre, offered the defendant a rent concession if it kept the supermarket open until someone else could be found to take over the lease. No reply was heard from the defendant and so the claimant sought specific performance to keep the supermarket open.

HELD: The House of Lords refused to grant specific performance. The House provided several justifications for its decision.

1. Granting such an order would require the court's constant supervision.

2. Granting such an order would, in effect, be compelling a person to continue running a business subject to the threat of contempt of court proceedings if he were to cease carrying on business. The House thought it inappropriate to use such a threat to compel a person to carry on a business that he had decided to close for commercial reasons.

3. Such cases would likely to be very expensive and time-consuming. Conversely, a simple award of damages is likely to be much simpler and cheaper overall.

COMMENT: Whilst this case confirmed the orthodox approach that specific performance will not be granted where it would require the court's constant supervision, Lord Hoffmann, *obiter*, did make a distinction between:

* contracts that require a person to continue an activity over a period of time; and

* contracts for results (for example, building contracts).

In the former, specific performance will not be ordered, because it would require constant supervision. As regards the latter, however, constant supervision would not be required, because the court 'only has to examine the finished work'.[81] In a number of cases, the courts have ordered specific performance where the purpose of the business was to achieve a particular result.[82]

See HY Yeo, 'Specific Performance: Covenant to Keep Business Running' [1998] JBL 254

Where there is a lack of mutuality

In order for specific performance to be granted, it must be a mutual remedy (that is, it must be available to both parties), as the following example demonstrates.

---

81. *Co-operative Insurance Society Ltd v Argyll Stores (Holdings) Ltd* [1998] AC 1 (HL) 13 (Lord Hoffmann).
82. See, e.g., *Jeune v Queens Cross Properties Ltd* [1974] Ch 97 (Ch); *Rainbow Estates Ltd v Tokenhold Ltd* [1998] 2 All ER 860 (Ch).

> ### Eg The requirement of mutuality
>
> Roger enters into a contract with Mike. Mike indicates that he does not intend to fulfil his obligations and so Roger applies to the court for specific performance. The court will only grant specific performance in favour of Roger, if it could similarly grant specific performance in favour of Mike. Therefore, if Roger was a minor and the contract was of a type not binding on him because of a lack of contractual capacity, he would be unable to obtain specific performance against Mike, because Mike could not obtain it against Roger, due to Roger's lack of contractual capacity.[83] Put simply, a claimant will be unable to obtain specific performance against the defendant if the defendant could not obtain specific performance against the claimant.

An important question to answer is at what point in time mutuality must exist. Mutuality may exist when the contract is created, but may not exist at the time of the court hearing, or vice versa. The courts have clearly established that mutuality must exist at the time of the hearing, not when the contract was made.[84] Accordingly, applying this to our example above, if Roger was aged 17 when he entered into the contract, but had turned 18 years old by the time of the hearing, he would be able to obtain specific performance.[85]

The nature of the equitable discretion

Even if a claim does not come within the above categories, there is no guarantee that specific performance will be ordered. Whereas the common law remedy of damages is available as of right (subject to an effective exclusion clause), specific performance, like all equitable remedies, is discretionary and, as such, is subject to the equitable maxims discussed in Chapter 1. The court's discretion is not exercised arbitrarily, but is 'governed as far as possible by fixed rules and principles',[86] including the following.

- Specific performance may be denied where a contract was procured by unfair (although not invalid) means.[87] This is simply an application of the principle that 'He who comes to Equity must come with clean hands'.
- Specific performance is unlikely to be granted where it would cause severe hardship for the defendant,[88] or where the cost of performance is wholly out of proportion to any benefit.[89]
- Specific performance is likely to be denied where the defendant has made a mistake *and* enforcing the mistake would lead to injustice.[90]
- The maxim 'Delay defeats Equity' means that specific performance may be denied where the claimant took so long to bring the claim for specific

---

83. *Flight v Bolland* (1828) 4 Russ 298.
84. *Price v Strange* [1978] Ch 337 (CA).
85. *Clayton v Ashdown* (1714) 9 Vin Abr 393.
86. *Lamare v Dixon* (1873) LR 6 HL 414 (HL) 423 (Lord Chelmsford).
87. *Walters v Morgan* (1861) 3 DF & J 718.
88. *Denne v Light* (1857) 8 DM & G 774; *Patel v Ali* [1984] Ch 283 (Ch).
89. *Tito v Waddell (No 2)* [1977] Ch 106 (Ch).
90. *Webster v Cecil* (1861) 30 Beav 62.

performance that, in the meantime, the defendant altered his position to such an extent that enforcing the contract would be unjust.[91]

- Because 'Equity will not assist a volunteer', specific performance will not be ordered where a claimant has not provided any consideration.[92]

 Key points summary

- Specific performance is an order of the court requiring the defendant to fulfil his contractual obligations.

- Failure to comply with an order for specific performance constitutes contempt of court.

- Specific performance is not available where:
  - damages would be an adequate remedy;
  - the contract involved is one for personal services;
  - the contract would require constant court supervision; and
  - there is a lack of mutuality.

- Whereas the common law remedy of damages is available as of right, the equitable remedy of specific performance is only available at the court's discretion.

Injunctions

Injunctions come in two types and the injunction sought by a claimant will depend upon the type of term that has been breached.

- Where the term imposes a positive obligation (that is, to do something) and the defendant has not performed the positive act, the claimant will seek an injunction requiring the claimant to perform the act in question. This is known as a 'mandatory injunction' and is clearly very similar to an order for specific performance. A mandatory injunction can also be used to order the remedying of a breach that has already occurred (that is, to restore the situation to what it would have been but for the breach). Mandatory injunctions are rare and will only be granted if the defendant has deliberately flouted the claimant's rights,[93] or if the claimant would be gravely prejudiced if the mandatory injunction were not granted.[94]

- Where the term imposes a negative obligation (that is, to refrain from doing something) and the defendant engages in the prohibited act, the claimant will seek an injunction preventing the defendant from carrying on the prohibited act. This is known as a 'prohibitory injunction'.

---

91. *Stuart v London and North Western Rly Co* (1852) 1 De GM & G 721; *Lazard Bros & Co Ltd v Fairfield Properties Co (Mayfair) Ltd* (1977) 121 Sol Jo 793.

92. *Penn v Lord Baltimore* (1750) 1 Ves Sen 444; *Cannon v Hartley* [1949] Ch 213 (Ch).

93. *Luganda v Service Hotels* [1969] 2 Ch 209 (CA).

94. *Shepherd Homes v Sandham* [1971] Ch 340 (Ch).

As with specific performance, breaching the terms of an injunction constitutes contempt of court. Because injunctions are an equitable remedy and therefore discretionary, the equitable maxims applicable to orders for specific performance will also apply to injunctions.

The relationship between prohibitory injunctions and specific performance

The courts will not issue a prohibitory injunction if this would amount to an indirect form of specific performance. This issue has arisen most commonly in employment cases, especially where contracts contain a restraint of trade clause. The rule is that injunctions will not be used to compel a defendant to work for the claimant, but they can be used to prevent a defendant working for anyone other than the claimant. The distinction is a fine, but important, one.

 Lumley v Wagner (1852) 1 De GM & G 604

FACTS: Wagner contracted to sing at Lumley's theatre for a three-month period. The contract contained a negative obligation—namely, that she could not sing at any other theatre without Lumley's written consent. She abandoned the contract with Lumley and entered into a contract to sing at Gye's theatre. Lumley applied for an injunction to prevent her from singing at Gye's theatre.

HELD: The court granted Lumley the injunction restraining Wagner from singing for Gye.

COMMENT: Had the contract provided that Wagner could sing only for Lumley, the court would have not granted the injunction. But the contract did not say that she had to work for Lumley, only that she could not work for anyone else. Nonetheless, is this distinction justifiable? The contract may not have forced Wagner to sing for Lumley, but it did provide that she could not earn a living by singing for anyone else. From a practical viewpoint, it has be argued that such an injunction could place so much economic pressure on a defendant as to compel him to work for the claimant in order to earn a living.[95]

Given the above criticism of *Lumley*, more recent cases have indicated that where an injunction would, 'as a practical matter',[96] force the defendant to continue working for the claimant, then an injunction would not be granted. Such an injunction would, in effect, amount to an order for specific performance. In order for an injunction to be granted, it should not compel, in law or in fact, the defendant to work for the claimant. The question for the court is therefore whether the injunction would place undue pressure on the defendant to work for the claimant.

---

95. CD Ashley, 'Specific Performance by Injunction' (1906) 6 Colum LR 82, 90.
96. *Page One Records Ltd v Britton* [1968] 1 WLR 157 (Ch) 166 (Stamp J).

Page One Records Ltd v Britton [1968] 1 WLR 157 (Ch)

FACTS: The defendants, a pop group named The Troggs, employed the first of two claimants as their manager. The agreement was to last five years. It contained a term stating that, during this time, the defendants would not appoint anyone else as manager. Shortly after, the defendants sought to replace the claimants with another manager. The claimants could not obtain specific performance, because this was a contract for personal service. Accordingly, they applied to the court for an injunction preventing the defendants from employing anyone else as their manager.

HELD: Stamp J stated:

> These groups, if they are to have any great success, must have managers. Indeed, it is the [claimant's] own case that the Troggs are simple persons, of no business experience, and could not survive without the services of a manager. As a practical matter on the evidence before me, I entertain no doubt that they would be compelled, if the injunction was granted, on the terms that the [claimants] seek, to continue to employ the first [claimant] as their manager and agent . . . [97]

Because the defendants would have been compelled to continue to employ the claimant, this would have amounted to an order for specific performance. Accordingly, the High Court refused the application for an injunction.

 Key points summary

- Whereas the common law remedy of damages is available as of right, the equitable remedy of injunction is only available at the court's discretion.

- Failure to comply with an injunction constitutes contempt of court.

- Injunctions may be mandatory (requiring the defendant to do something) or prohibitory (requiring the defendant to refrain from doing something).

- A prohibitory injunction will not be granted where its effect would amount indirectly to an order for specific performance.

- Damages may be awarded in addition to, or instead of, an injunction or specific performance.

The relationship between damages, specific performance, and injunctions

When the courts of common law and the courts of equity were distinct, they retained remedial exclusivity (that is, the courts of equity could not award damages and the common law courts could not grant injunctions or specific performance). This

---

97. *Page One Records Ltd v Britton* [1968] 1 WLR 157 (Ch) 166.

changed with the passing of the Chancery Amendment Act 1858 (known as 'Lord Cairns' Act'), s 2, which provided the Court of Chancery with the ability to award damages instead of specific performance. Today, the Supreme Court Act 1981, s 50, provides:

> Where the Court of Appeal or the High Court has jurisdiction to entertain an application for an injunction or specific performance, it may award damages in addition to, or in substitution for, an injunction or specific performance.

Limitation periods

A claimant who has suffered loss due to a breach of contract does not obtain an immortal right to sue on that breach. The case must be brought within a certain timeframe, or it will be barred. The rationale behind this is that, as time passes, available evidence becomes more unreliable.

Accordingly, the following limitations apply.

- Actions concerning a simple contract (that is, one not made by deed) cannot be brought after six years, beginning with the date on which the cause of action arose.[98] This date is normally the date of the breach and is never the date when the damage is suffered. But if the action includes a claim for damages for personal injury, then the time limit is reduced to three years[99]—although it may be extended when it is equitable to do so.[100]

- Actions concerning a contract made by deed cannot be brought after twelve years, beginning with the date on which the action arose.[101] As above, however, if the claim involves damages for personal injury, the period is still reduced to three years.

The effect of the expiry of the above limitation periods is not to extinguish the claimant's right under the contract. Thus, for example, if a debtor pays a statute-barred debt, he cannot recover the payment back as money not due.[102]

Exceptions

Minors and the mentally disabled

If the claimant is a minor (that is, under the age of 18) when the cause of action arises, the above time limits will not begin to run until the claimant reaches the age of 18 or dies. If the claimant is mentally disabled (that is, lacks mental capacity to conduct legal proceedings) when the cause of action arises, the time limit will not begin to run until he ceases to be mentally disabled or dies.[103] If the claimant is mentally sound, and the limitation period commences, however, the countdown will not be suspended simply because the claimant then becomes mentally disabled.

---

98. Limitation Act 1980, s 5.
100. Ibid, s 33.
102. *Bize v Dickason* (1786) 1 Term Rep 285.
99. Ibid, s 11(4).
101. Ibid, s 8(1).
103. Limitation Act 1980, s 28(1).

The effect of fraud, concealment, or mistake

The general rule is that the limitation period will start to run irrespective of whether or not the claimant realizes that he has a cause of action. Where the Limitation Act 1980, s 32, applies, however, this general rule does not apply. Section 32 applies to cases in which:

- the action is based upon the fraud of the defendant, or the defendant's agent;
- any fact relevant to the claimant's right of action has been deliberately concealed from him by the defendant, or the defendant's agent; or
- the action is for relief from the consequences of a mistake, whether of fact or law.

Where s 32 applies, the limitation period will not start running until the claimant has discovered (that is, he knows of, and not simply suspects)[104] the fraud, deliberate concealment, or mistake, or could, with reasonable diligence, have discovered it.[105] A deliberate breach of duty in circumstances in which it is unlikely to be discovered amounts to a deliberate concealment of the facts involved in breach of that duty.[106] For this purpose, 'breach of duty' excludes a breach of duty that the actor was not aware that he was committing. It follows that an act that was intentional, but was not done with knowledge that it amounted to a breach of duty, does not constitute deliberate concealment, despite being done in circumstances in which it was unlikely to be discovered. In order to be deliberate, a concealment does not have to be dishonest.[107]

Extending the limitation period

The Limitation Act 1980, s 29(5), provides an instance in which the limitation period can be extended. Section 29(5) basically provides that where the debtor acknowledges the debt, or provides part-payment of a debt or other liquidated (that is, agreed) pecuniary claim, the limitation period starts again from this date. The period will start afresh with each acknowledgement or part-payment. In order for acknowledgement to be effective, it must be in writing and signed by the person making it (or his agent), and must be made to the person (or his agent) whose claim is acknowledged. But s 29(5) will only apply where the acknowledgement or part-payment occurs while the limitation period is still running; once the limit has expired, the right of action will become statute-barred and cannot be revived.[108]

Equitable relief

The limitation periods discussed above do not apply to certain claims for equitable relief;[109] instead, equitable remedies are subject to the doctrine of laches. The word 'laches' basically upholds the equitable maxim 'Delay defeats Equity', and refers to a situation in which an equitable remedy is denied to a party on the grounds that

---

104. *Barnstaple Boat Co Ltd v Jones* [2007] EWCA Civ 727, [2008] 1 All ER 1124.
105. Limitation Act 1980, s 32(1).
106. Ibid, s 32(2).
107. *Cave v Robinson, Jarvis & Rolf* [2002] UKHL 18, [2003] 1 AC 384.
108. Limitation Act 1980, s 29(7).
109. Ibid, s 36(1).

there has been so substantial a delay between the cause of action accruing and the claimant initiating his claim that it is unconscionable for him to be permitted to assert his rights.[110]

 Key points summary

- A contractual cause of action does not exist forever. After a certain period of time, it will become statute-barred.

- Actions concerning simple contracts (that is, those not made by deed) must be brought within six years, beginning with the date on which the action arose.

- Actions concerning contracts made by deed must be brought within twelve years, beginning with the date on which the action arose.

- If the claimant is a minor, the above periods do not start to run until the claimant reaches the age of 18. If the claimant is mentally disabled, the period will not begin to run until he ceases being mentally disabled.

- Acknowledgement or part-payment of a debt will cause the limitation period to begin afresh.

- Generally, the limitation periods contained in the Limitation Act 1980 do not apply to equitable remedies—but unreasonable delay will bar the granting of an equitable remedy.

Chapter conclusion

A business that is party to a contract, which sustains loss due to the other party's breach of contract, potentially has access to a number of remedies. In order to obtain the best possible result, those who run the business would be wise to be aware of the advantages, disadvantages, and limitations of the remedies available. In many cases, an award of damages will be adequate to compensate the claimant for the loss sustained, but it is important to determine correctly for what type of damages to claim. As we saw, the calculation of the various forms of damages can result in significantly differing amounts and if no loss is suffered, it is likely that the damages awarded will be nominal only. In some cases, damages will not be an adequate remedy and the claimant will want either the other party to comply with its contractual obligations, or to cease engaging in an action that amounts to a breach. In such cases, seeking an order for specific performance or an injunction is likely to provide a more appropriate remedy than an award of damages. It should be remembered, however, that whereas damages are available as of right, specific performance and injunctions (being equitable remedies) are granted at the court's discretion.

This chapter concludes our discussion of the law of contract. In the next chapter, we begin our discussion of another major area of civil liability—namely, the law of torts.

---

110. For example, *Frawley v Neill* [2000] CP Rep 20 (CA).

Self-test questions

1. Define the following:
    (a) double recovery;
    (b) pecuniary;
    (c) mitigation;
    (d) restitution;
    (e) *quantum meruit*;
    (f) specific performance.

2. Explain the distinction between expectation and reliance loss, and the circumstances in which a clamant would prefer to claim one over the other.

3. What course of action is there for a company that has cancelled a contract, but finds that the other party performs the contract despite the cancellation?

4. Explain the distinction between a liquidated damages clause and a penalty clause.

5. What advantages does an action for the price have over a claim for damages?

6. Johnny Cab is a comedian who agrees to perform at The Happy Club in Cardiff. The contract provides that he will perform three shows a week for one month and that he will not perform at any other venues in Wales for the duration of the contract. Johnny receives a lucrative offer to perform at the Millennium Centre in Cardiff. The owners of The Happy Club hear of this and seek an injunction to prevent Johnny from performing there. What would be the most appropriate remedy for the owners of The Happy Club to seek? Would your answer differ if the agreement between Johnny and The Happy Club were to state that he could only work for The Happy Club for the duration of the contract?

Further reading

Cartwright, J, 'Remoteness of Damage in Contract and Tort: A Reconsideration' (1966) 55 CLJ 488
Analyses the rules relating to remoteness, focusing on the differences between the rules in contract and tort

Graham, M, 'Restitutionary Damages: The Anvil Struck' (2004) 120 LQR 26
Discusses the Experience Hendrix *case; argues that it has resulted in a full resurrection of the 'hypothetical release' approach of* Wrotham Park

Koffman, L, and Macdonald, E, *The Law of Contract* (6th edn, OUP, Oxford, 2007) ch 21
A clear account of the remedies available for breach of contract, especially in relation to the recovery of profits made through unjust enrichment

Phang, A, 'The Crumbling Edifice? The Award of Contractual Damages for Mental Distress' [2003] JBL 341
Discusses in depth the general prohibition of recovery of damages for non-pecuniary loss and the exceptions to the general prohibition

Poole, J, *Textbook on Contract Law* (9th edn, OUP, Oxford, 2008) ch 10
A detailed, but accessible, analysis of actions for the price, and equitable and restitutionary remedies

 Remember to visit the **Online Resource Centre** at **<http://www.oxfordtextbooks.co.uk/roach>** to access the following resources on Chapter 10, 'Remedies for breach of contract': more **practice questions** and answers; a **glossary** of key terms; **multiple-choice questions**; **revision summaries**; and **audio updates** when relevant.

PART III

the law of torts

11

An introduction to the law of torts

- What is a tort?
- The aims of the law of torts
- The tortious duty

- Breach of duty
- The claimant and defendant
- Tort and human rights

INTRODUCTION

In 2007–08, 732,750 individuals claimed nearly £142 million in compensation for accidents and diseases.[1] There were nearly 9,000 cases of clinical negligence, 550,000 claims in relation to motor vehicle use, and over 87,000 claims made against employers. In 2007, 233 individuals obtained compensation for defamation—forty-five of them being awarded over £50,000 compensation.[2] In all of these cases, individuals were able to claim compensation, because they were victims of a civil wrong known as a 'tort'.

Along with contract law, tort law forms the backbone of the UK's civil justice system and is, accordingly, of immense importance to the business community. Businesses can potentially be liable for significant sums if they commit tortious acts that harm others. Businesses that negligently release harmful products onto the market may be liable for injuries caused, with several infamous instances in which thousands of persons were harmed by a negligently manufactured product. Every year, thousands of employees are injured due to the tortious acts of their employers, resulting in substantial compensation payments. Businesses that interfere in the business activities of others may find themselves liable under what are known as the 'economic torts'. Accordingly, tort represents a significant source of legal exposure for businesses and it is fundamental that they understand the duties placed upon them, so as to best avoid tortious liability.

What is a tort?

Numerous definitions exist regarding what constitutes a tort, but, as has been noted, these definitions have 'varying degrees of lack of success'.[3] As this comment indicates, no single definition can fully capture the nature of what a tort is. Understanding what

---

1. Statistics derived from the Compensation Recovery Unit website, <http://www.dwp.gov.uk/cru/performance.asp>.
2. Secretary of State for Justice, *Judicial and Court Statistics 2007* (TSO, London, 2008) 47, Table 3.2.
3. WVH Rogers, *Winfield & Jolowicz on Tort* (17th edn, Sweet & Maxwell, London, 2006) 1.

constitutes a tort is best approached by examining the nature of liability imposed and the aims of the law of torts.

The word itself derives from the Latin word *tortus* ('twisted' or 'wrong')—but this does not mean that all wrongful acts constitute a tort.

1. The law of torts[4] relates only to civil wrongs—but this is not to say that tortious acts cannot result in criminal proceedings, because certain acts can result in both criminal and civil liability. For example, **battery** is both a crime and a tort, which could result in the perpetrator being prosecuted and punished under the criminal law, and, in separate proceedings in a different court, being sued and ordered to pay the victim compensation under civil law.

2. Even though torts can result in civil liability, it does not follow that all civil liability results from torts. Tort is merely one type of civil liability, with other notable instances of civil liability being breach of contract and unjust enrichment. In fact, it has been argued that tort constitutes 'our residual category of civil liability',[5] meaning that liability is likely to result from a tort if breach of contract and unjust enrichment have been discounted. But the differing forms of civil liability are not mutually exclusive and the existence of a contractual relationship between the parties does not preclude the existence of a tortious duty. In fact, a significant overlap between contract and tort is relatively common, with numerous acts constituting simultaneously a tort and a breach of contract.

3. The law of torts protects only certain interests. Certain acts caused by another will be regarded as compensatable, whilst other acts may not. It is not always easy to understand why the law of torts protects certain losses but not others. Losses that are not protected by the law are deemed *damnum sine injuria esse potest*.

4. The principal function of the law of torts is to compensate the victim for harm caused by the act or omission of the **tortfeasor**. But the mere fact that a party has harmed another is insufficient per se to result in the payment of compensation. A tortious remedy will only exist if the party causing the harm owed the victim a legal duty not to cause that harm and was in breach of this duty. The existence of a legal duty is a question of law, whereas breach of duty is a question of fact.

➡ **battery:** the direct application of unlawful violence to another

➡ *damnum sine injuria esse potest:* 'loss can be without legal wrong'

➡ **tortfeasor:** anyone who commits a tort

The aims of the law of torts

Compensation

Perhaps the principal aim of the law of torts is to compensate those who have suffered harm via an award of damages (although, as we shall see, compensation for certain torts can be recovered where no harm occurs). Theoretically, tort law shifts the loss from those who suffer harm to those who cause it; in reality, it can be argued that the imposition of damages does not shift the loss, but rather spreads the loss. In

---

4. Because there are numerous types of tort, it is more appropriate to refer to the law of torts, as opposed to the law of tort. It has been estimated that there may be as many as forty torts in the English legal system: see NJ McBride and R Bagshaw, *Tort Law* (2nd edn, Pearson, Dorset, 2005) 21.

5. G Gilmore, *The Death of Contract* (Ohio State University Press, Columbus, OH, 1974) 87.

TABLE 11.1 The average time taken to reach a small claims hearing or trial

Year	Time between issue of case and start of hearing/trial (weeks)	
	Small claims	Fast and multi-track
2000	29	74
2001	28	73
2002	31	58
2003	27	52
2004	27	52
2005	27	52
2006	27	50
2007	28	49

Source: Secretary of State for Justice, *Judicial and Court Statistics* 2007 (HMSO, London, 2008) 73, Table 4.14

the majority of cases, tortfeasors are insured against liability (for example, motor insurance), therefore it is the insurance company that usually compensates the victim,[6] using its own funds derived from premiums paid by the tortfeasor and other customers. The loss is therefore not borne by the insurance company alone, but is spread throughout the insurance company's customers.

The ability of the tort system to provide an efficient system for the payment of compensation has been doubted for several reasons. Firstly, historically, the system has been extremely expensive. In his review of the civil justice system, Lord Woolf noted that, in cases of lower value (in which the claim was £12,500 or below), the costs of one party exceeded the compensation paid out in 40 per cent of cases,[7] leading him to conclude that 'the present system provides higher benefits to lawyers than to their clients'.[8]

Secondly, the civil system is regarded as slow, with tort cases proving the slowest. There is, however, evidence that the Woolf reforms are having an effect in this area (at least, in relation to fast and multi-track cases), as Table 11.1 demonstrates.

Deterrence

Potential tortfeasors, realizing that they may be required to pay damages for any breach of duty, will reform their behaviour so as not to cause any harm. In this sense, the law of torts is preventative, because it encourages potential defendants to alter their behaviour and comply with any duties of care to which they are subject. In practice, however, the deterrent effect of tort law has been doubted, largely due to the prevalence of insurance. Individuals realize that if they breach certain tortious duties and

---

6. According to T Goriely, R Moorhead, and P Abrams, *More Civil Justice? The Impact of the Woolf Reforms on Pre-action Behaviour* (The Law Society and Civil Justice Council, London, 2002) 90, 94 per cent of compensation is paid out by insurance companies.

7. Lord Woolf, *Access to Justice: Final Report to the Lord Chancellor on the Civil Justice System in England and Wales* (HMSO, London, 1996) Annex III [16].

8. Ibid, [10].

cause harm to others, it will usually be covered by their insurance policy. Therefore, where the potential tortfeasor is insured, the deterrent value of an award of damages is emasculated, because he will realize that he may not bear the loss. It is no coincidence that the vast majority of tort cases occur in relation to road traffic accidents and accidents at work—two of the few areas in which insurance is compulsory.[9]

The protection of interests

As noted, sustaining harm is not enough per se to establish a claim in tort; the claimant will also need to establish that the defendant breached a duty owed to him. One could argue that duties are imposed upon persons to protect the rights or interests of others. In this sense, the law of torts provides a means whereby our interests are protected and, if breached, a remedy provided. Our right to enjoy our property (whether land or goods) is protected by the torts of trespass and nuisance. Our right to personal safety is protected by the torts of negligence and trespass to the person (assault and battery). Our right not to have our reputation falsely harmed is protected by the torts of libel, slander, and malicious falsehood.

Certain interests are afforded greater protection than others and are deemed so important that compensation may be recovered for their breach even where no actual harm is suffered. These interests are subject to the maxim *injuria sine damno* and their breach is likely to amount to a tort even though no harm is caused. For example, the tort of battery (which seeks to protect our physical safety) can be actionable even though no physical harm has been sustained. But the opposite is also true, with some interests deemed so important that no tortious liability will result even though they cause harm to others. For example, a business that cuts its prices in order to harm a competitor, or even to drive a competitor out of business, will not commit a tort (unless several businesses act in concert to force a competitor out of business, which could constitute the tort of conspiracy).

➡ *injuria sine damno*: 'injury without harm'

 The tort of conspiracy is discussed at p 463

‹› Key points summary

- A tort is a civil wrong, but not all civil wrongs are torts.

- Although tort is a form of civil liability, tortious acts can give rise to both civil and criminal consequences.

- In order to prove the commission of a tort, it is necessary to show that the defendant owed the claimant a duty of care and breached that duty. Whether the duty exists is a question of law. Whether the duty was breached is a question of fact.

- The aims of tort law are:

  - to compensate those who suffer harm;
  - to deter conduct that causes harm; and
  - to protect legitimate interests.

---

9. Road Traffic Act 1988, s 143, makes it a criminal offence to drive on a road without insurance. Employers' Liability (Compulsory Insurance) Act 1969, s 1, provides that every employer must insure his employees against 'liability for bodily injury or disease'.

The tortious duty

As noted, a tortious remedy will lie only if there exists a tortious duty not to cause a particular harm. Liability in tort is similar to liability in contract, in that both are civil cases in which the usual remedy is an award of damages. But there is a notable difference—namely, the source of the duty differs in contract and tort. Under a contract, parties choose to undertake contractual obligations and so the legal duty is largely self-imposed;[10] conversely, tortious duties are imposed upon the parties by the law (that is, common law or statute), although, in some cases, it will be possible for the parties to modify the duty owed (for example, via the use of exclusion or limitation clauses or notices). Figure 11.1 illustrates the two sources of tortious duties and offers several examples.

Basically, all torts derive either from the judiciary (common law) or from Parliament (statute). As society evolves, new forms of harm may arise that require the imposition of new duties and the creation of new torts. It has been argued for some time that the UK requires the creation of a tort of privacy and, whilst it does not yet exist as a recognized tort, tentative steps have been taken by the judiciary to improve individuals' rights to privacy by extending the scope of the **equitable wrong** of **breach of confidence**.

> → **equitable wrong:** breach of a duty created by the courts of equity

> → **breach of confidence:** the unauthorized disclosure and use of confidential information

Just as changes in society may require the creation of new torts, they may also render certain torts out of date and in need of abolition. For example, in the nineteenth century, all men were placed under a statutory duty not to commit adultery with another man's wife[11]—a duty imposed to reflect the notion that a man's 'wife was … regarded by the common law as the property of her husband'[12] and that adultery with a wife therefore constituted an unlawful violation of that property (the tort was quaintly termed 'criminal conversation'). As society came to realize that wives could not be regarded as the property of their husbands, the imposition of this duty became regarded as anachronistic and so the duty was abolished.[13]

Very often, both parties in a tortious case will have legitimate interests that are deserving of protection by the law. In this case, the courts need to determine which interest is protected and which is not. A classic example of competing, legitimate interests is the media's right to free speech (protected by the European Convention on Human Rights, Art 10) and the right to not have one's reputation ruined by the revelation of private information (protected by Art 8). Reconciling these arguably irreconcilable interests has been the main reason for the reluctance of the UK to create a tort of privacy, but the following high-profile case indicates that the courts are willing to protect an individual's reasonable expectations of privacy.

---

10. This is not always the case, because terms may be implied into the contract irrespective of, or even completely against, the wishes of the parties (e.g. the implied terms found in Sale of Goods Act 1979, ss 12–15, which are discussed in the chapter entitled 'The sale of goods', available in the Online Resource Centre).

11. Matrimonial Causes Act 1837, s 33.

12. *Butterworth v Butterworth and Englefield* [1920] P 126, 130 (McCardie J).

13. Law Reform (Miscellaneous Provisions) Act 1970, s 4, provides that damages may not be claimed on the ground of adultery.

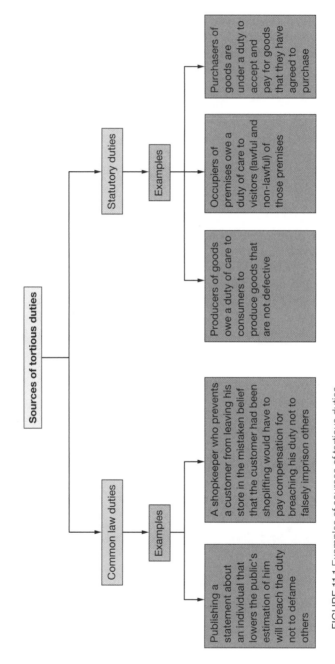

FIGURE 11.1 Examples of sources of tortious duties

Mosley v News Group Newspapers Ltd [2008] EWHC 1777 (QB)

FACTS: The claimant was the president of the Fédération Internationale de l'Automobile (the governing body for Formula One). The defendant was the publisher of the *News of the World*, which had published a story with the headline 'F1 Boss has Sick Nazi Orgy with 5 Hookers' in which it revealed (in lurid detail) that the claimant had engaged in sadomasochistic acts with a group of prostitutes. The claimant sued for breach of confidence and sought damages. The defendant argued that the revelations were in the public interest.

HELD: The claimant succeeded. Eady J stated that the law affords persons a reasonable expectation of privacy, but that such expectations could be overridden where it was in the public interest. Eady J did not believe that the publication of the story was in the public interest and therefore awarded the claimant £60,000 in damages—the highest award to date for a privacy case.

COMMENT: Eady J also held that the sadomasochistic activities of the clamant had no Nazi connotations. As a result of this, the claimant has indicated that he will commence libel proceedings against the defendant.

> ★ See S Foster, 'Balancing Sexual Privacy with the Public Right to Know: The Decision in *Mosley v MGN*' (2008) 172 JPN 627

Historically, legitimate tortious duties have been denied on the ground of public policy—notably in cases against public authorities, which received blanket immunities from prosecution. With the passing of the Human Rights Act 1998, many of these blanket immunities have started to be removed. But even where the 1998 Act has no effect, policy reasons change constantly, resulting in new immunities being created and old immunities abolished. For example, it used to be the case that barristers owed no duty of care to their clients in negligence on public policy grounds, because allowing clients to sue their barristers would, in effect, result in the reopening of their original case.[14] Changes in the laws relating to negligence and the administration of justice have resulted in this immunity being abolished.[15]

But immunities still do exist. For example, because of the rebuttable presumption that statutes do not apply to the Crown, it is still the case that the Crown cannot be made liable under any statute unless such statute expressly or impliedly states that the Crown may be liable.[16]

> 🔗 The presumptions made in relation to the scope of statutes are discussed at p 65

‹› Key points summary

- Tortious duties are imposed upon parties by the law, not by the parties themselves.
- Duties may derive from common law or statute.
- As society evolves, new torts may arise and existing torts may cease to exist.

---

14. *Rondel v Worsely* [1969] 1 AC 191 (HL).
15. *Hall v Simons* [2002] 3 All ER 673 (HL). Interestingly, whilst solicitors and barristers may have had their immunity revoked, the Arbitration Act 1996, s 29, still provides arbitrators with a blanket immunity unless they have acted in bad faith.
16. Crown Proceedings Act 1947, s 40(2)(f).

🔗 Breach of duty
is examined in more
detail at p 408

Breach of duty

Once the court has determined that the defendant owed a tortious duty to the claimant, it must then determine whether that duty was breached, thereby causing the claimant harm. In relation to certain torts, establishing breach of duty may also require establishing a particular state of mind on the part of the defendant. The mental state depends upon the tort in question: some torts require that the defendant was acting negligently; some torts will require proof of a mental element, or a degree of fault higher than negligence. The tort of trespass to land requires an intention to enter the land of another.[17] The tort of malicious falsehood requires that a false statement be made with malice. Those lacking the requisite mental element will not have breached their duty of care.

In some cases, however, no mental element or proof of fault is required—this is known as 'strict liability'. There are numerous examples of statutes that impose strict liability in specific situations, such as the Nuclear Installations Act 1965[18] and the Animals Act 1971.[19] Similarly, the common law can impose strict liability: the tort of defamation is a strict liability tort, because the defendant is not required to know that the statement is defamatory, nor is he required to have intended to refer to the claimant.[20]

The claimant and defendant

Who can sue?

As a general rule, any victim of a tort has a cause of action in respect of the harm caused to him. There are, however, several specific instances in which individuals other than the victim may commence proceedings:

- In respect of harm suffered by a minor, the action will be brought by 'the next friend' (usually the child's parent or guardian). If the harm to the minor is caused before birth, the minor's action is limited to cases in which the alleged tortfeasor was responsible for an event affecting the parent and would have been liable to that parent in tort.[21]

- Except in cases of defamation, the death of a tort victim does not cause the claim to fail.[22] Further, if legal proceedings have not commenced upon the death

---

17. Note that it does not require an intention to trespass. Therefore, even if a defendant did not know that he was trespassing, he will still be liable if he intended to enter the land in question.

18. Nuclear Installations Act 1965, s 7, imposes strict liability on licensees of nuclear installations for damage caused by nuclear matter or the escape of radiation.

19. Animals Act 1971, s 2(1), imposes strict liability for any damage on a keeper of an animal belonging to a dangerous species, unless the keeper satisfies one of the defences in s 5.

20. *Hulton & Co v Jones* [1910] AC 20 (HL). Note, however, that such cases could breach the European Convention on Human Rights, Art 10 (the right to freedom of expression).

21. Congenital Disabilities (Civil Liability) Act 1976, s 1.

22. Law Reform (Miscellaneous Provisions) Act 1934, s 1. There are, however, exceptions to this (e.g. where exemplary damages are sought).

of the victim, the deceased's **personal representatives** have six months from the date of death in which to initiate a claim.[23]

- Where the death of a family member is caused by tort, this can have serious financial implications for the deceased's dependants. Accordingly, the Fatal Accidents Act 1976, s 1, allows the deceased's dependants to initiate a claim against the tortfeasor, provided that, had the deceased lived, he would have had a claim. Additionally, the spouse, civil partner, or parents may bring an additional claim for 'bereavement'. Currently, this figure is fixed by statute at £11,800.[24]

> ➡ personal representative: an administrator or executor whose function it is to settle the affairs of deceased persons

Special mention needs to be made regarding the role of insurance companies in tort cases. In a significant proportion of tort cases, the victim's loss will be recovered by claiming on his insurance policy. For this reason, it has been stated that liability insurance is the 'primary medium for the payment of compensation and tort law [is] a subsidiary part of the process'.[25] This will mean, however, that the victim's insurance provider is bearing the loss resulting from the tortfeasor's actions (although, as we saw when we discussed the aims of tort law, this can be doubted). Therefore, via a long-established[26] process known as **subrogation**, the victim's insurance provider is permitted to take over the legal rights of the policyholder in relation to the claim and initiate proceedings against the tortfeasor to recoup any monies paid out by it to the victim. For this reason, in reality, the claimants in many tort cases are not the victims of the tort, but their insurance companies seeking to recover monies paid out.

> ➡ subrogation: the ability to take on the legal rights of others

Who can be sued?

As a general rule, any tortfeasor is capable of being sued in tort, although there are exceptions. Further, except in the case of defamation, the tortfeasor's death does not prevent the continuance of the action. Problems can arise where a claimant's loss is caused by two or more tortfeasors. In such a situation, there are a number of possible consequences, depending on the nature of the liability involved.

Joint tortfeasors

If two or more persons commit a joint tort, or commit a tort whilst in pursuance of a common design, they will be regarded as 'joint tortfeasors'. In *Brooke v Bool*,[27] Bool had leased a shop to Brooke, but retained the right to enter the premises to ensure that they were secure. Bool was informed by a lodger of the shop that he could smell gas. Whilst investigating, Bool told the lodger to light a match, which caused an

---

23. Limitation Act 1980, s 2. But s 11(5) provides that where the victim's death is the result of personal injury, the limitation period is three years, beginning with the date of death or the date on which the victim's representatives knew of his death.

24. Fatal Accidents Act 1976, s 1A(3).

25. P Cane, *Atiyah's Accidents, Compensation and the Law* (6th edn, Cambridge University Press, Cambridge, 1999) 191.

26. As far back as 1782, subrogation was a common occurrence: see *Mason v Sainsbury* (1782) 3 Doug KB 61, 64, in which Lord Mansfield states that '[e]very day the insurer is put into the shoes of the assured'.

27. *Brooke v Bool* [1928] 2 KB 578 (KB).

explosion. The court held that the lodger and Bool were engaged in a concerted enterprise, and so were jointly liable.

In the case of joint tortfeasors, all tortfeasors are jointly and severally liable. This gives the claimant several options. He may elect to sue some (or all) of the tortfeasors in a joint action. He may also elect to claim the entire value of the loss from one tortfeasor (usually the tortfeasor with the most money, or the one who is covered by insurance). At common law, it was the case that the tortfeasor proceeded against could not, in the absence of an express agreement, recover an indemnity or contribution from the other tortfeasors. Statute has now reversed this and the Civil Liability (Contribution) Act 1978, s 1, allows a tortfeasor to obtain a contribution from his fellow tortfeasors in respect of the 'same damage'.[28] Section 2 provides that the amount of the contribution will be 'just and equitable having regard to the extent of that person's responsibility for the damage in question'.

The following case provides a straightforward example of s 2 in practice.

 Fitzgerald v Lane [1988] 2 All ER 961 (HL)

FACTS: The claimant stepped into traffic at a busy road. He was struck by a car being negligently driven by the first defendant, which knocked him into the path of a car being driven negligently by the second defendant.

HELD: The House of Lords held that the defendants were both liable and total damages were assessed at £596,553. The House then had to decide how to apportion liability. The House held that the claimant was 50 per cent to blame by stepping into the traffic, leaving the two defendants jointly 50 per cent to blame. The House held that, as between the two defendants, both were equally to blame and ordered each of them to contribute £149,138 (25 per cent of the total loss).

Several concurrent tortfeasors

Two or more persons may inflict the same damage upon the claimant, but through independent actions. For example, two separate newspapers may publish a defamatory statement about an individual. In such a case, the tortfeasors will be known as 'several concurrent tortfeasors'. As with joint tortfeasors, liability is joint and several.

Separate or independent tortfeasors

Finally, two or more tortfeasors may independently cause different damage to the same claimant. In such a case, the tortfeasor's liability is limited to the damage caused by his own tortious act and liability is not joint.

---

28. It should be noted that this principle is not limited to tort cases, but can also apply to other civil wrongs, such as breach of contract.

Key points summary

- Once the claimant has established that the defendant owed him a duty of care, he will need to establish that the defendant breached that duty.

- Some torts can be established via negligent acts; others may require a higher degree of fault or an intention to commit the tort. Some torts impose strict liability and require no proof of fault.

- Generally, only victims of the defendant's tort may sue—but exceptions exist where the harm is suffered by a minor, or the victim of the tort dies.

- Two persons who commit a joint tort, or commit a tort whilst engaged in a common design, are known as 'joint tortfeasors', and are jointly and severally liable. Where two persons are acting independently, but cause the same damage, they are known as 'concurrent tortfeasors', and are jointly and severally liable. Where different forms of damage are created by two or more tortfeasors, each is liable for the damage caused by his act.

Tort and human rights

Prior to October 2000, the impact of the European Convention on Human Rights on UK citizens was limited in the sense that those who believed their human rights had been infringed could only obtain a remedy by taking their case to the European Court of Human Rights in Strasbourg—a costly and time-consuming process. On 2 October 2000, this changed, with the coming into force of the Human Rights Act 1998, which provides that most of the rights contained in the Convention can now be enforced directly in a domestic court.

Section 6 of the Act (which, in relation to tort, is probably the most significant provision) provides that '[i]t is unlawful for a public authority to act in a way which is incompatible with a Convention right'. Therefore, if any public body infringes an individual's human rights, the individual may bring a claim against that public body and obtain, at the court's discretion, a remedy that is 'just and appropriate', including damages.[29] Already, we have seen tortious cases succeeding under the Human Rights Act 1998, s 6, that would have probably failed prior to the Act's commencement.

The Human Rights Act 1998, s 6, is discussed in more detail at p 122

D v East Berkshire Community NHS Trust [2003] EWCA Civ 1151

FACTS: The defendant NHS Trust made accusations of child abuse against a number of parents. The motivation behind the accusations was the protection of the children. The accusations turned out to be untrue. The parents and one of the children suffered psychiatric harm as a result of the accusations, and so initiated a claim against the

---

29. Human Rights Act 1998, s 8(1).

defendant in negligence. The court at first instance dismissed the claims, because there existed a House of Lords' case that held that the imposition of a duty of care on the Trust in these circumstances was not fair, just, and reasonable.[30] The claimants appealed to the Court of Appeal.

HELD: The Court of Appeal dismissed the parent's claims,[31] but it upheld the claim of the child. Lord Phillips stated that the previous House of Lords' case 'cannot survive the Human Rights Act [1998]'.[32] Section 6 made it unlawful for public authorities to act in a manner that is inconsistent with the Convention. Because the defendant's acts had breached the child's Convention rights, the child was entitled to a remedy.

COMMENT: This case clearly demonstrates the impact of the 1998 Act. Here, the Court of Appeal declined to follow a House of Lords' decision on the ground that it was incompatible with the Human Rights Act 1998.

★ See P Case, 'The Accused Strikes Back: The Negligence Action and Erroneous Allegations of Child Abuse' (2005) 21 PN 214

But s 6 goes further than this. Section 6(3) states that a definition of a 'public authority' also includes courts and tribunals. Therefore, these bodies are also under a duty to act in a manner that is compatible with the Convention and, if they fail to do so, a victim might be able to obtain a remedy. As regards infringements of the Convention committed by courts and tribunals, however, the available remedies are limited. In particular, s 9(3) provides that 'in respect of a judicial act done in good faith, damages may not be awarded otherwise than to compensate a person to the extent required by Article 5(5) of the Convention'. Article 5(5) relates to a person's ability to claim compensation for arrest or detention that contravenes the Convention.

Chapter conclusion

The issues discussed in this chapter were designed simply to provide an introduction to a number of aims and concepts that occur throughout the law of torts. In subsequent chapters, much that is discussed in this chapter is expanded upon greatly. For example, when we discuss tortious remedies in Chapter 15, the aims of compensation and deterrence are very much in evidence.

In the next chapter, we will discuss the most important tort of all—namely, the tort of negligence—in relation to which the concepts of duty of care and breach of duty, briefly discussed in this chapter, are of fundamental importance.

Self-test questions

1. How do torts differ from other wrongful acts?

2. What are the aims of tort law?

---

30. *X v Bedfordshire County Council* [1995] 2 AC 633 (HL).
31. The parents appealed to the House of Lords, but their appeal was dismissed: [2005] UKHL 23, [2005] 2 AC 373.
32. *D v East Berkshire Community NHS Trust* [2003] EWCA Civ 1151, [2004] QB 558, [83].

3. In the following situations, identify whether the tortfeasors are joint, concurrent, or independent.

   (a) *The Daily Sun* publishes a story accusing a member of Parliament of taking cash from big businesses in return for proposing legislation favourable to big business. The same story is run by *The Daily Post*. The stories are defamatory.

   (b) The board of Microtech plc is about to launch a takeover bid for NanoCorp Ltd. The bid is being handled by Baker & Chance LLP (a firm of solicitors) and Cooper & Young (a firm of accountants). The documentation is drafted based on negligent input from both parties. Consequently, the documentation omits key information and, as a result, the bid cannot go ahead. NanoCorp ends up being taken over by another party.

4. In what circumstances can someone other than the victim make a tortious claim?

5. What does the Human Rights Act 1998, s 6, state and why is it significant in the area of tort?

Further reading

Bermingham, V, and Brennan, C, *Tort Law: Directions* (OUP, Oxford, 2008) chs 1 and 2
A clear and accessible account of what tort is and the operation of the tort system

Buxton, R, 'The Human Rights Act and Private Law' (2000) 116 LQR 48
Examines the nature of the rights provided for under the Human Rights Act 1998 and argues that the Act does not provide rights that can be enforced against private individuals; also examines the controversial case of Osman v UK and argues that the Act does not create a tort of privacy

Lewis, R, 'Insurance and the Tort System' (2005) 25 LS 85
Examines the role of insurance law on the law of torts, and presents the views of judges and academics; argues that insurance is the 'lifeblood of the [tort] system'

Lewis, R, Morris, A, and Oliphant, K, 'Tort Personal Injury Claim Statistics: Is There a Compensation Culture in the UK?' (2006) 2 JPIL 87
Presents and analyses statistics relating to the number and costs of personal injury claims; refutes the claim that the UK has developed a damaging 'compensation culture'

Rogers, WVH, *Winfield & Jolowicz on Tort* (17th edn, Sweet & Maxwell, London, 2006) ch 1
A highly detailed, but readable, account on the nature and functions of the law of torts

Websites

<http://www.dwp.gov.uk/cru/index.asp>
The website of the Compensation Recovery Unit; provides the most accurate statistics in relation to the number of personal injury claims every year

 Remember to visit the **Online Resource Centre** at **<http://www. oxfordtextbooks.co.uk/roach>** to access the following resources for Chapter 11, 'An introduction to the law of torts': more **practice questions** and answers; a **glossary** of key terms; **multiple-choice questions**; **revision summaries**; **audio updates** when relevant; and **diagrams** in pdf.

12 The tort of negligence

- The requirements for negligence
- The duty of care
- Breach of duty
- Causation
- Remoteness

INTRODUCTION

Despite the importance of the tort of negligence, it is of relatively recent origin. Prior to negligence becoming a generally recognized tort in its own right, any wrongs committed against a person or his property were regarded as examples of trespass. Negligence was recognized as a cause of action in specific and highly limited circumstances (for example, innkeepers were under a duty to look after the property of their guests and breaching this duty could amount to negligence). The Industrial Revolution introduced widespread mechanization and a consequent increase in the number of persons injured by emerging inventions. The development of the railway network enabled persons to purchase products from manufacturers hundreds of miles away, thereby increasing the scope of damage that could be caused by defective products. The welfare state or insurance markets of today did not exist, so the only way for claimants to obtain redress for their losses was to commence legal proceedings. The recognition of negligence became a method of transferring loss from injured claimants to negligent defendants — but there still did not exist a unified, generally recognized, tort of negligence. Then, in 1928, in a cafe just outside Glasgow, a woman found a snail in her bottle of ginger beer, and the resulting litigation[1] established the modern tort of negligence and radically altered the English system of tort law forever.

Since 1932, the tort of negligence has expanded rapidly to become easily the most important and frequently occurring tort in the English legal system. Further, it is not only a tort in its own right, but is also a method of committing other torts (for example, the negligent use of land can result in the commission of the tort of nuisance).

→ nuisance: the unreasonable interference with the use or enjoyment of another person's land (see p 475)

The requirements for negligence

Negligence can be defined as 'a breach of a legal duty to take care which results in damage to the claimant'.[2] Within this simple definition exist the four requirements that must be proven by the claimant, as follows.

---

1. *Donoghue v Stevenson* [1932] AC 562 (HL).
2. WVH Rogers, *Winfield & Jolowicz on Tort* (17th edn, Sweet & Maxwell, London, 2006) 132.

1. The defendant must owe the claimant a duty of care.
2. The defendant must have breached that duty.
3. The defendant's breach of duty must cause the claimant loss (negligence cannot exist where loss is not sustained).
4. The loss must not be too remote.

Each of these four requirements will now be discussed in detail.

The duty of care

One aim of the law of negligence is to impose limits upon our liability to other persons. If we were to be liable to anyone who was affected by any act of carelessness in which we may engage, this would impose an intolerable burden on our personal freedom, not to mention subject us to excessive and unpredictable liability. Accordingly, the law imposes a number of what Mullis and Oliphant term 'control devices',[3] which serve to limit the extent of our liability for negligence. The most important control device is the requirement that the claimant will need to establish that the defendant owed him a duty of care. A motorist will owe a duty of care to passing pedestrians, but he will not owe a duty of care to somebody working in the twenty-fifth floor of an office block that he happens to drive by. In other words, we do not owe a duty of care to the world, but only to those classes of persons that the court deems to be deserving of protection.

It should be stated that, in many cases, the establishment of a duty of care is actually not needed, since once the court has determined that a duty of care exists in a particular relationship, a duty will be presumed to exist in all subsequent similar cases. Returning to the example mentioned above, it is settled law that motorists owe pedestrians a duty of care. Accordingly, a pedestrian who is injured due to the negligent driving of the defendant motorist will not need to establish the existence of a duty of care. Other examples of established duties include:

- the duty of care that manufacturers of products owe to the ultimate users of their products;[4]
- the duty that employers have to take reasonable care of their employees' safety;[5]
- the duty of care that parents owe to their children to take reasonable care of them;
- the duty of care that providers of a service (for example, carpenters, solicitors, accountants) owe to the recipient of that service to exercise reasonable skill and care in its performance.

The 'neighbour' test

The starting point for any discussion of the duty of care is the case that established the modern tort of negligence, as follows.

---

3. A Mullis and K Oliphant, *Torts* (3rd edn, Palgrave, Basingstoke, 2003) 12–13.
4. *Donoghue v Stevenson* [1932] AC 562 (HL).
5. Health and Safety at Work etc. Act 1974, s 2(1) and (2).

⚷ Donoghue v Stevenson [1932] AC 562 (HL)

FACTS: The claimant and her friend entered a cafe. The claimant's friend purchased a bottle of ginger beer. The ginger beer was in an opaque bottle. The claimant poured half of the bottle's contents into a glass and drank it. When she proceeded to pour the remaining ginger beer into the glass, the remains of a decomposed snail fell out. The claimant suffered from shock at the sight of the snail and gastroenteritis as a result of consuming the contaminated ginger beer. The claimant could not sue the cafe owner, because she had no contractual relationship with him (her friend bought the ginger beer). Accordingly, the claimant sued the manufacturers of the ginger beer.

HELD: By a majority of three to two, the House of Lords held that the defendant owed the claimant a duty of care. Manufacturers owed a duty of care to users of their products and this duty was breached. Lord Atkin stated:

> The rule that you are to love your neighbour becomes in law, you must not injure your neighbour; and the lawyer's question, Who is my neighbour? receives a restricted reply. You must take reasonable care to avoid acts or omissions which you can reasonably foresee would be likely to injure your neighbour. Who, then, in law, is my neighbour? The answer seems to be persons who are so closely and directly affected by my act that I ought reasonably to have them in contemplation as being so affected when I am directing my mind to the acts or omissions which are called in question.[6]

The neighbour test was only the first part of a two-part test. The second part of the test required that there should be a close and direct relationship of proximity between the person causing the harm and the person who suffers injury. Again, quoting Lord Atkin:

> I think that this sufficiently states the truth if proximity be not confined to mere physical proximity, but be used ... to extend to such close and direct relations that the act complained of directly affects a person whom the person alleged to be bound to take care would know would be directly affected by his careless acts.[7]

Donoghue v Stevenson was a revolutionary decision for several reasons, as follows.

⚷ Privity of contract is discussed at p 143

- It established the independence of tort from contract and created a tortious cause of action in situations in which the doctrine of privity of contract would bar a contractual action. This doctrine basically states that rights and obligations only arise between the parties to the contract. Because Mrs Donoghue's friend purchased the ginger beer, privity of contract would prohibit Mrs Donoghue from making a contractual claim. Related to this, the case also eliminated the 'privity fallacy'. This basically stated that where a defendant was liable to the claimant for breach of contract, he could not be liable to a third party for any torts resulting from the breach.[8]

⚷ The 'narrow rule' of *Donoghue v Stevenson* is discussed at p 445

- It established that manufacturers of goods owe a duty of care to the ultimate users of those goods. This is undoubtedly the *ratio* of the case, but because it is considerably narrower than Lord Atkin's neighbour test, it is known as the 'narrow rule' of *Donoghue v Stevenson*.

---

6. *Donoghue v Stevenson* [1932] AC 562 (HL) 580.   7. Ibid, 581.
8. *Winterbottom v Wright* (1842) 10 M & W 109.

- Although attempts had been made prior to *Donoghue* to devise a general test for the determination of negligence liability, they were never fully accepted.[9] Whilst Lord Atkin's test can be criticized, there is little doubt that it provided the foundations for the modern law of negligence.

The neighbour test evolves

Lord Atkin's neighbour test, perhaps the most quoted judgment in *Donoghue*, was obviously far wider than was necessary for the purposes of determining the case and, as such, was only *obiter*. It is interesting that such a bedrock of the modern tort of negligence could be born from a statement that never formed part of the case's *ratio*. Given this, it may be the case that the greater reliance was placed upon the neighbour test that was intended by Lord Atkin and that 'it is probable that Lord Atkin never intended it to be an exact or comprehensive statement of law'.[10] Further, the test suffered from a number of problems, as follows.

- Lord Atkin's test refers to 'acts or omissions', yet it is generally recognized that the law of tort does not normally impose liability for negligent omissions, although, as we shall see later in the chapter, there are exceptions to this rule.

The law relating to omissions is discussed at p 391

- The test is somewhat vague. It does not indicate to what types of damage the test applied. For this reason, subsequent courts were extremely reluctant to apply it to situations in which a duty of care had been previously denied (for example, negligent statements).

Given that it could be argued that Lord Atkin's test 'had been called upon to bear a weight…manifestly greater than it could support',[11] it therefore came as little surprise when subsequent courts attempted to reformulate the test. The most ambitious and optimistic reformulation came in the following case, but, as we will see, the reformulation was severely criticized and subsequently overruled.

Anns v Merton LBC [1978] AC 728 (HL)

FACTS: The facts are not directly relevant.

HELD: Lord Wilberforce established a new two-stage test to determine whether or not a duty of care existed. He stated:

> [T]he question has to be approached in two stages. First one has to ask whether, as between the alleged wrongdoer and the person who has suffered damage there is a sufficient relationship of proximity or neighbourhood such that, in the reasonable contemplation of the former, carelessness on his part may be likely to cause damage to the latter—in which case a prima facie duty of care arises. Secondly, if the first question is answered affirmatively, it is necessary to consider whether there are any considerations which ought to negative, or to reduce or limit the scope of the duty or the class of person to whom it is owed or the damages to which a breach of it may give rise.[12]

---

9. The most notable example being Brett MR's formulation in *Heaven v Pender* (1883) 11 QBD 503 (CA) 509.

10. J Murphy, *Street on Torts* (12th edn, OUP, Oxford, 2007) 25.

11. RVF Heuston, 'Donoghue v Stevenson in Retrospect' (1957) 20 MLR 1, 23.

12. *Anns v Merton LBC* [1978] AC 728 (HL) 751, 752.

COMMENT: Lord Wilberforce's test had a number of effects. Firstly, Lord Atkin's test, which previously applied in a number of specific areas, was expanded to have universal application. The result was that negligence liability expanded in unpredictable and uncontrollable ways.

Secondly, the test abolished proximity as a separate requirement and made it part of the neighbour test. It has been argued that this downplayed the importance of proximity and could lead to the court ignoring key policy considerations that would not have been ignored had proximity been retained as a separate requirement.[13]

Thirdly, prior to *Anns*, policy reasons were used to justify an expansion of liability. Following *Anns*, liability could be expanded unless there was a policy reason for not doing so. But the courts were extremely reluctant to let policy restrict the scope of liability. As a result, Lord Wilberforce's test was much easier to satisfy than that of Lord Atkin.

The effect of *Anns* was to increase greatly the number of successful negligence actions and dramatically expand the scope of negligence liability, and it succeeded in doing so. The neighbour test, which originally only applied to physical injury, was expanded to cover economic loss[14] and psychiatric injury.[15] The courts greatly expanded the categories of established duties and even created duties that previous courts had denied.

The modern duty of care

Come the mid-1980s, however, concerns were starting to be expressed regarding the breadth of the test in *Anns*, and the courts started to retreat from Lord Wilberforce's universal test and instead started advocating a more incremental approach. Eventually, in the following case, the House of Lords overtly stated that Lord Wilberforce's test in *Anns* was no longer to be used and established a new approach, which forms the current basis for determining the existence of a duty of care.

 Caparo Industries plc v Dickman **[1990] 2 AC 605 (HL)**

FACTS: The facts are not directly relevant as regards the quotation below. The facts and decision are discussed at p 401.

HELD: Lord Bridge (with whom the other judges agreed) stated:

> [I]n addition to the foreseeability of damage, necessary ingredients in any situation giving rise to a duty of care are that there should exist between the party owing the duty and the party to whom it is owed a relationship characterised by the law as one of 'proximity' or 'neighbourhood' and that the situation should be one in which the court considers it fair, just and reasonable that the law should impose a duty of a given scope upon the one party for the benefit of the other. But it is

---

13. R Kidner, 'Resiling from the *Anns* Principle: The Variable Nature of Proximity in Negligence' (1987) 7 LS 319, 323, 324.

14. *Hedley Byrne & Co Ltd v Heller & Partners Ltd* [1964] AC 465 (HL).

15. *McLoughlin v O'Brian* [1983] 1 AC 410 (HL).

implicit in the passages referred to that the concepts of proximity and fairness embodied in these additional ingredients are not susceptible of any such precise definition as would be necessary to give them utility as practical tests, but amount in effect to little more than convenient labels to attach to the features of different specific situations which, on a detailed examination of all the circumstances, the law recognises pragmatically as giving rise to a duty of care of a given scope. Whilst recognising, of course, the importance of the underlying general principles common to the whole field of negligence, I think the law has now moved in the direction of attaching greater significance to the more traditional categorisation of distinct and recognisable situations as guides to the existence, the scope and the limits of the varied duties of care which the law imposes.[16]

COMMENT: Initially, it would appear that the House in *Caparo* established a three-stage test, involving:

1. foreseeability of damage;

2. proximity; and

3. that the imposition of a duty must be fair, just, and reasonable.

But a closer look reveals that this is not the case. Firstly, Lord Bridge labelled the above elements as 'ingredients', not tests. Accordingly, they are 'not susceptible of any such precise definition as would be necessary to give them utility as practical tests, but amount in effect to little more than convenient labels'[17] that enable the court to articulate why, in that given situation, it has chosen to impose a duty of care.

Secondly, unlike in *Anns*, in which foreseeability was the prime requirement, the three ingredients in *Caparo* have equal status. Accordingly, proximity and policy are resurrected from the subsidiary role that they played under *Anns*.

Thirdly, the House re-emphasized the importance of an incremental approach, whereby cases are decided on a case-by-case basis, having regard to established duties. This will avoid the creation of unpredictable duties; instead, the law of negligence will evolve step by step, 'rather than allowing huge leaps into unknown territory',[18] as was the case under *Anns*.

Despite the above comment, it is almost universally, if incorrectly, believed by both judges and commentators that *Caparo* has established a three-stage test, and it is probably too late to reverse this belief. The three ingredients or tests will now be discussed.

Reasonable foreseeability

Lord Bridge stated that the damage suffered by the claimant must be foreseeable. In practice, this imposes two requirements, as follows.

1. The claimant must be within a class of persons who could foreseeably be damaged by the negligence of the defendant.

---

16. *Caparo Industries plc v Dickman* [1990] 2 AC 605 (HL) 617, 618.
17. Ibid, 618 (Lord Bridge).
18. J Steele, *Tort Law: Text, Cases and Materials* (OUP, Oxford, 2007) 157.

2. The type of damage inflicted must be reasonably foreseeable. (This is also a condition for establishing that the damage suffered was not too remote. The requirements of duty, breach, and causation often overlap this way.)

Turning to the first requirement: a duty will only exist if it can be shown that the claimant was within a class of persons who could foreseeably be harmed by the defendant's negligence.

The following case illustrates this requirement well.

 Haley v London Electricity Board [1965] AC 778 (HL)

FACTS: The defendant was carrying out electrical maintenance and had dug a 60-foot trench along a pavement. To warn passers-by, it had put up a sign and created a makeshift barrier using hammers, pickaxes, and shovels. These measures were sufficient to warn sighted passers-by, but, unfortunately, the claimant was blind. Accordingly, he did not see the makeshift barrier. He tripped over one of the tools and fell into the trench, suffering serious injuries that resulted in him becoming deaf. The defendant denied liability on the ground that, given the low percentage of people who are blind, it was not foreseeable that a blind person would be walking along that street.

HELD: The House of Lords held that the defendant was under a duty to take reasonable care of the safety of all persons who used the pavement. This duty extends to blind persons if it was reasonably foreseeable that blind persons would use the pavement. The fact that blind people constitute a small percentage of the population does not make them unforeseeable. Accordingly, the claimant could recover damages for his injuries.

 See AGS Pollock, 'Negligence: Duty of Care to Blind' (1964) CLJ 189

The second requirement is that the type of damage suffered must be reasonably foreseeable. A tortious act can result in several different types of loss. For example, a motorist negligently mounts the pavement and runs over a pedestrian. Obviously, the pedestrian's physical injuries are foreseeable, but other foreseeable injuries might include damage to any property that the defendant hit, psychiatric injury to those who witnessed the accident, and loss of earnings of those suffering injury. Those losses that are reasonably foreseeable are recoverable. Losses not reasonably foreseeable are not, as the following case demonstrates.

Bourhill v Young [1943] AC 92 (HL)

FACTS: A motorcyclist negligently drove into a motorcar and was killed. The claimant, a pregnant lady standing about 45 feet away, heard the collision, but did not see it, although she did subsequently see a pool of blood on the road. As a result, she suffered nervous shock and a back injury (a month later, her baby was delivered stillborn, but it could not be established that this was due to the back injury or the nervous shock). She claimed damages against the estate of the motorcyclist.

> **HELD:** Her claim failed. It was certainly foreseeable that the negligence of the motorcyclist would result in injury to some people, and a duty of care would be established to those persons. The claimant, however, was outside the foreseeable area of potential danger and so the House of Lords held that she could not recover damages.

Proximity

Under *Caparo*, proximity is once again a separate requirement and, in many cases, it is a decisive one. But despite the independence of the test, it cannot be denied that there is a strong connection between foreseeability and proximity, and, in many cases, the establishment of one will establish the other. In *Bourhill v Young* (discussed above), the injuries sustained to the claimant were not foreseeable, because she was not within the potential area of danger—that is, she was not sufficiently proximate.

'Proximity', in a legal sense, does not simply refer to closeness in terms of distance or time. For example, in the following case, proximity referred to the nature of the relationship between the parties.

 Goodwill v British Pregnancy Advisory Service [1996] 1 WLR 1397 (CA)

FACTS: The defendant performed a vasectomy on MacKinlay. He was told that the operation was successful and that he was permanently sterile. Three years later, he entered into a relationship with Goodwill (the claimant). Knowing that MacKinlay was sterile, the couple did not use contraception. MacKinlay's vasectomy reversed itself and the claimant became pregnant, eventually giving birth to a healthy daughter. She claimed damages from the defendant for the costs of raising her daughter. The defendant argued that her claim should be stricken out as frivolous or vexatious.

HELD: Her claim failed and was struck out by the Court of Appeal. The relationship between the defendant and the claimant was not sufficiently proximate to establish the existence of a duty of care. It was suggested, *obiter*, that had the claimant been MacKinlay's wife or partner at the time of the vasectomy and had the doctor known that the operation was to confer a benefit on both of them, then the result might have been different. But the claimant was not his wife or partner; she was merely part of an indeterminate class of persons—namely, women with whom MacKinlay might have sex in the future.

COMMENT: This case also demonstrates that proximity may not exist even where foreseeability is present. Doctors are aware that vasectomies can spontaneously reverse themselves, so whilst such an event was unlikely, it was foreseeable.

In some cases, proximity will be a greater determining factor than in others. In cases in which the defendant negligently and directly inflicts physical injury on the claimant, proximity is not likely to be a major issue. Conversely, in other cases, proximity will be a central issue. For example, a professional who provides negligent advice could foreseeably cause economic damage to a wide number of people. In such a case, the courts are likely to use proximity to limit the number of potential claimants.

Yuen Kun Yeu v A-G of Hong Kong [1988] AC 175 (PC)

FACTS: The defendant was the Attorney General of Hong Kong, who was sued as representing the Commissioner of Deposit-taking Companies in Hong Kong. The Commissioner's role was to determine which companies should be registered on the register of deposit-taking companies. If a company was deemed unfit, he should refuse or revoke registration. The claimant had deposited money with a registered company, which went into liquidation, largely because it was run in a fraudulent manner. The claimant argued that, by registering the company, the Commissioner had represented that the company was fit to receive funds.

HELD: The Privy Council held that the Commissioner owed no duty of care to the claimant. The loss suffered might have been reasonably foreseeable, in that the Commissioner could foresee that the continued registration of an uncreditworthy company might lead to the loss of investors' money, but an unspecified group of potential investors could not be regarded as sufficiently proximate in the circumstances.

There is an extremely strong relationship between proximity and policy. In a number of cases, the courts have given effect to policy concerns by holding that a particular relationship is insufficiently proximate. We will discuss a number of examples in the following sections, but the following case clearly demonstrates how the requirement of proximity can be used to reflect policy concerns.

Hill v Chief Constable of West Yorkshire [1989] AC 53 (HL)

FACTS: The claimant's daughter was the final victim of Peter Sutcliffe—a serial killer known as the 'Yorkshire Ripper', who was convicted of murdering thirteen women between 1975 and 1980. The claimant argued that the police had been negligent in their investigations and that, had they not been negligent, they would have apprehended Sutcliffe before he could have murdered their daughter.

HELD: The House of Lords struck out the claim. Although it was reasonably foreseeable that, if Sutcliffe were not caught, he would continue to murder women, there was nothing to indicate that the claimant's daughter was especially at risk. Accordingly, the relationship between her and the police lacked proximity. Although this argument was enough to deal with the case, the House went on to state that, as a matter of public policy, imposing a duty on the police to catch criminals would be undesirable in so much as it could 'lead to the exercise of a function being carried on in a detrimentally defensive frame of mind'.[19] Therefore, the House stated that the police were immune from negligence actions when investigating or suppressing crime.

---

19. *Hill v Chief Constable of West Yorkshire* [1989] AC 53 (HL) 63 (Lord Keith). In legal jargon, this has become known as 'overkill'.

> **COMMENT:** Subsequent decisions extended the police's immunity to other functions, including the inspection of crime scenes[20] and the dispersal of violent protesters.[21] As we shall see later, however, this immunity came into question following the passing of the Human Rights Act 1998: in particular, claimants alleged that such immunity was not compatible with the right to a fair trial under the European Convention on Human Rights, Art 6.

Fairness, justice, and reasonableness

The court will only impose a duty where it is fair, just, and reasonable to do so. Like the requirement of proximity, policy plays a significant role, but it appears that, in relation to the third requirement of the *Caparo* test, policy considerations are less established and more ad hoc. As Lunney and Oliphant state:

> Whereas the tendency is to use proximity as the heading for relatively well-settled rules limiting liability for certain types of loss, ... the third stage of the *Caparo* approach can be regarded as the general repository for the miscellaneous set of policy arguments, undefined in nature and unlimited in number, which are invoked haphazardly and in an ad hoc fashion by the courts in determining whether a duty of care should arise.[22]

The requirement of fairness, justice, and reasonableness can be used by the courts in one of two ways:

- to deny the existence of a duty of care (even where the claimant has established foreseeability and proximity); or
- to argue that a new duty should be created, or an existing duty extended.

The following two cases show this in action. In the first case, the courts used conceptions of fairness and justice to deny the existence of a duty; in the second case, these justifications were used to establish a duty.

Marc Rich & Co v Bishop Rock Marine Co Ltd [1996] AC 211 (HL)

FACTS: The defendant was the owner of a ship transporting the claimant's cargo. En route, the ship's hull developed a crack, so the ship anchored in Puerto Rico. The ship's classification society, NKK, sent a surveyor to assess the damage. The surveyor allowed the ship to set off after making temporary repairs. A few days later, the ship sank and the claimant's cargo was lost. The claimant sued the shipowners and the case was settled for US$500,000. But the value of the cargo was over US$6 million, so the claimant sued NKK for the remainder.

HELD: The claimant successfully established the requisite foreseeability and proximity. But the House of Lords held that, in the interests of fairness and justice, a duty of care should not be imposed. Classification societies such as NKK are independent, non-profit-making

---

20. *Alexandrou v Oxford* [1993] 4 All ER 328 (CA).

21. *Hughes v National Union of Mineworkers* [1991] 4 All ER 278 (QB).

22. M Lunney and K Oliphant, *Tort Law: Text and Materials* (3rd edn, OUP, Oxford, 2008) 143.

★ See M Wood and DH Reisner, 'No Duty of Care Owed by Classification Societies' (1996) 4 Int ILR 30

organizations, the sole purpose of which is to promote the collective welfare of ships and mariners. If a duty were to be imposed, the survival of these classification societies might be jeopardized, and without these societies' classifications, ships would be almost impossible to insure. Accordingly, NKK was not liable for the remaining damages.

 ### *Arthur JS Hall & Co v Simons* [2002] 1 AC 615 (HL)

FACTS: Three claimants were alleging negligence against their former solicitors. The claimants argued that a rule established in 1969,[23] which provided that advocates would enjoy immunity from negligence actions, should be overruled.

HELD: The House of Lords unanimously ruled that advocate immunity should be abolished in civil cases and a majority of four to three ruled that it should be abolished in criminal cases. Accordingly, advocates will now owe their clients a duty of care. The reasons for the creation of this new duty were largely driven by considerations of fairness and justice. The House stated that the policy considerations that first justified the immunity were no longer present and that therefore, from a policy point of view, the immunity could not be justified. Lord Steyn argued that other professionals do not enjoy an immunity from negligence claims, so why should advocates?

COMMENT: This was not simply a case of using fairness and justice to create a new duty of care. The House actually created a duty, even though a previous House of Lords had specifically stated that a duty should not exist. The result is that solicitors and barristers are no longer immune to negligence claims. Judges are, however, still immune. Accordingly, a judge who decides a case in a negligent manner (for example, by not reading the case notes or evidence properly) cannot be sued.[24] Witness also have immunity and cannot be proceeded against if their testimony is negligent.[25]

 ## Key points summary

- The current test to establish duty of care requires:
  - foreseeability of damage;
  - proximity; and
  - that the imposition of a duty must be just, fair, and reasonable.
- Reasonable foreseeability requires that:
  - the claimant was within a class of persons who could foreseeably be damaged; and
  - the type of damage must be reasonably foreseeable.
- Proximity can refer to time and space, but it may also refer to the relationship between the parties.

---

23. *Rondel v Worsley* [1969] 1 AC 191 (HL) granted this immunity in relation to presenting their client's case in court. *Saif Ali v Sidney Mitchell & Co* [1980] AC 198 (HL) extended the immunity to cover pre-trial work.

24. See A Nicol, 'Judicial Immunity and Human Rights' (2006) 5 EHRLR 558, who argues that absolute judicial immunity should be abolished.

25. *Hinds v Liverpool County Court* [2008] EWHC 665 (QB), [2008] 2 FLR 63.

Problematic areas

Now that we have discussed the duty of care in a general sense, we will move on to examine a number of specific instances in which the courts have had difficulty in determining whether or not a duty of care should be imposed.

Omissions

The majority of negligence cases concern some form of negligent act that has caused the claimant to suffer loss. But is it possible to be liable in negligence for failing to perform an act (that is, an omission)? In *Donoghue v Stevenson*,[26] Lord Atkin stated: 'You must take reasonable care to avoid acts or omissions which you can reasonably foresee would be likely to injure your neighbour.'[27] Despite this, it generally regarded that 'the common law does not impose liability for what are called pure omissions'.[28] Accordingly, if you witness a car accident, you are under no obligation to provide aid, or if you see a person being attacked, you are under no obligation to help the victim to fight off their attackers. The general method of expressing this is that the law does not require people to be good Samaritans. Referring to the biblical parable, Lord Diplock stated that the priest and the Levite who walked on the other side would not incur civil liability under English law.[29] The question arising is why the law does not impose liability on those who fail to prevent harm.

Several potential answers were provided by Lord Hoffmann in *Stovin v Wise*,[30] in which he stated that the justifications for the rule could be expressed in political, moral, and economic terms:

> In political terms it is less of an invasion of an individual's freedom for the law to require him to consider the safety of others in his actions than to impose upon him a duty to rescue or protect. A moral version of this point may be called the 'why pick on me?' argument. A duty to prevent harm to others or to render assistance to a person in danger or distress may apply to a large and indeterminate class of people who happen to be able to do something. Why should one be held liable rather than another? In economic terms, the efficient allocation of resources usually requires an activity should bear its own costs. If it benefits from being able to impose some of its costs on other people...the market is distorted because the activity appears cheaper than it really is....Except in special cases (such as marine salvage) English law does not reward someone who voluntarily confers a benefit on another. So there must be some special reason why he should have to put his hand in his pocket.[31]

The following case provides an example of the general rule in practice.

---

26. *Donoghue v Stevenson* [1932] AC 562 (HL).   27. Ibid, 580.

28. *Smith v Littlewoods Organisation Ltd* [1987] 2 AC 241 (HL) 271 (Lord Goff).

29. *Home Office v Dorset Yacht Co Ltd* [1970] AC 1004 (HL) 1060.   30. *Stovin v Wise* [1996] AC 923 (HL).

31. Ibid, 943–4.

> ## 🔑 *Sutradhar v National Environmental Research Council* [2006] UKHL 33
>
> **FACTS:** The British Geological Survey (BGS, a department of the defendant organization) was testing water samples in Bangladesh. The tests employed were designed to test for the presence of a number of toxic substances, but they would not indicate if arsenic was present in the water. The report published based on the tests did not, however, state that arsenic was not tested for. The claimant drank water that had been tested and subsequently developed arsenic poisoning. He alleged that the BGS had breached its duty to test for arsenic.
>
> **HELD:** The House of Lords dismissed the claimant's action, with Lord Hoffman describing it as 'hopeless'.[32] He later stated that the BGS 'can be liable only for the things they did and the statements they made, not for what they did not do'.[33]

In practice, distinguishing between acts and omissions may not be easy. Bankes LJ provides the example of a 'medical man who diagnoses a case of measles as a case of scarlet fever may be said to have omitted to make a correct diagnosis; he may equally well be said to have made an incorrect diagnosis'.[34] A useful distinction is advanced by Lunney and Oliphant, who contend that a negligent act 'makes things worse', whereas an omission 'fails to make things better'.[35]

The principle is not absolute, however. In *Smith v Littlewoods Organisation Ltd*,[36] Lord Goff provided a number of principles that could be used to determine when a duty of care would be imposed.

- The relationship between the claimant and defendant may give rise to an undertaking or imposition of responsibility to prevent the harm in question (for example, owners of premises owe a duty to the occupiers of those premises and prison authorities owe a duty to take reasonable care of prisoners).[37] One would suppose that certain familial relationships—notably, parent and child—would qualify, but there is no authoritative law on the point.

- A duty may arise based on the relationship between the defendant and a third party, especially where the defendant is responsible for the actions of the third party. In *Carmarthenshire County Council v Lewis*,[38] the defendant council ran a nursery school. A 4-year-old boy ran out of the school and into the road. The claimant's husband swerved to avoid the boy, hit a lamp post, and was killed. The House held that the defendant Council and the teachers had been in control of the boy, and so owed the claimant's husband a duty of care to prevent him from causing harm.

- A duty may arise where the defendant creates, or permits to be created, a source of danger and it is reasonably foreseeable that third parties may interfere

---

32. *Sutradhar v National Environmental Research Council* [2006] UKHL 33, [2006] 4 All ER 490, [2].
33. Ibid, [27].   34. *Harnett v Bond* [1924] 2 KB 517 (HL) 541.
35. M Lunney and K Oliphant, *Tort Law: Text and Materials* (3rd edn, OUP, Oxford, 2008) 464–5.
36. [1987] AC 241 (HL).
37. *Reeves v Commissioner of Police for the Metropolis* [2000] 1 AC 360 (HL).
38. *Carmarthenshire County Council v Lewis* [1955] AC 549 (HL).

with that danger, thereby causing harm. In *Haynes v Harwood*,[39] the defendant's employee left a horse-drawn van unattended in a crowded street. A stone was thrown at the horses and they bolted. The claimant, a police officer, managed to stop the runaway horses, but was injured in doing so. The claimant could recover damages for his injuries from the defendant.

Psychiatric injury

An act of negligence that physically injures the claimant may have associated mental effects. The courts have long held that mental injury consequential upon physical injury is recoverable under the head of damage known as 'pain and suffering'. The courts have not, however, been so forthcoming in relation to acts of negligence that cause psychiatric injury alone. Historically, the courts have been reluctant to impose a duty of care where the claimant's injury has been purely psychiatric, for which three reasons can be advanced, as follows.

1. The courts did not regard psychiatric injury as serious as physical injury.
2. Whereas the extent of a physical injury was readily discernable, psychiatric injury was extremely difficult to diagnose and could be feigned.
3. The courts were concerned that establishing a duty of care to victims of psychiatric injury would flood the courts with claims.

Accordingly, up until the beginning of the twentieth century, the courts were relatively dismissive of such claims for 'nervous shock'.[40] As time progressed, however, the courts' prejudices regarding psychiatric damage began to fade, and they recognized that such damage was 'no less real and frequently no less painful and disabling'[41] than physical injury. Further, modern diagnostic techniques make it increasingly difficult to fake psychological conditions. But the court was still wary and two limitations were introduced, both of which survive today.

- The claimant must suffer from a medically recognized psychiatric condition. Accordingly:

  > Grief, sorrow, deprivation and the necessity for caring for loved ones who have suffered injury or misfortune must…be considered as ordinary and inevitable incidents of life which…must be sustained without compensation.[42]

- The psychological damage must be sustained due to a sudden event, or must arise in the immediate aftermath of a sudden event (this is why such damage was originally termed 'nervous shock'). Accordingly, parents who witness the slow death of their child, who has been injured due to the defendant's negligence, would be unable to obtain damages for any resultant psychological damage that they suffer.[43]

---

39. [1935] 1 KB 146 (CA).

40. In *Attia v British Gas plc* [1988] QB 304 (CA) 318, Bingham LJ dubbed the phrase 'nervous shock' as a 'misleading and inaccurate expression', and instead recommended that the term 'psychiatric damage' be used.

41. *McLoughlin v O'Brian* [1983] AC 410 (HL) 433 (Lord Bridge).

42. *Alcock v Chief Constable of South Yorkshire Police* [1992] 1 AC 310 (HL) 416 (Lord Oliver).

43. *Taylorson v Shieldness Produce Ltd* [1994] PIQR P329 (CA); *Sion v Hampstead Health Authority* [1994] 5 Med LR 170 (CA).

Initially, the courts would only establish a duty of care in relation to 'primary' victims, of which there were two types, as follows.

1. A person who sustains physical injury due to an incident caused by the defendant's negligence can recover damages for his physical injuries and for any psychiatric damage that he might have suffered.

2. Where a person is directly involved, as a participant, in an incident caused by the defendant's negligence and personal injury (whether physical or psychiatric) is foreseeable, then that person can recover damages for psychiatric injuries sustained, even if he did not sustain any physical injuries.[44]

This restrictive approach meant that 'secondary' victims (that is, those who witnessed the defendant's negligence, or were told about it, but did not fear for their physical safety) were unable to claim. This rule was first relaxed when the court established that psychological damage caused to those who witnessed shocking events whilst attempting to rescue others was claimable.

Chadwick v British Railways Board [1967] 1 WLR 912 (QB)

FACTS: Due to the defendant's negligence, ninety people were killed in a train crash. Chadwick lived 200 yards from the scene of the crash and, upon hearing of the accident, he immediately went to help. Being a small man, he was able to negotiate his way into small nooks and administer medical treatment to injured persons, which he did all night. As a result of what he witnessed, he developed what would today be termed post-traumatic stress disorder. Chadwick died before he could initiate a claim (his death was unrelated to the incident above). His wife, as **administratrix** of his estate, initiated a claim against the defendant for the psychiatric damage caused to her late husband.

HELD: A claimant could recover damages even where he was not in fear of his own safety—but it must be reasonably foreseeable that psychological injury could occur. The defendant, by putting the train passengers in danger, could reasonably foresee that people might attempt to help those passengers. It was also reasonably foreseeable that such rescuers might be injured in the process. Accordingly, in such a case, the High Court held that the defendant would owe a duty of care to any rescuers.

COMMENT: This case demonstrates that the line between primary and secondary victims is not always clear. Given that Chadwick was crawling inside damaged train carriages, it could be argued that he was a primary victim, because he doubtless had concerns for his own physical well-being.

➡ administratrix: a female administrator—a person appointed to manage the property of another

In time, the courts expanded the duty to cover those who had witnessed a shocking event, provided that there was a sufficiently proximate relationship both between the witness and the primary victim, and between the witness and the event in question, in terms of time and space.

The foundations for the modern approach were established in the following case.

---

44. *Page v Smith* [1996] 1 AC 155 (HL).

McLoughlin v O'Brian [1983] 1 AC 410 (HL)

FACTS: The claimant's husband and three children were involved in a car accident, due to the negligent driving of the defendant. At the time of the incident, the claimant was at home, some two miles away. Around two hours later, a neighbour told the claimant of the accident and she immediately drove to the local hospital. There, she learned that her youngest daughter had been killed, she saw her husband and another daughter covered in oil and dirt, and she heard her badly injured son screaming. She alleged that witnessing this caused her to become depressed and altered her personality, affecting her abilities as a wife and mother. Both at first instance and on appeal, the courts held that, because she was not a primary victim, the defendant did not owe her a duty of care.

HELD: The House of Lords unanimously held that the defendant owed her a duty of care. The psychological damage suffered by the claimant was a reasonably foreseeable result of the injuries caused to her family by the defendant's negligence. In order to claim, however, the claimant would either need to witness the shocking event or come upon its 'immediate aftermath'. The House held that she had witnessed the immediate aftermath and so could recover damages for her psychiatric injuries.

The modern law on when a duty of care is imposed in relation to cases involving pure psychological injury can be found in the following case, one of many to arise from the Hillsborough disaster.

 Alcock v Chief Constable of the South Yorkshire Police [1992] 1 AC 310 (HL)

FACTS: Hillsborough stadium in Sheffield was to be the venue for a FA Cup semi-final match between Liverpool and Nottingham Forest. The match was sold out, and received extensive television and radio coverage. Many stadia at the time had a wire fence separating the crowd from the pitch. After six minutes, the match was stopped when it became apparent that the police had admitted too many fans into the Liverpool end of the stadium. The weight of numbers resulted in fans being crushed against the wire fences. As a result, ninety-six Liverpool fans died and over 400 were injured. A number of people who witnessed or heard about the disaster suffered psychological damage. A **test case** was brought to determine the extent of the duty of care owed by the negligent police force. Test claimants included witnesses who were present inside the stadium, those who witnessed the events on television, those who heard about the events on the radio, and one claimant who was outside the stadium, but later had to identify the body of a friend at a makeshift mortuary. The test claimants also covered numerous relationships (for example, parents of disaster victims, spouses, friends, etc.). The defendant admitted negligence, but denied owing a duty of care to the test claimants.

➡ **test case:** a case that is brought and the result applied to similar cases that are not litigated

HELD: None of the test claimants were owed a duty of care by the police. The House of Lords laid down an extensive list of requirements that would all need to be met before a duty of care would exist, as follows. Most of these requirements revolve around establishing proximity.

- *Proximity of relationship* The claimant will need to establish sufficiently 'close ties of love and affection'[45] with the person injured or endangered. The House deliberately left open the types of relationship that would qualify, but certain relationships (for example, parent and child, husband and wife, engaged couples) would raise a rebuttable presumption of sufficient closeness. This would appear categorically to conclude that a duty is not owed to bystander, but Lords Keith and Ackner thought that a duty could exist to bystanders who witnessed an accident that was 'particularly horrific'.[46] It has been noted that the problem with this is that 'it is not clear how any "scale of horrors" could be devised'.[47] If the Hillsborough disaster did not qualify, what would?

- *Geographical and temporal proximity* The claimant will need to be sufficiently proximate in both time and space. Directly witnessing or hearing the event will be sufficient, but is not necessary. Coming upon the 'immediate aftermath' of an event will also suffice,[48] but their Lordships refused to define exactly what this meant. In *Alcock*, identifying a body in a morgue nine hours after the disaster did not qualify.[49] Claimants who witnessed the disaster on television were also not sufficiently proximate.

- *Proximity of communication* The event must have been communicated to the claimant in a sufficiently proximate way (that is, he must have directly seen or heard the event or its immediate aftermath). Accordingly, a person who was informed of the event by a third party would lack proximity,[50] as would a person who saw the event on television or read about it in a newspaper. Identifying a body at a mortuary would similarly lack sufficient proximity, but the courts have shown inconsistency here.

- *Foreseeability* The claimant must establish that it was reasonably foreseeable that a person of normal or reasonable fortitude would have suffered psychiatric damage as a result of the event.

- *Shock* The damage caused to the claimant must be caused by shock. A series of gradual events that eventually cause psychological damage will not suffice to establish a duty of care. But this does not mean that the 'shock' must derive from a single disastrous negligent act. For example, the courts held that psychological damage caused by the death of the claimant's son due to a series of negligent acts and medical misdiagnoses over a 36-hour period constituted sufficient 'shock'.[51]

- The primary victim does not owe a duty of care to a secondary victim where the primary victim is injured through his own negligence.[52] Accordingly, a secondary victim cannot sue a primary victim who is contributorily negligent.

---

45. *Alcock v Chief Constable of the South Yorkshire Police* [1992] 1 AC 310 (HL) 397 (Lord Keith).
46. Ibid.
47. M Lunney and K Oliphant, *Tort Law: Text and Materials* (3rd edn, OUP, Oxford, 2008) 346.
48. See, e.g., *Benson v Lee* [1972] VR 879 (a duty was owed to a mother who was told her son was involved in an accident, and ran 100 yards to discover his unconscious body); *Fenn v City of Peterborough* (1976) 73 DLR (3d) 177 (a duty was owed to a claimant who arrived home minutes after a gas explosion killed his children).
49. Contrast *Galli-Atkinson v Seghal* [2003] EWCA Civ 697, [2003] Lloyd's Rep Med 285, in which a duty was established where a father identified his daughter's body in a morgue several hours after a motor accident that caused her death.
50. *Ravenscroft v Rederiaktiebolaget Transatlantic* [1992] 2 All ER 470 (Note) (CA).
51. *North Glamorgan NHS Trust v Walters* [2002] EWCA Civ 1792, [2003] PIQR P16.
52. *Alcock v Chief Constable of the South Yorkshire Police* [1992] 1 AC 310 (HL) 418 (Lord Oliver); *Greatorex v Greatorex* [2000] 1 WLR 1970 (QB).

COMMENT: Given the extensive nature of the above tests, it is hardly surprising that none of the test claimants could pass all of the tests. It is clear that the law treats psychological damage far more strictly than physical damage.

★ See B Lunch, 'A Victory for Pragmatism? Nervous Shock Reconsidered' (1992) 108 LQR 367

There is almost universal dissatisfaction with the current state of the law regarding psychological damage. Todd argues that 'it is not very controversial to assert that the law concerning liability for causing mental injury is in a dreadful mess'.[53] The judiciary seems to have given up on finding a series of workable rules: Lord Hoffmann, in *White v Chief Constable of South Yorkshire Police*,[54] conceded that '[i]t seems to me that in this area of the law, the search for principle was called off'.[55] Opinion regarding the way forward is divided. Some commentators have argued that the restrictive treatment of psychological damage should be abandoned and that it should be regarded as the same as physical injury.[56] Others have gone so far as to argue that the law relating to psychological damage should be abolished completely, on the ground that acceptable boundaries will never be found.[57] In the foreseeable future, it is unlikely that either view will become reality. The Law Commission did propose a statutory duty of care[58] that could be viewed as a compromise between these two extremes, but it was never acted upon. A governmental Consultation Paper, published in May 2007, rejected the Law Commission's proposals and recommended that this area of the law continue to develop through the common law.[59] Based on the above, it appears that neither the courts themselves, nor commentators, share the government's confidence in the ability of the common law effectively to develop sound principles for the recovery of compensation for psychiatric damage.

'Pure' economic loss

Based on the discussion thus far, it can be seen that negligence is largely concerned with compensating victims of physical damage, whether to their person or property. Economic loss is recoverable if it is consequential upon physical damage (for example, loss of earnings due to physical injury, or the costs of repairing damaged property). As a general rule, however, 'pure' economic loss (that is, financial loss unassociated with physical injury or property damage) is not recoverable and the courts enforce this principle by finding that a duty of care does not exist,[60] as demonstrated clearly in the following case.

---

53. S Todd, 'Psychiatric Injury and Rescuers' (1999) 115 LQR 345, 349.
54. [1999] 2 AC 455 (HL).   55. Ibid, 511.
56. For example, P Handford, *Mullaney & Handford's Tort Liability for Psychiatric Damage* (2nd edn, Law Book Co, Ryde, NSW, 2006) [30.40].
57. For example, J Stapledon, 'In Restraint of Tort' in P Birks (ed), *The Frontiers of Liability, Vol 2* (OUP, Oxford, 1994).
58. Law Commission, *Liability for Psychiatric Illness* (Law Com No 249, HMSO, London, 1998).
59. Department of Constitutional Affairs, *The Law on Damages* (CP 9/07, HMSO, London, 2007) [94].
60. *Cattle v Stockton Waterworks Co* (1875) LR 10 QB 453.

Spartan Steel & Alloys Ltd v Martin & Co Ltd [1973] QB 27 (CA)

FACTS: The defendant's employees were carrying out roadworks when they negligently cut a power cable. The cable was the direct supply of electricity to the claimant's factory, which was engaged in the smelting of steel alloys. As a result of the power cut, the claimant suffered three distinct types of damage, as follows.

1. Molten metal could not be kept at the correct temperature and thus became damaged.

2. The damage to the metal meant that it depreciated in value.

3. As a result of the power cut, the claimant could not melt any further metal, resulting in a loss of profit.

HELD: The Court of Appeal held that the claimant could recover in relation to (1), because this constituted physical damage. It could also recover (2), because this loss was consequential upon the physical damage. It could not, however, recover (3), because this loss was purely economic and was not based upon damage to any property.

See JA Jolowicz, 'Negligence: Loss of Profits—Economic Loss' (1973) 32 CLJ 20

The obvious question to ask at this point is why the law protects those who suffer consequential economic loss (that is, loss that is the result of physical injury or property damage), but will not protect those who suffer pure economic loss. Numerous reasons have been advanced, as follows.

- 'The law should provide greater protection to personal safety and health than to purely economic interests.'[61] This argument is certainly true and physical injury should be afforded greater protection than pure economic loss,[62] but that does not mean that pure economic loss should be completely irrecoverable.

- Permitting widespread recovery of pure economic loss would result in indeterminate liability. In *Spartan Steel* above, if the power cable had been connected to a wide geographical area, the extent of the loss would be unpredictable in terms of the number of claimants and the size of potential claims. Conversely, the extent of physical damage will normally be limited and relatively predictable.

- Persons concerned with potential pure economic losses should obtain protection via contract, either by contracting with the potential tortfeasors directly or by taking out insurance against economic loss. Contract is preferable because, as established above, the extent of potential loss is unknown to the tortfeasors, but may be more accurately assessed by the victims.

- Perhaps the most-cited argument is that if pure economic loss were generally recoverable, it would open the 'floodgates', thereby exposing defendants to widespread liability and inundating the courts with claims. It is, however, highly unlikely that this would occur. As we will see later in the chapter, there are

---

61. S Deakin, A Johnston, and B Markesinis, *Markesinis and Deakin's Tort Law* (6th edn, OUP, Oxford, 2008) 158.

62. Compare this with the view of Stevenson J in *Canadian National Railway v Norsk Pacific Steamship Co* (1992) 91 DLR (4th) 289 (Supreme Court of Canada) 383, who states that '[s]ome argue that there is a fundamental distinction between physical damage (personal and property damage) and pure economic loss and that the latter is less worthy of protection…but I am left unconvinced'.

extensive rules relating to causation and remoteness that, in many cases, would substantially limit the liability of a tortfeasor. Further, why do the courts invoke the 'floodgates' argument in relation to pure economic loss, but not invoke it in relation to defective products that could result in unpredictable litigation?

Like many legal principles, the rule that pure economic loss cannot be recovered is not absolute. There exists one major exception to the rule—namely, where the defendant has made a negligent misstatement that causes the claimant pure economic loss, this loss can be recovered. Negligent misstatements will be examined in the next section.

For a time, it did appear that the courts had crafted a second exception—namely, where pure economic loss was caused as a result of defective property. This exception was initially crafted in the case of *Dutton v Bognor Regis Urban District Council*,[63] and confirmed by the House of Lords in *Anns v Merton LBC*[64] and *Junior Books v Veitchi Co Ltd*.[65] But the courts have since moved away from *Anns* (in very much the same way as they did in relation to Lord Wilberforce's two-stage test to establish a duty of care) and *Junior Books* has been confined to its own facts. Subsequent cases reasserted the principle that pure economic loss is not recoverable, even if it consequential upon defective property.[66]

As we shall see, however, the law relating to negligent misstatement has provided the impetus for an expansion in the instances in which pure economic loss can be recovered, although these instances are not so numerous as to jeopardize the general rule that damages are not recoverable for it. These instances are covered under the heading of 'extended' *Hedley Byrne* liability, but before we can discuss these, we need to examine the law relating to negligent misstatements.

Negligent misstatements

Historically, a claimant could only recover damages against a defendant who had committed a negligent act. Losses as a result of negligent statements were not recoverable for two reasons.

1. As noted in the previous section, a negligent act (especially if the damage is physical) will usually result in fairly limited and predictable damage. Conversely, negligent statements may be spoken to, or repeated to, many persons, thereby resulting in unpredictable and indeterminate liability.

2. Negligent statements do not tend to result in physical damage and, as discussed above, the general rule is that damages can only be recovered for physical damage, or loss that is consequential upon physical damage.

The law did acknowledge that certain damaging statements were deserving of compensation (for example, the **tort of deceit** provided the claimant with a remedy in tort if the statement was fraudulent).[67] But prior to 1964, damage caused by negligent statements was irrecoverable. This changed after the following seminal case.

➡ tort of deceit: a false statement made knowingly, or recklessly careless of whether it is true or false, with the intent that another relies on it to his detriment

---

63. [1972] 1 QB 373 (CA).   64. [1978] AC 728 (HL).

65. [1983] 1 AC 520 (HL).

66. *D & F Estates Ltd v Church Commissioners for England* [1989] AC 177 (HL); *Murphy v Brentwood District Council* [1991] 1 AC 398 (HL).

67. *Derry v Peek* (1889) LR 14 App Cas 337 (HL).

Hedley Byrne & Co Ltd v Heller & Partners Ltd [1964] AC 465 (HL)

FACTS: The claimant was an advertising agent. It began to express doubts regarding the financial viability of a client company called Easipower. The claimant therefore asked its bankers to inquire into Easipower's financial status. The claimant's bankers sought this information from the defendant's bankers, who replied that Easipower was a properly constituted company that could be considered good for its normal business engagements (this advice was subject to a disclaimer abdicating responsibility for the advice). Relying on this, the claimant procured advertising space on Easipower's behalf—but the nature of the contract meant that if Easipower failed to pay for the advertising, the claimant would be liable. Easipower subsequently became insolvent and the claimant became liable for Easipower's debt of £17,661. The claimant alleged that the defendant's advice had been negligent and sued accordingly. The defendant argued that, because the loss was purely economic, it did not owe the claimant a duty of care.

HELD: The House of Lords held that the defendant was not liable. The reason for this was that the disclaimer prevented a duty of care from arising. The House also stated *obiter* that the defendant owed the claimant a duty of care, notwithstanding that the loss was purely economic. The House was not, however, prepared to extend the general duty of care (as was determined at the time by *Donoghue v Stevenson*) to cover negligent misstatements. The House instead established a test that was much narrower than Lord Atkin's 'neighbour' test: in addition to satisfying the requirement of reasonable foreseeability, the claimant (the recipient of the statement) also had to demonstrate that there was a 'special relationship' between himself and the defendant (the maker of the statement).

COMMENT: The part of the decision referred to above was *obiter* because, on the facts of the case, the House held that the defendant was not liable. This case was decided prior to the passing of the Unfair Contract Terms Act 1977. If *Hedley Byrne* were to be decided today, it is possible that the disclaimer would be regarded as unreasonable and therefore invalid.[68]

See R Stevens, 'Hedley Byrne v Heller: Judicial Creativity and Doctrinal Possibility' (1964) 27 MLR 121

The requirement of reasonable foreseeability has been examined in depth already. Accordingly, we will focus on the second requirement established in *Hedley Byrne*— namely, that there must be a 'special relationship' between the maker of the statement and the recipient of the statement. Unfortunately, there exists no unanimous or authoritative statement as to what constitutes a 'special relationship', leading the High Court of Australia to comment that '[s]ince the decision in *Hedley Byrne & Co Ltd v Heller & Partners Ltd*, confusion bordering on chaos has reigned in the law of negligence'.[69]

An analysis of the judgments in *Hedley Byrne* reveals that the judges involved could not precisely agree what was needed to establish a special relationship. Lord Morris stated:

> [I]t should now be regarded as settled that if someone possessed of a special skill undertakes, quite irrespective of contract, to apply that skill for the assistance of another person who relies upon such skill, a duty of care will arise.[70]

---

68. See Unfair Contract Terms Act 1977, s 2, and *Smith v Eric S Bush* [1990] 1 AC 831 (HL).
69. *Woolcock Street Investments v CDG Pty Ltd* [2004] HCA 16 (High Court of Australia) [45] (McHugh J.)
70. *Hedley Byrne & Co Ltd v Heller & Partners Ltd* [1964] AC 465 (HL) 502, 503.

It can be seen that Lord Morris laid down two requirements: firstly, the defendant must possess a special skill; secondly, the claimant must reasonably rely upon that skill. But two other members of the House thought that a third requirement was needed—namely, that there must also be 'a voluntary undertaking to assume responsibility'[71] by the defendant. The problem that arises is that these three requirements have not been applied consistently, with subsequent courts even stating that certain requirements are not necessary. Some cases have regarded the requirement of reliance as crucial, while others have completely ignored it. In one case in 1990, Lord Griffiths stated: 'I do not think that voluntary assumption of responsibility is a helpful or realistic test for liability.'[72] Conversely, in a 1995 case, Lord Goff stated: '[A]n assumption of responsibility coupled with reliance by the plaintiff which, in all the circumstances, makes it appropriate that a remedy in law should be available ...'[73] More recently, in 2006, Lord Bingham has stated that 'it is correct to regard an assumption of responsibility as a sufficient but not a necessary condition of liability'.[74]

Given this confusion, it is hardly surprising that an examination of the cases reveals a very real lack of consistency. For example, in *Mutual Life and Citizens' Assurance Co Ltd v Evatt*,[75] Lord Diplock stated that 'there is, in general, no duty to take care imposed on an adviser who is not acting in the course of his business or professional activities'.[76] But in *Chaudhry v Prabhakar*,[77] the Court of Appeal imposed liability on a young man who gave advice to his friend regarding which car to buy. The defendant was not an expert on motor cars (although he considered himself to be) and was not acting in any form of professional or business capacity; his advice was free and was given simply to help a friend, yet his advice resulted in him having to pay over £5,500 in damages to that friend.

Given these inconsistencies, subsequent cases have attempted to specify more accurately what is required to establish a special relationship. We have already noted that the following case established the modern test for the establishment of a duty of care, but it also laid down specific guidance on what a claimant would need to establish in order to recover pure economic loss.

 ## Caparo Industries plc v Dickman [1990] 2 AC 605 (HL)

FACTS: The claimant (Caparo) was considering initiating a takeover bid of a company called Fidelity plc. Before making the bid, Caparo scrutinized Fidelity's annual accounts, which had been prepared for Fidelity by the defendant firm of auditors, Touche Ross. The accounts indicated that Fidelity's pre-tax profits were £1.2 million, and, on this basis, the claimant purchased further shares and took the company over. The claimant then discovered that the accounts were inaccurate and that Fidelity was actually running at a loss of £400,000. It also appeared that a number of Fidelity's directors were engaging in

---

71. Ibid, 529 (Lord Devlin). See also [1964] AC 465 (HL) 486 (Lord Reid).

72. *Smith v Eric S Bush* [1990] 1 AC 831 (HL) 862.

73. *Henderson v Merrett Syndicates Ltd* [1995] 2 AC 145 (HL) 186, 187.

74. *Customs and Excise Commissioners v Barclays Bank plc* [2006] UKHL 28, [2007] 1 AC 181, [4].

75. [1971] AC 793 (PC).   76. Ibid, 813.   77. [1989] 1 WLR 29 (CA).

fraudulent activities. Caparo sued Touche Ross, alleging that the auditors owed it a duty of care.

HELD: The House of Lords held that the auditors were not liable. Lord Oliver stated:

> What can be deduced from the *Hedley Byrne* case, therefore, is that the necessary relationship between the maker of a statement or giver of advice ('the adviser') and the recipient who acts in reliance upon it ('the advisee') may typically be held to exist where (1) the advice is required for a purpose, whether particularly specified or generally described, which is made known, either actually or inferentially, to the adviser at the time when the advice is given; (2) the adviser knows, either actually or inferentially, that his advice will be communicated to the advisee, either specifically or as a member of an ascertainable class, in order that it should be used by the advisee for that purpose; (3) it is known either actually or inferentially, that the advice so communicated is likely to be acted upon by the advisee for that purpose without independent inquiry, and (4) it is so acted upon by the advisee to his detriment.[78]

⭐ See R Martyn, 'Categories of Negligence and Duties of Care: *Caparo* in the House of Lords' (1990) 53 MLR 824

The annual accounts were prepared in order to enable Fidelity's shareholders to determine whether or not the company was being run effectively. Accordingly, it was clear that the auditors owed a duty to Fidelity. The House went on to say that the auditors did not prepare accounts in order to inform those who might wish to make investment decisions. Accordingly, no duty was owed to Caparo.

It will be noted that Lord Oliver's formulation makes no reference to the 'voluntary assumption of responsibility' that certain judges in *Hedley Byrne* regarded as essential. It would appear, therefore, that Lord Oliver in *Caparo* 'fatally weakened'[79] the requirement of voluntary assumption—but this may not be the case. All of the above cases concerned the provision of negligent advice (although negligent misstatement need not only relate to advice) and, as noted, this constitutes the principal exception to the rule that pure economic loss is not recoverable. The possibility always existed that the *Hedley Byrne* principles would be extended beyond cases concerning the provision of advice. This possibility has now occurred and is generally known as 'extended' *Hedley Byrne* liability, and many cases involving this extended liability have confirmed the importance of the 'assumption of responsibility'.

'Extended' Hedley Byrne *liability*

Hedley Byrne created the principal exception to the rule that pure economic loss could not be recovered—namely, where the claimant had suffered loss due to the defendant's negligent misstatement. Soon after *Hedley Byrne* was decided, a key issue arose—namely, whether the principles laid down in *Hedley Byrne* were confined to cases concerning the provision of advice. It is now clear that the answer is 'no' and the courts have extended the *Hedley Byrne* principle to other areas—notably to cases concerning the provision of services. This extension to services is a logical one. It would be incongruous if a professional could be liable in tort for negligent advice, but not for negligently providing a service. As Lunney and Oliphant state: 'It would

---

78. *Caparo Industries plc v Dickman* [1990] 2 AC 605 (HL) 638.
79. J Steele, *Tort Law: Text, Cases and Materials* (OUP, Oxford, 2007) 376.

be an odd result if a solicitor could be liable under *Hedley Byrne* for careless advice but not for carelessly drafting a document.'[80]

 ## White v Jones [1995] 2 AC 207 (HL)

FACTS: Barratt quarrelled with his two daughters (the claimants). The quarrel was so serious that he cut them both out of his will. A few months later, Barratt and his daughters were reconciled, and he instructed his solicitor, Jones (the defendant), to draft a new will restoring his daughter's legacies, which amounted to £9,000 each. The solicitor negligently delayed drafting the new will and Barratt died before the will was completed, with the result that Barratt's daughters did not receive their legacies. Barratt's daughters sued Jones. Jones argued that, because the loss was purely economic, he did not owe the daughters a duty of care.

HELD: By a three to two majority, the House of Lords held that Jones owed the daughters a duty of care. But the reasoning of the majority differed. Lord Goff—in many cases, the champion of the 'assumption of responsibility' test—acknowledged that, factually, there is little doubt that the defendant had not assumed responsibility towards the claimants, only to his client. But Lord Goff stated that if the claimants were not provided with a remedy, there would be 'a lacuna in the law'.[81] Accordingly, based on little more than an 'impulse to do practical justice',[82] Lord Goff held that whilst an assumption of responsibility was only factually owed to Barratt and not the claimants, 'the assumption of responsibility by the solicitor towards his client should be held *in law* to extend to the intended beneficiary'.[83] Conversely, Lord Browne-Wilkinson did not appear to believe that an assumption in law was needed, because he found that, factually, Jones had voluntarily assumed responsibility towards the claimants and that this assumption of responsibility created the *Hedley Byrne* 'special relationship' between the parties. Although subsequent courts have indicated that Lord Goff's judgment expresses the reasoning of the majority,[84] the divergent reasoning of the judges involved makes finding the *ratio* of this case extremely difficult.

★ See T Weir, 'A *Damnosa Hereditas?'* (1995) 111 LQR 357

It can be seen, from the above discussion relating to pure economic loss, negligent misstatement, and 'extended' *Hedley Byrne* liability, that the law in this area is far from certain and principled. Numerous tests have been advocated, but the exact requirements for recovery of pure economic loss are far from certain, especially in relation to cases outside established duty situations. Accordingly, in the following case, the House of Lords considered the differing tests and attempted to provide guidance on their application.

---

80. M Lunney and K Oliphant, *Tort Law: Text and Materials* (3rd edn, OUP, Oxford, 2008) 430.
81. *White v Jones* [1995] 2 AC 207 (HL) 265.   82. Ibid, 259.
83. Ibid, 268 (emphasis added).
84. See, e.g., *Carr-Glynn v Frearsons* [1999] Ch 326 (CA) 335, in which Chadwick LJ stated that the 'reasoning in Lord Goff's speech—and only that reasoning—that can be said to have received the support of the majority in the House of Lords'.

Customs and Excise Commissioners v Barclays Bank plc [2006] UKHL 28

FACTS: The claimant sought to recover outstanding VAT payments from two companies. To this end, injunctions were obtained freezing the assets of the two companies involved. The companies involved held their bank accounts at the defendant bank. The defendant was informed of the injunctions, but it failed to prevent the companies from drawing on the accounts. The claimant sought damages from the defendant in respect of the sums paid out and it was necessary to determine if the defendant owed the claimant a duty of care.

HELD: The House of Lords held that the defendant did not owe the claimant a duty of care. Because the bank was obliged to comply with the injunction and could be held in contempt of court if it did not, there was no voluntary assumption of responsibility so as to give rise to a duty of care. Their Lordships were all agreed that 'there is no single common denominator, even in cases of economic loss, by which liability may be determined'.[85] What then followed was a series of speeches indicating that the established tests provided 'no more than a helpful channelling for judicial thought'.[86] All five Law Lords involved provided a judgment, but Lord Walker's was largely in agreement with those of the others. The other four judgments all provided useful guidance as to when pure economic loss is recoverable.

The key points from each judgment are set out below.

Lord Bingham

1. The assumption of responsibility test is 'a sufficient, but not necessary condition of liability, a first test which, if answered positively, may obviate the need for further enquiry. If answered negatively, further consideration is called for'.[87] This further consideration would appear to be an application of the three-stage *Caparo* test (see p 384).

2. The assumption of responsibility test is to be applied objectively and is not concerned with what the defendant actually thought or intended.

3. The general three-stage duty of care test established in *Caparo* does not provide a straightforward answer in cases involving novel situations.

4. The incremental test is little use alone and it should be combined with other tests.

5. The outcomes of the leading cases were sensible and just, irrespective of what test was applied.

Lord Hoffmann

1. In cases involving economic loss, reasonable foreseeability is not enough to establish a duty of care.

2. The purpose of the assumption of responsibility test is to determine if the relationship between the parties was sufficiently proximate.

---

85. Ibid, [93] (Lord Mance).
86. S Gee, 'The Remedies Carried by a Freezing Injunction' (2006) 122 LQR 535, 536.
87. [2006] UKHL 28, [2007] 1 AC 181, [4].

Lord Rodger

1. Although some cases have indicated that the assumption of responsibility test is the 'touchstone' for establishing liability for pure economic loss, this is not the case.

2. In the absence of a single 'touchstone', the court should apply the three-stage test in *Caparo* to novel situations.

Lord Mance

1. The differing approaches often (although not invariably) lead to the same result.

2. 'Assumption of responsibility is on any view a core area of liability for economic loss.'[88]

3. '[T]here is no single common denominator, even in cases of economic loss, by which liability may be determined. In my view the threefold test of foreseeability, proximity and fairness, justice and reasonableness provides a convenient general framework although it operates at a high level of abstraction.'[89]

 See S Gee, 'The Remedies Carried by a Freezing Injunction' (2006) 122 LQR 535

⟨⟩ Key points summary

- Generally, liability is not imposed for omissions—but a duty of care may arise depending upon the relationship between the parties, or between the parties and a third party.

- A claimant may recover damages for psychiatric injury that is consequential upon physical injury.

- A 'primary victim' is a person who fears for his physical safety due to another's negligence. A 'secondary victim' is a person who witnesses an act of negligence, but does not fear for his personal safety.

- A secondary victim may only claim damages for psychiatric injury where:

  - the damage is reasonably foreseeable;
  - it is caused by a 'shock' and not a gradual series of events; and
  - there is sufficiently proximity in terms of time, space, relationship, and communication.

- As a general rule, a claimant cannot recover damages for 'pure' economic loss (that is, financial loss unassociated with physical injury or property damage).

- Economic loss is recoverable if it is consequential upon physical injury or property damage.

- A claimant can recover damages for 'pure' economic loss caused by the defendant's negligent misstatement, or his negligent performance of a service.

---

88. Ibid, [83].   89. Ibid, [93].

The effect of the Human Rights Act 1998

🔗 The general effects of the Human Rights Act 1998 are discussed at p 117

The final issue to discuss in relation to the duty of care is the effect of the Human Rights Act 1998. We have already examined the general effects of the passing of the Act in previous chapters; here, we will focus on the specific effects on tort law. The most significant effect has been in relation to the duty of care, where, for a time, it appeared that the 1998 Act would seriously jeopardize the survival of the *Caparo* test. The European Convention on Human Rights, Art 6, provides for the right to a fair trial. Any procedural rule or substantive law that interferes with an individual's right to a fair trial may infringe Art 6.

We noted above that the third part of the *Caparo* test (fair, just, and reasonable to impose a duty) has, in a number of cases, resulted in certain groups receiving immunity from negligence claims via the courts' refusal to impose a duty of care. It was the imposition of such an immunity that the European Court of Human Rights found to be in breach of Art 6 in the following case.

⊙ *Osman v UK*, App no 23452/94 (2000) 29 EHRR 245

FACTS: Paget-Lewis, a teacher, had developed an infatuation with a pupil named Osman (to the extent that Paget-Lewis eventually changed his surname to 'Osman' by deed poll). Over the course of the next few months, Paget-Lewis harassed Osman and his family, including engaging in acts of property damage. The harassment was reported to the police and, after a series of interviews, it was decided that a strong enough case existed to arrest Paget-Lewis. Unfortunately, Paget-Lewis had fled the area. A few months later, he returned and, using a stolen shotgun, he killed Osman's father and seriously injured Osman. The claimants (Osman and his mother) argued that the police had been negligent in failing to capture Paget-Lewis and prevent him from carrying out the attack. The Court of Appeal, applying *Hill v Chief Constable of West Yorkshire* (discussed above), held that no duty existed and struck out the Osmans' claim.[90] The Osmans took their case to the European Court of Human Rights.

⭐ See G Monti, *'Osman v UK:* Transforming English Negligence into French Administrative Law?' (1999) 48 ICLQ 757

HELD: The European Court of Human Rights (ECtHR) held that the Osmans' Art 6 rights had been infringed. In applying a blanket immunity, the Court of Appeal had failed to balance the policy factors identified in *Hill* with any other factors existing in Osman's case that could merit the imposition of a duty (for example, the seriousness of the harm suffered and the extent of Paget-Lewis' wrongdoing). Therefore, the automatic imposition of a blanket immunity was a disproportionate measure.

The effect of the ruling appears to be that the striking out of a claim based on the lack of a duty of care would infringe the claimant's Art 6 rights. Certainly, in the period following *Osman*, domestic courts were much more reluctant to strike out a negligence claim, especially based on the third part of the *Caparo* test. There is little doubt that, domestically, the decision was not popular. One commentator stated

---

90. *Osman v Ferguson* [1993] 4 All ER 344 (CA).

that there were 'few who were favourably disposed to the judgment'[91] and one judge branded the decision as 'extremely difficult to understand'.[92]

Fortunately, more recent decisions have indicated that the ECtHR has retreated from its openly hostile stance towards *Caparo* and there is now a recognition that the ECtHR in *Osman* failed to understand properly the nature of the *Caparo* test.

Z v UK, App no 29392/95 (2002) 34 EHRR 3

FACTS: The claimants were four young siblings. They were neglected and poorly treated by their parents. Reports from a string of concerned parties detailed practices that included locking the children out of the house all day, that the children were poorly fed, that one child had an abrasion which could have been a cigarette burn, and that there was a perceived risk of sexual abuse. Social services visited the house and, despite the blatantly poor conditions, the children were not placed on the child protection register. Some five years later, during which time there were continued reports of abuse and neglect, the council eventually placed the children on the child protection register and the children found foster homes. The children sued the council on the basis that its failure to act more promptly affected their psychical and emotional well-being. The House of Lords held that their negligence claim should fail on the ground that it would not be fair, just, and reasonable to impose a duty on the council.[93] The claimants took their claim to the ECtHR.

HELD: Retreating from *Osman*, the ECtHR held that 'the inability of the [claimants] to sue the local authority flowed not from an immunity but from the applicable principles governing the substantive right of action in domestic law'.[94] Accordingly, Art 6 was not infringed.

COMMENT: It would appear that the effect of this case and subsequent cases[95] is to confine Art 6 complaints to breaches of procedure, not complaints against substantive law. Accordingly, it would appear that a claimant would be unable to succeed on an argument based on Art 6 where the courts have used the third part of the *Caparo* test to refuse to impose a duty of care.

⭐ See ACL Davies, 'The European Convention and Negligence Actions: *Osman* "Reviewed"' (2001) 117 LQR 521

The retreat from *Osman* will doubtless be welcomed by many, especially the higher courts. But it is hoped that the courts do not revert completely to a pre-*Osman* position. One commentator has argued that *Osman* has resulted in two benefits that should be retained. Firstly, one benefit of the 'courts' post-*Osman* approach is their readiness to scrutinize the various policy factors involved in the "fair, just and reasonable" test much more carefully than in the past'.[96] Secondly, the courts have been much more reluctant to strike out applications brought against public

---

91. TR Hickman, '"Uncertain Shadow": Throwing Light on the Right to a Court Under Art 6(1) ECHR' [2004] PL 122, 133 fn 65.

92. *Barrett v London Borough of Enfield* [2001] 2 AC 550 (HL) 558 (Lord Browne-Wilkinson).

93. *X v Bedfordshire County Council* [1995] 2 AC 633 (HL).

94. *Z v UK*, App no 29392/95 (2002) 34 EHRR 3, [100].

95. See, e.g., *Matthews v Ministry of Defence* [2003] UKHL 4, [2003] 1 AC 1163, [42] (Lord Walker).

96. ACL Davies, 'The European Convention and Negligence Actions: "*Osman*" Reviewed' (2001) 117 LQR 521, 523.

authorities. The benefit of this is that cases are decided based upon their specific facts, as opposed to a (potentially incorrect) presumption that a duty does, or does not, exist.[97]

Breach of duty

Establishing a duty of care is only the first step in proving liability for negligence. The justification for the imposition of liability is that the duty has been breached (that is, that the defendant has acted negligently). This will be determined by discussing the two questions that the court will ask once it has been established that a duty is owed.

1. What is the standard of care owed by the defendant?
2. Has he met that standard?

For the courts, these are questions of law and fact, and the test established to determine the existence of breach of duty is an objective, 'reasonable man' test.

The standard of care

The duties of care that we owe to others are not absolute: we are not required to guarantee the safety of others, nor are we required never to cause damage to others. The standard imposed is one of reasonableness, not perfection. This is derived from the often-quoted statement of Alderson B in *Blyth v Birmingham Waterworks Co*:[98]

> Negligence is the omission to do something which a reasonable man, guided upon those considerations which ordinarily regulate the conduct of human affairs, would do, or doing something which the prudent and reasonable man would not do.[99]

So, who is the 'reasonable man'? Put simply, he is an ordinary citizen or, according to Greer LJ: '... "the man in the street," or "the man in the Clapham omnibus," or…"the man who takes the magazines at home, and in the evening pushes the lawn mower in his shirt sleeves." '[100] It is apparent, therefore, that the standard imposed is an objective one. Accordingly, it is not a defence for the defendant to claim that he did his best or that he honestly believed that his actions were not negligent. In this sense, it is 'an impersonal test. It eliminates the personal equation and is independent of the idiosyncrasies of the particular person whose conduct is in question'.[101] This is the case even where those idiosyncrasies contribute towards the alleged negligence, as the following cases demonstrate.

---

97. Ibid, 524. 98. (1856) 11 Ex 781 (Ex).
99. Ibid, 784. 100. *Hall v Brooklands Auto Racing Club* [1933] 1 KB 205 (CA) 224.
101. *Glasgow Corporation v Muir* [1943] AC 448 (HL) 457 (Lord Macmillan).

Nettleship v Weston **[1971] 2 QB 691 (CA)**

FACTS: The claimant, an experienced driver (but not a driving instructor), agreed to provide some driving lessons to the defendant—a friend's wife. On her third lesson, the defendant panicked and hit a lamp post. Although the car was moving at walking pace when it collided with the lamp post, the claimant suffered a broken kneecap. A duty of care was easily established and the claimant had to show that this duty was breached.

HELD: The claimant succeeded. The Court of Appeal held that the fact that the defendant was a learner driver was irrelevant. Lord Denning MR stated: 'The learner driver may be doing his best, but his incompetent best is not good enough. He must drive in as good a manner as a driver of skill, experience and care …'[102]

 Roberts v Ramsbottom **[1980] 1 WLR 823 (QB)**

FACTS: The 73-year-old defendant unknowingly suffered a cerebral haemorrhage. He did not realize that he was unfit to drive and that his consciousness was impaired. He collided with a stationary van, but still did not realize that he was unfit to drive. He continued to drive and collided with a parked vehicle belonging to the first claimant (the father). The second claimant (the mother) was slightly injured, but the third claimant (her daughter, who was in the car during the crash) was seriously injured.

HELD: The High Court held that the defendant was liable to pay damages to all three claimants. The fact that the defendant's reasoning was impaired was no defence: the standard to be applied was that of a driver of skill, experience, and care. Neill J stated that the defendant would have escaped liability if he had sustained a complete loss of consciousness, or such a sudden and complete loss of control as to amount to **automatism.** In the present case, the defendant's consciousness was merely impaired.

➡ automatism: a complete loss of voluntary control

The decisions in the above cases may appear harsh, but they can be justified. Oliver Wendell Holmes Jr, regarded by many as one of the finest justices ever to sit in the US Supreme Court, stated that:

> The standards of the law are standards of general application. The law takes no account of the infinite varieties of temperament, intellect, and education which make the internal character of a given act so different in different men.… [W]hen men live in society, a certain average of conduct, a sacrifice of individual peculiarities going beyond a certain point, is necessary to the general welfare. If, for instance, a man is born hasty and awkward, is always having accidents and hurting himself or his neighbors, no doubt his congenital defects will be allowed for in the courts of Heaven, but his slips are no less troublesome to his neighbors than if they sprang from guilty neglect. His neighbors accordingly require him, at his proper peril, to come up to their standard, and the courts which they establish decline to take his personal equation into account.[103]

---

102. *Nettleship v Weston* [1971] 2 QB 691 (CA) 699.
103. O Wendell Holmes Jr, *The Common Law* (The Lawbook Exchange, New Jersey, 2004) 108.

The courts have, however, acknowledged that, in certain circumstances, a completely objective approach may lead to injustice. Accordingly, in a number of specific instances, the courts will allow an element of subjectivity into their deliberations.

Children

It would clearly be unfair to apply an objective reasonable man test to the actions of a child, because children cannot be expected to meet the same standard of care as adults. The law still imposes an objective standard, but the standard in most cases is that of a reasonable and prudent child of the same age as the defendant.

 Mullin v Richards [1998] 1 WLR 1304 (CA)

FACTS: The claimant and the defendant were both 15-year-old schoolgirls. Whilst in class, they engaged in a mock swordfight using plastic rulers. One of the rulers snapped and a shard of plastic entered the claimant's right eye, causing her to become virtually blind in that eye. The claimant sued the defendant.

HELD: The claim failed. The Court of Appeal asked whether an ordinarily prudent and reasonable 15-year-old schoolgirl would have realized the risk of injury. On the facts, the answer was 'no'. The game was a commonplace one in the school and members of staff had not warned the pupils of any dangers.

COMMENT: Mullis and Oliphant note that the fact that the schoolgirls were engaged in a child's game was crucial. Had they been undertaking an adult's activity, the result might have been different and the standard reasonable man test would likely have been applied: 'If a 15-year-old tearaway were to hot-wire a motor-car and drive it off, she would be measured against the standard of care reasonably to be expected of a qualified adult driver without any allowance for her age.'[104]

Mental and physical disability or incapacity

We discussed above the case of *Roberts v Ramsbottom* and saw that a defendant who crashed his car due to a cerebral haemorrhage was found liable based on the standard reasonable man test. But this does not mean that the court will never take into account the physical and mental factors that may have contributed towards the defendant's negligence.

 Mansfield v Weetabix Ltd [1998] 1 WLR 1263 (CA)

FACTS: A lorry driver employed by the defendant was unaware that he was suffering from a malignant insulinoma. The effect of this was to starve his brain of glucose and oxygen, which resulted in a gradual loss of consciousness. In the course of a 40-mile journey, he was involved in a series of minor accidents. He failed to negotiate a bend in the road properly and crashed into the claimant's shop.

---

104. A Mullis and K Oliphant, *Torts* (3rd edn, Palgrave, Basingstoke, 2003) 122.

HELD: The defendant was not liable. The Court of Appeal held that the applicable standard was that which was to be expected of 'a reasonably competent driver unaware that he is or may be suffering from a condition that impairs his ability to drive'.[105] Applying this, the Court held that the driver was not negligent; the crash was not his fault and there was therefore no liability.

COMMENT: Why was the result in this case different from the result in *Roberts*? In both cases, the car accidents were directly attributable to the drivers having an undiscovered mental condition. This distinction was stated by Legatt LJ, who stated: 'There is no reason in principle why a driver should not escape liability where the disabling event is not sudden, but gradual, provided that the driver is unaware of it.'[106] In *Roberts*, the haemorrhage was sudden and the defendant admitted to 'feeling queer' before the crash. In *Mansfield*, the loss of consciousness was more gradual and the driver had no way of knowing that his function had been impaired.

Skill or expertise

In relation to children and physical or mental disability, the introduction of an element of subjectivity serves to lower the standard of care. But it may be the case that a characteristic of the defendant demands the raising of the standard of care. This is the case where the defendant has some special skill or expertise that 'the man in the Clapham Omnibus' would not normally possess. As we shall see, many of the cases in this area have involved medical negligence.

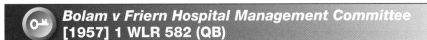

Bolam v Friern Hospital Management Committee [1957] 1 WLR 582 (QB)

FACTS: The claimant was a voluntary patient at the defendant's mental hospital. The claimant was undergoing electroconvulsive therapy (ECT), which involved passing an electric current through the brain. If a muscle relaxant was not administered, the shocks could be accompanied by violent spasms. In accordance with normal practice, the ECT therapy was administered without a muscle relaxant. The claimant convulsed and fractured a bone in his hip. The claimant sued.

HELD: The High Court held that the defendant was not liable. McNair J stated:

> [W]here you get a situation which involves the use of some special skill or competence, then the test as to whether there has been negligence or not is not the test of the man on the top of a Clapham omnibus, because he has not got this special skill. The test is the standard of the ordinary skilled man exercising and professing to have that special skill. A man need not possess the highest expert skill; it is well established law that it is sufficient if he exercises the ordinary skill of an ordinary competent man exercising that particular art.[107]

Applying this, the defendant was not liable, because it was common practice to administer ECT without the use of a muscle relaxant.

---

105. *Mansfield v Weetabix Ltd* [1998] 1 WLR 1263 (CA) 1268 (Legatt LJ).
106. Ibid, 1267.
107. *Bolam v Friern Hospital Management Committee* [1957] 1 WLR 582 (QB) 586.

But the application of the '*Bolam* test' can be problematic where the defendant is highly specialized. For example, if a patient is alleging negligence against an oncologist (a doctor who specializes in diagnosing and treating cancer), is the defendant to be judged by the standard of a reasonable doctor, or is he to be judged by the standard of a reasonable oncologist?

The answer came in the following case.

 Wilsher v Essex Area Health Authority [1988] AC 1074 (HL)

FACTS: The claimant was a baby, born at the defendant's hospital. He was born three months' premature and was placed in a special baby care unit. The most significant problem faced by premature babies is that their underdeveloped lungs cannot take in enough oxygen, making death through brain damage a serious threat. To combat this, the claimant's oxygen supply was increased—but due to a junior doctor inserting the catheter into the wrong vein, the claimant was given too much oxygen and he developed retrolental fibroplasia, a condition that affects the eyes. The claimant became completely blind in one eye and his vision was seriously impaired in the other. The claimant sued the defendant hospital.

HELD: The House of Lords held that it was irrelevant that the doctor in question was a junior doctor. No allowance would be made for inexperience. The relevant standard of care is not based upon the individual defendant, but rather the post that he holds. This would appear to indicate that the doctor was negligent, but the House held that there was no liability on causation grounds.

★ See A Grubb, 'Causation and Medical Negligence' (1988) 47 CLJ 329

Accordingly, where a person is a professional or has a special skill, the standard of care is that of the reasonably competent person occupying the same post, or carrying out the same function, as the defendant. The problem that arises is that the post in question might be a highly technical or specialized one. Are the courts qualified to determine the liability of such persons? The *Bolam* test stated that a defendant would not be negligent where his actions were considered appropriate by a body of competent persons exercising the same function as the defendant. Referring specifically to medical negligence cases, Lord Scarman has stated that 'the law imposes the duty of care; but the standard of care is a matter of medical judgment'.[108] This statement would seem to indicate that the courts have abdicated determination of the standard of care to the professionals (especially in medical negligence cases)—a sentiment echoed by several commentators who contend that the courts have 'elevated to the status of an unquestionable proposition of law…that professional practice will *not* be reviewed by the courts'.[109]

Thankfully, more recent decisions have indicated that professional practice will be reviewed by the courts.

---

108. *Sidaway v Board of Governors of Bethlehem Royal Hospital* [1985] AC 871 (HL) 881.
109. I Kennedy and A Grubb, *Medical Law: Text with Materials* (2nd edn, Butterworths, London, 1994).

Bolitho v City and Hackney Health Authority [1998] AC 232 (HL)

FACTS: A 2-year-old child was admitted to the defendant's hospital suffering from breathing difficulties. Over the course of the next day, he suffered two episodes of respiratory difficulty. On both occasions, a doctor was called to attend, but did not, and the child apparently recovered after both attacks. Half an hour after the second attack, he suffered acute respiratory failure, which resulted in cardiac arrest. The child suffered brain damage and later died. The claimants (the child's parents) alleged that the doctor should have attended the child and that he should have been intubated (a procedure that opens the airways) following the second episode. Medical evidence submitted was inconclusive: five of the eight expert witnesses called thought that intubation was appropriate; three thought that it was inappropriate. Applying *Bolam*, the Court of Appeal upheld the trial judge's decision that, because a body of medical opinion thought that intubation was inappropriate, the defendant was not liable for the child's death. The claimants appealed.

HELD: The appeal was dismissed by the House of Lords. But in a key passage, Lord Browne-Wilkinson stated:

> The court is not bound to hold that a defendant doctor escapes liability for negligent treatment or diagnosis just because he leads evidence from a number of medical experts who are genuinely of the opinion that the defendant's treatment or diagnosis accorded with sound medical practice....[T]he court has to be satisfied that the exponents of the body of opinion relied upon can demonstrate that such an opinion has a logical basis....in cases of diagnosis and treatment there are cases where, despite a body of professional opinion sanctioning the defendant's conduct, the defendant can properly be held liable for negligence....In the vast majority of cases the fact that distinguished experts in the field are of a particular opinion will demonstrate the reasonableness of that opinion....But if, in a rare case, it can be demonstrated that the professional opinion is not capable of withstanding logical analysis, a judge is entitled to hold that the body of opinion is not reasonable or responsible.[110]

Related to the skill or expertise of the defendant is the state of scientific or expert knowledge at the time of the alleged breach of duty. As the following case demonstrates, the level of such knowledge can have a significant impact upon a case.

 Roe v Minister of Health [1954] 2 QB 66 (CA)

FACTS: Roe (the claimant) was admitted to hospital for a minor operation. An anaesthetist employed by the defendant would administer an anaesthetic called nupercaine. The nupercaine was contained in a glass ampoule that was, in turn, kept in a phenol solution. To ensure that no phenol had leaked into the nupercaine, the anaesthetist inspected the ampoule for cracks. Not finding any, he injected the nupercaine into Roe's spine. After the operation, Roe developed spastic paraplegia, which rendered him permanently paralysed from the waist down. The paraplegia had been caused by phenol seeping through invisible

110. *Bolitho v City and Hackney Health Authority* [1998] AC 232 (HL) 241, 243.

cracks in the ampoule into the nupercaine. Administering a coloured agent to the phenol could have revealed the presence of invisible cracks.

HELD: The Court of Appeal held that the anaesthetist had not acted negligently. The operation took place in 1947, yet the risk of 'invisible cracks' was not made known to the medical profession until 1951. Accordingly, a reasonable man in the anaesthetist's position would not have been aware of the danger and so could not be held to have breached his duty.

The defendant's circumstances

The courts have acknowledged that whilst the standard to be met is that of the reasonable man, what is reasonable may depend upon the circumstances facing the defendant. For example, conduct that normally would be regarded as unreasonable may be regarded as reasonable in an emergency situation.[111] Accordingly, the standard to be applied that that of the reasonable man in the defendant's position.

Harris v Perry [2008] EWCA Civ 907

FACTS: Two parents (the first and second defendants) hired a bouncy castle and a bungee run for their triplets' tenth birthday party. The second defendant was supervising a number of children on the bouncy castle. At one stage, she went to help at the bungee run and turned her back on the bouncy castle. One child (who was older and larger than the other children) performed a somersault and his foot struck another child (the claimant) on the head, causing his skull to fracture, and leaving him with permanent cognitive and behavioural difficulties. The claimant alleged that the defendants had breached their duty of care. In particular, he drew attention to the bouncy castle hire agreement, which stated that children of different sizes should not play on the bouncy castle and that it should be supervised at all times.

HELD: The Court of Appeal held that the defendants had not breached their duty of care. They were required to take such care as a reasonably careful parent would take for the safety of his child of the claimant's age playing on a bouncy castle. A reasonably careful parent could foresee that boisterous children playing on a bouncy castle would run the risk of injury, but a reasonable parent would not foresee the severity of such injury. The standard of care requires parents to protect children from foreseeable harm and the injuries suffered by the claimant were not foreseeable. In relation to the precautions stated in the hire agreement, the Court said that no significance should be attached to them. Instead, the Court should:

> identify the standard of care required in the circumstances of this case on the basis of the facts of which the defendant knew or ought to have known. These could not include the contents of documents that the defendant neither saw nor ought to have seen.[112]

★ See N Dobson, 'Accidents Do Happen' (2008) 158 NLJ 1318

---

111. *Jones v Boyce* (1816) 171 ER 540.
112. *Harris v Perry* [2008] EWCA Civ 907, [2009] 1 WLR 19, [36] (Lord Phillips CJ).

Factors determining breach of duty

In the US case of *United States v Carroll Towing Co*,[113] Learned Hand J established a formula to determine the existence of breach of duty—namely, $B < PL$, where B represented the cost of the precautions needed to eliminate the risk of injury, P represented the probability of injury, and L represented the seriousness of the likely loss. Whilst English courts have not adopted the 'Learned Hand formula' itself, the factors identified within it have been adopted by the courts and added to, resulting in a number of factors that the court will take into account when determining whether the duty has been breached:

- the likelihood of injury;
- the seriousness of the injury;
- the cost of precautions;
- the usefulness of the defendant's conduct.

Likelihood of injury

The courts will attempt to determine the extent to which injury was likely as a result of the defendant's actions. It follows that the more foreseeable the injury, the more the law will expect of a defendant. Put another way, the greater the likelihood of injury, the more probable it is that the defendant's conduct was negligent.

Two contrasting cases with similar facts demonstrate this approach in practice.

 Bolton v Stone [1951] AC 850 (HL)

FACTS: The claimant was standing outside her house, which was adjacent to a cricket ground. A cricket ball cleared the 17-foot-high fence surrounding the ground and hit the claimant, causing her injury. Evidence at the trial indicated that on only six occasions in the previous thirty years had a ball left the cricket ground and that the claimant was the first person actually to be hit by a ball. The claimant contended that the defendant should have done more to guard against the possibility of a ball leaving the cricket ground.

HELD: The House of Lords held that the defendant was not liable for the claimant's injuries. Although the risk of a ball leaving the ground was foreseeable, the risk was so small that a reasonable person would not have anticipated it. Accordingly, the measures taken by the cricket ground were adequate.

 Miller v Jackson [1977] QB 966 (CA)

FACTS: As in *Bolton*, the claimants owned a house adjacent to a cricket ground. A ball did not hit the claimant, but balls did strike the claimant's property, causing damage. Further, the claimants alleged that the fear of a ball hitting their property or themselves caused them to become extremely apprehensive of danger, resulting in a loss of enjoyment of their

---

113. 159 F 2d 169 (1947).

property. Evidence presented at trial indicated that, in the previous season alone, a ball had entered their garden five times.

HELD: Because the risk was much greater and more foreseeable than in *Bolton*, the Court of Appeal held that the defendant was liable in negligence for damage caused by balls entering the claimants' property.

Seriousness of injury

If the court is of the opinion that injury is likely and foreseeable, it will then fall to it to determine how serious that injury is likely to be. The greater the potential injury, the greater the likelihood that the defendant was negligent, and the greater will be the steps required to prevent against such injury. In other words, the more serious the potential harm, the more that the defendant will have to do to guard against such harm—or, as Singleton LJ put it: 'The law expects of a man a great deal more care in carrying a pound of dynamite than a pound of butter.'[114]

 ***Paris v Stepney Borough Council* [1951] AC 367 (HL)**

FACTS: The claimant was employed as a mechanic at the defendant's garage. The claimant only had one eye and the defendant was aware of this. Whilst striking a bolt with a hammer, a metal chip flew off and struck him in his good eye, blinding him completely. At the time of the injury, he was not wearing goggles, and argued that his employer was negligent in failing to require him to wear, and to provide him with, a pair of goggles. The defendant argued that it was not normal practice to provide its mechanics with goggles.

HELD: The House of Lords held that the defendant was liable. Whilst failing to provide safety goggles to a normal employee might not constitute a breach of duty, it does constitute a breach of duty where the claimant has only one good eye and would accordingly suffer greater injury if his good eye were lost. This warranted an increase in the level of care owed to him and the defendant should have taken extra precautions—namely, to provide goggles.

COMMENT: Initially, this may appear to be an application of the 'eggshell skull' rule that we will discuss later on (see p 440). But it is not, because the application of the 'eggshell skull' rule is not determined by reasonable foreseeability, whereas in the above case, reasonable foreseeability was clearly a determining factor. Further, because the 'eggshell skull' rule is a principle of causation, it only comes into effect once breach of duty has been established.

Cost of prevention

Just as the court will balance usefulness against risk, so too will it balance risk against cost: the greater the risk, the greater the precautions that the court will require the defendant to take, even if the cost of such precautions is considerable. Basically, the greater the risk, the less willing the courts will be to accept cost as factor negativing the existence of a breach of duty. But where the cost of precautions is out

---

114. *Beckett v Newalls Insulation Co Ltd* [1953] 1 WLR 8 (CA) 16.

of proportion to the magnitude of the risk, then the courts will not hold that the defendant's duty has been breached.

 Latimer v AEC Ltd [1953] AC 643 (HL)

FACTS: An unusually heavy rainstorm flooded the defendant's factory. The defendant did all that it could to eliminate the effects of the flooding, but some areas of the flooring were still flooded and slippery. The claimant (an employee of the defendant) slipped and injured his ankle. He sued the defendant, alleging that it should have shut the factory down until it was completely safe.

HELD: His claim failed. The House of Lords held that the defendant had done all that it could reasonably do. The majority of the factory floor was rendered safe, so the risk of injury was minimal. Accordingly, the cost of shutting the factory down would have been wholly out of proportion to the risk involved.

What, however, is the situation where the cost of prevention is not disproportionate, but the defendant lacks the resources to take the necessary precautions? In such a case, it is clear that the activity in question that is generating the risk of injury should not be engaged in (that is, that lack of resources will not be an excuse if injury ensues because the defendant lacked the resources to make an act reasonably safe).[115] It would appear, however, that this rule is relaxed in the case of public authorities.

 Knight v Home Office [1990] 3 All ER 237 (QB)

FACTS: A patient in a prison mental hospital was placed on 'suicide watch' and observed every 15 minutes. Despite this, he still managed to kill himself. His widow claimed against the prison.

HELD: The High Court acknowledged that had the medical facility in question been a National Health Service facility, it is likely that the defendant's conduct would have amounted to a breach of duty. But Pill J (as he then was) stated that 'the resources available for the public service are limited'.[116] Given this, it was held that checking on the patient every 15 minutes was a reasonable precaution.

Usefulness of the defendant's conduct

An act that causes injury to another might not be regarded as a breach of duty if the act is of significant benefit to the public, or even to the claimant. The court has to balance the risk of injury with the usefulness of the act in question, of which the following case provides a clear example.

---

115. *Latimer v AEC Ltd* [1953] AC 643 (HL).   116. *Knight v Home Office* [1990] 3 All ER 237 (QB) 243.

Watt v Hertfordshire County Council [1954] 1 WLR 835 (CA)

FACTS: The claimant was an on-duty fireman. An emergency arose whereby a woman was trapped under a car and heavy-lifting equipment would be needed to rescue her. Only one fire engine was equipped to carry heavy-lifting equipment, but it was on call at another emergency. Accordingly, the equipment was loaded onto a lorry, which lacked the means to secure the equipment adequately. On the way to the trapped woman, the driver was forced to brake suddenly. The lifting equipment slid along the lorry's floor and seriously injured the claimant's ankle. He sued his employer.

HELD: The Court of Appeal held that the employer was not liable. The fire brigade was under a duty to provide proper equipment and to take reasonable care not to expose its firemen to unreasonable risks. But the saving of life and limb justifies exposing its firemen to abnormal risk, and so there was no liability.

COMMENT: Initially, it would seem correct that firemen be required to expose themselves to risk—but is it fair that firemen (and others who work for the emergency services) are less likely to recover compensation for work-related injuries than those in other occupations? Such concerns have been raised. In *King v Sussex Ambulance Service Ltd*,[117] Buxton LJ argued that if the public interest compels those who work for the emergency services to offer aid, should it not also be regarded as in the public interest to compensate those who are foreseeably injured when protecting the public?[118]

Despite Buxton LJ's comment, the principle in *Watt* has now been given statutory force by the Compensation Act 2006, s 1, which states:

> A court considering a claim in negligence or breach of statutory duty may, in determining whether the defendant should have taken particular steps to meet a standard of care (whether by taking precautions against a risk or otherwise), have regard to whether a requirement to take those steps might—
>
> (a) prevent a desirable activity from being undertaken at all, to a particular extent or in a particular way, or
>
> (b) discourage persons from undertaking functions in connection with a desirable activity.

Aside from placing the principle evidenced in *Watt* on a statutory footing, it is difficult to determine the purpose of s 1. The government claimed that it was enacted to combat the perceived 'compensation culture' that had developed. It is, however, difficult to see how it will have this effect, given that it merely codifies existing judicial practice. For this reason, s 1 has been justifiably described as 'an unnecessary solution to a non-existent problem'.[119]

---

117. [2002] EWCA Civ 953, [2002] ICT 1413.
118. Ibid, [47].
119. K Williams, 'Legislating in the Echo Chamber?' (2005) 155 NLJ 1938, 1938.

Proof of breach of duty

The above factors help the court to establish the standard of care owed by the defendant. It is for the claimant to prove, on the balance of probabilities, that the defendant breached his duty of care (that is, that he has fallen below the standard of care). In establishing this, the claimant is aided by:

- the application of the maxim *res ipsa loquitur*; and
- the Civil Evidence Act 1968.

Res ipsa loquitur

The claimant's task of establishing breach of duty may be rendered easier in cases in which the maxim *res ipsa loquitur* ('the thing speaks for itself') can be applied. In cases in which it applies, the defendant's breach of duty will be inferred.

The classic example and exposition of the maxim can be seen in the following case.

Scott v London and St Katherine's Dock Co (1865) 3 H & C 596 (Ex)

FACTS: Six bags of sugar fell from the defendant's warehouse onto the claimant, causing him injury. The claimant could not explain how the sugar fell on him, so the trial judge directed the jury to dismiss his claim, which it did. The claimant appealed.

HELD: His appeal was allowed and a retrial was ordered. Erle CJ stated:

> There must be reasonable evidence of negligence. But where the thing is shown to be under the management of the defendant or his servants, and the accident is such as in the ordinary course of things does not happen if those who have the management use proper care, it affords reasonable evidence, in the absence of explanation by the defendants, that the accident arose from want of care.[120]

Accordingly, where the maxim applies, a presumption of negligence is inferred. But *res ipsa loquitur* does not reverse the burden of proof. The burden of proof is still placed upon the claimant—*res ipsa loquitur* merely assists him in discharging that burden of proof.[121]

In order for *res ipsa loquitur* to apply, three requirements must be met. The first requirement is that the incident causing the claimant's damage is one that would not normally occur if proper care were being taken. *Scott* (discussed above) is a clear example of this: if proper care is taken, bags of sugar do not normally fall from warehouses. Other examples of incidents that were held not to occur if proper care had been taken include:

- the damaging of teeth following the finding of a stone in a bun;[122]

---

120. *Scott v London and St Katherine's Dock Co* (1865) 3 H & C 596 (Ex) 601.
121. *Ng Chun Pui v Lee Chuen Tat* [1988] RTR 298 (PC).
122. *Chapronière v Mason* (1905) 21 TLR 633 (CA).

- a hospital patient dying following an operation and the autopsy discovering a surgical swab inside the deceased's body;[123]
- injury caused by a flour barrel that fell from a window and struck the claimant.[124]

The second requirement is that there must be no complete explanation for the incident that causes the claimant's loss. If, based on the evidence, the court can discern how and why the incident occurred, there is no scope for inferring a breach of duty; the breach of duty will be established regardless. Thus, where a tyre on a bus bursts, causing the bus to career down an embankment, and it was proven that the tyre defect was the result of the defendant's negligent tyre inspection system, *res ipsa loquitur* will not be needed to establish the defendant's breach of duty.[125] Where only a partial explanation for the incident can be provided, *res ipsa loquitur* may still be used by the claimant to aid his case.

The final requirement is that the cause of the incident must have been under the defendant's control, or the control of those for whom the defendant is responsible. If it can be demonstrated that the cause of the incident could be attributable to someone else, *res ipsa loquitur* cannot be used, as the following contrasting examples demonstrate.

> ### Eg Res ipsa loquitur and train doors
>
> A 4-year-old child falls through the door of a train, seven miles after the last station stop. *Res ipsa loquitur* will not apply, because the train could have been opened by any of the passengers in the intervening seven miles. Accordingly, the defendant lacks sufficient control of the door.[126]
>
> Conversely, where a claimant falls through a train door moments after it leaves the train station, *res ipsa loquitur* could apply, because the door was very recently under the control of the defendant and was much more unlikely to have been interfered with.[127]

The Civil Evidence Act 1968

Whereas the maxim *res ipsa loquitur* will make proving negligence considerably easier for the claimant, the Civil Evidence Act 1968, s 11, completely relieves the clamant of the burden of proof in certain cases. Section 11 provides that where a defendant has been convicted of a criminal offence (for example, driving without due care and attention) and a civil action arises out of the same facts that led to the conviction, that conviction will be prima facie evidence of the defendant's civil liability. But it only constitutes prima facie proof, so it is open for the defendant to adduce proof denying his civil liability. Put another way, s 11 creates a rebuttable presumption that a defendant who has been convicted of a criminal offence is also liable in civil

---

123. *Mahon v Osborne* [1939] 2 KB 14 (CA).
124. *Byrne v Boadle* (1862) 2 H & C 722; cf *Larson v St Francis Hotel* 188 P 2d 513 (1938), in which a chair that fell out of a window onto the claimant did not pass the test. The court held that such an act was more likely the result of a malicious or maddened guest, than of the hotel's negligence.
125. *Barkway v South Wales Transport Co Ltd* [1950] AC 185 (HL).
126. *Easson v London & North Eastern Railway* [1944] 1 KB 421 (CA).
127. *Gee v Metropolitan Railway* (1873) LR 8 QB 161 (Ex).

proceedings in respect of any consequences that flow from that offence. Section 11 applies only to criminal convictions; acquittals cannot be adduced as evidence of innocence in subsequent civil proceedings.

 Key points summary

- Once the claimant has established that a duty of care exists, he will need to establish that the defendant breached that duty.

- The standard of care owed is that of the reasonable man. If the defendant is a child, the standard is that of a reasonable and prudent child of the defendant's age.

- The court may take into account the defendant's mental disability, provided that the defendant was unaware of it.

- If the defendant has a special skill or expertise, the standard of care will be raised to the standard of an ordinary skilled man exercising and professing to have that skill.

- The standard will take into account the position in which the defendant finds himself.

- Four factors are relevant when determining breach of duty:
  - the likelihood of injury;
  - the seriousness of the injury;
  - the cost of precautions; and
  - the usefulness of the defendant's conduct.

- The defendant's breach of duty will be inferred where the loss could not normally have occurred in the absence of negligence (*res ipsa loquitur*).

- The Civil Evidence Act 1968, s 11, provides that where the defendant has been convicted of a criminal offence and a negligence action arises out of the same facts, the conviction will be prima facie evidence of the defendant's civil liability.

Causation

In Chapter 10, we noted that a claimant who had suffered damage due to the defendant's breach of contract would need to establish a causal link between the breach and the damage suffered. The same rule applies in tort: even when the duty of care has been breached, the claimant must still show, on the balance of probabilities, that the defendant's negligence caused, in fact and in law, the damage in question.

The requirement of causation (unlike the rules relating to remoteness discussed later) applies to all torts, not only negligence. But because virtually all of the principles of causation were laid down in negligence cases, it is appropriate to discuss the issue in this chapter.

The 'but for' test

A negligence case may involve a mass of facts: some relevant to determining causation; some irrelevant. The courts screen out the irrelevant facts by applying what is known as the 'but for' test. This test basically asks whether the claimant would have suffered the loss 'but for' the defendant's breach of duty. If the claimant is to succeed, the answer must be 'no'. If the answer is 'yes', this would mean that the loss would have happened anyway and the claim will fail.

An application of the test can be seen in the following cases.

Barnett v Chelsea and Kensington Hospital Management Committee [1969] 1 QB 428 (QB)

FACTS: Barnett and two others drank some tea. Shortly after, they started vomiting and were admitted to the defendant's casualty department. A nurse telephoned the duty doctor to inform him of the men's condition. The doctor did not examine the patients, but instead told the nurse to send them home with instructions to consult their own doctors. Five hours later, Barnett died from arsenic poisoning. The poison was subsequently found in his tea. Barnett's widow initiated proceedings against the hospital.

HELD: The duty doctor was negligent in not examining Barnett, but the High Court held that the defendant was not vicariously liable. Even if the doctor had examined Barnett, it would have been too late to administer an antidote. Therefore, he would have died even if the doctor did not act negligently. Accordingly, the doctor's breach was not the factual cause of Barnett's death.

McWilliams v Sir William Arrol & Co Ltd [1962] 1 All ER 623 (HL)

FACTS: McWilliams was a steel erector. He fell 70 feet to his death. This would have been avoided if he had been wearing a safety harness, but his employer (the defendant) had not provided him with one. Witness testimony from his work colleagues indicated, however, that even if a harness had been provided, McWilliams would not have worn it.

HELD: The defendant had been negligent in failing to provide a harness, but the House of Lords held that McWilliams' widow could not recover damages, because the defendant's breach had not caused McWilliams' death: had it provided a harness, he probably would not have worn it and so he would have fallen anyway.

In *McWilliams*, the House could not be certain that McWilliams would not have worn the harness if provided—but the evidence clearly indicated that he would most likely not have worn a harness. So what is the situation if the evidence is not so helpful? What is the court to do if the actions of the claimant are much more uncertain?

Such a situation faced the House of Lords in the following case.

Chester v Afshar [2004] UKHL 41

FACTS: The claimant complained of back pain and was advised by the defendant (a neurosurgeon) to undergo a surgical procedure on her spine. The defendant failed to inform the claimant that, even if the operation was performed perfectly, there was still a 1–2 per cent chance that she could develop cauda equina syndrome (a neurological condition affecting all motor ability below the spinal cord). The surgery was performed competently, but the claimant developed the syndrome. She alleged the defendant's failure to warn her of the risk amounted to negligence. Evidence indicated that had the claimant been warned of the risk, she would not have undertaken the surgery immediately, but would have sought further advice.

HELD: A majority (by a three to two split) of the House of Lords held that the claimant could obtain compensation. Lord Steyn stated that the 'but for' test had been satisfied: had she undergone the surgery at a later date, the risk would still only have been 1–2 per cent; had she not had the surgery at all, the risk would have been 0 per cent. Either way, the defendant's breach could be argued to have caused the loss. But this was not the reason behind the House's decision. The House based its decision on public policy—namely, that if the claimant could not recover damages in this case, the surgeon's duty to disclose material information would be rendered impotent.

★ J Stapleton, 'Occam's Razor Reveals an Orthodox Basis for *Chester v Afshar*' (2006) 122 LQR 426

In such uncertain cases, the standard of proof becomes important. The claimant will need to establish, on the balance of probabilities, that the defendant's negligence caused the claimant's loss.

Problematic applications of the 'but for' test

In many cases, the application of the 'but for' test will be unproblematic. In certain cases, however, the courts have struggled to apply the test in a consistent and accepted manner. In particular, the 'but for' test results in considerable problems where there are several possible causes for the defendant's loss, only one of which is the claimant's breach of duty. In some cases, it is impossible to determine which of the multiple causes actually caused the defendant's loss. So what should the court do in such circumstances?

The following sections discuss the courts' approach.

Multiple causes

Multiple causes can arise in a number of ways:

- concurrent multiple causes (several negligent causes occur *at the same time*);
- successive multiple causes (a negligent act causes loss and a second subsequent negligent act causes the same loss, or greater loss);
- cumulative multiple causes (where several negligent acts contribute over time to the claimant's loss, but it may be inconclusive which of the multiple negligent acts actually caused the loss).

The law relating to cumulative causes will be examined in the next section, when we discuss negligent acts that materially increase the risk of loss. Here, we will focus on concurrent causes and successive causes.

Applying the 'but for' test is problematic where the claimant's loss was the result of concurrent (occurring at the same time) multiple acts of negligence. The problem is clearly demonstrated by the following Canadian case.

Cook v Lewis [1952] 1 DLR 1 (Supreme Court of Canada)

FACTS: The two defendants were hunting. They both simultaneously fired their guns, but instead of hitting their intended target, one of them hit the claimant. Because it was impossible to establish which of the two defendants had shot the claimant, the 'but for' test was useless.

HELD: The Canadian Supreme Court held that both defendants were liable. The onus of proof was on them to show that they had not been negligent. Neither of them was able to show this.

The following much-cited example demonstrates the problem with applying the 'but for' test to cases involving multiple concurrent causes.

Eg Causation and arson

Ricky negligently lights a fire. Half a mile away, Karl also negligently lights a fire. The two instances are unrelated. Both fires spread, merge, and burn down Steve's house. If we were to apply the 'but for' test, neither Ricky nor Karl would be liable. If we were to ask 'but for Ricky's negligence, would Steve have suffered loss?', the answer would be 'yes', because Karl's fire would still have caused the house to burn down, thereby rendering Ricky not liable. If we were to ask 'but for Karl's negligence, would Steve have suffered loss?', the answer would again be 'yes', rendering Karl not liable. Such a situation would clearly be unacceptable.

It has been argued that this is the major weakness of the 'but for' test—namely, that it assumes that only one negligent act brings about the claimant's loss.[128] Accordingly, where two unrelated acts of negligence cause the claimant's loss, the 'but for' test will not apply and instead the claimant is free to sue either one, or both, of the tortfeasors (therefore, liability is joint and several), but obviously, will not be permitted to recover full damages twice. Therefore, in the above example, Steve could:

- sue Ricky for the full loss;
- sue Karl for the full loss; or;
- sue Ricky for 50 per cent of the loss and Karl for 50 per cent of the loss (or a different percentage if the court were to think that Ricky or Karl was more to blame).[129]

It may be thought unfair that Steve could recover the full loss from one party only, given that both Ricky and Karl contributed to Steve's loss. To alleviate this, if Steve

---

128. HLA Hart and T Honoré, *Causation in the Law* (2nd edn, OUP, Oxford, 1985) 113.
129. *Holtby v Brigham & Cowan (Hull) Ltd* [2000] 3 All ER 421 (CA).

does claim the full loss from one party, that party may bring a claim against the other wrongdoer and seek a contribution from him.[130]

Where the negligent acts are successive (occurring one after the other), the application of the 'but for' test is more straightforward. If the negligent act of *B* causes *exactly the same loss* as the prior negligent act of *A*, then, applying the 'but for' test, *B* will not be liable because the rule is that the first cause in time is treated as the operative cause to the exclusion of others.

 Performance Cars Ltd v Abraham [1962] 1 QB 33 (CA)

FACTS: The first defendant negligently collided with the claimant's Rolls Royce, thereby requiring the front wing to be resprayed. Before the repairs could be performed, the second defendant also negligently collided with the Rolls Royce, also damaging the front wing, but caused no greater damage than the first collision.

HELD: 'But for' the second defendant's negligence, would the claimant have suffered loss? Because the car already needed a respray, the answer is 'yes', and so the Court of Appeal held that the second defendant was not liable for the cost of the respray.

⭐ See A Samuels, 'Scratching a Rolls: Consecutive Tortfeasors' Liability for Damages' (1962) 25 MLR 345

In the above case, the second act of negligence caused no greater damage than the first. But what would the situation be if the second act of negligence were to cause *greater* damage than the first?

The following case demonstrates the courts' approach.

Baker v Willoughby [1970] AC 467 (HL)

FACTS: In 1964, the claimant was crossing the road when the defendant negligently ran him over in his car, thereby causing injury to the claimant's left leg and reducing his earning capacity. The claimant sued the defendant, but, in 1967, before the case reached court, the claimant was shot in his left leg during an armed robbery. The leg had to be amputated. The defendant argued that his liability only extended up until the time of the robbery (that is, between 1964 and 1967). After that time, the original injury no longer existed, because the claimant's leg was removed, and so the defendant contended that he should not be liable for any loss of earnings following that date.

HELD: The House of Lords held that the second injury would not obliterate the effects of the first. Lord Reid treated the two torts as examples of concurrent causes (even though they were factually successive). Accordingly, the House awarded damages on the basis that the defendant's negligence ensured that the claimant had lost the use of his left leg for the rest of his life. This would include any loss of earning that occurred after the leg had been amputated.

COMMENT: The defendant's negligence only caused the claimant to lose the use of his left leg for three years. Even if the defendant had not been negligent, the claimant would

---

130. Civil Liability (Contribution) Act 1978, ss 1 and 2.

still have lost his leg in 1967. Therefore, why did the House quantify damages based on the defendant losing the use of his leg for the rest of his life? It is clear that the House was concerned about under-compensating the claimant. Had it limited damages up to the date of the shooting, the claimant could not have recovered damages for the loss of earnings occurring after 1967. Even if the armed robbers were caught, the claimant could not sue them, because his leg was already useless at the time that he was shot. Further, the defendant suffered no extra loss due to the amputation. Had the shooting not occurred, he would still have been liable for any loss of earnings occurring after the date of the first injury.

In *Baker*, the House refused to recognize that the effects of the first tort were overtaken by the second tort. Shortly after the decision in *Baker*, a notable query amongst academics[131] was whether the court would take the same approach if the original loss were overtaken by a non-tortious act. The answer came in the following case.

Jobling v Associated Dairies Ltd [1982] AC 794 (HL)

FACTS: In 1973, the claimant suffered an injury to his back due to the defendant's negligence. This injury reduced the claimant's earning capacity by 50 per cent—something that he intended to claim for in the upcoming litigation. But in 1976, before the trial could take place, the claimant was found to be suffering from a spinal disease called myelapothy—a condition that would render him totally unfit for work by the end of 1976.

HELD: The House of Lords held that the defendant was only liable for the losses caused between 1973 and 1976.

COMMENT: In *Baker*, the House's decision was clearly intended to avoid the claimant being under-compensated for his loss. In *Jobling*, the House was keen to avoid overcompensating the claimant. So, where does this leave *Baker*? Although the House in *Jobling* was critical of the reasoning employed in *Baker*, it did appear to believe that the actual result was 'acceptable on its own facts'.[132] It would appear therefore that the courts do distinguish between cases involving successive torts and cases in which the original loss is overtaken by a neutral, non-tortious event.

Figure 12.1 explains the effect of the above two cases.

Negligent acts that materially increase risk

The claimant's loss may have been caused by a number of cumulative causes. In some cases, all of the causes are tortious; in other cases, there is a mixture between tortious and non-tortious causes. A common thread amongst many of these cases is that it is impossible to state with certainty which one of the causes actually caused the loss in question. In such a case, the court has recognized that the 'but for' test is insufficient and will instead adopt a test based on which cause 'materially contributed' to the loss

---

131. See, e.g., H McGregor, 'Variations on an Enigma' (1970) 33 MLR 378, 382.
132. *Jobling v Associated Dairies Ltd* [1982] AC 794 (HL) 808, 809 (Lord Edmund-Davies).

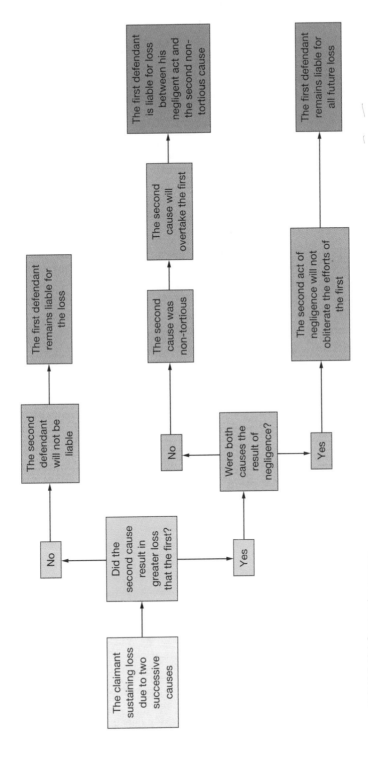

FIGURE 12.1 Successive causes

in question. As we shall see, virtually all of the key cases in this area have occurred in relation to the claimant's ability to claim for negligent exposure to asbestos. But the case that established the 'material contribution' test did not concern an asbestos-related condition; rather, it related to the contraction of dermatitis.

McGhee v National Coal Board [1973] 1 WLR 1 (HL)

FACTS: The claimant worked in the defendant's brick kilns. Conditions were extremely dusty, but the defendant failed to provide on-site facilities to wash away the brick dust. Accordingly, the claimant was unable to remove the dust until he got home, thereby prolonging his exposure. He contracted dermatitis and sued the defendant. The medical evidence could not, however, establish whether the dermatitis was caused by the prolonged exposure to brick dust (due to a lack of washing facilities), or whether it was caused by the innocent exposure to brick dust that was part of his everyday job. Because this could not be established, the 'but for' test could not be applied.

HELD: The House of Lords found for the claimant. Whilst it could not be established that the prolonged exposure caused the dermatitis, it could be established that the defendant's negligence materially contributed to an increase in the risk of contracting dermatitis. The material contribution to the increased risk could be regarded as a material contribution towards the claimant's loss. Therefore, a material contribution to an increase in risk will be regarded as a material contribution towards the injury caused.

★ See GR Rubin, 'Employer's Breach of Duty and Cause of Accident' (1973) 2 ILJ 96

COMMENT: The evidential uncertainty in *McGhee* was considerable. The dermatitis could have been caused by the innocent exposure to brick dust (that is, exposure during working hours) or the negligent exposure to brick dust (that is, exposure after working hours on his journey home). It was even acknowledged that its cause could have been completely unrelated to the claimant's job. But it was nowhere near as uncertain as the next case.

Fairchild v Glenhaven Funeral Services Ltd [2002] UKHL 22

FACTS: The claimant had contracted mesothelioma, an incurable form of cancer that, in the vast majority of cases, is lethal within a year of diagnosis. It is caused by asbestos exposure. Unlike asbestosis, however, it is not caused by long-term exposure; it can be contracted through an encounter with a single fibre of asbestos and, once contracted, subsequent exposure will not exacerbate or accelerate the condition. The problem was that the claimant had been negligently exposed to asbestos whilst working for a number of different employers and it was impossible to determine which employer had negligently exposed him to the asbestos fibre that caused his cancer (accordingly, the 'but for' test was of little use). Further, a number of his previous employers had since become insolvent and so could not be proceeded against.

HELD: The House of Lords held that the claimant could recover damages from any of the employers that were still solvent (the employers were jointly and severally liable). In cases such as this, the 'but for' test could be departed from and a less stringent causal test could be used.

COMMENT: This is a case in which injustice could not be avoided. Had the House ruled that the claimant could not recover damages, it would disadvantage individuals who worked for multiple employers. By ruling in favour of the claimant, it ensures that an employer may be liable even if it did not cause the claimant's loss. This would be especially harsh on an employer that employed a claimant only briefly. Lord Nicholls freely admitted the House's dilemma and stated that its decision was a policy one aimed at securing justice:

> The unattractive consequence, that one of the [defendants] will be held liable for an injury he did not in fact inflict, is outweighed by the even less attractive alternative, that the innocent plaintiff should receive no recompense even though one of the negligent [defendants] injured him. It is this balance…which justifies a relaxation in the standard of causation required. Insistence on the normal standard of causation would work an injustice.[133]

The House in *Fairchild* stated that, in cases such as this, 'the court is applying a different and less stringent test'[134] than the 'but for' test, but the exact nature of this different test was never truly made clear. Further, the approach of the majority differed considerably. Lord Bingham laid down a specific six-part test. Lord Rodger also laid down a six-part test, but it was much more general and little more than an expanded account of the test established in *McGhee*. Lord Hoffmann's five-part test was different again.

⭐ See J Morgan, 'Lost Causes in the House of Lords: *Fairchild v Glenhaven Funeral Services*' (2003) 66 MLR 277

It can be seen that the House in *Fairchild* was concerned about securing fairness and justice. Such concerns were also at the heart of the following case.

🔲 *Barker v Corus Group Ltd* [2006] UKHL 20

FACTS: Barker had died after contracting mesothelioma. He contracted it through being exposed to asbestos in three different working environments:

- while working for the defendant;
- while working for a company that had since become insolvent; and
- while self-employed.

The claimant (Barker's widow) initiated a claim against the defendant. At first instance and in the Court of Appeal, it was held that the claimant could recover the full amount of damages from the defendant.

HELD: With one dissentient, the House of Lords reversed the decision of the Court of Appeal in part. Although the House upheld *Fairchild*, it stated that while each employer could be held liable for exposing the claimant to asbestos dust, even though it could not be proved to have caused the mesothelioma, the approach in *Fairchild* (that is, imposing joint and several liability) was unfair to defendants. Accordingly, it held that a person responsible for the exposure to asbestos could be liable for the exposure only according to his relative degree of contribution to the cause of the claimant contracting mesothelioma. In other words, an individual defendant would only be liable for the extent that he contributed to

---

133. *Fairchild v Glenhaven Funeral Services Ltd* [2002] UKHL 22, [2003] 1 AC 32, [39].
134. Ibid, [45] (Lord Nicholls).

the risk. Therefore, liability was several only and defendants would not be liable for the increase in risk contributed by other parties.

COMMENT: Whilst the House may have been of the opinion that several liability provided a fair compromise between the interests of the claimant and defendant, it was soon apparent that Parliament did not share its opinion. Shortly after the decision, the Compensation Act 2006, s 3, reversed the decision of the House of Lords in *Barker* in relation to mesothelioma. Where a claimant is negligently exposed to asbestos by a number of employers and it is impossible to determine which employer's exposure resulted in the mesothelioma, s 3 provides that the claimant can recover the full damages from any one defendant; ergo joint and several liability is restored. It must be emphasized, however, that whilst s 3 has restored joint and several liability, it applies only in relation to mesothelioma cases. In any other case, the principle in *Barker* will continue and the defendant will be liable only for the increase in the risk to which it contributed. Therefore, if *McGhee* were to be heard today, the owner of the brick kilns would be liable only for the increase in risk that his breach of duty caused.

⭐ See A Kramer, 'Smoothing the Rough Justice of the *Fairchild* Principle' (2006) 122 LQR 547

The above cases concerned mesothelioma, which is a condition that can be contracted from exposure to one asbestos fibre. A more common condition is asbestosis, a serious lung disease that is caused by long-term exposure to asbestos. If the claimant suffering from asbestosis only worked for one employer, causation is unproblematic, but where he worked for several employers, all of whom negligently exposed the claimant to asbestos, it becomes extremely difficult to determine which employer 'caused' the asbestosis. In cases in which multiple negligent defendants successively and cumulatively contribute to the claimant's loss, the courts may be able to determine the extent that the defendant contributed towards the loss and apportion compensation accordingly.

🔑 Holtby v Brigham & Cowan (Hull) Ltd [2000] 3 All ER 421 (CA)

FACTS: Between 1942 and 1981, Holtby (the claimant) worked as a marine fitter—a job that exposed him to dangerous amounts of asbestos dust. He carried out work for the defendant and a number of other employers, none of which supplied him with any safety equipment. In 1996, he was diagnosed with asbestosis. He sued the defendant.

HELD: The Court of Appeal determined that had the defendant provided the claimant with breathing equipment, his asbestosis would have been 75 per cent less severe. Because 75 per cent of his condition was due to the defendant, the Court required the defendant to pay compensation only for the damage caused by it. Accordingly, the Court ordered a 25 per cent reduction of the damages claimed by Holtby.

⭐ See L Gullifer, 'One Cause After Another' (2001) 117 LQR 403

Loss of a chance

If the claimant cannot establish that the defendant's tort materially contributed to his damage, there is an alternative argument. The claimant can argue that whilst the tort did not materially contribute to the damage itself, it did contribute to the loss of a chance to avoid that damage. Such an approach would avoid the 'all or nothing' outcome in which most of the above cases resulted, as the following example demonstrates.

Eg The loss of a chance

Scott is involved in a car crash and suffers injuries to his spine. Helen, a surgeon, is due to perform an operation to correct the spinal injury. The operation is performed negligently and Scott is paralysed from the waist down. Scott cannot establish that Helen's negligence was the material cause of his paralysis, because the initial car crash may have been the cause. But he can establish that, had Helen correctly performed the operation, he would have had a 50 per cent chance of retaining the use of his legs. Accordingly, he could argue that Helen's negligence robbed him of a chance to avoid the loss. If his argument is accepted, Helen will not be liable for the full loss; she will be liable only for the loss of the chance of avoiding paralysis (that is, 50 per cent).

In practice, however, the courts have been reluctant to take such an approach, as the following two cases demonstrate.

Hotson v East Berkshire Area Health Authority [1987] AC 750 (HL)

FACTS: The claimant, a 13-year-old boy, fell out of a tree. He was taken to the defendant's hospital, at which his knee was X-rayed but no injury found, and so he was sent home. Five days later, the claimant returned to the hospital and the defendant discovered the claimant's hip was injured. In the trial, the claimant, now an adult, argued that, as a result of the five-day delay, his hip had become permanently deformed, and claimed damages totalling £46,000. The defendant argued that the hip deformity would have occurred even if it had been diagnosed immediately. The trial judge held that, based upon the medical evidence presented, immediate diagnosis would have resulted in a 25 per cent chance of avoiding the hip deformity. Accordingly, he awarded the claimant 25 per cent of the damages claimed (£11,500) on the ground that the defendant's breach of duty had turned a 75 per cent risk into an inevitability. The Court of Appeal approved the decision.

HELD: The House of Lords rejected the approach adopted by the trial judge and the Court of Appeal, and applied the orthodox material contribution test. The claimant could not establish, on the balance of probabilities, that the defendant's negligence was a material cause of the hip deformity. Therefore, his claim failed and the defendant was not liable.

COMMENT: Whilst the House of Lords may have rejected the claimant's claim for a loss of a chance in this case, it did not reject the concept universally. Croom-Johnson LJ even cited one case, *Kitchen v Royal Air Force Association*,[135] in which damages for loss of a chance were justifiably awarded.

★ See Y Cripps, 'Negligence, Causation and Probability Theory' (1987) 46 CLJ 389

---

135. [1958] 1 WLR 563 (CA).

Gregg v Scott [2005] UKHL 2

FACTS: In 1994, the claimant discovered a lump under his arm and sought the advice of his GP (the defendant). The defendant diagnosed the lump as a benign lipoma and, accordingly, saw no need to refer the claimant to an oncologist. In 1995, the claimant moved home and registered with a new GP. Upon seeing the lump, the GP referred the claimant to an oncologist, who confirmed that the lump was a symptom of a malignant form of cancer known as non-Hodgkin's lymphoma. In January 1996, it was discovered that the cancer had spread to his chest. Had the claimant been treated in 1994, he would have had a 42 per cent chance of surviving for ten years. The nine-month delay in diagnosing the cancer reduced this to 25 per cent and the claimant claimed for the loss of this chance.

HELD: By a majority of three to two, the House of Lords dismissed the claimant's action for damages. In *Hotson*, there was a 25 per cent chance that immediate action could have cured the claimant; in *Gregg*, immediate action would merely increase his chances of a cure (defined as living beyond ten years) to 42 per cent. It was therefore, more likely than not that even if treatment was received in 1994, the claimant would still have died within ten years. It therefore could not be established, on the balance of probabilities, that even if the claimant had received immediate treatment, he would have been cured.

COMMENT: As in *Hotson*, the majority were not completely dismissive to the possibility of awarding damages for the loss of a chance. Lord Phillips MR indicated that awarding damages for loss of a chance may be appropriate where the defendant's negligence leads to an 'adverse outcome'.[136] But Lord Phillips was not convinced that the defendant's negligence had resulted in an adverse outcome. The fact that, when the case was heard in May 2004, the claimant was still alive and had been in remission for six years could be taken as evidence that the defendant's negligence had not resulted in an adverse outcome for the claimant.

★ See E Peel, 'Loss of a Chance Revisited: *Gregg v Scott*' (2003) 66 MLR 623

Despite the above cases, the courts are willing to award compensation for loss of a chance in limited circumstances—namely, where the claimant's loss depends on the hypothetical action of a third party.

Allied Maples Group Ltd v Simmons & Simmons [1995] 1 WLR 1602 (CA)

FACTS: The defendant firm of solicitors advised the claimant to purchase several businesses from a third party. The proposed contract effecting the purchase contained a term that provided that the businesses were not subject to any outstanding liabilities, but this term was absent from the final contract. The claimant purchased the businesses and, due to the term being absent from the final contract, it became liable for the losses of one of the businesses. The claimant alleged that the defendant's negligence in omitting the term had deprived it of the chance to avoid the loss.

HELD: The Court of Appeal held that the claimant could recover compensation for the loss of the chance to avoid the loss.

---

136. *Gregg v Scott* [2005] UKHL 2, [2005] 2 AC 176, [190].

COMMENT: Why was the Court willing in this case to compensate the claimant for the loss of a chance? The answer is not strictly clear. The Court in *Allied Maples* favoured the view that compensation for loss of a chance can be recovered where the claimant's loss depends upon the acts of a third party. But the weight of academic opinion appears to favour the view that the courts are more open to recovery for loss of a chance in cases involving economic loss. Certainly all of the cases in which compensation for loss of a chance has been recovered concern economic loss[137]—but this would appear to be out of line with the general view that physical injury is more deserving of compensation than economic loss.

★ See T Church, 'Where Causation Ends and Quantification Begins' (1996) 55 CLJ 187

Intervening acts or events

The discussion so far has focused on whether the defendant's breach of duty was the factual cause of the claimant's loss. The claimant will also need to establish that the defendant's breach of duty was the cause in law of the claimant's loss. In Chapter 15, we noted that a defendant may not be liable for a breach of contract because some intervening event occurred between the breach and the suffering of the loss, which serves to break the chain of causation. The same principle applies in tort: the defendant may commit a tortious act, but before the claimant suffers loss, an event may occur that affects—or even exacerbates—the loss that the claimant subsequently suffers. The question for the court is whether the defendant is still liable for the loss, or whether the intervening act breaks the chain of causation, thereby relieving the defendant of liability.

An act that breaks the chain of causation is known as a *novus actus interveniens*. Such acts fall into one of three well-established categories:

➡ *novus actus interveniens*: 'new intervening act'

1. natural events (otherwise known as 'acts of God');
2. acts of third parties; or
3. acts of the claimant.

The first category of *novus* concerns natural events (for example, storms, lightning, earthquakes, etc.). In relation to such events, the courts have to strike a delicate balance. On the one hand, it would seem unfair to require a defendant to compensate the claimant for damage the immediate cause of which is a natural event; on the other hand, if the courts regard such events as breaking the chain of causation, it will leave the claimant without any source of redress.

 Carslogie Steamship Co v Royal Norwegian Government [1952] AC 292 (HL)

FACTS: The claimant's ship was damaged in a collision with the defendant's ship. The collision was caused by the defendant's negligence. The claimant's ship altered course towards a port where it could obtain repairs—but on the way to port, it encountered a

---

137. For example, *Kitchen v Royal Air Force Association* [1958] 1 WLR 563 (CA) (failure of a solicitor to bring a claim within the limitation period); *Spring v Guardian Assurance plc* [1995] 2 AC 296 (HL) (inaccuracies in an employment reference).

violent storm, which rendered the ship unseaworthy. When it arrived at port, it took thirty days to repair the collision and storm damage. Had the ship not been damaged in the storm, the collision damage alone could have been repaired in ten days. The claimant alleged that it should be able to claim thirty days' lost profits on the grounds that it would not have been caught in the storm had it not sustained the damage due to the collision with the defendant.

HELD: The House of Lords disagreed. It held that the storm damage was not the result of the collision. The storm broke the chain of causation between the defendant's negligence and the storm damage. Accordingly, the defendant was liable only for the damage caused by the original collision.

The second category of *novus* concerns intervening acts of third parties. This usually arises where the defendant's negligence provides an opportunity for a third party to act. The third party's acts may be beneficial (for example, a rescue), or they may be detrimental (for example, the commission of a crime). Whether a third-party act will constitute a *novus* will very much depend on the facts of the case, but it is relatively well established that if the third-party act constitutes a tort, it will be regarded as an intervening cause (especially if the act was unreasonable or deliberate).[138]

The following two cases demonstrate the court's approach.

 The Oropesa [1943] 1 All ER 211 (CA)

FACTS: A ship, *The Manchester Regiment,* collided with the defendant's ship, *The Oropesa.* The collision was caused partly by the negligence of the defendant. *The Manchester Regiment* was badly damaged, but its master thought that it could be saved. Accordingly, he and sixteen other men set out in a lifeboat towards *The Oropesa* to discuss how to save *The Manchester Regiment.* Unfortunately, before they could reach *The Oropesa,* the weather became worse and the lifeboat capsized, drowning nine of the crew (including the claimant's son). *The Manchester Regiment* subsequently sank. The issue was whether the defendant was liable for the deaths of the crewmen, or whether the master's decision to sail to *The Oropesa* in a lifeboat constituted a *novus actus interveniens.*

HELD: The master's actions were reasonable. Therefore, the Court of Appeal held that the deaths were not caused by the master's actions, but by the collision. Accordingly, the defendant was liable for the death of the claimant's son.

⭐ See W Freidman, *'The Manchester Regiment*: Chain of Causation—Alternative Danger' (1943) 6 MLR 237

 Knightley v Johns [1982] 1 WLR 349 (CA)

FACTS: The defendant negligently overturned his car in a one-way tunnel. The police inspector in charge forgot to close the tunnel and so a police motorcyclist (the claimant) was ordered to close the tunnel. The claimant drove back to the tunnel against the flow of traffic, believing this to be the quickest way to close the tunnel and avoid a further incident. Whilst driving around a blind bend, the claimant (who was found by the Court not to have been negligent) collided with another motorist and was injured. The issue before the Court was whether the defendant was liable for the claimant's injuries, or whether the inspector's acts were negligent and, if so, whether his negligence constituted a *novus actus interveniens*.

HELD: Stephenson LJ stated: 'Negligent conduct is more likely to break the chain of causation than conduct which is not.'[139] The Court of Appeal held that the actions of the police inspector were negligent and therefore constituted an intervening act that broke the chain of causation. Accordingly, the defendant was not liable for the claimant's injuries. The Court of Appeal further stated that an act of a third party would not break the chain of causation if it were a reasonably foreseeable consequence of the defendant's negligence. The inspector's negligence could not be regarded as reasonably foreseeable.

The third category of *novus* concerns acts of the claimant. Normally, cases in which the claimant contributes to his loss will concern contributory negligence, not causation. In some cases, however, it may be argued that the claimant's actions were such that they broke the chain of causation. The advantage of such a claim is that it would provide a complete defence, whereas contributory negligence only provides a partial defence. The general rule seems to be that the court will be more likely to regard the claimant's own conduct as a *novus* if it can be shown to be so unreasonable as to wipe out the defendant's original wrongdoing.

The following two cases show this test in practice.

McKew v Holland & Hannen & Cubitts (Scotland) Ltd [1969] 3 All ER 1621 (HL)

FACTS: The claimant's leg was injured due to the negligence of the defendant, his employer. As a result, without warning, he occasionally lost control of his leg and it would give way. Three weeks later, he was inspecting a house that he was considering renting. He attempted to walk down some steep stairs, while holding a small child by the hand. The stairs had no handrail for him to hold onto with the other hand. His leg gave way and, to avoid falling, he jumped to the bottom of the stairs, breaking his ankle in the process. The claimant alleged that the defendant was also responsible for this injury.

HELD: The House of Lords held that the defendant was not responsible for the second injury. The claimant's unreasonable conduct had broken the chain of causation. Note that it was not the act of jumping down the stairs that was deemed unreasonable: it was his decision to walk down a steep staircase without assistance that was held to constitute the *novus*.

---

139. *Knightley v Johns* [1982] 1 WLR 349 (CA) 366.

> ### 🔑 Wieland v Cyril Lord Carpets Ltd [1969] 3 All ER 1006 (HL)
>
> **FACTS:** The claimant was injured in a car accident due to the defendant's negligence. Her neck was injured and so she had to wear a support collar, which made the use of her bifocal spectacles difficult, because she could not tilt her head. Due to this, she did not wish to use public transport and asked her son to drive her home. Whilst being assisted down a flight of stairs by her son, she fell and fractured her ankles.
>
> **HELD:** The House of Lords held that the defendant was liable for the injury to the claimant's ankles. Because the claimant was being assisted by her son, her actions were not unreasonable and therefore did not constitute a *novus*.

> ### ‹› Key points summary
>
> - The claimant will need to establish that the defendant's negligence was the factual and legal cause of his loss.
>
> - The court will ask whether the claimant would have suffered the loss 'but for' the defendant's negligence. A positive answer means that the loss would have occurred anyway and the defendant will not be liable.
>
> - Where there are multiple concurrent negligent causes of loss, liability is joint and several.
>
> - Where there are successive negligent causes and the later causes do no more damage than the first, only the first defendant will be liable.
>
> - A defendant will be liable where his negligence materially increases the risk of the claimant suffering loss, even where it cannot be proved that the defendant actually caused the loss.
>
> - The courts are reluctant to allow a claimant to recover damages where the defendant's act causes the claimant to lose a chance to avoid loss.
>
> - Natural acts, acts of a third party, and acts of the claimant may break the chain of causation and free the defendant of liability for a negligent act. Such an act is known as a *novus actus interveniens* ('newly intervening act').

Remoteness

🔗 The contractual rules of remoteness are discussed at p 337

Having established that the defendant's negligence was the factual and legal cause of the claimant's loss, it needs to be determined whether that loss was too remote—a concept that we have already examined in relation to contract law and so readers should be familiar with the basic concept. There, we established that a defendant will not be liable for all losses that result from his breach of contract: some losses will be deemed too remote. The same principle applies in tort. The rules relating to remoteness serve to limit the liability of a defendant for his acts of negligence.

Such limitations may be justified on policy reasons; other limitations may be simply practicable. As Winfield stated: 'The line must be drawn somewhere…not on the grounds of pure logic, but simply for practical reasons.'[140]

The need to 'draw a line' can be seen in the following example.

Eg **The need for rules on remoteness**

On 5 September, Charlotte is walking along the pavement, when Joe, a drunk driver, negligently mounts the pavement and collides with her. Charlotte is seriously injured. She has to spend a month in hospital and her mobility will be impaired for the rest of her life. She was due to get married on 9 September, but the wedding and honeymoon had to be cancelled. Due to the short notice of cancellation, refunds of monies paid were unavailable. Further, she had applied for a promotion within her firm and was shortlisted for an interview to take place on 23 September. Because she was unable to attend, the promotion was awarded to someone else. The above events have resulted in Charlotte becoming depressed and she is receiving private psychiatric treatment.

In this relatively simple example, a substantial number of losses occur, as follows.

1. *Physical injury* Obviously, Charlotte sustained injury in the initial collision, but her mobility will also be impaired for the rest of her life.

2. *Property damage* The collision may also have caused damage to property on her person (for example, clothes, mobile phone, laptop, etc.).

3. *Loss of earnings* Charlotte was off work for a period of time. Her lack of mobility may affect her ability to do her job or to gain future employment.

4. *Economic loss* Cancelling the wedding and honeymoon has resulted in significant economic loss. Further, she has lost out on a chance of gaining a promotion. She is also paying for private psychiatric treatment.

5. *Distress* The injuries sustained would have caused significant distress, as would the occurrence of the subsequent events.

Should Joe have to compensate Charlotte for all of the above losses, or should a 'line be drawn'? Should damages be limited to the direct consequences of Joe's negligence? Should it matter that Joe could not have known the consequences of his actions would cause so much loss? The law relating to remoteness aims to answer these questions.

Reasonable foreseeability

It used to be the case that a claimant could recover all direct losses resulting from the tort, even if such losses were unforeseeable.[141] In 1961, this changed and the courts held that the defendant would only be liable for those types of loss that were a reasonably foreseeable consequence of his negligence.

---

140. WVH Rogers, *Winfield & Jolowicz on Tort* (17th edn, Sweet & Maxwell, London, 2006) 291.
141. *Re Polemis and Furness, Withy & Co* [1921] 3 KB 560 (CA).

Overseas Tankship (UK) Ltd v Morts Dock & Engineering Co (The Wagon Mound) (No 1) [1961] AC 388 (PC)

FACTS: The defendant's ship, *The Wagon Mound*, was moored in Sydney Harbour. Whilst taking on oil, the defendant's negligence resulted in a large quantity of oil being discharged into the harbour. The oil spread to a wharf owned by the claimant, where it contaminated the slipways (known as 'fouling'). The claimant was a shipbuilder and repairer, and it was concerned that its welding could ignite the oil. The wharf manager, after consulting the manager of an oil company, informed the defendant that it could carry on welding. A piece of molten metal dripped onto a floating cloth, which caught fire and ignited the oil. There was no way that the defendant could have known that this could happen. The fire damaged the claimant's wharf and several ships being repaired there.

HELD: The defendant was not liable for the fire damage. In overturning *Re Polemis*, the Privy Council held that the defendant would only be liable if the type of damage suffered by the claimant were reasonably foreseeable. The fire damage was not reasonably foreseeable, so the claim failed. The damage caused to the wharf by fouling was foreseeable, however, and was therefore recoverable.

★ See RWM Dias, 'Negligence: Remoteness—The *Polemis* Rule' (1961) CLJ 23

Type of harm

As established above, a claimant can only recover loss due to the negligence of another if the type of harm suffered was reasonably foreseeable. The issue for the courts to determine is how wide or narrow should be the interpretation of the phrase 'type of harm'. Unfortunately, the approach of the courts—especially the lower courts—has been somewhat inconsistent.

In the following case, the Court of Appeal adopted a somewhat narrow approach.

Tremain v Pike [1969] 1 WLR 1556 (CA)[142]

FACTS: The claimant was employed as a herdsman by the defendant farmer. The defendant had negligently allowed rats to infest a number of the farm buildings. The claimant contracted leptospirosis (better known as 'Weil's disease')—a disease caused by exposure to rat's urine.

HELD: The claimant could not recover damages. The Court of Appeal stated that whilst it was reasonably foreseeable that the claimant could suffer injury due to the rat infestation (for example, rat bites, food contamination), the contraction of Weil's disease was not regarded as reasonably foreseeable and was therefore too remote.

★ See RWM Dias, 'Kind and Extent of Damage in Negligence' (1970) 28 CLJ 28

Conversely, in the next case, the House of Lords adopted a much more generous approach.

---

142. See also *Doughty v Turner Manufacturing Co Ltd* [1964] 1 QB 518 (CA).

Jolley v Sutton London Borough Council [2000] 3 All ER 409 (HL)

FACTS: For two years, a boat had been left abandoned on a piece of land owned by the defendant council, beside which stood a block of flats. The council knew of the boat and planned to remove it, but never did. The claimant, a 14-year-old boy, and his friend jacked up the boat in order to repair it. The jack gave way and the boat fell on the claimant, causing him to suffer serious spinal injuries and rendering him a paraplegic. The Court of Appeal held that the damage was too remote. It held that the only reasonably foreseeable risk resulting from the council's failure to remove the boat was that children might climb on it and fall through the rotten deck. Accordingly, injury caused by a jack giving way was not reasonably foreseeable. The claimant appealed.

HELD: The House of Lords reversed the decision of the Court of Appeal and awarded damages. The House held that the foreseeable risk was a mere general one of children meddling with the boat and being injured in the process. The harm to the claimant was therefore recoverable.

⭐ See R Williams, 'Remoteness: Some Unexpected Mischief' (2001) 117 LQR 30

It would appear that, currently, the more accepted view is the claimant-friendly approach evidenced in *Jolley*. Weight was lent to this by the following recent decision of the House of Lords.

Corr v IBC Vehicles Ltd [2008] UKHL 13

FACTS: Corr was employed by the defendant as an engineer. Due to a malfunctioning machine of the defendant, Corr suffered severe injuries that left him disfigured. He developed post-traumatic stress disorder and, following a suicide attempt, he was admitted to a psychiatric hospital to undergo electroconvulsive shock therapy. The treatment did not work and he remained depressed. Six years after the original incident, he committed suicide. Prior to his death, he had commenced proceedings against the defendant for the injuries that he suffered. His widow was substituted as claimant and continued the proceedings. The defendant admitted that the accident was caused by its negligence, but argued that it was not liable for Corr's suicide, because the suicide constituted a *novus actus interveniens*.

HELD: The House of Lords held that the defendant was liable for Corr's suicide and that the claimant could therefore recover compensation under the Fatal Accidents Act 1976. Lord Bingham stated that 'the inescapable fact is that depression, possibly severe, possibly very severe, was a foreseeable consequence of this breach'[143] and that 'it was not incumbent on [the claimant] to show that suicide itself was foreseeable'.[144] He went on to state:

> The rationale of the principle that a novus actus interveniens breaks the chain of causation is fairness.... It is in no way unfair to hold the employer responsible for this dire consequence of its breach of duty, although it could well be thought unfair to the victim not to do so.[145]

⭐ See J O'Sullivan, 'Employer's Liability for Injured Employee's Suicide' (2008) 67 CLJ 241

---

143. *Corr v IBC Vehicles Ltd* [2008] UKHL 13, [2008] 1 AC 884, [13].   144. Ibid.
145. Ibid, [15] and [16].

The 'eggshell skull' rule

The 'eggshell skull' rule constitutes a major exception to the reasonable foreseeability rule. Currently, the 'eggshell skull' rule arises in the following situation. *A* commits a tort that causes *B* injury, but, due to *B* having some form of weakness or pre-existing condition, the harm suffered by *B* is much greater than could foreseeably be expected. The question arising is whether *A* should be liable for the damage caused, or only for that damage which could be foreseen.

The rule was established in the following case.

 Dulieu v White & Sons [1901] 2 KB 669 (DC)

FACTS: The claimant was a pregnant woman, who worked behind the bar in a pub. An employee of the defendant negligently drove a horse-drawn van through the doors of the pub. The shock of witnessing this caused the claimant to become ill and she gave birth prematurely. As a result, the child was born with learning difficulties (although the statement of the claim worded it less delicately, stating 'the said child was born an idiot').[146] The claimant sought damages for her illness and for the premature birth of her child (damages for the child's mental difficulties were not sought). The defendant argued that, because there was no immediate physical injury, but only psychiatric illness resulting from shock, the illness was too remote and could not be recovered.

HELD: The court rejected the defendant's argument, and awarded the claimant damages for her illness and the premature birth of her child. Kennedy J stated:

> If a man is negligently run over or otherwise negligently injured in his body, it is no answer to the sufferer's claim for damages that he would have suffered less injury, or no injury at all, if he had not had an unusually thin skull or an unusually weak heart.[147]

Accordingly, a defendant is fully liable to a claimant whose injuries are aggravated by an inherent defect (for example, a thin skull), even though the defendant could not reasonably have foreseen this. Where the aggravated injury is of the same type, the defendant could equally be liable on the basis that the extent of the damage need not be foreseeable. But the eggshell skull rule also extends to cases in which the secondary injury due to the inherent defect is of a different type, on the basis of the rule that a tortfeasor must take his victim as he finds him.

The following case (which also held that the eggshell skull rule survived the decision in *The Wagon Mound (No 1)*) provides the classic example of a secondary injury of a different type from the original injury.

 Smith v Leech Brain & Co [1962] 2 QB 405 (QB)

FACTS: Smith was burnt on the lip by a piece of molten metal, due to the negligence of his employer (the defendant). Unknown to both Smith and the defendant, the tissue in Smith's lips was pre-cancerous. The burn triggered the cancer and he died three years later. Had the

---

146. *Dulieu v White & Sons* [1901] 2 KB 669 (DC) 670. 147. Ibid, 679.

burn not occurred, his cancer might never have arisen, although it was likely that it would. Smith's widow claimed damages for his death from the defendant. The defendant argued that it could not reasonably have foreseen that Smith would contract cancer due to the burn.

HELD: The High Court stated that the correct test was not whether the defendant could foresee the cancer, but whether it could foresee the type of injury that was suffered— namely, the burn. The answer to this was 'yes'. Once that was established, the eggshell skull rule meant that the defendant was also liable for the results of the burn. Accordingly, the claimant was awarded damages for her husband's death.

> ⭐ See G Dworkin, 'A Negligent Tortfeasor Still Takes His Victim as He Finds Him' (1962) 25 MLR 471

To date, the vast majority of cases have involved physical injury. Whether some form of the eggshell skull rule could apply universally to non-physical injury (for example, property damage) has yet to be decided. The closest that the courts have come to applying the eggshell skull rule to property damage has been in cases involving the claimant's impecuniosity. If the defendant's tort causes the claimant to suffer loss, but this loss is then increased by the claimant's financial inability to minimize the loss, is the defendant liable for the increased loss? Initially, in *The Liesbosch Dredger v SS Edison*,[148] the House of Lords held that such increased losses were too remote and could not be recovered. But this case was distinguished on a number of occasions on unconvincing grounds[149] in cases in which a court has held that increased damages could be recovered. The decision of the House in *The Liesbosch Dredger v SS Edison* has now been overruled,[150] and it appears that the eggshell skull rule can apply to cases involving the claimant's impecuniosity.

> ➡ impecuniosity: the state of having little, or no, money

Other torts

Whilst the reasonable foreseeability test establishes the test to determine the remoteness of loss in negligence, it does not follow that this test applies to all torts. In particular, this test does not appear to apply in the case of torts that can only be committed intentionally (for example, malicious falsehood, conspiracy, and deceit). In such cases, the claimant can recover all losses directly caused by the tort, irrespective of their foreseeability.

Key points summary

- The claimant will need to establish that the harm suffered was not too remote from the defendant's negligent act.

- The defendant is only liable for those types of harm that are a reasonably foreseeable consequence of his negligence.

- Provided that the type of harm caused is foreseeable, it does not matter that it was caused in an unforeseeable way, or that it caused greater damage than could be reasonably foreseen.

---

148. [1933] AC 448 (HL).
149. For example, *Dodd Properties (Kent) Ltd v Canterbury County Council* [1980] 1 WLR 433 (CA).
150. *Lagden v O'Connor* [2003] UKHL 64, [2004] 1 AC 1067.

Chapter conclusion

There is little doubt that negligence is the most important tort and is central in allowing victims of accidents to obtain compensation for injuries that they suffer. Given the breadth of the tort and the potential for liability under it, it is therefore important that businesses understand to what extent they can be liable for their negligent acts (and, as we shall see in Chapter 14, for the negligent acts of their employees). At the very least, this involves a sound understanding of the duties of care that businesses owe. Indeed, given the scope of a business' activities, the duty of care that it owes will be considerably wider than that owed by an individual and the potential for liability that much greater.

However important negligence might be, it is not the only tort that can affect businesses. In the next chapter, we examine a number of other torts that can be committed by businesses, as well as torts that aim to protect businesses from the interference of others.

Self-test questions

1. What are the requirements for establishing negligence?

2. Gabriel is considering purchasing shares in Digisoft plc, a software company. He acquires a copy of the company's annual accounts, which show the company to be extremely profitable. He therefore purchases a thousand shares in Digisoft at a price of £6 per share. A week later, it is announced that Digisoft have entered voluntary liquidation. It transpires that the company was not actually profitable, but was running at a loss, and that the directors had been siphoning away company funds for personal use. The company's auditors, who signed off on the company's accounts, discovered none of this. Advise Gabriel. Would your answer differ if Gabriel had not relied on the company's accounts, but on a report that Gabriel commissioned a firm of accountants to prepare for his use alone?

3. Explain the difference between a 'primary' victim and a 'secondary' victim in cases of psychiatric injury. Why does the law distinguish between the two?

4. Are damages recoverable in the following situations?
    (a) Peter works as a porter at an airport. A plane crashes into the runway, due to the malfunction of a component negligently manufactured by AviaTech plc. Peter witnessed the crash, but was safely inside the terminal when it happened. The next day, he discovers that his girlfriend Joanne, an air hostess, was on board the plane when it crashed and was killed. Peter becomes clinically depressed.
    (b) BioMed plc (a pharmaceutical company) and MedCare Ltd (a company running a number of private hospitals) agree that BioMed will provide drugs and medical equipment to MedCare for the next five years. Both parties instruct Evans & Grimwood LLP (a firm of solicitors) to draft a contract based on what has been agreed, emphasizing that the contract needs to be drawn up and signed one month before the opening of a new private hospital in London. Evans & Grimwood fails to draft the contract on time and the hospital is opened, but cannot take any patients, because it lacks the equipment that would have been obtained from BioMed.

5. Why, historically, has the law of negligence been reluctant to allow recovery for 'pure' economic loss?

Further reading

Barker, K, 'Wielding *Occam*'s Razor: Pruning Strategies for Economic Loss'
(2006) 26 OJLS 289
*Discusses the three main approaches to the recovery of pure economic loss, and
examines the combination approach evidenced in Customs and Excise Commissioners
v Barclays Bank*

Cartwright, J, 'Remoteness of Damage in Contract and Tort: A Reconsideration'
(1966) 55 CLJ 488
*Analyses the rules relating to remoteness, focusing on the differences between the rules in
contract and tort*

Murphy, J, *Street on Torts* (12th edn, OUP, Oxford, 2007) ch 5
An excellent discussion of the rules relating to causation and remoteness

Nolan, D, 'Psychiatric Injury at the Crossroads' (2004) JPI Law 1
*Provides a clear and comprehensive analytical overview of the law relating to psychiatric
injury*

Rogers, WVH, *Winfield & Jolowicz on Tort* (17th edn, Sweet & Maxwell, London, 2006)
ch 5
*A detailed, but clear and well-written, discussion of the law relating to the duty of care and
breach of duty*

 Remember to visit the **Online Resource Centre** at **<http://www.
oxfordtextbooks.co.uk/roach>** to access the following resources
on Chapter 12, 'The tort of negligence': more **practice questions** and
answers; a **glossary** of key terms; **multiple-choice questions**; **revision
summaries**; **audio updates** when relevant; **diagrams** in pdf; and **audio
exam advice** on this key topic.

13 Business-related torts

- Product liability
- Wrongful interference with goods
- Interference with contract, trade, or business (the 'economic torts')
- Employers' liability

- Occupiers' liability
- Nuisance and *Rylands v Fletcher*
- Defamation
- Breach of statutory duty

INTRODUCTION

Whilst there is no doubt that, from a business perspective, negligence is the most important tort, there are many other torts that can be committed by and against businesses. Some of these are not torts in their own right, but rather specific forms of broader torts (for example, product liability at common law is a specific form of negligence). Others are applications of existing torts that have developed their own rules due to the identity of the tortfeasor (for example, employers' liability). A detailed examination of the numerous torts that can arise in a business context is beyond the scope of this text. Here, we will focus only on the principal torts that can affect businesses, beginning with one of the most important—namely, liability for defective products.

Product liability

🔗 Visit the Online Resource Centre 🌐 for more on terms implied under the Sale of Goods Act 1979 in the chapter entitled 'The sale of goods'

🔗 The doctrine of privity and the 1999 Act are discussed at p 143

The primary remedy for a person who has purchased a defective product will be a claim for breach of contract (especially where the implied terms found in the Sale of Goods Act 1979 apply). Privity will, however, ensure that such an action can only be brought against the seller by the person who purchased the goods, unless the Contracts (Rights of Third Parties) Act 1999 is applicable. A claimant third party who has sustained loss due to a defective product will therefore usually be unable to bring a claim in contract against the seller, but might be able to succeed in tort, where he will have a choice between an action against the manufacturer under the common law and/or an action under the Consumer Protection Act 1987. The availability of these actions is also important where the seller is insolvent.

Common law

We discussed in Chapter 12 how Lord Atkin, in the case of *Donoghue v Stevenson*,[1] laid down the 'neighbour test' that was to form the basis of the modern tort of negligence. But the neighbour test was *obiter*; the *ratio* of the case related specifically to defective products and is known as the 'narrow rule'.

Donoghue v Stevenson and the 'neighbour test' are discussed in more detail at p 382

The narrow rule was also laid down by Lord Atkin, who stated that:

> A manufacturer of products, which he sells in such a form as to show that he intends them to reach the ultimate consumer in the form in which they left him with no reasonable possibility of intermediate examination, and with the knowledge that the absence of reasonable care in the preparation...of the products will result in an injury to the consumer's life or property, owes a duty to the consumer to take reasonable care.[2]

The narrow rule still forms the basis of a claim for product liability at common law, and contains a number of phrases and terms that require further discussion.

Who is a 'manufacturer'?

Lord Atkin's narrow rule imposed a duty of care upon 'manufacturers' of products, but subsequent cases have expanded the scope of potential defendants to include virtually anyone who is involved in the supply chain, not simply those who 'made' the 'product'. This could include erectors,[3] fitters,[4] repairers,[5] and assemblers.[6] A supplier or distributor of goods will not normally owe a duty of care, unless the circumstances are such that he ought reasonably to have checked the goods. A second-hand car dealer, for example, can reasonably be expected to check the steering of a used car or, at least, to warn a prospective buyer that he has not done so.[7]

What are 'products'?

The word 'products' originally applied only to food and drink, but has since has been interpreted just as widely as the word 'manufacturer' to include virtually any product (for example, motor vehicles,[8] lifts,[9] hair dye,[10] computer software,[11] chemicals,[12] and tombstones).[13] Because the test includes the 'preparation' of products, it follows that negligent packaging, labelling, or instructions of use can also result in liability.[14]

---

1. [1932] AC 562 (HL).   2. Ibid, 599.
3. *Brown v Cotterill* (1934) 51 TLR 21 (KB).
4. *Malfroot v Noxal Ltd* (1935) 51 TLR 551 (KB).
5. *Haseldine v CA Daw & Son Ltd* [1941] 2 KB 343 (CA).
6. *Howard v Furness-Houlder Argentine Lines Ltd* [1936] 2 All ER 296 (KB).
7. *Andrews v Hopkinson* [1957] 1 QB 229 (QB).
8. *Herschtal v Stewart and Ardern Ltd* [1940] 1 KB 155 (KB).
9. *Haseldine v CA Daw & Son Ltd* [1941] 2 KB 343 (CA).
10. *Watson v Buckley, Osborne, Garrett & Co Ltd* [1940] 1 All ER 174.
11. *St Albans City and District Council v International Computers Ltd* [1996] 4 All ER 481 (CA).
12. *Vacwell Engineering Co Ltd v BDH Chemicals Ltd* [1971] 1 QB 88 (QB).
13. *Brown v Cotterill* (1934) 51 TLR 21 (KB).
14. *Distillers Co (Biochemicals) Ltd v Thompson* [1971] AC 458 (PC).

'Sells'

Lord Atkin's test refers to a manufacturer who 'sells' a product and while it is probable that liability under the narrow rule would not be imposed on a gratuitous provider of goods,[15] it is likely that liability could be imposed where goods are given away in the course of a business (for example, free samples[16] or promotional gifts). Whilst the narrow rule may not apply to purely gratuitous transfers of goods, there is no reason why the 'neighbour test' of Lord Atkin should not apply to such transfers.

Who is the 'ultimate consumer'?

In keeping with the breadth of the above definitions, the courts will permit a wide array of persons to bring a claim under Lord Atkin's narrow rule. This will obviously include users of the product,[17] but will also include anyone who could be foreseeably injured by the product[18] and anyone within physical proximity to the product.[19]

The effect of an 'intermediate examination'

According to Lord Atkin's test, a manufacturer will only owe a duty if the consumer could not reasonably be expected to carry out an intermediate examination. The mere possibility of an examination is not enough to deny the existence of a duty,[20] nor is the opportunity to examine the goods. In order for a duty of care to be denied, the manufacturer will need to show that an examination was a reasonable expectation. This could occur where the seller specifically warned or recommended that the buyer examine the product.[21] Because reasonable expectation is the crucial test, it follows that an unexpected examination will not result in the denial of the duty.

Breach of duty and causation

Once it is established that the manufacturer owes a duty of care to the ultimate consumer, it must be established that this duty was breached. The burden of proof is placed upon the claimant, who will need to establish that the defendant manufacturer failed to take reasonable care. Establishing this under *Donoghue v Stevenson* was 'verging on impossible',[22] because Lord Macmillan stated that the claimant must prove that the defect that caused the injury was present when the product left the defendant's control and that the defect was not caused by the defendant's carelessness. He added that there was no presumption of negligence, nor any justification for applying the maxim *res ipsa loquitur*. This harshness has now been mitigated by the apparent application of *res ipsa loquitur* to product liability cases.[23]

Res ipsa loquitur is discussed at p 419

---

15. J Murphy, *Street on Torts* (12th edn, OUP, Oxford, 2007) 404.

16. *Hawkins v Coulsdon and Purley Urban District Council* [1954] 1 QB 319 (CA) 333 (Denning LJ).

17. *Grant v Australian Knitting Mills* [1936] AC 85 (PC).

18. *Stennett v Hancock and Peters* [1939] 2 All ER 578 (KB).

19. *Brown v Cotterill* (1934) 51 TLR 21 (KB).

20. *Driver v William Willett (Contractors) Ltd* [1969] 1 All ER 665.

21. *Kubach v Hollands* [1937] 3 All ER 907 (KB).

22. J Murphy, *Street on Torts* (12th edn, OUP, Oxford, 2007) 406.

23. *Grant v Australian Knitting Mills Ltd* [1936] AC 85 (PC). Although the Privy Council never actually used the phrase '*res ipsa loquitur*' itself, the language used makes it virtually certain that *res ipsa loquitur* will apply.

Establishing breach of duty will still prove a most formidable task, because the claimant will need to establish that it was the defendant's breach of duty that caused his loss and not the intervening act of an intermediate person. This will require the claimant to adduce sufficient evidence indicating that the defect existed when it left the control of the defendant and did not subsequently arise.

The following case demonstrates how difficult this can be to establish.

Evans v Triplex Safety Glass Co Ltd [1936] 1 All ER 283 (KB)

FACTS: The claimant purchased a car, the windscreen of which was made of 'Triplex Toughened Safety Glass', which was manufactured by the defendant. A year after the car was purchased, with no warning and with no apparent cause, the windscreen shattered whilst the claimant was driving, injuring him, his wife, and his son. The claimant sued for damages.

HELD: The claim failed and the manufacturer was not liable. The claimant could not establish that the windscreen was defective when it left the defendant's control. Accordingly, the High Court stated that it was possible that the glass could have been weakened when it was being attached to the car, or that the glass could have broken due to some other non-manufacturing defect.

Where the claimant uses the product in an unforeseeable or materially different purpose from that for which it was designed, then it is likely that causation will not be established. In such a case, the injury may not be caused by the product's defect, but by the claimant's misuse of the product. Where both a defect in the product and misuse are present, causation is likely to be proven, but the defendant will be likely to be able to plead contributory negligence successfully.[24]

The defence of contributory negligence is discussed at p 529

Injury

In order to recover damages, the manufacturer's negligence must result in 'injury to the consumer's life or property'. Accordingly, product liability at common law is concerned with physical loss caused by dangerous goods. It would appear that loss caused by defective goods is not covered: as Winfield and Jolowicz note, if Mrs Donoghue's bottle of ginger beer were to have contained pure water, her claim would be likely to have failed.[25] Where goods that are not dangerous, but merely unsatisfactory, have been sold, the buyer's only remedy is to obtain compensation via an action under the Sale of Goods Act 1979.

Whilst damage to property is recoverable, this does not include damage to the product itself, because such loss amounts to pure economic loss (reduction in value of the product), which, as we have seen, is generally not recoverable. This is a problematic limitation, because it is not always easy to determine whether a product is itself a product or is merely part of a larger, more complex product, as the following example demonstrates.

---

24. *Griffiths v Arch Engineering Co Ltd* [1968] 3 All ER 217.
25. WVH Rogers, *Winfield & Jolowicz on Tort* (17th edn, Sweet & Maxwell, London, 2006) 447.

Damage to the product itself

Eddie purchases a brand new Ferrari F430. After he has driven the car a mere five miles, one of the tyres bursts, causing Eddie to skid and drive into a wall. The car is a write-off, but Eddie sustains no injuries. Would the tyre itself count as a product, which caused property damage to the rest of the car? Or, would the car be regarded as the product and the tyre a mere component? The former interpretation would allow Eddie to claim for the damage to the car. The latter interpretation would bar Eddie's claim in tort, because damage to the product itself is not recoverable.

The issue is a divisive one. Lord Lloyd stated *obiter*, in *Aswan Engineering Establishment Co v Lupdine Ltd*,[26] that, in such a case, his 'provisional view'[27] would be that the tyre would be a product in its own right (that is, separate from the car) and the damage to the car would constitute recoverable property damage. But several commentators[28] contend that the opposite is the case and that the tyre would merely be part of an overall defective product (the car), thereby rendering the damage irrecoverable in tort.

Imagine that, instead of the new tyres bursting, they function perfectly. Two years later, as part of routine maintenance, TyreChange Ltd replaces all four tyres. If one of these tyres were to burst, causing the car to crash, it is much more likely that the replacement tyre would be regarded as a product in its own right, thereby allowing Eddie to claim for the damage sustained to his car.[29]

The line between property damage and economic loss is a difficult one to draw, and there is little concrete authority on the subject—and what authority does exist is relatively superficial, with a notable number of split decisions.

‹› Key points summary

- Product liability at common law is based upon Lord Atkin's narrow rule from *Donoghue v Stevenson*. It is therefore a species of negligence.

- The narrow rule applies to 'manufacturers', which means not only those who 'made' the product, but also people such as repairers, assemblers, fitters, and erectors.

- A manufacturer of a product will not owe a duty of care if the consumer could be reasonably expected to examine the product prior to purchasing it.

- The claimant will need to establish that the defect existed when the product left the defendant's control. The claimant can be aided by the application of *res ipsa loquitur*.

- Causation may not be established where injury was caused by the claimant's misuse of the product.

---

26. [1987] 1 WLR 1 (CA).   27. Ibid, 21.
28. For example, J Murphy, *Street on Torts* (12th edn, OUP, Oxford, 2007) 406; S Deakin, A Johnston, and B Markesinis, *Markesinis and Deakin's Tort Law* (6th edn, OUP, Oxford, 2008) 743.
29. *Andrew Weir Shipping Ltd v Wartsila UK Ltd* [2004] EWHC 1284 (Comm), [2004] 2 Lloyd's Rep 337; WVH Rogers, *Winfield & Jolowicz on Tort* (17th edn, Sweet & Maxwell, London, 2006) 448.

- The defect in the product must cause 'injury to the consumer's life or property'. It can therefore be seen that product liability at common law is concerned with dangerous goods as opposed to unsatisfactory goods.

- Damage to the product itself cannot be recovered in tort, because it amounts to pure economic loss.

The Consumer Protection Act 1987

In the 1950s and 1960s, thousands of pregnant women were prescribed a drug called Thalidomide to help to alleviate their morning sickness. An unforeseen side effect of the drug resulted in thousands of these women giving birth to babies with severe deformities. The Thalidomide tragedy created a wave of public concern leading to the Law Commission[30] recommending the introduction of a strict liability regime in relation to product liability, whereby manufacturers would be liable merely because a product was defective: there would be no need to establish fault, as is required under the common law discussed above. Around the same time, the European Commission had presented a draft directive on product liability to the Council of Ministers, and the Council of Europe had published a Convention on Product Liability. Both of these European proposals aimed to harmonize EU product liability law by recommending the introduction of a strict liability regime. But there were deep divisions within the member States, which could not agree on the appropriate extent of manufacturer's liability, with the controversial 'development risks' defence proving a particularly troublesome issue. As a result, it was not until 1985 that Council Directive 85/374/EEC was passed, which required each EU member State introduce a system of strict liability in relation to defective products. In the UK, this Directive was implemented by the Consumer Protection Act 1987 (CPA 1987), Pt I (ss 1–9).

The development risks defence is discussed at p 453

It is important to note that the provisions of the CPA 1987 do not replace the common law rules discussed above, or the implied terms to be found in the Sale of Goods Act 1979; rather, the regime introduced by the CPA 1987 exists alongside existing measures. Where the injured party has a contract with the manufacturer of the defective product, the CPA 1987, Pt I, will be largely redundant, because the Sale of Goods Act 1979 will be considerably more useful. But where no contract exists, the strict liability regime of the 1987 Act was expected to be of more use than the negligence-based approach of the common law. To date, however, there has been little litigation under Pt I of the Act.

In order to understand the regime introduced by the 1987 Act, it is essential to answer a series of questions, beginning with who is liable under the Act.

Who is liable?

The 1987 Act imposes liability upon four classes of persons. Firstly, under s 2(2)(a), liability may be imposed upon the 'producer' of the product. Section 1(2) defines a producer as one of the following.

1. *The person who manufactured it* The Directive expressly included manufacturers of component parts within the definition of 'producer', but this was not

---

30. Law Commission, *Liability for Defective Products: Report of the Two Commissions* (Law Com No 82, Cmnd 6831, HMSO, London, 1977).

included in the 1987 Act. But the manufacturer of a component is a producer, because components are within the Act's definition of 'product'.[31]

2. *In the case of a substance that has not been manufactured, but has been won or abstracted, the person who won or abstracted it* 'Abstract', in this sense, means 'to extract or remove' and therefore usually refers to substances that have been mined or quarried (for example, stone or metals).

3. *In the case of a product that has not been manufactured, won, or abstracted (for example, agricultural products), but which has essential characteristics that are the result of some process (for example, a sausage), the person who carried out this process* Unfortunately, the Act does not provide definitions of 'process' and 'essential characteristics', leading to a degree of uncertainty in this area.

By s 2(2)(b), the second class of persons liable under the Act are those persons who hold themselves out as the product's producer by putting their name on the product or some other distinguishing mark (such persons are known as 'own-branders'). This is a common business practice whereby companies will purchase goods manufactured by a third party and then affix their name or logo onto the product. It should be noted that liability would only be imposed on such persons if they were to hold themselves out as the producer. Therefore, simply fixing a name or logo to the product is unlikely to suffice. A party who does, in some way, hold itself out as being the producer can counter this by stating on the product that it was manufactured by someone else.

By s 2(2)(c), the third class of persons liable are importers within the EU who have imported products from outside the EU. The following example demonstrates the rationale behind imposing liability on such persons.

Eg Importers and product liability

Rachel purchases a new SamSharp television from TV-Mart Ltd, a company based in London. The televisions are manufactured in China, before being sent to Japan, where SamSharp affixes its logo onto the televisions and packages them. TV-Mart then imports the televisions from Japan and sells them. The television that Rachel purchases is defective and electrocutes her.

In this case, both the manufacturer and the own-brander are outside Rachel's jurisdiction. Litigating in either Japan or China is likely to be an extremely expensive and time-consuming affair. Thankfully, she will not have to resort to this: she can proceed against TV-Mart, because it imported the goods into the EU.

Section 2(3) deals the fourth and final class of persons who may be liable. It may be the case that the consumer obtained the product from a supplier who is a retailer or intermediary distributor not falling within s 2(2)(a), (b), or (c). In such a case, s 2(3) provides that such a supplier will be liable unless he informs the claimant of the identity of the person who comes within the previous three classes. This is

---

31. CPA 1987, s 1(2).

important because someone who buys from a retailer or intermediary distributor may well not know the name of the manufacturer, etc.

Who can recover damages?

For an action to succeed under the common law tort of negligence, the claimant must prove that the defendant owed him a duty of care under the rules previously discussed. The list of potential claimants under the CPA 1987 is considerably wider. The Act itself does not specifically identify who may sue; it merely refers to 'the person who suffered the damage'. This means that anyone who has suffered damage due to a defective product may initiate a claim. The claimant does not need to be the purchaser of the product, nor does he need to be a consumer of the product, and it is irrelevant that the damage caused was not reasonably foreseeable. This is evidenced in s 6(3), which provides that if a product causes damage to a foetus, the child, once born, may sue for any disabilities caused.

What is a 'product'?

The defective product must be a 'product' within the meaning of the Act. Section 1(2) provides that a product 'means any goods or electricity and…includes a product which is comprised in another product, whether by virtue of being a component part or raw material or otherwise'.

Eg Components within products

ElectroTech Ltd provides electrical components to TeleBuild Ltd, which incorporates these components into its new range of plasma televisions. Telebuild sells one of these televisions to Cassie. It transpires that the components manufactured by ElectroTech are defective and tend to melt if the television remains on for over an hour. Cassie places the television on an antique oak table, which is damaged by a melting component.

In this case, Cassie will be able to claim against either ElectroTech or TeleBuild, because both are producers of a 'product' within the definition of s 1(2).

Section 45(1) expands the definition by defining 'goods' as including 'substances, growing crops and things comprised in land by virtue of being attached to it and any ship, aircraft or vehicle'. In turn, the words used in s 45(1) have often required further definition by the courts (for example, whether blood constitutes a substance).[32] Land clearly falls outside the definition of a 'product'. Buildings are excluded from the operation of the Act,[33] although products that are incorporated into buildings (for example, bricks, boilers, and washbasins) are within the scope of the Act.

---

32. In *A v National Blood Authority* [2001] 3 All ER 289 (QB), the High Court held that blood did constitute a substance and is therefore covered under the Act.
33. CPA 1987, s 45(1). Someone who defectively constructs a building may be liable under the Defective Premises Act 1972 and the tort of negligence.

When will a product be 'defective'?

The claimant will need to establish that the product is 'defective'. Section 3(1) provides that 'there is a defect in a product…if the safety of the product is not such as persons are generally entitled to expect'. As with the common law, the 1987 Act is not concerned with unsatisfactory goods, but with unsafe goods. Further, the definition of 'defective' focuses entirely on users of the product; the conduct of the producer is not mentioned. It follows that even if the producer has not acted negligently and has done all that could reasonably be done, he will still be liable if the product did not meet the objective standard of expectation.

When determining the safety of a product, s 3(2) provides that the court should take into account all of the circumstances of the case, as follows.

- *The way in which, and the purposes for which, the product was marketed* Because the test of safety is based upon what persons can expect, it follows that what they were led to believe by the product's marketing is of considerable importance.

- *The product's instructions and any warnings with respect to it* A suitably worded warning may make an inherently unsafe product safe. For example, many medicines can be harmful, but a warning stating what constitutes a safe dosage and a warning not to exceed this dosage would ensure that the product was not defective.

- *What might reasonably be expected to be done with, or in relation to, the product* Where reasonable or normal usage of a product causes damage, liability will be imposed. But misuse of a product might still result in liability, provided that such misuse was reasonably foreseeable.

- *The time at which the producer (or another) supplied the product* Clearly, the time at which a product was put into circulation is extremely relevant for several reasons:
  - the defect may have been caused by 'wear and tear', in which case the producer would not be liable;
  - it would be unfair to judge older products in the same way as newer products (for example, a vintage car would not be judged unsafe simply because it did not have airbags fitted). The safety of the product will be based on the knowledge and safety standards at the time that the product was supplied. The true importance of this factor will be seen later, when the 'development risks' defence is discussed.

Because the CPA 1987, Pt I, imposes strict liability, it is irrelevant that the producer has not acted in a negligent or careless manner. Provided that the product is defective and that the defect caused the claimant damage, liability will be imposed. It is important, however, to note that the type of damage suffered by the claimant must be within the meaning of the Act.

What damage is required?

The claimant can only recover damages if the defect in a product, wholly or partly, causes 'damage', as defined by the Act. Section 5(1) provides that 'damage' 'means 'death or personal injury or any loss of or damage to any property (including land)'. But where the damage is to property, there are several further limitations, as follows.

1. As under the common law, damage to the product itself cannot be recovered.[34]

2. The Act does not apply to damage caused to business property. The property must be 'ordinarily intended for private use, occupation or consumption'.[35]

3. Damages are not recoverable where the property damage is less than £275.[36] This is not a particularly strict limitation, because in cases concerning such small amounts, most lawyers would advise their clients not to initiate proceedings.

What defences are available?

Section 4 provides for a number of relatively straightforward defences including:

- the defect is attributable to compliance with a legal obligation;
- the defect arose after the product was supplied;
- the defective product was not supplied by the defendant (for example, where it is stolen);
- the defective product was not supplied to another by the supplier in the course of a business.

One defence contained in s 4(1)(e) has proven to be extremely controversial. This is the 'development risks' defence (sometimes known as the 'state of the art' defence), which states that a producer of a defective product can escape liability where:

> the state of scientific and technical knowledge at the relevant time was not such that a producer of products of the same description as the product in question might be expected to have discovered the defect [...]

The following is an example of a situation in which this defence might be relevant.

Eg The development risks defence

In January 2009, BioTech plc releases a new drug onto the market, which it claims will cure the common cold. The drug appears to work as claimed. But three years later, a small proportion of those who took the drug start to develop colds again. Further, the symptoms are more severe and occur more often. It is discovered that around 2 per cent of those who took the drug suffered a side effect that caused their immune system to become compromised, making them more susceptible to colds and infections.

BioTech may be able to avoid liability if it can establish that the state of scientific and technical knowledge in January 2009 was such that it could not be expected to have discovered the side effect.

The controversy surrounding the defence arose due to the UK's implementation. The defence in the Directive was wholly objective, whereas the defence is s 4(1)(e) is based on when the producer 'might be expected to have discovered the defect'. It was argued that this made the defence wider, more subjective, and more pro-producer than the defence under the Directive. Both the European Court of Justice[37]

---

34. Ibid, s 5(2).   35. Ibid, s 5(3).
36. Ibid, s 5(4).   37. *Commission of the EC v United Kingdom* [1997] All ER (EC) 481.

and the High Court[38] has, however, held that s 4(1)(e) does not establish a lower standard than under the Directive. Evidence for this can be found in the fact that, to date, the development risks defence has yet to be successfully pleaded. In the High Court, the judge concluded that once the potential hazard was known to the producer, the development risks defence could not apply.

Whilst the correctness of the UK's implementation may have been determined, the defence itself is still highly problematic for several reasons. Firstly, the court will have to determine the level of scientific and technical knowledge at the date that the product was supplied. This will not be easy to determine and the court may have to rely heavily on expert witnesses.

Secondly, the defence is based on the discoverability of the defect—but it could be argued that, with enough testing, any defect is discoverable. The key question will be how much testing is required and the Act provides no answer to this question.

Thirdly, it could be argued that the development risks defence does not fit well within a statute that imposes strict liability. In fact, it could be argued that the inclusion of the defence has turned a strict liability regime into a quasi-negligence-based regime.

Limitation periods

The limitation period for actions under the above provisions of the CPA 1987, Pt I, is three years from the date on which the damage was caused, or the date on which the claimant knew of the relevant facts, whichever is the later.[39] Either way, no action may be brought after the expiration of the period of ten years from the relevant time.[40] Where the action is brought against a person who falls within the CPA 1987, s 2(2), then the 'relevant time' is the time at which the product was supplied to another. Where an action is brought against someone who is outside the scope of s 2(2), then the relevant time is the time at which the product was last supplied by a person to whom s 2(2) does apply in relation to the product.

> ### ‹› Key points summary
>
> - The Consumer Protection Act 1987 was enacted to comply with a European directive that required member States to introduce a system whereby manufacturers of defective products could be liable even though they were not at fault.
>
> - Liability can be imposed upon:
>   - the product's 'producer;
>   - anyone who holds himself out as the product's producer by putting his name or other distinguishing mark on it;
>   - anyone who imports the product into the EU; and
>   - suppliers who do not fall within the above categories who fail to inform the claimant of the identity of the person who comes within those categories.

---

38. *A v National Blood Authority* [2001] 3 All ER 289 (QB).   39. Limitation Act 1980, s 11A(4).
40. Ibid, s 11A(3).

- Any person who suffered damage due to a defective product may commence an action under the 1987 Act.

- A product is defective under the Act if 'the safety of the product is not such as persons are generally entitled to expect'.

- The Act applies only to defective products that cause death, personal injury, or loss of, or damage to, non-business property. Damage to the product cannot be recovered and the Act does not apply to property damage valued at less than £275.

- Actions under the Act must be brought within three years from the date on which the damage was caused, or the date on which the claimant discovered the relevant facts.

Wrongful interference with goods

Product liability under the CPA 1987, Pt I, is not the only tort in relation to goods. Other torts exist that do not relate to the condition of goods, but relate to persons who interfere with goods belonging to others. Historically, a number of such torts existed and these torts were partially amalgamated by the Torts (Interference with Goods) Act 1977, which places them under the collective term 'wrongful interference with goods'.[41] For our purposes, the two principal torts to be discussed are:

- trespass to goods; and
- conversion.

Trespass to goods

Trespass to goods comprises any direct physical interference with goods that are in the possession of another person, without the consent of the person in possession, unless there is lawful justification for the interference. Several aspects of this definition require more detailed discussion.

Interference

The first question to ask is what type of action constitutes direct physical interference with the goods. Given the sheer number of goods, it is unsurprising that interference can take many forms. Examples would include:

- taking goods from another person who has lawful possession of them;[42]
- moving goods in the lawful possession of another;[43]
- scratching the panel of a vehicle;[44]
- unlawfully clamping the wheel of a car;[45]
- beating[46] or killing[47] an animal.

---

41. Torts (Interference with Goods) Act 1977, s 1. 42. *Brewer v Dew* (1843) 11 M & W 625 (Ex).
43. *Kirk v Gregory* (1876) 1 Ex D 55. 44. *Fouldes v Willoughby* (1841) 8 M & W 540.
45. *Vine v Waltham Forest London Borough Council* [2000] 1 WLR 2383 (CA).
46. *Wright v Ramscot* (1667) 1 Saund 84. 47. *Sheldrick v Abery* (1793) 1 Esp 55.

The interference must be direct. Accordingly, placing out poison for an animal to eat would probably not constitute trespass to goods,[48] nor would locking a room containing the claimant's goods.[49] The defendant's actions must be intentional or negligent and, provided that they are, liability is strict, and it is irrelevant that the defendant did not realize that his actions constituted a trespass.[50] Thus, if a person genuinely, but mistakenly, believes that goods belong to him and removes them from the possession of another, this will constitute trespass to goods because the interference was intentional.[51]

Although not entirely clear, the weight of opinion favours the view that trespass to goods is actionable per se (that is, proof of damage to the goods is not required). Of course, if no damage is suffered, then the claimant will usually only be able to recover nominal damages.[52]

Possession

Unlike conversion, trespass to goods will only be established if the claimant was in possession of the goods at the time of the alleged interference. Ownership of the goods is irrelevant and in fact, an owner of goods may be liable if he interferes with those goods whilst they are in the lawful possession of another.

Consent

No trespass will occur if the person in possession of the goods consented to the interference. In recent years, the issue of consent has arisen regularly in relation to the clamping of the wheels of cars.

🔑 *Arthur v Anke* [1997] QB 564 (CA)

FACTS: The owners of a piece of land engaged the defendant to prevent unauthorized parking on the land. The defendant displayed a number of prominent notices on the land indicating that the land was private and that vehicles parked without authority would be clamped. The claimant parked his car on the land and the defendant clamped it. The claimant alleged that the clamping constituted a trespass to goods.

HELD: The Court of Appeal held that no trespass to goods had occurred. By parking where he did, the claimant voluntarily accepted the risk that his car might be clamped and this amounted to implied consent to the interference.

★ See T Weir, 'Clamping' (1996) 55 CLJ 423

---

48. WVH Rogers, *Winfield & Jolowicz on Tort* (17th edn, Sweet & Maxwell, London, 2006) 748.
49. *Hartley v Moxham* (1842) 3 QB 701.
50. Direct physical interference might not, it seems, constitute trespass where the person interfering with the goods had no means of knowing the goods were present (accidental interference). For example, in *National Coal Board v JE Evans (Cardiff) Ltd* [1951] 2 KB 861 (CA), the defendant, who was excavating a trench, damaged a cable belonging to the claimant. The defendant was not liable in trespass since it had no means of knowing the cable was present at the site of the dig.
51. *Wilson v Lombank Ltd* [1963] 1 WLR 1294.
52. *Kirk v Gregory* (1876) 1 Ex D 55.

Conversion

Conversion is an intentional act[53] of dealing with goods in a manner that inconsistent with another's possession, or in a way that serves to deny another's right to immediate possession. As such, an action for conversion can be brought by anyone who has possession of goods, or a right to immediate possession of goods,[54] irrespective of whether such a person is the owner of the goods.

There are numerous situations in which an individual has possession or a right to immediate possession of goods, including the following.

- *Ownership* Note, however, that an individual who owns goods may lawfully lose the right to possession (for example, if he hires them to another for a fixed period, without providing for the right to repossession before the term of hire).

- *Bailment at will* A bailment at will occurs where one person (the 'bailor') temporarily transfers possession of goods to another (the 'bailee') for some purpose and is entitled to the return of the goods on demand. Because the bailee has possession and the bailor has the right to immediate possession,[55] either of them (but not both) may claim against a third party if the goods are converted.

- *Sale* A purchaser of goods can sue if ownership of the goods has passed to him, even though he does not yet have possession of the goods.[56]

- *Lien* A person who has possession of goods under a **lien** can sue if those goods are converted, provided that title to those goods has not passed to a third party.[57]

> ➡️ **lien:** the right to hold the property of another until an obligation is satisfied

Only material, tangible goods can be converted; a **chose in action** is usually incapable of conversion.[58]

> ➡️ **chose in action:** an asset (other than land) that cannot be possessed or which has no physical existence (e.g. a share in a company)

What acts amount to conversion?

Many different types of act can amount to conversion, such as:

- the theft or intentional destruction of goods;

- taking possession of goods via some legal process without appropriate justification;[59]

- possessing goods belonging to another, but refusing to allow the owner to collect them;[60]

- purchasing goods from a person who has no title to them;

---

53. Conversion cannot be committed by omission: *Ashby v Tolhurst* [1937] 2 KB 242 (CA).

54. *The Future Express* [1993] 2 Lloyd's Rep 542 (CA).

55. *Nicolls v Bastard* (1835) 2 Cr M & R 659 (Ex). The situation is different in the case of a contractual bailment for a term (e.g. a hire contract), because, during the term, the bailor will not be entitled to immediate possession.

56. *North West Securities Ltd v Alexander Breckon Ltd* [1981] RTR 518 (CA).

57. *Pendragon plc v Walon Ltd* [2005] EWHC 1082 (QB).

58. *OBG Ltd v Allan* [2005] EWCA Civ 106, [2005] QB 762. An exception to this rule is that a cheque can be converted: *Hounslow LBC v Jenkins* [2005] EWHC 315 (QB).

59. *Tinkler v Poole* (1770) 5 Burr 2657.

60. *Howard E Perry & Co Ltd v British Railways Board* [1986] 1 WLR 1375 (Ch).

- dealing with goods in a manner that is inconsistent with the rights of another (for example, an auctioneer selling the goods of a vendor who had no right to sell them);[61]
- using goods belonging to another as if they were one's own;[62]
- refusal of a bailee to return goods to the bailor, or the damage to or loss of the goods by the bailee.[63]

Intention

Like trespass to goods, liability in conversion is strict. All that is required is that the defendant intended to carry out the act in question. It is irrelevant:

- whether or not the defendant realized that the act interfered with the rights of the claimant;[64]
- whether or not the defendant was acting in good faith;[65] or
- whether or not the defendant was ignorant or mistaken.

Remedies

An individual whose goods have been wrongly interfered with may have access to several remedies, as follows.

- The principal remedy is an award of damages, the amount awarded being assessed so as to compensate the claimant for the destruction, damage, or deprivation of the goods, and for any consequential loss.
- Where the defendant is in possession of the goods, the court can:
  (i) order the return of the goods;
  (ii) order the return of the goods, but give the defendant the alternative of paying damages by reference to the value of the goods; or
  (iii) order the payment of damages.[66]
- Along with (i) and (ii), the court can also order the payment of consequential damages.
- In some cases, a claimant may simply be able to retake the goods wrongly taken from his possession. Like all self-help remedies, however, this remedy must be carefully exercised.

In *BBMB Finance (Hong Kong) Ltd v Eda Holdings Ltd*,[67] the Privy Council held that the general rule that should be adopted by the courts is that, where the claimant's property has been irreversibly converted, he has a right to damages measured by the value of the property at the date of conversion. The Privy Council also held that, where the claimant has got his property back, damages should be assessed as the difference between the value of the property when the wrongful interference occurred and its value on its return.

---

61. *RH Willis & Son v British Car Auctions Ltd* [1978] 1 WLR 438 (CA).
62. *Lancashire and Yorkshire Rly Co v MacNicoll* (1918) 88 LJ KB 601.
63. Torts (Interference with Goods) Act 1977, s 2(2).
64. *Caxton Publishing Co Ltd v Sutherland Publishing Co* [1939] AC 178 (HL).
65. *Fowler v Hollins* (1872) 7 QB 616.
66. Torts (Interference with Goods) Act 1977, s 3(2).
67. [1990] 1 WLR 409 (PC).

If the defendant improves the converted goods, thereby increasing their value, the claimant normally cannot recover the increased value. Damages will be assessed based on the market value of the goods minus the amount spent on improving them.[68]

 Key points summary

- Trespass to goods comprises any direct physical interference with goods that are in the possession of another person, without the consent of the person in possession, unless there is lawful justification for the interference.

- Conversion is an intentional act dealing with goods in a manner that is inconsistent with another's possession, or which serves to deny another's right to immediate possession.

- An individual whose goods have been wrongly interfered may:

  - seek damages;
  - apply to the court for an order remedying the interference; or
  - in certain cases, simply retake the goods wrongly taken from his possession.

Interference with contract, trade, or business (the 'economic torts')

Here, we are discussing a group of torts that were established to protect the interests of businesses from unlawful interference by others. These include:

- inducing breach of contract;
- unlawful interference with trade;
- conspiracy; and
- passing off.

A detailed examination of these torts is beyond the scope of this text, but their basic operation will be briefly discussed.

Inducing breach of contract

The law does not readily tolerate interference with the contractual relationships of other persons. The law holds liable those who interfere in the contracts of others via the tort of inducing breach of contract.[69] This tort occurs when the defendant intentionally causes someone who is a party to a contract with the claimant to breach it. The requisite level of intention required has been the subject of a substantial body of case law. What is clear is that:

- liability will not be imposed for negligently inducing another party to breach his contract, no matter how gross the negligence may be;[70] and
- there is no need to establish that the defendant intended to harm the claimant.

---

68. *Reid v Fairbanks* (1853) 13 CB 692.   69. *Lumley v Gye* (1853) 2 E & B 216.
70. *Cattle v Stockton Waterworks Co* (1875) 10 QB 453 (QB).

In a recent case, Lord Hoffmann stated that:

> To be liable for inducing breach of contract, you must know that you are inducing a breach of contract. It is not enough that you know that you are procuring an act which, as a matter of law or construction of the contract, is a breach. You must actually realize that it will have this effect. Nor does it matter that you ought reasonably to have done so.[71]

The key issue therefore is whether a person knows that he is inducing a breach of contract—but what level of knowledge is required?

Lord Hoffmann answered this question, stating:

> Intentional interference presupposes knowledge of the contract. With that knowledge the defendant proceeded to induce the other contracting party to act in a way the defendant knew was a breach of that party's obligations under the contract. If the defendant deliberately turned a blind eye and proceeded regardless he may be treated as having intended the consequence he brought about. A desire to injure the claimant is not an essential ingredient of this tort.[72]

The tort can be committed in a number of different ways.

Direct inducement

Where the defendant, without lawful justification or excuse, directly and intentionally persuades someone (*X*) to breach his (*X*'s) contract with the claimant, he will have committed the tort of inducing breach of contract.

Lumley v Gye (1853) 2 E & B 216

FACTS: The claimant had secured the services of Johanna Wagner, a famous opera singer. The terms of the contract stated that she would sing at the claimant's opera house and nowhere else. The defendant, who wished Ms Wagner to sing at his opera house, persuaded her to refuse to perform for the claimant. The claimant sued the defendant.

HELD: The majority of the court held that knowingly inducing breach of contract was a tortious act. On the facts, however, the claimant's action failed, because the court was not convinced that the defendant knew the agreement between the claimant and Ms Wagner was binding.

Direct intervention or preventing performance

The defendant does not have to directly persuade the third party to breach his contract in order to be liable. Any form of direct intervention that the defendant knows will prevent a party from performing his contractual obligations will constitute the tort of inducing breach of contract.

---

71. *OBG Ltd v Allan* [2007] UKHL 21, [2008] 1 AC 1, [39].
72. Ibid, [192].

GWK Ltd v Dunlop Rubber Co Ltd (1926) 42 TLR 376 (KB)

FACTS: The claimant manufactured tyres. A car manufacturer (*X*) was exhibiting a number of vehicles at an upcoming car show. The claimant contracted with *X* that it would provide the tyres for the cars being exhibited. The defendant, a rival tyre company, unlawfully removed the claimant's tyres from *X*'s cars and replaced them with its own tyres.

HELD: The High Court held that the defendant was liable to the claimant for inducing breach of contract and to *X* for trespass to goods.

Indirect intervention

Initially, only direct inducement or interference would result in liability. As time progressed, the courts came to realize that indirect interference with a contract could be just as damaging as direct interference. Indirect interference occurs where the defendant persuades someone (*Y*) to do a wrongful act, usually breaching a contract of employment to which *Y* is a party, in order to prevent performance of another contract (for example, a contract between *Y*'s employer and the employer's customer). In order for liability to be established, it must be demonstrated that the defendant intended a specific contract to be breached.[73]

 JT Stratford & Sons Ltd v Lindley [1965] AC 269 (HL)

FACTS: The claimant ran a business hiring out barges to the public. When hiring barges, the hirer was under a contractual obligation to return the barge to the claimant's moorings. This was achieved by sending individuals (known as 'watermen') to retrieve the barges and return them to the claimant. The defendants were officials of a trade union who were involved in a dispute with the claimant. This trade union also happened to represent the watermen. In order to place pressure on the claimant, the defendants instructed the watermen not to return the barges to the claimant. Because barges were not being returned, the claimant's business soon came to a stop. The claimant sued.

HELD: The House of Lords held that the defendant had committed the tort of inducement to breach. By instructing the watermen not to return the barges, they had indirectly caused the hirers to breach their contract with the claimant.

Inconsistent dealing

This occurs where the defendant is aware of a contract between two other parties, and has dealings with one of those parties (*Z*), which he knows are inconsistent with their contract and which cause *Z* to breach his contract.

---

73. *Mainstream Properties v Young* [2005] EWCA Civ 125, [2005] IRLR 964. An appeal to the House of Lords was dismissed ([2007] UKHL 21, [2008] 1 AC 1).

The following provides an example of such inconsistent dealing.

Eg Inconsistent dealing

The Rolls Royce Owners Club Ltd has a number of vintage Rolls Royces that it wishes to sell. It sells one of these cars to Keith. Because the club is keen to ensure that the cars remain in the right hands, it is a term of the contract with Keith that, should he decide to sell the car, he must first offer it to the Rolls Royce Owners Club before offering to sell to anyone else. Lisa is fully aware of this term, but wishes to own the particular Rolls Royce and modify it by adding a spoiler to the rear, large speakers in the boot, and spinning alloy wheels. She therefore offers to purchase Keith's Rolls Royce and offers him double what it is worth. Without first offering the car to the Club, Keith agrees and sells the car to Lisa.

In this case, Lisa would have committed the tort of inducing breach of contract through her inconsistent dealings with Keith. She was aware that her actions would cause Keith to breach the contract between himself and the Rolls Royce Owners Club.[74]

The court will only hold the defendant liable where his inconsistent dealing is the cause of the breach of contract. Thus, where a father sold a quarry and covenanted not to set up a rival quarry, but financially helped his sons in the setting up of a rival quarry, the father's dealings were not inconsistent, because the sons had decided to set up a rival quarry before their father provided financial assistance.[75]

Unlawful interference with trade

The other economic torts discussed in this chapter are relatively specific. There also exists a much more general economic tort—namely, the tort of 'interfering with the trade or business of another person by doing unlawful acts'.[76] For this tort to occur, the claimant will need to establish that the defendant intended to injure him, as *dicta* in the following case suggest.

Douglas v Hello! Ltd (No 3) [2007] UKHL 21

FACTS: Michael Douglas and Catherine Zeta-Jones had signed an exclusive deal with *OK!* magazine to publish their wedding photographs. A number of photographs were covertly taken by a freelance photographer and published in *Hello!* magazine. The owners of *OK!* sued the owners of *Hello!* for, inter alia, interference with trade by unlawful means. The claimant argued that the fact that the photos were no longer an exclusive for *OK!* had harmed their business interests by preventing them from full exploitation of the deal signed with the Douglases. The Court of Appeal dismissed the claim on the ground that *Hello!* had not intended to cause harm to *OK!*. The claimant appealed.

---

74. See *British Motor Trade Association v Salvadori* [1949] Ch 556 (Ch).
75. *Batts Combe Quarry Ltd v Ford* [1943] Ch 51 (CA).
76. *Merkur Island Shipping Corporation v Laughton* [1983] 2 AC 570 (HL) 608 (Lord Diplock).

HELD: The appeal succeeded. Lord Hoffmann stated that '[t]he injury to "OK!" was the means of attaining [*Hello!*'s] desired end and not merely a foreseeable consequence of having done so'.[77] The defendant's gain and the claimant's loss were 'inseparably linked',[78] in so much as '[t]he defendant cannot obtain one without bringing about the other'.[79]

COMMENT: The claimant actually succeeded on the ground of breach of confidence, not unlawful interference with trade, the House of Lords holding that the level of interference was insufficient to establish the latter tort. The comments mentioned above, however, do apply to the tort of unlawful interference with trade, but because liability was established based on another tort, Lord Hoffmann's comments are merely *obiter*.

★ See G Black, '*OK!* for Some: *Douglas v Hello!* in the House of Lords' (2007) 11 Edin LR 402

Examples of the types of unlawful act that could establish the tort include the following.

- *Violence or the threat of violence* In *Messenger Group Newspapers v NGA*,[80] employees on strike physically threatened employees who had decided not to strike. The court held that this constituted an unlawful interference with the claimant's business.
- *Breach of contract* Threatening to breach a contract or inducing breach of contract can constitute unlawful interference with trade.[81]
- *Misrepresentation* Where the defendant's misrepresentation interferes with the claimant's business interests, the tort of unlawful interference with trade will be committed.[82]

Conspiracy

Conspiracy is both a tort and a crime, although the scope of the crime is much narrower than that of the tort. Tortious conspiracies are divided into two types, dependent upon whether the actions of the defendant were lawful or unlawful.

Conspiracy to injure

Conspiracy to injure is also known as 'lawful means conspiracy', or 'simple conspiracy'. In a business context, conspiracy to injure occurs where the defendant joins forces with a third party and both parties then act in a manner that damages the business interests of another—this damage being their predominant purpose. The acts of the defendant and the third party need not be unlawful for the tort to be committed. Where the defendant and third party causes the claimant loss in order to protect or promote their own business interests, however, they will not be liable for conspiracy.

---

77. *Douglas v Hello! Ltd (No 3)* [2007] UKHL 21, [2008] 1 AC 1, [134].
78. Ibid, [167] (Lord Nicholls).　　　　79. Ibid.
80. [1984] ICR 397 (QB).
81. *JT Stratford & Son v Lindley (No 1)* [1965] AC 296 (HL).
82. *National Phonograph Co Ltd v Edison Bell Co Ltd* [1908] 1 Ch 335 (CA).

Mogul Steamship Co v McGregor, Gow & Co [1892] AC 25 (HL)

FACTS: A group of shipowners formed an association, the purpose of which was to secure exclusive control of the China shipping market for tea by forcing rival companies out of the market. The association offered discounts to those parties who only ever transacted with members of the association. Further, whenever non-members docked at a port in order to obtain tea to transport, the association would send ships to that port to undercut the rates being offered by the non-member, even if this meant having to transport the tea at a loss. The claimant was a former member of the association who had been excluded. As a result of the association's actions, the claimant was forced to transport cargo at a loss in order to attract any business. The claimant contended that the association's actions amounted to a conspiracy.

HELD: The House of Lords rejected the claimant's action. The association was set up in order to protect and extend the scope of its members' trade, and to increase their profits. Although this had the effect of injuring the clamant, this was a subservient purpose of the association.

COMMENT: As can be seen from this case, provided that the defendant and third party (or parties) act predominantly in order to protect or promote their own business interests, they will not be liable, no matter how selfish their actions were. For this reason, very few actions in conspiracy succeed.

Whilst the existence of this tort is undoubted,[83] it can be criticized on the ground that it appears questionable that parties to who join together to cause loss to another can be held liable for acts that would not result in liability if they were to be committed individually.

'Unlawful means' conspiracy

Conspiracy to injure is concerned with the end result or purpose of an association. Conversely, 'unlawful means' conspiracy is more concerned with the means used to achieve a particular result. Where the defendant uses unlawful means to harm the claimant, it is irrelevant that the harming of the claimant was not the dominant purpose; all that the claimant need establish is that his injury is an intended consequence of the defendant's actions and that unlawful means were used to achieve this end.[84]

Marrinan v Vibart [1963] 1 QB 528 (CA)

FACTS: The claimant was a disbarred barrister. He alleged that the two defendants, who were police officers, had conspired to defame him in a report submitted to the Director of Public Prosecutions, in evidence given during a criminal trial at the Old Bailey and in testimony at the inquiry that led to the barrister's disbarment.

---

83. *Lonrho Ltd v Shell Petroleum Co* [1982] AC 173 (HL).
84. *Lonrho plc v Fayed* [1992] 1 AC 448 (HL).

HELD: The claimant's action was dismissed by the Court of Appeal. The documents and testimony given by the defendants were privileged. Therefore, no legal action could ever arise from them. Accordingly, the defendant's actions were not unlawful.

Today, unlawful means conspiracy is largely redundant, due to the fact that if unlawful means are used to interfere with another's trade, the tort of unlawful interference with trade will automatically be committed.

Passing off

The tort of passing off occurs where the defendant makes a misrepresentation aimed at damaging the claimant's business or goodwill. This usually takes one of the following forms.

- *The defendant uses the trade name*[85] *or trade mark*[86] *(or a similar name or mark) of the claimant*   The purpose behind this is to make the claimant's customers believe that the defendant's product was manufactured by the claimant, thereby taking advantage of any goodwill attached to the claimant's reputation.
- *The defendant manufactures goods that imitate the appearance of the claimant's goods*   In *Reckitt & Colman Products Ltd v Borden Inc*,[87] the claimant had, for over thirty years, sold lemon juice in a distinctive yellow plastic container that was shaped like a lemon. The defendant began selling its lemon juice in a similar container and the House of Lords held that this constituted passing off.
- *False advertising*   Where a biscuit manufacturer advertised a chocolate biscuit called 'Puffin' that was packaged in a similar manner to the leading biscuit 'Penguin', the court held that this constituted passing off.[88]
- *Exploitation of popular characters, especially television characters*   Bootleg or unlicensed products created to cash in on a character's popularity can constitute passing off (for example, printing the Teletubbies onto T-shirts and then selling them to the public without the appropriate permission).[89]

⟨⟩ Key points summary

- Liability can be imposed upon parties who directly, or indirectly, and intentionally induce others to commit breach of contract.

- A person who uses unlawful acts with intent to interfere with the trade or business of another may be liable in tort.

- Liability can be imposed where two or more parties conspire to cause injury to the business interests of others. Where the parties use unlawful means to harm another,

---

85. *Powell v Birmingham Vinegar Brewery Co* [1897] AC 710 (HL).
86. *Millington v Fox* (1838) 3 My & Cr 338 (Ch).
87. [1990] 1 WLR 491 (HL).
88. *United Biscuits (UK) Ltd v Asda Stores Ltd* [1997] RPC 513 (Ch).
89. *BBC Worldwide Ltd v Pally Screen Printing Ltd* [1998] FST 665 (Ch).

> it is irrelevant that the injury to the claimant was not the principal purpose of the unlawful act.
>
> - Where a defendant makes a misrepresentation designed to damage another's business or goodwill, the tort of passing off will be committed.

Employers' liability

The Pearson Commission[90] of 1978 estimated that 1,300 employees were killed and that over 700,000 were injured in the course of employment. With the increased focus on safety and the enactment of health and safety legislation, these figures have been reduced considerably, but they could be lower. In 2007–08, 229 employees were killed whilst at work and 299,000 suffered reportable injuries,[91] while 2.1 million employees were at that time suffering from an illness that they believed was caused, or exacerbated, by their current, or previous, employment.[92]

An employee who is harmed in the course of his employment will normally become entitled to a range of social security benefits if his injuries affect his ability to work. But such payments will not compensate the employee fully for his injury and will generally be considerably lower than the employee's wage. The employee may therefore decide to obtain additional compensation by suing his employer.

Employers may be liable to pay their employees compensation on a number of grounds, all of which are discussed elsewhere in this text:

- breach of an express or implied contractual term;
- breach of statutory duty (discussed later in this chapter);
- the employer might be vicariously liable for the acts of employees that injure other employees;
- the employer might have breached the duty of care owed to his employees (that is, under the tort of negligence).

Health and safety legislation is discussed in Chapter 24

Terms implied into employment contracts are discussed in Chapter 23

Vicarious liability is discussed in Chapter 14

An employer's duty of care is discussed in Chapter 24

Occupiers' liability

Occupiers of premises owe a statutory duty of care towards persons on those premises, whether they are there lawfully (for example, visitors) or unlawfully (for example, trespassers), in respect of the *state* of the premises.[93] In relation to *activities* carried out on the premises, the occupier owes both a statutory and common law duty to lawful visitors, and a common law duty to non-lawful visitors. The common

---

90. *Report of the Royal Commission on Civil Liability and Compensation for Personal Injury* (Cmnd 7054, HMSO, London, 1978).

91. Health and Safety Executive, *Health and Safety Statistics 2007/08* (Office for National Statistics, London, 2008) 5.

92. Ibid.

93. In respect to activities carried out on premises, the occupier owes a common law duty.

law duties are owed under the tort of negligence, which was discussed in the previous chapter. Accordingly, here, we will focus on those duties of care imposed by statute.

This area of the law is largely dominated by two different Acts:

- liability in relation to lawful visitors is governed by the Occupiers' Liability Act 1957 (OLA 1957);
- liability in relation to non-lawful visitors is governed by the Occupiers' Liability Act 1984 (OLA 1984).

Scope

Occupier

Neither Act provides a definition of 'occupier', each preferring to state that the common law definition should be used,[94] as provided in the following case.

Wheat v E Lacon & Co Ltd [1966] AC 552 (HL)

FACTS: The defendant owned a public house, which was run by a manager and his wife, both of whom were employed by the defendant. The agreement provided that the manager would sell drinks in the licensed portion of the building (the ground floor) and could live rent-free in living accommodation on the first floor of the building. The defendant allowed the manager's wife to take in paying guests, who would stay in the living accommodation. There was no direct access between the ground floor and the first floor, but there was a separate emergency staircase leading to the first floor, which was barred by a door marked 'private'. A paying guest fell down this staircase and was killed. The deceased's widow commenced proceedings and the House of Lords had to determine who was the occupier.

HELD: The House of Lords held that the whole of the premises was in the defendant's occupation through the manager as its employee. Therefore, the defendant was the occupier of the emergency staircase for the purposes of the OLA 1957. It stated *obiter* that the manager and his wife were also the occupiers of the first-floor flat. Lord Denning stated that anyone with a 'sufficient degree of control over [the] premises'[95] could be an occupier. Based on this definition, both the defendant and manager were held to be occupiers (although, on the facts, neither was liable). Lord Denning stated that other persons who could constitute occupiers include landlords, tenants, and independent contractors.

★ See RC Gardner, 'Vicarious Occupation?' (1965) 28 MLR 721

Both Acts impose duties not only on occupiers of premises, but also on occupiers of any fixed or moveable structure.[96] This expands the definition of occupier

---

94. OLA 1957, s 1(2); OLA 1984, s 1(2).
95. *Wheat v E Lacon & Co Ltd* [1966] AC 552 (HL) 577. Accordingly, ownership or physical possession of the land is not necessary.
96. OLA 1957, s 1(3); OLA 1984, s 1(2).

considerably and has been held to include scaffolding,[97] a ship in dry dock,[98] a large mechanical digger,[99] and a lift.[100] With respect to the latter three cases, all of which involved not merely movable, but also self-propelling objects, items of this type will only fall within the scope of the Acts in respect of their defective condition and not their defective operation.[101]

Lawful visitors and non-lawful visitors

As we shall see, the duty of care owed to lawful visitors is different from that owed to non-lawful visitors. It is therefore important to distinguish between the two.

A person is a lawful visitor if:

- he has been invited by the occupier (or the occupier's authorized agent) on to the occupier's premises; or
- he has a contractual right to be on the premises; or
- he is on the premises as of right (for example, under a statutory power of entry, such as that possessed by the police or firemen);[102] or
- he is on the premises because he has been expressly or impliedly permitted by the occupier (or the occupier's authorized agent) to be on them.

A lawful visitor may become a non-lawful visitor if he visits parts of the premises of the occupier to which he has not been invited or allowed to enter, or if he stays beyond a specified time.

More difficult to determine are those situations in which a person claims to have implied permission to be on the occupiers' premises. Where such permission exists, the visitor is said to have an 'implied licence' to be on the premises. Certain implied licences are well established (for example, the right to visit a public library to borrow books). In all other cases, the existence of an implied licence is one of fact and it will be for the claimant to prove that he had an implied licence to be on the premises.[103] The mere toleration of non-lawful visitors incurring on premises is not normally enough to grant an implied licence, but if the occupier acts in such a way as to indicate assent to such incursions, then an implied licence might result.[104] Where children are 'allured' onto the premises by some feature of the premises (for example, shiny red berries),[105] then the child might have an implied licence to be on the premises. Prior to 1984, if the court were to hold that a person was not a lawful visitor, that person would be highly unlikely to obtain a remedy. The use of the implied

---

97. *Kearney v Eric Waller Ltd* [1967] 1 QB 29 (QB).

98. *London Graving Dock Co Ltd v Horton* [1951] AC 737 (HL). This case was decided at common law, but is still applicable.

99. *Bunker v Charles Brand & Son Ltd* [1969] 2 QB 480 (QB).

100. *Haseldine v Daw & Son Ltd* [1941] 2 KB 343 (CA). This case was decided at common law, but is still applicable.

101. Ibid.

102. OLA 1957, s 2(6). This does not extend to those lawfully using a public right of way: *McGeown v Northern Ireland Housing Executive* [1995] 1 AC 233 (HL). Such persons are also not owed a duty under the OLA 1984. Persons using a private right of way are not owed a duty under the OLA 1957: *Holden v White* [1982] QB 679 (CA), but are owed a duty under the OLA 1984, s 1(1)(a).

103. *Edwards v Railway Executive* [1952] AC 737 (HL).

104. *Lowery v Walker* [1911] AC 10 (HL).

105. *Glasgow Corporation v Taylor* [1922] 1 AC 44 (HL).

licence could be seen as a way of circumventing this limitation in cases in which the claimant deserved a remedy. With the passing of the OLA 1984, this limitation no longer exists and so the need to find the existence of an implied licence is reduced. The courts today may therefore be less generous in finding an implied licence than they were in the past.

It is often stated (incorrectly) that the OLA 1984 imposes duties on occupiers only in relation to trespassers. This is not true, because the OLA 1984 imposes a duty on occupiers in relation to persons other than lawful visitors. This will obviously include trespassers, but can also include persons who are not trespassing (for example, those using a private right of way).

Liability to lawful visitors

The common duty that the occupier of premises owes towards the person and property of his lawful visitors is defined, under OLA 1957, s 2(2), as:

> a duty to take such care as, in all the circumstances of the case, is reasonable to see that the visitor will be reasonably safe in using the premises for the purposes for which he is invited or permitted by the occupier to be there.

The common duty of care imposed by the statute closely resembles the standard and duty of care that are the bases of the common law tort of negligence.

The operation of the duty imposed by s 2(2) can be seen in the following case.

Murphy v Bradford Metropolitan Council [1992] PIQR P68 (CA)

FACTS: The defendant council occupied and managed a school, at which the claimant worked as a teacher. Snow fell several inches deep and the council initiated clearance work at around 6.30 a.m. A sloping path leading to the school was cleared and salt was placed down. At around 8.40 a.m., whilst walking on the path, the claimant slipped and was injured. Following the accident, a handrail was built along the path. The clamant sued the council.

HELD: The Court of Appeal held that, although the work to clear the snow was begun early, the actual steps taken were insufficient, given the prevailing conditions and the nature of the area in question. The sloping path on which the claimant fell was a likely source of an accident and was therefore 'a candidate for special attention'. The subsequent building of the handrail, although not evidence of an omission on the defendant's behalf, was evidence that the path was deserving of special measures.

The OLA 1957 elaborates upon the duty in several ways. Section 2(3)(a) provides that the occupier must be prepared for children to be less careful than adults. Accordingly, the duty will require the premises to be safe for a child of that age, but in *Phipps v Rochester Corporation*[106]—a case decided before the OLA 1957, but still of

---

106. [1955] 1 QB 450 (CA).

relevance—the Court of Appeal held that, in cases involving very young children (in this case, children of the ages of 5 and 7), primary responsibility for the safety of such children rests with their parents, and it would be socially undesirable to allow parents to shift the burden of looking after their children to those who have accessible premises. Provided that it is reasonably foreseeable that children will play on premises and be injured, it is irrelevant that their actual behaviour was unforeseeable, as the following case demonstrates.

Jolley v Sutton London Borough Council [2000] 1 WLR 1082 (HL)

FACTS: The claimant, who was aged 14, and a friend found an old boat abandoned on the estate where they lived. They jacked up the boat, hoping to restore it, but the jack collapsed and the boat fell on the claimant, injuring him extremely severely. The claimant sought to recover damages. The defendant council (the occupier of the estate) admitted that it should have moved the boat, but argued that, while it was foreseeable that children might play on the boat and fall through rotten boards, the conduct of the claimant was not foreseeable.

HELD: The House of Lords, in upholding the claimant's action, held that it was foreseeable that children would meddle with the boat and that it was not necessary for the precise method by which the claimant had put himself at risk to be foreseeable in order to hold that the defendant had breached its duty toward the claimant.

★ See R Williams,
'Remoteness: Some
Unexpected Mischief'
(2001) 117 LQR 30

Section 2(3)(b) provides that 'an occupier may expect that a person, in the exercise of his calling, will appreciate and guard against any special risks ordinarily incident to it, so far as the occupier leaves him free to do so'. Should this person fail to guard against such risks and be injured, the occupier will not be liable.

Roles v Nathan [1963] 1 WLR 1117 (CA)

FACTS: Premises occupied by the defendant contained two chimney flues that required sealing. This was to be carried out by two chimney sweeps. They were warned about the danger of carbon monoxide poisoning. Part of the work was completed, but the flues could not be fully sealed, because the sweeps had run out of concrete. It was agreed that the work would be completed the following day. In fact, the sweeps, without informing the defendant, decided to complete the work late that same night. The next day, both sweeps were found dead near the flues and the cause of death was found to be carbon monoxide poisoning. The sweeps' widows alleged that the defendant had breached the duty imposed by the OLA 1957.

HELD: The Court of Appeal held that the duty had not been breached. The sweeps should have been aware of the risk of carbon monoxide poisoning and should have guarded against it.

Section 2(4)(b) provides that:

> where damage is caused to a visitor by a danger due to the faulty execution of any work of construction, maintenance or repair by an independent contractor employed by the occupier, the occupier is not to be treated without more as answerable for the danger if in all the circumstances he had acted reasonably in entrusting the work to an independent contractor and had taken such steps (if any) as he reasonably ought in order to satisfy himself that the contractor was competent and that the work had been properly done.

Even if the occupier has taken reasonable steps to ensure that the independent contractor is competent, he still needs take steps to ensure that the contractor's work has been properly completed. If, however, the nature of the contractor's work is technical or specialized, the occupier will usually not be required to check the contractor's work, as the following example demonstrates.

 Independent contractors and specialized work

Dean, the landlord of a block of flats, contracts with ServiceLift Ltd to maintain the lifts within the flats. An employee of ServiceLift fails to replace a component satisfactorily, causing it to fracture when used. The result is that, when Caroline uses the lift the next day, it falls to the bottom of the lift shaft, severely injuring her. Caroline seeks compensation from Dean, alleging that, in failing to check the work of the engineer, he has breached that duty imposed by the OLA 1957.

In this case, it is highly likely that a court will hold that Dean has not breached the duty imposed by the OLA 1957, s 2(2). The technical nature of the work carried out by the engineer was such that Dean could not be expected to check that it had been properly done. Dean had discharged the duty by taking reasonable steps to employ a competent firm of engineers and Caroline's claim would therefore be likely to fail.

Warnings

If an occupier warns his lawful visitors of a danger, he discharges his duty of care, provided that the notice in itself is enough to render a visitor reasonably safe.[107] Whether a notice is sufficient is a question of fact. It is generally thought that a notice must specify the nature and location of the danger, so that a prudent visitor can take steps to avoid it. Hence a notice that simply says 'Danger' would not discharge the occupier's duty unless the danger were obvious—but if the danger is obvious, there may be no need to warn at all, because any visitor exercising reasonable care for his own safety should recognize and avoid the hazard.

---

107. OLA 1957, s 2(4)(a).

> ### ⊶ *Darby v National Trust* [2001] EWCA Civ 189
>
> **FACTS:** The defendant occupied a piece of National Trust property that contained a number of ponds. There was a (somewhat inconspicuous) sign in the car park forbidding persons visiting the property from bathing and boating. The claimant's husband drowned whilst swimming in one of the ponds. She contended that the ponds should have 'No Swimming' signs displayed around them and that the lack of such signs amounted to a breach of duty by the defendant.
>
> **HELD:** The Court of Appeal held that the duty had not been breached. The water in the pond was murky and the risks posed in bathing in the pond were obvious. Accordingly, the defendant was not under a duty to warn against them.

Exclusion of the duty of care

An occupier may seek to exclude or restrict the duty that he would otherwise owe under the OLA 1957, either by a term in a contract with his visitor, or by means of a notice indicating that those who enter do so at their own risk. Whilst such terms and notices are permitted by s 2(1), there are limitations upon such terms and notices, as follows.

- An occupier cannot exclude or restrict, by contract, the common duty of care owed to those lawful visitors who enter by virtue of a contract, but who are not parties to that contract.[108]

The common law rules relating to exclusion or restriction of liability are discussed at p 970

- Any exclusion or restriction of liability by an exclusion clause must satisfy the common law rules relating to the exclusion or restriction of liability.

- An occupier of business premises cannot, by an exclusion clause or notice, exclude or restrict the duty of care imposed by the OLA 1957, s 2(2), in respect of death or personal injury to visitors, and he can only exclude or restrict liability for causing other types of injury (for example, damage to property) if such exclusion or restriction is reasonable.[109]

The requirement of reasonableness under the Unfair Contract Terms Act 1977 is discussed at p 983

Defences

A defendant has access to two principal defences.

- Section 2(5) provides that the duty imposed by s 2(2) does not impose on an occupier 'any obligation to a visitor in respect of risks willingly accepted as his by the visitor'. In other words, the defence of *volenti non fit injuria* is available.

→ *volenti non fit injuria*: 'to a willing person, nor harm is done' (see p 521)

- Section 2(3) provides that, in determining whether the s 2(2) duty has been breached, the court should take into account 'the degree of care, and of want of care, which would ordinarily be looked for in ... a visitor'. Therefore, a want of care will entitle the defendant to raise the defence of contributory negligence.

The defence of contributory negligence is discussed at p 529

Liability to non-lawful visitors

The OLA 1984 provides that occupiers owe a duty to all persons other than lawful visitors (for example, trespassers). But s 1(3) provides that this duty only arises if:

(a) he is aware of the danger or has reasonable grounds to believe that it exists;

---

108. OLA 1957, ss 2(1) and 3(1).   109. Unfair Contract Terms Act 1977, s 2.

(b) he knows or has reasonable grounds to believe that the other is in the vicinity of the danger concerned or that he may come into the vicinity of the danger (in either case, whether he has lawful authority for being in that vicinity or not); and

(c) the risk is one against which, in all the circumstances of the case, he may reasonably be expected to offer the other some protection.

In relation to s 1(3)(a) and (b), 'reasonable grounds to believe' require that the occupier should actually know the relevant fact, or know facts that provide grounds for a relevant belief established by evidence; it is not enough simply that he ought to have known.[110] In short, the occupier is not in breach of his duty if a non-lawful visitor is injured by a danger of which the occupier was reasonably unaware, but the occupier must protect a non-lawful visitor adequately from those dangers of which he is aware or ought reasonably to have been aware. Even when the occupier is aware of some danger to non-lawful visitors, his duty is not to render them safe, but to take reasonable care to see that the danger does not cause injury to that non-lawful visitor.[111] Moreover, even if the occupier is in breach of his duty under the OLA 1984, a non-lawful visitor can recover damages only for certain injuries—namely, death and personal injury—and not for damage to his property.[112]

The standard of care

The standard of care expected in respect of non-visitors to whom a duty is owed is set out in the OLA 1984, s 1(4), which provides that the occupier is to take such care as is reasonable in all of the circumstances to see that the entrant does not suffer injury on the premises by reason of the danger concerned.

The following two cases demonstrate the scope of this duty.

Platt v Liverpool City Council [1997] CLY 4864 (CA)

FACTS: The defendant council engaged in a rehousing programme, which involved the emptying, repairing, and, in some cases, the demolition of properties. The council had secured one such property against intruders by fixing metal sheets over the doors and windows. In addition, an employee of the council routinely checked the property. Following one such check, it was discovered that the property was so badly vandalized that it would need to be demolished. The council arranged for an eight-foot fence to be placed around the building. A group of boys entered the property. It collapsed and one of the boys was killed. The boy's father commenced proceedings against the council.

HELD: The Could of Appeal held that the duty imposed by s 1(4) was to take such care as was reasonable in all of the circumstances of the case. When the boys entered the property, it was surrounded by an eight-foot fence, which could only be overcome by climbing over it or by wriggling through a small gap. There was no evidence that, prior to the boys entering the property, anyone else had overcome the fence. Accordingly, the council had done what was reasonable to prevent injury and so was not liable.

---

110. *Swain v Natui Ram Puri* [1996] PIQR P442 (CA). 111. OLA 1984, s 1(4).
112. Ibid, s 1(8) and (9).

Ratcliff v McConnell **[1999] 1 WLR 670 (CA)**

FACTS: The claimant, a 19-year-old college student, had been drinking with friends, but he was not drunk. They agreed to go swimming in the college's open-air swimming pool. The pool was surrounded by walls and fences, and secured by a locked gate. The claimant climbed over these and dived into the shallow end of the pool. Because the pool was closed for the winter, however, it contained very little water and the claimant hit his head on the bottom, causing him to sustain severe injuries that rendered him tetraplegic. He sued the college governors.

HELD: The Court of Appeal held that the defendants had not breached the duty imposed by the OLA 1984, s 1(4). The danger in question (that is, hitting one's head when diving into the shallow end of a swimming pool) was common to all swimming pools and was obvious to any adult (indeed, the claimant admitted knowing of this danger). The duty imposed by s 1(4) did not require occupiers to protect non-lawful visitors from dangers of which they should have been fully aware.

Warnings

The OLA 1984, s 1(5), states:

> Any duty owed by virtue of this section in respect of a risk may, in an appropriate case, be discharged by taking such steps as are reasonable in all the circumstances of the case to give warning of the danger concerned or to discourage persons from incurring the risk.

Under the OLA 1957, a warning will discharge the duty only if it enables the visitor to be reasonably safe. There is no such requirement in the case of the OLA 1984 and therefore warnings are more likely to discharge a duty owed to a non-lawful visitor than to a visitor.

The following example demonstrates the distinction in practice.

 Warnings under the OLA 1957 and OLA 1984

Dewi owns a disused factory surrounded by a large fence. On the fence and around the factory are signs stating 'Warning! Factory floor unsafe'. Dewi asks John, a structural engineer, to visit the factory and assess what renovations need to be completed to make the factory safe. Whilst at the factory, the floor gives way and John is injured. The presence of the warning will not discharge Dewi's liability, because the signs have not enabled John to be reasonably safe.

A day after Dewi's accident, Owen climbs the fence and forces his way into the factory. Another portion of the floor gives way and Owen is injured. The warning will discharge Dewi's duty, because the signs warn of the danger and discourage persons from incurring the risk.

Exclusion of the duty of care

An occupier may seek to exclude or restrict the duty that he would otherwise owe under the OLA 1984 by means of a notice indicating that those who enter do so at their own risk. The 1984 Act does not indicate whether such exclusion of liability is permissible, but it might be thought odd if liability to lawful visitors could be excluded, but not liability to non-lawful visitors. The Unfair Contract Terms Act 1977 does not apply to the duty imposed by the OLA 1984, s 1(4). Consequently, it appears that any occupier can exclude or restrict the duty owed to non-lawful visitors, unless any breach of duty also constitutes common law negligence.

Defences

As under the OLA 1957, the defences of *volenti* and contributory negligence are available.

 Key points summary

- Occupiers of premises owe a statutory duty towards persons on those premises, whether they are there lawfully or unlawfully.

- An occupier is a person who has a sufficient degree of control over the premises.

- A person is a lawful visitor if:

    - the occupier invites him onto the premises, or expressly or impliedly permits him to be on the premises;
    - he has a contractual right to be on the premises; or
    - he is on the premises as of right.

- The Occupiers Liability Act 1957, s 2(2), provides that an occupier is under a duty to take such care as is reasonable, in all of the circumstances of the case, to see that the visitor will be reasonably safe in using the premises for the purposes for which he is invited or permitted by the occupier to be there.

- The duty to a lawful visitor is discharged if the occupier warns the visitor of the danger, provided that the warning is enough to render the visitor reasonably safe.

- The Occupiers Liability Act 1984, s 1(4), provides that an occupier is under a duty to take such care as is reasonable, in all of the circumstances, to see that the non-lawful visitor does not suffer injury on the premises by reason of the danger concerned.

- The duty to a non-lawful visitor is discharged if the occupier takes reasonable steps to warn of the danger or to discourage persons from incurring the risk.

Nuisance and *Rylands v Fletcher*

The ownership or occupation of land imposes an obligation on the owner and/or the occupier to take due care to ensure that the state of the land or activities carried out on it do not cause injury to others. If injury is caused to others, the owner or occupier of the land may be liable in negligence. Additionally, there are two other torts (which overlap with negligence) that impose obligations on those who own or occupy land—namely, nuisance and the rule in *Rylands v Fletcher*. As we shall

TABLE 13.1 Private and public nuisance

	Private nuisance	Public nuisance
Legal status?	Only a tort	Both a crime and a tort
Interest in land?	The claimant will require an interest in the land	No interest in the land is required to bring a claim
Damages recoverable?	Property damage and loss of enjoyment of rights over property	Property damage, loss of enjoyment of rights over property, personal injury, and economic loss
Defences	*Volenti*; contributory negligence; prescription; statutory authority	*Volenti*; contributory negligence

see, nuisance can be further subdivided into private nuisance and public nuisance. Table 13.1 briefly highlights the differences between the two.

It should be noted that the two forms of nuisance are not mutually exclusive, and that an act can amount to both a public and private nuisance.

Private nuisance

Every occupier of property must expect his property and his enjoyment of it to be affected to some degree by the activities of his neighbours or the physical state of adjoining land. But if this interference exceeds what one can reasonably be expected to endure, it is an actionable private nuisance.

The classic definition of a private nuisance is provided by Winfield and Jolowicz, who define it as 'an unlawful interference with a person's use or enjoyment of land, or some right over, or in connection with it'.[113] This interference can take a number of different forms, including the following.

- *Physical interference*   Physical damage to the property of another can constitute a private nuisance. This could include damage to crops caused by fumes from a neighbouring copper-smelting works,[114] the collapse of the defendant's property onto the claimant's land,[115] and damage resulting from vibrations caused by neighbouring machinery.[116]

- *Encroachment*   If some feature of a person's land encroaches on the land of another and causes damage (for example, damage caused to the foundations of the claimant's property by roots encroaching from a tree on the defendant's land),[117] this can constitute a private nuisance.

- *Interference with the enjoyment of land (known as 'amenity nuisance')*   This is by far the widest category of private nuisance, and can include acts as diverse

---

113. WVH Rogers, *Winfield & Jolowicz on Tort* (17th edn, Sweet & Maxwell, London, 2006) 646. The courts have adopted this definition on numerous occasions: see, e.g., *Read v Lyons & Co Ltd* [1945] KB 216 (CA) 236 (Scott LJ).

114. *St Helen's Smelting Co v Tipping* (1865) 11 HL Cas 642 (HL).

115. *Wringe v Cohen* [1940] 1 KB 229 (CA).

116. *Grosvenor Hotel Co v Hamilton* [1894] 2 KB 836 (CA).

117. *Masters v Brent London Borough Council* [1978] QB 841 (QB).

as the crowing of cockerels,[118] the opening of a sex shop in a residential area,[119] and the opening of a fish-and-chip shop in a fashionable street.[120]

The point to be drawn is that private nuisance requires the claimant to show proof of damage. The above examples indicate that the damage need not be physical, but it must be present.

When is interference unlawful?

It can be very difficult to distinguish between an act that amounts to the lawful use or land and an act that amounts to private nuisance. The courts are required to engage in a fine balancing act. As Lord Wright stated: 'A balance has to be maintained between the right of the occupier to do what he likes with his own [land], and the right of his neighbour not to be interfered with.'[121] This balance is reflected in the fact that the interference must be substantial: 'The law does not regard trifling inconveniences: everything is to be looked at from a reasonable point of view.'[122] An obvious example is noise pollution. One must expect a certain amount of noise from one's neighbours, but it is only when that noise becomes excessive that an actionable nuisance might have been committed.

Given the breadth of activities that could potentially amount to a private nuisance, the courts have adopted a broad approach, determining unlawfulness by reference to a reasonableness test. In determining whether an interference is reasonable or not, the court will take into account a number of factors. The first factor is the extent of the damage suffered by the claimant as a result of the interference. The extent of the interference is highly dependent upon the facts of the case. The playing of loud music in the middle of the day might be a minor inconvenience, or no inconvenience at all if the neighbours are out at work. Conversely, playing loud music at 2 a.m. will constitute a more substantial interference. But no action would arise if the person bringing the claim was deaf, because there would be no damage caused.

A second factor is the duration of the interference: the more persistent an interference, the more likely it is to constitute an actionable private nuisance. Isolated or infrequent acts are highly unlikely to constitute a private nuisance. Students who host one noisy party are highly unlikely to commit an actionable private nuisance—but students who host such parties every night almost certainly will have committed a private nuisance. Isolated or infrequent acts can, however, be actionable if they are extremely disruptive. This will usually arise in the context of property damage. For example, an isolated incident of defective wiring that caused a neighbour's house to burn down constituted a private nuisance.[123]

Related to the duration and extent of the interference is the third factor—namely, the issue of locality. The submission of fumes or the making of noise by a factory in a heavy industrial area would be much less likely to amount to a nuisance than if the

---

118. *Leeman v Montagu* [1936] 2 All ER 1677.
119. *Laws v Florinplace Ltd* [1981] 1 All ER 659 (Ch). See also *Thompson-Schwab v Costaki* [1956] 1 WLR 335 (CA) (use of residential premises as for the purposes of prostitution).
120. *Adams v Ursell* [1913] 1 Ch 269 (Ch).
121. *Sedley-Denfield v O'Callaghan* [1940] AC 880 (HL) 903.
122. *St Helen's Smelting Co v Tipping* (1865) 11 HL Cas 642 (HL) 653.
123. *Spicer v Smee* [1946] 1 All ER 489 (KB).

factory were close to a residential area. As Thesiger LJ famously stated: 'What would be a nuisance in Belgrave Square would not necessarily be so in Bermondsey.'[124] But where property damage is caused, the issue of locality is less relevant, because no one should expect to have his property damaged by the acts of another.

A fourth factor is the sensitivity of the claimant or his property, of which the following case provides an example. If the damage is attributable to the claimant's sensitivity to a greater degree than to the conduct of the defendant, no nuisance will be committed.

 Robinson v Kilvert (1889) 41 Ch D 88 (CA)

FACTS: The defendant landlord used the cellar of his building as a place in which to manufacture cardboard boxes. This required the cellar to be hot and dry, so he purchased a heating apparatus for that purpose. The floor above the cellar had been let to the claimant who used it, inter alia, to store delicate brown paper. The use of the defendant's heaters caused the temperature to rise in the floor occupied by the claimant and, while the people who worked there were in no way inconvenienced by the rise in temperature, the heat caused the brown paper to dry and decrease in value. The claimant alleged that the defendant's actions amounted to a private nuisance.

HELD: The Court of Appeal dismissed the claimant's action. The heat did not cause discomfort to the claimant's workforce, nor would it have affected normal paper. The damage was caused more by the paper's delicacy than by the defendant's actions.

A fifth factor is motive. An act that would normally be lawful and reasonable might become an actionable nuisance if it were to be motivated by malice—as the following case clearly exemplifies.

 Hollywood Silver Fox Farm Ltd v Emmett [1936] 2 KB 468 (KB)

FACTS: The claimant was in the business of breeding silver foxes. During the breeding season, the vixens were very nervous and, if disturbed, they would refuse to breed or would miscarry, or might even kill their young. The defendant occupied land adjoining that of the claimant and was concerned that the presence of the fox farm might affect the value of his property. He therefore caused his son to discharge guns near the claimant's land with the express purpose of disturbing the claimant's business.

HELD: The defendant discharged the guns on his own land. Normally, this would not amount to a nuisance. But the Court of Appeal held that, because the defendant's actions were motivated by malice, an actionable nuisance was committed, and the claimant was granted an injunction and damages.

---

124. *Sturges v Bridgman* (1879) 11 Ch D 852 (CA) 865.

The final factor to be discussed is fault. Nuisance is not a strict liability tort, but neither does the claimant need to establish negligence. In *The Wagon Mound (No 2)*, Lord Reid stated that 'fault of some kind is almost always necessary and fault generally involves foreseeability'.[125] But given that negligence is fault-based, how can it be said that negligence is not required? The answer lies in that Lord Reid stated that 'negligence in the narrow sense is not essential'.[126] What this means is that the defendant need not show that the claimant broke his duty or care; all that need be established is that the claimant failed to meet the standard of a reasonable man.

In 1994, the House of Lords revisited the requirement of fault and stated that:

> [T]he fact that the defendant has taken all reasonable care will not of itself exonerate him.…But it by no means follows that the defendant should be held liable for damage of a type which he could not reasonably foresee…[127]

Accordingly, no nuisance will be committed if the damage is not reasonably foreseeable, but if it is foreseeable, the fact that the defendant took reasonable steps to avoid the damage will not exonerate him.

Who can sue?

The occupier of property affected by the nuisance is the usual claimant, and he can recover damages for injury to the property and to his enjoyment of the property. Alternatively, or in addition, he may seek an injunction, which is a discretionary remedy, to prevent the nuisance continuing (injunctions are discussed below). An owner of property who is not in occupation can also sue in nuisance, but only for damage to the property.

Because the tort of nuisance is designed to protect land and the enjoyment of land, the claimant must have a proprietary interest in the land affected. Despite the criticism levelled against this requirement and a brief departure from it by the Court of Appeal,[128] the House of Lords has reaffirmed the requirement.[129] This requirement may not survive for long. The European Convention on Human Rights, Art 8(1), provides that '[e]veryone has the right to respect for his private and family life, his home and his correspondence'. This right is granted irrespective of proprietary rights, so limiting nuisance actions to those persons who have a proprietary interest could be viewed as contrary to Art 8 and the retention of the requirement could be viewed as a breach of the Human Rights Act 1998, s 6.

The Human Rights Act 1998, s 6, is discussed at p 122

Who can be sued?

The person in occupation of the property from which the nuisance emanates is liable if either:

- he created the nuisance and was 'at fault' in so doing.[130] 'Fault' in nuisance means that the creator of the nuisance deliberately engaged in conduct that caused the nuisance (whether or not he intended to cause a nuisance) and

---

125. *Overseas Tankship (UK) Ltd v Miller Steamship Co Pty Ltd (The Wagon Mound)* [1967] 1 AC 617 (PC) 639.
126. Ibid.
127. *Cambridge Water Co Ltd v Eastern Counties Leather plc* [1994] 2 AC 264 (HL) 300 (Lord Goff).
128. *Khorasandjian v Bush* [1993] QB 727 (CA).   129. *Hunter v Canary Wharf Ltd* [1997] AC 655 (HL).
130. *Overseas Tankship (UK) Ltd v Miller Steamship Co Pty Ltd (The Wagon Mound (No 2))* [1967] 1 AC 617 (PC).

the injury suffered by the claimant was either reasonably foreseeable or was a 'real risk'. A 'real risk' seems to mean that the injury to the claimant could have been foreseen, even if it was not *reasonably* foreseeable, and that the injury, if it occurred, was likely to be serious;[131] or

- the nuisance was created by a third party (for example, a trespasser),[132] or arose naturally (for example, a tree struck by lightning),[133] and the person in occupation cannot prove that he was not negligent in failing to prevent the nuisance affecting the claimant. In deciding whether the defendant has done enough to prevent the injury to the claimant, the courts have regard to the defendant's personal circumstances, such as his age, financial circumstances, etc. Thus, unusually, the standard of care imposed on the defendant is that of a reasonable person in the *defendant's* circumstances—perhaps to reflect the fact that the hazard has been thrust on to the defendant through no fault of his own.

If a person other than the occupier of the property from which it emanates created the nuisance, the person creating the nuisance is also liable. A landlord is not, however, responsible for nuisances committed by his tenants unless the nuisance is in some way connected with their occupation of the property and the landlord has authorized or adopted it.[134]

Defences

A defendant has access to several defences, as follows.

- *Prescription* The defence of prescription arises where the defendant has committed an actionable nuisance for twenty years and action has not been taken during that period. Note that the act itself must have been actionable for twenty years. If there were periods during which the act was not actionable, the defence of prescription will not succeed.[135]

Volenti is discussed at p 521

- Volenti non fit injuria Where the claimant voluntarily consents to the act that amounts to an actionable nuisance, the defendant may be able successfully to raise the defence of *volenti*.

Contributory negligence is discussed at p 529

- *Contributory negligence* If the defendant contributes in some way to the act that amounts to an actionable nuisance, his damages may be reduced on the ground of his contributory negligence.

Statutory authority is discussed at p 526

- *Statutory authority* The defendant may have the defence of statutory authority if the act in question is authorized by statute. The mere fact that statute authorizes an act will not provide the defence; the courts will still have to consider other factors, as the following case demonstrates.

---

131. Ibid.

132. *Sedleigh-Denfield v O'Callaghan* [1940] AC 880 (HL). The third party who created the nuisance was also liable.

133. *Holbeck Hall Hotel v Scarborough Council* [2000] QB 836 (CA). Here, the local authority was in occupation of cliffs abutting the sea front. The cliffs slipped, removing support from neighbouring land occupied by the hotel, which subsequently collapsed in spectacular fashion. Since the local authority could not have discovered without expensive surveys that slippage on its land would adversely affect the adjoining land, it was not liable in nuisance.

134. *Hussain v Lancaster City Council* [2000] QB 1 (CA) (council not liable for harassment and racist abuse committed by tenants of its property).

135. *Sturges v Bridgman* (1879) 11 Ch D 852 (CA).

Allen v Gulf Oil Refining Ltd **[1981] AC 1001 (HL)**

FACTS: The defendant operated an oil refinery. The claimant alleged that the operation of the refinery was a nuisance, in so much as it expelled gases that produced a noxious smell, generated offensive levels of noise, and caused vibrations on the claimant's property.

HELD: The House of Lords stated that the Gulf Oil Refining Act 1965 gave the defendant the power to operate a refinery in the area. Once this was established, the defendant needed to demonstrate that it was impossible to construct and operate a refinery that conformed to Parliament's intentions without causing the nuisance alleged or any nuisance. The defendant could establish this. Consequently, there was no nuisance.

Remedies

Several remedies may be available to the victim of an actionable private nuisance, as follows.

- *Injunction*   The primary remedy is the granting of an injunction to stop the nuisance. An injunction is not available as of right; rather, it is a discretionary remedy and the courts may refuse to grant an injunction even if the nuisance is actionable. The injunction may be granted wholly or in part (for example, where the claimant contended successfully that nearby powerboating constituted a nuisance, the Court held that no powerboats creating a noise of over 75 decibels could be used and that no more than six boats could go on the water at any one time).[136]

- *Damages*   Damages can be sought instead of, or in addition to, an injunction. Because private nuisance is concerned only with protecting the claimant's interest in land, or his right to use and enjoy the land, it follows that damages will compensate the claimant only for the loss in the value of the land and/or the loss of the ability to use or enjoy the land. Damages for other losses (for example, personal injury or economic loss) are not recoverable under the tort of nuisance. Only foreseeable losses can be claimed and the test of remoteness in nuisance is the same as in negligence.

  The rules relating to remoteness in negligence are discussed at p 436

- *Abatement*   Abatement involves the claimant taking steps to prevent or stop the nuisance himself (for example, by cutting off overhanging branches).[137] Abatement, like all self-help remedies, needs to be exercised cautiously and its exercise is usually advised against. Further, the Court has limited its usage by stating that it is usually only appropriate in clear and simple cases, or in an emergency.[138]

Public nuisance

A private nuisance is a tort only and is concerned with protecting an individual's right in land. Conversely, a public nuisance is both a crime and a tort, and, as its name suggests, is concerned with protecting a wider group of persons. A public nuisance has been defined as one that 'materially affects the reasonable comfort and convenience of life of a class of the public who come within the sphere or neighbourhood of

---

136. *Kennaway v Thompson* [1981] QB 88 (CA).   137. *Lemmon v Webb* [1895] AC 1 (CA).
138. *Burton v Winters* [1993] 1 WLR 1077 (CA).

its operation'.[139] What constitutes a class of the public will depend upon the facts of the case. Examples of public nuisances include obstruction of the highway, selling food unfit for human consumption, the carrying on of an offensive trade, or the expulsion of noxious fumes over a wide area.

There are several significant limitations on the scope of what constitutes a public nuisance:

- the claimant must prove the existence of widespread harm;
- the act must cause a common injury to the class of persons concerned;[140]
- the claimant must prove that he suffered special damage (that is, damage greater than that suffered by the class of persons affected by the act). This requirement does not apply in relation to actions brought by local authorities or the Attorney General.

Who can sue and be sued?

It would appear that proceedings may be commenced by the following.

- *Local authorities* A local authority may commence proceedings for an injunction in its own name for the purposes of 'promotion or protection of the interests of the inhabitants of their area'.[141] This can obviously include situations in which its inhabitants are affected by a public nuisance.

➡ Attorney General: the principal law officer of the Crown, whose duties include, inter alia, commencing prosecutions on behalf of the Crown

- *The Attorney General* Because public nuisance is a crime, the Attorney General can bring a **relator action** seeking an injunction to prevent the nuisance. The Attorney General will only consider such an action if the applicant has suffered special harm.

- *Private citizens* A private citizen can commence proceedings for an injunction or for damages in two situations:

➡ relator action: an action brought by the Attorney General upon application from a private person, inviting him to join in bringing proceedings

  - where the nuisance in question appears to be a private nuisance, but affects a much larger group of persons (the requisite number of persons will vary, depending on the facts);
  - even where the nuisance does not affect the claimant's land, he can still bring a claim if it affects the public, but it affects him to a greater degree (that is, he suffers special damage).

Persons who can be liable for public nuisance are the same as those who can be liable for private nuisance.

Defences

The available defences for a public nuisance are broadly the same as those for a private nuisance—but:

- because a public nuisance constitutes a crime, the defence of prescription is not available;
- the Law Reform (Contributory Negligence) Act 1945 does not apply to criminal liability.

---

139. WVH Rogers, *Winfield & Jolowicz on Tort* (17th edn, Sweet & Maxwell, London, 2006) 643.
140. *R v Rimmington and Goldstein* [2005] UKHL 63, [2006] 1 AC 459 (HL).
141. Local Government Act 1972, s 222(1).

Remedies

Two remedies are available, as follows.

- *Injunction* As with private nuisance, an injunction may be available requiring the defendant to stop the nuisance. This may be sought by a local authority, the Attorney General, or a private citizen.
- *Damages* Like private nuisance, damages are recoverable by a private person for damage to property, but, unlike private nuisance, damages are also recoverable for personal injury[142] and economic loss.[143]

Rylands v Fletcher

The rule in *Rylands v Fletcher* is a distinct tort in its own right, although it bears an extremely close resemblance to private nuisance. Where it differs is that a person with neither an interest in land nor exclusive possession of it could also have a cause of action. The rule was created in response to the infliction of harm caused to land by increased industrialization brought about by the Industrial Revolution. The courts' response was to impose strict liability on those who damage the land of others in certain circumstances, as the case of *Rylands v Fletcher* itself demonstrates.

 Rylands v Fletcher (1868) LR 3 HL 330 (HL)

FACTS: The defendant owned land upon which he operated a mill. The mill was serviced by a small reservoir, but more water was required. The defendant therefore engaged a reputable firm of engineers (acting as independent contractors) to build a larger reservoir. When building the reservoir, the contractors discovered a number of disused mine shafts, which would have to be sealed. Unfortunately, the contractors sealed the mineshafts negligently, and, when the reservoir was completed, one of the seals broke and the water flooded the mineshaft, and, travelling through a series of underground passages, also flooded a nearby colliery belonging to the claimant. The claimant commenced proceedings against the defendant.

HELD: The clamant succeeded. The House of Lords affirmed the rule established by the first-instance judge, who stated that:

> [A] person who for his own purposes brings on his lands and collects and keeps there anything likely to do mischief if it escapes, must keep it in at his peril, and, if he does not do so, is prima facie answerable for all the damage which is the natural consequence of its escape.[144]

This was so, even though the defendant was entirely blameless. The House of Lords added an additional requirement—namely, that the defendant's **user** of his land should be non-natural.

➡ **user:** the use or enjoyment of a thing

COMMENT: As we shall see, the requirement that the defendant is liable for damage that is the natural consequence of escape has been modified by the House of Lords, which held that the claimant would need to establish foreseeability.

---

142. See, e.g., *Castle v St Augustine's Links* (1922) 38 TLR 615 (KB) (taxi driver hit by golf ball).
143. See, e.g., *Fritz v Hobson* (1880) 14 Ch D 542 (Ch) (loss of profits caused by obstruction of highway).
144. (1866) LR 1 Ex 265 (Ex) 279 (Blackburn J).

In order for liability to arise, a number of requirements must be satisfied.

Accumulation

The defendant must bring something onto, or allow something to accumulate, on his land. In *Rylands*, the defendant brought water onto his land. Things naturally on the land will not result in liability; rather, the thing in question must have been brought onto, or accumulated, on the land artificially.

Likely to do mischief

Note that liability is not dependent upon the thing being dangerous.[145] Water is not dangerous per se, yet it resulted in liability in *Rylands*. What is required is that the thing, if it were to escape, would be likely to do mischief. Clearly, this is strongly linked to the issue of foreseeability, which will be discussed shortly. Examples of things that have been held as likely to do mischief include water,[146] fire,[147] noxious fumes,[148] sewage,[149] electricity,[150] and piles of waste material.[151]

Escape

The claimant must demonstrate that the thing likely to do mischief escaped (either accidentally or intentionally) from 'a place which the defendant has occupation of, or control over, to a place which is outside his occupation or control'.[152] Accordingly, where a person in a factory is killed due to an explosion in the factory, liability under *Rylands* cannot arise if the thing that caused the explosion is also in the factory.[153] But liability can be imposed if a thing brought onto, or allowed to accumulate on, the land remains on the land, but causes another thing to escape (for example, explosives brought onto land, which explode, causing a rock slide that damages adjoining land).[154]

Non-natural user

When Blackburn J first laid down the rule in *Rylands*, he said that it would apply only to a thing that 'was not naturally there'. On appeal, the House of Lords amended this requirement to state that the bringing of the thing onto the land, or the accumulation of the thing, should be a non-natural user of the land. This phrase has caused a measure of confusion, but the House of Lords in *Transco plc v Stockport Metropolitan Borough Council*[155] attempted to provide a measure of clarity. Whether it succeeded is arguable.

In this case, Lord Bingham stated:

> I think it clear that ordinary user is a preferable test to natural user, making it clear that the rule in *Rylands v Fletcher* is engaged only where the defendant's use is shown to be extraordinary and unusual. This is not a test to be inflexibly applied: a use

145. *Cambridge Water Co v Eastern Counties Leather plc* [1994] 2 AC 264 (HL).
146. *Rylands v Fletcher* (1868) LR 3 HL 330 (HL).
147. *Jones v Festiniog Rly Co* (1868) 3 QB 733.
148. *West v Bristol Tramways Co* [1908] 2 KB 14 (CA).
149. *Humphries v Cousins* (1877) 2 CPD 239.
150. *National Telephone Co v Baker* [1893] 2 Ch 186 (Ch).
151. *Attorney General v Cory Bros and Co Ltd* [1921] 1 AC 521 (HL).
152. *Read v J Lyons & Co Ltd* [1947] AC 156 (HL) 168 (Viscount Simon LC).
153. Ibid.   154. *Miles v Forest Rock Granite Co* (1918) TLR 500.
155. [2003] UKHL 61, [2004] 2 AC 1.

may be extraordinary and unusual at one time or in one place but not so at another time or in another place.... [T]he question is whether the defendant has done something which he recognises, or ought to recognise, as being quite out of the ordinary in the place and at the time when he does it. In answering that question, I respectfully think that little help is gained (and unnecessary confusion perhaps caused) by considering whether the use is proper for the general benefit of the community.[156]

But Lord Hoffmann appeared not to favour a test based on ordinary usage,[157] stating instead that non-natural usage was based on whether or not 'the damage which eventuated was something against which the occupier could reasonably be expected to have insured himself'.[158] To add more confusion, Lord Hobhouse was critical of an approach based on the availability of insurance.[159]

The issue is still unclear. What is clear is that the requirement for non-natural user limits considerably the scope of the rule, especially if Lord Bingham's formulation of the test as non-ordinary is regarded as correct. For example, building a series of properties on a piece of land cannot be regarded as natural, but it could very well be regarded as ordinary.

Foreseeability

The following case has further limited the scope of the rule by providing that foreseeability is an essential requirement for liability.

> ### Cambridge Water Co v Eastern Counties Leather plc [1994] 2 AC 264 (HL)
>
> **FACTS:** The defendant operated a leather tannery and used a chemical—perchloroethylene (PCE)—to degrease the animal pelts. Some 1.3 miles away from the tannery was a borehole owned by the claimant, which was used to provide water to residents of the Cambridge area. It was discovered that, over a period of time, PCE spilt at the defendant's tannery had seeped into the soil and contaminated an underground water flow that, in turn, contaminated the water being abstracted by the claimant's borehole. The water became unfit for consumption, and the claimant had to shut the borehole down and find an alternative source of water. It was estimated that this cost the claimant around £900,000. The claimant commenced proceedings against the defendant.
>
> **HELD:** The House of Lords dismissed the claimant's action. Whilst the storage of PCE on the defendant's premises constituted a non-natural user of the land, the defendant could not have reasonably foreseen that spillage of the chemical would pollute the claimant's borehole.
>
> **COMMENT:** There can be little doubt that the imposition of a foreseeability requirement significantly weakens the strict liability nature of the rule in *Rylands*. But the requirement has introduced yet more uncertainty into the law. The House did not make clear whether the method of escape must be reasonably foreseeable, or the harm sustained, or both. The House of Lords in *Transco* has subsequently made clear that the requirement of foreseeability relates to the harm caused, not the method of escape.[160]

★ See RFV Heuston, 'The Return of *Rylands v Fletcher*' (1994) 110 LQR 185

---

156. Ibid, [11].   157. Ibid, [37].
158. Ibid, [46].   159. Ibid, [60].
160. *Transco plc v Stockport Metropolitan Borough Council* [2003] UKHL 61, [2004] 2 AC 1, [10] (Lord Bingham).

Defences

A defendant has access to a number of defences, as follows.

- Volenti   If the claimant expressly or impliedly consents to the accumulation of the thing, he cannot obtain a remedy if that thing escapes and causes damage to his land.[161]

- *Common benefit*   Where the thing that, if it were to escape, would be likely to cause mischief is on the defendant's land for the common benefit of both the defendant and the claimant, then the defendant will not be liable if the thing escapes. It is arguable that this is not an independent defence, but rather an example of *volenti*.

- *Default*   If the claimant's loss is caused entirely by his own act, he will have no remedy.[162]

- *Contributory negligence*   Where the claimant's loss is caused partially by his own act, the defendant can raise the defence of contributory negligence, which will serve to reduce the amount of damages payable.

- *Statutory authority*   It is relatively common for certain companies (especially utility companies) to be excluded from the operation of *Rylands* by statute, provided that they exercise reasonable care and skill. Each case will depend upon the facts and the nature of the statutory authority in question.

- *Act of God*   If the escape is caused by an unforeseeable, natural act (for example, extreme weather conditions), then no liable will be imposed.

- *Acts of a stranger*   If the escape is caused by the actions of an unknown third party, then no liability will arise.[163]

*Volenti,
contributory
negligence, and
statutory authority are
discussed in more
detail in Chapter 15*

⟨⟩ Key points summary

- An unlawful interference with a person's use or enjoyment of land or some right over, or in connection with, it may constitute a private nuisance. A private nuisance is a tort only.

- In relation to private nuisance, an individual can only bring a claim if he has a proprietary interest in the land affected.

- A person alleged to have committed a private nuisance has access to several defences, including prescription, *volenti non fit injuria*, contributory negligence, and statutory authority.

- A public nuisance is one that materially affects the reasonable comfort and convenience of life of a class of the public that comes within the sphere or neighbourhood of its operation. A public nuisance is both a tort and a crime.

- The claimant must show that he suffered special damage, but he will not require a proprietary interest in the land affected.

- The defence of prescription is not available in cases of public nuisance.

---

161. *Attorney General v Cory Bros and Co Ltd* [1921] 1 AC 521 (HL).
162. *Ponting v Noakes* [1894] 2 QB 281 (QB).
163. *Box v Jubb* (1879) 4 Ex D 76.

- The tort of *Rylands v Fletcher* occurs where a person brings a thing onto his land, or allows a thing to accumulate on his land, that, if it were to escape, would be likely to do mischief.

- The thing must amount to a non-natural user of the land and the harm sustained must be reasonably foreseeable.

Defamation

As noted in Chapter 11, one of the principal functions of the law of torts is to protect a person's interests. Not only will this include a person's physical well-being and financial interests, but it can also include less tangible interests, such as a person's reputation. Defamation seeks to protect a person's reputation and occurs where the defendant publishes a statement referring to the claimant that lowers the claimant in the estimation of right-thinking members of society generally, or which would tend to make them shun or avoid him. Today, the majority of defamation cases tend to relate to statements made on television or in newspapers about celebrities or other persons in the public eye, but defamation can have a strong commercial aspect too. For example, an auditor who states in his report that the directors are untrustworthy and engaged in suspect commercial transactions may be liable for defamation if such statements are untrue.

Libel and slander

Defamation is a collective term for the torts of libel and slander, and the distinction between them relates to the medium of publication:

- *libel* is a defamatory statement published in a permanent form (for example, a film, newspaper or statute);
- *slander* is a defamatory statement published in a non-permanent form (for example, through spoken words or gestures).

At a basic level, defamatory statements that are *seen* constitute libel and defamatory statements that are *heard* constitute slander (although permanent audio statements may amount to libel). For example, imagine that an auditor dictates a defamatory statement to his secretary, intending it to be included in his report. The dictation of the defamatory statement could constitute slander, but the publication of the statement in the auditor's report could constitute libel. It should always be remembered, however, that the key distinguishing feature is permanence and that defamatory spoken words can constitute libel if they are spoken in a permanent medium (for example, on television).[164]

It is important to be able to distinguish between slander and libel for two reasons. Firstly, slander per se is only ever a tort,[165] whereas libel can also amount to a crime.

---

164. Broadcasting Act 1990, s 166(1).

165. Slanderous words accompanied by other more serious wrongs (e.g. blasphemy) may constitute a crime.

Secondly, libel is actionable even if the libel has not caused any damage to the claimant. Conversely, slander is generally not actionable unless damage has been caused to the claimant, but an exception to this occurs where the slander imputes that:

- the claimant has committed a criminal offence for which he could be imprisoned;[166]
- the claimant is dishonest or unfit for his office, trade, or profession;[167]
- the claimant has some infectious or contagious disease (the continuing validity of which exception has been questioned, especially given that the last reported case concerning this exception occurred in 1844);[168]
- a woman is unchaste or an adulteress.[169]

Who can sue?

In Chapter 11, we discussed who can bring a claim in tort and noted that the death of the claimant will not normally cause the right of action to lapse. Defamation is the sole exception to this: it is impossible to defame the dead and the death of the claimant will extinguish an existing cause of action. Accordingly, any living person (natural or legal) can sue for defamation.

An important limitation was, however, established in the following landmark case.

Derbyshire County Council v Times Newspapers Ltd [1993] AC 534 (HL)

FACTS: The defendant published two newspaper articles in which it questioned the propriety of investments made in relation to the claimant's superannuation fund. The claimant commenced libel proceedings.

HELD: The House of Lords held that local authorities and other organs of the State cannot sue for defamation.[170] The rationale behind this restriction was stated by Lord Keith:

> It is of the highest public importance that a democratically elected governmental body, or indeed any governmental body, should be open to uninhibited public criticism. The threat of a civil action for defamation must inevitably have an inhibiting effect on freedom of speech.[171]

★ See B Bix and A Tomkins, 'Local Authorities and Libel Again' (1993) 56 MLR 738

The requirements for defamation

A party who is alleging defamation will need to establish:

- that the statement was defamatory;
- that it was published; and
- that it was published with reference to the claimant.

These requirements will be briefly discussed.

---

166. *Webb v Beavan* (1883) 11 QBD 609 (QB).   167. Defamation Act 1952, s 2.
168. *Bloodworth v Gray* (1844) 7 Man & G 334.   169. Slander of Women Act 1891, s 1.
170. This is extended to political parties, but individual members of Parliament may sue: *Goldsmith v Bhoyrul* [1998] QB 459 (QB).
171. [1993] AC 534 (HL) 547.

The statement was defamatory

A defamatory statement is one that tends 'to lower the clamant in the estimation of right-thinking members of society generally'.[172] Although many defamatory statements attack the morality or character of a person, this is not a requirement. In commercial cases involving defamation, often, the claimant's character has not been defamed, but the statement will 'impute lack of qualification, knowledge, skill, capacity, judgment or efficiency in the conduct of his trade or business or professional activity'.[173]

A statement in itself may not be generally defamatory, but when coupled with facts known only to certain persons, it may become defamatory.[174] Such a statement is known as an 'innuendo' and can be defamatory if the claimant can establish that the words have this hidden meaning known only to certain persons.

Reference to the claimant

The statement must refer to the claimant. This does not require that the statement refer to the claimant by name or that the defendant intended to refer to the claimant;[175] all that is required is that reasonable people would believe that the statement referred to the claimant.[176] So, for example, a statement may refer to the occupier of a particular office, or to a group of persons that includes the claimant. But where the group is large, the claimant will need to demonstrate that the statement in some way points specifically to him.[177]

Publication

In relation to defamation, the word 'publication' does not bear its ordinary meaning; rather, it refers to the communication of the statement to at least one person other than the claimant. It follows that if the statement is sent only to the claimant, then no defamation has occurred.[178] This reinforces the notion that defamation is concerned with protecting the claimant's reputation in the eyes of others and not with protecting the claimant's own sense of self-esteem.

The effect of the Human Rights Act 1998

In relation to defamation, the law has always had to strike a fine balance between two conflicting legitimate principles—namely, the protection of reputation and the preservation of freedom of expression. With the passing of the Human Rights Act 1998 and the consequent ability to enforce the European Convention on Human Rights (ECHR) in a domestic court, striking the correct balance has become even more important.

The two competing principles are both enshrined in the ECHR.

- Article 8 provides: 'Everyone has the right to respect for his private and family life, his home and his correspondence.' Accordingly, a person has a right not to have private information revealed that could damage his reputation.

---

172. *Sim v Stretch* [1936] 2 All ER 1237 (HL) 1240 (Lord Atkin).
173. *Drummond-Jackson v British Medical Association* [1970] 1 WLR 688 (CA) 698, 699 (Lord Pearson).
174. For example, *Cassidy v Daily Mirror Newspapers Ltd* [1929] 2 KB 331 (CA).
175. *Houlton & Co v Jones* [1910] AC 20 (HL).   176. *Hayward v Thompson* [1982] QB 47 (CA).
177. *Knupffer v London Express Newspaper Ltd* [1944] AC 16 (HL).
178. *Pullman v W Hill & Co Ltd* [1891] 1 QB 524 (CA).

- Article 10 provides: 'Everyone has the right to freedom of expression. This right shall include freedom to hold opinions and to receive and impart information and ideas without interference by public authority and regardless of frontiers.' But this right is not absolute and signatory States may restrict freedom of expression to the extent that it is necessary in a democratic society to protect the reputation of others.

Even where issues of privacy are not involved, Art 10 can still conflict with the general aim of tort in this area—namely, to protect a person's reputation. Defendants in defamation cases frequently invoke Art 10 and the courts will have to determine in each case which of the competing, but legitimate, rights is more deserving of protection. It is generally believed that the courts tend to protect freedom of expression to a greater degree than a person's reputation. The following case provides an example.

O'Shea v Mirror Group Newspapers Ltd [2001] EMLR 40 (QB)

FACTS: The first defendant published the *Sunday Mirror*. The second defendant ran a pornographic website, which it advertised in the *Sunday Mirror*. The advertisement contained a picture of a glamour model who closely resembled the claimant. The claimant had stated that several people had believed that she was the woman in the advertisement. She commenced libel proceedings.

★ See J Coad, ' "Pressing Social Need" and Strict Liability in Libel' (2001) 12 Ent LR 199

HELD: The High Court dismissed her claim. Morland J stated that, under the common law, her claim would have succeeded (because unintentional defamation is based on strict liability).[179] But such a result could not stand with Art 10 and it would 'impose an impossible burden on a publisher if he were required to check if the true picture of someone resembled someone else who because of the context of the picture was defamed'.[180]

Defences

A number of defences are available to a person who is alleged to have made a defamatory statement.

Justification

It will be a complete defence for the defendant to demonstrate that the statement was true, irrespective of whether the statement was maliciously or spitefully made. But the defence of justification will fail in relation to a malicious statement made in relation to another person's 'spent' convictions.[181]

Fair comment

This defence applies to comments made about the claimant or the claimant's conduct. In order for the defence of fair comment to arise, the comment must be made

---

179. *Houlton & Co v Jones* [1910] AC 20 (HL).   180. [2001] EMLR 40 (QB) [43].
181. Rehabilitation of Offenders Act 1974, s 8.

without malice, must be in the public interest, and must be an honest expression of opinion on matters of fact that have been accurately stated.

Consent

A person who consents to publication of a defamatory statement cannot sue for defamation.

Responsibility for publication

The Defamation Act 1996, s 1, provides that a person who is not the author, editor, or commercial publisher of the statement complained of (for example, a printer or distributor) has a defence to a defamation action if he can show that he took reasonable care in relation to its publication and that he did not know, and had no reason to believe, that what he did caused or contributed to the publication of a defamatory statement.

Offer to make amends

The Defamation Act 1996, s 2, introduced this defence, which allows a person who has published a statement alleged to be defamatory to offer to make amends. The party who published the allegedly defamatory material does so by issuing a suitable correction of the statement complained of, making a sufficient apology, and paying the aggrieved party such compensation (if any) and such costs as are agreed or determined to be payable. The person to whom the offer is made can accept it or reject it. If the offer is accepted, the party accepting the offer cannot continue defamation proceedings, but can enforce the offer to make amends.[182] If the offer is rejected, the offer is a complete defence unless the claimant can show that, when publishing the defamatory material, the defendant knew, or had reason to believe, that it referred to the claimant, and was both false and defamatory.

Absolute privilege

A limited number of statements are absolutely privileged and cannot, normally, form the basis of an action for defamation. Examples of such statements include:

- statements made in Parliament;[183]
- fair and accurate contemporaneous reports of court proceedings in the UK or of the European Court of Human Rights;[184]
- statements made in judicial proceedings, irrespective of whether they are untrue or malicious;
- communications between certain officers of State (for example, government ministers).[185]

---

182. Defamation Act 1996, s 3(2).
183. Bill of Rights 1688, art 9. Note, however, that the Defamation Act 1996, s 13, allows a member of Parliament to waive parliamentary privilege.
184. Defamation Act 1996, s 14(1).
185. *Chatterton v Secretary of State for India* [1895] 2 QB 189 (CA).

Qualified privilege

Where a statement is subject to a qualified privilege, the privilege disappears if the statement is made maliciously. The Defamation Act 1996, Sch 1, provides a non-exhaustive list of statements to which qualified privilege attaches. It includes fair and accurate reports of parliamentary proceedings, and fair and accurate reports of proceedings before courts anywhere in the world, other than reports that are absolutely privileged. Qualified privilege also exists where, on the basis of the facts known by the defendant at the time of publication,[186] there is a duty (legal or moral) to make a statement and the recipient has a legitimate interest in receiving it (for example, when an existing or former employer gives a reference for an employee to a prospective employer).

Remedies

Damages

Defamation is an extremely rare tort, in the sense that it is a civil action still tried by jury[187] and it is the jury that determines the quantum of damages. As with virtually all awards of damages, the amount awarded should compensate the claimant for the loss suffered, but it has long been believed that juries award defendants damages in excess of their actual loss. Accordingly, a number of steps have been taken to ensure that the damages awarded by juries better reflect the claimant's loss, including:

- a judge may direct the jury regarding the quantum of damages in defamation cases;[188]
- juries can be referred to conventional compensation awards in personal injury cases by way of comparison;[189]
- where the Court of Appeal considers a jury's award of damages to be excessive, it can set aside the award of damages and either order damages to be reassessed by a new jury,[190] or substitute the award of the jury for 'such sums as appears to the court to be proper'.[191]

Exemplary damages are discussed at p 539

Exemplary damages may be awarded in libel cases in which the defendant publishes a libel believing that the revenue generated by the published item will exceed the likely award of damages payable.[192]

---

186. *Loutchansky v Times Newspapers Ltd* [2001] EWCA Civ 536, [2001] 4 All ER 115.

187. Supreme Court Act 1981, s 69(1)(b). The Defamation Act 1996, s 8, introduced a summary procedure whereby: (i) the claimant's claim can be dismissed if it has no realistic chance of success; or (ii) summary judgment can be made in the claimant's favour where there is no defence that has a reasonable chance of success.

188. *Rantzen v Mirror Group Newspapers* [1994] QB 670 (CA).

189. *John v Mirror Group Newspapers Ltd* [1997] QB 586 (CA).

190. *Sutcliffe v Pressdram Ltd* [1991] 1 QB 153 (CA).

191. Courts and Legal Services Act 1990, s 8(2).

192. *Cassell & Co Ltd v Broome* [1972] AC 1136 (HL).

Injunctions

A person who believes that he has been defamed may attempt to restrain publication of the allegedly defamatory statement by means of an interim injunction until the jury can determine whether the statement is defamatory or not. Again, competing interests are involved: should the law favour the individual who may have been defamed or the freedom of the press to publish statements the nature of which has not yet been determined? Regarding the granting of injunctions, it is clear that the law favours the freedom of expression and that an interim injunction restraining publication will not be granted unless the court is satisfied that 'the applicant is likely to establish that publication should not be allowed'.[193]

Key points summary

- Defamation occurs where the defendant publishes a statement referring to the claimant that lowers the claimant in the estimation of right-thinking members of society generally, or which would tend to make them shun or avoid him.

- A defamatory statement published in permanent form constitutes libel, whereas a defamatory statement published in a non-permanent form constitutes slander. Slander per se is only a tort, whereas libel can be both a tort and a crime.

- There are a number defences for defamation, including justification, fair comment, consent, offer to make amends, and absolute or qualified privilege.

- The principal remedies for defamation are an award of damages and/or an injunction restraining publication.

Breach of statutory duty

Statute may impose duties on persons, breach of which will result in sanctions set out in statute. Alternatively, the statute may not provide for any sanctions at all. Increasingly, aspects of business life are being regulated by statute (for example, legislation imposing duties upon employers to safeguard the health and safety of their employees). Much of this legislation imposes criminal liability if the duty is breached. The question that arises is whether a person who has suffered loss due to another's breach of statutory duty can commence a private action in tort to recover damages for that loss. Where such an action is permissible, the defendant may have committed a tort know as 'breach of statutory duty'. An action for breach of statutory duty can be advantageous, especially where the duty imposed is strict. In such a case, the claimant will not need to establish negligence or fault. But in order for such a clam to succeed, a number of issues need to be addressed, beginning with whether the breach of the statutory duty gives rise to an action in tort.

---

193. Human Rights Act 1998, s 12(3).

Does the breach give rise to an action in tort?

Not every breach of a statutory duty gives a person injured by that breach the right to bring an action in tort for breach of statutory duty. The reason is that statutory provisions imposing a duty on organizations or people normally have a public purpose to achieve (for example, an orderly system of educational provision) and provide sanctions for breach of the duty. Hence, the courts may think it inappropriate to hold that such a statute should also create private rights allowing individuals to sue for its breach. Thus, the first task of the court is to determine whether breach of the particular statutory duty that has caused injury is actionable in tort. In determining this, the court will seek to ascertain the intention of Parliament. In some cases, the statute itself may expressly indicate Parliament's intention by providing that:

- breach of a statutory duty does not give rise to civil proceedings;[194]
- breach of a statutory duty can specifically give rise to a private civil action by any person who suffers loss due to the breach.[195]

In the majority of cases, however, the statute will be silent on this issue and the court will need to seek Parliament's implied intention.

The following case demonstrates how an implied intention can manifest.

Atkinson v Newcastle and Gateshead Waterworks Co (1877) 2 Ex D 441 (CA)

FACTS: The Waterworks Clauses Act 1847 placed a duty on the defendant to maintain a level of pressure in water pipes used to supply water to Newcastle. Breach of this duty resulted in a £10 fine, which would go to the overseers of the parish. Breaches of other duties in the 1847 Act were punishable with fines, part of which could be paid to those who suffered injury. The claimant's premises caught fire, but there was insufficient pressure in the pipes to expel water at a fast enough rate and so the premises burnt down. The defendant paid the £10 fine to the parish and the claimant brought a claim in damages for his loss.

HELD: The Court of Appeal held that no action in tort could arise for breach of the statutory duty. The Court was heavily influenced by the fact that the statute did not provide for payment to persons who suffered loss due to insufficient water pressure, but did provide payment to those who suffered loss as regards other breaches. The implied intention of Parliament was therefore that persons who suffer loss due to insufficient water pressure should not be able to recover compensation.

---

194. For example, Health and Safety at Work etc. Act 1974, s 47(1)(a), Medicines Act 1968, s 133(2)(a), and Guard Dogs Act 1975, s 5(2)(a).

195. For example, Financial Services and Markets Act 2000, s 150(1), Consumer Protection Act 1987, s 41(1), and Mineral Workings (Offshore Installations) Act 1971, s 11.

The courts take a restrictive view of when a statutory duty is actionable in tort. The courts will require that:

- the duty imposed protects a limited class of the public[196] (as opposed to the public generally); and
- Parliament intended to confer on members of that class a private right of action for breach of the duty.

In determining this, a number of factors may be relevant, as follows.

- If there exists a common law duty in respect of particular activities, the courts may be inclined to find that breach of a statute dealing with similar activities is also tortious (and vice versa)[197] in so far as the civil action for breach of statutory duty complements the common law.
- If a statute is designed to prevent a particular type of injury and it is that type of injury that the claimant has suffered, an action in tort is more likely to exist.[198] But if the loss suffered is pure economic loss, it is unlikely that the courts will impose civil liability on the party bearing the statutory duty.[199]
- If a statute provides no sanction for its breach, a civil action in tort may lie, because, unless such an action were available, breach of that statute would escape all punishment.[200] Hence, if the statute provides for a penalty or an alternative remedy for a person adversely affected by breach of a statute, there is a presumption against giving a civil remedy to individuals.[201]
- The fact that some part of a fine levied for breach of statutory duty can be used to compensate the victim of that breach militates against, but does not preclude, a right to sue in tort.[202]
- Where a statute imposes an administrative function on a public body that has a discretion as to how that function should be exercised, the courts are unlikely to find that there is a cause of action for breach of statutory duty vested in individuals, provided that the way in which the body exercised its discretion was within the ambit of the statute.[203] It is important to note, however, that, when the public body has made its policy decision, the negligent implementation of that decision can be actionable.[204]
- The fact that a statute, although designed to benefit a section of the public, has a community or social welfare remit (for example, the provision of education or housing) has tended to militate against the imposition of civil liability.[205] In such cases, it has been suggested that a remedy under the judicial review jurisdiction, rather than an action in tort, should be sought.

---

196. *X v Bedfordshire County Council* [1995] 2 AC 633 (HL).
197. *Cutler v Wandsworth Stadium Ltd* [1949] AC 398 (HL).
198. *Monk v Warbey* [1935] 1 KB 75 (CA).
199. *Murphy v Brentwood District Council* [1991] 1 AC 398 (HL); cf *Invercargill City Council v Hamlin* [1996] AC 624 (PC).
200. *Thornton v Kirklees Metropolitan Borough Council* [1979] QB 626 (CA).
201. See *Olotu v Home Office* [1997] 1 WLR 328 (CA).
202. *Groves v Lord Wimborne* [1898] 2 QB 402 (CA).
203. *X v Bedfordshire County Council* [1995] 2 AC 633 (HL). If, however, an exercise of discretion was so unreasonable that it fell outside the ambit of the discretion, that could itself be negligence.
204. *Phelps v London Borough of Hillingdon* [2000] 4 All ER 504 (HL).
205. *O'Rourke v Camden London Borough Council* [1998] AC 188 (HL).

To whom is the duty owed?

Once it is determined that a statutory duty can give rise to an action in tort, the claimant will need to establish that the duty was owed to him.[206] Accordingly, a duty imposed upon railway authorities to fasten level-crossing gates securely was not owed to a train driver who was injured when an unfastened gate swung across the line.[207] But if a statute imposes a duty, but does not define the class that the statute is designed to protect, the courts will tend to hold that the duty is owed to anyone adversely affected by the breach.[208]

In addition, the injury sustained by the claimant must have been of the kind that the statute sought to prevent.

 Gorris v Scott (1874) 9 LR Exch 125

FACTS: The Contagious Diseases (Animals) Act 1869, s 75, placed a duty on the defendant to provide pens for any livestock being transported on his ship. He failed to do this and the claimant's sheep were washed overboard. The claimant sued.

HELD: The court held that the purpose of the duty contained in s 75 was to prevent the spread of disease amongst livestock and not to prevent them being washed overboard. Accordingly, the injury sustained by the claimant was not of the type the statute sought to protect and his claim failed.

Breach of duty

As with negligence, once a duty is established, the claimant will need to demonstrate that the duty was breached. The standard that a person who is under a statutory duty must reach in order to avoid liability is determined by reference to the statute in question. The courts will determine the precise nature of the duty imposed and then measure the defendant's conduct against that duty. In addition to defining the scope of the duty, a court must also, by reference to the statute, consider the degree of fault that the defendant must have displayed if he is to incur liability. For example, if a statute provides that an employer must do something, it must be done, and any failure to comply with the Act in question, however innocent, will constitute a breach of statutory duty.[209]

Causation

 Causation in tort is discussed at p 421

In order to succeed in an action for breach of statutory duty, the claimant must establish that the breach caused his injuries. If the breach caused his injuries (at least partially), the claimant can recover damages even if he is also in breach of a statutory duty. Thus, if an employer fails to encourage his employees to wear safety goggles

---

206. *Hartley v Mayoh & Co Ltd* [1954] 1 QB 383 (CA).
207. *Knapp v Railway Executive* [1949] 2 All ER 508 (CA).
208. *Westwood v Post Office* [1974] AC 1 (HL).
209. *John Summers and Sons Ltd v Frost* [1955] AC 740 (HL).

that he has provided and this failure is a breach of a statutory duty, an employee who suffers eye injuries while not using his goggles can recover damages. This is the case even if the employee was in breach of a statutory duty owed by him to wear the goggles.[210] On the other hand, if the claimant's breach of statutory duty is the sole cause of his injuries, he cannot recover damages even though the defendant was also in breach of a statutory duty.[211]

Defences

An employer can raise the defence of contributory negligence when sued by his employees for breach of statutory duty. But it is the policy of the courts, in deciding whether an employee has contributed to his injuries:

 Contributory negligence is discussed at p 529

> to give due regard to the actual conditions under which men work in a factory or mine, to the long hours and the fatigue, to the slackening of attention which naturally comes from constant repetition of the same operation, to the noise and confusion in which the man works, to his preoccupation in what he is actually doing at the cost perhaps of some inattention to his own safety.[212]

To do otherwise would be to deprive employees of the protection of much of the safety legislation that is designed to protect them.

The defence of *volenti* (consent) is also available, but in relation to employment cases involving breach of statutory duty, the courts adopt a paternalistic approach. It is settled law that an employer who is personally in breach of a statutory duty (for example, by providing unfenced machinery) cannot rely on this defence at all.[213] An employer who is in breach of statutory duty because he is held vicariously responsible for the actions of another one of his employees can, however, raise this defence.[214]

Volenti is discussed at p 521

⟨⟩ Key points summary

- Not all breaches of statutory duty will give rise to liability in tort. Whether an action in tort can be founded will be ascertained by reference to Parliament's intention. This intention can be express or implied.

- Once the existence of a duty is established, the claimant will need to establish that the duty was breached and that the breach of duty was the case of his loss.

- The defences of contributory negligence and *volenti non fit injuria* are available.

---

210. *Bux v Slough Metals Ltd* [1973] 1 WLR 1358 (CA). In this case, the employee's damages were reduced by 40 per cent to reflect his partial responsibility for his injuries.
211. *Ginty v Belmont Building Supplies Ltd* [1959] 1 All ER 414 (QB).
212. *Caswell v Powell Duffryn Associated Collieries Ltd* [1940] AC 152 (HL) 178 (Lord Wright).
213. *Baddeley v Earl Granville* (1887) 19 QBD 423 (DC).
214. *ICI Ltd v Shatwell* [1965] AC 656 (HL).

Chapter conclusion

This chapter has discussed a number of torts that can be committed by, and against, businesses. They range from torts committed in relation to goods (for example, product liability and trespass to goods), to torts committed in relation to land (for example, nuisance and occupiers' liability). Some of the torts discussed are based on a party taking reasonable care (for example, occupiers' liability), whereas others are based on strict liability (for example, product liability under the Consumer Protection Act 1987). Some are designed to regulate the activities of businesses (for example, product liability), whereas others actually seek to product businesses from interference from others (for example, the economic torts). The point to note is that the variety of business-related torts is substantial and, whilst negligence is undoubtedly the principal tort, businesses must be aware of the full scope of tortious liability in which their actions can result.

In many cases, the party liable for the commission of a tort is not actually the party who committed it. In the next chapter, we discuss when one party can be liable for the tortious acts of another.

Self-test questions

1. Define the following:
   (a) strict liability;
   (b) own-brander;
   (c) inconsistent dealing;
   (d) passing off;
   (e) trespass to goods;
   (f) conversion;
   (g) conspiracy;
   (h) prescription.

2. In the following scenarios, can liability be imposed under the Consumer Protection Act 1987, Pt I? Explain the reasons behind your answer.
   (a) John purchases a new flat-screen television from his local branch of Asteroid Ltd, a countrywide chain of electrical retailers. A circuit board in John's television is defective causing sparks to be omitted from the rear of the television. John removes the rear casing of the television to try to fix the problem himself. John is electrocuted in the attempt and sustains severe burns to his hand. Can John sue Asteroid Ltd?
   (b) Perdita is employed as a test driver for ALV plc, a car manufacturer. She is test-driving a new prototype car with an electric engine on the company's test track. The brakes are defective and Perdita crashes, sustaining severe injuries.

3. Explain the distinction between the following.
   (a) Conspiracy to injure and unlawful means conspiracy.
   (b) A visitor and a non-visitor.
   (c) Public nuisance and private nuisance.
   (d) Libel and slander.
   (e) Absolute privilege and qualified privilege.

4. 'The existence of the tort of nuisance means that the rule in *Rylands v Fletcher* is now of no practical importance and should be abolished.' Do you agree with this statement? Provide reasons for your answer.

5. Discuss whether or not the following acts constitute a nuisance.
    (a) A neighbour keeps chickens that crow noisily at around 1 p.m.
    (b) A factory emits fumes. The fumes would not normally damage flowers and plants, but a nearby resident grows rare and delicate roses that are damaged by the fumes.
    (c) An errant golf ball struck from a golf course leaves the course and strikes a person walking along a pavement.

Further reading

Deakin, S, Johnston, A, and Markesinis, B, *Markesinis & Deakin's Tort Law* (6th edn, OUP, Oxford, 2008) chs 6 and 7
Provides an indepth discussion of occupiers' liability and breach of statutory duty

Lunney, M, and Oliphant, K, *Tort Law: Text and Materials* (3rd edn, OUP, Oxford, 2008) ch 12
An excellent account of the torts of nuisance and Rylands v Fletcher; *provides useful commentary on many key cases*

Murphy, J, *Street on Torts* (12th edn, OUP, Oxford, 2007) ch 16
A clear and well-structured discussion of product liability at common law and under the Consumer Protection Act 1987

Newdick, C, 'The Development Risks Defence of the Consumer Protection Act 1987' [1988] CLJ 455
Discusses the background to, and offers an analysis of, the development risks defence

Rogers, WVH, *Winfield & Jolowicz on Tort* (17th edn, Sweet & Maxwell, London, 2006) ch 18
An extremely detailed, but highly readable, account of the torts relating to interference with contract or trade

Stilitz, D, and Sales, P, 'Intentional Infliction of Harm by Unlawful Means' (1999) 115 LQR 411
Discusses the rationale and ambit of the tort of interfering with trade or business by unlawful means, and its relationship with other torts

Strong, SI, and Williams, L, *Tort Law: Text, Cases, and Materials* (OUP, Oxford, 2008) ch 14
Contains an extremely accessible and easy-to-understand account of the law relating to defamation

 Remember to visit the **Online Resource Centre** at <http://www. oxfordtextbooks.co.uk/roach> to access the following resources on Chapter 13, 'Business-related torts': more **practice questions** and answers; a **glossary** of key terms; **multiple-choice questions**; **revision summaries**; and **audio updates** when relevant.

14 Vicarious liability

- The fundamental principles
- Justifying vicarious liability
- The requirements for an employer to be vicariously liable
- The employer–employee relationship

- Vicarious liability outside the area of employment
- Defences and obtaining a contribution

INTRODUCTION

- A pedestrian is negligently knocked over by a lorry driver who was not insured by his employer to drive company vehicles.
- A cleaner in a hospital fails to indicate that a patch of flooring is wet, causing a patient to slip and injure himself.
- A trainee journalist writes a defamatory article in a local newspaper.
- A junior accountant fails to notice that the directors of a company he audits are engaged in fraud.

In all of these cases, the ability of the tortfeasor to compensate the victims fully for any loss is doubtful. It is here that the doctrine of vicarious liability is of crucial importance, because it allows the victim to claim compensation from the tortfeasor's employer for acts of his employees. Accordingly, it is crucial that businesses understand the extent of their liability for acts of their employees.

The fundamental principles

➡ battery: the direct application of unlawful violence to another

In August 2000, Mr Hawley visited a nightclub in Essex. Upon leaving the nightclub, he was, without apparent cause, assaulted by a doorman, who thereby committed the tort of battery. Mr Hawley commenced legal proceedings for battery, not against the doorman, but against the company (Luminar Leisure Ltd) that owned the nightclub and employed the doorman. His action succeeded and the owner of the nightclub was required to pay damages to Mr Hawley. The case of *Hawley v Luminar Leisure*

TABLE 14.1 *Hawley* and the fundamental principles of vicarious liability

Principle	Application in *Hawley*
An employer (or certain other types of person) may be liable in tort for the wrongful acts of another	In *Hawley*, the employer was vicariously liable for the wrongful acts of the doorman
Generally, liability in tort is only imposed on a party if there is some degree of fault or blameworthiness. Vicarious liability can be regarded as an exception to this principle and an employer (or certain other types of person) may be vicariously liable even though he is not, in any way, at fault	In *Hawley*, the fault lay with the doorman, yet his blameless employer was held liable
Vicarious liability is not a tort in itself and therefore does not create a cause of action; rather, it enables the claimant to sue on an existing cause of action (e.g. negligence) against a party other than the tortfeasor, provided that the other party has a particular relationship with the tortfeasor and the tort committed was referable to that relationship	In *Hawley*, the claimant had an existing cause of action in negligence against the doorman. The doctrine of vicarious liability simply allowed the claimant to pursue this cause of action against the doorman's employer
The word 'vicarious' is somewhat misleading, because it derives from the Latin *vicarius* meaning 'substitute'. This would seem to indicate that the tortfeasor's liability is substituted onto another party, thus extinguishing the liability of the tortfeasor. This is not the case, because *both* the tortfeasor and the other party are jointly liable to compensate the claimant and the claimant is free to proceed against whoever he wishes	In *Hawley*, the claimant had already received compensation from the doorman before he commenced proceedings against the doorman's employer. Vicarious liability provides an additional defendant, not an alternative one

Ltd[1] clearly demonstrates the fundamental principles behind the doctrine of vicarious liability that had been established in previous decisions, as outlined in Table 14.1.

It is important to be able to distinguish vicarious liability from personal liability. In *Hawley*, the doorman was personally liable because he committed the tort and caused Mr Hawley to suffer loss. The nightclub owner's liability was vicarious, because it did not actually commit the tort, but was held liable as if it had.

It is worth mentioning at the outset that the concept of vicarious liability does not only apply to common law torts, but can also apply to a breach of any statutory obligation (where the breach can result in damages) imposed upon the employee. As Lord Nicholls stated: 'Unless the statute expressly or impliedly indicates otherwise, the principle of vicarious liability is applicable where an employee commits a breach of a statutory obligation sounding in damages while acting in the course of his employment.'[2] This broadens the scope of the concept of vicarious liability significantly.

---

1. [2005] EWHC 5 (QB), [2005] Lloyd's Rep IR 275. The case was subject to an appeal on an unrelated procedural point.
2. *Majrowski v Guy's and St Thomas' NHS Trust* [2006] UKHL 34, [2007] 1 AC 224, [17].

Justifying vicarious liability

As noted, an employer may be held vicariously liable for the tortious act of an employee even though the employer lacks blameworthiness. It is therefore apparent that '[v]icarious liability is a species of strict liability'.[3] The question that arises is why, in the case of the employer–employee relationship, the law departs from the standard principle of fault-based liability and imposes strict liability upon the employer.

Numerous justifications have been advanced over time,[4] but the main justifications are as follows.

- The leading justification is the so-called 'deep pockets' argument. The employer is likely to have access to greater funds than the employee and is therefore a more reliable source of compensation. Further, it is more sensible that the employer bears the loss, because the employer will be better able to absorb any losses, either by passing the cost on to customers in the form of a price increase, or by providing insurance for the workforce.[5]

- Because employers derive an economic benefit from the acts of their employees, they should also bear any loss deriving from such acts. As Fleming stated: '[A] person who employs others to advance his own economic interest should in fairness be placed under a corresponding liability for losses incurred in the course of the enterprise ...'[6]

- Vicarious liability encourages employers to monitor their employees to ensure that they act in a proper manner. If this were a valid justification, however, the law would limit the employer's liability to those instances in which it could have prevented the employee's commission of the tort.[7] The law has never imposed such a limitation.

Irrespective of the above justifications, it can be argued that the ultimate aim of vicarious liability is to provide for the fairest system of apportioning loss, and to provide:

> a compromise between two conflicting policies: on the one end, the social interest in furnishing an innocent tort victim with recourse against a financially responsible defendant; on the other, a hesitation to foist any undue burden on business enterprise.[8]

In this sense, it has been argued that the doctrine of vicarious liability has now 'degenerated into a rule of expediency'.[9]

---

3. *Lister v Hesley Hall Ltd* [2001] UKHL 22, [2002] 1 AC 215, [65] (Lord Millett).

4. See T Baty, *Vicarious Liability. A Short History of the Liability of Employers, Principals, Partners, Associations and Trade Unions etc* (Clarendon Press, Oxford, 1916), which advanced nine justifications for the doctrine.

5. Under the Employers' Liability (Compulsory Insurance) Act 1969, s 1, every employer must insure his employees against 'liability for bodily injury or disease'.

6. JG Fleming, *The Law of Torts* (9th edn, LBC, Sydney, 1998) 410.

7. NJ McBride and R Bagshaw, *Tort Law* (3rd edn, Pearson, Harlow, 2008) 653.

8. JG Fleming, *The Law of Torts* (9th edn, LBC, Sydney, 1998) 409–10.

9. RVF Heuston and R Buckley, *Salmond & Heuston on the Law of Torts* (21st edn, Sweet & Maxwell, London, 1996) 431.

Key points summary

- Vicarious liability generally involves the imposition of liability on employers for the tortious acts of their employees.

- The imposition of vicarious liability does not depend upon the employer being at fault.

- Vicarious liability does not create a cause of action; rather, it allows an existing cause of action to be relied on against the tortfeasor's employer.

- Making the employer vicariously liable is justified on the basis that:
    - the employer is likely to have more money;
    - the employer can better absorb the loss;
    - because employers derive economic benefits from their employees, they ought also to bear the burden of their actions; and
    - it encourages employers to monitor their employees.

The requirements for an employer to be vicariously liable

The requirements for the imposition on an employer of vicarious liability are as follows.

1. There must be an employer–employee relationship.
2. The employee must have committed a tort.
3. The tort must have been committed in the course of the employee's employment.

Each of these requirements will now be discussed.

The employer–employee relationship

The imposition of vicarious liability is generally dependent upon there being an employer–employee relationship between the tortfeasor and his purported employer. It follows that if the employer can establish that the tortfeasor is, in fact, not an employee, vicarious liability cannot normally be imposed. It is therefore necessary to determine exactly who is an employee. In the majority of cases, determining whether the tortfeasor is an employee or not will be straightforward. But in a number of cases, establishing an employer–employee relationship can be problematic.

The requirement of employment

It is crucial that we draw a distinction between employees and independent contractors, because employers are not vicariously liable for torts committed by their independent contractors. The justification behind this is that an employer will have less control over the actions of an independent contractor and so should not be liable for his actions. It is worth noting that the distinction between employees and independent contractors is not only relevant in relation to tort, but is also crucial in a number of other areas, notably employment law.

The importance of the distinction in employment law purposes is discussed at p 780

Distinguishing employees from independent contractors

The starting point is to define what an 'employee' is. The Employment Rights Act 1996, s 230(1), defines an employee as an 'individual who has entered into or works under...a contract of employment'. We therefore need to define what a 'contract of employment' is and this is defined in s 230(2) as 'a contract of service or apprenticeship, whether express or implied, and (if it is express) whether oral or in writing'. An employee therefore is someone who operates under a contract *of* service, as opposed to an independent contractor who operates under a contract *for* services. But this distinction provides little aid, and so the responsibility of determining how to distinguish between employees vand independent contractors has been left to the courts and employment tribunals.

The courts have been unable to devise a single test that can differentiate between an employee and an independent contractor. Instead, a number of differing tests have been used. Here, we will briefly outline the evolution of the tests used by the courts. Readers who wish to examine the tests in more depth are referred to Chapter 23, where all three tests are discussed in detail.

These tests are discussed in considerably more detail at p 782

In the nineteenth century, the courts adopted the 'control' test. This basically involved the court asking whether the employer controlled where the employee worked, what he did, when he did it, and how he did it. If the answer was 'yes', the contract was one of employment.

As workers became more skilled, however, the control test became less useful and led to the development of the 'integration' test. This asks to what extent the worker was integrated into the employer's business. The more integrated a worker, the more likely he was to be an employee.

Whilst the integration test was useful for professional workers, the lack of a coherent definition of 'integration' led to the courts abandoning any one test and instead recognizing that all of the facts of the case need to be taken into account. This has come to be known as the 'multiple' test.

Who is an employer?

The majority of cases in this area have focused on attempting to identify whether or not the tortfeasor was an employee or not. In certain situations, however, there may be doubt as to the identity of the employer. This arises most commonly when an employer (known as the 'permanent employer') lends or hires an employee to another employer (known as the 'temporary employer'). If the employee commits a tort, which employer is vicariously liable?

Guidance came in the following case.

Mersey Docks and Harbour Board v Coggins & Griffith (Liverpool) Ltd [1947] AC 1 (HL)

FACTS: The Harbour Board (the permanent employer) employed a crane driver named Newall. It hired Newall and a crane to Coggins (the temporary employer) under a contract that provided that Newall would be an employee of Coggins, although he would continue to be paid by the Harbour Board. Coggins instructed Newall as to what goods needed unloading, but did not instruct him on how to unload them. While unloading the goods, Newall negligently injured the claimant. The question was whether the Harbour Board or Coggins was vicariously liable for Newall's negligence.

HELD: The House of Lords held that the Harbour Board was vicariously liable. The House made the following statements.

- The presumption was that the permanent employer would be the employer unless he could clearly establish otherwise. In other words, the burden of proof is placed upon the permanent employer.

- A term in the contract providing that the employee is to be an employee of the temporary employer will not avoid the imposition of vicarious liability on the permanent employer.[10]

- The most important factor in determining which of the two undertakings is the employer is who controlled the way in which the employee was to work. Coggins (the temporary employer) could only tell Newall what to load and unload; it could not tell him how to do it. Clearly, this is an application of the 'control' test, mentioned earlier.

The position established in *Mersey Docks* has, however, been disturbed somewhat by the following case, in which the Court of Appeal held that the permanent and temporary employers could both be vicariously liable.

Viasystems (Tyneside) Ltd v Thermal Transfer (Northern) Ltd [2005] EWCA Civ 1151

FACTS: The claimant had engaged the first defendant to install air conditioning in one of its factories. The first defendant subcontracted the fitting of air ducts to the second defendant. The ducting work itself would be carried out by a fitter and his mate (the tortfeasors), supplied to the second defendant (the temporary employer) by the third defendant (the permanent employer). Whilst carrying out the ducting work, the fitter and his mate negligently fractured the fire protection sprinkler system, causing the factory to flood. The issue was who was the fitter's employer for the purposes of establishing vicarious liability.

HELD: The Court of Appeal stated that, whilst there was a long-standing assumption that dual vicarious liability was not possible, it provided a coherent solution to cases involving

---

10. Although it may be construed by the courts as an indemnity clause entitling the permanent employer to seek an indemnity from the temporary employer if the permanent employer is held vicariously liable for the employee's tort: see *Thompson v T Lohan (Plant Hire) Ltd* [1987] 2 All ER 631 (CA).

borrowed employees. Accordingly, both the second and third defendants were held vicariously liable for the acts of the fitter and his mate.

COMMENT: Two comments can be made of this case. Firstly, the Court held the fitter and his mate to be employees even though there was no contract of employment. Secondly, whilst both judges involved agreed as to the result, their reasoning differed. For May LJ, 'the core question is who was entitled, and in theory obliged, to control the employee's relevant negligent act so as to prevent it',[11] and if the answer was that the both employers had control of the employee, then dual vicarious liability should be imposed. But Rix LJ stated:

> I am a little sceptical that the doctrine of dual vicarious liability is to be wholly equated with the question of control...[W]hat one is looking for is a situation where the employee in question, at any rate for relevant purposes, is so much a part of the work, business or organisation of both employers that it is just to make both employers answer for his negligence.[12]

⭐ See D Brodie,
'The Enterprise and
the Borrowed Worker'
(2006) 35 ILJ 87

The subsequent case of *Hawley v Luminar Leisure Ltd*,[13] discussed at the beginning of this chapter, affirmed the view that dual vicarious liability was permissible, but failed to clarify whether the 'control' test of May LJ or the 'integration' test of Rix LJ was to be preferred.

Personal liability

Having discussed the difference between employees and independent contractors, it is worth noting that whilst employers are not *vicariously* liable for the acts of independent contractors, they may be *personally* liable for the acts of their independent contractors in certain situations.

- An employer can be personally liable for the acts of his independent contractor if he fails to take adequate care in the selection or instruction of that contractor.[14]

- An employer can be personally liable for the acts of his independent contractor if the contractor is undertaking a 'non-delegable duty'. A non-delegable duty is not a duty that cannot be delegated by an employer; rather, it simply means that if the employer does delegate the duty to another, the employer cannot escape liability if the duty is improperly performed by that other person. For example, the common law duty placed upon an employer to take reasonable steps to provide and maintain a safe system of work has been classified as non-delegable.[15]

- An employer can be personally liable if he authorizes or ratifies the commission of a tort by his independent contractor.[16]

- An employer can be personally liable for the acts of an independent contractor if that contractor is engaged in particularly hazardous activities.[17]

---

11. *Viasystems (Tyneside) Ltd v Thermal Transfer (Northern) Ltd* [2005] EWCA Civ 1151, [49].
12. Ibid, [79].
13. [2005] EWHC 5 (QB), [2005] Lloyd's Rep IR 275.
14. *Pinn v Rew* (1916) 32 TLR 451 (DC).
15. *Wilsons & Clyde Coal Co Ltd v English* [1938] AC 57 (HL); *McDermid v Nash Dredging and Reclamation Co* [1987] AC 906 (HL).
16. *Ellis v Sheffield Gas Consumers Co* (1853) 2 E & B 767.
17. *Biffa Waste Services Ltd v Maschinenfabrik Ernst Hese GmbH* [2008] EWCA Civ 1257, [2009] PNLR 12.

Key points summary

- Various tests have been used to determine what an employer is, including the 'control' test and the 'integration' test, but the courts today acknowledge that all of the facts are relevant and so are unlikely to adopt any one test.

- Where an employer lends an employee to another employer, the presumption is that the employee is the employee of the permanent employer, unless the permanent employer can establish otherwise.

- Where the permanent and temporary employers exercise the right to control over an employee, the courts may impose vicarious liability on them both for any tortious acts of the employee.

- Employers cannot be vicariously liable for the acts of their independent contractors, but in certain circumstances, they may be personally liable.

The commission of a tort

As we have seen, the first requirement for the imposition of vicarious liability is that the alleged tortfeasor be an employee. The second requirement is that the employee must have committed a tort. Vicarious liability is usually imposed for the negligent acts of an employee, but it also covers other torts. Thus, in *Poland v John Parr & Sons*,[18] an employee of the defendant hit and seriously injured a schoolboy that he honestly believed was stealing from his employer. The Court of Appeal held that the employer was vicariously liable in respect of the employee's battery of the schoolboy.

The tort must be in the course of employment

The final requirement for the imposition of vicarious liability is that the employee committed the tort in the course of his employment. The existence of this requirement indicates that an employer–employee relationship is insufficient per se to establish vicarious liability: there must also be a sufficient connection between the tort and the employer's enterprise to justify the imposition of vicarious liability. It therefore follows that an employee who commits a tort outside the scope of his employment will be personally liable for the tort, but his employer will not be vicariously liable.

 Beard v London General Omnibus Co [1900] 2 QB 530 (CA)

FACTS: A bus conductor drove a bus when the normal bus driver became ill. The conductor drove into a cyclist and injured him. The cyclist commenced proceedings against the conductor's employer.

---

18. [1927] 1 KB 236 (CA).

HELD: The Court of Appeal held that the employer was not vicariously liable, because the conductor was not employed to drive the bus and was therefore not acting in the course of his employment.

COMMENT: If the bus driver were negligently to have *allowed* the conductor to drive, the employer would have been vicariously liable, because the driver would have been performing an authorized task in an unauthorized manner. Thus, in one case,[19] the Court imposed vicarious liability upon the employer of a lorry driver who had allowed an incompetent person to drive the lorry.

The Salmond test

Until the House of Lords decision in *Lister v Hesley Hall Ltd*,[20] the courts used exclusively what was known as the 'Salmond test' to determine whether or not a tort was committed in the course of employment. This test did not derive from a case, but rather from the first edition of Sir John Salmond's *Law of Torts*, in which he stated that a tort will be committed in the course of employment if it was either:

1. a wrongful act authorized by the employer; or
2. a wrongful and unauthorized mode of doing some act authorized by the employer.[21]

The test revolved around what the employee was (expressly or impliedly) authorized to do by his employer, and covered both authorized wrongful acts and authorized legitimate acts carried out in a wrongful or unauthorized manner.

Table 14.2 clarifies the two elements of the Salmond test.

Acts prohibited by the employer

Will an employee still be acting in the course of his employment if he disregards an express prohibition or instruction from his employer? This is a difficult question to answer and will involve the court attempting to determine whether the employee's disregard of instructions distances his act from his employment to such an extent that it would be unreasonable to impose liability upon the employer. What is certainly true is that an express prohibition will not automatically take the employee's act outside the course of his employment and absolve the employer from vicarious liability. If this were not the case, employers could avoid vicarious liability simply by instructing their employees to obey the law or never to act negligently.

In determining the effect of an express prohibition, the court has drawn a distinction between prohibitions that limit the manner in which the employee should perform his duties and prohibitions that limit the scope of his duties, with only the latter serving to absolve the employer from liability. The following case demonstrates this approach in practice.

---

19. *Ilkiw v Samuels* [1963] 2 All ER 879 (CA).
20. [2001] UKHL 22, [2002] 1 AC 215.
21. J Salmond, *Law of Torts* (Sweet & Maxwell, London, 1907) 83; RVF Heuston and R Buckley, *Salmond & Heuston on the Law of Torts* (21st edn, Sweet & Maxwell, London, 1996) 443.

TABLE 14.2 The Salmond test

Salmond test	Example
(i) An authorized wrongful act	With the aim of increasing sales, the senior executive editor of a newspaper specifically authorizes a journalist to print a story that is defamatory
(ii) An authorized legitimate act carried out in a wrongful or unauthorized manner	Whilst delivering petrol, the driver of a petrol tanker carelessly discards a lighted match at a petrol station, causing an explosion. He was carrying out an authorized act (delivering petrol), but was undertaking it in a wrongful manner by carelessly discarding the match (*Century Insurance Co v Northern Ireland Road Traffic Board* [1942] AC 509 (HL))

 Limpus v London General Omnibus Co Ltd (1862) 1 H & C 526 (CA)[22]

FACTS: An employer instructed his employees not to race other buses. Despite this, an employee raced another driver to a bus stop so that he could pick up all of the passengers who were waiting. During the race, one the drivers overturned the bus of the other.

HELD: The Court of Appeal held that the employer was vicariously liable. The prohibition merely limited the way in which he performed his job; it did not alter the scope of his employment—namely, to drive a bus.

COMMENT: This case should be contrasted with *Iqbal v London Transport Executive*,[23] in which a bus conductor who had been prohibited from driving buses, ignored the prohibition and drove a bus, injuring a fellow employee whilst doing so. Because the prohibition limited the scope of his employment, ignoring it took his activities outside the course of his employment and so the employer was not vicariously liable.

Employee's 'frolics'

In a number of cases, employees have committed torts whilst engaged in activities designed to benefit themselves. The question for the court is whether the employee was acting in the course of his employment or whether he was engaged in a 'frolic of his own'.[24] This will be a question of fact in each case.

Contrasting two similar cases demonstrates how the facts can have a bearing on the decision.

 Harvey v RG O'Dell Ltd [1958] 2 QB 78 (QB)

FACTS: The claimant's workplace had no canteen, so he and a fellow employee, named Galway, travelled five miles to obtain lunch. They travelled in a motorcycle and sidecar, with the claimant travelling in the sidecar. On the return journey, a crash occurred due to Galway's negligent driving, injuring the claimant and killing Galway. The claimant

---

22. See also *Rose v Plenty* [1976] 1 All ER 97 (CA).   23. [1976] 1 WLR 141 (CA).
24. *Joel v Morrison* (1834) 6 C & P 501, 503 (Parke B).

See JA Jolowicz, 'Master and Servant: Vicarious Liability—Master's Indemnity Against Servant' (1958) CLJ 157

commenced proceedings against his employer, arguing that it was vicariously liable for Galway's negligence. The employer argued that, at the time, Galway was not acting in the course of employment, but was engaged in a frolic of his own.

HELD: The High Court held that obtaining a meal was incidental to Galway's employment and so the claimant's employer was vicariously liable for Galway's negligence.

Hilton v Thomas Burton (Rhodes) Ltd [1961] 1 All ER 74

FACTS: Two employees decided to finish work early, in order that they might visit a cafe around seven miles away from their place of work. They drove to the cafe in a van belonging to their employer, which they were authorized to drive. On the return journey, the van crashed due to the negligence of the driver. The passenger was killed. The passenger's widow commenced proceedings against her husband's employer for the negligent driving of his fellow employee.

HELD: The claimant's husband and his fellow employee were held to be acting outside the course of their employment. The court was influenced by the fact that the employees had decided to finish work early and decided to visit the cafe before going home. This was enough to convince the court that the visit to the cafe constituted a frolic of the employees and so the employer was not vicariously liable.

The adoption of the 'close connection' test

At first glance, applying the Salmond test appears relatively straightforward. But as Atiyah noted, in practice, the Salmond test is 'an apparently simple test whose simplicity is largely deceptive'.[25]

The problems with the test are several, as follows.

- Although the first element of the test (wrongful acts authorized by the employer) is straightforward to apply, it is arguable that, in such cases, the liability of the employer is not vicarious, but personal. We noted above that an employer is personally liable if he authorizes an independent contractor to commit a tort—so surely the same principle applies to authorized torts committed by employees?

- The second element of the test (authorized legitimate acts carried out in an unauthorized or wrongful manner) proved extremely difficult to apply in practice.

- It is apparent that the Salmond test was designed to cover negligent acts of the employee; it was not designed to cover intentional torts and criminal acts, and, in such cases, the strained application of the test often led to highly unsatisfactory decisions.[26]

---

25. PS Atiyah, *Vicarious Liability in the Law of Torts* (Butterworths, London, 1967) 172.
26. See, e.g., *Morris v CW Martin & Sons Ltd* [1966] 1 QB 716 (CA).

It was therefore unsurprising when the House of Lords eventually decided to move away from the Salmond test in the following case.

 Lister v Hesley Hall Ltd [2001] UKHL 22

FACTS: The claimants were pupils at a boarding school owned and managed by the defendant. The defendant employed a warden named Grain, who, between 1979 and 1982, sexually abused the claimants who, during that period, were aged between 12 and 15. The defendant was unaware of the abuse. Grain was eventually sentenced to seven years' imprisonment for multiple offences, including sexual abuse. The claimants initiated a claim against the defendant for the personal injuries suffered whilst at its boarding school. Applying the Salmond test, the Court of Appeal found the employer not liable, because the acts of Grain were neither authorized wrongful acts, nor were they authorized legitimate acts carried out in an unauthorized manner. The claimants appealed.

HELD: The House of Lords allowed the appeal and found the defendant vicariously liable. It moved away from the Salmond test and instead stated:

> The question is whether the warden's torts were so closely connected with his employment that it would be fair and just to hold the employers vicariously liable. On the facts of the case the answer is yes. After all, the sexual abuse was inextricably interwoven with the carrying out by the warden of his duties …[27]

★ See P Giliker, 'Rough Justice in an Unjust World' (2002) 65 MLR 269

The close connection test in *Lister* basically states that if an employee commits a tort, the court should consider the task the employee was undertaken to perform, and whether there was so close a connection between that task and the tort that he committed that it would be fair and just to impose vicarious liability on the employer. The close connection test is undoubtedly broader and more claimant-friendly than the Salmond test, but it is arguable that, in the majority of cases, it will produce the same result as under the Salmond test.[28] For this reason, the Salmond test, although of decreased importance, has not been overruled by the introduction of the close connection test and it is still used by the courts to determine whether an act is in the course of employment. Where the Salmond test is not met, the court may then apply the close connection test. Where the tort is committed intentionally, the Salmond test is of limited aid and the close connection test becomes the dominant, if not the exclusive, test.

The close connection test has been applied in a number of recent cases. It can be argued, however, that the court's application of the 'close connection' test has been just as controversial and problematic as the application of the Salmond test. Two cases in particular are worthy of examination.

---

27. *Lister v Hesley Hall Ltd* [2001] UKHL 22, [2002] 1 AC 215, [28] (Lord Steyn).

28. Lord Steyn in *Lister* admitted that the close connection test was not entirely dissimilar from the Salmond test, in that the latter test provided the 'germ' for the former. But this admission could have been made simply to calm those who believed that reforming a principle as well established as the Salmond test is a task best left for Parliament.

Dubai Aluminium Co Ltd v Salaam [2002] UKHL 48[29]

FACTS: Amhurst was a senior partner in two successive firms of solicitors (collectively referred to by the House as 'the Amhurst firm'). He assisted two other individuals (Salaam and Tajir) in defrauding Dubai Aluminium out of almost US$50 million by drafting certain agreements. But Amhurst himself did not benefit personally from the fraud. It was accepted that Amhurst's co-partners were entirely innocent. The Amhurst firm settled with Dubai Aluminium and paid it US$10 million. The Amhurst firm then sought a contribution from Salaam and Tajir. But it could only obtain this contribution if it could show that it was responsible for the wrongs committed by Amhurst. Therefore, the Amhurst firm argued that it was vicariously liable.

HELD: The House of Lords held the firm to be vicariously liable for Amhurst's actions. Lord Nicholls stated:

> Drafting these particular agreements is to be regarded as an act done within the ordinary course of the firm's business even though they were drafted for a dishonest purpose. Those acts were so closely connected with the acts Mr Amhurst was authorised to do that for the purpose of the liability of the... firm they may fairly and properly be regarded as done by him while acting in the ordinary course of the firm's business.[30]

Accordingly, Salaam was ordered to contribute US$7.5 million and Tajir US$2.5 million.

COMMENT: *Dubai Aluminium* is a unique case in that the Amhurst firm was actually arguing that it was vicariously liable for Amhurst's actions. The unique nature of the case is a major contributory factor to the outcome, as were the policy considerations of the case. Had the Amhurst firm not been deemed vicariously liable, it could not have sought a contribution from Salaam and Tajir, who would have been permitted to keep any monies resulting from their fraudulent activities. Unfortunately, the House of Lords did not provide any meaningful further guidance on the application of the close connection test.

The ability to obtain a contribution is discussed at p 516

★ See C Mitchell, 'Partners in Wrongdoing?' (2003) 119 LQR 364

Mattis v Pollock (t/a Flamingos Nightclub) [2003] EWCA Civ 887

FACTS: Cranston was employed as a doorman at a nightclub belonging to Pollock (the defendant). Cranston was involved in a fight at the nightclub, which ended with him fleeing, following the involvement of Mattis (the claimant). Cranston fled to his home, armed himself with a knife, and returned to the vicinity of the nightclub. Mattis had left the club, but was eventually found by Cranston, who stabbed him, severing his spinal cord and rendering him a paraplegic. Cranston was subsequently convicted of causing grievous bodily harm and sentenced to eight years' imprisonment. Mattis initiated a civil claim against Pollock, alleging that he was vicariously liable for Cranston's actions.

---

29. This was a case concerning the vicarious liability of a partnership for the actions of one of its partners (i.e. not an employer–employee relationship). Non-employment relationships that can give rise to vicarious liability are discussed at p 515.

30. *Dubai Aluminium Co Ltd v Salaam* [2002] UKHL 48, [2003] 2 AC 366, [36].

HELD: Pollock was vicariously liable for Cranston's attack. The Court of Appeal placed great emphasis on the fact that Pollock had encouraged Cranston to act in a threatening and intimidatory manner if necessary. This was enough to establish that the assault was sufficiently connected to Cranston's employment.

COMMENT: The decision in *Mattis* can be criticized on a number of grounds. On the facts alone, it appears odd that Pollock should be liable for an employee's act of personal vengeance that took place around 100 metres away from the nightclub. The Court placed great weight on the fact that Pollock was aware that, on two previous occasions, Cranston had behaved violently towards customers and that, instead of admonishing him, Pollock had actually encouraged him to intimidate customers. It also transpired that Pollock had acted unlawfully in employing a doorman that he knew was not licensed by the relevant authority.[31] In emphasizing these facts, the Court of Appeal appears to be indicating that Pollock was somehow at fault for the incident that led to Mattis' injuries. But, as noted, vicarious liability is not concerned with fault, because it imposes strict liability. Therefore, it can be argued that evidence of fault per se is not a sufficient justification for the imposition of vicarious liability.

> ★ See R Weekes, 'Vicarious Liability for Violent Employees' (2004) 63 CLJ 53

The principal problem of the 'close connection' test is its breadth and ambiguity. In cases applying the test, the courts themselves have acknowledged this: in the *Dubai Aluminium* case discussed above, Lord Nicholls stated that the test 'affords no guidance on the type or degree of connection which will normally be regarded as sufficiently close'[32] to impose vicarious liability. Indeed, it may well be the case that the test was made purposely broad in order to service the open-ended nature of vicarious liability scenarios. Again quoting Lord Nicholls, '[t]his lack of precision is inevitable, given the infinite range of circumstances where the issue arises'.[33] The courts' discretion is increased further in that they have to consider whether or not the closeness of the connection makes it 'fair and just' to impose vicarious liability. Whilst this may provide the courts with the flexibility to take into account the idiosyncrasies of a case, by adopting such a broad test, it has been argued that the courts have 'disregarded the primary responsibility that they owe the public at large, which is to ensure that the law is stated in clear and certain terms, so that we can all know where we stand when we get involved in disputes with other people'.[34]

In a recent Court of Appeal decision, the close connection test was reviewed and the Court attempted to provide some much-needed clarification.

Gravil v Carroll [2008] EWCA Civ 689

FACTS: Both the claimant and first defendant were semi-professional rugby players. The first defendant's contract of employment with his rugby club (the second defendant) provided that he would not assault opposing players and that the second defendant might

---

31. At the time, the London Local Authorities Act 1995, s 31, required all 'door supervisors' to be registered with the local authority.
32. *Dubai Aluminium Co Ltd v Salaam* [2002] UKHL 48, [2003] 2 AC 366, [25].
33. Ibid, [26].
34. NJ McBride and R Bagshaw, *Tort Law* (3rd edn, Pearson, Harlow, 2008) 667–8.

be liable for acts of the first defendant committed in the course of employment. Following a scrum, an altercation developed in which the first defendant punched the claimant, causing the claimant to sustain an orbital fracture near his right eye. The trial judge found the first defendant liable, but refused to impose vicarious liability on the second defendant. The claimant appealed.

HELD: The Court of Appeal allowed the appeal. When the battery occurred, it was during the type of altercation that frequently occurs during rugby matches. The punch was regarded by the Court as an ordinary incident of a rugby match and was expressly prohibited by the defendant's contract of employment. It was therefore so closely connected with his employment as to be in the course of employment, thereby rendering the second defendant vicariously liable.

COMMENT: Sir Anthony Clarke MR reviewed the relevant authorities and laid down a number of propositions, as follows.

- The essential question is 'whether the tort is so closely connected with the employment, that is with what was authorised or expected of the employee, that it would be fair and just to hold the employer vicariously responsible'.[35]

- In answering this question, the court must take into account all of the circumstances of the case.

  > It will ordinarily be fair and just to hold the employer liable where the wrongful conduct may fairly and properly be regarded as done while acting in the ordinary course of the employee's employment...This is because an employer ought to be liable for a tort which can fairly be regarded as a reasonably incidental risk to the type of business being carried on.[36]
  >
  > It is not appropriate to ask...whether in all the circumstances of the case it would be fair and just to hold the club liable. The critical factor is the nature of the employment and the closeness (or otherwise) of the connection between the employment and the tort. The question what is fair and reasonable must be answered in the context of the closeness or otherwise of that connection.[37]

Key points summary

- In order for vicarious liability to arise, the employee's tortious act must have been committed in the course of his employment.

- An employer who establishes prohibitions limiting the *scope* of the employee's duties will not be vicariously liable if the employee acts beyond that scope. If the prohibition merely limits the *manner* of the employee's duties, the employer will remain vicariously liable.

- Under the Salmond test, an employee will be acting in the course of employment if he engages in either:
  - a wrongful act authorized by the employer; or
  - a wrongful and unauthorized mode of doing some act authorized by the employer.

- The Salmond test is not appropriate in cases involving intentional torts. In such cases, an employee will be acting in the course of employment if his tort was so closely

---

35. *Gravil v Carroll* [2008] EWCA Civ 689, [2008] ICR 1222, [21].　　36. Ibid.
37. Ibid, [22].

connected to his employment that it would be fair and just to hold the employer vicariously liable.

- The close connection test asks whether there was so close a connection between that task and the tort committed by the employee that it would be fair and just to impose vicarious liability on the employer.

- The creation of the close connection test has resulted in a move away from the Salmond test, but because the tests produce the same result in the majority of cases, the Salmond test is likely to remain valid for some time.

Vicarious liability outside the area of employment

In the previous section, we stated that in order for various liability to be imposed, there must be an employer–employee relationship. To state that the tortfeasor *must* be an employee is not strictly accurate. It is certainly true that the vast majority of vicarious liability cases involve torts committed by employees, but there are several examples that fall outside of the traditional employer–employee relationship:

- partners in a partnership are vicariously liable for the acts of each other provided that they are 'acting in the ordinary course of the business of the firm';[38]

- a principal will be vicariously liable for torts committed by his agent provided that the agent is acting within the scope of his authority[39]—but personal liability is likely to be imposed upon the agent if he assumes a personal responsibility towards the third party[40] or if he knowingly makes a false statement;[41]

  The law of agency is discussed in Chapter 27

- the owner of a vehicle may be vicariously liable for torts committed in that vehicle if:
  - he authorizes another to drive it; or
  - he allows another to drive it in his presence.[42]

Defences and obtaining a contribution

If the above requirements have been satisfied, vicarious liability can be imposed on an employer. At this point, the employer has two options to avoid or limit liability— namely, to rely of a defence, or to obtain a contribution from the tortfeasor.

---

38. Partnership Act 1890, s 10. This provision is discussed at p 576.

39. *Lloyd v Grace, Smith & Co* [1912] AC 716 (HL).

40. *Williams v Natural Life Health Foods Ltd* [1998] 2 All ER 577 (HL).

41. *Standard Chartered Bank v Pakistan National Shipping Corporation (Nos 2 and 4)* [2002] UKHL 43, [2003] 1 AC 959.

42. *Ormrod v Crossville Motor Services Ltd* [1953] 1 WLR 1120 (CA).

Defences

➡ *volenti non fit injuria*: 'to a willing person, no harm is done'

Employers found liable for torts committed by their employees may rely on the defences of *volenti non fit injuria* and contributory negligence. These defences are examined in more depth in Chapter 15.

Obtaining a contribution

➡ contributory negligence: the reduction of damages due to the claimant's own negligence

Because vicarious liability imposes joint and several liability upon the employer and employee, the claimant may elect to sue either party for the full amount. Given that the employer will be insured against such loss and will have 'deeper pockets' than the employee, it is almost always the employer that is sued and which ends up paying damages. Because the employee is a joint tortfeasor, however, statute permits the employer to obtain a contribution from the employee[43] that is 'just and equitable having regard to the extent of that person's responsibility for the damage in question'.[44]

Lister v Romford Ice & Cold Storage Ltd [1957] AC 55 (HL)

FACTS: The claimant employed Lister (Lister Jr) as a lorry driver. On one journey, Lister was accompanied by his father (Lister Sr), who was also a fellow employee. Lister Sr got out of the lorry whilst his son parked it. While parking the lorry, Lister Jr negligently drove into his father, injuring him. Lister Sr commenced proceedings against his son's employer, alleging that it was vicariously liable for his son's negligence. His claim succeeded and his son's employer's insurance company paid Lister Sr £1,600. Exercising its right to

➡ subrogation: the ability to take on the legal rights of others

subrogation, the insurance company sued Lister Jr for a contribution.

HELD: The insurance company's claim succeeded. The House of Lords held that the insurance company could recover the full £1,600 from Lister Jr.

★ See JA Jolowicz, 'The Right to Indemnity Between Master and Servant' (1956) CLJ 101

COMMENT: The *ratio* in *Lister* strongly favours insurance companies. It allows them to continue to receive insurance premiums from employers and to obtain a full contribution from their client's joint tortfeasors. In other words, it allows them to compensate themselves fully for the risk that their clients are paying them to bear.

The controversy surrounding the pro-insurance company stance evident in *Lister* was such that, following a committee of inquiry, all members of the British Insurance Association entered into a gentleman's agreement, which stated:

> Employers' Liability Insurers agree that they will not institute a claim against the employee of an insured employer in respect of the death of or injury to a fellow-employee unless the weight of evidence clearly indicates (i) collusion or (ii) wilful misconduct on the part of the employee against whom a claim is made.[45]

---

43. Civil Liability (Contribution) Act 1978, s 1.   44. Ibid, s 2.
45. Reproduced in *Morris v Ford Motor Co* [1973] QB 792 (CA) 799.

The scope of *Lister* has been qualified further by the case of *Morris v Ford Motor Co*,[46] in which the Court of Appeal prevented a subrogated claim from proceeding on the ground that it was not 'just and equitable',[47] even though such a requirement had never been imposed before.

It has been argued that, in the context of subrogation, such a vague and subjective standard is 'unworkable'.[48] Now that the right to subrogate is contained in statute, the courts' ability to impose such limitations is curtailed. Because the quantum of the contribution is limited to what is 'just and equitable', however, the court can limit the contribution to nil if it wishes to deny the insurer's right to subrogation.

 Key points summary

- An employer deemed vicariously liable still has access to certain tortious defences (for example, *volenti non fit injuria* and contributory negligence).

- As vicarious liability is joint and several, the claimant can sue either the employer or the employee.

- An employer deemed vicariously liable can seek a contribution from the employee who committed the tort.

Chapter conclusion

Vicarious liability is not a tort in its own right, but is a means whereby one party can be liable for the tortious acts of another. Vicarious liability can arise through a number of relationships, but by far the most common is that of employer and employee. Vicarious liability therefore greatly increases the legal exposure faced by the business community. Further, liability can be imposed even where the employer is in no way to blame for the loss sustained. The legal exposure created by the concept of vicarious liability is exacerbated by the fact that, although the claimant may sue either the employer or employee, it will almost always be the employer that is sued, because it will have access to greater funds or more comprehensive insurance. Given the level of exposure that vicarious liability can place upon employers, it is vital that businesses with employees have measures in place to minimize the opportunities that its employees have to commit negligent acts (for example, adequate supervision and the prohibition of certain acts). Where an employer is sued for the tortious acts of an employee, the employer may be able to obtain a contribution from the employee, but given the employee's comparative lack of funds, any such contribution might not offset the damages that the employer was required to pay to the claimant. Further, unless the employer dismisses the employee in question, obtaining a contribution would be likely to sour the employer–employee relationship—although it would certainly send a signal to other employees not to engage in tortious acts.

46. [1973] QB 792 (CA).
47. Ibid, 801 (Lord Denning MR).
48. R Hasson, 'Subrogation in Insurance Law: A Critical Evaluation' (1985) 5 OJLS 416, 435.

Self-test questions

1. Why may the word 'vicarious' provide a misleading understanding of the nature of vicarious liability?

2. What are the requirements for the imposition of vicarious liability?

3. Can vicarious liability be imposed in the following cases?
   (a) Charlotte is employed as a courier for Regal Mail plc. On a Sunday, she uses a company van to give her friend a lift to the airport. On the return trip home, she decides to make a number of deliveries to locations between the airport and her house. After making one such delivery, she negligently crashes into a car being driven by Pat.
   (b) Charles is employed as a doorman by Lion Lion plc, a company that owns a chain of nightclubs throughout the UK. One night, whilst working at one of Lion Lion's clubs, he is alerted to a drunken customer who has been kicking the toilet doors and has caused substantial property damage. Charles ejects the customer, but in doing so, he breaks the customer's arm. Would your answer differ if Charles had been expressly prohibited from manhandling troublesome customers?

4. What rights does an employer have against an employee who has committed a tort that results in the employer having to pay compensation?

Further reading

Deakin, S, 'Enterprise Risk: Economic and Legal Conceptions of the Firm' (2003) 32 ILJ 97
Discusses the 'enterprise risk' analysis of vicarious liability used in Canadian cases and argues it is preferable to the 'close connection' test established in Lister

Kidner, R, 'Vicarious Liability: For Whom Should the Employer Be Liable?' (1995) 15 LS 47
An excellent article that discusses how the emergence of new forms of employment has affected the definition of 'employee'

McIvor, C, 'The Use and Abuse of the Doctrine of Vicarious Liability' (2006) 35 CLWR 268
Examines recent vicarious liability cases and provides clear criticism; argues that these decisions have been based on a mistaken understanding of the doctrine's theoretical foundations

McKendrick, E, 'Vicarious Liability and Independent Contractors: A Re-examination' (1990) 53 MLR 770
Examines the legal relationship between employers and independent contractors; argues that the test for the existence of employment should be context-specific, and that one test should not cover tort and employment law

Murphy, J, *Street on Torts* (12th edn, OUP, Oxford, 2007) ch 24
Provides a clear, well-structured, and up-to-date discussion of vicarious liability

Weekes, R, 'Vicarious Liability for Violent Employees' (2004) 63 CLJ 53
*Analyses various rationales for imposing vicarious liability and uses them to criticize the
court's decision in* Mattis v Pollock

Case

Lister v Hesley Hall Ltd [2001] UKHL 22, [2002] 1 AC 215
*The leading case on how to determine whether an employee is 'acting in the course of his
employment'*

 Remember to visit the **Online Resource Centre** at **<http://www.
oxfordtextbooks.co.uk/roach>** to access the following resources
on Chapter 14, 'Vicarious liability': more **practice questions** and
answers; a **glossary** of key terms; **multiple-choice questions**; **revision
summaries**; and **audio updates** when relevant.

15 Tortious defences and remedies

- Defences
- Remedies

INTRODUCTION

Once the claimant has established that the prima facie requirements of a tort are present, this does not mean that he is guaranteed a remedy. It may be the case that the defendant can fully excuse or lessen the impact of his tort by successfully raising a defence. It is vital that parties involved in commercial dealings understand not only what types of activity are tortious, but also what defences can render such acts lawful. It may be the case that a business may need to engage in an act that, in the absence of a defence, would constitute a tort. In such a case, knowing the nature and extent of a defence is extremely important if liability and the payment of compensation are to be avoided. A business that suffers loss due to another's tort will also need to be aware, before it commences legal proceedings, of whether or not the tortfeasor has a potential defence.

If the defendant is unable successfully to raise a defence, the claimant will be entitled to a remedy. From the perspective of a party that has suffered harm, the overriding concern is what remedy can be obtained and, ultimately, the principal purpose of tort law is to compensate those who have suffered harm due to the tortious acts of another. The scope and purpose of tortious remedies is therefore of immense importance. But damages will not always be sufficient and, in such cases, the claimant may seek an injunction, or may even be able to exercise a remedy himself without the courts' involvement.

In this final chapter on the law of torts, we discuss the defences available to a defendant and the remedies sought by a claimant.

Defences

Even if the claimant can establish that the defendant's actions fulfil the requirements of the tort alleged, it may still be the case that the claim will fail (or damages will be reduced) because the defendant can successfully raise a defence. Certain defences are classified as general defences and can be pleaded in relation to any tort. Examples of general defences include *volenti non fit injuria* (voluntary assumption of risk) and *ex turpi causa non oritur actio* (illegality). But the majority of defences either apply only to certain torts (for example, the defence of contributory negligence applies to most torts, but does not apply to actions in deceit or some other actions),[1] or they will be specific to a certain tort (for example, self-defence can only be pleaded in cases involving trespass to the person).

Consent and voluntary assumption of risk

An individual may have been caused harm by the breach of duty of another, but may be denied a legal remedy on the ground that he in some way consented to the act that caused him harm. In such a case, the tortfeasor can raise the defence of *volenti non fit injuria*. Unlike contributory negligence, *volenti* operates as complete defence, fully exonerating the tortfeasor for the harm that he has caused.

> ➡ *volenti non fit injuria*: 'to a willing person, no harm is done'

Volenti can arise in two situations, as follows.

1. A party may decide voluntarily to assume the risk of being injured without having any subsequent legal redress (for example, by accepting a lift in a plane with a drunk pilot).[2] This is more likely to arise in torts involving negligence and strict liability.

2. A party may consent to the act that causes his injury. This is more likely to arise in the case of intentional torts such as **trespass to the person**. An obvious example of this would be consenting to a medical procedure (performing a medical procedure on a person who has not consented amounts to assault). Consent can act as a defence to such trespasses within the limits of public policy (for example, a patient cannot lawfully consent to a medical act that is designed to kill him in order to relieve suffering, known as 'euthanasia').[3] In such cases, the claimant may consent to the act that causes injury, but does not consent to having no legal redress if the person to whom consent is given performs some other act of wrongdoing (for example, the medical procedure is performed negligently).

> ➡ trespass to the person: a group of torts relating to the intentional and direct application of force to a person, including assault, battery, and false imprisonment

Because torts involving negligence and strict liability occur much more frequently than intentional torts, it is in relation to the voluntary assumption of risk (that is, the first type of *volenti*) that much of the case law has arisen. Therefore, we will discuss *volenti* in its capacity as a defence to negligence (that is, a voluntary assumption of risk).

In *Nettleship v Weston*,[4] Lord Denning MR stated:

> Now that contributory negligence is not a complete defence…the defence of *volenti*…has been closely considered and, in consequence, it has been severely limited. Knowledge of the risk of injury is not good enough. Nor is a willingness to take the risk of injury. Nothing will suffice short of an agreement to waive any claim for negligence. The [claimant] must agree, expressly or impliedly, to waive any claim for any injury that may befall him due to the lack of reasonable care by the defendant.[5]

---

1. *Standard Chartered Bank v Pakistan National Shipping Corporation* [2002] UKHL 43, [2003] 1 AC 599.
2. *Morris v Murray* [1991] 2 QB 6 (CA).
3. *Airedale NHS Trust v Bland* [1993] AC 789 (HL).
4. *Nettleship v Weston* [1971] 2 QB 691 (CA).   5. Ibid, 701.

From this passage, Lord Denning established that *volenti* requires three conditions to be fulfilled:

- the claimant must have known of the risk;
- the claimant must have voluntarily assumed the risk of having no legal redress; and
- the claimant must have agreed to waive the right to claim in negligence if the risk results in injury.

We will now examine each requirement in turn.

Knowledge of the risk

The defendant must show that the claimant actually knew of the risk, because a claimant cannot voluntarily consent to a risk of which he knew nothing.[6] This requirement is subjective, which means that the claimant must actually know of the risk; claiming that he ought to know of the risk, but did not, will cause *volenti* to fail.[7] But simply because a claimant knows of the risk, it does not follow that he automatically consents to it.

 Smith v Charles Baker & Sons [1891] AC 325 (HL)

FACTS: The claimant was employed by the defendant railway contractors to drill holes in a rock cutting. He worked near a crane, which, from time to time, would pass over the claimant's position carrying crates of heavy stones. The claimant was aware of this and had worked under these conditions for several months, although he had complained about the danger of falling stones. A stone fell from the crane, seriously injuring the claimant. He sued and his employer raised *volenti* as a defence.

HELD: The defence of *volenti* was rejected by the House of Lords. Although he claimant knew of the danger, mere knowledge was insufficient. The defendant would need to show that the claimant had voluntarily consented to the risk. On the evidence, this was not established.

The rule that mere knowledge of the risk does not automatically prove the existence of consent also has a policy justification. If knowledge were to result in consent, those who willingly engaged in dangerous activities designed to benefit others (the obvious example being rescuers) would never be able to recover damages for losses suffered and would be deterred from engaging in such socially beneficial conduct. Thankfully, knowledge of the risk will not bar such persons from claiming damages, due to the requirement of voluntary assumption of risk.

Voluntary assumption of risk

This requirement produces a measure of confusion. It is widely believed that all that the defendant has to establish is that the claimant voluntarily assumed the risk

---

6. *Harrison v Vincent* [1982] RTR 8 (CA).   7. *Smith v Austin Lifts Ltd* [1959] 1 WLR 100 (HL).

of injury, but this is not the case. *Volenti* requires more than this. What is required is that the claimant also voluntarily assumed the risk of having no legal redress.

The distinction can be seen in the following case.

Nettleship v Weston [1971] 2 QB 691 (CA)

FACTS: The claimant, an experienced driver (but not a driving instructor), agreed to provide driving lessons to the defendant (a friend's wife). Before agreeing to provide the lessons, the claimant checked that the defendant was suitably insured. On her third lesson, the defendant panicked and drove into a lamp post, resulting in the claimant breaking his kneecap. Shortly after, the defendant was convicted of driving without due care and attention, but the claimant also initiated a claim for damages, alleging negligence. The defendant pleaded *volenti*.

HELD: The defence of *volenti* failed and the Court of Appeal ordered that the claimant be compensated. In teaching a learner driver, the claimant had accepted that there was a risk of injury. But he had not accepted the risk of having no legal redress, which was evidenced by him ensuring that, in the event of him being injured, he would be adequately compensated by the defendant's insurance company.

COMMENT: Today, the defence of *volenti* is statute-barred in cases involving drivers of road vehicles and their passengers.[8]

★ See WVH Rogers, 'Trouble with Learners' (1972) 30 CLJ 24

The defendant will need to demonstrate that the claimant voluntarily consented. If the claimant's consent is forced in any way, the defence of *volenti* will fail. Accordingly, consent procured by fraud or duress will not establish *volenti*. With one exception,[9] the defence of *volenti* has failed in all cases involving injured rescuers, because it cannot be said that rescuers freely volunteer to run the risk of having no legal redress.

The defence of *volenti* will be extremely difficult to establish in the context of an employment relationship. In the early nineteenth century, this was not the case and employees were assumed to consent voluntarily to any risk involved in the course of their employment.[10] As time progressed, the courts began to accept that, given the inequality of power between employer and employee, in many cases, an employee will continue to work in dangerous conditions not because he has accepted the risk, but because he does not wish to lose his job. This was doubtless why the claimant in *Smith v Charles Baker & Sons* (discussed above) continued to work in such dangerous circumstances. It is now accepted that 'it must be shown that a servant who is asked or required to use dangerous plant is a volunteer in the fullest sense; that, knowing of the danger, he expressly or impliedly said he would do the job at his own risk, and not that of his master'.[11] Because this requirement is extremely difficult to meet, the

---

8. Road Traffic Act 1988, s 149.

9. *Cutler v United Dairies (London) Ltd* [1933] 2 KB 297 (CA). *Volenti* was permitted in this case, because the defendant's negligence posed no real danger and it was not reasonably necessary for the claimant to attempt a rescue.

10. See, e.g., *Woodley v Metropolitan District Railway Co* (1877) 2 Ex D 384 (CA).

11. *Bowater v Mayor, Aldermen and Burgesses of the Borough of Rowley Regis* [1944] KB 476 (CA) 481 (Goddard LJ).

defence of *volenti* plays almost no part in cases involving employer and employee. But where an employee chooses an especially dangerous method of performing an act that requires no such danger, or where an employee is injured through the tortious act of a fellow employee, the defence of *volenti* may succeed.

 ICI Ltd v Shatwell [1965] AC 656 (HL)

FACTS: The claimant was one of a team of three shot-firers employed by the defendant in one of its quarries. They were required to test detonators and were instructed to carry out such tests from a properly constructed shelter (indeed, statutory regulations passed at the time required as much). On one occasion, the wire was not long enough to reach the shelter and one of the shot-firers went to obtain a longer wire. The claimant and the remaining shot-firer decided not to wait for their colleague to return, and tested the detonators whilst in the open. Both men were injured, with the claimant sustaining severe injuries. The claimant sued the defendant and the defendant pleaded *volenti*.

HELD: The defence of *volenti* succeeded and the claimant's action failed. The House of Lords held that the claimant had voluntarily undertaken to act in a needlessly dangerous, not to mention unlawful, manner and had therefore voluntarily assumed the risk of having no legal redress. The defendant had not pressured the claimant to take such a risk and had, in fact, expressly prohibited the claimant from acting in such a way.

★ See P Brodetsky, 'Employers' Joint Breach of Statutory Duty' (1964) 27 MLR 705

Agreement

The final requirement stated by Lord Denning MR is that the claimant has expressly or impliedly agreed to waive any claim for the injury that may befall him. This requirement has been the subject of much criticism and is undoubtedly a severe restriction on the ability to establish *volenti*. Where an express and effective agreement exists (for example, via an effective exclusion clause), *volenti* can be successfully pleaded. An agreement to waive liability might also be implied by the courts, although they are extremely reluctant to do this.

The following case provides an instance in which an agreement was implied.

Morris v Murray [1990] 2 QB 6 (CA)

FACTS: The claimant and a friend had been drinking in a number of bars. The friend, who held a pilot's licence, suggested that they go for a fly in his private plane. Both parties were drunk, but the friend was exceptionally drunk (the subsequent autopsy revealed that he had drunk the equivalent of seventeen whiskies). The claimant knew that his friend was drunk, but agreed to the flight anyway. The plane crashed, killing the friend and severely injuring the claimant. The claimant alleged negligence against the deceased's estate. The defendant pleaded *volenti*.

HELD: The defence of *volenti* succeeded. The Court of Appeal held that knowingly accepting a plane ride from a drunken pilot was so dangerous that it created an implied waiver of any liability that resulted.

COMMENT: This case can be contrasted with prior cases[12] in which the claimant agreed to be a passenger in a car being driven by a drunk driver. In *Morris*, the defence of *volenti* succeeded on the apparent ground that drunken flying is more dangerous than drunken driving. In *Morris*, Fox LJ stated: 'Flying in intrinsically dangerous and flying with a drunken pilot is great folly. The situation is very different from what has arisen in the motoring cases.'[13]

See K Williams, 'Defences for Drunken Drivers: Public Policy on the Roads and in the Air' (1991) 54 MLR 745

It has been argued that the requirement for agreement 'is very difficult to reconcile with the case law without resort to fiction, because the parties typically give no thought to the matter'.[14] In *Morris*, the implication of an agreement was clearly fictitious, because both parties had not given the matter a moment's thought. In distinguishing between cases involving drunken flying and drunken driving, the Court's focus was clearly on the recklessness of the claimant. It has been argued that this is a preferable determinant of success that the requirement for an agreement to waive liability.[15]

Consent and the standard of care

We have seen that establishing *volenti* is not easy and that many defendants will be unable to meet the three requirements discussed above. But, provided that the claimant had knowledge of the risk, this may serve to lower the standard of care expected of the defendant to such an extent that breach of duty cannot be established. If this occurs, the defendant will not need to rely on any defence, because no tort will be committed, as the following case demonstrates.

The law relating to breach of duty and the standard of care is discussed in Chapter 12

 Wooldridge v Sumner **[1963] 2 QB 43 (CA)**

FACTS: The defendant was a horseman competing at a horse show. The defendant lost control of the horse after taking a corner too quickly. The claimant was struck by the horse and was seriously injured. At first instance, the defendant's actions were held to be negligent and the claimant recovered damages. The defendant appealed pleading, inter alia, *volenti*.

HELD: The Court of Appeal held that the defence of *volenti* did not apply in this case, because the defence presupposes the existence of a tort. It held that the actions of the defendant were not negligent and that, accordingly, *volenti* was inapplicable. Diplock LJ (as he then was) indicated that where the claimant has knowledge of a risk, this will affect the standard of care owed by the defendant:

> A person attending a game or competition takes the risk of any damage caused to him by any act of a participant done in the course of and for the purposes of the game or competition notwithstanding that such act may involve an error of judgment or a lapse of skill, unless the participant's conduct is such as to evince a reckless disregard of the spectator's safety.[16]

Accordingly, the defendant's appeal was allowed.

---

12. See, e.g., *Dann v Hamilton* [1939] 1 KB 509 (KB).

13. *Morris v Murray* [1990] 2 QB 6 (CA) 17.

14. WVH Rogers, *Winfield & Jolowicz on Tort* (17th edn, Sweet & Maxwell, London, 2006) 1068.

15. A Mullis and K Oliphant, *Torts* (3rd edn, Palgrave, Basingstoke, 2003) 167.

16. *Wooldridge v Sumner* [1963] 2 QB 43 (CA) 68.

Key points summary

- *Volenti non fit injuria* means 'to a willing person, no harm is done', and applies where the claimant consents to the act that causes his injury, or runs the risk of injury being caused and having no legal redress for such injury.

- The defendant will need to establish that the claimant actually knew of the risk. But knowledge of the risk does not automatically result in the claimant voluntarily assuming the risk.

- The claimant must voluntarily assume the risk of having no legal redress. Consenting to the risk of injury is not enough per se to establish *volenti*.

- The claimant must expressly or impliedly agree to waive any liability for the injury that may befall him. The courts are extremely reluctant to imply such an agreement.

- If the defendant cannot establish *volenti*, the claimant's knowledge of the risk may still serve to lessen the standard of care expected of the defendant, so that he is not liable for negligence, because no breach of duty has occurred.

Exclusion of liability

Many businesses may attempt to exclude or limit their liability via a contractual exclusion clause or notice. Because signing a contract that contains an exclusion clause is tantamount to agreeing to waive the right to legal redress, contractual exclusions of liability are often regarded as forming part of the defence of *volenti*. In fact, the express exclusion of liability is a separate and distinct defence, as is indicated by the Unfair Contract Terms Act 1977 (UCTA 1977), s 2(3), which states that a person's agreement to, or knowledge of, an exclusion clause is not of itself to be taken as indicating his voluntary assumption of any risk.

The operation and regulation of exclusion clauses is discussed at p 969

Exclusion clauses are paternalistically regulated by statute. These statutes will be discussed in depth later in the book. Here, we will limit discussion to the effect that statutory regulation has had on the ability to exclude liability for negligence, which, thanks to the UCTA 1977, s 2, is heavily limited. Section 2(1) provides that no one may, via a notice or exclusion clause, exclude or limit his liability for negligent acts that cause death or personal injury. In the case of all other losses (that is, damage to property and economic loss), an exclusion clause or notice will only be valid provided that it is reasonable.[17] The defendant is required to establish that the clause is reasonable.[18]

How the courts determine 'reasonableness' is discussed at p 983

Statutory authority

In some cases, statute may specifically authorize an act that would, in the absence of the statute, constitute a tort. A claimant who sustains loss due to such an authorized act has no remedy other than that provided for by the relevant Act.

nuisance: the unreasonable interference with the use or enjoyment of another person's land (see p 475)

The majority of cases in this area concern actions in nuisance, as did the following leading case.

---

17. Unfair Contract Terms Act 1977, s 2(2).   18. Ibid, s 11(5).

Allen v Gulf Oil Refining Ltd [1981] AC 1001 (HL)

FACTS: The defendant operated an oil refinery. The claimant alleged that the operation of the refinery was a nuisance, in so much as it expelled gases that produced a noxious smell, generated offensive levels of noise, and caused vibrations on the claimant's property.

HELD: The House of Lords stated that the Gulf Oil Refining Act 1965 gave the defendant the power to operate a refinery in the area. Once this was established, the defendant needed to demonstrate that it was impossible to construct and operate a refinery that conformed to Parliament's intentions, without causing the nuisance alleged, or any nuisance. The defendant could establish this, so there was no nuisance.

⭐ See RA Buckley, 'Nuisance, Negligence and Statutory Authorisation' (1980) 43 MLR 219

As can be seen from the decision in *Allen*, the existence of a statutory authorization does not provide a blanket immunity. Before holding that the acts did not constitute a tort, the courts will consider numerous factors that might include the following.

- Was the commission of the tort expressly or impliedly authorized by statute?
- Is the authorization total, or does it operate only in the absence of negligence?
- Could the tort have been avoided (for example, by engaging in the activity elsewhere, or by doing it in a different manner)?
- Has planning permission been granted for the act in question? Planning permission does not amount to statutory authority and will not directly excuse the commission of a tort,[19] but planning permission may alter the character of the neighbourhood to such an extent that a previously tortious act becomes non-tortious.[20]

Illegality

The claimant might be denied a remedy on the ground that he was engaged in an illegal act when he sustained loss. In such a case, the courts will apply the maxim *ex turpi causa non oritur actio* to hold that the defendant did not owe the claimant a duty of care.

The following case demonstrates the principle in practice.

➡ *ex turpi causa non oritur action:* 'an action does not arise from a base cause'

 Clunis v Camden and Islington Health Authority [1998] QB 978 (CA)

FACTS: Mr Clunis (the claimant) was a patient at the defendant's mental hospital. After his release from the hospital, he failed to attend aftercare appointments. Three months after his release, he carried out an unprovoked attack on a man at a London Underground station and stabbed him to death. He was later convicted of manslaughter. He alleged that the loss that he suffered (deprivation of liberty) was caused by the defendant's failure to provide him with adequate treatment, which resulted in his mental state, which, in turn, resulted in the unprovoked attack. The defendant pleaded *ex turpi causa*.

HELD: The defence succeeded. The Court of Appeal held that the loss that the claimant sustained was not due to the acts of the defendant, but due to his own criminal act.

⭐ See CA Hopkins, '*Ex Turpi Causa* and Mental Disorder' [1998] 57 CLJ 444

---

19. *Hunter v Canary Wharf Ltd* [1997] 2 All ER 426 (HL).
20. *Gillingham Borough Council v Medway (Chatham) Dock Co Ltd* [1993] QB 343 (QB).

The courts appear to take into account the culpability of the claimant when determining the availability of *ex turpi causa* and will ask the question: 'Were the losses sustained by the claimant the result of his own crime?' If the answer is 'yes' (as in *Clunis* above), the defence is likely to be available—but if the answer is 'no', then the defence may fail, as in the next case.

Revill v Newbury [1996] QB 567 (CA)

FACTS: The defendant owned an allotment shed in which he slept in order to protect his property from thieves and vandals. The claimant attempted to break into the shed. In an attempt to frighten the claimant, the defendant fired his shotgun through a hole in the door, but the blast hit the claimant, injuring him. The claimant sought damages in negligence and under the Occupiers' Liability Act 1984 for the injuries that he suffered. The defendant pleaded *ex turpi causa*.

HELD: The Court of Appeal did not accept the defence. The claimant's loss was not caused by his own criminal act, but by the defendant's unreasonable and disproportionate act. The claimant recovered damages, but they were reduced by two-thirds on the ground of contributory negligence, resulting in an award of £4,100.

Occupiers' liability is discussed at p 466

See T Weir, 'Swag for the Injured Burglar' [1996] CLJ 182

The courts have now overtly acknowledged the link between the loss sustained and the criminal act. In *Cross v Kirkby*,[21] Beldam LJ stated that *ex turpi causa* will apply 'when the claimant's claim is so closely connected or inextricably bound up with his own criminal or illegal conduct that the court could not permit him to recover without appearing to condone that conduct'.[22]

A recent case has highlighted an interesting issue in relation to the defence—namely, to what extent it can be relied on by a company. Where the directors of a company use it to conduct some manner of fraudulent activity, is the company to be regarded as the perpetrator of the crime (so that, if it commences a claim, the defence of *ex turpi causa* can be pleaded by the other party), or is the company to be regarded as the victim of the unmeritorious acts of its directors (in which case, the other party could not plead *ex turpi causa*)?

This issue arose in the following case.

Stone & Rolls Ltd v Moore Stephens [2008] EWCA Civ 644

FACTS: The claimant company was owned, controlled, and managed by a rogue named Stojevic. He employed the defendant firm of accountants to act as the claimant's auditor. Stojevic had been engaging in numerous acts of dishonesty, which basically involved him using the claimant company to defraud banks of substantial sums of money, which were then dispersed to Stojevic and others who were party to the fraud. The banks successfully brought an action for deceit against the claimant company and Stojevic, but the company

---

21. The Times, 18 February 2000 (CA).   22. Ibid, [76].

could not pay, because Stojevic had dispersed its assets. The banks therefore petitioned for the claimant's liquidation. The liquidator alleged that the defendant firm should have detected the fraud and that, in not doing so, it had acted negligently. The liquidator therefore caused the claimant company to commence an action in negligence against the defendant firm. The defendant firm alleged that the company had acted illegally and petitioned to strike out the claim on the basis of *ex turpi causa*.

HELD: The Court of Appeal held that Stojevic was the 'directing mind and will' of the claimant company and that his illegal acts were therefore attributable to it. Thus, because the claimant company's action was based on illegal acts attributable to it, the principle of *ex turpi causa* applied and the claimant company's action was struck out.

COMMENT: At the time of writing, the case is on appeal to the House of Lords.

 The attribution of directors' acts to the company is discussed at p 603

★ See P Watts, 'Auditors and Corrupt Clients' (2009) 125 LQR 38

‹ › Key points summary

- Parties may, via a notice or contractual exclusion clause, exclude or restrict liability for the commission of a tort.

- Liability cannot be excluded or restricted for negligence that causes personal injury or death. Where the negligence causes property damage or economic loss, a notice or exclusion clause will only be valid in so far as the defendant proves that it is reasonable.

- Statute may authorize the commission of certain normally tortious acts. Where this occurs, the claimant will have no remedy other than that provided by the statute in question.

- *Ex turpi causa non oritur actio* means 'an action does not arise from a base cause' and applies where the claimant sustained harm whilst engaging in a criminal act.

Contributory negligence

A claimant's loss may be caused by a number of parties, one of whom is the claimant himself. Where the claimant' negligence has, in some way, contributed to his own loss, the defendant can plead contributory negligence.[23] Prior to 1945, the common law provided that a successful pleading of contributory negligence would, like the defence of *volenti*, provide a complete defence, rendering the defendant not liable to pay damages.[24] Today, the defence is governed by the Law Reform (Contributory Negligence) Act 1945, s 1(1) of which provides that:

> Where any person suffers damage as the result partly of his own fault and partly of the fault of any other person or persons, a claim in respect of that damage shall not be defeated by reason of the fault of the person suffering the damage, but the damages recoverable in respect thereof shall be reduced to such extent as the court thinks just and equitable having regard to the claimant's share in the responsibility for the damage.

23. The defendant bears the burden of proof of establishing that the claimant was negligent.
24. *Butterfield v Forrester* (1809) 11 East 60.

From this, it can be seen that contributory negligence is a partial defence only, serving to reduce the damages payable by the defendant. The Act does not apply to the tort of wrongful interference with goods,[25] to actions in deceit,[26] or to other actions in which the essence of the particular claim is the defendant's dishonesty.[27] In such cases, contributory negligence will therefore operate as a complete defence. The 1945 Act applies only where the claimant has suffered 'damage', which 'includes loss of life and personal injury'.[28] The use of the word 'includes' indicates that the Act is not confined to cases involving bodily injury, and can include damage to property and economic loss.[29]

The tort of wrongful interference with goods is discussed at p 455

Standard of care

The 1945 Act applies only where both the claimant and the defendant are at 'fault'. Therefore, to plead contributory negligence successfully, the defendant will need to demonstrate the claimant's fault. The Act defines 'fault' widely as 'negligence, breach of statutory duty or other act or omission which gives rise to liability in tort'.[30] This definition is wide enough also to cover strict liability torts, with certain statutory strict liability torts expressly bringing themselves within the scope of the 1945 Act.[31] Because the majority of contributory negligence cases involve the claimant's own negligence, the defendant will need to establish that the claimant's actions were negligent. Normally, the first step towards this is to establish the existence of a duty of care, but it is clear that, to establish contributory negligence, the defendant does not have to establish that the claimant owed him a duty of care; all that need be established by the defendant is that the claimant failed to meet the requisite standard of care (that is, he failed to take reasonable care for his own safety).[32] When determining whether or not this standard has been met, the court will have regard to the same factors as are applicable in determining whether or not a defendant has breached his duty of care.

The factors relating to a breach of the duty of care are discussed at p 408

Examples of cases in which the courts have found the claimant to have breached the standard include the failure to wear a car seat belt[33] or a motorcycle crash helmet,[34] accepting a lift with a driver who one knows to be drunk[35] or whose car one

---

25. Torts (Interference with Goods) Act 1971, s 11.

26. *Standard Chartered Bank v Pakistan National Shipping Corp (Nos 2 and 4)* [2002] UKHL 43, [2003] 1 AC 959.

27. *Corporacion Nacional de Cobre de Chile v Sogemin Metals Ltd* [1997] 1 WLR 1396 (Ch).

28. Law Reform (Contributory Negligence) Act 1945, s 4.

29. *Platform Home Loans Ltd v Oyston Shipways Ltd* [2000] 2 AC 290 (HL).

30. Law Reform (Contributory Negligence) Act 1945, s 4.

31. The notable example being the tort of product liability: see the Consumer Protection Act 1987, s 6(4).

32. *Nance v British Columbia Electric Rly* [1951] AC 601 (PC).

33. *Froom v Butcher* [1976] QB 286 (CA) (damages reduced by 20 per cent). Today, failing to wear a seat belt is also criminal offence under the Motor Vehicles (Wearing of Seat Belts) Regulations 1982, SI 1982/176.

34. *O'Connell v Jackson* [1972] 1 QB 270 (CA) (damages reduced by 15 per cent). This includes a failure to fasten the helmet correctly: see *Capps v Miller* [1989] 2 All ER 333 (CA) (damages reduced by 10 per cent).

35. *Owens v Brimmell* [1977] QB 859 (QB) (damages reduced by 20 per cent).

knows to be dangerously defective,[36] crossing the road at a pelican crossing when the lights are green for cars,[37] and continuing to smoke cigarettes after being diagnosed with ischemic heart disease, angina, and emphysema.[38]

As with negligence, the standard of care imposed is an objective one. In certain cases, however, the courts will permit an element of subjectivity to enter their deliberations and affect the standard of care.

- *Children* As a strict matter of law, contributory negligence can be pleaded against a child of any age, although Lord Denning MR stated that '[a] very young child cannot be guilty of contributory negligence'.[39] When the claimant is a child, the question for the court is whether an ordinary child of the claimant's age would have taken any more care than the claimant.[40]

- *Dilemma* If the defendant's negligence places the claimant in a dilemma and, in the agony of the moment, he chooses a course of action that contributes to his damage, contributory negligence will not succeed, provided that the course of action that he took was a reasonable one. Thus, where a coach passenger, fearing that the coach was about to crash, jumped out of the coach and broke his leg, the court held that there was no contributory negligence, even though the coach did not crash and, had the passenger remained on board, he would not have been injured.[41]

- *Employees* Where the claimant is an employee and is suing his employer for breach of statutory duty, the courts will not so quickly allow contributory negligence to succeed. The rationale for this is that the employee's sense of danger is likely to have been dulled by repetition, noise, fatigue, and preoccupation with work. Accordingly, the standard that the employee will need to meet is that of the ordinary prudent workman in the position of the claimant.[42]

Causation

In order for contributory negligence to succeed, the defendant must show that the claimant's conduct contributed to the *damage suffered*. It is not enough to show that the claimant's conduct contributed to the *incident that caused the damage*.

The distinction can be seen in the following case.

 ***Froom v Butcher* [1976] QB 286 (CA)**

FACTS: A collision occurred between the defendant and claimant, due to the defendant's negligent driving. The claimant was not wearing a seat belt, and suffered head and chest injuries, as well as a broken finger. The accident was caused solely by the defendant's

---

36. *Gregory v Kelly* [1978] RTR 426 (QB) (failure to wear a seat belt and knowledge that the car had faulty brakes; 40 per cent reduction in damages).
37. *Fitzgerald v Lane* [1989] AC 328 (HL) (reduction of damages by 50 per cent).
38. *Badger v Ministry of Defence* [2005] EWHC 2941, [2006] 3 All ER 173 (reduction of damages by 20 per cent). The claimant's eventual cause of death was lung cancer caused by continued smoking and the negligent exposure to asbestos.
39. *Gough v Thorne* [1966] 1 WLR 1387 (CA) 1390.   40. Ibid.
41. *Jones v Boyce* (1816) 171 ER 540.
42. *Flower v Ebbw Vale Steel, Iron and Coal Co Ltd* [1934] 2 KB 132 (KB) 139 (Lawrence J).

negligence, but had the claimant been wearing a seat belt, he would probably not have suffered the head and chest injuries. The defendant pleaded contributory negligence.

HELD: The claimant's conduct was not a cause of the collision—but the Court of Appeal stated that, in contributory negligence cases, this was irrelevant. What is important is whether the claimant's conduct was a cause of the injury suffered and there was no doubt that the claimant's failure to wear a seat belt contributed towards his injuries. Accordingly, the defence succeeded and because wearing a seat belt would have prevented the injuries suffered by the claimant, the damages were reduced by 20 per cent.

COMMENT: Lord Denning MR suggested *obiter* that the courts adopt fixed reductions. He stated that, regarding injuries that would have been prevented by the wearing of a seat belt, damages should be reduced by 25 per cent. Regarding those injuries that would have been rendered less severe by the wearing of a seat belt, damages should be reduced by 15 per cent. This suggestion has not yet been accepted as a binding rule even in relation to accidents involving seat belts, although the Court of Appeal has stated that Lord Denning's guidelines should ordinarily be adhered to.[43]

Such fixed reductions are useful for two reasons: firstly, they help to make the law in this area more certain; secondly, they allow claimants to predict what their likely damages will be and lessen the likelihood that they will be coerced by the defendant's lawyers into accepting a low settlement.

★ On this case and other cases involving the failure to wear a seat belt, see A Palmer, 'Failure to Wear a Seat Belt and Contributory Negligence' (2001) 2 JPI Law 149

In addition, in order for contributory negligence to be present, the damage suffered must be within the scope of the risk to which the claimant exposed himself. If the damage suffered is outside the scope of the risk, then causation will not be established, as the following case demonstrates.

Jones v Livox Quarries Ltd [1952] 2 QB 608 (CA)

FACTS: The claimant, contrary to instructions from the defendant, was riding on the rear tow bar of one of the defendant's 'traxcavator' vehicles. Another of the defendant's vehicles negligently collided with the rear of the traxcavator, causing injury to the claimant. The claimant sued and the defendant alleged that the claimant had contributed towards his own injuries.

HELD: The Court of Appeal held that although the principal risk resulting from the claimant's actions was the risk of injury through falling off the traxcavator, he had also exposed himself to the risk of the injury that had, in fact, occurred. Accordingly, his damages were reduced by 20 per cent. Singleton LJ stated that had the claimant been sitting on an unsafe wall and sustained injury through a vehicle negligently colliding with the wall, contributory negligence would not be present, because the claimant's act would not be within the scope of the risk to which he exposed himself.

---

43. *Capps v Miller* [1989] 1 WLR 839 (CA).

Identification

In certain cases, one party (*A*) may be 'identified' with an act of contributory negligence committed by another (*B*). Where this is so, the damages recoverable by *A* may be reduced due to the contributory negligence of *B*.

The following example demonstrates this in practice.

 Identification and contributory negligence

Phil is employed as a lorry driver by ParcelQuick Ltd. Whilst driving one of ParcelQuick's lorries, Phil is involved in a collision with a van being driven by Clive. The collision is the result of the negligence of both drivers. Should ParcelQuick seek to recover damages from Clive for the damage of its lorry, the damages recoverable will be reduced, because ParcelQuick will be identified with Phil's contributory negligence.

The doctrine of identification will apply where the relationship between *A* and *B* is sufficient to impose vicarious liability. It will also apply to claims by dependants under the Fatal Accidents Act 1976 where the deceased was partly to blame for his own death.

Apportionment

The ability to apportion damages has existed in relation to disputes concerning collisions at sea since 1911.[44] The passing of the 1945 Act provided the courts with a general power to reduce damages based on what they think is 'just and equitable having regard to the claimant's share in the responsibility for the damage'.[45] Because the Act reduces damages based on what is just and equitable, it follows that the courts take a case-by-case approach and that there is no general test used to determine the extent that damages should be reduced. This can create a certain amount of uncertainty, which, in turn, may encourage a claimant to accept a low settlement. The adoption of a system of fixed reductions (as suggested by Lord Denning MR in *Froom v Butcher*, discussed above) would alleviate this to an extent.

Because each case is dependent upon its facts, appeal courts are reluctant to interfere with a trial judge's decision and will only do so if they consider it plainly wrong.[46] Whilst there is no single test, it does appear that the courts will take into account two significant factors:

- the extent to which the claimant's act caused the damage; and
- the blameworthiness of the claimant's conduct.

It would appear that the court's discretion is not unlimited, because it has been stated *obiter* that the court cannot order a 100 per cent reduction in damages.[47] There would

---

44. Maritime Conventions Act 1911, s 1(1).
45. Law Reform (Contributory Negligence) Act 1945, s 1(1).
46. *Hannam v Mann* [1984] RTR 252 (CA).
47. *Pitts v Hunt* [1990] 1 QB 24 (CA) 48 (Beldam LJ), cf *Reeves v Commissioner of Police of the Metropolis* [1999] QB 169 (CA) 195 (Morritt LJ).

appear to be two reasons behind this: firstly, because the 1945 Act presupposes fault by both the claimant and defendant, it follows that a claimant cannot be 100 per cent contributorily negligent; secondly, a 100 per cent reduction would permit contributory negligence to act as a complete defence in a manner similar to *volenti*.

⟨⟩ Key points summary

- Contributory negligence is a partial defence only, resulting in a reduction in the claimant's damages.

- The defence is regulated by the Law Reform (Contributory Negligence) Act 1945. The Act applies to most torts, but does not apply to the tort of wrongful interference with goods, actions in deceit, and actions in which the essence of the particular claim is the defendant's dishonesty.

- The defendant will need to establish that the claimant failed to take reasonable care of his own safety.

- The defendant will also need to establish that the claimant's conduct contributed to the damage suffered. It is not necessary to show that the claimant's conduct contributed to the incident that caused the damage.

- The court will reduce damages based on what is 'just and equitable having regard to the claimant's share in the responsibility for the damage'.

Limitation of actions

As with claims in contract, tortious actions must be brought within a specified period, and, as in contract, claims brought outside this period are not barred from being initiated and will be allowed to proceed if the defendant fails to raise the passing of the limitation period as a defence. But there are more generous limitation rules for claims in tort than for claims in contract. The reason for this is that, in breach of contract cases, the loss sustained by the claimant usually arises during the lifetime of the contract, or shortly afterwards. Conversely, in tort cases, the harm might not arise for many years after the conduct in question.

 Contractual limitation periods are discussed at p 360

Eg The time span of a tort

Examples of torts that can cause damage years after their commission include the following.

1. A pharmaceutical company releases a new drug onto the market without properly testing its long-term effects. Years later, people who took the drug start to develop adverse reactions.

2. As we saw in Chapter 12, many claimants negligently exposed to asbestos did not develop asbestosis and mesothelioma until many years after their exposure.

3. An architect may negligently design a building, but the structural flaws in his plans may not become evident until many years after the building is built.

The most significant benefit is perhaps the date on which the limitation period starts running. The Limitation Act 1980, s 2, provides that time begins running 'from the date on which the cause of action accrued'. This date will depend upon the tort in question. Where a tortious claim can be brought without establishing that damage occurred (for example, trespass), the limitation period will commence on the date of the defendant's act. But where proof of damage is required (for example, negligence), the limitation period will commence when the first damage is sustained, thereby allowing for the situations mentioned above in which damage occurs many years after the conduct in question. It can be seen that this rule is more generous than in contract, in which the limitation period generally starts running on the date of breach.

The general limitation period in tort is six years[48] from the date on which the period begins to run. Statute has, however, created a number of exceptions to this general rule, the main ones being as follows.

- Where the claimant's claim includes damages for personal injury, the limitation period is reduced to three years.[49] But the court does have an unfettered power to extend this period if it appears equitable to do so.[50] If the claimant dies of his injuries before the three years expire, then the three-year limitation period will begin again, starting on the date of death or the date on which the claimant's death was made known to his representatives (whichever is later).[51]

- In cases involving libel, slander, and malicious falsehood, the limitation period is reduced to one year.[52] But the court is free to disregard this period where it considers that it would inequitably prejudice the claimant.[53]

- Claims brought under the Consumer Protection Act 1987 must be brought within three years of the date on which the damage was first sustained or the date of knowledge of the defect (whichever is later).[54]

  Claims brought under the Consumer Protection Act 1987 are discussed at p 449

- In maritime cases (for example, collisions at sea, damage to cargo, loss of life at sea), the limitation period is reduced to two years,[55] although the court may extend this period if it deems fit.[56]

As in contract, if the claimant is subject to a legal disability (for example, he is a minor or mentally disabled) when the cause of action (that is, the right to sue) accrues, then the action may be brought at any time within the period of six years (three years in personal injury cases) after he ceases to be disabled (that is, reaches the age of 18, or is cured of his mental disability), or he dies, whichever occurs first.[57] If the action is based on the fraud of the defendant (or his agent), or if any such person conceals facts relevant to the claimant's cause of action, or if the action is one for relief from the consequences of a mistake, then the limitation period will not begin to run until the date on which the claimant discovered, or ought to have discovered, the fraud, concealment, or mistake.[58]

---

48. Limitation Act 1980, s 2.
49. Ibid, s 11(4). Unless the injury is caused by an intentional trespass to the person, when the six-year period will remain: *Stubbings v Webb* [1993] AC 498 (HL).
50. Limitation Act 1980, s 33(1).   51. Ibid, s 11(5).
52. Ibid, s 4A.   53. Ibid, s 32A(1).
54. Ibid, s 11A(4).   55. Merchant Shipping Act 1995, s 190(3).
56. Ibid, s 190(5).   57. Limitation Act 1980, s 28(1).
58. Ibid, s 32(1).

Where the tortious act is one that continually causes *recurring* damage (for example, the continuous commission of a nuisance,[59] or a breach of statutory duty by the continuing failure to implement an EU directive),[60] then, as long as the damage continues, a fresh cause of action accrues every day. Once the damage ceases, the claimant has the right to claim for any harm that was caused within the previous six years (three if the harm involved personal injury).

Latent damage

The word 'latent' means 'existing, but hidden or not yet developed'. The commission of a tort may result in latent damage, which does not manifest itself until many years after the tort was committed (see above for several examples). In such cases, the rules relating to limitation periods are modified, depending upon the type of loss sustained.

- *Personal injury* In cases involving negligence, nuisance, or breach of duty, the three-year limitation period will commence only once the claimant acquires certain 'knowledge'. This includes the knowledge that:
  - an injury has been suffered;
  - the injury is significant;
  - the injury was caused by negligence, nuisance, or breach of duty; and
  - the injury can be attributed to an identified defendant.[61]
- *Other damage* In cases involving negligence resulting in damage other than personal injury or death (for example, property damage or economic loss), the claimant can elect either the standard six-year limitation period, or a three-year period commencing on the date on which the claimant had both the right to bring an action and knowledge of the material facts.[62] But no action may lie fifteen years after the commission of the breach that caused the damage[63] (this is known as the 'longstop' provision).

The above rules relating to legal disabilities and fraud, concealment, or mistake also apply to cases involving latent damage.

‹ › Key points summary

- If the tort does not require proof of damage, the limitation period starts running on the date of the tortious act. Where the tort does require proof of damage, time starts running on the date on which the damage is first sustained.

- The general limitation period in tortious cases is six years.

- In personal injury cases, the limitation period is reduced to three years. The period is reduced to one year in cases of defamation and malicious falsehood.

---

59. *Earl of Harrington v Corporation of* Derby [1905] 1 Ch 205 (Ch).
60. *Phonographic Performance Ltd v DTI* [2004] EWHC 1795 (Ch), [2004] 1 WLR 2893.
61. Limitation Act 1980, s 14(1).   62. Ibid, s 14A(4)(b) and (5).
63. Ibid, s 14B(1).

- Where the claimant is subject to a legal disability at the time that the cause of action accrues, then the action may be brought at any time within the period of six years (three years in personal injury cases) after he ceases to be disabled.

- In cases involving latent (hidden) damage, the rules relating to when the limitation period commences are based upon the claimant acquiring certain knowledge.

Remedies

If the claimant has established that a tort has been committed and the defendant has failed successfully to raise a defence, or has only managed to raise a partial defence (for example, contributory negligence), the final issue to be determined is what remedy should the claimant be awarded. As in contract, the principal remedy will be an award of damages, although, as we shall see, damages in tort may operate in a very different manner from damages in contract. In certain cases, however, financial compensation will not adequately compensate the claimant. In these cases, the court may be willing to grant an injunction. Finally, it may be that the claimant need not involve the court at all, because certain torts can be remedied by the claimant taking matters into his own hands. As we shall see, however, such self-help remedies are limited in number and are used at the claimant's peril, lest he end up committing a tort, or even a crime, himself.

Damages

The basic aim of an award of damages is to compensate the claimant for any injury or loss caused by the defendant's tort. As we shall see later, this will include both his pecuniary (financial) and non-pecuniary losses. The rules relating to the calculation of tortious damages are extremely complex and a detailed examination is beyond the scope of this text. Readers who wish to learn more on the calculation of damages are advised to read a more specialist text.

The recovery of pecuniary and non-pecuniary loss is discussed at p 541

Traditionally, damages are awarded only once for each tort in the form of a single lump sum, assessed at the date of trial. The rationale behind this approach is that it provides the defendant with 'closure'. But the principal problem with a lump-sum award is that damages will frequently need to compensate the claimant for future losses (especially in personal injury cases), which will result in the judge having to estimate the extent of the future loss. If the judge underestimates the loss, the lump sum cannot be subsequently corrected and the claimant will be under-compensated. To combat this, the courts have established a number of devices, including postponed or split trials, interim or provisional damages, structured settlements, and periodic or reviewable payments. These are all beyond the scope of this text and will not be discussed further.[64]

---

64. Students who wish to explore these alternatives to a lump-sum payment are advised to read S Deakin, A Johnston, and B Markesinis, *Markesinis & Deakin's Tort Law* (6th edn, OUP, Oxford, 2008) 965–75.

TABLE 15.1 Compensatory and non-compensatory damages for tort

Type of damages	Compensatory?	Non-compensatory?
Compensatory	Yes	No
Contemptuous	No	Yes
Nominal	No	Yes
Aggravated	Yes	No
Exemplary	No	Yes

Although damages for breach of contract are always compensatory and damages in tort are usually compensatory, their measure is different.[65] Damages for breach of contract normally will aim to put the claimant in the position in which he would have been had the contract been performed properly. In tort, the aim of damages is to put the claimant in the position in which he would have been before the tort was committed (this is known as *restitutio in integrum* and would equate with the aim of reliance loss in contract). But unlike damages for breach of contract, which are always compensatory, there are several types of damages for tort that are non-compensatory in nature, as Table 15.1 clarifies.

➡ *restitutio in integrum*: 'restoration to the original position'

Contemptuous damages

Contemptuous damages constitute probably the lowest award of damages that the court can make and traditionally consist of an amount equal to the lowest value coin of the realm (currently 1 pence). Contemptuous damages are awarded where the claimant's legal rights have technically been infringed, but where the action is frivolous, or where the claimant has acted in a manner that the court deems entirely lacking in merit. Claimants who receive contemptuous damages will almost always have to pay their own costs (which will certainly result in them being out of pocket) and may also be ordered to pay the costs of the other party. Today, contemptuous damages are almost only ever awarded in defamation cases.[66]

Nominal damages

Nominal damages are awarded in both contract and tort where the claimant's legal rights have been infringed, but no actual loss has occurred. Specifically in tort, they are awarded in relation to torts that do not require proof of damage and will constitute a minimal sum only (typically £2). For example, in *Grobbelaar v News Group Newspapers Ltd*,[67] the claimant (a goalkeeper for Liverpool Football Club) was libelled by *The Sun*, which stated that he had fixed football matches. He had not fixed any matches, but he had agreed to concede goals deliberately in return for payment. The jury awarded him £85,000 damages. On appeal, this was reduced to £1. Given that he was a proven cheat, the libel had not caused him any further loss and so

---

65. Note, however, that damages under the Misrepresentation Act 1967, s 2(1), are assessed on a tortious basis.
66. See, e.g., *Reynolds v Times Newspapers Ltd* [1998] 2 WLR 862 (HL).
67. [2002] UKHL 40, [2002] 1 WLR 3024.

nominal damages were appropriate. Grobbelaar was also order to pay two-thirds of the defendant's legal costs (around £1 million).

Aggravated damages

Although there is debate on the issue, aggravated damages tend to be regarded as a special form of compensatory damages. They are awarded to compensate the claimant for hurt feelings or injured pride, usually in situations in which the defendant's actions have been improperly motivated, or are spiteful, malicious, or oppressive. As such, traditionally, they have not been awarded in negligence cases,[68] and tend to be limited to cases involving deceit, defamation, malicious falsehood and prosecution, false imprisonment, and trespass.

Examples of cases in which aggravated damages have been awarded include the following.

- A dentist who carried out expensive and unnecessary treatment on patients was ordered to pay an extra 15 per cent in aggravated damages for the distress and annoyance that he had caused.[69]

- Where claimants are victims of false imprisonment or malicious prosecution, aggravated damages should be awarded. These damages will rarely be less than £1,000, but will normally not exceed twice the normal compensatory damages.[70]

- *Private Eye* accused the wife of Peter Sutcliffe (a serial killer known as the 'Yorkshire Ripper') of agreeing to sell her story to a national newspaper for £250,000. After the wife initiated proceedings against *Private Eye* for defamation (which she subsequently won), it continued to publish further allegations about her. She was awarded aggravated damages.[71]

Although aggravated damages take into account the conduct of the defendant, they are not awarded in order to punish the defendant. If the courts wish to punish the defendant for his behaviour, they will award exemplary damages.

Exemplary damages

As we noted in Chapter 11, the law of torts is not only compensatory; it is also meant to act as a deterrent. Contract law does not have this function, which is why exemplary damages are not available. Nowhere is the deterrent value of tort law clearer than in cases in which exemplary damages are awarded. Exemplary damages (also known as 'punitive' damages) are not compensatory; rather, they are awarded in order to punish the defendant for his unacceptable, outrageous, or reprehensible conduct.

Because these cases involve the claimant gaining a windfall, exemplary damages will only be awarded in three types of case, as follows.[72]

- *Where the claimant has been the victim of oppressive, arbitrary, or unconstitutional action by employees of the government (including local government,*

---

68. *Kralj v McGrath and St Theresa's Hospital* [1986] 1 All ER 54 (QB); *AB v South West Water Services Ltd* [1993] QB 507 (CA).

69. *Appleton v Garrett* [1996] PIQR P1 (QB).

70. *Thompson v Commissioner of Police of the Metropolis* [1998] QB 498 (CA).

71. *Sutcliffe v Pressdram Ltd* [1991] 1 QB 153 (CA).

72. *Rookes v Barnard* [1964] AC 1129 (HL).

the police and prison officers) This could include acts of false imprisonment or malicious prosecution by the police. In such cases, exemplary damages would rarely be less that £5,000. Conduct that was 'particularly deserving of condemnation' could result in an award of up to £25,000. A figure of £50,000 would be the absolute maximum.[73] These limitations were imposed as a result to the increasing number of complaints being brought against the police.

- *Where the defendant calculates that the profit from the commission of a tort will exceed the compensation payable to a claimant* For example, where a publisher published a book, relying on the libellous content to sell enough copies to offset any compensation payable, the House of Lords awarded exemplary damages of £25,000.[74]

- *Where statute authorizes exemplary damages* It would appear that only one statute exists that expressly allows exemplary damages—namely, the Reserve and Auxiliary Forces (Protection of Civil Interests) Act 1951, s 13(2).

Exemplary damages can also be awarded against a defendant who is vicariously liable for the acts of another, as the following case demonstrates.

 Rowlands v Chief Constable of Merseyside Police [2006] EWCA Civ 1773

FACTS: The claimant had called the police to the scene of a neighbourhood dispute. An altercation occurred between her and a police officer, resulting in her arrest. She was handcuffed, which she claimed caused excruciating pain on her wrists and, when requested to loosen the handcuffs, the officer tugged at them, causing further pain. She was acquitted of all charges and brought a claim against the chief constable[75] for assault, false imprisonment, and malicious prosecution. At first instance, she succeeded and was awarded basic damages, but the issue of payment of exemplary damages was withdrawn from the jury. She therefore appealed. The chief constable contended that because exemplary damages were designed to punish the wrongdoer, they were not appropriate in cases involving vicarious liability.

HELD: The Court of Appeal allowed the appeal and held that awarding exemplary damages in this case was merely the Court's way of indicating its disapproval of the conduct of the police, even though such damages did not punish the wrongdoer. Accordingly, she was awarded exemplary damages of £7,500, bringing her total compensation to £19,850.

General and special damages

In the next few sections, we will discuss in more detail the rules relating to the calculation and recovery of pecuniary and non-pecuniary losses. But before that can be done, it is important to understand the distinction between general and special damages.

---

73. *Thompson v Commissioner of Police of the Metropolis* [1998] QB 498 (CA).

74. *Cassell & Co Ltd v Broome* [1972] AC 1027 (HL).

75. The Police Act 1996, s 88, provides that chief constables are liable for the unlawful acts of constables under their direction and control.

General and special damages relate to losses that may be pecuniary or non-pecuniary, and the distinction between them is based upon whether they can be precisely quantified or not.

- *General damages* compensate losses that are an inevitable result, or which are presumed to flow from the commission, of the tort. In personal injury cases, examples of general damages would include pain and suffering, loss of amenity, and loss of future earnings. Because such losses cannot be quantified precisely (that is, they are unliquidated), they do not need to be specifically pleaded.

- *Special damages* compensate particular losses that cannot be presumed to flow from the tort and which result from the particular facts of the case. This could include property damage, the cost of medical treatment, or loss of earnings up to the trial. Because such losses can be quantified precisely, they must be specifically pleaded and proved separately.

Pecuniary losses

Pecuniary losses include loss of earnings (before and after the trial), and the payment of medical treatment, care, and supervision (including adapting the claimant's surroundings to any disability).

Regarding past loss of earnings, the courts will simply calculate how much the claimant has lost between the tort and the date of the trial, and deduct any payments that would have been made for tax and National Insurance. Where relevant, the calculation of future loss of earnings is obviously more complicated. The court will first fix a figure that could be said to represent the claimant's annual income (this figure is known as the multiplicand). This will not simply be his salary at the date of trial, because that will fail to take into account future events. For example, the claimant may argue that he was climbing up a career ladder and would have been promoted several times during his working life, thereby increasing the multiplicand. Once this figure is reached, the court will deduct any tax that would be paid and also any amounts based on the claimant's current and future earnings (if the claimant is unable to work, this is likely to be nothing). This figure will constitute the final multiplicand. The court will then determine for how long the claimant would have continued working, taking into account the claimant's employment prospects, injuries or diseases, or any reduced life expectancy (this is known as the multiplier and will rarely exceed twenty-five years). But if the defendant's tort has resulted in a shortening of the claimant's life expectancy, the court will award an amount to compensate the claimant for the years that he will lose.[76] Multiplying the multiplicand by the multiplier will result in the amount of damages needed to compensate the claimant for his losses.

> **multiplicand**: a figure representing the annual amount per head of loss

> **multiplier**: the length of time for which each head of loss is likely to be payable

The above principles apply equally to the cost of future medical care. The court will determine the annual cost of medical care that the claimant will require (the multiplicand) and will multiply it by the number of years for which such medical treatment will be required (the multiplier).

---

76. *Pickett v British Rail Engineering Ltd* [1980] AC 136 (HL).

Non-pecuniary losses

Non-pecuniary losses will include compensating the claimant for any pain and suffering that was caused by the defendant's tort, as well as any loss of amenity (for example, loss of faculty or the inability to enjoy certain activities or hobbies).

The claimant can recover damages for pain and suffering caused by the tort itself, and for pain and suffering caused by any future medical treatment needed as a result of the tort. Compensation is recoverable for periods up to the trial, and for any future pain and suffering. Although suffering causing grief and sorrow is not recoverable,[77] recognized psychiatric damage is recoverable,[78] including mental distress caused by a realization that one's life expectancy has been shortened.[79] Damages for pain and suffering cannot, however, be recovered if the claimant does not actually suffer (for example, because he is in a coma).[80]

Damages for loss of amenity are awarded based upon the objective fact that the faculty has been lost, not upon the realization of such loss. Accordingly, a claimant who is placed into a persistent vegetative state by the defendant's tort is entitled to damages for loss of amenity. But this principle has proven to be controversial, as the following case demonstrates.

 H West & Sons v Shephard [1964] AC 326 (HL)

FACTS: The defendant negligently ran over the claimant with a lorry. The claimant sustained severe head injuries, leading to cerebral atrophy that resulted in paralysis in all four limbs. She could not speak and it was unknown whether she appreciated the extent of her situation. She required full-time medical care and the lack of such care would be fatal. There was no prospect of her condition improving and her life expectancy was reduced to five years.

HELD: The House of Lords awarded the claimant £500 for the reduction in life expectancy and £17,500 general damages for loss of amenity.

COMMENT: This case has proven controversial. In *West* itself, Lords Reid and Devlin (dissenting) thought that the award of damages was far too high because the claimant did not appreciate the true extent of her loss (if she appreciated it at all). Lord Reid stated: 'It is no more possible to compensate an unconscious man than it is to compensate a dead man.'[81] The counter-argument to this is that a claimant may not remain unconscious forever and that permanent unconsciousness is extremely difficult to diagnose.[82] The law is understandably reluctant to regard a living person as if he were dead. Although valid arguments have been submitted for both views, the current weight of opinion seems to be that the current rule should remain.[83]

---

77. *Kerby v Redbridge Health Authority* [1994] PIQR Q1 (QB).

78. *James v Woodall Duckham Construction Co Ltd* [1969] 1 WLR 903 (CA).

79. Administration of Justice Act 1982, s 1(1)(b).

80. *Wise v Kaye* [1962] 1 QB 638 (CA); *Lim v Camden Area Health Authority* [1980] AC 174 (HL).

81. *H West & Sons v Shephard* [1964] AC 326 (HL) 341.

82. Law Commission, *Damages for Personal Injury: Non-Pecuniary Loss* (Law Com No 257, HMSO, London, 1999) [2.14].

83. Ibid. Over two-thirds of consultees to the Law Commission's review favoured retention of the current rule.

Losses of amenity deemed compensatable by the courts includes the loss of sexual function,[84] the inability to enjoy a hobby,[85] and the loss of a partner due to the claimant's disfigurement.[86] These few examples indicate that the courts will award damages for a wide range of subjective losses.

The calculation of non-pecuniary losses is based upon a tariff system. These tariffs are drafted and reviewed by the Judicial Studies Board,[87] and while the tariffs are usually followed, the court may depart from them when it feels appropriate to do so (for example, where personal injury was caused by rape).[88] The following lists some of the current tariffs.

- *Quadriplegia — £206,750–£257,750*
- *Very severe brain damage — £180,000–£257,750*
- *Amputation or total loss of both legs — £154,000–£180,000*
- *Amputation of one arm above elbow — £70,000–£83,500*
- *Loss of a hand — £61,500–£70,000*
- *Total loss of index finger — £12,000*
- *Severe facial scarring — up to £42,000 (males) and £62,000 (females)*
- *Total blindness — £172,500*
- *Loss of one eye — £35,000–£42,000*
- *Total deafness — £58,000–£70,000*

Property damage

The general principle of *restitutio in integrum* (restoration to the original position) applies to property damage in very much the same manner as it applies to personal injury. Where property is destroyed or damaged beyond repair, damages are normally equal to the market value of the destroyed goods at the time of destruction.[89] This will allow the claimant to purchase substitute goods, thereby restoring him to his pre-tort position. It is irrelevant that the market value of the goods may be more than the claimant originally paid for them.[90] Where the destroyed property is business property (for example, machinery), the claimant may also be able to recover any profits lost due to the property's unavailability.[91]

Where the property is not destroyed, but merely damaged, damages are usually measured based on the cost of reasonable repair,[92] but it is irrelevant whether or not the damages are actually used to repair the goods.[93] As with the destruction of goods, if the property was profit-earning, the claimant can recover lost profits, or the cost of

---

84. *H West & Sons v Shephard* [1964] AC 326 (HL).
85. *Moeliker v A Reyrolle & Co Ltd* [1977] 1 All ER 9 (CA) (fishing).
86. *Oakley v Walker* (1977) 121 SJ 619.
87. Judicial Studies Board, *Guidelines for the Assessment of General Damages in Personal Injury Cases* (9th edn, OUP, Oxford, 2008).
88. *Griffiths v Williams*, The Times 24 November 1995 (CA).
89. *Liesbosch Dredger v SS Edison* [1933] AC 449 (HL).
90. *Dominion Mosaics Co Ltd v Trafalgar Trucking Co* [1990] 2 All ER 246 (CA).
91. *Liesbosch Dredger v SS Edison* [1933] AC 449 (HL).
92. *The London Corporation* [1935] P 70 (CA).
93. *The York* [1929] P 78 (CA).

obtaining temporary replacement (for example, rental) of the property. Even if the property is not profit-earning, damages may still be recoverable for loss of use,[94] or for the cost of hiring a substitute.[95] Where the cost of repair is greater than the value of the property in its undamaged state (for example, a car that is a write-off), the courts will award only damages based on the market value of a replacement,[96] unless the property is unique (so that the market value of a replacement is irrelevant).[97]

→ chattel: any property other than land

The above principles relate to chattels. When dealing with non-chattels (that is, buildings and land), the measure of damages is largely the same, but the application of the above principles takes into account the unique features of land. As a general rule, where the claimant intends to continue to use the land or building, damages will be quantified based on the cost of amelioration. Where the claimant does not intend to continue using the land (for example, by selling it), damages will be quantified based on the diminution in the market value of the land.

→ amelioration: the act of improving or making something better

'Pure' economic loss

🔗 The recovery of pure economic loss is discussed at p 397

We have already discussed the courts' reluctance to permit damages to be recovered for 'pure' economic loss. Where economic loss is recoverable, then the court will attempt to put the claimant in the position in which he was before the tort was committed, as the following case demonstrates.

> ### ⚙ *Watts v Morrow* [1991] 1 WLR 1421 (CA)
>
> **FACTS:** The claimants, a husband and wife, purchased a property for £177,500 based on the strength of a surveyor's report completed by the defendant. The claimants required the property to be reasonably trouble-free and the report indicated that the defects in the house could be easily repaired by routine maintenance. Upon purchasing the house, the claimants discovered that the property contained a number of substantial defects. The cost of repair was £33,961. At first instance, the judge awarded the cost of repair, along with an additional amount of £4,000 each for distress caused. The surveyor appealed the quantum of damages.
>
> **HELD:** The Court of Appeal allowed the appeal. The trial judge's quantification of damages did not achieve the restoration of the claimant's position, but put the claimants in the position in which they would have been had the tort not been committed. The correct measure of damages was the difference between the price paid for the property and its true value. Accordingly, damages were reduced to £15,000 and the damages for distress caused were reduced to £750 each.

★ See E Macdonald, 'Negligent Valuations and Lost Opportunities' (1992) 142 NLJ 632

Injunctions

🔗 On the rules relating to the granting of injunction in contract cases, see p 357

When we discussed remedies in contract, we noted that damages would not always adequately compensate the claimant for his loss and that the granting of an injunction might be a more suitable remedy. The same is true of tortious cases—especially

94. *The Mediana* [1900] AC 113 (HL).
95. *HL Motorworks (Willesden) Ltd v Alwahbi* [1977] RTR 276 (CA).
96. *Darbishire v Warran* [1963] 1 WLR 1067 (CA).
97. *O'Grady v Westminster Scaffolding Ltd* [1962] 2 Lloyd's Rep 238 (QB).

cases involving the tort of nuisance. Many of the rules regarding the equitable and discretionary nature of injunctions that we discussed in relation to contractual cases will apply equally in cases involving torts. Here, we will simply note the types of injunction that tend to be granted in cases involving torts.

🔗 Nuisance is discussed at p 475

- **Quia timet** *injunction*   Normally, injunctions are granted after a tort has been committed, with the aim of preventing repeated commissions of the tort—but in rare cases, the court may grant an injunction where no tort has yet been committed. In order for the court to grant a *quia timet* injunction, it will need to be satisfied that the damage is almost certain to occur[98] and will occur imminently.[99]

➡ *quia timet:* 'because he fears'

- *Interim injunction*   Formerly known as 'interlocutory' injunctions, these are granted where a tort may have been committed. They are temporary only and are imposed in order to restrain the continuance of an act the validity of which is to be determined by the court. If the court then decides that the act in question is tortious, it may replace the temporary interim injunction with a permanent final injunction. A common use of interim injunctions is where a newspaper is to publish an allegedly defamatory statement. The court can issue an interim injunction restraining publication until it can determine whether the statement is defamatory or not.

- *Final injunction*   As noted when we discussed injunctions in contractual cases, an injunction may be prohibitory (requiring the defendant to refrain from committing a tort), or mandatory (requiring the defendant to take positive steps to rectify the negative effects of his tort).

Self-help

In certain cases, the courts have recognized the claimant's right to remedy the tort himself. This will usually involve the commission of an act that, were it not classified as self-help, would probably constitute a tort. For this reason, individuals exercising self-help do so at their own peril and the courts are generally reluctant to permit unestablished self-help remedies to succeed.

Despite this, the following are examples of instances in which the court will normally, if reluctantly, permit self-help.

- The victim of a nuisance may attempt to **abate** it.[100]

➡ abate: lessen, reduce, or remove

- A victim of false imprisonment may attempt to escape.

- A chattel that has caused damage to the claimant's land may be seized until the owner of the chattel has paid compensation for the damage caused (known as 'distress damage feasant').

- A trespasser may be repelled or ousted using reasonable force.[101]

- Where the defendant has wrongfully taken the claimant's goods, or has wrongfully detained the claimant's spouse, child, or employee, the goods, spouse, child, or employee may be peacefully reclaimed by the claimant (known as 'recaption').[102]

---

98. *Attorney General v Nottingham Corporation* [1904] 1 Ch 673 (Ch).
99. *Lemos v Kennedy Leigh Developments* (1961) 105 SJ 178 (CA).
100. *Lemmon v Webb* [1895] AC 1 (HL).
101. *McPhail v Persons, Names Unknown* [1973] Ch 447 (CA).
102. *Blades v Higgs* (1865) 11 HL Cas 621.

Key points summary

- In tort, the general aim of compensatory damages is to put the claimant in the position in which he was before the tort was committed.

- Although damages are normally compensatory, certain damages (for example, contemptuous and exemplary damages) also take into account the claimant's conduct.

- In personal injury cases, damages will be pecuniary (loss of earnings, medical expenses) or non-pecuniary (pain and suffering, loss of amenity).

- Where the defendant's tort destroys the claimant's chattel, damages will be based on the market value of the chattel. Where the chattel is merely damaged, damages are usually based on the cost of repair.

- Injunctions may be granted before a tort is committed (*quia timet* injunction), but are usually granted after a tort has taken place (interim and final injunctions).

- In certain cases, the claimant may be able to remedy the tort himself by exercising a self-help remedy.

Chapter conclusion

It is vital that parties involved in commercial dealings understand not only what types of activity are tortious, but also what defences can render such acts lawful. It may be the case that a business needs to engage in an act that, in the absence of a defence, would constitute a tort. In such a case, knowing the nature and extent of a defence is extremely important if liability and the payment of compensation are to be avoided. A business that suffers loss due to another's tort will also need to be aware, before it commences legal proceedings, of whether or not the tortfeasor has a potential defence. As we have seen, certain defences are complete and will fully exonerate the defendant, thereby rendering him free of any liability. Other defences are only partial, serving merely to reduce the damages that he will be required to pay.

If the defendant is unable to raise a defence successfully, the claimant will be entitled to a remedy. Usually, this will be an award of damages that is designed to compensate him for his loss. But unlike in contract, the damages may go beyond what is required to compensate the claimant and may be designed to punish the defendant. Further, damages in tort may have to compensate the claimant for damage that may last the rest of his life. Indeed, the tort may actually serve to reduce severely the life expectancy of the claimant. For this reason, an award of damages in tort can be very different from an award of damages for breach of contract. Where damages are not sufficient, the court may be prepared to impose an injunction. Finally, the claimant may not need to rely on the court for a remedy at all, because certain torts permit the claimant to obtain his own remedy.

This chapter marks the conclusion of our analysis of the system of tort in England and Wales. Having examined legal topics that can affect businesses, we now move onto examine those legal topics that aim to define what businesses are and how they are run—namely, partnership law and company law.

Self-test questions

1. Define the following legal words and phrases:
    (a) *volenti non fit injuria*;
    (b) *ex turpi causa non oritur actio*;
    (c) contributory negligence;
    (d) latent damage;
    (e) multiplicand;
    (f) multiplier;
    (g) *quia timet* injunction.

2. Matthew is the getaway driver for an armed robbery. Whilst driving away from the bank, Matthew's car is involved in an accident with another vehicle, being driven by Katie. Although Matthew was driving quickly, the accident was the result of Katie's negligent driving. Matthew and his fellow criminals sustain severe injuries. Discuss the imposition of liability and the availability of any defences.

3. Explain the differences between the defences of contributory negligence and the voluntary assumption of risk.

4. Define and explain the differences between the following types of damages. Which types are compensatory and which are not?
    (a) Contemptuous.
    (b) Nominal.
    (c) Aggravated.
    (d) Exemplary.
    (e) General.
    (f) Special.

5. How do damages in tort differ from damages in contract?

6. Les is injured due to the negligence of his employer. Based on the following facts, calculate the amount of damages to which Les would be entitled. Where damages cannot be quantified precisely (because you do not have all of the facts), indicate what additional heads of damages can be recovered.
    (a) One of Les' arms has to be amputated and he loses the sight in one eye. The injury that caused him to lose the use of the eye also caused visible scarring on Les' face. This results in Les' wife leaving him.
    (b) Les is unable to work for two years. He worked as a barrister and earned around £65,000 per year. When he returns to work, his injuries mean that he is only able to work part-time (he works around a third of the hours he used to). Les plans to retire in eight years' time.
    (c) As a result of the accident, Les will require medical care for the next ten years. This medical treatment can be extremely painful. The cost of this treatment is estimated at £6,000 per year.
    (d) At the time of the accident, Les was holding his laptop. The accident caused the laptop to become damaged beyond repair. At the time of the accident, the laptop cost around £1,500, but, at the date of the trial, the same model laptop could be purchased for £700.

Further reading

Bartlett, A, 'Attribution of Contributory Negligence: Agents, Company Directors and Fraudsters' (1998) 114 LQR 460
Discusses the extent to which contributorily negligent acts of directors, agents, or other professionals can be attributed to the companies for which they work

Beever, A, 'The Structure of Aggravated and Exemplary Damages' (2003) OJLS 97
Discusses the distinctions between aggravated and exemplary damages; argues that exemplary damages are inconsistent with the goals of civil liability and should be abolished

Deakin, S, Johnston, A, and Markesinis, B, *Markesinis & Deakin's Tort Law* (6th edn, OUP, Oxford, 2008) ch 24
Provides a clear, yet detailed, discussion of all of the defences discussed in this chapter, including several defences not discussed, such as necessity and 'acts of God'

Jaffey, AJE, *'Volenti non fit injuria'* [1985] CLJ 87
Provides an indepth discussion of whether or not an agreement is needed in order to establish volenti; argues that such an agreement is necessary, and provides several methods of establishing such an agreement

Judicial Studies Board, *Guidelines for the Assessment of General Damages in Personal Injury Cases* (8th edn, OUP, Oxford, 2006)
Sets out the tariffs for the quantification of general damages in personal injury cases

Law Commission, *The Illegality Defence in Tort: A Consultation Paper* (Law Com CP No 160, HMSO, London, 2001)
Examines the defence of illegality and provides suggestions for possible reform; like all Law Commission papers, the discussion of the law is very clear and readable

Murphy, J, *Street on Torts* (12th edn, OUP, Oxford, 2007) chs 26 and 27
Examines the various remedies available; provides an accessible account of the complex principles relating to the quantification of damages

 Remember to visit the **Online Resource Centre** at <http://www.oxfordtextbooks.co.uk/roach> to access the following resources on Chapter 15, 'Tortious defences and remedies': more **practice questions** and answers; a **glossary** of key terms; **multiple-choice questions**; **revision summaries**; and **audio updates** when relevant.

PART IV

partnership law and company law

16 Unincorporated business structures

- Sole proprietorship
- Partnership

INTRODUCTION

This chapter is the first of seven chapters that aims to discuss the law relating to the various structures through which business can be conducted and how they are regulated. In these chapters, the formation, regulation, and dissolution of businesses will be discussed in depth. Before the regulation of businesses can be discussed, it is important to have a thorough understanding of the various business structures available.

An individual who wishes to engage in some form of business activity will need to do so via some form of business structure. Such structures can provide the proposed business with a number of significant advantages. Whereas some countries allow for the creation of dozens of forms of business structure, businesses in England and Wales conduct business through one of four principal business structures:

- the sole proprietorship;
- the partnership;
- the limited liability partnership (LLP); and
- the company.

Two of these structures (the LLP and the company) are created via a process called 'incorporation'. This process and these incorporated business structures are discussed in detail in the next chapter. This chapter will focus only on the two unincorporated structures—namely, sole proprietorship and partnership.

Sole proprietorship

The simplest and most popular method of carrying on business is sole proprietorship. At the beginning of 2007, there were an estimated 3 million sole proprietors in the UK.[1] A sole proprietor is normally defined as a single person carrying on some form of business activity. But this definition can be slightly misleading in that, whilst

---

1. Department for Business, Enterprise and Regulatory Reform, *Enterprise Directorate: Small and Medium Enterprise Statistics for the UK and Regions* (BERR, London, 2007), available online at <http://stats.berr.gov.uk>.

a sole proprietorship will be created by a single person and will be run largely for the benefit of that person, sole proprietors are completely free to take on employees.[2] The key point to note is that the business is not incorporated, nor does the sole proprietor undertake business activity in partnership with anyone else.

Sole proprietorships come in two forms:

- where the sole proprietor is a professional (for example, solicitor, accountant, etc.), then he will be known as a 'sole practitioner';
- where the sole proprietor is not a professional, then he will be known as a 'sole trader'. Although it is common to refer to all single person businesses as sole traders, sole practitioners are not actually sole traders.

🔗 The concept of 'legal persons' is discussed at p 600

Unlike companies and limited liability partnerships, there is no separation between a sole proprietor and his business, and sole proprietorships are not legal persons. Therefore, the sole proprietor owns all of the assets of the business and is also entitled to all of the profits that the business generates.

Formation

Setting up business as a sole proprietor is extremely simple and involves much less formality than creating a company. All that an individual need do to commence business as a sole proprietor is register[3] himself with HM Revenue and Customs (HMRC) as self-employed. Failure to register within three months of commencing business is punishable by a £100 fine. Once the turnover of the sole proprietorship reaches £68,000, the sole proprietor will need to register his business for value-added tax (VAT). Being self-employed, sole proprietors are required to complete their own tax returns. They should therefore ensure that they keep clear and accurate records of all sales and purchases, so that the process of self-assessment can be completed quickly and easily.

The name of the business

One of the few areas in which a sole proprietorship can be subject to stringent regulation is in relation to its name. The Business Names Act 1985 imposed a number of restrictions on what names could and could not be used, the provisions of which have been fully transplanted into the Companies Act 2006, which repeals the Business Names Act 1985. It is important to note that the restrictions contained in the 2006 Act only apply where the sole proprietorship has a 'business name'. A business name is a name other than the surname (including forenames or initials) of the sole proprietor.[4] For example, the Act will not apply where a name of the business is simply the name of the sole proprietor (for example, 'Smith', or 'J Smith', or 'John Smith'). But if the business were to be called 'Smith's Construction', then the name would be a business name and the Act would apply. It should be noted that these restrictions apply not only to sole proprietorships, but also to partnerships, limited liability partnerships, and companies.[5]

---

2. Around 316,000 sole proprietorships (10.6 per cent of the total) have employees.
3. A copy of the registration form can be found online at <http://www.hmrc.gov.uk/forms/cwf1.pdf>.
4. Companies Act 2006, s 1192(2)(a).
5. Ibid, s 1192(1).

Examples of the restrictions include the following.

- A name cannot be used if, in the opinion of the Secretary of State,[6] its use would be illegal or offensive.[7]

- The use of certain words may constitute a criminal offence, unless permission is obtained from the relevant body (for example, it is an offence for businesses to use the name 'credit union' without obtaining permission from the Financial Services Authority).[8]

- Use of a name that is identical, or deliberately similar, to the name of another business may constitute the tort of passing off.

- The Act gives the Secretary of State the power to specify what letters, characters, signs, symbols, or punctuation may be used in a business' name.[9] For example, the business' name cannot be longer than 160 characters, including spaces.[10]

The tort of passing off is discussed at p 465

Finance

In terms of raising enough finance to start a business, sole proprietors are at a disadvantage compared with other business structures. A partnership can raise finance by admitting new partners; a company (especially public companies) can raise finance by selling shares. Neither of these options is available to a sole proprietor who wishes for his business to remain a sole proprietorship. A sole proprietor will either need to invest his own money into the business, or obtain a loan. Given that many sole proprietorships are small affairs, banks are cautious when lending to sole proprietors and obtaining large sums of debt capital is usually impossible.

➡ debt capital: capital raised through borrowing

Liability

The principal disadvantage of carrying on business as a sole proprietorship is that the liability of the sole proprietor is personal and unlimited. Whereas both partnerships and companies can be limited, it is impossible to create a limited sole proprietorship. All of the assets (including private assets, such as the sole proprietor's house, car, and bank accounts) belonging to the sole proprietor can be seized and sold in order to satisfy the debts of the sole proprietorship. Further, if the sole proprietor attempts to prevent assets from being seized by transferring them to another person, the court can set aside the transfer and order that the assets be returned to the sole proprietor.

Dissolution

The dissolution of a sole proprietorship may be imposed upon the sole proprietor via certain court orders (for example, an administration order). Should a sole proprietor voluntarily decide to bring the sole proprietorship to an end, this can be

---

6. In relation to business matters, the relevant Secretary of State is usually the Secretary of State for Business, Enterprise and Regulatory Reform. (BERR replaced the Department of Trade and Industry in 2007.)

7. Companies Act 2006, s 53(1).   8. Credit Union Act 1979, s 3.

9. Companies Act 2006, s 57(1).

10. Company and Business Names (Miscellaneous Provisions) Regulations 2009, SI 2009/1085, reg 2(4).

achieved very easily. The first step is simply to cease acquiring any new business. Once this is done, the sole proprietor can then begin to tie up any loose ends, such as collecting any debts owed, paying the businesses' creditors, laying off employees, etc. Once this is done, any money left over belongs to the sole proprietor. Unless the sole proprietor is intending to form another sole proprietorship, he should inform HMRC that he is no longer self-employed. Of course, the sole proprietor is perfectly free to sell the business as a going concern to another person instead of dissolving it.

➡ going concern: a business that those who run it believe will continue in operational existence for the foreseeable future

---

‹› Key points summary

- A sole proprietorship is a non-incorporated business created by a single person. If the person is a professional, he will be a sole practitioner; if he is otherwise, he will be a sole trader.

- If the sole proprietorship is to have a business name, it will need to comply with the naming requirements imposed by the Companies Act 2006.

- A sole proprietor may keep the profits generated by the sole proprietorship, but he is also personally liable for the business' debts and this liability is unlimited.

- A sole proprietorship may be dissolved by the court or may be dissolved voluntarily simply by ceasing business. Alternatively, the sole proprietorship may be sold as a going concern.

Partnership

A group of persons who wish to carry on business together cannot do so as a sole proprietorship for obvious reasons. For such persons, a partnership may be a more appropriate business structure. At the beginning of 2007, there were an estimated 507,000 partnerships operating in the UK.[11]

Partnerships come in one of three forms, as follows.

- *Unlimited partnerships*   The vast majority of partnerships are unlimited partnerships (that is, as with sole proprietorships, the partners are personally liable for the debts of the business).

- *Limited partnerships*   Created under the Limited Partnerships Act 1907, these permit the partners to limit their liability to the amount contributed.

- *Limited liability partnerships (LLPs)*   Although LLPs are technically partnerships, they are formed through incorporation and have more in common with companies than with standard partnerships. Accordingly, they are discussed in the next chapter.

🔗 Limited partnerships are discussed at p 561

🔗 Limited liability partnerships are discussed at p 619

---

11. Department for Business, Enterprise and Regulatory Reform, *Enterprise Directorate: Small and Medium Enterprise Statistics for the UK and Regions* (BERR, London, 2007), available online at <http://stats.berr.gov.uk>.

What is a 'partnership?'

The Partnership Act 1890 (PA 1890), s 1(1), provides the following definition of partnership:

> Partnership is the relation which subsists between persons carrying on a business in common with a view of profit.

Although this definition is short and apparently straightforward, it contains a number of words and phrases that have proven deceptively complicated to define in practice. The definition contained in the 1890 Act therefore needs to be broken down into its constituent parts.

'The relation which subsists'

The PA 1890, s 1(1), makes clear that a partnership is based upon the relationship between the partners. This is a key difference between a partnership and a company. Whereas the creation of a company requires permission from the State (for example, acceptance of registration, enactment of an Act of Parliament, or the granting of a royal charter), a partnership is created simply by the agreement between the partners. There is no requirement that this agreement take any particular form: it may be written, oral, or implied through conduct. But to avoid disputes, it is common that the agreement be in writing. The basis of the partnership agreement is in contract, and the majority of partnership agreements are usually executed by deed and will contain written terms setting out the terms under which the partnership is to be run, with the 1890 Act providing a number of implied terms that can be varied or excluded by the partnership agreement.

The various methods of forming a company are discussed at p 590

The terms implied under the Partnership Act 1890 are discussed at p 564

Defining a partnership as a form of contractual relationship makes clear that a partnership (unlike a company) does not have a separate legal personality[12] and therefore cannot acquire rights or incur obligations in its own name, nor can it own assets. Further, a partner cannot be an agent for his firm, because this would require the firm to act as principal and this would also require separate personality. But the language used by partnerships and the 1890 Act does not reinforce this. It is common for the name of a partnership to end with the suffix '& Co', but use of this phrase has no legal significance (unlike the use of 'plc' and 'Ltd' in a company's name). Further, the 1890 Act provides that persons who have entered into a partnership are collectively called a 'firm'.[13] As a result of this potential confusion, the Law Commission has argued that defining a partnership as a 'relation' is 'out of touch with ordinary usage'[14] and that the word 'relation' should be replaced with the phrase 'voluntary association'.[15] This recommendation has not, however, been acted upon.

---

12. Unlike in Scotland, where a partnership is 'a legal person distinct from the partners of whom it is composed': see PA 1890, s 4(2).

13. Partnership Act 1890, s 4(1).

14. Law Commission, *Partnership Law: A Joint Consultation Paper* (Law Com CP No 159, HMSO, London, 2000) [5.14].

15. Ibid, [5.16].

'Between persons'

Under the PA 1890, s 1(1), a partnership is a relationship that exists 'between persons'. The use of the word 'persons' is important for two reasons:

- it indicates that a single person cannot establish a partnership; and
- it indicates that a partnership can consist of both natural and legal persons. Therefore, a natural person is free to enter into partnership with a legal person, such as a company.

The concept of a company being a person at law is discussed at p 600

The only limitation on the ability of natural and legal persons to enter into a partnership is their capacity to contract. Because the partnership relationship is one of contract, all partners must have the requisite contractual capacity. We have already discussed contractual capacity in a previous chapter, and noted that special rules apply to minors and mentally unsound persons. Where a minor enters into a partnership agreement, it is voidable at the minor's insistence during his minority, or for a reasonable time after attaining the age of majority.[16] A person of unsound mind who enters into a partnership and subsequently seeks to avoid the agreement, can do so only if, in addition to proving his mental incapacity, he can show that his partners knew, at the time that he entered into the partnership, that he was of such unsound mind as not to be capable of understanding what he was doing. As long as a person of unsound mind is a partner, he incurs liability on the partnership's contracts and for its debts, unless the person seeking to enforce a contract or debt knew of his incapacity at the time of its creation.

The rules relating to contractual capacity are discussed at p 137

The contractual capacity of a company may also be limited via restrictions contained in the company's constitution. Such restrictions may limit the company's ability to become a partner. A company's contractual capacity is discussed in the next chapter.

The contractual capacity of a company is discussed at p 615

'Carrying on'

The 1890 Act, s 1(1), requires the persons to be 'carrying on a business'. The use of the phrase 'carrying on' would appear to imply that some form of continuous activity is required, thereby prohibiting the creation of a partnership for a one-off transaction. The courts, however, have not sought to limit the creation of partnerships in this manner and have held that a partnership may be formed for a one-off transaction.[17] But where a partnership agreement is entered into on such a basis, the partnership will exist only in relation to that one transaction.[18]

Does a 'contemplated partnership' (that is, an agreement to carry on business in the future) constitute 'carrying on' business for the purposes of the Act? Provided that some form of business activity is being undertaken, a partnership will be created, even though it has yet to start trading. The court will, however, require a certain level of activity to exist and this will be a question of fact in each case.

---

16. *Goode v Harrison* (1821) 5 B & Ald 147.   17. *George Hall & Sons v Platt* [1954] TR 331.
18. *Mann v D'Arcy* [1968] 1 WLR 893 (Ch).

Khan v Miah [2000] 1 WLR 1232 (HL)

FACTS: The claimant agreed to finance the opening of an Indian restaurant that would be run by the defendant. A joint bank account was opened and a bank loan was obtained (in both transactions, the parties were described as 'partners'). Premises were leased, building work was undertaken, and equipment was purchased. Finally, an advertisement was placed in the local press. Before the restaurant opened, the parties fell out and their agreement ended. In order to determine the dispersal of assets and capital, the Court had to determine whether or not a partnership had been formed. The trial judge held that a partnership did exist. The Court of Appeal held that no partnership existed, because the business was not in operation.

HELD: The House of Lords reversed the decision of the Court of Appeal and held that a partnership had existed. Lord Millett stated:

> There is no rule of law that the parties to a joint venture do not become partners until actual trading commences....The question is not whether the restaurant had commenced trading, but whether the parties had done enough to be found to have commenced the joint enterprise in which they had agreed to engage.[19]

Given the level of activity undertaken, the House of Lords confirmed the trial judge's decision. But Lord Millett did make clear that a mere agreement to become a partner would be insufficient, as is merely describing oneself as a partner to a third party. There must be clear evidence that the parties have 'embarked upon the venture' and this will be a question of fact in each case.

★ See T Vollans, 'Partnership Defined?' (2001) 6 Cov LJ 93

Accordingly, parties who wish to form a partnership may do so before it actually starts trading. In contract, where the parties intend to form a company, their activities as promoters prior to the company's formation will not result in the creation of a partnership.

Keith Spicer Ltd v Mansell [1970] 1 WLR 333 (CA)

FACTS: Two individuals, Mansell (the defendant) and Bishop, agreed to form a company, which would run Mansell's restaurant. Prior to the company's formation, Bishop ordered £147 worth of goods from the claimant, which would be used by the newly formed company. The goods were never paid for. Recovering the £147 from Bishop would be impossible, because he had become insolvent. Therefore, the claimant brought an action against Mansell, alleging that Mansell and Bishop were in partnership (thereby making Mansell liable for Bishop's debts).

HELD: The Court of Appeal held that no partnership existed. Mansell and Bishop were not carrying on a business in line with the 1890 Act; they were merely working together to form a company.

---

19. *Khan v Miah* [2000] 1 WLR 1232 (HL) 2127, 2128.

'A business'

Section 1(1) of the PA 1890 requires that the partnership must be carrying on 'a business' and the 1890 Act defines 'business' to include 'every trade, occupation or profession'.[20] This does not, however, prevent the rules of a particular profession or trade prohibiting its members to practise or operate in a partnership. For example, the barristers' Code of Conduct forbids them from forming partnerships.[21]

'In common'

The mere fact that a business is carried on jointly with a view to profit is not in itself enough to make it a partnership. In order for persons to be carrying on business as a partnership, they must be carrying on business 'in common'. Factors relevant in determining whether persons are carrying on business 'in common' include:

- that any profits of the business earned, or any of its losses, accrue to them. Thus, executors carrying on the business of a testator in accordance with his will were held not be acting 'in common', because any benefits passed to the testator's estate;[22]
- that the concern is being carried on by, or on behalf of, all of them. A person may be carrying on a business in common despite taking no active role in running the business (for example, a sleeping partner)—but this is not always the case (for example, a supplier of goods who is paid with a share in the firm's profits will not be acting 'in common' with the firm's partners);[23]
- a person who does not participate in or have any control over the business is unlikely to be acting 'in common'.

Several of these factors were evidenced in the following case.

 Saywell v Pope [1979] STC 824 (Ch)

FACTS: From 1960 to 1972, Mr Saywell and Mr Prentice were partners in a firm that repaired machinery. Their wives were employed by the firm and carried out minor roles, for which they received a small salary. In 1973, the firm acquired a lucrative contract from Fiat and, in April 1973, a new partnership agreement was drawn up, which stated that Mr and Mrs Saywell, and Mr and Mrs Prentice, had gone into partnership. The wives never contributed any capital to the firm and never received a share of the firm's profits. Although their role increased, they played no role in its management. The partnership agreement was not, however, signed until 1975. The question was whether between 1973 and 1975, the wives should be taxed as employees of the firm or as partners. The Inland Revenue contended that the wives only became partners in 1975.

HELD: The High Court held that the wives did not become partners until 1975. Although the agreement provided that the wives were partners from April 1973 onwards, the reality of the situation did not reflect this. Between 1973 and 1975, the wives did not exercise any managerial powers, nor did they share in the firm's profits (although profits were credited to them, they did not draw upon them). Accordingly, they had not acted 'in common' with their husbands.

---

20. PA 1890, s 45.
21. Barristers' Code of Conduct 2004, r 403.1, available online at <http://www.barstandardsboard.org.uk>.
22. *Re Fisher & Sons* [1912] 2 KB 491 (KB).
23. *Strathearn Gordon Associates Ltd v Commissioners of Customs and Excise* [1985] VATTR 79.

'With a view to profit'

The final requirement of the PA 1890, s 1(1), is that the business be carried on 'with a view to profit'. A business in which no financial return is anticipated will not constitute a partnership: unlike companies, partnerships cannot be formed for altruistic or benevolent purposes. It used to be the case that the entitlement to a share in the firm's profits was enough to establish the existence of a partnership.[24] This is no longer the case, with s 2(3) of the 1890 Act indicating that receipt of a share in the profits is merely prima facie evidence that a person is a partner.

The fact that a profit is not actually made does not mean that the business is not a partnership; rather, what is required is that the parties *intended* to make a profit. It has been argued that the wording of the 1890 Act does not require persons actually to receive a share in the profits to be partners, provided that they intended that a profit be made. Historically, the courts have not favoured this argument and have held that not only is a profit motive required, but also that the partners should receive a share of the profits.[25] It will be remembered that, in *Saywell v Pope* (discussed above), the wives never drew on the profits to which they were entitled and therefore did not receive a share of the profits. In the following case, however, the Court of Appeal has (for the time being) settled the issue and held that an individual may be a partner even though he does not receive a share of the profits.

 M Young Legal Associates Ltd v Zahid (A Firm) [2006] EWCA Civ 613

FACTS: Bashir (one of the defendants) wished to set up a firm of solicitors. He had, however, only been qualified for two years and the Solicitors' Practice Rules required that every firm have a supervisory solicitor who has been qualified for three years or more.[26] He therefore asked an experienced solicitor, Lees (another defendant), to act as the supervisory solicitor. The parties agreed that Lees would not receive a share of the profits, but would instead be paid a fixed annual salary of around £18,000. The firm of solicitors began practising as 'Zahid Solicitors' (another defendant) in 2002. The claimant was a claims-handling company that alleged, in 2003, that it was owed money by Zahid Solicitors, but in 2004, Zahid Solicitors was dissolved. The claimant therefore sought to recover the money owed from Bashir and Lees. Lees argued that, because he did not share in the profits of the firm, he was not a partner and so not liable for the firm's debts.

HELD: The Court of Appeal held that Lees was a partner. There was nothing in s 1(1) of the 1890 Act that indicated that partners should share in the profits of the firm, and the partners could therefore remunerate themselves in any way they deemed fit.

COMMENT: As we shall see later, when we discuss the various types of partner, there has been an element of doubt as to whether salaried partners are actually partners at all. This case confirms that they are and states clearly that such partners will be exposed to the same liability as general partners, irrespective of how they are paid.

★ See P Breakey, 'Fair Share' (2006) 156 NLJ 1195

---

24. *Waugh v Carver* (1793) B Bl 235.   25. *Pooley v Driver* (1877) 5 Ch D 458 (CA).
26. Solicitors Practice Rules 1990, r 13.2. This rule can now be found in the Solicitor's Code of Conduct 2007, r 5.02(2)(b).

Types of partner

A partnership may have several different types of partner, with each type having different rights and responsibilities. The rights and responsibilities of each type of partner will be discussed shortly, but, first, it is important that the distinction between partners and employees is understood.

Around 37 per cent of partnerships take on employees,[27] but the distinction between a partner and an employee is not always straightforward. Partnership and employment are mutually exclusive: it is impossible to be a partner of the firm and its employee. It is vital to distinguish between the partners of the firm and its employees because:

- the partners are usually entitled to the profits of the firm, whereas the employees are not—but the employees are not liable for the firm's debts in the way that the partners are;

🔗 Employment rights are discussed in Chapter 24

- employees are granted a substantial number of rights by statute (for example, the right not to be unfairly dismissed, the right to receive redundancy pay). Such rights are not granted to partners.

🔗 Unfair dismissal and redundancy are discussed in Chapter 26

There is no standard test to determine whether or not a person is a partner or an employee, although certain factors (for example, the right to share in the firm's profits)[28] may constitute prima facie evidence that a person is a partner; rather, each case must be decided on its facts.

The following case provides an example of the sort of facts that can blur the dividing line between a partner and an employee.

🔑 *E Rennison & Son v Minister of Social Security* (1970) 10 KIR 65 (QB)

FACTS: A firm of solicitors terminated the employment contracts of a group of employees and formed new contracts, whereby the dismissed persons were regarded as self-employed and could work for other firms if they so chose. The dismissed employees entered into an agreement, which was described as a 'deed of partnership'. The agreement provided that the partnership business (that is, under the deed just referred to) would be carried on at the solicitors' offices, and that the profits and losses would be divided among the partners. Subsequently, the firm of solicitors agreed to pay the partnership a weekly sum based on the same hourly rate of work as their previous contracts of employment. The issue arose as to whether the solicitors firm had to pay National Insurance contributions—that is, whether the dismissed persons were partners (under the deed of partnership referred to above) or employees of the solicitors firm.

HELD: The High Court held that they were employees of the solicitors firm. Each person had an individual contract of service that was identical to the previous contract. That they were described as partners in the deed of partnership was irrelevant, because they were, in reality, still employees.

---

27. The exact figure is 36.8 per cent: see Department for Business, Enterprise and Regulatory Reform, *Enterprise Directorate: Small and Medium Enterprise Statistics for the UK and Regions* (BERR, London, 2007), available online at <http://stats.berr.gov.uk>.
28. PA 1890, s 2(3).

Having established the importance of the distinction between partners and employees, we can now discuss the different forms of partner that exist. It is perfectly permissible and increasingly common for a single firm to have several different types of partner.

General partners

Those partners who do not fall within the specialist types of partner discussed in subsequent sections (and few do) are known simply as 'partners', or 'general partners'. The rights of general partners are set out in the Partnership Act 1890, s 24, which provides for, inter alia, a right to be involved in the management of the firm and the right to an equal share in the profits of the firm. But these rights are subject to the partnership agreement, so it is perfectly permissible, for example, for a partner's right to manage the firm to be limited in some way.

General partners are not required by law to contribute capital to the firm, but are required to contribute equally to the debts and liabilities of the firm.[29] A partner will not be liable for debts that arose before he became a partner,[30] however, unless he chooses to accept responsibility for them.

Sleeping partners

Sleeping partners (also known as 'dormant partners') are not mentioned anywhere in the 1890 Act. The term has arisen to describe those partners who contribute capital to the firm (although this may not be the case), but currently play no part in the firm's management. Because the Act does not overtly recognize sleeping partners, they will have the same liabilities as general partners.

Limited partners

The Limited Partnerships Act 1907 provides for the ability to form limited partnerships, the partners of which are not subject to the unlimited levels of liability to which general and sleeping partners are subject. Limited partnerships are extremely rare, largely because limited liability is more readily obtainable by forming a limited liability partnership, or by incorporating the business. By 2008, there were only 10,142 limited partnerships registered in England and Wales.[31]

Limited liability partnerships are discussed at p 619

Limited partnerships can consist of any number of limited partners, but there must be at least one general partner, whose liability will be unlimited.[32] Unlike standard partnerships, limited partnerships are not formed via the partnership agreement, but, like companies, are formed by registering specified documents to the Registrar of Companies. The registration document (known as a 'Form LP5') consists of a statement indicating that the firm is to be a limited partnership, and provides the details of the firm and its partners. Until such registration is accepted, the firm will remain a standard partnership and its partners will be general partners.[33] Upon successful

---

29. PA 1890, s 24(1).
30. Ibid, s 17(1).
31. Companies House, *Statistical Tables on Companies Registration Activities 2007–08* (HMSO, London, 2008) 23, available online at <http://www.companieshouse.gov.uk>.
32. Limited Partnerships Act 1907, s 4(2).
33. Ibid, s 5.

registration, a limited partnership will be formed and the limited partners will be liable only for the capital that they have already contributed.

Provided that a limited partner complies with the 1907 Act, his liability will remain limited. But failure to comply with the Act will result in the limited partner becoming a general partner with unlimited liability. In practice, failure to comply with the Act occurs in two ways.

1. Limited partners are not permitted to take part in the management of the firm, nor do they have the power to bind the firm.[34] A limited partner who does take part in management will be liable for the debts and liabilities of the firm as if he were a general partner.

2. The registration documents will state how much capital each limited partner must contribute. A limited partner who has not contributed this amount (for example, by guaranteeing to pay this amount in the future) will be regarded as a general partner.[35]

Salaried partners

The growth of professional partnerships (for example, solicitors firms, accountancy firms, etc.) has been accompanied by an increase in the number of salaried partners. The typical salaried partner is a relatively young person who does not wish, or cannot afford, to contribute capital to the firm in the way that a general partner does. Instead, he will be represented as a partner (for example, his name will appear on the list of partners) and he may have some of the normal powers of a partner (for example, the power to bind the firm), but he will be paid a salary instead of receiving a share of the firm's profits (although it is possible for a salaried partner to receive a bonus based on the amount of profit).

For a considerable period of time, the law has struggled to state precisely the legal position of salaried partners, especially in relation to the extent of their liability. Because such persons do not contribute capital to the firm or receive a share of the profits, are they actually partners, or are they more accurately described as employees? The distinction is crucial, because partners have unlimited liability, whereas employees are in no way liable for the debts of the firm.

The courts' approach to determining the liability of a salaried partner was laid down in the following case.

Stekel v Ellice [1973] 1 WLR 191 (Ch)

FACTS: The defendant (Ellice) was a partner in an accountancy firm of two partners. The other partner died. The defendant therefore took on the claimant (Stekel) as a salaried partner in October 1968. The agreement was to last until April 1969, at which point, a new agreement would be made wherein the claimant would become a general partner. The temporary agreement also provided that the defendant would provide all of the capital and would be entitled to the profits of the firm. The claimant's name appeared on the list of partners on the firm's letters and he acted as a partner within the firm. In April 1969, the

---

34. Ibid, s 6(1).   35. *Rayner & Co v Rhodes* (1926) 24 Ll L Rep 25 (KB).

claimant had not been made into a general partner and no new agreement was made. The temporary agreement continued, but by August 1970, the two parties had fallen out and separated. The claimant sought to dissolve the firm and contended that he was merely an employee. The defendant argued that the claimant was a partner and that the partnership agreement only provided him with the right of dissolution in specified events, none of which had occurred in this case.

HELD: In the High Court, Megarry J stated that: 'It seems to me impossible to say that as a matter of law a salaried partner is or is not necessarily a partner in the true sense. He may or may not be a partner, depending on the facts.'[36] This would depend upon the substance of the relationship, as opposed to the label that the parties attached to it. On the facts, the claimant was held to be a partner. Aside from the capital requirements, the claimant acted and appeared to outsiders as a partner. Therefore, he could not dissolve the company, because he was bound by the original partnership agreement.

Stekel, along with *M Young Legal Associates* discussed earlier, places salaried partners in a somewhat precarious position. Both cases indicate that the fact that a person does not share in the profits does not prevent him being classified as a partner. In such a case, the salaried partner does not reap the full benefits of being a partner, but may be liable to the full extent of the law for the debts and liabilities of the partnership. Perhaps for this reason, more recent cases have tended to lean towards salaried partners being classified as employees.[37] Even so, salaried partners wishing to avoid unlimited liability should take steps to indicate that they are not general partners (for example, omitting their name from the firm's letterhead and describing themselves as a 'salaried partner').

 Key points summary

- A partnership is 'the relation which subsists between persons carrying on a business in common with a view of profit'.

- There are three types of partnership:

  - general partnerships (known simply as partnerships);
  - limited partnerships; and
  - limited liability partnerships (discussed in Chapter 17).

- General partnerships do not have separate personality and their partners do not have limited liability. Their liability is unlimited.

- All partnerships must have a partnership agreement, but it need not be in writing. The partnership agreement forms a contract between the partners. The partnership agreement can be altered with the consent of the all of the partners, and this consent can be express or inferred.

---

36. *Stekel v Ellice* [1973] 1 WLR 191 (Ch) 199.
37. See, e.g., *Casson Beckman & Partners v Papi* [1991] BCC 68 (CA); *Nationwide Building Society v Lewis* [1998] Ch 482 (CA).

- A partnership can be formed between natural and legal persons.

- Partnerships must be carried on with a view to a profit. Partnerships cannot be formed for altruistic or philanthropic purposes.

- Partners are not employees and are not entitled to protection under employment legislation.

- There are several types of partner:

  - general partners (simply known as partners);
  - sleeping (or dormant) partners;
  - limited partners; and
  - salaried partners.

The relationship between the partners

The partnership agreement is a contract unlike most others, and imposes duties and obligations upon the partners that can have a significant impact on the relationship between them. In addition to these duties, the PA 1890 implies additional rights and duties into the partnership agreement that aim to regulate the relationship between the partners.

Implied terms

Most partners would do well to have in place, before the partnership begins conducting business, a written and comprehensive partnership agreement that clearly sets out the rights and obligations of the partners. But where such an agreement does not exist, the 1890 Act implies a number of fundamental rights and obligations into whatever agreement does exist. Further, even where a written agreement does exist, the implied terms will continue to apply, except where they are inconsistent with the agreement. Section 24 implies nine terms into the partnership agreement (with s 25 implying a tenth term), which can broadly be divided into two categories:

- implied terms relating to the financial affairs of the firm; and
- implied terms relating to the management and composition of the firm.

Table 16.1 sets out the nine implied terms based on these two categories.

An examination of all ten terms will not be undertaken here. Instead, the principal implied terms will be discussed. The first term examined is contained in s 24(1), and provides that all of the partners will share equally in the capital and profits of the firm, and will also share equally in the losses of the firm. This applies even where the partners have not contributed equal amounts of capital. If a partner is to receive more capital or profit than his fellow partners, or if he is to bear less of the firm's losses, the partnership agreement must provide for this.[38] It is common for partnership agreements to provide that the capital or profits received by the partners will be proportional to the capital that they contribute, or that partners who contribute less capital will contribute less to the firm's losses. The Law Commission recommended

---

38. *Popat v Schonchhatra* [1997] 1 WLR 1367 (CA).

TABLE 16.1 Terms implied into the partnership agreement

Implied terms relating to the financial affairs of the firm	<ul><li>Right to equal share in the profits and capital of the firm</li><li>Right to an indemnity</li><li>Right to interest payments for advances made</li><li>No right to interest on capital prior to ascertainment of profits</li><li>Right to inspect and copy the firm's books</li></ul>
Implied terms relating to management and the composition of the firm	<ul><li>Right to take part in management</li><li>No right to remuneration</li><li>No person may be introduced as a partner without the consent of all of the other partners</li><li>A change in the nature of the partnership business requires the consent of all of the partners</li><li>Differences relating to ordinary matters may be decided by majority</li><li>The majority cannot expel a partner unless an express power to do so has been agreed on by all of the partners</li></ul>

that, in relation to capital, the presumption regarding equal return of capital be abolished,[39] but this recommendation has yet to be accepted.

Section 24(2) implies a term providing that partners are to be indemnified by the firm for any payments made or personal liabilities incurred:

- in the ordinary conduct of the business; or
- in or about anything necessarily done for the preservation of the business or property of the firm.

This is a consequence of the partners' joint and several liability for the firm's debts. Where one partner pays out money in the ordinary conduct of the firm, or pays off a debt of the firm, it is only proper that the firm indemnify him. The same is true in relation to payments made, or liabilities incurred, in preserving the firm's survival.

Perhaps the most crucial implied term can be found in s 24(5), which simply provides that every partner may[40] take part in the management of the firm. As noted above, when we discussed what constitutes a partnership, partners are persons carrying on business 'in common'. A consequence of this is that all partners should have a right to manage the firm, because they all have a common interest in it. A partner who is denied the right to participate in the management of the firm may be able to dissolve the firm on 'just and equitable grounds'. Whilst the partners may have a right to manage the firm, s 24(6) states that the partners do not have a right to be remunerated (receive a salary) for acting in the partnership business. This is because the partners will be rewarded via the distribution of profits. The increasing prevalence of salaried partners in recent years demonstrates that these implied terms are default rules only and can be ousted by an express contrary provision in the agreement. But in order to displace s 24(6), clear evidence must be provided. The mere fact that one or several partners perform all of the work is not enough to entitle them to any more than an equal share in the profits.

---

39. Law Commission, *Partnership Law* (Law Com No 283, Cm 6015, HMSO, London, 2003) [10.23].

40. Note that s 24(5) states 'may', and not 'should' or 'must'. Partners are not required to take part in management and, as we have seen, sleeping partners have long been recognized.

Section 24(7) provides that no new partners may be admitted to the firm without the consent of all of the other partners. This is a sensible requirement. The admission of a new general partner will dilute the share of the profits received by the other partners. Further, because the partners are liable for each other's acts, they will be keen to ensure that new partners are not going to impose severe financial burdens in the future. Given the potential liabilities, it would be unfair to permit the majority of partners to impose a new partner on the minority. But unanimity will not be required if the partnership agreement provides that one or more partners may introduce a new partner.

Section 24(8) provides that where the partners are in disagreement in relation to *ordinary* matters connected with the firm's business, the view of the majority will prevail. Where the disagreement concerns the nature of the firm's business (for example, alteration of the agreement), unanimity will be required. In practice, distinguishing between ordinary matters and matters that change the nature of the firm's business may not always be clear.

There is one additional implied term that is not contained in s 24, but is found in s 25. The implied terms in s 24 can be excluded or modified expressly or impliedly; conversely, the term contained in s 25 can only be excluded by an express agreement between the partners. Section 25 provides that '[n]o majority of the partners can expel any partner unless a power to do so has been conferred by express agreement between the partners'. Where a partnership agreement does contain an expulsion clause, this will not necessarily validate the expulsion.

The courts will consider three factors, as follows.

1. Was the expulsion covered by the clause? If the answer is 'no', the expulsion will be invalid. Thus, where an expulsion clause provided for expulsion upon the commission of fraud, the expulsion of a partner for repeated acts of adultery was invalid.[41]

2. Has the expelled partner been informed of the reason for the expulsion and had the opportunity to defend himself? The extent of this requirement is unclear. In one case, the court held that failure to inform the expelled partner of the reason for his expulsion would render the expulsion unlawful.[42] But in a later case, in which a partner was expelled for flagrant and repeated breaches of the partnership agreement, the court held that failure to inform him of the reason for expulsion did not invalidate the expulsion.[43] It has been argued that the latter case was not a true expulsion case, but a dissolution case (as we shall see, repeated breaches of the partnership agreement constitute grounds for dissolution), and that the general principle is that an expulsion will be unlawful where reasons for expulsion are not provided.[44]

3. Did the partners conducting the expulsion act in good faith? If they did not, the expulsion will be invalid. Thus, where the partners used an expulsion clause to obtain a partner's share in the firm at a discount, the expulsion was deemed invalid.[45]

---

41. *Snow v Milford* (1868) 18 LT 142.   42. *Barnes v Young* [1898] 1 Ch 414 (Ch).

43. *Green v Howell* [1910] 1 Ch 495 (CA).

44. B Davies, 'The Good Faith Principle and the Expulsion Clause in Partnership Law' (1969) 33 Conv NS 32.

45. *Blisset v Daniel* (1853) 10 Hare 493.

Alteration of the partnership agreement

Whilst the 1890 Act may imply a number of terms into partnership agreements, it may be the case that the partners wish to exclude these terms by express provision, or that they need to alter the original agreement. The ability to alter the partnership agreement is contained in s 19, which provides that the agreement may be altered by the consent of all of the partners and that such consent can be express or inferred from the partner's conduct.

An example of such inferred consent is provided below.

Eg **Inferred alteration of the partnership agreement**

Johnson & Sons is a partnership consisting of twenty-five partners. The agreement provides that only one of the partners, Louis, may enter into negotiations with outside parties and that only Louis has the power to bind the firm contractually. The firm becomes very profitable and Louis cannot meet with all of the parties who wish to transact with the firm. Accordingly, it becomes common practice for Bill, another partner, also to take part in negotiations and to enter into contracts on the firm's behalf. The other partners accept this practice and the firm thrives. In such a case, the court is likely to hold that it can be inferred from the actions of the partners that they wished the agreement to be altered to allow Bill to bind the firm in the same manner as Louis. Therefore, unanimous acquiescence to an alteration may operate as inferred consent to that alteration.

Utmost good faith

In Chapter 8, it was noted that certain types of contract (for example, insurance contracts) are branded of the utmost good faith (*uberrimae fidei*). Partnership agreements constitute a contract of the utmost good faith, the result of which is to impose a number of fiduciary duties upon the partners, irrespective of whether such duties are contained in the partnership agreement or not.

The 1890 Act itself provides for three such duties:

- the duty to render accounts;
- the duty to account for private profits; and
- the duty to account for profits made whilst competing with the firm.

The first duty is contained in s 28 and states that partners[46] are 'bound to render true accounts and full information of all things affecting the partnership to any partner or his legal representatives'. The duty imposed is a strict one, which means that an innocent failure to disclose will suffice; breach of duty is not dependent upon the presence of fraud or negligence.

The following case demonstrates the potential consequences of breaching the duty.

---

46. This duty applies not only to partners, but also to parties negotiating the partnership agreement: see *Conlon v Simms* [2006] EWCA Civ 1749, [2008] 1 WLR 484.

Law v Law [1905] 1 Ch 140 (CA)

FACTS: The four Law brothers carried on business as a partnership, based in Halifax. Two of the brothers died. One of the remaining brothers (the claimant) lived in London and took little part in the running of the business. The other brother (the defendant) offered to purchase the claimant's share in the business for £21,000, to which the claimant agreed. The claimant subsequently discovered that the firm had assets worth around £80,000 that the defendant had failed to disclose. The claimant initiated an action, contending that the purchase for £21,000 was voidable on the ground of non-disclosure.

HELD: The Court of Appeal held that the contract between the claimant and defendant was voidable at the claimant's option. The defendant was under a duty to disclose the true value of the firm and had breached that duty in concealing the true value of the firm's assets.

The second duty imposed by the Act could be regarded as a mere extension of the duty to account. Section 29(1) states that:

> Every partner must account to the firm for any benefit derived by him without the consent of the other partners from any transaction concerning the partnership, or from any use by him of the partnership property name or business connexion.

The obvious example of a breach of s 29(1) would be where a partner acts on behalf of a partnership, and in doing so, obtains some form of secret profit.

 Bentley v Craven (1853) 18 Beav 75

FACTS: Four individuals had formed a partnership refining sugar in Southampton. The defendant acted as the firm's buyer and was able to obtain sugar at a discounted price. Instead of purchasing the sugar on behalf of the firm at the discounted rate, on several occasions and unbeknownst to the other partners, he personally purchased the sugar at the discounted rate and then sold it to the firm at wholesale price, making a profit on each occasion. When the partners discovered this, one of them brought a claim against the defendant for the profit made.

HELD: The defendant was ordered to account to the firm for the profit made. It was irrelevant that, without the defendant, the firm would have to pay the wholesale price. All that mattered was the defendant had made a personal and secret profit from a transaction involving the partnership.

In many of the cases involving s 29(1), the profit is made through the use of some asset belonging to the partnership. In *Bentley* above, the defendant had used an asset of the partnership—namely, his position as the firm's buyer—to make an unauthorized profit. Where a partner uses a partnership asset to make a personal profit, the requirement to account for that profit is uncontroversial. But where the asset in question is information, the issue is more complex. The question is whether a partner is

liable to account for a profit made whilst engaged in an activity that has no connection to his firm, but which arose due to information obtained whilst acting as a
partner (that is, whether the profit derives from the partner's use of the partnership's
business connection for the purposes of s 29).

In the following case, the Court stated that the partner did not need to account
for such profit.

 Aas v Benham [1891] 2 Ch 244 (CA)

FACTS: The defendant was a partner in a firm of shipbrokers. He was involved in setting
up a shipbuilding company, and used information and experience gained whist acting as
a partner for his firm of shipbrokers. He was paid a fee for his assistance and was made a
director of the board of the new company. The partners of his firm sought to recover the
fee paid and the salary paid for acting as director.

HELD: The Court of Appeal stated that the defendant could keep the profit made. The
information used by the partner was employed in a venture outside the scope of the firm.
The key determinant was the use of the information, not from where it derived.

The decision in *Aas* was doubted (but not overruled) in cases involving other
types of fiduciary—namely, solicitors[47] and company directors.[48] In these cases, the
House of Lords held that the defendant had to account for the profit obtained by use
of information derived as a fiduciary even though the acts of the defendant had not,
in any way, deprived the other party of a benefit. These cases have been criticized
for being unduly harsh, but they cast significant doubt upon the extent to which *Aas*
can be relied upon as a general principle.

The third and final duty contain in the 1890 Act can be found in s 30, which states
that:

> If a partner, without the consent of the other partners, carries on any business of
> the same nature as and competing with that of the firm, he must account for and
> pay over to the firm all profits made by him in that business.

Clearly, a partner engaged in competition with his firm will not be acting in good
faith and there would be a substantial conflict of interest. There is a considerable
overlap between ss 29(1) and 30, and, very often, cases may involve an alleged breach
of both duties.[49] There is, however, a clear distinction between the two duties. Breach
of the duty in s 29(1) is dependent upon a profit being made through use of an asset
belonging to the partnership, but there is no need to establish that the profit was
made whilst in competition with the firm. Conversely, s 30 is not dependent upon
use of a partnership asset, but does require that the profit be made whilst engaged in
competition with the firm.[50]

---

47. *Boardman v Phipps* [1967] 2 AC 46 (HL).
48. *Regal (Hastings) Ltd v Gulliver* [1967] 2 AC 134 (HL).
49. See, e.g., *Trimble v Goldberg* (1906) 95 LTR 163 (PC).
50. *Rochwerg v Truster* (2002) 212 DLR (4th) 498 (Ontario Court of Appeal).

Partnership property

Because partnerships do not have separate personality, it follows that they cannot own property in the way that a company and a limited liability partnership can. The 1890 Act does refer to 'partnership property',[51] but this does not refer to property belonging to the partnership. An express agreement may exist stating what amounts to partnership property, but where such an agreement does not exist, the PA 1890, s 20(1), provides three ways in which property becomes partnership property:

- where property is originally brought into the partnership stock, by purchase or otherwise, on account of the firm (that is, using the firm's money),[52] it shall be called partnership property;
- where property is acquired, by purchase or otherwise, on account of the firm, it shall be called partnership property;
- property acquired for the purposes and in the course of partnership business shall be called partnership property. It is not enough that property is merely used by the firm; it must be essential to the viability of the firm, as the following case demonstrates.

 Miles v Clarke **[1953] 1 WLR 537 (Ch)**

FACTS: The defendant wished to establish a firm of photographers. He leased premises for such a purpose, and purchased furniture and photographic equipment. Because the defendant was not a photographer, he entered into partnership with the claimant, an experienced freelance photographer. It was agreed that the two partners were entitled to an equal share of the profits and that the claimant could draw £125 per month as his share of the profits. The claimant was able to attract a considerable amount of custom to the firm and it prospered. But the two partners fell out and the firm was wound up. The claimant brought an action claiming a share in all of the assets of the firm. The defendant alleged that certain items of property were not partnership property.

HELD: The lease of the premises, the furniture, and the equipment purchased were not regarded as partnership property, but the property of the defendant. Accordingly, the High Court held that the claimant was not entitled to a share of these assets. Items merely used by the firm should not be regarded as partnership property, unless regarding them as such is essential to the business efficacy of the firm.

In practice, it can be difficult to distinguish between partnership property and property that belongs to individual partners (for example, where a partner uses personal property for the purposes of the firm), but the distinction must be made for several reasons. Table 16.2 clarifies the practical importance of the distinction.

In interpreting s 20(1), the courts have indicated that they will not be bound by a literal interpretation that serves to defeat the commercial intentions of the parties. Instead, the courts have adopted a more purposive approach that emphasizes the commercial realities of a situation, as the following case demonstrates.

---

51. Partnership Act 1890, s 20.   52. Ibid, s 21.

TABLE 16.2 Distinguishing between partnership property and the property of individual partners

	Partnership property	Property belonging to a partner
Use of property	Must be used exclusively for the purposes of the firm and in accordance with the partnership agreement	Can be used for whatever lawful purposes the partner deems fit
Change in value of the property	The change in value belongs to the partnership (i.e. all of the partners)	The change in value belongs to the individual partner
Availability of property to creditors	Available to the partnership's creditors upon insolvency	Not available to the partnership's creditors, but is available to the individual partner's creditors
Sale upon dissolution	Upon dissolution, partners can insist on sale of partnership property and are entitled to the proceeds of sale	Can only be sold by the individual partner, who is entitled to the proceeds of sale

Don King Productions Inc v Warren [2000] Ch 291 (CA)

FACTS: The defendant (Frank Warren) was a boxing manager and promoter, focusing primarily on boxers based in the UK. The claimant (Don King) was a boxing promoter, focusing on boxers based in the USA. Their respective companies formed a partnership, and the defendant purported to assign to the partnership his management and promotion agreements with boxers. But the agreements could not be assigned, because they were contracts of personal service and/or contained non-assignment clauses. A second agreement was therefore entered into, which provided that the partners should hold all promotion agreements for the benefit of the partnership. The defendant entered into a multi-fight deal that would benefit only himself, which caused the parties to fall out and the partnership to be dissolved. The claimant claimed a share in the property of the partnership. The defendant contended that the management and promotion agreements did not constitute partnership property, because they were not validly assigned to the firm. As such, the claimant was not entitled to a share in them.

HELD: The Court of Appeal rejected the defendant's argument and held that the non-assignable contracts constituted partnership property. The Court affirmed Lightman J's first-instance judgment, in which he stated that the task of the court is to determine 'the commercial purpose which the businessman and entities...must as a matter of business common sense have intended to achieve'[53] and that 'the Court may have to require what may appear to be errors or inadequacies in the choice of language to yield to that intention'.[54]

★ See R Azim-Khan, 'Contract: Boxing' (1999) 10 Ent LR N66

---

53. *Don King Productions Inc v Warren* [1998] 2 Lloyd's Rep 176 (Ch) 176, 177.
54. Ibid, 177.

Duty of care

Because the liability of the partners is joint, the acts of one partner can result in liability being imposed upon all of the partners.[55] Where one partner causes the other partners to become liable to a third party through some act of wrongdoing (for example, negligence), can that partner be liable to the other partners? In other words, do partners owe a duty of care to each other? There is little doubt that the answer is 'yes', but the exact nature of this duty of care is unclear and there is little English law on the subject. What authority (English or otherwise) does exist leans towards the standard of the duty of care being an objective one (that is, the standard is that of a 'reasonable businessmen in the situation',[56] or that the partner must exercise 'reasonable care in all the relevant circumstances').[57] But there is no definitive judgment of a higher court indicating the exact scope of the duty of care and, until there is, the position will remain unclear. Placing the duties of care owed by partners on a statutory footing (as has happened in the case of company directors) would have provided much clarity in this area, but the Law Commission has recommended that the duties of care owed by partners to each other should not be placed in statute.[58]

🔗 The general duties of company directors are discussed in Chapter 20

Dissolution

Later in the chapter, the situations in which a partnership can be dissolved will be discussed. Here, the effects of dissolution amongst the partners themselves will be examined. Certain events capable of causing the firm's dissolution (for example, the death or bankruptcy of a partner) may not, in fact, cause the business to end. Where this is the case, the firm will need to account for the departing partner. This will normally involve valuing the partner's assets and paying the appropriate sum to the departing partner or his estate.

Where the firm is dissolved, the debts of the partnership must be paid. The partners are entitled to sell the partnership property and to use the proceeds to pay off the firm's debts.[59] Valuing and selling the physical assets of the firm (for example, equipment, plant, and vehicles) is straightforward, but other assets of the firm are more complex—notably, the firm's 'goodwill'.

Goodwill is likely to be one of the firm's major assets, although it will never show up in the firm's accounts. The concept of goodwill was defined by Lord Macnaghten as 'the reputation and connection of the firm, which may have been built up by years of honest work or gained by lavish expenditure of money'.[60] In more modern terms, it is usually defined as 'the difference between the value of the business as a going concern and the value of its assets'.[61] These definitions indicate that valuing the goodwill of a firm is a highly complex and specialized issue.

---

55. PA 1890, s 12.
56. *Winsor v Schroeder* (1979) 129 NLJ 103.
57. *Ross Harper & Murphy v Banks* 2000 SC 500 (OT) 510 (Lord Hamilton).
58. Law Commission, *Partnership Law* (Law Com No 283, Cm 6015, HMSO, London, 2003) [11.56].
59. PA 1890, s 39.
60. *Trego v Hunt* [1896] AC 7 (HL) 24.
61. G Morse, *Partnership Law* (6th edn, OUP, Oxford, 2006) 223.

In summary, the effect of a sale of goodwill is that:

- only the buyer may represent himself as continuing or succeeding to the seller's business;[62]
- the buyer has the exclusive right to use the former partnership's name, although the seller is free to set up a similar business in competition with the rival[63] (unless the seller covenanted not to do so in the contract of sale);
- the seller may advertise his new business, but he may not solicit or canvass the customers of the former partnership.[64]

When goodwill is sold, covenants are usually entered into that set out the rights of the seller and buyer after the sale. This is a wise precaution, especially from the point of view of the buyer, because the seller may be tempted to usurp or recover in some way the goodwill that he has sold.

Once the assets of the partnership have been realized, there must occur a final account, which will consist of a record of all transactions from the date of the last account up to the date of the dissolution. Once this final account has been made, the proceeds realized by the sale of the firm's assets can be distributed. The partnership agreement may state how the proceeds are to be distributed, but in the absence of such an agreement, s 44 (and decided case law) provides as follows.

1. The losses, including losses and deficiencies of capital, of the partnership must be paid, first, out of the firm's profits and, once the profits are gone, out of the firm's capital. If this fails to meet the firm's losses, the remainder is borne by the partners in proportion to their profit-share entitlement. If a partner is unable to pay his contribution towards to the partnership's losses, the other partners must pay his contribution between them in the same proportion as profits were divided.[65]

2. The assets of the partnership (including any contributions by partners to make up losses or deficiencies of capital) must be applied in the following manner and order.

   (a) Outside creditors are to be paid first.

   (b) The assets should be used to pay back any partners who made loans to the firm.

   (c) The costs of the dissolution are paid.[66]

   (d) Each partner is repaid the capital contribution that he made.

   (e) Any remaining assets are divided amongst the partners in proportion to the division of profits.

The dissolution of the firm can also result in several other consequences, including:

- any partner may give public notice of the firm's dissolution, and can require the other partners to join him in so doing;[67]
- once the firm is dissolved, the authority of each partner to bind the firm continues, but only in so far as to complete transactions begun, but unfinished, at the time of the dissolution;[68]

---

62. *Churton v Douglas* (1859) 28 LJ Ch 841.
64. *Curl Bros Ltd v Webster* [1904] 1 Ch 685 (Ch).
66. *Potter v Jackson* (1880) LR 13 Ch D 845 (Ch).
68. Ibid, s 38.

63. *Trego v Hunt* [1896] AC 7 (HL).
65. *Garner v Murray* [1904] 1 Ch 57 (Ch).
67. PA 1890, s 37.

- a partner may pay a premium in order to join a partnership. Such a sum will not constitute a contribution to partnership capital, but may instead be thought of as a 'joining fee'.[69] If the partnership is dissolved, the court may order that this premium (or some part of it as the court deem fit) can be recovered, but only if the partnership is for a fixed term, or it has been prematurely dissolved for reasons other than the death of a partner. The premium cannot be recovered where the dissolution was wholly or chiefly due to the misconduct of the partner who paid the premium, or where the partnership was dissolved by an agreement containing no provision for a return of any part of the premium.[70]

The relationship between partners and third parties

The PA 1890, ss 5–18, regulate the relationship between the partners and third parties. This will most obviously include the extent to which the partners can contractually bind the firm and the other partners to a third party, but it also lays down rules to establish when the firm and the partners can be liable for the unlawful acts of a single partner that have caused loss to a third party.

Agency

Regarding a partner's ability to bind the partnership and his co-partners, the key provision is s 5, which provides that:

> Every partner is an agent of the firm and his other partners for the purpose of the business of the partnership; and the acts of every partner who does any act for carrying on in the usual way business of the kind carried on by the firm of which he is a member bind the firm and his partners...

Accordingly, each partner is an agent of the firm and of his co-partners. The concept of agency is discussed in detail in Chapter 27, but a brief summary will be helpful here.

An agency relationship is simply a relationship between two parties, whereby one party (known as the 'agent') carries out some task on behalf of another party (known as the 'principal'). The ability of the agent to act on the principal's behalf will be limited by the authority that his principal grants him. The important point to note is that the agent can contractually bind the principal to a third party, provided that the agent acts within his authority.

The following example clarifies how an agency relationship might work.

Eg An agency relationship

Anna (the principal) instructs Jo (the agent) to purchase an item at an upcoming auction. Jo must not bid any more than £10,000 (this constitutes her authority). Jo goes to the auction and obtains the item with a bid of £9,000. Because Jo as acted within her authority, a binding contract exists between Anna and the auction house. If Jo were to have obtained the item with a bid in excess of £10,000, however, she would have breached her authority, and the contract would most likely have been between her and the auction house.

---

69. G Morse, *Partnership Law* (6th edn, OUP, Oxford, 2006) 253.
70. PA 1890, s 40.

Concerning partners, provided that a partner acts within his authority, he is able to bind his firm and his co-partners to a third party. Clearly, the central factor is the partner's authority. An agent's authority is a complex affair and it will not be discussed here.

🔗 The authority of an agent is discussed at p 937

A partner may be able to bind his firm and his co-partners even where he has no authority. Section 5 also provides that a partner cannot bind his firm and his co-partners where 'the partner so acting has in fact no authority to act for the firm in the particular matter, and the person with whom he is dealing either knows that he has no authority, or does not know or believe him to be a partner'. What this is saying is that a partner who has no authority to carry out an act can nevertheless bind the firm and his co-partners provided that:

- the third party is not aware that the partner lacks authority; or
- the third party believed the partner to be a partner of the firm.

Where a third party is aware of the partner's lack of authority, or believes that the partner is not, in fact, a partner, the firm and the co-partners will not be bound. This is reinforced by s 8, which provides:

> If it has been agreed between the partners that any restriction shall be placed on the power of any one or more of them to bind the firm, no act done in contravention of the agreement is binding on the firm with respect to persons having notice of the agreement.

It should be remembered that a partner's ability to bind his firm and co-partners only applies to 'an act for carrying on in the usual way business of the kind carried on by the firm'. This requires us to define:

- an 'act for carrying on in the usual way'; and
- 'business of the kind carried on by the firm'.

In determining whether an act arose 'in the usual way', the courts distinguish between trading and non-trading firms. A trading firm is one the business of which involves the buying and selling of goods.[71] Table 16.3 sets out what acts are within and beyond the scope of the usual authority of trading and non-trading firms.

The courts have held that the phrase 'business of the kind carried on by the firm' should be interpreted in exactly the same way as the phrase 'ordinary course of business', as found in s 10.[72] The interpretation of this phrase is discussed later, but a summary of the courts' approach to s 10 will be of aid. Applying the approach used in s 10, an act will be 'of the kind carried on by the firm' if it is so closely connected to what the partner is authorized to do that, for the purpose of determining the firm's liability, it may fairly be regarded as 'business of the kind carried on by the firm'.

Because each partner has the power to bind his co-partners contractually, it follows that every partner is liable jointly (but not severally) for all debts and obligations of the firm incurred while he is a partner. Partners, however, differ from other joint debtors in that the estate of a deceased partner is severally liable for any of

---

71. *Wheatley v Smithers* [1906] 2 KB 321 (CA).
72. *JJ Coughlan Ltd v Ruparelia* [2003] EWCA Civ 1057, [2004] PNLR 4.

TABLE 16.3 The usual authority of trading and non-trading firms

	Usual authority	No usual authority
Non-trading firm	• To sell partnership property • To purchase goods necessary for the firm's business • To employ and dismiss employees • To accept or indorse cheques • To instigate proceedings on the firm's behalf • To employ an agent	• To borrow money • To pledge partnership property as security • To accept or indorse negotiable instruments (except cheques) • To give a guarantee in the firm's name • To submit a dispute to arbitration • To make an outsider a partner, or to put co-partners into partnership with others
Trading firm	• To sell and pledge partnership property • To purchase goods necessary for the firm's business • To borrow money and pay debts • To employ and dismiss employees • To accept or indorse negotiable instruments • To instigate proceedings on the firm's behalf • To employ an agent	• To give a guarantee in the firm's name • To submit a dispute to arbitration • To make an outsider a partner, or to put co-partners into partnership with others

the firm's debts incurred while the deceased was a partner.[73] These rules have been supplemented by the Civil Liability (Contribution) Act 1978, which provides that the mere fact that one partner has been sued (successfully or not) on a contract does not preclude an action on that contract against another partner.[74] A partner successfully sued on a contract can seek a contribution from his co-partners.[75]

Liability for tortious and other wrongful acts

The above provisions deal with a partner's liability in contract, although the rules of agency are wide enough to cover non-contractual liability. Partners may also be liable in tort or even held guilty of a criminal offence. The PA 1890, s 10, provides that:

> Where, by any wrongful act or omission of any partner acting in the ordinary course of the business of the firm, or with the authority of his co-partners, loss or injury is caused to any person not being a partner in the firm, or any penalty is incurred, the firm is liable therefor to the same extent as the partner so acting or omitting to act.

➡ **vicarious liability:** liability imposed on a person for the acts of another (see Chapter 14)

What s 10 basically states is that the partnership and each partner is vicariously liable in tort for the wrongful acts or omissions of another partner, provided that the partner was acting within his authority, or that the act was done whilst in the ordinary course of the firm's business.

---

73. PA 1890, s 9.   74. Civil Liability (Contribution) Act 1978, s 3.
75. Ibid, s 1.

The following example demonstrates s 10 in operation.

 The operation of the PA 1890, s 10

Price & Young is a firm of accountants consisting of fifty partners. One of the firm's partners, Greg, is conducting a financial audit of KP Coopers Ltd—but he conducts the audit negligently. Under s 10, Price & Young and the other forty-nine partners face liability for Greg's act of negligence.

What constitutes the ordinary course of the firm's business was discussed in detail in the following case.

 Dubai Aluminium Co Ltd v Salaam [2002] UKHL 48

FACTS: Salaam defrauded the claimant company out of US$50 million. Salaam was the client of a law firm and it was alleged that the senior partner of the firm assisted Salaam in defrauding the claimant company by drafting certain documents. This was true, but neither the senior partner, nor any other partners of the firm, received any of the fraudulent proceeds. Were the co-partners liable for the acts of the senior partner? The Court of Appeal said 'no', on the ground that drafting documents in order to assist the commission of a fraud was not in the course of the firm's business.

HELD: The House of Lords reversed the decision and held the co-partners liable. The House held that, provided that the act itself was within the firm's business, it did not matter that it was carried out in an unauthorized or unlawful way. Drafting documents was within the firm's business; the fact the documents were drafted for an unlawful purpose did not take the acts outside the scope of the firm's business. Lord Nicholls stated:

> Drafting these particular agreements is to be regarded as an act done within the ordinary course of the firm's business even though they were drafted for a dishonest purpose. These acts were so closely connected with the acts [the senior partner] was authorised to do that for the purpose of the liability of the [law] firm they may fairly and properly be regarded as done by him while acting in the ordinary course of the firm's business.[76]

COMMENT: Accordingly, whether an act is within the course of the firm's business will depend on the closeness of the connection between the act of wrongdoing and what the partner is authorized to do. This will be a question of fact in each case. Lord Millett stated clearly that s 10 does not apply only to actions in tort, but can also apply to any fault-based common law or statutory wrong.

★ See C Mitchell, 'Partners in Wrongdoing?' (2003) 119 LQR 364

An act will not be within the ordinary course of the firm's business if the partner committed the act in a personal capacity and not as a member of the firm,

---

76. *Dubai Aluminium Co Ltd v Salaam* [2002] UKHL 48, [2003] 2 AC 366, [36].

even if the act itself is one that he is authorized to perform—as can be seen in the following case.

 Chittick v Maxwell (1993) 118 ALR 728

FACTS: The claimant built a house on land belonging to his daughter and son-in-law (the defendant). All of the parties agreed that the claimant would be permitted to live in the house until he died, whereupon it would pass to the defendant and his wife. The defendant, being a solicitor, drew up the agreement, but omitted to protect the claimant's right to possession. The defendant repeatedly mortgaged the land, and, when he failed to repay, the mortgagees obtained a possession order and evicted the claimant. The claimant sued the defendant and his firm for the negligent drafting of the agreement.

HELD: The defendant's firm and his co-partners were not liable. Although drafting agreements of this nature was within the ordinary business of the firm, it was clear that the defendant was engaged in this activity in a personal capacity, not in his capacity as a member of the firm.

An act that is not within the ordinary course of the firm's business may still result in liability under s 10 if it is within the partner's authority.

 Hamlyn v John Houston & Co [1903] 1 KB 81 (CA)

FACTS: The defendant was a firm of grain merchants consisting of two partners. One of the partners obtained confidential information on the claimant (a rival firm) by bribing one of the claimant's employees. The claimant lost money due to the information being divulged and it sued the defendant.

HELD: The Court of Appeal held that obtaining information on rival businesses was a legitimate business aim and within the authority of the partner. The fact that he obtained this information illegitimately was not enough to place it outside the partner's authority.

Liability imposed under s 10 is joint and several, which means that the claimant can sue each partner in turn, or all of the partners at the same time, until he has recovered the full amount of his loss. This differs from liability under s 9, which, as we saw, is joint only, meaning that the claimant has only one cause of action against all of the partners, who are jointly liable for his loss.

Holding out

The PA 1890, s 14(1), which overlaps with s 5 and with normal agency rules, provides that any person who, by words or conduct, represents himself, or knowingly suffers himself to be represented, as a partner in a partnership is liable as if he were a partner to any third party who has 'given credit' (that is, incurred any liability) to the partnership on the faith of that representation.

Section 14(1) applies to a person who is not, and has never been, a partner in a partnership, but it can equally well apply to a former partner. The effect of s 14(1) is that the person held out as being a partner is estopped from denying that he was a partner if that was the impression created, by a representation to that effect, in the mind of the person who relied on that representation in his dealing with the partnership. In order for a third party to rely on s 14(1) and obtain a remedy against the person holding himself out as a partner (X), he will need to establish that:

- a representation was made, indicating that X was a partner. The representation can be made by X or by another person, provided that X is aware that the other person is holding him out as a partner. Whether the representation indicates that X is a partner in an actual firm or a non-existent firm is irrelevant;
- the representation was made to the third party directly, or to another who subsequently repeated it to the third party; and
- the third party acted on the representation by giving credit to the partnership. All that he need establish is that he believed the representation and acted on it; he does not need to show that he would not have given credit had he known the truth.

Section 14(2) applies where a partner dies and the partnership continues under the old firm's name. In such a case, the continued use of that name, or of the deceased partner's name as part thereof, shall not, of itself, make his executors' or administrators' estate or effects liable for any partnership debts contracted after his death.

Liability following a change in the partnership's composition

The composition of a partnership will alter over time: new partners will be admitted to the firm and old partners may leave or retire. So how do these changes in composition affect the liability of the partners? Are new partners liable for acts committed before they joined the firm? Are existing partners liable for acts committed prior to their leaving the firm?

The liability of new partners

Determining the liability of new partners appears straightforward. The PA 1890, s 17(1), provides that '[a] person who is admitted as a partner into an existing firm does not thereby become liable to the creditors of the firm for anything done before he became a partner'. But the situation can be more complex than it appears, as the following example demonstrates.

 The liability of new partners

In November 2009, a firm enters into a contract. In January 2010, Ron becomes a partner of the firm. In March 2010, the firm breaches the contract. Is Ron liable? The contract was entered into before he became a partner, but the breach occurred while he was a partner.

Section 17(1) does not appear to provide an answer to the question of Ron's liability, so the issue has been left to the courts. The issue revolves around the phrase 'anything done before he became a partner'. In Ron's case (above), does 'anything done' refer to the entering of the contract or the breach of contract? Where the contract requires the firm to perform a single continuous act, it would appear that 'anything done' would refer to the contract being entered into[77] and that, accordingly, the new partner will not be liable. Where the contract involves a number of repeated acts, if liability arises following the new partner joining the firm, the phrase 'anything done' would appear to relate to the act of wrongdoing[78] and so the new partner would be liable.

The following example clarifies the distinction.

Eg **Single and repeated acts**

Single continuous act

In January 2009, a firm enters into a contract with a Jo, a solicitor, to recover a debt owed to it. In February 2009, Marc becomes a partner in the firm. In March 2009, the firm indicates that it is not happy with Jo's progress in recovering the debt and terminates the contract without paying her. Jo sues the firm for breach of contract. Because the contract provides for a single continuous act (recovery of the debt), the entering into the contract will constitute 'anything done' under s 17(1). Accordingly, Marc is not liable for the firm's breach of contract.

Repeated acts

In January 2009, a firm enters into a contract to supply consignments of goods to a company based in the USA. The contract provides that the consignments shall be supplied as and when the US firm requests them. In February, several consignments are delivered. In March 2009, Paul becomes a partner of the firm and several more consignments are delivered. In April 2009, more consignments are delivered, but one of them fails to meet the standard specified in the contract. Because the contract provides for repeated acts (supplying goods on request), the delivery of the unsatisfactory goods will constitute 'anything done' under s 17(1). Accordingly, Paul will be liable for the firm's breach.

Liabilities existing on retirement

Consider the following example.

Eg **Liabilities existing on retirement**

A firm enters into a contract to purchase goods. The firm will pay for the goods in twelve monthly instalments. After two months, one of the partners retires from the firm. Is he liable for the remaining payments?

---

77. *Court v Berlin* [1897] 2 QB 396 (CA).   78. *Bagel v Miller* [1903] 2 KB 212 (KB).

The PA 1890, s 17(2), provides that '[a] partner who retires from a firm does not thereby cease to be liable for partnership debts or obligations incurred before his retirement'. But this is a prima facie rule only and the court will apply the same rule as applies to new partners. If the contract requires a single continuous act by the firm, the retiring partner will remain liable. If the contract requires a series of repeated acts by the firm, the partner is only liable for those acts that arose before his retirement. The partner will not, however, be liable to a third party for debts occurring after he retires if the partnership agreement provides that he shall not be liable, or if he enters into an agreement with the other partners and the third party that provides that he shall not be liable.[79]

Liabilities incurred after retirement

The PA 1890, s 36(1), provides that '[w]here a person deals with a firm after a change in its constitution he is entitled to treat all apparent members of the old firm as still being members of the firm until he has notice of the change'. Accordingly, if a retired partner appears to be a partner and a third party has no notice that the partner has retired, the partner will remain liable to that third party. To avoid liability to the third party for any debts that are incurred after retirement, the partner should make the fact of his retirement known to the third party (although an advertisement placed in the *Gazette* will provide notice to persons who have not had dealings with the firm prior to the dissolution or the date of the advertisement).[80] If the third party did not know that the retiring partner was a partner in the first place, the partner will not be liable to the third party for any debts that accrue after his retirement.[81] This will also be the case where the partner leaves the firm through death or bankruptcy.[82]

➡️ *Gazette*: the official newspaper of record for the UK

Dissolution

A partnership can be brought to an end in numerous ways, but whereas the creation of a partnership is a straightforward affair, the dissolution of a partnership can be a lengthy and complex matter. Here, the principal methods and causes of dissolution will be discussed, but, before that, it is worth categorizing the various methods. A partnership can be dissolved:

- as a result of a provision in the partnership agreement;
- as a result of some rule of law; or
- by an order of the court.

Express and implied terms, and dissolution by agreement

Because a partnership agreement is merely a form of contract, many of the rules relating to the termination of contract will apply here. For example, in Chapter 9, we noted that a contract may be simply brought to an end upon the agreement of the parties. This agreement may be express, but it can also be implied through the acts of the partners.

🔗 The law relating to discharge by agreement is discussed at p 296

---

79. PA 1890, s 17(3).   80. Ibid, s 36(2).
81. Ibid, s 36(3).   82. Ibid.

TABLE 16.4 Categories of dissolution

Contractual dissolution	Dissolution by operation of law	Dissolution by court order
• Express terms • Implied terms (could include rules relating to death and bankruptcy) • Mutual agreement of the parties • Rescission • Repudiation	• Illegality • Death or bankruptcy of a partner (could be regarded as implied terms)	• Mental or permanent incapacity • Prejudicial conduct • Wilful or persistent breaches of the partnership agreement • Carrying on the business at a loss • Just and equitable

Alternatively, the partnership agreement itself may contain a number of terms specifying when the partnership will be dissolved (for example, if a partner is convicted of a serious criminal offence,[83] or is found to be committing professional misconduct).[84] The PA 1890 also implies six terms into the agreement that provide for dissolving events.

1. If the partnership is entered into for a fixed term, it will be dissolved at the end of that term, subject to any agreement otherwise by the parties.[85] This could be viewed as discharge by performance.

The law relating to discharge by performance is discussed at p 290

2. If the partnership is for a single adventure or undertaking, it will dissolve once the adventure or undertaking is completed or terminated, subject to any agreement otherwise between the partners.[86] This could also be viewed as discharge by performance.

3. If a partnership agreement is entered into for an undefined period, it can be dissolved by a partner by giving notice to the other partners of his intention to dissolve, subject to any agreement otherwise between the partners[87] (for example, by providing that termination may only occur by mutual agreement).

4. The death of a partner (except a limited partner) will dissolve the partnership, unless the partners agree otherwise.[88] If the partner is a body corporate, its dissolution will be treated as death. Due to the inconvenience caused by the death of a partner, most partnership agreements will provide that, upon the death of a partner, the firm will continue (although, technically, the firm is still dissolved, but is immediately replaced by a new firm).

5. The bankruptcy of a partner will dissolve the partnership, unless the partners agree otherwise.[89]

6. Where a partner, in order to satisfy his private debt, grants a charge over his share of the firm's assets, then the firm can be dissolved at the option of the other partners.[90]

---

83. *Essel v Hayward* (1860) 30 Beav 158.   84. *Clifford v Timms* [1908] AC 112 (HL).

85. PA 1890, s 32(a).   86. Ibid, s 32(b).

87. Ibid, s 32(c). Section 26(1) provides an identical right in cases in which a partnership has no fixed term of duration.

88. Ibid, s 33(1).   89. Ibid.

90. Ibid, s 33(2).

Illegality

The six events discussed above will, by default, result in the dissolution of the partnership. But dissolution can be avoided by excluding the implied terms via an agreement between the partners. What cannot be excluded is that the partnership will be dissolved where it becomes tainted by illegality.[91] Note that this applies to partnerships that are untainted by illegality, but subsequently become tainted: a partnership formed for an illegal purpose will be regarded as void *ab initio* on the ground of illegality.

The effect of illegality on a contract is discussed at p 276

The taint of illegality need not affect all of the partners, as the following case demonstrates.

 Hudgell Yeates & Co v Watson [1978] QB 451 (CA)

FACTS: The partnership in question was a firm of solicitors. The firm consisted of three solicitors, all of whom were partners. One of the solicitors forgot to renew his practising certificate. Without a certificate, the solicitor was not legally entitled to practise.[92]

HELD: The Court of Appeal held that the partnership had become tainted with illegality and was automatically dissolved, even though all three partners were unaware of the illegality.

Rescission

Because the partnership agreement is a contract, it follows that is can be rescinded just like any other contract. For example, if a person is induced to become a partner based upon another person's misrepresentation, this will provide grounds for the rescission of the partnership agreement.

In addition to the right to rescind, the representee also has access to other remedies, as follows.

- If the misrepresentation is fraudulent or negligent, damages can be recovered.
- Once the partnership's liabilities have been met, the representee will acquire a lien over any remaining assets in relation to any capital paid by him.[93]
- The creditors' rights will be subrogated to the representee (that is, the representee will be able to stand in the place of the partnership's creditors for payments made by him in respect of the partnership's liabilities).[94]
- The representee is entitled to be indemnified by the person who committed the fraud or misrepresentation against all of the debts and liabilities of the firm.[95]

➡ lien: the right to hold the property of another until an obligation is satisfied

➡ subrogation: the ability to take on the legal rights of others

Repudiation

One of the partners may breach the partnership agreement to such an extent that the other partners are entitled to terminate it (that is, the breach is repudiatory). Where the non-breaching party accepts the breach, the partnership agreement will

---

91. Ibid, s 34.
93. PA 1890, s 41(a).
95. Ibid, s 41(c).
92. Solicitors Act 1974, s 1(c).
94. Ibid, s 41(b).

be rescinded. But the effect of rescission here is more complex. Whilst repudiation may terminate the partnership agreement, it does not follow that it terminates the partnership itself.

🔑 *Hurst v Bryk* [2002] 1 AC 185 (HL)

FACTS: The firm in question was a solicitors firm comprising twenty partners. The claimant was one of the partners. Eighteen of the partners served retirement notices and gave nine months' notice, as required by the partnership agreement. But before the nine months had expired, all of the partners, except the claimant, entered into an agreement terminating the partnership. The actions of the nineteen other partners (the defendants) amounted to a repudiatory breach of the partnership agreement. The claimant accepted the breach and sought a declaration from the court stating that he was not liable for the liabilities of the partnership that accrued after the date of repudiation, especially the payment of rent on a lease of the partnership.

HELD: The House of Lords refused to make such a declaration. Although the acceptance by the claimant of the repudiatory breach of the other partners discharged all of the partners from further performance of their obligations, it did not operate to divest rights already unconditionally acquired. Therefore, the claimant remained liable for the debts of the partnership and remained liable to contribute upon its winding up.

COMMENT: Whilst this decision might appear odd at first, it does have a powerful justification. As we shall see, wilful or persistent breaches of the partnership agreement can result in dissolution at the discretion of the court. If, in *Hurst*, the claimant's repudiation were automatically to result in the dissolution of the firm, it would strongly undermine the courts' discretion to grant dissolution orders.

The current position therefore is that repudiation of the partnership agreement does not automatically dissolve the partnership itself. This does, however, result in one significant criticism—namely, that upon termination of the partnership agreement, the partnership will become a 'partnership at will'. A partnership at will is simply a partnership that has no fixed duration (which, by definition, a partnership without a partnership agreement must be). The point to note is that one partner serving notice on another may terminate such partnerships immediately.[96] Therefore, following the dissolution of the agreement, the partnership itself can be dissolved by mere notice.

Mental or permanent incapacity

Where a partner lacks mental capacity, the partnership is not automatically dissolved; instead, the other partners can petition the court for an order dissolving the partnership.[97] Such an order is granted entirely at the discretion of the court. The same applies where the partner is rendered in any other way 'permanently incapable of performing his part in the partnership contract'.[98] But it is vital that

---

96. PA 1890, s 26(1).   97. Mental Incapacity Act 2005, ss 16 and 18(1)(e).
98. PA 1890, s 35(b).

the incapacity be permanent. If the possibility exists that the partner's condition will improve (for example, where medical evidence indicates an improvement in the medical condition of a partner who suffered a stroke),[99] the court is unlikely to grant a dissolution order. For this reason, it is common for partnership agreements to contain a term permitting dissolution once a partner has been incapacitated for a specified period.[100]

Prejudicial conduct and wilful, or persistent, breaches of the partnership agreement

Where a partner engages in activity that is 'calculated to prejudicially affect the carrying on of the business', any of the other partners may petition the court for a dissolution order.[101] This could include adverse activities occurring within the firm (for example, a partner misappropriating of the firm's assets),[102] but can also include activity outside the firm (for example, a partner committing a crime).[103] Lawful, but immoral, conduct is unlikely to suffice unless it adversely affects the partnership.[104]

Innocent partners may also petition the court where one partner:

> wilfully or persistently commits a breach of the partnership agreement, or otherwise so conducts himself in matters relating to the partnership business that it is not reasonably practicable for the other partner or partners to carry on the business in partnership with him.[105]

Note that the conduct required will normally need to be of sufficient seriousness, so minor squabbles amongst the partners will not suffice. But minor breaches may warrant dissolution where they are persistent. Thus, in *Cheesman v Price*,[106] one partner had, on seventeen occasions, failed to document properly in the firm's books monies received. Although the amounts of money were small, the persistent nature of the breach warranted dissolution.

Loss-making

As was noted previously, a key requirement of a partnership is that it is carried on with 'a view to a profit'. It follows that where the making of a profit becomes impossible (that is, where the business of the partnership can only be carried on at a loss), the partners may apply to the court for a dissolution order.[107] The partners will, however, need to demonstrate the impossibility of making a profit. Thus, where a firm failed to make a profit because its senior partner was ill, a dissolution

---

99. *Whitwell Arthur* (1863) 35 Beav 140.
100. In *Peyton v Mindham* [1972] 1 WLR 8 (Ch), the partnership agreement provided that the partnership would be dissolved if any partner were to be incapacitated for more than nine consecutive months.
101. PA 1890, s 35(c).
102. *Essel v Hayward* (1860) 30 Beav 158.
103. *Carmichael v Evans* [1904] 1 Ch 486 (Ch) (travelling on the railway whilst intending to avoid paying the fare).
104. *Snow v Milford* (1868) 16 WTR 554 (persistent adultery).
105. PA 1890, s 35(d).
106. (1865) 35 Beav 142.
107. PA 1890, s 35(e).

order was not granted, because the other partners could still operate the firm at a profit.[108]

Just and equitable

🔗 The rules relating to the dissolution of companies on just and equitable grounds are discussed in more detail at p 740

The final ground for a dissolution order is where the court feels that it is 'just and equitable that the partnership be dissolved'.[109] Many of the cases in this area do not concern partnerships, but so-called 'quasi-partnerships'—small, private companies that bear all of the hallmarks of a partnership.[110]

Examples of instances in which the courts have dissolved a business on just and equitable grounds include:

- where the business had reached a deadlock, because the two directors refused to speak to one another;[111]
- where a business was formed on the basis that everyone involved would have a say in managing the business, but one individual was excluded from management;[112]
- where the objects of the firm could not be achieved.[113]

Reform

In November 1997, the Department of Trade and Industry—now the Department for Business, Enterprise and Regulatory Reform (BERR)—requested the Law Commission and the Scottish Law Commission to undertake a joint review of partnership law. A report was published in November 2003,[114] in which the two Commissions recommended that a number of changes be made to the PA 1890 and to the Limited Partnerships Act 1907. In July 2006, the government announced that the reforms of the 1890 Act would not be considered at this time, but that the reforms of the 1907 Act would be implemented. In August 2008, BERR published a consultation document[115] indicating the government's intention to pass a legislative reform order that would repeal the Limited Partnerships Act 1907 and replace its provisions with additions to the Partnership Act 1890. At the same time, a number of minor reforms will be introduced (including a requirement that limited partnerships add the suffix 'LP' to their name), but the Law Commission's recommendation that limited partnerships be granted separate personality will not be implemented.

---

108. *Handyside v Campbell* (1901) 17 TLR 623 (Ch).
109. PA 1890, s 35(f). This is also a ground for winding up a company: see Insolvency Act 1986, s 122(1)(g).
110. In *Re Yenidje Tobacco Co Ltd* [1916] 2 Ch 426 (CA) 432, Cozens-Hardy MR described a quasi-partnership as 'a partnership in the form or the guise of a private company'.
111. Ibid.
112. *Ebrahimi v Westbourne Galleries Ltd* [1973] AC 360 (HL).
113. *Baring v Dix* (1786) 1 Cox Eq Cas 213.
114. Law Commission, *Partnership Law* (Law Com No 283, Cm 6015, HMSO, London, 2003).
115. Department for Business, Enterprise and Regulatory Reform, *Legislative Reform Order to Repeal and Replace the Limited Partnerships Act 1907* (BERR, London, 2008).

Key points summary

- The Partnership Act 1890 implies a number of terms into the partnership contract, but these terms can be varied or excluded by the agreement itself.

- The partnership agreement constitutes a contract of utmost good faith, and imposes duties on the partners not to compete with the firm and to account for any secret profits made.

- The partners are agents of the firm and of each other, meaning that each partner can bind the firm and his co-partners, provided that he acts within his authority. Partners can also be vicariously liable for the wrongful acts of their co-partners.

- A person who is not a partner may be held liable as if he were a partner if he held himself out as being a partner.

- Partnerships can be dissolved due to an express contractual provision, by the operation of law, or by court order.

Chapter conclusion

An individual who wishes to commence business, but wishes to avoid complex formation procedures and extensive regulation, will be well served by conducting business as a sole proprietor. He will retain full control over the activities of the business and will be entitled to all of the profits. But he will also be solely liable for the business' debts to an unlimited amount. Similar benefits are available to those who conduct business through a partnership. Partnerships are easy to set up and subject to much less regulation than companies or limited liability partnerships—but the liability of the partners is joint and unlimited, and ending a partnership is much more complex than ending a sole proprietorship. For those persons who wish to avoid unlimited liability, it is possible to set up business as a limited partnership, but limited partners are not permitted to manage the firm. Accordingly, for many persons wishing to set up business, the disadvantages of unincorporated structures outweigh the advantages. For such persons, setting up business through a body corporate will be a much more advantageous proposition.

Self-test questions

1. Define the following:
    (a) sole proprietorship;
    (b) sole practitioner;
    (c) sole trader;
    (d) partnership;
    (e) *uberrimae fidei*;
    (f) partnership property;
    (g) holding out.

2. Jeff has an idea for a new business. His friend, Ryan, offers to help Jeff set up business. Jeff is unsure whether to commence business on his own, or to enter into partnership with Ryan. Advise Jeff on the advantages and disadvantages of conducting business as a sole proprietor and through a partnership.

3. Explain the distinction between: (i) a general partner; (ii) a sleeping partner; (iii) a limited partner; and (iv) a salaried partner.

4. Discuss the following.

   (a) In May 2009, Card & Co, a firm of solicitors, undertakes to recover a debt for Vincent. In July 2009, Shane becomes a partner of the firm. In November 2009, Vincent informs Card & Co that it will be impossible to recover the debt, because the debtor has become insolvent. Had the firm acted more quickly, Vincent might have been able to recover the money owed. Vincent alleges that the firm has been negligent and commences proceedings. Does Shane face any liability?

   (b) Tom and Dave are partners in a firm that has a number of female employees. Tom sexually harasses one of these females and she commences legal proceedings. To what extent is Dave liable for Tom's act?

   (c) Helen is a partner in a firm of accountants. Her sister, Emma, asks her if she would audit her company's accounts as a personal favour. Helen conducts the audit using her firm's premises and staff, but does not charge Emma a fee. The audit is negligently conducted and Emma sues Helen's firm. Are the firm and Helen's co-partners liable?

5. Richard has been a partner in a trading firm for over forty years. He is due to retire next month and is keen to ensure that, upon his retirement, he does not share in the liabilities of the firm. Advise him of his legal position and what steps should be taken to ensure that his liability as a partner will end upon his retirement.

6. Explain the three broad categories by which a firm can be dissolved and give examples from each category.

Further reading

Department for Business, Enterprise and Regulatory Reform, *Legislative Reform Order to Repeal and Replace the Limited Partnerships Act 1907* (BERR, London, 2008)
A consultation document proposing that the Limited Partnerships Act 1907 be repealed and the provisions relating to limited partnerships be inserted into the Partnership Act 1890

Law Commission, *Partnership Law* (Law Com No 283, Cm 6015, HMSO, London, 2003)
As with all Law Commission reports, the current law is stated clearly and with impressive depth; good criticism of current law and suggestions for reform

Morse, G, *Partnership Law* (6th edn, OUP, Oxford, 2006)
A popular, accessible, and well-structured account of the law and practicalities relating to partnerships

Websites

<http://stats.berr.gov.uk>
Provides extensive statistics on the number of sole proprietors and partnerships in the UK; also provides data on their composition

<http://www.companieshouse.gov.uk>
The official website of Companies House; provides useful statistical data relating to the number of limited partnerships

Remember to visit the **Online Resource Centre** at **<http://www. oxfordtextbooks.co.uk/roach>** to access the following resources on Chapter 16, 'Unincorporated business structures': more **practice questions** and answers; a **glossary** of key terms; **multiple-choice questions**; **revision summaries**; and **audio updates** when relevant.

17 Incorporation and bodies corporate

- Methods of incorporation
- Types of registered company
- The advantages and disadvantages of incorporation
- Corporate personality and 'lifting the veil'
- The constitution of a company
- Limited liability partnerships

INTRODUCTION

In the previous chapter, we discussed the advantages and disadvantages of conducting business through an unincorporated structure, such as a sole proprietorship or a partnership. We noted that such associations, whilst extremely suitable for certain forms of business, contain several inherent disadvantages—namely, unlimited liability—that will render them unsuitable or undesirable for other forms of business. Where this is the case, conducting business through a body corporate will be more suitable. Bodies corporate come in two forms:

- companies;[1] and
- limited liability partnerships (LLPs).[2]

Such business entities are known as 'bodies corporate' because they are bodies created via the process of incorporation and have corporate personality. In this chapter, we will examine both of these bodies corporate, and the various advantages and disadvantages that incorporation can bring. Our discussion begins with the principal body corporate—namely, the registered company.

Methods of incorporation

There are three principal methods by which a company can be created:

- incorporation by Act of Parliament;
- incorporation by royal charter; and
- incorporation by registration.

---

1. The Companies Act 2006, s 16(2), provides that a registered company is a 'body corporate'.
2. The Limited Liability Partnerships Act 2000, s 1(2), provides that a LLP is a 'body corporate'.

It is important to note at the outset that the provisions of the Companies Act 2006 (CA 2006) apply only to companies incorporated by registration,[3] but the Secretary of State does have the power to extend specified provisions of the CA 2006 to unregistered companies.[4] Because registered companies vastly outnumber unregistered companies, this book will concentrate only on the law that applies to registered companies. But an understanding of the two methods of creating an unregistered company is still of aid.

Act of Parliament

Parliament may create companies by passing an Act of Parliament. Such companies may be created by a public or private Act. Companies created as the result of a public Act are usually created to serve some public need (for example, the British Railways Board,[5] the Post Office,[6] and the National Assembly of Wales).[7] The organization of the 2012 London Olympics is the responsibility of the Olympic Delivery Authority—a company created by a public Act of Parliament.[8]

Companies may also be created by a private Act and such companies are known as 'statutory companies'. These companies are normally created to facilitate the petitioner's commercial dealings (for example, many former public utilities became statutory companies,[9] although many of them have since become standard registered public companies).

The distinction between public and private Acts of Parliament is discussed at p 58

➡ public Act: an Act of national importance that applies to the entire UK, unless stated otherwise

➡ private Act: an Act that applies to specific individuals, groups of individuals, companies, or localities

Royal charter

A company may be created by royal charter. Historically, the monarch granted these charters to further some aim that was beneficial to the country. At the time of writing, there are 977 chartered companies (although many are defunct),[10] the first of which was the University of Cambridge, which was granted its charter in 1231. Between the sixteenth and nineteenth centuries, royal charters were granted to trading companies engaged in activities that the monarch or government wished to encourage (for example, exploration, colonization, and overseas trade). Virtually all of the early joint-stock companies (for example, the East India Company and the South Sea Company) were created by royal charter. Today, royal charters tend to be fewer in number (in 2008, only eight companies were created by royal charter) and are exclusively granted, upon advice from the Privy Council, to bodies engaged

---

3. CA 2006, s 1.

4. Ibid, s 1043. For example, see the Companies Acts (Unregistered Companies) Regulations 2007, SI 2007/318.

5. Created by the Transport Act 1962, s 1 (repealed by the Transport Act 1969, but repeal not yet in force).

6. Created by the Post Office Act 1969, s 6 (repealed by the Postal Services Act 2000).

7. Created by the Government of Wales Act 1998, s 1.

8. The Olympic Delivery Authority was created by the London Olympic Games and Paralympic Games Act 2006, s 3(1).

9. Examples include British Telecom (Telecommunications Act 1984; repealed by the Communications Act 2000), British Gas (Gas Act 1972; repealed by the Gas Act 1986), and the regional water authorities (Water Act 1973; repealed by the Water Act 1989).

10. A full list of chartered companies is available from the website of the Privy Council Office, <http://www.privycouncil.gov.uk>.

in charitable, educational, or non-profit-making activities. Examples of such chartered companies include the Bank of England (1694), the Law Society (1845), the Royal College of Music (1883), the Institute of Chartered Accountants of England and Wales (1880), the British Broadcasting Corporation (1926), and the Chartered Institute of Management Accountants (1975).

Registration

Petitioning for a royal charter or the creation of an Act of Parliament is not exactly the most accessible or efficient way to create a company. Between 2004 and 2008, the average annual number of new incorporations in England and Wales was around 381,000.[11] There is no way that this many companies could ever be created by the mechanisms discussed above. Accordingly, to meet demand, a simple, quick, and efficient method of incorporation was required; with the passing of the Joint Stock Companies Act 1844, such a method was created—namely, incorporation by registration. Today, the vast majority of new companies are created by registration in accordance with the CA 2006. Any individual(s) who wish to create a company (such individuals are known as **promoters**) need only register certain documents with their respective Registrar of Companies to bring a company into existence.

→ promoter:
a person who
undertakes and enters
into the process of
setting up a company

The registration process

Incorporation by registration is so called because it is based upon the registration of certain documents. These documents, once registered and authorized, bring a registered company into existence. But before these documents can be drafted and registered, the promoters have some important decisions to make.

- Will the proposed company be public or private?
- Will the proposed company be unlimited or limited (if limited, will it be limited by shares or guarantee)?
- What will the company's name be?

These issues are discussed later in the chapter.

Once these decisions have been made, the promoters can begin to prepare the registration documents. A number of documents are required, but, historically, the most important were the memorandum and articles of association (collectively, these documents were known as the 'constitution' of the company). These documents and the substantial effects of the CA 2006 on them are discussed later in the chapter, when we discuss the constitution of the company.

🔗 The constitution
of the company is
discussed at p 614

In addition to the memorandum and articles, other documents need to be registered:

- a registration application detailing the proposed company name, whether the company's registered office is to be situated in England and Wales (or in Wales), in Scotland, or in Northern Ireland, whether the members will have limited liability

---

11. Information extrapolated from Companies House, *Annual Report and Accounts 2007/08* (BERR, London, 2008) 48.

and, if so, whether will it be limited by shares or guarantee, and whether the company will be public or private;[12]

- if the company is to have a share capital, a statement of capital and initial share-holdings—but if the company is limited by guarantee, a statement of guarantee will be required instead;[13]
- a statement identifying the company's proposed officers,[14] including the first directors and, if applicable, the first company secretary;[15]
- a statement of compliance, indicating that the requirements of the CA 2006 have been met.[16]

These documents must then be delivered to the appropriate Registrar of Companies,[17] who will, if satisfied that the documents contain the required information, issue a certificate of incorporation upon payment of the registration fee. Currently, the cost of a non-electronic registration is £20 (£15 if registration is electronic), but if the promoters wish to incorporate quickly, they can pay £50 for same-day incorporation (£30 for same-day electronic incorporation). Once registered, the new company will be allocated a 'registration number', which will appear on the certificate of incorporation. This certificate constitutes conclusive proof that a company is registered under the relevant Act. From the date of registration, the company has all of the powers and obligations of a registered company, including corporate personality. The promoters will formally become directors, subject to a range of statutory duties.

Off-the-shelf companies

Registration of the above documents is not an unduly burdensome process—but it does require a relatively serious layperson's knowledge of the procedures by which a company is run. Further, preparation of the required documents can be time-consuming, especially if the promoters require bespoke articles that cater for the particular needs of the proposed company. Persons who lack such knowledge or wish to gain access to the benefits of incorporation quickly may therefore prefer to purchase an 'off the shelf' company.

There are businesses and individuals (known as 'incorporation agents', or 'company formation agents') that specialize in creating companies and selling them onto others. They will register the necessary documents with the Registrar and then leave the company 'on the shelf' until such time as it is purchased. When this occurs, the incorporation agent will notify the Registrar of the relevant changes (for example, change of directors, registered office, etc.). It has been estimated that incorporation agents are responsible for around 60 per cent of all new company formations.[18]

---

12. Ibid, s 9(2).
13. Ibid, s 9(4)(a) and (b).
14. Ibid, s 9(4)(c).
15. Ibid, s 12(1).
16. Ibid, ss 9(1) and 13.
17. The UK has three such Registrars: (i) the Registrar of England and Wales, based in Cardiff; (ii) the Registrar of Scotland, based in Edinburgh; and (iii) the Registrar of Northern Ireland, based in Belfast.
18. Company Law Review Steering Group, *Modern Law for a Competitive Economy: Developing the Framework* (DTI, London, 2000) [11.32].

The use of an incorporation agent brings several benefits, chief amongst them being speed and lack of expense. Many incorporation agents operate online only and can provide purchasers with an off-the-shelf company for as little as £25 (although this is likely not to include hard copies of the relevant documentation). There is, however, one major drawback to purchasing an off-the-shelf company: because the company was created months, or even years, before it was purchased, it will not be tailored to meet the needs of the new business. In such cases, purchasers may find that the articles require alteration—a process that will be examined later in the chapter. If the promoters are willing to spend more money and wait a little longer, however, incorporation agents will create a bespoke company that meets the promoter's needs.

A company's ability to alter its articles is discussed at p 616

Pre-incorporation contracts

Prior to incorporation and the obtaining of the certificate of incorporation, the promoters may need to enter into contractual agreements with third parties in order to cater for the needs of the company to be incorporated (for example, the incorporators may attempt to interest others in contributing capital to the proposed company, or will enter into contracts for premises, supplies, etc.). As we shall see, a company has contractual capacity, but this capacity only comes into effect upon incorporation. Until the company is incorporated, it will not exist as a separate entity and so will have no capacity. Are such pre-incorporation contracts void or, because they are clearly for the benefit of the company-to-be, are they regarded as valid? Prior to the UK joining the EU, the common law provided the answer—but it was based upon a technical and often complex distinction, as follows.

1. Where a promoter entered into a contract signing the contract as the company's agent, or on behalf of the company, the promoter would be held personally liable for the contract.[19]

2. Where the promoter entered into the contract by signing the contract using the company's name or merely adding his own name to authenticate that of the company, then the supposed contract would be held to be with the non-existent company and therefore no contract would be formed.[20]

As a consequence of the entry of the UK into the EU, it was obliged to implement the First EU Company Law Directive,[21] Art 7 of which states:

> If, before a company has acquired legal personality (that is, before being formed) action has been carried out in its name and the company does not assume the obligations arising from such action, the persons who acted shall, without limit, be jointly and severally liable therefore, unless otherwise agreed.

This has been implemented by the CA 2006, s 51(1), which states:

> A contract that purports to be made by or on behalf of a company at a time when the company has not been formed has effect, subject to any agreement to the contrary, as one made with the person purporting to act for the company or as agent for it, and he is personally liable on the contract accordingly.

19. *Kelner v Baxter* (1866) LR 2 CP 174.   20. *Newborne v Sensolid* [1954] 1 QB 45 (CA).
21. Council Directive 68/151/EEC.

The basic effect of s 51 is to do away with the common law distinction and to render a promoter personally liable for a pre-incorporation contract, irrespective of whether the promoter signed the contract in the company's name or on behalf of the company. This obviously benefits the third parties who contracted with the promoter, because they will now be able to sue the promoter—but can the promoter enforce the contract against the third party? The Court of Appeal has stated that the promoter can enforce the contract,[22] but the fact that clarification was required from the courts is an indication of a flaw in the drafting of s 51.

Even after the company is incorporated, it cannot ratify or adopt the contract made on its behalf.[23] The only way in which the company can take benefit from the pre-incorporation contract is to discharge the pre-incorporation contract and enter into a new contract with the third party in respect of the same subject matter.[24] This discharge and re-creation of the contract can occur expressly or by implication, but it will not arise merely by virtue of the company acting on the pre-incorporation contract.[25] It will be noted that Art 7 permitted a company to 'assume the obligations' of the pre-incorporation contract, but that s 51 confers no such power on the company. One could therefore argue that s 51 only partially implements Art 7.

Where the promoters enter into a contract before purchasing an 'off the shelf' company, s 51 will not apply, provided that the company was in existence at the time that the contract was entered into.

 Key points summary

- A company can be created by Act of Parliament, royal charter, or registration. Virtually all companies are incorporated by registration and, unless extended by the Secretary of State, the provisions of the Companies Act 2006 apply only to registered companies.

- Under the Companies Act 1985, the two crucial documents needed to form a company were the articles of association and the memorandum. Under the CA 2006, the memorandum has lost much of its importance.

- Upon registering the necessary documents and paying the registration fee, the Registrar will issue a certificate of incorporation, thereby bringing the company into existence.

- The majority of new companies are created by incorporation agents and are subsequently purchased 'off the shelf' by those willing to engage in business through a company.

- Promoters of a company will be personally liable for any contracts entered into prior to the company being fully incorporated.

---

22. *Braymist Ltd v Wise Finance Co Ltd* [2002] EWCA Civ 127, [2002] Ch 273.
23. *Re Northumberland Avenue Hotel Co Ltd* (1886) 33 Ch D 16 (CA).
24. *Howard v Patent Ivory Manufacturing Co* (1888) 38 Ch D 156 (Ch).
25. *Re Northumberland Avenue Hotel Co Ltd* (1886) 33 Ch D 16 (CA).

Types of registered company

The CA 2006 provides for a number of different forms of registered company that are classifiable by reference to certain characteristics, as follows.

1. Is the company public or private?
2. Is the liability of its members to be limited or unlimited? If liability is to be unlimited, the company must be private.
3. Does the company have a share capital or not? A public company must have a share capital.

The vast majority of companies incorporated by registration are created with a share capital. In 2007–08, 343,000 new companies were registered, only 9,500 of which did not have a share capital.[26] A limited company that does not have a share capital will be known as a 'company limited by guarantee' (although such companies can have a share capital) and will have no shareholders, but will instead have 'members'. In a company limited by shares, however, shareholders will also normally qualify as members. Because companies limited by shares vastly outnumber companies limited by guarantee, this book will focus almost entirely on companies with a share capital and therefore the term 'shareholder' should be regarded as synonymous with the term 'member', unless otherwise stated.

Because we are focusing on companies limited by shares, it is the first two characteristics mentioned above that are of crucial importance, beginning with the difference between public and private companies.

Public and private companies

When creating a company, its promoters are required to state whether the company is to be registered as a private company or a public company. The public–private distinction forms the principal division of registered companies.

Public

A public company is a company limited by shares, or limited by guarantee and having a share capital, the certificate of incorporation of which states that it is a public company.[27]

Public companies differ from private companies in four principal ways, as follows.

1. Unlike private companies, a public company may offer its shares to the public and, to this end, may list its shares on a stock market (such companies are known as **listed, or quoted, companies**)—the principal market in the UK being the London Stock Exchange. Doing this allows the company to raise massive amounts of capital very quickly. Public companies are required to add the suffix 'plc' (meaning 'public limited company') to their name.[28]

➡ listed, or quoted, company: a public company, the shares of which are listed on a stock exchange

---

26. Companies House, *Statistical Tables on Companies Registration Activities 2007–08* (BERR, London, 2008) 8.
27. CA 2006, s 4(2).
28. Welsh public companies may use the Welsh equivalent—namely, 'ccc' (*cwmni cyfyngedig cyhoeddus*).

2. Whilst private companies can be created with a trivial amount of capital, public companies are required to have a minimum allotted share capital of £50,000[29] or €65,600.[30]

3. Both public and private companies can be created with only one shareholder[31] (the Companies Act 1985 prohibited one-member public companies). But whereas a private company can be formed with only one director,[32] a public company must have a minimum of two directors.[33]

4. Public companies are required by law to appoint a company secretary.[34]

This minimum capital requirement is discussed in more detail at p 683

The functions of a company secretary are discussed at p 654

Other differences do exist, but these will be discussed during the course of the following chapters. Private companies vastly outnumber public companies. As of the beginning of May 2009, there were 2,540,456 registered companies in England and Wales, of which only 10,806 were public companies.[35] But even though public companies constitute only 0.4 per cent of the total number of companies, such is their size that their combined assets are still greater than those of the private companies.

Private

A private company is defined simply as any company that is not a public company.[36] Table 17.1 demonstrates how private companies differ from public companies.

TABLE 17.1 The principal distinctions between public and private companies

	Public	Private
Can offer shares to the public and list shares on a stock exchange?	Yes	No[1]
Minimum capital requirement?	£50,000 or €65,600	No minimum requirement
Minimum number of directors?	Two	One[2]
Suffix?	Plc (or ccc, in Wales)	Ltd (or Cyf,[3] in Wales)
Required to appoint a company secretary?	Yes	No, but may appoint one if it chooses[4]

[1] CA 2006, s 755(1); Financial Services and Markets Act 2000, s 74
[2] CA 2006, s 154(1)
[3] Short for *Cyfyngedig*, meaning 'limited'
[4] CA 2006, s 270(1)

Limited and unlimited companies

Where the promoters have decided to form a private company, they will then need to decide whether the company's members will have limited or unlimited liability. The vast majority of private companies formed are limited. Where the promoters

---

29. Ibid, s 763.
30. Companies (Authorised Minimum) Regulations 2008, SI 2008/729, reg 2.
31. CA 2006, s 7(1).
32. Ibid, s 154(1).
33. Ibid, s 154(2).
34. Ibid, s 271.
35. Statistics available from the Companies House website, <http://www.companieshouse.gov.uk>.
36. CA 2006, s 4(1).

have decided to create a public company, then its shareholders must have limited liability. It is impossible to create an unlimited public company.[37]

Limited

🔗 Limited liability is discussed in more detail at p 600

Forming a limited company does not mean that the company itself has limited liability, but rather that its members will have limited liability. The extent of the limitation will depend upon the method of limitation. The concept of limited liability is discussed in more depth later in this chapter.

Unlimited

At the end of the period 2007–08, there were 2,412,700 private limited companies, compared to only 5,400 unlimited companies (just over 0.1 per cent).[38] The reason why there are so few unlimited companies is simple: in an unlimited company, upon winding up, the liability of its members is personal and unlimited. Unlimited companies may have a share capital, but that share capital will not provide a limit to liability.

➡ winding up: the process whereby a company is, voluntarily or by court order, brought to an end

The obvious question therefore is why a company would choose unlimited liability. Unlimited companies do have one notable advantage over limited companies to offset the loss of limited liability—namely, they do not need to file their accounts with the Registrar of Companies,[39] although they will still need to furnish their members with copies of the accounts. Accordingly, unlimited companies are subject to slightly fewer formalities and have more privacy than limited companies—but this is unlikely to be a fair trade-off for the loss of limited liability.

Not-for-profit companies

When we discussed partnerships, we noted that partnerships must be formed 'with a view to a profit'. It is impossible to form a charitable or non-profit-making partnership. Conversely, companies can be formed for non-profitable or charitable purposes. The problem is that both company law and the provisions of charities legislation historically regulated such companies. It was therefore recommended that a specialized corporate form be created for such companies.

As a result, it is now possible to create the following.

- A limited company known as a *community interest company* (CIC),[40] which is regulated by the Companies (Audit, Investigations and Community Enterprise) Act 2004, Pt 2. This Act provides a body of rules into which the CIC can opt, which are more suited for not-for-profit companies. As of May 2009, there were 2,807 CICs registered in the UK.[41]

- Alternatively, where the company is also a charity, it will be possible to register[42] as a *charitable incorporated organization* (CIO). CIOs are not governed by the CA 2006, but by the Charities Act 1993, which provides for a regulatory regime more suited to such entities (although much of the regulation of charities will be

---

37. Ibid, s 4(2).

38. Statistics available from the Companies House website, <http://www.companieshouse.gov.uk>.

39. CA 2006, s 448(1).   40. Ibid, s 6.

41. See <http://www.cicregulator.gov.uk>.

42. Note that registration will not be with the Registrar of Companies, but with the Charity Commissioners: see Charities Act 1993, s 69E.

familiar to company lawyers). At the time of writing, the regulations required to permit the registration of CIOs have not yet been drafted.

Societas Europaea (SE)

Even before the EU was formed, the idea of a Europe-wide company structure had been debated. It was hoped that such a company could better facilitate cross-border trade, but agreement on the form that such a company would take proved controversial, especially in relation to worker participation. After several failed attempts to reach a consensus, the European Company Statute[43] was finally passed, which allowed for the registration in any European Economic Area (EEA) country of a form of company known as a 'Societas Europaea' (SE). The SE is a Europe-wide form of public limited company, but it has yet to become popular in the UK. In fact, as of 31 March 2008, only five SEs had registered with Companies House.[44]

Given their extreme rarity, further discussion of SEs is not required for the purposes of this book.

 Key points summary

- Public companies may offer shares to the public, are subject to minimum capital requirements, must have at least two directors, and are legally required to appoint a company secretary.

- Private companies cannot offer shares to the public, have no minimum capital requirements, can be formed with one director, and do not need to appoint a company secretary.

- The members of a private company may have limited or unlimited liability. The members of a public company must have limited liability.

- Private companies comprise 99.6 per cent of companies in the UK; public companies comprise only 0.4 per cent.

- The members of an unlimited company are personally liable to contribute to the company's debts for an unlimited amount.

The advantages and disadvantages of incorporation

Having discussed the processes by which a company can be created and the various types of company, the next question to ask is what consequences flow from engaging in business through a company. What are the advantages and disadvantages of incorporation?

---

43. Council Regulation (EC) No 2157/2001.
44. Companies House, *Statistical Tables on Companies Registration Activities 2007–08* (BERR, London, 2008) Table E3.

Advantages

Carrying on business though a company has a number of significant benefits over carrying on business through an unincorporated association.

Corporate personality

🔗 The concept of corporate personality is discussed in more depth at p 606

The primary advantage of incorporation, from which most other advantages flow, is that the company acquires corporate personality. This means that the company is regarded as a separate person. It is not a biological person like you or me, but a legal or juridical person (that is, a person created by the law). As we shall see, the result of this is that a company can do many things that a biological person can do, such as own property and enter into contracts. Because corporate personality is such a fundamental characteristic of a company, it will be examined separately and in more detail later in the chapter.

Limited liability

Because the company is a legal entity separate from its members, it follows that its members are not normally personally liable for its debts. As we saw in the previous chapter, the imposition of personal and unlimited liability is a key weakness of sole proprietorships and partnerships. Does this mean that the members of a company are required to contribute nothing?

The answer depends on the type of company. As noted above, the majority of companies are limited companies, in which the members will have what is known as 'limited liability'. This means that the liability of each member is limited to the amount unpaid on his shares (in the case of a company limited by shares), or to an amount specified in the statement of guarantee (in the case of a company limited by guarantee). Accordingly, limited liability refers to the ability of a member to limit his liability and not to that of the company.

Because companies limited by shares vastly outnumber companies limited by guarantee, the following example will demonstrate the operation of limited liability in a company limited by shares.

Eg **Limited liability**

🔗 The nominal value of shares will be discussed at p 675

🔗 Liquidation will be discussed at p 756

Technosoft plc issues a new batch of shares with a nominal value of £1 each. The terms of subscription state that shares may be fully paid up immediately, or that subscribers may pay half of their value now and remain liable for the remainder. Tom purchases a hundred shares on such terms and pays £50. A year later, before Tom has fully paid for the shares, Technosoft goes into voluntary liquidation. The liquidator will be able to recover from Tom the amount that has yet to be paid (£50). Had Tom fully paid for the shares when they were issued (as is the case normally), or subsequently paid the remainder prior to liquidation, the liquidator would not be able to recover any monies from Tom.

It can therefore be seen that, where a company has limited liability, incorporation remedies the principal weakness of a partnership—namely, personal and unlimited liability.

Perpetual succession

Because the company is a legal person, it is not subject to 'the thousand natural shocks that flesh is heir to',[45] and has 'no soul to be saved and no body to be kicked'.[46] In other words, legal persons are not subject to the physical weaknesses that biological persons endure and can continue forever.[47] Even if a company loses all of its shareholders, it can still continue.[48] The advantages of this are obvious: shareholders and directors may come and go, but the company will continue. (This can be contrasted with a partnership, which, as we saw in the previous chapter, will be dissolved upon the death of a partner.)

Despite the apparent immortality of a company, if the Registrar of Companies has reasonable cause to believe that a company is no longer carrying on business (for example, because of an unexplained failure to file annual accounts for some time), he has the power to strike the company off the Register,[49] thereby dissolving it.

Contractual capacity

The company, as a person, has capacity to enter into contracts. This means that the company can enter into contracts with those outside and within the company.

The following case provides the classic example of this point.

The concept of contractual capacity is discussed at p 137

Lee v Lee's Air Farming Ltd [1961] AC 12 (PC)

FACTS: Lee was employed as a pilot by a company in which he held 2,999 shares (out of a total 3,000) and of which Lee was the only director. Whilst engaged in the company's business, his plane crashed and he was killed. His widow sought compensation for his death from the company, which, under the relevant legislation, was payable to the widows of deceased employees. The company's insurers argued that Lee was not an employee of the company, on the basis that he was synonymous with the company and had therefore made a contract with himself (which is not possible, since an agreement requires two parties).

HELD: The Privy Council held that Lee's widow was entitled to compensation. Lee had not made a contract with himself; rather, he had made a contract with the company, which was a separate entity. The fact that he owned virtually all of the shares and was the only director did not change the fact that the company was the employer and he was its employee.

---

45. This quotation is taken from the famous 'to be or not to be' soliloquy in Shakespeare's *Hamlet* (Act III, Scene I) and has been used by judges on numerous occasions to indicate the perpetual nature of the company.

46. *Stepney Corporation v Osofsky* [1937] 3 All ER 289 (CA) 291 (Greer LJ).

47. Although disagreement exists, many regard Stora Kopparberg (now known as 'Stora Enso') as the oldest existing corporation in the world. It can be found in Sweden and was established by charter in 1347. But documents referring to the company's mining activities date back to 1288.

48. See, e.g., the Australian case of *Re Noel Tedman Holdings Pty Ltd* [1967] Qd R 561, in which the company's two shareholders were killed in a car crash, yet the company continued.

49. CA 2006, s 1000.

🔗 The extent of a company's contractual capacity is discussed at p 615

The extent of a company's contractual capacity is discussed in more detail later in the chapter.

Ownership of assets

The company's property belongs to the legal person. This allows for a clear delineation between the property of the company and the property of its members, and establishes that the members have no proprietary interests in the assets of the company.

Macaura v Northern Assurance Co Ltd [1925] AC 619 (HL)

FACTS: Macaura owned a timber yard. He set up a company and transferred all of the timber to this new company, in return for which he obtained a number of fully paid-up shares in the company. He then insured the timber, in his own name, against loss caused by fire. Subsequently, the timber was destroyed in a fire and the insurance company refused to pay out. Macaura sued.

HELD: The House of Lords rejected Macaura's claim. In order to claim successfully, the insured party must have an insurable interest in the property in question. Macaura had no such interest, because the property did not belong to him; it belonged to the company.

It is important to be able to determine which property belongs to the company for two reasons:

- any capital borrowed by the company will be secured against the company's assets, not the assets of the members; and
- if the company fails to repay the loan, the creditors can bring claims against the assets of the company, not the assets of the members.

The ability to commence legal proceedings

As we noted in the previous chapter, determining who can sue in cases involving unincorporated businesses has historically proven to be an extremely troublesome issue. No such problems exist in relation to companies, because it is clear that where a company is wronged, the company, as an entity, is the proper claimant.[50]

Transferable shares

In a partnership, the transfer of a partner's interest can be a complex exercise and is dependent upon the existence of an express agreement. Conversely, the transfer of interests in a company is relatively straightforward due to the transferable nature of shares. A shareholder who wishes to transfer his interest to another need only sell his shares for his interest in the company to come to an end. Shareholders can transfer shares between one another without affecting the operation of the company.

---

50. For example, where a defamatory statement is made against the company: see *Metropolitan Saloon Omnibus Co Ltd v Hawkins* (1859) 4 Hurl & N 87.

Floating charges

A company has access to a specific form of security known as a 'floating charge'. The detailed operation of these charges will be discussed in a later chapter. All that need be noted here is that access to this form of security makes it easier for companies to acquire debt capital than it is for sole proprietorships and partnerships, which, despite their unlimited liability, can face difficulties when attempting to do so.

Floating charges are discussed at p 669

➜ debt capital: capital borrowed from another

Disadvantages

Whilst incorporation carries some notable benefits, a promoter considering incorporation should also be aware of several disadvantages.

Increased formality, regulation, and publicity

Companies are subject to substantially more formality and regulation than unincorporated businesses. The formalities involved in setting up a company are much more complex than is the case when creating a partnership. These formalities extend beyond formation and will apply throughout the company's existence. There are lengthy and complex rules relating to the conduct of meetings and the passing of resolutions. Company directors are subject to a raft of statutory duties that do not apply to partners and sole proprietors. Incorporation also results in a loss of privacy, because companies are required to make certain financial information available to the public throughout their existence.

Directors' duties are discussed in Chapter 20

Civil liability

Just as the company can commence legal proceedings where it has been wronged, so too can it be subject to proceedings where it has committed a wrong. In certain cases (for example, breach of contract), imposing liability on the company poses no problems, but in other cases, the fact that the company acts through natural persons (namely, its directors and employees) can cause problems. Establishing the vicarious liability of the company is one method of solving this problem, but certain civil wrongs require defendants to have a certain level of knowledge that the company will lack, for obvious reasons. In such a case, vicarious liability cannot be imposed.

Vicarious liability is discussed in Chapter 14

The courts' answer is, in certain cases, to attribute the knowledge of certain persons (usually its directors, but not always) to the company. This is known as 'identification theory', and the courts will usually attribute the knowledge of a person to a company where that person is the 'directing mind and will' of the company.

The following case demonstrates how identification theory operates in practice.

Lennard's Carrying Co Ltd v Asiatic Petroleum Co Ltd [1915] AC 705 (HL)

FACTS: The Merchant Shipping Act 1894, s 502, provided that the owner of a British seagoing ship was not liable for 'any loss or damage happening without his actual fault or privity' in relation to goods on board the ship that were lost or damaged by fire. The defendant company owned a ship, the cargo hold of which contained a cargo of benzine that belonged to the claimant. The ship's boilers were in a poor state of disrepair and failed en route, grounding the ship upon a reef. The ship's grounding damaged the cargo hold and the benzine escaped. It came into contact with the boiler's combustion chambers and caused an explosion, completely destroying the ship and its cargo. The claimant sued for the loss of the cargo. It transpired that one of the directors of the defendant knew that the ship was unseaworthy. The defendant argued that the company had no knowledge and could not be held liable.

HELD: The House of Lords found the defendant liable. Viscount Haldane LC stated that:

> a corporation is an abstraction. It has no mind of its own any more than it has a body of its own; its active and directing will must consequently be sought in the person of somebody who for some purposes may be called an agent, but who is really the directing mind and will of the corporation, the very ego and centre of the personality of the corporation...[I[f [the director] was the directing mind of the company, then his action must, unless a corporation is not to be liable at all, have been an action which was the action of the company itself within the meaning of s. 502...It must be upon the true construction of that section in such a case as the present one that the fault or privity is the fault or privity of somebody who is not merely a servant or agent for whom the company is liable...but somebody for whom the company is liable because his action is the very action of the company itself.[51]

The question that arises is who can constitute the 'directing mind and will' of the company. The position has been best stated by Lord Reid:

> Normally the board of directors, the managing director and perhaps other superior officers of a company carry out the functions of management and speak and act as the company. Their subordinates do not. They carry out orders from above and it can make no difference that they are given some measure of discretion. But the board of directors may delegate some part of their functions of management giving to their delegate full discretion to act independently of instructions from them. I see no difficulty in holding that they have thereby put such a delegate in their place so that within the scope of the delegation he can act as the company. It may not always be easy to draw the line but there are cases in which the line must be drawn.[52]

Criminal liability

The company can be convicted of a crime in just the same way as can a natural person—but there are limits to this. A company cannot be imprisoned, so a company cannot be convicted of a crime for which the only offence is imprisonment.[53] It used to be thought that a company could not be convicted of a crime that had a *mens rea* requirement. But this is no longer the case and, applying identification theory (discussed above), the courts will be prepared to attribute *mens rea* to those who are the 'directing mind and will' of the company.

➡ *mens rea:* 'guilty mind'; the mental element required for the commission of certain crimes

Public disquiet over the lack of successful prosecutions of companies following high-profile incidents causing death resulted in repeated calls for the introduction of a statutory crime of corporate manslaughter. Although companies could be convicted for

---

51. *Lennard's Carrying Co Ltd v Asiatic Petroleum Co Ltd* [1915] AC 705 (HL) 713, 714.
52. *Tesco Supermarkets Ltd v Nattrass* [1972] AC 153 (HL) 171.
53. *R v ICR Haulage Ltd* [1944] KB 551.

manslaughter,[54] such convictions were rare, because the court would convict only if it could be established that the death was the result of the actions and gross negligence of an identifiable member of the directing mind and will within the company.[55] The difficulty of securing a conviction was a source of significant criticism and so Parliament passed the Corporate Manslaughter and Corporate Homicide Act 2007. Under this Act, corporate manslaughter (or corporate homicide in Scotland) is committed by an organization[56] if the way in which its activities are managed or organized:

1. causes a person's death; and
2. amounts to a gross breach of the relevant duty of care owed by the organization to that person.[57]

But liability will be imposed only if the way in which the organization is managed or organized by its senior management is a substantial element in that breach. These rules constitute a notable relaxation of the common law requirement that an individual's actions need to be identified as the cause of the death.

The offence is triable on indictment, but only after permission has been obtained from the Director of Public Prosecutions[58] and is punishable by a fine only.[59] The appropriateness of this punishment can be questioned, because it will not serve to punish the 'senior management' who have breached their duty of care, but will instead punish the company's shareholders, who will find that the resultant reduction in profits may affect their dividend payments. Ultimately, the greater punishment may be found in s 10, which empowers the court to make a 'publicity order' requiring the company to publicize that it has committed the offence, the facts involved, and the amount of the fine. The effect of such publicity on the company's reputation may prove more damaging than the imposition of a fine. At the time of writing, however, s 10 is not yet in force, although it is expected to come into force by summer 2009.

➡ Director of Public Prosecutions: the head of the Crown Prosecution Service (CPS), whose permission is required before certain designated offences can be prosecuted

Key points summary

- All companies have corporate personality, which means that a company is a legal person, with many of the same rights and abilities as a natural person.

- In a company limited by shares, a shareholder's liability is limited to the amount unpaid on their shares. Where the company is limited by guarantee, a guarantor's liability is limited to a specified amount.

---

54. The notable example being *R v P and O European Ferries (Dover) Ltd* (1990) 3 Cr App R 72, in which the company was convicted of manslaughter following the sinking of the *Herald of Free Enterprise*, resulting in the loss of 193 lives.
55. *Attorney General's Reference (No 2 of 1999)* [2000] QB 796 (CA).
56. For the purposes of the Act, an 'organization' will include both a partnership and a company: Corporate Manslaughter and Homicide Act 2007, s 1(2).
57. Ibid, s 1(1).
58. Ibid, s 17. Such permission is not required in Scotland.
59. Ibid, s 1(6). This fine may be unlimited in amount.

- A company can continue forever. It can survive even when it has no members.

- A company has contractual capacity to enter into contracts with persons outside and inside the company.

- A company can sue or be sued for a legal wrong.

- A company is able to own assets and the members of the company have no legal interests in the assets of the company.

- The price for the above benefits is that companies are subject to more regulation, more formality, and have less privacy than an unincorporated business. Further, companies can be found liable for civil wrongs and can be convicted of certain crimes.

Corporate personality and 'lifting the veil'

As we noted above, upon incorporation, a company becomes a legal person in its own right. In company law terms, this is known as 'corporate personality' (or 'separate personality', or 'legal personality'). The practical consequences of the company having its own personality have already been examined. Here, we will examine the true significance of corporate personality and to what extent this separate personality can be disregarded.

It is often argued that the following case established the concept of corporate personality, but this is not true. The existence of corporate personality was clearly envisaged by the Joint Stock Companies Act 1844. It was, however, only in the following case that the courts finally appreciated the true significance of corporate personality—namely, that promoters, directors, and shareholders could legitimately use a company's separate personality to shield themselves from certain liabilities.

 Salomon v A Salomon and Co Ltd [1897] AC 22 (HL)

FACTS: Salomon was a sole trader engaged in the business of bootmaking. He decided to incorporate and, to that end, he created a company (A Salomon and Co Ltd) and sold the bootmaking business to the newly created company in return for £39,000. This payment came in a number of forms:

- 20,000 £1 shares;

- £10,000 worth of **debentures**, secured by a floating charge over all of the assets of the company; and

- the balance in cash.

Legislation at the time required that a company have a minimum of seven members. Accordingly, the company's 20,007 shares were divided up, with Salomon holding

➡ debenture: a document evidencing a loan to the company

20,001[60] shares, and his wife and five children each holding one share. Very shortly thereafter, the company business failed and went into liquidation. The company owed money to several creditors, including Salomon (the £10,000 in debentures). Because Salomon had secured his loan (via a floating charge), he enforced this and claimed the £10,000 that he was owed. Unfortunately, this meant that there were no more assets to pay the other creditors. The company liquidator chastised Salomon and argued on behalf of the other creditors, stating that, instead of taking money from the company, Salomon should be personally liable for its debts. At first instance, the judge held that the company was Salomon's agent and that he was therefore liable for its debts. In the Court of Appeal, it was held that, by appointing six 'dummy' shareholders, the company was not incorporated within the spirit and intent of the legislation. Accordingly, the Court held that the company acted as a trustee for Salomon and he should be liable for its debts. Salomon appealed to the House of Lords.

HELD: The House of Lords allowed his appeal. Whilst it could be said that the company does carry on business for the benefit of its shareholders, it does not follow that this creates a principal–agent relationship, or a trustee–beneficiary relationship. Further, the relevant legislation did not require the seven members all to be active members. Accordingly, Salomon had complied fully with the requirements for incorporation and was therefore not liable to pay the company's debts.

COMMENT: Many regard *Salomon* as the most famous and important case in company law, for three reasons, as follows.

1. It recognized that an incorporated company could legitimately be used to shield its members from liability.

2. It implicitly recognized the validity of the 'one-man company' (that is, a company run only by one person, with a number of dormant nominee shareholders).

3. The fact that an individual holds shares in a company (even all of the shares) is not enough to establish a relationship of agency or trusteeship.

Salomon is now regarded by many as an 'unyielding rock'[61] and 'the cornerstone of English company law'.[62] But the ability to shield oneself from liability by incorporating a company is clearly open to abuse. Therefore, both statute and the courts have the ability to ignore a company's corporate personality and impose personal liability on the directors or members. This has become known as 'piercing', or 'lifting', the 'veil'—referring to the 'corporate veil' that hides the directors and members from view. There is no single principle or test used to determine when the veil will be pierced and, traditionally, instances in which the veil is pierced are discussed in relation to whether it is statute or the courts that have set aside a company's corporate personality.

---

60. The 20,000 £1 shares plus the one share to which he subscribed when he registered the company.
61. Lord Templeman, 'Forty Years On' (1990) 11 Co Law 10, 10.
62. D French, S Mayson, and C Ryan, *Mayson, French & Ryan on Company Law* (25th edn, OUP, Oxford, 2008) 123.

Statute

Because corporate personality is bestowed upon a registered company by statute,[63] it follows that statute can brush aside corporate personality and impose liability on those behind the veil.

Examples include the following.

- *Insolvency Act 1986, ss 213–214* Where, in the course of a winding up, it appears that the company has been run with intent to defraud the creditors, the courts will lift the veil and impose personal liability to contribute to the assets of the company upon the directors (or any other persons) who were knowingly parties to carrying on the business in such a way (fraudulent trading).[64] Where a company has gone into insolvent liquidation, the directors may be personally liable if they continued trading when they knew, or ought to have known, that there was no prospect of the company avoiding liquidation (wrongful trading).[65]
- *CA 2006, s 767* The directors will be personally liable where their company carries on business or exercises any borrowing powers prior to the company being issued with a trading certificate.

Common law

Because corporate personality is granted to registered companies by statute, it is understandable that the courts are reluctant to pierce the veil and impose liability on the directors or members, as the current leading case demonstrates.

 Adams v Cape Industries plc [1990] Ch 443 (CA)

FACTS: This case concerned a large multinational group of companies engaged in the mining, marketing, and selling of asbestos. The parent company (Cape) was based in England. The asbestos was mined by a subsidiary company based in South Africa. The asbestos was marketed and sold by two companies: one based in Illinois, USA (NAAC); the other in England (Capasco). The asbestos was sold to a factory in Texas, the employees of which subsequently developed medical conditions caused by exposure to asbestos. A number of actions were initiated against, inter alia, Cape, Capasco, and NAAC, and were settled out of court for around US$20 million. Cape then decided to place NAAC in liquidation and a new company (CPC) was set up to continue NAAC's work. This new company was not a subsidiary of Cape, but did receive financial support from Cape. A further 206 claimants from the Texas factory initiated proceedings against Cape and Capasco, and a US court ordered that damages of just over US$15 million be paid. The claimants therefore sought to enforce the judgment in the UK against Cape and Capasco. The only way in which this could be achieved was if these companies were held to be present in the USA. The claimants argued that Cape and Capasco were present in the USA through their subsidiaries, NAAC and CPC. For this argument to succeed, the separate corporate personalities of each company would need to be disregarded, and Cape, Capasco, and NAAC/CPC treated as one entity.

---

63. CA 2006, s 16(2).   64. Insolvency Act 1986, s 213.
65. Ibid, s 214.

HELD: The Court of Appeal refused to lift the veil. The US subsidiaries were separate and distinct from their English parent. Accordingly, Cape and Capasco were not present in the USA, and so the US judgment could not be enforced against them. The reason why Cape had created subsidiaries in the USA was so that liability would fall on those subsidiaries. *Salomon* recognized that this was a valid use of the company and nothing in the case convinced the Court that the principle in *Salomon* should not be followed.

★ See S Griffin, 'Holding Companies and Subsidiaries: The Corporate Veil' (1991) 12 Co Law 16

In *Adams*, the claimants put forward a number of arguments in favour of lifting the veil:

- the subsidiary was a fraud or a sham;
- the group of companies was, in fact, one 'single economic unit';
- the subsidiary was an agent of Cape; and
- lifting the veil was fair and just given the circumstances of the case.

All of these arguments will be discussed in more detail below. In *Adams*, they all failed (the first three failed on the facts, and the fourth argument was not deemed a sufficient reason to lift the veil), and the Court of Appeal strongly reaffirmed the principle in *Salomon* and indicated that a company's corporate personality will not be lightly cast aside.

Our discussion of judicial lifting of the veil begins with the most accepted and least problematic justification for lifting the veil—namely, where the company has been used to perpetrate a fraud, or is being used to evade a legal obligation.

Fraud, sham, or cloak

In *Adams*, the Court stated that 'there is one well recognised exception to the rule prohibiting the piercing of the "corporate veil"'.[66] This is where the company is used to perpetrate a fraud, or where the company is a facade or a sham. A common theme amongst these cases is that the company is used to evade a contractual obligation, such as a restrictive covenant, or even to avoid the sole purpose of a contract entirely.

⊙━ *Gilford Motor Co Ltd v Horne* [1933] Ch 935 (CA)[67]

FACTS: The defendant was the managing director of the claimant company. His employment contract contained a restrictive covenant that provided that, upon leaving the claimant's employment, he would not attempt to solicit any of its customers. The defendant's contract was terminated, but he convinced his wife to set up a company in her name, which was nonetheless under the defendant's control. This new company competed directly with the claimant. The claimant sought an injunction to enforce the restrictive covenant and prevent the new company from soliciting the claimant's customers. The defendant argued that the covenant was binding on him only, not on the company.

---

66. *Adams v Cape Industries plc* [1990] Ch 443 (CA) 539 (Slade LJ).
67. See also *Jones v Lipman* [1962] 1 WLR 832 (Ch).

HELD: The Court of Appeal granted the injunction preventing the defendant and the new company from soliciting the claimant's customers. Lord Hanworth MR stated that the new company was 'formed as a device, a stratagem, in order to mask the effective carrying on of a business of [the claimant]'.[68]

'Single economic unit'

As we saw in *Adams*, it is common for larger companies to carry out their various functions via a number of smaller subsidiary companies. Are the various companies to be regarded as having separate corporate personalities or are they to be treated as one 'single economic unit'?

The general rule can be found in the following case.

 ### The Albazero [1977] AC 774 (HL)

FACTS: The defendant company owned a ship called *The Albacruz*. The claimant (Concord, a subsidiary of Occidental Petroleum Co) chartered *The Albacruz* to transport a cargo of oil from Venezuela to Antwerp. During the journey, Concord transferred ownership of the oil to RBP, another subsidiary of Occidental. Sometime after the transfer, *The Albacruz* sank and the cargo of oil was lost. Concord initiated legal proceedings against the defendant for loss of the cargo (estimated at around £137,000). The defendant argued that, because Concord no longer owned the cargo, it could not sue the defendant; only RBP could sue for the loss. But it was not possible for RBP to sue at this point, because the limitation period had expired. Therefore, the only way for Concord to succeed was if the separate personalities of Concord and RBP were ignored, and they were treated as one 'single economic unit'.

HELD: In the House of Lords, Roskill LJ stated that it was 'long established and now unchallengeable by judicial decision...that each company in a group of companies...is a separate legal entity possessed of separate legal rights and liabilities'.[69] Therefore, as a matter of company law, there was no reason to ignore the separate personalities of Concord and RBP.

COMMENT: Concord actually won the case, but on a special point of maritime law— namely, that a shipowner could be held liable to pay substantial damages for loss of cargo, irrespective of who owned it at the time of the loss.[70] On the facts, however, the House did not believe that this rule of maritime law should be extended to cover the facts of *The Albazero* and so Concord only recovered nominal damages.

Roskill LJ's statement in *The Albazero* was designed to affirm the principles established in *Salomon* and to ensure that the law in this area remained certain. Unfortunately, the following case, reported after *The Albazero*, but actually decided four months before it, has introduced a measure of unwelcome uncertainty into the law.

---

68. *Gilford Motor Co Ltd v Horne* [1933] Ch 935 (CA) 956.
69. *The Albazero* [1977] AC 774 (HL) 807.
70. *Dunlop v Lambert* (1836) 6 Cl & F 600.

DHN Food Distributors Ltd v Tower Hamlets London Borough Council [1976] 1 WLR 852 (CA)

FACTS: DHN was the holding company that included two other wholly owned subsidiaries. One of the subsidiaries (Bronze Investments Ltd) did not carry on any business activity, but it did own the land upon which DHN carried out business (DHN occupied the land as a **bare licensee**). The local authority compulsorily purchased this land and £360,000 was paid to Bronze, as the owner of the land. DHN could not find alternative premises, so all three companies went into liquidation, thereby entitling the holder of a legal or equitable interest in the land to receive compensation for disturbance to the business. The claimant (DHN) argued that it was entitled to such compensation. The defendant (the local authority) argued that Bronze Investments owned the land, that Bronze Investments had not been disturbed, and that DHN was not entitled to any compensation for disturbance because it had no legal or equitable interest in the land (a bare licence not conferring such an interest).

→ holding company: a company that controls a subsidiary company (or companies)

→ bare licensee: someone who is permitted to be present on another's land, but is required to leave if the owner withdraws permission

HELD: The Court of Appeal awarded DHN compensation for the disturbance to the business that the compulsory purchase caused. In a much-criticized passage, Lord Denning MR stated:

> The subsidiaries are bound hand and foot to the parent company and must do just what the parent company says.... This group is virtually the same as a partnership where all the three companies are partners.... The three companies should, for present purposes, be treated as one, and the parent company, DHN, should be treated as that one.[71]

COMMENT: Although the judges involved were unanimous that the three companies should be treated as one, there was no clear test established to determine when groups of companies should be regarded as one single economic unit. Denning MR's passage above indicates the lack of clarity, because he described the subsidiaries as 'bound hand and foot' before going onto to describe them as 'partners'. A subsidiary that 'must do just what the parent company says' cannot realistically be regarded as a 'partner'.

★ See D Hayton, 'Contractual Licenses and Corporate Veils' (1977) 36 CLJ 12

The validity of *DHN* has been questioned by subsequent courts, but not over-ruled. In *Adams*, Slade LJ stated:

> The relevant parts of the judgment in the *DHN* case must...be regarded as deci-sions on the relevant statutory provisions for compensation, even though these parts were somewhat broadly expressed, and the correctness of the decision was doubted by the House of Lords in *Woolfson v Strathclyde Regional Council*.[72]

More recently, however, there are slight indications that the courts are more will-ing to regard groups of companies as one 'business enterprise'. In *Beckett Investment Management Group Ltd v Hall*,[73] the Court of Appeal approved the words of Lord Denning MR in a previous case in which he stated that 'the law today has regard

---

71. *DHN Food Distributors Ltd v Tower Hamlets London Borough Council* [1976] 1 WLR 852 (CA) 860.
72. *Adams v Cape Industries plc* [1990] Ch 443 (CA) 536.
73. *Beckett Investment Management Group Ltd v Hall* [2007] EWCA Civ 613, [2007] ICR 1539.

to the realities of big business. It takes the group as being one concern under one supreme control'.[74]

Agency

🔗 The authority of an agent is discussed at p 937

As is discussed in Chapter 27, where two parties (known as the 'principal' and the 'agent') are involved in an agency relationship, the principal is responsible for the acts of the agent, provided that the agent acts within his actual or apparent authority. In the corporate context, this means that if two companies are in an agency relationship, the principal (normally the parent company) could be liable for the acts of its agent (normally a subsidiary company). In effect, the corporate personality of the agent is ignored and the principal made liable.

This can be seen in the following case.

⊶ Smith, Stone and Knight Ltd v Birmingham Corporation [1939] 4 All ER 116 (QB)

FACTS: The business of the claimant company was the manufacturing of paper. It acquired a partnership that was involved in the waste paper business. The claimant set up a subsidiary company to run this waste paper business, but never transferred ownership of the business to the subsidiary and retained ownership of the land upon which the subsidiary operated. The land upon which the subsidiary conducted business was compulsorily purchased by the defendant, who planned to pay the subsidiary compensation for the loss of the land and the disturbance caused to the business. The claimant contended that it was entitled to the compensation. The defendant argued that, because the subsidiary was a separate entity, it should receive the compensation.

HELD: The High Court held that the subsidiary was the agent of the claimant and, as such, the claimant recovered the compensation. The crucial factor was that the waste paper business and the land upon which it operated still belonged to the claimant.

It should be noted that cases such as *Smith, Stone & Knight* are extremely rare. In *Adams* (discussed above), the Court stressed that, in the absence of an express agreement of agency,[75] it is highly unlikely that a relationship of agency will exist between a parent and subsidiary.[76] In *Smith, Stone & Knight*, the level of domination that the parent exhibited over the subsidiary was a crucial factor in the court's decision. The parent owned the subsidiary's business and the land upon which it conducted business. The parent also owned 497 of the subsidiary's 502 shares and nominees of the parent held the remaining five shares. This is important, because the actual relationship of agency was deemed to be between the subsidiary and its principal shareholder (that is, its parent).

---

74. *Littlewoods Organisation Ltd v Harris* [1977] 1 WLR 1472 (CA) 1482.
75. For a case in which an express agreement existed, see *Southern v Watson* [1940] 3 All ER 439 (CA).
76. *Adams v Cape Industries plc* [1990] Ch 443 (CA) 545–9 (Slade LJ).

Justice or convenience

Several judges have contended that the court should have a general power to ignore a company's corporate personality where justice demands. In *Re a Company*,[77] the Court of Appeal stated that 'the court will use its powers to pierce the corporate veil if it is necessary to achieve justice'.[78] But the Court in *Adams* firmly rejected this, stating that 'the court is not free to disregard the principle of *Salomon*…merely because it considers that justice so requires'.[79]

Whilst this has been upheld in a number of cases,[80] there are still those who advocate a more wide-ranging ability to pierce the veil. In *Conway v Ratui*,[81] Auld LJ (with whom Laws LJ expressed his 'emphatic agreement'[82] and Sedley LJ agreed) referred to 'the readiness of the courts, regardless of the precise issue involved, to draw back the corporate veil to do justice when common-sense and reality demand it'.[83] Because these judges did not refer to *Adams* or any other similar cases, however, it is likely that their comments are to be regarded as *per incuriam*. Whilst the view in *Adams* is doubtless currently the authoritative view, a substantial body of the judiciary clearly believes that the courts should be free to disregard corporate personality where they feel that it is just to do so.

➤ *per incuriam*: 'through want of care'; where the court did not discuss relevant authority

Whilst the courts lack a general power to pierce the veil in the interests of justice, in a number of cases, the courts have indicated that they are willing to do so as a matter of convenience and to minimize legal costs, as can be seen in the following case.

Re H (Restraint Order: Realizable Property) [1996] 2 All ER 391 (CA)

FACTS: The three defendants owned 100 per cent of the shares in two family-run companies. The Commissioners of Customs and Excise alleged that the defendants had, through the two companies, evaded excise duty to the amount of £100 million. Accordingly, the Commissioners had obtained an order restraining the use of certain properties belonging to the company. The defendants argued that the company's property could not be restrained, because it was they who had been charged with tax evasion, not the company.

HELD: Had the company's corporate personality been stringently observed, the Court of Appeal would have lacked the jurisdiction to grant the restraining orders. The two companies could have been charged with tax evasion, but Rose LJ stated that 'it seems to me that no useful purpose would have been served by introducing into criminal proceedings the additional complexities as to the corporate mind and will which charging the companies would have involved'.[84] Accordingly, the Court of Appeal treated the restrained property as if it belonged to the defendants and the order was upheld.

---

77. *Re a Company* [1985] BCLC 333 (CA).   78. Ibid, 337, 338.

79. *Adams v Cape Industries plc* [1990] Ch 443 (CA) 536 (Slade LJ).

80. See, e.g., *Re Polly Peck International plc (No 3)* [1996] 2 All ER 433 (Ch).

81. *Conway v Ratiu* [2005] EWCA Civ 1302, [2006] 1 All ER 571.   82. Ibid, [186].

83. Ibid, [75].

84. *Re H (Restraint Order: Realizable Property)* [1996] 2 All ER 391 (CA) 402.

Key points summary

- A company's corporate personality can be set aside, or pierced, by statute or the courts.

- The courts will pierce the corporate veil where the company is a sham or a fraud, or is being used to evade a legal or contractual obligation.

- Depending upon the construction of a particular statute or contract, the courts may be willing to ignore the separate corporate personalities of a group of companies and regard them as a 'single economic unit'.

- The courts may pierce the corporate veil where a company is regarded as the agent of another.

- The courts will not pierce the veil purely in the interests of fairness or justice, but they might pierce the veil in order to save costs or to make litigation more convenient.

The constitution of the company

As noted above, historically, the two most important documents requiring registration with the Registrar of Companies were the memorandum and articles. Collectively, these two documents formed the constitution of the company. But with the passing of the CA 2006, the role of these documents has changed substantially.

- *Memorandum* Under the Companies Act 1985 (CA 1985), the memorandum was of immense importance. It would contain key information, including the name of every corporate officer, the location of its registered office, the aims of the company (known as its 'objects'), whether the company was public or private, whether the liability of its members was limited or unlimited, and the company's authorized share capital. Under the CA 2006, the memorandum, whilst still a necessary document, has lost much of its importance. Under the 2006 Act, the memorandum will simply contain a statement indicating that the subscribers wish to form a company under the 2006 Act and agree to become members of the company.[85] Most of the information that was contained in memorandum under the 1985 Act can now be found in other registration documents. Under the 2006 Act, therefore, the memorandum is simply an 'historical snapshot', indicating the state of affairs at the time that the company was set up.

- *Articles* Under the 1985 Act, the articles were extremely important and would set out the internal rules of the company, such as the appointment and powers of the directors, how general meetings should be conducted, and rules relating to share capital. Under the 2006 Act, the articles are now the principal document of importance. Whilst they still contain the internal rules mentioned, they can also contain, if a company wishes, a statement setting out the objects of the company.[86] These objects were formerly contained in the memorandum. The reason for the change of location is that, under the 1985 Act, the limitations on the company's power were found in two documents. Placing all of the limitations

---

85. CA 2006, s 8(1). Where the company is to have a share capital, the memorandum must also state that the subscribers have agreed to take at least one share each.

86. By default, a company's objects are unrestricted (CA 2006, s 31(1)).

in one document is much simpler and clearer. Accordingly, the memorandum no longer forms a part of the company's constitution.

As a result, the articles now form the company's most important constitutional document and every company must have a set of articles.[87] The articles form the principal rules by which the company is to be run, focusing on the internal rules that bind the company and its shareholders. Promoters are free to draft their own articles and submit them upon registration. But drafting articles can be a complex and time-consuming business, and many small business owners will lack the knowledge required to draft appropriate articles. Therefore, for many years, statutory instruments have provided a set of model articles that limited companies may adopt if they choose. The Companies (Model Articles) Regulations 2008[88] provide model articles for public companies[89] and private limited companies.[90] Unlimited companies, being relatively rare, are not provided with model articles and will therefore need to register their own articles.[91] Where promoters of a limited company do not submit their own set of articles as part of the registration process, these model articles will form the articles of their proposed company.[92] Even if the promoters do register their own articles, the model articles will still form part of the company's articles unless the registered articles exclude or modify them.[93] Companies formed under pre-2006 companies legislation (which are usually governed by the old Table A model articles)[94] will not be governed by the new model articles, but can adopt them if they so choose. Because the articles regulate the internal workings of the company, they are of particular importance to the company's shareholders. Accordingly, the CA 2006, s 32(1), provides that all companies are required to supply their members with up-to-date copies of the articles free of charge.

Extent of a registered company's contractual capacity

Previously, it was noted that, because the company is a legal person with its own distinct personality, it can enter into contracts in much the same way as can a natural person. But the contractual capacity of the company is subject to a major limitation to which natural persons are not: a natural person may enter into any contract that he chooses, but a company can only enter into contracts that fall within its objects. The objects of a company basically set out the purposes for which the powers of the company may be exercised. Under the 1985 Act, the company's objects clause would be located in its memorandum, but the 2006 Act provides that the objects will now become part of the articles.[95] Accordingly, the articles can act as an important limitation upon the company's ability to enter into contracts.

Any act that is beyond the objects of the company will be ultra vires. Historically, the ultra vires doctrine has been regarded as overly technical and complex, and

➡ ultra vires: 'beyond one's powers'

---

87. Ibid, s 18(1).   88. SI 2008/3229.

89. Ibid, Sch 3.

90. Ibid, Schs 1 ('Model Articles for Private Companies Limited by Shares') and 2 ('Model Articles for Private Companies Limited by Guarantee').

91. CA 2006, s 18(2).   92. Ibid, s 20(1).

93. Ibid, s 20(1)(b).

94. Companies (Tables A to F) Regulations 1985, SI 1985/805.   95. CA 2006, s 28.

numerous ad hoc reforms did little to improve matters. Accordingly, the CA 2006 provides that, unless the company chooses to restrict its objects, the objects will be unrestricted,[96] with the result that the contractual capacity of the company will also be unrestricted. For such companies, the ultra vires doctrine has been effectively abolished. Further, whereas the 1985 Act[97] provided that all public companies must have an object clause at all times, the 2006 Act has abolished this requirement. Companies may still restrict their objects if they so choose, however, and, for such companies, the ultra vires doctrine will still be relevant.

Today, with one exception,[98] the effect of the ultra vires doctrine has been nullified. This is because the CA 2006, s 39(1), provides that the validity of an act may not be called into question on the ground of lack of capacity because of anything in a company's constitution. This means that if the company enters into a contract that is ultra vires, the contract will still be binding and enforceable. Because the directors are subject to a statutory duty to act in accordance with the company's constitution,[99] however, causing the company to enter into an ultra vires transaction will result in them being in breach of duty.

The duty to act within the company's powers is discussed at p 699

Alteration of the articles

As a company—or the market within which it operates—evolves, it may become necessary for it to alter its articles and s 21(1) provides that the company may amend its articles by passing a **special resolution**. It is noteworthy that this power is vested in the company, because it means that the contract between the members and the company can only be altered by the company (albeit acting through the shareholders). It also means that the minority may be bound by article provisions to which they object. The ability to alter the articles is not boundless, and both the CA 2006 and the common law impose restrictions upon the company's ability to alter its articles.

➡ **special resolution:** a vote requiring no less than a 75 per cent majority

Statutory restrictions under the CA 2006

Certain statutory provisions will limit the ability to alter the articles, of which the following are examples.

- The ability to alter the articles is limited by the provisions of the Companies Acts.[100]
- A member is not bound by any change in the articles made after he became a member if, and in so far as it:
  - requires him to take or subscribe for more shares than the amount he had at the date of alteration; or

---

96. Ibid, s 31(1).   97. CA 1985, s 2(1)(c).

98. Where a person deals with a company that is a charity, the CA 2006, s 42, provides that s 39 will not apply unless: (i) the person was unaware that the company was a charity; or (ii) the company has received full consideration in respect of the act done, and the person was unaware that the act in question was beyond the company's capacity or beyond the powers of the directors.

99. CA 2006, s 171(1)(a).

100. *Allen v Gold Reefs of West Africa Ltd* [1900] 1 Ch 656 (CA) 671 (Lindley MR).

– in any way increases his liability to contribute to the company share capital or otherwise to pay money to the company, unless, in either case, the member expressly agrees in writing to be bound.[101]

- In certain situations (for example, where the members object to a public company re-registering as private),[102] statute empowers the courts to prohibit a company altering its articles without the courts' leave.

Common law restrictions

The most important limitation on the company's ability to alter its articles is not found in statute, but was introduced by Lindley MR in *Allen v Gold Reefs of West Africa Ltd*,[103] who stated that the power to alter the articles must:

> like all other powers, be exercised subject to those general principles of law and equity which are applicable to all powers conferred on majorities and enabling them to bind minorities. It must be exercised, not only in the manner required by law, but also bona fide for the benefit of the company as a whole...[104]

It has been argued at first instance that 'bona fide' and 'for the benefit of the company as a whole' are two separate requirements that must be satisfied, with the first test being subjective and the second being objective.[105] But the Court of Appeal, whilst not overruling these cases, has confirmed that Lindley MR's test imposes a single criterion only[106] and it is clear that the test is subjective. This means that, provided that the majority believed the alteration to be for the benefit of the company as a whole, the court will not invalidate it simply because it disagrees with the members' assessment.[107]

A minority shareholder who wishes to challenge an article alteration on this ground will face a difficult task. Given that the principle of majority rule is fundamental to the operation of the company, the courts are extremely reluctant to strike down changes in the articles, as the following case demonstrates.

Greenhalgh v Arderne Cinemas Ltd [1951] Ch 286 (CA)

FACTS: The claimant was a minority shareholder in a company, the articles of which provided that a shareholder should not sell his shares to an outsider if an existing shareholder was willing to purchase them (this is known as a 'pre-emption right'). The managing director, who was also the company's majority shareholder, wished to sell his shares to an outsider. He therefore (in his capacity as a shareholder) altered the articles to permit the selling of shares to an outsider, provided that it was approved by an ordinary resolution (which would be a certainty, given that he owned the majority of the company's shares). The claimant challenged the alteration, on the ground that it was not for the benefit of the company as a whole. The majority shareholder admitted that he had not acted in

---

101. CA 2006, s 25.   102. Ibid, ss 97 and 98(6).
103. [1900] 1 Ch 656 (CA).   104. Ibid, 671.
105. See, e.g., *Brown v British Abrasive Wheel Co* [1919] 1 Ch 290 (Ch).
106. *Sidebottom v Kershaw, Leese & Co Ltd* [1920] 1 Ch 154 (CA).
107. *Shuttleworth v Cox Brothers & Co (Maidenhead) Ltd* [1927] 2 KB 9 (CA).

the interests of the company, but argued that the company had no interest in who its shareholders were.

HELD: Evershed MR stated:

> the phrase, "the company as a whole" [in *Allen v Gold Reefs*] does not…mean the company as a commercial entity, distinct from the corporators: it means the corporators as a general body. That is to say, the case may be taken of an individual hypothetical member and it may be asked whether what is proposed is, in the honest opinion of those who voted in its favour, for that person's benefit.

Applying this 'hypothetical member' test, the Court of Appeal held that the alteration was valid. If an outsider offers to purchase the shares of a hypothetical member for a fair price, the ability to sell to the outsider might very well be of benefit and the hypothetical member would be justified in acting in a manner that benefits himself as an individual. Further, the alteration of the articles was not discriminatory, in that the advantage obtained by the majority (the ability to sell shares to outsiders) was also obtained by the minority (the fact that the majority shareholder could determine whether or not approval was given was deemed irrelevant).

COMMENT: As can be seen, Lord Evershed MR established two tests in this case:

* the hypothetical member test; and
* the discrimination test.

The discrimination test has, however, been somewhat ignored and it is the hypothetical member test that has become prominent. The problem is that the courts have never fully articulated who the hypothetical member actually is. To what extent does the hypothetical member differ from the real member in question? Are the hypothetical member's interests purely financial? If the actual shareholder in question has a non-financial reason to challenge an alteration, to what extent will this be relevant? Evershed MR's test fails to answer these questions.

Entrenched article provisions

It is a long-held principle of company law that a company cannot contract out of its ability to alter the articles and thereby make certain article provisions unalterable.[108] For the first time, however, the 2006 Act does allow companies to entrench in their articles article provisions. Such entrenchment cannot make the articles unalterable, but it does make it more difficult to alter them, by requiring that additional conditions to be met (for example, by requiring unanimity instead of the normal special resolution), or more restrictive procedures to be adhered to (for example, certain identified shareholders must approve the alteration in order for it to be valid).[109]

To combat possible abuse, several safeguards are imposed, as follows.

* Entrenchment will not prevent alteration of the articles where:
  - all of the members of a company agree to the alteration; or

---

108. *Walker v London Tramways Co* (1879) 12 Ch D 705 (Ch).   109. CA 2006, s 22(1).

- – the court, or some other authority having power to alter the articles, makes an order altering the articles.[110]

- Potential investors and shareholders may wish to inspect the articles. Clearly, it is vital that such parties know if any article provisions are entrenched. Therefore, the company will need to notify the Registrar of Companies if its article provisions permit entrenchment.[111]

- If a company wishes to entrench an article provision after it has been formed, it can only do so with the agreement of *all* of the members of the company.[112]

Key points summary

- A company's constitution is found principally in its articles of association.

- The articles provide the internal rules of the company.

- If promoters do not register their own articles, statute will provide a default set of articles that will be used.

- The purpose of a company may be limited by placing a restrictive objects clause in the company's articles. In the absence of such objects, the company has unrestricted contractual capacity.

- A company that acts beyond the scope of its objects clause will be acting ultra vires, which is likely to constitute a breach of the director's statutory duties.

- A company may alter its articles by passing a special resolution. But statute may limit the company's ability to alter its articles and any alterations must be exercised bona fide for the benefit of the company as a whole.

- The company may make alteration of certain article provisions more difficult by entrenching them.

Limited liability partnerships

With the passing of the Limited Liability Partnerships Act 2000 (LLPA 2000), it is now possible for two or more persons to conduct business through an entity called a 'limited liability partnership' (LLP).[113] Initially, one might wonder why this discussion is not taking place in the previous chapter, in which partnerships were discussed—but it is more appropriate to discuss LLPs alongside registered companies for four reasons, as follows.

1. Like a registered company, a LLP is incorporated through registration.

2. Like a registered company, a LLP is a 'body corporate' and therefore has corporate personality.

---

110. Ibid, s 22(3).   111. Ibid, s 23(1).

112. Ibid, s 22(2).

113. LLPs should not be confused with limited partnerships, which were discussed at p 561. As will be seen, LLPs bear virtually no similarities to limited partnerships.

3. Like most registered companies, a LLP has limited liability.

4. Generally, LLPs are regulated by company law, although there are notable areas in which they are regulated by partnership law.

LLPs are often described as a 'hybrid' business structure, because they combine the characteristics of a company and a partnership. Whilst this is true, there is little doubt that LLPs have more in common with registered companies than with partnerships. In fact, their resemblance to companies is so apparent that it has been argued that describing LLPs as partnerships is 'misleading'.[114]

In order to understand the true function and purpose of LLPs, it is necessary to discuss briefly the origins of the LLP and the reasons behind the passing of the LLPA 2000.

For many years, the partnership and the provisions of the Partnership Act 1890 (PA 1890) provided businesses with a flexible method of conducting business for firms that wished to avoid the regulation and inflexibility that comes with conducting business through a registered company. As time progressed and the size of partnerships (especially professional firms) grew, certain firms came more to resemble companies and the partnership was no longer entirely suitable for their needs, with the principal weakness being the imposition of unlimited joint and several liability upon the partners. Additionally, certain professions (notably, auditors) were prohibited from contractually excluding or limiting their liability.[115] Accordingly, large accountancy firms (notably, the then 'Big Six')[116] began lobbying for a partnership structure that provided for limited liability. In 1996, Jersey enacted legislation allowing firms to register as LLPs. Fearing that large firms would register in Jersey, the UK government capitulated and, in 1997, published proposals for the introduction of LLPs into UK law. Following a protracted consultation period, the LLPA 2000 was eventually passed and came into force in April 2000.

The above discussion indicates that the LLP was never designed to be a business structure of mass appeal and, certainly, it was not intended to be a vehicle for small businesses, as some at the time argued that it could be. It was created largely to cater for the needs of those who lobbied for it—namely, large professional firms. This is indicated by the fact that, as of May 2009, there were only 37,263 LLPs registered in the England and Wales.[117] Virtually all large accountancy and solicitors firms have adopted LLP status.

The LLPA 2000, s 1(2), provides that a LLP shall be a body corporate, meaning that, like a company, it will have a legal personality separate from that of its members. Accordingly, the consequences of having separate personality discussed earlier in relation to companies will also apply to LLPs. The LLP itself will be liable for its debts and will be vicariously liable for the acts of its agents. Where a member of a

---

114. PL Davies, *Gower & Davies' Principles of Modern Company Law* (8th edn, Sweet & Maxwell, London, 2008) 6.

115. Today, limitation is possible through 'liability limitation agreements', which are discussed at p 663.

116. The 'Big Six' were: Arthur Andersen; Coopers & Lybrand; Deloitte Touche Tohmatsu; Ernst & Young; KPMG; and PriceWaterhouse. These firms were segregated from the rest due to the significant size gap between them and other firms. With the merger of PriceWaterhouse and Coopers & Lybrand, and the dissolution of Arthur Andersen, they are now known as the 'Big Four'.

117. Statistics derived from the Companies House website, <http://www.companieshouse.gov.uk>.

LLP is liable to any person (other than another member of the LLP) as a result of a wrongful act or omission of his in the course of the business of the limited LLP or with its authority, the LLP is liable to the same extent as the member.[118] All LLPs have unlimited capacity,[119] so a LLP cannot act ultra vires.

The LLPA 2000 and the regulation of LLPs

The LLPA 2000 itself is a short Act, comprising only nineteen sections and one Schedule. The reasons for the shortness of the Act are twofold: firstly, unless otherwise stated in the Act, LLPs are not subject to partnership law;[120] secondly, detailed regulation of LLPs is contained in a series of statutory instruments (the principal one being the Limited Liability Partnership Regulations 2001),[121] which were passed subsequent to the LLPA 2000. These Regulations basically provided that large parts of the CA 1985 and Insolvency Act 1986 were also to apply to LLPs. With the passing of the CA 2006, the government had to decide whether to keep the existing regulatory framework or to pass new regulations that apply the reforms contained in the CA 2006 to LLPs. At the time of writing, the government has laid draft regulations[122] before Parliament that will apply significant parts of the CA 2006 to LLPs. These Regulations are due to come into force by 1 October 2009.[123]

Formation

Like a registered company, a LLP is formed through incorporation by registration with the Registrar of Companies. The LLPA 2000, s 2(1), provides three basic requirements for registration:

- two or more persons associated for carrying on a lawful business with a view to profit must have subscribed their names to an incorporation document;
- there must have been delivered to the Registrar either the incorporation document or a copy authenticated in a manner approved by him; and
- there must be delivered to the Registrar a statement of compliance indicating that two or more persons associated for carrying on a lawful business with a view to profit must have subscribed their names to an incorporation document.

The two or more persons who wish to form a LLP need not be natural persons; they may be companies or other LLPs. Unlike a company, it is impossible to form a single-member LLP. But whereas when the membership of a normal partnership drops to one, it will cease to exist, where the membership of a LLP drops to one, it will continue—although if that member carries on the business of the LLP for over six months, he will become jointly and severally liable, along with the LLP, for the LLP's debts.[124]

---

118. LLPA 2000, s 6(4).   119. Ibid, s 1(3).
120. Ibid, s 1(5).   121. SI 2001/1090.
122. Limited Liability Partnerships (Application of Companies Act 2006) Regulations 2009.
123. Ibid, reg 2.
124. This requirement currently arises by applying the CA 1985, s 24, to LLPs. By 1 October 2009, however, s 24 will be repealed and so this requirement will be inserted into the LLPA 2000 via a new s 4(3A).

The incorporation document is the LLP equivalent of a company's pre-2006 memorandum. The LLPA 2000, s 2(2), states that the incorporation document must state:

The restrictions on names are discussed at p 552

- the name of the LLP (the limitations that apply to the names of partnerships and companies will also apply to LLPs);
- whether the registered office of the limited liability partnership is to be situated in England and Wales, in Wales, or in Scotland;
- the address of that registered office;
- the name and address of each of the persons who are to be members of the LLP on incorporation (persons who do not wish their residential address to be made public can apply for a confidentiality order and thereby register an alternative service address);[125]
- which of those persons are to be designated members, or that every person who, from time to time, is a member of the LLP is a designated member. This requirement has no parallel in company law. The designated members are the members of the LLP charged by the legislation with ensuring that the requirements of the legislation as to disclosure and notification to the Registrar have been satisfied. A LLP must always have at least two designated members.

If the Registrar of Companies is satisfied that the above requirements have been complied with, he must register the incorporation and issue a certificate of incorporation.[126] The certificate provides conclusive evidence that the LLP has been incorporated.[127]

The financing of LLPs

A LLP can raise money for its business either from its members or by borrowing (either from a third party or from a member), including issuing debentures. Where a LLP borrows from a third party, it can give security for the loan, including the granting of a floating charge (normal partnerships cannot grant floating charges). A register of debenture holders must be kept[128] and any charges must be registered with the Registrar of Companies.[129]

Management of a LLP

A LLP, unlike a company, can adopt whatever structure for managing the entity the members choose. The LLP agreement is likely to specify the decision-making arrangements within the LLP. As we shall see, where no agreement exists, the

---

125. Currently, confidentiality orders are granted under the CA 1985, s 732B, but from 1 October 2009, the CA 2006, ss 240–246 (which relate to protected information) will also apply to LLPs.
126. LLPA 2000, s 3(1).
127. Ibid, s 3(4).
128. The CA 2006, s 743, which requires companies to keep a register of debenture holders, will also apply to LLPs by virtue of the Limited Liability Partnerships (Application of Companies Act 2006) Regulations 2009, reg 18.
129. The CA 2006, s 860, which requires charges to be registered, will also apply to LLPs by virtue of the Limited Liability Partnerships (Application of Companies Act 2006) Regulations 2009, reg 29.

default rules provide that every member may participate in management and that no member is to be paid for acting in the business or management of the LLP.

Particularly in larger LLPs, it is likely that management functions will be delegated to a management committee, and the LLP agreement should make plain how the relationship of the members and the managing members (or managers who are not members) is to be structured. One of the default rules provides that where there are differences between members 'as to ordinary matters connected with the business of the LLP', a majority decision will prevail. It is not entirely clear what constitute 'ordinary matters', but decisions that affect members but not the LLP (for example, profit sharing) will not fall within this provision.

Membership of a LLP

Unlike in a normal partnership, those who form LLPs are not known as partners, but as 'members' (another indication of how closely LLPs resemble companies). The term 'member' is used loosely throughout the various pieces of LLP legislation to refer to roles that, in companies legislation, would apply more specifically to directors, officers, or shareholders. Indeed, there is a presumption that, in companies legislation that also applies to LLPs, the terms 'director' and 'officer' apply also to members of a LLP.

There are two ways in which to become a member of a LLP:

- by subscribing to the incorporation document;
- by subsequently joining with the agreement of all of the existing members.[130]

Rights and duties

Unlike a normal partnership, there is no requirement for a LLP to have some form of agreement in place, although the frequent reference to such an agreement in the LLPA 2000 indicates that such an agreement is envisaged and encouraged. Where no agreement exists, however, the law will impose a number of default rights and duties upon the members, in very much the same way that the PA 1890, s 24, implies terms into the partnership agreement. Even where the members do have a LLP agreement, the default provisions will still apply, unless they are inconsistent with the express provisions of the agreement.

There are eleven default provisions in total: the first ten derive from the Limited Liability Partnerships Regulations 2001, reg 7, and the eleventh derives from reg 8. It will be seen that they resemble closely the terms implied by the PA 1890.

1. All of the members are entitled to share equally in the capital and profits of the LLP.
2. The LLP must indemnify each member in respect of payments made and personal liabilities incurred by him:
   (a) in the ordinary and proper conduct of the business of the LLP; or
   (b) in or about anything necessarily done for the preservation of the business or property of the LLP.

---

130. LLPA 2000, s 4(1) and (2).

3. Every member may take part in the management of the LLP.

4. No member shall be entitled to remuneration for acting in the business or management of the LLP.

5. No person may be introduced as a member or voluntarily assign an interest in a LLP without the consent of all existing members.

6. Any difference arising as to ordinary matters connected with the business of the LLP may be decided by a majority of the members, but no change may be made in the nature of the business of the LLP without the consent of all the members.

7. The members have the right to inspect and take copies of the books and records of the LLP.

8. Each member shall render true accounts and full information of all things affecting the LLP to any member or his legal representatives.

9. If a member, without the consent of the LLP, carries on any business of the same nature as, and competing with, the LLP, he must account for and pay over to the limited LLP all profits made by him in that business.

10. Every member must account to the LLP for any benefit derived by him without the consent of the LLP from any transaction concerning the LLP, or from any use by him of the property of the LLP, name or business connection.

11. No majority of the members can expel any member unless a power to do so has been conferred by express agreement between the members.

A member's duties to his co-members, other than those specified in the LLP agreement, are not entirely clear. It is uncertain whether members owe each other a duty of good faith, but comparison with company law suggests that they might do so—at least in certain circumstances (for example, a member might be required to vote in good faith and for the benefit of the LLP, and not for an ulterior motive). Whether there can be fiduciary duties between members is also uncertain. Perhaps, as in the case of directors, a member may owe a fiduciary duty to a fellow member in a particular situation in which he has voluntarily assumed such a responsibility, but not otherwise.

The members as agents

As noted, a LLP has unlimited capacity and thus has the same capacity to enter into any transaction as a natural legal person. But like other bodies corporate, the LLP can act only through others and it is important to determine to what extent the actions of others can bind the LLP.

The law of agency is discussed in Chapter 27

Under normal principles of agency, any authorized agent can bind the LLP. In addition, the LLPA 2000, s 6(1), provides that every member of a LLP is the agent of the LLP. But the LLP will not be bound by a member's actions where:

- the member had no authority to perform the act in question; or
- the person with whom the member dealt knows that he has no authority, or does not know or believe him to be a member of the LLP.[131]

---

131. Ibid, s 6(2).

A former member of the LLP who deals with a person will still be regarded as a member (and so can bind the firm) unless:

- the person has notice that the former member has ceased to be a member of the LLP; or
- notice that the former member has ceased to be a member of the limited liability partnership has been delivered to the Registrar of Companies.[132]

Minority protection

The law provides a substantial amount of protection for minority shareholders of companies. Such protection is also available to members of a LLP under the following circumstances.

🔗 Minority shareholder protection is discussed in Chapter 21

- At common law, the members of a LLP were entitled to bring a derivative action for wrongs committed against the LLP.[133] It is likely that this entitlement will continue to apply to the statutory derivative action under the CA 2006, s 260.
- A member of a LLP may petition the court where he feels that the LLP's affairs are being conducted in a manner that is unfairly prejudicial to his interests.[134] But the right to petition the court can be excluded by agreement, provided that all of the members of the LLP agree and that the agreement is set out in writing.
- A member of a LLP can petition to court to have the LLP wound up on just and equitable grounds.[135]

Cessation of membership

The LLPA 2000, s 4(3), provides that a person who wishes to cease his membership of a LLP can do so in accordance with an agreement with the other members (presumably, this agreement can be in the LLP agreement or agreed from time to time) and, in the absence of such a provision or agreement, on the giving of reasonable notice. What constitutes reasonable notice will be a question of fact.

Where a member ceases to be a member for other reasons, including his death or bankruptcy, or where he assigns his share in the LLP to another, then neither he, nor his personal representative, trustee in bankruptcy, or assignee, can interfere in the management or business affairs of the LLP.[136]

Liability of the members to contribute

In the event of a partnership being dissolved, the partners are liable for the debts of the firm, with such liability being unlimited; conversely, the members of a LLP need contribute nothing when it is wound up. There are, however, three notable exceptions to this. Firstly, the members of a LLP can be found liable for fraudulent

---

132. Ibid, s 6(3).

133. *Feetum v Levy* [2005] EWCA Civ 1601, [2006] Ch 585.

134. This remedy is provided to shareholders by virtue of the CA 2006, s 994. The draft Limited Liability Partnerships (Application of Companies Act 2006) Regulations 2009, reg 45, provides that s 994 will also apply to members of LLPs.

135. Limited Liability Partnerships Regulations 2001, Sch 3.

136. LLPA 2000, s 7.

and wrongful trading in exactly the same way as company directors can, and may therefore be required to contribute upon a winding up.[137]

Secondly, the LLPA 2000, s 1(4), provides that the members of a LLP have such liability to contribute to its assets in the event of its being wound up 'as is provided for in the Act'. Regulations created under the Act have imposed additional liability on the members by virtue of modifying the Insolvency Act 1986, s 74, which provides that a member is liable to contribute on the winding up of the LLP such sum as has been agreed between the members of the LLP. Where such an agreement exists, the liability of the members is similar to the liability of the members of a company limited by guarantee (that is, to pay what they have agreed to pay), except that the members of a LLP are not obliged to make such an agreement.

Thirdly, the Insolvency Act 1986, s 214A (known as the 'clawback' provision), allows the court to order the member to contribute an additional sum where:

- within a two-year period ending on the date of the winding up, the member withdrew any property of the LLP (including a share of the profits, drawing a salary or taking a repayment);
- it is proved by the liquidator that, at the time of the withdrawal, the member knew, or had reasonable ground for believing, that the LLP:
  - was unable to pay its debts; or
  - would become unable to pay its debts as a result of the withdrawal, and any other withdrawals made by the members contemporaneously;
- that, at the time of the withdrawal, the member knew, or ought to have known, that there was no reasonable prospect that the LLP would avoid insolvent liquidation. Like the test for wrongful trading, when determining what the member knew or ought to have known, the court will apply a dual test, taking into account what could be known by a reasonably diligent member with:
  - the knowledge and skill that could be expected from a person in that position; and
  - the knowledge and skill that the member actually had.

Disqualification

A member of a LLP can be disqualified from being a LLP member or company director under the Company Directors Disqualification Act 1986.[138] The maximum period of disqualification is fifteen years. Breaching a disqualification order constitutes a criminal offence. On summary conviction, the maximum punishment is six months' imprisonment and/or a fine not exceeding the statutory maximum (currently £5,000). On conviction on indictment, the maximum penalty is two years' imprisonment and/or a fine.[139]

⚲ The disqualification of directors is discussed at p 652

---

137. Limited Liability Partnerships Regulations 2001, reg 5.
138. Ibid, reg 4(2).
139. Company Directors Disqualification Act 1986, s 13.

Termination

Virtually all of the provisions of the Insolvency Act 1986 apply to LLPs as well as companies.[140] Therefore, its members can wind up a LLP; alternatively, it can be struck off by the Registrar of Companies (for example, where it appears to have ceased to carry on a business, is put into administration or receivership, or is wound up by a creditor).

 Various provisions of the Insolvency Act 1986 are discussed in Chapter 22

‹ › Key points summary

- Two or more persons who wish to carry on a lawful business with a view to profit can create a body corporate known as a 'limited liability partnership' (LLP).

- Generally, company law regulates LLPs and substantial portions of the CA 2006 will apply to LLPs.

- Unlike companies, LLPs can adopt any management structure that they wish.

- Members of a LLP have rights and owe duties that are similar to those of partners.

- Every member of a LLP is an agent of the LLP.

- Provisions that provide protection to minority shareholders also provide protection to members of LLPs.

- A member who wishes to leave the LLP can do so in accordance with the LLP agreement. Where no agreement exists, the member can leave by giving reasonable notice.

- Members of a LLP normally will not need to contribute if the event of the LLP being wound up. But a contribution may be required where the member is liable for fraudulent or wrongful trading, where the agreement provides for a contribution, or where the member withdraws property from the LLP.

Chapter conclusion

Incorporation and its consequent benefits—notably, corporate personality and limited liability—have contributed hugely to the social, financial, and technological developments of the last century. In 1911, Nicholas Murray Butler, then President of Colombia University, in a much-quoted passage stated: '[T]he limited liability corporation is the single greatest discovery of modern times.... Even steam and electricity are far less important than the limited liability corporation, and would be reduced to comparative impotence without it.'[141] There is little doubt that the proliferation of companies (in both size and number) is due to a massive increase in the number of persons (natural and legal) willing to invest in companies. Investment on such scope would not have occurred if a company's members were liable for the debts of the company, or if the members' liability were unlimited.

---

140. Limited Liability Partnerships Regulations 2001, SI 2001/1090, reg 5.
141. N Murray Butler, *Why Should We Change Our Form of Government?* (Girvin Press, 2007) 82.

Carrying on business through a company has a significant number of fundamental benefits. In fact, it has been argued that incorporation is too easily obtainable,[142] and that the consequent regulation, publicity, and formality are too low a price for the key benefits of corporate personality and limited liability. Such a contention is debatable. What is not debatable is that easy access to the corporate form has altered the global business landscape in a way that could never have been predicted when incorporation by registration was first introduced in 1844.

Having discussed the advantages and disadvantages of conducting business through a registered company, the next chapter will move on to discuss the role played by the various constituents that contribute to the running of the company.

Self-test questions

1. Define the following words and phrases:
   (a) corporate personality;
   (b) limited liability;
   (c) perpetual succession;
   (d) promoters;
   (e) single economic unit;
   (f) ultra vires.

2. Explain the difference between the following.
   (a) A public company and a private company.
   (b) A limited company and an unlimited company.
   (c) A company limited by shares and a company limited by guarantee.

3. Sam is the chief executive officer of AeroFlight plc, a large airline. He owns 99 per cent of the company's shares. The company owns a fleet of private airplanes, one of which is only ever used by Sam. In his will, Sam bequeaths this private plane to his son. Sam is killed in a car crash and the company refuses to let the executor's of Sam's will give the plane to Sam's son. Advise the executors.

4. The characteristics of public or private, limited or unlimited, and limited by shares or guarantee can be combined to produce five possible forms of company. Bearing in mind the restrictions that exist (for example, that a public company cannot be unlimited), what are these five possible types of company?

5. Cathryn is the sole director and shareholder of Shoes in the City Ltd, a company that sells ladies' designer shoes. Cathryn runs the business in an inefficient manner and the company is liquidated, owing a number of creditors substantial amounts of money. Two months later, Cathryn starts up a new company, also called Shoes in the City Ltd. She acquires the stock of the previous company at a considerable discount and carries on business much as before. Do the creditors have a claim against Cathryn? Will the courts pierce the veil?

6. 'The Limited Liability Partnerships Act 2000 was passed to create a business structure that was suitable for small businesses.' Do you agree with this quote? Provide reasons for your answer.

---

142. See, e.g., JS Ziegal, 'Is Incorporation (With Limited Liability) Too Easily Available?' (1990) 31 Cahiers de Droit 1075.

Further reading

Cross, SR, 'Limited Liability Partnerships Act 2000: Problems Ahead?' (2003)
JBL 268
*Discusses the background and operation of the Limited Liability Partnerships Act 2000,
and highlights a number of problem areas that are likely to impede the general
usefulness of limited liability partnerships*

Davies, PL, *Gower & Davies' Principles of Modern Company Law* (8th edn, Sweet &
Maxwell, London, 2008) ch 2
An excellent discussion of the advantages and disadvantages of incorporation

French, D, Mayson, S, and Ryan, C, *Mayson, French, & Ryan on Company Law* (25th
edn, OUP, Oxford, 2008) ch 5
*An indepth examination of the concept of corporate personality and the instances in which
the court will pierce the corporate veil; also provides an extremely useful account of
corporate law theory*

Morse, G, *Partnership Law* (6th edn, OUP, Oxford, 2006) ch 9
*Provides a detailed, yet accessible, account of the law relating to limited liability
partnerships (but note that this text was written before the passing of the Companies
Act 2006 and may be out of date in parts)*

Ottolenghi, S, 'From Peeping Behind the Corporate Veil to Ignoring It Completely'
(1990) 53 MLR 338
*Examines the way in which judicial piercing of the corporate veil can be classified; provides
an alternative classification based on the extent to which the veil is set aside*

Pickering, MA, 'The Company as a Separate Entity' (1968) 31 MLR 481
Provides a detailed analysis of the nature and extent of corporate personality

Rixon, FG, 'Competing Interests and Conflicting Principles: An Examination of
the Power of Alteration of Articles of Association' (1986) 49 MLR 446
*Provides an indepth analysis of the power to alter the articles and examines the limitations
upon this power; also discusses what remedies are available to those who wish to
challenge an alteration to the articles*

Remember to visit the **Online Resource Centre** at **<http://www.
oxfordtextbooks.co.uk/roach>** to access the following resources
on Chapter 17, 'Incorporation and bodies corporate': more **practice
questions** and answers; a **glossary** of key terms; **multiple-choice
questions**; **revision summaries**; and **audio updates** when relevant.

18 The constituents of a company

- The shareholders
- The directors
- The company secretary

- The auditor
- Creditors

INTRODUCTION

Although a company is a legal person, it is highly dependent upon other legal persons and natural persons to operate it, and to provide it with the resources that it needs to continue. Certain persons are required by all companies (for example, all companies must have at least one director) and there are other persons who will be required by most companies (for example, most companies will need to appoint a company auditor and most companies will have shareholders). Finally, certain persons are required by some companies (for example, public companies are required to appoint a company secretary). Without these various constituents, companies could not exist. Accordingly, this chapter will discuss the principal constituents who make up, and contribute to, the success of the company, beginning with the most numerous constituent—namely, the shareholders.

The shareholders

Shareholders play two vital roles. Firstly, through the purchase of shares, they contribute capital to the company. The nature of shares and share capital is discussed in detail in Chapter 19. In this chapter, we will focus instead on the second vital role of the shareholders—namely, their ability to make decisions. As will be seen, a significant amount of power is placed in the hands of the shareholders and numerous key decisions are reserved for them alone. But before we discuss the shareholder's ability to exercise this power, it is important to understand the difference between a company's shareholders and its members.

Shareholders and members

In the previous chapter, we briefly noted that the terms 'shareholder' and 'member' are used interchangeably, and, in the vast majority of cases, a shareholder will also be a member and vice versa. But there is a difference and it is important that this difference is understood. The most obvious difference occurs in a company that does not have a share capital (for example, a company limited by guarantee): such companies have members, but they do not have shareholders.

But the distinction exists even in companies that have a share capital. Purchasing shares might make a person a shareholder, but it does not automatically make him a member. What constitutes membership of the company is stated in the Companies Act 2006 (CA 2006), s 112, which provides that:

- the subscribers of a company's memorandum are deemed to have agreed to become members of the company, and, on its registration, become members and must be entered as such in the register of members;
- every other person who agrees to become a member of the company and whose name is entered in its register of members is a member of the company.

Therefore a person may purchase shares in a company (thereby making him a shareholder), but he will not become a member until he has agreed to become a member and his name has been entered in the register of members. It will be noted that the definition of 'member' in s 112 does not actually refer to the purchase of shares. This means that a company is free to enter persons in the register of members who have not purchased shares, although this would be highly unusual.

Because in the vast majority of cases, a member will also be a shareholder and vice versa, the practice of using the terms interchangeably will continue.

Resolutions

As we shall see, the general power to manage the company is usually vested in the directors by the company's articles. Despite this, there are still a number of extremely important powers that may be exercised by the members, including:

- only the members can amend the company's articles;[1]
- approval of the members is required if the company wishes to:
  - convert from a private company to a public company,[2] or vice versa;[3] or
  - convert from an unlimited company to a limited company;[4]
- the members have the power to remove a director (or directors) from office;[5]
- numerous loans and other transactions involving directors require the approval of the members;

  Transactions involving the directors that require approval of the members are discussed at p 710

- the members must approve a director's service contract if it is over two years in length;[6]
- the members may ratify conduct of the directors that amounts to negligence, default, breach of duty, or breach of trust;[7]
- the members may petition the court to have the company wound up.[8]

The company's members exercise these powers via the passing of resolutions. A resolution is simply a more formal word for a vote, whereby the members resolve themselves to a particular decision or course of action.

→ *resolutions: decisions arrived at by a formal vote*

---

1. CA 2006, s 21(1).　　2. Ibid, s 90(1).

3. Ibid, s 97(1).　　4. Ibid, s 105(1).

5. Ibid, s 168(1).　　6. Ibid, s 188.

7. Ibid, s 239.　　8. Insolvency Act 1986, s 122(1)(a).

Types of resolution

The CA 2006 provides for two different types of resolution, as follows.

1. *Ordinary resolution* An ordinary resolution of the members is one passed by a simple majority[9] (that is, over 50 per cent—remembering that an exact 50 per cent split means that the resolution is lost).

2. *Special resolution* A special resolution of the members is one passed by a majority of not less than 75 per cent.[10] Special resolutions tend to be reserved for more important decisions and constitutional changes.

Where the resolution is tabled at a meeting, the above majorities refer to those persons present at the meeting, not to the total members of the company. Often, the CA 2006 will simply state that a resolution is required, without specifying its type. Where this is the case, the resolution required will be an ordinary resolution, but the company is free to require a higher majority (or unanimity) by inserting a provision in its articles to that effect.[11] Where the CA 2006 specifies that an ordinary or special resolution is required, the articles cannot alter the majority required.

Regarding public companies, resolutions can only be passed at a meeting of the members.[12] If the company is private, the members can pass resolutions at a meeting, or they can take advantage of what is known as a 'written resolution'.[13]

Written resolutions

The convening of a meeting and the passing of a formal resolution at the meeting involves compliance with a substantial body of procedures that can prove onerous and potentially costly, especially for smaller companies. Further, where the number of members is small or where the directors are the members, convening a meeting in order to pass resolutions seems a somewhat redundant exercise. Accordingly, the CA 2006 allows private companies to pass a written resolution in substitute for a resolution passed at a meeting and the ability to substitute a written resolution cannot be excluded by the articles.[14]

The written resolution procedure can be used for any resolution, except two:[15]

1. a resolution to remove a director before the expiry of his office[16] must be passed at a meeting; and

2. a resolution to remove an auditor before the expiry of his office[17] must be passed at a meeting.

In both cases, the director or auditor whose removal is sought has a statutory right to be heard at (in the case of a director), or to make written representations to (in the case of an auditor), the meeting that seeks his removal, so a written resolution would be inappropriate, because it would deny this right. Written resolutions require the

---

9. CA 2006, s 282(1). 10. Ibid, s 283(1).
11. Ibid, s 281(3). 12. Ibid, s 281(2).
13. Ibid, s 281(1). 14. Ibid, s 300.
15. Ibid, s 288(2). 16. Ibid, s 168.
17. Ibid, s 510.

same majorities, and have the same force, as resolutions passed at meetings.[18] Where the company has a share capital, each shareholder has one vote per share. As regards companies without a share capital, each member has one vote.[19] The procedures for the passing of a written resolution depend on whether the directors or the members propose the resolution.

Where the directors propose a written resolution, the company must send a copy of the proposed resolution (in hard-copy form, by electronic means, or by means of a website) to every member eligible to vote.[20] This must be accompanied by a statement informing the member how to signify agreement to the resolution and the date by which the resolution must be passed.[21] Failure to comply with these requirements constitutes an either-way offence by every officer of the company who is in default,[22] but a failure to comply with these requirements will not affect the validity of the resolution if passed.[23]

The members of a private company may also require a written resolution if they hold 5 per cent of the total voting rights in the company, or some other lower percentage specified in the articles.[24] If a company is required to circulate a resolution, the resolution proposed by the members must be circulated by the company along with, if the members so desire, a statement of no more than 1,000 words supporting the resolution.[25] The resolution and accompanying statement can be in either hard-copy or electronic form, but must be circulated to all eligible members within twenty-one days of the company receiving the proposal from the members.[26] As with written resolutions proposed by the directors, the resolution must be accompanied by a statement informing the member how to signify agreement to the resolution and the date by which the resolution must be passed.[27] Failure to comply with these requirements constitutes an either-way offence,[28] but a failure to comply with these requirements will not affect the validity of the resolution if passed. The expense of circulating the resolution and accompanying statements is borne by the members who requested the circulation of the materials, unless the company resolves otherwise.[29]

A written resolution may not be proposed by the members if:

- if passed, it would be ineffective (for example, because it is inconsistent with legislation or the company's constitution);

---

18. Ibid, s 288(5). Under the CA 1985, all written resolutions required unanimity.
19. Ibid, s 284(1). As we shall see, this differs from resolutions passed at a general meeting, where the general rule is one vote per shareholder.
20. Ibid, s 291(2) and (3)(a).
21. Ibid, s 291(4).
22. Ibid, s 291(5) and (6). On summary conviction, the offence is punishable by a fine not exceeding the statutory maximum (currently £5,000). On conviction on indictment, there is no limit on the fine that can be imposed.
23. Ibid, s 291(7).
24. Ibid, s 292(1), (4), and (5).
25. Ibid, s 292(3).
26. Ibid, s 293(2)(a) and (3).
27. Ibid, s 293(4).
28. Ibid, s 293(5) and (6). On summary conviction, the offence is punishable by a fine not exceeding the statutory maximum (currently £5,000). On conviction on indictment, there is no limit on the fine that can be imposed.
29. Ibid, s 294(1).

- it is defamatory; or
- it is frivolous or vexatious.[30]

Irrespective of who proposed the written resolution, it must be passed within a certain period or it will lapse. This period can be specified in the company's articles, but if it is not, the resolution will lapse twenty-eight days after the copy of the resolution was first circulated to the company's members.[31]

The procedure for signifying agreement to a written resolution is found in the CA 2006, s 296(1), which provides that a member signifies his agreement to a proposed written resolution when the company receives from him (or from someone acting on his behalf) an authenticated document:

- identifying the resolution to which it relates; and
- indicating his agreement to the resolution.

This document can be sent as hard copy or, if the company agrees (generally or specifically),[32] in electronic form.[33] Once a member has signified agreement, it cannot be revoked.[34]

Company meetings

The resolutions of public companies must be passed at meetings; resolutions of private companies must be passed by meeting unless the written resolution procedure is used. Other than to remove a director or an auditor before the expiry of his term of office, a private company may go its entire existence without ever having to call a meeting. Conversely, public companies must have at least one meeting every financial year and this meeting is known as the 'annual general meeting' (AGM). Resolutions passed at general meetings are only valid if the procedural requirements laid down in the CA 2006 are complied with,[35] and these procedures cannot usually be excluded or modified by the articles.

These procedural requirements are extensive and, after their discussion, it will be easier to appreciate why the written resolution procedure is so valued by private companies.

The calling of meetings

The general power to call a general meeting is vested in the directors,[36] but the CA 2006, s 303, grants members the power to require that the directors call a general meeting of the company. The directors are required to call a meeting only if the request derives from:

- members representing 10 per cent of the company's paid-up share capital; or
- if the company does not have a share capital, members representing 10 per cent of the voting rights of all the members.[37]

---

30. Ibid, s 292(2).   31. Ibid, s 297(1).
32. Ibid, s 298(1).   33. Ibid, s 296(2).
34. Ibid, s 296(3).   35. Ibid, s 301.
36. Ibid, s 302. This power, like all powers of the directors, must be exercised for the purpose for which it was conferred (s 171).
37. Ibid, s 303(2) and (3).

But where the company is a private company and more than twelve months has elapsed since the last general meeting at which the members had the right to circulate a resolution, then the qualifying threshold is reduced to 5 per cent.[38]

The members' request must state the general nature of the business to be dealt with at the requested meeting and may also include any resolutions proposed to be voted on at the meeting.[39] But a resolution cannot be proposed if:

- it would, if passed, be ineffective;
- it is defamatory; or
- it is frivolous or vexatious.[40]

The members' request may be in hard copy or, if the company agrees, in electronic form, and must be authenticated by the member(s) making it.[41]

Once a valid request from the members has been received, the directors must, within twenty-one days, call a general meeting, which must be held within twenty-eight days of the date of the notice convening the meeting.[42] If the request proposes a resolution intended to be voted on at the meeting, the notice of the meeting must also include notice of the resolution.[43] If a special resolution is proposed, the notice must include the text of the special resolution and must indicate that it is a special resolution.[44]

If the directors fail to comply with a valid request from the members to call a meeting, then the CA 2006, s 305, grants those members who requested the meeting, or any of them representing over half of the total voting rights of the company, the power to call a meeting themselves at the company's expense, provided that such expenses are reasonable.[45] This meeting must take place within three months of the date on which the directors became subject to the requirement to call a meeting.[46]

Where it is not practicable to call a meeting in accordance with the above provisions, then the court may, of its own volition or upon the application of a director or member, order a meeting to be called, held, and conducted in any manner that it deems fit.[47] The purpose of this is to prevent members or directors from frustrating meetings through their own conduct (for example, by refusing to attend, so that the meeting is inquorate).

Notice of meetings

Resolutions passed at general meetings are only valid if adequate notice of the meeting and of the resolution is provided to those entitled to such notice.[48] All of the members (irrespective of whether or not they are entitled to vote) are entitled to notice of a meeting, including those to whom shares have been transmitted through death or bankruptcy.[49] In addition, notice must be provided to all of the company's

38. Ibid, s 303(3).
39. Ibid, s 303(4).
40. Ibid, s 303(5).
41. Ibid, s 303(6).
42. Ibid, s 304(1).
43. Ibid, s 304(2).
44. Ibid, ss 304(4) and 283(6).
45. Ibid, s 305(1) and (6).
46. Ibid, s 305(3).
47. Ibid, s 306.
48. Ibid, s 301.
49. Ibid, s 310(1)(a) and (2).

directors[50] and its auditor.[51] Except in relation to the company's auditor, these entitlements of notice may be modified by the company's articles.[52]

Notice of a meeting must state the time, date, and place of the meeting, and, subject to the articles, the general nature of the business to be dealt with at the meeting.[53] It is usual for this information to be sent to all members in the form of a 'circular', which is also likely to contain a brief agenda setting out the business of the meeting. The members have the power to require the company to circulate a statement of not more than 1,000 words in relation to a matter referred to in a proposed resolution, or any other business dealt with at the meeting.[54] But this power only arises if a sufficient number of members require the statement to be circulated:

- members representing at least 5 per cent of the total voting rights of all the members who have a relevant right to vote (that is, to vote on a proposed resolution); or

- at least a hundred members who have a relevant right to vote and hold shares in the company on which there has been paid up an average sum, per member, of at least £100.

Paid-up capital is discussed at p 677

Notice can be provided:

- in hard-copy form (for example, a letter sent out to the members informing them of the meeting);
- in electronic form (for example, an email sent to the members);
- by means of a website;[55] and
- partly by one of these means and partly by another.[56]

Notice must also be provided within a sufficient period prior to the meeting. Notice of a meeting must generally be provided at least fourteen days prior to the meeting, rising to twenty-one days in the case of the AGM of a public company.[57] The company's articles are free to specify a longer notice period,[58] but they cannot specify a shorter notice period. It is possible to shorten the notice period of a meeting, but only with the agreement of the majority of the shareholders having the right to attend and vote at the meeting, who, together, hold not less than the requisite percentage in nominal value of the shares.[59] In the case of a private company, the requisite percentage is 90 per cent (or higher if the articles specify, subject to a maximum of 95 per cent) of the nominal value of the shares, or, if the company does not have a share capital, of the total voting rights at that meeting. In the case of a public company, the requisite percentage is 95 per cent.[60] The notice period of a public company's AGM

---

50. Ibid, s 310(1)(b).　　51. Ibid, s 502(2)(a).
52. Ibid, s 310(4)(b).　　53. Ibid, s 311.
54. Ibid, s 314(1).
55. Notice placed on a website must remain on the site throughout the period beginning on the date of notification and ending with the conclusion of the meeting (s 309(3)).
56. CA 2006, s 308.
57. Ibid, s 307(1) and (2). The day on which notice is given and the day of the meeting are excluded (s 360).
58. Ibid, s 307(3).
59. Ibid, s 307(4) and (5)(a).
60. Ibid, s 307(6).

can only be shortened if all of the members entitled to attend and vote agree to the shorter notice period.[61]

If, at the meeting, a resolution is proposed that purports to do any of the following, then special notice of that resolution is required:

- remove a director under CA 2006, s 168;
- appoint a person to fill the vacancy caused by the removal of a director under s 168; or
- remove or replace an auditor under CA 2006, s 510 or 515.

In such cases, those entitled to notice must receive notice of the resolution at least twenty-eight days before the meeting at which the resolution is to be voted on.[62]

Procedure at meetings

In addition to the procedures relating to the calling of general meetings and the provision of notice, the actual meeting itself is also subject to a raft of procedural requirements. A meeting (and any decisions made at it) will only be valid if a quorum is present. In relation to company meetings, a quorum is the minimum number of 'qualifying persons' required in order validly to conduct business. A qualifying person is:

- a member of the company;
- a representative of a corporate member; or
- a proxy of the member.[63]

proxy: someone appointed by a member to vote on his behalf

Where a limited company has only one qualifying member, that member constitutes a quorum.[64] In all other cases, two qualifying persons constitute a quorum, unless the articles provide otherwise.[65] The members need not be in the same place to establish a quorum.[66]

If a quorum is not present, the meeting is said to be 'inquorate' and no business may be conducted at the meeting, except the appointment of a chair for the meeting.[67] The CA 2006, s 319, provides that a member may be elected to act as the chairman of a company meeting, but this is subject to the articles, and the model articles for both private and public companies provide that, normally, the chair will be appointed by the directors. If the directors have not appointed a chairman, however, or if their chairman is unwilling to chair or is not present within 10 minutes of the start of the meeting, then the directors or members may appoint a director or shareholder to chair the meeting.[68] The choice of chair can be crucial for two reasons: firstly, it is the responsibility of the chair to supervise the meetings and to resolve

---

61. Ibid, s 337(2).
62. Ibid, s 312(1).
63. Ibid, s 318(3). In all cases, the member in question must be entitled to vote (*Henderson v James Loutitt and Co Ltd* (1894) 21 R 674).
64. Ibid, s 318(1).
65. Ibid, s 318(2). If one member appoints two proxies or two representatives, the two proxies or representatives will not constitute a quorum (s 318(2)(a) and (b)).
66. The Companies (Model Articles) Regulations 2008, SI 2008/3229, Sch 1, para 38, and Sch 3, para 30.
67. Ibid, Sch 1, para 37(4), and Sch 3, para 29(4).
68. Ibid, Sch 1, para 39, and Sch 3, para 31.

any disputes that arise; secondly, it is common for a company's articles to provide the chair with the casting vote in the event of split vote (although the model articles contain no such provision in relation to company meetings).

Regarding the passing of resolutions at the meeting, there are two methods of voting:

- on a show of hands; or
- by poll.

The general rule is that resolutions are taken on a show of hands and so each member will have one vote. The model articles for both private and public companies provide that a resolution at a meeting will be decided on a show of hands unless a poll is demanded in accordance with the articles.[69] Unless the articles provide otherwise, where a vote is taken on a poll, each member will have one vote per share (unless the company has no share capital, in which case, each member has one vote).[70] The members have the right to demand that a vote be taken on a poll and any provision in the articles that purports to exclude this right is void, unless it relates to the election of a chair or the adjournment of the meeting.[71] A company's articles may stipulate that a certain number of members are required to demand a poll, but this cannot be greater than:

- five members entitled to vote;
- a member or members representing 10 per cent of the total voting rights of member entitled to vote on the resolution; or
- a member or members representing at least 10 per cent of the company's paid-up share capital.[72]

Members need not attend the meeting to exercise their voting rights. The CA 2006, s 324, grants members the right to appoint another person (who may or may not be a member) to exercise their rights to attend, speak, and vote at general meetings, and this person is known as a 'proxy'. Members with multiple shares are free to appoint multiple proxies. In large public companies, the appointment of proxies is especially important, because only a small minority of the company's members will actually attend the meeting. When public companies send out notice of a meeting, it is common for the notice to contain a document allowing the member to appoint a proxy who can exercise the member's vote. Unsurprisingly, the person nominated by the company to act as proxy is usually one of the directors.

The annual general meeting

Under the CA 1985, both public and private companies were required to hold an annual general meeting (AGM), although private companies could opt out of this requirement. The CA 2006 does not require private companies to hold an AGM, although they may do so. Public companies must hold an AGM every year within a six-month period ending on the date of the company's financial year.[73] Failure to

---

69. Ibid, Sch 1, para 42, and Sch 3, para 34.   70. CA 2006, s 284(3).
71. Ibid, s 321(1).   72. Ibid, s 321(2).
73. Ibid, s 336(1).

hold an AGM in the required period constitutes an either-way offence on the part of every officer of the company who is in default.[74]

The AGM is subject to its own procedures, which must be complied with by any company that holds an AGM. As noted above, the normal notice period for a meeting is fourteen days, but where the meeting is an AGM of a public company, this is extended to twenty-one days.[75] This notice period can be reduced, but only with the consent of all of the members entitled to attend and vote.[76] The notice of any AGM must state that the meeting is an AGM.[77]

The CA 2006 does not prescribe what business must be dealt with at the AGM, but it is customary that certain matters be dealt with there—namely, the laying out of the accounts and the directors' report, and the reappointment of the directors and/or auditor. In listed companies, the 'board should use the AGM to communicate with investors and to encourage their participation'.[78] In such companies, the AGM is likely to constitute the only opportunity that the members will have to question the board.

Records of meetings and resolutions

Every company must keep, for a period of ten years, records comprising:

- copies of all resolutions passed otherwise than at a general meeting;
- the minutes of all proceedings at general meetings; and
- if the company is a limited company with a single member, any decisions of that member (except written resolutions) that may be taken by the company in general meeting and which may have effect as if they were taken in general meeting.[79]

Failure to keep such records constitutes a summary offence by each officer who is in default.[80] These records must be kept at the company's registered office or at a place specified by the Secretary of State, and can be inspected, free of charge, by any member of the company.[81] Failure to allow inspection constitutes a summary offence by every officer in default.[82]

Unanimous consent

Convening meetings and passing resolutions can be a complex issue and failing to comply with the numerous procedural requirements could invalidate any decisions made. To mitigate this stringency, the common law has long provided that if all of

---

74. Ibid, s 336(3). On summary conviction, the offence is punishable by a fine not exceeding the statutory maximum (currently £5,000). On conviction on indictment, there is no limit on the fine that can be imposed (s 336(4)).
75. Ibid, s 307(2)(a).
76. Ibid, s 337(2).
77. Ibid, s 337(1).
78. Financial Reporting Council, *The Combined Code on Corporate Governance* (June 2008) [D.2].
79. CA 2006, ss 355(1), (2), and 357(2).
80. Ibid, s 355(3) and (4). The offence is punishable by a fine not exceeding level 3 on the standard scale (currently £1,000).
81. Ibid, s 358(1)–(3).
82. Ibid, s 358(5) and (6). The offence is punishable by a fine not exceeding level 3 on the standard scale (currently £1,000).

the members entitled to vote on a matter agree on the matter, then that agreement is valid even if no meeting was convened and no resolution took place.[83] This rule tends to be known as the *Duomatic* principle, named after the case of *Re Duomatic Ltd*,[84] in which Buckley J stated:

> ...where it can be shown that all shareholders who have a right to attend and vote at a general meeting of the company assent to some matter which a general meeting of the company could carry into effect, that assent is as binding as a resolution in general meeting would be.[85]

Because the procedural rules relating to the passing of resolutions and the convening of meetings are put in place to protect the members as a whole, it is unsurprising that the ability of the members to make a decision through unanimous consent is closely watched. Restrictions on the rule include the following.

- Nothing less than unanimity will suffice. Thus a member who held 99 per cent of a company's shares could not take advantage of the *Duomatic* principle by himself.[86]
- Unanimous consent will not suffice where the decision in question could not have been taken at a meeting.[87]
- Unanimous consent cannot be used to circumvent prohibitions imposed by the CA 2006.
- It is likely that decisions that cannot be taken by written resolution (namely, the removal of a director or auditor) also cannot be taken by unanimous consent.

Earlier in the chapter, we noted that all resolutions of the company must be registered with the Registrar of Companies. It is likely that any decisions taken by means of unanimous agreement would also need to be registered with the Registrar.

‹› Key points summary

- Shareholders make important decisions regarding the company's activities via the passing of resolutions.

- An ordinary resolution requires a simple majority (that is, over 50 per cent) to pass. A special resolution requires not less than 75 per cent to pass.

- Resolutions of public companies must be passed at general meetings, but private companies can pass most resolutions via a written resolution without the need for a meeting.

- The general power to call meetings is vested in the directors.

- Resolutions passed at meetings are valid only if adequate notice of the meeting is provided to persons entitled to such notice.

---

83. *Baroness Wenlock v The River Dee Co* (1883) 36 Ch D 675 (CA).
84. [1969] 2 Ch 365 (Ch).
85. Ibid, 373.
86. *Re D'Jan of London* [1994] 1 BCLC 561 (Ch).
87. *Re New Cedos Engineering Co Ltd* [1994] 1 BCLC 797 (Ch).

- A meeting, and any resolutions passed at it, will only be valid if a quorum is present. A quorum is the minimum number of persons needed to conduct business.

- Public companies must hold an AGM each financial year. Private companies may hold an AGM, but are not required to.

- Many decisions normally requiring a resolution may be passed without a meeting and without passing a resolution, provided that all of the members agree to the decision.

The directors

A company may be a legal person possessing its own rights and powers, but it requires human intermediaries in order to exercise the powers granted to it. As we have seen, certain powers of the company are exercisable only by the members, but the power to run the company generally is vested in the directors. The CA 2006 provides that every private company must have at least one director and that every public company must have at least two directors.[88] A director can be a natural person or a body corporate, but every company must have at least one director who is a natural person.[89]

The definition of 'director'

A company may be run by individuals who are described by the articles, or describe themselves, as 'governors' or 'managers'. Conversely, the practice is growing whereby individuals who are not involved in management at board level are called 'directors'. Are such persons actually directors? Answering this question is crucial, because many provisions in the CA 2006 are aimed squarely at directors of the company.

The CA 2006 does not define what a director is; rather, it provides who is included within the office of director. Section 250 provides that a director 'includes any person occupying the position of director, by whatever name called'. This encompasses those who have been validly appointed to the office of director (who are known as *de jure* directors), but also encompasses persons who have not been validly appointed, but who act as directors (such persons are known as *de facto* directors). De facto directors, although not validly appointed, are directors, and are subject to the obligations and duties of that office (for example, they are subject to the general duties imposed on directors).[90]

➡ *de jure*: 'in law'

➡ *de facto*: 'in fact'

Shadow directors

A person who has neither been appointed a director, nor acted as director, may, for certain purposes, be treated as a director if he is 'a person in accordance with whose directions or instructions the directors of the company are accustomed to act',[91] other

---

88. CA 2006, s 154.
89. Ibid, s 155(1).
90. *Re Canadian Land Reclaiming and Colonizing Co* (1880) 14 Ch D 660 (CA).
91. CA 2006, s 251(1).

than where that advice is given in a professional capacity.[92] Such a person is termed a 'shadow director'. It is vital that shadow directors can be identified, because the CA 2006 often expressly states that a particular duty or obligation is also imposed upon shadow directors (for example, regarding the rules relating to directorial transactions that require shareholder approval, a shadow director is to be treated as a director).[93] In practice, however, determining who constitutes a shadow director is not always straightforward. That the courts often give inconsistent guidance does not help the issue.[94]

Two cases provide the principal guidance.

 Transactions involving directors that require shareholder approval are discussed at p 710

 Secretary of State for Trade and Industry v Deverell [2001] Ch 340 (CA)

FACTS: The facts are not relevant for our purposes.

HELD: Morritt LJ established five propositions, as follows.[95]

1. The definition of a shadow director should not be strictly construed.

2. It is not necessary for a shadow director to give directions or instructions over the whole field of the company's activities.

3. Whether a communication by a shadow director constitutes a direction or instruction is to be assessed objectively.

4. Non-professional advice can constitute a direction or instruction.

5. It is not necessary to show that the *de jure* directors acted in a subservient manner or surrendered their respective discretions.

★ See J Payne, 'Casting Light into the Shadows: *Secretary of State for Trade and Industry v Deverell*' (2001) 22 Co Law 90

 Ultraframe (UK) Ltd v Fielding [2005] EWHC 1638 (Ch)

FACTS: The facts are not relevant for our purposes.

HELD: Lewison J provided the following guidance.

- It is insufficient that some of the *de jure* directors follow the directions or instructions of the purported shadow director. In order for a person to be a shadow director, a governing majority of the board must be accustomed to acting on his directions and instructions.[96]

---

92. Ibid, s 251(2).
93. Ibid, s 223(1).
94. For example, in *Secretary of State for Trade and Industry v Hollier* [2006] EWHC 1804 (Ch), [2007] Bus LR 352, the High Court stated that shadow directorships and de facto directorships were alternatives. But in *Secretary of State for Trade and Industry v Aviss* [2006] EWHC 1846 (Ch), [2007] BCC 288 (Ch), the High Court held that a person could simultaneously be a shadow director and *de facto* director.
95. *Secretary of State for Trade and Industry v Deverell* [2001] Ch 340 (CA) 354.
96. *Ultraframe (UK) Ltd v Fielding* [2005] EWHC 1638 (Ch), [2006] FSR 17, [1272].

- The *de jure* directors must be 'accustomed' to a person's directions and instructions for that person to be a shadow director. Accordingly, there may be an initial period during which a person who gives directions and instructions is not a shadow director. Further, transactions entered into before the *de jure* directors become accustomed cannot be retrospectively invalidated.[97]

- A person will not become a shadow director until the directors actually act in accordance with his directions and instructions.[98] The mere giving of directions and instructions is insufficient.

- Shadow directors are not subject to the same duties as *de jure* and *de facto* directors.[99]

⭐ See DD Prentice and J Payne, 'Directors' Fiduciary Duties' (2006) 122 LQR 558

Chairman and managing director

Senior members of the board may undertake additional services for the company, which could include being appointed to positions of seniority over their fellow directors. Two positions are of importance:

- a director may be appointed as the 'managing director' (also known as the 'chief executive officer', or CEO), the exact role of whom will depend upon the company in question;

- a director may be appointed as the 'chairman', whose role is to chair board meetings and, in the event of deadlock, usually to have the casting vote.

Historically, it was common for one person to act as both managing director and chairman. But fearing that this concentrated too much power in one person, the Combined Code now provides that listed companies must:

- split the roles of chairman and managing director;[100] and
- appoint a chairman who is an independent non-executive director.[101]

Executive and non-executive directors

It is important that students understand the distinction between executive and non-executive directors, especially given the recent prominence of non-executive directors as a governance mechanism. It is worth stressing at the outset that the CA 2006 does not recognize the distinction, and that it treats executive and non-executives alike (the phrase 'non-executive director' does not appear anywhere in the CA 2006).

🔗 Visit the **Online Resource Centre** 🌐 for more on non-executive directors as a mechanism for improving standards of corporate governance in the chapter entitled 'Corporate governance'

Executive directors work for the company full-time and are responsible for the company's day-to-day management. Conversely, non-executive directors are

---

97. Ibid, [1274]–[1277].
98. Ibid, [1278].
99. Ibid, [1279]–[1356].
100. Financial Reporting Council, *The Combined Code on Corporate Governance* (June 2008) [A.2.1].
101. Ibid, [A.2.2].

part-time directors, devoting around one or two days a month to the company,[102] and tend to be paid considerably less than their executive counterparts (around £30,000 per year). Although non-executive directors will be involved in management, from a governance standpoint, their key role is monitoring (from a theoretically neutral standpoint) the activities of the executives. The Combined Code provides that, except for smaller companies, at least half of the board should comprise independent non-executive directors.[103]

Eligibility and appointment

Eligibility

Generally, anyone can be appointed to the office of director, but statute does impose certain restrictions.

- An individual under the age of 16 cannot be appointed as a director,[104] unless the appointment is not to take effect until the individual's sixteenth birthday,[105] or the appointment is within an exception specified by the Secretary of State.[106]
- A company's auditor is disqualified from acting as its director.[107]
- An undischarged bankrupt who acts as a director commits an either-way offence,[108] unless leave has been obtained from the court.[109]

Who appoints the directors?

In Chapter 17, we noted that the registration documents submitted to the Registrar of Companies will need to include details of the company's proposed officers.[110] Accordingly, a company's first directors are nominated when the company is first registered and such persons will be appointed to the office of director upon the company's registration.[111] Following the company's incorporation, directors may vacate office or the board may wish to expand its number. The power to appoint directors post-incorporation is usually a matter for the company's articles, but where the articles are silent on this, the power to appoint directors is vested in the members[112] and is usually exercised by passing an ordinary resolution.

The model articles for private companies limited by shares[113] and the model articles for public companies[114] provide that directors may be appointed:

- by an ordinary resolution of the members; or
- by a decision of the directors.

---

102. In many cases, non-executives spend the rest of their time acting as executives in other companies.
103. Financial Reporting Council, *The Combined Code on Corporate Governance* (June 2008) [A.3.2].
104. CA 2006, s 157(1).   105. Ibid, s 157(2).
106. Ibid, s 158.   107. Ibid, s 1214(1) and (2).
108. On summary conviction, the maximum punishment is six months' imprisonment and/or a fine not exceeding the statutory maximum (currently £5,000). On conviction on indictment, the maximum penalty is two years' imprisonment and/or a fine (Company Directors Disqualification Act 1986, s 13).
109. Ibid, s 11(1).   110. CA 2006, s 9(4)(c).
111. Ibid, s 16(6).
112. *Worcester Corsetry Ltd v Witting* [1936] Ch 640 (CA).
113. The Companies (Model Articles) Regulations 2008, SI 2008/3229, Sch 1, para 17(1).
114. Ibid, Sch 3, para 20(1).

When appointing directors, the members must exercise their power of appointment for the benefit of the company as a whole.[115] Regarding public companies, two or more persons cannot be appointed by one resolution, and any such appointment is void unless the general meeting has unanimously approved such a procedure.[116] A director appointed by the directors of a public company will only hold office until the next AGM, whereupon he must vacate office and may offer himself for reappointment.[117]

Where the company is listed, the appointment of directors should be led by a nomination committee, which should consist predominantly of independent non-executive directors.[118] This rule was introduced to combat the perception of the 'old boys' network' that many believe operated amongst larger public companies. This nomination committee will make recommendations to the board regarding appointments.

Any appointment will only become effective once the person in question has agreed to act as director.[119] Lack of capacity or understanding may vitiate such agreement.

Service contracts

A person who is appointed as an executive director will almost certainly have a contract with the company known as a 'service contract'. Such a service contract could:

- derive entirely from any conditions of service set out in the articles of the company; or
- be a separate contract, which, expressly or impliedly, incorporates any conditions of service set out in the articles; or
- be a self-contained contract.

The final type of service contract offers the greatest protection to an executive director (or other executive officer). This is because a contract that derives from the articles, or which incorporates the articles, may be changed by the company in accordance with the usual rules for the alteration of a company's articles. Consequently, because the articles change, the service contract changes,[120] although a change in the articles cannot deprive a director of rights that had accrued before the change.[121] The law imposes restrictions regarding the length of a director's service contract—namely, that it cannot provide be for over two years in length, unless it has been approved by the company's members.[122]

The limitation on the length of a director's service contract is discussed in more detail at p 710

---

115. *Re HR Harmer Ltd* [1959] 1 WLR 62 (CA).
116. CA 2006, s 160.
117. The Companies (Model Articles) Regulations 2008, SI 2008/3229, Sch 3, para 21(2).
118. Financial Reporting Council, *The Combined Code on Corporate Governance* (June 2008) [A.4.1].
119. *Re British Empire Match Co Ltd* (1888) 59 LT 291.
120. *Read v Astoria Garage (Streatham) Ltd* [1952] Ch 637 (CA).
121. *Swabey v Port Darwin Gold Mining Co Ltd* (1889) 1 Meg 385 (CA). Hence if a director's entitlement to be paid derives from the articles, he could have his salary for the future reduced, but could not be deprived of sums already earned.
122. CA 2006, s 188.

The board

Board meetings

Collectively, the directors are referred to as the 'board' and, as we shall see, much of a company's power is concentrated in its board. The board exercises its power via board meetings (not to be confused with general meetings of the members) and the procedures relating to the function of board meetings are found in the company's articles. Decisions of the directors are only valid if made at a board meeting, unless all of the directors agree with, or acquiesce to, a decision.[123] The general rule is that decisions at board meetings are made by majority vote,[124] but a decision can be made via a written resolution if all of the directors agree to the decision in writing. Where the number of votes is equal, the chairman or other director chairing the meeting will have the casting vote.

The model articles allow any director to call a board meeting by giving notice to the other directors.[125] It is not necessary that all of the directors are present at the meeting, but decisions at board meetings are only valid if a quorum can be obtained. The model articles for public and private companies set the quorum at two,[126] but companies are free to increase (but not decrease) this number if they choose. Decisions taken at a meeting that lacks a quorum (known as an 'inquorate meeting') are invalid.[127]

The proceedings of the board meeting must be recorded[128] (these proceedings are known as the 'minutes') and kept for at least ten years from the date of the meeting.[129] Failure to take minutes, or to keep them for the requisite period, constitutes a summary offence by every officer who is in default,[130] but decisions taken at an unminuted meeting are not invalidated by the failure to take minutes.[131] Once the chairman authenticates the minutes, they will provide evidence of the proceedings of that meeting.[132]

Powers of management

A company, while a legal person, can only operate and be operated through human intermediaries. This raises the issue of who has the power to run the company. The power to run the company is initially vested in the members of the company. But in all but the smallest companies (in which the directors and members are normally the same persons), it is impractical for the members to exercise day-to-day control over the company's affairs and their powers are therefore delegated to surrogates. Since

---

123. *Charterhouse Investment Trust Ltd v Tempest Diesels Ltd* [1986] BCLC 1 (Ch).

124. The Companies (Model Articles) Regulations 2008, SI 2008/3229, Sch 1, para 7(1), and Sch 3, para 13(1).

125. Ibid, Sch 1, para 9(1), and Sch 3, para 8(1).

126. Unless the company is private and has only one director (ibid, Sch 1, para 7(2)).

127. *Re Greymouth Point Elizabeth Railway and Coal Co Ltd* [1904] 1 Ch 32 (Ch).

128. CA 2006, s 248(1).

129. Ibid, s 248(2).

130. Ibid, s 248(3) and (4). The offence is punishable by a fine not exceeding level 3 on the standard scale (currently £1,000).

131. *Re North Hallenbeagle Mining Co (Knight's Case)* (1867) 2 Ch App 321 (CA).

132. CA 2006, s 249(1).

all companies must have at least one director,[133] the directors are usually the members' appointees. The issue then arises as to who has the right to determine what the company will do: the members or the directors?

The directors have only such power as is delegated to them by the members. Most companies have in their articles a provision vesting day-to-day control of the company in the directors as a body, or in a managing director. Where power has been vested in the directors, the members have no right to interfere in management, unless that power has been reserved to the members in the articles or by statute.

Automatic Self-Cleansing Filter Syndicate Co Ltd v Cuninghame [1906] 2 Ch 34 (CA)

FACTS: The articles of the claimant company conferred general powers of management on the directors and provided that they could sell any property of the company on such terms as they deemed fit. The company's members passed an ordinary resolution resolving to sell the assets and undertakings of the claimant company, but the directors did not believe such a sale to be in the interests of the company and so refused.

HELD: The Court of Appeal held that the right to manage the company and the right to determine which property to sell was vested in the directors. Accordingly, the directors were not compelled to comply with the resolution unless the articles so provided.

Because the division of power between the members and directors is a matter for the articles, the provisions of the model articles are of considerable importance. Article 3 of both the model articles for private companies limited by shares and the model articles for public companies provides that, '[s]ubject to the articles, the directors are responsible for the management of the company's business, for which purpose they may exercise all the powers of the company'. Clearly, this places a significant amount of power in the hands of the directors, but, because it is subject to the articles, provisions can be inserted that alter this balance of power, as the following case demonstrates.

Salmon v Quin & Axtens Ltd [1909] 1 Ch 311 (CA); aff'd [1909] AC 442 (HL)

FACTS: The articles of the defendant company conferred general powers of management upon the directors, but such powers were subject to the articles. Article 80 provided that resolutions of the directors relating to the acquisition or letting of certain premises would not be valid if two named members (who were also the company's managing directors) were to dissent. The directors passed a resolution resolving to acquire certain property, but one of the named members vetoed the resolution. An extraordinary meeting was called and the member passed an ordinary resolution resolving similar to the one the

---

133. As discussed, public companies require two directors (ibid, s 154(2)).

directors attempted to pass. The member who vetoed the original resolution commenced proceedings, seeking an injunction to restrain the property acquisitions.

HELD: The Court of Appeal held that, whilst the directors had a general power of management, it was subject to the articles. Accordingly, the veto exercised by the claimant was valid and the company could not override it by passing an ordinary resolution.

In both *Automatic Self-Cleansing* and *Salmon*, ordinary resolutions passed by the members could not affect the powers conferred in the articles, because this would permit the members to alter the articles indirectly by ordinary resolution. It follows from this that a direction from the members passed by special resolution should be valid and this is reflected in the model articles, art 4(1) of which states that '[t]he members may, by special resolution, direct the directors to take, or refrain from taking, specified action'. Accordingly, whilst power is vested in the directors, the members retain a specific supervisory power exercisable by passing a special resolution. This supervisory power is not retrospective, however, and cannot be used to invalidate anything that the directors have done prior to the resolution. In practice, this power is rarely used on the ground that there is little need to pass a special resolution compelling the directors to act a certain way, when it is easier to pass an ordinary resolution removing them from office.

🔗 The members' ability to remove the directors from office is discussed at p 650

Article 4 confers a specific power upon the members, but the general power to run the company is still vested in the directors by art 3. But where the directors are unwilling or unable to exercise the powers conferred by art 3, then the general power to manage reverts to the members.[134] It should be noted that the default powers of the general meeting operate only where the board is completely incapable of making decisions and not when a minority of directors use any power that they may have been given by the articles to block the implementation of a decision by the majority of the board (as in *Salmon v Quin & Axtens Ltd*, discussed above). In the latter case, the board is precluded from acting by the operation of the articles, not by any incapacity to act.

Unitary and two-tier boards

Mention should briefly be made of board structures. Although the UK system of corporate governance has several different types of director, they all sit on a single board (although this board may have several satellite committees devoted to determining remuneration, nominating directorial candidates, etc.). The UK therefore has what is known as a 'unitary' board structure. Conversely, other countries segregate their directors into multiple boards, or multiple tiers of a single board. The dual-board system found in Germany provides the classic example. German companies will have a management board (the *Vorstand*), which is responsible for managing the company and in whom much of the company's power is concentrated. There will also be a supervisory board (the *Aufsichtsrat*), which will consist of non-executives and employee representatives. This board will play a role in management, but will also supervise and approve many decisions of the management board.

---

134. *Barron v Potter* [1914] 1 Ch 895 (Ch).

Remuneration

Generally, directors are office holders, rather than employees (although a director can be an employee if he has an employment contract). A consequence of this is that they are not generally entitled to be remunerated for acting as a director.[135] This general rule is, in practice, however, normally excluded either by providing for remuneration in a director's service contract, or by including a provision in the articles entitling the directors to remuneration for their services. The model articles for both public and private companies provide that directors are to be paid for their services as directors, and for any other services that they undertake for the company.[136]

Where the company is listed, it should establish a remuneration committee consisting entirely of non-executive directors, the function of which will be to determine the remuneration of the executives.[137]

Visit the Online Resource Centre for more on the effectiveness of remuneration committees in the chapter entitled 'Corporate governance'

Termination of office

A director's term of office may be terminated in one of several different ways.

Termination in accordance with the articles

A company's articles may lay down a number of instances that will cause a director to cease to hold office. The model articles[138] state that a person will instantly and automatically cease to be a director upon the occurrence of certain events, including:

- the person being prohibited by law from being a director (for example, where he has been disqualified from acting as a director);
- where a bankruptcy order is made against the person;[139] and
- where a registered medical practitioner has written to the company stating that the person has become physically or mentally incapable of acting as a director and may remain so for more than three months.

A director may be reappointed as a director once the event has passed, but whilst the event is current, he cannot hold office as a director and the other directors cannot waive the effects of any article provision causing a director to cease to hold office.[140]

Resignation

A director may, at any time, relinquish office by giving notice to the company and the company must accept his resignation. The articles or the director's service contract may provide restrictions on the director's ability to resign, but in the absence of such restrictions, resignation is effective as soon as it is given and cannot be retracted

135. *Hutton v West Cork Railway Co* (1883) 23 Ch D 654 (CA).
136. The Companies (Model Articles) Regulations 2008, SI 2008/3229, Sch 1, para 19, and Sch 3, para 23.
137. Financial Reporting Council, *The Combined Code on Corporate Governance* (June 2008) [B.2.1].
138. The Companies (Model Articles) Regulations 2008, SI 2008/3229, Sch 1, para 18, and Sch 3, para 22.
139. The Company Directors Disqualification Act 1986, s 11(1), provides that it is a criminal offence for an undischarged bankrupt to act as a director, except with leave of the court.
140. *Re Bodega Co Ltd* [1904] 1 Ch 276 (Ch).

without the consent of the company.[141] Where the articles or service contract do not provide for a notice period, the courts will imply a term into the service contract requiring a reasonable period of notice.[142]

Retirement

A company's articles may provide for the retirement of the directors by rotation. In practice, it is only public companies that tend to require retirement by rotation and art 21 of the model articles for public companies[143] requires that the directors of a public company retire at its first AGM. At every subsequent AGM, any directors appointed by the directors since the last AGM, or any directors who were not appointed or reappointed at one of the preceding two AGMs, must retire from office and may offer themselves for reappointment. In practice, this means that directors of public companies must be re-elected every three years. This is in line with the recommendations of the Combined Code.[144]

Removal

The CA 2006, s 168(1), provides that '[a] company may by ordinary resolution at a meeting[145] remove a director before the expiration of his period of office, notwithstanding anything in any agreement between it and him'. Despite the wording of s 168, the resolution can seek the removal of multiple directors. Special notice (twenty-eight days) is required for the resolution and the company must send a copy of the resolution to the director(s) concerned.[146]

The director(s) whose removal is sought has a right to be heard at the meeting where the resolution is to take place (even if he is not a member).[147] The director(s) may make written representations to the company and, if such representations are received in time, the company must send them to every member to whom notice of the meeting has been sent.[148] If the representations are sent too late, the director(s) can require that the representations be read out at the meeting.[149]

Section 168(5)(b) provides that s 168 should not be construed as derogating from any power to remove a director that exists outside s 168. Accordingly, the power to remove a director under s 168 exists alongside any other power. This can allow a removal to be effected more easily, as the following example demonstrates.

 Removal of a director other than through s 168

Computech Ltd has a provision in its articles that states that 'a director of the company may be removed by passing an ordinary resolution'. Because this provision makes no mention of the resolution requiring special notice, such notice is not required. Because

---

141. *Glossop v Glossop* [1907] 2 Ch 370 (Ch).

142. *CMS Dolphin Ltd v Simonet* [2002] BCC 600 (Ch).

143. The Companies (Model Articles) Regulations 2008, SI 2008/3229, Sch 3.

144. Financial Reporting Council, *The Combined Code on Corporate Governance* (June 2008) [A.7.1].

145. Because the resolution must be at a meeting, the written resolution procedure cannot be used to effect a removal under s 168.

146. CA 2006, ss 168(1) and (2), 169(1), and 312(1).   147. Ibid, s 169(2).

148. Ibid, s 169(3).   149. Ibid, s 169(4).

the provision does not require the resolution to be passed at a meeting, it can be passed using the written resolution procedure. Finally, the provision does not provide the directors with a right to make representations, so none may be made. Where a company has such an article provision, the members have a choice between removing the director via the s 168 procedure or the procedure under the articles. The articles can even provide for a method of removal that does not involve the members (for example, removal upon a vote of the directors).

Once a director has been removed, the only remaining remedies available to him would be to petition the court for a winding-up order, or (if he is also a member) to bring a claim alleging that the removal was unfairly prejudicial to his interests as a member. This latter remedy is only likely to have a chance of success if the company is a quasi-partnership.

These remedies and the concept of the quasi-partnership are discussed in Chapter 21

Initially, the power granted to members under s 168 appears extremely substantial, but, in practice, the effectiveness of s 168 is emasculated in two ways. Firstly, a removal under s 168 does not deprive the director of any compensation payable as a result of the removal. For example, a director removed under s 168 who still has a period of his service contract left to run will be able to obtain damages for breach of contract. If the director's remuneration is high and/or the period remaining on his service contract is lengthy, removing him may be extremely costly to the company.

Statutory restrictions on the length of a director's service contract are discussed at p 710

Secondly, s 168 does not prohibit the company from including in its articles a weighted voting clause. Such a clause usually provides that, in the event of a vote to remove a director from office, the voting power of the director shall be increased (usually to such an extent as to enable him to defeat any resolution seeking his removal).

The following case demonstrates how a weighted voting clause operates in practice and how it severely emasculates the power granted to the members by s 168.

Bushell v Faith [1970] AC 1099 (HL)

FACTS: A company had 300 shares, equally divided between three siblings. Two of the siblings (the claimant and defendant) were the company's only directors. The company's articles contained a weighted voting clause that provided that, in relation to resolutions to remove a director, the director involved would have his voting power trebled (that is, each share would carry three votes). Two of the siblings (one of whom was the claimant) sought to remove the third sibling director (the defendant). But the weighted voting clause meant that the defendant's shares were worth 300 votes, whereas the claimant and the other sibling could only muster 200 votes between them. Accordingly, the defendant argued that the resolution was defeated. The claimant contended that the resolution was passed by 200 votes, compared to the defendant's 100 votes, and she sought an injunction preventing the defendant from acting as a director.

HELD: The House of Lords held that the weighted voting clause was effective and the resolution was therefore validly defeated. The Companies Acts did not expressly state that such clauses were invalid and there was therefore no reason to imply such an intention.

COMMENT: Unsurprisingly, the decision in *Bushell* has proved controversial on the ground that a weighted voting clause could serve to entrench a director and make him irremovable. In practice, the effect of *Bushell* may be more limited than many realize. Firstly, it has been argued that the decision was justified on the ground that the company in question was a quasi-partnership, in which all of the members will expect to be involved in management. It may therefore be the case that such clauses are effective only in relation to such companies (although there are no *obiter dicta* or *rationes* to this effect).

Secondly, such clauses probably breach the Listing Rules and so will not be adopted by public companies.

Thirdly, a weighted voting clause could be removed by passing a special resolution (although admittedly, members with 75 per cent of the company's votes could probably defeat even a director with weighted voting rights).

⭐ See D Prentice, 'Removal of Directors from Office' (1969) 32 MLR 693

Finally, it should be noted that the members are not the only party granted the power to remove a director. The Insolvency Act 1986, Sch B1, para 61, provides that where a company is in administration, the administrator has the power to remove a director.

Disqualification

The shareholders can decide to dismiss a director, but the Company Directors Disqualification Act 1986 (CDDA 1986) grants a court the power to make a disqualification order disqualifying a person from promoting, forming, or taking part in the management of a company (or LLP) without the leave of the court. Alternatively, since 2000, instead of obtaining a disqualification order from a court, the Secretary of State may, if it is in the public interest, accept from a person a disqualification undertaking, whereby that person undertakes not to do anything prohibited by a disqualification order.[150] The majority of disqualifications are made this way. From April 2007 to March 2008, there were 1,145 disqualifications, 897 (78 per cent) of which were obtained through a disqualification undertaking.[151]

The CDDA 1986 provides numerous grounds for disqualification, including the following.

- Section 2 provides for disqualification upon conviction of an indictable offence[152] in connection with the promotion, formation, or management of a company.
- Section 3 provides for disqualification for persistent breaches of companies legislation requiring returns, accounts, or other documents to be filed, delivered, or sent to the Registrar. Three or more defaults in a five-year period are regarded as persistent.
- Section 4 provides for disqualification where the director is guilty of fraudulent trading[153] in relation to the company at a time when the company is in liquidation.
- Section 5 provides for disqualification where the director has, within a five-year period, been convicted of three or more summary offences in relation to requiring

---

150. CDDA 1986, s 1A.

151. The Insolvency Service, *Annual Report and Accounts 2007–08* (HMSO, London, 2008) 14.

152. Disqualification can occur irrespective of whether the indictable offence was tried summarily or on indictment.

153. The offence of fraudulent trading is found in the CA 2006, s 993.

a return, account, or other document to be filed with, delivered, or sent, or notice of any matter to be given, to the Registrar of Companies.

- Section 9A provides for disqualification where the director commits a breach of competition law and that breach renders him unfit to be concerned in the management of a company.
- Section 10 provides for disqualification where a person has been required to contribute to the company's assets under the Insolvency Act 1986, s 213 (director's liability for fraudulent trading), or 214 (wrongful trading).

The most wide-ranging ground for disqualification (and the ground that most disqualification cases concern) can be found in s 6, which provides for disqualification where a person is a director of a company that has become insolvent (whether while he was a director or subsequently), and his conduct as a director makes him unfit to be concerned in the management of the company. Conduct need not be unlawful or dishonest in order to be unfit.[154]

In the following case, the Court of Appeal provided guidance on what constitutes unfitness.

 Re Sevenoaks Stationers (Retail) Ltd [1991] Ch 164 (CA)

FACTS: The facts are not directly relevant.

HELD: Dillon LJ stated that it was 'beyond dispute'[155] that the purpose of s 6 was to protect the public and creditors from losing money through companies becoming insolvent. The words of s 6 should be treated as ordinary English words and what amounts to unfitness will turn on the facts of each case. Incompetence or negligence will not normally result in disqualification, but they may do where they are to 'a very marked degree'.[156]

COMMENT: Dillon LJ's comments appear to be somewhat inconsistent. If the purpose of s 6 is to protect the public and creditors from directors whose conduct could cause the company to lose money, then surely incompetence and negligence should both merit disqualification under s 6, even where they are not to a 'very marked degree'.

The possible length of disqualification depends upon the ground of disqualification. Breaches of s 3 or 5 can result in a maximum disqualification period of five years. Breaches of s 2, 4, 6, 9A, or 10 can result in a maximum disqualification period of fifteen years. Breach of s 6 is also subject to a minimum disqualification period—namely, two years. In *Re Sevenoaks Stationers* (discussed above), Dillon LJ divided s 6 cases into three brackets.

1. Disqualification periods of ten years or more should be reserved for particularly serious cases. This may include a case in which a director already has one period of disqualification imposed upon him and is disqualified a second time.

---

154. *Re Deaduck Ltd* [2000] 1 BCLC 148 (Ch).
155. *Re Sevenoaks Stationers (Retail) Ltd* [1991] Ch 164 (CA) 176.
156. Ibid, 184.

2. Disqualification periods of between six and ten years should be reserved for serious cases that do not fall into (1) above.

3. Disqualification periods of two to five years should apply where disqualification is mandatory, but the case is, relatively, not very serious.[157]

Breach of a disqualification order constitutes an either-way offence.[158] Further, a director who contravenes a disqualification order by taking part in the management of a company can be personally liable for the debts and liabilities of the company incurred during the duration of the contravention.[159] A director subject to a disqualification order can become involved again in corporate management if he obtains leave from the court. Leave will only be granted where the company has need of the director's services and the public is adequately protected.[160]

 Key points summary

- Every private company must have at least one director and every public company must have at least two directors.

- The directors (except the first directors) may be appointed by the members or the directors.

- Collectively, the directors are referred to as the 'board'.

- The company's articles normally vest day-to-day control of the company in the board of directors.

- A director, or directors, may be removed by the passing of an ordinary resolution.

- Directors may be disqualified from acting as directors on a number of grounds. The length of disqualification depends upon the ground of disqualification.

The company secretary

The company secretary is an officer of the company,[161] whose function is to carry out the administrative tasks imposed on companies by the Companies Acts (although the CA 2006 itself does not specifically require these tasks to be carried out by the secretary). Common administrative tasks include:

- ensuring the timely filing of accurate documents with the Registrar of Companies;

---

157. Ibid, 174.
158. CDDA 1986, s 13. On summary conviction, the maximum punishment is six months' imprisonment and/or a fine not exceeding the statutory maximum (currently £5,000). On conviction on indictment, the maximum penalty is two years' imprisonment and/or a fine.
159. Ibid, s 15.
160. *Re Gibson Davies Ltd* [1995] BCC 11 (Ch).
161. CA 2006, s 1121(2).

- maintaining the statutory registers (for example, the register of members that is kept at the company's registered office);
- preparing the agenda for, and minuting, board meetings; and
- ensuring that general meetings are conducted according to the procedures laid down in the CA 2006 (for example, providing members with adequate notice).

In relation to these sorts of administrative tasks, the secretary has apparent authority to bind the company, as the following case demonstrates.

 Apparent authority is discussed at p 940

Panorama Developments (Guildford) Ltd v Fidelis Furnishing Fabrics Ltd [1971] 2 QB 711 (CA)

FACTS: The defendant's company secretary was a man named Bayne. Using the defendant's notepaper, Bayne hired a number of cars from the claimant, telling the claimant that they would be used to transport important customers of the defendant. The agreement of hire stated that Bayne was the hirer and he was described as 'Company Secretary'. Bayne used the cars for personal purposes and not for the company's business. The hire charges were not paid and the claimant sued the defendant for the outstanding charges. The defendant, unsurprisingly, denied liability.

HELD: The Court of Appeal held that the defendant was liable to pay the hire charge. Lord Denning MR stated that a company secretary is not:

> a mere clerk. He regularly makes representations on behalf of the company and enters into contracts on its behalf which come within the day-to-day running of the company's business. So much so that he may be regarded as held out as having authority to do such things on behalf of the company.[162]

The company secretary must also obey the lawful orders of the directors, but he is not normally to be regarded as being involved in the company's management. His ability to bind the company will not therefore extend to commercial matters, unless he has been expressly authorized to engage in such matters.

Appointment and dismissal

A company secretary may be a natural person or a body corporate. Every public company must appoint a company secretary,[163] and the Secretary of State may direct a public company that has failed to appoint a company secretary to do so.[164] Failure to comply with this direction will constitute a summary offence on the part of the company and every officer of the company who is in default, punishable by a maximum fine of level 5 on the standard scale (currently £5,000).[165] Not only must a public company appoint a company secretary, but its directors are also under a duty

---

162. *Panorama Developments (Guildford) Ltd v Fidelis Furnishing Fabrics Ltd* [1971] 2 QB 711 (CA) 716, 717.
163. CA 2006, s 271. Although not stated by the Act, one of the company's directors may act as company secretary.
164. Ibid, s 272(1).
165. Ibid, s 272(6) and (7).

to take all reasonable steps to ensure that the secretary has the requisite knowledge and experience, and also the appropriate qualifications.[166] Appropriate qualifications include:

- holding the office of secretary of a public company for at least three of the five years preceding the appointment;
- being a member of certain professional bodies (for example, the Institute of Chartered Accountants, the Institute of Chartered Secretaries and Administrators, or the Chartered Institute of Management Accountants);
- being a barrister, advocate, or solicitor.[167]

The Company Law Review Steering Group and the government initially intended to abolish the office of company secretary in relation to private companies, but the government subsequently altered its position. Accordingly, a private company may appoint a company secretary, but is not required to do so[168] unless its articles provide that a company secretary must be appointed. It is anticipated that larger private companies will retain a company secretary. Where a private company does not appoint a company secretary, anything authorized or required to be given or sent to, or served on, the company by being sent to its company secretary is satisfied if it is sent to or served on the company.[169] A director, or a person authorized on behalf of the directors, can undertake anything that must be authorized or done by the company secretary.[170]

The Companies (Tables A to F) Regulations 1985,[171] Table A, art 99, provided that a company secretary may be appointed and dismissed by the directors. Curiously, the new model articles[172] contain no references whatsoever to the appointment or dismissal of company secretaries.

Legal duties and liabilities

Company secretaries are subject to a number of duties and liability can be imposed upon them in a number of ways. In one, notable, Canadian case, the Canadian Supreme Court held that the duties placed upon directors can also apply to those in senior management positions[173] (this would presumably include company secretaries, because they are officers of the company). English courts have not yet adopted this view and there is little doubt that the general duties of directors are not imposed on company secretaries. But it is settled that company secretaries owe fiduciary duties to the company that are similar to those owed by directors (for example, not to compete and not to make a secret profit).

In addition, the CA 2006 imposes numerous obligations upon the company, breach of which can result in liability being imposed upon the company and its officers, which would include the company secretary. In fact, breach of many of these

🔗 The general duties of directors are discussed in Chapter 20

---

166. Ibid, s 273(1).   167. Ibid, s 273(2) and (3).
168. Ibid, s 270(1).   169. Ibid, s 270(3)(a).
170. Ibid, s 270(3)(b).   171. SI 1985/805.
172. The Companies (Model Articles) Regulations 2008, SI 2008/3229.
173. *Canadian Aero Service v O'Malley* [1973] 40 DLR 3d 371 (Canadian Supreme Court).

obligations constitutes a criminal offence punishable by a fine, which, in certain cases, may be payable by the company secretary.

If the company secretary is an employee of the company, he will be subject to the normal duties imposed upon employees (for example, the duty of mutual trust, confidence, and respect, and the duty of fidelity). Should a company secretary place himself in an agency relationship with the company, he will be subject to the fiduciary duties imposed on an agent.

The duties imposed upon employees are discussed at p 794

The duties imposed upon agents are discussed at p 954

The register of secretaries

Every public company and every private company that appoints a company secretary must maintain and keep available for inspection, usually at its registered office, a register of secretaries.[174] The register must contain the secretary's name and (if applicable) former name, and his address (which may be stated as the company's registered office).[175] Where the secretary is a body corporate, the register must contain the corporate or firm's (that is, LLP's) name, its registered or principal office, and the legal form of the company or firm.[176]

Where a company changes its secretary, or changes the particulars of the register of secretaries, it must notify the Registrar of Companies of the change within fourteen days of the date of the change.[177] Failure to do so constitutes a summary offence by every officer of the company who is in default, punishable by a maximum fine of level 5 on the standard scale (currently £5,000).[178]

‹› Key summary points

- The company secretary is an officer of the company responsible for carrying out the administrative tasks imposed by the Companies Acts.

- In relation to these administrative functions, the secretary has the power to bind the company.

- All public companies must appoint a secretary and the directors are under a duty to appoint a secretary with sufficient skill, experience, and qualifications.

- Private companies do not need to appoint a secretary, but may do so if they choose.

- Company secretaries are subject to fiduciary duties similar to those imposed on directors.

- Every public company and every private company that appoints a company secretary must maintain and keep available for inspection, usually at its registered office, a register of secretaries.

---

174. CA 2006, s 275. 175. Ibid, s 277.
176. Ibid, s 278. 177. Ibid, s 276(1).
178. Ibid, s 276(3) and (4).

The auditor

For each financial year, the directors are under a duty to prepare 'individual accounts' providing information relating to the company's financial position.[179] Although the directors must not approve such accounts unless they give a true and fair view of the company's financial position,[180] the directors may nevertheless be tempted to present these accounts in an overly favourable way in order to encourage investment. To discourage such behaviour, the law requires that these accounts be subject to an independent third-party verification by a statutory auditor.

Appointment, eligibility, and remuneration

As a general rule, all companies must appoint (or reappoint) an auditor each financial year[181] and such persons are known as 'statutory auditors'. Where the law requires that an auditor be appointed, but one is not, the company in question must notify the Secretary of State, who has the power to appoint an auditor on the company's behalf.[182] Failure to notify the Secretary of State constitutes a summary offence by the company and every officer of the company who is in default, punishable by a fine not exceeding level 3 on the standard scale (currently £1,000).[183] Not all auditors are eligible to act as statutory auditors.

Because the effectiveness of the audit rests on the skill and independence of the auditor, the CA 2006 imposes the following eligibility requirements.

- A person is ineligible for appointment as a statutory auditor if:
  - he is an officer or employee of the company; or
  - he is the partner, or in partnership with such a person.[184]
- An individual or firm (that is, partnership) may only act as statutory auditor if he or it is a member of a recognized supervisory body (for example, the Institute of Chartered Accountants in England and Wales), and he is eligible for appointment under the rules of that body.[185]
- A recognized statutory body must have rules to the effect that a person is not eligible for appointment as a statutory auditor, unless:
  - in the case of an individual, he holds a recognized qualification;[186] or
  - in the case of a firm, each individual responsible for statutory audit work on behalf of the firm is eligible for appointment as a statutory auditor, and the firm is controlled by qualified persons.[187]

Any ineligible person who acts as a statutory auditor commits an either-way offence,[188] punishable on summary conviction by a fine not exceeding the statutory maximum (currently £5,000). On conviction on indictment, there is no limit to the

---

179. Ibid, s 394.
180. Ibid, s 393(1).
181. Ibid, ss 485 and 489.
182. Ibid, ss 486(1) and 490(2).
183. Ibid, ss 486 and 490.
184. Ibid, s 1214(1).
185. Ibid, s 1212(1).
186. Ibid, Sch 10, para 6(1)(a).
187. Ibid, Sch 10, para 6(1)(b). A qualified person is defined in Sch 10, para 7.
188. Ibid, ss 1213(3) and 1215(2).

fine that can be imposed. But it is a defence for him to show that he did not know and had no reason to believe that he was ineligible for appointment.[189]

Private companies

A private company must appoint an auditor each financial year, unless the directors reasonably resolve otherwise on the ground that audited accounts are unlikely to be required.[190] The directors can make the appointment of an auditor for the first financial year, but, to encourage independence, subsequent appointments must be made by the members passing an ordinary resolution.[191] Other than in the company's first financial year, the appointment must be made within twenty-eight days of the date by which the company's accounts must be sent out to the members, or, if earlier, the date on which the accounts actually are sent out.[192] Unless reappointed, an auditor loses office at the end of his term of appointment. But s 487(2) provides that reappointment is automatic unless:

- he was appointed by the directors;
- the company's articles require actual reappointment;
- 5 per cent (or some other percentage as specified in the articles) of the company's members present a notice to the company stating that the auditor should not be reappointed;
- the members have resolved that he should not be reappointed; or
- the directors have resolved that no auditor(s) should be appointed for the financial year in question.

Public companies

A public company must appoint an auditor each financial year, unless the directors reasonably resolve otherwise on the ground that audited accounts are unlikely to be required.[193] The rules relating to the appointment of a statutory auditor for a public company are exactly the same as those for a private company, except that:

- because public companies are required to lay their accounts out to the general meeting, the appointment of the auditor must take place before the end of the meeting in which the accounts are laid out;[194]
- there is no provision for the automatic reappointment of a public company's statutory auditor.

Exemptions

Two types of company are exempt from the requirement to appoint an auditor, as follows.

- *Dormant companies* A company that has been dormant since its formation, or which has been dormant since the end of the previous financial year, is exempt from the requirement to appoint an auditor.[195]

---

189. Ibid, ss 1213(8) and 1215(7).   190. Ibid, s 485(1).
191. Ibid, s 485(3) and (4).   192. Ibid, s 485(2).
193. Ibid, s 489(1).   194. Ibid, s 489(2).
195. Ibid, s 480(1).

- *Small companies*   Companies deemed small companies under the CA 2006 are exempt from the requirement to appoint an auditor. The CA 2006 defines a small company as one that meets two of the following three criteria:
  - it has a turnover of no more than £6.5 million;
  - it has a balance sheet total of not more than £3.26 million; and
  - it has no more than fifty employees.[196]
- A public company cannot be a small company under the CA 2006.[197]

Remuneration

Once appointed, the auditor will need to be paid. Section 492(2) provides that the remuneration of an auditor appointed by the directors can be fixed by the directors. In all other cases, the auditor's remuneration must be fixed by either:

- the members passing an ordinary resolution; or
- some other method, as determined by the members by passing an ordinary resolution.[198]

In practice, the auditor's remuneration is usually determined by the directors, because the members pass a resolution allowing them to do so.

Powers of investigation

The principal function of an auditor is to examine the annual accounts prepared by the directors and to prepare an auditor's report, which is then sent out to the members (in the case of a private company), or laid before the general meeting (in the case of a public company).[199] The auditor's report must state whether, in the auditor's opinion, the annual accounts give a true and fair view of the company's financial position, and whether they have been prepared in accordance with the CA 2006. If the auditor is of the opinion that the company has kept inadequate records, or that the records are inconsistent with the annual accounts, then this must be stated in his report.[200] Preparing an auditor's report will therefore involve a substantial amount of investigative work and, indeed, auditors are under a duty to carry out such investigations.[201]

To aid auditors in complying with this duty, the Act grants auditors significant investigative powers, including:

- the right of access, at all times, to the company's books and accounts;[202]
- the right to require certain persons (for example, officers and employees of the company) to provide him with such information and explanations as he thinks necessary;[203]

---

196. Ibid, ss 477 and 382(3). Note that it is possible that these amounts will rise in April 2009.
197. Ibid, s 478.   198. Ibid, s 492(1).
199. Ibid, s 495(1).   200. Ibid, s 498(2).
201. Ibid, s 498(1).   202. Ibid, s 499(1)(a).
203. Ibid, s 499(1)(b).

- the right to view all notes and communications relating to any general meeting, and also to attend and be heard at any general meetings.[204]

A person who fails to comply with the auditor's right to information without delay commits a summary offence punishable by a fine not exceeding level 3 on the standard scale (currently £1,000).[205] But no offence will be committed where it was not reasonably practicable for him to provide the information or explanations.[206] A person who knowingly or recklessly provides to the auditor any information or explanation that is misleading, false, or deceptive commits an either-way offence, punishable on conviction on indictment with imprisonment for up to two years and/or a fine.[207]

Liability of an auditor

Contractual liability

A contractual relationship exists between the company and its auditor. As with any provider of a service, there will be an implied contractual term placing a duty upon the auditor to carry out his functions with reasonable care and skill.[208] Accordingly, an auditor may be liable to pay damages to a company if his audit is conducted in a negligent manner.

It is clear from established cases that, historically, the contractual duty placed upon auditors was not an onerous one. This is evident from the following statement of Lopes LJ:

> It is the duty of an auditor to bring to bear on the work he has to perform that skill, care, and caution which a reasonably competent, careful, and cautious auditor would use...An auditor is not bound to be a detective, or...to approach his work with suspicion or with a foregone conclusion that there is something wrong. He is a watch-dog, but not a bloodhound. He is justified in believing tried servants of the company in whom confidence is placed by the company. He is entitled to assume that they are honest, and to rely upon their representations, provided he takes reasonable care. If there is anything calculated to excite suspicion he should probe it to the bottom; but in the absence of anything of that kind he is only bound to be reasonably cautious and careful.[209]

This statement indicates that, in the absence of suspicious circumstances, the auditors are free to rely on information provided by the directors. It is debatable whether this is still the case. In *Fomento (Sterling Area) Ltd v Selsdon Fountain Pen Co Ltd*,[210] Lord Denning stated that the auditors should carry out their functions 'with an inquiring mind—not suspicious of dishonesty...but suspecting that someone may have made a mistake somewhere and that a check must be made to ensure that there has been none'.[211]

---

204. Ibid, s 502. Where the auditor is a firm, the right to attend or be heard at a meeting is exercisable by an individual authorized by the firm in writing to act as its representative at the meeting (s 502(3)).
205. Ibid, s 501(3) and (5).
206. Ibid, s 501(3).
207. Ibid, s 501(1).
208. Supply of Goods and Services Act 1982, s 13.
209. *Re Kingston Cotton Mill Co (No 2)* [1896] 2 Ch 279 (CA) 288, 289.
210. [1958] 1 WLR 45 (HL).
211. Ibid, 61.

The Auditing Practices Board's International Standards on Auditing state that the auditor should:

> plan and perform an audit with an attitude of professional scepticism recognizing that circumstances may exist that cause the financial statements to be materially misstated. An attitude of professional scepticism means the auditor makes a critical assessment, with a questioning mind, of the validity of audit evidence obtained and is alert to audit evidence that contradicts or brings into question the reliability of documents or management representations.[212]

Given that such professional standards constitute 'very strong evidence as to what is the proper standard which should be adopted',[213] it is almost certainly the case that auditors cannot rely blindly on information provided to them by the directors and will need to engage in a certain amount of independent research.

Tortious liability for negligent misstatement

➡ proper claimant principle: the principle that, where the company is wronged, only the company can sue on that wrong (see p 726)

The doctrine of privity of contract, alongside the proper claimant principle, ensures that, if the auditor breaches his contractual duty of care and skill, only the company may initiate a claim for loss. The same is not true in relation to the auditor's liability in tort, under which, depending upon the facts of the case, the auditor may owe a duty of care to third parties as well as to the company.

The requirements for the imposition of a duty of care to third parties were set down in the case of *Caparo Industries plc v Dickman*,[214] a case that we have already examined when we discussed negligent misstatement. The House of Lords examined the existing authorities and reformulated the requirements to establish negligent misstatement in a way that was much more acceptable to auditors than to third parties. The House reiterated that the auditors owe a duty of care to the company the accounts of which are being audited. But the company is not the only party who may rely on the audited accounts: potential investors will also examine the accounts before deciding whether or not to invest. The House made clear that, as a general rule, the auditor's duty of care will not extend to potential investors who rely on the audited accounts. But the House acknowledged that there may be situations in which auditors do owe a duty of care to third parties.

🔗 The facts and decision in *Caparo* are discussed at p 401

In order for a third party to establish that the auditor owed him a duty of care, he will need to prove the existence of a 'special relationship' between himself and the auditor. In relation to claims against auditors, this would require the claimant to show that the following four factors were present:

1. that the audited accounts were required for a purpose, which was made known to the auditor;
2. that the auditor knew that the audited accounts would be communicated to the claimant, either specifically or as part of a ascertainable class, for the purpose made known;

---

212. Auditing Practices Board, *International Standard on Auditing: Objective and General Principles Governing An Audit of Financial Statements* (2006) [6], available online at <http://www.frc.org.uk/apb>.
213. *Lloyd Cheyham and Co Ltd v Littlejohn and Co* [1987] BCLC 303 (QB) 313 (Woolf J).
214. [1990] 2 AC 605 (HL).

3. that the auditor knew that, upon publication of the audited accounts, the claimant was likely to act upon the audited accounts; and

4. that the claimant acted on the audited accounts to his detriment.

These four factors establish that there will need to be a sufficient degree of proximity between the claimant and the auditor. In the absence of even one of the four factors, the relationship will not be sufficiently proximate and will almost certainly result in the claimant's action failing. But even if the claimant can establish that these four factors are present, this will merely establish that sufficient proximity exists. The court may still hold that a duty should not be imposed on the ground of fairness and reasonableness.

Assuming that a claimant can establish that the auditor owed him a duty of care, he will then need to establish that the auditor breached the standard of care. The standard that an auditor is required to meet is not a particularly high one. In *Saif Ali v Sydney Mitchell & Co*,[215] Lord Diplock stated:

> No matter what profession it may be, the common law does not impose…any liability for damage resulting from what in the result turn out to have been errors of judgment, unless the error was such as no reasonably well-informed and competent member of that profession could have made.[216]

Further, auditors are unlikely to have breached their duty of care where they acted in accordance with a practice that a body of skilled and professional persons would regard as proper.[217]

Limitation and relief of liability

From a legal point of view, auditors have historically occupied a vulnerable position due to their joint and several liability. The following example demonstrates this vulnerability in practice.

Eg **The joint and several liability of auditors**

Fearne & Conway LLP is engaged to audit the accounts of Hammond plc. The directors of Hammond have been defrauding the company, but Fearne & Conway negligently fails to discover the fraud, which eventually leads to the company's insolvency. Thousands of shareholders and a number of creditors sustain significant losses, and are looking for legal redress.

Fearne & Conway and the directors of Hammond plc are jointly and severally liable for the losses sustained, meaning that a claimant may elect to sue either of them for the full extent of his loss (even if one party is significantly less blameworthy). Because Fearne & Conway is likely to have greater access to funds and more comprehensive insurance cover than the directors of Hammond plc, it will almost always be the auditor who is sued. The auditor can obtain a contribution from the directors, but by this time, the directors may be financially wiped out.

---

215. [1980] AC 198 (HL).
216. Ibid, 220.
217. *Lloyd Cheyham and Co Ltd v Littlejohn and Co* [1987] BCLC 303 (QB).

The auditors' vulnerability was exacerbated in that, historically, they were prohibited absolutely from contractually restricting their liability via an exclusion clause.[218] Generally, the prohibition still exists, with the CA 2006, s 532, declaring void any provision that seeks to exempt or restrict an auditor's liability for negligence, default, breach of duty, or breach of trust. Concerted lobbying from the 'Big Four' accounting firms[219] resulted in the government relenting (as it did regarding limited liability partnerships), and s 534 provides that s 532 will not apply in the case of 'liability limitation agreements' (LLAs), the terms of which comply with the provisions of the CA 2006, s 535, and which are authorized by the members of the company. The original aim behind LLAs was to provide a system of proportionate liability whereby an auditor would be liable only for the proportion of loss that he caused. Auditors believed this to be a much fairer than the imposition of joint and several liability.

But it could be argued that LLAs do not, in fact, introduce proportionate liability in the way that many believe they do. Under s 534(1), a LLA is an agreement that 'purports to limit the amount of a liability owed to a company by its auditor'. The key word is 'amount' and this indicates that liability can be limited to a fixed amount, although s 535(4) indicates that this is not a necessary requirement. Given this, one could argue that the Act does not introduce proportionate liability, because that would involve the court determining the amount of loss that the auditor should bear, based upon its culpability, once the loss has been sustained. Conversely, the use of the word 'amount' indicates that the amount would be determined before any loss occurred. Therefore, it could be argued that what the Act introduces is not, in fact, proportionate liability, but rather a liability cap. In this sense, the auditing profession may actually have received considerably more than it asked for. Upon seeing the proposed limitation, an in-house lawyer at KPMG stated: 'It's almost a Holy Grail that the auditors never thought they would get…We were expecting some mechanism for proportionate liability.'[220]

⚲ The general regulation of exclusion clauses is discussed at p 969

Under general contract law, exclusion clauses are strictly regulated and this paternalism is evident in the requirements for an effective LLA. Section 536(1) requires that the agreement be authorized by an ordinary resolution of the members.[221] Section 537(1) states that the agreement can only limit liability to an amount that is 'fair and reasonable in all the circumstances'. Section 538 requires that the agreement to be disclosed to persons stated in subsequent regulations (these regulations have now come into force and require the company to disclose, in a note to the company's annual accounts, the principal terms of the agreement).[222] Section 535(1)(a)

---

218. CA 1985, s 310 (now repealed).

219. Namely, PriceWaterhouseCoopers, KPMG, Ernst & Young, and Deloitte Touche Tohmatsu. These firms are segregated from the rest due to the significant size gap between them and other firms. For example, in the period 2006–07, the fourth largest auditor, Ernst & Young, had a UK fee income of £1.1 billion; the fifth largest firm, Grant Thornton, had a UK income of only £387 million (including the increased income generated by the merger with another significant firm, Robson Rhodes).

220. Quoted in 'On the Audit Trail' (2005) *The Lawyer* 11.

221. A public company must authorize the LLA in general meeting, whereas a private company may use the written resolution procedure.

222. Companies (Disclosure of Auditor Remuneration and Liability Limitation Agreements) Regulations 2008, SI 2008/489, reg 8.

provides that such agreements cannot be made in relation to audit accounts for more than one financial year, and s 536(5) provides that the members can terminate the agreement by ordinary resolution before the agreement is entered into, or before the beginning of the financial year to which the agreement relates.

Finally, it should be mentioned that the courts have a general power to relieve, wholly or partly, the liability of any auditor for negligence where they consider the auditor to have acted honestly and reasonably, and, given the circumstances of the case, that he ought fairly to be excused.[223]

Criminal liability

An auditor commits an either-way offence if he knowingly or recklessly causes an auditor's report to include any matter that is misleading, false, or deceptive, or if he knowingly or recklessly omits a required statement.[224] On summary conviction, the offence is punishable by a fine not exceeding the statutory maximum (currently £5,000), and on conviction on indictment, there is no limit to the fine that can be imposed.[225] Clearly, such liability is not covered by a LLA and so cannot be excluded.

Leaving office

An auditor may cease to hold office in three ways:

- resignation;
- removal; or
- replacement (that is, he is not reappointed).

It may be the case that the auditor has ceased to hold office because he has conducted a thorough investigation of the company's affairs and has discovered inconsistencies in the reports, and the directors have removed him in an attempt to silence him. To avoid this, where an auditor of an unquoted company ceases to hold office, he must deposit at the company's registered office a statement setting out the circumstances surrounding his cessation of office, unless he considers that there are no circumstances in connection with his ceasing to hold office that need to be brought to the attention of members or creditors of the company.[226] An auditor who considers that there are no circumstances in connection with his ceasing to hold office that need to be brought to the attention of members or creditors of the company must make a statement to that effect.[227] If the company is quoted, the auditor must deposit this statement stating the circumstances connected to his leaving office.[228] Failure to deposit the statement constitutes an either-way offence, punishable on summary conviction by a fine not exceeding the statutory maximum (currently £5,000), and on conviction on indictment, to a fine of any amount.[229] But it will be a defence for the auditor to show that he took all reasonable steps to avoid the commission of

---

223. CA 2006, s 1157(1).   224. Ibid, s 507(1) and (2).
225. Ibid, s 507(4).   226. Ibid, s 519(1).
227. Ibid, s 519(2).   228. Ibid, s 519(3).
229. Ibid, s 519(7).

the offence.[230] Where the auditor of a quoted company ceases to hold office, s 527 provides that the members of the company (provided that they hold 5 per cent of the total voting rights, or at least a hundred members who have a relevant right to vote and hold shares in the company on which there has been paid up an average sum, per member, of at least £100) can require the company to publish on its website a statement setting out the circumstances surrounding the auditor's loss of office.

Resignation

Section 516 provides that an auditor of a company may resign his office by depositing a notice in writing to that effect at the company's registered office, but the resignation will not be effective unless it is accompanied by the statement discussed above.

Removal

Section 510(1) and (2) provides that the members of a company may remove an auditor at any time by passing an ordinary resolution at a meeting (therefore the written resolution procedure cannot be used). Special notice (twenty-eight days) must be given of the resolution.[231] Notice of the meeting must also be provided to the auditor whose removal is sought.[232] The auditor has the right to make written representations to the company and (unless the representations are received too late) the company must send a copy of the representations to all of the members to whom notice of the resolution has been sent.[233] But copies of the representations need not be sent out if an application is made to the court and the court is satisfied that the auditor has made the representations in order to secure needless publicity for a defamatory matter.[234]

An auditor removed under s 510 is not deprived of any compensation payable to him in respect of the removal.[235]

Replacement

Finally, an auditor may lose office by not being reappointed. This may happen in one of two ways:

- a private company may pass a written resolution, the effect of which is to replace the existing auditor with a new auditor once the existing auditor's term of office has expired;[236] or
- any company may pass an ordinary resolution, the effect of which is to replace the existing auditor with a new auditor once the existing auditor's term of office has expired.[237] Special notice (twenty-eight days) is required.[238]

In both cases, the outgoing auditor is entitled to make representations, copies of which must be circulated to the members (unless they are received too late, or an application is made alleging that the auditor has made the representations in order to secure needless publicity for defamatory matter).[239]

---

230. Ibid, s 519(6).
231. Ibid, s 511(1).
232. Ibid, s 511(2).
233. Ibid, s 511(3) and (4).
234. Ibid, s 511(6).
235. Ibid, s 510(3).
236. Ibid, s 514(1) and (2).
237. Ibid, s 515(1).
238. Ibid, s 515(2).
239. Ibid, ss 514(4), (5), and (7), and 515(4), (5), and (7).

Key points summary

- A company's auditor verifies that the annual accounts provide a true and fair view of the company's financial position.

- All companies (except dormant companies and companies classified as 'small' under the Companies Act 2006) are required to appoint an auditor each financial year and the law imposes restrictions on who can act as a company's statutory auditor.

- The auditors are given substantial powers of investigation and persons who supply false information to an auditor, or omit required information, commit a criminal offence.

- A negligent auditor can be liable in both contract and tort, but auditors can exclude or limit their liability via liability limitation agreements.

- An auditor may cease to hold office if he:

  - resigns;
  - is removed by the members; or
  - is not reappointed once his term of office expires.

Creditors

A company needs capital in order to function and most companies have two principal sources of capital, as follows.

- Capital obtained through the selling of shares is known as 'share capital', or 'equity capital'.

- Capital obtained through borrowing is known as 'loan capital', or 'debt capital'.

Share capital is discussed in Chapter 19

It may be the case that a company can obtain all of the capital that it needs through selling shares, but in most companies, this is not the case and extra capital will need to be obtained by borrowing it from others. Those who lend money to the company are known as its 'creditors' and they form an important class of persons. Accordingly, in this section, the company's ability to borrow and grant security for such borrowing is discussed.

A company can obtain loan capital in a number of different ways, including:

- making use of an overdraft facility;
- obtaining a loan from a bank; or
- by mortgaging the property of the company.

Virtually all companies will have a power to obtain loan capital in these various forms,[240] but some forms of loan (especially loans involving directors) may require the passing of a resolution.

The document by which a company creates or acknowledges a debt is known as a 'debenture'.[241] One popular method of raising substantial amounts of loan capital is

---

240. *General Auction Estate and Monetary Co v Smith* [1891] 3 Ch 432 (Ch).
241. The CA 2006, s 738, states that a debenture includes 'debenture stock, bonds and any other securities of a company, whether or not constituting a charge on the assets of the company'.

for a company to issue debenture stocks or bonds, which are similar to shares, except that the holder is a creditor of the company and not a member.

A creditor of a company has such rights as are given by the contract creating the loan. Typically, the contract will include provisions for repayment of the loan, the payment of interest (if any), and the ability of the creditor to attend company meetings or otherwise influence company policy (generally, none). A debenture holder should be sent a copy of the company's annual accounts and reports,[242] and is entitled to ask for the company's accounts. A debenture is transferable (unless the contract creating it prohibits transfer), and a transfer may be affected by simple delivery from the current holder to the new holder (a bearer debenture), or by delivery and the completion of a transfer document.

It is not a legal requirement, but a prudent lender may insist on having some claim upon the assets of the company, so that if the company defaults on the loan, he will have some security that he can sell to repay his debt. Where the contract of loan, or a linked contract, provides that if the company fails to meet its obligations the creditor can have recourse to the company's assets and can obtain the sums outstanding by selling the assets or receiving income generated by those assets, the loan is said to be 'secured'. Should the company be wound up, the secured creditors will have the right to be paid before the unsecured creditors. The assets of the company covered by this security are said to be 'charged' and the creditor who obtained the charge is called the 'chargee'. The person (the company) that granted the charge and the assets of which are secured by the charge is known as the 'surety', or 'chargor'.

Charges

Any charge created by a company over an asset may be a legal charge or an equitable charge.

- *Legal charges* potentially bind any person who acquires a charged asset from the company, even if that person is unaware of the charge. But as we shall see, the position is different where the charge is required to be registered.

- In contrast to a legal charge, an *equitable charge* does not bind a person who subsequently acquires an interest in the charged asset bona fide, for value, and without notice of the existence of the charge. But because most charges created by companies have to be registered in compliance with the CA 2006, s 860, and registration gives constructive notice of the existence of the charge, a person acquiring an interest in a charged asset will generally have notice of its existence.

➡ constructive notice: notice implied by law based on what a person ought to know

The two principal types of charge are fixed charges (which can be legal or equitable) and floating charges (which are equitable only).

Fixed charges

A fixed charge is the simplest form of charge and is simply a charge over a fixed, identifiable asset of the company (for example, a building, vehicle, or machine). Should the company default on the loan, the creditor may look to the charged asset to satisfy the debt (usually by selling it and recovering the proceeds). A classic example of a

---

242. CA 2006, s 423(1)(b).

fixed charge is a mortgage: should the mortgagor (the company) fail to keep up with the mortgage repayments, the mortgagee (the creditor) can seize possession of the mortgaged asset and sell it.

Fixed charges are very useful, from the creditor's point of view, because they allow it to secure its loan over an identifiable and quantifiable asset. Further, the company can only deal with the charged asset to the extent permitted by the charge contract, which will normally prohibit the company from disposing of the charged asset. Unless the charge contract provides otherwise, the company may create multiple fixed charges over one specific asset, with prior charges having priority over subsequent ones (unless the terms of the first charge provide that subsequent fixed charges can be made that take priority).

Floating charges

Whilst fixed charges provide certainty, they are also highly inflexible, in that the company's ability to deal with the charged assets is highly limited. As a result, certain assets that fluctuate (for example, raw materials) are not appropriate subjects of a fixed charge. A more flexible form of charge was therefore required and the floating charge provides this flexibility.

In *Re Yorkshire Woolcombers' Association Ltd*,[243] Romer LJ identified three factors that point to a charge being a floating charge, which also indicate the flexible nature of the charge.

1. A floating charge is normally taken over a class of assets (for example, plant, machinery, raw materials, or even the entire undertaking), as opposed to a specific asset.
2. The class of asset charged is normally constantly changing (for example, raw materials will be used and replenished).
3. A floating charge leaves the company free to use and deal with those assets.

The third factor is what makes the floating charge so flexible. A floating charge 'floats' over the class of assets charged, but is not fixed on them, and so the company is free to deal with those assets. The company may also grant subsequent fixed charges over the assets that the charge floats over, which may (depending on the terms of the floating charge) rank ahead of the floating charge.[244] But the company cannot create a subsequent floating charge over the exact same class of assets as a prior floating charge that has priority over the first charge, unless the first chargee agrees.[245] The company may create subsequent floating charges over *part* of the assets charged by a prior floating charge and the general rule is that later floating charges rank behind earlier ones (although the terms of the first charge may provide that later charges can take priority).[246]

Upon the occurrence of certain events, the charge will cease to float and will become a fixed charge over the charged assets, and the company's ability to deal

---

243. [1903] 2 Ch 284 (CA).
244. *Wheatley v Silkstone and Haigh Moor Coal Co* (1885) 29 Ch D 715 (Ch).
245. *Re Benjamin Cope and Sons Ltd* [1914] 1 Ch 800 (Ch).
246. *Re Automatic Bottle Makers Ltd* [1926] Ch 415 (CA).

freely with the charged assets will disappear (this process is known as 'crystalliza-tion'). Certain events will always cause a floating charge automatically to crystallize:

- the appointment of an administrator or receiver by the court or the chargee;
- the company going into liquidation;[247]
- the company ceasing to carry on business as a going concern;[248]
- an event that a clause (known as an 'automatic crystallization' clause) in the security contract specifies as causing automatic crystallization.[249]

Additionally, it is common for the security contract to provide that the chargee (the creditor) can bring about crystallization by giving notice to that effect. In cases in which the chargee seeks to crystallize the charge by notice, strict compliance with the security contract is necessary for crystallization to occur.[250] Where assets are sub-ject to two floating charges and the later charge crystallizes before the first charge, then the later charge takes priority.[251]

Despite their flexibility, floating charges do suffer from some notable disadvan-tages, as follows.

Preferential debts and winding up are discussed in Chapter 22

- Upon winding up, a floating charge ranks behind preferential debts.
- A floating charge attaches only to assets of the relevant class that belong to the company. Consequently, where a floating chargee has a charge over raw materials to be used in production, he may find that the supplier of the goods has retained title to them until he is paid (via what is known as a 'retention of title' clause). Such a clause allows the supplier, if unpaid, to remove the goods from the company's premises and out of the grasp of the floating charge. Additionally, the company may have disposed of much, or all, of the class of charged assets when the charge crystallizes.

The liquidator's ability to set aside defective floating charges is discussed at p 767

- The Insolvency Act 1986, s 245, provides that a floating charge created within twelve months of winding up—or two years if the charge holder is a connected person (for example, a director of the company)—is invalid unless the company was solvent at the time that the charge was granted.

Registration

For obvious reasons, prior to providing a company with capital, a potential creditor will want to know of any charges over the company's assets. Accordingly, the CA 2006 provides for two ways in which potential creditors can discover to what extent a company's assets have been charged. Firstly, ss 876 and 877 provide that all limited companies must keep a register of charges listing all charges affecting the property of the company and that this register must be kept at either the company's regis-tered office, or at some other place specified in regulations. Any creditor may inspect this register free of charge. Failure to comply with these requirements constitutes a criminal offence.

---

247. *Wallace v Universal Automatic Machines Co* [1894] 2 Ch 547 (CA).
248. *Re Woodroffes (Musical Instruments) Ltd* [1986] Ch 366 (Ch).
249. Ibid.
250. *Re Brightlife Ltd* [1987] Ch 200 (Ch).
251. *Griffiths v Yorkshire Bank plc* [1994] 1 WLR 1427 (Ch).

Secondly, s 860 provides that most charges[252] (but not all) must be registered with the Registrar of Companies within the registration period, which is twenty-one days beginning with the day after that on which the charge was created.[253] This registration must provide the details of the charge, including its date of creation, the amount secured by the charge, and short particulars of the property charged.[254] The Registrar will then register the charge in the register of charges kept at Companies House, which can be inspected by any person who pays the requisite fee.[255] The result of this is that there will be a period (of up to twenty-one days) during which the company's assets will be charged, but the register of charges at Companies House will not reflect this. Accordingly, a creditor would be wise also to check the register of charges kept at the company's registered office. The effect of registration is to give constructive notice to the whole world of the existence of the charge, but registration does not provide notice of the charge's terms.[256] Obviously, those who inspect the register have actual notice of both the charge and its terms.

Several consequences flow from the failure to register a registrable charge within the registration period:

- an either-way offence, punishable by a fine, will be committed by the company and all officers in default;[257]
- the charge itself becomes void against any liquidator, administrator, or creditor.[258] The debt remains payable, of course, but it loses any secured status granted by the charge.

⟨⟩ Key points summary

- Creditors provide a company with capital, known as 'debt capital, or 'loan capital'.

- A prudent creditor will secure the loan, usually through the creation of a charge.

- A fixed charge is taken over a tangible, identifiable asset, and allows the creditor to seize the asset and sell it should the company default. The company may not deal with the charged asset.

- A floating charge is usually taken over a class of assets that is constantly changing. Companies are free to deal with the charged assets.

- Certain events will cause a floating charge to become a fixed charge. This process is known as 'crystallization'.

- Most charges must be registered. Failure to register a registrable charge will render the charge void and will also constitute a criminal offence.

---

252. The list of charges requiring registration can be found at CA 2006, s 860(7).
253. CA 2006, s 870(1).   254. Ibid, s 869(4).
255. Ibid, s 869(7).   256. *Wilson v Kelland* [1910] 2 Ch 306 (Ch).
257. CA 2006, s 860(4) and (5).   258. Ibid, s 874(1).

Chapter conclusion

For centuries, academics have been attempting to conceptualize what a company is. A prominent theory (known as the 'new economic theory of the firm', or the 'nexus of contracts' theory) contends that a company is simply a collection of contracts and inputs deriving from various persons. Whether we regard this theory as accurate or not, it emphasizes the importance of the persons who contribute to the company's well-being. In this chapter, we have discussed five groups of person who, in differing ways, are essential to the effective running of the company. Certain groups (for example, the directors) are essential from a legal point of view, whereas others (for example, creditors) may be essential from a financial point of view.

There is one important advantage of conducting business through a company on which we only touched in this chapter—namely, the ability to raise money through investment and borrowing. How a company raises capital and—more importantly, from the perspective of the company's creditors—how the law requires levels of capital to be maintained are the focus of the next chapter.

Self-test questions

1. Define the following:
    (a) resolution;
    (b) annual general meeting (AGM);
    (c) shadow director;
    (d) non-executive director;
    (e) charge;
    (f) crystallization.

2. Explain the distinction between a shareholder and a member.

3. Explain the division of power between the board of directors and the members.

4. Do you agree with the position taken by the Companies Act 2006 regarding the appointment of company secretaries in private companies? Provide arguments both for and against.

5. 'The law affords auditors too much protection.' Do you agree with this statement? Provide arguments both for and against.

6. Explain the differences between a fixed and a floating charge. What are the advantages and disadvantages of each?

Further reading

Birds, J, Boyle, A, MacNeil, I, McCormack, G, Twigg-Flesner, C, and Villiers, C, *Boyle & Birds' Company Law* (6th edn, Jordans, Bristol, 2007) ch 12
Discusses in detail the rules and procedures applicable to company meetings

Davies, PL, *Gower & Davies' Principles of Modern Company Law* (8th edn, Sweet & Maxwell, London, 2008) chs 14 and 32
Chapter 14 discusses the role, structure, appointment, and removal of the board of directors; ch 32 provides a detailed, but readable, account of the benefits of taking security and the rules relating to company charges

French, D, Mayson, S, and Ryan, C, *Mayson, French, & Ryan on Company Law* (25th edn, OUP, Oxford, 2008) ch 15 and pp 507–21
Chapter 15 provides a very thorough account of the role, appointment, and remuneration of the directors, and how their office may be terminated; pp 507–21 discuss the company secretary and the statutory auditor

Hicks, A, 'Director Disqualification: Can It Deliver?' (2001) JBL 433
Discusses the general effectiveness of the Company Directors Disqualification Act 1986 and highlights a number of notable weaknesses

Statutes

Companies Act 2006, Explanatory Notes
Provide a clear and straightforward account of each section of the Companies Act 2006; extremely useful if a particular section is difficult to understand

 Remember to visit the **Online Resource Centre** at <http://www.oxfordtextbooks.co.uk/roach> to access the following resources on Chapter 18, 'The constituents of a company': more **practice questions** and answers; a **glossary** of key terms; **multiple-choice questions**; **revision summaries**; and **audio updates** when relevant.

19 Shares and capital maintenance

- Shares and share capital
- Capital maintenance

INTRODUCTION

The vast majority of companies can function only if they can obtain capital. The *Oxford English Dictionary* defines 'capital' as 'of or pertaining to the original funds of a trader, company or corporation'.[1] Capital can be obtained from several sources, (for example, loan capital can be obtained from creditors). Whilst the word 'capital' may have a broad meaning, in company law terms, it is used to refer to a very specific form of capital—namely, the capital received by the company in payment for shares. Although share capital is only one form of capital (and, in many companies, it may not even be a major source of capital), the law has always made special provision for the raising and maintaining of share capital. In many cases, breach of the provisions relating to share capital can result in significant civil and criminal liability. It is therefore of substantial importance that companies with a share capital are fully aware of the complex procedures relating to raising and maintaining share capital. This chapter will therefore examine the nature of shares and share capital, and the provisions for the maintenance of capital as they apply to companies with a share capital.

🔗 The importance of loan capital is discussed at p 667

Shares and share capital

The Companies Act 2006 (CA 2006), s 540(1), defines a 'share' as a 'share in the company's share capital', but this definition grossly undervalues the full nature of a share. A share is an item of property,[2] known as a 'chose in action'. A 'chose' is simply an asset other than land and a 'chose in action' is simply an intangible chose,[3] which, being intangible, can only be claimed or enforced by legal action, as opposed to by taking possession of it.[4] A share has no physical existence, but rather confers a number of rights and liabilities upon its holder, including providing evidence of the existence of a contract between the shareholder and the company. Because shares are items of property, they can be transferred from person to

---

1. See the Oxford English Dictionary Online, <http://www.oed.com>.
2. CA 2006, s 541.
3. Tangible choses are known as 'choses in possession'.
4. *Torkington v Magee* [1902] 2 KB 427 (KB) 430 (Channell J).

person, with the process of transfer subject to the rules specified in the company's articles, which may, in the case of a private company, restrict transferability.[5] A share does not give a shareholder a proprietary right over the assets of the company.[6] A shareholder may own 50 per cent of the shares in a company, but he is not entitled to 50 per cent of the assets, nor can he demand 50 per cent of the profits. Shares in quoted public companies are used principally as an investment: the investor is looking for income or capital growth, and may not expect to exercise any significant control over the actions of the directors. Shareholders in private companies, many of which are small and/or family-run, may well be involved in management or may otherwise work for the company. For such companies, the shares are more significant as a measure of the degree of control that an individual has over the company.

Irrespective of the type of company, being a shareholder brings about several basic rights:

- the right to vote at general meetings;
- provided that the company's creditors have been paid, shareholders are entitled to any surplus capital upon the winding up of the company.

> ✎ The voting power of shareholders and the conduct of general meetings are discussed in Chapter 18

Classifications of share capital

The law relating to share capital and capital maintenance abounds with terminology, which can render the subject complex. Before we can discuss the legal nature of shares and capital maintenance regime, it is essential to explain the various classifications of share capital.

> ✎ The distribution of assets upon winding up is discussed at p 768

Nominal value

All shares in a limited company with a share capital are required to have a fixed 'nominal' value,[7] (also known as 'par' value) and failure to attach a nominal value to an allotment of shares will render the allotment void.[8] The nominal value represents a notional value of the shares' worth, but, in reality, the nominal value may bear no resemblance whatsoever to the share's actual value. The nominal value of a share represents the minimum price for which the share can be bought and also sets the level of liability of a shareholder if the company is wound up. In other words, once the shareholder had paid the nominal value, he cannot be required to contribute more.

Whilst shares cannot be allotted for less than their nominal value, it is common for shares to be sold for more than their nominal value and the excess is known as the 'share premium'. Where the company in question is a public company, the premium must be fully paid at the time of allotment.[9] The premium is placed in a separate account in the company's balance sheet, called the 'share premium account',

> ✎ The prohibition on allotting shares at a discount is discussed at p 680

---

5. For example, the Companies (Model Articles) Regulations 2008, SI 2008/3229, Sch 1, para 26(5), allows the directors to refuse to register a share transfer.

6. *Borland's Trustee v Steel Bros & Co Ltd* [1901] 1 Ch 279 (Ch).

7. CA 2006, s 542(1).

8. Ibid, s 542(2).

9. Ibid, s 586(1). One quarter of the nominal value of the shares must also be paid at the time of allotment.

⌖ The law relation to distributions is discussed at p 692

and is treated as capital for distribution purposes, but it can be used inter alia to pay write-off expenses associated with the issuing of shares.[10]

Authorized share capital

The concept of authorized share capital has been abolished by the CA 2006, but it regularly appears in pre-2006 cases, so it is a concept that is worth understanding.

Prior to the CA 2006, companies were required to state in their memoranda the total nominal value of shares that may be issued by the company and this value would represent the company's authorized share capital.

Eg Authorized share capital

MicroTech plc has an authorized share capital of £1 million. Thus, the maximum number of shares that it could allot could not have a combined nominal value of over £1 million. So, for example, it could allot:

1. a million shares with a nominal value of £1; or

2. 500,000 shares with a nominal value of £2, etc.

In practice, the requirement to state the authorized share capital was largely pointless. Companies would choose an arbitrary and inflated figure, confident that it would never be reached. Even if it were, passing an ordinary resolution could increase the authorized share capital. Accordingly, in the CA 2006, there is no requirement to state the authorized share capital, and companies can now simply create and allot shares, subject to the limitations discussed in this chapter.

Issued and unissued share capital

The authorized share capital used to represent the maximum nominal value of shares that could be allotted. The nominal value of the shares that actually has been allotted and issued is known as the 'issued' share capital.

Eg Issued share capital

BioCom plc has issued 3 million shares with a nominal value of £3 each. Accordingly, its issued share capital is £9 million. Prior to the CA 2006, a company's issued share capital could never exceed its authorized share capital.

'Unissued' share capital represented the difference between the authorized share capital and the issued share capital. With the abolition of authorized share capital, the concept of unissued share capital has also been abolished.

---

10. Ibid, s 610(2).

Paid-up, called-up, and uncalled share capital

Shareholders may not be required to pay fully for their shares upon allotment (for example, as noted, the shares in public companies need only have a quarter of their nominal value paid at the time of allotment). Shares may be partly paid for at allotment (that is, the payment made is less than the nominal value), with the remainder to be paid at a later date. The combined total of the nominal share capital that has actually been paid is known as the 'paid-up' share capital.

 Paid-up share capital

TechSoft plc has issued a million shares with a nominal value of £1 each (its issued share capital is therefore £1 million). But the company allows allottees to pay 50 pence on allotment and the remainder at a later date to be specified by the company. All of the million shares are allotted and purchased, and every shareholder pays the required 50 pence per share. No shareholder pays more than 50 pence at allotment. The paid-up capital is therefore £500,000.

If shares are not fully paid for, the company may call for any outstanding amounts to be paid, or the company may require payment in instalments and an instalment may have become due. The paid-up share capital plus the amount called for or the instalment due is known as the 'called-up' share capital.

 Called-up share capital

Following on from the TechSoft example above, the company then calls for an additional 25 pence per share to be paid. The called-up share capital is therefore £750,000—that is:

£500,000 + (£1,000,000 x £0.25)

Paid-up share capital + (no of shares issued x amount called for)

Note that the amount called for forms part of the called-up capital irrespective of whether it is actually paid or not.

The difference between the company's issued capital and its called-up capital is known as the 'uncalled' share capital.

The issuing and allotment of shares

There are two principal ways in which a person can become a shareholder in a company:

- because shares are freely transferable (subject to any limitations contained in the articles),[11] he can become a shareholder by purchasing shares from an existing shareholder; or

---

11. Ibid, s 544(1).

- he can become a shareholder by purchasing from the company shares that it has issued.

The latter process is considerably more complex, and the remainder of this section will examine the various rules relating to the issuing and allotment of shares.

The terms 'issue' and 'allotment' are often used interchangeably, but there is a distinction:

- *issuing* refers to the process whereby shares are created and taken;
- shares are only *allotted* 'when a person acquires the unconditional right to be included in the company's register of members in respect of the shares'.[12]

The power to allot shares

The directors must not allot shares except in accordance with the procedures set out in the CA 2006, and any director who knowingly contravenes, permits, or authorizes an unlawful allotment commits an offence triable either way,[13] although the allotment itself will remain valid.[14] On summary conviction, the maximum fine is the statutory maximum (currently £5,000), and on conviction on indictment, there is no limit on the fine that can be imposed. Where a private company has only one class of share, the power to allot shares is vested in the directors, subject to any limitations contained in the company's articles.[15] Regarding any other form of company, whether public or private, the directors may only allot shares if they are authorized to do so by the company's articles or by a resolution of the company.[16] This authority (whether granted by the articles or by resolution) can be general or for the purposes of a particular allotment, and can be subject to conditions or unconditional.[17]

All forms of authority are, however, subject to the following limitations and requirements.

- The authorization must state the maximum number of shares that can be allotted under it.[18]
- The authorization must specify a date on which it is to expire and this date cannot be longer than five years after authorization is granted. Authorization can be renewed, but the renewal is also subject to the five-year maximum.[19]
- The authorization can be revoked or varied at any time by passing an ordinary resolution.[20] This is still the case where revocation or variation results in the articles being altered.
- Any resolution granting, varying, or revoking authority must be sent to the Registrar of Companies within fifteen days of its passing.[21] Failure to do so constitutes a summary offence, punishable by a maximum fine of level 3 on the standard scale (currently £1,000).[22]

---

12. Ibid, s 558.   13. Ibid, s 549(4) and (5).
14. Ibid, s 549(6).
15. Ibid, s 550. The Companies (Model Articles) Regulations 2008, SI 2008/3229, Schs 1 and 2, contain no such limitations.
16. Ibid, s 551(1).   17. Ibid, s 551(2).
18. Ibid, s 551(3)(a).   19. Ibid, s 551(3)(b) and (4)(a).
20. Ibid, s 551(4)(b).   21. Ibid, ss 30(1) and 551(9).
22. Ibid, s 30(2) and (3).

Once the allotment has taken place, the company must, within two months, complete and have ready for delivery share certificates for all of the shares allotted,[23] unless the conditions of allotment provide that no certificate will be issued, or the shares are to be allotted in uncertificated form through a central securities depository such as Euroclear. The share certificate provides prima facie evidence that the person named in the certificate has title to the shares specified in the certificate,[24] but this can be rebutted if evidence can be adduced establishing that the bearer's title is defective. For example, the company might seek to disclaim all liability for a share certificate on the basis that the person who had issued it on behalf of the company was not authorized so to do,[25] or that the share certificate was forged.

When exercising the power to allot shares, directors are under a statutory duty to exercise this power for the purpose for which it was conferred.[26] As we shall see, many cases involving improper uses of directors' powers relate to the allotment of shares.

The 'proper purpose' doctrine is discussed at p 699

Pre-emption rights

An unavoidable consequence of an allotment of new shares is the dilution of the shareholdings of existing shareholders, or the possibility of control being transferred to a new shareholder. To combat these consequences, existing shareholders are given a right of pre-emption, whereby any new allotment of shares must be offered first to the existing shareholders in proportion with their existing shareholdings.

But the shareholders' pre-emption rights are limited in several ways:

- pre-emption rights only apply to the allotment of equity securities, defined as ordinary shares, or the right to subscribe to, or convert securities into, ordinary shares;[27]

- pre-emption rights do not apply to an allotment of **bonus shares**,[28] or shares to be held under an employees' share scheme;[29]

- pre-emption rights do not apply where shares are to be paid up, wholly or partly, otherwise than in cash.[30]

bonus shares: shares allotted to existing shareholders and paid for out of the company's distributable profits

Pre-emption rights can be completely excluded or disapplied in certain situations, including:

- private companies may include a provision in their articles excluding pre-emption rights;[31]

- the directors of a private company with only one class of shares may allot shares ignoring the pre-emption rights of the members if they have been so authorized by the articles or by special resolution;[32]

- a general power of disapplication is given to directors of any company if they are generally authorized by s 551 to allot shares and the power of disapplication

---

23. Ibid, s 769.
24. Ibid, s 768(1).
25. *Ruben v Great Fingall Consolidated* [1906] AC 439 (HL).
26. CA 2006, s 171(b).
27. Ibid, s 560(1).
28. Ibid, s 564.
29. Ibid, s 566.
30. Ibid, s 565.
31. Ibid, s 567(1). The Companies (Model Articles) Regulations 2008, SI 2008/3229, Schs 1 and 2, contain no such provision.
32. Ibid, s 569(1).

is contained in the articles, or is granted to the directors by passing a special resolution.[33]

An allotment that contravenes the pre-emption rights of existing shareholders is still valid, but the company and every officer who knowingly authorized or permitted the contravention are jointly and severally liable to compensate the shareholders who would have benefited from the pre-emptive offer.[34]

Prohibition on allotting shares at a discount

The common law has long held that shares cannot be allotted at a discount (that is, below their nominal value)[35] and this general prohibition can now be found in the CA 2006, s 580. A contract that purports to allot shares at a discount is void.[36] Where discounted shares actually are allotted, the allottee is liable to pay to the company an amount equal to the discount including interest.[37] In addition, the company and every officer in default commit an either-way offence.[38] On summary conviction, the maximum fine is the statutory maximum (currently £5,000), and on conviction on indictment, there is no limit on the fine that can be imposed

In relation to private companies, however, the effectiveness of the prohibition in s 580 is seriously weakened by the fact that shares do not have to be paid for in cash. Section 582(1) provides that shares can be paid for in 'money or money's worth (including goodwill and know-how)', and it is reasonably common to pay for shares with goods, property, services, or even by transferring an existing business to a company in return for shares (as Mr Salomon did).

The Salomon case is discussed at p 606

By overvaluing the non-cash payment, the shares are effectively being issued at a discount. This problem could be remedied if the courts were willing to query the value of the non-cash consideration, but the courts have stated that, as regards private companies, they will only inquire where the consideration is illusory or manifestly inadequate.[39] As a result, it is likely to be rather easy for a private company to issue shares at a discount if it so chooses.

Regarding public companies, the rules are much more stringent. Firstly, public companies cannot accept payment for shares in the form of services.[40] Secondly, where a public company allots shares for non-cash consideration, that consideration must have been independently valued[41] as being equivalent to the value of the amount paid up on the shares. An independent person eligible for appointment as the company's auditor must have made the valuation.[42] The valuation report must have been made available during the six months immediately preceding the allotment and must also have been sent to any proposed allottees.[43] If an allottee has not received a valuation report, or he knew or ought to have known that the provisions applicable to public companies have been contravened, then he is liable to pay to the

---

33. Ibid, s 570(1).   34. Ibid, s 563(2).
35. *Ooregum Gold Mining Co of India Ltd v Roper* [1892] AC 125 (HL).
36. *Re Almada & Tirito Co* (1888) 38 Ch D 415 (CA).   37. CA 2006, s 580(2).
38. Ibid, s 590.   39. *Re Wragg Ltd* [1897] 1 Ch 796 (CA).
40. CA 2006, s 585(1).   41. Ibid, s 593(1).
42. Ibid, s 1150(1).   43. Ibid, s 593(1).

company an amount equal to the aggregate of the nominal value of the shares and the whole of any premium.[44]

Classes of share

Many companies (including most private companies) will only have one class of shareholder, who will hold 'ordinary shares', with the usual rights attributable to a shareholder. But provided that the articles so authorize, companies are free to have different classes of share, conferring different rights upon the holder,[45] examples of which could include:

- differing nominal values for different classes of share;[46]
- shares with increased or decreased voting rights (shares that entitled the holder to receive a dividend if declared and to surplus assets on winding up, but do not entitle the holder to vote at meetings, are known as 'non-voting ordinary shares');
- shares that provide that the holder will only receive a dividend once the ordinary shareholders have received a certain amount (these are known as 'deferred shares').

A common form of share class is the preference share. The precise rights granted to preference shareholders will change from company to company, but preference shares normally provide the holder with preferential claims on any surplus assets on winding up and/or entitle the holder to a predetermined percentage dividend before anything is payable to the ordinary shareholders.

The rights attached to a particular class of shares are known as 'class rights' and shareholders of one class may attempt to deprive shareholders of another class of some beneficial class right, especially if the right grants them some form of preference over the other shareholders. Accordingly, the variation of class rights will only be effective if it complies with the requirements laid down in the CA 2006.

The variation of class rights

Before looking at the procedures for varying class rights, it is important to define what constitutes a 'variation'. It is clear that abrogation of a right constitutes variation. Section 630(5) provides that '[a]ny amendment of a provision contained in a company's articles for the variation of the rights attached to a class of shares, or the insertion of any such provision into the articles, is itself to be treated as a variation of those rights'. Whether or not an alteration constitutes a variation is a matter for the courts and the courts are generally reluctant to hold that an alteration is a variation, as the following case demonstrates.

➡ abrogation: abolishing, or putting an end to

---

44. Ibid, s 593(3).

45. Differing classes of shares are permissible under the Companies (Model Articles) Regulations 2008, SI 2008/3229, Sch 1, para 22, and Sch 3, para 43(1). In both cases, an ordinary resolution is required.

46. *Re Scandinavian Bank Group plc* [1988] Ch 87 (Ch).

> ### ⊙— *Re Mackenzie and Co Ltd* [1916] 2 Ch 450 (Ch)
>
> **FACTS:** The company had issued preference shares, each with a nominal value of £20. Owners of these preference shares were entitled to a 4 per cent dividend on the amount paid up and, because the preference shares were fully paid up, this worked out at 80 pence per share. The company then amended the articles to reduce the nominal value of the preference shares to £12, thereby reducing the dividend to 48 pence per share.
>
> **HELD:** The High Court held that that the alteration of the articles did not constitute a variation of the class right, because the right had remained the same (that is, 4 per cent of the amount paid up).
>
> **COMMENT:** This case demonstrates that, provided that the right remains the same, an alteration will not be classified as a variation if its effect is to render the right less valuable or even to render the right worthless.[47]

There are only two ways in which class rights can be varied, as follows.

1. Where the company's articles contain a class rights variation clause, a variation is valid if it complies with that clause.[48]
2. Where the articles contain no variation clause, a variation will be valid if it is:
   (a) approved by the written consent of the holders of three-quarters in nominal value of the issued shares of the relevant class (not merely three-quarters of those voting);[49] or
   (b) approved by the passing of a special resolution at a meeting of holders of that class.

Where class rights are varied, the holders of not less than 15 per cent of the class of shares in question may apply to the court to have the variation cancelled, provided that they did not consent in writing to the variation, or vote in favour of the resolution approving the variation.[50] The application must be made within twenty-one days of the written consent being given or the resolution being passed,[51] and the variation will have no effect until it has been confirmed by the court.[52] The court must refuse to confirm a variation if it would unfairly prejudice the shareholders of the relevant class.[53] There are very few cases on this provision. Consequently, it is difficult to determine what constitutes 'unfair prejudice' in this context. The court's decision is final and once a variation has been made, the company must, within one month of the variation, inform the Registrar of Companies of the variation.[54] Failure to do so constitutes a summary offence, punishable by a maximum fine of level 3 on the standard scale (currently £1,000).

---

47. *Dimbula Valley (Ceylon) Tea Co Ltd v Laurie* [1961] Ch 353 (Ch).
48. CA 2006, s 630(2)(a). The Companies (Model Articles) Regulations 2008, SI 2008/3229, Schs 1–3 contain no such clauses.
49. Ibid, s 630(4).   50. Ibid, s 633(2).
51. Ibid, s 633(4).   52. Ibid, s 633(3).
53. Ibid, s 633(5).   54. Ibid, s 637(1).

Minimum capital requirements imposed on public companies

Whilst private companies may trade with only a nominal amount of capital, the law imposes minimum capital requirements upon public companies. A public company cannot conduct any business, nor can it exercise any borrowing powers, until the Registrar of Companies has issued it with a trading certificate.[55] The Registrar will not issue a certificate unless he is satisfied that the nominal value of the company's allotted share capital is not less than the authorized minimum, which is currently set at £50,000,[56] or €65,600.[57] A company that conducts business or exercises borrowing powers without a trading certificate commits an offence triable either way, and so does every officer in default. On summary conviction, the maximum fine is the statutory maximum (currently £5,000), and on conviction on indictment, there is no limit on the fine that can be imposed

The rationale behind the imposition of minimum capital requirements upon public companies is to attempt to ensure that there is always a minimum level of capital available to satisfy the company's debts. But it is widely acknowledged that, in practice, the minimum capital requirement does little to aid creditors for several reasons, as follows.

- The authorized minimum is simply too low to offer creditors any real security, and has been described as 'derisory'[58] and 'paltry.'[59]

- The shares do not even need to be fully paid up. Only one quarter of the nominal value and the whole of the premium need be paid up at the time of allotment.[60]

- The authorized minimum is measured at the time that the company wishes to commence trading, but little account is taken of the possibility that it will be reduced once trading commences. Once the company has commenced trading, the only safeguard imposed is that should the company's assets fall to half or less than its called-up share capital, then the directors must call a general meeting to consider what steps, if any, should be taken.[61] By the time that the assets reach this level, it is highly likely that some form of insolvency procedure is already in place, thereby rendering the general meeting largely useless.

 The various insolvency procedures are discussed in Chapter 22

‹ › Key points summary

- Shares are items of personal property that provide their holders with certain rights, but provide no proprietary rights over the company's assets.

- All shares have a fixed nominal value, and this can be used to calculate the company's issued capital, paid-up capital, called-up capital, and uncalled capital.

---

55. Ibid, s 761(1).
56. Ibid, s 763(1)(a).
57. Companies (Authorised Minimum) Regulations 2008, SI 2008/729, reg 2.
58. PL Davies, *Gower & Davies' Principles of Modern Company Law* (8th edn, Sweet & Maxwell, London, 2008) 261.
59. J Birds, AJ Boyle et al, *Boyle & Birds' Company Law* (6th edn, Jordans, Bristol, 2007) 218.
60. CA 2006, s 568(1).
61. Ibid, s 656.

- The directors of private companies with one class of share are empowered to allot shares. As regards other companies, directors can only allot shares in compliance with the provisions set out in the articles.

- Generally, when a company allots shares, it must first offer them to existing shareholders (this is known as a 'pre-emption right').

- Companies are free to issue different classes of shares with differing rights. A variation in those rights is only valid if it complies with the rules in the articles, or, in the absence of such rules, if three-quarters of the class in question approves the variation.

- A public company will not be issued with a trading certificate unless the nominal value of its allotted share capital is not less than £50,000 or €65,600.

Capital maintenance

Having obtained share capital via the allotment of shares, the law requires that the company 'maintain' that capital by not distributing it in unauthorized ways. The principal reason for this is that it is the company's capital to which the creditors look for payment in the event of a winding up and any depreciation in the company's capital could increase the risk of the company defaulting. Of course, creditors appreciate that the company's capital will increase and decrease in the normal course of business based on the company's fortunes, but the creditors will not expect the company to return share capital to the shareholders. Accordingly, the law generally prohibits companies from returning capital to their shareholders, thereby providing protection to the creditors and helping to ensure that certain assets remain inviolate for the payment of the company's creditors. These rules are known collectively as the 'capital maintenance regime' and the principal rules are explained below.

The restructuring of share capital

A company may seek to restructure its share capital in a number of ways, including:

- increasing its share capital by allotting new shares;
- subdivision (that is, taking existing shares and subdividing them into shares of a smaller nominal value than the existing shares, thereby creating an overall increase in the number of shares);[62]
- consolidation (that is, consolidating existing shares into shares with a larger nominal value than the existing shares, thereby producing an overall decrease in the number of shares).[63]

None of these restructurings of capital adversely affect the level of share capital and therefore they pose no danger to the creditors' interests. Accordingly, these are matters to be decided on by the shareholders alone. On the other hand, a reduction of share capital does have the potential to affect the creditors' interests adversely. Consequently, such a reduction is regulated by statute. The general position is that

---

62. Ibid, s 618.   63. Ibid.

a reduction of capital is unlawful unless authorized by the CA 2006, ss 641–653.[64] That statute permits a company to reduce its share capital is recognition of the fact that a reduction can be beneficial in certain circumstances and, whilst the CA 2006 does not limit the ways in which a company can reduce its capital, s 641(4) provides a non-exhaustive list of examples of ways it can do so.[65]

A company may:

- extinguish or reduce the liability on any of its shares in respect of share capital not paid up;
- cancel any paid-up share capital that is lost or unrepresented by available assets;
- repay any paid-up share capital in excess of the company's wants.

The cancellation of paid-up share capital is designed to reflect reality: there is little point in a company having a high nominal capital when trading losses have reduced its net assets to a lower figure. Reduction of capital in such a case would allow a company to resume dividend payments. Paying off unneeded share capital involves returning money to the shareholders and is most often encountered when a company is scaling down its trading activities (a common occurrence in the past following nationalization).

Under the now-repealed Companies Act 1985 (CA 1985), s 135, a company could only reduce its share capital if the articles permitted a reduction, if a special resolution was obtained authorizing the reduction, and if the court approved the reduction. But requiring private companies to obtain court approval imposed substantial regulatory burdens on private companies, as well as the courts. Accordingly, the CA 2006 no longer requires private companies to obtain court approval and provides for the following two methods of effecting a reduction.

Special resolution and court confirmation

The first method of effecting a reduction of capital is available to all types of company, and provides that a reduction is valid where the members authorize the reduction by passing a special resolution and the company then applies to the court for an order confirming the reduction.[66] Where a public company wishes to reduce its share capital below the authorized minimum discussed earlier (£50,000, or €65,600), then an expedited procedure is provided, allowing the public company to re-register as a private company without the usually required special resolution.[67]

The requirement of court approval is the source of creditor protection, because the courts' principal concern is to protect the interest of the company's creditors. Under the CA 1985, creditors were arguably overprotected, because virtually any creditor could object to a reduction. The result of this was that, prior to many reductions, the company would settle or secure the creditor's claims thereby placing the creditors in a better position than that in which they would have been

---

64. Ibid, s 617(2)(b).
65. Ibid, s 641(3) provides that, subject to s 641(2), a company may reduce its share capital in any way.
66. Ibid, s 641(1)(b).
67. Ibid, s 651. Unless the public company re-registers as private, the Registrar must not register the reduction unless the court so directs (s 650(2)).

had the reduction never been proposed. The protection afforded to creditors under the CA 1985 was therefore reduced by providing that the only creditors who could object were those who could demonstrate 'a real likelihood that the reduction would result in the company being unable to discharge [their] debt or claim when it fell due'.[68]

This limitation has not, however, been preserved in the CA 2006. Accordingly, where a reduction involves a diminution of liability in respect of unpaid share capital or the payment to a shareholder of unpaid share capital, every creditor has the right to object to the reduction. Where a creditor does object, the court will draw up a list of creditors entitled to object and provide that those creditors should come forward by a certain date. Creditors who fail to meet the deadline will be unable to object to the reduction. Once the date has passed, the reduction cannot proceed unless all of the creditors who came forward have agreed to the reduction, or their claims have been settled or secured—although the court can dispense with the consent of certain creditors as it sees fit. This procedure places considerable pressure on the company to settle the creditor's claims prior to effecting the reduction. This is demonstrated in the fact that, since 1949, the courts have not had to resort to this procedure, because the companies have usually settled with the creditors. The court does have the power to direct that the provisions regarding the rights of creditors are not to apply as regards any class or classes of creditors,[69] but the Act is silent on when this would be appropriate.

In addition to the interests of creditors, the court will also take into account the interests of existing shareholders, with two factors being of particular importance, as follows.

- The reduction should be fair and equitable between the different classes of shareholder,[70] and between shareholders of the same class,[71] unless such shareholders consent to be treated differently.
- The company should ensure that, when explaining to the shareholders why a reduction is desired, any information presented is accurate and enables the shareholders to make an informed choice.[72]

Special resolution supported by a solvency statement

The second method of effecting a reduction of capital is available to private companies only and does not require court approval. A private company can effect a reduction of capital by passing a special resolution authorizing the reduction, supported by a statement of solvency from the directors.[73] This statement must be made no more than fifteen days before the special resolution is passed[74] and will provide that each of the directors has formed the opinion that:

---

68. CA 1985, s 136(3)(b), inserted by the Companies (Reduction of Capital) (Creditor Protection) Regulations 2008, SI 2008/719, reg 2.
69. CA 2006, s 645(3).
70. *Poole v National Bank of China Ltd* [1907] AC 229 (HL).
71. *British and American Trustee and Finance Corporation Ltd v Couper* [1894] AC 399 (HL).
72. *Re Jupiter House Investments (Cambridge) Ltd* [1985] 1 WLR 975 (Ch).
73. CA 2006, s 641(1)(a).
74. Ibid, s 642(1)(a).

- there is no ground on which the company could then be found to be unable to pay (or otherwise discharge) its debts; and
- the company will be able to pay (or otherwise discharge) its debts as they fall due during the year immediately following the date of the statement. If it is intended to commence the winding up of the company within twelve months of the date of the statement, each director must be of the opinion that the company will be able to pay (or otherwise discharge) its debts in full within twelve months of the commencement of the winding up.[75]

Within fifteen days of the resolution being passed, a copy of the statement , along with a statement of capital (which will indicate the share capital of the company following the reduction) and a copy of the resolution must be delivered to the Registrar of Companies.[76] The resolution will not take effect until the Registrar registers these documents.[77]

If the directors make a solvency statement without reasonable grounds for the opinions expressed within it and the statement is delivered to the Registrar of Companies for registration, every director who is in default commits an offence triable either way,[78] although this will not affect the validity of the resolution. On summary conviction, the offence carries a maximum penalty of up to six months' imprisonment[79] and/or a fine not exceeding the statutory maximum (currently £5,000). On conviction on indictment, the maximum penalty is two years' imprisonment and/or a fine.

The acquisition of own shares

Under the common law, a company was prohibited absolutely from purchasing its own shares, on the ground that such a purchase would result in a return of capital to the shareholders and a consequent reduction in the capital available to pay creditors.[80] The CA 2006, s 658, continues to take a strict approach and provides that a company cannot purchase its own shares, except in accordance with the methods set down in the CA 2006. Where s 658 is contravened, the purported acquisition is void, and the company and every officer of the company who is in default commits a criminal offence triable either way. On summary conviction, the offence carries a maximum penalty of up to six months' imprisonment[81] and/or a fine not exceeding the statutory maximum (currently £5,000). On conviction on indictment, the maximum penalty is two years' imprisonment and/or a fine.

The CA 2006 provides the following exceptions to the general prohibition.

Redeemable shares

A limited company has the power to issue redeemable shares (that is, shares that are issued, but which can be redeemed by the company at the insistence of either the

---

75. Ibid, s 643(1).   76. Ibid, s 644(1).

77. Ibid, s 644(4).   78. Ibid, s 643(4).

79. This will rise to twelve months' imprisonment if or when the Criminal Justice Act 2003, s 154(1), comes into force.

80. *Trevor v Whitworth* (1887) 12 App Cas 409 (HL).

81. This will rise to twelve months' imprisonment if or when the Criminal Justice Act 2003, s 154(1), comes into force.

company or the shareholder).[82] But a public company can only issue redeemable shares if its articles so provide.[83] Private companies require no authorization by the articles,[84] but the articles may exclude or restrict redeemable shares being issued.[85]

The issuing and redemption of redeemable shares is subject to a number of restrictions, as follows.

- Redeemable shares can only be issued at a time when the company has issued shares that are not redeemable.[86]

- Redeemable shares can only be redeemed if they are fully paid up.[87] Therefore the company cannot purchase unissued or partly paid-up redeemable shares.

- When redeeming shares, the company must pay fully for them at the time of redemption, unless the terms of redemption provide for a later date.[88]

- The redeemable shares of public companies must be paid for out of distributable profits of the company, or out of the proceeds of a fresh issue of shares made for the purposes of redemption.[89] This will ensure that the company's share capital is not reduced by the redemption. As we shall see later, however, there is a procedure whereby private companies can redeem their own shares out of capital.

Shares that are redeemed are treated as cancelled.[90] Within one month of the redemption, the company must inform the Registrar of Companies of the redemption. Failure to notify the Registrar constitutes a criminal offence by the company and every officer in default. The offence is punishable summarily by a fine not exceeding level 3 on the standard scale (currently £1,000).[91]

Purchase by a company of its own shares

Whilst issuing redeemable shares does provide the company with the ability to acquire its own shares, its flexibility is limited in two ways: firstly, the company will need to decide, prior to issue, that the shares are to be redeemable; secondly, the company can only then purchase those additional shares. What companies wanted was a general power to purchase any shares; such a power was introduced by the Companies Act 1981 and can now be found in the CA 2006, s 690.

A number of general restrictions are imposed, as follows.

- Only limited companies may purchase their own shares.

- The company may not purchase its own shares if to do so would result in there being no member holding any shares other than redeemable shares or treasury shares.[92]

➡ treasury shares: shares held in the company's own treasury

- The shares purchased must be fully paid and where the company purchases its own shares, the shares must be paid for on purchase.[93]

---

82. CA 2006, s 684(1).

83. Ibid, s 684(3). The Companies (Model Articles) Regulations 2008, SI 2008/3229, Sch 3, para 43(2), permits public companies to issue redeemable shares.

84. Although the Companies (Model Articles) Regulations 2008, SI 2008/3229, Sch 1, para 22(2), provides such authorization.

85. CA 2006, s 684(2). 86. Ibid, s 684(4).

87. Ibid, s 686(1). 88. Ibid, s 686(2) and (3).

89. Ibid, s 687(2). 90. Ibid, s 688.

91. Ibid, s 689. 92. Ibid, s 690(2).

93. Ibid, s 691.

- Authorization in the articles for the purchase is not required (as was required under the CA 1985), but the articles can restrict or exclude the company's ability to purchase its own shares.[94]
- Purchase of the shares must be paid for out of distributable profits, or out of the proceeds of a fresh issue of shares made for the purpose of financing the purchase.[95] As we shall see later, however, there is a procedure whereby private companies can purchase their own shares out of capital.

Additional requirements are imposed, but these depend on whether the purchase is to be a market purchase or an off-market purchase. As we shall see, the basic difference is that, because market purchases are conducted through a recognized investment exchange with its own safeguards, they are less regulated by the CA 2006 than are off-market purchases.

An 'off-market purchase' is:

- a purchase otherwise than on a recognized investment exchange; or
- a purchase on a recognized stock exchange, but not subject to a marketing arrangement on that exchange.[96]

The terms of purchase of an off-market purchase will need to be authorized in advance by the members by passing a special resolution,[97] and in the case of a public company, such authorization will last for a maximum of eighteen months.[98] This authorization can be varied, revoked, or renewed by another special resolution.[99] The votes of the shareholders whose shares are to be purchased will not count towards the special resolution.[100] Even where the company has the requisite votes, the special resolution will not be passed until a copy of the contract of purchase (or a memorandum of its terms, if the contract is not in writing) is made available to the members of the company. This will be satisfied either by having the contract available for inspection at the meeting at which the resolution is passed, or by having the contract available for inspection at the company's registered office for at least fifteen days before the date of the meeting.[101]

A 'market purchase' is a purchase made on a recognized investment exchange (for example, the London Stock Exchange), otherwise than a purchase on a recognized stock exchange that is not subject to a marketing arrangement on the exchange.[102] Like an off-market purchase, a market purchase requires authorization from the general meeting, but only an ordinary resolution is required.[103] The resolution must state the maximum number of shares that may be acquired by the company, and the maximum and minimum prices that may be paid for those shares.[104] This authorization can last for a maximum of eighteen months, but can be varied, renewed, or revoked by passing another ordinary resolution. A copy of the authorizing resolution must be forwarded to the Registrar within fifteen days of the resolution being passed.[105] Failure to do so constitutes a summary offence by the company and every

---

94. Ibid, s 690(1)(b).
95. Ibid, s 692(2).
96. Ibid, s 693(2).
97. Ibid, s 694(1) and (2).
98. Ibid, s 694(5).
99. Ibid, s 694(4).
100. Ibid, s 695(2) and (3).
101. Ibid, s 696(2).
102. Ibid, s 693(4).
103. Ibid, s 701(1).
104. Ibid, s 701(3).
105. Ibid, ss 30(1) and 701(8).

officer who is in default, punishable by a maximum fine of level 3 on the standard scale (currently £1,000).[106]

Irrespective of whether the purchase is market or off-market, once the purchase has been made, the company must, within twenty-eight days beginning on the date on which the shares were delivered, deliver to the Registrar a return indicating the number and nominal value of the shares sold. Where the company is public, it must also indicate the aggregate amount paid by the company for the shares, and the maximum and minimum prices paid.[107] Failure to deliver the return to the Registrar constitutes an either-way offence by the company and every officer in default.[108] On summary conviction, the maximum fine is the statutory maximum (currently £5,000), and on conviction on indictment, there is no limit on the fine that can be imposed

Redeeming or purchasing shares out of capital

Normally, a company that wishes to purchase its own shares must, in order to avoid returning capital to the shareholders, pay for such shares out of distributable profits or via a fresh issue of shares. But private companies may often lack distributable profits and may not wish to issue new shares. The only other option was formerly to reduce share capital, but, prior to the 2006 Act, court approval was required, thereby making the process potentially expensive. Given that, in many private companies, the capital maintenance regime is of limited practical usefulness, it was decided to permit private limited companies to redeem or purchase their own shares out of capital and such a power is now provided for by s 709. But such a payment will only be valid if stringent requirements are complied with, as follows.

- Before payment can come out of capital, the company must first use any distributable profits or any proceeds from a fresh issue of shares made for the purpose of redemption or purchase (this is known as the 'permissible capital payment').[109]

- The directors must make a statement similar to the solvency statement discussed above. Annexed to this statement must be a report from the company's auditor, stating that there is nothing to indicate that the opinions expressed by the directors in the statement are unreasonable.[110]

- Within a week of the statement being made, the company must pass a special resolution authorizing payment out of capital.[111]

- Within a week following the resolution, the company must publish in the *Gazette* a notice stating that the company has approved payment out of capital for the purpose of redeeming or purchasing its own shares. It must also state the same in an advertisement in a national newspaper, or notify all of its creditors by letter of the same.[112]

- The directors' statement and the auditor's report must be delivered to Companies House on or before the day on which the notice or advertisement appears.[113] From that day onwards, for a period of five weeks, the statement and report must be made available for inspection (usually at the company's

---

106. Ibid, s 30(2) and (3).   107. Ibid, s 707(4).
108. Ibid, s 707(7).   109. Ibid, s 710.
110. Ibid, s 714.   111. Ibid, s 716.
112. Ibid, s 719(2).   113. Ibid, s 719(4).

registered office) to any shareholder or creditor who wishes to do so. Failure to allow inspection constitutes a summary offence by the company and every officer in default, punishable by a fine not exceeding level 3 on the standard scale (currently £1,000).[114]

Any creditor or any shareholder of the company who did not vote for the resolution may, within five weeks following the resolution, apply to the court for cancellation of the resolution. The court can confirm or cancel the resolution on such terms as it sees fit.[115]

Financial assistance to acquire shares

Under the CA 1985, all companies were generally prohibited from providing financial assistance to another to purchase it shares. Exceptions did exist, but they were narrow and strictly regulated. The problem that arose was that the prohibition served to prevent perfectly innocent and beneficial transactions, especially as regards private companies. Accordingly, for private companies, the prohibition on providing financial assistance has been abolished. Sections 678 and 679 preserves the prohibition for public companies, and provides that a public company may not provide financial assistance for the acquisition of its own shares, or for the acquisition of the shares in a private company of which the public company is a subsidiary. Contravention of the prohibition constitutes an either-way offence by the company and any director in default.[116] On summary conviction, the offence carries a maximum penalty of up to six months' imprisonment[117] and/or a fine not exceeding the statutory maximum (currently £5,000). On conviction on indictment, the maximum penalty is two years' imprisonment and/or a fine.[118] Any agreement to provide financial assistance unlawfully will be unenforceable[119] and any assistance received may also be held on trust for the company where the recipient knew or ought to have known of the illegality.[120] Additionally, any directors involved may be found to have breached their duties and could be subject to a disqualification order.[121]

This disqualification of directors is discussed at p 652

The prohibition, however, is not absolute and there are instances in which a public company can provide financial assistance, including the following.

- Financial assistance given in good faith in the interests of the company is permitted where:
  - the principal purpose of the assistance is not for the acquisition of shares; or
  - where the purpose of the assistance is to acquire shares, but it is part of some larger purpose of the company.[122]

---

114. Ibid, s 720.   115. Ibid, s 721.
116. Ibid, s 680(1).
117. This will rise to twelve months' imprisonment if or when the Criminal Justice Act 2003, s 154(1), comes into force.
118. CA 2006, s 680(2).
119. *Brady v Brady* [1989] AC 755 (HL).
120. *Belmont Finance Corporation v Williams Furniture Ltd* [1980] 1 All ER 393 (CA).
121. See, e.g., *Re Continental Assurance Co of London plc* [1997] 1 BCLC 48 (Ch).
122. CA 2006, s 678(2).

- Certain transactions are unconditionally excluded from the prohibition, including:
  - the distribution of the company's assets by way of dividend lawfully made, or by way of a distribution in the course of the company's winding up;
  - the allotment of bonus shares;
  - a reduction in capital; and
  - a redemption or purchase of shares.[123]
- Certain transactions are conditionally excluded from the prohibition, with the condition being that the assistance does not reduce its net assets, or is paid out of distributable profits. These transactions include:
  - the provision of financial assistance where the lending of money is part of the ordinary business of the company; and
  - employees' share schemes.[124]

Distributions out of profits

As is discussed in Chapter 20, a director is under a duty to promote the success of the company for the benefit of its members.[125] The imposition of such a duty is recognition of the fact that the principal purpose of most commercial companies is to make a profit. In turn, the shareholders will expect to receive a share in the profits, usually via the distribution of a payment known as a 'dividend'. Dividends are simply the distribution, usually in cash,[126] of profits to the shareholders, usually at a fixed amount per share. Accordingly, the more shares held, the greater the dividend payment. Normally, companies will retain a portion of the profits to reinvest in the company and will distribute the remainder in the form of dividends. But it is important to note that, until the company is wound up, companies are not under a legal obligation to distribute profits to their shareholders[127] and that therefore shareholders have no 'right' to a dividend. A failure to pay a dividend could, however, constitute unfairly prejudicial conduct,[128] or possibly justify winding up on just and equitable grounds.[129]

These shareholder remedies are discussed in Chapter 21

A dividend can only be paid if it is properly declared and authorized, with the applicable procedures being found in the company's articles. The normal procedure contained in the model articles[130] is as follows.

1. The directors must first recommend the amount of profits to be distributed by way of dividend.
2. The company will then 'declare' a dividend by passing an ordinary resolution. This resolution cannot be passed until the directors have made their recommendation and the shareholders cannot declare an amount greater that that

---

123. Ibid, s 681.   124. Ibid, s 682.

125. Ibid, s 172.

126. Non-cash payments may only be made if the articles permit: *Wood v Odessa Waterworks Co* (1889) 42 Ch D 636 (Ch). The Companies (Model Articles) Regulations 2008, SI 2008/3229, Sch 1, para 34, and Sch 3, para 76, allow for non-cash distributions.

127. *Burland v Earle* [1902] AC 83 (PC).

128. *Re Sam Weller & Sons Ltd* [1990] Ch 682 (Ch).

129. *Re a Company, ex p Glossop* [1988] BCLC 570 (Ch).

130. See the Companies (Model Articles) Regulations 2008, SI 2008/3229, Sch 1, para 30, and Sch 3, para 70.

recommended by the directors. Once the dividend has been declared, it becomes a debt of the company owed to the shareholders.

3. The responsibility for paying out the dividend in accordance with the rights of the shareholders is placed upon the directors.

Profits available for distribution

From a capital maintenance perspective, the key restriction is established in s 830(1), which provides that a 'company may only make a distribution out of profits available for the purpose', with such profits defined as 'its accumulated, realised profits, so far as not previously utilised by distribution or capitalisation, less its accumulated, realised losses, so far as not previously written off in a reduction or reorganisation of capital duly made'.[131]

Two words used in this definition deserve elaboration.

- *Accumulated* The inclusion of the word 'accumulated' indicates that when determining 'profits available for the purpose' of paying a dividend, the company cannot ignore previous years' trading performance and must include any losses sustained in previous years. This is to prevent a situation in which a company has several years' poor performance, but then has a profitable year and pays out dividends, even though the profitable year has not replaced the losses sustained in previous years.

- *Realized* The inclusion of the word 'realized' is to prevent the company paying a dividend based on estimated profits. Companies used to be able to pay out dividends based on estimated profits;[132] if those profits were never to materialize, the payment would have come out of capital. Companies are now required to determine profits based on gains and losses realized. 'Realized' is to be defined in accordance with generally accepted accounting principles,[133] and realized profits are therefore defined as profits 'in the form of either cash or of other assets, the ultimate cash realisation of which can be assessed with reasonable certainty'.[134]

Payment by the company of an unlawful distribution, or part of one, to one of its shareholders can result in several consequences, although the CA 2006 itself only provides for one—namely, that if the shareholder, at the time of the distribution, knew or had reasonable grounds to believe that the distribution was unlawful, he is required to repay it, or part of it, to the company.[135] A shareholder will not avoid liability where his lack of knowledge of the illegality was due to his ignorance of the legal limitations discussed above.[136] The directors who authorized the payment are liable under the common law to repay to company the money if they knew, or ought to have known, that the distribution was illegal.[137] The subsequent resolution

---

131. CA 2006, s 830(2).

132. *Dimbula Valley (Ceylon) Tea Co Ltd v Laurie* [1961] Ch 353 (Ch).

133. CA 2006, s 853(4).

134. Accounting Standards Board, *Financial Reporting Standard 18: Accounting Policies*, [28], available online at <http://www.frc.org.uk>.

135. CA 2006, s 847(1) and (2).

136. *It's a Wrap (UK) Ltd v Gula* [2006] EWCA Civ 554, [2006] BCC 626.

137. *Re National Funds Assurance Co* (1878) 10 Ch D 118 (Ch).

of the members does not constitute ratification.[138] This is a substantial deterrent. For example, in *Bairstow v Queens Moat Houses plc*,[139] the directors of the company were required to pay back an unlawful distribution of £26.7 million plus an additional £15.2 million in interest. If an unlawful distribution is made based on erroneous accounts, the company's auditor, if negligent in failing to identify the error, is also liable under the common law to the company for such negligence and is liable to repay the amount of the unlawful distribution.[140]

It is clear that the above rules are primarily designed to protect creditors by prohibiting a distribution out of capital. The creditors have no right to commence an action to restrain a wrongful distribution,[141] however, although they can seek to have the company wound up.

Key points summary

- All companies may reduce their capital by passing a special resolution, which is then confirmed by the court. Private companies need not obtain court approval provided that a statement of solvency supports the special resolution.

- Companies are generally prohibited from purchasing their own shares, but may do so where the shares are redeemable shares, or where the procedures relating to market and off-market purchases are complied with.

- Subject to certain exceptions, public companies are normally prohibited from providing financial assistance for the acquisition of their shares. Private companies are free to provide such financial assistance.

- Distributions (for example, dividends) may be made only out of profits available for the purpose.

Chapter conclusion

There is little doubt that the rules relating to the raising and maintenance of share capital have been simplified by the CA 2006, but the rules are still complex and highly technical. Certain areas of the law have been deregulated, but share capital remains a paternalistically regulated area of company law. Such complexity and heavy regulation would be justified if the rules were to provide effective protection for creditors, but it has been doubted that the rules offer much protection in practice. The concept of the nominal value of a share has been heavily criticized and might well have been abolished were it not a requirement of the Second Company Law Directive.[142] The minimum capital requirement imposed on public companies is of little practical use and private companies easily sidestep the rules prohibiting the allotment of shares at a discount. For public companies,

---

138. *Re Exchange Banking Co (Flitcroft's Case)* (1882) 21 Ch D 519 (CA).
139. [2001] EWCA Civ 712, [2002] BCC 91.
140. *Leeds Estate Building and Investment Co v Shepherd* (1887) 36 Ch D 787 (Ch).
141. *Mills v Northern Rly of Buenos Ayres* (1870) 5 Ch App 621 (CA).
142. Council Directive (EC) 77/91/EEC.

effecting a reduction in capital, even for a wholly sensible and beneficial reason, is still an onerous undertaking. A company wishing to acquire its own shares will need to ensure that a raft of procedures is complied with and the law relating to distributions requires a serious layperson's knowledge of accounting principles. Whilst it cannot be doubted that creditor protection is an essential feature of any system of company law, the extent to which the capital maintenance regime actually protects the interests of creditors is open to discussion.

Self-test questions

1. Define the following:
    (a) chose in action;
    (b) nominal value;
    (c) pre-emption rights;
    (d) preference shares;
    (e) redeemable shares;
    (f) dividend.

2. Explain the distinction between:
    (a) called-up and uncalled share capital;
    (b) the allotment and issue of shares;
    (c) the subdivision and consolidation of shares.

3. MultiSoft plc was incorporated in 2006. Its memorandum states that it has an authorized share capital of £2 million. Since then, it has issued 1.2 million shares, all with a nominal value of £1.50. The terms of all allotments to date have provided that shares can be partly paid for with a minimum 90 pence payable at allotment and the remainder due when called for. Of the 1.2 million shares, 500,000 have 90 pence paid up, 400,000 have £1.20 paid up, and the remainder are fully paid up. The company calls for 10 pence per share on all unpaid shares. Based on the information provided, calculate Multisoft's:
    (a) issued share capital;
    (b) unissued share capital;
    (c) paid-up capital;
    (d) called-up capital;
    (e) uncalled capital.

4. 'The rules relating to capital maintenance are overly complex and too technical and the Companies Act 2006 has done little to improve the protection afforded to creditors.' Do you agree with this statement? Provide reasons for your answers.

Further reading

Alcock, A, Birds, J, and Gale, S, *Companies Act 2006: The New Law* (Jordans, Bristol, 2007) chs 14 and 16
Clearly sets out the new law and explains how the current capital maintenance provisions differ from those of the Companies Act 1985

Armour, J, 'Share Capital and Creditor Protection: Efficient Rules for a Modern Company Law' (2000) 63 MLR 355
Discusses the rationale behind the capital maintenance provisions from an economic viewpoint

French, D, Mayson, S, and Ryan, C, *Mayson, French, & Ryan on Company Law* (25th edn, OUP, Oxford, 2008) chs 6 and 10
A comprehensive and detailed account of the nature of shares and the rules relating to capital maintenance

Myners, P, *Pre-Emption Rights: Final Report* (DTI, London, 2005)
Analyses the law relating to pre-emption rights and discusses why such rights are needed

Pennington, RR, 'Can Shares in Companies Be Defined?' (1989) 10 Co Law 140
Discusses the nature of the share since the first chartered companies up to the proliferation of the registered company

Remember to visit the **Online Resource Centre** at <http://www.oxfordtextbooks.co.uk/roach> to access the following resources on Chapter 19, 'Shares and capital maintenance': more **practice questions** and answers; a **glossary** of key terms; **multiple-choice questions**; **revision summaries**; **audio updates** when relevant; and audio exam advice on this key topic.

20 Directors' duties

- Codification
- The general duties
- Transactions requiring shareholder approval

- Limitation periods
- Relief from liability

INTRODUCTION

In Chapter 18, we noted that the directors of the company are vested with a substantial amount of discretionary power. The problem with such a concentration of power is that the directors may be tempted to engage in self-benefiting acts, acts for an improper purpose, or other acts that are not in the company's interests. In this chapter, we will discuss the principal method by which such acts are discouraged and remedied—namely, the imposition of duties upon directors.

By and large, the duties of directors were not changed by the Companies Act 2006, but this Act did introduce a major alteration in that, after over a century of discussion on the topic, the duties of directors have finally been codified.

Codification

Historically, the duties of directors were derived from a mass of case law based on the common law of negligence and equitable duties analogous to those imposed on trustees. The result was that this area of the law was unclear, inaccessible, and out of date. Accordingly, as far back as 1895,[1] it had been suggested that directors' duties should be codified in some manner, but it was only following a 1999 Law Commission report[2] and a review of company law[3] that it was finally decided to enact a statutory statement of directors' duties. The result can be found in the Companies Act 2006 (CA 2006), ss 170–181, which codify the common law and

➡️ codification: the process whereby law is collected and restated in statute

---

1. Davey Committee, *Report of the Departmental Committee to Inquire what Amendments are Necessary in the Acts Relating to Joint Stock Companies Incorporated with Limited Liability* (C 7779, HMSO, London, 1895).
2. Law Commission, *Company Directors: Regulating Conflicts of Interest and Formulating a Statement of Duties* (Law Com No 261, Cm 4436, HMSO, London, 1999).
3. Company Law Review Steering Group, *Modern Company Law for a Competitive Economy: Final Report, Vol 1* (DTI, London, 2001).

equitable duties, and sets them out in a more accessible and up-to-date manner. In addition, the law relating to directorial transactions requiring shareholder approval has also been restated.

The general duties

The restated duties are referred to in the Act as the 'general duties' and are 'based on certain common law rules and equitable principles as they apply in relation to directors'.[4] It is clear therefore that codification has not radically altered the duties in any way, but has rather restated them in a more appropriate manner (although several notable reforms have been made, as we shall see). Doubtless, this is to ensure that the authoritative and extremely useful body of case law that has developed should remain highly relevant—an assertion that is backed up by s 170(4), which provides that 'regard shall be had to the corresponding common law rules and equitable principles in interpreting and applying the general duties'.[5] These duties are in addition to any duties that the director might have in his capacity as an agent or employee. These duties apply to shadow directors to the same extent as did the corresponding common law rules.[6]

> 🔗 The duties of an agent are discussed at p 954

> 🔗 The duties of an employee are discussed at p 794

Before examining these duties, it is important to understand to whom these duties are owed, because, generally, only that person can sue the directors for breach of duty. Statute preserves the common law position[7] by providing that the general duties 'are owed by a director of a company to the company'.[8] Generally therefore, directors do not owe their duties to shareholders,[9] creditors,[10] employees, or anyone else, and only the company (and those who can act on its behalf) can sue for breach of such a duty. But exceptions do exist and in two limited circumstances, the directors may owe a duty directly to the shareholders:

- where a director undertakes to act as agent for one or more shareholders, he will owe a duty directly to those shareholders,[11] but such a duty derives from his position as an agent and not by virtue of him being a director;
- where the company is the target of a takeover bid, the directors may owe a direct duty to the shareholders to provide honest advice regarding the bid and not to prevent the shareholders from obtaining the best price for their shares.[12]

> 🔗 Derivative claims are considered at p 726

In addition, in limited circumstances, the shareholders might be able to sue for breach of duty via a derivative claim.

Although the general duties themselves are set out in statute, the specific remedies for their breach are not stated in the CA 2006. Instead, s 178(1) provides that the

---

4. CA 2006, s 170(3).
5. Ibid, s 170(4).
6. Ibid, s 170(5).
7. *Percival v Wright* [1902] 2 Ch 421 (Ch).
8. CA 2006, s 170(1).
9. *Multinational Gas and Petrochemical Co v Multinational Gas and Petrochemical Services Ltd* [1983] Ch 258 (CA).
10. Ibid.
11. *Allen v Hyatt* (1914) 30 TLR 444 (PC).
12. *Heron International Ltd v Lord Grade* [1983] BCLC 244 (CA).

consequences of breaching the general duties are the same as those that would apply if the corresponding common law or equitable principle were to have been breached. These remedies are discussed alongside the corresponding general duty.

Duty to act within the company's powers

The first general duty is contained in s 171 and is an amalgam of two prior common law duties:

- a duty to act in accordance with the company's constitution; and
- a duty to exercise powers only for the purposes for which they are conferred.

Duty to act in accordance with the constitution

As we discussed in Chapter 17, the powers of the company will predominantly be set out in the company's articles and the default position is that companies created under the 2006 Act will have unrestricted articles. It is common, however, for companies to impose some form of limitation on the power of the directors and directors who breach such limitations will breach the general duty contained in s 171. It is important to note that, under the CA 2006, s 17, the company's constitution is not only its articles, but also includes any resolution or agreement that would need to be notified to the Registrar.[13] In addition, references to the company's constitution in the part of the CA 2006 dealing with the company's directors include:

- any decision agreed by the shareholders, or a class of the shareholders, which is treated in law as equivalent to a decision of the company;[14]
- any resolution or other decision arrived at in accordance with the constitution.[15]

Where the directors cause the company to enter into a transaction with a third party that is outside the scope of its constitution, the transaction cannot be set aside and will bind the company.[16] Where such a transaction is due to occur, but has not yet been entered into, however, a shareholder can apply to the court for an injunction restraining the proposed act.[17] Where the company enters into such a transaction with a director, or someone connected to a director, the transaction is voidable by legal proceedings brought at the company's instance.[18] Irrespective of whether the transaction is avoided or not, the director will be required to account for any gains made and to indemnify the company for any losses resulting from the transaction. It would appear that the shareholders cannot ratify this element of the duty, especially where the directors act outside the scope of the articles. To permit ratification would, in effect, allow the directors to alter the articles indirectly by ordinary resolution, whereas, as we have noted, a special resolution is required to alter the articles.

The 'proper purpose' doctrine

The second strand of the s 171 duty is based on the common law 'proper purpose' doctrine and requires that directors exercise their powers for the purposes

---

13. CA 2006, ss 17, 29, and 30.   14. Ibid, s 257.

15. Ibid.

16. Ibid, s 39. Note that where a company is a charity, s 39 will apply only in certain circumstances.

17. Ibid, s 40(4).   18. Ibid, s 41(2).

for which they are conferred. A purpose outside this scope is usually known as an 'improper purpose' and many cases involving improper purposes relate to directors using their powers to benefit themselves financially or to retain control of the company. Determining whether an exercise of power breaches this duty can be difficult, because the directors will often exercise their powers for several purposes, some of which are proper and others improper.

The courts' approach to ascertaining the propriety of the exercise of a power was established in the following case.

Howard Smith Ltd v Ampol Petroleum Ltd [1974] AC 821 (PC)

FACTS: The claimant controlled 55 per cent of the shares in company X and wished to take it over. A rival bid was made by the defendant, but was rejected by X's majority shareholder—namely, the claimant. The directors of X (who were also defendants) favoured the defendant's bid, largely because it was higher than that offered by the claimant, but given that the claimant was X's majority shareholder, the defendant's bid could never succeed. The directors of X therefore decided to issue US$10 million worth of new shares to the defendant, the purpose of which was twofold: firstly, it would allow X to raise much-needed finance for the building of two oil tankers; and secondly, it would relegate the claimant's holdings to 37 per cent, thereby making it a minority shareholder. The claimant alleged that the issuing of the shares was for an improper purpose.

HELD: The Privy Council stated that the court should consider first the nature of the power in question (that is, why this power was conferred on the directors). The court should then objectively determine the substantial or dominant purpose for which the power was exercised. If the dominant purpose is proper, no breach will occur. Conversely, if the dominant purpose is improper, a breach will occur irrespective of the fact that other subservient proper purposes exist. Here, the dominant purpose was to reduce the shareholding of the claimant, thereby manipulating the voting power of one shareholder over another. This was, unsurprisingly, deemed to be an improper purpose.

COMMENT: The majority of cases relating to the proper purpose doctrine relate to the directors' power to issue shares and the courts have categorically stated that where the dominant purpose of an issue of shares is to manipulate shareholder voting power, or to enable the directors to keep themselves in office, then the exercise of power will be for an improper purpose.

⭐ See JH Farrar, 'Abuse of Power by Directors' (1974) 33 CLJ 221

Where the directors act for an improper purpose, such acts are voidable at the company's instance and the director in breach may be required to compensate the company for any loss sustained. But these consequences are avoided where the shareholders ratify the breach of duty.[19]

---

19. *Hogg v Cramphorn* [1967] Ch 254 (Ch).

Duty to promote the success of the company

Of the seven general duties, the duty contained in s 172 is perhaps the most fundamental and contains a reformulation of the common law duty to act bona fide in the interests of the company.[20] Section 172(1) requires the director to 'act in the way he considers, in good faith, would be most likely to promote the success of the company for the benefit of its members as a whole'. It is immediately clear that this duty is subjective, meaning that what matters is what the directors honestly believed would promote the success of the company. It is not the courts' place to substitute their beliefs for those of the directors. As Lord Wilberforce famously stated: 'There is no appeal on merits from management decisions to courts of law: nor will courts of law assume to act as a kind of supervisory board over decisions within the powers of management honestly arrived at.'[21] It follows that, provided that the decision of the directors was honest, it does not matter that it was unreasonable.[22]

'Success of the company for the benefit of its members'

The use of the phrase 'success of the company for the benefit of its members' is interesting. In many cases, acts that benefit the company as a separate entity will also benefit its members, but this is not always the case. In certain cases decided before the CA 2006, the courts have recognized that, where the interests of the company and its members conflicted, preference should be given to the interests of the company as a separate entity.[23] The formulation in s 172(1) appears also to give primacy to the interests of the company as a separate entity. But the Act provides no guidance as to what 'success of the company' might mean, so definitive statements as to the operation of s 172 are impossible until a body of case law develops.

Because this formulation is based on the common law requirement to act bona fide in the interests of the company, acts that breached the common law duty are likely to also be regarded as a breach of s 172. For example, shortly before the passing of the 2006 Act, the Court of Appeal held that a director who had breached his duty to the company was under an obligation to disclose the breach to the company and that failure to disclose could constitute another breach of duty.[24]

Relevant factors

A common criticism levelled at the previous common law formulation was that it overly prioritized the interests of the shareholders and failed to acknowledge the effects that directors' actions can have on other constituents (for example, creditors, employees, the environment, etc.). To remedy this, one approach considered by the Company Law Review Steering Group was a 'pluralist' approach, whereby the interests of employees, creditors, the community, etc. would be given equal weight to the interests of the shareholders and the directors would be required to balance the various interests. The Steering Group ultimately rejected the pluralist approach,

---

20. *Re Smith and Fawcett Ltd* [1942] Ch 304 (CA).
21. *Howard Smith Ltd v Ampol Petroleum Ltd* [1974] AC 821 (PC) 832.
22. *Extrasure Travel Insurance Ltd v Scattergood* [2003] 1 BCLC 598 (Ch).
23. For example, *Mutual Life Insurance Co of New York v Rank Organisation Ltd* [1985] BCLC 11 (Ch) 21 (Goulding J).
24. *Item Software (UK) Ltd v Fassihi* [2004] EWCA Civ 1244, [2005] ICR 450.

largely on the ground that enforcing such a standard would prove impossible, and instead adopted the 'enlightened shareholder value' approach, whereby the interests of the shareholders would retain priority, but the directors would be required to take into account other wider factors. This approach was adopted by Parliament and s 172(1) provides that when directors are considering what would promote the success of the company for the benefit of its members, regard must be had (amongst other things) to:

- the likely consequences of any decision in the long term. This is an important inclusion, because the long-term interests of the company (for example, research and development, or engaging in environmentally sustainable activities) might conflict with the short-term interests of the members (for example, to receive a dividend and to increase the value of their shares). Companies are now free to sacrifice short-term profits for long-term gains;
- the interests of the company's employees;
- the need to foster the company's business relationships with suppliers, customers, and others;
- the impact of the company's operation on the community and the environment;
- the desirability of the company maintaining a reputation for high standards of business conduct;
- the need to act fairly as between members of the company.

This list contains a notable omission—namely, the company's creditors (although, of course, suppliers, customers, and employees may be creditors). Prior to the 2006 Act, there were several notable *dicta* requiring the directors to take into account the interests of creditors when the company neared insolvency.[25] Section 172(3) preserves these principles by stating that s 172 'has effect subject to any enactment or rule of law requiring directors, in certain circumstances, to consider or act in the interests of creditors of the company'.

Remedies for breach

Where the court finds that an act of the directors has not been exercised in good faith to promote the success of the company for the benefit of its members, that act is voidable at the company's instance. Where the act also causes loss to the company, any directors in breach will be required to indemnify the company for such loss. Breach of the common law duty upon which s 172 is based was unratifiable by the members. Section 180(4)(a) preserves any common law rules enabling ratification. Whether that provision also preserves rules prohibiting ratification is unclear.

Duty to exercise independent judgment

The duty to exercise independent judgment imposed by s 173(1) is a reformulation and encapsulation of the common law duty placed upon directors not to fetter their discretion when exercising their powers.[26] But this duty was not absolute. Under the

---

25. For example, *West Mercia Safetywear Ltd v Dodd* [1988] BCLC 250 (CA). In fact, the Court stated that where a company is insolvent, the interests of the creditors completely displace those of the members.
26. *Re Englefield Colliery Co* (1878) LR 8 Ch D 388 (CA).

common law, the courts recognized that directors could fetter their discretion and bind themselves to act in a certain way when they bona fide believed such action to be in the interests of the company.

Fulham Football Club Ltd v Cabra Estates plc [1992] BCC 863 (CA)

FACTS: A subsidiary of the defendant owned the freehold of the home football ground of the claimant's football team. The subsidiary wished to redevelop the ground, which would require the football club to move, but planning permission was not granted, because the council wished the club to remain at the ground. Undeterred, the subsidiary entered into an agreement with the claimant whereby, in return for substantial payments, the claimant would support the subsidiary's scheme. Later, the claimant changed its mind and wished to remain at the football ground. The claimant therefore sought a declaration that the agreement was invalid, because it was based on its directors fettering their own discretion.

HELD: The Court of Appeal refused to make such a declaration and held the agreement valid. The agreement conferred substantial benefits on the claimant and the claimant's directors honestly believed it to be in the interests of the company when they entered into it. Accordingly, the agreement was not an improper fettering of their discretion.

★ See A Griffiths, 'The Best Interests of Fulham FC: Directors' Fiduciary Duties in Giving Contractual Undertakings' (1993) JBL 576

The *ratio* of *Fulham Football Club* appears to be preserved by s 173(2)(a), which states that the duty to exercise independent judgment will not be breached where the directors act 'in accordance with an agreement duly entered into by the company that restricts the future exercise of discretion by its directors'. The presence of the word 'duly' indicates that such an agreement should be in the interests of the company, but this requirement could have been made more prominent. Section 173(2)(b) adds a second case in which the duty to exercise independent judgment is not breached—namely, where the director acts in a way that is authorized by the company's constitution.

Remedies for breach

Any agreement entered into that contravenes the duty to exercise independent judgment will be voidable at the company's instance. Any directors in breach will be required to account for any gains made and to indemnify the company for any loss sustained as a result of the agreement.

Duty to exercise reasonable care, skill, and diligence

A duty to exercise skill and care, now imposed by s 174(1), had been imposed upon the directors by the common law long before the 2006 Act was passed.[27] Until relatively recently, however, the standard of care imposed was a subjective one, based on the skills and experience that the director actually had. Accordingly, a director

---

27. *Re City Equitable Fire Insurance Co Ltd* [1925] Ch 407 (CA).

with no skills and no experience would be subject to an extremely low standard of care, as the following case demonstrates.

Re Cardiff Savings Bank [1892] Ch 100 (Ch)

FACTS: The Marquis of Bute was appointed a director of a bank at the age of six months. He attended one board meeting over the course of the next thirty-eight years and took no part in the business of the bank. A number of the bank's officials were engaging in financial irregularities, which ultimately led to the bank's liquidation. The liquidator sought to hold the Marquis liable for failing to notice the irregularities being committed by the bank's officials.

HELD: The High Court dismissed the liquidator's claim. Whilst the Marquis might have neglected to attend meetings, this was not the same as neglecting his duty. He was appointed at a time when he could take no part in the business and it was understood that this state of affairs would continue. The standard of care should reflect this, so he had not breached his duty.

The effect of a subjective duty was to allow incompetent, unskilled, or inexperienced directors to use such deficiencies as a shield against liability. Accordingly, the courts introduced an objective element into the standard of care[28] and this dual objective–subjective test has been codified into s 174(2), which provides that the standard of care, skill, and diligence expected from a director is based on that of a reasonably diligent person with:

(a) the general knowledge, skill and experience that may reasonably be expected of a person carrying out the functions carried out by the director in relation to the company, and

(b) the general knowledge, skill and experience that the director has.

The test contained in s 174(2)(a) imposes an objective minimum standard of care, skill, and diligence that will apply to all directors, irrespective of their individual capabilities. But it will take into account the functions of the director, so the standard is likely to alter depending on whether the director is executive or non-executive, or whether a director sits on the board of a large or small company. Section 174(2)(b) imposes a subjective standard that will apply where the director in question has some special skill or ability (for example, he is a lawyer, or accountant, etc.), and will therefore serve to raise the standard of care expected. The rationale behind imposing a higher standard of care upon such directors is that, because they were appointed to bring such skills to bear (and are likely to be paid more for having such skills), a higher standard will require them to use such skills. The counter-argument is that the higher standard could deter qualified persons from undertaking directorial office.

In determining whether or not the standard is met, pre-CA 2006 case law will doubtless remain relevant, and one notable case, concerning the collapse of

---

28. *Norman v Theodore Goddard* [1992] BCC 14 (Ch).

Barings Bank, laid down a series of principles that are likely to remain of significant importance in determining the scope of the statutory duty of care and skill.

 Re Barings plc (No 5) [2000] 1 BCLC 523 (CA)

FACTS: Barings Bank collapsed in 1995 following the unauthorized trading activities of a single trader named Nick Leeson, which resulted in the bank sustaining losses of £827 million. The case concerned disqualification proceedings issued against three directors, who, it was alleged, had made serious errors of management in relation to Leeson's activities that warranted disqualification. At first instance, Jonathan-Parker J held that disqualification was justified. The directors appealed.

HELD: The Court of Appeal dismissed the appeal, and, more significantly, it affirmed a series of principles laid down by Jonathan Parker J in relation to the directors' duties of skill and care. He stated that:

- directors have a continuing duty to acquire, and maintain, a sufficient knowledge and understanding of the company's business;

- whilst directors are entitled to delegate functions to those below them, and to trust their competence and integrity to a reasonable extent, delegation does not absolve the director from the responsibility of supervising those to whom he has delegated. Whether the duty has been breached will be a question of fact in each case.

★ See A Walters, 'Directors' Duties of Skill, Care and Diligence' (1999) 20 Co Law 142

Remedies for breach

A director who causes his company to sustain loss due to his failure to exercise reasonable skill, care, and diligence will be liable to compensate the company for such loss.

Duty to avoid conflicts of interest

Under the common law, directors were subject to two equitable principles known as the 'no conflict' rule and the 'no profit' rule. Both of these rules are reformulated in s 175, with s 175(1) providing that '[a] director of a company[29] must avoid a situation in which he has, or can have, a direct or indirect that conflicts, or possible may conflict, with the interests of the company'. Section 175(2) provides that this duty arises in particular to 'the exploitation of any property, information or opportunity (and it is immaterial whether the company could take advantage of the property, information or opportunity)'. Focusing on these specific forms of conflict indicates that the statutory duty is based on what is known as the 'corporate opportunity' doctrine.

The corporate opportunity doctrine

The corporate opportunity doctrine is based upon the premise that the director breaches his duty if he personally takes advantage of an opportunity that rightly belongs to the

---

29. The duty also applies to former directors in relation to any property, information, or opportunities of which they may have become aware in their former directorship (CA 2006, s 170(2)(a)).

company. Where the director does this, he will be liable to account for any profit that he makes.

The strictness of the court's approach can be seen in the following relatively recent case.

⊙ *Bhullar v Bhullar* [2003] EWCA Civ 424

FACTS: For over fifty years, the families of two brothers (M and S) had run a company that, inter alia, let commercial property. The families fell out and it was decided that they would go their separate ways. M's family (the claimants) decided that the company would not acquire any further properties and S's family (the defendants) agreed. A director of the company who was part of the defendant's family discovered, by chance and not whilst acting in the course of the company's business, a piece of property adjacent to property owned by the company. Through another company that they owned, the defendants acquired this property without informing the claimants. The claimants discovered the acquisition and alleged that the defendants had breached their fiduciary duties.

HELD: The Court of Appeal held that the defendants had breached their fiduciary duties. Despite the fact that the defendants had acquired knowledge of the property in a 'private' capacity, the Court held that the opportunity to purchase the property was one that belonged to the company. There was doubt as to whether it was 'worthwhile' for the company to acquire the property, given that it was in the process of being wound up. The Court stated that whether or not the company could, or would, have acquired the property was irrelevant.

COMMENT: Understandably, this case has been criticized—notably, because the company agreed (at the claimants' behest) not to acquire any more properties. The Court, in effect, allowed the claimants to change their minds opportunistically at the moment that an attractive commercial opportunity arose.

★ See DD Prentice and J Payne, 'The Corporate Opportunity Doctrine' (2004) 120 LQR 198

There is little doubt that s 175 preserves the strict and inflexible position evidenced in *Bhullar*, but pre-CA 2006 law did contain an important exception to the above rules—namely, where the conflict was authorized.

Authorization

The harshness of the rule was mitigated in one important respect—namely, that a director who engaged in a conflict could keep any profit made where the act in question was disclosed and authorized. In effect, disclosure and authorization would exclude the operation of the no-conflict and no-profit rules.

Section 175 preserves this, but the requirement of authorization is different. Under pre-CA 2006 law, authorization would occur where the director disclosed the conflict and obtained consent from the company in general meeting,[30] but it was common for companies to provide in their articles that disclosure to the board was sufficient.[31] Under the 2006 Act, where the company is a private company, the

---

30. *Aberdeen Rly Co v Blaikie Bros* (1854) 2 Eq Rep 1281 (HL).
31. Companies (Tables A to F) Regulations 1985, SI 1985/805, Table A, art 85.

directors alone can give authorization, provided that there is nothing to the contrary in the company's constitution.[32] Conversely, whilst directors of public companies can give authorization, they can only do so if the articles so provide.[33] For obvious reasons, the vote of the director in conflict will not count in determining authorization.[34]

Remedies for breach

Where a director fails to disclose a conflict or fails to obtain valid authorization, any resulting contract is voidable at the company's instance, provided that the third party involved has notice of the director's breach.[35] In addition, the company can require the director to account for any profit made as a result of the conflict.[36] Where the directors refuse to authorize a conflict, the director engaging in the conflict can avoid the above consequences by obtaining ratification from the shareholders in general meeting.[37]

Duty not to accept benefits from third parties

Section 176(1) places a duty on a director not to accept from a third party a benefit conferred by reason of his being a director, or by doing (or not doing) anything as a director. As with the s 175 duty, *mala fides* is not a requirement and it will therefore be no defence for the director to argue that he acted in good faith. A 'third party' is defined as 'a person other than the company, an associated body corporate or a person acting on behalf of the company or an associated body corporate'.[38] The duty extends to former directors in relation to acts or omissions prior to his ceasing to be a director.[39]

➜ *mala fides*: 'bad faith'; cf bona fides, meaning 'good faith'

    Initially, the inclusion of this duty appears odd, because s 176(4) provides that this duty is not breached 'if the acceptance of the benefit cannot reasonably be regarded as likely to give rise to a conflict of interest'. Because this duty covers only benefits that are likely to give rise to a conflict, it would be thought that such benefits would be adequately covered by the duty to avoid conflicts of interest contained in s 175. Indeed, there is considerable overlap between the two duties. But there is a notable difference—namely, that a conflict under s 175 can be authorized by the directors, but the receipt of a third-party benefit under s 176 cannot be authorized by the directors and must instead be authorized by the shareholders in general meeting.[40] This clearly indicates that the receipt of third-party benefits constitutes a much greater danger to board impartiality than the conflicts covered by s 175 (indeed, as we shall see in Chapter 27, under the rules of agency, such benefits would be classed

---

32. CA 2006, s 175(4)(b) and (5)(a).
33. Ibid, s 175(4)(b) and (5)(b).
34. Ibid, s 175(6).
35. *Hely-Hutchinson & Co Ltd v Brayhead Ltd* [1968] 1 QB 549 (CA).
36. *Aberdeen Rly Co v Blaikie Bros* (1854) 2 Eq Rep 1281 (HL).
37. CA 2006, s 180(4)(a).
38. Ibid, s 176(2).
39. Ibid, s 170(2)(b).
40. Authorization by the shareholders is not expressly stated, but is a consequence of s 180(4)(a).

as 'bribes'). It has been argued that the requirement of shareholder authorization amounts to a 'near-ban on the receipt of third party benefits'.[41]

Remedies for breach

The consequences of breaching the s 176 duty can be severe. Where a director accepts an unauthorized third-party benefit, the company can rescind the contract[42] and the benefit can be recovered. Instead of recovering the benefit, the company may claim damages in fraud from either the director in breach or the third party.[43] In addition, the company can summarily terminate the director's service contract and dismiss him.[44]

Duty to declare interest in proposed transactions or arrangements

Section 177(1) provides that '[i]f a director of a company is in any way, directly or indirectly, interested in a proposed transaction or arrangement with the company, he must declare the nature and extent of that interest to the other directors'. The declaration must be made before the company enters into the transaction or arrangement.[45] Under the pre-CA 2006 common law, disclosure and authorization by the company in general meeting was required, although the articles could modify this to require mere disclosure.

Several points need be noted in relation to this duty, as follows.

- The duty imposed by s 177 relates to *proposed* transactions or arrangements only. *Existing* transactions or arrangements are covered by s 182, which is discussed later.
- The duty relates only to transactions or arrangements between the director and his company. Transactions between directors and outsiders are covered by the duties relating to conflict of interests and third-party benefits, discussed above.
- The duty relates only to transactions or arrangements that could reasonably be regarded as giving rise to a conflict of interest.[46]
- Because the duty covers indirect transactions or arrangements, a director need not be party to the transaction or arrangement in order for the duty to arise.
- A declaration is not required where the director in question is not aware of the interest, or of the transaction or arrangement as the case may be,[47] or where the other directors are aware of it.[48]

---

41. PL Davies, *Gower & Davies' Principles of Modern Company Law* (8th edn, Sweet & Maxwell, London, 2008) 575.

42. *Shipway v Broadwood* [1899] 1 QB 369 (CA).

43. *Mahesan v Malaysia Government Officers' Co-operative Housing Society Ltd* [1979] AC 374 (PC).

44. *Boston Deep Sea Fishing Co v Ansell* (1888) 39 Ch D 39 (CA).

45. CA 2006, s 177(4).

46. Ibid, s 177(6)(a).

47. Ibid, s 177(5).

48. Ibid, s 177(6)(b). In this context, the directors are treated as being aware of anything of which they ought reasonably be aware.

- Where a company only has one director, a declaration is not required.[49] Where the company has only one member, who is also a director, the transaction or arrangement must either be in writing, or be set out in a written memorandum and recorded in the company's minutes.[50] Failure to comply with these requirements constitutes a criminal offence.
- The requirement of disclosure to the directors constitutes the minimum requirement. A company, if it so chooses, can impose more exacting requirements in its constitution[51] (for example, by inserting a provision in the articles requiring authorization by the general meeting).

The declaration can take any form, but it is not enough for a director merely to state that he has an interest in a proposed transaction or arrangement; he must also declare the nature and extent of the interest.[52] If a declaration proves to be, or becomes, inaccurate or incomplete, then if the company has not yet entered into the transaction or arrangement, the director must make a further declaration correcting the previous one before the company enters into the transaction or arrangement.[53]

Existing transactions or arrangements

The s 177 duty relates to *proposed* transactions or arrangements, whereas s 182 contains separate rules relating to *existing* transactions or arrangements.[54] Section 182(1) provides that '[w]here a director of a company is in any way, directly or indirectly, interested in a transaction or arrangement that has been entered into by the company, he must declare the nature and extent of the interest to the other directors'. Whether this is a distinct general duty or simply a duty supplementary to s 177 is unclear (although its location in ch 3 of Pt 10 would indicate that it is a supplementary duty), but it is clear that if a declaration under s 177 takes place, a subsequent declaration under s 182 is not required once the transaction comes into effect.[55]

The declaration requirements in s 182 largely mirror those of s 177, except that a declaration under s 182 must be made 'as soon as is reasonably practicable',[56] whereas, as already stated, under s 177, a declaration need only occur at a time prior to the transaction or arrangement being entered into.[57]

Remedies for breach

Where the director enters into a proposed transaction or arrangement with the company in contravention of s 177, the transaction or arrangement is voidable at the company's instance. Where the director enters into an existing transaction or arrangement with the company in contravention of s 182, he commits a criminal

---

49. Ibid, Explanatory Notes [352].

50. Ibid, s 231(2).

51. Ibid, s 180(1).

52. Ibid, s 177(1).

53. Ibid, s 177(3).

54. It should be noted that s 182 does not come under the umbrella of the 'general duties', but is so closely related to the duty contained in s 177 (which is one of the general duties) that it makes sense to discuss it alongside s 177.

55. CA 2006, s 182(1).

56. Ibid, s 182(4).

57. Ibid, s 177(4).

offence.[58] The offence is triable either way and, on summary conviction, is punishable by a fine not exceeding the statutory maximum (currently £5,000). On indictment, the maximum fine is unlimited.

> ### ‹› Key points summary
>
> - Directors are under a duty to act in accordance with the company's constitution and to exercise their powers for the purposes for which they are conferred.
>
> - Directors are under a duty to promote the success of the company for the benefit of its members, but in doing so, they must also have regard to the wider interests, such as those of the employees, suppliers, consumers, and the environment.
>
> - Directors are under a duty to exercise independent judgment, but they can enter into an agreement binding themselves to a certain course of action where they believe it to be in the interests of the company.
>
> - Directors are under a duty to exercise reasonable care, skill, and diligence when performing their functions.
>
> - Directors are under a duty to avoid conflicts of interest, but a conflicting act will not constitute a breach of duty where the other directors authorize it.
>
> - Directors must not accept benefits from third parties. Receipt of such a benefit cannot be authorized by the directors, but it can be authorized by the members.
>
> - Directors are under a duty to declare an interest in any proposed or existing transaction or arrangement. Failure to declare an interest in an existing transaction or arrangement will constitute a criminal offence.

Transactions requiring shareholder approval

The law imposes 'specific statutory duties'[59] on directors in relation to certain transactions and arrangements into which they enter with the company. In relation to such transactions or arrangements, compliance with the general duties discussed above is insufficient[60] and shareholder approval is generally required.

Four such transactions or arrangements can be identified.

Service contracts

Historically, directors would attempt to negotiate lengthy service contracts in order to entrench their position. The following example explains how this would occur.

---

58. Ibid, s 183.
59. A Alcock, J Birds, and S Gale, *Companies Act 2006: The New Law* (Jordans, Bristol, 2007) [12.30].
60. CA 2006, s 180(3).

> **Eg** **Entrenchment through lengthy service contracts**
>
> Danny is appointed as CEO of BioTech plc. He has negotiated a ten-year service contract and is to be paid £4 million per year. After one year, it is apparent that he is incompetent. The company wishes to remove him from office, but to do so would breach Danny's service contract, enabling him to recover £36 million in damages (£4 million x the number of years left on his contract). Danny's position is entrenched by making it prohibitively expensive to remove him.

In order to curtail this practice, s 188 provides that a director cannot have a guaranteed term of employment of over two years[61] in length unless it has been approved by resolution of the company's members. An ordinary resolution is required, but the company is free to insert a provision into its articles requiring a higher majority or unanimity.[62] As a result of s 188 (and its predecessor), directors now tend to have rolling contracts, whereby, once their service contract ends, they are reappointed on similar terms—and where the contract specifies, such reappointment can be automatic.

Remedies for breach

A provision in a service contract that provides a director with guaranteed employment for over two years is void if shareholder approval has not been obtained.[63] Further, the contract will also be deemed to contain a term allowing the company to terminate it at any time by giving reasonable notice.[64]

Substantial property transactions

Where a director has a conflict or an interest in a proposed or existing transaction or arrangement, the general duties require him to declare that conflict or interest to the other directors. But where an arrangement[65] amounts to a 'substantial property transaction', disclosure to the directors is insufficient and a company may not enter into such an arrangement unless it has been approved in advance by an ordinary resolution of the shareholders (or a higher majority or unanimity if required by the company's articles),[66] or is conditional on such approval being obtained.[67]

Two types of arrangement require shareholder approval:

- where a director of the company or of its holding company, or a person connected with such a director, acquires, or is to acquire, from the company (directly or indirectly) a substantial non-cash asset;

---

61. Where the company is listed on a stock exchange, the period is reduced to one year: see Financial Reporting Council, *The Combined Code on Corporate Governance* (June 2008) [B.1.6].

62. CA 2006, s 281(3).

63. Ibid, s 189(a).

64. Ibid, s 189(b).

65. The use of the word 'arrangement' in s 190 includes an agreement or understanding that does not have contractual effect: *Re Duckwari plc* [1999] Ch 253 (CA).

66. CA 2006, s 281(3).

67. Ibid, s 190.

- where the company acquires, or is to acquire, a substantial non-cash asset (directly or indirectly) from such a director or a person so connected.

A 'non-cash asset' is 'any property or interest in property, other than cash'[68] and a non-cash asset is substantial if it:

- is over £100,000; or
- exceeds 10 per cent of the company's asset value and is more than £5,000.[69]

Remedies for breach

A substantial property transaction entered into without shareholder approval is voidable at the company's instance, unless:

- restitution is impossible;
- the company has been indemnified; or
- avoidance would affect the rights of a person who had acquired those rights bona fide for value and without actual notice of the contravention.[70]

In addition, irrespective of whether the arrangement was avoided, any director or connected person who was involved in the arrangement (including any directors who authorized the arrangement) will be liable to account for any direct or indirect gains made, and is also required to indemnify the company for any losses sustained as a result of the arrangement.[71] But a connected person or director who authorized the arrangement can escape liability if he shows that, at the time that the arrangement was entered into, he was unaware of the relevant circumstances constituting the contravention.[72]

Loans, quasi-loans, and credit transactions

Under the CA 1985, a company was prohibited from making any form of loan to one of its directors (subject to several exceptions) and breach of this prohibition constituted a criminal offence. The CA 2006 adopts a very different approach that is dependent upon the type of loan and the type of company in question, as follows.

- No company can make a loan to its directors unless the transaction has been approved by an ordinary resolution.[73] A higher majority or unanimity will be required if the company's articles so provide.[74]
- A public company cannot make a quasi-loan to its directors unless the transaction has been approved by an ordinary resolution.[75] A higher majority or unanimity will be required if the company's articles so provide.[76] Section 199(1) provides that a quasi-loan occurs where the company agrees to pay a sum on behalf of the director, or where it reimburses expenses incurred by another party due to actions of the director.
- A public company cannot enter into a credit transaction with a director of the company unless the transaction has been approved by an ordinary resolution.[77]

---

68. Ibid, s 1163(1).
70. Ibid, s 195(2)
72. Ibid, s 195(7).
74. Ibid, s 281(3).
76. Ibid, s 281(3).

69. Ibid, s 191(2).
71. Ibid, s 195(3).
73. Ibid, s 197(1).
75. Ibid, s 198(2).
77. Ibid, s 201(2).

A higher majority or unanimity will be required if the company's articles so provide.[78] Examples of credit transactions include hire purchase or conditional sales agreements, the leasing or hiring of goods, and the disposition of land, goods, or services on the understanding that payment is to be deferred.[79]

In the case of quasi-loans and credit transactions, the requirement of shareholder approval also applies to any company 'associated with' a public company[80]—the obvious example being a private subsidiary of a public holding company.[81]

The requirements for approval of loans, quasi-loans, and credit transactions do not apply in a number of situations, including:

- loans, quasi-loans, or credit transactions of up to £50,000 to meet the director's expenditure on company business;[82]
- loans or quasi-loans that do not exceed £10,000;[83]
- credit transactions that do not exceed £15,000;[84]
- loans and quasi-loans made by money-lending companies, where the loan or quasi-loan is entered into by the company in the ordinary course of its business and its value is not greater, and its terms are not more favourable, than it is reasonable to expect the company would have offered to a person of the same financial standing, but unconnected with the company.[85]

Remedies for breach

Any transaction or arrangement that contravenes s 197, 198, or 201 is voidable at the company's instance, unless:

- restitution is impossible;
- the company has been indemnified; or
- avoidance would affect the rights of a person who had acquired those rights bona fide for value and without actual notice of the contravention.[86]

Irrespective of whether the transaction or arrangement has been avoided, any director, or person connected with the director involved, is liable to account to the company for any gains made and is also liable to indemnify the company for any losses sustained as a result of the transaction or arrangement.[87] The company's right to rescind the transaction or arrangement will be lost if the members ratify the transaction or arrangement.[88]

Payments for loss of office

The law requires that the shareholders approve certain voluntary payments made by the company to directors losing office. 'Payment for loss of office' is generally defined as a payment made to a director or past director:

- by way of compensation for loss of office;

---

78. Ibid, s 281(3).
80. Ibid, ss 200(1)(b) and 201(1)(b).
82. Ibid, s 204.
84. Ibid, s 207(2).
86. Ibid, s 213(2).
88. Ibid, s 214.

79. Ibid, s 202(1).
81. Ibid, s 256.
83. Ibid, s 207(1).
85. Ibid, s 209(1).
87. Ibid, s 213(3).

- by way of compensation for loss, while a director, of any other office or employment in connection with the management affairs of the company (or of a subsidiary undertaking of the company); or

- as consideration for, or in connection with, his retirement as director or an officer or employee involved in the management of the affairs of the company (or of a subsidiary undertaking of the company).[89]

A company may not make a payment for loss of office to a director unless the payment has been approved by an ordinary resolution of the members (or higher majority or unanimity if the articles require). This would include payments for:

- loss of office;[90]

- loss of office in connection with the transfer of the undertaking or property of the company;[91]

- loss of office in connection with a transfer of shares in the company (for example, a takeover).[92] In this case, the approval must be made by the holders of the shares to which the bid relates and any holders of shares of the same class as any of those shares.

The requirement of shareholder approval does not apply to:

- a payment made in good faith to discharge a legal obligation, or to compensate another for breach of such obligation, or to settle a claim arising from termination of a person's office or employment, or by way of a pension in respect of past services;[93]

- a payment that does not exceed £200.[94]

Remedies for breach

Where shareholder approval is not obtained for payment for a general loss of office, the recipient will hold the payment on trust for the company, and any director who authorized the payment is jointly and severally liable to indemnify the company for any loss resulting from the payment.[95] Where the unapproved payment for loss of office is in connection with a transfer of the undertaking, the recipient will hold the payment on trust for the company the undertaking or property of which is being, or is proposed to be, transferred.[96] Where the payment for loss of office is in connection with a share transfer, the recipient will hold the payment on trust for the persons who have sold their shares.[97]

 Key points summary

- A director cannot have a guaranteed term of employment for over two years, unless it has first been approved by an ordinary resolution of the members.

- Where a director wishes to enter into a substantial property transaction with the company, the transaction will first need to be approved by the members by ordinary resolution.

---

89. Ibid, s 215(1). 90. Ibid, s 217.
91. Ibid, s 218. 92. Ibid, s 219.
93. Ibid, s 220(1). 94. Ibid, s 221(1).
95. Ibid, s 222(1). 96. Ibid, s 222(2).
97. Ibid, s 222(3).

- A substantial property transaction occurs where the director acquires, or is to acquire, from the company a non-cash asset that either:
  - is worth over £100,000; or
  - exceeds 10 per cent of the company's asset value and is worth more than £5,000.
- No company can make a loan to one of its directors without first obtaining approval by ordinary resolution from the members. Public companies cannot make a quasi-loan to, or enter into a credit transaction with, a director without first obtaining approval by ordinary resolution from the members.
- Generally, a company cannot provide a payment for loss of office to a departing director for loss of office unless the members first approve that payment by ordinary resolution.

Limitation periods

The Limitation Act 1980, s 21(3), provides that an action alleging breach of duty must normally be brought within six years of the date on which the action accrued, unless any other provision in the Act applies that provides for a different limitation period. But s 21(1) provides that, in two cases, there will be no limitation period and an action can be brought at any time:

- where the director was party to a fraud or fraudulent breach of trust; or
- where the director is in possession of the company's property or proceeds of the company, or where the directors has received company property and converted it to his use.

Relief from liability

A director who is liable for breaching the duties discussed above may be able to obtain relief from such liability in several ways.

Exclusion and indemnity clauses

A director may attempt to obtain relief from liability for negligence, default, breach of duty, or breach of trust via a provision (either in the articles or in his service contract) excluding such liability. Section 232(1) provides that such a provision is void. The director may try to obtain relief via a provision requiring the company to indemnify the director for any loss or liability sustained by him due to his breach of duty. Again, such a provision will be void,[98] except:

- where the company purchases and maintains insurance for a director in relation to liability for breach of duty;[99]

---

98. Ibid, s 232(2).   99. Ibid, s 233.

- where the company indemnifies directors in respect to proceedings brought by third parties;[100] and

- where the company, which is a trustee of an occupational pension scheme, indemnifies the director for liability incurred in connection with the company's activities as a trustee for an occupational pension scheme.[101]

Ratification

The CA 2006, s 239, puts in place, for the first time, a statutory scheme concerning the ratification of acts committed by directors (including former directors and shadow directors) that amount to negligence, default, breach of duty, or breach of trust. Where effective ratification occurs, any cause of action that the company had in respect of the breach is extinguished. But this new scheme does not affect any previous rules of law denying the ability to ratify. Accordingly, an act that could not be ratified under the pre-2006 law cannot be ratified under the CA 2006. Unratifiable acts would therefore include illegal acts,[102] acts not bona fide in the interests of the company, and acts that involved a 'fraud on the minority'.[103]

Ratification requires an ordinary resolution of the company's members, unless the company's articles require a higher majority or unanimity.[104] Where the director is also a shareholder of the company, his votes will be disregarded, although he may attend the meeting.[105] This is in contrast to the pre-2006 position, which permitted a director's votes to count, provided that they were made in good faith.[106] In order for ratification to be valid:

- the directors must have fully disclosed their interest in the transaction in breach;[107]

- the ratification by the members must be informed;[108] and

- the ratification 'must not be brought about by unfair or improper means, and is not illegal or oppressive towards the shareholders who oppose it'.[109]

Relief from the court

A director who is unable to obtain authorization or ratification from the directors or the shareholders has one last option for avoiding liability—namely, the ability of the court to grant relief. Section 1157(1) allows a court that has found an officer or auditor of the company liable for negligence, default, breach of duty, or breach of trust to grant

---

100. Ibid, s 234.
101. Ibid, s 235.
102. *Re Exchange Banking Co (Flitcroft's Case)* (1882) 21 Ch D 519 (CA).
103. *Burland v Earle* [1902] AC 83 (PC).
104. CA 2006, s 281(3).
105. Ibid, s 239(4).
106. *North-West Transportation Co Ltd v Beatty* (1887) 12 App Cas 589 (PC).
107. *Kaye v Croydon Tramways Co* [1898] 1 Ch 358 (CA).
108. *Knight v Frost* [1999] 1 BCLC 364 (Ch).
109. *North-West Transportation Co Ltd v Beatty* (1887) 12 App Cas 589 (PC) 593, 594 (Sir Richard Baggallay), affirmed by *Franbar Holdings Ltd v Patel* [2008] EWHC 1534 (Ch), [2008] BCC 885.

that officer, either wholly or partly, relief from liability[110] on such terms as it sees fit. Section 1157(2) allows an officer or auditor to petition the court for such relief where he has reason to believe that such a claim for negligence, etc. will be made against him.

In both cases, relief will only be granted where the court is of the opinion that the officer:

- has acted honestly—a test that is subjective, meaning that the crucial factor is whether the officer actually believed that he acted honestly;[111]
- has acted reasonably, which, unlike honesty, must be assessed objectively;[112]
- given all of the circumstances of the case, ought fairly to be excused. Given that *all* of the circumstances of the case need to be examined, it is very rare that a case involving the granting of relief under s 1157 will be **struck out** and, usually, a full trial should occur.[113]

➡ striking out: the dismissal by the court of all or part of a statement of a case

The following case provides a classic example of the courts' discretion to grant relief from liability.

 ### Re Duomatic Ltd [1969] 2 Ch 365 (Ch)

FACTS: A company had three directors, E, H, and T, who owned all of the company's ordinary shares. E and T were critical of H's performance, and wished to remove him. H threatened to sue if they tried to dismiss him, so, instead, E and T paid H £4,000 to leave the company. H did so and transferred his shares to E. The company's articles provided that the directors' remuneration had to be authorized by the company's members, but no such resolution was ever passed. Instead, the directors drew sums from the company as needed, and, at the end of the year, the sums drawn were totalled and entered into the company's accounts as 'directors' salaries'. These sums were drawn with the knowledge and approval of all of the members who were entitled to vote at the company's meetings. This practice continued until the year prior to the company's liquidation, when E, who by now was the majority shareholder, drew £9,000 before the company's final accounts had been prepared. The company entered voluntary liquidation and the liquidator sought to claim:

1. sums drawn by E and T as salary;

2. the £9,000 drawn by E in the final year; and

3. the £4,000 loss-of-office payment paid to H.

HELD: Buckley J (as he then was) held that there was little doubt that all three payments were in breach of duty; the question arising was whether relief could be obtained. Regarding (1), the court held that relief should be granted and the payments remained valid. Buckley J stated that:

> where it can be shown that all shareholders who have a right to attend and vote at a general meeting of the company assent to some matter which a general meeting

---

110. This will include liability to account for profits gained as well as liability to pay damages: see *Coleman Taymar Ltd v Oakes* [2001] 2 BCLC 749 (Ch).
111. Ibid.
112. *Re MDA Investment Management Ltd* [2004] EWHC 42 (Ch), [2005] BCC 783.
113. *Equitable Life Assurance Society v Bowley* [2003] EWHC 2263 (Comm), [2004] 1 BCLC 180.

of the company could carry into effect, that assent is as binding as a resolution in general meeting would be.[114]

The court also granted relief for (2), stating that E was merely following a practice that had been followed in preceding years.

But Buckley J refused to grant relief for (3), and held that E and T were jointly liable to pay back the £4,000. There was no disclosure or authorization under what, today, would be CA 2006, s 217, and it was therefore a misapplication of the company's funds.

‹ › Key points summary

- Clauses excluding liability for breach of duty are void and clauses requiring the company to indemnify the directors for liability for breach of duty are generally void.

- The members can ratify liability for most breaches of duty by passing an ordinary resolution.

- The courts can grant relief to an officer of the company for liability, provided that the director has acted honestly and reasonably, and that, given all of the circumstances of the case, the officer ought to be excused.

Chapter conclusion

The codification of directors' duties is arguably the most significant reform contained in the Companies Act 2006, and has greatly clarified the content and scope of the duties owed. Prior to the CA 2006, an analysis of this area would have involved a discussion of a mass of common law rules and equitable principles. But the general duties set out in the Act are broad indicators, at best, of how the directors should manage the company. Recourse to the substantial body of prior case law will still be essential in order for directors to understand fully the duties to which they are subject and how best to comply with them. Still, there can be little doubt that the restatement of the duties in the CA 2006 is a considerable improvement in terms of accessibility and clarity. It remains to be seen, however, whether the codification is clear enough for directors to understand sufficiently. It has been argued, quite correctly, that the codification contained in the CA 2006 is not as clear as that recommended by the Law Commission.[115] Only time will tell whether or not the codification of directors' duties will have a notable impact.

Self-test questions

1. Define the following:
   (a) improper purpose;
   (b) substantial property transaction;

---

114. *Re Duomatic Ltd* [1969] 2 Ch 365 (Ch) 373.
115. J Birds, AJ Boyle, et al, *Boyle & Birds' Company Law* (6th edn, Jordans, Bristol, 2007) 606.

    (c)   quasi-loan;

    (d)   credit transaction.

2. Discuss the advantages and disadvantages of codifying the duties of directors.

3. AssetStrip Ltd launches a takeover bid for MicroCorp plc. The directors of MicroCorp are aware that if the takeover is successful, AssetStrip will break up MicroCorp and sell its assets off to various interested parties. The directors of MicroCorp believe that the takeover will be highly detrimental to the company's shareholders. The directors therefore issue a large batch of shares, thereby making the takeover prohibitively expensive. AssetStrip retracts its takeover bid. Has a breach of duty occurred?

4. 'The duty to promote the success of the company for the benefit of its members preserves the view that UK company law is based on a narrow, shareholder-centred approach. Instead the law should allow the courts to balance equally the interests of shareholders and non-shareholder constituents.' Do you agree with this statement? Provide reasons for your answer.

5. Read the following cases and discuss whether or not each would be decided differently today under the CA 2006.

    (a)   *Re Brazilian Rubber Plantations and Estates Ltd.*[116]

    (b)   *Regal (Hastings) Ltd v Gulliver.*[117]

    (c)   *West Mercia Safetywear Ltd v Dodd.*[118]

Further reading

Clark, B, 'UK Company Law Reform and the Directors' Exploitation of 'Corporate Opportunities' (2006) 17 ICCLR 231

Discusses the corporate opportunity doctrine and argues that the retention by the Companies Act 2006 of a strict approach is the correct approach

Edmunds, R, and Lowry, J, 'The Continuing Value of Relief for Directors' Breach of Duty' (2003) 66 MLR 195

Discusses the court's ability to grant relief for breach of duty and argues that a more radical approach is required than that contained in s 1157

Fisher, D, 'The Enlightened Shareholder: Leaving Stakeholders in the Dark—Will Section 172(1) of the Companies Act 2006 Make Directors Consider the Impact of Their Decisions on Third Parties?' (2009) 20 ICCLR 10

Discusses the likely impact of the duty imposed by s 172 and argues that, in practice, it will not make directors consider the interests of stakeholders; contends that the pluralist approach could provide a more inclusive approach

French, D, Mayson, S, and Ryan, C, *Mayson, French, & Ryan on Company Law* (25th edn, OUP, Oxford, 2008) ch 16

A highly detailed and analytical discussion of the general duties and those transactions requiring shareholder approval

---

116. [1911] 1 Ch 425 (Ch).   117. [1967] 2 AC 134 (HL).

118. (1988) 4 BCC 30 (CA).

Keay, A, 'The Duty of Directors to Exercise Independent Judgment' (2008) 29 Co
  Law 290
*Discusses the common law background to the duty to exercise independent judgment and
  explores to what extent, if any, the duty contained in the Companies Act 2006 will adopt
  a different approach*

Law Commission, *Company Directors: Regulating Conflicts of Interest and
  Formulating a Statement of Duties—Consultation Paper* (Law Com CP No 153,
  HMSO, London, 1998)
*Discusses all of the duties and requirements examined in this chapter; provides a clear, yet
  detailed, analysis of the law and recommends a number of options for reform*

Statutes

Companies Act 2006, Explanatory Notes, paras 298–445
*Explains clearly the operation of each duty and indicates how the Act has changed the law;
  also provides useful background information on the decision to codify the duties*

Remember to visit the **Online Resource Centre** at **<http://www.
oxfordtextbooks.co.uk/roach>** to access the following resources
on Chapter 20, 'Directors' duties:' more **practice questions** and
answers; a **glossary** of key terms; **multiple-choice questions**; **revision
summaries**; **audio updates** when relevant; and **audio exam advice** on
this key topic.

21 Shareholders' remedies

- The constitution as a contract
- Derivative claims
- Unfairly prejudicial conduct
- The petition for winding up

INTRODUCTION

In previous chapters, we have discussed the civil and criminal liability of a company, the limits on the company's contractual capacity, the powers of the directors, and the general duties contained in statute. Where the company, its directors, or its majority shareholders have committed some form of maladministration or breach of duty, or some other act that has caused loss, how can redress be obtained? The problem that arises is that, very often, the parties who have standing to commence proceedings to obtain redress are the very parties who have caused the harm. Shareholders, especially minority shareholders, who sustain loss due to the wrongdoer's acts or omissions would, without the law's aid, be left without a remedy. Accordingly, several shareholder remedies are provided for by common law and statute, of which the principal four are:

- the ability to enforce the provisions of the constitution;
- the ability to commence a statutory derivative claim;
- the unfair prejudice remedy; and
- a petition to wind up the company.

➡ standing: the right to be heard in a court

The constitution as a contract

The courts have long held that a company's articles of association constitute a contract between the company and its members, and between the members *inter se*.[1] The Companies Act 2006 (CA 2006), s 33(1), expands the scope of this contract to include not only the articles, but also those resolutions and agreements that, by virtue of s 17, together with the articles, make up the constitution of the company. Section 33(1) provides that '[t]he provisions of a company's constitution bind the company and its members to the same extent as if there were covenants on the part of the company and

➡ *inter se*: between, or amongst, themselves

---

1. *Re Tavarone Mining Co (Pritchard's Case)* (1873) LR 8 Ch App 956 (CA).

of each member to observe those provisions'. The company's constitution therefore forms what is known as a 'statutory contract' and imposes obligations upon:

- the company when dealing with its members;
- the members when dealing with the company; and
- the members when dealing with each other.

Breach of certain obligations contained in the constitution will therefore constitute breach of contract, thereby allowing the non-breaching party to obtain a remedy. As we shall see, however, only those provisions of the articles relating to membership rights can be enforced.

Before discussing the ability of the parties to enforce the statutory contract, it is important to note that the statutory contract is a highly unusual one and differs from standard contracts in several notable ways.

The statutory contract

In Chapters 6, 7, and 9, we discussed the formation, content, and termination of contracts—but the statutory contract created by s 33 is a highly unusual one and does not follow many standard contractual rules discussed in previous chapters. Notable differences include the following.

- Standard contracts derive their binding force from the agreement between the parties; the statutory contract derives its binding force from statute.
- The terms of the statutory contract can be altered by the company[2] against the wishes of minority shareholders party to it. This can be particularly harsh where an employee of the company has an employment contract based on the articles. For example, if the articles provide that a director is to be paid £100,000 per year and the company alters the articles to reduce his pay to £1 per year, then £1 per year is all that he will be entitled to. This is why directors should have self-contained service contracts.
- Breach of any term in a standard contract will allow the non-breaching party to commence an action for breach of contract. But the shareholders' right to sue for breach of the statutory contract is limited to those provisions that provide 'membership rights'.
- Unlike a standard contract, the courts will not rectify the statutory contract if it fails to give effect to the intentions of the parties, or contains a mistake.
- The statutory contract is not defeasible on the grounds of misrepresentation, undue influence, or duress.

It can therefore be seen that several standard rules of contract law do not apply to the statutory contract. One rule that does apply, however, is the doctrine of privity. The statutory contract is formed between a company and its members, and outsiders are therefore not permitted to enforce the constitution, as the following case demonstrates.

The doctrine of privity of contract is discussed at p 143

---

2. By passing a special resolution (CA 2006, s 21(1)) and, if applicable, by complying with any additional requirements in relation to entrenched provisions (ibid, s 22).

Eley v Positive Government Security Life Assurance Co (1876) LR 1 Ex D 88 (CA)

FACTS: The claimant solicitor drafted the defendant company's articles, which were then duly registered. The articles provided that the claimant would act as its solicitor and would not be removed from office unless he were to engage in some form of misconduct. The claimant did not subscribe for any shares upon registration, but did purchase shares about a year later. The claimant acted as the company's solicitor for a period, but the company then ceased to employ him and employed other solicitors. The claimant brought an action alleging that the defendant had breached the contract formed by the articles.

HELD: The Court of Appeal dismissed the claimant's action. He was not a party to the statutory contract and so could not sue for its breach.

COMMENT: Two points are worthy of note.

1. The Court paid no attention to the fact that the claimant had actually become a member by the time of the hearing (although, as we shall see, this was irrelevant, because the right in question was not a membership right).

2. It might be thought that, because the defendant had obtained a valuable benefit from the acts of the claimant, the Contracts (Rights of Third Parties) Act 1999, s 1, would apply, thereby allowing the doctrine of privity to be avoided. But para 108 of the Explanatory Notes to the CA 2006 provides that the s 33 contract is not subject to s 1 of the 1999 Act.[3]

The contract between the company and its members

Because the constitution of the company forms a contract between the company and its members, both parties can enforce compliance with the terms of the constitution. In the following case, the company enforced the constitution against one of its members.

Hickman v Kent or Romney March Sheepbreeders' Association [1915] 1 Ch 881 (Ch)

FACTS: The articles of the defendant company provided that any dispute between it and a member should be referred to arbitration. The defendant purported to expel one of its members (the claimant), but instead of referring the dispute to arbitration, the claimant petitioned the High Court for an injunction restraining his expulsion.

HELD: The articles formed a contract between the company and its members. The company was therefore permitted to enforce the provisions and require disputes to be referred to arbitration. The High Court therefore stayed the legal proceedings and the claimant was subsequently expelled.

COMMENT: Today, the same outcome could be achieved as a result of the Arbitration Act 1996, s 9, which provides that legal proceedings can be stayed where a party commences proceedings in contravention of an arbitration agreement.

---

3. The Contracts (Rights of Third Parties) Act 1999, s 6(2), provides that it does not apply to the CA 1985, s 14 (the predecessor to s 33). It is unusual that the 1999 Act has not been amended to reflect the passing of the CA 2006.

The opposite is also true, so a member can enforce compliance of a term of the constitution against the company.

Pender v Lushington (1877) 6 Ch D 70 (Ch)

FACTS: The company's articles provided that its members would have one vote for every ten shares held, up to a maximum of a hundred votes. Consequently, shareholders with over 1,000 shares would not have voting power commensurate with their shareholdings. To remedy this, members with over 1,000 shares transferred some of their excess shares to several nominees (including the claimant), thereby unlocking the votes within them. The chairman of the company (the defendant) refused to accept the votes of the nominees. The claimant alleged that his votes were improperly rejected.

HELD: The High Court upheld the claim. The shares were properly transferred and registered, so refusing to accept the nominee's votes constituted a breach of the articles. The court therefore issued an injunction restraining the rejection of the nominee's votes.

It is important to note, however, that not all of the terms of the constitution will form a contract between the company and its members. As Buckley LJ stated: 'The purpose of the [constitution] is to define the position of the shareholder as shareholder, not to bind him in his capacity as an individual.'[4] Therefore, only the terms of the constitution that relate to the members in their capacity as members (that is, those that relate to membership rights) will form part of the statutory contract. Accordingly, in *Eley* (discussed above), the fact that the claimant solicitor had subsequently become a member of the defendant company would be irrelevant, because the article provision did not relate to his rights as a member.

The following case provides an example of a claim that failed because the member was not seeking to enforce a membership right.

Beattie v E and F Beattie Ltd [1938] Ch 708 (CA)

FACTS: The claimant company's articles contained a provision providing that any disputes between the company and its members would be referred to arbitration. It was alleged that one of the defendants (a director of the company who also held shares in the company) had been improperly drawing a salary without the authorization of the company or the general meeting. The claimant therefore initiated legal proceedings to recover the unauthorized payments. The defendant alleged that, because he was a member, the matter should be referred to arbitration.

HELD: Lord Greene MR stated that 'the contractual force given to the [constitution] by [s 33] is limited to such provisions…as apply to the relationship of the members in their capacity as members'.[5] Accordingly, because the defendant was relying on the articles in his capacity as a director and not as a member, the Court of Appeal held that the defendant could not enforce the arbitration agreement.

---

4. *Bisgood v Henderson's Transvaal Estates Ltd* [1908] 1 Ch 743 (CA) 759.
5. *Beattie v E and F Beattie Ltd* [1938] Ch 708 (CA) 721.

Accordingly, provisions of the constitution that relate to the rights of directors will not normally form part of the statutory contract. But in certain types of company classified as 'quasi-partnerships', the dividing line between member and director is blurred, because the members may have an expectation to be involved in management. In such companies, provisions conferring rights upon directors will be regarded as membership rights in relation to those members who have such an expectation.[6]

 What constitutes a quasi-partnership is discussed at p 741

The contract between the members *inter se*

Just as the constitution forms a contract between the company and its members, so too does it form a contract between the members themselves. Accordingly, a breach of the statutory contract by a member can be enforced by another member, provided that the provision breached concerns a membership right.

⊙ *Rayfield v Hands* [1960] Ch 1

FACTS: The company's articles provided that if a member were to wish to sell his shares, he should inform the directors of this and they would then 'take the said shares equally between them at a fair value'. The claimant wished to sell his shares and notified the directors (the defendants) of this, but the directors refused to purchase his shares. The directors were all members of the company (in fact, the articles required that the directors be members). The claimant sought a court order requiring the directors to purchase his shares.

HELD: The High Court made such an order and the defendants were required to purchase the claimant's shares at fair value. Vaisey J stated that the provision in question affected the directors in their capacity as members and that therefore the claimant could enforce it.

COMMENT: Vaisey J's assertion that the provision affected the directors in their capacity as members is not wholly convincing and it is submitted that the decision should be confined to the facts. In the context of the company in question (which was akin to a quasi-partnership), blurring the line between director and member might be justified, but in many companies, there will be a clear demarcation between the rights of the directors and the rights of the members.

 See LCB Gower, 'The Contractual Effect of Articles of Association' (1958) 21 MLR 401

‹› Key points summary

- The constitution of a company forms a statutory contract between:
    - the company and its members; and
    - the members themselves.

- The doctrine of privity ensures that outsiders cannot enforce the provisions of the company's constitution and the Contracts (Rights of Third Parties) Act 1999 does not apply.

- Only those provisions relating to membership rights will form part of the statutory contract.

---

6. *Rayfield v Hands* [1960] Ch 1 (Ch).

Derivative claims

A particular problem arises where a director breaches his general duties, or commits some other act that causes the company loss. Because the company has suffered the loss, only the company as a separate entity can generally commence proceedings to remedy it. But because a company can only function through human actors and the power to commence proceedings on the company's behalf is usually vested in the board of directors,[7] a problem arises where the directors or majority shareholders themselves have committed the wrong and they are reluctant to sue a member of their board.

So can the shareholders ever commence litigation on the company's behalf where the directors are unwilling to do so? The general answer was provided in the following case.

The rule in *Foss v Harbottle*

In the following case, the Court of Chancery established one of the cardinal rules in company law.

 Foss v Harbottle (1843) 2 Hare 461

FACTS: The facts are not required for our purposes.

HELD: The court established three principles, which have collectively come to be known as 'the rule in *Foss v Harbottle*'.

1. *The 'proper claimant' principle* This provides that only the company can commence proceedings for wrongs committed against it. Accordingly, shareholders cannot sue on the company's behalf. As we shall see, the proper claimant principle is subject to exceptions.

2. *The 'internal management' principle* This provides that where a company is acting within its powers, the courts will not interfere in matters of internal management unless the company itself commences proceedings.

3. *The 'irregularity' principle* This provides that where some procedural irregularity is committed, an aggrieved member cannot commence proceedings where the irregularity is one that can be ratified by a simple majority of the members. This principle applies both to rights vested in the company and to personal rights of the members. Accordingly, even where the right to commence proceedings is vested personally in a member, proceedings cannot be commenced if the irregularity in question can be ratified by the members.

---

7. The Company (Model Articles) Regulations 2008, SI 2008/3229, Sch 1, para 3, Sch 2, para 3, and Sch 3, para 3, provide that the directors may 'exercise all the powers of the company', which would include the right to litigate on behalf of the company. Where an insolvency procedure has been initiated, the liquidator also acquires the right to commence proceedings on the company's behalf.

The three principles are natural corollaries of three fundamental pillars of company law:

- the proper claimant principle is a natural corollary of the company's corporate personality;
- the internal management principle is indicative of the courts' long-established reluctance to become involved in the internal affairs of businesses; and
- the irregularity principle is simply a natural extension of the principle of majority rule.

Each principle therefore has an accompanying rationale, but there is an additional rationale behind all three principles—namely, the often-cited 'floodgates' argument. It has been argued that if members were to have the right to commence litigation on the company's behalf, then every minor irregularity would be litigated, thereby flooding the court with claims.[8]

'Exceptions' to the rule

The rule in *Foss v Harbottle* is not absolute; were it to be so, wrongs committed by the directors or majority shareholders would rarely be subject to litigation. Accordingly, there are exceptions to the rule whereby the members are permitted to bring an action on the company's behalf. Such actions are known as 'derivative' actions, because the members are bringing an action based on rights derived from the company. This derivation is reinforced by the fact that, if the derivative action succeeds, the remedy is granted to the company, not to the member who brought the action. With the creation of the statutory derivative claim and the consequent abolition of the common law derivative action, the common law exceptions to *Foss* have lost a measure of their relevance, but parallels do exist between these exceptions and the scope of the statutory derivative claim, so a basic knowledge of the common law exceptions will be of aid.

Historically, it has been stated that there were four exceptions to the rule in *Foss v Harbottle.*[9]

1. where the act complained of was illegal[10] or **ultra vires**.[11] Because ultra vires acts cannot be ratified by a simple majority (a special resolution is required), they would not be caught by the irregularity principle;

   ➡ ultra vires: 'beyond one's powers'

2. where the act complained of infringed the personal rights of a member. There are numerous examples of breaches of personal rights, including the failure to provide sufficient notice of meetings,[12] the failure to provide dividends in the manner provided for by the articles,[13] and the improper rejection of votes;[14]

---

8. See the classic statement of Mellish LJ in *MacDougall v Gardiner* (1875) 1 Ch D 13 (CA) 25.

9. See the judgment of Jenkins LJ in *Edwards v Halliwell* [1950] 2 All ER 1064 (CA).

10. See, e.g., *Taylor v National Union of Mineworkers (Derbyshire Area)* [1985] BCLC 237 (unlawful strike action).

11. See, e.g., *Simpson v Westminster Palace Hotel Co* (1860) 8 HL Cas 712 (HL).

12. *Baillie v Oriental Telephone and Electric Co Ltd* [1915] 1 Ch 503 (CA).

13. *Wood v Odessa Waterworks Co* (1889) 42 Ch D 636 (Ch).

14. *Pender v Lushington* (1877) 6 Ch D 70 (Ch)

3. where the act complained of could only be done or sanctioned by the passing of a special resolution;[15] and

4. where the act complained of constituted a 'fraud on the minority'.

Today, it is generally acknowledged that the only 'true' exception to *Foss* was the fraud on the minority exception. The reason for this is the first three so-called exceptions do not concern rights vested in the company, but concern personal rights belonging to the member. Accordingly, they were not 'exceptions' to *Foss*, but rather areas in which *Foss* had no application.

The fraud on the minority exception was created specifically for those instances in which those who control the company (including those having the right to commence litigation on the company's behalf) have committed some form of fraud. 'Fraud' is defined widely to include actual fraud (for example, breach of the Theft Act 1968, or the Fraud Act 2006) and equitable fraud (for example, conduct tainted with impropriety). For example, although the courts have maintained that negligence, however gross, is not a fraud on the minority,[16] where an act of negligence benefits those who control the company (thereby tainting it with impropriety), this can constitute a fraud on the minority.[17]

A court will, however, deny a member a right to sue on behalf of the company, even though there is fraud on the minority, if it would not serve the interests of justice. Examples of cases in which a member has been denied the chance to bring a derivative action include where the conduct of the shareholder seeking to sue is itself tainted by impropriety,[18] or where the independent shareholders (that is, not the wrongdoer or the applicant) have already indicated that they do not wish there to be litigation on behalf of the company.[19] In one case,[20] the Court denied *locus standi* to a shareholder who sought to bring an action on behalf of the company against a director, her ex-son-in-law, when it became clear that she was really pursuing a personal vendetta against the director for deserting her daughter rather than displaying concern for the interests of the company.

➡ *locus standi*: 'place of standing'; the right to appear and be heard before a court

The statutory derivative claim

Whilst the Law Commission agreed with the underlying approach of the rule in *Foss v Harbottle* (that is, that shareholders should rarely be able to commence actions for wrongs done to the company), it was also of the opinion that the rules relating to derivative actions had become 'complicated and unwieldy'.[21] As a result of the Law Commission's recommendations (which were largely adopted by the Company Law Review Steering Group), the CA 2006, Pt 11, now allows for the making of a statutory derivative claim. The provisions contained in Pt 11 do not actually affect

---

15. *Edwards v Halliwell* [1950] 2 All ER 1064 (CA).
16. *Pavlides v Jensen* [1956] Ch 565 (Ch).
17. *Daniels v Daniels* [1978] Ch 406 (Ch).
18. *Nurcombe v Nurcombe* [1985] 1 WLR 370 (CA), in which a shareholder, who had, to her knowledge, benefited from the fraud of the director who controlled the company, was denied the right to sue on the company's behalf.
19. *Smith v Croft (No 2)* [1988] Ch 114 (Ch).
20. *Barrett v Duckett* [1995] 1 BCLC 243 (CA).
21. Law Commission, *Shareholder Remedies* (Law Com No 246, Cm 3759, HMSO, London, 1997) [6.4].

the rule in *Foss v Harbottle* itself, which retains much of its forcefulness (especially in relation to personal clams); rather, the provisions of Pt 11 now replace the common law rules relating to when a derivative action may be brought. Accordingly, the common law derivative action is abolished.

Scope

Section 260(1) defines a derivative claim as one brought by a member[22] in respect of a cause of action vested in the company, seeking relief on behalf of the company. This reiterates that any benefits obtained as a result of the claim accrue to the company and not to the derivative claimant. Section 260(2) provides that a derivative claim can only be brought under Pt 11 of the Act, or in pursuance of a court order under s 994. Section 260(3) provides that a claim can only arise from an actual or proposed act or omission involving one of the following.

> 🔗 The unfair prejudice remedy found in s 994 is discussed at p 733

- *Negligence* It will be remembered that negligence could not found a common law derivative action unless the wrongdoer gained some form of benefit from the negligent act. This limitation is not preserved by the Act.

- *Default* 'Default' is a general term used in many pieces of legislation that refers to a failure to perform a legally obligated act (for example, to appear in court when required).

- *Breach of duty* Accordingly, a member will have standing to commence a derivative claim for breach of the general duties discussed in Chapter 20.

- *Breach of trust.*

The act or omission must be by a director.[23] Under the common law, the actions of members could found a derivative action,[24] but this is no longer the case. Where a member commits a wrong, a claim under s 994 or a winding-up order will constitute the appropriate remedies. But even though the act or omission must be by a director, the derivative claim may be brought against a director or another person (or both).[25] This would allow a claim to be brought against members or other persons who are somehow involved in the director's act or omission.

Section 260(4) provides that it is immaterial whether the cause of action arose before or after the person seeking to bring or continue the derivative claim became a member of the company. The timing of membership is irrelevant, because the claim belongs to the company and not the member.

Permission from the court

Section 261(1) provides that a member who brings a derivative claim must apply to the court for permission to continue it. If the member cannot establish a prima facie case for permission, the court must either dismiss the application or make any

---

22. Section 260(5)(c) provides that, for the purposes of Pt 11, a member will also include a person who is not a member, but to whom shares in the company have been transferred or transmitted by operation of law (e.g. through inheritance).

23. For the purposes of Pt 11, 'director' also includes former directors and shadow directors: CA 2006, s 260(5)(a) and (b).

24. See, e.g., *Estmanco (Kilner House) Ltd v Greater London Council* [1982] 1 WLR (QB).

25. CA 2006, s 260(3).

consequential order that it considers appropriate.[26] If a prima facie case is established, the court will direct the company to provide evidence. After hearing the application, the court may:

- give permission to continue the claim on such terms as it deems fit;
- refuse permission and dismiss the claim; or
- adjourn proceedings and give such directions as it sees fit.[27]

The rationale behind this procedure is to screen out unmeritorious claims before the defendant becomes involved.

The directors may attempt to forestall a possible derivative claim by causing the company to bring a claim in respect of the wrongdoing, but with no intention of diligently pursuing it. Where this occurs, s 262(2) allows a member to apply to the court for permission to take over the company's claim as a derivative claim on the grounds that:

- the manner in which the company commenced or continued the claim amounts to an abuse of the process of the court;
- the company has failed to prosecute the claim diligently; and
- it is appropriate for the member to continue the claim as a derivative claim.

Section 262(2) is subject to the same rules as s 261 regarding the obtaining of permission from the court.[28]

Key to the exercise of the court's discretion is s 263, which provides the court with guidance on the granting of permission under s 261 or 262. Section 263(2) provides that the court *must* refuse permission if it is satisfied that any one of the following three conditions is satisfied.

1. *That a person acting in accordance with s 172 (director's duty to promote the success of the company) would not seek to continue the claim* This reinforces the fact that a derivative claim should be for the benefit of the company. Permission must be refused where a claim does not benefit the company and, in relation to derivative claims, this will be judged by reference to whether a hypothetical director would not seek to continue the claim.

2. *Where the cause of action arises from an act or omission that is yet to occur, that the act or omission has been authorized by the company* An act or omission that has been authorized is no longer a wrong done to the company, so no claim should arise.

3. *Where the cause of action arises from an act or omission that has already occurred, that the act or omission was authorized by the company before it occurred, or has been ratified by the company since it occurred* Authorization or ratification will prevent the act or omission from constituting a wrong done to the company.

Section 263(3) provides that when considering whether or not to grant permission, the court must take into account a number of factors (several are which are highly relevant to the refusal of permission under s 263(2)), including:

- whether the member is acting in good faith in continuing the claim;

⟜ The duty imposed upon directors by s 172 is discussed at p 701

---

26. Ibid, s 261(2).   27. Ibid, s 261(4).
28. Ibid, s 262(3)–(5).

- the importance that a person acting in accordance with s 172 (director's duty to promote the success of the company) would attach to continuing with the claim;
- where the cause of action arises from an act or omission that is yet to occur, whether the act or omission could be, and in the circumstances would be likely to be:
  - authorized before it occurs; or
  - ratified after it occurs;
- where the cause of action arises from an act or omission that has already occurred, whether the act or omission could be, and in the circumstances would be likely to be, ratified;
- whether the company has decided not to pursue the claim;
- whether the act or omission in respect of which the claim is brought gives rise to a cause of action that the member could pursue in his own right rather than on behalf of the company.

An additional factor was added late in the Bill's passage through the House of Lords and can be found in s 263(4), which provides that '[i]n considering whether to give permission…the court shall have particular regard to any evidence before it as to the views of members of the company who have no personal interest, direct or indirect, in the matter'. This resembles the 'majority of the minority' test that existed under the common law and is of particular relevance where the company has decided not to pursue the claim. The company may have perfectly legitimate reasons for not pursuing a claim (for example, waste of time and expense), and seeking the views of members with no interest in the matter may aid the court in determining whether to allow the action to go ahead even though the company does not wish it to.

The 'no reflective loss' principle

The ability to bring a derivative claim is further limited by what is known as the 'no reflective loss' principle. A loss sustained by the company's members may simply be reflective of the loss sustained by the company itself. In such a case, the members will not be permitted to bring a derivative claim for recovery of the reflective losses that could be recovered by the company.[29]

The following example clarifies the principle.

Eg The 'no reflective loss' principle

The directors of Undercard Ltd commit an act of negligence that causes a substantial reduction in the company's profits. This, in turn, reduces significantly the dividends paid to the members. Marc, a member of Undercard, wishes to commence a derivative claim against the directors involved. He will be unable to do so, because the loss sustained by the members is merely a reflection of the loss sustained by the company. The members' loss is embodied in the loss of the company.

---

29. *Prudential Assurance Co Ltd v Newman Industries Ltd (No 2)* [1982] Ch 204 (CA).

The rationale behind the 'no reflective loss' principle is to prevent double recovery by ensuring that a defendant can only be sued once for the loss that he caused. It could be argued, however, that the same result could be achieved by preventing one party from recovering where another party has already obtained recovery. Why should a rule exist that always subordinates the claims of members to those of the company? One argument is that the rule protects creditors by ensuring that any money recovered stays within the company, as opposed to being distributed to a shareholder, but as has been correctly argued,[30] where a company has distributable profits, the 'no reflective loss' principle will in no way prejudice the creditors' interests.

The following case is the leading authority on reflective loss, and clarifies when the principle will and will not prevent a derivative claim.

Johnson v Gore Wood & Co [2002] AC 1 (HL)

FACTS: The claimant owned all but two shares in a company. On behalf of the company, he instructed the defendant firm of solicitors to exercise an option to purchase land. The defendant exercised the option negligently and the claimant's company had to go to court to acquire the land. These legal proceedings were expensive and lengthy, and by the time that the land was acquired, the property market had crashed and the value of the land had dropped considerably. The defendant settled with the company, but the claimant then commenced proceedings for the losses that he sustained as a result of the defendant's negligence.

HELD: The House of Lords struck out the claimant's action, because his loss was reflective of that of the company. Lord Bingham established three propositions, as follows.

1. Where a company suffers loss due to another's breach of duty, only the company may sue to recover compensation for its loss. A shareholder cannot bring a claim where the company's loss could be recovered by an action brought by the company, irrespective of whether the company actually decides to commence the action or not.

2. Where a company suffers loss due to the acts or omissions of another, but has no cause of action against the person, a shareholder may bring a claim against that person to recover the loss sustained by the company if he has a cause of action, even though the loss sustained is a diminution in the value of his shareholding.

3. Where a company suffers loss caused by a breach of duty to it, and a shareholder suffers a separate and distinct loss caused by a breach of duty owed independently to the shareholder, each may sue to recover its loss, but neither can sue to recover the loss caused to the other caused by the breach of duty owed to the other.

★ See E Ferran, 'Litigation by Shareholders and Reflective Loss' (2001) 60 CLJ 245

Lord Bingham's propositions greatly clarified the law, but uncertainties still existed. To a large extent, subsequent decisions have clarified the law and have established qualifications to Lord Bingham's propositions. For example, Lord Bingham

---

30. PL Davies, *Gower & Davies' Principles of Modern Company Law* (8th edn, Sweet & Maxwell, London, 2008) 625.

clearly stated that the 'no reflective loss' principle applies even where the company declines to recover its loss. But the Court of Appeal has subsequently held that the principle will not apply where the company is unable to sue due to the defendant's wrongdoing[31] (for example, where the defendant's wrongdoing has forced the company into insolvency and it cannot afford to commence proceedings).

Key points summary

- The 'proper claimant' principle provides that only a company can sue in respect of wrongs committed against it.

- The 'internal management' principle provides that the courts will not interfere in the internal management of a company.

- The 'irregularity' principle provides that a member cannot bring an action for an irregularity that could be ratified by a simple majority of the members.

- In certain circumstances, the rule in *Foss v Harbottle* did not apply and a member could commence a derivative action on the company's behalf.

- Today, the only form of derivative action available is known as a 'statutory derivative claim' and may be brought where a director commits an act or omission involving negligence, default, breach of duty, or breach of trust.

- A derivative claimant will require the permission of the court in order to continue with the claim and the claim will be dismissed if the claimant cannot establish a prima facie case.

- The courts will not allow a derivative claim to succeed where the member's loss is merely reflective of the loss of the company.

Unfairly prejudicial conduct

The CA 2006, Pt 30, consists of a mere six sections, yet it provides what is perhaps the most important shareholder remedy. Section 994 allows a member[32] to petition the court for a remedy on the ground that the company's affairs will be, are being, or have been conducted in a manner that is unfairly prejudicial to the interests of members generally, or of some part of its members (including at least himself).

Section 994 re-enacts almost identically the Companies Act 1985 (CA 1985), s 459, so case law decided under s 459 is still highly relevant. Section 459 was regarded as an extremely useful and popular shareholder remedy, largely because of the courts' willingness to interpret it in a liberal manner. Key to the effectiveness of s 994 has been the courts' interpretation of the phrases 'unfairly prejudicial' and 'the interests of members' in the CA 1985, s 459.

---

31. *Giles v Rhind* [2002] EWCA Civ 1428, [2003] Ch 618.
32. As with statutory derivative claims, transferees of shares are classified as members where the transfer or transmission is by the operation of law: CA 2006, s 994(2).

'Unfairly prejudicial'

The conduct complained of must be 'unfairly prejudicial'. The courts take an objective approach when determining whether conduct is unfairly prejudicial.[33] Accordingly, there is no requirement for the petitioner to 'come with clean hands', but unmeritorious behaviour on the part of the petitioner might lead the court to conclude that the conduct complained of was not unfair, or that the remedy granted should be reduced.[34]

The starting point in determining what constitutes unfairly prejudicial conduct is the much-quoted passage from Neill LJ, who stated that:

> The words 'unfairly prejudicial' are general words and they should be applied flexibly to meet the circumstances of the particular case....The conduct must be both prejudicial (in the sense of causing prejudice or harm to the relevant interest) and also unfairly so: conduct may be unfair without being prejudicial or prejudicial without being unfair, and it is not sufficient if the conduct only satisfies one of these tests.[35]

Because the words 'unfairly prejudicial' are general words, the courts have not sought to impose a general standard or test, but it has been emphasized that the court's discretion must be judiciously exercised. In *O'Neill v Phillips*,[36] Lord Hoffmann (who, as will be seen, was involved in many of the major cases concerning the unfair prejudice remedy) stated that Parliament chose the concept of fairness to:

> free the court from technical considerations of legal right and to confer a wide power to do what appeared just and equitable. But this does not mean that the court can do whatever the individual judge happens to think fair. The concept of fairness must be applied judicially and the content which it is given by the courts must be based upon rational principles....Although fairness is a notion which can be applied to all kinds of activities its content will depend upon the context in which it is being used. Conduct which is perfectly fair between competing businessmen may not be fair between members of a family.[37]

Accordingly, whether conduct is unfairly prejudicial or not is a matter for each case.

Examples of conduct that the courts have held capable of being unfairly prejudicial include:

- non-payment of dividends,[38] or payment of low dividends;[39]
- exclusion from the management of a quasi-partnership company;[40]

---

33. *Re Guidezone Ltd* [2000] 2 BCLC 321 (Ch).
34. *Re London School of Electronics Ltd* [1986] Ch 211 (Ch).
35. *Re Saul D Harrison and Sons plc* [1995] 1 BCLC 14 (CA) 30, 31.
36. [1999] 1 WLR 1092 (HL).
37. Ibid, 1098.
38. *Re a Company (No 00370 of 1987)* [1988] 1 WLR 1068 (Ch).
39. *Re Sam Weller & Sons Ltd* [1990] Ch 682 (Ch).
40. *Re RA Noble & Sons (Clothing) Ltd* [1983] BCLC 273 (Ch).

- serious mismanagement[41]—the requirement of *serious* mismanagement being crucial (mismanagement will not normally constitute unfairly prejudicial conduct);[42]
- preventing the members from obtaining the best price for their shares;[43]
- the payment of excessive remuneration;[44]
- the improper transfer of assets.[45]

'Interests of members'

The conduct must unfairly prejudice the 'interests of members'. Defining the extent of members' interests has proven to be a complex issue that has generated a substantial body of case law. Historically, the courts imposed a member *qua* member requirement similar to that imposed upon members when attempting to enforce the constitution. As time progressed, however, the courts have eroded this requirement more and more, with the following case indicating how far away from the member *qua* member rule the court is prepared to go in order to achieve a just result.

 qua: 'in the capacity of'

 Gamlestaden Fastigheter AB v Baltic Partners Ltd [2007] UKPC 27

FACTS: The claimant company entered into a joint venture with a man named Karlsten. The venture operated through a company (the first defendant). The claimant company held 22 per cent of the shares in the first defendant and, in order to finance the joint venture, it had also made substantial loans to the first defendant over a two-year period. The claimant company alleged that Karlsten and others had withdrawn substantial funds from the venture with the approval of the first defendant's directors (who were also defendants), but that no consideration had been provided for the withdrawals. The claimant company alleged that this constituted unfairly prejudicial conduct and argued that the first defendant's directors should compensate the first defendant (not the claimant company) for the withdrawals that they authorized. At the time of the hearing, the first defendant had become insolvent and its directors therefore argued that the payment of compensation to the first defendant would benefit the claimant company *qua* creditor, but would not benefit it *qua* member and, as such, the conduct did not affect its interests as a member.

HELD: The Privy Council rejected the director's arguments and found for the claimant company. Lord Scott stated:

> in a case where an investor in a joint venture company has, in pursuance of the joint venture agreement, invested not only in subscribing for shares but also in advancing loan capital, the investor ought not…to be precluded from the grant of relief…on the ground that the relief would benefit the investor only as loan creditor and not as member.[46]

---

41. *Re Macro (Ipswich) Ltd* [1994] 2 BCLC 354 (Ch).
42. *Re Elgindata Ltd* [1991] 1 BCLC 959 (Ch).
43. *Re a Company (No 008699 of 1985)* [1986] BCLC 382 (Ch).
44. *Re Cumana Ltd* [1986] BCLC 430 (CA).
45. *Re London School of Electronics Ltd* [1986] Ch 211 (Ch).
46. *Gamlestaden Fastigheter AB v Baltic Partners Ltd* [2007] UKPC 27, [2007] BCC 272, [37].

COMMENT: This case is significant for two reasons: firstly, the claimant company succeeded, even though the case was brought in its capacity as a creditor and not as a member of the first defendant; secondly, the claimant company did not seek compensation for itself, but on behalf of the first defendant. The claimant therefore enforced a right on behalf of the defendant company, which would normally be prohibited by the rule in *Foss v Harbottle*. A prior derivative claim had failed on the ground that the case did not come within any of the common law exceptions to *Foss*. To allow the claimant to use the unfair prejudice remedy to obtain relief for the first defendant confirms that a principal reason for the remedy's creation was to outflank the rule in *Foss v Harbottle* where fairness requires.

 See T Singla, 'Unfair Prejudice in the Privy Council' (2007) 123 LQR 542

But the courts have only been prepared to go so far and the member *qua* member requirement has not been fully abandoned. The court will still require the petitioner's interest to be sufficiently related to his membership. Thus, the courts have rejected claims where the petitioner has brought a claim in his capacity as an employee of the company,[47] or where a claim is brought in the capacity of a freeholder of land upon which a business was run, as opposed to a member of the company that runs the business.[48]

Equitable considerations

Section 994 focuses on the members' interests, as opposed to their rights. The members' rights are found in the company's constitution, but their interests are wider than this.[49] In particular, in certain types of company, the members may agree that the company is to be run in a certain way, but that agreement may never be formalized or inserted into the constitution. The courts have indicated that the majority may not be permitted to rely on the articles if reliance unfairly prejudices the interests of the members by defeating the 'legitimate expectations'[50] to which such agreements may give rise.

The courts' approach was stated in the first (and so far, only) case involving unfair prejudice to reach the House of Lords.

O'Neill v Phillips [1999] 1 WLR 1092 (HL)

FACTS: The defendant owned all of the shares (a hundred) in a company, but in 1985, he gave twenty-five shares to the claimant (who was an employee) and made him a director. The defendant also retired from the board, leaving the claimant as *de facto* managing director. The company's profits were split between the defendant (75 per cent) and the claimant (25 per cent), but the defendant voluntarily gave up 25 per cent of his profits, so that their share of the profits was equal. It was also discussed between them that the claimant's shareholding might be increased to 50 per cent. In 1991, the business experienced difficulties and the defendant returned to oversee management. He offered

---

47. *Re John Reid & Sons (Strucsteel) Ltd* [2003] EWHC 2329 (Ch), [2003] 2 BCLC 319.
48. *Re JE Cade & Son Ltd* [1992] BCLC 213 (Ch).
49. *Re a Company (No 00477 of 1986)* [1986] BCLC 376 (Ch).
50. This phrase was first used by Lord Hoffmann in *Re Saul D Harrison and Sons plc* [1995] 1 BCLC 14 (CA). He has since indicated in *O'Neill v Phillips* [1999] 1 WLR 1092 (HL) that the term should not be used.

the claimant the opportunity to manage, under the defendant's direction, either the English or German branch of the business—the claimant choosing the German branch. Later in the year, the defendant claimed to be entitled once again to receive 75 per cent of the profits and the claimant left the company, claiming unfair prejudice. The Court of Appeal held that the claimant had a legitimate expectation that he would receive 50 per cent of the profits and would receive 50 per cent of the shares. The defendant appealed.

HELD: The House of Lords allowed the defendant's appeal. Lord Hoffmann stressed that:

> a member of a company will not ordinarily be entitled to complain of unfairness unless there has been some breach of the terms on which he agreed that the affairs of the company should be conducted. But…there will be cases in which equitable considerations make it unfair for those conducting the affairs of the company to rely upon their strict legal powers. Thus unfairness may consist in a breach of the rules or in using the rules in a manner which equity would regard as contrary to good faith.[51]

On the facts, the House held that the claimant had not been excluded from management, nor had the defendant promised to transfer any shares to the claimant (even if the claimant had hopes of such a transfer). Further, the defendant had not promised that the claimant would always receive 50 per cent of the profits; rather, the claimant had, at most, been promised 50 per cent of the profits whilst he remained *de facto* managing director. The defendant had not breached the articles or memorandum, nor was there anything giving rise to the equitable considerations of which Lord Hoffmann spoke.

★ See DD Prentice and J Payne, 'Section 459 of the Companies Act 1985: The House of Lords' View' (1999) 115 LQR 587

Although the category of equitable considerations is open-ended, the majority of cases in this area have involved members being excluded from management. The exclusion from management is a very good example of when equitable considerations will be relevant. In public companies and most private companies, the members will have no expectations beyond those found in the company's constitution[52] and they will certainly not expect to manage. Conversely, in quasi-partnerships, the members are likely to have an expectation that they will participate in management and such an expectation may derive from an informal agreement, as opposed to the constitution. Exclusion from management in such companies is likely to amount to unfairly prejudicial conduct. But it must be noted that the expectation must be legitimate: a mere hope that the company's affairs will be run in a certain way will be insufficient and the court will only seek to enforce what was actually agreed. As Lord Hoffmann stated, the unfair prejudice remedy 'enables the court to give full effect to the terms and understandings on which the members of the company become associated but not to rewrite them'.[53]

⌗ Quasi-partnerships are discussed in more detail at p 741

Remedies

Where a s 994 petition is successful, the court has significant remedial flexibility, being able to make 'such order as it thinks fit for giving relief in respect of the

---

51. *O'Neill v Phillips* [1999] 1 WLR 1092 (HL) 1098, 1099.
52. *Re Blue Arrow plc* [1987] BCLC 585 (Ch); *Re Elgindata Ltd* [1991] 1 BCLC 959 (Ch).
53. *Re Postgate and Denby (Agencies) Ltd* [1987] BCLC 8 (Ch) 14.

matters complained of.[54] Section 996(2) provides examples of orders that the court could make, including:

- an order regulating the conduct of the company's affairs in the future (in *Re HR Harmer Ltd*,[55] the Court of Appeal allowed an elderly director, who snooped on staff, ignored board decisions, and insulted customers, to remain as chairman of the company, but deprived him of any executive role);
- an order requiring the company to:
  - refrain from doing an act complained of; or
  - to perform an act that it has failed to perform;
- an order authorizing civil proceedings to be brought in the name and on behalf of the company by such person(s), and on such terms, as the court may direct;
- an order requiring the company not to make any, or any specified, alterations in its articles without the leave of the court;
- an order providing for the purchase of the shares of any members of the company by other members or by the company itself and, in the case of a purchase by the company itself, a reduction of the company's capital accordingly.

A share purchase order is by far the most common remedy ordered under s 996 and it is usually the majority shareholders who are ordered to purchase the petitioner's shares.[56] The issue that then arises is how the shares should be valued. If the articles contain a price-fixing formula, the court will use it, unless there is a risk that this method of valuation will depreciate the value of the interest to be acquired.[57] In many cases, however, the articles will not contain such a formula and the price will need to be fixed by the courts. The principal issue that has arisen is whether the shares should be valued pro rata (based on the value of the company), or whether their value should be discounted to reflect that they were a minority holding and therefore lacked control of the company (as would most likely be the case where such a holding were sold voluntarily).

The valuation depends upon the type of company, as follows.

- Where a company is a quasi-partnership, the presumption is that the minority holding will be bought on a pro rata basis,[58] because the buying out of a partner in a partnership would be on a similar basis. But the shares of a quasi-partnership may be discounted where the court feels that the petitioner's conduct requires the shares to be discounted.[59]
- As regards other companies, although the House of Lords has stated that unfair prejudice may not be founded where the majority offered to purchase the minority's shares at fair value (with fair value defined as 'a value representing an equivalent proportion of the total issued share capital, that is, without a discount

---

54. CA 2006, s 996(1).

55. [1959] 1 WLR 62 (CA).

56. In rare cases, however, the majority may be ordered to sell their shares to the petitioner: *Re Brenfield Squash Racquets Club Ltd* [1996] 2 BCLC (Ch).

57. *Re a Company (No 00330 of 1991), ex p Holden* [1991] BCLC 597 (Ch).

58. *Re Bird Precision Bellows Ltd* [1986] Ch 658 (CA).

59. *Larvin v Phoenix Office Supplies Ltd* [2002] EWHC 591 (Ch), [2003] BCC 11.

for its being a minority holding'),[60] the High Court has not extended this to cover share purchase orders and has held that:

> a minority shareholding…is to be valued for what it is, a minority shareholding, unless there is some good reason to attribute to it a pro-rata share of the overall value of the company. Short of a quasi-partnership or some other exceptional circumstance, there is no reason to accord to it a quality which it lacks.[61]

* A definitive appellate court ruling is required.

A petition under s 994 is not subject to a limitation period, but because the granting of relief is discretionary, the court may refuse to grant a remedy where a substantial period has elapsed between the unfairly prejudicial conduct and the petition being brought.[62] The lack of a limitation period has been criticized on the ground that it encourages counsel to trawl through the company's history and adduce excessive amounts of evidence to back up any claims. This has resulted in s 994 claims gaining a reputation for being overly lengthy and expensive. For example, in one case concerning shares worth around £24,600, the legal costs amounted to £320,000.[63] The case of *Re Freudiana Music Co Ltd*[64] took over 165 days of court time, with the successful respondent awarded costs of £2 million.

 Key points summary

* Section 994 allows a member to petition the court where the conduct of the company's affairs has unfairly prejudiced his interests as a member.

* The conduct complained of must be both unfair *and* prejudicial to the interests of the members.

* The courts have interpreted very liberally what amounts to an interest of the member and the requirement that the member must bring a claim *qua* member has lost much of its force.

* In most companies, the members' interests will not extend beyond the rights found in the company's constitution, but in certain cases, the members may have legitimate expectations not found in the constitution that are deserving of protection.

* The court has significant remedial powers for breaches of s 994, but the most common remedy is to order the majority to purchase the petitioner's shares for fair value.

* In a quasi-partnership, a fair value will normally be determined on a pro rata basis, but in other types of company, the value will usually be discounted to reflect the nature of the minority holding.

---

60. *O'Neill v Phillips* [1999] 1 WLR 1092 (HL) 1107 (Lord Hoffmann).
61. *Irvine v Irvine* [2006] EWHC 583 (Ch), [2007] 1 BCLC 445, [11] (Blackburne J).
62. For example, *Re Grandactual Ltd* [2005] EWHC 1415 (Ch), [2006] BCC 73 (nine-year delay between conduct and petition).
63. *Re Elgindata Ltd* [1991] 1 BCLC 959 (Ch).
64. The Times 4 December 1995 (CA).

The petition for winding up

Perhaps the most extreme remedy available to an aggrieved shareholder is to petition the court for an order winding up the company. Despite the remedial flexibility afforded to the court in cases involving unfairly prejudicial conduct, winding up is not available under CA 2006, s 996. A shareholder desiring the winding up of the company will need to petition a county court,[65] or the High Court under the Insolvency Act 1986 (IA 1986), s 122(1), which lists eight circumstances in which a winding up may be ordered.

For our purposes, two of these are of relevance. A company may be wound up where the company passes a special resolution resolving that the company should be wound up.[66] But this will clearly be of no use to an aggrieved minority shareholder. The key provision here, then, is s 122(1)(g), which allows the court to wind up a company where it is 'of the opinion that it is just and equitable that the company should be wound up'. A single shareholder may petition the court[67] under s 122(1)(g), thereby making it an extremely significant minority shareholder remedy.

Since the introduction of the unfair prejudicial remedy (now found in the CA 2006, s 994), the number of s 122(1)(g) petitions has decreased. But the precise relationship between the two remedies has never been truly clear. There is no doubt that the remedies overlap and that unfairly prejudicial conduct might also justify winding up under s 122(1)(g). Indeed, it is common for a winding-up order to be pleaded alongside a petition under s 994. The IA 1986, s 125(2), provides that the court will not order a winding up where an alternative remedy is available and the petitioner is acting unreasonably in seeking winding up as opposed to the alternative remedy. This indicates that the remedies are complementary, as opposed to mutually exclusive, but also recognizes that winding up is a much more drastic remedy that will be ordered only rarely.[68]

The relationship between the two remedies was, however, the subject of a controversial decision in *Re Guidezone Ltd*,[69] in which Jonathan Parker J (as he then was) stated that the scope of s 122(1)(g) was no wider than that of the CA 2006, s 994, and that conduct that was not unfairly prejudicial under s 994 would not justify winding up under s 122(1)(g). This would seem to be a bizarre ruling,[70] because the courts have long held (albeit at first instance only) that '[t]he words "just and equitable" are words of the widest significance, and do not limit the jurisdiction of the court to any case'.[71]

---

65. IA 1986, s 117(2), provides that the county court will have concurrent jurisdiction with the High Court where the company's paid-up share capital does not exceed £120,000. Where the paid-up capital is over this amount, jurisdiction is granted solely to the High Court.

66. Ibid, s 122(1)(a).

67. Petitions may also be brought by the company itself, a director, a creditor, or a liquidator.

68. This is backed up by a Practice Direction ([1990] 1 WLR 490), which provides that petitioners should not apply under both ss 994 and 122(1)(g), unless a winding-up order is genuinely preferred.

69. [2001] 1 BCC 692 (Ch).

70. Stephen Acton, counsel for the petitioner in *Re Guidezone Ltd* has unsurprisingly criticized the decision: see 'Just and Equitable Winding Up: The Strange Case of the Disappearing Jurisdiction' (2001) 22 Co Law 134.

71. *Re Blériot Manufacturing Aircraft Co Ltd* (1916) 32 TLR 253 (Ch) 255.

Despite this, certain instances can be identified in which the court is more likely to order a winding up, including:

- where the company is fraudulently promoted[72] or set up for a fraudulent purpose;[73]
- where the company is deadlocked[74] (that is, where management or the shareholders are divided and refuse to be reconciled), meaning that it is unable to make any decisions, and the court will therefore order its winding up;
- where a company's objects clause indicate that it has been formed for a particular purpose (this purpose is known as the company's 'substratum'), a winding-up order will be appropriate if that purpose can no longer fulfilled. Thus, where a company was set up to manufacture goods based on a patent application, the fact that the patent was never granted constituted a loss of substratum sufficient to justify the company's winding up.[75] Cases involving a loss of substratum are likely to disappear over time, because companies created under the CA 2006 have unrestricted objects by default;[76]
- where the directors displays a lack of probity[77] (that is, honesty or decency). Note that inefficiency or negligence will not be enough.[78]

Quasi-partnerships

Section 122(1)(g) acquires an increased importance where the company in question is a 'quasi-partnership'. Indeed, as we have seen, other shareholder remedies also acquire increased importance in relation to such companies.

What constitutes a quasi-partnership and the importance of s 122(1)(g) to such companies was the subject of the following case.

Ebrahimi v Westbourne Galleries Ltd [1973] AC 360 (HL)

FACTS: In 1945, E (the claimant) and N formed a partnership that sold fine rugs and carpets. In 1958, they incorporated the business, and E and N became its first directors, but shortly afterwards, G (N's son) also became a director. Between them, N and G held the majority of the company's shares. In 1969, a dispute arose, and N and G used their majority shareholding to vote E out of office. At the time, the remedy found in the CA 2006, s 994, did not exist, so E petitioned the court for a winding-up order.

HELD: The House of Lords stated that, in many companies, the rights of the members would be exhaustively stated in the company's constitution. But certain companies, known as 'quasi-partnerships', also conducted business based on legitimate expectations and

---

72. *Re London and County Coal Co* (1866) LR 3 Eq 355.

73. *Re Walter Jacob Ltd* [1989] BCLC 345 (CA).

74. *Re Yenidje Tobacco Co Ltd* [1916] 2 Ch 426 (CA).

75. *Re German Date Coffee Co* (1882) 20 Ch D 169 (CA).

76. CA 2006, s 31(1).

77. *Loch v John Blackwood Ltd* [1924] AC 783 (PC).

78. *Re Five Minute Car Wash Service Ltd* [1966] 1 WLR 745 (Ch).

agreements made between the members, and, in such companies, effect should be given to such expectations and agreements.

Although the characteristics of quasi-partnerships cannot be exhaustively stated, the House stated that, typically, quasi-partnerships would display all, or some, of the following characteristics:

- the company will be an association formed on the basis of mutual trust and confidence;

- there will be an agreement that some, or all, of the shareholders will be involved in management; and

- the shares of the company will not be freely marketable, thereby locking an aggrieved shareholder into the company.

The defendant company was clearly a quasi-partnership and had been formed on the understanding that all of the shareholders would participate in management. Because this understanding had been breached, the House ordered the company to be wound up.

COMMENT: This case demonstrates that where a company is a quasi-partnership, the conduct of the majority should not be judged purely based on the rights of the parties, but also by the legitimate expectations of the parties and any informal agreements that existed between them. The courts have confirmed on multiple occasions that, in most quasi-partnerships, there will be an expectation that all of the shareholders will participate in management and that exclusion of a shareholder from management will be likely to justify the winding up of the company.[79]

 See DD Prentice, 'Winding Up on the Just and Equitable Ground: The Partnership Analogy' (1973) 89 LQR 107

Key points summary

- The Insolvency Act 1986, s 122(1)(g), allows the court to wind up a company where it considers it just and equitable to do so.

- The court will not wind up a company where an alternative remedy is available and the petitioner is acting unreasonably in seeking the winding up.

- Winding up may be appropriate where:
  - the company is fraudulently promoted or set up for a fraudulent purpose;
  - the company is deadlocked;
  - it becomes impossible for the company to fulfil its objects; or
  - the directors display a lack of probity.

- Where the company is a quasi-partnership, the court may order a winding up where the legitimate expectations of the shareholders are denied. In many cases, this would involve the shareholder's expectation to be involved in the management of the company.

---

79. See, e.g., *Re Davis and Collett Ltd* [1935] Ch 693 (Ch); *Tay Bok Choon v Tahansan Sdn Bhd* [1987] 1 WLR 413 (PC).

Chapter conclusion

The law relating to shareholder remedies can be complex and there is considerable overlap between the four remedies discussed. The ability to enforce the provisions of the constitution is useful, but only those provisions relating to membership rights can be enforced and determining what constitutes a membership right is not always straightforward, especially where the company is a quasi-partnership. The instances in which a member can commence an action on behalf of the company have been slightly extended and clarified by the introduction of the statutory derivative claim, but whether it encourages derivative claimants to commence proceedings remains to be seen. The unfair prejudice remedy remains the same as it was under the CA 1985, and is likely to remain the most popular and broad shareholder remedy. But the CA 2006 has done nothing to remedy the practical problems associated with unfair prejudice claims—namely, excessive length and cost. Finally, a member has the option of petitioning the court for a winding-up order. Such a remedy will almost always be a remedy of last resort and certain decisions of the courts have further narrowed its scope in practice. The introduction of the unfair prejudice remedy has had a marked impact upon the other remedies. One could argue that the time may be approaching for the consolidation of shareholder remedies, but, at the moment, such a reform is unlikely. The Law Commission recommended that the courts should be able to make a winding-up order in cases of unfair prejudice,[80] thereby effectively consolidating s 994 and s 122(1)(g) into one remedy, but it was felt by the Company Law Review Steering Group that this remedy would be open to abuse and so the recommendation was never adopted.

Self-test questions

1. Define the following:
   (a) qua;
   (b) derivative claim;
   (c) reflective loss;
   (d) legitimate expectations;
   (e) quasi-partnership.

2. Explain how the contract created by the company's constitution differs from a normal contract. What limits are placed upon the parties' ability to enforce the other to observe the provisions of the constitution?

3. The articles of Sims Ltd provide that a director can only be removed from office by special resolution. Jeremy, who is a director and member of Sims Ltd, is removed at a general meeting, but the resolution removing him was an ordinary one. Is the removal valid and does Jeremy have a remedy?

4. 'The unfair prejudice remedy is the principal source of redress for an aggrieved shareholder. In fact the remedy under the CA 2006, s 994 is so useful that the derivative claim and the winding up remedy are no longer required.' Do you agree with this statement? Provide reasons for your answer.

---

80. Law Commission, *Shareholder Remedies* (Law Com No 246, Cm 3759, HMSO, London, 1997) [4.35].

Further reading

Chesterman, MR, 'The "Just and Equitable" Winding Up of Small Private Companies' (1973) 36 MLR 129
Discusses the winding-up remedy found in the Insolvency Act 1986, s 122(1)(g), focusing on its use in relation to quasi-partnerships

Davies, PL, *Gower & Davies' Principles of Modern Company Law* (8th edn, Sweet & Maxwell, London, 2008) ch 20
A detailed, yet lucid, account of the unfair prejudice remedy and the ability to petition the court for a winding-up order on just and equitable grounds

French, D, Mayson, S, and Ryan, C, *Mayson, French, & Ryan on Company Law* (25th edn, OUP, Oxford, 2008) pp 76–89
Discusses the legal effect of the constitution and the extent to which the provisions of the constitution can be enforced

Law Commission, *Shareholder Remedies: Consultation Paper* (Law Com CP No 142, HMSO, London, 1996)
A Consultation Paper that discusses the contract created by the constitution, the rule in Foss v Harbottle, *the unfair prejudicial remedy, and the winding up remedy*

Mitchell, C, 'Shareholders' Claims for Reflective Loss' (2004) 120 LQR 457
Provides a readable and analytical account of the 'no reflective loss' principle

Poole, J, and Roberts, P, 'Shareholder Remedies: Efficient Litigation and the Unfair Prejudice Remedy' (1999) JBL 38
Discusses the Law Commission's proposed reforms of the unfair prejudice remedy, focusing on those measures designed to make s 994 cases less lengthy and costly

Von Nessen, P, Goo, SH, and Keong Low, C, 'The Statutory Derivative Action: Now Showing Near You' (2008) JBL 627
Discusses the worldwide proliferation of the statutory derivative claim and examines how such derivative claims operate in the UK, Commonwealth countries, the USA, and Hong Kong

Wedderburn, KW, 'Shareholders' Rights and the Rule in *Foss v Harbottle*' [1957] CLJ 194
Despite its age, this remains a seminal article on the ability of a member to enforce the constitution and how this ability relates to the rule in Foss v Harbottle

 Remember to visit the **Online Resource Centre** at **<http://www. oxfordtextbooks.co.uk/roach>** to access the following resources on Chapter 21, 'Shareholders' remedies': more **practice questions** and answers; a **glossary** of key terms; **multiple-choice questions**; **revision summaries**; **audio updates** when relevant; and **audio exam advice** on this key topic.

22 Corporate rescue, insolvency, and dissolution

- Fostering a 'rescue culture'
- Administration
- Company voluntary arrangements
- Receivership
- Liquidation
- Dissolution

INTRODUCTION

This final chapter relating to company law discusses the various procedures available to companies that are experiencing financial difficulties that could jeopardize their survival. A company need not utilize any of these procedures and may simply attempt to trade its way out of difficulty, but, in many cases, such a strategy will not prove successful, and the company will either need the aid of the law in order to become profitable again, or it will decide that there is no prospect of avoiding insolvency and enter into a process whereby it is brought to an end. This chapter discusses those procedures that:

- aim to help struggling companies;
- allow creditors of the company to recover monies owed; and
- bring about the death of a company and provide for the distribution of its remaining assets.

Fostering a 'rescue culture'

The failure of a company and its subsequent liquidation can have a substantial effect on a significant number of persons:

- the company's employees will lose their jobs;
- the company's creditors are unlikely to recover the full extent of the debt owed to them;
- the company's members will lose the value of their investment and their shares are likely to become worthless;
- suppliers that relied on the company may be forced into liquidation;
- retailers that sold the company's goods may be adversely affected;

- if the company is a large national or multinational company, it can even adversely affect the national economy in which it is based.

One would therefore assume that the law would be keen to prevent companies from becoming insolvent and would put mechanisms in place to help companies in a financially precarious position. But prior to the passing of the Insolvency Act 1985 and its replacement by the Insolvency Act 1986 (IA 1986), the law did little to help, and struggling companies were basically 'left to die'.

The problem is one of balancing interests. The pre-1985 law protected creditors by seeking to ensure that the creditors received as much of the money owed to them as possible. But the result of this was invariably that the company was liquidated and dissolved, even where it could have been saved. Alternatively, one can contend that the law should seek to aid financially vulnerable companies by creating a 'rescue culture', whereby such companies are encouraged to attempt to return to profitability. Of course, if the attempt fails, the company's assets will be depleted further and the creditors will receive even less than they would have done had the company been promptly liquidated.

The 1982 Cork Report[1] firmly favoured the fostering of a rescue culture, and this was reflected in the Insolvency Acts of 1985 and 1986, which established a number of mechanisms primarily aimed at providing a means 'for the preservation of viable commercial enterprises capable of making a useful contribution to the economic life of the country',[2] the principal one of which being administration. Whilst it is still the case that most insolvent companies are liquidated, administration has been used successfully either to rescue a company, or to result in a more advantageous winding up.

Administration

In January 2009, the UK officially entered a recession for the first time since 1991. The preceding few months were notable for the unprecedented number of prominent high-street companies that went into administration (for example, The Pier, Woolworths, Zavvi, USC, Whittard of Chelsea, and MFI). In such difficult economic times, the value of the administration procedure is greater than ever. Administration was introduced by the IA 1986 and is a clear example of the law's desire to foster an increased rescue culture. Indeed, the procedure itself is very similar to the pro-rescue provisions of ch 11 of the US Federal Bankruptcy Code.

The pro-rescue nature of the procedure is evidenced in the hierarchy of objectives that the administrator is appointed to realize:

(i) rescuing the company as a going concern, or
(ii) achieving a better result for the company's creditors as a whole than would be likely if the company were wound up (without first being in administration), or
(iii) realising property in order to make a distribution to one or more secured or preferential creditors.[3]

---

1. *Report of the Review Committee on Insolvency Law and Practice* (Cmnd 8558, HMSO, London, 1982).
2. Ibid, [198].
3. IA 1986, Sch B1, para 3(1).

The principal purpose of administration is therefore objective (i) (that is, to rescue the company as a going concern) and the administrator must perform his functions with this objective solely in mind unless he believes that rescue is not a reasonably practicable objective, or that objective (ii) would achieve a better result for the company's creditors as a whole.[4] An administrator should only aim to achieve objective (iii) if it is not reasonably practicable to achieve objectives (i) or (ii), and he does not unnecessarily harm the interests of the creditors as a whole.[5]

Certainly, when compared with liquidation, administration can have a number of beneficial effects:

- it is likely to be cheaper than liquidation;
- it may allow the sale of a going concern, rather than a 'fire sale' on liquidation, during which the assets are sold off for whatever price the liquidator can get;
- it allows a company currently trading profitably, but burdened by debt from past unsuccessful enterprises, to trade on with some form of debt moratorium or restructuring operating; and
- it means that creditors (including directors and employees) may have better prospects of payment than they do in a liquidation.

The appointment of an administrator

The appointment of an administrator places the company 'in administration'. An administrator may be appointed in one of several ways, as follows.

- *Appointment by the court*   A court may make an administrative order appointing a person as the administrator of a company.[6] Only the company, its directors, or one or more of the company's creditors may make an application for an administration order.[7] Prior to the Enterprise Act 2002, this was the only method of appointing an administrator. The court may only make an administration order if it is satisfied that:
  - the company is likely to become unable to pay its debts; or
  - that the administration order is reasonably likely to achieve the purpose of administration.[8]
- *Appointment by a floating charge holder*   An administrator may be appointed out of court by the holder of a qualifying floating charge (that is, the holder of one or more debentures of the company secured by such a charge).[9] A qualifying floating charge is one that, alone or in combination with other floating charges, relates to the whole, or substantially the whole, of the company's property and the instrument creating which states that:
  - IA 1986, Sch B1, para 14 (the provision that governs appointment by a floating charge holder), applies to the floating charge;
  - the charge holder is purported to be empowered to appoint an administrator; and

Floating charges are discussed at p 669

---

4. Ibid, para 3(3).   5. Ibid, para 4(4).
6. Ibid, para 10.   7. Ibid, para 12(1).
8. Ibid, para 11.   9. Ibid, para 14.

   – the charge holder is purported to be empowered to appoint an administrative receiver.[10]

- *Appointment by the company or its directors* An administrator may be appointed out of court by either the company or its directors.[11] At least five business days' written notice must be given to anyone who is, or may be entitled to, appoint an administrative receiver and to floating charge holders, and this notice must identify the proposed administrator.[12] The proposed administrator can be appointed as the actual administrator upon the expiry of the notice, or before that time, if each person to whom written notice has been given has given written consent.[13] The appointment must be made within ten business days, beginning on the date on which notice of intention to appoint has been filed with the court.[14] To prevent the company or its directors from abusing the procedure and obtaining a continuous moratorium, this procedure cannot be used within twelve months of the ending of a previous administration.[15]

The powers of an administrator

The effect of an administrator's appointment is substantial. The administrator will manage the company's affairs and the directors can no longer exercise any managerial powers without the administrator's consent.[16] In effect, the administrator becomes the board. Accordingly, an administrator is given extremely wide-ranging powers. IA 1986, Sch B1, para 59(1), provides that '[t]he administrator of a company may do anything necessary or expedient for the management of the affairs, business and property of the company'. Schedule 1 then provides an extensive list of specific powers afforded to the administrator, including the power to:

- take possession of, collect, and get in the property of the company, and, for that purpose, to take such proceedings as may seem to him expedient;
- sell or otherwise dispose of the property of the company by public auction or private contract;
- raise or borrow money and grant security therefor over the property of the company;
- bring or defend any action or other legal proceedings in the name and on behalf of the company;
- use the company's seal;
- draw, accept, make, and endorse any bill of exchange or promissory note in the name and on behalf of the company;
- make any payment that is necessary or incidental to the performance of his functions;
- carry on the business of the company and establish subsidiaries of the company;
- present or defend a petition for the winding up of the company.

All of these powers are granted to the administrator so that he may achieve the objectives of administration discussed above.

---

10. Ibid, para 14(2) and (3).   11. Ibid, para 22.
12. Ibid, para 26.   13. Ibid, para 28(1).
14. Ibid, para 28(2).   15. Ibid, para 23.
16. Ibid, para 64(1).

The administrator must make a statement setting out how he proposes to achieve these objectives.[17] This statement must be sent to:

- the Registrar of Companies;
- every creditor of whose claim and address the administrator is aware; and
- every member of whose address the administrator is aware.[18]

Within ten weeks of the company entering into administration, the administrator's proposals must be put to a meeting of the company's creditors.[19] A failure to hold such a meeting without reasonable excuse constitutes a criminal offence,[20] punishable by a fine not exceeding one fifth of the statutory maximum (that is, £1,000).[21] The meeting may approve, modify, or reject the proposals, but whatever the outcome, the result of the meeting must be reported to the court. If the creditors approve the proposals, the administrator is under a duty to exercise his powers in accordance with the approved proposals.[22] But if the proposals are rejected, the court may:

- terminate the administrator's appointment;
- adjourn the hearing conditionally or unconditionally;
- make an interim order;
- make an order on a petition for winding up; or
- make any other order (including an order making consequential provision) that it thinks appropriate.[23]

The statutory moratorium

Perhaps the most beneficial aspect of administration is the imposition of the statutory moratorium. The principal objective of administration (that is, to rescue the company as a going concern) would be frustrated if the company's creditors were then able to enforce their security. Accordingly, Sch B1, para 43, provides that, unless permission has been obtained from the administrator or the court, no creditor may, during the period of the administration:

- take steps to enforce security over the company's property;
- take steps to repossess goods in the company's possession under a hire-purchase agreement;
- institute or continue any legal process (including legal proceedings, execution, and distress) against the company or property of the company.

In addition, during the period of administration, an administrative receiver cannot be appointed[24] and a winding-up order cannot be made (except a public interest winding-up order made on application by the Secretary of State).[25] The purpose of the moratorium is clear: it grants the company vital breathing space, and allows the

17. Ibid, para 49(1). 18. Ibid, para 49(4).
19. Ibid, para 51(2). 20. Ibid, para 51(5).
21. Ibid, Sch 10. 22. Ibid, Sch B1, para 53(1).
23. Ibid, para 55(2). 24. Ibid, para 43(6A).
25. Ibid, para 42.

administrator to put his proposals into effect and enter into arrangements with the creditors, with the aim of rescuing the company.

The termination of administration

A company can exit administration in a number of different ways, including the following.

- A creditor or member may apply to the court for a remedy on the grounds that:
  - the administrator's actions are unfairly harming (or his proposed actions will unfairly harm) the applicant's interests; or
  - the administrator is not performing his functions as quickly or as efficiently as is reasonably practicable.
- In either case, the court may order the termination of the administrator's appointment.[26]
- The appointment of an administrator will automatically end after one year from the date of appointment, but this can be extended:
  - by the court; or
  - with the consent of the creditors.[27]
- Upon an application from the administrator, the court can terminate an administrator's appointment.[28]
- An administrator's appointment will be terminated where he files a notice with the court and the Registrar of Companies stating that the purpose of the administration has been sufficiently achieved.[29]
- A creditor can apply for a court order terminating the administrator's appointment on the grounds of improper motive on the part of the administrator, or on the part of the person who appointed the administrator.[30]
- The administrator's appointment must be terminated where the court orders a winding up on public interest grounds.[31]
- The administrator's appointment will cease if he sends notice to the Registrar of Companies indicating that he intends to place the company into a creditors' voluntary liquidation,[32] or that he intends to dissolve it.[33]
- As already noted, the court may terminate the administrator's appointment if the creditors fail to approve the administrator's proposals.

‹› Key points summary

- The principal aim of administration is to rescue the company as a going concern. If this is not reasonably practicable, the administrator should aim to achieve a better result for the company's creditors than would be available if the company were to be wound up.

26. Ibid, para 74(1), (2), and (4)(d).   27. Ibid, para 76.
28. Ibid, para 79.   29. Ibid, para 80.
30. Ibid, para 81.   31. Ibid, para 82.
32. Ibid, para 83.   33. Ibid, para 84.

- The appointment of an administrator places the company 'in administration'. An administrator may be appointed by:
  - the court;
  - a floating charge holder; or
  - the company or its directors.

- A company in administration is subject to a statutory moratorium, which prevents creditors from enforcing security, repossessing goods, or continuing any legal process against the company or its property.

Company voluntary arrangements

The company voluntary arrangement (CVA) is an important, but much underused,[34] rescue procedure that basically allows a company to enter into a binding scheme or arrangement with its creditors. There are two types of CVA:

- the standard CVA, which does not provide a moratorium; and
- a CVA available to 'eligible companies', which does provide a moratorium.

Commencement of a CVA

The proposal

The first step in entering into a CVA is the proposal of a scheme or arrangement. The creators of the proposal will depend upon the status of the company. If the company is in administration, the administrator will propose the arrangement.[35] If the company is in liquidation, the liquidator will propose the arrangement.[36] If the company is in neither administration nor liquidation, the directors will make the proposal.[37] Neither the company's members nor its creditors can propose a CVA. An arrangement proposed by an administrator or liquidator can be supervised by that administrator or liquidator, but if it is not, or if the arrangement is proposed by the directors, it will need to be supervised by a qualified insolvency practitioner or by some other authorized person,[38] who is known as the 'nominee'.

Within twenty-eight days of receiving notice of the directors' proposal (or such longer period as the court may allow), the nominee must submit a report to the court stating:

- whether, in his opinion, the proposed voluntary arrangement has a reasonable prospect of being approved and implemented;
- whether, in his opinion, meetings of the company and of its creditors should be summoned to consider the proposal; and

---

34. Companies House, *Statistical Tables on Companies Registration Activities 2007–08* (BERR, London, 2008). Table C2 states that, in 2007–08, there were 19,215 liquidations, compared with only 462 CVAs.
35. IA 1986, s 1(3)(a).   36. Ibid, s 1(3)(b).
37. Ibid, s 1(1).   38. Ibid, s 1(2).

- if in his opinion such meetings should be summoned, the date on which, and time and place at which, he proposes that the meetings should be held.[39]

Approval

Where the nominee's report states that meetings of the company (that is, a meeting of the members) and creditors should be convened, the nominee should convene such meetings, unless the court directs otherwise.[40] These meetings, which are normally chaired by the nominee, must decide whether to approve, modify, or reject the proposal. But no proposal or modification can be approved if it:

- affects the right of a secured creditor of the company to enforce his security, except with the concurrence of the creditor concerned;[41]
- affects the priority of any preferential debt, unless the preferential creditor concerned concurs.[42]

Approval is granted if:

- at the creditors' meeting, a majority in excess of three-quarters in value of the creditors present in person or by proxy vote on the resolution;[43] and
- at the meeting of the company, a majority in excess of half in value of the members present in person or by proxy vote on the resolution.[44]

If the decisions of the two meetings conflict, the decision of the creditors' meeting prevails.[45] But a member may, within twenty-eight days, apply to the court, which may order that the decision of the members' meeting shall have effect, or make any other order that it sees fit.[46] If the proposal is approved, it binds every person who was entitled to vote at, or who would have been entitled to vote at had they had notice of, the creditors' meeting.[47] But within twenty-eight days of the relevant report of the meeting being given to the court, an application to the court may be made on the grounds that the CVA:

- unfairly prejudices the interests of a creditor, member, or contributory of the company; or
- that there has been some material irregularity at or in relation to either of the meetings.[48]

Such an application can be made by the nominee, the liquidator, or administrator (if the company is in liquidation or administration, respectively), or anyone who had the right to vote at any of the meetings.[49] If the court agrees with the applicant, it can

---

39. Ibid, s 2(2).
40. Ibid, s 3(1). Where the nominee is the administrator or liquidator who proposed the arrangement, such meetings must be convened: s 3(2).
41. Ibid, s 4(3).
42. Ibid, s 4(4).
43. The Insolvency Rules 1986, SI 1986/1925, r 1.19.1.
44. Ibid, r 1.20.1.
45. IA 1986, s 4A(2).
46. Ibid, s 4A(3)–(6).
47. Ibid, s 5(2).
48. Ibid, s 6(1) and (3)(a).
49. Ibid, s 6(2).

revoke or suspend any decision approving the CVA, or give directions for a further meeting to be convened to consider a revised proposal.[50]

'Eligible companies' and the moratorium

As noted, CVAs are useful, but underused. One significant reason for this is that it is relatively easy for an aggrieved creditor to derail an arrangement proposed by the directors by appointing an administrator or receiver, or by petitioning the court for a winding-up order. To combat this, a new form of CVA was introduced that is identical to the one above, but which provides for a 28-day moratorium (which may be extended by a further two months) whilst the proposal is being considered.

During this moratorium:

- no petition may be presented, or resolution passed, that orders the winding up of the company;
- an administrator or administrative receiver may not be appointed;
- no other steps may be taken to enforce any security over the company's property, or to repossess goods in the company's possession under any hire-purchase agreement, except with the leave of the court and subject to such terms as the court may impose.[51]

A CVA with a moratorium is, however, only available to 'eligible companies'— namely, companies that satisfy any two of three criteria for being a small company:

1. a turnover of no more than £6.5 million;
2. a balance sheet total of no more than £3.26 million; and
3. employees numbering no more than fifty.[52]

The moratorium is certainly useful, but it could be argued that its usefulness is outweighed by the complex nature of the procedures for obtaining it and the fact that administration appears to be a much more effective (and certainly much more popular) procedure. From the point of view of the directors, however, the obvious advantage of a CVA over administration is that they remain in control of the company.

 Key points summary

- A company voluntary arrangement allows the company to enter into a binding scheme or arrangement with its creditors.

- In order for a CVA to come into effect, a proposal will need to be created and approved. The creator of the proposal depends on the status of the company (for example, if the company is in administration, the administrator will create the proposal).

- A CVA with a 28-day moratorium is available to companies defined as small by the Companies Act 2006.

---

50. Ibid, s 6(4).   51. Ibid, Sch A1, para 12.
52. Ibid, para 3; CA 2006, s 382.

Receivership

Receivership is a mechanism by which a secured creditor can recover payment owed. The usual procedure is that the secured creditor appoints a receiver, who then takes control of the charged assets and uses them to satisfy the debt of the creditor who appointed him.

A receiver can be appointed in one of two ways, as follows.

- The court can appoint a receiver upon an application from a creditor. If the application is successful, the Official Receiver attached to the court will act on behalf of the applicants.[53]

- The instrument creating the charge confers upon the charge holder the power to appoint a receiver without the need to apply to the court. The majority of receivers are appointed this way.

There are restrictions on who can be appointed as a receiver, as follows.

- A body corporate (that is, a company or limited liability partnership) is not qualified for appointment as a receiver and a body corporate that acts as a receiver is liable, on summary conviction, to pay a fine not exceeding the statutory maximum (currently £5,000). On conviction on indictment, there is no limit to the fine that can be imposed.[54]

- An undischarged bankrupt commits an offence if he acts as a receiver, unless the court has appointed him.[55] On summary conviction, the offence is punishable by a term of imprisonment not exceeding six months and/or a fine not exceeding the statutory maximum (currently £5,000).[56] On conviction on indictment, the maximum prison sentence is two years and there is no limit to the fine that can be imposed.[57]

Once a receiver has been appointed, every invoice, order for goods or services, business letter, or order form (whether in hard copy, electronic, or any other form) issued by or on behalf of the company, or the receiver, or manager, or the liquidator of the company, and all of the company's websites, must contain a statement stating that a receiver has been appointed.[58] Failure to make such a statement constitutes a criminal offence committed by the company and any officer of the company, liquidator, receiver, or manager who knowingly and wilfully authorizes or permits the default.[59] The offence is punishable by a fine not exceeding one fifth of the statutory maximum (that is, £1,000).[60]

The role of a receiver

The role of the receiver and the obligations that he owes depend upon the nature of his appointment. Where a person is appointed solely to act as a receiver, his principal duty will be to realize the charged assets and to satisfy the debt of the creditor who appointed him. He will have power only to deal with the charged assets and will have no general powers of management (in turn, the directors will lose the

---

53. IA 1986, s 32.   54. Ibid, s 30 and Sch 10.
55. Ibid, s 31.   56. Ibid, Sch 10.
57. Ibid.   58. Ibid, s 39(1).
59. Ibid, s 39(2).   60. Ibid, Sch 10.

power to deal with the charged assets if they had such a power). But it is usual for the instrument creating the security to provide that the receiver will be an agent of the company, and he will therefore be able to enter into contracts and engage in other acts on the company's behalf. The receiver's principal duty is to the creditor who appointed him[61] and he is free to subordinate the interests of the company, or the other creditors, to those of his client. This can be contrasted with an administrator, whose principal function is to rescue the company, or, if that is not reasonably practicable, to secure a result that is beneficial to the creditors as a whole.

It is increasingly common for a person to be appointed as both receiver and manager. In such a case, the person will have the normal powers of a receiver discussed above, but will also have a general power to manage the company (and this power displaces that of the directors, although the directors still retain office). Because the receiver's powers are limited to the charged assets, however, a general power of management arises only in relation to a floating charge taken over the whole of the undertaking.

Administrative receivership

A special form of receiver must be mentioned—namely, an administrative receiver. The office of administrative receiver was created by the Insolvency Act 1985 and has been largely abolished by the Enterprise Act 2002. The right to appoint an administrative receiver is granted only to floating charge holders who registered their charges before 15 September 2003 and whose charge covers the whole, or substantially the whole, of the company's property.[62] Floating charge holders whose charges were registered after this date cannot appoint an administrative receiver, but, as noted above, can appoint an administrator.[63] This is a significant reform and a clear indication of the law's desire to foster a rescue culture.

The administrative receiver has the sole right to deal with the charged assets. Given the breadth of the charges that permitted the appointment of an administrative receiver, this usually means that the directors cease to manage the company, although they remain in office. Administrative receivers are agents of the company[64] and so can engage in acts on the company's behalf, but unlike other agents, administrative receivers are personally liable for any contracts entered into by them in the carrying out of their functions (except in so far as the contract of appointment provides otherwise).[65] Like a normal receiver, an administrative receiver is tasked with realizing the charged assets and satisfying the debt of the floating charge holder who appointed him. But certain debts rank ahead of those of floating charge holders (for example, preferential debts) and these debts must be paid out of the proceeds of the charged assets before the floating charge holder can be paid.

The ranking of debts and the distribution of assets are discussed at p 768

---

61. Where a receiver is appointed by the court, he is accountable to the court and so need not obey the instruction of the creditor who applied for his appointment.
62. IA 1986, s 29(2).
63. Ibid, Sch B1, para 14(1). Floating charge holders with the right to appoint an administrative receiver also have the right to appoint an administrator.
64. Ibid, s 44(1)(a). The agency ends if the company goes into liquidation.
65. Ibid, s 44(1)(b). But an administrative receiver can obtain an indemnity from the company in respect of such liability (s 44(1)(c)).

Once his task is complete, the administrative receiver's relationship with that company ends and the directors regain their powers (although, by this time, the company usually has few assets left to manage and its liquidation is likely).

 Key points summary

- Receivership is a mechanism whereby a secured creditor can recover payment owed.

- The court can appoint a receiver, or the instrument creating the charge can grant the holder the power to appoint a receiver.

- It is a criminal offence for a body corporate or an undischarged bankrupt to act as a receiver.

Liquidation

In many cases, corporate rescue is not possible and a company that cannot trade out of its difficulties will usually be liquidated (also known as 'winding up'). Liquidation is the final step before a company's death. It is the process whereby the assets of the company are collected and realized, its debts and liabilities paid, and the surplus distributed to the members. Liquidations come in two forms:

1. compulsory; and
2. voluntary.

Compulsory winding up

A compulsory winding up occurs where a specified party petitions the court to have a company wound up on specified grounds. The court then has the discretion whether or not to order the company's winding up. In 2007–08, there were 5,882 compulsory winding-up orders made by the courts in England and Wales.[66] The court has no ability to wind up a company on its own initiative: a compulsory winding-up order can only be made following a petition.

The IA 1986 states that the following may petition the court for a compulsory winding-up order:

- the company itself;[67]
- the directors of the company;[68]
- any creditor(s) of the company (including contingent or prospective creditors);[69]

---

66. Companies House, *Statistical Tables on Companies Registration Activities 2007–08* (BERR, London, 2008) Table C2.
67. IA 1986, s 124(1).
68. Ibid.
69. Ibid.

- a contributory of the company[70] (that is, any person who is liable to contribute to the assets of the company in the event of it being wound up,[71] an obvious example being a member of the company);
- the Secretary of State, provided that:
  - where the company is a public company, it has not been issued with a trading certificate and more than a year has expired since the company was registered;[72] or
  - the company is not already in the process of being compulsorily wound up and it appears to the Secretary of State that it is in the public interest that the company be wound up;[73]
- an official receiver, but only if the company is in the process of being voluntarily wound up;[74]
- an administrative receiver;[75]
- an administrator.[76]

The court will only consider a petition from the above parties on specified grounds.

Grounds for winding up

Section 122(1) provides specified grounds upon which a compulsory winding-up order may be made:

- where the company has, by special resolution, resolved that the company be wound up by the court;
- where a public company has not been issued with a trading certificate and more than a year has expired since its registration;
- where a company is an 'old public company';[77]
- where the company does not commence its business within a year from its incorporation, or suspends its business for a whole year;
- where the company is unable to pay its debts;
- where a moratorium attached to a CVA ends and there is no approved voluntary arrangement in effect;
- where the court is of the opinion that it is just and equitable that the company should be wound up.

Winding up on just and equitable grounds is discussed at p 740

The vast majority of compulsory winding-up orders made are made on the ground that the company is unable to pay its debts and, of orders sought under this ground, the vast majority of the petitions made are by a creditor (usually the one whose debt the company has been unable to meet).

---

70. Ibid.
71. Ibid, 79(1).
72. Ibid, s 124(4)(a).
73. Ibid, ss 124(4)(b) and 124A.
74. Ibid, s 124(5).
75. Ibid, s 42(1) and Sch 1, para 21.
76. Ibid, Sch B1, para 60, and Sch 1, para 21.
77. The Companies Consolidation (Consequential Provisions) Act 1985, s 1(1), defines an 'old public company' as a company that existed on 22 December 1980 and has not, since that date or the date of its registration, re-registered as a public or private company.

Despite the wording used, a creditor will not need to establish that the company cannot pay any of its debts; rather, failure to pay one debt will suffice. This is reinforced by the s 123(1), which states that a company will be unable to pay its debts if:

- a creditor who is owed a sum exceeding £750 makes a written demand for payment and, three weeks later, the sum has not been paid, or security acceptable to the creditor has not been given; or

- execution or other process issued on a judgment, decree, or order of any court in favour of a creditor of the company is returned unsatisfied in whole or in part; or

- it is proved to the satisfaction of the court that the company is unable to pay its debts as they fall due.

Again, however, it should be stressed that the court is not bound to make a winding-up order if any of the above requirements are met. For example, a creditor may decide to petition the court for a winding-up order on the ground that petitioning for a winding-up order may, in terms of recovering monies owed, be less troublesome than commencing a direct action to recover the debt. The court may regard this as an abuse of the system and refuse to make such an order.[78] In any case, the court may want to determine the wishes of the creditors or contributories, and, to this end, the IA 1986, s 195(1), allows the court to call meetings of the creditors or contributories to determine whether or not such parties would wish for the company to be wound up.

Consequences of a compulsory winding up

If the court orders that a company should be wound up, the Official Receiver attached to the court will become the company's liquidator until such time as another is appointed.[79] The role and powers of a liquidator will be discussed later, but his function is to gather in the assets of the company and distribute them to persons entitled to such assets. It may be the case that the company's assets are insufficient even to cover the liquidator's fees. In such a case, the liquidator will usually— provided that the affairs of the company do not require further examination—apply to the Registrar of Companies for early dissolution of the company.[80] The creditors and contributories also have the power to appoint a liquidation committee,[81] and this committee, as we will see, is granted various powers under the IA 1986.

If a court decides to order a winding up, depending on the facts, a number of consequences may follow.

- In all cases, the company must forward a copy of the winding-up order to the Registrar of Companies,[82] who will then publish notice of the winding up in the *Gazette*.

- The court may stay any proceedings currently outstanding against the company.[83]

---

78. *London Wharfing Co* (1866) 35 Beav 37.
79. IA 1986, s 136(2).
80. Ibid, s 202.
81. Ibid, s 141(1).
82. Ibid, s 130(1).
83. Ibid, s 126.

- In all cases, once a winding up has been commenced, any disposition of the company's property, and any transfer of shares, or alteration in the status of the company's members, are void unless authorized by the court.[84]

- Although not expressly stated in the IA 1986, the powers of the directors will cease upon the appointment of a liquidator,[85] and, whilst it is not settled, the weight of authority would appear to indicate that the directors cease to hold office upon the appointment of a compulsory liquidator.[86] Given this, the directors have the right to appeal the winding-up order, because the cessation of their powers derives from the order, which they may wish to contest.[87]

- The company's employees are dismissed, although the liquidator may reappoint them.

- The business of the company will normally cease, although the liquidator may, upon obtaining permission from the court, carry on the business of the company in order to realize the most beneficial distribution of assets.[88]

- Any floating charges taken over the company's assets will crystallize.

Floating charges are discussed at p 669

Voluntary winding up

The majority of windings up do not occur due to an order from the court, but occur voluntarily. In 2007–08, of the 19,215 company liquidations in England and Wales, 12,245 were voluntary.[89]

A company can be voluntarily wound up in one of two ways:

- a members' voluntary winding up; or
- a creditors' voluntary winding up.

In both cases, the winding up is commenced by the members passing a special resolution stating that the company is to be wound up voluntarily.[90] The distinction lies in whether or not a declaration of solvency is made. Where a majority of the company's directors make such a declaration, the winding up will be a members' winding up and the creditors will likely be paid in full. Where no such declaration is made, the winding up will be a creditors' winding up[91] and the creditor may not be paid in full.

The declaration of solvency

In order for a winding up to be a members' winding up, a majority of the directors must, within the five weeks preceding the passing of the resolution,[92] make a declaration of solvency. This declaration must state that the directors have made a full

---

84. Ibid, s 127.

85. *Re Farrow's Bank Ltd* [1921] 2 Ch 164 (CA).

86. *Measures Brothers Ltd v Measures* [1910] 2 Ch 248 (CA); cf *Madrid Bank Ltd* (1866) 2 QB 37.

87. *Re Diamond Fuel Co* (1879) 13 Ch D 400 (CA).

88. IA 1986, s 167(1)(a).

89. Companies House, *Statistical Tables on Companies Registration Activities 2007–08* (BERR, London, 2008) Table C2.

90. IA 1986, s 84(1)(b).

91. Ibid, s 90.

92. Ibid, s 89(1) and (2).

inquiry into the company's affairs and that, having done so, they have formed the opinion that the company will be able to pay its debts in full, together with interest at the official rate, within such period, not exceeding twelve months from the commencement of the winding up, as may be specified in the declaration.[93] The declaration must be delivered to the Registrar of Companies within fifteen days of the resolution being passed.[94] Failure to do so constitutes a summary offence by every officer in default,[95] punishable by a fine not exceeding one fifth of the statutory maximum[96] (that is, £1,000).

Any director who makes a declaration of solvency without reasonable grounds for the opinion expressed in it commits an either-way offence.[97] On summary conviction, the maximum penalty is six months' imprisonment and/or a fine not exceeding the statutory maximum (currently £5,000).[98] On conviction on indictment, the maximum penalty is two years' imprisonment and/or a fine.[99]

The appointment of a liquidator

In the case of a members' voluntary winding up, it is the members in general meeting who will appoint a liquidator[100] and this will normally take place at the meeting at which the general meeting resolved to wind up the company.

In the case of a creditors' winding up, the members may also appoint a liquidator, but, no more than fourteen days after the resolution winding up the company was passed, the company must summon a meeting of its creditors.[101] If, at this meeting, the creditors do not approve of the members' choice of liquidator, they may nominate a person to replace the member's choice and this person will become the liquidator.[102] The creditors also have the power to appoint a liquidation committee of not more than five persons.[103] Where such a committee is appointed, the company may also nominate five persons to sit on the committee, but the creditors may veto any or all of the company's nominations, whereupon they will not form part of the liquidation committee unless the court directs otherwise. The court can also appoint other persons to act in place of the company's nominees.[104]

Consequences of a voluntary winding up

Once the resolution has been passed, the voluntary winding up is deemed to commence,[105] and several consequences follow.

- The company ceases to carry on business, except so far as may be required for its beneficial winding up.[106]
- Any transfer of shares is void, unless authorized by the liquidator.[107]
- Any alteration in the status of the company's members is void.[108]
- Upon the appointment of a liquidator, the powers of the directors cease. If the winding up is a members' voluntary winding up, the directors may continue

---

93. Ibid, s 89(1).   94. Ibid, s 89(3).
95. Ibid, s 89(6).   96. Ibid, Sch 10, para 1.
97. Ibid, s 89(4).   98. Ibid, Sch 10, para 1.
99. Ibid.   100. Ibid, s 91(1).
101. Ibid, s 98(1).   102. Ibid, s 100(1) and (2).
103. Ibid, s 101(1).   104. Ibid, s 101(2) and (3).
105. Ibid, s 86.   106. Ibid, s 87(1).
107. Ibid, s 88.   108. Ibid.

to exercise such powers as may be determined by the general meeting or the liquidator.[109] If the winding up is a creditors' voluntary winding up, the directors may continue to exercise such powers as may be determined by the liquidation committee or, if no such committee exists, the creditors.[110]

- The company's employees are dismissed, although the liquidator may reappoint them.
- Any floating charges taken over the company's assets will crystallize.

The crystallization of floating charges is discussed at p 669

The role and powers of a liquidator

As can be seen from above, the liquidator occupies an extremely important position. The liquidator's role is basically to gather in all of the assets of the company, to pay off the company's debts and liabilities, and to distribute any remaining assets to persons entitled to them in the correct order. To this end, the liquidator is granted a wide array of general powers, including the following.

The distribution of assets is discussed at p 768

1. The ability to pay any creditors in full.
2. The power to enter into compromises or arrangements with the creditors.
3. The power to compromise in relation to any claims or debts (and liabilities capable of resulting in debts) owed to the company.
4. The power to bring legal proceedings under certain sections of the IA 1986.
5. A general power to bring or defend legal proceedings on behalf of the company.
6. The power to carry on the business in order to obtain a beneficial winding up.
7. The power to sell any of the company's property by public auction or private contract.
8. The power to do all acts and to execute, in the name and on behalf of the company, all deeds, receipts, and other documents, and for that purpose to use, when necessary, the company's seal.
9. The power to draw, accept, make, and indorse any bill of exchange or promissory note in the name and on behalf of the company.
10. The power to raise security on the assets of the company.
11. The power to appoint an agent to conduct business that the liquidator himself cannot conduct.
12. The power to do all such other things as may be necessary for winding up the company's affairs and distributing its assets.

The powers granted under (1)–(4) can only be exercised if sanctioned. In the case of a compulsory winding up, the sanction of the court or liquidation committee is required.[111] In the case of a members' voluntary winding up, a special resolution is required.[112] The sanction of the court or liquidation committee (or the creditors, if no liquidation committee exists) is required in the case of a creditors' voluntary winding up.[113] The powers granted under (5) and (6) require no sanction if the winding

---

109. Ibid, s 91(2).   110. Ibid, s 103.
111. Ibid, s 167(1)(a).   112. Ibid, s 165(2)(a).
113. Ibid, s 165(2)(b).

up is voluntary,[114] but will require the sanction of the court or liquidation committee if the winding up is compulsory.[115] The powers granted under (7)–(12) do not require sanction, irrespective of the type of winding up.[116]

In addition to these powers, the liquidator can maximize the size of the pool of assets by requiring certain persons to make contributions, or by preventing assets from being removed. In the case of misfeasance proceedings, the liquidator himself may be required to make a contribution.

Misfeasance

The IA 1986, s 212, applies where, during the course of a winding up, it appears that an officer of the company, a liquidator, an administrative receiver, or other person involved in the promotion, formation, or management of the company has misapplied or retained, or become accountable for, any money or other property of the company, or has been guilty of any misfeasance or breach of any fiduciary or other duty in relation to the company. In such a case, the court may examine the conduct of one of the above persons, but only upon an application from:

➡ misfeasance: the improper or unlawful performance of a lawful act

- the liquidator;
- the official receiver;
- a creditor; or
- a contributory.[117]

If the court is of the opinion that misfeasance has occurred, it may order the misfeasor to:

- repay, restore, or account for the money or property, or any part of it, with interest at such rate as the court thinks just; or
- contribute such sum to the company's assets by way of compensation in respect of the misfeasance or breach of fiduciary or other duty as the court thinks just.[118]

Fraudulent trading

Section 213 provides that if, in the course of the winding up[119] of a company, it appears that any business of the company has been carried on with intent to defraud creditors of the company or creditors of any other person, or for any fraudulent purpose, then the court, on the application of the liquidator,[120] may declare that any

---

114. Ibid, s 165(3).

115. Ibid, s 167(1)(a).

116. Ibid, ss 165(3) and 167(1)(a).

117. Ibid, s 212(3). A liquidator and a contributory may only make an application with the leave of the court: s 212(4) and (5).

118. Ibid, s 212(3).

119. Fraudulent trading under s 213 only applies in the course of a winding up. It should not be confused with the offence of fraudulent trading found in the CA 2006, s 993, which can apply at any time. But it is perfectly possible for one fraudulent transaction to breach both provisions, and civil and criminal liability to be imposed.

120. If fraudulent trading has occurred, but the liquidator fails to take action, the victims of the fraud may have the right to bring an action under the tort of deceit: *Contex Drouzhba Ltd v Wiseman* [2007] EWCA Civ 1201, [2008] BCC 301.

persons who were knowingly parties to the carrying on of the business in such a manner are liable to make such contributions to the company's assets as the court thinks proper.

The first question that arises is what constitutes 'fraudulent activity'. In an often-quoted passage, Maugham J defined it as 'actual dishonesty involving, according to current notions of fair trading among commercial men, real moral blame'.[121] Whether or not a person has an 'intent to defraud' is heavily dependent upon the facts of the case, but the courts have indicated that certain conduct is highly likely to involve an intent to defraud (for example, inducing a person to provide a company with credit, when it is known that the company will be unable to repay).[122] Finally, it must be shown that the parties involved were knowing parties to the fraud. What the liquidator will need to show to establish this was stated by Patten J in *Morris v Bank of India; Re BCCI Ltd*,[123] in which he stated that:

- a liquidator will need to show that the defendant knew that the relevant transactions were being entered into to defraud, or for a fraudulent purpose;
- the liquidator will not need to know every detail of the fraud, or how it was carried out, but he will have to know, either through observation or through being told, that the company was intent on a fraud;
- the liquidator must have actual contemporaneous knowledge of the fraud (a failure to realize that a fraud is being committed is not enough to breach s 213, no matter how obvious the fraud might be with hindsight);
- a defendant will have knowledge where it 'shuts its eyes to the obvious because of a conscious fear that to enquire further will confirm a suspicion of wrongdoing which already exists'.[124]

Where a director is found to have engaged in fraudulent trading, the court may also make a disqualification order against the director, for a maximum period of fifteen years.[125]

Wrongful trading

Because fraud must be proved beyond reasonable doubt and the liquidator must prove subjective knowledge of the fraud, actions under s 213 rarely succeed. The Jenkins Committee[126] and the Cork Committee[127] (the recommendations of which led to the IA 1986) therefore recommended that a lesser form of civil liability be introduced, and this was implemented by s 214, which allows the court to require current and former directors of a company who have engaged in 'wrongful trading' to contribute to the assets of that company, provided that, during the course of a winding up, it appears that:

- the company has gone into insolvent liquidation;

---

121. *Re Patrick and Lyon Ltd* [1933] Ch 786 (Ch) 790.
122. *R v Grantham* [1984] QB 675 (CA).
123. [2004] EWHC 528 (Ch), [2004] BCC 404.
124. Ibid, [13].
125. Company Directors Disqualification Act 1986, s 10.
126. *Report of the Company Law Committee* (Cmnd 1749, HMSO, London, 1962).
127. *Report of the Review Committee on Insolvency Law and Practice* (Cmnd 8558, HMSO, London, 1982).

- at some time before the commencement of the winding up of the company, that person knew, or ought to have concluded, that there was no reasonable prospect that the company would avoid going into insolvent liquidation; and
- that person was a director of the company at that time.[128]

Trading whilst insolvent does not, in itself, constitute wrongful trading. As Chadwick J (as he then was) stated:

> The companies legislation does not impose on directors a statutory duty to ensure that their company does not trade while insolvent; nor does that legislation impose an obligation to ensure that the company does not trade at a loss.... Directors may properly take the view that it is in the interests of the company and of its creditors that, although insolvent, the company should continue to trade out of its difficulties. They may properly take the view that it is in the interests of the company and its creditors that some loss-making trade should be accepted in anticipation of future profitability. They are not to be criticised if they give effect to such views, properly held.[129]

Liability will be imposed only if a person knew, or ought to have known, that there was no reasonable prospect of avoiding insolvent liquidation. But no liability under s 214 will lie if, after the person concerned first knew, or ought to have concluded, that there was no reasonable prospect of the company avoiding insolvent liquidation, he took every step to minimize the potential loss to the company's creditors that he ought to have taken.[130]

For the purposes of s 214, the facts that a director of a company ought to know or ascertain, the conclusions that he ought to reach, and the steps that he ought to take are those that would be known or ascertained, or reached or taken, by a reasonably diligent person having both:

   (a) the general knowledge, skill and experience that may reasonably be expected of a person carrying out the same functions as are carried out by that director in relation to the company, and

   (b) the general knowledge, skill and experience that that director has.[131]

⚯ The director's duty of care, skill, and diligence is discussed at p 703

It will be remembered that this dual objective–subjective test is identical to the test used to determine whether or not a director has breached the duty of care, skill, and diligence under the CA 2006, s 174. The objective test in s 214(4)(a) applies to all directors, irrespective of their skills and qualifications, and therefore represents the minimum level expected. The subjective test in s 214(4)(b) applies to those directors whose subjective abilities raise them above the standard expected in s 214(4)(a) (for example, those who are highly qualified or highly experienced). Therefore, all directors are judged by the standard of a reasonably competent hypothetical director, except directors who are better qualified than this hypothetical director—such directors are judged by reference to their own qualifications.

---

128. IA 1986, s 214(2).
129. *Secretary for State and Industry v Taylor* [1997] 1 WLR 407 (Ch) 414.
130. IA 1986, s 214(3).
131. Ibid, s 214(4).

The first ever reported case regarding s 214 is still one of the most important and illuminating regarding the operation of that section.

> ## Re Produce Marketing Consortium Ltd [1989] BCLC 520 (Ch)
>
> **FACTS:** The company in question imported fruit and was incorporated in 1964. It was profitable until 1980. Between 1980 and 1984, its profitability and turnover decreased, it built up a large overdraft, its liabilities exceeded its assets, and it was trading at a loss. Between 1984 and the company's liquidation in October 1987, these losses continued. By February 1987, one of the directors realized that liquidation was inevitable, but the company continued to trade until October 1987. The rationale behind the decision to continue trading was to dispose of the fruit that had been stored in the company's cold storage. Upon the company's liquidation, the liquidator sought a contribution from the two directors under s 214.
>
> **HELD:** The Companies Court held that the directors should have concluded by July 1986 that liquidation was inevitable. Over a period of seven years, the company went from being profitable, having excess assets and no overdraft, to trading at a loss, having liabilities that exceeded its assets and regularly exceeding the overdraft limit. Further, the directors had failed to take all steps to minimize loss. The Court estimated that prompt liquidation could have saved the company £75,000, so it ordered the two directors to contribute this amount.

★ See LS Sealy, 'Insolvent Company: Wrongful Trading' (1989) 48 CLJ 375

Transactions at an undervalue

Clearly, companies that are nearing insolvency should be engaged in acts designed to increase the assets of the company. But the directors of such companies may cause their companies to sell off their assets cheaply (usually to the directors or other connected persons) in order to place them out of the control of a future liquidator. To combat this, s 238 provides that where, at a 'relevant time', a company has gone into liquidation (or administration), the liquidator (or administrator) may apply to the court for a remedy on the ground that the company has entered into a transaction at an undervalue. If the application is successful, the court will make such order as it thinks fit for restoring the position to that which it would have been had the company not entered into that transaction.[132]

A company enters into a transaction at an undervalue with a person if:

- the company makes a gift to that person, or otherwise enters into a transaction with that person on terms that provide for the company to receive no consideration; or
- the company enters into a transaction with that person for a consideration the value of which, in money or money's worth, is significantly less than the value, in money or money's worth, of the consideration provided by the company.[133]

---

132. Ibid, s 238(3).   133. Ibid, s 238(4).

An application for an order can, however, only be made in relation to transactions at an undervalue that occurred at the 'relevant time'. What constitutes the relevant time will depend upon with whom the company transacted:

- if the company entered into a transaction with someone 'connected with the company',[134] the relevant time is two years, ending on the date of insolvency;
- in all other cases, the period is six months, ending on the date of insolvency.[135]

Even if a company does enter into a transaction at an undervalue at the relevant time, no order shall be made if:

- the company entered into the transaction in good faith and for the purposes of carrying on the business; and
- at the time, there were reasonable grounds to believe that the transaction would benefit the company.[136]

Preferences

As we noted, a principal role of the liquidator is to distribute surplus assets to persons entitled to them in the event of a company being wound up. As we shall see, this distribution of assets is hierarchical, with certain types of creditor ranking ahead of others. A company may attempt to avoid this hierarchy by paying off certain low-ranking creditors prior to insolvency. As a result, there may be insufficient assets to pay the high-ranking creditors. This is known as a 'preference' and where a company has provided a creditor with a preference, the liquidator may apply to the court, which may make such order as it thinks fit for restoring the position to that which it would have been had the company not given that preference.[137]

A company provides a person with a preference if:

- that person is one of the company's creditors, or a surety or guarantor for any of the company's debts or other liabilities; and
- the company does anything or suffers anything to be done that (in either case) has the effect of putting that person into a position that, in the event of the company going into insolvent liquidation, will be better than the position in which he would have been had that thing not been done.[138]

Like transactions at an undervalue, a preference must be given at the 'relevant time' in order to obtain a remedy. What constitutes a relevant time is defined in exactly the same way as it is in relation to transactions at an undervalue.

The decision to make a preference must have been influenced by the desire to place a person in the advantageous position described above.[139] There is no need for such a desire to be the sole, or even the dominant, influence, provided that it is present to some degree.[140] Where a preference is given by a company to a connected

---

134. Ibid, s 249, provides that connected persons are directors, shadow directors, and 'associates' of the company. Section 435 states that associates would include the husbands, wives, civil partners, business partners, employers, and employees of connected persons.

135. Ibid, s 240(1).   136. Ibid, s 238(5).

137. Ibid, s 239(3).   138. Ibid, s 239(4).

139. Ibid, s 239(5).   140. *Re MC Bacon Ltd* [1990] BCC 78 (Ch).

person other than an employee, this influence is presumed to exist unless the contrary can be shown.[141] In all other cases, the liquidator will need to establish such influence.

Extortionate credit transactions

Section 244 allows a liquidator (or administrator) to petition the court for a remedial order where, within a three-year period ending on the date of insolvency (or the granting of the administration order), the company entered into an 'extortionate credit transaction'. Unless the contrary is proven, a credit transaction will be presumed to be extortionate if:

- the terms of it are, or were, such as to require grossly exorbitant payments to be made (whether unconditionally or in certain contingencies) in respect of the provision of the credit; or
- it otherwise grossly contravened ordinary principles of fair dealing.[142]

If the court is of the opinion that a credit transaction is extortionate, it may make an order containing one or more of the following provisions as it thinks fit:

- a provision setting aside all, or part, of the transaction;
- a provision varying the terms of the transaction, or varying the terms on which any security for the purposes of the transaction is held;
- a provision requiring any person who is, or was, a party to the transaction to pay to the liquidator (or administrator) any sums paid to that person, by virtue of the transaction, by the company;
- a provision requiring any person to surrender to the office holder any property held by him as security for the purposes of the transaction;
- a provision directing accounts to be taken between any persons.[143]

Avoidance of floating charges

The directors of a company may cause the company to grant them a floating charge over the assets of the company, thereby prioritizing themselves over other creditors in the event of the company's liquidation. To prevent this, s 239 invalidates floating charges created within the relevant time prior to insolvency.[144] The relevant time is:

- two years, where the charge was granted to a person connected with the company;
- twelve months for an unconnected person[145]—but a floating charge to an unconnected person will not be invalidated, even if created within the relevant time, if the company was able to pay its debts at the time that the charge was granted and did not become unable to pay its debts due to the granting of the charge.[146]

---

141. IA 1986, s 239(6).   142. Ibid, s 244(3).
143. Ibid, s 244(4).   144. Ibid, s 245(2).
145. Ibid, s 245(3).   146. Ibid, s 245(4).

A floating charge apparently invalidated by the above rules will remain valid if it falls within s 245(2)(a) or (b), which provides that the charge is valid to the extent of the total of:

- the value of so much of the consideration for the creation of the charge as consists of money paid, or goods or services supplied, to the company at the same time as, or after, the creation of the charge; and
- the value of so much of that consideration as consists of the discharge or reduction, at the same time as, or after, the creation of the charge, of any debt of the company.

‹› Key points summary

- Liquidation is the process whereby the assets of the company are collected and realized, its debts and liabilities paid, and the surplus distributed to the members. The company is then usually dissolved.

- A winding up can be ordered by the court (known as a 'compulsory winding up') upon a petition from certain persons. This petition must be made based on defined grounds, the most common of which is that the company is unable to pay its debts.

- A company may voluntarily wind itself up (known as a 'voluntary winding up'). If the winding up is accompanied by a statement of solvency, it will be a members' voluntary winding up. If no statement is made, it will be a creditors' voluntary winding up.

- A liquidator will be appointed, whose task it is to realize the company's assets, pay off the company's debts and liabilities, and distribute any remaining assets to those entitled to them.

- Persons who have engaged in misfeasance (the improper performance of a lawful act) may be required to contribute to the company's assets.

- The liquidator may be able to obtain a contribution from those who have carried on the business of the company with the intent to defraud the creditors.

- The liquidator may be able to obtain a contribution from a director, or directors, where the company has entered insolvent liquidation and, at some time before the commencement of the winding up, the directors knew, or ought to have known, that there was no prospect of avoiding insolvent liquidation.

- The liquidator may be able to obtain a contribution where the company has entered into a transaction at an undervalue, or has granted a creditor a preference.

- The liquidator may be able to obtain a remedy if the company has entered into an extortionate credit transaction, or he may be able to set aside certain floating charges.

Distribution of assets

In relation to a voluntary winding up, s 107 states that:

the company's property in a voluntary winding up shall on the winding up be applied in satisfaction of the company's liabilities pari passu and, subject to that application, shall…be distributed among the members according to their rights and interests in the company.

In relation to compulsory windings up, similar provisions can be found in the Insolvency Rules.[147] The *pari passu* rule generally means that creditors receive an equal share of the company's assets—but it is subject to a number of important qualifications, as follows.

➡ *pari passu*: 'with equal step'

- Creditors who have taken security over the company's assets (for example, fixed or floating charges) can usually recover monies owed without relying on the liquidator by taking the charged assets and selling them. As we shall see, whilst this is true regarding fixed charges, the issue is more complex regarding floating charges.
- The expenses of liquidation are paid out of the assets realized by the liquidator.
- Certain creditors are classified by statute as 'preferential creditors' whose claims rank above those of others.

Charge holders

The principal reason for taking a charge over the company's assets is to acquire a means by which to recover monies owed without having to rely on the liquidation process. Where an individual has secured a debt of the company by way of fixed charge, upon the company's liquidation, he may take the charged asset, sell it, and use the proceeds to satisfy the debt owed to him. Of course, if the proceeds exceed the sum owed, the remainder must be returned to the company and will be added to the pool of assets to be distributed by the liquidator.

🔗 Fixed and floating charges are discussed at p 668

Regarding floating charges, the position is slightly more complex, in that charges created after 15 September 2003 are subject to new rules introduced by the Enterprise Act 2002. Regarding such charges, once the liquidator has determined the assets that would go to the floating charge holders, he must then set aside a percentage of those assets to pay off the unsecured creditors.[148] The prescribed percentage is:

- 50 per cent of the first £10,000;
- 20 per cent of the remainder, up to a limit of £600,000.[149]

But this rule will not apply where the company's net property is worth less than £10,000,[150] or where the liquidator, administrator, or receiver thinks that the cost of making a distribution to unsecured creditors would be disproportionate to the benefits.[151]

Preferential debts

Statute classifies certain debts as preferential debts, meaning that they rank ahead of all other debts (except the liquidation expenses). The categories of preferential debts can be found in the IA 1986, Sch 6, but it is worth noting that Crown debts (for

---

147. The Insolvency Rules 1986, SI 1986/1925, rr 4.179–4.181.
148. IA 1986, s 176A.
149. Insolvency Act 1986 (Prescribed Part) Order 2003, SI 2003/2097, art 3.
150. IA 1986, s 176A(3)(a); Insolvency Act 1986 (Prescribed Part) Order 2003, SI 2003/2097, art 2.
151. IA 1986, s 176A(3)(b).

example, debts owed to HM Revenue and Customs) are, following the passing of the Enterprise Act 2002, no longer classified as preferential.

The current preferential debts include:

- pension scheme contributions;
- remuneration owed to employees (but only remuneration earned in the four months prior to the relevant date,[152] up to a maximum of £800,[153] will rank as preferential—the remainder will rank as unsecured);
- any amount owed by way of accrued holiday pay;
- levies on coal and steel production.

Preferential debts rank equally among themselves, meaning that if there are insufficient assets to pay all of the preferential debts, the preferential creditors will all receive an equal proportion.[154] Of course, this means that creditors who rank below the preferential creditors will receive nothing.

The order of distribution

The order of distribution of assets is as follows.

1. *Debts secured by fixed charge* Those who have secured assets via a fixed charge can simply take the charged asset and sell it to recover the proceeds. Accordingly, fixed charge holders do not need to rely on the liquidator to satisfy their debt.

2. *Liquidation expenses* Expenses properly incurred during the liquidation rank ahead of all debts, except those of fixed charge holders.[155]

3. *Preferential debts*.[156]

4. *Debts secured by floating charge* Floating charge holders rank behind preferential creditors. The abolition of the preferential status of Crown debts has benefited the floating charge holders most—although remember the provisions discussed above regarding the setting aside of floating charge assets to pay the unsecured creditors.

5. *Unsecured debts*.

6. *Deferred debts* This would include certain sums due to the members before liquidation (for example, any dividends declared prior to liquidation, but not yet paid).

7. *Surplus distributed to members* If, once the above groups have been fully paid, there are still assets remaining (which is highly unlikely), the surplus is distributed *pari passu* to the company's members[157] (although the company's articles may provide that certain classes of member have priority).

The groups are paid off one by one, so the higher a debt ranks, the more chance it has of being paid. Once a group is paid in full, the remaining assets are used to pay

---

152. What constitutes the relevant date will depend upon the type of administration procedure. The IA 1986, s 387, provides a list of the relevant dates.
153. Insolvency Proceedings (Monetary Limits) Order 1986, SI 1986/1996, art 4.
154. IA 1986, s 175(2).
155. Ibid, s 175(2)(a).
156. Ibid.
157. Ibid, ss 107 and 154.

the next group. If there are insufficient assets to pay a group fully, each creditor amongst that group will receive the same percentage of their debt (that is, the *pari passu* rule operates amongst members of each group).

Key points summary

- Fixed charge holders can normally recover the charged assets without the liquidator's involvement.

- The liquidator will distribute assets in the following order:
  - liquidation expenses;
  - preferential debts;
  - debts secured by floating charge;
  - unsecured debts;
  - deferred debts; and
  - debts to the members.

Dissolution

None of the procedures discussed above actually brings about the death of a company (although liquidation is certainly the final step in bringing about a company's demise). In order for a company to cease to exist, it must be removed from the Register of Companies (this is known as 'dissolution'). Dissolution ends a company's separate personality, and terminates the relationship between a company and its members.

A company may be dissolved in a number of different ways, including the following.

- The Registrar of Companies may strike a company from the Register if he believes it to be 'defunct' (that is, if it is not carrying on business).[158] Before doing this, he must send a letter to the company's registered address enquiring whether it is still carrying on business. If no reply is received within one month, he will send a second letter. If no reply is received, or if the company replies stating that it is not carrying on business, he will publish a notice in the *Gazette* stating that, in three months' time, the company will be struck off the Register and dissolved.[159] The majority of companies that are dissolved are defunct.

- The decision of the Registrar to register a company is subject to judicial review, provided that the application for judicial review is brought by the Attorney General. The court may order the Registrar to cancel the registration and remove the company from the Register.[160]

---

158. CA 2006, s 1000(1).
159. Ibid, s 1000(2)–(6).
160. See, e.g., *R v Registrar of Companies, ex p Attorney General* [1991] BCLC 476 (DC).

- Three months after the Registrar has been notified that a winding up has been completed, the company will be automatically struck off the Register.[161]
- If an administrator of a company thinks that the company has no property that can be distributed to its creditors, he must send a notice to that effect to the Registrar. The Registrar will register the notice and, three months later, the company will be deemed to be dissolved.[162]
- An Act of Parliament may dissolve a company (for example, the HSBC Investment Banking Act 2002).

Restoration

It may be necessary to restore to the Register of Companies a company that has been dissolved (for example, where further assets of the dissolved company are discovered). A company may be restored by:

- applying to the Registrar on the ground that a company has been incorrectly struck off as defunct.[163] Only a former member or director may make such an application,[164] and it must be made within six years of the date of dissolution;[165]
- applying to the court for restoration. Such an application can be made where:
  - the company was struck off by the Registrar for being defunct, but at the time of the striking off, it was actually carrying on business;
  - the company was voluntarily struck off, but the relevant requirements for such a striking off were not complied with; or
  - in any other case the court considers it just to do so.;[166]
- an application must normally be made within six years of the date of dissolution,[167] but there is no time limit where the application is made for the purpose of bringing proceedings against the company for damages for personal injury.[168]

Chapter conclusion

Liquidation still lies at the heart of our insolvency law regime. In fact, it is worth remembering that, in many cases, liquidation occurs even though a company is solvent or even financially healthy. In all cases, it is vital that there is a clear procedure in place regarding who can wind up a company and how the assets of the company are distributed. Despite the importance of liquidation, the growth of the UK's rescue culture should not be underestimated. Administration and, to a lesser extent, company voluntary arrangements have radically affected the underlying philosophy behind our insolvency law regime. The result is that companies facing serious financial difficulties now have a number of options available to them, ranging from attempting to trade back into profitability, to liquidating and distributing the assets of the company.

---

161. IA 1986, ss 201 and 205.
163. CA 2006, ss 1024 and 1025.
165. Ibid, s 1024(4).
167. Ibid, s 1030(4).

162. Ibid, Sch B1, para 84.
164. Ibid, s 1024(3).
166. Ibid, s 1031(1).
168. Ibid, s 1030(1).

Self-test questions

1. Define the following:
   (a) rescue culture;
   (b) administration;
   (c) moratorium;
   (d) receivership;
   (e) liquidation;
   (f) misfeasance;
   (g) preference;
   (h) *pari passu.*

2. What procedures are designed to help companies survive as going concerns? To what extent has the Insolvency Act 1986 introduced a rescue culture into English law?

3. Other than through selling the assets of the company, how else can a liquidator maximize the pool of assets to be distributed?

4. In September 2009, Ethos plc enters insolvent liquidation. Below is a list of Ethos' creditors.
   (a) Around fifty of Ethos' employees have not been paid in the last six months. Each is owed around £9,000.
   (b) Ethos owes around £5,000 in tax to HM Revenue and Customs.
   (c) Your fee for conducting the liquidation is around £3,000.
   (d) Andrew, who is owed £60,000, has taken out a fixed charge over Ethos' fleet of company cars. The cars have a market value of £90,000. He also took out, in June 2009, a floating charge over all of the company's assets.
   (e) Ceri, the wife of one of Ethos' directors, lent the company £3,000. One month before Ethos entered liquidation, Ethos paid Ceri back the full £1,000.

   Skene & Jordan Ltd is Ethos' auditor and it transpires that it advised the directors of Ethos in January 2009 that the company's insolvency was inevitable. The assets of Ethos have been collected in and amount to around £75,000. You have been appointed as Ethos' liquidator. Explain what your role is and how you would go about performing it in relation to Ethos plc.

5. In what ways can a company be dissolved?

Further reading

Cook, C, 'Wrongful Trading: Is It a Real Threat to Directors or Is It a Paper Tiger?' (1999) Insolv L 99
Discusses the effectiveness of s 214 and examines a number of cases concerning the provision; argues that several decisions of the courts prevent s 214 from reaching its full potential

Goods, R, *Principles of Corporate Insolvency Law* (Sweet & Maxwell, London, 2005)
A detailed, but highly readable, account of insolvency law in England and Wales; examines in depth all of the insolvency procedures discussed in this chapter

Hunter, M, 'The Nature and Functions of a Rescue Culture' [1999] JBL 491
Discusses in depth what constitutes a rescue culture and whether such a culture is justified

Websites

<http://www.companieshouse.gov.uk>
*The official website of Companies House; provides information and guidance booklets on
    liquidation and company charges*

<http://www.insolvency.gov.uk>
*The official website of the Insolvency Service; provides a substantial amount of information
    on the various insolvency procedures*

 Remember to visit the **Online Resource Centre** at **<http://www.
oxfordtextbooks.co.uk/roach>** to access the following resources
on Chapter 22, 'Corporate rescue, insolvency, and dissolution': more
practice questions and answers; a **glossary** of key terms; **multiple-
choice questions**; **revision summaries**; and **audio updates** when
relevant.

PART V

employment law

23 The contract of employment

- Employment tribunals and the Employment Appeal Tribunal

- Employees and independent contractors

- The terms of the employment contract

INTRODUCTION

One of the most long-standing debates in employment law concerns the issue of how to determine whether an individual is an employee or not. Recent years have witnessed an increase in the debate's intensity and complexity as new forms of worker have emerged. Arguably, the historical distinction between employees and the self-employed is becoming less important due to the increasing trend of employment law statutes offering protection to 'workers', but it can be argued that the addition of this new class has served to make the issue even more complex. Even if we can establish that an individual has a contract of employment, the terms of that contract can derive from a number of vastly differing sources. This chapter aims to clarify these complex issues.

But before these issues are discussed, it is worth moving away from the contract of employment for a moment to discuss how disputes in employment law are resolved. The majority of employment disputes are resolved not in courts of law, but in the various employment tribunals. It is therefore important that students understand how these various tribunals work and how they fit into the administrative structure of the English legal system.

Employment tribunals and the Employment Appeal Tribunal

Employment tribunals

Employment tribunals are classified as First-tier Tribunals under the Tribunals, Courts and Enforcement Act 2007. They were originally called 'industrial tribunals' when established by the Industrial Training Act 1964. In 1998, they were renamed as employment tribunals.[1] The majority of employment litigation is handled by

---

1. Employment Rights (Dispute Resolution) Act 1998, s 1(1).

employment tribunals and, in recent years, their jurisdiction has increased dramatically, to encompass hearings on a wide array of employment issues (all of which are discussed in subsequent chapters), including:

- allegations of unfair dismissal (discussed at p 904);
- contraventions of legislation relation to discrimination (discussed in Chapter 25);
- equal pay claims (discussed at p 802);
- breaches of the Working Time Regulations 1998[2] (discussed at p 841);
- breaches of the National Minimum Wage Act 1998 (discussed at p 811);
- cases involving breaches of the contract of employment.

This increase in jurisdiction has been accompanied by an increased caseload. Between April 2004 and March 2005, employment tribunals accepted 86,181 cases. Between April 2007 and March 2008, this had increased to 189,303 cases.[3]

A typical employment tribunal will consist of three persons:[4] a legally qualified chairman (who may be known as an 'employment judge') and two lay members (known as 'wing members'). In order to obtain a balanced bench, one of the lay members will be drawn from a list of persons representing employers (for example, the Confederation of British Industry); the other, from a list representing workers (for example, the Trades Union Congress). To combat the rise in the employment tribunals' caseload, certain cases (for example, those involving breach of contract) can be heard by a chairman alone, or with only one lay member.[5] Decisions of employment tribunals are based on a majority and the votes are equal, meaning that the two lay members may outvote the chairman—although this is extremely rare and most employment tribunal decisions are unanimous.

➡ legal aid: the system of publicly funded legal advice and representation

The various forms of legal aid are not available in employment tribunals, although trade unions or the various anti-discrimination bodies (for example, the Equality and Human Rights Commission) might provide financial assistance. Unlike the position in civil courts, costs are not usually awarded: each party pays his own costs. But an employment tribunal does have the power to award costs where a party has acted 'vexatiously, abusively, disruptively or otherwise unreasonably, or the bringing or conducting of the proceedings by the paying party has been misconceived'.[6] In 2007–08, employment tribunals awarded costs in only 461 cases, the average amount being £2,095.[7]

Employment tribunals are not courts and the parties are not required to have legal representation. This results in a number of advantages—namely, that employment tribunals tend to hear cases more quickly than the courts, and that cases tend to be decided more quickly and with less formality (although formalities are increasing

---

2. SI 1998/1833.

3. Tribunals Service, *Employment Tribunal and EAT Statistics (GB) 1 April 2007 to 31 March 2008* (HMSO, London, 2008) Table 1, available online at <http://www.employmenttribunals.gov.uk>.

4. Employment Tribunals Act 1996, s 4(1).

5. Where this is the case, the parties are entitled to know if the lay member was drawn from the employer list or the employee list: see *Rabahallah v BT Group plc* [2005] ICR 440 (EAT).

6. Employment Tribunals (Constitution and Rules of Procedure) Regulations 2004, SI 2004/1861, reg 41(3).

7. Tribunals Service, *Employment Tribunal and EAT Statistics (GB) 1 April 2007 to 31 March 2008* (HMSO, London, 2008) Table 12.

and the rapidly rising caseload has increased delays). But lacking the status of a court means that decisions of employment tribunals are not binding on any other court or tribunal, and that they cannot enforce their decisions. Research conducted by the Citizens Advice Bureau indicates that 10 per cent of those whose case succeeds at an employment tribunal do not obtain the compensation ordered.[8] If a court order is breached, it will constitute contempt of court, but if an order of the employment tribunal is breached, it will not constitute contempt and the aggrieved party may need to initiate a claim in a county court to have the employment tribunal's decision enforced—and such proceedings may be lengthy and expensive.

Whilst employment tribunals are not courts, they are, however, bound by the decisions of certain courts—namely, the Court of Appeal and the House of Lords or Supreme Court. Employment tribunals are also bound by decisions of the Employment Appeal Tribunal, which will now be examined.

The Employment Appeal Tribunal

Decisions of employment tribunals can be appealed to an Upper Tribunal known as the 'Employment Appeal Tribunal' (EAT), which was set up by the Employment Protection Act 1975, s 87. The jurisdiction of the EAT is exclusively appellate and, in 2007–08, it disposed of 466 appeals, with an additional 184 cases being disposed of at a preliminary stage.[9] It will not hear first-instance cases and it will generally only hear appeals on points of law—a policy introduced to minimize the number of appeals. For this reason, legal representation is highly recommended, although it is not compulsory. As with employment tribunals, costs are not normally awarded, but can be awarded where the proceedings are 'unnecessary, improper, vexatious or misconceived or that there has been unreasonable delay or other unreasonable conduct in the bringing or conducting of proceedings'.[10] Unlike the position in employment tribunal hearings, however, legal aid is available in the EAT.

Like employment tribunals, most EAT cases are heard by three persons, two of whom will be lay members (rising to four lay members in certain exceptional cases).[11] But the chairman will either be a High Court judge, a circuit judge, or a judge of the Scottish Court of Session. Where the chairman of an employment tribunal heard the case alone, the judge in the EAT may also hear the appeal alone.

Although the EAT is not technically a court, it is a superior 'court of record', meaning that its decisions are reported and form precedents that must be followed by employment tribunals. The EAT is not bound by its own decisions,[12] but is bound by decisions of the Court of Appeal and the House of Lords or Supreme Court. Decisions of the EAT can be appealed to the Court of Appeal, although, strictly speaking, it is the first-instance decision of the employment tribunal that is appealed. Leave to appeal is required, either from the EAT or from the Court of Appeal. From

---

8. Citizens Advice Bureau, *Justice Denied: The Deliberate Non-Payment of Employment Tribunal Awards By Rogue Employers* (CAB, London, October 2008) 1, available online at <http://www.citizensadvice.org.uk>.

9. Tribunals Service, *Employment Tribunal and EAT Statistics (GB) 1 April 2007 to 31 March 2008* (HMSO, London, 2008) Tables 13 and 14.

10. Employment Appeal Tribunal Rules 1993, SI 1993/2854, reg 34A(1).

11. Employment Tribunals Act 1996, s 28(2).

12. *Secretary of State for Trade and Industry v Cook* [1997] ICR 288 (EAT).

the Court of Appeal, an appeal would lie to the House of Lords or Supreme Court in the normal way.

 Key points summary

- The majority of employment law disputes are dealt with by employment tribunals, which usually consist of a legally qualified chairman and two lay members.

- Decisions of employment tribunals do not constitute precedent and can be appealed to the Employment Appeal Tribunal. The EAT has no first-instance jurisdiction.

- Appeals in the EAT are also heard by a chairman and two lay members, but the chairman will be a legally qualified judge.

- Decisions of the EAT are binding upon employment tribunals.

Employees and independent contractors

The importance of the distinction

➡ vicarious liability: liability imposed on an employer for torts committed by his employee (see Chapter 14)

We have already noted that establishing vicarious liability is largely dependent upon the existence of an employer–employee relationship. We therefore need to determine who qualifies as an employee and who does not. The significant distinction to be made is between employees and independent contractors (also known as 'self-employed persons'). Distinguishing between the two is crucial, not only for the purposes of establishing liability in tort, but also because the distinction is of immense practical significance in relation to employment law, as follows.

- Employees pay tax under Schedule E, whereas independent contractors are taxed under Schedule D.[13] This allows independent contractors to set off business expenses for tax purposes and to pay tax off in arrears. In relation to National Insurance (NI), employees pay Class 1 contributions, whereas independent contractors pay their own contributions under Class 2 (and Class 4 if profits are high enough).[14] Employers hiring independent contractors are thus relieved of the administrative burdens of deducting tax and NI, because this is the responsibility of the independent contractor.

- As we shall see, many statutory employment rights are reserved solely for 'employees' (for example, only employees have the right to claim for unfair dismissal). Similarly, the common law may impose duties of care or imply terms that protect only employees.

---

13. As a strict matter of law, the terminology of 'Schedules D and E' was abolished by the Income Tax (Earnings and Pensions) Act 2003, but the terminology is still used and is likely to be for some time.
14. Because NI contributions entitle the payer to Jobseeker's Allowance and statutory sick pay, it follows that self-employed persons are not entitled to these allowances.

- In relation to health and safety issues, the duty owed to employees is stronger than that owed to independent contractors.
- Several important EU directives offer protection only to employees (for example, the Acquired Rights Directive).[15]

It is therefore of immense practical importance that the law can distinguish between an employee and an independent contractor.

But these are not the only classes of persons that need to be defined, with legislation increasingly serving to protect 'workers'. It may be the case that the parties attempt to gain the above benefits by defining their status themselves and labelling themselves as employees, workers, or independent contractors. So to what extent is such self-classification valid?

Self-classification of the relationship

 Ferguson v John Dawson & Partners Ltd [1976] 1 WLR 1213 (CA)

FACTS: The claimant was informally hired by the defendant to work as part of a 'lump labour force' (that is, a labour-only subcontractor and not an employee). He was required to obey the instructions of the defendant regarding the timing of work and the manner of its performance. Whilst working on an unguarded roof, he fell and was injured. He claimed damages for breach of statutory duty under the now-repealed Construction (Working Places) Regulations 1996,[16] but the relevant provision applied only to employees. The defendant argued that both parties operated under the belief that the claimant was to be a contractor only and so the Regulations did not apply.

HELD: In the Court of Appeal, Megaw LJ stated: 'I find difficulty in accepting that the parties, by a mere expression of intention as to what the legal relationship should be, can in any way influence the conclusion of law as to what the relationship is.'[17] The classification adopted by the parties is but one factor to be taken into account. Given the level of control that the defendant exercised over the claimant, the Court believed that, in reality, the relationship was more akin to that of employer and employee, and so the claimant recovered compensation for his injuries.

See P. Russell, 'The "Lump" and Safety' (1977) 40 MLR 479

Clearly, Megaw LJ believed that it is for the courts to determine the employment relationship, not the parties themselves. But this does not mean that the intention of the parties is not relevant. The courts will consider the parties' classification of the relationship, but only if other factors do not help resolve the issue.[18] As we noted above, there are tax benefits to being classified as an independent contractor and legal benefits to being classified as an employee. The approach of the courts prevents workers from changing their status on a whim to obtain these benefits.

---

15. Council Directive No 77/187/EEC.
16. SI 1996/1592.
17. *Ferguson v John Dawson & Partners Ltd* [1976] 1 WLR 1213 (CA) 1222.
18. *Massey v Crown Life Assurance* [1978] 1 WLR 676 (CA).

Distinguishing between employees and independent contractors

The starting point is to define what an 'employee' is. The Employment Rights Act 1996 (ERA 1996) defines an employee as an 'individual who has entered into or works under…a contract of employment'.[19] We therefore need to define what a 'contract of employment' is, and this is defined in s 230(2) as 'a contract of service or apprenticeship, whether express or implied, and (if it is express) whether oral or in writing'. An employee therefore is someone who operates under a contract *of* service, as opposed to an independent contractor who operates under a contract *for* services. But this distinction provides little aid, and so the responsibility of determining how to distinguish between employees and independent contractors has been left to the courts and employment tribunals. The courts and employment tribunals have, however, been unable to articulate a single test, and what tests have been devised tend to be vague and difficult to apply to marginal cases.

The 'control' test

In the nineteenth century, the court adopted the 'control' test, which defined an employee as 'a person subject to the command of his master as to the manner in which he shall do his work'.[20] In *Performing Right Society Ltd v Mitchell & Booker (Palais de Danse) Ltd*,[21] a band was engaged to play in a dance hall owned by the defendant. On one occasion, the band played several songs protected by a copyright owned by the claimant. The claimant argued that the defendant was vicariously liable for the band's infringement of copyright and the court had to determine were the band employees or independent contractors. Applying the control test, the court held that the band were employees, because the defendant had 'continuous, dominant, and detailed control on every point, including the nature of the music to be played'.[22]

At this time, when the workforce was largely based on agrarian and manual work, this test was perfectly acceptable. But as technology and industry progressed, skilled workers were increasingly employed whose actions were not under the direct control of their employers. Noted examples include a surgeon[23] or a ship's captain.[24] In such cases, the control test lost much of its effectiveness[25] (although, in certain cases, it will still be relevant and even decisive) and new tests had to be created to supplement it. This led to the development of the 'integration' test.

The 'integration' test

The weaknesses of the control test led to the development of the 'integration' test by Denning LJ (as he then was), who stated that an individual would be an employee

➔ copyright: the exclusive right to reproduce certain works

---

19. ERA 1996, s 230(1).
20. *Yewens v Noakes* (1880–81) LR 6 QBD 530 (CA) 532, 533 (Bramwell LJ).
21. [1924] 1 KB 762 (KB).
22. Ibid, 771 (McCardie J).
23. *Cassidy v Ministry of Health* [1951] 2 KB 343 (CA).
24. *Gold v Essex County Council* [1942] 2 KB 293 (CA).
25. In *Nora Beloff v Pressdram Ltd* [1973] FSR 33 (Ch) 42, Ungoed-Thomas J stated 'the greater the skill required for an employee's work, the less significant is control in determining whether the employee is under a contract of service'.

if he 'is employed as part of the business and his work is done as an integral part of the business'.[26] Conversely, an individual would not be an employee if 'his work, although done for the business, is not integrated into it but only accessory to it'.[27] Whilst the integration test better catered for skilled workers than the control test, it was rarely used, largely due to the vagueness of the terms used (for example, what it means to be 'an integral part of the business'). The problems were best laid out by MacKenna J, who stated that the integration test 'raises more questions than I know how to answer'.[28]

The 'multiple' test

Following the failures of the control and integration tests, the courts soon came to realize that no single test could categorically determine whether an individual was an employee or self-employed. The courts will therefore now look at all of the facts of a case and weigh up all of the relevant factors.

Ready Mixed Concrete (South East) Ltd v Minister of Pensions & National Insurance [1968] 2 QB 497 (QB)

FACTS: Ready Mixed Concrete introduced an 'owner-driver' scheme, whereby the company's lorry drivers were dismissed and re-employed after they had purchased their lorries. Certain terms in the contract indicated the drivers were employees (they had to wear uniforms and could only use the lorries for company business), whereas other terms indicated that they were self-employed (they had no set hours of work and, if they were unable to work, they could substitute others to work in their place). A dispute arose over who had to pay the NI contributions and the court had to determine if the drivers were employees or independent contractors.

HELD: The drivers were independent contractors. The High Court was heavily influenced by the fact that, in the event of sickness or unavailability, the drivers could employ another to take their place. Further, the risk of the venture was placed upon the drivers, not the company. Given this, the court favoured the view that the drivers were self-employed.

★ See BA Hepple, 'Servants and Independent Contractors' (1968) 26 CLJ 227

In *Ready Mixed Concrete*, the court listed three factors that might be relevant in determining the case. In *O'Kelly v Trust House Forte plc*,[29] it has been argued that the court listed *seventeen* possible factors that might be relevant.[30] Whilst the multiple test grants the courts the flexibility to take into account a wide variety of factors, it also increases uncertainty, because it allows judges to weigh the relevant considerations subjectively. One judge may regard a certain factor as crucial, whereas, in

---

26. *Stevenson, Jordan & Harrison Ltd v Macdonald and Evans* (1952) 69 RPC 10 (CA) 22.
27. Ibid.
28. *Ready Mixed Concrete (South East) Ltd v Minister of Pensions and National Insurance* [1968] 2 QB 497 (QB) 524.
29. [1984] QB 90 (CA).
30. M Sargeant and D Lewis, *Employment Law* (4th edn, Pearson, London, 2008) 45.

another case, it may be regarded as trivial. The scope for inconsistent decisions is considerable.

In more recent years, the courts have attempted to introduce a measure of certainty by referring to the 'irreducible minimum' required for a person to be contract of employment to exist. Several such irreducible minimum requirements have been stated by the courts, including:

- the need for personal service by the employee;[31]
- a mutuality of obligation between the employer and employee;[32] and
- that the employee should be subject to the control of the employer.[33]

Atypical workers

The use of the multiple test has proved effective in dealing with what have been termed 'atypical' workers. These are workers who may work outside the normal working hours of many employees and who are likely to work from home. Here, we will focus on two principal types of atypical worker—namely, homeworkers and agency workers.

Homeworkers

As we shall see, a significant number of cases involving homeworkers relate to those working in the clothing industry, but, in recent years, with the advent of modern communications, we have seen a new form of homeworker known as a 'teleworker'. Homeworkers do have certain specific rights under statute,[34] but to qualify for more general rights, they would need to be classified as employees.

 Nethermere (St Neots) Ltd v Taverna [1984] ICR 612 (CA)[35]

FACTS: The claimant was a homeworker sewing pockets onto trousers using a machine provided by the defendant company. She had no set hours, was paid according to how much work she did, and was not obliged to carry out a minimum amount of work. She was dismissed and initiated an unfair dismissal claim. The defendant company alleged that she was not an employee and that she therefore could not claim for unfair dismissal.

★ See J Warburton, 'The Employment of Home Workers' (1984) 13 ILJ 251

HELD: The Court of Appeal held that she was an employee. The Court focused on the mutuality of obligations between the parties. These obligations were never written down, but, during the course of a number of years, they gave rise to sufficient obligations on both sides to justify the existence of a contract of employment.

---

31. *Express & Echo Publications Ltd v Tanton* [1999] ICR 693 (CA).
32. *Carmichael v National Power plc* [1999] 1 WLR 2042 (HL).
33. *Montgomery v Johnson Underwood Ltd* [2001] EWCA Civ 318, [2001] ICR 819.
34. Notably, the right to a minimum wage under the National Minimum Wage Act 1998, s 35.
35. See also *Airfix Footwear Ltd v Cope* [1978] ICR 1210 (CA).

Agency workers

Over 8,000 recruitment agencies (and 6,000 recruitment professionals) in the UK assign work to nearly 1.4 million temporary workers every week in an industry worth over £26 billion.[36] There is limited statutory protection for agency workers in the form of the Employment Agencies Act 1973 and the Conduct of Employment Agencies and Employment Business Regulations 2003.[37] These are primarily aimed at regulating the activities of recruitment agencies, as opposed to providing protection for agency workers, but regs 14 and 15(a) of the 2003 Regulations are notable in that they aim to clarify the employment status of an agency worker by requiring the agency to provide the worker with a copy of terms and conditions before he starts work, which state whether the worker is employed or self-employed. Agency workers are entitled to the national minimum wage under the National Minimum Wage Act 1998[38] and agency workers who are not self-employed are also covered by Working Time Regulations 1998, reg 36. A proposed Directive on Working Conditions for Temporary Employees was published by the European Commission in 2002, which aims to provide agency workers with similar rights and benefits to those of permanent employees. At the time of writing, objections from the UK have resulted in a delay to the passing of the legislation and the possibility of an agreed draft in the near future seems unlikely, with two commentators even describing the possibility of significant legislative change as a 'non-starter'.[39]

The National Minimum Wage Act 1998 and the Working Time Regulations 1998 are discussed in Chapter 24

Outside of the above specific statutory measures, it has been left to the courts, in individual cases, to determine the status of the worker. The courts have emphasized that there is no single test or factor that could point towards the legal status of an agency worker. Instead, they have to take into account the individual facts of the case to determine one of a possible number of outcomes:

- the agency worker is employed by the recruitment agency;[40]
- the agency worker is employed by the client of the agency (known as the 'end-user');[41]
- the agency worker is employed by both the recruitment agency and the end-user, and the duties of an employer are shared between them;
- the agency worker is not employed by either the recruitment agency or the end-user.[42]

The following two cases demonstrate how important the particular facts of the case can be.

---

36. Figures derived from the website of the Recruitment and Employment Confederation, <http://www.rec.uk.com>.

37. SI 2003/3319.

38. Agency workers qualify as 'workers' under s 54(3). Section 34 states that the responsibility for paying the minimum wage is placed upon the person who pays the wages or salary of the agency worker.

39. P Leighton and M Wynn, 'Temporary Agency Working: Is the Law on the Turn?' (2008) 29 Co Law 7, 8.

40. *McMeechan v Secretary of State for Employment* [1997] ICR 549 (CA).

41. *Dacas v Brook Street Bureau (UK) Ltd* [2004] EWCA Civ 217, [2004] ICR 1437.

42. *Wickens v Champion Employment* [1984] ICR 365 (EAT).

Dacas v Brook Street Bureau (UK) Ltd [2004] EWCA Civ 217

FACTS: The defendant recruitment agency had assigned Dacas to clean a hostel owned and run by Wandsworth Council (the end-user). Although Wandsworth Council exercised day-to-day control over her activities, the recruitment agency paid her wages, deducted tax and NI, and had the power to discipline and terminate her contract. After six years, the local authority asked the agency not to assign her to it, following an allegation that she had been rude to a visitor of the hostel. The agency informed Dacas that it would not assign her any further work. She alleged unfair dismissal against both the recruitment agency and Wandsworth Council—but only an employee can allege unfair dismissal.

HELD: The Court of Appeal held that Dacas was an employee of Wandsworth Council, but not of the recruitment agency. The recruitment agency was not required to provide her with work, nor was she under an obligation to accept work from it. It did not exercise day-to-day control over Dacas—that was the role of Wandsworth Council. The Court agreed that no express contract of employment existed, but that did not preclude the Court from finding the existence of an implied employment contract between Dacas and the end-user.

⭐ See F Reynold, 'Negligent Agency Workers: Can There Be Vicarious Liability?' (2005) 34 ILJ 270

James v London Borough of Greenwich [2008] EWCA Civ 35

FACTS: James had worked for the end-user for three years, having been assigned to it by two successive recruitment agencies. A contract existed between James and the agency, which contained clauses denying her employee status with the agency and provided that she or the agency could terminate the agreement. A second contract existed between the agency and the end-user, which stated that James was under the full control of the end-user. Following a period of illness, the end-user decided that it no longer required her services and the agency terminated her agreement. She could not allege unfair dismissal against the agency, because it lacked the requisite control over her and had an express term stating that she was not an employee. She therefore alleged that there was an implied contract between her and the end-user and that, as such, she was the end-user's employee.

HELD: James was not an employee of the end-user. The Court of Appeal stated that it would be rare to imply a contract between a worker and an end-user where no pre-existing contract existed. Further, working for one end-user for a significant period is not enough to justify the implication of a contract.

⭐ See M Wynn, 'End of the Line for Temps?' (2008) 158 NLJ 352

The consequence of the above decisions is that many agency workers are unable to demonstrate the existence of a contract of employment, either due to a lack of mutuality or control, or because the court is unwilling to imply a contract of employment. It may be the case, however, that, in certain fields of employment law, agency workers can gain protection by bringing themselves within the definition of 'worker'.

Distinguishing 'workers' and 'employees'

It can be argued that the divide between employees and independent contractors can be significant, and that the UK workforce is too diverse to be shoehorned into one of these two categories.[43] What is required is an intermediate category for those who do not fit neatly into the definition of 'employee' or 'self-employed'. It can be argued that such a category has existed for some time—namely, the concept of the 'worker'. The definition of 'worker' is important on both a European and domestic level.

From a European perspective, English translations of directives have used the term inconsistently, with certain directives applying to workers,[44] whilst others apply to employees.[45] The European Court of Justice (ECJ) has stated that how these terms are defined is a matter for the individual member States, unless the ECJ (or Court of First Instance) considers that a Community meaning of the term is required in order to create uniform harmonization.[46] The lack of uniformity is apparent in domestic law, too, but there is little doubt that the term 'worker' is gradually replacing the term 'employee' in employment legislation.[47] It is therefore of vital importance to define what a worker is.

The ERA 1996, s 230(3), defines a worker as:

- someone who has entered into a contract of employment; or
- someone who has not entered into a contract of employment, but who undertakes to perform personally work or services for another, provided that these services are not being provided for a professional client.

The leading judicial discussion of the term 'worker' can be found in the case of *Byrne Bros v Baird*.[48] The case concerned the Working Time Regulations 1998 and the EAT articulated why these Regulations apply to workers and not only employees, stating: 'The reason why employees are thought to need such protection is that they are in a subordinate and dependent position vis-à-vis their employers: the purpose of the Regulations is to extend protection to workers who are, substantively and economically, in the same position.'[49] The EAT also indicated that, in determining whether an individual was a worker or not, it would use the same considerations used when determining whether an individual is an employee or self-employed, 'but with the boundary pushed further in the [assumed] worker's favour'.[50]

---

43. I Smith and G Thomas, *Smith & Wood's Employment Law* (9th edn, OUP, Oxford, 2008) 87.
44. For example, the Health and Safety Directive (Council Directive No 89/391/EC) and the Working Time Directive (Council Directive No 93/104/EC).
45. For example, the European Works Council Directive (Council Directive No 94/45/EC) and the Insolvency Directive (Council Directive No 80/987/EC).
46. Case C-53/81 *DM Levin v Staatssecretaris van Justitie* [1982] ECR 1035.
47. For example, the National Minimum Wage Act 1998, ss 1 and 54, and the Working Time Regulations 1998, SI 1998/1833, reg 2(1).
48. [2002] ICR 667 (EAT).
49. Ibid, 677. It could be argued that such individual extensions of protection are unnecessary, because the ERA 1999, s 23, allows the Secretary of State to extend the protection offered by employment legislation to persons not covered by that legislation, or even persons expressly excluded. But this power has not been regularly used.
50. Ibid.

It is argued that the increasing use of the term 'worker' is a welcome one. Too often, employers are able to avoid their obligations by convincing a court or tribunal that an individual is not an employee under the relevant legislation. There is little doubt that the wider notion of the 'worker' will result in an extension of protection to previously unprotected individuals. Further, it will avoid the need for the court to force the individual into one of two polarized possibilities: employee or self-employed.

 Key points summary

- Self-labelling of an employment relationship is not conclusive and the courts will only take such labels into account if the issue is ambiguous.

- Historically, the courts developed several tests to distinguish employees and independent contractors. But the modern view is that this distinction now depends upon the individual facts of the case.

- Atypical workers include agency workers and homeworkers. Atypical workers often work outside normal working hours or may work from home.

- Increasingly, statutes are expanding the scope of the protection offered by providing rights to 'workers' instead of 'employees'.

The terms of the employment contract

Historically, the existence on an employer–employee relationship derived from the status of master and servant. Today, it is clear that the basis of the employment relationship is to be found in the contract of employment. Judges and academics have stated repeatedly that an employment contract 'is but an example of contracts in general, so that the general law of contract will be applicable'.[51] Certainly, it is true that contracts of employment are subject to the normal rules of contract, but it is also true that the contract of employment is subject to so much statutory regulation and implied terms that 'it is certainly open to doubt whether we should still accept that contract law alone provides the underlying structure of employment law'.[52]

The sources and content of the terms of the contract of employment will now be considered.

Express terms

Subject to limitations imposed by statute, the parties may (either orally or in writing) specify terms to be included in the contract. Since 1963, employees have been entitled to receive a copy of the written particulars of the contract following the

---

51. *Laws v London Chronicle* [1959] 2 All ER 285 (CA) 287 (Evershed MR).
52. I Smith and G Thomas, *Smith & Wood's Employment Law* (9th edn, OUP, Oxford, 2008) 89.

commencement of employment.[53] Today, the right is found in the ERA 1996, s 1, which provides that employees have a general right to receive a written statement of the particulars of employment no later than two months following the commencement of employment. The Act also prescribes exactly what particulars must be included:

- the names of the employer and employee;
- the date on which employment began and the date on which the contract of employment commences (known as the 'date of continuous employment');
- the employee's scale or rate of remuneration, or its method of calculation, and the frequency of payment;
- the employee's hours of work;
- information concerning holiday entitlements and pay, sick pay, and pension schemes;
- notice requirements;
- the job title and/or description;
- the length of employment if the contract is not permanent;
- the place of work or, where the employee is required or permitted to work at various places, an indication of that, and the address of the employer;
- collective agreements that directly affect the terms and conditions of employment (see below); and
- where the employee is required to work outside the UK for a period of more than one month, the period for which he is to work outside the UK and any additional payment that he is to receive for working outside the UK.

Under s 11, if the statement is not provided within two months, or if the statement is incomplete, the employee has the right to refer the issue to an employment tribunal, which can determine what should be included in the statement (although it cannot invent terms).[54] The tribunal will also award the employee a minimum of two weeks' pay,[55] unless the failure to receive a statement is connected to unfair dismissal or discrimination, in which case the minimum award is increased to four weeks' pay.

The above particulars are relatively straightforward. One does require further explanation, however—namely, collective agreements. Collective agreements are agreements (usually relating to working conditions, holiday entitlements, etc.) made between employers and trade unions,[56] and, unless expressly stated in writing,[57] they are not presumed to be legally enforceable. But if the parties expressly incorporate them into the contract, they will become enforceable as express terms and will be required to form part of the written statement discussed above. It is also possible for collective agreements to be implied into a contract, but simply belonging to the union or association that negotiated the collective agreement is insufficient to

---

53. Contracts of Employment Act 1963, s 4.

54. *Eagland v British Telecommunications plc* [1993] ICR 644 (CA).

55. Employment Act 2002, s 38(4)(a).

56. The precise definition and scope of collective agreements can be found in the Trade Union and Labour Relations (Consolidation) Act 1992, s 178.

57. Ibid, s 179(1).

justify implication its implication.[58] If, however, it can be demonstrated that, during bargaining, it was the intention of the parties that the final agreement would be binding, the court may imply the agreement into the contract.[59] The terms of a collective agreement may also be implied into a contract if it can be demonstrated that there is a reasonable, certain, and notorious custom to that effect.[60] Where such a custom exists, the provisions of a collective agreement may be implied into the contract of an employee who is not a member of the union.[61]

Implied terms relating to the conduct of the employer

The implication of terms is discussed at p 213

The concept of implying terms into a contract has already been examined in relation to contract law. In relation to employment law issues, terms may be implied from a number of sources:

- by the courts, as a matter of fact based upon the intentions of the parties;
- by the courts as a matter of law;
- by statute;
- by custom and practice.

We will now examine a selection of the main duties placed upon employers.

Duty to provide work

In *Collier v Sunday Referee Publishing Co Ltd*,[62] a newspaper sub-editor was hired, but not given any work to do. He initiated a claim for breach of contract against his employer. In a much-quoted passage, Asquith J stated: 'It is true that a contract of employment does not necessarily, or perhaps normally, oblige the master to provide the servant with work. Provided I pay my cook her wages regularly she cannot complain if I choose to take any or all of my meals out.'[63] But whilst no general duty to provide work exists, specific duties will arise in certain circumstances:

- where the employee is paid by commission,[64] because refusal to provide work will mean that the employee will earn no money;
- where the job in question requires regular practice in order to maintain skills;[65]
- where the lack of a job would lead to loss of publicity or reputation (for example, that of an actor or actress).[66]

---

58. *Hamilton v Futura Floors Ltd* [1990] IRLR 478.
59. *Rookes v Barnard* [1964] AC 1129 (HL).
60. *Henry v London General Transport Services Ltd* [2002] EWCA Civ 488, [2002] ICR 910.
61. Ibid. But in the absence of such a custom, it is highly unlikely that the terms of a collective agreement will be implied into a non-member's contract of employment: *Singh v British Steel Corporation* [1974] IRLR 131 (IT).
62. [1940] 2 KB 647 (KB).
63. Ibid, 650.
64. *Turner v Goldsmith* [1891] 1 QB 544 (CA).
65. *William Hill Organisation Ltd v Tucker* [1999] ICR 291 (CA).
66. *Marbé v George Edwardes (Daly's Theatre) Ltd* [1928] 1 KB 269 (CA).

Duty to pay the employee

In *Beveridge v KLM (UK) Ltd*,[67] Beveridge, after a long-term period of illness and having exhausted her right to sick pay, announced that she was fit to return to work. But her employer would not let her return to work until its own doctor deemed her fit to return—a process that took six weeks, during which time Beveridge was not being paid, even though she was willing to work. The EAT held that, in the absence of a contractual provision, employees who offer work to their employers are entitled to be paid. But this duty to pay the employee will not apply where the lack of work is due to circumstances outside the control of the employer (for example, a strike,[68] or the closure of a workplace due to a natural disaster).[69]

Duty to indemnify the employee

The employer is under a duty to indemnify the employee for any expenses reasonably incurred during the course of his employment. This would not only include obvious examples such as travelling expenses, but may also include indemnifying the employee for any costs incurred in defending a legal action.[70] This duty will not apply, however, where the employee has incurred costs defending his own negligence.

Duty of mutual trust, confidence, and respect

Because the employment relationship is based upon confidence and trust, it follows that employers are under a duty not to act in a manner that would jeopardize this relationship. Examples of breach of this duty include requiring an employee to relocate at short notice[71] and referring to an employee as an 'intolerable bitch'.[72] Virtually all cases in this area are constructive dismissal cases, but the first case not involving constructive dismissal provided the duty with a renewed prominence.

➡ **constructive dismissal:** an employee's termination of his employment as a result of the negative actions of the employer

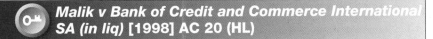

Malik v Bank of Credit and Commerce International SA (in liq) [1998] AC 20 (HL)

FACTS: In 1991, BCCI entered insolvent liquidation amidst allegations of fraud, corruption, and criminal activity. The liquidator dismissed two employees named Malik and Mahmud. Both men claimed that, due to the stigma surrounding the collapse of BCCI, their reputations had been damaged to such an extent that they could not obtain alternative employment. This, they argued, amounted to a breach of the implied duty of mutual trust and confidence.

HELD: The claimants succeeded and the House of Lords awarded them 'stigma damages'. The House of Lords held that, by acting in a dishonest and corrupt manner, BCCI had damaged the claimant's employment prospects. This, in turn, had damaged the relationship of trust and confidence, entitling the claimants to compensation.

⭐ See M Jefferson, 'Stigma Damages Against Corrupt Companies' (1998) 19 Co Law 21

---

67. [2000] IRLR 765 (EAT).
68. *Miles v Wakefield MDC* [1987] AC 539 (HL).
69. *Browning v Crumlin Valley Collieries Ltd* [1926] 1 KB 522 (KB) (flooding in a mineshaft).
70. *Re Famatina Development Corporation Ltd* [1914] 2 Ch 271 (CA).
71. *United Bank v Akhtar* [1989] IRLR 507 (EAT).
72. *Isle of Wight Tourist Board v JJ Coombes* [1976] IRLR 413 (EAT).

Duty to take reasonable care of employees' health and safety

As we shall see in Chapter 24, employers are under both a common law and statutory duty to take reasonable care of the health and safety of their employees. What is important to note here is that this implied term may actually override any express terms of the contract (for example, if an employee's contract requires him to work a number of hours that can be damaging to health).[73]

Duty to deal with grievances

Employers are under a duty to put into place measures to deal effectively and promptly with the grievances of their employees. In *WA Goold (Pearmak) v McConnel*,[74] a change in sales methods resulted in the reduction of commission due to two salesmen. The company had no grievance procedure, so they tried to raise the matter informally with their manager, the managing director, and, ultimately, the chairman. When this failed, they resigned, alleging constructive dismissal.[75] The EAT held that their employer had breached an implied term to provide a reasonable opportunity to obtain redress for any grievances.

Duty of confidentiality

As we shall see, it is well established that an employee owes a duty of confidentiality to his employer; it has only recently been accepted that the employer may owe a similar duty to his employees. Thus, in *Dalgleish v Lothian and Borders Police Board*,[76] an injunction was granted to stop the defendant disclosing to a local council details of its employees to ascertain if they had paid their community charge.

Statute also provides employees with rights relating to the use of their personal information. Extensive regulation can be found in the Data Protection Act 1988. It is a criminal offence to intercept employee communications in the course of transmission[77] (for example, monitoring telephone calls). But employers are able to access, without consent, the employee's email account and other forms of communication in a number of circumstances.[78]

Duty to provide references

Employers may be reluctant to provide references, largely because of the potential imposition of liability for defamation or negligent misstatement.[79] In *Spring v Guardian Assurance plc*,[80] the House of Lords held that employers have both a tortious

---

73. See the judgment of Stuart-Smith LJ in *Johnstone v Bloomsbury Area Health Authority* [1992] QB 333 (CA).

74. [1995] IRLR 516 (EAT).

75. Today, grievances resulting in constructive dismissal would need to adhere to the statutory grievance procedure set out in the Employment Act 2002, Sch 2, Pt 2.

76. 1992 SLT 721. It should be noted that, because this is a Scottish case, it provides only persuasive authority.

77. Regulation of Investigatory Powers Act 2000, s 1. Such interception is allowed if an 'interception warrant' is obtained.

78. Telecommunications (Lawful Business Practice) (Interception of Communications) Regulations 2000, SI 2000/2699, reg 3. Reasons include to protect national security, to aid in the detection of a crime, and to discover whether the communications are being used for business purposes.

79. *Hedley Byrne & Co Ltd v Heller & Partners Ltd* [1964] AC 465 (HL).

80. [1994] ICR 596 (HL).

and contractual duty not to produce a negligent reference. Note that this does not prevent the employer from writing an unflattering reference; rather, it simply places a duty on the employer not to write a negligent reference.

Cox v Sun Alliance Life Ltd [2001] EWCA Civ 649

FACTS: Cox (the claimant) was promoted to office manager, but, following an altercation with several members of staff who, according to Rix LJ, had 'mutinied against him',[81] he was suspended. During his suspension, allegations were made that Cox had engaged in improper conduct—namely, receiving a number of improper payments totalling £1,250. The employer's own investigation was not particularly thorough and an audit investigation found no evidence of dishonesty. Cox resigned, upon the agreement that his employers would provide him with an agreed reference making no mention of the alleged and unproven dishonesty. Subsequently, however, Cox's former employer spoke to two employers who had agreed to employ Cox, informing them of the allegations of dishonesty. Both employers dismissed Cox.

HELD: The Court of Appeal held that Cox's ex-employer had breached its duty of care to provide Cox with an accurate and fair reference. His ex-employer had acted without objectivity and its conduct was 'wholly unfair'.

See J Gidney, 'Walking the Reference Tightrope' (2001) 151 NLJ 1274

The question that arises is whether the employer is now under a positive duty to provide a reference if one is requested. The existence of a general duty is unlikely, but specific duties may exist. In *Spring*, Lords Hadley and Woolf indicated that a duty would exist where the current occupation of the employee is of the type that normally requires a reference. Lord Woolf even stated that the duty could continue to exist for a reasonable time after the employee's contract has ended. This is undoubtedly an area in which the law will develop.

Duties in relation to trade unions

Statute imposes a number of duties upon the employer in relation to trade unions. It is unlawful to refuse to employ a person on the ground that he belongs to, or refuses to join a union,[82] and dismissal of an employee on the ground that he belongs to, or refuses to join or to take part in the activities of, a trade union is automatically regarded as unfair dismissal.[83]

If a trade union wishes to bargain with an employer collectively, it can do this only if it is 'recognized' by the employer. Recognition can be voluntary, but unions can ensure recognition by following the statutory rules relating to recognition found in the Trade Union and Labour Relations (Consolidation) Act 1992, Sch A1. Employers are under a duty to disclose to recognized unions material information to enable them to engage in collective bargaining.[84] Agreements made between unions and employers as a result of collective bargaining are known as 'collective

---

81. *Cox v Sun Alliance Life Ltd* [2001] EWCA Civ 649, [2001] IRLR 448, [26].
82. Trade Union and Labour Relations (Consolidation) Act 1992, s 137(1).
83. Ibid, s 152(1).
84. Ibid, s 181.

agreements',[85] and the contents of such agreements may be incorporated into the contract of employment as express terms. Such terms affect the employee even if he is not a member of the union.

Implied terms relating to the conduct of the employee

Duty of obedience

An employee is under a duty to obey any reasonable instructions from the employer and failure to do so will constitute a breach of contract, allowing the employer to dismiss the employee without notice. Thus, in *Pepper v Webb*,[86] a gardener who refused who put plants into a garden was validly dismissed. The duty of obedience will also include reasonable requests to relocate[87] and the adaptation of new working methods.[88] This duty is, however, subject to a number of qualifications, as follows.

- The instructions must be lawful. Therefore, an employee will not breach this duty if he refuses to drive an uninsured vehicle,[89] or refuses to falsify records.[90]
- The instructions must not place the employee in danger. In *Ottoman Bank v Chakarian*,[91] an employee who was under a death sentence in Turkey disobeyed his employer, which had order him to remain in Constantinople (now Istanbul). The employee had not breached his duty of obedience. But the belief in the danger must be reasonable and personal. Thus an employee was validly dismissed for refusing to go to Wexford, Eire, based upon an unsubstantiated belief that it was a seat of terrorist activity.[92]
- The instructions must not relate to activities outside the scope of the employee's contract.

Duty of fidelity

The duty of fidelity (or of good faith, as it if often referred) is an extremely wide-ranging duty that encompasses a number of activities that could validly be regarded as duties in their own right. Here, several key aspects of the duty will be discussed.

The employee will breach the duty of fidelity if he acts in a manner that disrupts the employer's business. Thus, in *British Telecommunications plc v Ticehurst*,[93] Ticehurst (a BT manager) organized and took part in a strike and a withdrawal of goodwill. The company informed its employees that further strike action would be regarded as a breach of their employment contracts. Ticehurst continued to strike and BT refused to pay her for the duration of the strike, leading Ticehurst to claim for the deducted pay. Her claim failed: by refusing to work in a normal manner, her actions had disrupted and inconvenienced her employer, and breached her duty of fidelity.

---

85. The definition and content of a collective agreement can be found in ibid, s 178.
86. [1969] 1 WLR 514 (CA).
87. *United Kingdom Atomic Energy Authority v Claydon* [1974] ICR 128 (NIRC).
88. *Cresswell v Inland Revenue Commissioners* [1984] ICR 508 (Ch) (employees refused to adapt to computer-based tax system).
89. *Gregory v Ford* [1951] 1 All ER 121.
90. *Morrish v Henlys (Folkestone)* [1973] ICR 482 (NIRC).
91. [1930] AC 277 (PC).
92. *FG Walmsley v UCED Refrigeration Ltd* [1972] IRLR 80.
93. [1992] ICR 383 (CA).

The duty of fidelity can also be breached if an employee has an interest that conflicts with those of his employer. Such conflicts can arise in a number of ways. For example, an employee may make a profit by virtue of his employment and not disclose it to his employer. In such a case, the employee will be in breach of duty and the employer will be able to recover the profit made.[94] The principal conflict of interest arises where the employee's activities compete with the interests of his employer. The courts are normally reluctant to impose limits on what the employee does in his spare time, but if the employee is engaged in an activity in his spare time that causes harm to his employer, it is likely to constitute a breach of duty. In *Hivac Ltd v Park Royal Scientific Instruments Ltd*,[95] employees of the claimants made hearing aids. In their spare time, they did exactly the same work for a rival firm. The Court found them in breach of duty and granted an injunction preventing them from working for the rival firm. Note, however, the existence of a breach of duty will depend on the nature of the work (for example, it is likely that the result in *Hivac* would have differed if the employees were to have been engaged in manual or non-skilled work).

Does this duty extend beyond the employee's employment? Can an employee be prevented from resigning and setting up a rival business or joining a rival firm? Employers may try and achieve this via a restrictive covenant or a 'garden leave' clause.

- *Restrictive covenants* are simply contractual undertakings requiring a party to refrain from something (for example, competition with the other party). They are, however, strictly regulated, and such a covenant will be void unless it is reasonably in the interests of the parties and the public.[96]

- *Garden leave clauses* simply impose lengthy notice periods on employees, during which time they receive full pay, but are unable to work for anyone. Therefore, an employee with skills that could be useful to a rival may have such a clause imposed upon him, requiring a notice period of six months or a year, during which time he will be unable to work for a rival firm. Such clauses are, however, enforced via the granting of an injunction,[97] which is a discretionary remedy. The courts may, therefore, deny a garden leave clause by refusing to enforce it if they feel that it is unreasonable (for example, where allowing an employee to leave would not harm the business interests of the employer).[98]

The validity of restrictive covenants that restrain trade is discussed at p 282

Duty to use reasonable skill and care

It is a long-established principle that, when an individual is employed, 'there is on his part an implied warranty that he is of skill reasonably competent to the task he undertakes'.[99] Breach of this duty allows the employer to dismiss the employee and to claim damages for any loss. Thus, in *Janata Bank v Ahmed (Qutubuddin)*,[100] a bank manager who lent substantial sums to individuals without checking their

---

94. *Reading v Attorney General* [1951] AC 507 (HL).

95. [1946] Ch 169 (CA).

96. *Thorsten Nordenfelt v The Maxim Nordenfelt Guns and Ammunition Company* [1894] AC 535 (HL).

97. As occurred in *Evening Standard Co Ltd v Henderson* [1987] ICR 588 (CA), in which the Court enforced a year-long garden leave clause and prevented a newspaper production manager from taking up employment with a rival newspaper.

98. *Provident Financial Group plc v Hayward* [1989] ICR 160 (CA).

99. *Harmer v Cornelius* [1843–60] All ER Rep 624, 625 (Willes J).

100. [1981] ICR 791 (CA).

creditworthiness was held to have breached this duty and was required to compensate his employer.

The significance of this duty arises where an employee commits a tort that causes loss to a third party and the third party commences proceedings against the employer via the doctrine of vicarious liability. We have already noted that an employer can obtain a contribution from the employee under the Civil Liability (Contribution) Act 1978, s 1, but it is also open for the employer to claim damages for breach of the implied term to exercise reasonable skill and care.[101]

The ability to claim a contribution under the Civil Liability (Contribution) Act 1978 is discussed at p 376

Duty of confidentiality

Some regard the duty of confidentiality as an aspect of the duty of fidelity[102] discussed above, but, given its recent prominence, it is beneficial to discuss it separately.

Issues of confidentiality can arise in a number of ways. An employee might pass on trade secrets belonging to his employer in return for payment or a job offer. This would clearly constitute a breach of duty. But what if an employee were to leave his employer and set up a new business using information acquired in his previous occupation? In other words, does the duty of confidentiality owed to an employer end once the employee leaves its employment? The answer is clearly 'no'. In *Roger Bullivant Ltd v Ellis*,[103] an employer who set up a new firm after acquiring technical data and customer lists from his previous employer was held to have breached his duty to his former employer. The courts have, however, distinguished genuinely confidential information from commercial 'know-how', with usage or disclosure of the latter not constituting a breach of duty.[104]

So what is the position if an employee wishes to disclose confidential *unlawful* acts of an employer? The employee is not legally obliged to disclose, but if he does, will he breach his duties of confidentiality? The 1980s and 1990s witnessed a number of instances of fatal accidents (for example, the Zeebrugge ferry disaster,[105] and the Clapham rail crash[106]) and instances of corporate corruption (for example, BCCI), which could have been prevented had certain employees been free to disclose what they knew without fear of retribution. Professor Stephen Bolsin of Bristol Royal Infirmary was forced to emigrate to Australia due to threats and discriminatory behaviour that followed his disclosure of the infirmary's high infant mortality rate. In response to such instances, the Public Interest Disclosure Act 1988 was passed, to allow so-called 'whistleblowers' to disclose freely instances of employer wrongdoing that are deemed 'protected'. This includes disclosure of criminal offences, failures to comply with a legal obligation, the endangerment of health and safety, or instances of miscarriages of justice.[107] Disclosure may be made to the employer, or, where it relates the employer's conduct, it may be made to an outside party (for example, a regulator).

Figure 23.1 sets out examples of the terms of the employment contract.

---

101. See *Lister v Romford Ice and Cold Storage Co Ltd* [1957] AC 555 (HL).
102. M Sargeant and D Lewis, *Employment Law* (4th edn, Pearson, London, 2008) 97.
103. [1987] ICR 464 (CA).
104. *Faccenda Chicken v Fowler* [1987] Ch 117 (CA).
105. In 1987, the ferry *Herald of Free Enterprise* sank, killing 193 passengers.
106. In 1988, two trains collided near Clapham Junction, killing thirty-five people and injuring another 500.
107. Employment Rights Act 1996, s 43B.

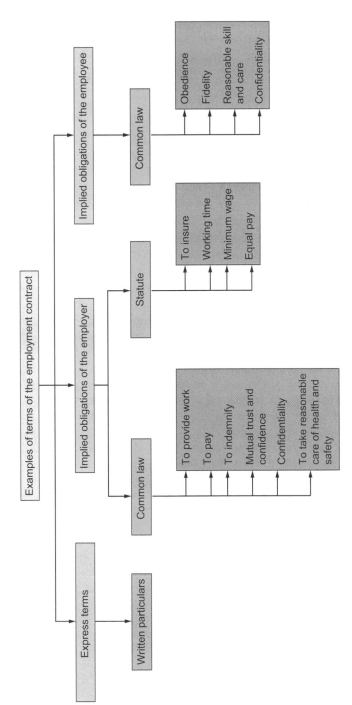

FIGURE 23.1 Terms of the employment contract

Key points summary

- Employees have a statutory right to receive written particulars of the contract within two months of commencing employment.

- Terms of the contract may be express or implied.

- Express terms may derive from the parties themselves or from a collective agreement (an agreement between an employer and a trade union).

- Implied terms may derive from the intentions of the parties, the courts, statute, and through trade and custom.

- Employers are, inter alia, subject to duties to provide work, to pay the employee, to indemnify the employee, to treat the employee with trust and confidence, to take reasonable care of the employees' health and safety, to deal with grievances, to provide a fair and accurate reference, to preserve confidentiality, and various duties in relation to trade unions.

- Employees are, inter alia, subject to duties of obedience, fidelity, to perform their jobs with reasonable skill and care, and not to breach confidentiality in relation to information belonging to their employer.

Chapter conclusion

There is a gradual move towards increasing the scope of employment law protection by providing it to 'workers', as opposed to the narrower category of 'employees'. When such a practice is universal, determining the scope of the protection offered by employment law legislation should become considerably easier. But that day has yet to arrive, and businesses and employers still need to be aware of the distinction between 'employees', 'independent contractors', and 'workers'.

Whilst employers will doubtless be aware of the express obligations imposed upon them in the contract of employment, they should also ensure they are fully aware of the considerable number of implied obligations that employment contracts contain. These implied terms impose a substantial number of duties upon employers and breach of these duties will also constitute breach of the employment contract, entitling the employee to a remedy. Employers should also be aware of the express and implied obligations placed upon employees, because breach of such obligations might allow the employer to remove an employee whose actions could cause harm to the business.

Self-test questions

1. Define the following:
   (a) Employment Appeal Tribunal;
   (b) garden leave;
   (c) whistleblower;
   (d) protected disclosure.

2. Explain the practical significance of the distinction between employees and independent contractors.

3. Explain the operation of the various tests used by the courts to determine the distinction between employees and independent contractors, and to what extent these tests have survived.

4. Christian is a marketing consultant. He contracts with MicroMart plc to carry out a review of the company's marketing strategy. The contract is based on standard terms drawn up by Christian. The contract provides that Christian is to be an employee of MicroMart for the duration of the review, and that he is not required to take orders from MicroMart's management and can cancel the contract without notice at any time. Christian's work proves to be unsatisfactory and MicroMart terminates the contract. Christian alleges that he has been unfairly dismissed, but the right not to be unfairly dismissed only extends to employees. MicroMart argue that Christian was never its employee. How would you advise Christian?

5. What is required to be included in the written statement of particulars provided to employees and when must this statement be provided?

6. Has a breach of the employment contract occurred in the following cases?
   (a) Dylan works in a factory. Due to the negligence of another employee, the factory catches fire and severe damage is caused. The factory will be closed for a week and, during this week, all employees (including Dylan) will not be paid.
   (b) John is employed as an area manager for CostMart Ltd. A rival company offers John a better job and more money, but only if John provides it with a reference from his current employer. CostMart wishes to keep John and so refuses to provide a reference.

Further reading

Baker, N, 'Employee Status: Ongoing Saga' (2006) 29 CSR 177
Discusses recent cases concerning the statutory definition of 'employee'

Brodie, D, 'Legal Coherence and the Employment Revolution' (2001) 117 LQR 604
Examines the employer's duty of mutual trust and confidence, and how it has been affected by statute

Davidov, G, 'Who is a Worker?' (2005) 34 ILJ 57
Discusses the philosophy behind, and the importance of the increased use of, the term 'worker' in UK legislation

Department of Trade and Industry, *Better Dispute Resolution: A Review of Employment Dispute Resolution in Great Britain* (DTI, London, 2004)
Examines the effectiveness of employment tribunals and the Employment Appeal Tribunal, and suggests a number of reforms aimed at improving dispute resolution in employment cases

Flannigan, R, 'The (Fiduciary) Duty of Fidelity' (2008) 124 LQR 274
Examines the origins and evolution of the employee's duty of fidelity

Fredman, S, 'Labour Law in Flux: The Changing Composition of the Workforce' (1997) 26 ILJ 337
Examines the response of the law to non-standard forms of work—especially casual, part-time, and temporary workers

Leighton, P, and Wynn, M, 'Temporary Agency Working: Is the Law on the Turn?' (2008) 29 Co Law 7
Detailed, but highly readable, examination of current developments relating to the employment law protection offered to agency workers

Middlemiss, S, 'The Truth and Nothing but the Truth? The Legal Liability of Employers for Employee References' (2004) 33 ILJ 59
Examines a number of recent cases concerning the employer's duty to provide a reference, and also looks at the human rights aspects and the role of exclusion clauses

Smith, I, and Thomas, G, *Smith & Wood's Employment Law* (9th edn, OUP, Oxford, 2008) chs 3 and 4
Provides a detailed, but readable, account of the differing forms of worker and the contents of the contract of employment

Websites

<http://www.direct.gov.uk/en/employment/employees/employmentcontractsand conditions/DG_10027916>
Accessible and up-to-date information on the contract of employment collated from a number of online governmental sources

<http://www.employmentappeals.gov.uk>
The official website of the Employment Appeal Tribunal; contains up-to-date information on the work of the EAT, as well as access to all judgments of the EAT since 1999

<http://www.employmenttribunals.gov.uk>
The official website of employment tribunals; contains a significant amount of up-to-date information and links to relevant legislation

Remember to visit the **Online Resource Centre** at **<http://www. oxfordtextbooks.co.uk/roach>** to access the following resources on Chapter 23, 'The contract of employment': more **practice questions** and answers; a **glossary** of key terms; **multiple-choice questions; revision summaries; audio updates** when relevant; and **diagrams** in pdf.

24 Employment rights, and health and safety

- Employment rights
- Health and safety

INTRODUCTION

Much of employment law is about protecting the rights of employees. In the previous chapter, we discussed the contract of employment and the rights within it. In this chapter, we will move on to examine what employment rights are provided by law to employees. Today, employees are granted numerous rights to which employers are required to adhere, including the right to equal pay and working conditions, and a raft of rights relating to the family. In addition to upholding these rights, businesses also have substantial requirements in terms of protecting the health and safety of their employees. For both employers and their employees, the losses caused by inadequate health and safety measures can be substantial. In 2007–08, 2.1 million employees suffered from an illness that they believed to be work-related. A further 229 employees were killed due to work-related accidents and 299,000 suffered work-related injuries. The combined result is that UK businesses lost over 34 million work days due to work-related illnesses and accidents in 2007–08.[1] The cost of such losses to society has been estimated at over £30 billion[2] and the actual cost will be even greater once the cost of settling or contesting any resultant litigation is included. Clearly, it is therefore vital that we have an effective system of regulation for health and safety at work in place in order to minimize such losses.

Employment rights

In addition to any rights contained in the employment contract, the law provides employees with a number of free-standing rights. Here, we will examine the principal rights, beginning with the right to equal pay.

---

1. Health and Safety Executive, *Health and Safety Statistics 2007/08* (HSE, London, 2008) 5.
2. Institute of Directors/Health and Safety Commission, *Leading Health and Safety at Work* (HSE, London, 2007) 1.

Equal pay

The EC Treaty places an obligation upon all member States to 'ensure that the principle of equal pay for male and female workers for equal work or work of equal value is applied'.[3] Even before the UK joined the EU, Parliament had enacted provisions relating to equal pay via the passing of the Equal Pay Act 1970 (EPA 1970), the aim of which is stated in the Act's long title—namely, 'to prevent discrimination as regards terms and conditions of employment between men and women'. The need for such legislation was evidenced by the fact that, at the time that the EPA 1970 was passed, a woman's hourly rate of pay was 63 per cent of that of a man.[4] Although the Act was passed in 1970, in order to provide employers with the necessary time to ensure compliance, the Act did not come into force until December 1975. The first few years of the Act's operation saw a significant levelling in the pay of men and women: by 1977, the gender pay gap that was 37 per cent in 1970 had been reduced to 24.5 per cent. Since then, however, progress has been slow and the pay of men and women is still far from equal. The pay gap between men and women is still 12.6 per cent and it has been estimated that, at the current rate of progress, the pay gap will not close until 2085.[5] Female part-time workers are paid around 40 per cent less per hour than their male counterparts.[6]

It should be noted at the outset that, although the EPA 1970 is framed with reference to the treatment of women relative to men, s 1(13) provides that such provisions will also apply to the treatment of men relative to women.

The equality clause

The EPA 1970, s 1(1), provides that if the terms of a contract under which a woman is employed at an establishment in Great Britain do not include an equality clause, they shall be deemed to include one. The effects of an equality clause are stated in s 1(2) as:

- if the women's employment contract contains a term that is less favourable than a similar term in a man's contract, then her contract shall be treated as modified so that it is not less favourable; and
- if a man's employment contract contains a term benefiting him, but such a term is not found in a woman's employment contract, then the beneficial term shall also be included in the woman's contract.

But in order for the equality clause to operate, the woman will need to pass *one* of the following three tests.

1. She must be employed in 'like work with a man in the same employment'.[7]
2. She must be employed in 'work rated as equivalent with that of a man in the same employment'.[8]

---

3. EC Treaty (Treaty of Rome, as amended) Art 141(1). In the original EC Treaty, this provision was contained in Art 119.
4. Equal Opportunities Commission, *Women and Men in Britain: At the Millennium* (EOC, London, 2000) 5.
5. Government Equalities Office, *Framework for a Fairer Future: The Equality Bill* (HMSO, London, 2008) 7.
6. Ibid.
7. EPA 1970, s 1(2)(a).
8. Ibid, s 1(2)(b).

3. She must be employed in work that, in terms of the demands made on her (for example, in terms of effort and skills), is 'of equal value to that of a man in the same employment'.[9]

Because the Act does not provide for a reversal of the burden of proof, the woman will need to show that she passes one of the three tests.[10] These three tests will now be examined in more depth.

'Like work'

The first test provides that the woman will need to establish that she is employed in 'like work with a man of the same employment'. A woman will be employed in 'like work' with that of men if 'her work and theirs is of the same or a broadly similar nature',[11] and as long as any differences that exist 'are not of practical importance in relation to terms and conditions of employment'.[12] The wording used indicates that the courts should not focus too heavily on minute and technical differences, and that the words used in s 1(4) should be interpreted broadly. Therefore, it will not be necessary for a woman to demonstrate that she performs an identical job to a man in order to satisfy the 'like work' test.

 ***Capper Pass Ltd v Lawton* [1977] ICR 83 (EAT)**

FACTS: The defendant employed the claimant as a cook and catering manager. She worked a forty-hour week in a kitchen (she was the only cook employed in the kitchen) during which she prepared daily lunches for between ten and twenty of the defendant's directors. In a different kitchen, two male assistant chefs provided lunches for the defendant's employees. The male chefs prepared around 350 meals (including breakfast, lunch, and tea) every day and they worked a forty-hour week, in addition to five-and-a-half hours' overtime and one Saturday in three. The male chefs' hourly rate of pay was higher than that of the claimant and their staff conditions were better. The claimant argued that she was entitled to an equality clause in her contract. An industrial tribunal allowed her claim, on the basis that she performed 'like work'. The defendant appealed.

HELD: The Employment Appeal Tribunal (EAT) dismissed the defendant's appeal and held that the claimant was entitled to an equality clause. Although the job performed by the claimant was not identical to that of the male chefs, the type of work was broadly similar and both parties required similar skills in order to perform their functions.

It would be thought that where a man and a woman perform identical tasks, the 'like work' test would be satisfied, but the following controversial decision of the European Court of Justice has indicated that this may not necessarily be the case.

---

9. Ibid, s 1(2)(c).

10. Except where the employer's pay system suffers from 'a total lack of transparency', in which case the employer will bear the burden of establishing that the disparity in pay is not discriminatory: C-109/88 *Handels-og Kontorfunktionaerernes i Danmark v Dansk Arbejdsgiverforening (acting for Danfoss)* [1991] ICR 74.

11. EPA 1970, s 1(4).

12. Ibid.

> ### C-309/97 *Angestelltenbetriebsrat der Wiener Gebietskrankenkasse v Wiener Gebietskrankenkasse* [1999] ECR I-2865
>
> **FACTS:** A health fund based in Vienna employed trainee physiotherapists (the majority of whom were female) and a number of qualified doctors (the majority of whom were male). Both parties performed identical functions, but the doctors received a higher salary. The trainees sought a declaration from the European Court of Justice that they were entitled to the same pay as the doctors.
>
> **HELD:** The Court refused to make such a declaration. Whilst the trainees and doctors might have performed identical tasks, the doctors could draw upon superior training and experience when performing their functions. Further, although not required by their contracts, the doctors could perform a much wider range of functions if needed.
>
> **COMMENT:** This case related to the 'same work' test found in the EC Treaty, Art 141. The case should not be considered to impose a general rule that a difference in qualifications will cause the test to fail. In fact, a difference in qualifications should be regarded as irrelevant, unless it results in a 'genuine material difference' between the work carried out by the men and the women.

In relation to any differences that exist, s 1(4) states that, in comparing a woman's work with that of a man, 'regard shall be had to the frequency or otherwise with which any such differences occur in practice as well as the nature and extent of the differences'. A key phrase here is 'in practice', because this indicates that the courts should focus on what the employees *actually* do, as opposed to what they *may* have to do or what their contract *requires* them to do.

The distinction is demonstrated in the following case.

> ### *Shields v E Coomes Holdings Ltd* [1978] ICR 1159 (CA)
>
> **FACTS:** The claimant was employed as a counterhand in a betting shop owned by the defendant. She was paid 92 pence per hour, whereas a male counterhand in the same betting shop was paid was paid £1.06 per hour. Both employees performed identical tasks, except that the male employee was required to provide physical assistance should any customers cause trouble or attempt to steal from the betting shop. There had, however, never been any trouble of this kind. The claimant brought a case, alleging that she was entitled to equal pay.
>
> **HELD:** The claimant's action succeeded. The Court of Appeal stated that the claimant performed 'like work' to that of the male employee, and that the differences between the employment were not of practical importance, because the man had not been called upon to exercise his additional duties.

This focus on the practical realities of employment means that, even if a man and a woman perform similar or identical functions, a disparity in pay may be justified where the man's level of responsibility is greater than that of the woman, or the consequences of his failure more severe. Thus, in *Eaton Ltd v Nuttall*,[13] a man and a woman were both employed as production schedulers, but the man earned £51.88 per week, whereas the woman earned £45.38 a week. The Employment Appeal Tribunal (EAT) held that the disparity in pay was justified, because the man handled packages worth between £5 and £1,000, whereas the woman handled packages worth a maximum of £2.50.

'Work rated as equivalent'

The second test is satisfied where the work of the woman is 'rated as equivalent' to that of a man. This will occur where a job evaluation study has been carried out and the work of the woman has been graded as equivalent to that of a man, based on various factors (for example, effort, skill, or decisions made).[14] In such cases, the functions performed by the man and woman may be very different (so the 'like work' test would not be satisfied), but if the job evaluation study grades them equally, the woman will be able to pass the test and the equality clause may come into operation. Whilst the EPA 1970 does not lay down any requirements for such an evaluation scheme, it has been held that it must be valid, meaning that it must be 'thorough in analysis and capable of impartial application'.[15] It follows that even where a study has been carried out, it can be challenged.

It is worth pointing out a flaw in the drafting of the EPA 1970 in relation to this test—namely, that the equality clause will operate where the work is rated as 'equivalent'. On a literal interpretation of the Act, the equality clause will not operate where the woman's work is rated more highly than a man's, because the rating is not equivalent. Fortunately, the Court of Appeal has rectified this and stated that a greater rating will qualify as equivalent,[16] but the fact that it required a decision of the Court demonstrates a notable flaw in the Act's drafting.

'Work of equal value'

The third test for the imposition of the equality clause is that the woman is employed on 'work of equal value' to that of a man. Originally, the EPA 1970 failed adequately to provide for this right in that it only allowed a woman to claim equal pay for equal work where her employer had voluntarily undertaken a job evaluation, as described above. But shortly before the Act came into force, the Equal Pay Directive[17] was passed, which provided women with a right to equal pay for equal work. In 1982, the European Court of Justice ruled that the limitation on this right that was contained in the original EPA 1970 failed to comply with the right contained in Art 141 and the Directive.[18] Accordingly, a year later, the government passed regulations[19] that amended the EPA 1970 by creating the third test discussed here.

---

13. [1977] ICR 272 (EAT).

14. EPA 1970, s 1(5).

15. *Eaton Ltd v Nuttall* [1977] ICR 272 (EAT) 277 (Phillips J).

16. *Redcar and Cleveland Borough Council v Bainbridge* [2007] EWCA Civ 929, [2008] ICR 238.

17. Council Directive No 75/117/EEC.

18. C-61/81 *EC Commission v UK* [1982] ICR 578.

19. Equal Pay (Amendment) Regulations 1983, SI 1983/1794.

The third test applies where a woman cannot satisfy the first two tests (that is, she does not provide 'like work' or 'work rated as equivalent'), but, based on the demands and obligations imposed upon her, she provides work of equal value to that of a man in the same employment. 'Like work' and 'work rated' are both concepts that can be determined without undue complexity. 'Equal work' is much more ambiguous, involving an examination of 'the almost religious mysteries of job evaluation'.[20] As a result, of the three tests, equal value claims are by far the most complex and initial cases took several years to resolve. In 1989, the then president of the EAT stated that the procedures resulted in 'delays which are properly described as scandalous and amount to a denial of justice to women seeking remedy through the judicial process'.[21] A series of regulations passed in 2004 aimed to streamline the procedures involved in these cases and equal value claims are now subject to an 'indicative timetable'—namely, twenty-five weeks where no independent expert is appointed and thirty-seven weeks where an independent expert is appointed.[22] Section 2A(4) defines an independent expert as a person on the panel on independent experts as designated by the Advisory, Conciliation and Arbitration Service (ACAS).

The new procedures provide that equal work claims will take place in two stages.

1. The tribunal will decide whether or not the woman has adequate grounds for complaint and, if so, whether the tribunal can deal with the claim, or if it requires the aid of independent experts. If a job evaluation scheme has been carried out and the woman graded lower than the man, her claim will be struck out at this stage.

2. The tribunal will determine, on the facts, whether or not the work carried out by the woman is, in fact, equal. It is important to note that the relevant test refers to the equality of individual terms. Therefore, provided that a single term is deemed unfavourable to a woman, it does not matter that the contract overall is equally favourable to men and women, as the following case demonstrates.

Hayward v Cammell Laird Shipbuilders Ltd [1988] AC 894 (HL)

FACTS: The claimant worked in a shipyard as a cook and was classified by the defendant as unskilled. She claimed that she was undertaking work of equal value compared to male shipyard workers (namely, a painter, a joiner, and an engineer), who were classified as skilled and so received higher pay. The defendant argued that whilst the men received better pay, the claimant received better sickness benefits and holiday pay, resulting in her overall contract being equally favourable.

HELD: The House of Lords allowed her claim. The EPA 1970, s 1(2)(c), referred to a specific term being unfavourable, not to the entire contract. Because the specific term regarding

---

20. I Smith and G Thomas, *Smith & Wood's Employment Law* (9th edn, OUP, Oxford, 2008) 299.

21. *Aldridge v British Telecommunications plc* [1989] ICR 790 (EAT) 799 (Wood J).

22. See the Annex to the Employment Tribunals (Constitution and Rules of Procedure) (Amendment) Regulations 2004, SI 2004/2351.

pay was unfavourable, it did not matter that the contract overall was equally favourable. The House accepted that the claimant performed equal work and so the equality clause became operational. The claimant's contract was improved so that her rate of pay was equal to that of the men.

COMMENT: As a result of this, the men would, in turn, become entitled to the improved sickness benefits and holiday pay that the claimant received.

⭐ See E Ellis, 'A Welcome Victory for Equality' (1988) 51 MLR 781

The male comparator

Although the above three tests have different meanings and functions, they all have one feature in common—namely, that they are based upon comparing the woman's pay to that of a man 'in the same employment'. The claimant will therefore, in addition to satisfying one of the three tests above, also have to locate a male employee (known as the 'male comparator') against whom the claimant's pay can be compared.[23] The male comparator must be 'in the same employment' as the claimant, which, according to the EPA 1970, s 1(6), means either:

- they are both employed by the same employer at the same establishment; or
- they both work for associated employers (that is, where one employer has direct or indirect control of the other, or both are controlled by a third person at the same establishment); or
- they both work for the same employer or associated employer on common terms and conditions, but work at different establishments in the UK.

Whilst the ability to choose her own male comparator, coupled with the above definitions of 'in the same employment', would seem to favour the claimant, finding a suitable male comparator may, in fact, be extremely difficult. Certain businesses (for example, textiles and secretarial services) may be dominated by women to such an extent that finding a male comparator within the meaning of s 1(6) may be impossible. Accordingly, a number of claimants contended that they should be able to choose a male comparator who used to be 'in the same employment', but was not at the time of the case. The Court of Appeal referred this issue[24] to the European Court of Justice, which held that a woman has the right to compare her pay to that of a male predecessor in the same job.[25] The Court of Appeal applied the decision of the European Court of Justice[26] and the EAT has since extended the principle to include a comparison with a successor.[27] But whilst the time of employment of the male comparator has been expanded, the claimant must still locate an actual comparator; the courts will not permit a comparison with a hypothetical comparator (as is permitted under the Sex Discrimination Act 1975).

The concept of the male comparator suffers from a flaw that goes to the heart of the EPA 1970. The EPA 1970 focuses on a woman's pay being less than that of

---

23. A court or tribunal cannot select the comparator; he must be selected by the claimant: *Ainsworth v Glass Tubes and Components Ltd* [1977] IRLR 74 (EAT).

24. *Macarthys Ltd v Smith* [1979] 1 WLR 1189 (CA).

25. C-129/79 *Macarthys Ltd v Smith* [1980] ECR 1275.

26. *Macarthys Ltd v Smith* [1981] QB 180 (CA).

27. *Diocese of Hallam Trustee v Connaughton* [1996] ICR 860 (EAT).

the male comparator. It follows that the EPA 1970 will be of no aid to a woman who is better qualified and more experienced than a male comparator, but is paid the same as him. Arguably, such women should be paid more. The EC Treaty, Art 141, is based on equal pay for equal work; arguably, if the work of the female is not equal, but superior, she should not have to settle for equal pay. Permitting a comparison with a hypothetical comparator could remedy this lacuna, and allow women to obtain a level of pay commensurate with their skills and experience.

Genuine material factors

If a woman can bring herself within one of the three tests described above and has located a suitable male comparator, then a presumption is raised that the disparity in pay is due to sex discrimination and the equality clause will come into effect, to provide parity between the contract of the woman and that of the male comparator. But the employer may be able to rebut the presumption by raising the defence that the disparity in pay is genuinely due to a 'material factor' other than the difference of sex.[28] The existence of this defence recognizes that there are reasons unrelated to sex that may justify a man receiving a higher rate of pay than a woman, including the following.

- *Qualifications*　A highly qualified man may be entitled to higher pay than a less-qualified woman.
- *Length of service*　A man who has worked for a company for a longer period of time than a woman may be entitled to higher pay.[29]
- *Geographical location*　A man based in a part of the country with a higher cost of living (for example, London) may be entitled to higher pay than a woman based in another part of the country, where the cost of living is much less.[30]

The above material factors are easy to justify. But a number of cases have proven more problematic—namely, cases involving part-time workers,[31] 'red-circling', and market forces.

Cases involving part-time workers being paid a lower hourly rate than full-time workers could be viewed as indirectly discriminatory on the ground that women constitute a high proportion of the part-time labour market. Early cases regarded part-time work as a genuine material factor, thereby entitling a full-time male employee to a higher hourly rate than a part-time female.[32] But more recent cases indicate that the tribunals and courts will not regard part-time work as a genuine material factor unless the higher pay of full-time workers is objectively justified by some reason other than sex.[33]

The following case demonstrates this more recent approach.

---

28. EPA 1970, s 1(3).

29. *Capper Pass Ltd v Lawton* [1977] ICR 83 (EAT).

30. *NAAFI v Varley*, The Times 1 January 1976 (EAT).

31. Part-time workers are now protected by the Part-Time Workers (Prevention of Less Favourable Treatment) Regulations 2000, SI 2000/1551, so recourse to the Equal Pay Act 1970 is likely to lessen in the future. The 2000 Regulations are discussed at p 885.

32. *Handley v H Mono Ltd* [1979] ICR 147 (EAT).

33. *Jenkins v Kingsgate (Clothing Productions) Ltd (No 2)* [1981] ICR 715 (EAT).

Barry v Midland Bank plc [1999] ICR 859 (HL)

FACTS: The claimant was employed by the defendant full-time between 1979 and 1990. From 1990 onwards, after giving birth, she continued to work part-time. In 1993, she accepted voluntary redundancy. The severance payment was calculated based on her salary at the date of redundancy (accordingly, her eleven years' full-time service was irrelevant). She contended that, in failing to take into account the fact that, for eleven years, her salary was that of a full-time worker, the defendant had indirectly discriminated against her on the ground of sex, which contravened the equality clause contained in her contract.

HELD: The House of Lords dismissed her claim. Because the severance payment was calculated based on pay at the time of redundancy, all employees were treated the same. Further, the defendant's actions were objectively justified, in that it sought to cushion the impact of the redundancies, which was a legitimate justification that was not based on sex.

The second problematic area relates to 'red-circling'. This usually occurs where an employee's job is downgraded, but to avoid breaching the employment contract, the employer protects (or 'red-circles') the pay of the downgraded employee. The following example demonstrates the problem that has arisen.

 The problem of 'red-circling'

John is employed in a factory as a 'Grade 1' engineer. His contract of employment entitles him to £25,000 per year and his current contract has another five years to run. He is downgraded to a 'Grade 2' engineer. Such engineers are only paid £20,000 per year, but to pay John this lower amount would constitute a breach of his employment contract. Accordingly, his employer protects (red-circles) John's salary and he continues to receive £25,000 per year. Kelly is employed as a 'Grade 2' engineer and receives £20,000 per year, even though she is performing exactly the same work as John, who is receiving £5,000 more.

The courts have stated that red-circling can constitute a genuine material factor, provided that the red-circling occurs for a reason not (directly or indirectly) related to sex,[34] as occurred in the following case.

 Methven v Cow Industrial Polymers Ltd [1980] ICR 463 (CA)

FACTS: The defendant company employed three clerks (one each for the mill, the press shop, and the trimming shop). The clerk of the press shop (a man) was paid more than the clerks of the mill and the trimming shop (both women). The reason for this was that, for the

---

34. *Snoxell v Vauxhall Motors Ltd* [1978] QB 11 (EAT).

previous twenty-five years, the clerk of the press shop was a long-standing employee who had been moved to the press shop due to age or ill health. As such, the clerk of the press shop was paid more, even though he did the same work as the other clerks (in effect, the post of clerk of the press shop was red-circled). The female clerks alleged that their lower pay was discriminatory.

HELD: The Court of Appeal held that the red-circling constituted a genuine material factor and so was not discriminatory. The post of clerk of the press room was not red-circled due to reasons of sex, but due to reasons of age and ill health.

The third and final problematic issue relates to market forces. This tends to occur where market forces dictate that an employer, in order to attract employees of sufficient calibre, will need to pay new employees more than existing employees. Where a new male employee is being paid more than an existing female employee, the female employee is likely to feel aggrieved. The question is whether the market forces that forced the employer to offer higher wages can constitute a genuine material factor.

In the following case, the House of Lords established that where a difference in pay exists for some sound economic reason, this will constitute a genuine material factor.

Rainey v Greater Glasgow Health Board [1987] AC 224 (HL)

FACTS: The defendant Health Board set up a prosthetic fitting service. In order to attract sufficient numbers of qualified prosthetists from the private sector, the Health Board stated that it would pay such prosthetists the same pay as they were earning in the private sector. Twenty new prosthetists were taken on, all of whom happened to be men. A woman prosthetist was taken on a year later, but because she was not previously employed in the private sector, she received £2,790 less than the men, even though she was doing the same work. She initiated an action, alleging that she was entitled to the same pay as the new male prosthetists.

HELD: The House of Lords rejected her claim and held that the genuine material factor defence was not limited to personal characteristics, but can also apply to other objective grounds. Here, the increased pay paid to the new prosthetists was based on a sound objective justification—namely, to expand the prosthetics fitting service. The fact that all of the new prosthetists employed were male was simply coincidental.

★ See P Schofield, 'Equal Pay: What's the Difference?' (1987) 50 MLR 379

Enforcement and remedies

A claim for equal pay may be referred to an employment tribunal[35] or a county court, provided that the claim is brought within six months of leaving the employment

---

35. EPA 1970, s 2(1).

in question.[36] A claimant whose case for equal pay succeeds will have the terms of her contract and pay placed on the same level as that of her male comparator, and will also be able to claim arrears in pay or damages[37] for breach of the equality clause. Originally, the EPA 1970 provided that the claimant could obtain arrears in pay and damages only in respect of two years prior to the date on which proceedings were commenced. But the European Court of Justice,[38] EAT,[39] and House of Lords[40] held that this contravened the EC Treaty, Art 119 (now Art 141) and the Equal Pay Directive, and so the period of recovery has now been extended to six years, ending on the date on which proceedings were commenced.[41]

‹› Key points summary

- The Equal Pay Act 1970 implies an equality clause into a contract where a woman carries out 'like work', 'work rated as equivalent', or 'work equal in value' to that of a man 'in the same employment'.

- In order to succeed, the woman employee will need to compare her work with that of an identifiable male comparator.

- The equality clause modifies the woman's employment contract to bring it in line with that of the male comparator.

- The pay and working conditions of a man may validly be more preferable than a woman's if the court considers that the difference is attributable to a genuine material factor other than gender.

- An equal pay claim must be brought within a six-month period, commencing on the last day of employment in the job in question. Arrears in pay and damages can be claimed for a period of six years ending on the date on which proceedings were commenced.

The national minimum wage

The concept of a national minimum wage is widespread around the world. Three-quarters of the EU member States have in place some form of statutory minimum wage. Forty-six of the USA's fifty states have enacted minimum wage laws, with twenty-one of those states enacting higher minimum wage rates than the federal minimum.[42] In England and Wales, the introduction of a national minimum wage is comparatively recent. The introduction of a national minimum wage had been proposed by the Labour Party for a number of years and, following its election victory

---

36. Ibid, s 2ZA(3).

37. General damages (e.g. non-economic loss such as injury to feelings) cannot be claimed under the EPA 1970: *Newcastle-upon-Tyne County Council v Allan* [2005] ICR 1170 (EAT).

38. C-78/98 *Preston v Wolverhampton Healthcare NHS Trust* [2000] 2 CMLR 837.

39. *Levez v TH Jennings (Harlow Pools) Ltd* [1999] 3 CMLR 715 (EAT).

40. *Preston v Wolverhampton Healthcare NHS Trust (No 2)* [2001] UKHL 5, [2001] 2 AC 455.

41. EPA 1970, s 2ZB(3).

42. Statistics derived from the US Department of Labor website, <http://www.dol.gov/esa/minwage/america.htm>.

in 1997, one of its first acts in government was to pass the National Minimum Wage Act 1998 (NMWA 1998). But much of the details, including the actual minimum rates of pay, are set out in the National Minimum Wage Regulations 1999.[43] Any attempt to contract out of the protection offered by the minimum wage legislation is void.[44] In November 2008, the Employment Act 2008 received Royal Assent. An effect of this Act is to amend key provisions of the NMWA 1998. The majority of the provisions of the 2008 Act came into force on 6 April 2009.

Entitlement

The NMWA 1998, s 1(1), sets out the basic entitlement—namely:

> A person who qualifies for the national minimum wage shall be remunerated by his employer in respect of his work in any pay reference period at a rate which is not less than the national minimum wage.

From this, two issues derive.

- Who is entitled to the minimum wage?
- How much is the minimum wage?

Turning to the first issue, the Act takes a very broad approach to entitlement, stating that a person will qualify for the minimum wage provided that he is a worker, is working (or ordinarily works) in the UK, and has ceased to be of compulsory school age.[45] Because the word 'worker' is used as opposed to 'employee', it follows that a contract of employment is not essential in order to claim the minimum wage, because a worker is defined as an individual who works under a contract of employment, or any other contract whereby the individual undertakes to do or perform personally any work or services for another party to the contract, whose status is not by virtue of the contract that of a client or customer of any profession or business undertaking carried on by the individual.[46] Agency workers,[47] home workers,[48] casual workers, output (or piece) workers,[49] workers paid on commission, and part-time workers are therefore all entitled to the minimum wage.

But certain workers are not entitled to the minimum wage, including:

- self-employed persons (independent contractors);[50]
- company directors (unless their contracts classify them as workers);
- voluntary workers (for example, workers employed by a charity);[51]
- prisoners who perform some form of paid work;[52]

---

43. SI 1999/584.
44. NMWA 1998, s 49(1).
45. Ibid, s 1(2).
46. Ibid, s 54(3).
47. Ibid, s 34.
48. Ibid, s 35.
49. An output worker is a worker who is paid not on the number of hours they work, but on the number of items produced, or tasks performed.
50. Self-employed persons do fit within the definition of 'worker' found in the NMWA 1998, s 54(3).
51. Ibid, s 44.
52. Ibid, s 45.

- workers under the age of 19 who are employed under a contract of apprenticeship, or apprentices aged 19 and over who are in the first twelve months of their apprenticeship;[53]
- workers on certain government schemes,[54] or certain European Community programmes;[55]
- students undertaking work placements not exceeding one year.[56]

Having determined whether or not a worker is entitled to the minimum wage, the second issue is to determine how much the minimum wage is. The 1998 Act established the Low Pay Commission,[57] an independent body, the sole function of which is to advise the government regarding the national minimum wage. The Low Pay Commission advises the Secretary of State for Employment, who, in turn, sets the minimum wage by amending the 1999 Regulations. The initial minimum wage (£3.60 per hour) was set well below what the trade unions were recommending, but it has increased every October (although the NMWA 1998 requires no such increase). As of 1 October 2008, the minimum wage is as set out in Table 24.1.

TABLE 24.1 The national minimum wage

Adult workers (22 years old and over)	Development rate (18–21 years old)	16–17-year-olds
£5.73 per hour[1]	£4.77 per hour[2]	£3.53 per hour[3]

[1] National Minimum Wage Regulations 1999, SI 1999/584, reg 11
[2] Ibid, reg 13(1)
[3] Ibid, reg 13(1A)

In order to determine whether or not a worker is being paid the minimum wage, the courts will first work out his hourly rate of pay and then compare it to the minimum rates above. Depending on the type of worker, the actual rules for determining a worker's hourly pay can be extremely complex and are beyond the scope of this book.[58]

Duty to keep records

To aid the process of quantifying the worker's pay, the 1998 Act requires that employers keep and preserve records relating to pay.[59] Officers appointed under the 1998 Act may enter premises and inspect these records, and can require an explanation of them from the employer.[60] The Employment Act 2008 increases the powers

---

53. National Minimum Wage Regulations 1999, SI 1999/584, reg 12(2)(b) and (c).
54. Ibid, reg 12(4A).
55. Ibid, reg 12(13)–(15).
56. Ibid, reg 12(9A).
57. NMWA 1998, s 8(9); see <http://www.lowpay.gov.uk>.
58. For a clear account of the rules relating to the scope and calculation of the minimum wage, see Department for Business, Enterprise and Regulatory Reform, *National Minimum Wage Guide* (BERR, London, September 2008), available online at <http://www.berr.gov.uk>.
59. NMWA 1998, s 9.
60. Ibid, s 14(1).

of these officers by allowing them to remove these records and take copies of them.[61] Workers are also entitled to inspect these records, provided they have reasonable grounds to believe that they are being paid less than the minimum wage.[62] Such workers who are denied the right to inspect the records may, within three months of the fourteen-day period during which the records have to be produced, apply to an employment tribunal, which may, if the complaint is founded, award the worker a sum equal to eighty times the national minimum wage.[63]

Enforcement

The provisions of the NMWA 1998 can be enforced in four different ways.

1. Because the right to the minimum wage is a contractual one,[64] the worker can claim arrears via an ordinary claim for breach of contract in a county court or employment tribunal.

2. The worker can bring a claim under the Employment Rights Act 1996 (ERA 1996), Pt II, on the ground that the underpayment constitutes an unlawful deduction in wages. In such a case, the burden of proof is reversed, so the worker will be presumed to qualify for the minimum wage and it will also be presumed that he has been paid less than the minimum wage.[65]

3. HM Revenue and Customs (HMRC) may issue an enforcement notice requiring the employer to pay the worker the minimum wage.[66] If this notice is not complied with, HMRC may bring a claim on the worker's behalf under the ERA 1996, Pt II, as described above.[67] Again, the burden of proof will be reversed. In addition, the employer may be subject to a financial penalty for failure to comply with the enforcement notice.[68]

4. The Employment Act 2008, s 9, inserts new provisions into the NMWA 1998 that allow an enforcement officer to serve a 'notice of underpayment' to any employer who is paying his employees less than the minimum wage. This notice will require the employer to pay the worker arrears in pay within twenty-eight days of the notice being served.[69] Failure to pay within this period will result in a financial penalty, which will amount to 50 per cent of the total underpayment, subject to a minimum penalty of £100 and a maximum of £5,000.[70]

In addition to the above civil remedies, the NMWA 1998 also provides for a number of summary criminal offences. For example, an employer who refuses, or wilfully neglects, to pay a worker the minimum wage will commit an offence.[71] The offence used to be a summary one, punishable only by a fine not exceeding the statutory minimum (currently £5,000). But the Employment Act 2008, s 11, has amended the 1998 Act so that the criminal offences within the Act will become either-way offences capable of more severe punishments on conviction on indictment—namely, an unlimited fine.[72]

If a worker is dismissed for any reasons relating to the entitlement to receive the minimum wage, or following an employer being convicted of a criminal offence

---

61. Ibid, s 14(3A).
63. Ibid, s 11(2).
65. Ibid, s 28.
67. Ibid, s 20(1)(a).
69. Ibid, s 19(2).
71. Ibid, s 31(1).

62. Ibid, s 10(1) and (2).
64. Ibid, s 17(1).
66. Ibid, s 19(1).
68. Ibid, s 21.
70. Ibid, s 19A.
72. Ibid, s 31(9).

under the 1998 Act, then that dismissal shall be regarded as unfair, irrespective of whether or not the worker's right to the minimum wage has been infringed.[73]

 Key points summary

- The majority of workers over school age are entitled to receive the national minimum wage.

- To aid the process of quantifying pay, employers are required to maintain adequate records relating to pay.

- The provisions of the NMWA 1998 can be enforced by an action for breach of contract, in an action for an unlawful deduction of wages, and via an enforcement notice issues by HM Revenue and Customs.

- Failure to pay the national minimum wage can also result in the commission of a criminal offence.

- The Employment Act 2008 has made a number of reforms of the 1998 Act, the majority of which came into force on 6 April 2009.

Transfer of undertakings

It is common for the ownership structure of a business to change during its lifetime: a business may be sold to another party; it may be subject to a takeover bid; or it may merge with another business to create a new commercial enterprise. The issue with which we are concerned here is, where such a change in ownership occurs, what effect this has on the employees' contracts of employment. Historically, such employees were placed in an extremely vulnerable position. At common law, where the ownership of a business changed, the employment contracts of the business were not transferred to the new owner.[74] This placed the new owner in an extremely advantageous position, because it could choose which employees to retain. Conversely, the employees were placed in an extremely vulnerable position, in so much as if the new owner were to decide not to take their contracts on, the employees would lose their jobs, with no legal redress.

The unfairness of this situation was remedied by the passing of the Acquired Rights Directive,[75] which protected the employees' contracts of employment by automatically transferring them to the new owner upon a transfer of ownership of the business. The Directive was belatedly implemented into national law by the Transfer of Undertakings (Protection of Employment) Regulations 1981.[76] But both the Directive and the Regulations were notoriously complex. Accordingly, the Directive was amended in 1998[77] and consolidated into a new Directive in 2001.[78]

---

73. ERA 1996, s 104A.
74. *Nokes v Doncaster Amalgamated Collieries Ltd* [1940] AC 1014 (HL).
75. Council Directive No 77/187/EC.
76. SI 1981/1794.
77. Council Directive No 98/50/EC.
78. Council Directive No 2001/23/EC.

The Regulations themselves have been amended four times, with the most recent version being the Transfer of Undertakings (Protection of Employment) Regulations 2006 (TUPE).[79]

Relevant transfer

TUPE only applies where the change in ownership amounts to a 'relevant transfer', of which there are two types. The first is where there is a:

> transfer of an undertaking, business or part of an undertaking or business situated immediately before the transfer in the United Kingdom to another person where there is a transfer of an economic entity which retains its identity.[80]

Several of the words and phrases within this provision require elaboration.

- *Undertaking* An 'undertaking' is simply another word for a trade or business. The original 1981 Regulations stated that non-commercial ventures (for example, charities) were not classified as 'undertakings', but, following the holding of the European Court of Justice that this was contrary to the Directive,[81] TUPE was amended and now specifically applies to 'public and private undertakings engaged in economic activities whether or not they are operated for gain'.[82]

- *Economic entity* The first type of relevant transfer occurs where there is a transfer of an 'economic entity', which is defined as 'an organized grouping of resources which has the objective of pursuing an economic activity, whether or not that activity is central or ancillary'.[83]

- *Retention of identity* In order to qualify, the undertaking must retain its identity following the transfer. This will require a measure of continuance post-transfer, so where a business was closed down upon transfer, or where the nature of its activity changes, it will not fall within TUPE. The new entity does not need to be identical to the prior one, but merely identifiable with it.[84]

The second 'relevant transfer' occurs where there is a 'service provision change'. This will occur in one of three situations set out in reg 3(1)(b). Firstly, reg 3(1)(b)(i) provides that a service provision change will occur where activities cease to be carried out by a person (a client) on his own behalf and are carried out instead by another person on the client's behalf (a contractor).

Eg A service provision change under reg 3(1)(b)(i)

MicroTech plc (the client) owns a number of warehouses that it uses to store computer equipment. At night, security guards employed by MicroTech guard the warehouses. MicroTech decides to contract out its security services to GuardCorp Ltd (the contractor). The security guards employed by MicroTech will have their contracts taken over by GuardCorp.

---

79. SI 2006/246.
80. TUPE, reg 3(1)(a).
81. C-29/91 *Dr Sophie Redmond Stichting v Bartol* [1992] IRLR 366.
82. TUPE, reg 3(4)(a).
83. Ibid, reg 3(2).
84. *Securicor Guarding Ltd v Fraser Security Services Ltd* [1996] IRLR 552 (EAT).

Secondly, reg 3(1)(b)(ii) provides that a service provision change will occur where activities cease to be carried out by a contractor on a client's behalf (whether or not those activities had previously been carried out by the client on his own behalf) and are carried out instead by another person (a subsequent contractor) on the client's behalf.

Eg **A service provision change under reg 3(1)(b)(ii)**

MicroTech (the client), not happy with the price charged by GuardCorp (the contractor), puts its security needs out to tender. The tender is obtained by KeepSafe Ltd (the subsequent contractor). The contracts of the security guards who worked for MicroTech, but now work for GuardCorp, will now be transferred to KeepSafe.

Thirdly, reg 3(1)(b)(iii) provides that a service provision change will occur where activities cease to be carried out by a contractor or a subsequent contractor on a client's behalf (whether or not those activities had previously been carried out by the client on his own behalf) and are carried out instead by the client on his own behalf.

Eg **A service provision change under reg 3(1)(b)(iii)**

Not happy with the service provided by KeepSafe (the subsequent contractor), MicroTech (the client) decides not to contract out its security needs and will once again arrange its own security. The security guards who originally worked for MicroTech will once again become employees of MicroTech.

The effect of a transfer

The key provision in TUPE is reg 4(1), which provides that, except where an objection is made under reg 4(7) (discussed later):

> a relevant transfer shall not operate so as to terminate the contract of employment of any person employed by the transferor…[and]…any such contract shall have effect after the transfer as if originally made between the person so employed and the transferee.[85]

Accordingly, where a relevant transfer takes place, the employees of the original owner become the employees of the new owner. Whereas the common law would terminate the employment contract, reg 4(1) transfers it to the new owner. Accordingly, the effect of reg 4(1) is to novate the employees' contracts. The novation is automatic: the views of the parties are irrelevant[86] (subject to reg 4(7), discussed later) and the contract will be transferred even where the employee is

➡ novate: substitute (one contract) for another

---

85. TUPE, reg 4(1).
86. C-144/87 *Berg and Busschers v Besselsen* [1989] IRLR 447.

unaware of the undertaking being transferred.[87] All of the rights, powers, duties, and non-criminal liabilities[88] of the original owner under, or in respect of, the employment contract are transferred to the new owner,[89] and any act or omission of the original owner in respect of that contract prior to the transfer are deemed to be an act or omission of the new owner.[90]

The protection afforded to employees by reg 4(1) applies not only to those employees employed 'immediately before the transfer', but also to employees who would have been so employed had they not been unfairly dismissed because of the transfer.[91] Such a dismissal occurs where an employee is dismissed before or after a relevant transfer and the dismissal is solely or principally due to the transfer itself.[92] But where the reason for the dismissal is solely or principally an economic, technical, or organizational reason, the dismissal may be valid. The onus of proof is placed upon the employer to demonstrate that such a reason exists and that it was why the employee was dismissed.[93] The aim of these provisions is to prevent an employer from avoiding reg 4(1) by dismissing his employees shortly before a transfer.[94]

Upon transfer, the new owner may seek adversely to alter the terms and condition of the novated employment contracts. This could occur for unmeritorious reasons (for example, the new owner is disgruntled at having to take on the prior owner's employees and wishes to force them to resign), or for valid reasons (for example, to avoid potential equal pay claims, especially where the novated contracts provide for a higher rate of pay than that received by the new owner's existing employees). The ability to alter the terms of the novated contracts is limited by reg 4(4), which provides that any purported alteration of the novated contract is void if the sole or principal reason for the alteration is due to the transfer itself. But an alteration is permitted where the sole or principal reason for it is unconnected with the transfer, or where it is connected to the transfer, but is due to an economic, technical, or organizational factor that entails changes in the workforce.[95]

Refusing a transfer

Although the transfer of the contract of employment is normally automatic, the employee can prevent the transfer from taking place by informing the new owner that he objects to being employed by the new owner.[96] Where this occurs, the contract of employment will be terminated, but the employee will not be regarded as dismissed,[97] thereby leaving him without any form of legal redress against either the original owner or the new owner. The harshness of this is partially mitigated

---

87. *Secretary of State for Trade and Industry v Cook* [1997] IRLR 150 (EAT).
88. TUPE, reg 4(6).
89. Ibid, reg 4(2)(a). Regulation 10 provides that rights and duties relating to pension schemes are excluded.
90. Ibid, reg 4(2)(b).
91. Ibid, reg 4(3).
92. Ibid, reg 7(1).
93. Ibid, reg 7(2) and (3).
94. Even before the passing of TUPE, the House of Lords had curtailed this activity: *Litster v Forth Dry Dock and Engineering Co Ltd* [1990] 1 AC 546 (HL).
95. TUPE, reg 4(5).
96. Ibid, reg 4(7).
97. Ibid, reg 4(8).

by reg 4(9), which provides that, where the employee does not wish to transfer his employment because it would involve a substantial and detrimental change in his working conditions, he may elect to treat the employment contract as terminated and will also be regarded as being dismissed, thereby entitling him to compensation.

‹› Key points summary

- Under the common law, the transfer of an undertaking did not result in the transfer of the employees' contracts of employment to the new owner.

- The Transfer of Undertakings (Protection of Employment) Regulations 2006 provide that, if the transfer is a relevant transfer, the employees' contracts of employment are transferred to the new owner.

- An employee will be unfairly dismissed if the sole or principal reason for his dismissal is the transfer. Where the reason is connected to the transfer, the dismissal will be unfair unless it was solely or principally for an economic, technical, or organizational reason.

- Any alteration of the transferred contracts is void unless it is for a reason unconnected to the transfer, or for an economic, technical, or organizational reason.

- An employee who does not wish his contract to be transferred can prevent the transfer, but he will normally lack any form of remedy against either the new or the previous owner.

Maternity and paternity rights

When the Labour Party came to power in 1997, it promised to increase the maternity and paternity rights of employees substantially and to introduce new rights. This promise has been kept. In the last ten years, the length of maternity leave has increased substantially, as has the amount of maternity pay. Paternity leave has been introduced, as has paternity pay. An additional right to parental leave has supplemented paternity and maternity leave, and a right to take time off for antenatal care has been introduced. Parents of children under six years old have also acquired the right to request flexible working hours.

The reforms are not yet complete. In the near future, the length of time for which maternity pay may be claimed is due to increase, as will the amount of paternity leave and paternity pay. Here, we will examine the principal maternity and paternity rights available to employees, beginning with maternity leave.

Maternity leave

All pregnant employees are entitled to maternity leave. The law in this area used to be extremely complex, but a raft of recent legislation has greatly simplified the determination of maternity leave.

The various pieces of legislation establish three different periods of maternity leave.

- *Ordinary maternity leave (OML)* All pregnant employees are entitled to OML, irrespective of how long they have worked for their employer. The length of OML is currently set at twenty-six weeks,[98] but can only be claimed if, by the end of the fifteenth week before the expected week of childbirth (EWC), the employee informs her employer of her pregnancy, the EWC, and when she intends the period of OML to start.[99] During this period, the employee is entitled to all of the benefits of the terms and conditions of her contract of employment[100] (for example, holiday entitlements, insurance, etc.), except in relation to remuneration.[101] Instead of her contractual rate of pay, she will receive maternity pay, which is discussed later.

- *Additional maternity leave (AML)* It used to be the case that AML was only available to pregnant employees who had served twenty-six weeks' continuous service, but this requirement has now been abolished. Now, all employees entitled to OML are also entitled to an additional twenty-six weeks' AML,[102] which will run immediately after the OML period has finished. It was the case that, during the period of AML, the employee could only receive the benefit of certain terms and conditions of the contract, but this limitation has been removed in respect of women whose babies are born after 5 October 2008. Now, as with OML, the employee is entitled to all of the benefits of her contract of employment,[103] except in relation to remuneration.[104] Instead of her contractual rate of pay, she will receive maternity pay, which is discussed later. It can therefore be seen that the distinction between OML and AML is much less important than it used to be.

- *Compulsory maternity leave (CML)* Any employer who permits an employee to work during her period of CML commits a criminal offence.[105] The period of CML begins on the day of childbirth and last for two weeks.[106]

Therefore, an employee is entitled to up to fifty-two weeks of statutory maternity leave (CML, being mandatory, is not an entitlement and so is not counted towards this period). The government wished to encourage employees on maternity leave and employers to keep in touch during the maternity period. Accordingly, the employee is permitted to work for up to ten days during her statutory maternity period, and such work will not cause her maternity leave to end,[107] nor will it extend the period of leave.[108]

Statutory maternity pay and maternity allowance

As noted above, during the period of maternity leave, an employee will not receive her contractual rate of pay, but will instead receive maternity pay. Whereas all pregnant employees will qualify for maternity leave (subject to the requirements of

---

98. Maternity and Parental Leave etc. Regulations 1999, SI 1999/3312, reg 7(1).
99. Ibid, reg 4(1)(a).
100. ERA 1996, s 71(4)(a).
101. Ibid, s 71(5)(b).
102. Maternity and Parental Leave etc. Regulations 1999, SI 1999/3312, reg 7(4).
103. ERA 1996, s 73(4)(a).
104. Ibid, s 73(5)(b).
105. Ibid, s 72.
106. Maternity and Parental Leave etc. Regulations 1999, SI 1999/3312, reg 8(b). Where the employee works in a factory, an offence is committed if she is allowed to return to work within a four-week period following childbirth: Factories Act 1961, s 61.
107. Ibid, reg 12A(1).
108. Ibid, reg 12A(7).

notice), the entitlement for maternity pay is dependent upon meeting the following requirements:

- prior to the fifteenth week before the EWC, the employee must have worked for the employer for a minimum period of twenty-six weeks;[109]
- in order to qualify for maternity pay, the employee must be earning enough to require her to make National Insurance (NI) contributions[110] (as of April 2009, this amount is £95 per week, although it is likely to change in April 2010);[111]
- the employee must notify the employer of her pregnancy, the EWC, and the date on which she intends her OML to commence. The employer can require the employee to produce medical evidence stating the EWC;[112]
- the employee must have reached the eleventh week before the EWC.[113]

Currently, employees meeting the above requirements will receive maternity pay for up to thirty-nine weeks. But this will be increased to fifty-two weeks at some point in the future,[114] thereby entitling employees to maternity pay for the entire period of statutory maternity leave.

The rate of maternity pay is fixed by statute. For the first six weeks of maternity leave, the employee will receive 90 per cent of her normal gross weekly earnings.[115] For the remaining weeks, the employee will receive either a flat rate of £123.06 per week[116] (as of April 2009, to rise in April 2010), or 90 per cent of her standard pay (if this is less than £123.06 per week).[117] The employer, in turn, is able to recover from the government most of the money paid in maternity pay by deducting it from PAYE and NI contributions.

Those employees not entitled to statutory maternity pay (for example, because they do not earn enough to make NI contributions) may be entitled to a maternity allowance. In order to qualify, the following conditions must be met:

- the employee must have reached the eleventh week before her EWC;[118]
- the employee must have been employed for at least twenty-six out of the sixty-six weeks prior to her EWC;[119]
- the employee's average weekly earnings must not be less than the maternity allowance threshold[120] (currently, £30 per week).

---

109. Social Security Contributions and Benefits Act 1992, s 164(2)(a).

110. Ibid, s 164(2)(b).

111. See <http://www.hmrc.gov.uk/rates/nic.htm>.

112. Maternity and Parental Leave etc. Regulations 1999, SI 1999/3312, reg 4(1).

113. Social Security Contributions and Benefits Act 1992, s 164(2)(c).

114. This extension, introduced by the Work and Families Act 2006, s 1, is intended to come into effect before the end of the current Parliament. The government has indicated that it will not come into effect before October 2009.

115. Social Security Contributions and Benefits Act 1992, s 166(1)(a) and (2).

116. Statutory Maternity Pay (General) Regulations 1986, SI 1986/1960, reg 6.

117. Social Security Contributions and Benefits Act 1992, s 166(1)(b).

118. Ibid, s 35(1)(a).

119. Ibid, s 35(1)(b).

120. Ibid, s 35(1)(c).

Maternity allowance is paid for the same period as statutory maternity pay (currently thirty-nine weeks)[121] and is paid at a flat rate of £123.06 per week (as of April 2009, to rise in April 2010), or 90 per cent of her standard pay (if this is less than £123.06 per week).[122]

Returning to work

Within twenty-eight days of maternity leave commencing, the employee must provide her employer with the date on which her maternity leave will end. If the employee wishes to return to work early from AML, she will need to provide her employer with at least eight weeks' notice of her return.[123] An employee returning from OML is entitled to return to the same job in which she was employed prior to her maternity leave.[124] An employee returning from AML is entitled to return to the same job or, where this is not reasonably practicable, to return to a suitable and appropriate job[125] on terms no less favourable than those to which she was subject prior to taking leave.[126]

The right to return to work also includes protection from redundancy and dismissal. It may be the case that, during an employee's period of maternity leave, her employer may need to make her redundant. In such a case, the employer is bound to offer the employee any suitable alternative vacancy under a new contract of employment.[127] Where the employee is dismissed and the principal reason for the dismissal is related to, inter alia, pregnancy, childbirth, or the taking of maternity leave, the employee shall be regarded as unfairly dismissed.[128] It is also likely that such a dismissal will constitute direct sex discrimination.

Sex discrimination is discussed at p 852

Antenatal care

Antenatal care refers to care and treatment administered during pregnancy. The right to time off to receive antenatal care was introduced in 1980 to combat the UK's alarmingly high perinatal mortality rate.[129] Today, the right to time off for antenatal care can be found in the ERA 1996, s 55, and is available to all women, irrespective of their length of service. The right to time off for antenatal care is dependent upon the employee making an appointment for antenatal care upon the advice of a registered medical practitioner, midwife, or nurse.[130] The employer can require the employee to provide proof of the appointment, and if such proof cannot be produced, the employee loses the entitlement to time off.[131] Where the employee obtains time

---

121. Ibid, s 35(2). As with statutory maternity pay, the right to maternity allowance will increase to fifty-two weeks when the Work and Families Act 2006, s 1, comes into force.
122. Social Security Contributions and Benefits Act 1992, s 35A(1).
123. Maternity and Parental Leave etc. Regulations 1999, SI 1999/1322, reg 11(1).
124. Ibid, reg 18(1).
125. Ibid, reg 18(2).
126. Ibid, reg 18A(1)(b).
127. Ibid, reg 10(2).
128. Ibid, reg 20.
129. The perinatal mortality rate (PMR) represents the number of stillbirths and neonatal deaths per thousand births. In 1973, the UK's PMR stood at twenty-one per thousand—one of the highest in Europe. Today, the PMR stands at 7.7 per thousand: see Office for National Statistics, *Population Trends* (ONS, London, 2008) 67.
130. Employment Rights Act 1996, s 55(1)(b).
131. Ibid, s 55(2)(b).

off to receive antenatal care, she is entitled to be paid at her normal rate of pay.[132] Should the employer refuse to provide the employee with time off, the employee may take her case to an employment tribunal. But it should be noted that the right to time off is not absolute and that an employer may be entitled to refuse time off for reasonable reasons (for example, where the employee could have obtained antenatal care outside working hours, but chose not to do so).[133]

Paternity leave and pay

Pregnant employees have long had the right to maternity leave, but only recently has a similar right been extended to expectant fathers. Prior to this, unless the employer had a voluntary scheme for paternity leave, fathers wishing to take time off were forced to use their holiday entitlement or to ask their employer for a period of unpaid leave. The Employment Act 2002, s 1, introduced the concept of 'paternity leave' by inserting a new s 80A into the ERA 1996. Paternity leave is obtainable upon satisfaction of several requirements:[134]

- the employee must have been employed for at least twenty-six continuous weeks prior to the fourteenth week of the EWC;
- the employee must be either:
  - the biological father of the child; or
  - if not the father, married to, or the partner (including civil partners) of, the child's mother;
- the employee must have, or must expect to have, responsibility for the child's upbringing.

Compared to maternity leave, the current right to paternity leave is modest. Whereas the mother has the right to up to fifty-two weeks' maternity leave, the father's right to maternity leave currently extends to one week's leave or two consecutive weeks' leave.[135] But the Work and Families Act 2006 inserts a new s 80AA into the ERA 1996, which provides for a period of additional paternity leave, to be no longer than twenty-six weeks in duration. This provision is expected to come into force before the end of the current Parliament, but not before October 2009.

During the period of paternity leave, a man is in a similar position to a woman on OML. He will be entitled to the benefit of all of the terms and conditions of employment that would have applied had he not been absent, except those terms relating to remuneration.[136] Instead of receiving his contractual rate of pay, if he is earning enough to make NI contributions (£95 per week, as of April 2009), he will be instead receive statutory paternity pay, which is set at the same amount as statutory maternity pay (123.06 per week, as of April 2009).[137] If he does not earn enough, the paternity leave will be unpaid, but he is likely to qualify for Income Support whilst on paternity leave.

---

132. Ibid, s 56(1).
133. *Gregory v Tudsbury* [1982] IRLR 267 (IT) [8].
134. These are found in the Paternity and Adoption Leave Regulations 2002, SI 2002/2788, reg 4(2).
135. Ibid, reg 5(1).
136. Ibid, reg 12.
137. When additional paternity leave comes into force, fathers will also be entitled to additional statutory paternity pay: see the Social Security Contributions and Benefits Act 1992, s 171ZEA, as inserted by the Work and Families Act 2006, s 6.

Many employers will have their own scheme of paternity leave. If these are less advantageous to the employee than the statutory scheme, the employee may choose the statutory scheme.

Parental leave

The right to parental leave is in addition to the right to maternity or paternity leave (and therefore is available to both mothers and fathers). It was introduced by the Maternity and Parental Leave etc. Regulations 1999,[138] which were enacted in order to comply with the Parental Leave Directive.[139] Entitlement to parental leave is dependent upon the satisfaction of the following conditions:

- the employee must have been continuously employed for not less than one year;[140]
- the employee must have, or expect to have, responsibility for a child.[141] 'Parental responsibility' is defined as 'all the rights, duties, powers, responsibilities and authority which by law a parent of a child has in relation to the child and his property'.[142]

Employees who meet these requirements are entitled to thirteen weeks' unpaid parental leave per child,[143] except where the child is disabled, when it is increased to eighteen weeks.[144] This leave must be taken before the child's fifth birthday,[145] except where the child is disabled, when it must be taken before his eighteenth birthday.[146]

In terms of procedural rules, where parental leave is not covered by the contract of employment or in any collective agreements, the statutory default rules will apply. These provide as follows.

- The employee must state when the parental leave is due to commence and provide the employer with at least twenty-one days' notice prior to leave being taken.[147]
- Each leave period must be for a minimum of one week and in weekly multiples.[148] Unlike maternity and paternity leave, the right to parental leave does not need to be exercised in one consecutive period—but it is still inflexible, in that a parent who merely requires one day off will have to take a full week's leave.
- The employee may not take more than four weeks' leave in respect of any individual child in any one year.[149]

Upon returning from parental leave, the employee is entitled to return to the same job in which she was employed before her absence,[150] except where leave is taken for over four weeks, or where parental leave is taken immediately following AML, in which case, the employee is entitled to return to the same job or, where this is not reasonably practicable, to return to a suitable and appropriate job.[151]

---

138. SI 1999/3312.   139. Council Directive No 96/34/EC.
140. Maternity and Parental Leave etc. Regulations 1999, SI 1999/1322, reg 13(1)(a).
141. Ibid, reg 13(1)(b).   142. Children Act 1989, s 3(1).
143. Maternity and Parental Leave etc. Regulations 1999, SI 1999/1322, reg 14(1).
144. Ibid, reg 14(1A).   145. Ibid, reg 15(1).
146. Ibid, reg 15(3).   147. Ibid, Sch 2, para 3.
148. Ibid, para 7.   149. Ibid, para 8.
150. Ibid, reg 18(1).   151. Ibid, reg 18(2).

Adoption leave

The basic right to adoption leave is similar to maternity leave—namely, a period of paid ordinary adoption leave of twenty-six weeks,[152] followed by a period of unpaid additional adoption leave for a further twenty-six weeks.[153] But whereas all employees are entitled to maternity leave, entitlement to adoption leave is different in the following ways:

- where a couple adopt a child, only one of the adoptive parents is entitled to adoption leave;
- adoption leave is only available where the employee has twenty-six weeks' continuous service, ending with the week in which the employee is informed that he has been matched with a child.[154]

During ordinary adoption leave, the employee will be entitled to the benefit of all of the terms and conditions of employment that would have applied had he not been absent, except those terms relating to remuneration.[155] Instead of his contractual rate of pay, the employee will receive statutory adoption pay at the same rate as maternity and paternity pay—namely, £123.06 per week (as of April 2000, to rise in April 2010), or 90 per cent of his standard pay (if this is less than £123.06 per week). As with maternity pay, employers can recover from the government the majority of adoption pay paid out. The rights upon return from work and protection from dismissal are the same as those for maternity leave.

Flexible working rights

Once maternity or paternity leave and parental leave have ended, employees will often find it difficult to return to work and raise their new child. To ease this difficulty, the Employment Act 2002 provided workers with increased flexible working rights. As we shall see, however, the rights conferred are somewhat weak. As with the other rights discussed above, flexible working rights apply only to employees who meet the conditions of entitlement:[156]

- the employee must have been continuously employed for at least twenty-six weeks;
- the employee must be a mother, father, adopter, guardian, special guardian, foster parent, or private foster carer. Partners, civil partners, and spouses of such persons also qualify;
- the employee must have, or expect to have, responsibility for the upbringing of a child who is under the age of 6 (or the age of 18, if the child is disabled).

Employees who meet these requirements may apply to their employer for a change in their terms of employment in relation to hours, times, and places of work.[157] The employee does not have a right to flexible working conditions, but only the right to apply to his employer for more flexible conditions. This significantly reduces the

---

152. Paternity and Adoption Leave Regulations 2002, SI 2002/2788, reg 18(1).
153. Ibid, reg 20(2).
154. Ibid, reg 15(2)(b).
155. Ibid, reg 19.
156. Flexible Working (Eligibility, Complaints and Remedies) Regulations 2002, SI 2002/3236, reg 3(1).
157. ERA 1996, s 80F(1)(a). Such an application may only be made once per year (s 80F(4)).

strength of the right. The application must be in writing[158] and, within twenty-eight days of receipt of the application, the employer must either accept the employee's request or hold a meeting with the employee to discuss the application.[159] Within fourteen days of this meeting, the employer must notify the employee of the decision made.[160]

Where the application is granted, the change will be permanent, unless the parties agree otherwise. Thus, if the employee finds the new arrangements to be disadvantageous, there is no automatic right to revert to the prior terms and conditions. Where the application is rejected, the notice must state why the application was rejected, and the ERA 1996, s 80G(1)(b), provides that only certain grounds for refusal are valid grounds for refusal (for example, the burden of additional costs, the inability to reorganize work among existing staff, etc.). The rejection notice must also inform the employee that he has a right to appeal. This right to appeal must be exercised within fourteen days of notice of the decision,[161] and such an appeal amounts to a simple re-run of the initial procedure. The employer must notify the employee of the result of the appeal within fourteen days.[162] Failure of the employer to adhere to these procedures can result in a complaint to an employment tribunal, which can award the employee compensation not exceeding eight weeks' pay.[163]

 Key points summary

- All pregnant employees are entitled to twenty-six weeks' ordinary maternity leave and another twenty-six weeks' additional maternity leave. For thirty-nine of these weeks (due to increase to fifty-two weeks), they are also entitled to receive statutory maternity pay.

- All pregnant employees are entitled to time off to receive antenatal care.

- Paternity leave off up to two weeks (due to increase to twenty-six weeks) is currently available to fathers (or spouses or civil partners), provided that they have served at least twenty-six weeks' continuous service.

- Employees with parental responsibility, who have served at least one year's continuous employment, are entitled to thirteen weeks' unpaid parental leave.

- Where a couple adopt a child, either one of them, provided that they have at least twenty-six weeks' continuous service, are entitled to twenty-six weeks' paid ordinary adoption leave and an extra twenty-six weeks' unpaid additional adoption leave.

- Employees who have been continuously employed for at least twenty-six weeks and have responsibility for a child are entitled to request more flexible working hours.

---

158. Flexible Working (Eligibility, Complaints and Remedies) Regulations 2002, SI 2002/3236, reg 4(a).
159. Flexible Working (Procedural Requirements) Regulations 2002, SI 2002/3207, reg 3.
160. Ibid, reg 4.
161. Ibid, reg 6.
162. Ibid, reg 9.
163. ERA 1996, s 80I.

Time off

In addition to maternity, paternity, parental, and adoption leave, an employee is entitled to time off in the following situations.

Dependant care

Employees have a right to reasonable time off to care for dependants. A dependant is defined as a spouse (or civil partner), child, parent, or someone who lives in the same household as the employee, but is not his employee, lodger, or tenant.[164] Examples of instances in which reasonable time off should be granted include where a dependant falls ill, gives birth, is injured or assaulted, or where a dependant dies.

Unlike other forms of leave, no period of leave is stated, because the leave required will depend upon the circumstances. The period of leave must be reasonable, but this will be very difficult to define in practice. Unlike maternity and paternity leave, there is no requirement to pay an employee who takes time off to care for a dependant. An employee who is refused time off may complain to an employment tribunal, provided that the complaint is brought within three months of the date of the refusal.[165]

Public duties

A substantial number of public bodies can only continue to operate through part-time contributors. Because the performance of such public duties is in the collective interests of the country, the ERA 1996, s 50, provides that employers must permit their employees to take reasonable time off if they wish to perform certain public duties including:

- acting as a Justice of the Peace (magistrate);
- working for a local authority or statutory tribunal;
- working for a health body or education body.

The right contained in s 50 is not dependent upon a minimum length of service, but employers are not required to pay employees for the time that they take off to perform public duties. An employee who is refused time off under s 50 may present a complaint to an employment tribunal, provided that the complaint is brought within three months beginning on the date on which the refusal occurred, or within whatever period the tribunal considers reasonable if the three-month period is not reasonably practicable.[166]

Although not covered by s 50, another public duty for which the employee is entitled to time off is jury service. Further, an employee who is dismissed due to absence caused by attending jury service is to be regarded as being unfairly dismissed.[167]

---

164. Ibid, s 57A(3).   165. Ibid, s 57B.
166. Ibid, s 51(2).   167. Ibid, s 98B(1).

Study or training

Certain employees are entitled to paid time off in order to undertake study or training leading to a relevant qualification. The ERA 1996, s 63A(1), provides that, in order to obtain this entitlement, the employee:

- must be aged 16 or 17;
- must not be receiving full-time secondary or further education; and
- must not have attained such minimum standards of education as prescribed by the Right to Time Off for Study and Training Regulations 2001,[168] reg 3 (for example, grades A* to C in five subjects at GCSE level).

Employees satisfying these requirements are entitled to a period of paid time off that is reasonable in all of the circumstances, having regard, in particular, to:

- the requirements of the employee's study or training; and
- the circumstances of the business of the employer or the principal and the effect of the employee's time off on the running of that business.

An employee entitled to such time off may make a compliant to an employment tribunal if his employer unreasonably refuses to allow him to take time off under s 63A, or refuses to pay him if he does take such time off.[169]

 Key points summary

- Employees are entitled to reasonable time off to care for dependants.
- Employees are entitled to take time off to perform certain public duties (for example, sitting as a magistrate or serving on a jury).
- Certain employees are entitled to take time off to engage in study or training.

Health and safety

In addition to the above employment rights, employees also have the right to have their health and safety protected. Employers who fail to protect the health and safety of their employees adequately may find themselves facing liability in three different ways.

1. *Tort* Employees who suffer illness or injury due to acts of their employers may be able to recover compensation under the tort of negligence.
2. *Contract* It is an implied term of the employment contract that employers will take reasonable care of the health and safety of their employees. Failure to do so can result in damages being awarded for breach of contract.
3. *Criminal liability* The Health and Safety at Work etc. Act 1974 places a duty on employers to take reasonable care, so far as is reasonably practicable, of

---

168. SI 2001/2801.   169. ERA 1996, s 63C(1).

their employee's health and safety. Employers who breach this duty commit a criminal offence.

These forms of liability are not mutually exclusive, and an employer who fails to protect the health and safety of his employees may be both civilly liable to pay compensation and guilty of a criminal offence.

Negligence

An employee who suffers some form of injury whilst at work will be able to recover damages if he can demonstrate that the injury was caused by his employer's negligence. The usual requirements of negligence apply—namely:

> The tort of negligence is discussed in Chapter 12

- Did the employer owe the employee a duty of care?
- Did the employer breach this duty of care?
- Was the employee's injury caused by the employer's breach of duty?

Issues of breach of duty, causation, and remoteness are the same as for general negligence. Here, we will focus on the scope of the duty of care owed by the employer and the available defences.

It is well established that the employer owes a duty of care to his employees, but what does this duty entail? The classic formulation of the employer's duty of care was laid down by Lord Wright in *Wilsons and Clyde Co Ltd v English*,[170] in which he stated that the duty of care was met by 'the provision of a competent staff of men, adequate material, and a proper system and effective supervision'.[171] Each of these three elements will be examined, along with a fourth element (namely, the duty to protect employees from psychiatric harm) that has been subsequently added. But before we discuss the scope of the duty, two points need to be made. Firstly, the duty is non-delegable, meaning that employers cannot avoid liability by arguing that they delegated responsibility for the employees' health and safety to someone else. Secondly, the duty is not owed to the employees collectively, but to each individual employee. This means that if an employer is aware that an employee is more susceptible to health risks whilst at work, the employer should take special precautions to ensure the employee's protection.[172]

'The provision of a competent staff of men'

The first element of Lord Wright's duty of care provides that employers are under a duty to provide competent fellow employees. Where an employee is injured due to the actions of an incompetent colleague, the employer will have breached his duty of care to the injured employee. Employers should ensure that their employees receive adequate training and should also curtail any undesirable practices of which they become aware.

---

170. [1938] AC 57 (HL).   171. Ibid, 78.
172. *Paris v Stepney Borough Council* [1951] AC 367 (HL).

Hudson v Ridge Manufacturing Co [1957] 2 QB 348

FACTS: An employee of the defendant had a reputation as a practical joker, and frequently made a nuisance of himself to the claimant and fellow employees. For over four years, the defendant was aware of the employee's activities, but beyond several formal reprimands, no further action was taken to curtail the employee's behaviour. On one occasion, the employee tripped up the claimant, a disabled man. The claimant sustained a broken wrist and claimed damages from the defendant employer.

HELD: The court held that the defendant had breached the duty of care that it owed to the claimant. The defendant was aware of the employee's disruptive and potentially dangerous conduct, and, in failing to prevent it, it had breached the duty of care. The claimant recovered damages for the injury sustained.

'Adequate material'

The second element of the duty states that employers should provide safe work equipment (for example, machinery, vehicles, protective clothing, etc.) and also safe premises (for example, effective lighting and ventilation, clear and unobstructed fire exits, etc.).

Bradford v Robinson Rentals Ltd [1967] 1 WLR 337

FACTS: The defendant employed the claimant, a 57-year-old man. During the winter of 1963, he was required to exchange a van for another, but this would involve a journey of around 450 miles, which would take around twenty hours (the motorway system at the time was much less extensive than it is today). The defendant knew that both vans were unheated (the heater in the first van was broken and the second van had no heater), but still required the claimant to engage in the journey. During the journey, the claimant contracted frostbite, causing permanent damage to his hands and feet.

HELD: The court held that the defendant knew that the claimant would be exposed to prolonged periods of extreme cold and that, by failing to provide him with a heated vehicle, it had breached the duty of care owed. Although contracting frostbite was unusual in England, the actions of the defendant had made it reasonably foreseeable.

The law relating to the provision of safe work equipment has been made substantially more stringent with the passing of the Employer's Liability (Defective Equipment) Act 1969. Section 1(1) of the 1969 Act provides that where an employee suffers personal injury in the course of his employment from a defect in equipment provided by his employer for the purposes of the business, and the defect is attributable wholly or in part to the negligence or other tort of a third party (for example, the manufacturer or supplier of the equipment), the injury shall be deemed also to be attributable to the negligence of the employer. Thus, the employee may sue his employer, rather than the manufacturer or other third party who was at fault; the employer, in turn, may then seek a contribution from the third party.

The effect of s 1(1) can be seen in the following case.

Knowles v Liverpool City Council [1993] 1 WLR 1428 (HL)

FACTS: The claimant was employed by the defendant to lay flagstones. One of the flagstones was defective and broke, crushing the claimant's right index finger. The flagstones were not manufactured by the defendant, but purchased from a third party.

HELD: The House of Lords held that the flagstones constituted 'equipment'. Although the defect was not due to the defendant's negligence, the 1969 Act deemed the defendant negligent for equipment that was defective due to the actions of a third party. Accordingly, the defendant was held negligent and was ordered to pay the claimant £3,092 in damages.

COMMENT: This case is notable for the width of the House's interpretation of the term 'equipment'. Lord Jauncey (with whom the other judges agreed) stated that the term 'equipment' could apply to any article provided by the employer for the purposes of the business, irrespective of whether the employee was required to, or had in fact, used the article.

⭐ See G Holgate, 'Employers' Liability and the Provision of Defective "Equipment"' (1993) 22 ILJ 214

The courts will not impose liability on an employer who has taken all reasonable precautions in avoiding the act that led to the claimant's injury. Where the employer would need to take precautions wholly out of proportion to the risk involved, the courts will not hold that failure to take such precautions constitutes a breach of the duty of care.

 Latimer v AEC Ltd [1953] AC 643 (HL)

FACTS: An unusually heavy rainstorm flooded the defendant's factory. The defendant did all that it could to eliminate the effects of the flooding, but some areas of the flooring were still flooded and slippery. The claimant (an employee of the defendant) slipped and injured his ankle. He sued the defendant, alleging that it should have shut the factory down until it was completely safe.

HELD: His claim failed. The House of Lords held that the defendant had done all that it could reasonably do. The majority of the factory floor was rendered safe, so the risk of injury was minimal. The only other option was to shut the factory down and the cost of such action would have been wholly out of proportion to the risk involved.

'A proper system and effective supervision'

The third element of the duty states that employers should provide a safe system of work. This duty is extremely wide and can overlap with the other duties. A safe system of work could include ensuring that the workplace is safe, ensuring that effective supervision is in place, ensuring that employees are trained to deal with work-related hazards and risks, and ensuring that proper safety equipment is available, etc. The provision of safety equipment has proven to be a troublesome issue—notably, where safety equipment is available, but the employee decides not to use it. Historically, in such cases, employers were not liable for injuries caused due to an employee's failure to use available safety equipment.[173] But more recent cases have moved away from this position and will impose liability where the employer acquiesces to the employee's decision not to use the available equipment.

⊶ *Bux v Slough Metals Ltd* [1973] 1 WLR 1358 (CA)

FACTS: The defendant employed the claimant as a die-caster. His work involved the pouring of molten metal into a die. Safety goggles were supplied to the claimant, but he did not wear them. When his superintendant questioned him on this, the claimant stated that the goggle were useless, because they misted up. The superintendant did not attempt to convince the employee to wear the goggles. Whilst pouring molten metal into a die, the metal splashed on the claimant's face, causing him to lose the sight fully in one eye and suffer partial blindness in the other. He claimed damages from the defendant.

HELD: The Court of Appeal held that the defendant should have instructed the claimant to wear the goggles 'in a reasonable and firm manner'[174] and then followed up the instruction to check that the goggles were being worn. The defendant's failure to do this was a breach of its duty of care. The claimant was awarded damages of just over £19,400.

COMMENT: The Health and Safety at Work Act 1974, s 7 (discussed later), places a duty on employees to take reasonable care for their own safety. Had this claim been brought under the 1974 Act, it would have been likely to have failed.

★ See B Barrett, 'Another Look at the Contribution to Occupational Safety of the "Safe System"' (1974) 37 MLR 577

Where the safety equipment becomes ineffective (not due to being defective) and the employee fails to take steps to obtain new equipment, however, the employer will not be liable.

⊶ *Smith v Scot Bowyers* [1986] IRLR 315 (CA)

FACTS: The claimant was required, as part of his job, to walk on floors covered in oil. To prevent him from slipping, he was provided with a pair of boots with ridged soles designed to grip slippery surfaces. Through use, however, the soles had become worn and failed to grip adequately, but the claimant failed to request a new pair from his employer. The claimant slipped and was injured.

HELD: The Court of Appeal held that the employer was not liable for the claimant's injuries. The employer had acted reasonably in providing boots and informing employees that replacement boots were available on request. The claimant should have taken responsibility for his own safety by requesting a replacement pair of boots.

★ See B Barrett, 'The Employers' Duty to Ensure that Safety Measures are Taken by Employees' (1987) 52 ILJ 57

A final point to note is that this duty still applies even where the employee's activities take place away from the employer's premises. Thus, an employee who worked

---

173. *McWilliams v Sir William Arrol & Co Ltd* [1962] 1 WLR 295 (HL).
174. *Bux v Slough Metals Ltd* [1973] 1 WLR 1358 (CA) 1372 (Stephenson LJ).

for a firm of window cleaners could claim damages for injuries caused by a defective safety belt, even though his work was not carried out on the defendant's premises.[175]

Duty to protect employees from psychiatric illness

The duty to protect employees from psychiatric illness was not part of Lord Wright's original threefold formation of the employer's duty of care; rather, it was established in the following case.

 Walker v Northumberland County Council [1995] ICR 702 (QB)

FACTS: The claimant had worked for the defendant for seventeen years. In 1986, he suffered a nervous breakdown due to stress caused from overwork. Several months later, he returned to work and informed the defendant that his workload would need to be reduced. The defendant agreed to provide extra assistance to the claimant and stated that this assistance would be available for as long as the claimant required. But after only one month, the assistance was withdrawn and, by September 1987, the claimant suffered from a stress-related condition. Shortly after, he suffered a second nervous breakdown and was dismissed on the ground of permanent ill health.

HELD: The High Court held that the defendant had breached its duty of care in relation to the second nervous breakdown. The possibility of a stress-related condition was foreseeable, given the claimant's level of work, and psychiatric illness became even more foreseeable following his first nervous breakdown. In withdrawing the extra assistance, the defendant had therefore breached the duty of care owed to the claimant and was ordered to pay damages.

★ See L Dolding and R Mullender, 'Law, Labour and Mental Harm' (1996) 59 MLR 297

This area of the law is still at an embryonic stage and is still developing, as is evidenced by the substantial number of recent cases on the topic. In determining the exact scope of the employer's duty to protect employees from psychiatric illness, a number of relevant questions and factors are starting to emerge, including:

- From what forms of psychiatric illness is the employer under a duty to protect the employee?
- To what extent is psychiatric illness foreseeable?
- How proximate must the employee be to the potential cause of psychiatric illness?
- At what stage should the employer act? Should the employer be reactive or proactive?
- Does the fact that counselling is available absolve the employer?

Whilst there is a growing body of case law on these issues, the response of the courts has not always been entirely consistent and this area of the law must be regarded as being far from settled.

---

175. *General Cleaning Contractors Ltd v Christmas* [1953] AC 180 (HL).

Defences

An employee who has suffered injury due to his employer's negligence may be denied a remedy if the employer can successfully raise a defence. The tortious defences have already been examined in detail in Chapter 15. Here, we will simply highlight the principal defences available.

Where the employer's negligence has caused the employee injury, but the employee's own conduct also contributed to that injury occurring, then the employer can plead the defence of contributory negligence. It will be remembered that contributory negligence is a partial defence only and will serve to reduce the damages recoverable, based on the extent to which the employee's actions contributed to his injury. For example, in the case of *Bux v Slough Metals Ltd* [176] (discussed above), the Court held that the employee, in refusing to wear the provided safety goggles, was 40 per cent to blame for his injuries and therefore his damages were reduced by 40 per cent.

If the employer can demonstrate that the employee consented to the actions that caused his injury, then he will be able to raise the defence of *volenti non fit injuria*. As discussed, *volenti* is a complete defence, serving to exonerate the defendant completely. [177]

 volenti non fit injuria: 'to a willing person, no harm is done' (see p 521)

 Key points summary

- The employer owes a duty of care to all of his employees to:

    - provide competent fellow employees;
    - provide safe equipment and premises;
    - provide a safe system of work; and
    - protect the employees from psychiatric illness.

- An employer who has breached the duty of care and thereby caused injury to an employee may lessen his liability if he can establish that the employee's negligence contributed to his own loss.

- An employer who has breached the duty of care and thereby caused injury to an employee may avoid liability completely if it can establish that:

    - the employee voluntarily undertook the act that caused his injury; or
    - the employer took all reasonable precautions to prevent the act that caused the employee's injury.

Breach of contract

In addition to a claim in negligence, an employee injured at work might also have a claim for breach of contract. There is an implied term in the contract of employment that imposes a duty on the employer to take reasonable care of his employees'

---

176. [1973] 1 WLR 1358 (CA).

177. *ICI Ltd v Shatwell* [1965] AC 656 (HL). This case is discussed at p 524.

safety.[178] The scope of this duty is largely similar to the tortious duty discussed above and, in the majority of cases, a tortious claim will be preferable.

Whether it is preferable to bring a claim in contract or tort, depends on a number of factors, as follows.

- As we have noted, the courts are reluctant to award damages for pure economic loss in tort. Contractual damages for pure economic loss, however, are freely recoverable.

  The law relating to pure economic loss is discussed at p 397

- The construction of the employment contract may, in some way, preclude a contractual claim. A claim in tort may not be limited by the terms of the contract.

- The limitation periods in tort are generally more generous than those in contract.

- The claimant may choose to bring a claim in contract to deny the employer access to certain tortious defences.

- Damages in contract and tort are calculated differently. Depending on the facts, choosing the correct claim might result in a higher award of damages.

The Health and Safety at Work etc. Act 1974

Prior to the passing of the Health and Safety at Work etc. Act 1974 (HSWA 1974), the law relating to the health and safety of employees was spread across a mass of legislation: over thirty Acts and 500 statutory instruments. A committee was set up, under the chairmanship of Lord Robens, to evaluate the state of the law and to suggest reform. The Robens Report[179] was published in 1972 and was highly critical of the state of the law relating to the health and safety of employees, branding it a 'haphazard mass of law which is intricate in detail, unprogressive, often too difficult to comprehend and difficult to amend and keep up to date'. The report recommended that the mass of legislation be swept away and replaced by a 'comprehensive and orderly set of revised provisions under a new enabling Act'. This Act would cover only the general duties of employers, with more detailed regulation coming in the form of subordinate legislation and non-statutory codes of practice. The rationale behind this reliance on subordinate legislation was the desire to ensure that the law was flexible and could be amended easily, thereby ensuring that it would remain up to date. The recommendations of the Robens Report were almost universally adopted, resulting in the passing of the HSWA 1974.

As envisaged by Robens, the Act is an enabling one, stating only the general duties of employers and other relevant parties (for example, manufacturers and suppliers). But unlike previous piecemeal legislation, it applies to all types of workplace and all types of employer. The Act does not provide employees with civil remedies for injuries caused in the workplace[180]—to obtain such remedies, the employee should bring a claim in tort or contract, as discussed above; rather, the Act imposes criminal liability upon employers that breach the duties owed to employees.

---

178. *Lister v Romford Ice and Cold Storage Co* [1957] AC 555 (HL).
179. Lord Robens, *Report of the Committee on Safety and Health at Work* (Cmnd 5034, HMSO, London, 1972).
180. HSWA 1974, s 47(1).

Duties owed by employers to employees

The overriding duty owed by employers to their employees can be found in s 2(1) of the 1974 Act, which provides that '[i]t shall be the duty of every employer to ensure, so far as is reasonably practicable, the health, safety and welfare at work of all his employees'. Section 2(2) then provides a non-exhaustive list of matters that come within the s 2(1) duty:

- the provision and maintenance of plant and systems of work that are, so far as is reasonably practicable, safe and without risks to health;
- arrangements for ensuring, so far as is reasonably practicable, the safety of, and absence of risks to health in connection with, the use, handling, storage, and transport of articles and substances;
- the provision of such information, instruction, training, and supervision as is necessary to ensure, so far as is reasonably practicable, the health and safety at work of employees;
- so far as is reasonably practicable as regards any place of work under the employer's control, the maintenance of that place of work in a condition that is safe and free from risks to health, and the provision and maintenance of means of access to and egress from that place of work that are safe and free from such risks;
- the provision and maintenance of a working environment for employees that is, so far as is reasonably practicable, safe, free from risks to health, and adequate as regards facilities and arrangements for the employees' welfare at work.

It will be noted that each of these matters is subject to a limitation—namely, that the employer need only comply with the duty 'so far as is reasonably practicable'.

The meaning of the phrase 'reasonably practicable' was considered in the following case.

 Edwards v National Coal Board [1949] 1 KB 704 (CA)

FACTS: A miner walking along a travelling road that led to a coal mine was killed by a fall of material from the side of the mine, caused by a latent defect in the side of the road. His widow claimed damages from the defendant, on the ground it had breached the now repealed Coal Mines Act 1911, s 49, which placed a duty on employers to make secure 'every travelling road and working place'. The Act provided that liability would not be imposed where it was 'not reasonably practicable to avoid a breach' of s 49. The defendant argued that, given that it was impossible to know when and where a fall could occur, it would have to prop and support every travelling road, the cost of which was not reasonably practicable.

HELD: The Court of Appeal stated that the risk of an accident had to be measured against the costs (in terms of money, time, or trouble) of precautions. Where the risk of injury is great, the issue of cost is given less weight. Asquith LJ stated:

> 'Reasonably practicable' is a narrower term than 'physically possible' and seems to me to imply that a computation must be made by the owner, in which the quantum of risk is placed on one scale and the sacrifice involved in the measures necessary

> for averting the risk (whether in money, time or trouble) is placed in the other; and
> that if it be shown that there is a gross disproportion between them—the risk being
> insignificant in relation to the sacrifice—the defendants discharge the onus on
> them.[181]
>
> Here, the risk was considerable and, because the employer had presented little
> evidence to support its assertion, the Court found in the claimant's favour.

Like the common law, the HSWA 1974 does not expect the impossible, nor does it impose strict liability. The Act permits employers to balance the need to comply with the s 2 duty with the costs required for compliance. But the normal burden of proof is reversed, so that the employer will need to demonstrate that compliance with the duty was not reasonably practicable.[182]

As the following case demonstrates, establishing this does not appear to be overly difficult.

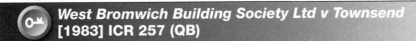

West Bromwich Building Society Ltd v Townsend
[1983] ICR 257 (QB)

FACTS: An environmental health inspector served an improvement notice on the defendant building society, alleging that it had contravened the HSWA 1974, s 2(1), by not installing anti-bandit screens to protect employees from attack. The defendant challenged the improvement notice. An industrial tribunal held that, because installing screens was well within the financial means of the defendant, the improvement notice was valid. The defendant appealed.

HELD: The High Court held that the tribunal had erred and that the correct question was not whether the installation of screens was financially viable, but whether the installation of screens was reasonably practicable, given the risk of a robbery occurring. Because the tribunal had erred in law, the Court allowed the appeal and quashed the improvement notice.

★ See R Howells, 'Criminal Attacks Upon Employees' (1983) 12 ILJ 182

Complying with the duty contained in s 2(1) might involve the provision of safety equipment, training, etc. In relation to this, s 9 imposes a further duty on employees not to charge their employees for any health and safety provision. But this duty extends only to provision provided to meet the statutory duties and employers may charge for provision if it goes beyond what is required by statute.

Duties owed by employers to persons who are not their employees

Employers also owe duties to persons who are not their employees (for example, employees of others, independent contractors, or members of the public). Section 3(1) provides that '[i]t shall be the duty of every employer to conduct his undertaking in such a way as to ensure, so far as is reasonably practicable, that persons not in

---

181. *Edwards v National Coal Board* [1949] 1 KB 704 (CA) 712.
182. HSWA 1974, s 40.

his employment who may be affected thereby are not thereby exposed to risks to their health or safety'. In the following case, it was noted that injury to health is not required to establish a breach of s 3(1), but only a breach that *exposes* persons who are not their employees to injury.

> ## R v Board of Trustees of the Science Museum [1993] 1 WLR 1171 (CA)
>
> **FACTS:** The defendant's air conditioning system was found to contain legionella pneumophila, the bacterium that causes legionnaires' disease. It was charged under the HSWA 1974, s 3(1), on the ground that members of the public could be exposed to the bacterium. The defendant argued that no harm had actually been caused and that there was no evidence to indicate that members of the public had inhaled the bacterium.
>
> **HELD:** The Court of Appeal rejected the defendant's argument and upheld the conviction. Actual damage to health was not required to be proved; only that the defendant's conduct had exposed persons other than its employees to the possibility of danger.
>
> **COMMENT:** This case demonstrates the difference in approach between the common law and the HSWA 1974. In order to succeed, a claim in contract or tort would require a claimant who had suffered loss. As regards the HSWA 1974, no loss need occur. This more stringent approach fits in with the Act's aim of preventing injury.

★ See B Barrett, 'Trends in Occupational Health and Safety' (1994) 23 ILJ 60

Duties owed by other persons

Although the principal duties contained in the HSWA 1974 are imposed on employers, the Act does impose duties on a number of other parties, including the following.

- A self-employed person is under a duty under s 3(2) to conduct his undertaking in such as way so as to ensure, as far as is reasonably practicable, that he and other persons (who are not his employees) who may be affected by the undertaking, are not exposed to risks to their health and safety.

- A duty is imposed by s 4 upon occupiers and controllers of premises (except domestic premises) to take care for the safety of persons who are not their employees on their premises.

- A duty is imposed by s 6 upon designers, manufacturers, importers, and suppliers of articles or substances for use at work to ensure, so far as is reasonably practicable, that such articles and substances do not pose a risk to health and safety.

- A duty is imposed by s 7 upon employees to take reasonable care of their own safety and to cooperate with employers or any other person so far as is necessary to enable them to fulfil their duties under the HSWA 1974 or a related provision.

- A duty is imposed by s 8 upon everyone not to interfere with, intentionally or recklessly, or to misuse anything provided in the interests of health and safety pursuant to the HSWA 1974 or a related provision.

The 'six-pack'

As noted, the HSWA 1974 is an enabling Act, meaning that it was always envisaged that the Act would be supplemented by a substantial amount of subordinate legislation. Over fifty pieces of subordinate legislation have been passed that provide more specific and detailed regulation, but there are six principal pieces of subordinate legislation that are collectively referred to as the 'six-pack', as follows.

1. *The Health and Safety (Display Screen Equipment) Regulations 1992*[183] These Regulations, aimed at protecting employees who have to work with display screens for long periods, provide that employers should carry out risk assessment of workstations, should provide their employees with free and regular eye tests (and special spectacles if necessary), should provide training to enable employees to use display screens without affecting their safety, and should ensure that their employees have regular breaks.

2. *The Manual Handling Operations Regulations 1992*[184] These Regulations aim to reduce the number of injuries caused through manual handling. Employers should carry out risk assessments and establish safety measures to minimize the risk of injury.

3. *The Workplace (Health, Safety and Welfare) Regulations 1992*[185] These Regulations place a duty upon employers to ensure that places of work are clean, well lit and well ventilated, and are maintained at an adequate temperature. Travel around the place of work should be safe, including safe lifts, doors, and vehicle routes. There should be adequate washing and toilet facilities, and designated eating areas and rest areas should be provided.

4. *The Personal Protective Equipment at Work Regulations 1992*[186] These Regulations provide that suitable personal protective equipment be provided to employees whose health and safety might be at risk. The equipment must be adequately maintained and employees must be trained in its use.

5. *The Provision and Use of Work Equipment Regulations 1998*[187] These Regulations provide that work equipment should be suitable, safe, routinely checked, and maintained in a state of good repair. Providers of equipment should also provide instructions on how to use such equipment.

6. *The Management of Health and Safety at Work Regulations 1999*[188] These Regulations require employers to undertake a health and safety risk assessment of the dangers facing their employees. Protective and preventative measures must be put in place, and must be routinely monitored and reviewed. Procedures must be put in place to deal with events resulting in serious or imminent danger, including the provision of a place of safety.

Enforcement

The Health and Safety Executive (HSE), a body created by the 1974 Act, primarily enforces the HSWA 1974 and accompanying regulations.[189] The HSE is assisted by local authority environmental health officers, who, along with HSE inspectors, have the power to:

- enter premises at any reasonable time or, if they believe that the situation is dangerous, enter premises at any time;
- be accompanied by a police officer if they believe that their entry will be obstructed;

---

183. SI 1992/2792.
184. SI 1992/2793.
185. SI 1992/3004.
186. SI 1992/2966.
187. SI 1998/2306.
188. SI 1999/3242.
189. HSWA 1974, s 10 and Sch 2.

- make such examination and investigation as is necessary;
- direct that premises be undisturbed to facilitate such investigations;
- take measurements, photographs, and samples within the premises;
- take possession of substances, articles, or equipment, and subject them to testing;
- require the production of books and records;
- require that persons answer questions and sign a declaration providing that such answers are true.

Anyone who obstructs an inspector in the performance of his duties commits a summary offence,[190] punishable by a term of imprisonment not exceeding six months[191] and a fine not exceeding the statutory maximum (currently £5,000).[192]

Once an examination has been carried out, inspectors have a number of powers available to them. Where the inspector believes that an employer is not meeting the requirements laid down by the HSWA 1974 and accompanying regulations, he may issue an improvement notice requiring the employer to take stated measures within twenty-one days of the notice being issued.[193] Where the employer's breach of legislation results, in the opinion of the inspector, in a risk of serious injury, a prohibition notice may be issued, which will require the employer immediately to cease the activity that is causing the risk.[194] This may involve closing down the employer's business until the breach is rectified. Employers have a right to appeal against an improvement or prohibition notice. Where an improvement notice is appealed, it will be suspended until the appeal is heard.[195] Prohibition notices are not suspended pending an appeal, unless an employment tribunal so directs.[196] Failure to comply with an improvement notice or prohibition notice constitutes a criminal offence.[197] The offence is either way and, on summary conviction, carries a penalty of up to six months' imprisonment and/or a £20,000 fine. On indictment, the maximum penalty is up to two years' imprisonment and/or a fine.

Breach of any of the duties under ss 2–9 discussed above constitutes an either-way offence.[198] A breach of a duty contained in ss 2–8 will, on summary conviction, result in a maximum penalty of six months' imprisonment[199] and/or a fine not exceeding £20,000.[200] On conviction on indictment, the maximum penalty is two years' imprisonment and/or a fine.[201] On summary conviction, a breach of the duty contained in s 9 can result in a fine not exceeding £20,000; on conviction on indict-

---

190. Ibid, s 33(1)(h).
191. This will increase to twelve months if or when the Criminal Justice Act 2003, s 154, comes into force.
192. HSWA 1974, Sch 3A, para 1.
193. Ibid, s 21.
194. Ibid, s 22.
195. Ibid, s 24(3)(a).
196. Ibid, s 24(3)(b).
197. Ibid, s 33(1)(g).
198. Ibid, s 33(1)(a).
199. This will rise to twelve months' imprisonment if or when the Criminal Justice Act 2003, s 154, comes into force.
200. HSWA 1974, Sch 3A. For breach of the duty imposed by s 7, the maximum fine is the statutory maximum (currently £5,000).
201. Ibid.

ment, there is no limit on the fine that can be imposed. Where an offence under the HSWA 1974 is committed by a body corporate with the consent or connivance of, or can be attributable to any neglect on the part of, any director, manager, secretary, or other similar officer of the body corporate, or a person who was purporting to act in any such capacity, he, as well as the body corporate, shall be guilty of that offence, and shall be liable to be proceeded against and punished accordingly.[202]

> **⟨ ⟩ Key points summary**
>
> - Breach of the duties contained in the Health and Safety at Work etc. Act 1974 constitutes a criminal offence. The Act provides no civil remedies.
>
> - Employers owe a duty to ensure, as far as is reasonably practicable, the health, safety, and welfare of their employees. The burden of proof is on the employer to establish that compliance with this duty is not reasonably practicable.
>
> - Employers also owe a duty not to expose non-employees to health and safety risks.
>
> - Employees are under a duty to take reasonable care of their own safety.
>
> - Other parties, such as designers, manufacturers, importers, and suppliers, also owe a duty not to expose those who use their products to health and safety risks.
>
> - Enforcement of the HSWA 1974 is carried out by the Health and Safety Executive and local authorities.

The Working Time Regulations 1998

There can be little doubt that the health and safety of an employee can be adversely affected by working long hours. But the UK was reluctant to recognize this. A restriction on the number of hours for which an employee may work was proposed by the EU Council but was blocked by the previous Conservative government. The other member States managed to circumvent the UK's veto and pass the Working Time Directive[203] by adopting it under the EC Treaty, Art 118a (now Art 137), which permits legislation relating to 'health and safety' to be passed by a qualified majority. The UK attempted to annul the Directive by arguing that the number of hours for which an employee works was not a health and safety issue, but the European Court of Justice disagreed.[204] A year later, the Labour Party came to power and implemented the Directive by passing the Working Time Regulations 1998 (the WTRs).[205]

Scope

The rights contained in the WTRs apply only to 'workers'. The definition of 'worker' is extremely wide and covers any individual who has entered into, or works under, a contract of employment, or any other contract (express or implied) whereby the individual 'undertakes to do or perform personally any work or services for another

---

202. Ibid, s 37(1).
204. C-84/94 *UK v Council of the EU* [1997] ICR 30.

203. Council Directive No 93/104/EC.
205. SI 1998/1833.

party to the contract whose status is not by virtue of the contract that of a client or customer of any profession or business undertaking carried on by the individual'.[206]

The WTRs differentiate between two different types of worker:

- a *young worker* is a worker who is over 15 years of age, but less than 18 years of age, and who is over compulsory school age;
- an *adult worker*, or simply *worker*, is any worker over the age of 18.

Exceptions to the obligations contained in the WTRs apply in respect of certain types of employee, including:

- generally, employees of the armed forces, the emergency services, and the police, who are not protected by the principal provisions of the WTRs (but certain provisions of the WTRs may apply where the worker is a young worker);
- workers whose working hours are governed by specific legislation (for example, workers on board seagoing fishing vessels and air transport workers are not covered by the WTRs);
- workers whose working time is not measured or predetermined, or workers who determine their own working hours, are not covered by the WTRs. The WTRs provide several examples of workers who *may* be excluded from the WTRs on these grounds, including managing executives and family workers.[207]

Any term in an agreement (whether the contract of employment or not) that attempts to exclude the provisions of the WTRs, or to preclude a person from bringing proceedings under the WTRs in an employment tribunal, shall be regarded as void.[208]

The 'forty-eight hours' restriction

The key provision in the WTRs is reg 4(1), which provides that a worker's working time, including overtime, must not exceed an average of forty-eight hours per week. The average is usually calculated over a seventeen-week reference period,[209] but this can be varied by a collective or workforce agreement up to a maximum period of fifty-two weeks.[210] The fact that the restriction is based upon the average working time is important, because this means that an employee can be made to work long hours for a sustained period, without a breach of the WTRs occurring, as the following example demonstrates.

Eg Average working hours

Fiona is employed at her local Royal Mail sorting office. The Christmas period is an extremely busy one in the sorting office and Fiona is, for four weeks leading up to Christmas and for two weeks after Christmas, required to work overtime. In these six weeks, she works around sixty-five hours per week. Once the backlog of mail is cleared, Fiona's hours are reduced to her normal contractual amount—namely, thirty-five hours per week.

---

206. WTRs 1998, reg 2. 207. Ibid, reg 20(1).
208. Ibid, reg 35(1). 209. Ibid, reg 4(3).
210. Ibid, reg 23(b).

A seventeen-week period that includes the six weeks of overtime will produce the following result. Six weeks at sixty-five hours per week totals 390 hours. Eleven weeks at thirty-five hours per week totals 385 hours. Therefore, across the seventeen-week reference period, Fiona worked 775 hours. Averaging this across the period will result in Fiona working an average of 45.6 hours per week, with the result that the WTRs have not been breached.

Days taken off as paid holiday leave, absence due to sickness, and maternity/paternity/parental/adoption leave do not count when determining the average.[211] The restriction contained in reg 4(1) ceases to apply where the employee has agreed in writing that it should not apply, provided that the worker's consent is free and with full knowledge of all of the relevant facts.[212] This agreement can be indefinite or for a specific duration, and the employee has the right to terminate the agreement upon providing notice to the employer. The default period of notice is seven days,[213] but the agreement itself can provide for a longer notice period, up to a maximum of three months.[214]

It has been argued that '[t]he individual opt-out is the principal means by which the potential impact of the Directive has been diluted'[215] and that it 'provides employers with a low-cost mechanism to avoid the 48-hour limit'.[216] Evidence would appear to indicate that the WTRs have had a limited impact on working hours in the UK. The ability to opt out is certainly not popular amongst the EU institutions. In 2005, the European Parliament voted in favour of abolishing the UK's right to allow its workers to opt out of the forty-eight-hour maximum, but this did not ultimately occur. In June 2008, a revised Working Time Directive was agreed upon in which the opt-out was preserved. But the Directive will only be passed if the European Parliament approves. In December 2008, its members voted in favour of ending the opt-out. The UK and several other EU member States are lobbying to retain the opt-out. The European Commission will examine the European Parliament's decision, but the final decision rests with the European Council, which has indicated that it will decide the matter in June 2009. If it does decide to abolish the opt-out, it must end within three years of the revised Directive coming into force.

Night workers

Special provision is made for workers who work during the night. Regulation 6 provides that employers are under a duty to take all reasonable steps to ensure that a night worker's normal hours of work in any seventeen-week period shall not exceed an average of eight hours in each twenty-four hours (that is, the average number of hours work at night should not exceed one third of the total hours worked during those seventeen weeks). Where the night work is hazardous, or involves physical or

---

211. Ibid, reg 4(7).
212. C-397/01 *Pfeiffer v Deutsches Rotes Kreuz Kreisverband Waldshut eV* [2004] ECR I-8835.
213. WTRs 1998, reg 5(2).
214. Ibid, reg 5(3).
215. C Barnard, S Deakin, and R Hobbs, 'Opting Out of the 48-Hour Week: Employer Necessity or Individual Choice?' (2003) 32 ILJ 223, 252.
216. Ibid.

mental strain, a limit of eight hours in *any* 24-hour period applies (that is, there is no averaging out).[217]

A 'night worker' is defined as a worker who normally works at least three hours of his daily working time during night-time, or who is likely, during night-time, to work at least such proportion of his annual working time as may be specified for in a collective agreement or a workforce agreement.[218] 'Night-time' is defined as a period of not less than seven hours that includes the entire period between midnight and 5 a.m.[219] Where the worker is a young worker, he is not permitted to work between the hours of 10 p.m. and 6 a.m.,[220] unless the work is of an 'exceptional nature'.[221]

No worker may be assigned to night work without the opportunity for a free health assessment, except where the employee has already had an assessment and the employer has no reasons to believe that the assessment is no longer valid.[222] In either case, the employee is entitled to future free health assessments at regular intervals.

Rest breaks

Workers are entitled to the following rest breaks:

- a daily rest period of not less than eleven consecutive hours each working day (where the worker is a young worker, the rest period is increased to twelve hours);[223]

- an uninterrupted weekly rest period of at least twenty-four hours in each seven-day period (where the worker is a young worker, the rest period is increased to forty-eight hours, which can be reduced to thirty-six hours if justified by technical or organizational reasons);[224]

- a rest break of at least 20 minutes where the worker's daily working time is more than six hours (young workers are entitled to a rest break of at least 30 minutes where their daily working time is over four-and-a-half hours).[225]

Annual leave

With the passing of the WTRs, employees became entitled, for the first time, to a period of paid annual leave. The period of leave is currently four weeks,[226] with an extra period of additional leave amounting to 1.6 weeks,[227] providing for a total of 5.6 weeks' annual leave. The entitlement to annual leave used to be conditional upon thirteen weeks' continuous service, but this requirement has been abolished and employees are now entitled to paid annual leave from their first day of work. The entitlement to annual leave is not additional to any entitlement contained in the contract of employment. Accordingly, where the contract of employment provides annual leave at an amount equal to, or greater than, that contained in the WTRs, no further leave need be provided.

---

217. WTRs 1998, reg 6(7).
219. Ibid.
221. Ibid, reg 7(4).
223. Ibid, reg 10.
225. Ibid, reg 12.
227. Ibid, reg 13A(2)(e).
218. Ibid, reg 2.
220. Ibid, regs 7(2) and 6A.
222. Ibid, reg 7(1)(a).
224. Ibid, reg 11.
226. Ibid, reg 13(1).

Enforcement

The responsibility for enforcing the WTRs is split amongst various bodies.

- The HSE and local authority environmental health departments enforce the provisions relating to the maximum weekly working time limit and night workers.

- The provisions relating to rest breaks and annual leave are enforced through employment tribunals. Employees must bring their claim within three months beginning on the date on which the alleged right should have been permitted, or within whatever period the tribunal considers reasonable if the three-month period is not reasonably practicable.[228] Where the tribunal holds that an employee's rights under the WTRs have been breached, it can award him such compensation as it deems just and equitable, given all of the circumstances.[229]

Employers who breach the WTRs commit a criminal offence.[230] The offence is either way and therefore can be tried summarily or on indictment. On summary conviction, the maximum penalty is a fine not exceeding the statutory maximum (currently £5,000), and on indictment, there is no limit to the amount that the defendant can be fined.[231] Where the offence is committed by a body corporate (that is, a company or limited liability partnership), not only is the body corporate guilty, but any director, manager, secretary, or other similar officer of the body corporate, or a person who was purporting to act in any such capacity, is also guilty of the offence if the offence was committed due to his consent, connivance, or neglect.[232]

A worker who is dismissed for refusing to comply with a policy that contravenes the WTRs, or for refusing to forgo a right conferred by the WTRs, is to be regarded as being unfairly dismissed.[233]

 Key points summary

- The Working Time Regulations 1998 apply to any worker who works under a contract of employment or any other contract, and performs personally any work or services for another.

- A worker who is over the age of 15, but under the age of 18, is known as a 'young worker'.

- The worker's working week should not exceed an average of forty-eight hours per week across the reference period (which is normally seventeen weeks). But this restriction shall not apply where the worker has agreed in writing that it should not apply.

- Night workers should not work more than an average of eight hours in each twenty-four hours across the reference period (usually seventeen weeks).

- Workers are entitled to daily and weekly rest breaks, with young workers entitled to longer breaks. Workers are also entitled to 5.6 weeks' annual leave.

- Enforcement of the WTRs is split amongst the Health and Safety Executive, local authorities, and employment tribunals.

- A breach of the WTRs constitutes an either-way offence.

---

228. Ibid, reg 30(2).   229. Ibid, reg 30(4).
230. Ibid, reg 29(1).   231. Ibid, reg 29(4).
232. Ibid, reg 29B(1).   233. ERA 1996, s 101A(1).

Chapter conclusion

The area of employment rights is perhaps the fastest moving area of employment law. In a relatively short period of time, the existing rights of employees have increased greatly and new rights have been created. These rights will continue to increase in scope and number in the near future. In many cases, these rights are protected by statute, and any business that fails to uphold these rights will be required to pay compensation and may even be guilty of a criminal offence. Accordingly, it is crucial that businesses and employers have a full understanding of their employees' rights.

The same is true of the obligations imposed upon employers in relation to safeguarding the health and safety of their employees. Given the importance of health and safety, it is hardly surprising that that law has chosen to go down the path of imposing criminal liability upon employers who fail adequately to protect their employees' well-being. But businesses should safeguard the health and safety of their employees not only to avoid criminal liability: as was stated in the introduction to this chapter, millions of work days are lost each year due to injuries sustained by employees whilst at work. Therefore, employers have both legal and economic reasons to ensure that their employees are not exposed to health and safety risks.

Self-test questions

1. Define the following:
   (a) male comparator;
   (b) red-circling;
   (c) undertaking;
   (d) young worker;
   (e) night worker.

2. Has there been a breach of employment rights in the following cases?
   (a) Rachel and Eddie work in a factory. They perform identical work, have identical duties, and work the same number of hours. But Eddie's contract provides that he may be required by his employer to work on the night shift. Eddie is paid £1,000 per year more than Rachel.
   (b) Carys, an 18-year-old school leaver, cleans the offices of Smith & Co, a small high-street firm of accountants, in return for which she is paid £4.50 per hour. She has, however, never signed an employment contract.

3. Explain the distinction between: (i) ordinary maternity leave; (ii) additional maternity leave; and (iii) compulsory maternity leave.

4. 'The recent increase in the scope and number of employment rights places intolerable burdens upon employers and businesses and therefore employers should be permitted to exclude these employment rights where it is reasonable to do so.' Discuss.

5. Has there been a breach of health and safety legislation in the following cases?
   (a) David has been employed by BuildCo Ltd as a labourer for the previous six months. He normally works a forty-hour week, but for five weeks, he was required to work an extra fifteen hours per week of overtime.

(b)   Olivia is employed as a trainee solicitor. The firm is engaged in a high-profile merger and, with the deadline for the merger approaching, the partners require the trainees to work longer hours than normal. In the period leading up to the merger deadline, Olivia is required to work for eight consecutive days.

Further reading

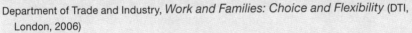

Department of Trade and Industry, *Work and Families: Choice and Flexibility* (DTI, London, 2006)
Sets out the imminent changes to be introduced in relation to family employment rights as a result of the Work and Families Act 2006

Equal Opportunities Commission, *Code of Practice on Equal Pay* (EOC, London, 2003)
Provides detailed, yet easy-to-understand, guidance on the right to equal pay and how to bring a claim

Health and Safety Executive, *Health and Safety Statistics 2007/08* (Office for National Statistics, London, 2008)
Provides detailed statistics of all work-related injuries and illnesses; also provides statistics relating to the issuing of improvement and prohibition notices

Institute of Directors/Health and Safety Commission, *Leading Health and Safety at Work* (HSE, London, 2007)
Sets out why health and safety is so important for companies, and what action should be taken by directors and board members to ensure that a company's statutory obligations are met

James, G, 'The Work and Families Act 2006: Legislation to Improve Choice and Flexibility?' (2006) 35 ILJ 272
Examines the reforms introduced by the 2006 Act and contends that such piecemeal reforms have little to offer interested parties

McMullen, J, 'An Analysis of the Transfer of Undertakings (Protection of Employment) Regulations 2006' (2006) 35 ILJ 113
Examines in depth the TUPE and argues that the aims set out in the Acquired Rights Directive have been met only in part

Simpson, B, 'The National Minimum Wage Five Years on: Reflections on Some General Issues' (2004) 33 ILJ 22
Discusses the early operation of the National Minimum Wage Act 1998 and argues that it plays a valuable, if limited, role

Smith, I, and Thomas, G, *Smith & Wood's Employment Law* (9th edn, OUP, Oxford, 2008) ch 7
An excellent and up-to-date discussion of employment law rights relating to the family

Websites

<http://www.hse.gov.uk>
The official website of the Health and Safety Executive; provides useful guidance of all health and safety legislation, as well as links to more detailed research publications

<http://www.lowpay.gov.uk>

The official website of the Low Pay Commission; contains useful guidance on the national minimum wage, and links to various reports and publications

 Remember to visit the **Online Resource Centre** at **<http://www. oxfordtextbooks.co.uk/roach>** to access the following resources on Chapter 24, 'Employment rights, and health and safety': more **practice questions** and answers; a **glossary** of key terms; **multiple-choice questions**; **revision summaries**; and **audio updates** when relevant.

25 Discrimination

- What is 'discrimination'?

- Sex discrimination

- Race discrimination

- Disability discrimination

- Age discrimination

- Discrimination on grounds of religion or beliefs

- Discrimination on ground of sexual orientation

- Discrimination against part-time workers and fixed-term workers

- The proposed Equality Bill

INTRODUCTION

Although discrimination law is still treated as an element of employment law, it could rightly be regarded as a subject in its own right. In the early nineteenth century, employees were not protected from the discriminatory acts of their employers and an employer was free to refuse a person employment 'for the most mistaken, capricious, malicious or morally reprehensible motives that can be conceived'.[1] The situation today is very different. In the last forty years, the volume of anti-discrimination legislation that has been enacted has been staggering—and the process is still far from over. In order to avoid liability, employers need to be aware of the duties and restrictions imposed upon them by this mass of legislation. But given its sheer bulk, understanding the differing forms and grounds of discrimination, and the distinctions that exist between them can be extremely difficult. Fortunately, the government has indicated that the various Acts and statutory instruments will be unified into a single Act at some point in the future. Until this occurs, employers will need to be aware of the various pieces of legislation that prohibit them from engaging in discriminatory acts against their workers.[2] In this chapter, this legislation will be discussed in depth, after which will be highlighted the government's proposals regarding the forthcoming Equality Bill.

---

1. *Allen v Flood* [1898] AC 1 (HL) 172 (Lord Davey).

2. Virtually all of the anti-discrimination legislation discussed in this chapter (the sole exception being the Fixed-Term Employees (Prevention of Less Favourable Treatment) Regulations 2002) protects workers, as opposed to employees. The importance of the distinction is discussed at p 787.

What is 'discrimination'?

Before discussing the various grounds of discrimination, it is first necessary to actually define what 'discrimination' is. Currently, the law recognizes three distinct forms of discrimination:

- direct discrimination;
- indirect discrimination; and
- victimization.

It is important, however, to note that not all of these forms of discrimination suffice under the various anti-discrimination statutes. For example, both the Sex Discrimination Act 1975 and the Race Relations Act 1976 expressly recognize all three forms of discrimination. The Disability Discrimination Act 1995, however, recognizes only direct discrimination and victimization; it does not deal with indirect discrimination on the ground of disability.

Direct discrimination

Direct discrimination is the archetypal form of discrimination whereby a person is treated less favourably on the grounds of sex, disability, race, etc.

Eg Direct discrimination

Helen is applying for a job as a PA to the managing director of a large corporate bank. She is shortlisted for an interview, along with two other candidates, Tom and Dave—but the bank's managing director instructs the personnel department not to invite Tom and Dave for an interview, because he would prefer his PA to be a woman, and to offer Helen the job.
    Tom and Dave have been directly discriminated against on the ground of their sex.

A specific form of direct discrimination has gained prominence in recent years— namely, harassment. The definition of 'harassment' differs slightly depending upon the ground of discrimination, but it basically occurs where *A*, on the grounds of sex, disability, etc. is the recipient of unwanted attention from *B* that serves to humiliate *A* or which creates a hostile or intimidating atmosphere.

Eg Harassment

Daphne suffers from early onset Parkinson's disease. The condition is in an early stage and she has almost full control over her body—but a few times a day, her hand will shake uncontrollably for a few seconds. Sometimes, the shaking spreads up her arm. She works in an office with four other people, all of whom are aware of her condition. Whenever her hand shakes, the office manager, Ian, tends to make disparaging comments about Daphne's condition and openly laughs when he sees Daphne having difficulty with everyday tasks.
    Daphne is being harassed on the ground of her disability.

Indirect discrimination

Indirect discrimination is more subtle than direct discrimination and occurs where a particular practice or restriction, whilst not overtly discriminating against anyone, indirectly discriminates against a certain group of persons by virtue of sex, race, etc. When we discuss the various grounds for discrimination, we shall see how insidious indirect discrimination can be.

 Eg **Indirect discrimination**

BioCorp plc advertises a vacancy for a managerial post, stating that only current full-time employees of BioCorp should apply. Initially, this advertisement does not appear discriminatory, but because the majority of part-time workers are women, refusing to consider applications from part-time employees may indirectly discriminate against women.

Victimization

The final form of discrimination is victimization, which occurs where *A* treats *B* less favourably because, at some point in the past, *B* has brought a complaint against *A*, or has given evidence against *A*, or engaged in other similar activity.

 Eg **Victimization**

Rasheed is alleging that her employer has discriminated against her on the ground of race. A colleague of hers, Adam, provides evidence backing up Rasheed's claim and, as a result of this evidence, an employment tribunal holds that Rasheed has been the victim of race discrimination. Appalled by his employer's apparent racism, Adam decides to seek employment elsewhere. He completes an application form and asks his employer to write him a reference. Even though Adam has been an outstanding employee, the employer writes a negative reference and Adam fails to get the job.

The writing of the negative reference constitutes victimization.

Having discussed the various forms of discrimination, we can now discuss the various grounds of discrimination, beginning with sex discrimination.

 Key points summary

- The law currently recognizes three forms of discrimination:

  - direct discrimination;
  - indirect discrimination; and
  - victimization.

- The law also provides for a specific form of direct discrimination known as 'harassment'.

- Direct discrimination occurs where a person is treated less favourably on the grounds of sex, disability, race, etc.

- Harassment occurs where *A*, on the grounds of sex, disability, etc. is the recipient of unwanted attention from *B* that serves to humiliate *A*, or which creates a hostile or intimidating atmosphere.

- Indirect discrimination occurs where a particular practice or restriction, whilst not overtly discriminating against anyone, indirectly discriminates against a certain group of persons by virtue of sex, race, etc.

- Victimization occurs where *A* treats *B* less favourably because, at some point in the past, *B* has brought a complaint against *A*, or has given evidence against *A*, or engaged in other similar activity.

Sex discrimination

Sex discrimination against men and women is prohibited by the Sex Discrimination Act 1975 (SDA 1975). Despite this, sex discrimination claims are the fourth most numerous and, in 2006–07, there were 28,153 claims accepted by employment tribunals.[3] Table 25.1 demonstrates the trend in the number of claims since 2000.

TABLE 25.1 Number of sex discrimination claims

	2006–07	2005–06	2004–05	2003–04	2002–03	2001–02	2000–01
No of claims	28,153	14,250	11,726	17,722	11,001	15,703	25,940

Source: Statistics collated from the Annual Reports of the Employment Tribunal Service and the Tribunal Service, available online at <http://www.employmenttribunals.gov.uk/Publications/publications.htm>

Before discussing this Act in detail, it is worth highlighting how it relates to another piece of legislation that aims to combat inequalities due to sex—namely, the Equal Pay Act 1970 (EPA 1970).

The relationship between sex discrimination and equal pay

The right to equal pay is discussed at p 802

In the previous chapter, we discussed the employees' right to equal pay under the EPA 1970, which came into force at almost exactly the same time as the SDA 1975. It might be thought that paying employees more or less based upon their sex would amount to sex discrimination under the SDA 1975, but this is unlikely to be the case. This is because the EPA 1970 applies to discriminatory contractual terms (for example, higher contractual rates of pay for men than women), whereas the SDA 1975 applies to discrimination that occurs outside the contract of employment (for

---

3. Tribunals Service, *Employment Tribunal and EAT Statistics (GB) 1 April 2006 to 31 March 2007* (Tribunals Service, London, 2007) Table 1.

example, refusing to employ a person because she is a woman). The two Acts are therefore mutually exclusive and a claim must be brought under one or the other. Given that the EPA 1970 is limited to matters concerning the contract of employment, the ambit of the 1975 Act is much wider, and can relate to sex discrimination in relation to appointments, promotion, dismissals, and other non-contractual issues that are outside the scope of the 1970 Act.

Although differentiating between the scopes of the two Acts is relatively straightforward, it does seem somewhat unnecessary to have two separate Acts dealing with separate aspects of sex discrimination. For this reason, the then Equal Opportunities Commission (now subsumed within the Equality and Human Rights Commission) recommended that the 1970 and 1975 Acts be repealed, and replaced with a single sex equality Act.[4] In June 2007, the government published a Consultation Paper, in which it set out its proposals for an Equality Bill.[5] This Bill goes further than unifying the EPA 1970 and the SDA 1975, and aims to unify *all* discrimination legislation into a single Act. This would be a welcome development. As we shall see, the various pieces of discrimination legislation often have identical rules and it is common for the *ratio* of a case involving one form of discrimination also to apply to other forms of discrimination. Having all of these rules incorporated into one Act instead of repeated rules throughout several Acts would simplify the law greatly. The proposals for this Act and the changes that it would introduce will be discussed at the end of this chapter, once the discrimination legislation that it aims to unify has been examined.

*The Equality Bill is discussed at p 886

Forms of sex discrimination

The SDA 1975 recognizes and provides for all three forms of discrimination.

Direct sex discrimination

The SDA 1975, s 1(2)(a), provides that a person directly discriminates against a woman if 'on the ground of her sex he treats her less favourably than he treats or would treat a man'. Section 2(1) indicates that s 1(2)(a) will apply equally to direct discrimination against a man.[6] This requires the claimant to establish two things:

1. that the discrimination was on the ground of sex; and
2. that the woman[7] was treated less favourably than a man. It is vital that the treatment be less favourable: treatment that is merely different from, but no less favourable than, that of a man will not amount to direct discrimination.[8]

---

4. Equal Opportunities Commission, *Equality in the 21st Century: A New Sex Equality Law for Britain* (EOC, London, 1998).

5. Department of Communities and Local Government, *A Framework for Fairness: Proposals for a Single Equality Bill for Great Britain* (HMSO, London, June 2007).

6. But s 2(2) states that special treatment received by women in connection with pregnancy or childbirth is not to be regarded as discriminatory against men.

7. Because the majority of cases concern alleged discrimination against women, feminine nouns and pronouns will be used to discuss sex discrimination, unless gender-specific pronouns are required. Accordingly, 'she', 'her', and 'woman' should also be taken to mean 'he', 'him', and 'man', and vice versa.

8. *Smith v Safeway plc* [1996] IRLR 456 (CA) 458 (Phillips J).

Turning to the first requirement, the claimant will need to establish that she was discriminated against on the ground of her sex. This will obviously cover situations in which a person is treated less favourably because she is a woman, but it will also cover discrimination against a person on the grounds that she is married,[9] or has undergone gender reassignment.[10]

The second requirement that the claimant will need to establish is that she was treated less favourably than a man would be treated. But s 1(2)(a) does not indicate whether intention is a requirement—does a person need to intend to treat others less favourably in order to directly discriminate against them?

In the following case, the House of Lords held that motive was irrelevant.

 ### James v Eastleigh Borough Council [1990] 2 AC 751 (HL)

FACTS: The defendant council adopted a policy of providing free swimming facilities to persons of pensionable age. Mr James and his wife, who were both aged 61, visited a swimming pool run by the defendant council. Because the pensionable age for women is 60 and 65 for men, this meant that Mrs James was admitted for free, whereas Mr James had to pay 75 pence. Mr James brought an action against the defendant council alleging that he had been treated less favourably because he was a man. The Court of Appeal rejected his claim on the ground that the reason for the policy was to encourage pensioners to swim, not to discriminate against men. Mr James appealed.

HELD: It was clear that the defendant did not intend to discriminate. But the House of Lords, by a majority of three to two, held that this was irrelevant and allowed the appeal. The test under s 1(2)(a) was objective. If it was satisfied, it was irrelevant whether the motive (that is, reason) for the discriminatory act was benign or not. The question to ask was: '[W]ould the complainant have received the same treatment but for his or her sex?'[11] But for Mr James' sex, he would have received the same treatment, and so direct discrimination was proven.

COMMENT: Lord Griffiths gave a powerful, if short, dissenting speech. He applauded the council's 'wholly admirable practice of treating old age pensioners with generosity'[12] and stated that he could not believe 'that it was the intention of Parliament that this benevolent practice should be declared to be unlawful'.[13] Lord Lowry agreed, stating that the free swimming facilities were provided to persons because they were of pensionable age, not because they were men or women. Ultimately, Lords Griffiths and Lowry were in the minority, and the principal result of *James* was to make it easier for a claimant to establish direct discrimination by preventing the defendant from using motive as a defence. A likely rationale for this is the desire to preserve the exclusive status of those instances in which the SDA 1975 itself permits sex discrimination.

🔗 Instances in which sex discrimination is permitted are discussed at p 860

⭐ See G Mead, 'The Role of Intention in Direct Discrimination' (1990) 19 ILJ 250

---

9. SDA 1975, s 3(1) and (2). This will also apply to civil partners.
10. Ibid, s 2A(1).
11. *James v Eastleigh Borough Council* [1990] 2 AC 751 (HL) 774 (Lord Goff).
12. Ibid, 767. 13. Ibid.

In order to establish that she was treated less favourably than a man, the claimant will need to compare her treatment to that of a man. It will be remembered that a similar requirement exists in relation to the EPA 1970. But a claimant bringing proceedings under that Act will need to identify an actual male comparator, whereas claimants under the SDA 1975 can compare their treatment to a hypothetical comparator (although they may also choose an actual comparator if a suitable one can be found).[14] Irrespective of whether the comparator is actual or hypothetical, the comparator's circumstances must be the same as, or not materially different from, those of the claimant.[15] Where the comparator's circumstances are materially different, the claim will fail, as can be seen in the following case.

The requirement for a male comparator under the EPA 1970 is discussed at p 807

Bullock v Alice Ottley School [1993] ICR 138 (CA)

FACTS: The defendant, a school for girls, operated a policy whereby teaching and domestic staff were forced to retire at the age of 60, whereas gardeners and maintenance staff retired at the age of 65. Because the majority of domestic staff were female, one of them brought an action alleging that being forced to retire earlier than gardeners and maintenance staff (who were predominantly male) constituted direct discrimination. The defendant argued that the disparity in retirement age was not due to sex, but to the fact that gardeners and maintenance staff were more difficult to recruit. The Employment Appeal Tribunal (EAT) held that the policy was discriminatory. The defendant appealed.

HELD: The Court of Appeal allowed the appeal. Because gardeners and maintenance staff were more difficult to recruit, the circumstances between the two comparators were materially different and did not provide a proper basis for comparison.

We noted above that harassment is a specific form of direct discrimination and the SDA 1975, s 4A(1), provides that a person subjects a woman to sexual harassment if:

- he engages in unwanted conduct relating to her sex, or the sex of another person, which has the purpose or effect of violating her dignity, or of creating an intimidating, hostile, degrading, humiliating, or offensive environment for her; or

- he engages in any form of unwanted verbal, non-verbal, or physical conduct of a sexual nature, which has the purpose or effect of violating her dignity, or of creating an intimidating, hostile, degrading, humiliating, or offensive environment for her; or

- on the ground of her rejection of, or submission to, unwanted conduct of a kind above, he treats her less favourably than he would treat her had she not rejected, or submitted to, the conduct.

Indirect sex discrimination

The SDA 1975, s 1(1)(b), contains a definition of indirect discrimination. But this definition is narrower and more difficult to establish than was probably intended,

---

14. If an actual comparator does not exist or cannot be located, the tribunal *must* compare the claimant's treatment to that of a hypothetical comparator: *Balamoody v United Kingdom Central Council for Nursing, Midwifery and Health Visiting* [2001] EWCA Civ 2097, [2002] IRLR 288.

15. SDA 1975, s 5(3).

and certain phrases used are somewhat vague. This definition is now limited to non-employment cases. In relation to employment-related cases, a new definition contained in s 1(2)(b) was inserted into s 1 in 2001. Because this is the requirement to which employers and businesses will be subject, it is this new definition that will be discussed.

Section 1(2)(b) provides that indirect sex discrimination occurs where an employer applies to a woman a provision, criterion, or practice that would apply equally to a man, but:

(i)   which puts or would put women at a particular disadvantage when compared with men;
(ii) which puts her at that disadvantage; and
(iii) which the employer cannot show to be a proportionate means of achieving a legitimate aim.

Whilst the new definition is doubtless an improvement, it does result in a problem. The definition contained in s 1(1)(b) was in force for over twenty-five years and a substantial body of authoritative case law had grown around it. The definition contained in s 1(2)(b), whilst not radically different, is different enough to cast doubt upon the usefulness of cases decided under the old definition. But what is known is that the new definition was inserted to comply with a series of reforms introduced by the Burden of Proof Directive.[16] Article 6 of this Directive states that implementation of the Directive shall not result in a reduction in the protection of workers in relation to sex discrimination. Accordingly, any case that fell within the scope of the previous definition must also fall within the scope of the new definition.[17] This will ensure that previous case law will remain relevant until a new body of authority has been developed.

The first element that the claimant will need to establish is that the alleged discrimination is the result of a 'provision, condition or practice' (PCP). This is wider than the previous definition, which used the phrase 'condition or requirement'. 'Condition or requirement' implies an absolute practice that must be adhered to, meaning that a discretionary practice or a set of criteria would not be covered by the Act,[18] whereas it would come under the heading of a PCP. A PCP that applies only to one employee will suffice.[19] Once the claimant has established the existence of a PCP, she will also need to establish that it applies to both sexes.

The claimant will then need to establish that the PCP puts women 'at a particular disadvantage when compared to men'. The question arising is how the courts can calculate whether a particular PCP adversely affects women more than it does men. The claimant will be required to identify a 'pool for comparison' and then the tribunal can determine whether, amongst that pool, the PCP disadvantages women more than men. This pool does not consist of all persons to whom the PCP is applied, but rather of those persons who can comply with the PCP. Once the pool is determined, the tribunal must determine whether or not the PCP proportionally affects women more than it does men.[20]

---

16. Council Directive No 97/80/EC.
17. *British Airways plc v Starmer* [2005] IRLR 683 (EAT) [4] (Burton J).
18. *Perera v Civil Service Commission (No 2)* [1983] ICR 428 (CA).
19. *British Airways plc v Starmer* [2005] IRLR 683 (EAT).
20. *Jones v University of Manchester* [1993] IRLR 218 (CA).

The following example demonstrates this method in practice.

 The 'pool for comparison'

BritSteel plc is a multinational construction company based in London. It has 5,000 employees, based in factories situated throughout the UK, 2,000 (40 per cent) of whom are women. BritSteel introduces a new policy (the PCP) whereby employees who have an undergraduate degree are entitled to a 3 per cent bonus at the end of the year. Of the 5,000 employees, only 2,000 qualify for this bonus. These 2,000 employees will therefore form the 'pool for comparison'. Of these 2,000 employees, only 800 are women—but because 800 is 40 per cent of 2,000, proportionally, the PCP does not affect women more than it does men and so is not indirectly discriminatory. If, of the 2,000 employees, only 400 were women, then this would represent only 20 per cent and therefore proportionally fewer women would gain the benefit of the PCP, thereby rendering it indirectly discriminatory.

The claimant must also demonstrate that the PCP actually caused her a disadvantage. The courts have adopted a wide approach in relation to this requirement and have held that the disadvantage need not be physical or financial. Examples of qualifying disadvantages would include a PCP that prevented a woman from applying for a job or gaining a promotion, or being able to obtain training.

The following case provides an example of a PCP that clearly caused a disadvantage.

 London Underground v Edwards (No 2) [1999] ICR 494 (CA)

FACTS: The claimant was a single mother, who had been employed by the defendant for almost ten years as a train driver on the London Underground. She worked on a shift system, which allowed her to organize her working hours to fit in with her parental responsibilities. The defendant introduced a new shift system (the PCP), which, due to her commitments to her child, would have resulted in her working excessively long hours during the day. She alleged that this amounted to indirect discrimination, and an employment tribunal and the EAT agreed. The defendant appealed.

HELD: The appeal was dismissed. The Court of Appeal held that, because there were only twenty-one female train drivers, compared to 2,023 male train drivers, the PCP adversely affected women more than it did men and that it clearly caused the claimant a substantial disadvantage.

Once the claimant has established the above, she will have established that indirect discrimination has occurred. But the employer may be able to avoid liability if it can establish that the PCP was introduced to meet a legitimate aim and that it was proportional to meeting this aim. Many of the cases in this area were decided under s 1(1)(b), which contained a similar defence—namely, where the employer had a justification irrespective of sex—an example of which can be seen in the following case.

> ### 🔑 Greater Glasgow Health Board v Carey [1987] IRLR 484 (EAT)
>
> **FACTS:** The defendant employed the claimant as a full-time health visitor. After maternity leave, she requested that she be allowed to work between two-and-a-half and three days a week. The defendant agreed that she could work part-time, but that she would have to work for part of five days a week. The claimant alleged that this constituted indirect discrimination. An employment tribunal held that it was not necessary for the claimant to be in work for every day of the working week and so the policy was not justified. The defendant appealed.
>
> **HELD:** The EAT allowed the appeal. Whilst the policy did affect women more than it would affect men, the policy was justified in that health visitors could only provide an efficient service if they were available to visit patients for all five days of the working week.

Discrimination by victimization

The SDA 1975, s 4(1), states that an employer discriminates against an employee (the person victimized) if it treats that employee less favourably than it treats, or would treat, other employees in those circumstances, because she has brought, or intends to bring, a case, or give evidence in a case, under the SDA 1975 or the EPA 1970, or has made (or intends to make) allegations in good faith[21] that one of these Acts has been breached. These acts (initiating a case, giving evidence, or making an allegation) are known as 'protected acts' and the claimant will not need to demonstrate that she received less favourable treatment because of her sex, but that she received less favourable treatment because she carried out a protected act.[22] Referring back to the example headed 'Victimization' (see p 851), Adam was not victimized because he was a man, but because he engaged in a protected act—namely, giving evidence against his employer. The question that arises is whether the employee would have been treated differently but for the commission of the protected act; if the answer is 'yes', victimization has occurred. To determine the difference in treatment, a comparator should be used and the appropriate comparator is another employee who has not engaged in the protected act in question.[23]

Sex discrimination in the employment field

In addition to the above general forms of sex discrimination, the SDA 1975, s 6, also contains more specific provisions relating to sex discrimination in the 'employment field'. Section 6(1) focuses on sex discrimination in relation to female applicants and provides that it is unlawful for a person, in relation to employment by him at an establishment in the UK, to discriminate against a woman:

- in the arrangements that he makes for the purpose of determining who should be offered that employment;

---

21. SDA 1975, s 4(2).
22. It therefore follows that discrimination and victimization are technically completely different causes of action: *Air Canada v Basra* [2000] IRLR 683 (EAT).
23. *Chief Constable of West Yorkshire v Khan* [2001] UKHL 48, [2001] ICR 1065.

- in the terms on which he offers her that employment; or
- by refusing or deliberately omitting to offer her that employment.

Section 6(2) goes on to state that it is unlawful for a person, in the case of a woman employed by him at an establishment in the UK, to discriminate against her:

- in the way in which he affords her access to opportunities for promotion, transfer or training, or to any other benefits, facilities, or services, or by refusing or deliberately omitting to afford her access to them; or
- by dismissing her, or subjecting her to any other detriment.

Section 6(2A) provides that it is unlawful for an employer, in relation to employment by him at an establishment in the UK, to subject to harassment a woman who he employs, or a woman who has applied to him for employment.

Vicarious liability

The SDA 1975, s 41(1), provides that an employer is vicariously liable for the discriminatory acts of its employees in the course of their employment, irrespective of whether such acts were carried out with the employer's knowledge or approval. When we discussed vicarious liability in Chapter 14, we noted that a crucial requirement for holding the employer vicariously liable was that the employee carried out the act in question 'in the course of his employment'. Applying this common law requirement to vicarious liability under the SDA 1975 proved problematic, especially in cases of sexual harassment. Employers do not employ persons to engage in discriminatory behaviour or victimization, so it can be argued that such activities are never committed 'in the course of employment'. To remedy this problem, the courts have adopted a purposive approach, whereby the words 'in the course of his employment' are to be given their ordinary, everyday meaning.[24] Accordingly, discriminatory acts or victimization that takes place whilst at work will result in vicarious liability being imposed. But the employer will have a defence if it can establish that it took such steps as were reasonably practicable to prevent the employee from committing the act in question.[25]

➜ vicarious liability: liability imposed on one person for the acts of another

Where vicarious liability is established, the employee responsible for the discriminatory act may be personally liable for aiding and abetting the employer's vicarious liability.[26] The utility of this can be seen in the following case.

Gilbank v Miles [2006] EWCA Civ 543

FACTS: Both the claimant and defendant were employed by the same company. Upon becoming pregnant, the claimant was subjected to a campaign of bullying and harassment by the defendant. The claimant brought a successful action for sex discrimination and was awarded £25,000 damages. Because the company had become insolvent, the defendant was personally liable to pay this sum. The defendant appealed.

---

24. *Jones v Tower Boots Co Ltd* [1997] ICR 254 (CA).
25. SDA 1975, s 41(3).
26. Ibid, s 42(1). Rather bizarrely, this means that the employee is being held liable for aiding his own act.

> **HELD:** The Court of Appeal dismissed the appeal. The defendant had 'fostered and encouraged a discriminatory culture'[27] targeted at the claimant and so it was correct that she should be jointly and severally liable to pay damages.

When is sex discrimination permitted?

The SDA 1975 (along with virtually all forms of discrimination legislation) permits sex discrimination where it is authorized by statute[28] and where it is in the interests of national security.[29] In addition to these standard exceptions, sex discrimination is permitted in the following situations.

'Genuine occupational qualification'

The SDA 1975, s 7(2), provides an exhaustive list of eight instances in which sex discrimination is permissible on the ground of sex being a 'genuine occupational qualification', including:

- where the essential nature of the job calls for a man for reasons of physiology (excluding physical strength or stamina), or, in dramatic performances or other entertainment, for reasons of authenticity (thus, a casting director would be free to demand that a male to be taken on to play King Lear);
- where the job must be performed by a man to preserve decency or privacy, such as where the job involves physical contact with males and such males would object to a female, or where the job involves seeing men in a state of undress;
- where the nature or location of the job makes it impracticable for the jobholder to live anywhere other than in premises provided by the employer, and such premises are normally lived in by men and are not equipped with suitable facilities for women, and it would not be reasonable to provide other premises for women;
- where the job is located in a single-sex establishment, such as a hospital or prison;
- where the job needs to be held by a man because it is likely to involve the performance of duties outside the UK in a country the laws or customs of which are such that the duties could not, or could not effectively, be performed by a woman.

These exceptions are not absolute. For example, where an employer already has a sufficient number of male employees who could carry out the task in question without undue disruption, then the exceptions contained in s 7(2) do not apply[30] and refusal to employ a woman would amount to discrimination. Section 7A provides that the above exceptions also apply in cases in which an employee has undergone gender reassignment.

Positive discrimination

In recent years, certain occupations that have historically been dominated by a single sex have attempted to redress this gender imbalance by encouraging the opposite sex to apply via positive discrimination policies. So far, we have examined situations

---

27. *Gilbank v Miles* [2006] EWCA Civ 543, [2006] ICR 1297, [50] (Sedley LJ).
28. SDA 1975, s 51A. 29. Ibid, s 52.
30. Ibid, s 7(4).

in which a person is treated *less* favourably due to sex, but positive discrimination treats persons *more* favourably if they are of a certain sex. The question is to what extent positive discrimination is unlawful.

The simple answer is that positive discrimination in favour of a woman is unlawful if it causes a man to be treated less favourably (and vice versa). But there are two instances in which positive discrimination is permissible, as follows.

1. Facilities and training can be provided to one sex only where, at any time within the last twelve months immediately preceding the act in question, there were no persons of that sex performing the work in question or the number of persons performing the work in question was comparatively small.[31]

2. Facilities and training can be provided to one sex only where such persons have been absent from full-time work because they were discharging domestic or family responsibilities (for example, persons returning from maternity leave).[32]

It should be noted that, as regards positive discrimination, the UK's approach differs in some respects from that of the EU. Several pieces of EU legislation[33] would appear to permit preferential treatment for women. Whilst such legislation may have laudable motives, the English courts have demonstrated that such a motive will not provide an employer with a defence to an allegation of discrimination. The case of *James v Eastleigh Borough Council*[34] (discussed at p 854) provides a perfect example of the English courts' refusal to acknowledge motive.

Enforcement

Any complainant who feels that she have been the victim of sex discrimination may make a complaint to an employment tribunal,[35] provided that the complaint is made within three months beginning on the date on which the act complained of was committed.[36] There are, however, a number of exceptions and modifications to this rule:

- a court or tribunal may consider a case outside this period if it considers it just and equitable to do so,[37] but this should only happen in exceptional circumstances;[38]
- where the discrimination is continuing, the three-month period begins to run once the discrimination ceases;
- where the discrimination is not continuing, but amounts to a series of repeated discriminatory acts, the three-month period begins to run from the occurrence of the last act;[39]

---

31. Ibid, s 47(1).
32. Ibid, s 47(3).
33. For example, EC Treaty, Art 141(4), and the Equal Treatment Directive, Council Directive No 76/207/EEC, Art 2(4).
34. [1990] 2 AC 751 (HL).
35. SDA 1975, s 63.
36. Ibid, s 76(1).
37. Ibid, s 76(5).
38. *Robertson v Bexley Community Centre* [2003] EWCA Civ 576, [2003] IRLR 434.
39. *Rovenska v General Medical Council* [1998] ICR 85 (CA).

- where an employee is aware of an act, but is not aware that it is discriminatory until a later date, the three-month period begins from this later date.[40]

In addition to a complaint before an employment tribunal, the Equality and Human Rights Commission may, if it is of the opinion that a person is about to commit an unlawful act, apply to a county court for an injunction restraining that act.[41] To enable it to perform this function, the Commission may also carry out investigations into the activities of employers and, where it believes that an unlawful act has been committed, it can issue an 'unlawful act notice'.[42] This notice will require the employer to prepare an action plan that indicates how the employer will avoid repetition or continuation of the unlawful act.[43] The Commission can then apply to a county court for an order requiring the employer to take the steps set out in the action plan.[44] These powers operate in relation to all forms of discrimination.

Remedies

If a tribunal is of the opinion that the claimant's case is founded, then it has access to three remedies.

Declaration of rights

The first remedy is an order declaring what the rights of the parties are in relation to the proven act of discrimination.[45] This remedy in itself is of little practical use, which is why it is almost combined with one (or both) of the other two remedies.

Compensation

 Damages in tort are discussed at p 537

The second remedy is the most common remedy—namely, an award of compensation.[46] Claims under the SDA 1975 are treated as statutory torts, meaning that damages are assessed on a tortious basis. Therefore, the courts will aim to put the claimant in the position in which she would have been had the discrimination not occurred. There is no limit to an award of compensation that can be made under the SDA 1975 and, in a number of cases, tribunals have made a number of substantial awards. A factor in the size of these awards is the fact that the SDA 1975 expressly permits tribunals to award damages for injured feelings[47] and that aggravated damages may also be awarded, although the EAT has stated that exemplary damages cannot be awarded.[48]

Table 25.2 demonstrates the highest single compensatory award made in each year since 2000 and the average award for each year.

Recommendation for corrective action

The final remedy is a recommendation that the defendant take, within a specified period, action aimed at reducing or eradicating the discrimination complained of.[49] A recommendation is just that: it is not binding and the tribunal cannot order the

---

40. *Clarke v Hampshire Electro-Plating Co* [1992] ICR 312 (EAT).
42. Ibid, s 21(1).
44. Ibid, s 22(6).
46. Ibid, s 65(1)(b).
48. *Deane v Ealing London Borough Council* [1993] ICR 329 (EAT).

41. Equality Act 2006, s 24(1)(a).
43. Ibid, s 21(4).
45. SDA 1975, s 65(1)(a).
47. Ibid, s 66(4).
49. SDA 1975, s 65(1)(c).

TABLE 25.2 Maximum and average awards for sex discrimination

	2006–07	2005–06	2004–05	2003–04	2002–03	2001–02	2000–01
Maximum award (£)	64,862	217,961	179,026	504,433	91,496	1,414,620	139,896
Average award (£)	10,052	10,807	14,158	12,971	8,787	19,279	15,484

Source: Statistics collated from the Annual Reports of the Employment Tribunal Service and the Tribunal Service, available online at <http://www.employmenttribunals.gov.uk/Publications/publications.htm>

employer to take remedial action.[50] If, without reasonable justification, the employer fails to implement the recommendation, the tribunal may increase the level of compensation if it considers it just and equitable to do so.[51]

 Key points summary

- The Sex Discrimination Act 1975 applies to sex discrimination that occurs outside the contract of employment. Sex discrimination within the contract of employment is regulated by the Equal Pay Act 1970.

- The SDA 1975 prohibits discrimination on the grounds of sex, marriage, or gender reassignment. The Act recognizes and prohibits direct and indirect discrimination, victimization, and harassment.

- An employer can be held vicariously liable for the discriminatory acts of his employees. Such employees also face personal liability for aiding the employer in committing discriminatory acts.

- Sex discrimination is permitted where a person's sex is a genuine occupational qualification. Positive discrimination is permitted in limited circumstances.

- A victim of sex discrimination may take her claim to an employment tribunal, and the tribunal may declare the rights of the parties, provide the victim with compensation, and/or recommend what steps the employer should take in order to avoid committing sex discrimination in the future.

Race discrimination

Legislation prohibiting racial discrimination was first introduced in 1965, with the passing of the Race Relations Act 1965. But this Act did not prohibit discrimination in the workplace and did not recognize indirect discrimination. Both of these flaws are remedied by the current Act—namely, the Race Relations Act 1976 (RRA 1976). The number of claims brought under this Act each year since 2000 is shown in Table 25.3.

---

50. *Ministry of Defence v Jeremiah* [1980] QB 87 (CA).   51. SDA 1975, s 65(3).

TABLE 25.3 Number of race discrimination claims

	2006–07	2005–06	2004–05	2003–04	2002–03	2001–02	2000–01
No of claims	3,780	4,103	3,317	3,492	3,638	3,889	4,238

Source: Statistics collated from the Annual Reports of the Employment Tribunal Service and the Tribunal Service, available online at <http://www.employmenttribunals.gov.uk/Publications/publications.htm>

Many of the provisions of the RRA 1976 are identical to the applicable provisions contained in the SDA 1975. Accordingly, we shall focus here on the major differences between race and sex discrimination.

Forms of race discrimination

Like the SDA 1975, the RRA 1976 recognizes and provides for all three forms of discrimination. In fact, the definitions of discrimination under the RRA 1976 are identical to those under the SDA 1975, except that the prohibition is on the ground of race as opposed to sex. Accordingly, these definitions will not be examined in depth and readers unfamiliar with these definitions should refer to the discussion of the forms of sex discrimination.

The various forms of sex discrimination are discussed at p 853

Direct racial discrimination

A person directly discriminates against another if, on racial grounds, he treats that other less favourably than he treats, or would treat, other persons.[52] This requires the claimant to establish two things:

- that the discrimination was 'on racial grounds'; and
- that he was less favourably treated.

Discrimination 'on racial grounds' means discrimination on the grounds of 'colour, race, nationality or ethnic or national origins'.[53] This definition is largely straightforward, but some clarification has been required from the courts and tribunals, and one notable amendment has been made. In terms of clarification, there has been some confusion regarding the relationship between race and religion. For example, are Jews protected under the RRA 1976? They have no country of origin, but many would include them within the above definition, due to their 'ethnic origins'. Clarity was provided in the following case, which, although concerning an allegation of indirect discrimination, provides guidance that applies to all forms of racial discrimination.

O⇩ *Mandla v Dowell Lee* [1983] 2 AC 548 (HL)

FACTS: The claimants were a Sikh father and son, who, in accordance with their religion, wore turbans over uncut hair. A school owned by the defendant refused to admit the son because he would not cut his hair and cease to wear a turban. The claimants alleged

---

52. RRA 1976, s 1(1)(a).   53. Ibid, s 3(1).

that this amounted to race discrimination. At first instance and in the Court of Appeal, the action was dismissed, because the discrimination was not on 'racial grounds'. The claimants appealed.

HELD: The House of Lords allowed the appeal. The RRA 1976 prohibited discrimination due to a person's 'ethnic origins' and Sikhs could be regarded as a group who were defined by their ethnic origins. To determine whether a group would qualify, two requirements were essential:

* a long-shared history; and

* a cultural tradition of its own.

Other relevant factors would include whether the group had a common geographical origin, common language (but not necessarily peculiar to the group), common literature peculiar to the group, or a common religion different from that of neighbouring groups or from the general community surrounding it. Being a minority, or an oppressed or dominant group, within a larger community would also be a relevant factor.

COMMENT: Since *Mandla*, it has been held that both Jews[54] and gypsies[55] are covered by the RRA 1976. But Rastafarians are not protected, because they lack a 'long-shared history'.[56]

⭐ See GT Pagone, 'The Lawyer's Hunt for Snarks, Religion and Races' (1984) 43 CLJ 218

The distinction between 'nationality' and 'national origin' is also worth noting. Although most persons' nationality and national origin will be the same, some people are born in one country, but subsequently gain national citizenship in another country. Prior to 1976, nationality was not part of the definition, meaning that discrimination on the ground of one's acquired nationality was not covered by the Act. This lacuna was filled in the RRA 1976, by including nationality within the definition of 'racial grounds'.

The claimant will also need to establish that he was 'less favourably treated' due to his race. This will be determined in exactly the same way as it was under the SDA 1975. But there is one major difference between direct discrimination under the RRA 1976 and the SDA 1975: under the RRA 1976, direct discrimination is prohibited if it is 'on racial grounds'; under the SDA 1975, it is prohibited if it is 'on the ground of her sex'. This means that, unlike the SDA 1975, the RRA 1976 can apply where a person is treated less favourably due to *another person's* race, as the following case demonstrates.

Showboat Entertainment Centre Ltd v Owens [1984] 1 WLR 384 (EAT)

FACTS: The claimant was a white man, who was employed as the manager of an entertainment centre owned by the defendant. The defendant instructed the claimant to exclude all black customers from the centre. The claimant refused and was dismissed.

---

54. *Seide v Gilette Industries* [1980] IRLR 427 (EAT).
55. *Commission for Racial Equality v Dutton* [1989] QB 783 (CA).
56. *Dawkins v Department of the Environment* [1993] IRLR 284 (CA).

> **HELD:** The EAT held that the term 'on racial grounds' could include discrimination due to the race of the claimant, or where the claimant was treated less favourably due to the race of a third party. Accordingly, the claimant had been directly discriminated against 'on racial grounds'.

The definition of harassment under the RRA 1976 is exactly the same as the definition contained in the SDA 1975, save that the harassment must be on the grounds of race, ethnic origin, or national origin.[57] It is notable that this definition would not include harassment due to skin colour or nationality. This is because the definition of harassment was added to the RRA 1976 in order to comply with the Race Directive,[58] which only applies to discrimination based on race, ethnic origin, or national origin. It is unclear whether the courts will extend the definition to include discrimination based on skin colour and nationality, but a failure to do so would constitute an unjustifiable and major omission.

Indirect racial discrimination

It will be remembered that the SDA 1975 contains two definitions of indirect discrimination:

- an 'old' definition that applies to non-employment cases; and
- a 'new' definition that applies to employment and related cases.

The RRA 1976 contains the identical definitions, but their scope is different:

- the 'old' definition can be found in the RRA 1976, s 1(1)(b), and can apply to any form of race discrimination;
- the 'new' definition can be found in the RRA 1976, s 1(1A), and applies to discrimination due to race, ethnic origin, or national origin, but does not apply to discrimination based on colour or nationality (in such cases, the employee must base his claim under s 1(1)(b)).

The new definition was examined in detail when we discussed indirect sex discrimination and so will not be discussed again. Here, we will focus on the old definition (which will also apply to non-employment sex discrimination cases).

The old definition defines 'indirect racial discrimination' as the application of a requirement or condition that applies equally to all racial groups, but which:

- is such that the proportion of persons of the same racial group as that claimant who can comply with it is considerably smaller than the proportion of persons not of that racial group who can comply with it;
- the employer cannot show to be justifiable irrespective of the colour, race, nationality, or ethnic or national origins of the person to whom it is applied; and
- is to the detriment of the claimant because he cannot comply with it.

The requirements are broadly similar to those under the new definition, but several differences should be noted, as follows.

- Whereas the new definition applies to 'provisions, criteria and practices', the old definition applies only to 'requirements and conditions'. This is narrower than the

---

57. RRA 1976, s 3A(1). 58. Council Directive No 2000/43/EC.

new definition and will only apply to policies that *must* be complied with. A discretionary policy will not constitute a requirement or a condition.

- Whilst both the old and new definitions will require the claimant to provide a 'pool for comparison', the old definition requires the claimant to show that the proportion of persons in a racial group who cannot comply is 'considerably smaller' than the proportion of persons not of that racial group. This appears to be more difficult to establish and would require the claimant to provide some form of statistical evidence.

- The new definition permits race discrimination where it is a genuine occupational qualification. The old definition permits race discrimination where it is justified for reasons other than colour, race, nationality, etc. In practice, it would appear that these two tests provide little difference.

A 'racial group' is defined as 'a group of persons defined by reference to colour, race, nationality or ethnic or national origins'.[59] In determining which groups qualify as a 'racial group', the principles established in *Mandla v Dowell Lee* (discussed above) will be of crucial importance, especially where the group alleges inclusion due to its 'ethnic origins'.

Discrimination by victimization

The definition of victimization under the RRA 1976 is identical to that under the SDA 1975, save that the victim must have brought proceedings under, given evidence in a case involving, or alleged a breach of, the RRA 1976.[60]

Race discrimination in the employment field

The RRA 1976, like the SDA 1975, contains specific provisions relating to discrimination in the 'employment field'. Section 4(1) focuses on race discrimination in relation to applicants and provides that it is unlawful for a person, in relation to employment by him at an establishment in the UK, to discriminate against a person:

- in the arrangements that he makes for the purpose of determining who should be offered that employment;
- in the terms on which he offers him that employment; or
- by refusing or deliberately omitting to offer him that employment.

Section 4(2) goes on to state that it is unlawful for a person, in the case of a person employed by him at an establishment in the UK, to discriminate against him:

- in the terms of employment that he affords him;
- in the way that he affords him access to opportunities for promotion, transfer, or training, or to any other benefits, facilities, or services, or by refusing or deliberately omitting to afford him access to them; or
- by dismissing him, or subjecting him to any other detriment.

Section 4(2A) provides that it is unlawful for an employer, in relation to employment by it at an establishment in the UK, to subject to harassment a person who it employs, or a person who has applied to it for employment.

---

59. RRA 1976, s 3(1).   60. Ibid, s 2(1).

Vicarious liability

As under the SDA 1975, an employer is vicariously liable for the discriminatory acts of its employees, irrespective of whether such acts were carried out with the employer's knowledge or approval.[61] But it will be a defence for the employer to show that it took such steps as were reasonably practicable to prevent the employee from engaging in the discriminatory act.[62] Where vicarious liability is established, the employee responsible for the discriminatory act may be personally liable for aiding and abetting the employer's vicarious liability.[63]

When is race discrimination permitted?

In addition to the standard exceptions relating to statutory authority[64] and national security,[65] the RRA 1976 provides a number of other instances in which race discrimination is permitted.

Genuine occupational qualification and requirement

The 'genuine occupational qualification' exception found in the SDA 1975 is also in the RRA 1976, s 5(2). But whereas the SDA 1975 has eight such exceptions, the RRA 1976 has only four.

Examples of exceptions include:

- where the job involves participation in a dramatic performance or other entertainment in a capacity for which a person of that racial group is required for reasons of authenticity (a classic example is that a casting director could insist on employing a black man to play Othello);
- where the job involves working in a place where food or drink is (for payment or not) provided to and consumed by members of the public, or a section of the public, in a particular setting for which, in that job, a person of that racial group is required for reasons of authenticity (for example, the owner of an Indian restaurant could insist on employing an Indian chef);
- where the holder of the job provides persons of that racial group with personal services promoting their welfare, and those services can most effectively be provided by a person of that racial group (for example, where a vacancy for a health visitor arises in an area that has population dominated by one ethnic group, the employer can insist on the successful applicant being from that ethnic group).

In order to comply with the Race Directive, a new s 4A was inserted into the RRA 1976, which permits racial discrimination where it is a 'genuine occupational *requirement*'. Because this derives from the Race Directive, it does not expressly apply to cases involving discrimination due to skin colour or nationality, although it is hoped that the courts will extend s 4A to cover such cases. Section 4A(2) provides that racial discrimination is permitted where:

- being of a particular race or of particular ethnic or national origins is a genuine and determining occupational requirement;
- it is proportionate to apply that requirement in the particular case; and

---

61. Ibid, s 32(1).   62. Ibid, s 32(3).
63. Ibid, s 33(1).   64. Ibid, s 41.
65. Ibid, s 42.

- either:
  - (i) the person to whom that requirement is applied does not meet it; or
  - (ii) the employer is not satisfied—and, in all of the circumstances, it is reasonable for him not to be satisfied—that the person meets the requirement.

Whether s 4A is wider or narrower in application than s 5 is unknown, because there have been no reported cases to date concerning s 4A.

Positive discrimination

As under the SDA 1975, positive discrimination is generally prohibited under the RRA 1976. But the exception in relation to training that is contained in the SDA 1975, s 45, can also be found in the RRA 1976, s 38.

Enforcement and remedies

The enforcement of the RRA 1976 is carried out in exactly the same way as the enforcement of cases under the SDA 1975—namely, by making a complaint to an employment tribunal.[66] The Equality and Human Rights Commission, in addition to subsuming the Equal Opportunities Commission, also took over the functions of the Commission for Racial Equality. Therefore the investigatory and enforcement powers of the Commission discussed in relation to cases under the SDA 1975 also apply to cases under the RRA 1976.

The three remedies available under the SDA 1975—namely, declaration, compensation, and recommendation—are also available under the RRA 1976.[67] One principal difference is that, under the RRA 1976, compensation cannot be awarded for unintentional indirect discrimination.[68] Such a limitation did exist under the SDA 1975, but was removed in 1996. The (then) Commission for Racial Equality, somewhat unsurprisingly, recommended that this limitation be abolished in relation to racial discrimination too.

As with the SDA 1975, there have been a number of notable compensatory awards. Table 25.4 demonstrates the highest single compensatory award made in each year since 2000 and the average award for each year.

◀◆▶ Key points summary

- The Race Relations Act 1976 prohibits discrimination on the grounds of race, colour, nationality, or ethnic or national group.

- The RRA 1976 recognizes and provides for direct and indirect discrimination, victimization, and harassment.

- As under the SDA 1975, discrimination is permitted where race is a genuine occupational qualification and relation to certain types of positive discrimination. Unlike the SDA 1975, the RRA 1976 also permits discrimination where race is a genuine occupational requirement.

- In many respects, the RRA 1976 is similar to the SDA 1975. Enforcement and remedies are the same, except that compensation cannot be awarded for unintentional indirect discrimination.

---

66. Ibid, s 54(1).   67. Ibid, s 56(1).
68. Ibid, s 57(3).

TABLE 25.4 Maximum and average compensatory awards for race discrimination

	2006–07	2005–06	2004–05	2003–04	2002–03	2001–02	2000–01
Maximum award (£)	123,898	984,465	170,953	635,150	814,877	66,086	201,260
Average award (£)	14,049	30,361	19,114	26,660	27,041	10,007	15,484

Source: Statistics collated from the Annual Reports of the Employment Tribunal Service and the Tribunal Service, available online at <http://www.employmenttribunals.gov.uk/Publications/publications.htm>

Disability discrimination

Despite the fact that there are around 10 million people in the UK classified as disabled,[69] legislation prohibiting disability discrimination was only enacted in 1995. Table 25.5 demonstrates the trend in the number of claims since 2000.

TABLE 25.5 Number of disability discrimination claims

	2006–07	2005–06	2004–05	2003–04	2002–03	2001–02	2000–01
No of claims	5,533	4,585	4,942	5,655	5,310	5,273	4,630

Source: Statistics collated from the Annual Reports of the Employment Tribunal Service and the Tribunal Service, available online at <http://www.employmenttribunals.gov.uk/Publications/publications.htm>

What constitutes a 'disability?'

Only disabled persons can claim under the Disability Discrimination Act 1995 (DDA 1995). The issue of what constitutes a 'disability' is therefore of central importance to the Act's scope and effectiveness. Section 1(1) of the Act provides that a person has a disability if he has 'a physical or mental impairment which has a substantial and long-term adverse effect on his ability to carry out normal day-to-day activities'.

In *Goodwin v Patent Office*,[70] the EAT stated that this definition established four conditions that would need to be satisfied.

1. Does the claimant have an impairment that is physical or mental?
2. Is this impairment adverse and does it affect the claimant's ability to carry out day-to-day activities?
3. Is the adverse effect substantial?
4. Is the adverse effect long-term?

'Physical or mental impairment'

The onus is on the claimant to establish that he has a 'physical or mental impairment'.[71] Many of the terms within the DDA 1995 are defined in the Act itself,

---

69. Disability Rights Commission, *Understanding the Disability Discrimination Act* (DRC, London, 2007).
70. [1999] ICR 302 (EAT).
71. *McNicol v Balfour Beatty Rail Maintenance Ltd* [2002] EWCA Civ 1074, [2002] IRLR 711.

but 'physical or mental impairment' is not defined, doubtless to allow the courts and tribunals a measure of flexibility given the number of existing and newly discovered medical conditions. The Court of Appeal has stated that the word 'impairment' should bear its 'ordinary and natural meaning',[72] and in many cases, there will be no dispute as to whether a claimant has an impairment or not. Whether the cause of the impairment is physical or mental is irrelevant; what matters is how the impairment affects the claimant. This approach can be useful in cases in which an impairment exists, but there is no discernable cause.[73]

Prior to 2005, it was a requirement that any mental impairment be 'clinically well recognized' in order to qualify, but this requirement no longer exists. The scope of mental impairment is, however, still watched closely. The EAT has stated that whether the claimant's mental condition constitutes mental impairment 'is very much a matter for qualified and informed medical opinion'.[74] It also stated that the claimant should obtain a written diagnosis from a suitably qualified medical practitioner of an illness specified in the World Health Organization's International Classification of Diseases, or some other proof that a body of respectable medical opinion recognizes the impairment.[75]

Examples of mental conditions deemed to qualify include:

- Asperger's syndrome;[76]
- depression (provided that it is not short-term);[77]
- dyslexia;[78]
- myalgic encephalomyelitis, or ME (also known as 'chronic fatigue syndrome');[79]
- paranoid schizophrenia;[80]
- epilepsy.[81]

The Disability Discrimination (Meaning of Disability) Regulations 1996,[82] regs 3 and 4, provide that certain mental impairments are not be classified as disabilities—namely, addictions to alcohol or other substances, pyromania (a tendency to start fires), kleptomania (the tendency to steal), the tendency to commit physical or sexual abuse, exhibitionism, voyeurism, and seasonal allergic rhinitis (that is, hay fever). But impairments caused by these conditions may qualify (for example, depression caused by alcoholism).[83]

---

72. Ibid, [17] (Mummery LJ).
73. See, e.g., *College of Ripon and York St John v Hobbs* [2002] IRLR 185 (EAT).
74. *Morgan v Staffordshire University* [2002] ICR 475 (EAT) 485 (Lindsay J).
75. Ibid, 479.
76. *Hewett v Motorola Ltd* [2004] IRLR 545 (EAT).
77. *Kapadia v Lambeth London Borough Council* [2000] IRLR 699 (CA).
78. *Whitbread Hotel Ltd v Bayley* [2006] WL 1078905 (EAT).
79. *O'Neill v Symm & Co Ltd* [1998] IRLR 233 (EAT).
80. *Goodwin v Patent Office* [1999] ICR 302 (EAT).
81. Department for Work and Pensions, *Disability Discrimination Act: Guidance on Matters to be Taken Into Account in Determining Questions Relating to the Definition of Disability* (HMSO, London, 2006) [A6].
82. SI 1996/1455.
83. *Power v Panasonic UK Ltd* [2003] IRLR 151 (EAT).

Finally, it should be noted that certain physical and mental impairments are so severe that they will be regarded as disabilities, even if they fail to satisfy the other criteria established by the DDA 1995, s 1(1):

- cancer, HIV/AIDS, and multiple sclerosis;[84] and
- certified blindness or partial sight.[85]

'Ability to carry out normal day-to-day activities'

The impairment must adversely affect the claimant's ability to carry out normal day-to-day activities. The DDA 1995, Sch 1, para 4(1), provides that this requirement will be met if the impairment adversely affects an exhaustive list of factors, including:

- mobility, manual dexterity, or coordination;
- the ability to lift, carry, or otherwise move manual objects;
- speech, hearing, or eyesight;
- memory, or the ability to concentrate, learn, or understand; and
- perception of the risk of physical danger.

All that the impairment need do is adversely *affect* the claimant's ability to carry out day-to-day tasks. It follows that even if the claimant can still carry out these tasks, he may still qualify as disabled, provided that the impairment makes these tasks more difficult in some way.

The courts and tribunals take a broad view of what constitutes a normal day-to-day activity, defining it as an activity 'which most people do on a frequent or fairly regular basis',[86] or 'anything which is not abnormal or unusual'.[87] But activities undertaken whilst at work will not normally qualify 'because no particular form of work is "normal" for most people'.[88]

'Substantial'

The impairment must have a 'substantial' effect on the claimant's ability to carry out normal day-to-day activities. The Guidance to the DDA 1995 rather unhelpfully defines that a 'substantial' effect is greater than a 'minor' or 'trivial' effect.[89] But it then goes on to list a number of factors to be taken into account when determining whether or not the effect of the impairment is substantial, including:

- the time taken to carry out an activity;
- the way in which the activity is carried out;
- the cumulative effects of an impairment;
- the effect that the environment has on the impairment.

---

84. DDA 1995, Sch 1, para 6A(1).
85. Disability Discrimination (Blind and Partially Sighted Persons) Regulations 2003, SI 2003/712, reg 3.
86. *Vicary v British Telecommunications plc* [1999] IRLR 680 (EAT) 682 (Morison P).
87. *Ekpe v Commissioner of the Police of the Metropolis* [2001] ICR 1084 (EAT) 1092 (Langstaff QC).
88. Department for Work and Pensions, *Disability Discrimination Act: Guidance on Matters to be Taken Into Account in Determining Questions Relating to the Definition of Disability* (HMSO, London, 2006) [D7].
89. Ibid, [B1].

When determining whether or not an impairment has a substantial effect, the tribunal should focus on those things that the claimant cannot do, or those that he can do only with difficulty, rather than focusing on what he can do, as the following case demonstrates.

 Goodwin v Patent Office [1999] ICR 302 (EAT)

FACTS: The claimant was a paranoid schizophrenic, who was dismissed by the defendant following complaints about his behaviour from fellow workers. He believed that other people could read his mind and he suffered from auditory hallucinations whilst at work. But his condition had little effect on his domestic life, in which he was able to cook, clean, and go shopping without help. On this basis, an employment tribunal dismissed his claim of disability discrimination, because his impairment was not substantial. The claimant appealed.

HELD: The EAT allowed his appeal. The employment tribunal had focused on what the claimant could do, whereas the focus should have been on what he could *not* do, or what he could do only with difficulty. Given that his impairment had most effect at work, this was the focus of the case, and his impairment clearly had a substantial adverse effect on his ability to work.

⭐ See S Taylor and R Allen, 'The Meaning of "Disability" ' (1999) 149 NLJ 10

An impairment that consists of severe disfigurement is always regarded as having a substantial effect.[90]

'Long-term'

An impairment will have a long-term effect if it has lasted, or is likely to last, at least twelve months, or, in the case of a terminal condition, it if is likely to last for the rest of the person's life.[91] Where an impairment has ceased to have a substantial effect (for example, because it is intermittent), it will be regarded as continuing if it is likely to reoccur.[92]

Forms of disability discrimination

Discrimination under the DDA 1995 differs from discrimination under the SDA 1975 and RRA 1976 in the following ways.

- The DDA 1995 does not classify the various forms of discrimination in the same way as the SDA 1975 and the RRA 1975. Instead, it contains two forms of discrimination specific to disability discrimination:
  - disability-related discrimination; and
  - discrimination through a failure to make reasonable adjustments.
- Further, under the DDA 1995, 'direct discrimination' is not a form of discrimination in itself, but rather a sub-form of disability-related discrimination, and harassment is a separate form of discrimination.

---

90. DDA 1995, Sch 1, para 3(1).   91. Ibid, para 2(1).
92. Ibid, para 2(2).

- There is no concept of indirect discrimination under the DDA 1995, although disability-related discrimination is similar.
- Under the SDA 1975 and RRA 1976, all forms of discrimination can be justified if it is a genuine occupation qualification. Conversely, under the DDA 1995, only disability-related discrimination can be justified, provided that it does not constitute direct discrimination.

As noted above, the DDA 1995 does not classify the forms of discrimination in the same manner as the SDA 1975 and RRA 1976. Whereas those pieces of legislation provide for three types of discrimination, the DDA 1995 provides for four.

Disability-related discrimination[93]

Under the DDA 1995, s 3A(1), a person engages in disability-related discrimination against a disabled person for the purpose of the employment-related provisions of the DDA 1995 if:

(a) for a reason which relates to the disabled person's disability, he treats him less favourably than he treats or would treat others to whom that reason does not or would not apply, and

(b) he cannot show that the treatment in question is justified.

The following is an example is disability-related discrimination.

Eg Disability-related discrimination

TechnoCorp plc operates within a building that has a strict 'no dogs' policy. John, a blind man who is dependent upon a guide dog, applies for a job at TechnoCorp, but is rejected because he would be required to bring his dog to work in contravention of the 'no dogs' policy. John has been rejected, not because of his disability, but because of the 'no dogs' policy. The rejection is clearly related to his disability and so could constitute disability-related discrimination.

This example also demonstrates that, whilst the DDA 1995 may not recognize indirect discrimination, disability-related discrimination is very similar to indirect discrimination.

Disability-related discrimination is the only form of disability discrimination that can be justified. In order for treatment to be justified, the reason for the treatment must be material to the circumstances of the particular case and substantial.[94] When determining the validity of a justification, the tribunal must balance the needs of the employer with the interests of the disabled employee.[95] Establishing a justification is not difficult, because what is material and substantial will be for the employer to decide, and provided that the decision fell within a 'band of reasonable responses' (a similar test to that used to determine whether a dismissal is unfair), the justification

The 'band of reasonable responses' test in relation to unfair dismissal is discussed at p 916

---

93. The DDA 1995 does not use the phrase 'disability-related discrimination', but this phrase is used by the Disability Code of Practice.

94. DDA 1995, s 3A(3).

95. *Baynton v Saurus General Engineers Ltd* [2000] ICR 375 (EAT).

will be established.[96] It has been argued by both judges[97] and academics[98] that this is an inappropriately low standard.

Disability-related discrimination cannot be justified if it amounts to direct discrimination.[99] As noted, direct discrimination under the DDA 1995 is not a separate form of discrimination, but is rather a sub-form of disability-related discrimination. It is defined almost identically to direct discrimination under the SDA 1975 and RRA 1976:

> A person directly discriminates against a disabled person if, on the ground of the disabled person's disability, he treats the disabled person less favourably than he treats or would treat a person not having that particular disability whose relevant circumstances, including his abilities, are the same as, or not materially different from, those of the disabled person.[100]

Because direct discrimination cannot be justified, it follows that the motive for direct discrimination is irrelevant, and many cases in this area involve employers discriminating against disabled employees due to ignorance surrounding the disability (for example, the mistaken belief that blind persons cannot use computers).

A comparator will be required and a recent case has significantly altered the law in this area in favour of the discriminating party. Until recently, it was well established that the treatment of the claimant should be compared to that of an able-bodied person who can perform the job in question.[101] This test is pro-claimant and is much more likely to result in a finding of disability discrimination, as the following example demonstrates.

 The comparator test from *Clark v Novacold Ltd*[102]

Cassie has severe arthritis and finds it difficult to type. She applies for an office job, but is rejected, because the job requires typing skills. Under *Clark*, Cassie's treatment by the employer would be compared to that of a person who could type and did not have arthritis. It is highly likely that Cassie has been treated less favourably than such a person.

In the recent case of *Malcolm v Lewisham London Borough Council*,[103] however, the House of Lords overruled *Clark* and held that the correct comparator was an able-bodied person who could not perform the same function. This makes the claimant's task much more difficult, as we can see if we apply the *Malcolm* test to Cassie's case.

---

96. *Jones v Post Office* [2001] EWCA Civ 558, [2001] ICR 805.
97. *Collins v Royal National Theatre Board Ltd* [2004] EWCA Civ 144, [2004] 2 All ER 851 [15] (Sedley LJ).
98. For example, J Davies, 'A Cuckoo in the Nest? A "Range of Reasonable Responses", Justification and the Disability Discrimination Act 1995' (2003) 32 ILJ 164.
99. DDA 1995, s 3A(4).
100. Ibid, s 3A(5).
101. *Clark v Novacold Ltd* [1999] ICR 951 (CA).
102. Ibid.
103. [2008] UKHL 43, [2008] 3 WLR 194.

> <table><tr><td>**Eg**</td><td>*The* comparator test from *Malcolm v Lewisham LBC*[104]</td></tr></table>
>
> Cassie has severe arthritis and finds it difficult to type. She applies for an office job, but is rejected, because the job requires typing skills. Under *Malcolm*, Cassie's treatment by the employer would be compared to that of a person who could not type and did not have arthritis. Because such a person would also be rejected, Cassie has not been treated less favourably.

The decision in *Malcolm* has been almost universally criticized by academics,[105] as well as by the Equality and Human Rights Commission. In response to *Malcolm*, the government has proposed that the Equality Bill will replace disability-related discrimination with a concept of 'indirect disability discrimination' that would move away from the pro-defendant position evidenced in *Malcolm*.[106] But these proposals are at the consultation stage only and may not be included in the final Bill.

Discrimination through a failure to make reasonable adjustments

An employer is under a duty to make reasonable adjustments where a PCP, or a physical feature of the employer's premises, places the disabled employee at a substantial disadvantage in comparison with an able-bodied person.[107] A failure to make these adjustments can constitute discrimination.[108] Like direct discrimination, a failure to make reasonable adjustments cannot be justified.[109]

The employer need only make reasonable adjustments. Section 18B(1) provides a list of factors to which the tribunal or court shall have regard when determining reasonableness, including:

- the extent to which taking the step would prevent the disadvantage;
- the extent to which it is practicable for the employer to take the step;
- the financial and other costs that would be incurred by the employer in taking the step, and the extent to which taking it would disrupt any of his activities;
- the extent of the employer's financial and other resources;
- the nature of the employer's activities and the size of the undertaking.

The DDA 1995, s 18B(2), also indicates what types of adjustment may have to be made to comply with the duty, including:

- making adjustments to premises;
- allocating some of the disabled person's duties to another person;

---

104. Ibid.
105. For example, R Horton, 'The End of Disability-related Discrimination in Employment?' (2008) 37 ILJ 376.
106. Office for Disability Issues, *Consultation on Improving Protection from Disability Discrimination* (Office for Disability Issues, London, 2008).
107. DDA 1995, s 4A(1).
108. Ibid, s 3A(2).
109. Ibid, s 3A(6).

- transferring him to fill an existing vacancy;
- altering his hours of working or training;
- assigning him to a different place of work or training;
- allowing him to be absent during working or training hours for rehabilitation, assessment, or treatment;
- acquiring or modifying equipment.

The burden of proof is placed upon the employer to demonstrate that the duty has been complied with. This burden will not be met if the employee did not suggest any adjustments and the employer did not consider what adjustments should be made.[110]

Whereas other forms of discrimination are about less favourable treatment, in order to comply with the duty to make reasonable adjustments, the employer might actually have to give preferential treatment to a disabled employee, as the following case demonstrates.

 Archibald v Fife Council [2004] UKHL 32

FACTS: The defendant employed the claimant as a road sweeper. Due to a complication following surgery, it became almost impossible for her to walk, which rendered her unable to continue sweeping roads. She asked the defendant if she could perform a more sedentary role and, being aware of the duty to make reasonable adjustments, the defendant sent her on several training courses. But despite applying for over a hundred jobs, she failed to impress the various interview panels (it was council policy that all candidates attend an interview). The defendant dismissed her, arguing that it had exhausted all options. The claimant brought an action alleging breach of the duty to make reasonable adjustments.

HELD: The House of Lords found in favour of the claimant. Baroness Hale stated that the 1995 Act does not require able-bodied persons and disabled persons to be treated the same way; instead, it 'necessarily entails an element of more favourable treatment'.[111]

 See P Hughes, 'Disability Discrimination and the Duty to Make Reasonable Adjustments: Recent Developments' (2004) 33 ILJ 358

Harassment

Under the DDA 1995, harassment is a separate form of discrimination,[112] and is defined in exactly the same way as under the SDA 1975 and RRA 1976.[113]

Discrimination by victimization

The definition of victimization under the DDA 1995 is identical to that found in the SDA 1975 and RRA 1976.[114] Like direct discrimination and discrimination through the failure to make reasonable adjustments, victimization cannot be justified.

---

110. *Cosgrove v Caesar and Howie* [2001] IRLR 653 (EAT).
111. *Archibald v Fife Council* [2004] UKHL 32, [2004] 4 All ER 303, [47].
112. Under the SDA 1975 and RRA 1976, harassment is a sub-form of direct discrimination.
113. DDA 1995, s 3B(1).
114. Ibid, s 55.

Disability discrimination in the employment field

Like the RRA 1976 and the SDA 1975, the DDA 1995 contains specific provisions relating to discrimination in the 'employment field', although the wording has been updated. Section 4(1) focuses on disability discrimination in relation to applicants and provides that it is unlawful for a person, in relation to employment by him, to discriminate against a disabled person:

- in the arrangements that he makes for the purpose of determining who should be offered that employment;
- in the terms on which he offers him that employment; or
- by refusing or deliberately omitting to offer him that employment.

Section 4(2) goes on to state that it is unlawful for a person to discriminate against a disabled person who he employs:

- in the terms of employment that he affords him;
- in the opportunities that he affords him for promotion, a transfer, training, or receiving any other benefit;
- by refusing to afford him, or deliberately not affording him, any such opportunity; or
- by dismissing him, or subjecting him to any other detriment.

Section 4(3) provides that it is unlawful for an employer, in relation to employment by him, to subject to harassment a disabled person who he employs, or a disabled person who has applied to him for employment.

Vicarious liability

As under the SDA 1975 and RRA 1976, an employer is vicariously liable for the discriminatory acts of its employees, irrespective of whether such acts were carried out with the employer's knowledge or approval.[115] But the employer will not be liable where it took reasonable steps to prevent the discriminatory acts of its employees.[116]

Enforcement and remedies

The enforcement of the DDA 1995 is carried out in exactly the same way as the enforcement of cases under the SDA 1975 and RRA 1976—namely, by making a complaint to an employment tribunal.[117] The Equality and Human Rights Commission, in addition to subsuming the Equal Opportunities Commission and the Commission for Racial Equality, also took over the functions of the Disability Rights Commission. Therefore the investigatory and enforcement powers of the Commission discussed in relation to cases under the SDA 1975 and RRA 1976 also apply to cases under the DDA 1995.

The three remedies available under the SDA 1975 and RRA 1976—namely, declaration, compensation, and recommendation—are also available under the

---

115. Ibid, s 58(1).   116. Ibid, s 58(5).
117. Ibid, s 17A(1).

DDA 1995.[118] Table 25.6 demonstrates the highest single compensatory award made in each year since 2000 and the average award for each year.

TABLE 25.6 Maximum and average compensatory awards for disability discrimination

	2006–07	2005–06	2004–05	2003–04	2002–03	2001–02	2000–01
Maximum award (£)	138,648	138,650	148,681	173,139	90,000	215,000	71,063
Average award (£)	15,059	19,360	17,736	16,214	10,157	23,365	12,978

Source: Statistics collated from the Annual Reports of the Employment Tribunal Service and the Tribunal Service, available online at <http://www.employmenttribunals.gov.uk/Publications/publications.htm>

 Key points summary

- The Disability Discrimination Act 1995 prohibits discrimination on the ground of disability. A disability is defined as a physical or mental impairment that has a substantial and long-term effect on a person's ability to carry out day-to-day activities.

- The DDA 1995 recognizes and provides for four forms of discrimination:

  - disability-related discrimination;
  - discrimination through a failure to make reasonable adjustments;
  - harassment; and
  - victimization.

- The DDA 1995 does not recognize indirect discrimination and direct discrimination is a sub-form of disability-related discrimination.

- Direct discrimination, discrimination through a failure to make reasonable adjustments, harassment, and victimization cannot be justified.

- Enforcement and remedies under the DDA 1995 are the same as under the SDA 1975.

Age discrimination

The UK has an increasingly ageing population. By mid-2007, there were just over 11.5 million persons over state pensionable age [119] (that is, the ages of 60 for women and 65 for men). It is estimated that this figure will reach over 16 million by 2032.[120] For the first time ever, the number of persons under the age of 16 has dropped below the number of persons over state pensionable age,[121] and the fastest-growing age category in the UK is those who are over the age of 80.[122] The ageing population

---

118. Ibid, s 17A(2).
119. Office for National Statistics, *Mid-2007 Population Estimates* (ONS, London, 2008) Table 1.
120. Office of National Statistics, *Population Trends No 134* (ONS, London, Winter 2008) 6.
121. Office of National Statistics, *News Release: UK Population Approaches 61 Million in 2007* (ONS, London, 2008) 3, available online at <http://www.statistics.gov.uk/pdfdir/popest0808.pdf>.
122. Ibid.

has had a marked impact on the UK's workforce, with persons staying in work and applying for jobs at a much later age than in previous decades. Age discrimination has consequently become an increasingly significant problem.

Prior to the 1997 election, the Labour Party indicated that it intended to legislate in this area, but initial efforts were lacklustre at best. Impetus for more effective legislation came in the form of the Equal Treatment Directive[123] in 2000. The controversial nature of age discrimination is evidenced in that the provisions of the Directive relating to age were given a six-year implementation period (as opposed to the more normal two). The Directive was implemented by the Employment Equality (Age) Regulations 2006 (EEAR 2006).[124]

Forms of discrimination

The definitions of direct and indirect discrimination under the SDA 1975 are discussed at p 853

The EEAR 2006 recognize and provide for direct discrimination (including harassment), indirect discrimination, and victimization, and, in many ways, the definitions mirror those contained in the SDA 1975 and RRA 1976. The definitions of direct and indirect discrimination contained in reg 3(1) are identical to those found in the SDA 1975 and RRA 1976, save for one notable exception. Under the 'new' definitions contained in the SDA 1975 and RRA 1976, indirect discrimination can be justified if it is a 'proportionate means of achieving a legitimate aim'; direct sex and racial discrimination cannot be justified in this way. Conversely, the EEAR 2006 allow both direct and indirect age discrimination to be justified if it is a 'proportionate means of achieving a legitimate aim'.

The definitions of victimization and harassment under the SDA 1975 are discussed at pp 855 and 858

The EEAR 2006 define victimization[125] and harassment[126] in exactly the same way as do the SDA 1975 and RRA 1976. The provisions relating to discrimination in the employment field[127] are the same as those found in the DDA 1995.

Vicarious liability

As under the SDA 1975 and RRA 1976, an employer is vicariously liable for the discriminatory acts of its employees, irrespective of whether such acts were carried out with the employer's knowledge or approval.[128] But the employer will not be liable where it took reasonable steps to prevent the discriminatory acts of its employees.[129]

When is age discrimination permitted?

In addition to those situations in which discrimination can be justified as being a 'proportionate means of achieving a legitimate aim', and the usual exceptions relating to statutory authority[130] and national security,[131] the EEAR 2006 provide a number of other instances in which age discrimination is permitted.

---

123. Council Directive No 2000/78/EC.
125. Ibid, reg 4(1).
127. Ibid, reg 7.
129. Ibid, reg. 25(3).
131. Ibid, reg 28.

124. SI 2006/1031.
126. Ibid, reg 6(1).
128. Ibid, reg 25(1).
130. Ibid, reg 27.

'Genuine occupation requirement'

The EEAR 2006 permit age discrimination where it is a 'genuine occupational requirement'. What constitutes a genuine occupational requirement is defined in exactly the same way as it is in the RRA 1976. The government has indicated that this is likely to be narrowly construed, especially given the number of other exceptions available. Note that, unlike the SDA 1975 and RRA 1976, the EEAR 2006 do not provide for an exception where age is a genuine occupational *qualification.*

Positive discrimination

As with sex and race discrimination, positive discrimination per se is prohibited—but 'positive action' is permitted. Positive action occurs where an employer allows persons of a certain age or age group access to certain training, or encourages them to do a particular form of work, and the reason for this action is to prevent or compensate for a disadvantage that such persons would have due to their age.[132]

Retirement age

Regulation 30 provides that dismissal of a person over the age of 65 shall not be unfair if the reason for the dismissal is retirement. A further exception is contained in reg 7(4), which provides that it is not unlawful to discriminate against applicants who, when they would become employees, would be over the employer's normal retirement age or, if the employer does not set such an age, over 65 years of age. This exception also applies to those within six months of these ages. Therefore any job applicant over 64.5 years of age may be turned down based on his age.

National minimum wage

When we discussed the National Minimum Wage Act 1998, we noticed that the national minimum wage was lower for 18–21-year-olds than for those aged 22 and over (and even lower again for those aged under 18). Obviously, this could be regarded as a form of age discrimination. Regulation 31 provides that employees between the ages of 18 and 21 can be paid a lower amount without it amounting to age discrimination.

The National Minimum Wage Act 1998 is discussed at p 811

Benefits based on length of service

It is common for many employers to provide additional benefits to employees who have worked for the employer for a certain period (for example, length of service increments, increase in holiday entitlements, etc.). The problem is that such benefits indirectly discriminate against younger employees. Regulation 32 therefore allows an employer to provide benefits based on length of service. Where an employee has worked for the employer for less than five years, the employer does not need to justify any differences based on length of service. Where the employee has worked for the employer for over five years, any differences in pay based on length of service will only be lawful if they fulfil a business need of the undertaking (for example, to encourage loyalty or to reward experience).[133] It has been argued that, given the

---

132. Ibid, reg 29(1).   133. Ibid, reg 32(2).

apparent subjectivity of this test, it will be extremely difficult to challenge and that virtually any benefit can be justified as rewarding experience.[134]

Enforcement and remedies

In relation to enforcement and remedies, the provisions of the EEAR 2006 are identical to those of the SDA 1975 and RRA 1976.

 Key points summary

- The Employment Equality (Age) Regulations 2006 prohibit discrimination on the ground of age. The Regulations recognize and provide for direct and indirect discrimination, victimization, and harassment.

- Unlike other anti-discrimination legislation, direct discrimination can be justified if it is a proportional means of achieving a legitimate aim.

- The Regulations have a number of exceptions not found in other anti-discrimination legislation, including exceptions relating to positive action, retirement, and benefits based on length of service.

Discrimination on grounds of religion or beliefs

As we have seen, discrimination against certain religions (for example, Sikhs and Jews) may be classified as race discrimination. But many religions have been unable to obtain protection under the RRA 1976, leaving them vulnerable to persecution in the workplace. Whilst many forms of discrimination were specifically prohibited by legislation, until relatively recently, religious discrimination was not one of them. The impetus for change came following the Treaty of Amsterdam, which introduced a new Art 13 into the EC Treaty. Article 13 gave the Council the power to take appropriate measures to combat a number of forms of discrimination, which led to the Council adopting the Framework Directive.[135] This Directive required member States to prohibit discrimination on a number of grounds, including discrimination on grounds of religion or beliefs. The provisions relating to religion and beliefs were implemented by the Employment Equality (Religion or Belief) Regulations 2003 (EERBR 2003)[136]

In virtually every respect, the protection offered under the EERBR 2003 is identical to that contained in the SDA 1975 and RRA 1976. The Regulations recognize and provide for direct discrimination (including harassment), indirect discrimination,

---

134. M Sargeant, 'The Employment Equality (Age) Regulations 2006: A Legitimisation of Age Discrimination in Employment' (2006) 35 ILJ 209, 222.
135. Council Directive No 2000/78/EC.
136. SI 2003/1660.

and victimization, and the definitions are identical to those found in the 1975 and 1976 Acts, with the exception that the EERBR 2003 only contain the 'new' definition of indirect discrimination.[137] The provisions relating to discrimination in the employment field,[138] vicarious liability,[139] and genuine occupational requirements[140] are similar to those under the SDA 1975. The procedures, enforcement, and remedies are the same as those under the SDA 1975, and so need not be repeated here.

What constitutes a religion or belief?

The EERBR 2003 prohibit discrimination on the grounds of religion or belief. The rationale behind the inclusion of the word 'belief' was doubtless to avoid the need to have to define what 'religion' meant and thereby limit the protection offered. 'Religion' is accordingly defined as 'any religion'[141] and belief means 'any religious or philosophical belief'.[142] These definitions are clearly extremely wide, and it will be left to the tribunals to determine exactly which religions and beliefs will qualify. What is clear is that protection is now offered to groups that did not qualify for protection under the RRA 1976. For example, we noted that Rastafarians are not protected under the RRA 1976[143]—but they are protected under the EERBR 2003.[144]

 Key points summary

- The Employment Equality (Religion or Belief) Regulations 2003 prohibit discrimination on the grounds of religion or beliefs. The Regulations recognize and provide for all three forms of discrimination.

- The words 'religion' and 'belief' are given a wide meaning, and their precise scope will be a matter for the tribunals to define.

- Groups unable to obtain protection under the RRA 1976 are more likely to gain protection under the EERBR 2003.

Discrimination on ground of sexual orientation

The Framework Directive also resulted in the passing of the Employment Equality (Sexual Orientation) Regulations 2003 (EESOR 2003).[145] This legislation was much needed, because both the European Court of Justice[146] and the House of Lords[147]

---

137. Ibid, reg 3(1)(b).   138. Ibid, reg 6.
139. Ibid, reg 22.   140. Ibid, reg 7.
141. Ibid, reg 2(1)(a).   142. Ibid, reg 2(1)(b).
143. *Dawkins v Department of the Environment* [1993] IRLR 284 (CA).
144. *Harris v NKL Automotive Ltd* [2007] WL 2817981 (EAT).
145. SI 2003/1661.
146. C-249/96 *Grant v South-West Trains* [1998] ECR I-621.
147. *AG for Scotland v Macdonald* [2003] UKHL 34, [2004] 1 All ER 339.

had steadfastly refused to grant gays and lesbians protection under the SDA 1975, thereby permitting employers to discriminate on grounds of sexual orientation. As with the EERBR 2003, the EESOR 2003 are modelled closely on the SDA 1975 and RRA 1976, in terms of the forms of discrimination, enforcement, and remedies.

Defining 'sexual orientation'

'Sexual orientation' is defined as a sexual orientation towards:

- persons of the same sex;
- persons of the opposite sex; or
- persons of the same sex and opposite sex.[148]

Therefore, not only does it cover gays, lesbians, and bisexuals,[149] but it will also cover heterosexuals if they are discriminated against for being heterosexual. Because the EESOR 2003 prohibit discrimination 'on grounds of sexual orientation', a person is protected if treated less favourably due a perception regarding his sexual orientation irrespective of whether such perceptions are correct or not.[150]

Genuine occupational requirement

The EESOR 2003 contain the standard genuine occupational requirement—namely, that discrimination will not occur where sexual orientation is a genuine occupational requirement.[151] But there is also a more controversial exception—namely, that discrimination will not occur where the employment is for the purposes of an organized religion and the employer imposes a requirement regarding sexual orientation so as to comply with the religion's doctrines, or to avoid conflicting with the beliefs of a significant number of the religion's followers.[152] This has understandably proved extremely unpopular with gay rights groups.

 Key points summary

- The Employment Equality (Sexual Orientation) Regulations 2003 prohibit discrimination on the ground of a person's sexual orientation. All three forms of discrimination are recognized and provided for.

- The Regulations protect gays, lesbians, bisexuals, and heterosexuals against discrimination on the ground of their sexual orientation.

---

148. EESOR 2003, reg 2(1).
149. It would appear that it does not cover asexuals (i.e. persons with no sexual orientation).
150. See, e.g., *English v Thomas Sanderson Ltd* [2008] EWCA Civ 1421, [2009] 153 SJLB 31, in which a claim of harassment was upheld involving a heterosexual man whose work colleagues subjected him to sexual innuendo suggesting that he was homosexual.
151. EESOR 2003, reg 7(2).
152. Ibid, reg 7(3).

Discrimination against part-time workers and fixed-term employees

Part-time workers

As of March 2009, there were almost 7.55 million part-time workers in the UK, of whom 5.68 million were women.[153] As we have noted, discrimination against part-time workers might amount to indirect sex discrimination. But not all part-time workers will be able to obtain protection under the SDA 1975 (usually because they are men). This was recognized by the EU when it passed the Part-Time Workers Directive,[154] which has since been implemented by the Part-Time Workers (Prevention of Less Favourable Treatment) Regulations 2000 (PTWR 2000).[155]

The PTWR 2000 only provide for direct discrimination—namely, that a part-time worker has the right not to be treated less favourably than a full-time worker.[156] But this only applies where the part-time worker is treated less favourably on the ground that he works part-time[157] and the employer cannot objectively justify his actions.[158] Whether a part-time employee is treated less favourably than a full-time employee will be determined on a pro rata basis, unless it is in appropriate to do so.[159]

The following example demonstrates the pro rata principle in practice.

> ### Eg The pro rata principle
>
> Steve works full-time, and his contract provides that he shall work forty hours per week and shall receive thirty days' holiday leave per year. Karl works part-time, and his contract provides that he shall work twenty hours per week and shall receive ten days' holiday leave per year. Because Karl works half the number of hours that Steve does, on a pro rata basis, he is entitled to half the benefits to which Steve is entitled. This would entitle Karl to fifteen days' holiday leave per year and, because he only has ten days' leave, he has a claim under the PTWR 2000.

In order to make a pro rata comparison, a full-time comparator will be required. The comparator must be:

- employed under the same type of contract as the part-time employee;
- engaged in identical or broadly similar work; and
- based in the same establishment, unless there is no full-time worker based in the same establishment, in which case a full-time worker from a different establishment will suffice.[160]

---

153. Office of National Statistics, *Labour Market Statistics* (ONS, London, March 2009) 2, available online at <http://www.statistics.gov.uk>.

154. Council Directive No 1998/23/EC.   155. SI 2000/1551.

156. PTWR 2000, reg 5(1).   157. Ibid, reg 5(2)(a).

158. Ibid, reg 5(2)(b).   159. Ibid, reg 5(3).

160. Ibid, reg 2(4).

The rules relating to enforcement and the remedies available are largely identical to those under the SDA 1975,[161] except that damages cannot be recovered for injured feelings.[162]

Fixed-term employees

The Fixed-Term Employees (Prevention of Less Favourable Treatment) Regulations 2002 (FTER 2002)[163] aim to protect employees on fixed-term contracts who receive less favourable treatment than those on permanent contracts. These Regulations provide employees on fixed-term contracts with an identical level of protection to that provided to part-time workers under the PTWR 2000. Accordingly, the right not to be treated less favourably is largely the same and less favourable treatment is determined in the same pro rata manner.

There is, however, a notable difference between the FTER 2002 and other pieces of anti-discrimination legislation: whereas other legislation protects 'workers', the FTER 2002 protect only 'employees'. We discussed in Chapter 23 how much narrower the term 'employee' is than the term 'worker'.

This distinction between an 'employee' and a 'worker' is discussed at p 787

The rules relating to enforcement and the remedies available are largely identical to those under the SDA 1975, except that damages cannot be recovered for injured feelings.[164]

> ### ‹› Key points summary
>
> - The Part-Time Workers (Prevention of Less Favourable Treatment) Regulations 2000 prohibit discrimination against workers on the ground that they work part-time. Part-time workers should be treated as favourably as full-time workers.
>
> - The PTWR 2000 only provide for direct discrimination and whether a part-time worker is treated less favourably will usually be determined on a pro rata basis.
>
> - The Fixed-Term Employees (Prevention of Less Favourable Treatment) Regulations 2002 prohibit discrimination against employees on the ground that they work under a fixed-term contract. Such employees should be treated no less favourably than permanent employees.
>
> - Whereas most anti-discrimination legislation applies to 'workers', the FTER 2002 apply to the narrower category of 'employees'.

The proposed Equality Bill

It can be seen that the law relating to discrimination is spread across a mass of primary, subordinate, and EU legislation. In 2000, it was calculated that, in order to obtain a full understanding of the law relating to the various forms of discrimination, a person would need to consult over thirty Acts of Parliament, thirty-eight statutory

---

161. Ibid, reg 8. 162. Ibid, reg 8(11).

163. SI 2002/2034. 164. Ibid, reg 7(10).

instruments, eleven codes of practice, and twelve EU directives and recommendations.[165] Today, that number has increased significantly and it has been estimated that the number of statutory instruments alone is around 100.[166] Whilst much of the legislation follows a similar format and uses similar definitions, there are notable differences that render the law confusing at best and inconsistent at worst. Accordingly, for some time, there have been growing calls for a Single Equality Act that unifies all of the anti-discrimination legislation in one single statute—an approach that has been adopted in Australia, Canada, the USA, and Ireland.

For a considerable period of time, the government did not seem interested in unifying the various Acts and statutory instruments, and even when it was persuaded that a single Act was the best way forward, the announcement of a Bill was delayed on several occasions. A Consultation Paper was finally published in June 2007, which set out the government's initial approach to the Bill,[167] and in December 2008, the government announced in the Queen's Speech that it intended to introduce into Parliament an Equality Bill that would unify the anti-discrimination legislation into one Act.

Details on the Bill are steadily being published and consultation is still ongoing, especially following the controversial decision of the House of Lords in *Malcolm v Lewisham LBC*[168] (discussed earlier). Given this, the proposed approach contained in the 2007 consultation document is likely to alter in a number of respects. The Government Equalities Office,[169] a free-standing governmental department responsible for devising the government's strategy on equality, has published a document[170] indicating the proposed aims of the Equality Bill, including:

- increasing transparency by requiring public bodies (such as local authorities, government departments, and universities) to report on equality issues (for example, gender pay, employment of disabled persons, etc.);
- public bodies will become subject to an equality duty, requiring them to consider how their policies, programmes, and services affect different groups within the community;
- increasing those instances in which positive discrimination (or 'positive action', as it has become known) is permitted;
- strengthening the enforcement powers of tribunals;
- simplifying the definitions of discrimination, especially the confusing definitions found in the DDA 1995;
- providing greater support for the Equality and Human Rights Commission, including launching a Commission inquiry into the financial sector and construction industries.

At the time of writing, the Bill is undergoing its second reading. Details of the Bill will be discussed in the Online Resource Centre when it becomes law.

---

165. B Hepple, M Coussey, and T Choudhury, *Equality: A New Framework* (Hart, Oxford, 2000) 21.

166. Government Equalities Office, *Framework for a Fairer Future: The Equality Bill* (HMSO, London, 2008) 6.

167. Department for Communities and Local Government, *A Framework for Fairness: Proposals for a Single Equality Act for Great Britain* (HMSO, London, 2007).

168. [2008] UKHL 43, [2008] 3 WLR 194.

169. See <http://www.equalities.gov.uk>.

170. Government Equalities Office, *Framework for a Fairer Future: The Equality Bill* (HMSO, London, 2008).

Chapter conclusion

The prevention of discrimination is a comparatively recent development and we are still struggling to discover the best method of preventing it. It could be argued that the various pieces of discrimination legislation are based around a core structure. It is clear that the core structure found in the SDA 1975 and RRA 1976 have provided a template for future legislation—but there are enough subtle, but nonetheless important, differences between the various forms of discrimination to cause confusion to businesses, employers, employees, and applicants. For example, disability discrimination occurs in a very different manner from the other forms of discrimination. It is hoped that the proposed Equality Bill will provide a unified framework that greatly simplifies and minimizes the amount of legislation in this complex area of the law. But more is needed. It could be argued that the law is not clear regarding the underlying purpose of anti-discrimination legislation. Should the law aim to prevent discrimination or promote equality? In many cases, the two aims will coincide, but in relation to topics such as positive action, the two aims may be contradictory. To promote equality, discrimination may have to occur. It will be interesting to see which of the two aims future legislation favours.

Self-test questions

1. Define the following:
   (a) direct discrimination;
   (b) indirect discrimination;
   (c) victimization;
   (d) harassment;
   (e) positive discrimination;
   (f) disability;
   (g) racial grounds.

2. Has discrimination occurred in the following cases?
   (a) A firm of solicitors advertises a job opening. The advertisement states that the successful applicant will have between five and seven years' post-qualifying experience and will be under the age of 30.
   (b) Mohinder emigrated from India to the UK when he was 28 years old. He is now aged 35 and in employment. He applies for a job, but is rejected, because the job requires the applicant to have ten years' experience working in the UK.
   (c) Sharon is employed to cover for another employee who is taking maternity leave. A few days into the job, Sharon discovers that she is pregnant. Sharon informs her employer, who promptly dismisses her.

3. 'The current legislation is modelled on standard terms that apply throughout the various grounds of discrimination and therefore an Equality Act is not necessary.' Discuss.

Additional reading

Clement, R, 'Happy Birthday RRA' (2006) 156 NLJ 875
On the thirtieth birthday of the Race Relations Act 1976, the author examines why there are still so many cases of racial discrimination

Oliver, H, 'Sexual Orientation Discrimination: Perceptions, Definitions, and Genuine Occupational Requirements' (2004) 33 ILJ 1
Discusses the Employment Equality (Sexual Orientation) Regulations 2003 and analyses in depth the genuine occupation requirements exceptions

Sargeant, M, 'The Employment Equality (Age) Regulations 2006: A Legitimisation of Age Discrimination in Employment' (2006) 35 ILJ 209
Sets out the main provisions of the Employment Equality (Age) Regulations 2006, paying particular attention to possible limitations to the Regulations' effectiveness

Smith, I, and Thomas, G, *Smith & Wood's Employment Law* (9th edn, OUP, Oxford, 2008) ch 6
Provides a detailed, yet engaging, discussion of all of the principal forms of discrimination

Vickers, L, 'The Employment Equality (Religion or Belief) Regulations 2003' (2003) 32 ILJ 188
Discusses the Employment Equality (Religion or Belief) Regulations 2003 and argues that the rights granted conflict with rights granted by other anti-discrimination legislation

Websites

<http://www.equalities.gov.uk>
The official website of the government Equalities Office

<http://www.equalityhumanrights.com>
The official website of the Equality and Human Rights Commission

Remember to visit the **Online Resource Centre** at **<http://www. oxfordtextbooks.co.uk/roach>** to access the following resources on Chapter 25, 'Discrimination': more **practice questions** and answers; a **glossary** of key terms; **multiple-choice questions**; **revision summaries**; **audio updates** when relevant; and **audio exam advice** on this key topic.

26 The termination of employment

- Termination not due to dismissal
- Forms of dismissal
- Unfair dismissal
- Redundancy

INTRODUCTION

The termination of employment constitutes an extremely litigious area of the law. Over half of the cases heard by employment tribunals concern the termination of employment, and owners and controllers of businesses are required to pay out millions of pounds each year in compensation to employees who have been wrongfully or unfairly dismissed. A termination of employment may also place an obligation upon the employer to provide dismissed employees with redundancy pay. Clearly, therefore, the termination of employment is an issue that businesses need to take extremely seriously. Both statute and the common law impose a raft of obligations upon employers when considering terminating contracts of employment, and detailed and complex procedures are in place to ensure that employees are treated fairly. In this chapter, these obligations and procedures will be discussed in detail. It will be seen that the protection provided is primarily aimed at employees who have been dismissed and it is therefore important that businesses are aware of what forms of termination constitute dismissal.

Termination not due to dismissal

For two reasons, it is vital to determine whether or not the termination of employment constitutes a dismissal or not: firstly, a claim for wrongful or unfair dismissal can only be brought if an employee is dismissed; secondly, only dismissed employees are entitled to redundancy pay. When the contract of employment is terminated for the following reasons, it will not normally constitute dismissal.

Resignation

An employee can end the contract of employment simply by resigning—but the employee will need to provide the employer with the requisite notice. The notice period is usually stated in the contract of employment, but the Employment Rights Act 1996 (ERA 1996), s 86(2), provides that the minimum notice period shall be one week (provided that the employee has worked for the employer for more than one month). This applies even if the contract provides for a shorter notice period, but it does not prevent a party from waiving the right to notice or accepting payment in lieu of notice.[1] It follows that an employee who fails to provide the requisite notice will be in breach of contract.

Because a resignation is the voluntary termination of the employment contract by the employee, it follows that it does not constitute a dismissal and the employee will not be entitled to redundancy pay, or to bring a wrongful dismissal or unfair dismissal claim. It is crucial, however, that the resignation is voluntary. If the resignation is not voluntary, it is most likely to constitute a dismissal.

 Essex County Council v Walker (1972) 7 ITR 280 (NIRC)

FACTS: The claimant was a school cook. She had a disagreement with her employer, who told her that, if she did not resign, she would be dismissed and that resigning was in her best interests. Accordingly, the claimant wrote a letter of resignation. She later claimed redundancy pay, but was refused, on the ground that she had not been dismissed. She appealed.

HELD: Brightman J stated that 'if an employee is told that she is no longer required in her employment and is expressly invited to resign, a court of law is entitled to come to the conclusion that, as a matter of common sense, the employee was dismissed'.[2] Accordingly, the claimant had been dismissed and was entitled to redundancy pay.

Frustration

As we saw when we discussed vitiating factors, frustration automatically results in the termination of a contract. Frustration will occur where the employment contract becomes impossible to perform or illegal, or where performance will produce a result that is radically different from that envisaged by the parties when the contract was made. Examples of events that could frustrate an employment contract include the employee being imprisoned,[3] or the employee being called up for military service.[4]

The law relating to frustration is discussed at p 311

The frustration of an employment contract has two principal effects, as follows.

1. The contract of employment is automatically terminated. The wishes of the parties are irrelevant and neither party need take any steps in order for their contractual relationship to end.

2. Because the contract is terminated by the operation of law, it follows that the employee has not been dismissed. This means that he will be unable to make a claim for unfair dismissal. But statute provides that if the frustrating event is an event affecting the employer, then the employee will be regarded as dismissed[5]

1. ERA 1996 s 86(3).
2. *Essex County Council v Walker* (1972) 7 ITR 280 (NIRC) 281.
3. *FC Shepherd & Co Ltd v Jerrom* [1987] QB 301 (CA).
4. *Morgan v Manser* [1948] 1 KB 184 (KB).
5. ERA 1996, ss 136(5) and 139(4).

and entitled to redundancy pay (but not entitled to bring a claim for unfair dismissal).

Three types of frustrating event are slightly more complex and warrant further discussion—namely, the death of an employer or employee, the dissolution of a business, and illness or injury of the employee.

Death

What effect does the death of an employee or employer have on the contract of employment? At common law, the death of the employee automatically brings the employment contract to an end by operation of law on the ground of frustration.[6] The same is true if the business ceases on the employer's death. It follows that the employee has not been dismissed and cannot claim unfair dismissal. But the employee is regarded as dismissed for the purposes of the redundancy provisions and is entitled to redundancy payment.[7] Where the employer's personal representatives or trustees continue the business and the employee continues to work for the business, however, there is deemed to be no termination and the employment continues unbroken.[8] If, following the employer's death, the business ceases, then, for the purposes of claiming redundancy pay, the employee is regarded as being dismissed.[9]

→ personal representative: an administrator or executor, whose function it is to settle the affairs of deceased persons

Dissolution

In many cases, the employer will be a company and so cannot 'die' in the literal sense of the word. Where the employer is a company, the method of the company's dissolution is an important factor. Certain events, such as the appointment of a receiver, will cause the employees' contracts to be terminated.[10] Commencement of a compulsory winding up will constitute notice to dismiss,[11] as will commencement of a voluntary winding up where there is no intention to carry on the business in any form.[12] Where a company is voluntarily wound up, but is to continue in some form (for example, where it is taken over), there will be no dismissal.[13]

Illness or injury

That illness or injury can result in the frustration of the employment contract is undisputed. The problem is that it is not clear what length or type of illness or injury is required in order for an employer to regard the contract as frustrated. Further, where the illness or injury amounts to a disability, any negative action taken by the employer could amount to disability discrimination. Mere absence from work is unlikely in itself to frustrate a contract. Thus, where a cabinetmaker was absent from work for two years, but continued to submit sick notes during that period, an

𝒮 Disability discrimination is discussed at p 870

---

6. *Stubbs v Holywell Rly Co* (1867) LR 2 Exch 311.

7. ERA 1996, ss 136(5) and 139(4).

8. Ibid, s 218(4).

9. Ibid, s 139(1).

10. *Reid v Explosives Co* (1887) 19 QBD 264 (CA).

11. *Re General Rolling Stock Co (Chapman's Case)* (1866) LR 1 Eq 346.

12. *Reigate v Union Manufacturing Co (Ramsbottom) Ltd* [1918] 1 KB 592 (CA).

13. *Midland Counties District Bank Ltd v Attwood* [1905] 1 Ch 357 (Ch).

industrial tribunal held that the contract was not frustrated, because his job was not the type that required filling by a permanent replacement.[14]

The Employment Appeal Tribunal (EAT) sought to establish guidance in the following case.

Egg Stores (Stamford Hill) Ltd v Leibovici [1977] ICR 260 (EAT)

FACTS: The claimant employee was injured in a car accident in November 1974 and was off work for five months. The defendant employer paid the claimant's wages until January 1975 and another employee completed his work. In April 1975, the claimant felt able to return to work, but was informed that his position had been filled. The claimant sought compensation for unfair dismissal or redundancy pay. The defendant argued that it was entitled to terminate his contract on the ground of frustration (even though it had not done so before the claimant asked to be re-engaged).

HELD: The EAT held that the contract had been frustrated. Phillips J stated that there may be illnesses or injuries that are so dramatic and shattering (for example, a crippling accident) that everyone is aware that the employment contract must be regarded as coming to an end. In most cases, however, the illness or injury will be less severe and its effects more uncertain. In such cases, a contract will become frustrated at that point at which 'the prospects for the future were so poor, that it was no longer practical to regard the contract as still subsisting'.[15]

When determining whether this point has arrived, the following should be taken into account:

• the length of the employment;

• how long the employment would have been likely to continue;

• the nature of the job;

• the nature, length, and effect of the illness or injury;

• the need of the employer for the work to be done, and the need for a replacement to do it;

• the risk to the employer of acquiring obligations in respect of redundancy payments or compensation for unfair dismissal to the replacement employee;

• whether wages have continued to be paid;

• the acts and the statements of the employer in relation to the employment, including the dismissal of, or failure to dismiss, the employee; and

• whether, in all of the circumstances, a reasonable employer could be expected to wait any longer.

★ See HG Collins, 'Frustration of the Contract of Employment' (1977) 6 ILJ 185

---

14. *Maxwell v Walter Howard Designs* [1975] IRLR 77 (IT).

15. *Egg Stores (Stamford Hill) Ltd v Leibovici* [1977] ICR 260 (EAT) 265.

Two further factors have since been added to the list outlined in the above case:

- the terms of the employment contract in relation to sick pay; and
- the employee's prospects of recovery.[16]

Agreement

 The law relating to discharge by agreement is discussed at p 296

Like any other contract, an employment contract may be discharged if both parties agree to the discharge. Because the employment contract is discharged by the consent of both parties, it follows that the employee is not dismissed.[17] But in order for the discharge to be valid, the employee must agree freely and there must be no coercion. This is a crucial requirement, because, without it, employers would pressure their employees into agreeing to a discharge to avoid the consequences that can result following a dismissal. A finding of discharge by agreement avoids the need to pay redundancy pay and will prevent a claim for unfair dismissal from being made. Accordingly, employers may try to argue that an agreement to discharge was present when it was clearly not, as the following case demonstrates.

McAlwane v Boughton Estates [1973] ICR 470 (NIRC)

FACTS: The defendant employer informed the claimant employee that his employment would be terminated on 19 April. The claimant asked the defendant if the employment could be terminated on 12 April, so that he could start a new job. The defendant agreed. The defendant refused to pay the claimant redundancy pay on the ground that, in agreeing to terminate the employment on 12 April, the employment had been terminated by agreement. Consequently, the claimant was not dismissed and so was not entitled to redundancy pay. At first instance, the industrial tribunal agreed with the employer. The claimant appealed.

HELD: The appeal was allowed. The claimant's request to bring forward the date of termination did not constitute a discharge by agreement; rather, it merely altered the terms of the dismissal. Accordingly, the claimant had been dismissed and was entitled to redundancy pay.

COMMENT: The ERA 1996, s 95(2), now expressly states that a request to terminate the employment on a date earlier than that stated by the employer still constitutes a dismissal.

Key points summary

- An employee whose employment contract is terminated in a manner that does not constitute dismissal cannot claim that he was wrongfully or unfairly dismissed and is not entitled to redundancy pay.

---

16. *Williams v Watson Luxury Coaches Ltd* [1990] ICR 536 (EAT).
17. *Strange Ltd v Mann* [1965] 1 WLR 629 (Ch).

- Where the employee voluntarily resigns, there will be no dismissal.

- Where the employment contract becomes frustrated, this will not constitute a dismissal for the purposes of unfair dismissal, but will constitute a dismissal for the purposes of redundancy payment.

- The death of the employer may constitute dismissal, depending on the circumstances.

- Where both parties agree freely to the discharge of the employment contract, this will not amount to a dismissal.

Forms of dismissal

Dismissal is the second most common form of termination, next to resignation. As indicated above, the importance of classifying a termination as a dismissal is that it will entitle the dismissed employee to redundancy pay and a possible remedy if the dismissal is wrongful or unfair. The ERA 1996, ss 95(1) and 136(1), provide that an employee is dismissed where:

- the employment contract is terminated by the employer (whether with or without notice);
- he is employed under a limited-term contract and that contract terminates by virtue of the limiting event, without being renewed under the same contract; or
- the employee terminates the contract (with or without notice) in circumstances under which he is entitled to terminate it without notice by reason of the employer's conduct (known as 'constructive dismissal').

The ERA 1996, s 95, relates to what constitutes a dismissal for the purposes of an unfair dismissal claim, whereas s 136 relates to dismissal for the purposes of determining entitlement to redundancy pay. The forms of dismissal discussed here are common to both claims. As we have seen, other forms of termination may constitute a dismissal for the purposes of a redundancy claim, but not another claim (for example, termination of employment due to a frustrating event that affects the employer constitutes dismissal for the purposes of a redundancy pay claim, but not for the purposes of unfair dismissal).

Notice

Either party can normally terminate an employment contract upon giving notice. If the employer gives notice of termination, this will constitute dismissal. Normally, where the employee gives notice, this will constitute resignation, which, as we saw above, does not normally constitute dismissal. As we shall see later, however, it is possible for an employee to give notice and still be regarded as dismissed.

The minimum notice period is normally stated in the employment contract. In the absence of such a period, the requisite notice period is subject to common law and statutory rules.

Common law

Where the notice period is not provided for by the contract and there is no minimum period established by custom or trade usage, the parties will need to provide 'reasonable notice' of termination.[18] What is reasonable will depend upon the facts in question, but it is common for a reasonable period to correspond with the period of payment (that is, weekly or monthly). The problem with this approach is that an employee paid monthly would be entitled to a month's notice irrespective of whether he had worked for the employer for a week or for thirty years. Long-serving employees should be entitled to longer periods of notice and this was eventually provided for by statute.

Statute

The ERA 1996, s 86(1), lays down the minimum period of notice that an employer must provide. These periods are the minimum and the courts may very well hold that the common law requirement for 'reasonable notice' requires a longer period. Under s 86(1), the minimum notice period depends upon the length of service, as follows.

- Employees employed for less than a month are not entitled to notice under the ERA 1996, but will be entitled to reasonable notice under the common law.
- Employees employed for one month or more, but less than two years, are entitled to no less than one week's notice.
- Employees employed for over two years, but less than twelve years, are entitled to an additional week's notice for every additional year of their employment.
- Employees employed for over twelve years are entitled to no less than twelve weeks' notice.

Because these constitute the minimum notice periods, the parties are free to provide for a longer period if they so wish. If they do so, the minimum notice period will be the longer period contained in the employment contract.

Either party may waive the right to notice or can accept payment in lieu of notice.[19]

Expiry of a limited-term contract

Employment contracts are usually deemed to continue indefinitely, but can be discharged by reasonable notice.[20] Parties are free to enter into limited-term contracts, however, with such limitations tending to occur in one of two ways.

1. The parties may provide that the employment contract will continue for a fixed period of time and, at common law, as soon as this period expires, the contract terminates automatically.[21]

---

18. *Richardson v Koefod* [1969] 1 WLR 1812 (CA).
19. ERA 1996, s 86(3). It was held in *Trotter v Forth Ports Authority* [1991] IRLR 419 (CA) that where a party waives the right to notice, he loses the right to be paid in lieu of notice.
20. *Richardson v Koefod* [1969] 1 WLR 1812 (CA).
21. *R v Secretary of State for Social Services, ex p Khan* [1973] 2 All ER 104 (CA).

2. If an employee is employed solely to complete a single specific task, then once that task is complete, the contract will automatically terminate.

In both cases, the employee is not technically dismissed, because his contract simply reaches its end. The termination of the contract could be regarded as a form of discharge by agreement or performance. But in order to prevent employers from avoiding the rules relating to redundancy payments and unfair dismissal, terminations due to expiry of a limited term are regarded as dismissals.[22]

Summary dismissal

Summary dismissal (also known as 'dismissal for cause') occurs where the employer dismisses the employee without notice.[23] Summary dismissal is permitted (that is, will not amount to wrongful or unfair dismissal) where the employee has committed an act that amounts to a repudiatory breach of the contract (that is, the employee has 'caused' his dismissal). The employer is entitled to accept the repudiatory act and treat the contract as immediately terminated.

➡️ repudiatory breach: a breach of contract that gives rise to the right to terminate

What amounts to a repudiatory act was set out by Lord Evershed MR when he stated:

> the question must be—if summary dismissal is claimed to be justifiable—whether the conduct complained of is such as to show the servant to have disregarded the essential conditions of the contract of service.[24]

Based upon this, the following have been held to constitute repudiatory breaches that justify summary dismissal:

- disclosure of confidential information;[25]
- taking part in strike action;[26]
- disobeying the employer's lawful orders;[27]
- Internet or email abuse;[28]
- gross negligence;[29]
- acts of dishonesty.[30]

It should be noted that the courts have indicated that summary dismissal will be justified only in exceptional circumstances. So, for example, mere negligence will normally not justify summary dismissal.[31] The courts have also indicated that summary dismissal will rarely be justified for a single act. Where an employer acquires the

---

22. ERA 1996, ss 95(1)(b) and 136(1)(b).
23. The introduction of minimum notice periods by the ERA 1996 does not deprive the employer of the right to dismiss summarily: see ERA 1996, s 86(6).
24. *Laws v London Chronicle (Indicator Newspapers) Ltd* [1959] 1 WLR 698 (CA) 700.
25. *Denco Ltd v Joinson* [1991] IRLR 63 (EAT).
26. *Simmons v Hoover Ltd* [1977] QB 284 (EAT).
27. *Pepper v Webb* [1969] 1 WLR 514 (CA).
28. *Thomas v Hillingdon London Borough Council*, The Times 4 October 2002 (EAT) (downloading pornography).
29. *Jupiter General Insurance Co Ltd v Shroff* [1937] 3 All ER 67 (PC).
30. *Sinclair v Neighbour* [1967] 2 QB 279 (CA).
31. *Gould v Webb* (1855) 4 E & B 933.

right to dismiss an employee summarily, it must do so within a reasonable period. Failure to do so will be regarded as a waiver of the right, entitling the employer to damages only.

Constructive dismissal

As noted above, where the employee terminates the employment contract, this will usually constitute resignation and not dismissal. But the ERA 1996, s 95(1)(c), provides that, for the purposes of unfair dismissal, an employee will be regarded as dismissed where:

> the employee terminates the contract under which he is employed (with or without notice) in circumstances in which he is entitled to terminate it without notice by reason of the employer's conduct.

In other words, where the employer's conduct is such that it entitles the employee to terminate the contract without giving notice, the employee is regarded as if he was dismissed. This is known as 'constructive dismissal' and is, in many respects, similar to summary dismissal, except that we are concerned with the employer's conduct. The question therefore is what conduct will entitle the employee to terminate without notice. Initially, the courts took a reasonably wide view and stated that an employee would be entitled to terminate without notice where the employer's conduct was 'of a kind which in accordance with good industrial relations practice no employee could reasonably be expected to accept'.[32] But this reasonable expectations test was firmly rejected and a narrower test introduced in the following case.

 Western Excavations (ECC) Ltd v Sharp [1978] QB 761 (CA)

FACTS: The claimant asked his defendant employer if he could have an afternoon off (in order to play cards). His request was refused, but he took the afternoon off anyway and was subsequently suspended from work without pay. As a result, his financial situation deteriorated and so he asked the defendant if he could have an advance of his accrued holiday pay. The defendant refused, and, in order to obtain this holiday pay, the claimant resigned and claimed that he was unfairly dismissed. An industrial tribunal held that the claimant had been constructively dismissed. The defendant appealed.

HELD: The Court of Appeal allowed the appeal. Lord Denning MR stated:

> If the employer is guilty of conduct which is a significant breach going to the root of the contract of employment, or which shows that the employer no longer intends to be bound by one or more of the essential terms of the contract, then the employee is entitled to treat himself as discharged from any further performance. If he does so, then he terminates the contract by reason of the employer's conduct. He is constructively dismissed. The employee is entitled in those circumstances to leave at the instant without giving any notice at all or, alternatively, he may give notice and

---

32. *George Wimpey & Co Ltd v Cooper* [1977] IRLR 205 (EAT) 224 (Phillips J).

say he is leaving at the end of the notice. But the conduct must in either case be sufficiently serious to entitle him to leave at once.[33]

Applying this test, the claimant had not been constructively dismissed, because the defendant had not breached or repudiated the contract.

COMMENT: Although Lord Denning MR's test is a narrow one, it should not be applied too rigidly. In applying the test, Lawton LJ stated that 'what is required for the application of this provision is a large measure of common sense'.[34] Subsequent decisions have further expanded the scope of the test by implying a term of mutual respect into the employment contract, so that unreasonable conduct by the employer can be regarded as a breach of this implied term.

The duty of mutual respect is briefly discussed at p 791

An employee will only be regarded as constructively dismissed where the employer has breached a term of the contract and the breach is so substantial that it constitutes a repudiatory breach. In applying Lord Denning MR's test, the tribunals and courts have held that the following conduct by the employer could justify the employee being regarded as constructively dismissed:

- instruction to discriminate against ethnic customers;[35]
- refusal to pay the employee's wages;[36]
- failure to follow grievance procedures,[37] or the imposition of disproportionate punishment;[38]
- failure to provide a safe system of work;[39]
- breach of the implied term of mutual trust and confidence;[40]
- unjustifiable demotion or suspension of an employee.[41]

An employee who has been the victim of such conduct has two options: firstly, he can resign and claim that he was constructively dismissed; secondly, he can continue to work for the employer, thereby affirming the employer's breach. If the employee does intend to resign, he must do so quickly. A failure to act quickly will lead an employment tribunal or court to infer that the employee has acquiesced to the employer's conduct and affirmed the breach, with the result that a subsequent resignation will not amount to constructive dismissal.[42]

A constructive dismissal is not necessarily an unfair dismissal. A constructive dismissal merely demonstrates that the employee was dismissed, and if the employer can justify his actions, then the constructive dismissal will be fair.

---

33. *Western Excavations (ECC) Ltd v Sharp* [1978] QB 761 (CA) 769.
34. Ibid, 772, 773.
35. *Weathersfield Ltd v Sargent* [1999] ICR 425 (CA).
36. *Cantor Fitzgerald International v Callaghan* [1999] ICR 639 (CA).
37. *Post Office v Strange* [1981] IRLR 515 (EAT).
38. *BBC v Beckett* [1983] IRLR 43 (EAT).
39. *Keys v Shoefayre* [1978] IRLR 476 (IT).
40. *Cortaulds Northern Textiles v Andrew* [1979] IRLR 84 (EAT).
41. *McNeill v Charles Crimm (Electrical Construction) Ltd* [1984] IRLR 179 (EAT).
42. *Jeffrey v Laurence Scott Electromotors Ltd* [1978] IRLR 466 (EAT).

> ### Savoia v Chiltern Herb Farms Ltd [1982] IRLR 166 (CA)
>
> **FACTS:** The claimant worked as a supervisor for the defendant. The claimant was off ill and so another employee took over his work. The defendant found this employee to be more cooperative than the claimant. Accordingly, when the production foreman died, the defendant offered the claimant this job, and offered the supervisor's job to the other employee. Although it was a promotion, the claimant refused, because he believed that the job would expose him to the risk of contracting conjunctivitis. The defendant wished to test this claim by having the claimant undergo a medical examination, but the claimant refused. The defendant refused to let the claimant act as supervisor and the claimant resigned, alleging that he had been constructively dismissed.
>
> **HELD:** The Court of Appeal agreed that the claimant had been constructively dismissed, but held that the dismissal was fair. The reorganization of the business was justified and the employer had offered the claimant a promotion, thereby taking reasonable steps to ease the transition.

Wrongful dismissal

Wrongful dismissal occurs where the employer, in breach of contract, dismisses the employee. Examples of such breaches could include:

- terminating the employee's contract without providing sufficient notice;
- terminating a fixed-term contract before the expiry of the contract; and
- summarily dismissing an employee without sufficient justification.

Wrongful dismissal is a common law claim and should not be confused with unfair dismissal, which is a claim under the ERA 1996. Unfair dismissal requires the dismissal to be unfair, whereas wrongful dismissal does not; all that need be established is that the dismissal was in breach of contract. The claims are not mutually exclusive, and it is common for an employee to allege that he was both unfairly and wrongfully dismissed.

Making a claim

An employee who believes that he has been wrongfully dismissed may either initiate a claim in a civil court, or in an employment tribunal (which cannot order payment of more than £25,000).[43] The usual limitation periods apply (that is, three months where the case is brought before an employment tribunal, and six years where the claim is brought before a court).

Damages

Because a wrongful dismissal claim is an action for breach of contract, it follows that damages will be the principal remedy and will be assessed on a contractual basis (that is, to put the claimant in the position in which he would have been had the

---

43. Employment Tribunals Extension of Jurisdiction (England and Wales) Order 1994, SI 1994/1623, art 10.

breach not occurred, in so far as money is able to do this).[44] This strongly limits the amount of damages that can be claimed, as the following example demonstrates.

The quantification of damages in contract claims is discussed at p 327

Eg Damages for wrongful dismissal

Hywel is employed by DataTech plc. His employment contract is to last five years and can be terminated by either party at any time by providing four weeks' notice. After two years, DataTech terminates Hywel's contract, but only provides him with two weeks' notice. Hywel makes a claim for wrongful dismissal.

There is no doubt that Hywel has been wrongfully dismissed—but what damages can he claim? He cannot claim for the remaining three years left on his contract, because DataTech was entitled to terminate the contract at any time upon providing four weeks' notice. Had the breach not occurred, Hywel would have received four weeks' notice. It follows that all that Hywel is entitled to is the wages and other benefits that he would have received had he been given sufficient notice (that is, two weeks' worth).

Accordingly, in cases in which inadequate notice if given, the damages recoverable are limited to what the employee would have obtained during the period of notice to which he was entitled or which he was denied. This would include pay and any benefits that the employee would have received had he worked the full notice period.[45]

A number of other limitations apply, as follows.

- Damages cannot be recovered for injured feelings or where the nature of the dismissal was humiliating.[46]

- Damages are not generally available for a loss of reputation caused by being dismissed. So called 'stigma damages' are only available for a loss of reputation caused by a breach *during* employment.[47]

- Damages cannot be recovered for discretionary payments that could have been made by the employer (for example, bonuses), even where the employee expected to receive such payments.[48] But the employer cannot simply refuse to pay the discretionary payment: the exercise of the decision to pay or not to pay must be rational and bona fide.[49]

- Where the wrongful dismissal causes the employee to lose the right to bring an unfair dismissal claim (for example, because the employee is dismissed before he has acquired one year's continuous service), damages cannot be recovered for this loss.[50]

- The normal rules regarding mitigation apply, so the employee's damages may be reduced if he failed to take reasonable steps to mitigate his loss (for example,

The rules relating to mitigation are discussed at p 340

---

44. *Robinson v Harman* (1848) 1 Ex 855 (Ex).
45. *Silvey v Pendragon plc* [2001] EWCA Civ 789, [2001] IRLR 685.
46. *Addis v Gramophone Co Ltd* [1909] AC 488 (HL).
47. *Johnson v Unisys Ltd* [2001] ICR 480 (HL).
48. *Lavarack v Woods of Colchester Ltd* [1967] 1 QB 278 (CA).
49. *Horkulak v Cantor Fitzgerald International* [2004] EWCA Civ 1287, [2005] ICR 402.
50. *Harper v Virgin Net Ltd* [2004] EWCA Civ 271, [2005] ICR 921.

by looking for another job). The burden of proof is placed upon the employer to demonstrate this.

- Where a claim is brought before a tribunal, the maximum damages that can be awarded are £25,000. Many have argued that this limit is too low, especially given that tribunals can award much higher sums in unfair dismissal cases.
- Where damages are over £30,000, the excess is taxable.[51] This is not the case regarding damages for unfair dismissal.

Accordingly, it can be seen that the courts take a strict and restrictive approach to the recovery of damages in wrongful dismissal cases.

There are, however, two notable exceptions to this approach. Firstly, where the dismissal is wrongful because an employee on a fixed-term contract that is not terminable by notice is dismissed before the expiry of the contract, the damages awarded will reflect what the employee would have earned had the contract run its stated length. Secondly, whilst damages are not normally recoverable for loss of reputation, where an employment is undertaken and it is envisaged that the employee will receive a greater benefit that a simple wage (such as an increase in reputation),[52] damages may be recoverable for the loss of this benefit.

Enforcing the contract

Injunctions and specific performance are discussed in Chapter 10

Given the limited ability to recover damages, a wrongfully dismissed employee may instead wish to have the employment contract enforced via an injunction or an order for specific performance. Such remedies will, in effect, compel both parties to continue working together (at least until the contractual notice period has been served, or the fixed term of the contract expires). The general rule is that the courts will not allow either party to enforce the contract. Statute prohibits the court from making any form of order that compels an employee to do any work or attend a place to do any work.[53] The courts have clearly indicated that, because employment contracts are personal contracts, they should not be enforced against any party who does not wish enforcement. As Fry LJ stated:

> I should be very unwilling to extend decisions the effect of which is to compel persons who are not desirous of maintaining continuous personal relations with one another to continue those personal relations. I have a strong impression and a strong feeling that it is not in the interest of mankind that the rule of specific performance should be extended to such cases.[54]

Employment contracts are based on mutual trust and confidence, and it would be wrong to enforce a contract where this trust and confidence was not present. Accordingly, it would appear to be the case that an order of specific performance will never be granted in cases of wrongful dismissal.

In a number of rare instances, however, the courts have been willing to grant an injunction to restrain the employer from committing the breach that caused the wrongful dismissal.

---

51. Income Tax (Earning and Pensions) Act 2003, ss 401, 403, and 404.
52. *Marbé v George Edwardes (Daly's Theatres) Ltd* [1929] 1 KB 536 (CA).
53. Trade Union and Labour Relations (Consolidation) Act 1992, s 236.
54. *De Francesco v Barnum* [1890] LR 45 Ch D 430 (Ch) 438.

Hill v CA Parsons & Co [1972] Ch 305 (CA)

FACTS: The defendant agreed with a trade union that, after one year, it should be a condition of service that all technical staff join the trade union. The claimant was an engineer who had worked for the defendant for thirty-five years. He refused to join the trade union and was dismissed. He was due to retire in two years' time and, because his pension was calculated based on his wages in the three years leading up to retirement, the dismissal had a substantial effect upon his pension rights. The claimant brought an action for wrongful dismissal and sought an interim injunction preventing the dismissal.

HELD: The Court of Appeal granted an interim injunction preventing the defendant from terminating the claimant's employment for six months. Lord Denning MR stated that the rule against enforcement an employment contract was not inflexible and that exceptions could be made. He said: 'It may be said that, by granting an injunction in such a case, the court is indirectly enforcing specifically a contract for personal services. So be it.'[55]

COMMENT: There were three reasons why the Court departed from the normal rule and enforced the contract.

1. There was no breakdown of trust and confidence between the parties; rather, the dismissal was due to pressure from the trade union.

2. Damages were an inadequate remedy, because they would not have compensated the claimant for the effect to his pension rights.

3. Finally, and this reason appears to be more influential, the Industrial Relations Act 1971 was due to come into force shortly after the case. This Act created the concept of unfair dismissal and the claimant's dismissal would certainly be regarded as unfair. By delaying the termination, the Court ensured that the claimant was an employee when the Act came into force and could bring an action for unfair dismissal.

The facts of *Hill* are unique and subsequent courts have restricted it by branding it as decided on its facts. It has not been overruled, however, and it has been applied in a small number of cases, resulting in injunctions being granted effectively to enforce a contract of employment.[56]

Declarations

The courts' reluctance to enforce the employment contract may be in the process of being outflanked by an increasingly important remedy—namely, a declaration. Under the Civil Procedure Rules, Pt 24, a court may give summary judgment on a number of issues, including a point of law, which would include the construction of a document. The court can then make a declaration on the issue in question.

---

55. *Hill v CA Parsons & Co* [1972] Ch 305 (CA) 315.
56. For example, *Irani v Southampton and South-West Hampshire Health Authority* [1985] ICR 590 (Ch); *Powell v Brent London Borough Council* [1988] ICR 176 (CA).

Jones v Gwent County Council [1992] IRLR 521

FACTS: The claimant, a college lecturer, was, on two separate occasions, accused of misconduct by the defendant (namely, that she lied about her qualifications). On both occasions, disciplinary committees found that she was not guilty of such misconduct. Despite this, the defendant sent a letter of dismissal to the claimant. The claimant alleged wrongful dismissal.

HELD: The High Court declared that a letter of dismissal was not valid, because it failed to comply with the terms of the employment contract—namely, a proper grievance procedure had not been followed and the defendant had no grounds on which to dismiss the claimant. Accordingly, an injunction was granted, preventing the defendant from enforcing the letter of dismissal.

COMMENT: It should be noted that declarations have no coercive effect, which was why the High Court had to grant an injunction in addition to the declaration. It was the injunction, and not the declaration, that prevented the defendant from enforcing the letter of dismissal.

‹› **Key points summary**

- Either party can terminate a contract by giving notice. Where the employer gives notice, the termination will amount to dismissal. Where the employee gives notice, the termination will usually not amount to dismissal.

- Where a limited-term contract expires without renewal, the employee will be regarded as dismissed.

- Summary dismissal without notice occurs due to the conduct of the employee. Constructive dismissal occurs where the employee resigns due to the conduct of the employer.

- Where, in breach of contract, the employer terminates the contract of employment, the termination may constitute a wrongful dismissal.

- The primary remedy for wrongful dismissal is damages, but in exceptional cases, the tribunal may be willing to enforce the contract by granting an injunction. A declaration can also be made.

Unfair dismissal

The concept of 'unfair dismissal' was first introduced by the Industrial Relations Act 1971 and can now be found in the ERA 1996, s 94(1), which provides that '[a]n employee has the right not to be unfairly dismissed by his employer'. Today, claims for unfair dismissal form the third most common form of complaint made to employment tribunals, with 40,941 unfair dismissal claims made between April 2007 and

March 2008.[57] Unfair dismissal claims far outnumber claims for wrongful dismissal for a simple reason: unlike wrongful dismissal, a claim for unfair dismissal does not depend upon the employment contract being breached. But whereas any employee who has been wrongfully dismissed may bring a claim for wrongful dismissal, the right not to be unfairly dismissed only extends to employees who meet the eligibility requirements.

Eligibility

Before an individual can claim that he has been unfairly dismissed, he will need to meet the eligibility requirements:

- he must have been an 'employee' of the employer;
- he must have been continuously employed by the employer for no less than one year; and
- he must have been dismissed.

'Employee'

In previous chapters, we noted that there is an increasing trend for employment legislation to provide rights to a wider category of persons known as 'workers'. Indeed, many rights under the ERA 1996 itself apply to workers—but the right to bring an unfair dismissal claim is not one of them and the individual concerned will be unable to bring a claim unless he is an 'employee'. Accordingly, an independent contractor will be unable to bring a claim and will have to resort to a claim for breach of contract or wrongful dismissal.

The distinction between workers and employees is discussed at p 787

One year's continuous service[58]

Normally, an employee will only be permitted to bring a claim if he has been 'continuously employed for a period of not less than one year ending with the effective date of termination'.[59] This demands definition of:

- what constitutes 'continuous employment'; and
- what constitutes the 'effective date of termination'.

The period of continuous employment usually begins on the day on which the employee starts work for the employer.[60] The employee's employment will be continuous for '[a]ny week during the whole or part of which an employee's relations with his employer are governed by a contract of employment'.[61] In other words, if the

---

57. Tribunals Service, *Employment Tribunal and EAT Statistics (GB) 1 April 2007 to 31 March 2008* (Tribunals Service, London, 2008) Table 1, available online at <http://www.employmenttribunals.gov.uk>.

58. It should be noted that the requirement of a minimum period of continuous service applies in relation to many statutory employment rights. The rules discussed here apply to all of these rights, not merely the right to claim for unfair dismissal.

59. ERA 1996, s 108(1). As we shall see, where the dismissal is automatically regarded as unfair, this requirement does not apply.

60. Ibid, s 211(1)(a).

61. Ibid, s 212(1).

employee does not work for the employer for a period of at least one week, then the period of service will be broken and will begin to run again when the employee does work. Time off work due to sickness, injury, family leave, or annual leave will not break the period of service, and will count toward the qualifying period. Provided that the employee works for the employer under a contract of employment, continuous service will not be broken by the employee changing roles or working in a different location within the UK. Continuous service will also not be broken by the undertaking being transferred to another employer.[62]

The employee must have one year's continuous employment ending on the 'effective date of termination'. Determining the exact date on which the employment ended is important for three reasons. Firstly, it allows the court to calculate exactly whether the employee has one year's continuous employment. Secondly, it allows the court to calculate whether the claim has been brought within the limitation period (an unfair dismissal claim must be brought within three months beginning on the effective date of termination, unless the court believes that it is just and equitable to extend this period).[63] Finally, it is used to calculate the amount of compensation that the employee will receive if his claim succeeds.

The ERA 1996 s 97 defines what constitutes the effective date of termination, as follows.

- Where the contract is terminated by notice (either by the employer or employee), the effective date of termination is the date on which the notice expires (irrespective of whether the notice was the proper length).
- Where the termination is without notice (for example, summary dismissal), the effective date of termination will be the date on which the termination takes effect. This will normally be the date on which the employer tells the employee that he has been dismissed.
- Where the employee is employed under a fixed-term contract, the effective date of termination will be the date on which the fixed-term expires.

It could be argued that the requirement of a minimum period of one year's continuous service is a harsh one. In effect, the requirement provides that employers may dismiss newer employees for any reason (provided that it is not a reason deemed automatically unfair) and the employee will lack a remedy. Further, provided that the employer provides the requisite period of notice, the employee will also be unable to bring a claim for wrongful dismissal. The initial reasons behind the rule (namely, to prevent part-timers from making a claim, and to allow employers to freedom to subject employees to lengthy probation periods and then dismiss them without fear of reprisal) were attacked by the EU and the qualifying period had to be lowered (it used to be two years). It could be argued that the time has come to remove the qualifying period requirement completely.

Dismissal

An employee who has served the qualifying period must then prove that he was actually dismissed. We have already discussed in some detail what constitutes dismissal,

---

62. Ibid, s 218(2)(b).   63. Ibid, s 111(2)(a).

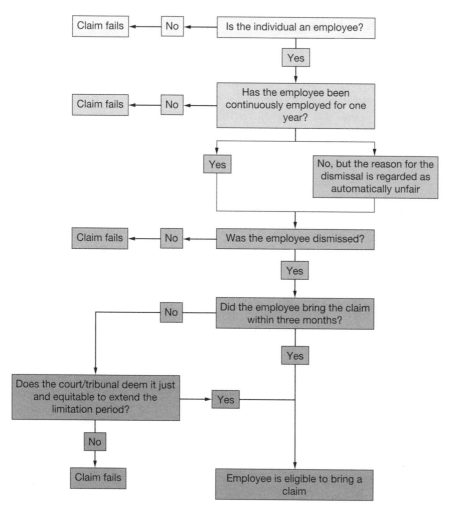

FIGURE 26.1 The eligibility requirements for bringing a claim of unfair dismissal

so this will not be repeated here, save to list the forms of dismissal that will qualify for the purposes of making an unfair dismissal claim:

- where the employer terminates the employment, with or without notice, this will qualify as a dismissal;[64]
- where a fixed-term employment contract expires and is not renewed, the employee will be regarded as dismissed;[65]
- where an employee resigns due to the conduct of the employer, this will constitute constructive dismissal;[66]

---

64. Ibid, s 95(1)(a).   65. Ibid, s 95(1)(b).
66. Ibid, s 95(1)(c).

- where an employee resigns, but the resignation is not voluntary, he will be regarded as dismissed.[67]

Once the employee has established that a dismissal took place, the eligibility requirements will be met. Figure 26.1 helps to clarify the steps that the employee will need to establish in order to meet the eligibility requirements.

Once an employee has established that he is eligible to bring a claim, the burden of proof is transferred to the employer, who must establish the reason (or, if more than one, the principal reason) for the dismissal.[68] If the employer cannot produce a reason for the dismissal, it will be regarded as unfair. An employee who wishes to discover the reason for his dismissal is aided by the ERA 1996, s 92(1), which entitles[69] a dismissed employee to a written statement from the employer, providing details regarding why the dismissal took place, provided that the employee has at least one year's continuous service.[70] Once the employer has provided a reason for the dismissal, the task of the employment tribunal is to determine if this was the real reason behind the dismissal. If the tribunal does not believe the employer, or holds that its reasons were inadequate, it may attempt to determine what the real reason for the dismissal was.

Once the employee has established that a dismissal took place and the reason for the dismissal has been determined, the next stage is to determine whether or not the dismissal was unfair. The burden of proof is placed upon the employer to establish that the dismissal was fair, but there are a number of cases in which the employer will be unable to argue that the dismissal was fair, because the law deems certain dismissals to be automatically unfair.

Automatically unfair reasons

A dismissal for certain reasons is automatically regarded as unfair and cannot be justified by the employer. Further, where such a dismissal occurs, the requirement of one year's continuous service does not apply.[71]

Automatically unfair reasons include the following.

Procedural fairness

The Employment Act 2002, Sch 2, Pt 1, lays down a series of dismissal and disciplinary procedures to which employers must adhere. Where a dismissal is made in breach of these procedures, it will automatically be regarded as unfair,[72] unless following these procedures would have made no difference to the decision whether or not to dismiss the employee.[73]

⨠ These procedures are discussed in more detail at p 918

---

67. *Essex County Council v Walker* (1972) 7 ITR 280 (NIRC).
68. ERA 1996, s 98(1)(a).
69. This entitlement only arises if the employee requests the written statement (ibid, s 92(2)).
70. Ibid, s 92(3).
71. Ibid, s 108(3).
72. Ibid, s 98A(1).
73. Ibid, s 98A(2).

Family reasons

The ERA 1996, s 99(1), provides that a dismissal will automatically be unfair if the sole or principal reason for the dismissal is that the employee took some form of family leave. A dismissal will be automatically unfair if its sole or principal reason is related to:

The right to take the various forms of family leave is discussed in Chapter 24

- pregnancy or childbirth;[74]
- the fact that the employee took ordinary or additional maternity leave;[75]
- the fact that the employee took parental leave,[76] or took time off to care for dependants;[77]
- the employee took paternity or adoption leave;[78]
- the fact that an employee applied to change his hours of work in order to care for a child.[79]

Health and safety cases

A dismissal will automatically be unfair if the sole or principal reason for the dismissal is that the employee carried out activities designed to prevent or reduce risks to health and safety, and had been designated to carry out such activities.[80] The same will apply where the employee is designated as a representative or member of a safety committee.

Working time cases

A dismissal will automatically be unfair if the sole or principal reason for the dismissal is that the employee refused to work hours that contravened the Working Time Regulations 1998,[81] or that he refused to forgo the rights granted by those Regulations.[82]

The rights granted under the Working Time Regulations 1998 are discussed at p 841

Assertion of a statutory right

A dismissal will automatically be unfair if the sole or principal reason for the dismissal is that the employee brought proceedings against the employer to enforce a statutory right.[83] Whether the employee actually had the statutory right and whether that right was infringed is irrelevant.[84] Applicable statutory rights would include:

- any right under the ERA 1996 that, if breached, could be remedied by making a complaint to an employment tribunal;
- the right to minimum notice;[85]

---

74. Maternity and Parental Leave etc. Regulations 1999, SI 1999/3312, reg 20(3)(a) and (b).
75. Ibid, reg 20(3)(d).
76. Ibid, reg 20(3)(e)(ii).
77. Ibid, reg 20(3)(e)(iii).
78. Paternity and Adoption Leave Regulations 2002, SI 2002/2788, reg 29(3)(a).
79. ERA 1996, s 104C.
80. Ibid, s 100(1)(a).
81. SI 1998/1833.
82. ERA 1996, s 101A(1).
83. Ibid, s 104(1).
84. Ibid, s 104(2).
85. Ibid, s 86(1).

- the right to take time off to engage in trade union activities;[86]
- rights conferred by the Working Time Regulations 1998, the National Minimum Wage Act 1998,[87] and the Transfer of Undertakings (Protection of Employment) Regulations 2006;[88]
- rights conferred by the Part-Time Workers (Prevention of Less Favourable Treatment) Regulations 2000[89] and the Fixed-Term Employees (Prevention of Less Favourable Treatment) Regulations 2002.[90]

Spent convictions

A principal aim of our penal system is to rehabilitate offenders and encourage them to make a valuable contribution to society. This aim would be frustrated if persons with criminal records were to find it impossible to obtain employment due to their criminal past. Accordingly, the Rehabilitation of Offenders Act 1974 introduced the concept of the 'spent' conviction, whereby, after a certain period of time, the conviction becomes spent and is regarded as if it never happened.[91] Consequently, an employee would not have to disclose the spent conviction when applying for a job or at an interview, and an employee who is dismissed for not disclosing a spent conviction will be regarded as unfairly dismissed.[92]

If and when a conviction becomes spent depends upon the sentence imposed (in the case of imprisonment, the amount of time actually served in prison is irrelevant). For example, a conviction that results in a person being sentenced to over thirty months' imprisonment will never be regarded as spent.[93] Where a person is sentenced to a period of imprisonment exceeding six months, but under thirty months, the conviction will be spent after ten years. In the case of a prison sentence not exceeding six months, the conviction will become spent after seven years.

There are, however, a number of professions that are excluded from the operation of the 1974 Act, including medical practitioners, barristers, accountants, nurses, any judicial appointments, police constables, and jobs involving the care of children and vulnerable adults.[94]

Other reasons

Other dismissals deemed automatically unfair include:

The rights of an employee upon the transfer of an undertaking are discussed at p 815

- where the dismissal is due to the undertaking being transferred, or where the dismissal is connected to the transfer of the undertaking and was not made for an organizational, technical, or economic reason;[95]

---

86. Trade Union and Labour Relations (Consolidation) Act 1992, s 168.

87. ERA 1996, s 104A.

88. SI 2006/246.

89. SI 2000/2551.

90. SI 2002/2034.

91. Rehabilitation of Offenders Act 1974, s 4(1).

92. Ibid, s 4(3)(b).

93. Ibid, s 5(1)(b).

94. Rehabilitation of Offenders Act 1974 (Exceptions) Order 1975, SI 1975/1023, Sch 1.

95. Transfer of Undertakings (Protection of Employment) Regulations 2006 (TUPE), SI 2006/246, reg 7(1).

- where a dismissal is related to trade union membership or activity;[96]
- where the dismissal is related to the employee making a 'protected disclosure' (that is, **whistleblowing**);[97]
- where the employee is dismissed for discriminatory reasons due to sex,[98] race,[99] disability,[100] age,[101] sexual orientation,[102] or religion or beliefs.[103]

→ **whistleblowing:** the reporting of alleged misconduct to a person or body inside or outside of the whistleblower's employment

Reasons that are prima facie fair

If the reason for the dismissal does not fall within the category of automatic unfair dismissals discussed above, the employer will be given the opportunity to establish that the dismissal was fair. This will require the employer to show that the dismissal fell within one of six reasons set down by the ERA 1996, s 98(1)(b) and (2). If the employer cannot establish this, the dismissal will be unfair. These six reasons will now be discussed, but it should be noted that they merely establish that a dismissal was prima facie fair. Once this is established, the tribunal will then determine the *actual* fairness of the dismissal.

🔗 All of these forms of discrimination are discussed in Chapter 25

🔗 How the tribunals and courts determine the fairness of a dismissal is discussed at p 916

Capability or qualifications

The first prima facie fair reason is that the employee was dismissed because he was incapable of performing the job, or because he lacked sufficient qualifications for it.[104] 'Capability' is determined by reference to 'skill, aptitude, health or any other physical or mental quality'.[105] The test employed is a subjective one—namely, that, provided that the employer had reasonable grounds to believe that the employee lacked capability, it will not be necessary to show that the employee actually was objectively incapable.[106] Where an employee lacks capability due to insufficient skill or aptitude (that is, he is incompetent), the tribunal must strike a balance between allowing the employer to protect its business by removing an incompetent employee and the need to treat the employee fairly. In practice, this means that the employer should investigate fully the facts that have led to the possibility of dismissal before dismissing the employee. It may be the case that the employee's incompetence is due to a lack of training or supervision, in which case, the tribunal may feel that immediate dismissal is inappropriate and that the employer should instead provide the requisite training.

---

96. Trade Union and Labour Relations (Consolidation) Act 1992, s 152(1).
97. ERA 1996, s 103A.
98. Sex Discrimination Act 1975, s 6(2)(b).
99. Race Relations Act 1976, s 4(2)(c).
100. Disability Discrimination Act 1995, s 4(2)(d).
101. Employment Equality (Age) Regulations 2006 (EEAR 2006), SI 2006/1031, reg 7(2)(d).
102. Employment Equality (Sexual Orientation) Regulations 2003 (EESOR 2003), SI 2003/1661, reg 6(2)(d).
103. Employment Equality (Religion or Belief) Regulations 2003 (EERBR 2003), SI 2003/1660, reg 6(2)(d).
104. ERA 1996, s 98(2)(a).
105. Ibid, s 98(3)(a).
106. *Taylor v Alidair Ltd* [1978] IRLR 82 (CA).

> ### 🔑 *Davison v Kent Meters* [1975] IRLR 145 (IT)
>
> **FACTS:** The claimant was employed by the defendant to assemble components. The supervisor demonstrated to the claimant how to assemble the components and then left her to get on with her work. Of the 500 components she assembled, 471 were faulty. She was dismissed.
>
> **HELD:** The dismissal was unfair. The supervisor should have instructed her more fully and then checked her work after she had assembled a small number of the components.

What should an employer do when faced with an incompetent employee? The Advisory, Conciliation and Arbitration Service (ACAS) provides a Code of Practice on Disciplinary and Grievance Procedures, which provides that:

> Where misconduct is confirmed or the employee is found to be performing unsatisfactorily, it is usual to give the employee a written warning. A further act of misconduct or failure to improve performance would normally result in a final written warning … If an employee's first misconduct or unsatisfactory performance is sufficiently serious, it might be appropriate to move directly to a final written warning. This might occur where the employee's actions have had, or are liable to have, a serious or harmful impact on the organisation … Some acts, termed gross misconduct, are so serious in themselves or have such serious consequences that they may call for dismissal without notice for a first offence.[107]

The courts have indicated that the employer should be slow to dismiss an employee, and that a warning and the chance to improve should usually be given. But where the incompetence is sufficiently severe, or where the job is one that requires a high degree of care, immediate dismissal may be justified. Thus, when an airline pilot performed a poor landing that damaged the aircraft, immediate dismissal was justified.[108]

🔗 The extent to which illness can frustrate an employment contract is discussed at p 892

A particularly controversial and litigious area is that in which an employee is deemed incapable due to prolonged or regular illness. A particularly severe illness could serve to frustrate the contract,[109] thereby remedying the employer's problem. Conversely, such an illness might also constitute a disability, so that if the employer dismisses the employee, the dismissal might be automatically regarded as unfair on discriminatory grounds.[110] It is reasonably settled that, in determining whether or not a dismissal due to illness was fair, the question that the tribunal should ask is whether it was reasonable for the employer to wait any longer before dismissing the employee.[111] The tribunals and courts have also indicated that usually a full review of the employee's case should be undertaken, which could include obtaining medical

---

107. ACAS, *Disciplinary and Grievance Procedures* (ACAS, London, 2009) [18]–[22]. The Trade Union and Labour Relations (Consolidation) Act 1993, s 207, provides that, where relevant, employment tribunals must take this Code of Practice into account.

108. *Taylor v Alidair Ltd* [1978] IRLR 82 (CA).

109. *Notcutt v Universal Equipment Co (London) Ltd* [1986] 1 WLR 641 (CA).

110. Disability Discrimination Act 1995, s 4(2)(d).

111. *East Lindsey District Council v Daubney* [1977] ICR 566 (EAT).

evidence. The employee should then be issued with an appropriate warning. Where this warning is not heeded, dismissal will usually be justified.[112]

'Qualifications' is defined as any degree, diploma, or other academic, technical, or professional qualification relevant to the position that the employee held.[113] In practice, very few cases arise in relation to a lack of qualifications, because unqualified applicants tend not to be offered the job in the first place.

Conduct

Dismissal may be justified due to the employee's conduct.[114] Clearly, the facts of the case are all important and examples of misconduct deemed sufficient to justify dismissal include:

- a refusal to obey reasonable and lawful orders (although, usually, the employee will need to be warned of the possibility of dismissal should he continue to disobey orders, unless the misconduct is so serious as to justify summary dismissal, and if the employee refuses to carry out acts that are not within his contractual duties, a dismissal on such grounds is likely to be unfair);[115]
- breach of confidentiality;[116]
- acts of dishonesty;[117]
- failure to disclose unspent convictions;[118] and
- inflicting violence upon another employee.[119]

Criminal conduct is likely to cause the employer to consider dismissal. Crimes committed whilst at work (for example, theft of company property) will almost always provide sufficient grounds for dismissal.[120] Crimes committed outside of work are not per se grounds for dismissal,[121] unless the commission of the crime renders the employee unsuitable to perform his job, as in the following case.

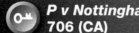

P v Nottinghamshire County Council [1992] ICR 706 (CA)

FACTS: The claimant was employed as a groundsman at a school run by the defendant council. The claimant's daughter, who was a pupil at the school, complained to a teacher that the claimant had indecently assaulted her. The defendant, upon discovering that the claimant intended to plead guilty to the offence, suspended him and then dismissed him. The clamant alleged that he was unfairly dismissed.

---

112. *International Sports Co Ltd v Thomson* [1980] IRLR 340 (EAT).
113. ERA 1996, s 98(3)(b).
114. Ibid, s 98(2)(b).
115. *Redbridge London Borough Council v Fishman* [1978] ICR 569 (EAT).
116. *Denco Ltd v Joinson* [1991] 1 WLR 330 (EAT).
117. *British Railways Board v Jackson* [1994] IRLR 235 (CA).
118. *Torr v British Railways Board* [1977] ICR 785 (EAT).
119. *Fuller v Lloyds Bank plc* [1991] IRLR 336 (EAT).
120. *Trust House Forte Hotels Ltd v Murphy* [1977] IRLR 186 (EAT).
121. ACAS, *Disciplinary and Grievance Procedures* (ACAS, London, 2009) [30].

★ See RA Watt,
'Unfair Dismissal: A
Duty to Redeploy in
Misconduct Cases?'
(1993) 22 ILJ 44

HELD: Even though the defendant had not investigated whether or not the claimant had committed the alleged crime, the dismissal was deemed fair. Where a defendant pleads guilty or is found guilty, the employer is entitled to believe that the offence was committed. Because the offence clearly rendered the claimant unsuitable for a job at a school, the Court of Appeal held that the dismissal was wholly justified.

Retirement

The third type of prima facie fair dismissal is where an employee is dismissed due to retirement.[122] Normally, the *actual* fairness of a dismissal will be determined in accordance with the test laid down in the ERA 1996, s 98(4) (which is discussed later)—but dismissal due to retirement as a prima facie fair ground for dismissal was only introduced in 2006, and so is subject to its own rules.[123] Before discussing these rules, one preliminary point should be made. Whilst the Employment Equality (Age) Regulations 2006 (EEAR 2006)[124] introduced a default retirement age of 65, employers are free to establish a different retirement age (which is known as the 'normal retirement age'),[125] but a retirement age of below 65 will need to be objectively justified.

The rules relating to retirement are as follows.

- Where the employee is dismissed whilst under the age of 65, and where the employer has not established a normal retirement age, then retirement must not be taken to be the reason for the dismissal.[126]

- Where the employee is dismissed whilst over the age of 65 after having been informed that he has the right to request not to retire, and where the employer has not established a normal retirement age, the dismissal must be taken to be on the ground of retirement and not for any other reason.[127]

- Where the employer has established a normal retirement age and where the employee is dismissed before this age, then retirement must not be taken to be the reason for the dismissal.[128]

- Where the employer has established a normal retirement age over the age of 65, and where the employee has been dismissed after reaching this age, then the dismissal shall be taken to be the ground of retirement and not for any other reason, provided that the employer notified the employee of the right to request not to retire.[129]

- Where the employer has established a normal retirement age under the age of 65, and where the employee has been dismissed after reaching this age, the dismissal must be taken to be the ground of retirement and not for any other reason, provided that the employer has objectively justified the lower retirement age and has notified the employee of the right to request not to retire.[130]

It can be seen that, in the majority of cases, a dismissal will only be regarded as due to retirement if the employee has been notified of certain rights. This is part of a wider obligation imposed by the EEAR 2006. These Regulations require the employer to

---

122. ERA 1996, s 98(2)(ba).
123. Ibid, s 98(3A).
124. SI 2006/1031.
125. ERA 1996, s 98ZH.
126. Ibid, s 98ZA.
127. Ibid, s 97ZB.
128. Ibid, s 98ZC.
129. Ibid, s 98ZD.
130. Ibid, s 98ZE.

notify an employee who is to be retired of the date on which the retirement is due to occur, and this notification must take place between six months and one year before the intended retirement date.[131] This notification must also inform the employee that he has the right to request to work beyond the statutory or normal retirement ages. If the employee makes such a request, the employer must consider it. Failure to do so may result in the dismissal being deemed unfair. Where an employer fails to notify the employee of the right to request to work beyond retirement, the employee may make a claim to an employment tribunal and, if successful, can receive compensation not exceeding six weeks' pay.[132]

Redundancy

What constitutes redundancy is considered later in this chapter. Dismissal due to redundancy is deemed prima facie fair.[133] In order to demonstrate that the dismissal is *actually* fair, the EAT has established[134] a number of principles that employers should follow, as follows.

⚓ Redundancy is discussed in detail at p 924

- The employer will seek to give as much warning as possible of impending redundancies.
- The employer will consult the union as to the best means by which the desired management result can be achieved fairly and will seek to agree the criteria to be applied in selecting the employees to be made redundant.
- The employer will seek to establish criteria for selection that, so far as possible, do not depend solely upon the opinion of the person making the selection, but can be objectively checked against such things as attendance record, efficiency at the job, experience, or length of service.
- The employer will seek to ensure that the selection is made fairly in accordance with these criteria.
- The employer will seek to see whether, instead of dismissing an employee, he could offer him alternative employment.

Where the employer fails to consult with either the trade union or the employee, the dismissal will normally be unfair, unless the employment tribunal is of the opinion that a reasonable employer would have believed consultation to be utterly futile.[135]

Illegality

A dismissal will be prima facie fair where continuing to employ the dismissed employee would have breached a statutory provision.[136] For example, continuing to employ a company director who had been disqualified under the Company Directors Disqualification Act 1986 would contravene that Act. Accordingly, dismissing the director would be prima facie fair.

---

131. EEAR 2006, Sch 6, para 2.
132. Ibid, para 11(3).
133. ERA 1996, s 98(2)(c).
134. *Williams v Compair Maxam Ltd* [1982] ICR 156 (EAT) 162 (Browne-Wilkinson J).
135. *Mugford v Midland Bank plc* [1997] ICR 399 (EAT).
136. ERA 1996, s 98(2)(d).

Some other substantial reason

The previous five categories of prima facie fair dismissals operate within relatively narrow confines. Conversely, the final category provides a 'catch-all' provision, which states that a dismissal will be prima facie fair if it is for 'some other substantial reason of a kind such as to justify the dismissal of an employee holding the position which the employee held'.[137] The reason for the breadth of this category is that Parliament 'can hardly have hoped to produce an exhaustive catalogue of all the circumstances in which an employer would be justified in terminating the services of an employee'.[138] The tribunals must strike a balance between permitting employees to dismiss employees for justifiable reasons whilst protecting employees from dismissal for trivial reasons. There is little doubt that, in striking this balance, the tribunals have leaned in favour of the employers and the majority of reasons advanced by employers have been accepted as sufficiently substantial.

Examples of dismissals deemed prima facie fair by legislation or case law under this category include:

- where an employee is employed in order to cover for another employee who is taking leave on medical grounds, or who is on maternity leave or adoption leave, and, upon that employee's return, the new employee is dismissed;[139]
- where an employee is dismissed following the transfer of an undertaking, and the reason for the dismissal is economic, technical, or organizational;[140]
- where an employee is dismissed because his personality clashes with others to such an extent that it causes the working atmosphere to become intolerable;[141]
- where an employee is dismissed due to his refusal to accept a pay cut that is necessary to avoid the company suffering severe financial difficulties.[142]

Fairness and reasonableness

Once the employer has established that the reason for the dismissal falls within one of the six prima facie fair categories discussed above, the tribunal will then decide whether or not the employer acted reasonably in dismissing the employee for this reason (that is, whether the dismissal was *actually* fair). Section 98(4)(a) provides that this will depend on 'whether in the circumstances (including the size and administrative resources of the employer's undertaking) the employer acted reasonably or unreasonably in treating the reason as a sufficient reason for dismissing the employee', and s 98(4)(b) provides that the determination of fairness 'shall be determined in accordance with equity and the substantial merits of the case'.

Determining reasonableness

The focus on 'reasonableness' in s 98(4)(a) would appear to indicate that tribunals should take an objective approach when determining the fairness of a dismissal, and

---

137. Ibid, s 98(1)(b).
138. *RS Components Ltd v Irwin* [1973] ICR 535 (NIRC) 540 (Sir John Brightman).
139. ERA 1996, s 106.
140. TUPE, reg 7(3)(b).
141. *Treganowan v Robert Knee & Co Ltd* [1975] ICR 405 (QB).
142. *St John of God (Care Services) Ltd v Brooks* [1992] IRLR 546 (EAT).

early cases did indeed take such an approach.[143] But there has been a move away from a purely objective test, towards a much more subjective test, as the following case demonstrates.

Iceland Frozen Foods Ltd v Jones [1983] ICR 17 (EAT)

FACTS: The claimant, a night-shift foreman, was dismissed by the defendant for forgetting to lock up the premises at the end of the night and for allegedly attempting to deceive the defendant into paying extra overtime payments. An industrial tribunal held that the dismissal was unfair, because, in its opinion, the claimant's conduct was not sufficiently serious to warrant dismissal. The defendant appealed.

HELD: The EAT held that the relevant test was not whether, in the tribunal's opinion, the dismissal was reasonable; the tribunal should consider the reasonableness of the employer's conduct, not simply whether it considers his actions to be fair or not. The tribunal should not substitute its decision as to the right course of action for that of the employer. In many cases, the employee's conduct could result in a band of reasonable responses, within which one employer might take one response, whereas another employer might take another. The function of the tribunal is to determine, based on the facts of the case, whether the decision to dismiss comes within this band of reasonable responses. If it does, the dismissal will be fair. If it does not, it will be unfair. Because the industrial tribunal had applied the wrong test, the case would be remitted to a new tribunal.

⭐ See A Freer, 'The Range of Reasonable Responses Test: From Guidelines to Statute' (1997) 27 ILJ 335

Subsequent cases were critical of this 'band of reasonable responses' test, including one case in which the EAT stated that '[t]here is, in reality, no range or band to be considered, only whether the employer acted reasonably in invoking that sanction'.[144] The chief criticism of the band of reasonable responses test was that it could result in a decision to dismiss being reasonable, and a decision not to dismiss also being deemed reasonable, provided that both reasons were within the band of reasonable responses. Polarized decisions could come within the band of reasonable responses, leading to a test that strongly favoured the employer, because only extreme conduct would fall outside the band.

But the Court of Appeal strongly disagreed with this criticism and reaffirmed that the band of reasonable responses test was correct.[145] It refuted the criticism that the band was overly broad by providing two examples:

1. an employee who is dismissed for burning down his employer's factory without good cause;
2. an employee who is dismissed for saying 'good morning' to his manager.

---

143. *Bessenden Properties Ltd v Corness* [1977] ICR 821 (CA).

144. *Haddon v Van Den Bergh Foods Ltd* [1999] ICR 1150 (EAT) 1160 (Morison J).

145. *Post Office v Foley; HSBC Bank plc v Madden* [2000] ICR 1283 (CA).

The Court argued that the 'band of reasonable responses' test would not apply in these cases, because the first dismissal is clearly fair and the second is clearly unfair. It is cases in between these two extremes in which there is room for disagreement and in which the band of reasonable responses test would be used.

Whether the Court's logic is accepted, there is little doubt that the test strongly favours the employer.

Procedural fairness

The ERA 1996 places great emphasis on procedural fairness. Historically, a large number of unfair dismissal cases were based on procedural unfairness (that is, the employee was deserving of dismissal, but the employer failed to comply with the correct procedures). In order to reduce the number of procedural cases reaching tribunals, the Employment Act 2002 introduced, for the first time, statutory disciplinary and dismissal procedures.[146] The ERA 1996, s 98A(1), provides that where these procedures apply and where, due to a failure wholly or partly attributable to the employer, these procedures are not complied with, the dismissal is automatically unfair, unless following these procedures would have made no difference to the decision whether or not to dismiss the employee. This is the case even if the dismissal is for a prima facie fair reason and is within the band of reasonable responses discussed previously.

It is an implied term of the employment contract that the employer will comply with the statutory disciplinary and dismissal procedures.[147] The procedures can be complex and a detailed discussion is outside the scope of this text, Instead, an outline of the procedures will be provided. Basically, the statutory disciplinary and dismissal procedures operate in three stages, as follows.

1. *The statement* The employer must set out in writing the employee's alleged conduct or characteristics, or other circumstances, which led to the employer contemplating dismissal or taking some other disciplinary measure. This statement must be sent to the employee and the employee must be invited to attend a meeting to discuss the matter.

2. *The meeting* The employer must not take any disciplinary action until the meeting takes place, except where such action consists of suspending the employee. The employee must be given a reasonable amount of time to consider the statement and the employee should take all reasonable steps to attend the meeting. If it is not reasonably practicable for either the employer or employee to attend the meeting, failure to attend does not constitute a breach of these procedures.[148] After the meeting, the employee must be informed of the employer's decision and, if he is not satisfied with the decision, that he has the right to appeal against it.

3. *The appeal* If the employee wishes to appeal, he must inform the employer. The appeal takes the form of a second meeting and, unlike the first meeting, the employer need not wait before dismissing the employee or taking any other disciplinary action. After the appeal meeting, the employee must be informed of the employer's decision.

---

146. Employment Act 2002, Sch 2, Pt 1.

147. Ibid, s 30(1).

148. Employment Act 2002 (Dispute Resolution) Regulations 2004, SI 2004/752, reg 13(1).

Figure 26.2 helps to clarify the process by which the tribunal determines whether a dismissal is fair or unfair.

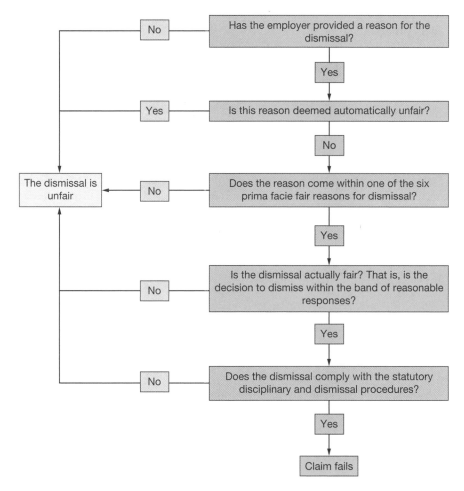

FIGURE 26.2 Is the dismissal unfair?

Remedies

The ERA 1996 specifies three remedies for unfair dismissal—namely, reinstatement, re-engagement, and compensation. Once a dismissal is deemed unfair, the tribunal will explain to the claimant that it has the power to order his reinstatement or re-engagement and will ask whether or not the claimant would want such a remedy. Should a tribunal fail to do this, it will not render a decision as to compensation a nullity, but if, as a result, unfairness or injustice is caused, then the case should be sent back to an employment tribunal.[149]

---

149. *Cowley v Manson Timber Ltd* [1995] ICR 367 (CA).

Reinstatement and re-engagement

The ERA 1996 provides that a tribunal or court may make an order for reinstatement or an order for re-engagement (collectively referred to as 're-employment orders'). Where the court makes an order for reinstatement, 'the employer shall treat the complainant in all respects as if he had not been dismissed'.[150] In other words, the claimant should be given his old job back on the same terms and conditions as before. He will be entitled to any benefits that he should have received whilst he was dismissed—notably, back pay.[151] The tribunal will specify a date on which the reinstatement is to occur.

But a tribunal will be unlikely to order reinstatement where the claimant does not wish to be reinstated, where it would be unjust to order reinstatement (for example, because the claimant contributed in some way to his dismissal), or where it is not practicable for the employer to reinstate the claimant.[152] If the tribunal considers that reinstatement is not appropriate, it should consider making an order for re-engagement (re-engagement should not be considered until reinstatement is ruled out).[153] Where an order for re-engagement is made, the employee will not get his old job back, but must be given 'employment comparable to that from which he was dismissed or other suitable employment'.[154] As with reinstatement, the claimant is entitled to any benefits that he would have received whilst he was dismissed.[155]

In practice, orders for reinstatement and re-engagement are not made very often for the same reasons that discourage the courts from enforcing the contract in wrongful dismissal cases—namely, that the relationship of mutual trust and confidence will usually have broken down to such an extent that forcing the two parties to work together would be inappropriate.

As noted in Chapter 23, a recurring problem faced by tribunals is the inability to enforce its decisions. If an employer refuses to re-employ the claimant or does not fully comply with a re-employment order, the tribunal cannot hold the employer in contempt of court or impose a fine. All that the tribunal can do is, upon an application from the claimant, increase the compensation ordered via an 'additional award', which will amount to between twenty-six and fifty-two weeks' gross pay.[156]

Compensation

Compensation awards for unfair dismissal consist of two parts:

1. the basic award, which aims to reward service (and discourage unfair dismissals); and

2. the compensatory award, which aims to compensate the claimant's actual loss.

---

150. ERA 1996, s 114(1).
151. Ibid, s 114(2)(a).
152. Ibid, s 116(1).
153. *Pirelli General Cable Works Ltd v Murray* [1979] IRLR 190 (EAT).
154. ERA 1996, s 115(1).
155. Ibid, s 115(2)(d).
156. Ibid, s 117(3). At the time of writing, a week's gross pay is limited to £350.

The basic award is calculated via a set formula, and is heavily dependent upon the length of the employee's service and his age. The basic award is calculated by multiplying the employee's weekly pay by the number of years' continuous service.

Three points should be noted, as follows.

1. The weekly pay is subject to a maximum limit and this is usually increased every February. At the time of writing, the maximum is £350.[157]

2. This weekly pay is multiplied by the number of years' continuous service accrued at the effective date of termination. This, too, is subject to a maximum limit—namely, twenty years.[158] Where an employee has over twenty years' continuous service, only those twenty years preceding the effective date of termination will count.

3. Older employees receive more basic compensation than younger employees, based on the following formula:[159]

   (a) for each year served during which the employee was under the age of 22, he shall receive half a week's pay;

   (b) for each year served during which the employee was aged 22 or over, but under the age of 41, he shall receive one week's pay;

   (c) for each year served during which the employee was aged 41 or over, he shall receive one-and-a-half weeks' pay.

For each age range, the following formula should be used:

Weekly wage × number of years continuous service × week's pay = basic award

The following examples demonstrate how the basic award is calculated.

Eg **Calculating the basic award**

Arthur

Arthur is unfairly dismissed at the age of 64, after working for his employer for thirty-five years. At the time of dismissal, he earned £550 per week. Arthur can claim for a maximum of twenty years, ending on the date of termination. He will therefore claim for the twenty years during which he was aged between 44 and 64. Because he was over the age of 41 during this period, he will receive one-and-a-half weeks' pay for each of the twenty years. Because he earns over the maximum weekly limit, the week's pay will be limited to £350 per week. Accordingly:

£350 (weekly wage) × 20 (number of year's service) × 1.5 (one-and-a-half weeks' pay)
= £10,500

Therefore, Arthur's basic award of compensation is £10,500.

---

157. Employment Rights (Increase of Limits) Order 2008, SI 2008/3055, Sch 1.
158. ERA 1996, s 119(3).
159. Ibid, s 119(2).

Gwen

Gwen is unfairly dismissed at the age of 43, after working for her employer for fifteen years. Her weekly wage is £300. Of these fifteen years, two were served after the age of 41, and the remaining thirteen were served over the age of 22. Accordingly:

£300 (weekly wage) × 2 (number of years served whilst over the age of 41)
× 1.5 (one-and-a-half weeks' pay) = £900

plus

£300 (weekly wage) × 13 (number of years served whilst over the age of 22
but under that age of 41) = £3,900
= £4,800

Therefore, Gwen's basic award of compensation is £4,800.

Whilst the basic award is subject to a maximum (currently £10,500),[160] it is generally not subject to a minimum amount. In certain situations (for example, where the employee is dismissed due to trade union, or health and safety activity), however, a minimum award is applicable.[161] At the time of writing, this minimum is £4,700.

In several cases, a tribunal has the power to reduce the basic award:[162]

- where the employer has offered to reinstate the employee and the employee has unreasonably refused the offer;
- where the tribunal considers that any conduct of the claimant before the dismissal was such that it would be just and equitable to reduce, or to reduce further, the amount of the basic award;
- where the employee has already received a redundancy payment, this must be deducted from the basic award.

The rules regarding mitigation of loss do not apply to the basic award (as opposed to the compensatory award, to which the rules relating to mitigation of loss do apply).

Whereas the basic award compensates the claimant for his years of service, the compensatory award aims to provide the claimant with an amount that is 'just and equitable in all the circumstances having regard to the loss sustained by the complainant in consequence of the dismissal'.[163] Currently, the maximum compensatory award that can be awarded is £66,200.[164]

The compensatory award is in addition to the basic award and, unlike the basic award, is not calculated by a fixed formula, but is an amount that is 'just and equitable'. Accordingly, a tribunal has considerable discretion, but, to avoid this discretion becoming overly vague, a number of heads of damage have been established

---

160. This figure is based on a person claiming the maximum weekly pay for the maximum number of years at one-and-a-half weeks' pay (as Arthur in the above example did).
161. ERA 1996, s 120.
162. Ibid, s 122.
163. Ibid, s 123(1).
164. Employment Rights (Increase of Limits) Order 2008, SI 2008/3055, Sch 1. The ERA 1996, s 124(1A), does provide that, in certain cases, this maximum will not apply (e.g. health and safety cases).

and tribunals should set out in their judgments the amount of compensation under each head.[165]

The principal heads of damage are as follows.

- *Immediate loss of earnings*   This would be the loss of pay that the employee has sustained from the date of dismissal up to the date of the hearing.

- *Manner of dismissal*   This would relate to the loss that the employee could sustain in the future due to being dismissed (for example, if the dismissal will make it more difficult for him to obtain employment). If the dismissal does not make the employee less likely to obtain work, no compensation should be awarded under this head.

- *Future loss of earnings*   The aim of this head of damage is to compensate the claimant for the period following the hearing during which he is likely to remain unemployed. The burden of proof in establishing this will be placed on the claimant. If the employee has already gained employment, no compensation should be awarded under this head, unless the salary being paid is less than that paid under the original employment. In that case, the tribunal should determine how long it will take to reach the salary that would have been paid had the employee not been dismissed.

- *Loss of rights*   Certain statutory rights (such as the right to claim unfair dismissal or the right to redundancy pay) are based on a minimum period of continuous service. Unfair dismissal breaks the period of continuous service and affects the availability of these rights. The claimant should be compensated for any rights lost due to the dismissal.

- *Loss of pension rights*   The claimant should be compensated for any loss caused to his pension entitlements due to the dismissal. Such losses can be significant, especially if the employee cannot transfer his existing pension rights to a new employer.

- *Loss of other benefits*   In addition to loss of earnings, the claimant is entitled to be compensated for the loss of any benefit that he would have expected to obtain but for the dismissal[166] (for example, company car, health insurance, etc.).

The claimant should take reasonable steps to mitigate the above losses and failure to do so may result in the compensatory award being reduced.[167] It follows that any reasonable expenses incurred in mitigating the loss (for example, travel expenses incurred in attending interviews) can also be recovered.

Key points summary

- Employees have the right not to be unfairly dismissed, provided that they have at least one year's continuous service. Where a dismissal is automatically unfair, this requirement does not apply.

- Unlike wrongful dismissal, unfair dismissal is not dependent upon the employment contract being breached.

---

165. *Norton Tool Co Ltd v Tewson* [1973] 1 WLR 45 (NIRC).   166. ERA 1996, s 123(2)(b).
167. Ibid, s 123(4).

- The employer must provide a reason for the dismissal. Failure to do so will make the dismissal unfair. The employer must then establish that the dismissal was for one of six prima facie fair reasons. If the dismissal was not for one of these reasons, it will be unfair.

- A prima facie fair dismissal can still be unfair if the decision to dismiss was not within the band of reasonable responses, or if the relevant statutory procedures were not followed.

- A tribunal may also order that the dismissed employee be reinstated to his old job or re-engaged to a similar job. The courts can order an additional award if an employer fails to comply with an order requiring the employee to be reinstated or re-engaged.

- The principal remedy for unfair dismissal is an award of compensation, which consists of a basic award that is based on length of service, and a compensatory award that is based on the employee's actual loss.

Redundancy

As noted previously, it may be the case that making an employee redundant constitutes unfair dismissal. Here, the focus is on the redundant employee's entitlement to receive redundancy pay. The entitlement to redundancy pay was first introduced by the Redundancy Payments Act 1965 and can now be found in the ERA 1996, s 135. The majority of redundancies are negotiated in advance, following consultation with trade unions and employees. In such cases, little dispute arises, and this is evidenced by the available statistics. In 2008, around 653,000 people were made redundant,[168] yet employment tribunals heard only 7,313 claims involving redundancy pay and an additional 4,480 claims in relation to the failure to consult.[169] Just like the right not to be unfairly dismissed, the right to receive redundancy pay is conditional upon eligibility requirements being satisfied.

Eligibility

A person wishing to claim redundancy pay must meet two eligibility requirements. The first requirement is that the employee has at least two years' continuous service ending with the relevant date.[170] The second requirement is that the employee was dismissed. The following will constitute dismissal for the purposes of claiming redundancy pay:

- where the employer terminates the employment, with or without notice, this qualifies as a dismissal;[171]

---

168. See Labour Force Survey Redundancy Tables, available online at <http://www.statistics.gov.uk>.
169. Tribunals Service, *Employment Tribunal and EAT Statistics (GB) 1 April 2007 to 31 March 2008* (Tribunals Service, London, 2008) Table 1, available online at <http://www.employmenttribunals.gov.uk>.
170. ERA 1995, s 155.
171. Ibid, s 136(1)(a).

- where a fixed-term employment contract expires and is not renewed, the employee is regarded as dismissed;[172]
- where an employee resigns due to the conduct of the employer, this constitutes constructive dismissal;[173]
- where an act of the employer or an event occurring to the employer causes the contract to be terminated by the operation of law (for example, frustration), the employee is regarded as dismissed.[174]

What constitutes redundancy?

Redundancy pay is only payable to persons dismissed 'by reason of redundancy'.[175] Accordingly, it is fundamental that employers are aware of what constitutes redundancy. The ERA 1996, s 139(1), provides that redundancy occurs where the dismissal is wholly or mainly attributable to:

- the fact that the employer has ceased, or intends to cease:
    (i) to carry on the business for the purposes of which the employee was employed by him; or
    (ii) to carry on that business in the place where the employee was so employed; or
- the fact that the requirements of the business for the following have ceased or diminished, or are expected to cease or diminish:
    (i) for employees to carry out work of that particular kind; or
    (ii) for employees to carry out work of a particular kind in the place where the employer employed the employee.

This definition indicates that a dismissal will amount to redundancy in three situations, which will now be examined.

Cessation of the business

Where the employer completely ceases the business in which the employees are employed, the resulting dismissals will constitute redundancies. Where the business is taken over by another, however, its employment contracts will also be taken on by the new owner, and there will be no dismissals and no redundancies.

The rules relating to employment contracts upon the transfer of a business are discussed at p 815

Cessation of the business at a particular location

Very often, businesses will operate in numerous locations. Where an employer ceases business in one location, any resulting dismissals will constitute redundancies even though the employer continues business elsewhere. In many cases, there will be no dispute, but where the employee's contract of employment contains a mobility clause, this issue is more complex.

A mobility clause is a term of the contract that can requires the employee to work at a different location from that at which he normally works. Where such employees work in several different locations, and one of these locations is closed down and the

---

172. Ibid, s 136(1)(b).   173. Ibid, s 136(1)(c).
174. Ibid, s 136(5).   175. Ibid, s 135.

employee is dismissed for refusing to move to another location, does the dismissal constitute a redundancy?

The courts used to take a strict approach to answering this question, as the following case demonstrates.

Rank Xerox Ltd v Churchill [1988] IRLR 280 (EAT)

FACTS: The defendant employed the six claimants in its London headquarters. The claimants' contracts of employment provided that they would be based in London, but added that they might be required to transfer to another location. The defendant decided to move its headquarters to Marlow, but the claimants refused to move. They left the employment and claimed redundancy.

HELD: The EAT held that the phrase 'the place where the employee was so employed' referred not to the actual place of work, but to where they could be required to work under their contract. Accordingly, the claimant's place of work still existed, meaning that they had not been made redundant. They had resigned.

In *Rank Xerox*, the EAT focused on the contract of employment to determine 'the place where the employee was so employed'. But recent cases have moved away from a contractual test and held that a geographical test is more appropriate.

Bass Leisure Ltd v Thomas [1994] IRLR 104 (EAT)[176]

FACTS: The claimant was employed by the defendant at a depot in Coventry, which was about 10 minutes' drive from her home. Her employment contract provided that she could be transferred to a suitable alternative place of work. The defendant closed the Coventry depot and the claimant was offered employment at another depot around 20 miles away. She refused to move, terminated her employment, and claimed redundancy pay.

HELD: The EAT held that she had been made redundant. The place of work could not be extended to anywhere she might be contractually required to work; instead, the place of work should be determined geographically by asking where the claimant actually works. Based on this test, she worked in the Coventry depot, and, because it had closed, her dismissal was due to the closure and so had been made redundant.

★ On how this case affects mobility clauses, see A Williamson, '*High Table v Horst*: Are Mobility Clauses Redundant?' (1998) 142 SJ 394

Diminution in the need for labour

The demand for a business' products or services may lessen to such an extent that the employer does not need, or cannot afford, to employ the current number of employees. Alternatively, certain employees may not be required for other reasons (for example, where certain processes become automated). Where employees are no longer required to carry out 'work of that particular kind', are such employees

---

176. Affirmed by *High Table Ltd v Horst* [1998] ICR 409 (CA).

made redundant or not? The question revolves around defining what 'work of that particular kind' means.

Initially, two tests were developed, as follows.

1. *The 'functional' test* This test focused on the work that the employee actually did and asked whether or not this type of work was still required. If it were not, the employee's dismissal would constitute redundancy.

2. *The 'contract' test* This test focused not on the work that the employee actually did, but on what work the employee could be required to do under the contract. Only where this contractual work was no longer required could the dismissal be said to amount to redundancy.

For a time, the contract test was the more favoured, but, in the following case, the EAT held that both tests were incorrect and a new, three-stage, 'statutory' test was introduced.

 Safeway Stores plc v Burrell **[1997] ICR 523 (EAT)**

FACTS: The defendant employed the claimant as the manager of a petrol station. The defendant reorganized the management structure. Under the new structure, the post of petrol station manager would disappear and be replaced by petrol station controller. This new post paid around £2,000 less than the post of manager. Accordingly, the claimant refused to apply for the post and terminated his employment. The claimant accepted the redundancy pay that he was offered, but subsequently alleged that he had not been made redundant and had been unfairly dismissed. The lay members of an industrial tribunal applied the function test and held that there was no redundancy, whereas the chairman applied the contract test and argued that the claimant had been made redundant. The defendant appealed.

HELD: The EAT held that both the functional test and the contract test were flawed. The correct approach was to adopt a three-stage 'statutory' test, as follows.

1. Was the employee dismissed?

2. If so, had the requirements of the employers' business for employees to carry out work of a particular kind ceased or diminished, or were they expected to cease or diminish?

3. If so, was the dismissal of the employee caused wholly or mainly by the cessation or diminution?

Because the industrial tribunal had applied the wrong test, the appeal was allowed, and the EAT held that a fresh industrial tribunal should hear the case and determine whether or not the dismissal was due to redundancy.

COMMENT: The House of Lords[177] has approved the three-stage statutory test established by the EAT in *Safeway Stores* and it must therefore be regarded as the correct test.

★ See C Barnard, 'Redundant Approaches to Redundancy' [2000] 59 CLJ 36

---

177. *Murray v Foyle Meats Ltd* [2000] 1 AC 51 (HL).

Redundancy selection procedures and consultation

The EAT has established[178] a number of principles that employers should follow when making redundancies. These were already discussed when we examined those instances in which a redundancy can constitute an unfair dismissal. Here, the procedure relating to consultation will be discussed in slightly more detail.

Where redundancies are to be made, the employer should consult the trade union as to the best means by which the desired management result can be achieved fairly and will seek to agree the criteria to be applied in selecting the employees to be made redundant. Statute has gone further and provided that, where an employer is to make redundant twenty or more employees within a period of ninety days or less, the employer is under a statutory duty to consult with the appropriate trade union representatives.[179] This consultation must take place at least thirty days before any redundancies are made, except where the employer proposes to make a hundred or more redundancies, in which case, this period increases to at least ninety days.[180] In both cases, the employer must notify the Secretary of State of the redundancy proposal and failure to do so constitutes a criminal offence punishable by a maximum fine not exceeding level 5 on the standard scale (currently £5,000).[181] The consultation must include discussions on avoiding the dismissals, reducing the number of dismissals, and mitigating the consequences of those dismissals that do have to be made.[182]

Where the employer or the trade union fails to comply with any of the above requirements, the claimant may make a complaint to an employment tribunal. If the complaint is upheld, the employment tribunal may make a declaration, or it may make a protective award, which requires the employer to pay the clamant remuneration during the protected period. This period begins on either the date on which the first of the redundancies are made or the date on which the award is made, whichever is the earlier.[183] The award will continue for such length as the tribunal thinks just and equitable, up to a maximum of ninety days.

Calculating and recovering redundancy pay

Redundancy pay is calculated in exactly the same way as the basic award of compensation for unfair dismissal,[184] except that there is no discretion to reduce the pay where the employee contributed to the dismissal. An employee who has been made redundant also has no right to compensatory pay (for example, along the lines of the compensatory award to which an unfairly dismissed employee is entitled). For this reason, given the choice, a claim for unfair dismissal can be preferable. An employer should provide the employee with a written statement indicating how the redundancy pay was calculated. An employer who fails to do this commits a criminal offence

⊘ The calculation of the basic award is discussed at p 921

---

178. *Williams v Compair Maxam Ltd* [1982] ICR 156 (EAT) 162 (Browne-Wilkinson J).
179. Trade Union and Labour Relations (Consolidation) Act 1992, s 188(1).
180. Ibid, s 188(1A).
181. Ibid, s 194(1).
182. Ibid, s 188(2).
183. Ibid, s 189(4)(a).
184. ERA 1996, s 162.

punishable by a maximum fine of level 1 on the standard scale (currently £200).[185] If, following this failure, the employee requests a written statement and the employer, without reasonable excuse, fails to provide one, a further offence is committed, punishable by a maximum fine of level 3 on the standard scale (currently £1,000).[186]

One of the principal reasons for making an employee redundant is because the employer lacks the financial means to continue to employ him. It is likely that such an employer also lacks the ability to pay the requisite redundancy pay. Where the employer has refused or failed to pay the requisite redundancy pay, and either the employee has taken all reasonable steps (other than legal proceedings) to recover payment or the employer is insolvent, the employee can apply to the Secretary of State for payment.[187] This payment will come from the National Insurance Fund and the employer will be required to pay the money back to the Secretary of State, who will pay any money received into the Fund.[188]

Loss of the right to redundancy pay

An employee who is entitled to redundancy pay may engage in acts that cause him to lose this entitlement, including the following.

- Where the employee commits an act that entitles his employer to terminate his employment contract without notice, he loses the right to redundancy pay, provided that the dismissal is:
    (i) without notice; or
    (ii) with a period of notice that is shorter than would be required but for the conduct; or
    (iii) by giving notice that includes, or is accompanied by, a statement in writing that the employer would, by reason of the employee's conduct, be entitled to terminate the contract without notice.[189]
- Where an employee, upon being made redundant, is offered suitable alternative employment or a renewal of the contract by his employer, and the employee unreasonably refuses, he loses his entitlement to redundancy pay.[190]
- Where an employer has given notice of termination and the employee, having then taken part in strike action during the period of notice, fails to comply with a notice extending the notice period for a number of days equivalent to those lost through strike action, he will lose his entitlement to redundancy pay.[191]

⟨⟩ Key points summary

- Redundancy occurs where an employee is dismissed because:

    - the business ceases;
    - the place of business at which the employee carries on work ceases to exist; or
    - the need for labour diminishes.

---

185. Ibid, s 165(2).   186. Ibid, s 165(4).
187. Ibid, s 166.   188. Ibid, s 167.
189. Ibid, s 140(1).   190. Ibid, s 141(2).
191. Ibid, s 143.

- Employees made redundant are entitled to redundancy pay provided that they have two years' continuous service.

- Prior to making any redundancies, the employer should (and, in some cases, must) consult with the trade union regarding the redundancies. If the employer fails to do this, the redundancy may amount to an unfair dismissal.

- The employer may be required to notify the Secretary of State of the proposed redundancies. Failure to do so will constitute a criminal offence.

- Redundancy pay is calculated in the same way as the basic award of compensation for unfair dismissal. Redundant employees are not entitled to an additional element of compensatory pay.

- The right to receive redundancy pay can be lost if the employee engages in certain conduct.

Chapter conclusion

With the exception of a claim for wrongful dismissal, the rights and obligations relating to the termination of employment derive almost exclusively from statute. In many cases, the obligations are absolute and cannot be avoided or excluded. Breach of these obligations will, in many cases, provide the claimant with the opportunity to obtain compensation from an employment tribunal. It is therefore crucial that any business or employer that is considering terminating a contract of employment has a thorough understanding of the obligations placed upon them and the accompanying rights of the dismissed employee. Failure to do so could cost the employer dear and may even constitute a criminal offence.

Self-test questions

1. Define the following:
   (a) resignation;
   (b) notice;
   (c) limited-term contract;
   (d) constructive dismissal;
   (e) summary dismissal;
   (f) redundancy.

2. Claire is a compensation consultant. She is employed by OmniCorp plc to review the remuneration packages of the directors. The contract of employment provides that the contract will last six months and that she will complete her review within that time. She will be paid £2,000 per month. She completes the review after only two months and hands it to the board of OmniCorp. Because OmniCorp no longer needs Claire's services, it terminates the contract of employment. Advise Claire of her legal position.

3. Explain the distinction between wrongful dismissal and unfair dismissal. When is it preferable to claim for one as opposed to the other?

4. What is the distinction between reinstatement and re-engagement? How does the calculation of redundancy pay differ from the calculation of compensation for unfair dismissal?

5. Food-Mart plc decides to make 150 employees redundant. The management selects the 150 employees and the employees are given six weeks' notice (the contracts of employment entitle them to eight weeks' notice) and are told that they will receive redundancy pay. Has Food-Mart complied with the law and should the employees accept the redundancy pay?

Further reading

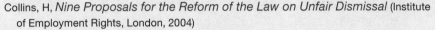

Collins, H, *Nine Proposals for the Reform of the Law on Unfair Dismissal* (Institute of Employment Rights, London, 2004)
Examines the strengths and weaknesses of the law relating to unfair dismissal, and suggests options for reform aimed at increasing the right not to be unfairly dismissed

Department of Trade and Industry, *Redundancy, Consultation and Notification: Guidance* (DTI, London, 2006)
Provides clear guidance on the procedures that an employer should follow when making redundancies, focusing on the statutory consultation and notification procedures

Freer, A, 'The Range of Reasonable Responses Test: From Guidelines to Statute' (1997) 27 ILJ 335
Discusses the 'reasonable responses' test used to determine whether a dismissal was fair and contends that the test heavily favours employers

Honeyball, S, *Honeyball & Bowers' Textbook on Employment Law* (10th edn, OUP, Oxford, 2008) ch 9
Analyses in depth the law relating to statutory redundancy payments and the accompanying procedures

Morris, G, 'The Employment Act 2002 and the Crisis of Individual Employment Rights' (2002) 31 ILJ 245
Discusses the reforms and procedures introduced by the Employment Act 2002, and argues that the Act downgrades the importance of procedural fairness

Smith, I, and Thomas, G, *Smith & Wood's Employment Law* (9th edn, OUP, Oxford, 2008) chs 8 and 9
Provides a detailed account of the law relating to the termination of employment and unfair dismissal

Websites

<http://www.acas.org.uk>
The official website of the Advisory, Conciliation and Arbitration Service; provides access to numerous useful reports and research publications

Remember to visit the **Online Resource Centre** at <http://www.oxfordtextbooks.co.uk/roach> to access the following resources on Chapter 26, 'The termination of employment': more **practice questions** and answers; a **glossary** of key terms; **multiple-choice questions**; **revision summaries**; **audio updates** when relevant; and **diagrams** in pdf.

PART VI

elements of
commercial law

27

The law of agency

- What is 'agency'?
- The creation of agency and the agent's authority
- Contracts effected through agency

- The duties of an agent
- The rights of an agent
- The termination of agency

INTRODUCTION

In various chapters throughout this text, reference has been made to the concept of 'agency' and to persons known as 'agents'. The words 'agency' and 'agent' are common words, but have a very specific and important meaning at law. At its most basic level, agency is a mechanism that helps to facilitate the process of contracting and, given the number of contracts entered into by businesses, it has become a fundamental component of commercial dealing. Without agency, those who run and manage businesses would be required to enter personally into contracts with each and every person with whom they had dealings. The inefficiency in terms of time and cost is obvious. Agency allows those who run businesses to authorize others to enter into contracts on their behalf, thereby greatly facilitating the contractual process, which, in turn, reduces costs and time spent in contractual negotiations. Directors can enter into contracts on behalf of their companies. Partners can enter into contracts on behalf of their firms. Accordingly, the UK's business landscape can only continue to function due to the law of agency. Therefore, our first step in examining this fundamental topic is to define exactly what 'agency' is.

What is 'agency'?

At law, agency is a specific form of legal relationship between two persons (who may be natural or legal—that is, companies and limited liability partnerships) whereby one person (known as the 'principal') appoints[1] another person (known as the 'agent') to act on his behalf. In most cases, this will involve negotiating and entering into contracts with third parties on behalf of the principal. Accordingly, the agent

---

1. Although, as we shall see, one type of agency—namely, agency by necessity—can arise without the need for appointment.

has the ability to affect the legal position of the principal and contractually bind him to a third party. Once the agent's task is complete, he usually 'drops out' of the transaction, leaving a binding contract between the principal and a third party. Therefore, a typical agency transaction usually involves three persons:

- the principal;
- the agent; and
- a third party.

The classic everyday example of an agency situation is that of an auction.

Eg **The auctioneer as an agent**

Jeremy (the principal) wishes to sell an antique oak cabinet. He decides to sell it at auction and instructs the auctioneer, Richard (the agent), to sell it for him, but not to sell it for less than £1,000. The highest bid is made by Ceri (the third party) and is for £1,300. The hammer falls and the sale is made. Richard, having obtained his commission from the sale, then drops out, leaving a valid and binding contract between Jeremy and Ceri.

Central to the concept of agency is the agent's authority. The various types of authority are discussed later. The point that should be noted here is that it is normal for the agent's authority to bind the principal to be limited in some way (in the example above, Richard's authority was limited by the imposition of a reserve price). Generally, the agent only has the ability to bind his principal where he acts within his authority. Where the agent acts outside his authority, the principal may not be bound and the agent may instead be contractually liable to the third party for breach of warranty of authority. Accordingly, had Richard sold the oak cabinet for less than £1,000, Jeremy might not have been bound to Ceri, but Richard could be liable to Ceri for breach of warranty of authority.

⊘ Breach of warranty of authority is discussed at p 951

Commercial agents

The law of agency has traditionally been regulated by the common law, which does not distinguish between different forms of agent. But due to a perceived fear that self-employed agents were vulnerable to exploitation by their principals, the Council passed the Commercial Agents Directive,[2] which was implemented by the Commercial Agents (Council Directive) Regulations 1993.[3] These Regulations provide additional rights to 'commercial agents', who are defined as:

> a self-employed intermediary who has continuing authority to negotiate the sale or purchase of goods on behalf of another person (the 'principal'), or to negotiate and conclude the sale or purchase of goods on behalf of and in the name of that principal[4]

---

2. Council Directive No 86/653/EC.   3. SI 1993/3053.
4. Ibid, reg 2(1).

This definition restricts the application of the Regulations in a number of ways, as follows.

- The Regulations apply only to self-employed agents. Therefore, agents who are agents by virtue of their employment will not be classified as commercial agents.
- The use of the phrase 'continuing authority' appears to envisage a long-term relationship. Accordingly, agents engaged for a short period of time, or to perform a single transaction, are unlikely to be classified as commercial agents.
- An agent involved in contracts for the provision of services (for example, insurance) will not be a commercial agent. Only agents involved in contracts for the sale and purchase of goods will qualify.
- The courts have interpreted the phrase 'negotiate and conclude' to mean that an agent who has no power to negotiate on the principal's behalf will not be a commercial agent.[5]

The various rights of commercial agents will be discussed as and when they arise in relation to a normal agency relationship.

The creation of agency and the agent's authority

A relationship of agency can be created in a number of different ways. It can be created by express or implied agreement between principal and agent, but it can also be created without the consent of the parties. Linked closely to the issue of creation of agency is the authority of the agent. Accordingly, both will be discussed together, but first, it is important to understand how the parties' contractual capacity can affect the agency relationship.

Capacity

Before discussing the various methods by which an agency relationship can be created, it is important to discuss whether or not the principal has contractual capacity to appoint an agent, and whether the person purporting to act as an agent has the capacity to do so. Where there is a lack of capacity, a relationship of agency can still arise, but the relationship may not be a contractual one.

Contractual capacity is discussed at p 137

The contractual capacity of companies is discussed at p 615

Capacity of the principal

An agent can be appointed to enter into any transaction for which the principal has capacity.[6] Where the principal has full contractual capacity, the issue is straightforward—but where the principal has no, or limited, capacity, the issue is

---

5. *Parks v Esso Petroleum Co Ltd* [2000] ECC 45 (CA).

6. An exception to this is where the principal is a company, because the Companies Act 2006, s 39(1), provides that 'the validity of an act done by a company shall not be called into question on the ground of lack of capacity'.

slightly more complex. As we saw in Chapter 5, the two principal groups of persons who can lack full capacity are minors and mentally disordered persons.

- A minor can appoint an agent to buy necessaries or make a beneficial contract of employment[7] for him, but a minor cannot enter into trading contracts merely by the interposition of an adult agent.[8]

- A mentally disordered person can appoint an agent to purchase or obtain necessaries, and an agent who incurs expense on behalf of a mentally disordered principal is entitled to reimbursement.

Capacity of the agent

Anyone not suffering from a mental disorder can act as an agent. A minor can act as agent in a transaction into which he would not have capacity to enter on his own behalf. For example, a father could appoint his 17-year-old son to purchase non-necessary goods on his behalf even though the son, being a minor, could not make a binding contract for non-necessary goods on his own behalf. But an agent who lacks full contractual capacity can only be made personally liable on those contracts that he would have had capacity to make on his own behalf[9] and may well not be liable on the contract of agency.

Appointment by express agreement

⚓ The rules relating to contractual formation are discussed in Chapters 5 and 6

A person may be appointed as an agent by express agreement with the principal. This agreement is usually, but not necessarily, a contract and the usual rules for the formation of contracts apply. For example, an agent who acts without payment (known as a 'gratuitous agent') will not be acting under a contract, because the principal has provided no consideration for the agent's actions.[10] The appointment can normally be made informally, even if the agent is to transact contracts that must be made, or evidenced in, writing.[11] All that is necessary is a desire to appoint A as agent and A's consent to act as such. Where an agent is appointed as a commercial agent, he is entitled to receive, on request, a signed, written contract setting out the terms of the agency agreement and any terms subsequently agreed.[12]

The agreement that appoints an agent will usually specify the authority (that is, powers) that the principal bestows on him, but this may be extended based on the relationship between the parties or their conduct.

Express actual authority

The simplest form of authority is express actual authority, whereby the agency agreement expressly delineates the authority of the agent. The extent of an agent's

---

7. *Doyle v White City Stadium* [1935] 1 KB 110 (CA).

8. *G (A) v G (T)* [1970] 2 QB 643 (CA).

9. *Smally v Smally* (1700) 1 Eq Cas Abr 6.

10. *Chaudhry v Prabhakar* [1989] 1 WLR 29 (CA). A contract for gratuitous agency can exist if executed by deed.

11. *Heard v Pilley* (1869) LR 4 Ch 548.

12. Commercial Agents (Council Directive) Regulations 1993, SI 1993/3053, reg 13(1). The principal has a similar right against the agent.

express actual authority is a matter of construction of the agency agreement, but the courts will not require every possible transaction to be expressly provided for in order for express authority to exist.[13] Where express authority is ambiguous and has several meanings, the agent may be deemed to have express authority if he acts on a bona fide interpretation.[14] But where the agent is capable of contacting the principal to clarify the meaning of the ambiguous provision, a failure to do so may very well place the act outside the scope of the agent's express authority.[15]

Implied actual authority

An agent expressly appointed by his principal is likely to have his authority expressly provided for in the agency agreement. The actual authority of the agent can, however, also be implied based on the relationship between the principal and agent, or based on their conduct.

 Hely-Hutchinson v Brayhead Ltd [1968] 1 QB 549 (CA)

FACTS: Richards (the agent) was chairman of the defendant company (the principal) and, although he was not formally appointed as the company's managing director, he acted in this role with the board's acquiescence. Richards, on the defendant company's behalf, agreed to indemnify the claimant (the third party) for any loss in relation to a number of loans made by the claimant to a company called Perdio Ltd. When Perdio Ltd went into liquidation, the claimant sought to obtain the indemnity from the defendant company. The defendant company refused to pay, arguing that Richards had no authority to enter into the indemnity agreement with the claimant.

HELD: The Court of Appeal held that Richards had no express actual authority to enter into the agreement with the claimant. Because the board had acquiesced to his acting as managing director, however, he had implied actual authority to enter into any transaction that this office allowed, including the agreement with the claimant. Lord Denning MR stated that:

> actual authority may be express or implied. It is *express* when it is given by express words, such as when a board of directors pass a resolution which authorises two of their number to sign cheques. It is implied when it is inferred from the conduct of the parties and the circumstances of the case, such as when the board of directors appoint one of their number to be managing director. They thereby impliedly authorise him to do all such things as fall within the usual scope of that office.[16]

⭐ See RS Nock, 'When Is a Director Not a Director?' (1967) 30 MLR 705

In the majority of cases, implied authority will serve to extend the express authority of the agent. Two more specific forms of implied actual authority demonstrate this, as follows.

- *Incidental authority* provides the agent with implied authority to engage in 'all subordinate acts incident to and necessary for the execution of [his express

---

13. *SMC Electronics Ltd v Akhter Computers Ltd* [2001] 1 BCLC 433 (CA).
14. *Ireland v Livingstone* (1872) LR 5 HL 395 (HL).
15. *European Asian Bank AG v Punjab and Sind Bank (No 2)* [1983] 1 WLR 642 (CA) 656 (Goff LJ).
16. *Hely-Hutchinson v Brayhead Ltd* [1968] 1 QB 549 (CA) 583.

actual] authority'.[17] This is a question of fact in every case. For example, an agent granted express authority to sell a house also has incidental authority to enter into and sign a contract of sale.[18] But an agent does not have incidental authority to enter into a contract of sale where he is granted authority to find a purchaser, but not to sell.[19]

- *Usual (or customary) authority* provides the agent with implied authority to do what is usual, given the post to which he is appointed, or based on what is usual in his trade or profession.[20] *Hely-Hutchinson* (discussed above) could be regarded as a case involving usual authority.

An agent's implied authority cannot conflict with his express authority. Accordingly, an agent who normally has implied authority to engage in an act will lack such authority if the agency agreement specifically prohibits the act in question. The principal therefore has the ability to limit or destroy completely an agent's implied authority. As we shall see, however, even where such acts are taken, the principal might still be bound to a third party.

Implied agreement

If the parties have not expressly agreed to become principal and agent, it may be possible to find an implied agreement based on their conduct or relationship. If the parties have so conducted themselves towards one another that it would be reasonable for them to assume that they have consented to act as principal and agent, they are deemed to be principal and agent.[21] For example, the agent of a finance company or of an insurance company may also be held to be the agent of the party seeking finance or insurance if the circumstances warrant an implication that the client agreed to such a relationship.[22] Factors that have been found relevant in determining whether agency has been created by implied agreement are whether one party acts for the other at the other's request and whether commission is payable. The House of Lords has rejected the notion that a spouse who negotiates a loan secured on the matrimonial home is necessarily an implied agent of the lender vis-à-vis his or her spouse.[23]

Where the existence of an agency agreement is implied, it follows that the authority of the agent cannot be express. The authority of the agent will therefore be implied, as discussed above.

Apparent (or ostensible) authority

A person may be estopped from claiming that a relationship of agency does not exist where his words or conduct indicate that such a relationship is apparent. In such a case, there is no agency agreement (express or implied), but the apparent agent will

---

17. *Collen v Gardener* (1856) 21 Beav 540.
18. *Rosenbaum v Belson* [1900] 2 Ch 267 (Ch).
19. *Earner v Sharp* (1874) LR 19 Eq 108.
20. *Bayliffe v Butterworth* (1847) 1 Exch 425.
21. *Ashford Shire Council v Dependable Motors Pty Ltd* [1961] AC 336 (PC).
22. *Newsholme Bros v Road Transport and General Insurance Co Ltd* [1929] 2 KB 356 (CA).
23. *Barclays Bank plc v O'Brien* [1994] 1 AC 180 (HL).

have the authority to bind the apparent principal to third parties who are unaware that the agent lacks actual authority.

The requirements for apparent authority were laid down by Slade J (as he then was), who stated that:

> apparent authority which negatives the existence of actual authority is merely a form of estoppel, indeed, it has been termed agency by estoppel, and you cannot call in aid an estoppel unless you have three ingredients: (i) a representation, (ii) a reliance on the representation, and (iii) an alteration of your position resulting from such reliance.[24]

Apparent authority can become extremely important where a principal has restricted (or terminated) the actual authority of his validly appointed agent, or where the apparent agent has never been appointed an agent at all (in which case, there can be no actual authority). As between principal and agent, a restriction (or termination) is binding, and an agent will be liable to his principal should he ignore it—but third parties who are entitled to rely on apparent authority are not bound by any restriction or termination of which they are unaware.

A representation

The first requirement is that the principal has represented to the third party that the agent has authority to engage in the act in question. Traditionally, the representation had to be one of fact, but following the *Kleinwort Benson*[25] decision, which, as we saw in Chapter 8, eventually led to mistakes and misrepresentations of law being recognized, this limitation might require reconsideration. The principal must make the representation; it cannot come from the agent.[26] To allow otherwise would permit the agent to self-authorize or to 'pull himself up by his own shoe laces'.[27] The representation has to indicate to the third party that the agent is authorized to act on the principal's behalf. This can be through words, but it will usually occur through conduct, such as placing the purported agent in a particular position.

The following case—the facts of which are easily confused with those of *Hely-Hutchinson* (discussed above)—demonstrates a representation by conduct.

Freeman & Lockyer v Buckhurst Park (Mangal) Properties Ltd [1964] 2 QB 480 (CA)

FACTS: Two gentlemen, Kapoor (the agent) and Hoon, formed the defendant company (the principal) to purchase a resell a large estate. Both were directors of the defendant company, along with a number of nominees. Kapoor acted as managing director with the board's acquiescence, even though he was not formally appointed to the role. He engaged a firm of architects (the claimant third party) on the defendant company's behalf. The claimant completed the work and claimed payment of its fees from the defendant.

---

24. *Rama Corporation Ltd v Proved Tin and General Investments Ltd* [1952] 2 QB 147 (QB) 149–50.

25. *Kleinwort Benson Ltd v Lincoln CC* [1999] 2 AC 349 (HL).

26. *Attorney General for Ceylon v Silva* [1953] AC 461 (PC).

27. *United Bank of Kuwait v Hammoud* [1988] 1 WLR 1051 (CA) 1066 (Donaldson MR).

The defendant refused to pay, arguing that Kapoor lacked the authority to engage the architects.

HELD: The Court of Appeal held that the defendant company was liable to pay the fees claimed. Diplock LJ (as he then was) stated that:

> The representation which creates "apparent" authority may take a variety of forms of which the commonest is representation by conduct, that is, by permitting the agent to act in some way in the conduct of the principal's business with other persons. By so doing the principal represents to anyone who becomes aware that the agent is so acting that the agent has authority to enter on behalf of the principal into contracts with other persons of the kind which an agent so acting in the conduct of his principal's business has usually "actual" authority to enter into.[28]

Accordingly, the defendant's acquiescence represented to the claimant that Kapoor had the authority to enter into the contract on the defendant's behalf.

⭐ See JL Montrose, 'The Apparent Authority of an Agent of a Company' (1965) 7 Malaya L Rev 253

The similarities between *Hely-Hutchinson* and *Freeman* are indicative of the similarities between implied actual authority and apparent authority. On the relationship between the two, Lord Denning MR stated that:

> apparent authority is the authority of an agent as it *appears* to others. It often coincides with actual authority. Thus, when the board appoints one of their number to be managing director, they invest him not only with implied authority, but also with ostensible authority to do all such things as fall within the usual scope of that office. Other people who see him acting as managing director are entitled to assume that he has the usual authority of a managing director. But sometimes ostensible authority exceeds actual authority.[29]

In the majority of cases involving apparent authority, the principal will make the representation before the contract is entered into. It is possible, however, for apparent authority to arise based on a subsequent representation, as the following case demonstrates.

Spiro v Lintern [1973] 1 WLR 1002 (CA)

FACTS: The husband (the principal and first defendant) wished to sell his house and instructed his wife (the agent and second defendant) to put the house in the hands of a firm of estate agents, but not to sell the property. The estate agents located a buyer (the claimant third party) and the wife entered into a contract of sale. The husband took no steps to indicate that the wife lacked authority to make the contract, even when the claimant visited him. The husband also allowed the claimant to incur related expenses and to commence building work on the house without dispute. Before going abroad, the defendant executed a power of attorney empowering his wife to complete the sale. But she instead transferred the property to another third party (the third defendant). The claimant sought to enforce the contract against the husband via specific performance.

---

28. *Freeman & Lockyer v Buckhurst Park (Mangal) Properties Ltd* [1964] 2 QB 480 (CA) 503, 504.
29. *Hely-Hutchinson v Brayhead Ltd* [1968] 1 QB 549 (CA) 583.

HELD: The Court of Appeal held that the husband's failure to disclose to the claimant that the wife lacked authority amounted to a representation by conduct indicating that she did, in fact, have authority to sell the property. Accordingly, the husband was estopped from denying that his wife lacked authority and the order for specific performance was granted.

Reliance

The second requirement is that the third party relied on the representation. The purpose of this requirement is to establish a link between the representation and the act of the third party. It follows that a third party who did not know of the representation, or who knew, or ought to have known, that the agent lacked actual authority, cannot be said to have relied on it.[30] Where a transaction is clearly not in the commercial interests of the principal, the third party will be put on notice that the agent is unlikely to have the requisite authority. In such a case, it will be 'very difficult for the [third party] to assert with any credibility that he believed the agent did have actual authority. Lack of such a belief would be fatal to a claim'.[31]

Alteration of position

The courts have demonstrated a glaring lack of consistency in relation to this requirement. Although Slade J (as he then was) stated in *Rama Corporation Ltd v Proved Tin and General Investments Ltd*[32] that an alteration of position is required, other cases have held that this, in itself, is not enough and that the third party will also need to show that he suffered a detriment due to his reliance on the representation.[33] Conversely, other cases have stated that an alteration of position is not required and that all that the third party need demonstrate is that the representation caused him to enter the contract.[34]

Usual authority

We have already discussed the concept of 'usual authority' and noted that it is a form of implied actual authority. But one difficult case has indicated that there also exists another form of usual authority that is distinct from any other form of authority and which can exist even where actual or apparent authority does not.

 Watteau v Fenwick **[1893] 1 QB 346 (QB)**

FACTS: The defendant firm of brewers (the principal) appointed a manager (the agent) to run a beerhouse. The liquor licence was taken out in the name of the manager, his name appeared over the door, and he had formerly owned the beerhouse. The defendant prohibited the manager from purchasing goods for the business, except bottled ales and water. In contravention of this, the manager purchased a consignment of cigars and other

---

30. *Overbrooke Estates Ltd v Glencombe Properties Ltd* [1974] 1 WLR 1335 (CA).
31. *Criterion Properties plc v Stratford UK Properties LLC* [2004] UKHL 28, [2004] 1 WLR 1846, [31] (Lord Scott).
32. [1952] 2 QB 147 (QB) 150.
33. For example, *Farquharson Bros & Co v King & Co* [1902] AC 325 (HL).
34. *Arctic Shipping Co Ltd v Mobilia AB (The Tantra)* [1990] 2 Lloyd's Rep 51 (QB).

articles from the claimant (the third party). The claimant believed the manager still to be the owner of the beerhouse. The claimant sought the contract price from the defendant.

HELD: The High Court held that a binding contract had been created between the claimant and the defendant, and so the defendant was liable to pay the contract price, because the manager had the usual authority to do such things that an agent of his type would usually have authority to do.

COMMENT: It is clear that the manager lacked actual authority, because he had been expressly prohibited from purchasing such goods. It is also clear that the manager lacked apparent authority, because the defendant had made no representation to the claimant. The claimant was not even aware that an agency relationship existed. Therefore, how did the court justify the decision? The court's answer was that the manager had usual authority to do such things 'usually confided to an agent of that character'.[35] This would clearly include buying goods for use in the beerhouse.

The existence of usual authority as a distinct form of authority can be doubted. The decision in *Watteau* has been heavily criticized by academics[36] and judges,[37] and has only been followed once.[38] It therefore seems unlikely that it will be followed in the future. It continues to be good law, however, and the possibility of a principal being bound by an agent who lacks both actual and apparent authority remains.

Ratification

Normally, a relationship of agency is created before the agent engages in any acts on behalf of the principal. An agency relationship can, however, be created retrospectively by ratification.

The following example demonstrates the typical way in which agency by ratification can come about.

Eg Agency by ratification

Brian purports to act as Freddie's agent. In fact, Brian is not Freddie's agent and has no authority to act on his behalf. Brian enters into an agreement with John on Freddie's behalf. Normally, Freddie would not be bound, because Brian has no actual authority and, because Freddie has not made a representation indicating that Brian has authority, Brian does not have apparent authority. But if Freddie chooses to do so, he can ratify Brian's act. In such a case, Freddie's ratification will retrospectively grant Brian actual authority to enter into the contract with John.[39] The contract will therefore be binding on Freddie if he ratifies what Brian has done.

---

35. *Watteau v Fenwick* [1893] 1 QB 346, 348 (Wills J).
36. For example, GHL Fridman, 'The Demise of *Watteau v Fenwick*: *Sign-O-Lite Ltd v Metropolitan Life Insurance Co*' (1991) 70 Can Bar Rev 329.
37. Bingham J (as he then was) described *Watteau* as 'a somewhat puzzling case' in *Rhodian River Shipping Co SA v Halla Maritime Corp* [1984] 1 Lloyd's Rep 373 (QB) 379.
38. *Kinahan & Co Ltd v Parry* [1910] 2 KB 389 (QB). But on appeal, the Court of Appeal held that there was no evidence of an agency relationship ([1911] 1 KB 459).
39. *Bolton Partners v Lambert* (1889) 41 Ch D 295 (CA).

The idea that an agent is granted retrospective authority is, of course, a 'wholesome and convenient fiction',[40] but it is a fiction that gives effect to the common wishes of the parties involved and is therefore justified. But the ability contractually to bind others without having the requisite authority could, if not monitored closely, have an adverse effect upon the doctrine of privity of contract. Accordingly, agency by ratification is subject to a number of restrictions and conditions, as follows.

Privity of contract is discussed at p 143

- The principal must exist at the time that the agent purported to act as an agent. Ratification will not occur where a purported agent enters into a contract on behalf of a principal who will exist in the future and who will ratify his actions. Thus, where a purported agent enters into a contract on behalf of a company that has not yet been formed, subsequent ratification by the company once incorporated will be ineffective[41] and the purported agent will be personally liable on the pre-incorporation contract, unless personal liability has been excluded by the agreement.[42] The company will need to create a new contract to take the benefit of it.[43]

- The agent must purport to act as an agent for a disclosed principal. Ratification will not occur where an agent has not revealed that he is acting as an agent (that is, he has not disclosed that he has a principal).[44]

- Only the principal can ratify the actions of the purported agent.[45] Where the ratification is by conduct, the principal must be aware of all of the material facts,[46] or intend to ratify irrespective of such facts.[47]

- In order to ratify, the principal must have had contractual capacity to enter into the contract on the date on which the agent entered into the contract[48] and at the time at which ratification takes place.[49]

- The principal must have a choice whether or not to ratify. Where the principal has no choice but to accept the benefit conferred by the acts of the purported agent, this will not constitute ratification. For example, where an agent has had unauthorized repairs done on a ship, merely retaking the ship with these repairs is not ratification by the principal.[50]

- An act that is void in law or an act contrary to statute cannot be ratified.[51]

- Ratification must take place within a reasonable time.[52] What is reasonable is a question of fact in every case, but if the time for performance of a contract has passed, ratification is impossible.[53]

---

40. *Keighley, Maxsted & Co v Durant* [1901] AC 240 (HL) 247 (Lord Macnaghten).
41. *Kelner v Baxter* (1866) LR 2 CP 174.
42. Companies Act 2006, s 51(1).
43. *Howard v Patent Ivory Manufacturing Co* (1888) 38 Ch D 156 (Ch).
44. *Keighley, Maxsted & Co v Durant* [1901] AC 240 (HL) 247.
45. *Wilson v Tumman* (1843) 6 Man & G 236.
46. *The Bonita; The Charlotte* (1861) 1 Lush 252.
47. *Marsh v Joseph* [1897] 1 Ch 213 (CA).
48. *Boston Deep Sea Fishing and Ice Co Ltd v Farnham* [1957] 1 WLR 1051 (Ch).
49. *Grover & Grover Ltd v Mathews* [1910] 2 KB 401 (KB).
50. *Forman & Co Pty Ltd v The Liddesdale* [1900] AC 190 (PC).
51. *Re Tiedemann and Ledermann Frères* [1899] 2 QB 66 (QB).
52. *Re Portuguese Consolidated Copper Mines Ltd, ex p Bosanquet* (1890) 45 Ch D 16 (CA).
53. *Metropolitan Asylums Board of Managers v Kingham & Sons* (1890) 6 TLR 217.

- Ratification will not be permitted where it would defeat the vested property right of a third party,[54] or unfairly prejudice him in some manner.[55]

Method and effect of ratification

The easiest form of ratification is express affirmation of the purported agent's unauthorized acts by the principal.[56] Ratification need not take any special form, except where the agent executed a deed. In such a case, ratification must also be by deed.[57] Ratification can also occur by conduct, but it would appear that passive acceptance or acquiescence may be insufficient.[58]

Where ratification takes place, the ratified act is regarded as authorized at the time the agent performed it and the agent is regarded as having actual authority to perform such an act.[59] But ratification only affects past acts of the agent. It does not provide him with authority to repeat such acts in the future,[60] although repeated ratification may provide the agent with implied or apparent authority to engage in the ratified acts.[61] Since the acts of the agent are retrospectively validated, the agent cannot be liable to a third party for breach of warranty of authority, nor can he be liable to the principal for acting outside the scope of his authority,[62] and he can claim commission and an indemnity.[63]

Agency of necessity

In certain, narrow circumstances, the operation of law can impose an agency relationship where none exists, or extend the authority of an agent. Agency of necessity arises where there is some pressing need for action to safeguard the interests of another. In such a case, the courts might be willing to deem that the person acted as an agent to safeguard the interests of a principal.

The following case provides an example.

China-Pacific SA v Food Corporation of India (The Winson) [1982] AC 939 (HL)

FACTS: The defendant cargo owner chartered a ship to carry a cargo of wheat from the USA to Bombay (now Mumbai). En route, the ship became stranded on a reef. The shipmaster entered into a salvage agreement with the claimant, who was a professional salvor. The claimant managed to salvage 15,429 tonnes of wheat and, to protect the

➡ salvor: a person engaged in the salvaging of a ship, or of items lost at sea

---

54. *Bird v Brown* (1850) 4 Ex 786.
55. *Smith v Henniker-Major* [2002] EWCA Civ 762, [2003] Ch 182.
56. *Soames v Spencer* (1822) 1 Dow & Ry KB 32.
57. *Hunter v Parker* (1840) 7 M & W 322.
58. *Hughes v Hughes* (1971) 221 Estates Gazette 145 (CA).
59. *Bolton Partners v Lambert* (1889) 41 Ch D 295 (CA).
60. *Irvine v Union Bank of Australia* (1877) 2 App Cas 366 (PC).
61. *Midland Bank Ltd v Reckitt* [1933] AC 1 (HL).
62. *Smith v Cologan* (1788) 2 Term Rep 188n.
63. *Hartas v Ribbons* (1889) 2 QBD 254 (CA).

wheat from deterioration, it stored it at its own expense. The claimant then sought to recover the storage expenses from the defendant cargo owner.

HELD: The House of Lords held that the claimant could recover the storage expenses from the defendant cargo owner.

COMMENT: The actual decision was based on the law relating to salvage, **bailment**, and **liens**, so the House did not need to find that the claimant was the defendant's agent. Because the case clearly involved facts in which an agency of necessity could exist, however, Lord Diplock wished to provide some clarification regarding the scope of agency of necessity. He distinguished between:

1. agents of necessity—namely. those who can create contracts between their principals and third parties; and

2. cases in which a party is merely seeking reimbursement for expenses (as in *The Winson*).

Lord Diplock believed that the phrase 'agency of necessity' should be confined to the first type of case.[64] The potential importance of this distinction will become apparent when we discuss the requirements for the creation of agency by necessity.

➡ lien: the right to hold property of another until an obligation is satisfied

★ See FD Rose, 'From Necessary to Restitution' (1982) 45 MLR 568

➡ bailment: the transfer of goods by one party to another, on the understanding that the goods will be returned once the purpose of the transfer is fulfilled

Agency by necessity, like agency by ratification, is closely monitored and strict requirements are in place—namely, that agency by necessity will only arise where:

- the agent has no practical way of communicating with the principal[65] (but given the technological advances in mobile communications, this requirement is now a difficult one to satisfy);
- the action of the agent is reasonably necessary to benefit the principal;[66]
- the agent acts bona fide in the interests of the principal;[67]
- there is, or at that time appears to be, some pressing reason for action, and such action is reasonable and prudent.[68]

Lord Diplock suggested that all of the above requirements would need to be met where there was a genuine agency of necessity (that is, the agent had authority to contractually bind his principal to a third party). But where an agent was merely seeking reimbursement for expenses, he felt that all of the above conditions need not necessarily apply.[69] In such a case, the dispute as to reimbursement could be dealt with by reference to the relationship between the parties (for example, where the parties, as in *The Winson*, were bailor and bailee), or even by resorting to the law of restitution. Lord Diplock's narrow interpretation of what constitutes agency by necessity has been divisive, with some commentators advocating its adoption[70] and

64. *China-Pacific SA v Food Corporation of India (The Winson)* [1982] AC 939 (HL) 958.
65. *Springer v Great Western Rly Co* [1921] 1 KB 257 (CA).
66. *Prager v Blatspiel, Stamp and Heacock Ltd* [1924] 1 KB 566 (KB).
67. Ibid.
68. *F v West Berkshire Health Authority* [1989] 2 All ER 545 (HL).
69. *China-Pacific SA v Food Corporation of India (The Winson)* [1982] AC 939 (HL) 958.
70. FMB Reynolds, *Bowstead & Reynolds on Agency* (18th edn, Sweet & Maxwell, London, 2006) [4.005].

others contending that we should retain a relatively wide conception of agency by necessity.[71]

Key points summary

- Agency can be created:
    - by express or implied agreement;
    - through the agent's apparent authority;
    - where the principal ratifies the purported agent's act; or
    - by necessity.
- In addition, there may be a separate category of usual authority.
- The authority based on the agreement between the principal and agent is called 'actual authority'. In addition, an agent may have 'apparent authority', based on a representation from the principal indicating that the agent has authority to act on the principal's behalf.
- An agent who has acted without sufficient authority, or even any authority, may have his act ratified by the principal. Such ratification only applies to prior acts.
- Agency by necessity may arise where there is some pressing need to safeguard the interests of another.

Contracts effected through agency

The agency relationship gives rise to legal effects between the three parties involved. Where all goes to plan and the agent effects an authorized contract, the key relationship is between principal and third party. But problems can arise and, in certain situations, the agent can become jointly liable alongside his principal to the third party.

This section explores the relationship between the three parties, beginning with the relationship between the principal and the third party.

Relationships between the principal and third party

Where the agent has authority to contract with a third party on behalf of his principal, the resulting contract is known as an 'authorized contract'. An authorized contract is deemed to be between the principal and the third party—the agent drops out of the picture once he has effected the contract. As a general rule, therefore, only the principal and third party can enforce the contract, but as we shall see, there are instances in which the agent can sue and be sued on the contract. It will depend primarily on whether or not the principal is disclosed or undisclosed.

---

71. E Peel, *Treitel on the Law of Contract* (12th edn, Sweet & Maxwell, London, 2007), 2007 771.

The disclosed principal

A disclosed principal is one whose existence, although not necessarily his identity, is known to the third party at the time that the agent makes the contract. In other words, where the third party knows that he is dealing with an agent, the principal will be disclosed.[72] Where the principal is disclosed, a contract is formed between the principal and the third party, on which the principal can sue and be sued.

There are, however, two exceptions to this rule, as follows.

1. Where the agent contracts by deed *inter partes*, the principal will not be a party to it unless it is executed in his name and he is described as being party to it.[73]

2. A principal cannot be made liable for any negotiable instrument that he has not signed.[74]

➡ *inter partes*: 'between the parties'

➡ negotiable instrument: a transferable document that promises to pay the bearer a sum of money at a future date (for example, a cheque)

Because the principal is disclosed, the doctrine of privity will normally prevent the third party from suing the agent or vice versa, but as we shall see, there are several situations in which an agent can enforce the contract against, or is jointly liable with his disclosed principal towards, a third party.

🔗 The liability of an agent to a third party is discussed at p 950

The undisclosed principal

Where the third party does not know the principal exists (that is, he is not aware that he is dealing with an agent), the principal is said to be 'undisclosed'. In such a situation, it would be assumed that no contract would be created between the third party and the undisclosed principal, and that neither party could commence enforcement proceedings against the other, but this is not the case. Where an agent enters into a contract on behalf of an undisclosed principal, a contract is formed between the undisclosed principal and the third party, which both can enforce.[75] Because the third party believed that he was dealing with the agent, allowing the principal to sue and be sued on the contract appears contrary to privity of contract. Because the principal is deemed to be a party to the contract, the Contracts (Rights of Third Parties) Act 1999 cannot apply, so how does the law justify a rule that 'is inconsistent with the elementary doctrines of the law of contract'?[76]

Although several reasons have been advanced, the accepted view appears to be the simplest—namely, that the rule relating to an undisclosed principal constitutes an exception to the privity rule created as a matter of 'commercial convenience'.[77] Given that the rule relating to the undisclosed principal existed before the doctrine of privity was fully established, this seems justified. But because this rule can result in a third party being contractually bound to a principal that he did not know existed, or with which he would not have wished to contract, the rule is subject to a number of conditions and restrictions:

- the principal cannot enforce the contract where it expressly[78] or impliedly[79] prohibits his intervention;

---

72. *Langton v Waite* (1868) LR 6 Eq 165.
73. *Re International Contract Co v Pickering's* (1871) LR 6 Ch App 525.
74. Bills of Exchange Act 1882, s 23.
75. *Montgomerie v United Kingdom Mutual Steamship Association* [1891] 1 QB 370 (QB).
76. Sir F Pollock (1887) 3 LQR 358, 359.
77. *Siu Yin Kwan v Eastern Insurance Co Ltd* [1994] 2 AC 199 (PC) 207.
78. *United Kingdom Mutual Steamship Assurance Association v Nevill* (1887) 19 QBD 110 (CA).
79. *Humble v Hunter* (1848) 12 QB 310.

- the principal cannot enforce the contract where he lacked capacity or, in the case of a body corporate, where it did not exist at the time that the agent contracted;
- the principal cannot enforce the contract if the third party can establish that he wanted to contract personally with the agent (for example, because the agent has a certain skill or reputation);[80]
- the principal cannot enforce the contract where his intervention would materially worsen the legal position of the third party;[81]
- the principal cannot enforce the contract against a third party where the third party has a defence against the agent;[82] and
- the principal cannot enforce the contract where the third party can demonstrate some good reason for not wanting to contract with the undisclosed principal, or where the principal knows that the third party would not wish to deal with him.

The following case provides an example.

 Said v Butt [1920] 3 KB 497 (KB)

FACTS: The claimant (the undisclosed principal) was a theatre critic, who wished to see the first-night performance of a play in a theatre managed by the defendant. But the claimant had previously made serious and unfounded allegations against members of the theatre staff, and so knew that his application for a ticket would be refused. He therefore asked a friend (the agent) to purchase a ticket for him, but not to disclose whom it was for. When the claimant attended the opening night of the play, the defendant refused him admission. The claimant alleged that, in refusing entry, the defendant had maliciously procured the proprietors of the theatre (the third party) to breach their contract with the claimant.

HELD: The High Court held that there was no contract between the claimant and the proprietors of the theatre. The identity of the undisclosed principal was a material factor and a ticket would not have been sold to him had his identity been disclosed.

Where the principal is undisclosed, the result is largely the same as where he is disclosed (that is, a contract exists between himself and the third party, which can usually be enforced by either party). But there is a notable difference—namely, that where the principal is undisclosed, the agent is also personally liable on the contract, and can sue and be sued on it.[83] This is entirely justifiable, because the third party believed that it was the agent that he was contracting with. The third party may elect to sue either the undisclosed principal or the agent.[84]

Relationships between the agent and third party

As discussed above, where the principal is disclosed, the agent is not party to the contract and cannot generally be sued on it. But this is subject to exceptions and there

---

80. *Collins v Associated Greyhounds Racecourses Ltd* [1930] 1 Ch 1 (CA).   81. Ibid.
82. *Isaac Cook & Sons v Eshelby* (1887) 12 App Cas 271 (HL).
83. *Siu Yin Kwan v Eastern Insurance Co Ltd* [1994] 2 AC 199 (PC).
84. *Paterson v Gandasequi* (1812) 15 East 62.

are several instances in which an agent is liable under, and can enforce, a contract either alone or jointly with his disclosed principal, as follows.

- An agent can be liable on a contract where the contract expressly or impliedly indicates this to be the intention of the parties. In some cases, statute will imply such an intention. For example, the Partnership Act 1890, s 5, provides that a partner who contracts on behalf of the partnership is jointly liable on that contract along with the other partners.

  The Partnership Act 1890, s 5, is discussed in more detail at p 574

- Where a contract is executed by deed, an agent will be liable on it, even where the third party knows that the agent is acting as an agent.[85] As discussed above, the principal will not be liable on such a contract unless it was executed in his name and it provides that he shall be a party to it.

- An agent will be liable on a contract where a trade or local custom provides that the agent should be liable.[86] But the courts will not give effect to the custom if it is inconsistent with the contract.

- An agent will be personally liable on a negotiable instrument if he signs his name as a party to the instrument, unless he indicates that he is signing on behalf of a principal.[87] But the principal will not be liable unless he has signed his name as a party to the instrument.[88]

- There may be instances in which an agent is acting for himself and not for his principal, even though he may purport to be acting for an unnamed principal. In such a case, the agent is liable on the contract.[89]

- Where the agent acts for a principal who does not yet exist, the agent is liable if he intended to assume personal liability.[90] Where the non-existent principal is a company that has yet to be incorporated, the agent will be liable on the contract unless he can establish an agreement to the contrary[91] and, as noted, the company cannot ratify the contract on incorporation.

Breach of warranty of authority

In addition to a right to sue on the contract, the third party might also be able to sue the agent for breach of warranty of authority. Such a breach occurs where a person, knowing that he has no actual authority, represents to a third party that he has authority[92] and the third party, in reliance on that representation, sustains a loss.[93] The rule is a strict one and, as the following case demonstrates, an agent will be in breach even where he honestly, but mistakenly, believes that he has authority.

⚖ *Yonge v Toynbee* [1910] 1 KB 215 (CA)

FACTS: The defendant (the principal) had been threatened with legal proceedings alleging that he had slandered and libelled the claimant (the third party). The defendant engaged a

Slander and libel are discussed at p 487

---

85. *Schack v Anthony* (1813) 1 M & S 573.

86. *Barrow & Bros v Dyster, Nalder & Co* (1884) 13 QBD 635 (DC).

87. Bills of Exchange Act 1882, s 26(1).   88. Ibid, s 23.

89. *Bickerton v Burrell* (1816) 5 M & S 383.

90. *Kelner v Baxter* (1886) LR 2 CP 174.   91. Companies Act 2006, s 51(1).

92. Simply acting as an agent will constitute such a representation.

93. *Collen v Wright* (1857) 8 E & B 647.

➡ interlocutory
proceedings:
proceedings that are
incidental to the main
object of the cause of
action

firm of solicitors (the agent) to defend the action. Before the action was commenced, and unknown to the solicitors, the defendant was certified as insane. The action proceeded and the solicitors delivered a defence in interlocutory proceedings. The solicitors and the claimant then discovered that the defendant principal had been certified insane. The claimant applied to have the defence and all subsequent proceedings struck out, and argued that the solicitors should personally pay his costs to date on the ground that they had acted without authority. At first instance, the proceedings were struck out, but costs were not awarded. The claimant appealed.

HELD: The Court of Appeal allowed the appeal and the solicitors were required to pay the claimant's costs. The defendant's certification of insanity had terminated their authority and they had accordingly breached their warranty of authority. The fact that they did not know their authority was terminated was irrelevant.

The harshness of the decision in *Yonge* is mitigated by several factors:

- no breach will lie where the third party knew, or ought to have known, that the agent lacked authority;[94]
- no breach will be committed where the principal ratifies the agent's act;
- the representation must be one of fact, not law[95]—although, given the abolition of the distinction in other areas of contract law (that is, misrepresentation and mistake), it remains to be seen whether this limitation will be upheld in the future.

Where a breach does occur, the third party will be entitled to damages, calculated by reference to the amount required to put the third party in the position in which he would have been had the representation been true.

The following case demonstrates this in practice.

 Simons v Patchett (1857) 7 E & B 568

FACTS: The defendant agent purchased for £6,000 a ship from the claimant (the third party), representing that he had authority to do so from his principal. In fact, the defendant had no such authority and the principal terminated the contract. The claimant resold the ship for £5,500 to another party. The claimant then brought an action against the defendant for breach of warranty of authority.

HELD: The claimant's action succeeded. Had the defendant's representation been true, the claimant would have received £6,000. Accordingly, to put the claimant in this position, the defendant was ordered to pay £500 damages.

Normally, damages are assessed on the date of the breach, but the courts will abandon this rule if they consider it appropriate to do so, as occurred in the following case.

---

94. *Halbot v Lens* [1901] 1 Ch 344 (Ch).   95. *Rashdall v Ford* (1866) LR 2 Eq 750.

Habton Farms v Nimmo **[2003] EWCA Civ 68**

FACTS: The defendant (the agent) was a bloodstock agent (that is, someone who purchases and sells horses on behalf of others). He purchased a horse from the claimant company (the third party) for £70,000, claiming that the purchase was on behalf of a certain racehorse owner named Williamson (the principal). The agent lacked the authority to purchase horses on Williamson's behalf and Williamson refused to accept the horse. The claimant refused to sell the horse to anyone else and continued to press for payment. Around four weeks later, after the delivery date, the horse contracted peritonitis and died. The claimant sued for recovery of the £70,000. The defendant argued that, at the time of his breach of warranty of authority, the horse was still worth £70,000, so the claimant had lost nothing and damages should therefore be nil.

HELD: The Court of Appeal awarded the claimant the full £70,000. Auld LJ stated that '[i]f the contract had proceeded, [the claimant] would have divested himself of the ownership, possession and risk of harm to the horse in return for the price some four weeks before the horse had to be put down'.[96]

COMMENT: In *Habton Farms*, the claimant refused to accept the principal's termination and therefore the normal rule of assessing damages at the date of breach was not appropriate. Conversely, where the claimant accepts the termination (as in *Simons v Patchett*, discussed above), assessing damages at the date of breach is likely to be more appropriate.

> ★ See CA Hopkins, 'Damages for Breach of Warranty of Authority' (2003) 62 CLJ 559

Tort

An agent may also be liable in tort to a third party (for example, for deceit or negligent misstatement), even where the principal is vicariously liable for the tortious act.

 Key points summary

- Where a third party knows that a principal exists (although not necessarily who he is), that principal will be disclosed. An agent who contracts for a disclosed principal is not normally liable on any authorized contract into which he enters on the principal's behalf.

- Where the principal is undisclosed, both the principal and agent are liable on the contract, and the third party may elect which one to sue. The ability of the principal to enforce the contract is limited.

- In a number of situations, an agent can be liable on a contract involving a disclosed principal (for example, where the contract provides for the agent's liability, where the agent acts for himself, etc.).

- An agent who acts outside his authority may be liable to the third party for breach of warranty of authority.

---

96. *Habton Farms v Nimmo* [2003] EWCA Civ 68, [127].

The duties of an agent

An agent will owe a number of duties to his principal. Irrespective of the type of agency, a number of duties are imposed on all agents by virtue of the fiduciary relationship that exists between principal and agent. Where agency is created by express agreement, the agency agreement is likely to contain other duties. But agency can be created through an implied agreement, or even where no agreement is present. Irrespective of how a relationship of agency is created, an agent will be subject to a number of duties imposed upon him by the law. Whilst the duties imposed by the law cannot conflict with the duties contained in an express agreement, they are nevertheless independent of such agreements and will apply even after a contract of agency has been terminated.[97] In the case of a commercial agent, the Commercial Agents (Council Directive) Regulations 1993 impose a number of duties, which cannot be excluded by the parties.

Failure to comply with a contractual duty or the general duties imposed by the law will normally disentitle the agent from any remuneration to which he would otherwise be entitled, and may also render him liable to pay damages for breach of contract (if there is an agency contract) or in tort.

Duty to act

A paid agent is under a duty to do any act required by the contract of agency, other than an act that is illegal or void,[98] and any loss suffered by the principal because of failure to fulfil this duty (either through non-performance or defective performance) is recoverable from the agent by the principal. Thus, where an agent was engaged to insure the principal's ship and he failed to do so, the principal could sue the agent for breach of contract when the uninsured ship was lost.[99]

Where the agent is a commercial agent, he is under a duty to 'make proper efforts to negotiate and, where appropriate, conclude the transactions he is instructed to take care of'.[100]

A gratuitous agent is not subject to the duty to act, but if he chooses to act and does so in a negligent manner, he will be liable in tort.[101]

Duty to perform personally

➡️ *delegatus non potest delegare*: 'delegated powers cannot be further delegated'

Related to the duty to act is the general requirement that the agent must perform the act personally and not delegate it to another. This rule derives from a general rule of administrative law expressed by the maxim *delegatus non potest delegare*. Sub-delegation is permitted, however, where it is expressly authorized by the

---

97. *Kelly v Cooper* [1993] AC 205 (PC).
98. *Cohen v Kittell* (1889) 22 QBD 680 (QB).
99. *Turpin v Bilton* (1843) 5 Man & G 455.
100. Commercial Agents (Council Directive) Regulations 1993, SI 1993/3053, reg 3(2)(a).
101. *Wilkinson v Coverdale* (1793) 1 Esp 74.

principal,[102] where such a power can be implied, where the act required is one of skill that requires the services of another, or where delegation becomes necessary.

Even where an agent is authorized to appoint a subagent to carry out his instructions, it is presumed that the person appointed is merely an agent of the agent. He does not, unless clear evidence indicates otherwise, become an agent of the principal.[103] As a result, the subagent has no claim against the principal for remuneration or indemnity, nor does he owe the principal any duty to act or to obey instructions. Conversely, it seems that a subagent who knew both of the existence and of the identity of the principal could owe the principal a duty of care under the normal principles of negligence,[104] and might owe the principal fiduciary duties.[105]

Duty to obey instructions

The primary obligation imposed on an agent is to act strictly in accordance with the instructions of his principal in so far as they are lawful and reasonable. Where the agent is a commercial agent, he is under a duty to 'comply with reasonable instructions given by his principal'.[106] An agent has no discretion to disobey his principal's instructions, even in what he honestly and reasonably regards to be his principal's best interests.[107] When an agent carries out his instructions, he cannot be liable for loss suffered by the principal because the instructions were at fault.[108] If the principal's instructions are not complied with, the agent will be responsible to his principal for any loss thereby suffered, even if the loss is not occasioned by any fault on his part.[109] If the instructions are ambiguous, however, the agent will not breach this duty if he makes a reasonable, but incorrect, interpretation of them.[110] If the instructions confer a discretion on an agent, he will not be liable for failure to obey them if he exercises that discretion reasonably.[111]

Duty to exercise care and skill

A paid agent is required to display reasonable care in carrying out his instructions and also, where appropriate, such skill as may reasonably be expected from a member of his profession.[112] Should he fail to do so, he will be liable for any consequential loss that his principal suffers. For example, an accountant acting as agent should acquaint himself with such relevant legislation as a competent accountant would do, as well as exercise proper care in pursuing his principal's instructions.

---

102. *De Bussche v Alt* (1878) 8 Ch D 286 (CA).

103. *Calico Printers' Association Ltd v Barclays Bank Ltd* (1931) 145 LT 51 (CA).

104. *Henderson v Merrett Syndicates Ltd* [1995] 2 AC 145 (HL).

105. *Powell and Thomas v Evan Jones & Co* [1905] 1 KB 11 (CA); cf *New Zealand and Australian Land Co v Watson* (1881) 7 QBD 374 (CA).

106. Commercial Agents (Council Directive) Regulations 1993, SI 1993/3053, reg 3(2)(c).

107. *Bertram, Armstrong & Co v Godfray* (1830) 1 Knapp 381 (PC).

108. *Overend, Gurney & Co v Gibb* (1872) LR 5 HL 480.

109. *Lilley v Doubleday* (1881) 7 QBD 510.

110. *Weigall & Co v Runciman & Co* (1916) 85 LJ KB 1187 (CA).

111. *Boden v French* (1851) 10 CB 886.

112. The Supply of Goods and Services Act 1982, s 13, makes the exercise of reasonable care and skill an implied term of all contracts of agency, provided that the agent is acting in the course of a business.

The standard of care that can be expected from a gratuitous agent is similar—namely, to exercise such care and skill as could reasonably be expected in the circumstances.

⊶ *Chaudhry v Prabhakar* [1989] 1 WLR 29 (CA)

FACTS: The claimant (the principal), who had just passed her driving test, asked the defendant (the gratuitous agent), a friend of hers, to locate for her a second-hand car, stipulating that the car should not have been involved in an accident. The defendant was not a mechanic, but was a keen amateur enthusiast. He located a car and recognized that the bonnet had been straightened or repaired, but did not enquire as to whether the car had been involved in an accident. He recommended the car to the claimant, who purchased it. Subsequently, it was discovered that the car had been involved in an accident and was a valueless insurance write-off.

HELD: The Court of Appeal held that, in failing to question the vendor regarding the repaired bonnet, the defendant had failed to fulfil the duty to exercise reasonable care and skill that he owed as a gratuitous agent.

COMMENT: Counsel for the defendant had conceded that the defendant was acting as a gratuitous agent and owed such a duty to the claimant, but May LJ thought that such a concession should not be made in a social context. This implies that a duty will not be owed in all circumstances, but May LJ did not specify when a duty would not be owed. It could be argued that, in such a case, there is no need to establish a relationship of agency and the matter could be dealt with via the law of negligence.

Duty to provide information

Since the agent has the ability to effect contractual relations between his principal and a third party, it is important that the agent provides adequate information to the principal. A commercial agent is also under a duty to 'communicate to his principal all the necessary information available to him'.[113] This duty could even extend to providing the principal with a right to inspect the books and records of his agent.[114]

Fiduciary duties

Unless excluded by the agency agreement,[115] every agent owes fiduciary duties to his principal. This is a consequence of the trust and confidence that should exist between a principal and his agent, and because the agent has the power to affect the principal's legal position. Whereas the other duties are positive duties (that is, they tell an agent what he should do), fiduciary duties are negative (that is, they tell

---

113. Commercial Agents (Council Directive) Regulations 1993, SI 1993/3053, reg 3(2)(b).
114. *Yasuda Fire and Marine Insurance Co of Europe Ltd v Orion Marine Insurance Underwriting Agency Ltd* [1995] QB 174 (QB).
115. The requirement imposed upon commercial agents to look after the interests of their principals and act in good faith (found in the Commercial Agents (Council Directive) Regulations 1993, SI 1993/3053, reg 3(1)) cannot be excluded by the agency agreement.

an agent what he should not do). It is important to note that an agent may breach his fiduciary duties, and be liable for such breach, even where he is acting completely innocently[116]—although, in some cases, an agent may be able to recover commission.

Four fiduciary duties can be identified.

Conflict of interest

Lord Cairns, in *Parker v McKenna*,[117] stated: 'No man can in…acting as an agent, be allowed to put himself into a position in which his interest and his duty will be in conflict.' Where an agent's own interests come into conflict with those of his principal, he must make a full disclosure to the principal of all relevant facts, so that the principal may decide whether to continue with the transaction. It is this rule that prevents an agent, in the absence of disclosure, from selling his own property to the principal,[118] purchasing the principal's property for himself,[119] acting as agent for both parties to a transaction,[120] or receiving commission from a third party.[121]

If the agent is in breach of this duty, the principal may have any resulting transaction set aside, claim any profit accruing to the agent, and refuse to pay commission.[122]

Secret profits and bribes

Where an agent, in the course of the agency, and without his principal's knowledge and consent, makes a profit for himself out of his position or his principal's property, or out of information with which he is entrusted by virtue of his agency, he must account for this profit to the principal.[123] Thus, an agent may not accept commission from both parties to a transaction,[124] nor keep for himself the benefit of a trade discount while charging his principal the full price,[125] without the principal's informed consent. It makes no difference that the agent has acted honestly throughout, nor even that his actions have conferred substantial benefits upon the principal.[126]

Where the secret profit takes the form of a payment from a third party, who is aware that he is dealing with an agent, it is called a 'bribe'—even if the payment is not made with any unmeritorious motive and even if the principal suffers no loss thereby.[127] Accordingly, acts of corporate hospitality could constitute bribes in this sense.

---

116. *Keppel v Wheeler* [1927] 1 KB 577 (CA).

117. (1874) LR 10 Ch 96, 118.

118. *Gillett v Peppercorne* (1840) 3 Beav 78.

119. *McPherson v Watt* (1877) 3 App Cas 254 (HL).

120. *Harrods Ltd v Lemon* [1931] 2 KB 157 (CA).

121. *Hurstanger Ltd v Wilson* [2007] EWCA Civ 299, [2007] 1 WLR 2351.

122. Note that in *Kelly v Cooper* [1993] AC 205 (PC), the court suggested, *obiter*, that an agent who committed an innocent breach of fiduciary duty could recover any commission otherwise payable. Whether this would be sufficient to disentitle a commercial agent to recover commission is uncertain.

123. *Regal (Hastings) Ltd v Gulliver* [1967] 2 AC 134n (HL).

124. *Andrews v Ramsay & Co* [1903] 2 KB 635 (KB).

125. *Hippisley v Knee Bros* [1905] 1 KB 1 (KB).

126. *Boardman v Phipps* [1967] 2 AC 46, [1966] 3 All ER 721 (HL).

127. *Industries and General Mortgage Co Ltd v Lewis* [1949] 2 All ER 573 (KB).

The taking of a bribe entitles the principal to:

- dismiss the agent;[128]
- recover either the amount of the bribe or his actual loss (if greater) from the agent or third party;[129]
- refuse to pay commission;
- repudiate any transaction in respect of which the bribe was given (provided that he can return to any third party any contractual benefits that he has received);[130]
- where an agent has taken a bribe and used the money to good effect so that he has increased its value, the principal is entitled to claim not only the amount of the bribe, but also any increase in its value.[131]

Duty to account

The agent is under a duty to keep his own property separate from that of his principal. Where the agent fails to do this, the principal will be entitled to all of the property, unless the agent can establish which property belongs to him. Related to this duty to account is a requirement that the agent maintains accurate records of his dealings and provides them to the principal upon request.[132] This duty will continue even after the agency has ended.

Duty of confidentiality

The agent is under a duty to keep confidential any information acquired whilst acting as an agent. This duty will continue even after the agency has ended.[133]

Key points summary

- Agents are under a duty to perform personally any acts required by the agency agreement and must obey the lawful instructions of the principal.

- Agents are under a duty to act with care and skill, and must provide their principals with all necessary information.

- Because the agency relationship is a fiduciary one, the agent must not have a personal interest that conflicts with that of his agency, he must account for any secret profits made or bribes received, and he must keep confidential any information acquired whilst acting as an agent.

---

128. *Boston Deep Sea Fishing and Ice Co v Ansell* (1888) 39 Ch D 339 (CA).
129. *Armagas Ltd v Mundogas SA* [1986] AC 717, [1986] 2 All ER 385 (HL).
130. *Shipway v Broadwood* [1899] 1 QB 369 (CA).
131. *AG of Hong Kong v Reid* [1994] 1 AC 324 (PC).
132. *Yasuda Fire and Marine Insurance Co of Europe Ltd v Orion Marine Insurance Underwriting Agency Ltd* [1995] QB 174 (QB).
133. *Bolkiah v KPMG* [1999] 2 WLR 215 (HL).

The rights of an agent

In addition to owing duties to a principal, an agent will also be granted a number of rights in relation to this principal. Compared to the duties owed by an agent, the rights an agent has under the common law are somewhat sparse. But the rights of commercial agents have been bolstered by statute—notably, a duty is imposed upon the principal to act dutifully and in good faith towards his agent.[134]

Payment

In the absence of an express agreement stating otherwise, commercial agents are entitled to be paid for their services.[135] Non-commercial agents have no common law right to be paid, but, in practice, most are. The right to be paid will only arise if there is an express or implied term to that effect, and the normal contractual rules regarding implication of terms will apply. The courts will not imply a term where it would conflict with an express term of the agreement.[136] Where the agent is a professional person, there is a very strong presumption that he will be paid for his services and the courts are likely to imply such a term where no express term provides otherwise.[137]

An agent employed under a contract of agency is entitled to be paid only if he has performed, precisely and completely, the obligations in the agency agreement, unless the contract otherwise provides. Consequently, when an agent does less than he is contractually required to do, he can recover nothing, unless the contract provides for payment for part-performance. The right of an agent to be paid depends upon the type of payment provided for, or implied into, in the agreement, with two types of payment identifiable—namely, remuneration and commission.

Remuneration

Payment by remuneration occurs where the agent is to be paid, irrespective of whether he enters into a transaction on behalf of the principal. Where such a term is express and provides the amount of remuneration, this is what the agent will receive. Where the agreement fails to provide the amount, the agent will be entitled to a reasonable amount.[138] Where no express term as to remuneration exists, the courts will imply such a term only where it was clearly the intention of the parties that the agent be remunerated.[139] Where no contract of agency exists, the agent may be entitled to a *quantum meruit*, provided that the agent has engaged in the acts required by the principal.[140]

➡ *quantum meruit:* 'as much as he has deserved'; a reasonable sum based on services provided

---

134. Commercial Agents (Council Directive) Regulations 1993, SI 1993/3053, reg 4(1).
135. Ibid, reg 6(1).
136. *Kofi Sunkersette Obu v A Strauss & Co Ltd* [1951] AC 243 (PC).
137. *Miller v Beal* (1879) 27 WR 403.
138. *Way v Latilla*]1937] 3 All ER 759 (HL).
139. *Reeve v Reeve* (1858) 1 F & F 280. See also the Supply of Goods and Services Act 1982, s 15.
140. *Howard Houlder & Partners Ltd v Manx Isles Steamship Co Ltd* [1923] 1 KB 110 (KB).

Commission

Payment by commission occurs where the agent is to be paid only if he complies fully and precisely with the requirements of the agency agreement. Failure to comply fully and precisely will entitle the agent to nothing. Further, the agent will only be entitled to commission if he brought about the act in question, unless the contract provides otherwise.[141] No commission need be paid where the act occurs without the agent's involvement. A non-commercial agent will not usually be able to recover commission where he failed to perform the required act due to the hindrance of the principal, nor can he sue the principal unless the agency contract contains a term providing that the principal will not hinder the agent in his efforts to earn commission. Further, if there is no express term to this effect, the courts will be reluctant to imply such a term.[142] A principal who hinders a commercial agent will certainly breach the duty of good faith mentioned earlier. An agent who acts outside his actual authority,[143] breaches his duties,[144] or who enters into a transaction rendered void or illegal by statute normally forfeits the right to commission.

Reimbursement and indemnity

Unless the contract provides otherwise, an agent who has suffered loss (for example, incurred expenses) or incurred liabilities (for example, in tort) in the course of carrying out authorized actions for his principal is entitled to be reimbursed or indemnified by the principal.[145] This entitlement is destroyed where the agent acts outside his actual authority,[146] where the loss or liability is the result of his negligence, default, or breach of duty,[147] or where he engages in a transaction that is rendered void or illegal by statute.[148]

Lien

Where an agent is entitled to payment, reimbursement, or an indemnity, and his principal refuses to pay, reimburse, or indemnify the agent, the agent will have a lien over any goods belonging to the principal that are in the lawful possession of the agent. The agent can then retain possession of the goods until payment or the indemnity is received, but cannot dispose of them. But no right to a lien will arise where it is inconsistent with, or is excluded by, the terms of the agency agreement.[149]

---

141. *Millar, Son & Co v Radford* (1903) 19 TLR 575 (CA).
142. *Luxor (Eastbourne) Ltd v Cooper* [1941] AC 108 (HL).
143. *Mason v Clifton* (1863) F & F 899.
144. *Salomons v Pender* (1865) 3 H & C 639. But the agent may still be entitled to commission where the breach is technical and the agent acted honestly: see *Keppel v Wheeler* [1927] 1 KB 577 (CA).
145. *Hooper v Treffry* (1847) 1 Exch 17.
146. *Barron v Fitzgerald* (1840) 6 Bing NC 201.
147. *Lage v Siemens Bros & Co Ltd* (1932) 42 Ll L Rep 252 (KB).
148. *Capp v Topham* (1805) 6 East 392.
149. *Wolstenholm v Sheffield Union Banking Co* (1886) 54 LT 746.

Information

English law has not formulated an obligation whereby a principal must provide his agent with relevant information, although a term to this effect might well be implied into a contract of agency. If the agent is a commercial agent, then the principal must provide his agent with the necessary documentation relating to the goods concerned and the information necessary for the performance of the agency contract.[150]

 Key points summary

- Commercial agents are entitled to payment for their services, unless the agreement provides otherwise. Conversely, non-commercial agents will only have a right to be paid if one is contained in the agency agreement.

- An agent entitled to payment who has not received payment, reimbursement, or an indemnity due, has the right to retain possession of the principal's goods that are lawfully in his possession until such time as payment is received.

- Unless the agreement provides otherwise, an agent is entitled to be reimbursed or indemnified for any losses or liabilities incurred in the course of carrying out his authorized acts.

- Commercial agents have the right to necessary information in order to be able to perform their functions.

The termination of agency

Like any other contract, a contract of agency may be terminated[151] by performance, agreement, repudiatory breach, or frustration. As we have seen, even where the contract of agency is terminated, the ability of the agent contractually to bind his principal may continue. In addition, there are the following special rules applicable to the termination of agency, some of which relate only to commercial agents.

The grounds of termination of contract are discussed in Chapter 9

Termination by one of the parties

Where both parties desire the agency relationship to end, it can be simply terminated by agreement. But what is the situation where only one party wishes to terminate the relationship?

Because an agency contract is one for personal services, the courts have indicated that they will not compel performance via an order for specific performance.[152] Consequently, either party may terminate the agency agreement at will, although such a termination is likely to amount to breach of contract (for example, where the

---

150. Commercial Agents (Council Directive) Regulations 1993, SI 1993/3053, reg 4(2).

151. Many cases and texts use the word 'determine' instead of the word' terminate'. 'Determine' is being used in its legal sense to mean 'to bring to an end or extinguish'.

152. *Chinnock v Sainsbury* (1860) 30 LJ Ch 409

agency agreement is for a fixed term, or where inadequate notice is given). In some cases, however, termination without notice will not amount to breach. Examples include:

- where an agent accepts a bribe, his contract can be terminated without notice;
- the contract may expressly, or through its construction, allow one of the parties to terminate without notice;[153]
- where the agent acts in a manner inconsistent with the continuation of the agency, his contract can be terminated without notice.[154]

Dissolution

Where the principal is a partnership, limited liability partnership, or company and it is wound up or dissolved, or where a sole proprietor ceases to carry on business, the contract of agency will be terminated.[155] But the ability of the agent to recover damages for breach of contract is a more complex issue. The agent will need to prove that either:

- the principal's action in dissolving the business amounts to breach of an express term; or
- the contract contained an implied term providing that the principal would not deprive the agent of the opportunity to earn his commission.

The courts are extremely reluctant to imply such a term, as the following case demonstrates.

Rhodes v Forwood (1876) LR 1 App Cas 256 (HL)

FACTS: The defendant colliery owner (the principal) appointed the claimant as the sole agent for the sale of the defendant's coal (that is, coal from his colliery) in Liverpool. The agreement provided that it would last for seven years, or as long as the defendant conducted business in Liverpool. After four years, the defendant sold the colliery and the agreement was terminated. The claimant sought damages for the loss of future commission, arguing that there was an implied term that the defendant would send coal to Liverpool to be sold by the claimant.

HELD: The House of Lords rejected the claimant's action. The defendant had not contracted, expressly or impliedly, to keep the claimant supplied with coal and therefore he was not liable for breach of contract.

In the following case, however, the Court of Appeal distinguished *Rhodes* and held the principal liable to pay damages for breach of contract.

---

153. For example, *Atkinson v Cotesworth* (1825) 3 B & C 647.
154. *EP Nelson & Co v Rolfe* [1950] 1 KB 139 (CA).
155. *Pacific and General Insurance Co Ltd v Hazell* [1997] BCC 400 (QB).

Turner v Goldsmith **[1891] 1 QB 544 (CA)**

FACTS: The defendant shirt manufacturer (the principal) expressly agreed to employ a travelling salesman (the agent) for five years. After only two years, the defendant's factory was destroyed by fire and the business was not resumed. The agent commenced legal proceedings for loss of commission.

HELD: The Court of Appeal distinguished *Rhodes* and awarded the claimant 'substantial damages'. In failing to send the claimant a reasonable amount of clothing to sell, the defendant had breached the implied term not to deprive the claimant of the opportunity to earn commission.

COMMENT: On what basis was *Rhodes* distinguished? In *Rhodes*, it was a term of the contract that the claimant would be supplied with coal from the defendant's colliery. Conversely, in *Turner*, there was no term in the contract providing that the defendant would supply the claimant with clothing from the destroyed factory. The defendant in *Turner* might have had other sources with which to supply the claimant. Therefore, whether a term is implied will depend very much on the construction of the contract—but one could question whether or not the distinction is significant enough to sustain such a different approach.

Death

The death of either the principal or agent will terminate the agency relationship, irrespective of whether the surviving party has notice of the other's death.[156] Where the principal dies, the actual authority of the agent (and probably his apparent authority too)[157] ceases, and any transactions entered into by the agent after the principal's death will contractually bind the agent and not the estate of the deceased principal, irrespective of whether the agent knows of the principal's death.[158]

Insanity

The agency relationship will be terminated where either party becomes insane. Where the principal becomes insane, however, the agent continues to have apparent authority and so he can contractually bind the principal to any third parties who were not aware of his insanity.[159]

Bankruptcy

The bankruptcy of the principal terminates the agency relationship.[160] But the bankruptcy of the agent does not terminate the relationship, unless his bankruptcy prevents him acting as an agent, or renders him unfit to perform his duties.[161]

---

156. *Blades v Free* (1829) 9 B & C 167.
158. *Blades v Free* (1829) 9 B & C 167.
160. *Elliott v Turquand* (1881) 7 App Cas 79 (PC).
161. *McCall v Australian Meat Co Ltd* (1870) 19 WR 188.

157. See *Watson v King* (1815) 4 Camp 272.
159. *Drew v Nunn* (1879) 4 QBD 661 (CA).

Effects of termination

The events described above will, in many cases, terminate the agency agreement, but it does not follow that the agent is robbed of his authority, or his ability to bind the principal. Termination of the agreement will terminate the agent's actual authority. This means that agents who have only actual authority can no longer bind their principals. Agents with apparent authority, or authority deriving from an agency of necessity, may, however, be able to continue contractually to bind the principal to a third party. To avoid being bound, the principal needs to inform the third party of the termination of the agency agreement.[162]

An agent is entitled to any commission or indemnity payments due prior to termination.[163] But the agent will lose his entitlement to commission or indemnity post-termination.[164]

Commercial agents

Additional rights are provided to commercial agents in relation to the termination of their agency by the Commercial Agents (Council Directive) Regulations 1993, Pt IV. The rights contained in Pt IV apply to all forms of termination by the principal, and can even apply to termination by the agent in limited circumstances. But the Regulations do not apply where the agent was terminated without notice due to his failure to carry out all, or part, of his obligations, or due to exceptional circumstances[165] (although the Regulations provide no guidance as to what circumstances are regarded as 'exceptional').

Notice periods

Regulation 14 provides that an agency agreement for a fixed period, which continues beyond the expiry of that period, shall be converted into an agency agreement of indefinite duration. The significance of this is found in reg 15, which establishes minimum notice periods for agency agreements of indefinite duration, as follows:

- one month for the first year of the contract;
- two months for the second year of the contract;
- three months where the contract has lasted longer than two years.

Where an agreement of fixed duration is converted into an agreement of indefinite duration by reg 14, the fixed period shall also be taken into account when determining the minimum notice period.[166] Parties cannot agree shorter notice periods than those contained in reg 15, but they can agree longer notice periods, provided that the notice period to be observed by the principal is not shorter than that to be observed by the agent.[167]

---

162. *AMB Generali Holding AG v SEB Trygg Liv Holding Aktiebolag* [2005] EWCA Civ 1237, [2006] 1 WLR 2276.
163. *Chappell v Bray* (1860) 6 H & N 145.
164. *Farrow v Wilson* (1869) LR 4 CP 744.
165. Commercial Agents (Council Directive) Regulations 1993, SI 1993/3053, reg 16.
166. Ibid, reg 15(5).
167. Ibid, reg 15(3).

The minimum notice periods will not apply where immediate termination could occur through frustration or repudiatory breach of the agency agreement.[168]

Compensation and indemnity

Regulations 17 and 18 provide the agent with the right to compensation or an indemnity upon termination of the agency agreement. The usual entitlement will be compensation, unless the agency agreement provides that an indemnity shall be paid instead.[169] The right to compensation or an indemnity cannot be excluded by the agency agreement,[170] but it will be lost in four situations:

1. where the agent does not inform the principal, within one year following the date of termination, that he intends to pursue his entitlement;[171]
2. where the principal has terminated the agency agreement for a reason that would justify immediate termination under reg 16 (that is, due to the agent's failure to carry out all, or part, of his obligations, or due to exceptional circumstances);[172]
3. where the agent himself has terminated the agreement, unless such termination was justified due to circumstances attributable to the principal, or was due to age, infirmity, or illness of the agent;[173]
4. where the agent, with the agreement of the principal, has assigned his rights to another person.[174]

Regulation 17 provides that an agent shall be entitled to compensation or an indemnity for the damage that he suffers as a result of the termination of his relations with his principal. According to normal compensatory principles, where no loss has been suffered, substantial compensation will not be awarded.

Regulation 17(7) provides two particular forms of damages for which reg 17(6) should provide compensation:

- where the termination deprives the agent of commission that he would have obtained had the agency agreement continued; and
- where the termination has deprived the agent with the opportunity to amortize the costs and expenses that he has incurred on the advice of his principal.

> → amortize: reduce or recoup an amount or debt

The Regulations (and the deriving Directive) provide no guidance as to how compensation is to be assessed. The issue has therefore been left to the courts, but for a significant period, the courts could not articulate a consistent approach[175]—until the House of Lords offered guidance in the following case.

---

168. *Crane v Sky-in-Home Service Ltd* [2007] EWHC 66 (Ch), [2007] All ER (Comm) 599.
169. Commercial Agents (Council Directive) Regulations 1993, SI 1993/3053, reg 17(2).
170. Ibid, reg 19.
171. Ibid, reg 17(9).
172. Ibid, reg 18(a).
173. Ibid, reg 18(b).
174. Ibid, reg 18(c).
175. See for example, the different approaches adopted in *Barret McKenzie v Escada (UK) Ltd* [2001] ECC 50 (QB) and *Ingmar GB Ltd v Eaton Leonard Inc* [2001] CLC 1825 (QB).

> ## 🔑 *Lonsdale v Howard & Hallam Ltd* [2007] UKHL 32
>
> **FACTS:** The facts are not directly relevant.
>
> **HELD:** The House of Lords stated that a two-part approach should be adopted. The first part was to ask for what the agent should be compensated. Regulation 17(6) answers this question—namely, the damage suffered as a result of the termination of his relations with the principal.
>
> The second, and more difficult, part is the question of how compensation should be assessed. Lord Hoffmann's answer was to assess compensation based on what a sale of the agency business would fetch on the open market. This would be determined by asking what a hypothetical purchaser would be willing to pay for the agency business at the time of termination, but also taking into account factors in the real world, such as whether the 'market for the product in which the agent dealt was rising or declining'.[176]

★ See S Saintier, 'Final Guidelines on Compensation of Commercial Agents' (2008) 124 LQR 31

An agent will receive an indemnity instead of compensation where the agency contract provides so, and only then if two conditions imposed by reg 17(3) are met:

- the agent has brought the principal new customers or has significantly increased the volume of business with existing customers,[177] and the principal continues to derive substantial benefits from the business with such customers; and
- the payment of this indemnity is equitable, having regard to all of the circumstances and, in particular, the commission lost by the commercial agent on the business transacted with such customers.

Regulation 17(4) limits the amount of the indemnity to a figure equivalent to an indemnity for one year. This one-year figure is calculated by determining the agent's average annual remuneration over the previous five-year period. Where the agent has worked for less than five years, the average shall be calculated based on the period for which he has worked.

Irrevocable agencies

The law provides for a number of irrevocable agencies. Any attempts to terminate such agencies will not only amount to breach of contract, but will also be ineffective and the agent's authority will remain intact.

Examples of irrevocable agencies include:

➡ power of attorney: a deed executed by one person granting authority for another person to represent him or act on his behalf

- where a **power of attorney** is given to secure a proprietary interest of, or the performance of an obligation owed to, the donee (the person who can exercise the power of attorney), then so long as the donee has that interest or the obligation remains undischarged, the power cannot be revoked without the consent of the donee, or by the death, insanity, or bankruptcy of the donor;[178]
- where the agent's authority is granted by deed, or for some other valuable consideration, for the purpose of securing an interest of the agent that is independent

---

176. *Lonsdale v Howard & Hallam Ltd* [2007] UKHL 32, [2007] 1 WLR 2055, [13].

177. The agent need not be the sole cause of the increase in customers or business volume, but he must have played an active role in obtaining the increase: *Moore v Piretta PTA Ltd* [1999] 1 All ER 174 (QB).

178. Power of Attorney Act 1971, s 4.

of the agency[179] (the earning of commission will not suffice, because this interest is not independent of the agency);

- where the agent incurs personal liability through the exercise of his authority for which he must be indemnified by the principal.[180]

 Key points summary

- Unless an agency is irrevocable, it can be terminated by one of the parties at any time, although such termination may amount to a breach of the agency agreement.

- Where the principal is a business, its dissolution will terminate the agency agreement.

- The death or insanity of either party will terminate the agency agreement. The bankruptcy of the principal will terminate the agreement, but the agent's bankruptcy will not, unless it prevents him from acting as an agent or renders him unfit to carry on as agent.

- Termination of the agency agreement will terminate the agent's actual authority, but the agent may continue to have apparent authority.

- Commercial agents have additional rights upon termination—namely, the right to notice, and the right to compensation or an indemnity.

- Certain agencies are irrevocable, and purported termination of such agencies will be invalid and will amount to a breach of contract.

Chapter conclusion

Having discussed what agency is and the relationships that it creates, its importance cannot be underestimated. Large businesses will enter into thousands of contracts every day with customers, suppliers, consumers, employees, accountants, lawyers, manufacturers, and creditors. Only through the use of agents can this contractual volume be met. Without agency, the number of contracts into which businesses could enter would fall drastically. Given its importance, it is therefore of no surprise that agency has become a legal topic in its own right, with agents subject to their own rights and duties, and a complex body of centuries-old case law in place to help to determine how the relationships between the various parties should operate. In recent years, however, statute has intervened and provided extra protection for commercial agents who enter into contracts for the sale of goods.

Self-test questions

1. Define the following terms:
   (a) principal;
   (b) commercial agent;

---

179. *Re Hannan's Empress Gold Mining and Development Company, ex p Carmichael* [1896] 2 Ch 643 (CA).
180. *Chappell v Bray* (1860) 6 H & N 145.

(c) gratuitous agent;

(d) actual authority;

(e) usual authority;

(f) agency of necessity;

(g) disclosed principal;

(h) commission.

2. Explain the various ways in which a relationship of agency can be created.

3. John owns a 1951 Mercedes SL that he wishes to sell. He instructs Ross to sell the car and, in return, Ross will be paid £5,000 commission. Ross manages to find a buyer, Paul, and introduces Paul to John. But John decides not to proceed with the sale. Advise Ross.

4. Explain the distinction between:

(a) implied actual authority and apparent authority;

(b) remuneration and commission;

(c) a disclosed principal and an undisclosed principal;

(d) a secret profit and a bribe.

Further reading

Brown, I, 'The Agent's Apparent Authority: Paradigm or Paradox?' [1995] JBL 360

Discusses the theoretical basis of apparent authority and argues that the theoretical basis of apparent authority stated by the court is not always in line with modern commercial reality

Dowrick, FE, 'The Relationship of Principal and Agent' (1954) 17 MLR 24

A seminal article discussing the distribution of power between, and the liability faced by, principals and their agents

Reynolds, F, *Bowstead & Reynolds on Agency* (18th edn, Sweet & Maxwell, London, 2006)

The leading text on agency and regularly referred to by the courts in agency cases

Sasse, S, and Whittaker, J, 'An Assessment of the Impact of the UK Commercial Agents (Council Directive) Regulations 1993' [1994] 5 ICCLR 100

Discusses the impact of the 1993 Regulations, and argues that they contain a number of uncertain and ambiguous terms

Sealy, LS, and Hooley, RJA, *Commercial Law: Text, Cases and Materials* (4th edn, OUP, Oxford, 2008) chs 3–6

Discusses the law relating to the creation, operation, and termination of agency; provides useful extracts from key cases and articles

 Remember to visit the **Online Resource Centre** at <http://www.oxfordtextbooks.co.uk/roach> to access the following resources on Chapter 27, 'The law of agency': more **practice questions** and answers; a **glossary** of key terms; **multiple-choice questions**; **revision summaries**; **audio updates** when relevant; and audio exam advice on this key topic.

Unfair commercial practices

- Exclusion clauses
- The Unfair Contract Terms Act 1977
- The Unfair Terms in Consumer Contracts Regulations 1999
- The Consumer Protection from Unfair Trading Regulations 2008
- The Business Protection from Misleading Marketing Regulations 2008
- Competition law
- Enforcement orders under the Enterprise Act 2002

INTRODUCTION

We have noted several times in previous chapters that many businesses, when contracting with others, will contract on pre-drafted standard terms designed to facilitate the businesses' aims. In consumer contracts, given the inequality of bargaining power between the consumer and the business, the business, if left unchecked, could impose all manner of onerous or unfair terms on the consumer. Businesses may engage in unfair practices in order to encourage persons to enter into contracts for its goods or services. The latter half of the twentieth century has witnessed an explosion in legislation designed to combat the use of unfair business practices. In some cases, the practice is prohibited and any contracts resulting from it are deemed unenforceable. In other cases, the law goes further and deems such practices to be criminal offences warranting substantial punishments.

In this chapter, we will examine a selection of the principal unfair and criminal commercial and consumer practices, and discuss how the law has attempted to curtail such practices, beginning with one of the most prevalent and potentially unfair practices—namely, the exclusion clause.

Exclusion clauses

As has been noted when we discussed contract law, nineteenth-century classical contract law theory was based on the notion that the parties should be free to determine the terms of their contracts. It was only a matter of time before parties began including terms that altered the nature of contractual liability itself in their favour as against the other party. This was the advent of the exclusion clause (also known as an 'exemption clause'). Exclusion clauses come in numerous different forms, but their basic effect is either to exclude completely liability for a legal wrong (for example, breach of contract, negligence, etc.), or to restrict such liability (for example, by limiting the amount of compensation payable).

Initially, it may seem bizarre to allow a party completely to exclude liability for breaching a term by which it has freely agreed to be bound, but the following example demonstrates the rationale behind upholding the validity of exclusion clauses.

Eg **Exclusion clauses and contractual bargaining**

MoneyCorp, a large bank, has been accused of fraud. Clifford & McKenzie, a large firm of solicitors, has agreed to defend the bank. Clifford & McKenzie wishes to insert a term into the proposed contract excluding its liability completely should it commit any acts of negligence in relation to the case. MoneyCorp will only permit such a term to be included if Clifford & McKenzie agrees to reduce its fee by 10 per cent. Clifford & McKenzie agree and a contract is drawn up.

In this case, both parties have equal bargaining power, and the negotiations are free and mutual. The exclusion clause was 'purchased' for a 10 per cent reduction in the fee charged. The risk of being unable to claim compensation for negligence has been offset by an immediate reduction in the fee. The negotiations have therefore led to a mutually beneficial outcome and an allocation of risk that is acceptable to both parties.

But a significant number of contracts—notably, consumer contracts—demonstrate a stark inequality of bargaining power between the parties. This allows the stronger party to impose its own standard terms on the weaker party, and such terms could contain extremely wide-ranging or potentially unfair exclusion clauses. It therefore became necessary to begin regulating the use of exclusion clauses. Initially, it was the courts that imposed limitations upon the use of exclusion clauses and we shall first focus on these common law limitations. Later, it will become clear that the principal source of regulation can now be found in statute.

The common law limitations fall into two categories:

- limitations relating to incorporation; and
- limitations relating to construction and interpretation.

Incorporation

➡ proferens: the party favoured by an exclusion clause

In order for the proferens to rely on an exclusion clause, he will need to demonstrate that the clause is actually part of the contract. Although the following rules relating to incorporation are discussed in relation to exclusion clauses, they are of general application and can apply to the incorporation of other forms of terms.

The effect of a signature

A person who signs a contract will generally be bound by the terms of that contract, irrespective of whether or not he has actually read them, as the following, somewhat harsh, decision demonstrates.

L'Estrange v Graucob Ltd [1934] 2 KB 394 (KB)

FACTS: The claimant purchased from the defendant a vending machine and placed it in her cafe. She signed, but did not read, an order form, which was written in standard sized print and which also contained 'in regrettably small print'[1] a term excluding liability for breach of any implied terms. The vending machine did not work and the claimant sued for breach of the implied term as to fitness for purpose.

HELD: The High Court rejected her claim. She had signed the contract and was bound by its terms. That she had not read the contract and therefore did not know of the exclusion clause was completely irrelevant.

The rule in *L'Estrange* is not absolute and the courts have mitigated its harshness to an extent by providing for several exceptions. A plea of *non est factum* will, in very limited circumstances, allow a party who has signed a contract containing an exclusion clause to escape the contract. More importantly, a person seeking to rely on an exclusion clause will be unable to do so if he misrepresented to the other person the effect of the exclusion clause.

Non est factum is discussed at p 264

 Curtis v Chemical Cleaning and Dyeing Co Ltd [1951] 1 KB 805 (CA)

FACTS: The claimant took her wedding dress to the defendant's shop to be cleaned. The dress was trimmed with beads and sequins. The claimant was presented with a receipt and asked to sign it. When she inquired why she was required to sign it, the defendant replied that it was required in order to exclude the defendant from liability for damage to the beads and sequins. In fact, the receipt contained a clause excluding liability for any damage howsoever caused. The dress was returned to the claimant, but it was badly stained. The claimant brought an action and the defendant sought to rely on the exclusion clause.

HELD: The Court of Appeal held that the defendant was not protected by the exclusion clause, because it had misrepresented the effect of the clause.

Is the document contractual?

A signature will bind the signatory only if the document signed constitutes a contractual document. Even where a document is not signed, some or all of the terms (including exclusion clauses) printed on it may be incorporated if the document is deemed to be a contractual document.

Determining whether a document is a contract or not is not always straightforward. Where an exclusion clause is located within a written contractual document, there is no difficulty in determining its incorporation. But very often, an exclusion clause will be contained in a separate document, such as a ticket or a receipt, or may be displayed on a sign or other notice. Such documents are unlikely to be signed, so

---

1. *L'Estrange v Graucob Ltd* [1934] 2 KB 394 (KB) 405 (Maugham LJ).

the rule in *L'Estrange* has no application. The approach of the courts is that a document will be regarded as contractual if a reasonable person would assume it to contain contractual terms, as the following case demonstrates.

 Chapelton v Barry UDC [1940] 1 KB 532 (CA)

FACTS: The defendant council hired deckchairs to the public. A notice near the deckchairs stated that members of the public hiring chairs should obtain a ticket from the deckchair attendant and keep it for inspection. The claimant hired two chairs and placed the tickets in his pocket without reading them. The tickets contained a clause excluding any liability for injury arising from the use of the chairs. The claimant's chair was defective and, when he sat on it, it collapsed, injuring him. The defendant sought to rely on the exclusion clause.

HELD: The Court of Appeal held that the exclusion clause was ineffective. The ticket was merely a voucher or receipt and no reasonable person would expect it to amount to more than this.

COMMENT: It is important to remember that the status of a document is highly dependent upon the facts of the case. Although, in *Chapelton*, a receipt was not deemed to constitute a contractual document, this does not mean that any document called a 'receipt' will fail to have contractual force and, based on the facts, terms located on a receipt could become incorporated into the contract.[2]

The requirement of notice

An exclusion clause will not be incorporated into the contract if it was not brought to the party's reasonable notice before or at the time that the contract was entered into (that is, the notice of the clause must be given before or contemporaneously with the contract and it must be reasonable). If the clause is brought to the party's notice after the contract is entered into, it will not become part of the contract.

 Olley v Marlborough Court Ltd [1949] 1 KB 532 (CA)

FACTS: The claimant and her husband arrived at the defendant's hotel, checked in, and paid for a week's stay in advance. They went up to their room, where a notice, displayed on a wall, stated that the defendant was not liable for any items lost or stolen. Due to the negligence of the hotel staff, property belonging to the claimant was stolen from the hotel room. The claimant sued and the defendant sought to rely on the exclusion clause.

HELD: The Court of Appeal held that the exclusion clause was ineffective. The contract was entered into at the checking-in desk. Accordingly, the notice was communicated to the claimant after the contract was entered into.

---

2. *Parker v South Eastern Rly Co* (1877) 2 CPD 416 (CA).

The requirement of prior notice is subject to two exceptions. Firstly, where there has been a consistent course of dealings[3] between the parties on the basis of documents incorporating similar terms excluding liability, then, provided that those dealings have been of a consistent nature, the courts may imply the exclusion clause into a particular contract where express notice is given too late.

🔓 *J Spurling Ltd v Bradshaw* [1956] 1 WLR 461 (CA)

FACTS: The defendant had, for many years, dealt with the claimant warehouseman. The defendant delivered eight barrels of orange juice to the claimant to store, in return for which he received a document acknowledging receipt of the barrels and referring to a number of terms located on the rear of the document, one of which excluded the claimant from any loss or liability caused by its negligence. The defendant did not read these terms. When the defendant came to collect the barrels, they were either empty or damaged to such an extent as to be useless. He refused to pay the storage charges. The claimant sued and the defendant counterclaimed for negligence.

HELD: The Court of Appeal held that the exclusion clause was effective and that therefore the claimant could recover the charges, and the defendant's counterclaim failed. Although the defendant never read the document, he had dealt with the claimant on such terms for many years.

COMMENT: The requirement of a consistent course of dealings means that incorporation through prior dealings is less likely to occur where a private party is involved, because such persons are unlikely to have had sufficient dealings for there to be a course of dealing. For example, in one case, the Court of Appeal held that three or four dealings over a five-year period did not establish a course of dealing.[4]

The second exception is where an exclusion clause is implied through trade usage or local custom. In such cases, prior notice of the clause will not be required and there is no need for parties within the particular trade or locality to have dealt with each other previously; all that matters is that the usage or custom existed when the contract was entered into and that it was used so frequently that the party affected must (as a reasonable person in that trade or locality) have known that it would be included in the contract.[5]

The requirement of notice does not require that the party actually knew of the existence of the clause prior to the contract being formed; all that is required is that the proferens did what was reasonable to bring the exclusion clause to the other party's attention.[6] This will depend upon the facts of the case, but the courts have held that the more onerous or unusual the clause, the higher the degree of notice required from the proferens. In one case, Denning LJ (as he then was) stated: 'Some

---

3. *McCutcheon v David MacBrayne Ltd* [1964] 1 WLR 125 (HL).
4. *Hollier v Rambler Motors (AMC) Ltd* [1972] 2 QB 71 (CA).
5. *British Crane Hire Corporation Ltd v Ipswich Plant Hire Ltd* [1975] QB 303 (CA).
6. *Parker v South Eastern Rly Co* (1877) 2 CPD 416 (CA).

clauses I have seen would need to be printed in red ink on the face of the document with a red hand pointing to it before the notice could be held to be sufficient.'[7]

The following case provides an example of a particularly onerous term (albeit not an exclusion clause).

Interfoto Picture Library Ltd v Stiletto Visual Programmes Ltd [1988] QB 433 (CA)

FACTS: The claimant ran a photographic transparency library. It loaned forty-seven transparencies to the defendant. The transparencies were accompanied by a delivery note containing nine conditions, one of which stated that the transparencies had to be returned within fourteen days of delivery and that failure to do so would result in a £5 penalty per transparency per day. The defendant had not contracted with the claimant before and did not read the conditions. It returned the transparencies some four weeks later, whereupon the claimant invoiced it for £3,783. The defendant refused to pay and the claimant commenced proceedings.

HELD: The Court of Appeal stated that, given how onerous the penalty clause was, the claimant should have done more to bring it to the defendant's attention. Accordingly, it held that the claimant could not recover the £3,783, but could recover a *quantum meruit*.

⭐ See JA Holland and PA Chandler, 'Notice of Contractual Terms' (1988) 104 LQR 359

➡ *quantum meruit*: 'as much as he has deserved'; a reasonable sum based on services provided

Construction and interpretation

Once it is established that an exclusion clause is a term of the contract, it must be determined whether or not the clause covers the liability in question. In construing exclusion clauses, the courts take a restrictive approach,[8] but the current approach is less restrictive than in years past. It used to be the case that the courts would not allow the proferens to rely on an exclusion clause that excluded or limited liability for a fundamental breach of contract. Today, the doctrine of fundamental breach has been abolished and the approach adopted by the courts can be seen in the following case.

Photo Productions Ltd v Securicor Transport Ltd [1980] AC 827 (HL)

FACTS: The claimant employed the defendant to patrol four of its factories at night, and to guard against fire and theft. The contract excluded the liability of the defendant for any injurious acts of its employees, unless such acts could be foreseen and prevented by the defendant's due diligence. It further excluded the liability of the defendant for any loss caused by fire, except in so far as such loss was solely attributable to the negligence of the defendant's employees acting within the scope of their employment. One of the defendant's employees deliberately started a fire in one of the claimant's factories and

---

7. *J Spurling Ltd v Bradshaw* [1956] 1 WLR 461 (CA) 466.
8. It should be noted that the courts will take a more restrictive approach in relation to exclusion clauses than they will in relation to limitation clauses, for obvious reasons.

his actions caused £615,000 worth of damage. The defendant sought to rely on the exclusion clause, but the claimant argued that it was invalid, because it excluded liability for a fundamental breach.

HELD: The House of Lords held that the doctrine of fundamental breach was no longer good law and that the correct approach was to determine, based on the construction of the exclusion clause, whether or not it covered the liability in question. Applying this approach, the House held that the exclusion clause covered the liability in question and that the defendant could therefore rely on it.

COMMENT: The effect of this decision was to permit the defendant to avoid liability, even though its employee's act destroyed the claimant's factory. It may be thought that this decision was a harsh one and that its application to consumer contracts containing imposed standard exclusion clauses would be highly detrimental, but it should be remembered that even where an exclusion clause covers the liability in question, it may still be subject to additional statutory safeguards—notably, the requirement of reasonableness imposed by the Unfair Contract Terms Act 1977. Accordingly, the relatively harsh approach evident in this case will tend to apply only to contracts between businesspersons, who should be capable of looking after their own interests.

Contra proferentem

The doctrine of fundamental breach might have been abolished, but the courts still construe and interpret exclusion clauses in a restrictive manner, and this is evidenced in what is known as the *contra proferentem* rule. The *contra proferentem* rule basically provides that where an exclusion clause contains an ambiguity, the courts will interpret it against the proferens. Thus, where an exclusion clause's ambiguity produces two possible meanings, one of which brings the liability within the clause and the other takes the liability outside the scope of the clause, the courts should choose the latter.

➜ *c ontra proferentem*: 'against a person who proffers a thing'; an ambiguous exclusion clause will be construed against the proferens

Although the rule is limited to cases involving an ambiguity, the courts have been creative in finding ambiguities, as the following case demonstrates.

⊙ *Houghton v Trafalgar Co Ltd* [1954] 1 QB 247 (CA)

FACTS: The claimant was involved in a car accident and claimed on his insurance policy. The policy contained an exclusion clause stating that the defendant insurance company would not be liable to pay out where the damage was 'caused or arising whilst the car is conveying any load in excess of that for which it was constructed'. Because the car was designed for five people and was carrying six at the time of the accident, the defendant relied on the clause and denied liability.

HELD: The Court of Appeal affirmed the trial judge's decision that the limitation imposed by the clause was based on excess weight, as opposed to an excess number of passengers. Accordingly, the exclusion clause did not apply.

Excluding liability for negligence

The restrictive approach of the *contra proferentem* rule is demonstrated clearly in relation to exclusion clauses that seek to exclude liability for negligence. The general approach is that the courts are reluctant to allow an exclusion clause to cover non-contractual liability (for example, liability in tort) unless the clause expressly provides that such liability is covered. The rationale behind this approach is the desire not to leave claimants without a remedy. The exact effect of this rule depends on the drafting of the exclusion clause and the type of obligation breached.

Where an exclusion clause expressly covers all forms of liability, or where the words used are wide enough to cover liability in contract and tort, effect must be given to it irrespective of the nature of liability[9] (subject to it satisfying the requirements of statute discussed later). But many clauses do not provide such blanket coverage and the effect of such clauses depends upon the types of obligation imposed by the contract, as follows.

- Where the proferens breaches a contractual term that imposes a strict obligation (that is, a person who breaches the term is liable despite the absence of negligence or fault), then the exclusion clause is normally construed so that it will protect him against liability in contract, but will not extend to cover liability in tort for negligence.[10]

- Where liability can be based only on negligence (whether only in tort, or for breach of a contractual term requiring the exercise of reasonable care and skill), the clause will normally be interpreted to extend to cover that liability (that is, negligence), because, otherwise, the clause would lack a subject matter and would be redundant.[11]

The need for clear words

For an exclusion clause to cover a particular liability, the words used must clearly cover that liability. The courts will apply this rule more strictly to exclusion clauses than to limitation clauses.[12]

The following case demonstrates the strictness of the courts' approach.

Andrews Bros (Bournemouth) Ltd v Singer & Co Ltd [1934] 1 KB 17 (CA)[13]

FACTS: The claimant entered into a contract to purchase a number of 'new Singer cars' from the defendant. The contract excluded the liability of the defendant for breach of all 'conditions, warranties and liabilities implied by common law, statute or otherwise'. One of the cars delivered had 550 miles on the odometer and the claimant brought an action for breach of contract, because the car was not new. The defendant sought to rely on the exclusion clause.

---

9. *Canada Steamship Lines v The King* [1952] AC 192 (PC).
10. *White v John Warwick & Co Ltd* [1953] 1 WLR 1285 (CA).
11. *Alderslade v Hendon Laundry Ltd* [1945] KB 189 (CA).
12. *Ailsa Craig Fishing Co Ltd v Malvern Fishing Co Ltd* [1983] 1 WLR 964 (HL).
13. See also *Wallis, Son and Wells v Pratt and Haynes* [1911] AC 394 (HL).

HELD: The Court of Appeal held that the clause did not protect the defendant, because it only excluded liability for breach of implied terms, whereas the requirement for the cars to be new was an express obligation.

 Key points summary

- Exclusion clauses seek to exclude or restrict liability for the commission of a civil wrong.

- An exclusion clause will only be effective if it is incorporated into a contract. An exclusion clause contained in a signed contract will be effective, irrespective of whether the signatory read it or not.

- An exclusion clause will be ineffective if the proferens misrepresents the effect of the clause.

- An exclusion clause will usually only be effective if it was brought to the other party's attention prior to the contract being formed.

- When interpreting an exclusion clause, the key issue is whether, based on the construction of the clause, it covers the liability in question.

The Unfair Contract Terms Act 1977

As discussed above, exclusion clauses were initially regulated by the common law alone, but, as time progressed, such clauses began to be subject to increasing levels of statutory regulation. At first, such regulation was piecemeal and applied only to specific contracts (for example, contracts involving the conveyance of passengers in public service vehicles),[14] but as time progressed, Parliament passed an Act that covered exclusion clauses in general. The Unfair Contract Terms Act 1977 (UCTA 1977), described by Furmston as 'the most important statute in the English contract law since the Statute of Frauds',[15] basically has two effects.

1. It renders certain exclusion clauses completely unenforceable.
2. It renders certain exclusion clauses unenforceable, unless they satisfy a requirement of reasonableness.

Before discussing the extent to which the UCTA 1977 affects the enforceability of exclusion clauses, it is important to understand the extent and scope of the Act.

---

14. Road Traffic Act 1960, s 151 (now repealed).
15. M Furmston, *Cheshire, Fifoot and Furmston's Law of Contract* (15th edn, OUP, Oxford, 2007) 253.

Scope

Naming the Act the 'Unfair Contract Terms Act 1977' would indicate that the Act has a wide remit and can apply to any form of unfair contractual term. In fact, this is not the case and it has been argued that the title of the Act is 'grossly misleading'[16] for two reasons:

1. the Act does not apply solely to contractual terms, but can also apply to exclusions contained in non-contractual notices; and

2. the Act does not seek to regulate unfair terms generally, but merely terms that limit or exclude 'business liability'.[17]

'Business liability' is defined as liability for breach of obligations or duties arising from:

- things done or to be done by a person in the course of a business; or
- the occupation of premises used for business purposes of the occupier.[18]

A 'business' is defined as 'a profession and the activities of any government department or local or public authority'.[19]

From these definitions, several consequences flow, as follows.

- It is apparent that the Act applies exclusively to contractual clauses and non-contractual notices that seek to exclude or limit liability. Section 13(1) indicates that the Act covers not only express exclusions of liability, but also covers clauses that aim to:

  (i) ake liability or its enforcement subject to strict or onerous conditions;

  (ii) exclude any right or remedy in relation to liability;

  (iii) subject persons to prejudice who exercise such a right or remedy; and

  (iv) exclude rules of evidence or procedure.

- The Act does not generally cover exclusion clauses in contracts between private individuals—but there are exceptions to this, as we shall see.

The Act applies to most forms of contract that contain a term seeking to exclude business liability, but several types of contract are excluded wholly or in part, including:

- Sch 1, para 1, excludes certain contracts from the operation of UCTA 1977, ss 2–4, including contracts of insurance, contracts for the creation and transfer of interests in land, and contracts relating to the dissolution of a company or the constitution, rights, or obligations of its members;

- contracts of employment are excluded from the operation of UCTA 1977, s 2, except where the clause operates in favour of the employee;[20]

- international supply contracts (that is, contracts for the sale of goods between parties whose places of business are in different states) are wholly outside the operation of the Act.[21]

---

16. Ibid, 232.
17. Not all of the terms are limited to the exclusion of business liability (e.g. UCTA 1977, s 6(1), (3), and (4)).
18. UCTA 1977, s 1(3).
19. Ibid, s 14.
20. Ibid, Sch 1, para 4.
21. Ibid, s 26(1).

Excluding liability for negligence

Section 1(1) defines 'negligence' as the breach of:

- any obligation, arising from the express or implied terms of a contract, to take reasonable care or exercise reasonable skill in the performance of the contract;
- any common law duty to take reasonable care or exercise reasonable skill; and
- the common duty of care imposed by the Occupiers' Liability Act 1957.

The Occupiers' Liability Act 1957 is discussed at p 466

Section 2(1) provides that a person cannot, by reference to an exclusion clause or notice, exclude or restrict his liability for death or personal injury (including any disease or impairment of physical or mental condition) resulting from negligence. Any clause purporting to do so will be ineffective. In relation to contract, the limitation contained in s 2(1) applies only to obligations to exercise reasonable care or skill (this is consequential upon the definition of negligence discussed above). Accordingly, liability for death and personal injury can be excluded where it is caused by breach of a strict obligation, provided that the clause or notice complies with s 3 (discussed later).

In relation to any other type of loss (for example, property damage or financial loss) caused by negligence, s 2(2) provides that such liability can be excluded, but 'only in so far as the term or notice satisfies the requirement of reasonableness'. The use of the words 'only in so far as' means that an unreasonable clause is not automatically unenforceable (although, in many cases, it will be); rather, the court may be able to keep part of the clause effective (the part of the clause that is reasonable) and hold ineffective the unreasonable part. As we shall see, this phrase is used several times throughout the Act.

The requirement of reasonableness is discussed at p 983

Excluding liability for breach of contract

We noted above that s 2 limits the ability to exclude liability for qualified contractual obligations (that is, those that require the exercise of reasonable care and skill) and tortious acts that amount to negligence, but it does not cover obligations that are not based on a duty to take reasonable care (that is, a strict obligation). An exclusion clause or notice that excludes liability for a breach of a strict contractual obligation is primarily regulated by s 3 (although it will be regulated by ss 6 and 7 in some cases). Section 3 only applies where:

- one party to the contract deals as a consumer; *or*
- the contract is formed based on the other's written standard terms of business.[22]

Both of these limitations require further discussion.

'Deals as a consumer'

Under UCTA 1977, a 'consumer' is defined as someone who neither makes the contract in the course of a business, nor holds himself out as doing so, and the other party does make the contract in the course of a business.[23] Based on this definition, it would be assumed that a business could never deal as a consumer and obtain the protection of s 3, but this is not so, as the following case established.

22. Ibid, s 3(2). 23. Ibid, s 12(1).

R & B Customs Brokers Co Ltd v United Dominions Trust Ltd [1988] 1 WLR 321 (CA)

FACTS: The claimant company was a freight forwarding and shipping agent. It purchased a car for one of its directors, which was used for both business and private purposes. The car was defective and the claimant alleged that the implied term relating to fitness for purpose in the Sale of Goods Act 1979, s 14(3), had been breached. The defendant sought to rely on an exclusion clause excluding liability for breach of s 14(3). But liability for breach of s 14(3) can only be validly excluded against a party not dealing as a consumer. The Court therefore had to determine whether or not the claimant dealt as a consumer.

HELD: In the Court of Appeal, Dillon LJ stated:

> there are some transactions which are clearly integral parts of the businesses concerned, and these should be held to have been carried out in the course of those businesses; this would cover, apart from much else, the instance of a one-off adventure in the nature of trade, where the transaction itself would constitute a trade or business. There are other transactions, however, such as the purchase of the car in the present case, which are at highest only incidental to the carrying on of the relevant business; here a degree of regularity is required before it can be said that they are an integral part of the business carried on, and so entered into in the course of that business.[24]

The purchase of the car was clearly not an integral part of the claimant's business, nor was it regular enough to be regarded as integral. Therefore, the claimant was regarded as a consumer and liability for breach of s 14(3) could not be excluded.

★ See DR Price, 'When Is a Consumer Not a Consumer?' (1989) 52 MLR 245

Unsurprisingly, the decision of the Court of Appeal in *R & B Customs Brokers* has proved controversial and has attracted considerable criticism. In the case of *Stevenson v Rogers*,[25] the Court of Appeal stated that, in the context of the law relating to contracts for the sale of goods, the test laid down in *R & B Customs Brokers* was not the correct test and that a sale would be in the course of business unless it was purely private. The Court distinguished *R & B Customs Brokers* and held that it applied solely to cases under UCTA 1977. Many believed the test laid down in *Stevenson* to be preferable to that established in *R & B*,[26] and it was hoped that, when the issue was litigated again, the test in *Stevenson* would be the one adopted. But when the Court of Appeal was invited to hold that the test in *Stevenson* was preferable to that in *R & B Customs Brokers*, it declined and applied the latter test.[27]

⌕ Visit the Online Resource Centre for more on *Stevenson v Rogers* in the chapter entitled 'The sale of goods'

Subsequently, the Law Commission considered the issue and recommended that a new regime should be created that applied to 'consumer contracts'.[28] A consumer contract would be between an individual (the consumer) who enters into it wholly or mainly for purposes unrelated to a business of his, and a person (the business)

---

24. *R & B Customs Brokers Co Ltd v United Dominions Trust Ltd* [1988] 1 WLR 321 (CA) 330, 331.
25. [1999] QB 1028 (CA).
26. See, e.g., E Macdonald, '"In the Course of a Business": A Fresh Examination' [1999] 3 Web JLI.
27. *Feldaroll Foundry plc v Hermes Leasing (London) Ltd* [2004] EWCA Civ 747, (2004) 101 LSG 32.
28. Law Commission, *Unfair Terms in Contracts* (Law Com No 292, Cm 6464, HMSO, London, 2005) Pt 3.

who enters into it wholly or mainly for purposes related to his business.[29] Under this definition, only natural persons could become consumers and, in order to be such, the contract would have to be for a purpose wholly or mainly unrelated to the person's business. In 2006, the government indicated that it was ready to go forward with the Law Commission's recommendations, but little progress has been made.

Under s 12(2), a buyer of goods will not be dealing as a consumer where he is an individual (that is, not a company or limited liability partnership) and the goods are second-hand goods sold at a public auction at which individuals have the opportunity of attending the sale in person. A buyer who is not an individual will not deal as a consumer where the goods are sold by auction or competitive tender.

'On the other's written standard terms of business'

Section 3 will apply where the consumer deals 'on the other's written standard terms of business'. It is crucial that the standard terms are those of the other party and not standard terms simply used by the other party, but drafted by someone else. For example, it is common for professional and trade associations to draft standard terms that are used by their members. These terms would not be regarded as the members' terms and so would not be subject to s 3,[30] which substantially limits the protection offered by s 3.

It is common for certain terms contained in a standard form contract to be amended following negotiation. So to what extent can such standard terms be amended before s 3 no longer applies? This question was considered in a number of cases and the following principles are evident.

- Whether the terms are still standard is a question of fact, taking into account the degree of negotiation and amendment, and the equality of bargaining power between the parties.[31]

- Where the exclusion clause itself is subject to negotiation, the terms will no longer be regarded as standard and s 3 will not apply.[32]

The effect of s 3

Section 3(2) provides that, as against the party dealing as consumer or on the other's written standard terms of business, the other party cannot, by reference to any contract term:

(a) exclude or restrict his liability for breach of contract, or;

(b) claim to be entitled:
  (i) to render a contractual performance substantially different from that which was reasonably expected of him, or
  (ii) in respect of the whole or any part of his contractual obligation, to render no performance at all

   except in so far as the contract term satisfies the requirement of reasonableness.

---

29. Draft Unfair Contract Terms Bill, cl 26.
30. *British Fermentation Products Ltd v Compare Reavell Ltd* [1999] 2 All ER (Comm) 389 (QB).
31. *Salvage Association v CAP Financial Services Ltd* [1995] FSR 654 (QB).
32. *St Albans City and District Council v International Computers Ltd* [1996] 4 All ER 481 (CA).

Unreasonable indemnity clauses

A contract may require one party to indemnify the other for any liability incurred in performance of the contract. The following example demonstrates how such a clause can operate in a manner identical to an exclusion clause.

 Eg Indemnity clauses

Anna hires a car from QuickHire Ltd. The hire agreement provides that Anna is obliged to indemnify QuickHire for any damage caused whilst driving the hire car. Should QuickHire be obliged to pay compensation for any damage caused by Anna whilst driving the hire car, the contract provides it with the right to be indemnified. In effect, the liability for causing damage is transferred from QuickHire to Anna. The practical effect of this is that it allows QuickHire indirectly to exclude its liability.

Because indemnity clauses can have the same practical effect as exclusion clauses, it is appropriate that they should be restricted by the UCTA 1977. Section 4 provides that a person dealing as consumer cannot, by reference to any contract term, be made to indemnify another person (whether a party to the contract or not) in respect of liability that may be incurred by the other for negligence or breach of contract, except in so far as the contract term satisfies the requirement of reasonableness. The definition of 'dealing as a consumer' is the same as that under s 3.

Excluding statutory implied terms

The Sale of Goods Act 1979 (SGA 1979) implies a number of terms into contracts for the sale of goods. It may be the case that a party will try to exclude liability for breaching one of these statutory implied terms, or the corresponding terms relating to hire-purchase agreements found in the Supply of Goods (Implied Terms) Act 1973 (SGITA 1973). It may be thought that, because such terms are implied by statute, they cannot be excluded by contract, but this is not the case. These terms can be excluded, but the ability to do so is heavily restricted.

*Visit the **Online Resource Centre** for more on the terms implied by the Sale of Goods Act 1979 in the chapter entitled 'The sale of goods'*

The implied terms as to title found in the SGA 1979, s 12, and the SGITA 1973, s 8, cannot be excluded or restricted by any contractual term.[33] The remaining implied terms (namely, those found in the SGA 1979, ss 13–15, and the SGITA 1973, ss 9–11) cannot be excluded or restricted by any contractual term against a person dealing as a consumer.[34] The definition of 'dealing as a consumer' is the same as that under ss 3 and 4, except that an additional requirement is added—namely, that the goods passing under, or in pursuance of, the contract are of a type ordinarily supplied

---

33. UCTA 1977, s 6(1).   34. Ibid, s 6(2).

for private use or consumption.[35] Where a person does not deal as a consumer, the implied terms found in the SGA 1979, ss 13–15, and the SGITA 1973, ss 9–11, can be excluded or restricted, but only so far as the term excluding or restricting liability satisfies the requirement of reasonableness.[36]

Section 7 deals with exemption clauses purporting to exclude or restrict liability for breach of statutorily implied terms into contracts such as those of hire or exchange, or for work and materials.[37] Section 7 applies to these contracts a regime that is broadly similar to that just mentioned in relation to sale of goods and hire purchase.

Sections 6 and 7 do not apply to the term implied into contracts for the supply of a service by the Supply of Goods and Services Act 1982, s 13—namely, that a supplier of a service acting in the course of a business will carry out that service with reasonable care and skill. Because such a term is implied into contracts for the supply of a service, however, and the exclusion of such a term constitutes the exclusion of liability for negligence, it will be subject to s 2.

The requirement of reasonableness

It can be seen that many types of exclusion clause are of no effect, except in so far as they satisfy the requirement of reasonableness. This requirement lies at the heart of the UCTA 1977, but by its very nature, it is inherently uncertain and it can be doubted that judges lack the expertise to determine what is reasonable in a business context. To aid the judges, the Act itself provides three sources of limited guidance. Firstly, s 11(1) provides that a term will be reasonable if it is a fair and reasonable one to be included, having regard to the circumstances that were, or ought reasonably to have been, known to or in the contemplation of the parties when the contract was made. From this, it can be seen that the courts should determine reasonableness based on the circumstances when the contract was made, not at the time when the case was heard. From an evidential perspective, this could cause problems, especially where there is a considerable period of time between the act complained of and the case being heard.

Secondly, s 11(2) provides that, in cases involving ss 6 and 7, the court is to have regard in particular to those matters specified in Sch 2. The use of the words 'in particular' indicates that the list of matters in Sch 2 is not exhaustive. The matters listed in Sch 2 are:

- the strength of the bargaining positions of the parties relative to each other;
- whether the customer received an inducement to agree to the term, or, in accepting it, had an opportunity of entering into a similar contract with other persons, but without having to accept a similar term;
- whether the customer knew, or ought reasonably to have known, of the existence and extent of the term;
- where the term excludes or restricts any relevant liability if some condition is not complied with, whether it was reasonable at the time of the contract to expect that compliance with that condition would by practicable;
- whether the goods were manufactured, processed, or adapted to the special order of the customer.

---

35. Ibid, s 12(1)(c).   36. Ibid, s 6(3).
37. Namely, the implied terms found in the Supply of Goods and Services Act 1982, ss 2–5 and 7–10.

Strictly speaking, the matters identified in Sch 2 apply only to cases involving ss 6 and 7, but, in practice, these matters are deemed relevant for all cases under UCTA 1977. As Lord Donaldson stated: 'Although Schedule 2 does not apply in the present case, the considerations there set out are usually regarded as being of general application to the question of reasonableness.'[38]

The third source of guidance can be found in s 11(4) and applies solely to clauses seeking to restrict liability to a specified sum of money (that is, s 11(4) does not apply to clauses that exclude liability). In such cases, the court should have regard in particular to:

- the resources that the party could expect to be available to him for the purpose of meeting the liability should it arise; and
- how far it was open to him to cover himself by insurance.

It cannot be overemphasized that, in all cases, it is the clause as a whole that must be reasonable in relation to the particular contract; the question is not whether its particular application in the particular case is reasonable. If a clause is drawn so widely as to be capable of applying in unreasonable circumstances, it will be deemed unreasonable, even though, in the actual situation that has arisen, its application is reasonable.[39] A clause may well have various parts to it, but, because the whole clause must be subjected to the test of reasonableness, it is not permissible to look only at that part of it on which the proferens relies.[40] A court will be particularly unwilling to find a clause reasonable if it purports to exclude all potential liability.[41] Persons claiming that a term is reasonable bear the burden of proof of establishing reasonableness.[42]

Where a term is found to be unreasonable, it cannot be relied on to exclude or restrict the liability of the proferens. In other words, the contract continues as normal, but without reference to the unreasonable exclusion clause.

Evasion of UCTA 1977 via a secondary contract

A party may try to evade the provisions of the UCTA 1977 by inserting the exclusion clause into a secondary contract. The following example provides a common instance in which such a situation could arise.

Eg Secondary contracts and UCTA 1977

Deborah purchases a car from MotorMart Ltd. She also enters into another contract with MotorMart, in which she upgrades the standard one-year warranty to a three-year warranty. This second contract contains a term excluding MotorMart's liability in the event that the car fails to comply with the terms implied by the Sale of Goods Act 1979. In this case, the second contract takes away rights that Deborah has under the first contract.

---

38. *Stewart Gill Ltd v Horatio Myer & Co Ltd* [1992] QB 600 (CA).
39. *Walker v Boyle* [1982] 1 WLR 495 (Ch).
40. *Stewart Gill Ltd v Horatio Myer & Co Ltd* [1992] QB 600 (CA).
41. *Lease Management Services Ltd v Purnell Secretarial Services Ltd* [1994] CCLR 127 (CA).
42. UCTA 1977, s 11(5).

Section 10 prevents such practices by providing that a person is not bound by any contract term prejudicing or taking away rights of his that arise under, or in connection with the performance of, another contract.

Key points summary

- The Unfair Contract Terms Act 1977 regulates exclusion clauses that exclude or restrict 'business liability'.

- The Act absolutely prohibits the exclusion or limitation of liability for death or personal injury caused by negligence. For other types of loss, an exclusion clause will only be effective in so far as it satisfies the requirement of reasonableness.

- Where standard terms exclude or restrict liability against a consumer for breach of contract, such terms will only be effective in so far as they satisfy the requirement of reasonableness.

- An indemnity clause will be ineffective, except in so far as it satisfies the requirement of reasonableness.

- The implied terms found in the Sale of Goods Act 1979 cannot be excluded against a consumer. Against a non-consumer, these implied terms (except the terms as to title) can be excluded in so far as they satisfy the requirement of reasonableness.

The Unfair Terms in Consumer Contracts Regulations 1999

In an effort to harmonize the law relating to unfair contractual terms, in 1993, the EU Council adopted the Directive on Unfair Terms in Consumer Contracts.[43] The Directive was implemented by the Unfair Terms in Consumer Contracts Regulations 1994,[44] which have since been repealed and replaced by the Unfair Terms in Consumer Contracts Regulations 1999 (UTCCR 1999).[45]

Scope

Given the relatively short deadline for implementation, the Directive was implemented without taking into account the potential overlaps or inconsistencies that exist between the Directive's provisions and those of the UCTA 1977. The result is that there is a considerable overlap between UCTA 1977 and the UTCCR 1999, with parties often having a claim under both pieces of legislation. As we shall see, however, in some respects, the Regulations are wider in scope then the UCTA 1977, but in other respects, the Regulations are noticeably narrower. Also, the tests established are different, with the result that a term could comply fully with the Act, but contravene the Regulations, or vice versa. To combat the potential confusion that

---

43. Council Directive No 93/13/EC.   44. SI 1994/3159.
45. SI 1999/2083.

can arise from having exclusion clauses subject to two differing pieces of legislation, the Law Commission has recommended[46] that a unified legislative regime be created that merges key provisions of UCTA 1977 and UTCCR 1999, and has even produced a Draft Unfair Contract Terms Bill. To date, however, its recommendations have not been acted upon.

Consumer contracts

Regulation 4(1) provides that the Regulations apply 'in relation to unfair terms in contracts concluded between a seller or a supplier and a consumer'. Immediately, it is apparent that, in this respect, the Regulations are narrower than UCTA 1997, in that the 1977 Act is not limited to consumer contracts, whereas the Regulations apply only to consumer contracts.

A 'seller', or 'supplier', is defined as 'any natural or legal person who, in contracts covered by these Regulations, is acting for purposes relating to his trade, business or profession, whether publicly owned or privately owned'.[47] A 'consumer' is defined as 'any natural person who, in contracts covered by these Regulations, is acting for purposes which are outside his trade, business or profession'.[48] Accordingly, under the Regulations, legal persons, such as companies and limited liability partnerships, can never be classified as a consumer,[49] whereas under the 1977 Act, such an entity could constitute a consumer provided that the transaction was not integral to its business. Sole proprietors and partners would qualify as natural persons, but would need to demonstrate that the contract is outside their trade, business, or profession.

Term not individually negotiated

The Regulations only apply to terms that have not been individually negotiated (that is, standard terms). Conversely, the 1977 Act applies to both standard and individually negotiated terms. The Regulations provide that a 'term shall always be regarded as not having been individually negotiated where it has been drafted in advance and the consumer has therefore not been able to influence the substance of the term'.[50] But reg 5(3) goes on to state that '[n]otwithstanding that a specific term or certain aspects of it in a contract has been individually negotiated, these Regulations shall apply to the rest of a contract if an overall assessment of it indicates that it is a pre-formulated standard contract'. Accordingly, a consumer who has been able to negotiate a minor amendment to the standard terms will still be covered by the Regulations. Where there is a dispute as to whether or not a term has been individually negotiated, the burden of proof is placed upon the seller or supplier to show that it was.[51]

The Law Commission's Draft Unfair Contract Terms Bill, cl 4, follows UCTA 1977, and applies to both standard and individually negotiated terms, the rationale

---

46. Law Commission, *Unfair Terms in Contracts* (Law Com No 292, Cm 6464, HMSO, London, 2005).
47. UTCCR 1999, reg 3(1).
48. Ibid.
49. There is one exception to this—namely, where the term is an arbitration agreement (i.e. a term that requires disputes to be referred to arbitration before commencing legal proceedings), then a legal person will constitute a consumer: see the Arbitration Act 1996, s 90.
50. UTCCR 1999, reg 5(2).
51. Ibid, reg 5(4).

behind this being that to follow the approach in the UTCCR 1999 would be to reduce the overall level of protection offered.[52]

Unfair terms

One area in which the 1999 Regulations are wider in scope than the 1977 Act is in relation to the terms covered. As noted, the 1977 Act applies only to terms that exclude, limit, or require indemnification of liability, whereas the Regulations apply to any potentially unfair term. But this breadth is limited in two ways:

- the Regulations relate only to unfair *contractual* terms and do not cover non-contractual notices, whereas the 1977 Act does cover such notices; and
- the Regulations do not apply to terms in relation to:
  (i) the definition of the main subject matter of the contract; or
  (ii) the adequacy of the price or remuneration, as against the goods or services supplied in exchange.[53]
- But both of these types of term will be covered by the Regulations if they are not in plain intelligible language.

The courts have indicated that the limitations found in reg 6(2) should be interpreted liberally: the object of the Regulations is to protect consumers against unfair terms and reg 6(2) should not be allowed to frustrate this objective.[54]

Excluded contracts

Another area in which the Regulations are wider is in relation to excluded contracts. Both the 1977 Act and the 1999 Regulations contain a list of contracts that are excluded from their operation, but the list in the Act is wider and contains contracts that are covered by the Regulations (for example, insurance contracts are not covered under the UCTA 1977, but are covered by the UTCCR 1999).

Unfairness

Regulation 5(1) provides that:

> A contractual term which has not been individually negotiated shall be regarded as unfair if, contrary to the requirement of good faith, it causes a significant imbalance in the parties' rights and obligations arising under the contract, to the detriment of the consumer.

Three potential elements are identifiable, as follows.

1. The term is contrary to the requirement of good faith.
2. The term causes a significant imbalance between the parties' rights and obligations arising under the contract.
3. The significant imbalance causes a detriment to the consumer.

---

52. Law Commission, *Unfair Terms in Contracts* (Law Com No 292, Cm 6464, HMSO, London, 2005) [3.55].
53. UTCCR 1999, reg 6(2).
54. *Director General of Fair Trading v First National Bank plc* [2001] UKHL 52, [2002] 1 AC 481.

But the relationship between these three elements is not clear. For example, will a significant imbalance automatically amount to a lack of good faith? No definitive answer has been provided. Accordingly, the three elements will be discussed separately.

Although not stated in the Regulations, the House of Lords has clarified that the burden of proof is placed upon the consumer to establish that a term is unfair.[55] This differs from the UCTA 1977, under which the party seeking to rely on the exclusion clause bears the burden of establishing the term's reasonableness.

A term held to be unfair under the Regulations is not binding on the consumer.[56] But the rest of the contract continues to bind the parties if it is capable of continuing in existence without the unfair term.[57] This appears similar to the 'blue pencil' test used to determine whether or not a term can be severed.

🔗 The severing of terms is discussed at p 286

Good faith

The Regulations provide no definition or guidance as to what amounts to good faith, doubtless due to the inability to define precisely such a vague and flexible concept. The House of Lords has provided general hints, stating that good faith is about 'fair and open dealing',[58] defining this as:

> the terms should be expressed fully, clearly and legibly, containing no concealed pitfalls or traps. Appropriate prominence should be given to terms which might operate disadvantageously to the customer. Fair dealing requires that a supplier should not, whether deliberately or unconsciously, take advantage of the consumer's necessity, indigence, lack of experience, unfamiliarity with the subject matter of the contract [or] weak bargaining position.[59]

Schedule 2 of the 1994 Regulations contained a list of relevant factors, but the 1999 Regulations do not contain this list. Because the list appears in Recital 16 of the Unfair Contract Terms Directive, however, it can still be properly relied upon by the judges. The factors included in Recital 16 were:

> the strength of the bargaining positions of the parties, whether the consumer had an inducement to agree to the term, whether the goods or services were sold or supplied to the special order of the consumer, and the extent to which the seller and supplier has dealt fairly and equitably with the consumer.

Significant imbalance

When determining whether or not a significant imbalance exists, the courts are directed to take into account:

> the nature of the goods or services for which the contract was concluded and by referring, at the time of conclusion of the contract, to all the circumstances attending the conclusion of the contract and to all the other terms of the contract or of another contract on which it is dependent.[60]

---

55. Ibid.
56. UTCCR 1999, reg 8(1).
57. Ibid, reg 8(2).
58. *Director General of Fair Trading v First National Bank plc* [2001] UKHL 52, [2002] 1 AC 481, [17] (Lord Bingham).
59. Ibid.
60. UTCCR 1999, reg 6(1).

The House of Lords has provided further guidance, stating that '[t]he requirement of significant imbalance is met if a term is so weighted in favour of the supplier as to tilt the parties' rights and obligations under the contract significantly in his favour'.[61]

Detriment to the consumer

The phrase 'detriment to the consumer' appears to be included simply to indicate who the significant imbalance should favour. In other words, a term that causes a significant imbalance by favouring the consumer will not be considered unfair.

Terms that may be unfair

Schedule 2 of the Regulations contains a non-exhaustive list of seventeen terms that may be regarded as unfair. A notable contrast can be drawn with the UCTA 1977, under which certain terms (that is, clauses that exclude liability for negligence that causes death or personal injury, and clauses that exclude the implied terms as to title) will always be regarded as ineffective. Conversely, the Regulations do not classify any terms as always being unfair, but merely indicates which terms *may* be unfair. Accordingly, a term that excludes liability for negligence that causes death or personal injury can be effective under the Regulations, provided that it does not breach the test of unfairness.

The list of terms that may be unfair includes terms that:

- exclude or limit liability for an act or omission that causes death or personal injury;
- inappropriately exclude or limit the legal rights of the consumer vis-à-vis the seller or supplier, or another party, in the event of total or partial non-performance or inadequate performance by the seller or supplier of any of the contractual obligations;
- require any consumer who fails to fulfil his obligation to pay a disproportionately high sum in compensation;
- authorize the seller or supplier to dissolve the contract on a discretionary basis where the same facility is not granted to the consumer, or permit the seller or supplier to retain the sums paid for services not yet supplied by him where it is the seller or supplier himself who dissolves the contract;
- enable the seller or supplier to terminate a contract of indeterminate duration without reasonable notice, except where there are serious grounds for doing so;
- irrevocably bind the consumer to terms with which he had no real opportunity of becoming acquainted before the conclusion of the contract.

Interpretation

Regulation 7(1) provides that terms of the contract must be expressed in plain intelligible language. But terms that fail to comply with reg 7(1) are still binding and valid; all that happens is that any ambiguity resulting from the lack of plain language

---

61. *Director General of Fair Trading v First National Bank plc* [2001] UKHL 52, [2002] 1 AC 481, [17] (Lord Bingham).

The *contra proferentem* rule is discussed at p 975

shall be interpreted in favour of the consumer.[62] This is simply a form of the *contra proferentem* rule established under the common law.

Enforcement and the Office of Fair Trading

The Regulations provide substantial enforcement powers to the Office of Fair Trading (OFT).[63] Regulation 10(1) provides that the OFT is under a duty to consider any complaint made to it, unless the complaint is frivolous or vexatious, or the complaint is heard by another body qualified[64] to hear such complaints. Both the OFT and these qualifying bodies may apply for an injunction to prevent the use, or the recommended use, of an unfair term in a consumer contract. In deciding whether or not to apply for an injunction, the OFT may have regard to any undertakings made not to continue to use the unfair term in question and, in many cases, the presence of such an undertaking will result in no injunction application being made.

The enforcement powers granted by the Enterprise Act 2002 are discussed at p 1012

A breach of the UTCCR 1999 can also be subjected to enforcement orders obtained by various bodies under the Enterprise Act 2002, Pt 8, because it amounts to a Community infringement.

> ### ‹› Key points summary
>
> - The Regulations apply to any type of term that could potentially be unfair, provided that the term is not individually negotiated and is contained in a consumer contract.
>
> - Unfair terms will be ineffective. A term will be unfair if, contrary to the requirement of good faith, it causes a significant imbalance in the parties' rights and obligations arising under the contract, to the detriment of the consumer.

The Consumer Protection from Unfair Trading Regulations 2008

The Consumer Protection from Unfair Trading Regulations 2008 (CPUTR 2008) have been described as 'one of the most significant changes in consumer protection for a generation'.[65] The origins of the Regulations lay in the Unfair Commercial Practices Directive[66] (UCPD), the principal aim of which is stated in Art 1:

> The purpose of this Directive is to contribute to the proper functioning of the internal market and achieve a high level of consumer protection by approximating

---

62. UTCCR 1999, reg 7(2).
63. The Regulations actually provide these enforcement powers to the Director General of Fair Trading (DGFT), but the office of DGFT was abolished and his powers transferred to the OFT by the Enterprise Act 2002, s 2.
64. A list of 'qualifying bodies' can be found in the UTCCR 1999, Sch 1.
65. WCH Ervine, 'The Consumer Protection from Unfair Trading Regulations 2008' (2008) 22 SLT 147, 147.
66. Council Directive No 2005/29/EC.

the laws, regulations and administrative provisions of the Member States on unfair commercial practices harming consumers' economic interests.

The Directive's commitment to harmonization is demonstrated in its unusual nature. Most directives lay down minimum standards that member States are free to implement in their own way, including the implementation of higher standards if they so wish. Conversely, the UCPD provides for maximum harmonization, meaning that member States cannot provide any more or any less protection than that specified by the UCPD. Maximum harmonization is controversial, but it does fit in with the UCPD's aim of facilitating cross-border trading by creating a 'level playing field'.

It is worth noting at the outset that the Regulations protect consumers from unfair commercial practices by imposing criminal liability on those who engage in such practices. But the Regulations do not provide any civil remedies for consumers who have suffered loss due to such practices and such redress must be obtained elsewhere.

Implementation and scope

The UCPD was implemented into English law by the CPUTR 2008.[67] In order to comply with the UCPD's goal of harmonization of standards, over twenty-two pieces of extremely important and well-established legislation had to be amended or repealed, with notable repeals including the Control of Misleading Advertisements Regulations 1988, the Consumer Protection Act 1987, Pt III, and most of the Trade Descriptions Act 1968.

The Regulations aim to provide a broad framework for determining the fairness of the commercial practices of traders. A 'trader' is 'any person who in relation to a commercial practice is acting for purposes relating to his business, and anyone acting in the name of or on behalf of a trader'.[68] Therefore, not only are the acts of traders covered, but also the acts of their agents and employees.

Regulation 2(1) defines a 'commercial practice' as:

> any act, omission, course of conduct, representation or commercial communication (including advertising and marketing) by a trader, which is directly connected with the promotion, sale or supply of a product to or from consumers, whether occurring before, during or after a commercial transaction (if any) in relation to a product.

'Product' is defined as 'any goods or service and includes immovable property, rights and obligations'.

The Regulations are concerned entirely with commercial practices that may affect consumers, with a 'consumer' being 'any individual who in relation to a commercial practice is acting for purposes which are outside his business'.[69] Business-to-business transactions are not covered, but practices that can affect both consumers and businesses are covered by the Regulations. There is no requirement for the trader to deal directly with the consumer: any commercial practice that could affect consumers

---

67. SI 2008/1277.   68. CPUTR 2008, reg 2(1).
69. Ibid.

is subject to the Regulations. The Regulations apply to commercial practices that occur before, during, and after a transaction.

The breadth of these definitions indicates that the Regulations aim to establish an extremely broad framework, within which the fairness of commercial practices can be determined. In order to understand the operation of the Regulations, there are two key terms we need to define first—namely, who is the 'average consumer' and what constitutes a 'transactional decision'.

The 'average consumer'

In determining whether or not a commercial practice is fair, great weight is placed upon how the practice would affect the 'average consumer'. The identity of the average consumer depends upon at whom the commercial practice in question is targeted, with there being three types of possible average consumer.

1. By default, the average consumer will simply be a 'reasonably well informed, reasonably observant and circumspect'[70] person at whom the commercial practice is addressed or whom it reaches.

2. Where, however, a practice is directed at a particular group of persons, the average person will be an average member of that group[71] (for example, where a television advertisement is targeted at children, the average consumer would be an average child).

3. Where a practice is targeted at a group of particularly vulnerable persons, the average consumer will be an average member of that vulnerable group[72] (for example, where a practice targets those in wheelchairs, the average consumer will be an average wheelchair-bound consumer).

A 'transactional decision'

Most commercial practices will breach the Regulations only if they 'impair the average consumer's ability to make an informed decision thereby causing him to take a transactional decision that he would not have taken otherwise'.[73] A 'transactional decision' is defined as any decision taken by a consumer, whether it is to act or to refrain from acting, concerning:

- whether, how, and on what terms to purchase, make payment in whole or in part for, retain, or dispose of a product; or

- whether, how, and on what terms to exercise a contractual right in relation to a product.

What is an 'unfair commercial practice'?

The Green Paper that led to the UCPD advocated a mixed approach to defining what would constitute an unfair commercial practice.[74] This would consist of a general prohibition, coupled with a number of more specific, detailed prohibitions. This

---

70. Ibid, reg 2(2).
71. Ibid, reg 2(4).
72. Ibid, reg 2(5).
73. Ibid, reg 2(1).
74. Commission of the EU, *Green Paper on European Union Consumer Protection* (COM (2001) 531) [3.4].

mixed approach was adopted, with the UCPD and the 2008 Regulations providing for a general prohibition and four additional specific prohibitions.

All five prohibitions will be discussed.

The general prohibition

The general prohibition can be found in reg 3(3) and is aimed at covering those practices that fall outside the scope of the specific prohibitions. It is therefore a legislative safety net, included in the 2008 Regulations due to the recognition that new commercial practices can evolve with which current legislation is unable to deal. The inclusion of the general prohibition therefore will hopefully make the 2008 Regulations 'future-proof'.[75]

Under the general prohibition, a commercial practice is unfair if:

1. it contravenes the requirements of professional diligence; and
2. it distorts materially, or is likely to distort materially, the economic behaviour of the average consumer with regard to the product.

It can be seen that (1) focuses on the commercial practice in dispute, whereas (2) focuses on the effect of the commercial practice. 'Professional diligence' is defined in reg 2(1) as:

the standard of special skill and care which a trader may reasonably be expected to exercise towards consumers which is commensurate with either—

(a) honest market practice in the trader's field of activity, or
(b) the general principle of good faith in the trader's field of activity.

Although the test imposes an objective standard, the phrase 'in the trader's field of activity' demonstrates that the standard will vary depending on the facts in question. The courts will not permit a breach of professional diligence simply because such a breach is widespread across the industry. Compliance with industry-specific codes of practice may provide evidence towards a practice being fair, but will not be conclusive in itself.

A practice that contravenes the requirements of professional diligence will not be prohibited unless it also distorts materially or is likely to distort materially the economic behaviour of the average consumer with regard to the product. This will occur where a practice appreciably impairs 'the average consumer's ability to make an informed decision thereby causing him to take a transactional decision that he would not have taken otherwise'.[76] This test is clearly objective and basically requires the practice to affect the consumer's ability to decide 'whether, how and on what terms to purchase, make payment for, retain or dispose of a product'.[77] There is a causative element, in that the transactional decision must be caused by the impairment. A practice that contravenes the requirement of professional diligence may cause the consumer to make a transactional decision, but unless his ability to make

---

75. G Abbamonte, 'The Unfair Commercial Practices Directive and its General Prohibition' in S Weatherill and U Bernitz (eds), *The Regulation of Unfair Commercial Practices Under EC Directive 2005/29 New Rules and New Techniques* (Hart, Oxford, 2007) 20.
76. CPUTR 2008, reg 2(1).
77. Ibid.

this decision was impaired by the commercial practice, the practice will not fall foul of the general prohibition. Smith[78] provides the example of a trader who offers to sell a number of fake Rolex watches and discloses clearly that the watches are fake. This will constitute a contravention of the requirements of professional diligence and could be likely to cause the consumer, in purchasing a watch, to make a transactional decision. Because the consumer knows that the watches are fake, however, his 'economic behaviour' has not been impaired and so the practice will not breach the general prohibition.

Misleading actions

The first of four more specific forms of unfair commercial practice are misleading actions. Note that we are concerned with misleading actions, not false actions. The word 'misleading' is wider and can include practices that are not false per se, but in some way mislead the consumer. A misleading action can occur in one of two ways and, in both cases, the action must cause the consumer to take a transactional decision that he would not have taken otherwise.

Firstly, a commercial practice will constitute a misleading action if it contains false information and is therefore untruthful, or if it, or its overall presentation, in any way deceives, or is likely to deceive, the average consumer, even if the information is factually correct.[79] The misleading information must relate to one of the matters contained in reg 5(4), which includes:

- the existence or nature of the product (for example, offering to sell a product that does not exist);
- the main characteristics of a product (for example, clocking a car's odometer);
- the price or the manner in which the price is calculated (for example, offering to sell a product for a certain price, but then requiring the claimant to purchase insurance for an extra amount);
- the existence of a specific price advantage (for example, a seller who claims that his prices 'cannot be beaten', when, in fact, items can be obtained cheaper elsewhere);
- the need for a service part, replacement, or repair (for example, a mechanic tells a consumer that the brakes on his car require replacing, when, in fact, they are perfectly safe).

The second method of committing a misleading action is found in reg 5(3), which provides two further forms of misleading action. The first occurs where a product is marketed in a way that creates confusion with any products, trademarks, trade names, or other distinguishing marks of a competitor. This would cover the situation in which a producer markets a product in a way that is similar to the marketing of an existing popular product (for example, using a similar name, using similar packaging, or advertisements, etc.). The second occurs where a trader fails to comply with a code of conduct by which he has indicated he is bound. The Guidance on the Regulations provides the example of a trader who agrees to be bound by a code of

---

78. V Smith, 'The Trade Descriptions Act 1968 is Dead: Long Live the Consumer Protection from Unfair Trading Regulations 2008—Part 2' (2008) 172 JPN 536, 536.
79. CPUTR 2008, reg 5(2)(a).

conduct that promotes the sustainable use of wood and prohibits the use of unsus-tainable hardwoods.[80] If the trader uses such hardwoods, then his actions could be construed as misleading.

Misleading omissions

An unfair commercial practice need not constitute a positive act; it is also possible to mislead others through omission. Being given false information may mislead a consumer, but he may also be misled if a trader fails to disclose material informa-tion. Regulation 6(1) provides that a commercial practice will constitute a mislead-ing omission, where:

- it omits or hides material information;
- it provides material information in a manner that is unclear, unintelligible, ambigu-ous or untimely; or
- it fails to identify its commercial intent, unless this is already apparent from the context.

The omission must also cause the consumer to take a transactional decision that he would not have taken otherwise.

In order for an omission to be misleading, the omission must be 'material'. The Regulations define 'material information' as 'the information which the average con-sumer needs, according to the context, to take an informed transactional decision',[81] which will also include any information requiring disclosure under EU legislation.

Eg Material information

The Guidance provides the following examples[82] of information that are likely to be material.

1. A trader omits that a contract is to run for a minimum period, or that further purchases are required.

2. A trader fails to disclose that goods sold are reconditioned or second-hand.

3. A trader who operates a car park fails to indicate the pricing before the consumer enters the car park.

4. A trader sells a television, but fails to disclose that it has an analogue tuner and will become useless once television signals switch from analogue to digital.

The definition of material information is expanded where the commercial prac-tice amounts to an 'invitation to purchase' (similar to an invitation to treat), which is defined as a 'commercial communication which indicates characteristics of the

Invitations to treat are discussed at p 154

---

80. Office of Fair Trading/Department for Business, Enterprise and Regulatory Reform, *Consumer Protection from Unfair Trading* (OFT, London, 2008) [7.11].

81. CPUTR 2008, reg 6(3)(a).

82. Office of Fair Trading/Department for Business, Enterprise and Regulatory Reform, *Consumer Protection from Unfair Trading* (OFT, London, 2008) [7.18].

product and the price in a way appropriate to the means of that commercial communication and thereby enables the consumer to make a purchase'.[83] Advertisements that simply draw attention to a new product or service without providing further details are unlikely to amount to invitations to purchase.

Eg Invitations to purchase

Examples of likely invitations to purchase would include the following.

1. Advertisements in newspapers or magazines that contain an order form allowing the advertised goods to be ordered.

2. An interactive television channel allowing orders to be placed via phone, the Internet, or through an interactive satellite television service.

3. Websites that allow consumers to order goods.

4. Products in shops that have a price displayed.

5. Menus in restaurants.

Where a practice constitutes an invitation to purchase, certain information will automatically be regarded as material, including the main characteristics of the product, the identity and geographical address of the trader, the price or the manner by which price is to be calculated, delivery charges, and, if applicable, any rights of withdrawal or cancellation.[84]

Aggressive practices

The third category of specific unfair commercial practices is aggressive practices. An 'aggressive practice' is one that impairs significantly, or is likely to impair significantly, the average consumer's freedom of choice or conduct in relation to the product concerned, through the use of harassment, coercion, or undue influence, and thereby causes or is likely to cause him to take a transactional decision that he would not have taken otherwise.[85] 'Harassment' and 'coercion' are not categorically defined in the Regulations, but would include most forms of physical and non-physical (for example, psychological) pressure.[86] 'Undue influence' is defined as 'exploiting a position of power in relation to the consumer so as to apply pressure, even without using or threatening to use physical force, in a way that significantly limits the consumer's ability to make an informed decision'.[87]

The following provides an example of a practice that is likely to constitute undue influence.

---

83. CPUTR 2008, reg 2(1).
84. Ibid, reg 6(4).
85. Ibid, reg 7(1).
86. Office of Fair Trading/Department for Business, Enterprise and Regulatory Reform, *Consumer Protection from Unfair Trading* (OFT, London, 2008) [8.3].
87. CPUTR 2008, reg 7(3)(b).

Eg Undue influence

Rhys takes his car to QuickFix Ltd to undergo its annual service. The service is carried out by Julian, who informs Rhys that the car will need an oil change and a new air filter, which will cost around £100. Rhys instructs Julian to change the oil and replace the filter, saying that he will pick the car up the following day. While carrying out the necessary repairs, Julian discovers that the car's gearbox is also faulty, and, without first informing Rhys, he repairs the gearbox and installs several new components. When Rhys arrives to pick up the car, Julian informs him of the repairs that he made to the gearbox and states that the costs have according increased by £300. Rhys refuses to pay, because he did not consent to the extra repairs. Julian informs Rhys that unless he pays the full £400, he will not be permitted to take his car.

When determining whether a practice is aggressive, reg 7(2) indicates several factors that should be taken into account including:

- the timing, location, nature, and persistence of the practice (for example, constant phone calls or late-night visits);
- the use of threatening or abusive language, or behaviour (for example, threatening violence against a person who refuses to purchase a particular product);
- the exploitation by the trader of any specific misfortune or circumstance, of such gravity as to impair the consumer's judgment and of which the trader is aware, to influence the consumer's decision with regard to the product (for example, placing pressure on a recently bereaved widow towards her buying an expensive coffin to avoid 'shaming the deceased's family');
- any threat to take action that cannot legally be taken (for example, threatening to send the bailiffs to collect on a debt when no such right exists).

Practices unfair in all circumstances

The fourth and final category of specific unfair commercial practices can be found in Sch 1 to the Regulations, which contains a 'blacklist' of thirty-one commercial practices that are always considered unfair. There is no requirement that such practices affect the transactional decision of the consumer; rather, they are automatically considered unfair in all circumstances. Many of these banned practices are extreme forms of unfair practices discussed above.

Examples of banned practices include:

- claiming to be a signatory to a code of practice when the trader is not, or claiming that a code has an endorsement that it does not;
- displaying a trust mark, quality mark, or equivalent without authorization;
- falsely stating that a product will only be available for a limited time in order to elicit an immediate decision;
- stating, or creating the impression, that a product can be legally sold when it cannot;
- promoting a product similar to a product made by a particular manufacturer in such a manner as deliberately to mislead the consumer into believing that the product is made by that same manufacturer when it is not;

- creating the impression that the consumer cannot leave the premises until a contract is formed.

Figure 28.1 indicates the issues to be determined when assessing the fairness of a commercial practice.

Enforcement

Responsibility for enforcing the CPUTR 2008 is placed upon local authority trading standards services and the OFT. To assist them in enforcing the Regulations, they are provided with a number of powers, including the power to make test purchases, and to enter premises without a warrant and conduct investigations. A principal aim of enforcement is to encourage compliance and the commencement of legal proceedings is usually the last resort, after the enforcement body has exhausted all 'established means'. Enforcers have access to both civil remedies (albeit not under the Regulations themselves) and the ability to pursue a criminal prosecution.

Civil remedies

The enforcement powers granted by the Enterprise Act 2002 are discussed at p 1012

The Regulations confer no rights upon those who have suffered loss due to an unfair commercial practice. Regulation 29 specifically states that '[a]n agreement shall not be void or unenforceable by reason only of a breach of these Regulations'. Persons looking to set aside an agreement or obtain compensation will need to obtain a remedy through other channels. In particular, breach of the Regulations will constitute a Community infringement and can therefore be subjected to enforcement orders obtained by various bodies under the Enterprise Act 2002, Pt 8,[88] in the same way as can the UTCCR 1999.

Criminal offences and mens rea

➡ *mens rea*: 'guilty mind'; the mental element required for the commission of certain crimes

A trader who engages in an unfair commercial practice will commit one or more of a number of criminal offences provided for under the CPUTR 2008. The *mens rea* requirements for these offences differ depending on the type of unfair commercial practice. Where the commercial practice is unfair by virtue of breaching the general prohibition, the offence requires proof of *mens rea*—namely, that the trader knowingly or recklessly engaged in a practice that contravenes the requirements of professional diligence.[89] 'Knowingly' is straightforward and will occur where the trader actually knows that his actions breach standards of professional diligence. The Regulations do not provide a full definition of 'reckless', but reg 8(2) does provide that:

> a trader who engages in a commercial practice without regard to whether the practice contravenes the requirements of professional diligence shall be deemed recklessly to engage in the practice, whether or not the trader has reason for believing that the practice might contravene those requirements.

This is an almost identical requirement to that imposed under the now-repealed Trade Descriptions Act 1968, s 14(2)(b).

---

88. Enterprise Act 2002, Sch 13, para 9C.   89. CPUTR 2008, reg 8(1)(a).

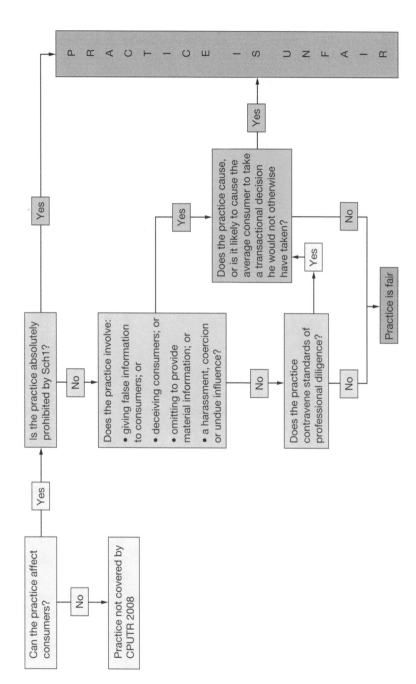

FIGURE 28.1 Is the commercial practice unfair?
Source: © Crown copyright. Reproduced from OFT and BERR, *Consumer Protection from Unfair Trading* (2008)

Under the 1968 Act, Widgery CJ stated that 'recklessly':

> does not involve dishonesty....I think it suffices for present purposes if the prosecution can show that the advertiser did not have regard to the truth or falsity of his advertisement even though it cannot be shown that he was deliberately closing his eyes to the truth, or that he had any kind of dishonest mind.[90]

It remains to be seen whether the courts will apply a similar interpretation to 'reckless behaviour' under the 2008 Regulations.

Where the trader engages in a misleading action, misleading omission, aggressive practice, or a banned practice under Sch 1, the offence is strict liability and there is no requirement to establish *mens rea*.[91]

Where an offence is committed by a body corporate and was committed with the consent or connivance, or attributable to the neglect of, an officer of the body corporate, that officer, as well as the body corporate, is guilty of the offence.[92]

Prosecutions of the above offences are subject to strict time limits. A prosecution cannot be brought after the end of a period of three years beginning with the date on which the offence was committed, or, if earlier, at the end of a period of one year, beginning with the date of the discovery of the offence by the prosecutor.[93] Irrespective of under which type of unfair practice the offence arises, the maximum punishment is the same—namely, on summary conviction, a fine not exceeding the statutory maximum (currently £5,000), and on conviction on indictment, a fine and/or imprisonment for up to two years.[94]

Defences

A trader prosecuted for committing an unfair commercial practice may nevertheless avoid conviction if he can successfully raise a defence. The Regulations provide for two defences:

- the due diligence defence; and
- the innocent publication defence.

These defences can be pleaded for all of the offences under the CPUTR 2008, except where the offence was committed by breaching the general prohibition.

Due diligence

A defence of due diligence is found in most pieces of consumer protection legislation, and provides that a trader shall have a defence where:

- the commission of the offence was due to a mistake, reliance on information supplied to him by another person, the act or default of another person, an accident, or any other cause beyond his control; and
- he took all reasonable precautions and exercised all due diligence to avoid the commission of such an offence by himself or any person under his control.[95]

---

90. *MFI Warehouses Ltd v Nattrass* [1973] 1 WLR 307 (QB) 313.
91. CPUTR 2008, regs 9–12.
92. Ibid, reg 15(1).
93. Ibid, reg 14(1).
94. Ibid, reg 13.
95. Ibid, reg 17(1).

The wording of this defence is identical to the defence contained in the Trade Descriptions Act 1968, s 24(1), and pre-2008 case law is likely to retain much of its authority. Such case law provided that, for the defence to succeed, it is essential that *all* reasonable precautions be taken.

 Simmons v Potter **[1975] RTR 347 (DC)**

FACTS: The defendant car dealer purchased a second-hand Jaguar with an odometer reading of 14,000 miles. He attempted to learn more about the car's history by telephoning the car's previous owner and the owner of the garage that serviced the car. The defendant displayed the car for sale in his showroom. The claimant purchased the car, and discovered that the odometer reading was false and that the car had, in fact, travelled 24,000 miles. The defendant was prosecuted under the Trade Descriptions Act 1968, s 1, and raised the due diligence defence.

HELD: The defendant passed the first part of the defence, because he had relied on information supplied by another person. But he had not undertaken all reasonable precautions, because he had not displayed a disclaimer regarding the accuracy of the odometer reading. Therefore the defence failed and the Divisional Court overturned the magistrates' acquittal.

Innocent publication

The innocent publication defence provides that a trader shall have a defence where:

- he is a person whose business it is to publish or to arrange for the publication of advertisements;
- he received the advertisement for publication in the ordinary course of business; and
- he did not know, and had no reason to suspect, that its publication would amount to an offence under the regulation to which the proceedings relate.[96]

'Advertisement' is defined broadly and will include catalogues, circulars, and price lists.[97]

 Key points summary

- The Consumer Protection from Unfair Trading Regulations 2008 were enacted to implement the Unfair Commercial Practices Directive.
- The Regulations aim to protect consumers from unfair commercial practices engaged in by traders and their agents or employees.
- There are five forms of unfair commercial practice:
  - breach of the general prohibition;
  - misleading actions;

---

96. Ibid, reg 18(1).   97. Ibid, reg 18(2).

- misleading omissions;
- aggressive practices; and
- practices unfair in all circumstances.

- Commission of an unfair commercial practice constitutes one or more of a number of strict liability criminal offences provided for by the CPUTR 2008. But where the practice breaches the general prohibition, the prosecution will need to establish that the practice was engaged in knowingly or recklessly.

The Business Protection from Misleading Marketing Regulations 2008

As noted, the CPUTR 2008 provides protection to consumers only. We also noted that, in order to implement the UCPD, certain pieces of legislation that provided protection to businesses had to be repealed—notably, key sections of the Trade Descriptions Act 1968 were repealed and the Control of Misleading Advertising Regulations 1988[98] were completely repealed. As a result of this, there were considerable gaps created in the protection afforded to businesses. In order to fill these gaps and to implement the Misleading and Comparative Advertising Directive,[99] a second set of regulations was passed—namely, the Business Protection from Misleading Marketing Regulations 2008 (BPMMR 2008).[100] These Regulations, as the name suggests, are concerned with the regulation of advertising, but 'advertising' is given an extremely wide meaning, as 'any form of representation which is made in connection with a trade, business, craft or profession in order to promote the supply or transfer of a product'.[101] These Regulations principally seek to prohibit misleading advertising and to regulate the scope of comparative advertising.

Misleading advertising

A trader who engages in misleading advertising commits a criminal offence.[102] Advertising is misleading that:

- in any way, including its presentation, deceives or is likely to deceive the traders to whom it is addressed or whom it reaches, and, by reason of its deceptive nature, is likely to affect their economic behaviour; or
- for those reasons, injures or is likely to injure a competitor.[103]

It is clear from this that the BPMMR 2008 is concerned solely with the relationship between traders.

When determining whether an advertisement is misleading, reg 3(3) provides that all of its features shall be taken into account and, in particular, any information

---

98. SI 1988/915.
100. SI 2008/1276.
102. Ibid, reg 6.
99. Council Directive No 2006/114/EC.
101. BPMMR 2008, reg 2(1).
103. Ibid, reg 3(2).

concerning the characteristics of the product, the price, or the manner in which the price is calculated, the conditions on which the product is supplied or provided, and the nature, attributes, and rights of the advertiser. Characteristics of the product would include its availability, nature, composition, fitness for purpose, etc.[104]

Comparative advertising

Businesses will often create advertisements in which they compare their products to those of their rivals (and, in doing so, indicate that their products are superior). This is known as 'comparative advertising' and it can have damaging consequences for a rival business, especially if the comparison is in any way misleading. Regulating the scope of comparative advertising is one of the principal aims of the BPMMR 2008 and reg 4 provides that comparative advertising is only permitted where a number of conditions are met, including that the advertisement:

- is not misleading under the BPMMR 2008, reg 3;
- does not constitute a misleading action or omission under the CPUTR 2008, regs 5 and 6;
- compares products meeting the same needs or intended for the same purpose;
- objectively compares one or more material, relevant, verifiable, and representative features of those products, which may include price;
- does not create confusion among traders.

Enforcement, offences, and defences

The enforcement, civil remedies (or lack thereof), penalties for offences, and available defences are the same as those available under the CPUTR 2008.

 Key points summary

- The Business Protection from Misleading Marketing Regulations 2008 only offer protection to businesses.
- A trader who engages in misleading advertising that injures, or is likely to injure, a competitor commits a criminal offence.
- Comparative advertising occurs where a trader compares its product to that of a rival. Comparative advertising is prohibited, unless:
  - it is not misleading;
  - it compares products meeting the same needs or intended for the same purpose;
  - it objectively compares features of the products; and
  - it does not create confusion among traders.

---

104. Ibid, reg 3(4).

Competition law

It is well established that a competitive marketplace results in a number of benefits. Because competitive markets offer consumers a choice of goods and services, manufacturers and suppliers will wish to make their goods or services seem more attractive than those of others by:

- offering to sell their goods or offering to provide their services at a lower price;
- producing goods of superior quality to those of their rivals; or
- offering a superior level of service compared to that of their rivals.

Strong competition encourages businesses to provide these benefits, and, as a consequence, it also encourages businesses to use and allocate their resources efficiently.

Conversely, where a market is oligopolistic or monopolistic, prices tend to be higher, goods may be of lower quality, and resources may not be optimally used or allocated. New producers may be unable to enter the market, thereby denying consumers the opportunity for greater choice, and the opportunity to purchase potentially new and superior products. Competition law exists to avoid the detrimental effects of oligopolistic and monopolistic markets by prohibiting certain anti-competitive activities. Competition law in the UK derives from three principal sources:

- the EC Treaty, Arts 81 and 82;
- the Competition Act 1998; and
- the relevant provisions in the Enterprise Act 2002.

EU competition law

The Commission's role is discussed in more detail at p 98

In Chapter 4, we noted that one of the principal tasks of the European Commission is to investigate and punish breaches of EU law. We also noted that, in relation to this role, the Commission has been extremely active in investigating and punishing breaches of EU competition law. The principal provisions relating to EU competition law can be found in the EC Treaty, Arts 81 and 82.

Article 81

Article 81(1) provides that certain conduct that may affect trade between member States and which has as its object or effect the prevention, restriction, or distortion of competition within the common market is prohibited. Because Art 81 is concerned with conduct that has as its 'object *or* effect' the reduction or distortion of competition, it follows that the conduct need not actually have this effect, provided that it aimed to have this effect.[105] The *de minimis* rule applies, so conduct that has only a minor effect on competition will not breach Art 81(1).[106]

Article 81 applies in the following cases.

- *Agreements between undertakings* Two or more persons agreeing to prevent, restrict, or distort competition would clearly fall within the prohibition contained

---

105. Commission Decision 86/398 *Polypropylene* (1986) OJ L230/1.
106. *Notice on Agreements of Minor Importance* (2001) OJ C368/13.

in Art 81. No formal agreement need actually exist and an agreement can be evidenced by conduct. What is essential is that two or more persons must be involved; entirely unilateral conduct is not covered by Art 81 (but is subject to Art 82).[107]

- *Decisions by associations of undertakings* Very often, industries will have their own trade association (for example, the Association of the British Pharmaceutical Industry, or the National Federation of Builders), which often engages in activities designed to benefit its members (for example, promotional campaigns, political lobbying, market research, etc.). Trade associations may also be used to coordinate activities designed to prevent, restrict, or distort competition (thereby allowing its members to deny that they have agreed to engage in such behaviour). Such activities by trade associations are also prohibited by Art 81.

- *Concerted practices* Concerted practices form a much more general and ambiguous category of prohibited conduct, and tend to apply where there is evidence of anti-competitive behaviour, but there is little evidence indicating the existence of an agreement between undertakings.

In addition to these general forms of prohibited conduct, Art 81(1) also provides a non-exhaustive list of conduct that could breach Art 81(1), including:

- directly or indirectly fixing purchase or selling prices or any other trading conditions;

- limiting or controlling production, markets, technical development, or investment;

- sharing markets or sources of supply;

- applying dissimilar conditions to equivalent transactions with other trading parties, thereby placing them at a competitive disadvantage;

- making the conclusion of contracts subject to acceptance by the other parties of supplementary obligations that, by their nature or according to commercial usage, have no connection with the subject of such contracts.

Any agreement or decision that breaches Art 81(1) is automatically void.[108] But an agreement between undertakings, a decision by an association of undertakings, or a concerted practice that prevents, restricts, or distorts competition may be excluded from the prohibition contained in Art 81(1) if it contributes to improving the production or distribution of goods, or to promoting technical or economic progress, while allowing consumers a fair share of the resulting benefit, and which does not:

- impose on the undertakings concerned restrictions that are not indispensable to the attainment of these objectives; or

- afford such undertakings the possibility of eliminating competition in respect of a substantial part of the products in question.[109]

Article 83(1)(b) allows the Council to 'lay down detailed rules for the application of Article 81(3), taking into account the need to ensure effective supervision on the one hand, and to simplify administration to the greatest possible extent on the other' and, to this end, the Council has drafted a list of agreements (known as 'block exemptions') that will automatically come under the ambit of the exclusion contained in

---

107. Case T-41/96 *Bayer AG v EC Commission* [2001] 4 CMLR 4.
108. EC Treaty (Treaty of Rome), Art 81(2).
109. Ibid, Art 81(3).

Art 81(3) (for example, certain concerted practices within the motor vehicle market are excluded from Art 81(1)).[110]

Article 82

Article 82 provides that '[a]ny abuse by one or more undertakings of a dominant position within the common market or in a substantial part of it shall be prohibited as incompatible with the common market in so far as it may affect trade between Member States'. An immediately apparent difference between Arts 81 and 82 is that Art 82 applies to abuse by 'one or more undertakings', meaning that unilateral action by one party is covered (unlike Art 81, under which conduct between two or more parties is required). In this sense, Art 82 is wider in scope than Art 81. Because Art 82 applies only to undertakings in a dominant position, however, cases involving Art 82 arise much less frequently than cases involving Art 81.

Regarding what constitutes a 'dominant position', the European Court of Justice has stated that:

> The dominant position referred to in [Art 82] relates to a position of economic strength enjoyed by an undertaking which enables it to prevent effective competition being maintained on the relevant market by giving it the power to behave to a appreciable extent independently of its competitors, customers and ultimately of its consumers.[111]

Dominance per se does not constitute a breach of Art 82; it is only breached when an undertaking abuses its dominant position. What constitutes 'abuse' is not defined, but Art 82 does provide a non-exhaustive list of examples of conduct that may constitute an abuse of a dominant position:

- directly or indirectly imposing unfair purchase or selling prices or other unfair trading conditions;
- limiting production, markets, or technical development to the prejudice of consumers;
- applying dissimilar conditions to equivalent transactions with other trading parties, thereby placing them at a competitive disadvantage; or
- making the conclusion of contracts subject to acceptance by the other parties of supplementary obligations that, by their nature or according to commercial usage, have no connection with the subject of such contracts.

The Competition Act 1998

Prior to 1998, UK competition law was spread across a number of different pieces of legislation and enforcement was the responsibility of a number of different bodies. In 1997, the government announced that it intended to streamline the competition law provisions into one Act that was more in harmony with the EC Treaty, Arts 81 and 82. The result was the Competition Act 1998, which came into force on 1 March 2000. The Competition Act 1998, Pt I, introduced two prohibitions (known

---

110. Regulation EC/1400/1202 (2002) OJ L203/30.
111. Case 27/76 *United Brands Co v EC Commission* [1978] ECR 207.

as the 'Chapter I' and 'Chapter II' prohibitions), which closely resemble those found in Arts 81 and 82. To ensure as much harmony as possible between domestic and EU law, the Competition Act 1998, s 60, provides that domestic courts should apply the 1998 Act in a manner consistent with the EC Treaty and decisions of the European courts, except in relation to those areas in which there is a 'relevant difference' between the provisions.

The 'Chapter I' prohibition

The 'Chapter I' prohibition can be found in s 2(1) and mirrors closely the prohibition found in the EC Treaty, Art 81. Section 2(1) provides the prohibition—unless they are exempt in accordance with Pt I of the Act—of agreements between undertakings, decisions by associations of undertakings, or concerted practices that:

- may affect trade within the UK; and
- have as their object or effect the prevention, restriction, or distortion of competition within the UK.

Section 2(2) provides a list of examples of activities that could breach s 2(1) and this list is identical to that found in Art 81(1).

Section 2(4) provides that any agreement or decision that breaches s 2(1) is void. As with Art 81, the *de minimis* rule applies and so-called 'small agreements' have limited immunity, in that they are not subject to the financial penalties that can be imposed by the Act, but they are subject to any other penalties. A 'small agreement' is one between undertakings, the combined applicable turnover of which for the business year ending in the calendar year preceding that during which the infringement occurred does not exceed £20 million.[112]

The Chapter I prohibition is subject to two types of exception, as follows.

- *Block exemptions* These are similar to those that operate under Art 81, except that block exemptions are made by the Secretary of State upon a recommendation from the OFT.[113] To date, it appears that only one such block exemption has been made.[114]
- *Parallel exemptions* These are the block exemptions provided for by the European Council under Art 81(3), discussed above.

The 'Chapter II' prohibition

The 'Chapter II' prohibition can be found in s 18(1) and provides that 'any conduct on the part of one or more undertakings which amounts to the abuse of a dominant position in a market is prohibited if it may affect trade within the United Kingdom'. Clearly, s 18(1) is virtually identical to Art 82 and the list of potential breaches of s 18(1) contained in s 18(2) is identical to that found in Art 82. The definition of 'dominant position' is virtually identical to that adopted under Community law, except the territorial scope is different—namely, the

---

112. Competition Act 1998 (Small Agreements and Conduct of Minor Significance) Regulations 2000, SI 2000/262, reg 3.
113. Competition Act 1998, ss 6, 8, and 9.
114. Namely, the Competition Act 1998 (Public Transport Ticketing Schemes Block Exemption) Order 2001, SI 2001/319.

undertaking(s) must occupy a dominant position in the UK, or any part of it. The limited immunity granted to 'small agreements' under the Chapter I prohibition also applies to the Chapter II prohibition, except that turnover threshold is increased to £50 million.[115]

Section 19 also provides for exclusions in relation to mergers and other more general matters.

Enforcement

Enforcement of the above provisions initially rests with the OFT, which is given substantial investigatory powers, as well as the ability to decide cases and enforce its decisions via a court order. Perhaps more importantly, the OFT has the power to refer cases to the Competition Commission (CC), a body created by the Competition Act 1998. The CC can be thought of as the competition law equivalent of an employment tribunal. It is important to note that the CC has no power to investigate cases on its own initiative; it can only investigate and decide on cases referred to it. Just as decisions of employment tribunals can be appealed to the Employment Appeal Tribunal, so can decisions of the CC be appealed to the Competition Appeal Tribunal (CAT). This appeal tribunal did not exist when the CC was created, but was established subsequently by the Enterprise Act 2002, which has had a significant effect upon the UK's competition law regime.

The Enterprise Act 2002

The Enterprise Act 2002 substantially altered the regulation and enforcement of certain competition law issues, and aimed to improve the effectiveness of the regulatory regime imposed by the Competition Act 1998. It introduced a number of reforms, perhaps the most important being the creation of the CAT.

Part 2—The Competition Appeal Tribunal

Part 2 of the Act (ss 12–21) establishes the CAT and the Competition Service (the job of which is to fund and provide support services to the CAT). The CAT was set up to hear appeals against decisions of the OFT, the CC, and the Secretary of State in relation to competition matters. The CAT consists of a president, who will be a judge of the Chancery Division of the High Court and will be appointed to the post by the Lord Chancellor following a recommendation from the Judicial Appointments Commission. In addition to the president, there are eighteen chairmen (sixteen of whom are also judges in the Chancery Division), and seventeen ordinary members (all of whom are senior lawyers, accountants, or have expertise in related fields). Like employment tribunal cases, a panel of three hears cases before the CAT, that panel comprising one chairman (or the president) and two ordinary members. Where an appeal is allowed, the decision of the OFT or CC is not quashed; rather, the matter is referred back to the OFT or CC, which is required to reconsider the matter.

---

115. Competition Act 1998 (Small Agreements and Conduct of Minor Significance) Regulations 2000, SI 2000/262, reg 4.

In 2007–08, the CAT handed down twenty-six judgments.[116] Like the Employment Appeal Tribunal, decisions of the CAT may be appealed on a point of law to the Court of Appeal.

Part 3—The regulation of mergers

Part 3 of the Act (ss 22–130) concerns the regulation of mergers. Prior to the Enterprise Act 2002, the Secretary of State took decisions regarding the control of mergers. The 2002 Act largely removes this power (except in relation to special public interest cases), and transfers it to the OFT and the CC. Where the target of a merger has a turnover of at least £70 million, or where a merger would result in the merging parties supplying at least 25 per cent of goods or services of a particular description in the UK or a substantial part of it, then the OFT is under a duty to investigate that merger. If it believes that the merger may result in a substantial lessening of competition, it is under a duty to refer the merger to the CC,[117] or to obtain from the merging parties an undertaking whereby the parties agree to remedy the expected adverse competition effects of the merger.[118]

If a merger is referred to the CC, it will investigate whether or not the merger will substantially lessen competition. If the CC believes that competition will be substantially lessened, it can prohibit the merger, impose a wide array of remedies (for example, requiring a firm to sell part of its business, or requiring it to behave in a manner that safeguards competition), or seek an undertaking from the parties.

Decisions of the OFT and the CC can be appealed to the CAT as discussed above.

Eg **The proposed merger of Lloyds TSB Group plc and the Abbey National Group plc**

In 2001, Lloyds TSB proposed to merge with Abbey National. The proposed merger came at the end of a period of intense merger activity amongst banks that left the UK banking sector with four dominant banks—namely, Barclays, HSBC, Lloyds TSB, and the Royal Bank of Scotland. There were few banks that could compete with these four, but the Abbey National was one of them. Fearing that the merger would adversely affect the banking market, the Secretary of State referred the merger to the CC.

After a thorough investigation, the CC concluded that the merger would have adverse effects of the banking market. Lloyds TSB was already the leading supplier of personal current accounts and the merger would have increased its share of the market. Given the concentration of the market, having strong rivals was vital and any reduction in the number of such rivals would adversely affect competition. Accordingly, the CC prohibited the merger.

---

116. CAT, *Annual Review and Accounts 2007/2008* (CAT, London, 2008) 41.
117. Enterprise Act 2002, ss 22 and 33. The duty to refer does not apply where the market is not important enough to justify a reference, or where there are obvious benefits to the consumer that outweigh the adverse effects on competition.
118. Ibid, s 73.

Part 4—Market investigation references

Part 4 of the Act (ss 131–184) relates to market investigation references. The OFT has the power to refer a market to the CC for investigation where it believes that the structure of the market, or the conduct of its suppliers or customers, is preventing, restricting, or distorting competition in connection with the supply or acquisition of goods and services within the UK.[119] The CC will, within two years, carry out an investigation into the market and, if adverse effects on competition are identified, it will determine what measures must be taken to remedy the adverse effects.

As under Pt 3, the OFT's decision to refer or the decision of the CC can be appealed to the CAT.[120]

Eg The market for groceries

In May 2006, the OFT referred the supply of groceries by retailers to the CC. In May 2008, the CC completed its investigation, concluding that, generally, the market works well and provides consumers with a good deal. But the CC did state that large grocery retailers (for example, Asda, Morrisons, Tesco, etc.) have very strong positions in local markets, and that consumers in these areas could face poorer service and higher prices. The CC therefore decided to implement a number of remedies including:

➡ restrictive covenant: a promise, usually made by deed, forbidding the commission of a certain act

1. requiring large grocery retailers to release restrictive covenants in a number of highly concentrated local markets and prohibiting the imposition of future covenants;

2. requiring large grocery retailers to notify the OFT of all acquisitions of existing grocery stores of 1,000 square feet and over; and

3. establishing a Groceries Supply Code of Practice, with an accompanying ombudsman, who will monitor and enforce the Code.

Tesco appealed the findings of the CC to the CAT, which, in March 2009, unanimously concluded that the CC failed to consider a number of relevant matters in relation to the package of remedies awarded. The CAT therefore upheld Tesco's appeal. The CC has stated that it will study the CAT's judgment closely before deciding what steps should be taken.

Part 6—The criminalization of cartels

Maintaining a market position through lower prices or the production of superior products can affect the profitability of a business. Accordingly, rival businesses may decide that the costs of competition are excessive, and that it is economically more viable for them to cooperate and try to control the market. They may try to achieve this by forming a cartel. A cartel operates where an individual dishonestly agrees with one or more other persons that undertakings will engage in one or more prohibited cartel activities, including price-fixing, limiting or preventing supply or production of a product or service, market-sharing (that is, dividing up a market between them), or bid-rigging.[121] Part 6 of the Act (ss 188–202) makes it a criminal offence to agree

---

119. Ibid, s 131(1).   120. Ibid, s 179.
121. Ibid, s 188.

to form a cartel. Whether the agreement is actually put into effect is irrelevant; the offence is committed once the agreement is made. The agreement must be horizontal (that is, the persons involved must be on the same level of the supply chain); vertical agreements (for example, agreements between manufacturers and suppliers) are not covered. To encourage those who have information on cartel activity to come forward, the OFT will offer a reward of up to £100,000 to anyone who provides such information. Where the person providing information has such information because he is involved in the cartel, he will usually wish to obtain immunity from prosecution. This can be obtained by the OFT issuing a written notice (known as a 'no-action letter'), which states that the individual will not be prosecuted.[122] The OFT will require the person to admit participation in the offence, to provide it with all of the information available until the investigation is concluded, and to cease further participation in the cartel.[123] Breach of these conditions will result in the revocation of the no-action letter.

The offence is triable either way and attracts a maximum penalty of six months' imprisonment[124] and/or a fine not exceeding the statutory maximum (that is, £5,000) on summary conviction. On conviction on indictment, the maximum penalty is five years' imprisonment and/or a fine.[125] Prosecutions are normally brought by the Serious Fraud Office, although the OFT also has the power to prosecute.

Section 204—Competition disqualification orders

Section 204 amends the Company Directors Disqualification Act 1986 (CDDA 1986) to allow the OFT to apply to the High Court for an order (known as a 'competition disqualification order') disqualifying a director who has committed a breach of competition law.[126] A breach of competition law relates to those competition law provisions discussed earlier in the chapter—namely, the Competition Act 1998, chs 1 and 2, and the EC Treaty, Arts 81 and 82.[127] But any court that convicts a director of the cartel offence discussed previously can itself impose an ordinary disqualification order under the CDDA 1986, s 2. The OFT will not apply for a disqualification order against a director who is the beneficiary of a no-action letter.[128]

The courts' ability to disqualify a director is discussed at p 652

The maximum period of disqualification is fifteen years (five years, in the case of a disqualification on summary conviction) and breaching a disqualification order constitutes an either-way offence, punishable on summary conviction by up to six months' imprisonment[129] and/or a £5,000 fine. On conviction on indictment, the maximum penalty is two years' imprisonment and/or a fine.[130]

---

122. Ibid, s 190(4).
123. OFT, *The Cartel Offence: Guidance on the Issue of No-Action Letters for Individuals* (OFT, London, 2003) [3.3].
124. This will rise to twelve months' imprisonment if or when the Criminal Justice Act 2003, s 154(1), comes into force.
125. Enterprise Act 2002, s 190(1).
126. Company Directors Disqualification Act 1986, s 9A.
127. Ibid, s 9A(4).
128. OFT, *Competition Disqualification Orders: Guidance* (OFT, London, 2003) [4.27].
129. This will rise to twelve months' imprisonment if or when the Criminal Justice Act 2003, s 154(1), comes into force.
130. Company Directors Disqualification Act 1986, s 13.

> **‹›** **Key points summary**
>
> - The EC Treaty, Art 81, prohibits agreements and decisions that prevent, restrict, or distort competition. Article 82 prohibits undertakings that occupy a dominant position from abusing that position.
>
> - The Competition Act 1998 imposes prohibitions that are virtually identical to those found in Arts 81 and 82. The prohibition that resembles Art 81 is known as the 'Chapter I' prohibition and is found in s 2(1). The prohibition that resembles Art 82 is known as the 'Chapter II' prohibition and is found in s 18(1).
>
> - Part 2 of the Enterprise Act 2002 established the Competition Appeals Tribunal, which hears appeals from decisions of the Office of Fair Trading, the Competition Commission, and the Secretary of State.
>
> - Part 3 of the 2002 Act allows the OFT and CC to investigate mergers to determine whether they could substantially lessen competition. Part 4 allows the OFT and CC to investigate market behaviour that prevents, restricts, or distorts competition. Part 6 makes it a criminal offence to engage in cartel activity.
>
> - Section 204 of the 2002 Act allows a competition disqualification order to be issued against a director who has breached competition law.

Enforcement orders under the Enterprise Act 2002

The passing of the Enterprise Act 2002, which we have already discussed in relation to competition law, was of immense importance to the enforcement of consumer law. It implemented the government's 2001 election manifesto pledge to increase the independence of the competition authorities and to provide greater enforcement powers to those who seek to eradicate practices that harm consumers. Of particular importance are the provisions found in Pt 8 (ss 210–236) of the 2002 Act, which greatly enhance the enforcement powers of certain bodies by allowing them to obtain 'enforcement orders' against businesses that breach their legal obligations towards consumers.

Domestic and Community infringements

The legal obligations enforceable under Pt 8 of the Act are divided into either 'domestic infringements' or 'Community infringements', but it is important to note that Pt 8 provides enforcement powers only where the infringement 'harms the collective interests of consumers'. Accordingly, Pt 8 does not allow individual consumers to obtain redress for breaches of consumer legislation.

Domestic infringement

A domestic infringement is an act or omission carried out in the course of a business that harms the collective interests of consumers in the UK and consists of an act or omission specified in s 211(2). Section 211(2) provides a comprehensive and extremely wide list of acts or omissions that can constitute a domestic infringement, including:

- contravention of an enactment that imposes a duty, prohibition, or restriction enforceable by criminal proceedings;
- an act done or omission made in breach of contract;
- an act done or omission made in breach of a non-contractual duty owed to a person by virtue of an enactment or rule of law and enforceable by civil proceedings;
- an act or omission in respect of which an enactment provides for a remedy or sanction enforceable by civil proceedings; and
- an act or omission by which a person supplying or seeking to supply goods or services purports, or attempts, to avoid (to any extent) liability relating to the supply in circumstances under which such avoidance is restricted or prevented under an enactment.

But the acts and omissions specified in s 211(2) apply only to breaches of law specified by the Secretary of State in subordinate legislation. The list specified by the Secretary of State[131] includes breaches of the common law, such as acts or omissions that breach a duty of care owed in tort.[132] The list also covers breaches of many major pieces of legislation discussed in this text, including the Misrepresentation Act 1967, the Consumer Credit Act 1974, the Torts (Interference with Goods) Act 1977, the Unfair Contract Terms Act 1977, the Sale of Goods Act 1979, and the Supply of Goods and Services Act 1982.[133]

Community infringement

A Community infringement is similar to a domestic infringement, except that the law breached is either:

- a piece of EU law specified in Sch 13 to the Act (laws covered include many major pieces of EU legislation discussed throughout this text, including the Unfair Terms Directive, which led to the UTCCR 1999, and the Unfair Commercial Practices Directive, which led to the CPUTR 2008); or
- a piece of domestic law that gives effect to a listed directive and provides for protection greater than that specified in the directive, provided that greater protection is permitted (examples include the UTCCR 1999 and the CPUTR 2008).[134]

Enforcers

The ability to obtain an enforcement order for a domestic or Community infringement is vested in 'enforcers'. Enforcers come in four forms, as follows.

1. *General enforcers* are the OFT and the Trading Standards Service.[135] General enforcers can apply for an enforcement order for any infringement under the Act.[136]

---

131. Enterprise Act 2002 (Part 8 Domestic Infringements) Order 2003, SI 2003/1593.
132. Ibid, Sch 1, Pt III.   133. Ibid, Pt I.
134. Enterprise Act 2002 (Part 8 Community Infringement Specified UK Laws) Order 2003, SI 2003/1374, Sch 1.
135. Enterprise Act 2002, s 213(1).
136. Ibid, s 215(2).

2. *Designated enforcers* are those bodies designated by the Secretary of State. They include the Office of Communications, the Gas and Electricity Markets Authority, and the Information Commissioner.[137] Designated enforcers can apply for an enforcement order only in relation to their designated area.[138]

➡ European Economic Area (EEA): a body that enables states to join the single market without joining the EU

3. *Community enforcers* are entities from other European Economic Area (EEA) states, which are listed in the Official Journal of the European Communities for the purposes of the Injunctions Directive, but which are not general, designated, or Community protection cooperation (see below) enforcers.[139] Accordingly, only bodies outside the EEA will be classified as community enforcers. Community enforcers can obtain an enforcement order only in relation to Community infringements.[140]

4. *Community protection cooperation (CPC) enforcers* were subsequently added in order to help to curtail cross-border infringements. CPC enforcers include the OFT, the Financial Services Authority, and the Office of Communications.[141] CPC enforcers can obtain an enforcement order only in relation to Community infringements.[142]

Enforcement orders

An enforcer can obtain an enforcement order against a person who has committed a domestic or Community infringement, or who is likely to commit a Community infringement.[143] Where the infringer is a body corporate (that is, a company or limited liability partnership), any act of connivance committed by a director, manager, or company secretary may also be subject to enforcement under Pt 8.[144]

Prior to applying for an enforcement order, the enforcer should first consult with the OFT and the business that has committed the infringement.[145] The consultation period is normally a minimum of fourteen days, but can be dispensed with where, in the opinion of the OFT, urgent action is required. The end result of the consultation may be that the business in question offers an undertaking, stating that it will not repeat the infringement. Enforcers are free to accept these undertakings[146] and, if the undertaking is complied with, the matter is resolved. If the undertaking is broken or if the business does not offer such an undertaking, the enforcer can move onto the option of last resort—namely, applying for an enforcement order. When an undertaking is made, the OFT should be notified of the terms of the undertaking and its compliance should be monitored.

Enforcers may apply to a county court or the High Court for an enforcement order. The court, instead of making an enforcement order, may accept an undertaking from the business that it will not repeat the infringement. Unlike an

---

137. Enterprise Act 2002 (Part 8 Designated Enforcers: Criteria for Designation, Designation of Public Bodies as Designated Enforcers and Transitional Provisions) Order 2003, SI 2003/1399, Sch 1.
138. Enterprise Act 2002, s 215(3).   139. Ibid, s 213(5).
140. Ibid, s 215(4).   141. Ibid, s 213(5A).
142. Ibid, s 215(4A).   143. Ibid, s 217.
144. Ibid, s 222(2) and (3).   145. Ibid, s 214(1).
146. Ibid, s 219.

undertaking given to an enforcer, if this undertaking is breached, it will constitute contempt of court. If no undertaking is offered, the court may make an enforcement order requiring the business to cease the infringement. Failure to comply with an enforcement order constitutes contempt of court. Where the enforcer obtains an enforcement order or an undertaking, the infringing business will normally pay the enforcer's costs. If the enforcer fails to prove its case, it will be ordered to pay the business' costs.

Figure 28.2 demonstrates the procedure for enforcing an infringement.

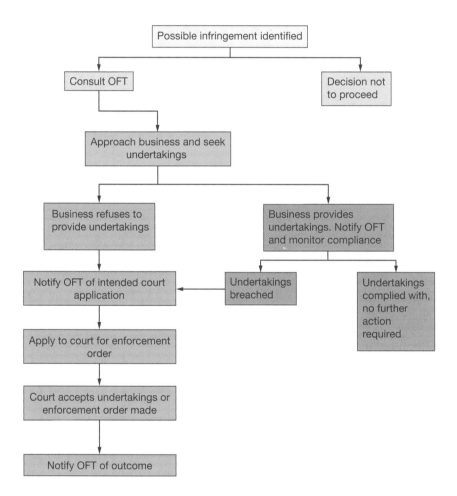

FIGURE 28.2 Enforcement procedures under the Enterprise Act 2002, Pt 8
Source: © Crown copyright. Reproduced from OFT, *Enforcement of Consumer Protection Legislation* (2003)

Key points summary

- Enforcement orders can be obtained for certain breaches of domestic law (known as 'domestic infringements') and breaches of Community law (known as 'Community infringements').

- Only enforcers may apply for an enforcement order to remedy a domestic or Community infringement. The types of enforcer are:
  - general enforcers;
  - designated enforcers;
  - Community enforcers; and
  - Community protection cooperation enforcers.

- Part 8 allows enforcers to obtain an enforcement order against a business that has committed a domestic or Community infringement.

 ## Chapter conclusion

Whilst profit maximization remains the dominant purpose of business, there will always be an incentive to engage in unfair commercial practices in order to increase profits. Such practices may aim to increase revenue through higher sales (for example, high-pressure sales techniques), whereas others will attempt to increase profits by lowering outgoings (for example, exclusion clauses will lower outgoings by reducing the amount of compensation payable). Either way, the business will attempt to use its dominant position to gain an advantage. Because the party dealing with the business can do little to protect itself, it falls to the law to provide protection. We have seen an explosion in consumer protectionist legislation in the latter half of the twentieth century, but it should also be remembered that smaller businesses may be just as vulnerable as consumers. The aim of the law should be to disincentivize unfair commercial practices, and the law has utilized both the civil and criminal law to achieve this aim. The law's commitment to discouraging unfair commercial practices is demonstrated by the passing of the Consumer Protection from Unfair Trading Regulations 2008, which have swept away and replaced a number of notable statutory provisions that have been in place for over forty years. To what extent the Regulations can prevent the use of unfair commercial practices remains to be seen.

Self-test questions

1. Define the following:
   (a) proferens;
   (b) *contra proferentem*;
   (c) maximum harmonization;
   (d) aggressive practice;
   (e) comparative advertising;
   (f) Community infringement.

2. Do you believe that enacting the Law Commission's draft Unfair Contract Terms Bill would be a beneficial development? Provide reasons for enacting the Bill and for retaining the current position.

3. Has an unfair commercial practice occurred in the following situations?
   (a) PC Components Ltd provides PC components to PC manufacturers. It manufactures a batch of transistors, but discovers that the transistors contain a defect and that a small proportion of them have ceased working without warning. It sells a batch of these transistors to CompuBuild Ltd, but fails to inform it of the defect.
   (b) HD Stuff Ltd sells high-definition audio-visual equipment. Patrick enters its shop and purchases a Blu-ray player. HD Stuff fails to tell Martin that he will need an HD television in order for the Blu-ray player to work correctly.

4. Explain whether the following would or would not constitute an 'invitation to purchase'. Provide reasons for your answer.
   (a) A wine list displayed on a wall-mounted board above a licensed bar.
   (b) A phone company sends a text to all of its customers stating that, if they reply to the text with the word 'ringtone', they can acquire five ringtones for £1.
   (c) A billboard poster advertises the new album by the girl group 'Pointless WAGs'.

5. 'The Enterprise Act 2002 has radically altered the enforcement of competition law in the UK.' Discuss this statement, paying particular attention to the relationship between the 2002 Act and the Competition Act 1998.

6. 'Given that consumer legislation in the UK provides its own rights of enforcement, the enforcement mechanisms found in the Enterprise Act 2002, Pt 8, are not required and offer little.' Do you agree with this statement? Provide reasons for your answer.

Further reading

Brownsword, R, and Adams, JN, 'The Unfair Contract Terms Act: A Decade of Discretion' (1988) 104 LQR 94
Discusses the operation of the Unfair Contract Terms Act 1977 and focuses on how the courts have applied the requirement of reasonableness

Furmston, M, *Cheshire, Fifoot & Furmston's Law of Contract* (OUP, Oxford, 2007) pp 202–57
Provides a clear, but detailed, account of the common law and statutory regulation of exclusion clauses and unfair terms

Furse, M, *Competition Law of the EC and UK* (6th edn, OUP, Oxford, 2008)
Provides a detailed and up-to-date analysis of domestic and European Community competition law

Law Commission, *Unfair Terms in Contracts* (Law Com No 292, Cm 6464, HMSO, London, 2005)
Recommends that the UCTA 1977 and the Unfair Terms in Consumer Contracts Regulations 1999 should be unified, and provides a draft Unfair Contract Terms Bill

Macdonald, E, 'Unifying Unfair Terms Legislation' (2004) 67 MLR 69
*Discusses the problems associated with having two pieces of legislation regulating unfair
terms; analyses the Law Commission's draft Unfair Contract Terms Bill*

Office of Fair Trading, *Enforcement of Consumer Protection Legislation: Guidance
on Part 8 of the Enterprise Act* (OFT, London, 2003)
*Provides easy-to-understand guidance on the enforcement of consumer law under the
Enterprise Act 2002, Pt 8*

Office of Fair Trading/Department for Business, Enterprise and Regulatory Reform,
Consumer Protection from Unfair Trading (OFT, London, 2008)
*Provides easy-to-understand guidance on the Consumer Protection from Unfair Trading
Regulations 2008*

Ramsay, I, *Consumer Law and Policy* (Hart, Oxford, 2007) ch 6
*Discusses in depth the reasons behind, and the provisions contained within, the Unfair
Commercial Practices Directive*

Websites

<http://www.catribunal.org.uk>
*The official website of the Competition Appeal Tribunal; provides detailed information on
the workings of the Tribunal and links to all of its judgments*

<http://www.competition-commission.gov.uk>
*The official website of the Competition Commission; provides information on the workings
of the Commission, and also details of past and current investigations*

<http://www.oft.gov.uk>
*The official website of the Office of Fair Trading; provides a substantial body of information
on consumer law issues and provides numerous case studies of the law in practice*

Remember to visit the **Online Resource Centre** at **<http://www.
oxfordtextbooks.co.uk/roach>** to access the following resources on
Chapter 28, 'Unfair commercial practices': more **practice questions** and
answers; a **glossary** of key terms; **multiple-choice questions; revision
summaries; audio updates** when relevant; and **diagrams** in pdf.

table of cases

table of statutes

table of european legislation

index

D